T0211829

# Lecture Notes in Computer Science    11861

More information about this series at http://www.springer.com/series/7412

Heung-Il Suk · Mingxia Liu ·
Pingkun Yan · Chunfeng Lian (Eds.)

# Machine Learning in Medical Imaging

10th International Workshop, MLMI 2019
Held in Conjunction with MICCAI 2019
Shenzhen, China, October 13, 2019
Proceedings

 Springer

*Editors*
Heung-Il Suk (iD)
Korea University
Seoul, Korea (Republic of)

Mingxia Liu (iD)
University of North Carolina
Chapel Hill, NC, USA

Pingkun Yan (iD)
Rensselaer Polytechnic Institute
Troy, NY, USA

Chunfeng Lian
University of North Carolina
Chapel Hill, NC, USA

ISSN 0302-9743            ISSN 1611-3349   (electronic)
Lecture Notes in Computer Science
ISBN 978-3-030-32691-3         ISBN 978-3-030-32692-0   (eBook)
https://doi.org/10.1007/978-3-030-32692-0

LNCS Sublibrary: SL6 – Image Processing, Computer Vision, Pattern Recognition, and Graphics

This Springer imprint is published by the registered company Springer Nature Switzerland AG
The registered company address is: Gewerbestrasse 11, 6330 Cham, Switzerland

# Preface

The 10th International Workshop on Machine Learning in Medical Imaging (MLMI 2019) was held in Shenzhen, China, on October 13, 2019, in conjunction with the 22nd International Conference on Medical Image Computing and Computer-Assisted Intervention (MICCAI 2019).

In the face of artificial intelligence making significant changes in both academia and industry, machine learning has always played a crucial role in the medical imaging field, including but not limited to computer-aided detection and diagnosis, image segmentation, image registration, image fusion, image-guided intervention, image annotation, image retrieval, image reconstruction, etc. The main scope of this workshop was to help advance the scientific researches within the broad field of machine learning in medical imaging. This workshop focused on major trends and challenges in this area and presented original works aiming to identify new cutting-edge techniques and their uses in medical imaging. The workshop facilitated translating medical imaging research, boosted by machine learning, from bench to bedside. Topics of interests included deep learning, generative adversarial learning, ensemble learning, sparse learning, multi-task learning, multi-view learning, manifold learning, and reinforcement learning, with their applications to medical image analysis, computer-aided detection and diagnosis, multi-modality fusion, image reconstruction, image retrieval, cellular image analysis, molecular imaging, digital pathology, etc.

Along with the great advances in machine learning, MLMI 2019 received an unprecedentedly large number of papers (158 in total). All the submissions underwent a rigorous double-blinded peer-review process, with each paper being reviewed by at least two members of the Program Committee, composed of 81 experts in the fields. Based on the reviewing scores and critiques, the 78 best papers (49.3%) were accepted for presentation at the workshop and chosen to be included in this Springer LNCS volume. It was a tough decision and many high-quality papers had to be rejected due to the page limit of this volume.

We are grateful to all Program Committee members for reviewing the submissions and giving constructive comments. We also thank all the authors for making the workshop very fruitful and successful.

September 2019

Heung-Il Suk
Mingxia Liu
Pingkun Yan
Chunfeng Lian

## Preface

# Organization

## Steering Committee

Dinggang Shen     University of North Carolina at Chapel Hill, USA
Kenji Suzuki     University of Chicago, USA
Fei Wang     Huami Inc., USA
Pingkun Yan     Rensselaer Polytechnic Institute, USA

## Program Committee

Arnav Bhavsar     Indian Institute of Technology Mandi, India
Chunfeng Lian     University of North Carolina at Chapel Hill, USA
Dan Hu     University of North Carolina at Chapel Hill, USA
Defu Yang     Hangzhou Dianzi University, China
Dongren Yao     Institute of Automation Chinese Academy of Sciences, China
Erkun Yang     Xidian University, China
Fan Yang     Inception Institute of Artificial Intelligence, UAE
Fengjun Zhao     Northwest University, USA
Gang Li     University of North Carolina at Chapel Hill, USA
Heang-Ping Chan     University of Michigan Medical Center, USA
Heung-Il Suk     Korea University, South Korea
Holger Roth     Nagoya University, Japan
Hongmei Mi     China Jiliang University, China
Hongming Shan     Rensselaer Polytechnic Institute, USA
Hoo-Chang Shin     NVIDIA Corporation, USA
Hyekyoung Lee     Seoul National University Hospital, South Korea
Hyunjin Park     Sungkyunkwan University, South Korea
Ilwoo Lyu     Vanderbilt University, USA
Islem Rekik     Istanbul Technical University, Turkey
Jaeil Kim     Kyungpook National University, South Korea
Janne Nappi     Massachusetts General Hospital, USA
Jianpeng Zhang     Northwestern Polytechnical University, China
Jie Wei     Northwestern Polytechnical University, China
Jinfan Fan     Beijing Institute of Technology, China
Jong-Min Lee     Hanyang University, South Korea
Joon-Kyung Seong     Korea University, South Korea
Kelei He     Nanjing University, China
Ken'ichi Morooka     Kyushu University, Japan
Kilian Pohl     SRI International, USA
Kim-Han Thung     University of North Carolina at Chapel Hill, USA
Kyu-Hwan Jung     VUNO Inc., South Korea

| Yuankai Huo | Vanderbilt University, USA |
| Yuxuan Xiong | Wuhan University, China |
| Ze Jin | Tokyo Institute of Technology, Japan |
| Yi Zhang | Sichuan University, China |
| Zhenghan Fang | University of North Carolina at Chapel Hill, USA |
| Zhengwang Wu | University of North Carolina at Chapel Hill, USA |
| Zhicheng Jiao | University of Pennsylvania, USA |
| Zhiguo Zhou | UT Southwestern Medical Center, USA |

# Contents

# Brain MR Image Segmentation in Small Dataset with Adversarial Defense and Task Reorganization

Xuhua Ren[1], Lichi Zhang[1], Dongming Wei[1,2], Dinggang Shen[2(✉)], and Qian Wang[1(✉)]

[1] Institute for Medical Imaging Technology, School of Biomedical Engineering, Shanghai Jiao Tong University, Shanghai 200030, China
wang.qian@sjtu.edu.cn
[2] Department of Radiology and Biomedical Research Imaging Center (BRIC), University of North Carolina at Chapel Hill, Chapel Hill, NC 27599, USA
dgshen@med.unc.edu

**Abstract.** Medical image segmentation is challenging especially in dealing with small dataset of 3D MR images. Encoding the variation of brain anatomical structures from individual subjects cannot be easily achieved, which is further challenged by only a limited number of well labeled subjects for training. In this study, we aim to address the issue of brain MR image segmentation in small dataset. First, concerning the limited number of training images, we adopt adversarial defense to augment the training data and therefore increase the robustness of the network. Second, inspired by the prior knowledge of neural anatomies, we reorganize the segmentation tasks of different regions into several groups in a hierarchical way. Third, the task reorganization extends to the semantic level, as we incorporate an additional object-level classification task to contribute high-order visual features toward the pixel-level segmentation task. In experiments we validate our method by segmenting gray matter, white matter, and several major regions on a challenge dataset. The proposed method with only seven subjects for training can achieve 84.46% of Dice score in the onsite test set.

## 1 Introduction

Brain MR segmentation plays a pivotally important role in clinical diagnosis. But manual segmentation is generally time-consuming and prone to errors due to inter- or intra-operator variability. Therefore, fully automated segmentation method is essential for brain image analysis, which has also drawn a lot of attention from the community. The MRBrainS18[1] challenge, for example, aims to find the optimal algorithm for

---

[1] https://mrbrains18.isi.uu.nl/.

This work was supported by the National Key Research and Development Program of China (2018YFC0116400) and STCSM (19QC1400600, 17411953300).

© Springer Nature Switzerland AG 2019
H.-I. Suk et al. (Eds.): MLMI 2019, LNCS 11861, pp. 1–8, 2019.
https://doi.org/10.1007/978-3-030-32692-0_1

automatic segmentation of individual regions of interest (ROIs) in 3T brain MR scans, including gray matter, basal ganglia, white matter, white matter lesions, cerebrospinal fluid, ventricles, cerebellum and brain stem. The challenge reflects a common circumstance, as the number of the labeled images available to training is often limited. Also, the ROIs in the brain can vary a lot in position, appearance, scale, and etc., making it hard for a single network to adapt to all segmentation tasks.

With the success of deep learning in medical imaging, supervised segmentation approaches built on 3D convolutional neural networks (CNNs) have produced superior segmentation result with satisfactory speed performance. Dolz et al. proposed Hyper-DenseNet [1], a 3D fully convolutional network (FCN), and extended the definition of dense connectivity to multi-modal brain segmentation. Roulet et al. [2] focused on training a single CNN for brain and lesion segmentation using heterogeneous datasets. Wang et al. [3] investigated how test-time augmentation can improve CNN's performance for brain tumor segmentation and used different underpinning network structures.

Although these studies provide new paradigms in automatic brain segmentation, it is still difficult to handle the large variation of the neuroanatomical structures from different individuals using only limited number of training subjects. Moreover, the task-level interaction with the prior knowledge of brain anatomies is mostly ignored. To this end, we propose a novel CNN based segmentation method for brain MR image segmentation in this work. Specifically, we deploy the adversarial defense framework, such that the adversarial examples combined with the original small training dataset can improve the robustness of the network. Then, we split the to-be-segmented brain ROIs into several groups according to the anatomical prior knowledge, and thus reorganize the segmentation tasks. Whereas the pixel-level segmentation task further benefits from an additional object-level classification task, which helps ease the difficulty in segmentation.

We summarize our main contributions as follows:

(1) We deploy the adversarial attack and defense framework on medical image segmentation, to alleviate the concern of small training dataset.
(2) We propose a task reorganization strategy to group the brain ROIs according to anatomical prior knowledge.
(3) We extend task reorganization to different semantic levels by incorporating an additional object-level classification task, such that the classification and segmentation tasks can interact with each other toward better segmentation performance.

## 2   Methods

In this section, we detail the proposed method for automatic brain MR segmentation, which is featured by two innovative components: **Adversarial Defense Module** and **Task Reorganization Module**. The whole pipeline of our method is shown in Fig. 1. The adversarial defense module is designed for generating adversarial examples by Fast Gradient Sign Method (FGSM) [4], aiming at increasing the robustness of the trained

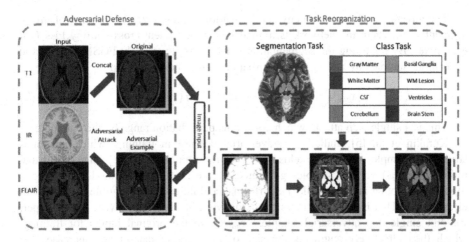

**Fig. 1.** Illustration of our proposed method. (1) Adversarial defense which combines adversarial examples with the original images to increase the robustness of model; (2) Task reorganization which reorganizes the multi-class segmentation task into several simple tasks following anatomical information. Moreover, it also reorganizes the single segmentation task into pixel-level segmentation and object-level classification tasks.

model (Sect. 2.1). For the task reorganization module, we first split the segmentation tasks of 8 ROIs (Fig. 1) into three groups based on the anatomical prior knowledge, such that all segmentation tasks can be solved from easy to hard (Sect. 2.2). Moreover, we incorporate an additional object-level classification task, which determines whether a certain ROI exists given a specific 2D slice. The object-level classification task is properly organized within the segmentation network, such that the pixel-level segmentation task benefits from the high-level semantic information learned in classification. Details of the task reorganization module are presented in Sect. 2.2.

## 2.1 Adversarial Defense

Adversarial attack causes a neural network to deviate from its correct prediction. An adversarial sample is often generated by modifying a real input very slightly, in order to fool a machine learning classifier toward misclassification. In many cases, these modifications can be so subtle that a human observer even cannot notice them at all. However, many existing machine learning classifiers are highly vulnerable to the attacks from adversarial samples. Considering an original input $x$, for a neural network $f$ parametrized by $\theta$ which maps the input $x$ to the output $y$, we can define an adversarial perturbation $r$ as follows:

$$r = \operatorname{argmin} |r|_2 \quad \text{s.t.} f(x+r; \theta) = y_t, \tag{1}$$

where $y_t$ is the target label of the adversarial sample $x_{adv} = x + r$ and thus differs from the label of the original input $x$.

The adversarial defense strategy can be naturally generalized to the case of image segmentation, where the network is trained with independent cross-entropy loss $L$ at each pixel. By regarding the segmentation network as $f$, we apply FGSM to generate adversarial samples by adding the perturbation $r$ into the input $x$ as:

$$x_{adv} = x + r = x + \epsilon \cdot \text{sign}(\nabla_x L(f(x; \theta), y)). \qquad (2)$$

This is a single-step attack, which constrains perturbation range by the parameter $\epsilon$.

Kurakin et al. [5] studied the adversarial defense in training, which generates adversarial samples online and adds them into the training set. They have found that training with adversarial samples generated by the single-step method can improve robustness to other attacks, while the performance difference is negligible if tested with clean inputs. That is, the robustness of the network has been improved. In this paper, we mix single-step adversarial samples ($x_{adv}$) with the original inputs for training, which then effectively augments the size of the training dataset and increases the robustness of our segmentation network.

## 2.2   Task Reorganization

**Splitting Segmentation Tasks from Easy to Hard.** In the task reorganization module, we first group different segmentation tasks corresponding to the 8 ROIs, which is the objective in the MRBrainS18 challenge. The ROI labels are presented in Fig. 1, where we design 3 individual classifiers to solve the segmentation from easy to hard. Specifically, we utilize the first classifier to segment the brain stem (*BS*), cerebellum (*C*) and cerebrospinal fluid (*CSF*), all of which occupy large portions in human brain. The first classifier also predicts the *locating* class (white region in Fig. 1) which merge the gray matter (*M*), white matter (*WM*), white matter lesions (*L*), basal ganglia (*B*), and ventricles (*V*) into one class. The cropped region of the input images based on the bounding box (yellow box in Fig. 1) which is obtained by the *locating* class is used as the input of the second classifier for *M, WM* and *L* segmentation. After the second classifier finishing the task, image region inside the other tissues, i.e., *B, V* which is obtained by the *locating* class in the second classifier is used as the input of the third network for *B* and *V* class segmentation. Here is our task reorganization module in object-level representation.

**Joint Learning of Pixel-Level Segmentation and Object-Level Classification.** Moreover, we aim to exploit the tasks of different semantic levels in the task reorganization module. While state-of-the-art segmentation methods often require large number of training data, it is possible to utilize the mutual dependency of the tasks of multiple semantic levels to ease the challenge faced by FCN for segmentation. Here, we propose two tasks, i.e., (1) pixel-wise image segmentation and (2) object-level classification which predicts the object classes within the image. These two sub-tasks are closely coupled, i.e., object-level classification is the high-level representation of pixel-wise image segmentation task.

For the high-level class tasks, we adopt the classification loss designed as:

$$L_{cla} = \sum_{x \in \Omega} \text{BCE}(C(x), \hat{C}(x)), \tag{3}$$

where BCE() is the binary cross entropy, $C$ and $\hat{C}$ are the ground-truth and estimated class labels for a single image $x \in \Omega$, and $\Omega$ is the training image set.

Moreover, we utilize a hybrid loss $L_{seg}$ to supervise the low-level segmentation task:

$$L_{seg} = \sum_{x \in \Omega} \text{CE}(Y(x), \hat{Y}(x)) + (1 - \text{Dice}(Y(x), \hat{Y}(x))), \tag{4}$$

where $\text{CE}(Y(x), \hat{Y}(x))$ is the cross entropy between the segmentation ground truth $Y$ and the estimated $\hat{Y}$ for a single image $x \in \Omega$, and $\Omega$ is the training image set. $\text{Dice}(Y(x), \hat{Y}(x))$ is the mean Dice score between $Y$ and $\hat{Y}$. The existence of a certain class in the image has strong correlation with the accuracy of pixel-wise segmentation task. So, the object-level classification task would have benefit for the segmentation task.

Both of object-level and semantic-level representations in task reorganization module could ease the difficulty of the main task by reorganizing the original task to several simple sub-tasks.

## 3   Experiments and Results

In this paper, we use MRBrainS18 challenge data to validate our method. The dataset has 21 subjects acquired on a 3T scanner at the UMC Utrecht (the Netherlands). Each subject contains fully annotated multi-sequence (T1-weighted, T1-weighted inversion recovery, and T2-FLAIR) scans. The subjects include patients with diabetes, dementia and Alzheimers, and matched controls (with increased cardiovascular risk) with varying degrees of atrophy and white matter lesions (age > 50). We use 7 subjects as our training and validation sets. Participants in this challenge were required to submit the segmentation results for onsite evaluation. The test data (14 subjects) were not released to the public. We utilized 5-fold cross-validation in hyper-parameters tuning. The network was trained and applied with a Titan X GPU on Tensorflow [8] and NiftyNet [9] platform.

### 3.1   The Role of Adversarial Defense

Table 1 shows the performance incurred by the adversarial defense module. First, we consider the single task of segmentation only ("*Base*"), derived from Cascaded Anisotropic Convolutional Neural Networks [10]. We also added the proposed semantic-level task reorganization ("*Class*") in this experiment. Then, we find mixing adversarial samples with the original dataset ("*Base + Class + Defense*") makes the network more robust to the clean inputs, compared with *("Base + Class")* model. In particular, we

**Table 1.** Comparisons of baseline with our proposed modules.

|  | Dice: % |
|---|---|
| *Evaluation of Adversarial Defense* | |
| Base + Class + Defense ($\epsilon$: 0.05) | 82.42 |
| Base + Class + Defense ($\epsilon$: 0.1) | 82.71 |
| Base + Class + Defense ($\epsilon$: 0.2) | 82.31 |
| *Evaluation of Task Reorganization* | |
| Base | 81.89 |
| Base + Class | 82.44 |
| Base + Class + Defense | 82.71 |
| **Base + Class + Defense + Coarse2Fine (Proposed)** | **83.12** |
| *Comparison with State-of-the-Art Methods* | |
| Unet [6] | 81.95 |
| Vnet [7] | 81.88 |
| **Base + Class + Defense + Coarse2Fine (Proposed)** | **83.12** |

tuned the parameters of $\epsilon$ in FGSM between 0.05 and 0.2. In both cases, the value of 0.1 shows greater performance, which is selected as the default parameter. Therefore, we conclude that the proposed adversarial defense module could improve the performance of model.

### 3.2   The Role of Task Reorganization

To validate the design of our framework with two levels of task reorganization representations, i.e., object-level (*"Coarse2Fine"*) and semantic-level (*"Class"*), we compare several different settings and report the results in Table 1. First, we consider the single task of segmentation only (*"Base"*). Second, we further verify the contribution of the proposed semantic-level task reorganization module. We add the class tasks (*"Class"*); the experimental results in the middle of Table 1 show that the semantic-level representation solution outperforms the single-task solution. Third, with the object-level representation (*"Coarse2Fine"*) added in the framework, the combination solution to semantic segmentation outperforms the (*"Base + Class + Defense"*) model. Therefore, we conclude that the proposed task reorganization module is beneficial to the segmentation task.

### 3.3   Comparison to State-of-the-Art Methods

Finally, we compare our proposed method with other state-of-the-art algorithms (Unet and Vnet) in Table 1. The results show that the proposed method outperforms all the methods under comparison in the validation set. We have also provided visual inspection of the typical segmentation results (Unet *vs.* our proposed method) with the ground truth in Fig. 2. The labeling result of the region inside the yellow box shows that, with the integration of our proposed module, the labeling accuracy of our model is improved.

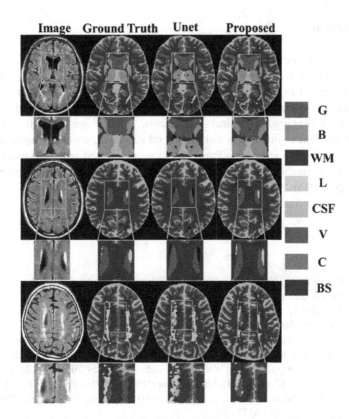

**Fig. 2.** Example segmentation results for MRBrainS18 by using the Unet and our proposed methods. Our proposed method produces significant accurate labels for the regions inside the yellow box. (Color figure online)

Furthermore, we compare our method with the winner solution to the MRBrainS18 challenge in Table 2. Though our method falls short of the top-two ranked teams, it is worth noting that our submission is indeed corresponding to the "*Base + Class*" model in Table 2. In this work, we have further substantially improved our method and achieved much better segmentation results, i.e., comparing "*Base + Class + Defense + Coarse2Fine*" to "*Base + Class*" in Table 1.

**Table 2.** Comparisons of the intermediate method result with other top-rank results submitted to on-site validation of MRBrainS18.

| Team | Dice: % | | | | | | | |
|---|---|---|---|---|---|---|---|---|
| | G | B | WM | L | CSF | V | C | BS |
| MISPL | 86.0 | 83.4 | 88.2 | 65.2 | 83.7 | 93.1 | 93.9 | 90.5 |
| K2 | 85.1 | 82.3 | 87.5 | 61.6 | 83.3 | 93.4 | 93.5 | 91.1 |
| "Base + Class" | 85.6 | 78.3 | **89.0** | 60.9 | **83.7** | 92.9 | **94.2** | **91.2** |

# 4  Conclusion

We have proposed an effective adversarial defense, task reorganization framework for semantic segmentation of brain MR image segmentation. Specifically, we proposed adversarial defense to penalize the noise and variance in small dataset for improving the robustness of network. Moreover, we reorganize multi-class segmentation to several sub-tasks following anatomical mechanism. Finally, we reorganize the very challenging semantic segmentation task to several sub-tasks, which are associated with low-level to high-level representations. We have conducted comprehensive experiments on popular medical image datasets. Our results are currently top-ranked in the challenge; specifically, we only addressed intermedia model (*"Base + Class"*) in the challenge.

# References

1. Dolz, J., Gopinath, K., Yuan, J., Lombaert, H., Desrosiers, C., Ayed, I.B.: HyperDense-Net: a hyper-densely connected CNN for multi-modal image segmentation (2018)
2. Roulet, N., Slezak, D.F., Ferrante, E.: Joint learning of brain lesion and anatomy segmentation from heterogeneous datasets (2019)
3. Wang, G., Li, W., Ourselin, S., Vercauteren, T.: Automatic brain tumor segmentation using convolutional neural networks with test-time augmentation. In: Crimi, A., Bakas, S., Kuijf, H., Keyvan, F., Reyes, M., van Walsum, T. (eds.) BrainLes 2018. LNCS, vol. 11384, pp. 61–72. Springer, Cham (2019). https://doi.org/10.1007/978-3-030-11726-9_6
4. Goodfellow, I.J., Shlens, J., Szegedy, C.: Explaining and harnessing adversarial examples. arXiv preprint arXiv:1412.6572 (2014)
5. Kurakin, A., Goodfellow, I., Bengio, S.: Adversarial machine learning at scale. arXiv preprint arXiv:1611.01236 (2016)
6. Çiçek, Ö., Abdulkadir, A., Lienkamp, S.S., Brox, T., Ronneberger, O.: 3D U-net: learning dense volumetric segmentation from sparse annotation. In: Ourselin, S., Joskowicz, L., Sabuncu, M.R., Unal, G., Wells, W. (eds.) MICCAI 2016. LNCS, vol. 9901, pp. 424–432. Springer, Cham (2016). https://doi.org/10.1007/978-3-319-46723-8_49
7. Milletari, F., Navab, N., Ahmadi, S.-A.: V-net: fully convolutional neural networks for volumetric medical image segmentation. In: 2016 Fourth International Conference on 3D Vision (3DV), pp. 565–571. IEEE (2016)
8. Abadi, M., et al.: TensorFlow: large-scale machine learning on heterogeneous distributed systems. arXiv preprint arXiv:1603.04467 (2016)
9. Gibson, E., et al.: NiftyNet: a deep-learning platform for medical imaging. Comput. Methods Programs Biomed. **158**, 113–122 (2018)
10. Wang, G., Li, W., Ourselin, S., Vercauteren, T.: Automatic brain tumor segmentation using cascaded anisotropic convolutional neural networks. In: Crimi, A., Bakas, S., Kuijf, H., Menze, B., Reyes, M. (eds.) BrainLes 2017. LNCS, vol. 10670, pp. 178–190. Springer, Cham (2018). https://doi.org/10.1007/978-3-319-75238-9_16

# Spatial Regularized Classification Network for Spinal Dislocation Diagnosis

Bolin Lai[1], Shiqi Peng[1], Guangyu Yao[2], Ya Zhang[1($\boxtimes$)], Xiaoyun Zhang[1],
Yanfeng Wang[1], and Hui Zhao[2]

[1] Cooperative Medianet Innovation Center, Shanghai Jiao Tong University,
Shanghai, China
ya_zhang@sjtu.edu.cn
[2] Department of Internal Oncology, Shanghai Sixth People's Hospital Affiliated
to Shanghai Jiaotong University, Shanghai, China

**Abstract.** Spinal dislocation diagnosis manifests typical characteristics
of fine-grained visual categorization tasks, i.e. low inter-class variance and
high intra-class variance. A pure data-driven approach towards an automated spinal dislocation diagnosis method would demand not only large
volume of training data but also fine-grained labels, which is impracti-
cal in medial scenarios. In this paper, we attempt to utilize the expert
knowledge that the spinal edges are crucial for dislocation diagnosis to
guide model training and explore a data-knowledge dual driven approach
for spinal dislocation diagnosis. Specifically, to embed the expert knowledge into the classification networks, we introduce a spatial regularization
term to constrain the location of the discriminative regions of spinal CT
images. Extensive experimental analysis has shown that the proposed
method gains 0.18%–4.79% upon AUC, and the gain is more significant
for smaller training sets. What's more, the spatial regularization brings
more discriminative and interpretable features.

**Keywords:** Spinal dislocation · Knowledge embedding · Spatial
regularization · Class activation maps

## 1 Introduction

Spinal dislocation is a serious disease and one of the common causes of paraple-
gia. The routine diagnosis of spinal dislocation requires evaluation of computed
tomography (CT) or magnetic resonance images (MRI) scans by radiologists.
However, dislocation usually occupies only a small local region of the entire
spine, leading to subtle visual differences between spines with and without dislocation, i.e. low inter-class variance. On the other hand, there is large variance in

---

**Electronic supplementary material** The online version of this chapter (https://
doi.org/10.1007/978-3-030-32692-0_2) contains supplementary material, which is available to authorized users.

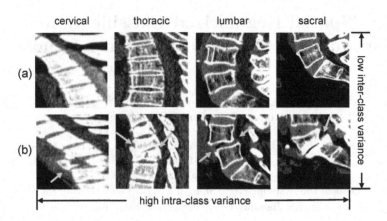

**Fig. 1.** Examples of spines (a) with dislocation and (b) without dislocation. Yellow arrows indicate the dislocation regions. (Color figure online)

appearance among different regions of spines such as cervical, thoracic, lumbar and sacral spines. Spinal dislocation diagnosis thus manifests characteristics of fine-grained visual categorization tasks. See Fig. 1 for an illustration.

Deep learning, succeeding in a wide spectrum of computer vision applications, has increasingly become the methodology choice of medical image analysis. With regard to spine analysis, convolutional neural networks have been designed for vertebral segmentation [10], vertebral localization [6], spinal fracture recognition [8], and scoliosis diagnosis [13]. To our best knowledge, there is no study on spinal dislocation so far.

In this paper, we seek a data-knowledge dual driven approach for spinal dislocation diagnosis. A pure data driven approach requires no feature engineering but demands significant amounts of labeled training data, which are prohibitive to collect in the medical domain. A pure knowledge driven approach provides interpretable results but requires a thoughtful set of complex rules and carefully handcrafted image features, which are often infeasible to obtain. A dual-driven approach is expected to have the advantages of both approaches, *i.e.* no feature engineering, less training data, and interpretable results. A close example is that sizes of cancerous regions have been successfully injected as prior knowledge for cancer region segmentation [4]. Regarding to spinal dislocation, a well trained radiologist makes the judgement mainly based on the shape and alignment of front and rear edges along a spine. We thus propose to incorporate the above expert knowledge into a classification network through a specifically designed spatial regularization term. The embedded knowledge is expected to guide the classification network to learn more discriminative and interpretable features for spinal dislocation.

We evaluate the proposed method on a dataset of spinal dislocation with 168 patients. We experiment with three well developed classification networks for natural images, AlexNet [5], Vgg [12], and ResNet [2], and demonstrate results

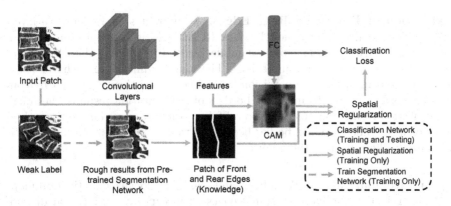

**Fig. 2.** The architecture of the proposed network. The expert knowledge is embedded as a spatial regularization (orange arrows) into the classification network (blue arrows) through CAM [11]. (Color figure online)

in Sect. 3 and supplemental material. The experimental results show that our method improves the AUC by 0.18%–4.79% than the original networks. We also show that our method has more gain when only smaller amount of training data is available. What's more important is that the discriminative location is more consistent with human interpretable visualization.

## 2  Spatial Regularized Classification Network

For the spinal dislocation diagnosis task, we utilize the middle sagittal view of CT volume images because doctors usually make decisions based on that view. Considering the fine-grained visual categorization nature of the task, to model it as a typical classification problem, patches covering at least 3 vertebrae are cropped from the sagittal images according to the rough segmentation results and the corresponding patch labels are inferred from the slice labels. In this way, we turn the task of spinal dislocation diagnosis to patch classification.

Figure 2 illustrates the architecture of the proposed spinal dislocation patch classification network. Its backbone could be any arbitrary convolutional neural network such as AlexNet [5], Vgg [12] and ResNet [2]. First of all, a coarse segmentation network is trained with weak labels (four corner landmarks) and employed to capture the expert knowledge in the form of front and rear edges. Then, to incorporate the knowledge about the spinal edges into the backbone classification network, we introduce a spatial regularization term to constrain the location of discriminative regions of images. Following previous studies, we employ Class Activation Map (CAM) [11] to indicate the discriminative regions of a particular category. The spatial regularization will guide the classification network so that the discriminative features learned will be close to the front and rear edges of spine and provide interpretable features for spinal dislocation.

**Extraction of Front and Rear Edges.** To extract spinal edges, we leverage previous well designed model, Mask RCNN [1], as segmentation network and train it with only four corner landmarks of 10% training data instead of time-consuming pixel-wise annotations. The four landmarks of each vertebrae are connected in order as supervision. Spinal edges are then extracted by connecting pixels on the left and right borders of segmentation results. The rough segmentation results may include several false positive regions on inter-vertebral disks or miss some vertebral bodies because of weak labels. But our approach is validated to be robust to these noise.

**Spatial Regularization.** With front and rear edges localized, activation maps are constrained to be close to spinal edges to incorporate dislocation diagnosis knowledge. Thus a spatial regularization term is designed based on common pixel-wise cross-entropy loss between the spinal edge patches and activation maps as demonstrated in Fig. 2. The spinal edge patch is a binary mask with '1' denoting pixels on spinal edges and '0' denoting pixels out of edges. The activation map can be regarded as a probability distribution with each value between 0 and 1. Let $p_{i,j}$ and $e_{i,j}$ denote the activation map and spinal edge patch, respectively. Spatial regularization can be written as

$$\mathcal{R}_{spatial} = -\left[ \frac{\sum_{i,j \in S_1} e_{i,j} \log p_{i,j}}{\sum_{i,j} e_{i,j}} + \frac{\sum_{i,j \in S_2} (1 - e_{i,j}) \log (1 - p_{i,j})}{\sum_{i,j} (1 - e_{i,j})} \right], \quad (1)$$

where $S_1$ denotes areas whose values are smaller than threshold $T$ on activation maps and $S_2$ denotes those whose values are larger than $T$, i.e. $S_1 = \{(i,j)|p_{i,j} < T\}$ and $S_2 = \{(i,j)|p_{i,j} > T\}$. In Eq. (1), the first term constrains regions on spinal edges and the second term constrains those out of edges. $S_1$ and $S_2$ are used seperately in the first term and second term. Threshold $T$ weakens the constraint of cross-entropy loss and makes the regularization more appropriate for the rough localization of edges. If $T$ equals 1, only the first term in Eq. 1 is effective because the probability is always between 0 and 1. Similarly, only the second term works if $T$ equals 0. Consequently, $T$ controls the degree of constraint of the two terms. Experiments in Sect. 3.2 indicate that, compared with standard cross-entropy regularization, our designed regularization brings 1.43% gains on AUC. Thus the classification loss of our method is

$$\mathcal{L}_{classification} = \mathcal{L}_{BCE} + \lambda \mathcal{R}_{spatial}, \quad (2)$$

where $\mathcal{L}_{BCE}$ is a standard binary cross-entropy loss and $\lambda$ is a balance factor set to control the contributions of the two terms.

## 3   Experiments

### 3.1   Dataset and Implementation Details

To our best knowledge, there is no public dataset for spinal dislocation. We collected a dataset consisting of 104 patients' CT images with spinal dislocation and

**Table 1.** Classification results of ResNet18, AG-ResNet18 and SR-ResNet18 trained with a quarter, a half and a full amount of training data, respectively.

| Model | Data size | SP (%) | SE (%) | AUC (%) |
|---|---|---|---|---|
| ResNet18 [2] | Quarter | **86.47 ± 4.59** | 81.63 ± 7.54 | 86.88 ± 4.14 |
| AG-ResNet18 [9] | | 86.26 ± 4.62 | 82.47 ± 5.92 | 87.90 ± 4.25 |
| SR-ResNet18 (Ours) | | 84.05 ± 4.13 | **87.69 ± 3.57** | **89.46 ± 3.11** |
| ResNet18 [2] | Half | **90.48 ± 4.82** | 88.29 ± 4.42 | 92.27 ± 2.52 |
| AG-ResNet18 [9] | | 87.60 ± 5.02 | 89.71 ± 4.72 | 92.61 ± 3.18 |
| SR-ResNet18 (Ours) | | 89.59 ± 4.15 | **90.40 ± 3.84** | **93.54 ± 2.28** |
| ResNet18 [2] | Full | 92.35 ± 4.32 | 93.33 ± 3.47 | 95.15 ± 1.83 |
| AG-ResNet18 [9] | | **92.46 ± 3.75** | 92.01 ± 2.27 | 95.34 ± 1.45 |
| SR-ResNet18 (Ours) | | 92.14 ± 3.14 | **94.48 ± 1.64** | **95.88 ± 1.49** |

64 patients' CT images without this disease. Labels of each image include image-level label and slices where the dislocation occurs. All images are annotated and examined by senior radiologists with at least 10 years of experience.

In all experiments, Adam optimizer is used in training phase and initial learning rate is $10^{-4}$. A weighted binary cross-entropy loss is used to overcome the imbalance between two categories. If not specifically mentioned, $\lambda$ in Eq. (2) and $T$ in Eq. (1) are empirically set to be 0.1 and 0.5, respectively. Three metrics are used in the following experiments: Specificity (SP), Sensitivity (SE) and Area Under Curve (AUC). Because of the limited amounts of training and testing data, we evaluate the performance of different networks on extracted patches through 5-fold cross validation as described in Sect. 2. We choose ResNet18 [2] as main backbone network which has relatively fewer parameters. We also experiment with AlexNet [5], Vgg16 [12] and ResNet50 [2] and demonstrate results in the supplemental material.

## 3.2 Results and Analysis

In this section, experiments validate three advantages of our model: (1) medical knowledge helps to improve the performance of classification networks, (2) our proposed spatial regularized (SR) classification networks provide more explainable evidence and localize the discriminative regions for spinal dislocation and (3) our approach can maintain its superiority when the amount of training data is limited.

**Comparison with Basic and Self-attention Classification Models.** Our approach is compared with ResNet18 [2] and attention-gate (AG) [9]. Attention-gate is an application of self-attention module [3] on medical images. All models are trained with different amounts of training data. Table 1 presents the classification results of the three networks. As can be observed, SR-ResNet18 out-

**Table 2.** Classification results of models with spinal edges information incorporated.

| Model | Data size | SP (%) | SE (%) | AUC (%) |
|---|---|---|---|---|
| ResNet18 [2] w/o BG | Quarter | 87.45 ± 3.38 | 80.18 ± 6.42 | 87.04 ± 3.65 |
| AG-ResNet18 [9] w/o BG | | **87.90 ± 3.24** | 81.63 ± 7.41 | 87.17 ± 4.55 |
| Multi-Task [7] | | 85.65 ± 4.84 | 83.29 ± 7.27 | 88.39 ± 2.02 |
| SR-ResNet18 (Ours) | | 84.05 ± 4.13 | **87.69 ± 3.57** | **89.46 ± 3.11** |
| ResNet18 [2] w/o BG | Half | 87.04 ± 4.45 | 89.56 ± 6.22 | 91.90 ± 3.04 |
| AG-ResNet18 [9] w/o BG | | 88.59 ± 4.96 | 86.31 ± 5.55 | 90.80 ± 3.50 |
| Multi-Task [7] | | 89.49 ± 4.88 | 88.58 ± 3.25 | 92.71 ± 2.04 |
| SR-ResNet18 (Ours) | | **89.59 ± 4.15** | **90.40 ± 3.84** | **93.54 ± 2.28** |
| ResNet18 [2] w/o BG | Full | 92.38 ± 2.24 | 88.41 ± 4.85 | 93.49 ± 3.25 |
| AG-ResNet18 [9] w/o BG | | **93.04 ± 2.95** | 89.43 ± 6.63 | 93.59 ± 3.62 |
| Multi-Task [7] | | 92.17 ± 3.74 | 91.54 ± 1.12 | 94.39 ± 0.92 |
| SR-ResNet18 (Ours) | | 92.14 ± 3.14 | **94.48 ± 1.64** | **95.88 ± 1.49** |

performs ResNet18 and AG-ResNet18 upon the AUC, showing the benefits of spatial regularization over basic network and self-attention network.

More importantly, when a quarter, a half and a full amount of data are separately used for training, gains of SR-ResNet18 to ResNet18 are 2.58%, 1.27% and 0.73%, respectively, regarding the AUC. This is a reasonable discovery that medical knowledge makes more contributions when less training data is available. If more data is provided, supplemental data compensates the lack of knowledge to some degree. This is a highly desirable advantage since medical images are usually in small-scale size. Besides, SR-ResNet18 provides higher SE, while the SP is relatively lower, indicating positive samples are easier to recognize when the model focuses on spinal edges. Models with higher SE are more needed clinically because missed diagnosis is more serious than misdiagnosis.

The discriminative localization of our model also presents more interpretable evidence as illustrated in Fig. 3. Activation maps of SR-ResNet18 mainly highlight the front and rear edges of spine, which leads to better causality and is more consistent with the diagnosis evidence of doctors. The reasonable CAM of SR-ResNet18 with a quarter amount of data shows that our model still works as expected when less data is provided. Although ResNet18 sometimes can capture a small part of edge, it is still likely to focus on some irrelevant regions, such as vertebral bodies and accessory structures of spine. CAM of AG-ResNet18 is relatively more explainable than ResNet18. However, the discriminative regions that AG-ResNet localizes concentrate more on vertebral bodies instead of edges.

**Comparison with Different Ways to Utilize Spinal Edges.** Besides comparison with basic classification networks, we conduct experiments that also incorporate edge information as follows: (1) the extracted edges are utilized to remove the background as shown in the second column in Fig. 4 and these patches

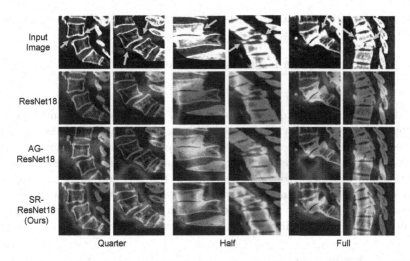

**Fig. 3.** Activation maps of ResNet18, AG-ResNet18 and SR-ResNet18. The yellow arrows on input image indicates the regions of dislocation. SR-ResNet18 provides better causality and more reasonable evidence than other networks. (Color figure online)

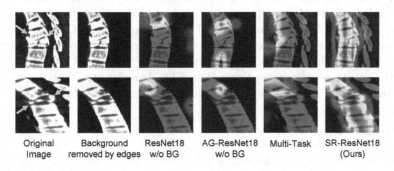

**Fig. 4.** Activation maps of models with spinal edge information incorporated. The second column show image whose background (BG) is removed by spinal edges.

without background (BG) are fed to ResNet18 [2] and AG-ResNet18 [9], and (2) the edge patches are inputted as segmentation annotations into a multi-task framework for simultaneous dislocation classification and edge segmentation. Y-Net [7] is adopted as multi-task framework in our experiments. By utilizing edge information, all experiments have the same input settings as our proposed method. The results are illustrated in Table 2.

We find that, with background removed, the AUC and SE of ResNet18 (ResNet18 w/o BG) and AG-ResNet18 (AG-ResNet18 w/o BG) are relatively lower in most cases compared with results in Table 1. The main reason is that the segmentation network is coarse due to weak annotations. This leads to some inaccurate localization of spinal edges. We can see that, in the second column in Fig. 4, some corners of spine may be cut out by the rough spinal edges, mak-

**Table 3.** AUC with different threshold values and cross-entropy (CE) regularization.

| T | 0 | 0.25 | 0.50 | 0.75 | 1.00 | CE |
|---|---|------|------|------|------|-----|
| AUC | 87.34 ± 4.40 | 87.56 ± 4.41 | **89.46 ± 3.11** | 88.88 ± 3.25 | 88.44 ± 3.78 | 88.03 ± 4.34 |

ing dislocation less discriminative. In contrast, both multi-task framework and our approach are trained with the original images and give higher AUC. Multi-task network mainly utilizes the potential correlation of classification and edge segmentation, while our approach explicitly regards spinal edges as spatial regularization and provides stronger supervision to the network. Thus the proposed SR-ResNet18 outperforms multi-task method, which validates that our approach is different from a simple multi-task framework. In Fig. 4, our approach also presents better visual findings and more explainable evidence.

**Influence of Different Hyper Parameters** In our model, a threshold $T$ is introduced into regularization term to cope with noise in edge localization and control the degree of two terms in Eq. 1. We show the AUC in Table 3 when $T$ takes different values. We also compare with standard cross-entropy (CE) regularization. All experiments are implemented with a quarter amount of training data. As illustrated, our method gives the highest AUC when $T$ equals 0.5. This indicates that the two terms in our spatial regularization reach the best balance at this point. AUC of our method when $T$ equals 0.5 is 1.43% higher than AUC of cross-entropy regularization. This demonstrates that threshold $T$ makes our method more robust to the rough localization of spinal edges.

## 4    Conclusion

In this paper, we develop a data-knowledge dual driven approach for spinal dislocation diagnosis. To incorporate the medical domain knowledge into classification networks, we design a spatial regularization term on class activation maps. Experiments show that the proposed method improves the performance upon AUC by 0.18%−4.79% with different backbone networks and the gain is more on smaller training sets. The incorporation of knowledge also provides activation maps with better interpretability.

## References

1. He, K., Gkioxari, G., Dollár, P., Girshick, R.: Mask R-CNN. In: Proceedings of the IEEE International Conference on Computer Vision, pp. 2961–2969 (2017)
2. He, K., Zhang, X., Ren, S., Sun, J.: Deep residual learning for image recognition. In: Proceedings of the IEEE Conference on Computer Vision and Pattern Recognition, pp. 770–778 (2016)
3. Jetley, S., Lord, N.A., Lee, N., Torr, P.: Learn to pay attention. In: International Conference on Learning Representations (2018). https://openreview.net/forum?id=HyzbhfWRW

4. Jia, Z., Huang, X., Eric, I., Chang, C., Xu, Y.: Constrained deep weak supervision for histopathology image segmentation. IEEE Trans. Med. Imaging **36**(11), 2376–2388 (2017)
5. Krizhevsky, A., Sutskever, I., Hinton, G.E.: ImageNet classification with deep convolutional neural networks. In: Advances in Neural Information Processing Systems, pp. 1097–1105 (2012)
6. Liao, H., Mesfin, A., Luo, J.: Joint vertebrae identification and localization in spinal CT images by combining short-and long-range contextual information. IEEE Trans. Med. Imaging **37**(5), 1266–1275 (2018)
7. Mehta, S., Mercan, E., Bartlett, J., Weaver, D., Elmore, J.G., Shapiro, L.: Y-Net: joint segmentation and classification for diagnosis of breast biopsy images. In: Frangi, A.F., Schnabel, J.A., Davatzikos, C., Alberola-López, C., Fichtinger, G. (eds.) MICCAI 2018. LNCS, vol. 11071, pp. 893–901. Springer, Cham (2018). https://doi.org/10.1007/978-3-030-00934-2_99
8. Roth, H.R., Wang, Y., Yao, J., Lu, L., Burns, J.E., Summers, R.M.: Deep convolutional networks for automated detection of posterior-element fractures on spine CT. In: Medical Imaging 2016: Computer-Aided Diagnosis, vol. 9785, p. 97850P. International Society for Optics and Photonics (2016)
9. Schlemper, J., et al.: Attention gated networks: learning to leverage salient regions in medical images. Med. Image Anal. **53**, 197–207 (2019)
10. Sekuboyina, A., et al.: Btrfly net: vertebrae labelling with energy-based adversarial learning of local spine prior. In: Frangi, A.F., Schnabel, J.A., Davatzikos, C., Alberola-López, C., Fichtinger, G. (eds.) MICCAI 2018. LNCS, vol. 11073, pp. 649–657. Springer, Cham (2018). https://doi.org/10.1007/978-3-030-00937-3_74
11. Selvaraju, R.R., Cogswell, M., Das, A., Vedantam, R., Parikh, D., Batra, D.: Grad-CAM: visual explanations from deep networks via gradient-based localization. In: Proceedings of the IEEE International Conference on Computer Vision, pp. 618–626 (2017)
12. Simonyan, K., Zisserman, A.: Very deep convolutional networks for large-scale image recognition. arXiv preprint arXiv:1409.1556 (2014)
13. Wu, H., Bailey, C., Rasoulinejad, P., Li, S.: Automatic landmark estimation for adolescent idiopathic scoliosis assessment using boostnet. In: Descoteaux, M., Maier-Hein, L., Franz, A., Jannin, P., Collins, D.L., Duchesne, S. (eds.) MICCAI 2017. LNCS, vol. 10433, pp. 127–135. Springer, Cham (2017). https://doi.org/10.1007/978-3-319-66182-7_15

# Globally-Aware Multiple Instance Classifier for Breast Cancer Screening

Yiqiu Shen[1]([⊠]), Nan Wu[1], Jason Phang[1], Jungkyu Park[1], Gene Kim[2],
Linda Moy[2], Kyunghyun Cho[1,3,4,5], and Krzysztof J. Geras[1,2]

[1] Center for Data Science, New York University, New York, USA
ys1001@nyu.edu
[2] Department of Radiology, New York University School of Medicine,
New York, USA
[3] Department of Computer Science, Courant Institute, New York University,
New York, USA
[4] Facebook AI Research, New York, USA
[5] CIFAR Azrieli Global Scholar, Toronto, Canada

**Abstract.** Deep learning models designed for visual classification tasks on natural images have become prevalent in medical image analysis. However, medical images differ from typical natural images in many ways, such as significantly higher resolutions and smaller regions of interest. Moreover, both the global structure and local details play important roles in medical image analysis tasks. To address these unique properties of medical images, we propose a neural network that is able to classify breast cancer lesions utilizing information from both a global saliency map and multiple local patches. The proposed model outperforms the ResNet-based baseline and achieves radiologist-level performance in the interpretation of screening mammography. Although our model is trained only with image-level labels, it is able to generate pixel-level saliency maps that provide localization of possible malignant findings.

**Keywords:** Deep learning · Neural networks · Breast cancer screening · Weakly supervised localization · High-resolution image classification

## 1 Introduction

As the second leading cause of cancer death among women in the US, breast cancer has been studied for decades. While studies have shown screening mammography has significantly reduced breast cancer mortality, it is an imperfect tool [8]. To address its limitations, convolutional neural networks (CNN) designed for computer vision tasks on natural images have been applied. For instance, VGGNet [11], designed for object classification on ImageNet [2], has been applied to breast density classification [13] and Faster R-CNN [9] has been adapted to localize suspicious findings in mammograms [10]. We refer the readers to [5] for a comprehensive review of prior work on machine learning for mammography.

© Springer Nature Switzerland AG 2019
H.-I. Suk et al. (Eds.): MLMI 2019, LNCS 11861, pp. 18–26, 2019.
https://doi.org/10.1007/978-3-030-32692-0_3

The compatibility between the models designed for natural images and the distinct properties of medical images remains an open question. Firstly, medical images are usually of a much higher resolution than typical natural images, so deep CNNs that work well for natural images may not be applicable to medical images due to GPU memory constraints. Moreover, for many applications, regions of interest (ROI) in medical images, such as lesions and calcifications, are proportionally smaller in size compared to those in natural images. Fine details, often only a few pixels in size, along with global features such as the spatial distribution of radiodense tissue determine the labels. In addition, while natural images can be aggressively downsampled and preserve the information necessary for classification, significant amounts of information could be lost from downsampling medical images, making the correct diagnosis unattainable.

**Contributions.** In this work, we address the aforementioned issues by proposing a novel model for the classification of medical images. The proposed model preserves global information in a saliency map and aggregates important details with a Multiple Instance Learning (MIL) framework. Unlike existing approaches that rely on pixel-level lesion annotations [10,14], our model only requires image-level supervision and is able to generate pixel-level saliency maps that highlight suspicious lesions. In addition, our model is equipped with an attention mechanism that enables it to select informative image patches, making the classification process interpretable. When trained and evaluated on more than 1 million high-resolution breast cancer screening exams, our model outperforms a ResNet-based baseline [14] and achieves radiologist-level performance.

**Related Works.** Existing methods have approached the breast cancer detection problem using techniques such as MIL [16] and 3D CNNs [12]. Our model is inspired by works on weakly supervised object detection. Recent progress demonstrates that CNN classifiers, trained with image-level labels, are able to perform semantic segmentation at the pixel level [3,4,15]. This is achieved in two steps. First, a backbone CNN converts the input image to a saliency map (SM) which highlights the discriminative regions. A global pooling operator then collapses the SM into scalar predictions which makes the entire model trainable end-to-end. To make an image-level prediction, most existing models rely on the SM which often neglects fine-grained details. In contrast, our model also leverages local information from ROI proposals using a dedicated patch-level classifier. In Sect. 3.2, we demonstrate that the ability to focus on fine visual detail is important for classification.

## 2    Methods

We formulate our task as a multi-label classification. Given a grayscale high-resolution image $\mathbf{x} \in \mathbb{R}^{H,W}$, we would like to predict the label $\mathbf{y}$, where $y^c$ denotes whether class $c \in \mathbb{C}$ is present. As shown in Fig. 1, the Globally-Aware Multiple Instance Classifier (GMIC) consists of three modules: (i) The localization module processes $\mathbf{x}$ to generate a SM, denoted by $\mathbf{A}$, which indicates

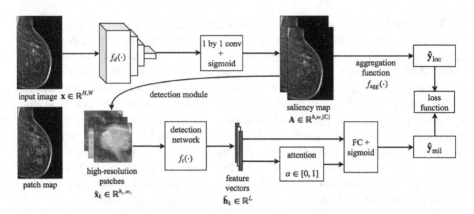

**Fig. 1.** Overall architecture of GMIC. The input image is annotated with true ROIs (red). The patch map indicates positions of ROI patches (blue squares) on the input. (Color figure online)

approximate localizations of ROIs. (ii) The detection module uses $\mathbf{A}$ to retrieve $K$ patches from $\mathbf{x}$ as refined proposals for ROIs. (iii) We use an MIL framework to aggregate information from retrieved patches and generate the final prediction.

## 2.1  Localization Module

As illustrated in Fig. 1, the localization module first uses a CNN $f_d(\cdot)$ to extract relevant features from $\mathbf{x}$. Due to memory constraints, input images are usually down-sampled before $f_d(\cdot)$ [15]. For mammograms, however, down-sampling distorts important visual details such as lesion margins and blurs small ROIs. In order to retain the original resolution, we parameterize $f_d(\cdot)$ as a ResNet-22 [14] and remove its global average pooling and fully connected layers. This model has fewer filters than the original ResNet architectures in each layer in order to process the image at the full resolution while keeping GPU memory consumption manageable. The feature maps obtained after the last residual block are transformed into the SM $\mathbf{A} \in \mathbb{R}^{h,w,|\mathbb{C}|}$ using $1 \times 1$ convolution with sigmoid non-linearity. Each element of $\mathbf{A}$, $\mathbf{A}_{i,j}^c \in [0,1]$, denotes a score that indicates the contribution of spatial location $(i,j)$ towards classifying the input as class $c$.

## 2.2  Detection Module

Due to its limited width, $f_d(\cdot)$ is only able to provide coarse localization. We propose using patches as ROI proposals to complement the localization module with fine-grained detail. We designed a greedy algorithm (Algorithm 1) to retrieve $K$ proposals for ROIs, $\tilde{\mathbf{x}}_k \in \mathbb{R}^{h_c,w_c}$, from the input $\mathbf{x}$. In our experiments, we set $K = 6$, and $w_c = h_c = 256$. The reset rule in line 12 explicitly ensures that extracted ROI proposals do not significantly overlap with each other.

---

**Algorithm 1.** Retrieve the ROIs

| | |
|---|---|
| **Require:** $\mathbf{x} \in \mathbb{R}^{H,W}$, $\mathbf{A} \in \mathbb{R}^{h,w,|\mathbb{C}|}$, $K$ | 7:  $f_c(l, \hat{\mathbf{A}}) = \sum_{(i,j) \in l} \hat{\mathbf{A}}[i,j]$ |
| **Ensure:** $O = \{\tilde{\mathbf{x}}_k | \tilde{\mathbf{x}}_k \in \mathbb{R}^{h_c, w_c}\}$ | 8:  **for** each $1, 2, ..., K$ **do** |
| 1:  $O = \emptyset$ | 9:      $l^* = \text{argmax}_l \, f_c(l, \hat{\mathbf{A}})$ |
| 2:  **for** each class $c \in \mathbb{C}$ **do** | 10:     $L = $ position of $l^*$ in $\mathbf{x}$ |
| 3:      $\tilde{\mathbf{A}}^c = \text{min-max-normalization}(\mathbf{A}^c)$ | 11:     $O = O \cup \{L\}$ |
| 4:  **end for** | 12:     $\hat{\mathbf{A}}[i,j] = 0, \forall (i,j) \in l^*$ |
| 5:  $\hat{\mathbf{A}} = \sum_{c \in \mathbb{C}} \tilde{\mathbf{A}}^c$ | 13: **end for** |
| 6:  $l$ denotes an arbitrary $h_c \frac{h}{H} \times w_c \frac{w}{W}$ rectangular patch on $\hat{\mathbf{A}}$ | 14: **return** $O$ |

---

## 2.3   Multiple Instance Learning Module

Since ROI patches are retrieved using a coarse saliency map, the information relevant for classification carried in each patch varies significantly. To address this, we apply an MIL framework to aggregate information from ROI patches. A detection network $f_t(\cdot)$ is first applied on every instance $\tilde{\mathbf{x}}_k$ and converts them into feature vectors $\tilde{\mathbf{h}}_k \in \mathbb{R}^L$. We use $L = 128$ in all experiments. We parameterize $f_t(\cdot)$ as a ResNet-18 (pretrained on ImageNet [2]). Since not all ROI patches are relevant to the prediction, we use the Gated Attention Mechanism proposed in [6] to let the model select informative patches. The selection process yields an attention-weighted representation $\mathbf{z} = \sum_{k=1}^{K} \alpha_k \tilde{\mathbf{h}}_k$, where attention score $\alpha_k \in [0,1]$ indicates the relevance of each patch $\tilde{\mathbf{x}}_k$. The representation $\mathbf{z}$ is then passed to a fully connected layer with sigmoid activation to generate a prediction $\hat{\mathbf{y}}_{\text{mil}} = \text{sigm}(\mathbf{w}_{\text{mil}}^T \mathbf{z})$, where $\mathbf{w}_{\text{mil}} \in \mathbb{R}^{L \times |\mathbb{C}|}$ are learnable parameters.

## 2.4   Training

It is difficult to make this model trainable end-to-end. Since the detection module is not differentiable, the gradient from the training loss $L(\mathbf{y}, \hat{\mathbf{y}}_{\text{mil}})$ will not flow into the localization module. Inspired by [3], we circumvent this problem with a scheme that simultaneously trains the localization module and the MIL module. An aggregation function $f_{\text{agg}}(\mathbf{A}^c) : \mathbb{R}^{h,w} \mapsto [0,1]$ is designed to map the SM for each class $c$ into a prediction $\hat{\mathbf{y}}_{\text{loc}}^c$. The design of $f_{\text{agg}}(\mathbf{A}^c)$ has been extensively studied [4]. Global Average Pooling (GAP) would dilute the prediction as most of the spatial locations in $\mathbf{A}^c$ correspond to background and provide little training signal. On the other hand, Global Max Pooling (GMP) only backpropagates gradient into a single spatial location which makes the learning process slow and unstable. In our work, we use a soft balance between GAP and GMP : $f_{\text{agg}}(\mathbf{A}^c) = \frac{1}{|H^+|} \sum_{(i,j) \in H^+} \mathbf{A}_{i,j}^c$, where $H^+$ denotes the set containing locations of top $t\%$ values in $\mathbf{A}^c$, and $t$ is a hyper-parameter. The prediction $\hat{\mathbf{y}}_{\text{loc}}^c = f_{\text{agg}}(\mathbf{A}^c)$ is a valid probability as $\mathbf{A}_{i,j}^c \in [0,1]$. To fine-tune the SM and prevent the localization module from highlighting irrelevant areas, we impose the following regularization on $\mathbf{A}^c$: $L_{\text{reg}}(\mathbf{A}^c) = \sum_{(i,j)} |\mathbf{A}_{i,j}^c|^\beta$, where $\beta$ is a hyper-parameter. In summary, the loss function used to train the entire model is:

$$L(\mathbf{y}, \hat{\mathbf{y}}) = \sum_{c \in \mathbb{C}} \text{BCE}(\mathbf{y}^c, \hat{\mathbf{y}}_{\text{loc}}^c) + \text{BCE}(\mathbf{y}^c, \hat{\mathbf{y}}_{\text{mil}}^c) + \lambda L_{\text{reg}}(\mathbf{A}^c), \qquad (1)$$

where $\text{BCE}(\cdot, \cdot)$ is the binary cross-entropy and $\lambda$ is a hyper-parameter. In the inference stage, the prediction is computed as $\hat{\mathbf{y}} = \frac{1}{2}(\hat{\mathbf{y}}_{\text{mil}} + \hat{\mathbf{y}}_{\text{loc}})$.

## 3   Experiments

The proposed model is evaluated on the task of predicting whether any benign or malignant findings are present in a mammography exam. The dataset includes 229,426 exams (1,001,093 images). Across the entire data set, malignant findings were present in 985 breasts and benign findings in 5,556 breasts. As shown in Fig. 2, each exam contains four grayscale images (2944 × 1920) representing two standard views (CC and MLO) for both left and right breasts. A label $\mathbf{y} \in \{0,1\}^2$ is associated with each breast where $y_c \in \{0,1\}$ ($c \in \{\text{benign, malignant}\}$) denotes the presence or absence of a benign/malignant finding in a breast. All findings are confirmed by a biopsy. In each exam, two views on the same breast share the same label. A small fraction (<1%) of the data are associated with pixel-level segmentation $\mathbf{M}^c \in \{0,1\}^{H \times W}$ where $\mathbf{M}_{i,j}^c = 1$ if pixel $i, j$ belongs to the findings of class $c$. In all experiments, segmentations are only used for evaluation.

### 3.1   Experimental Set-up and Evaluation Metrics

We adopt the same pre-processing as [14]. The dataset is divided into disjoint training (186,816), validation (28,462) and test (14,148) sets. In each iteration, we train the model using all exams that contain at least one benign or malignant finding and an equal number of randomly sampled negative exams. All images are cropped to 2944 × 1920 pixels and normalized. The training loss is optimized using Adam [7]. We optimize the hyper-parameters using random search [1]. Specifically, we search on a loga-rithmic scale for the learning rate $\eta \in 10^{[-5.5, -3.8]}$, the regularization weight $\lambda \in 10^{[-5, -2.8]}$, the regu-larization exponent $\beta \in e^{[-1.6, 1.6]}$, and the pooling threshold $t \in e^{[-5, -1.5]}$. We train 100 separate mod-els, each for 40 epochs.

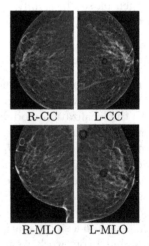

R-CC          L-CC

R-MLO        L-MLO

**Fig. 2.** Example exam for a patient. Benign findings are highlighted in green. (Color figure online)

For classification performance, we report the area under the ROC curve (AUC) on the breast-level. As our model generates a prediction for each image and each breast is associated with two images (CC and MLO), we define breast-level predictions as the average of the two image-level predictions. To quantitatively evaluate our model's localization ability, we use the continuous F1 score, where precision (P) and recall (R) are defined as: $P = (\sum_{i,j \in \mathbf{M}^c} \mathbf{A}_{i,j}^c)/(\sum_{i,j} \mathbf{A}_{i,j}^c)$ and $R = (\sum_{i,j \in \mathbf{M}^c} \mathbf{A}_{i,j}^c)/|\mathbf{M}^c|$, and $\mathbf{M}^c$ denotes the segmentation label and $\mathbf{A}^c$ is the SM for class $c$. On the test set, these metrics are averaged over images for which segmentation labels are available.

**Table 1.** AUCs of the baseline model and a few variations of GMIC

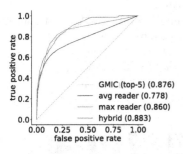

**Fig. 3.** Reader study

| Model | Malignant | Benign |
|-------|-----------|--------|
| ResNet-22 [14] | 0.827 | 0.731 |
| GMIC-loc | 0.885 | 0.777 |
| GMIC-mil | 0.878 | 0.766 |
| GMIC-noattn | 0.823 | 0.726 |
| GMIC-random | 0.757 | 0.692 |
| GMIC-loc-random | 0.889 | 0.776 |
| GMIC | **0.900** | **0.784** |

## 3.2 Classification Performance

In this section, we report the average test performance of the 5 models from the hyper-parameter search that achieved the highest validation AUC on malignant classification (referred to as *top-5*). In order to understand the impact of each module, we evaluate GMIC under a number of settings. GMIC-loc uses $\hat{y}_{loc}$ as its predictions and GMIC-mil uses $\hat{y}_{mil}$. As shown in Table 1, both variants of GMIC outperform the baseline, especially in predicting malignancy. The full model, GMIC, using the aggregated prediction $\hat{y} = \frac{\hat{y}_{loc} + \hat{y}_{mil}}{2}$, attains higher AUC than GMIC-loc and GMIC-mil. We attribute this improvement to the synergy of local and global information. To empirically validate this conjecture, we test three additional models: GMIC-noattn assigns equal attentions on each ROI patch; GMIC-random outputs prediction $\hat{y}_{random}$ by applying MIL module on patches randomly selected from the input image; GMIC-loc-random combines the predictions from GMIC-loc and GMIC-random $\hat{y} = \frac{\hat{y}_{loc} + \hat{y}_{random}}{2}$. As Table 1 shows, GMIC-noattn is less accurate than GMIC-mil, suggesting that the attention mechanism in MIL module is essential for classification. Moreover, GMIC-random is weaker than GMIC-mil and GMIC-loc-random does not demonstrate any performance gain on top of GMIC-loc. These observations confirm our hypothesis that applying the MIL module on high-resolution ROI patches supplements the global information extracted by SM and refines predictions.

To evaluate the clinical value of our model, we compare the performance of GMIC with radiologists using data from the reader study described in [14].

This reader study includes 14 radiologists, each providing a probability estimate of malignancy for 720 screening exams (1440 breasts). The radiologists were only shown images for each exam with no other data. To further improve our predictions, we ensemble the predictions of the *top-5* models. As shown in Fig. 3, the ensemble GMIC model achieves higher AUC (0.876) than the average (0.778) and the most accurate (0.860) among the 14 readers. GMIC obtains a marginally worse performance in the reader study than in the test set because the reader study contains a much larger portion of positive samples.

We also assess the efficacy of a human-machine hybrid, whose predictions are simply the average of predictions from the radiologists and the model. The human-machine hybrid achieves an AUC of 0.883. These results suggest that our model captures different aspects of the task compared to radiologists and can be used as a tool to assist in interpreting breast cancer screening exams.

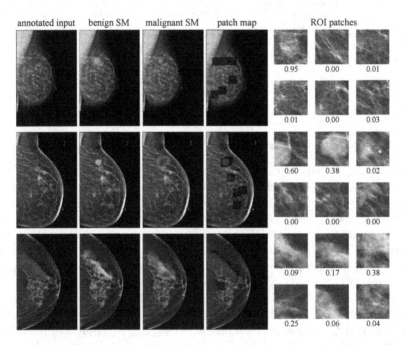

**Fig. 4.** Visualization of three examples. Input images are annotated with segmentation labels (green=benign, red=malignant). ROI patches are shown with their attention scores. (Color figure online)

### 3.3  Localization Performance

We select the model with the highest validation F1 for malignancy localization. At the inference stage, we upsample SMs using nearest neighbour interpolation to match the resolution of the segmentation labels. The average continuous F1/precision/recall on test set is 0.207/0.288/0.254 for malignant and

0.133/0.135/0.224 for benign. In addition, the best localization model also achieves a classification AUC of 0.886/0.78 for malignant/benign classes.

To better understand our model's behavior, we visualize SMs of three samples selected from the test set in Fig. 4. In the first two examples, the SMs are highly activated on the true lesions, suggesting that our model is able to detect suspicious lesions without pixel-level supervision. Moreover, the attention $\alpha_k$ is highly concentrated on ROI patches that overlap with the annotated lesions. In the third example, the malignant SM only highlights parts of a large malignant lesion. This behavior is related to the design of $f_{\text{agg}}$: a fixed pooling threshold $t$ cannot be optimal for all sizes of ROI. Furthermore, this observation also illustrates that while human experts are asked to annotate the entire lesion, CNNs tend to emphasize only the most informative part.

## 4  Conclusion

We present a novel model for breast cancer screening exam classification. The proposed method uses the input in its original resolution while being able to focus on fine details. Moreover, our model also generates saliency maps that provide additional interpretability. Evaluated on a large mammography dataset, GMIC outperforms the ResNet-based baseline and generates predictions that are as accurate as radiologists. Given its generic design, the proposed model is widely applicable to other image classification tasks. Our future research will focus on designing joint training mechanisms that would enable GMIC to improve its localization using error signals from the MIL module.

## References

1. Bergstra, J., Bengio, Y.: Random search for hyper-parameter optimization. J. Mach. Learn. Res. **13**(Feb), 281–305 (2012)
2. Deng, J., Dong, W., Socher, R., Li, L.J., Li, K., Fei-Fei, L.: ImageNet: a large-scale hierarchical image database. In: CVPR 2009 (2009)
3. Diba, A., Sharma, V., Pazandeh, A.M., Pirsiavash, H., Van Gool, L.: Weakly supervised cascaded convolutional networks. In: CVPR (2017)
4. Durand, T., Mordan, T., Thome, N., Cord, M.: Wildcat: weakly supervised learning of deep convnets for image classification, pointwise localization and segmentation. In: CVPR (2017)
5. Gao, Y., Geras, K.J., Lewin, A.A., Moy, L.: New frontiers: an update on computer-aided diagnosis for breast imaging in the age of artificial intelligence. Am. J. Roentgenol. **212**(2), 300–307 (2019)
6. Ilse, M., Tomczak, J.M., Welling, M.: Attention-based deep multiple instance learning. arXiv:1802.04712 (2018)
7. Kingma, D., Ba, J.: Adam: a method for stochastic optimization. In: ICLR (2015)
8. Kopans, D.B.: Beyond randomized controlled trials: organized mammographic screening substantially reduces breast carcinoma mortality. Cancer **94**(2), 580–581 (2002)
9. Ren, S., He, K., Girshick, R., Sun, J.: Faster R-CNN: towards real-time object detection with region proposal networks. In: NIPS (2015)

10. Ribli, D., Horváth, A., Unger, Z., Pollner, P., Csabai, I.: Detecting and classifying lesions in mammograms with deep learning. Sci. Rep. **8**(1), 4165 (2018)
11. Simonyan, K., Zisserman, A.: Very deep convolutional networks for large-scale image recognition. arXiv:1409.1556 (2014)
12. Wang, N., et al.: Densely deep supervised networks with threshold loss for cancer detection in automated breast ultrasound. In: Frangi, A.F., Schnabel, J.A., Davatzikos, C., Alberola-López, C., Fichtinger, G. (eds.) MICCAI 2018. LNCS, vol. 11073, pp. 641–648. Springer, Cham (2018). https://doi.org/10.1007/978-3-030-00937-3_73
13. Wu, N., et al.: Breast density classification with deep convolutional neural networks. In: ICASSP (2018)
14. Wu, N., et al.: Deep neural networks improve radiologists' performance in breast cancer screening. arXiv preprint arXiv:1903.08297 (2019)
15. Yao, L., Prosky, J., Poblenz, E., Covington, B., Lyman, K.: Weakly supervised medical diagnosis and localization from multiple resolutions. arXiv:1803.07703 (2018)
16. Zhu, W., Lou, Q., Vang, Y.S., Xie, X.: Deep multi-instance networks with sparse label assignment for whole mammogram classification. In: Descoteaux, M., Maier-Hein, L., Franz, A., Jannin, P., Collins, D.L., Duchesne, S. (eds.) MICCAI 2017. LNCS, vol. 10435, pp. 603–611. Springer, Cham (2017). https://doi.org/10.1007/978-3-319-66179-7_69

# Advancing Pancreas Segmentation in Multi-protocol MRI Volumes Using Hausdorff-Sine Loss Function

Hykoush Asaturyan[1]($\boxtimes$)(iD), E. Louise Thomas[2], Julie Fitzpatrick[2],
Jimmy D. Bell[2], and Barbara Villarini[1]

[1] School of Computer Science and Engineering, University of Westminster,
London, UK
h.asaturyan@my.westminster.ac.uk, b.villarini@westminster.ac.uk
[2] School of Life Sciences, University of Westminster, London, UK
{L.Thomas3,J.Fitzpatrick,J.Bell}@westminster.ac.uk

**Abstract.** Computing pancreatic morphology in 3D radiological scans could provide significant insight about a medical condition. However, segmenting the pancreas in magnetic resonance imaging (MRI) remains challenging due to high inter-patient variability. Also, the resolution and speed of MRI scanning present artefacts that blur the pancreas boundaries between overlapping anatomical structures. This paper proposes a dual-stage automatic segmentation method: (1) a deep neural network is trained to address the problem of vague organ boundaries in high class-imbalanced data. This network integrates a novel loss function to rigorously optimise boundary delineation using the modified Hausdorff metric and a sinusoidal component; (2) Given a test MRI volume, the output of the trained network predicts a sequence of targeted 2D pancreas classes that are reconstructed as a volumetric binary mask. An energy-minimisation approach fuses a learned digital contrast model to suppress the intensities of non-pancreas classes, which, combined with the binary volume performs a refined segmentation in 3D while revealing dense boundary detail. Experiments are performed on two diverse MRI datasets containing 180 and 120 scans, in which the proposed approach achieves a mean Dice score of $84.1 \pm 4.6\%$ and $85.7 \pm 2.3\%$, respectively. This approach is statistically stable and outperforms state-of-the-art methods on MRI.

**Keywords:** Automatic pancreas segmentation ·
Energy-minimisation · MRI · Hausdorff loss function

## 1 Introduction

Segmenting the pancreas in 3D radiological scans (e.g. an MRI volume) could provide significant insight into the severity or progression of type 2 diabetes [1] and ductal adenocarcinoma [2]. However, pancreas segmentation presents

© Springer Nature Switzerland AG 2019
H.-I. Suk et al. (Eds.): MLMI 2019, LNCS 11861, pp. 27–35, 2019.
https://doi.org/10.1007/978-3-030-32692-0_4

several challenges due to high structural and inter-patient variability in size and location. The greyscale intensity of the pancreas can be very similar to neighbouring tissue, and the boundary contrast can vary depending on the level of surrounding visceral fat. Differing from computer tomography (CT), the low resolution and slower imaging speed of MRI presents edge-based artefacts that blur the imaging boundaries between the pancreas and surrounding organs [3]. In existing research literature, pancreas segmentation tasks have been driven by two major methodologies: multi-atlas based [4,5] coupled with statistical shape modeling [6], and in more recent years, convolutional neural networks (CNNs) or deep learning [3,7,8]. While CNNs have achieved higher quantitative accuracy scores in 2D medical image segmentation, such methods can exhibit discontinuity in predicting pancreatic regions between consecutive slices for an input volume.

This paper presents a novel approach for automatic pancreas segmentation in MRI. As illustrated in Fig. 1, the proposed method consists of two successive stages. First, a CNN specialising in blurred boundary detection is trained to predict targeted pixel-wise pancreas tissue. This deep learning stage firstly identifies the main pancreas region (ROI) in a dataset of MRI volumes [8] by training a random forest on extracted texture and probability-wise features on image patches of $25 \times 25$ pixels. Next, inspired by the encoder-decoder architecture of SegNet [9] a new model termed Hausdorff Sine SegNet (HSSN) is developed using the ROI data. A novel loss function incorporates the modified Hausdorff distance metric and a sinusoidal component to capture local boundary information, enforce edge detection and thus raise the true pancreas prediction rate on a 2D (slice-by-slice) basis. The testing stage consists of two phases. First, the output of the trained HSSN for a given test MRI volume encodes spatial information to classify every pixel in each slice, thus forming a volumetric binary mask (VBM). The second phase generates dense contouring by further tackling the low dissimilarity between organ boundaries: a digital contrast enhancement model is utilised to improve the greyscale variation between surrounding background classes within close proximity to the pancreas. A 3D energy-minimising algorithm performs refined segmentation on the enhanced pancreas that is fused with the VBM, producing greater consistency in spatial smoothness and prediction among successive slices.

The proposed method, which is evaluated on two MRI datasets with varying noise, outperforms the state-of-the-art approaches [8,10–12], and moreover, surpasses the performance of readily employed deep learning-based loss functions. Although this approach has been tested on pancreas segmentation, the methodology is reproducible, scalable and generalisable to other organ segmentation tasks. The implementation is available at https://github.com/med-seg/p.

## 2   Methodology

### 2.1   Training the HSSN

The proposed HSSN model has an encoder-decoder topology, as illustrated in Fig. 2. The decoder network uses max-pooling indices to upsample low-resolution

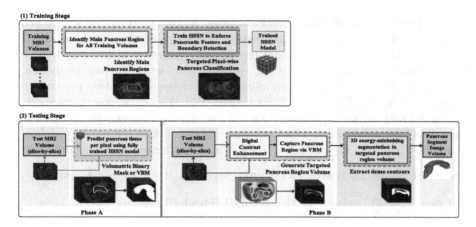

**Fig. 1.** Overview of proposed approach. (1) develop the HSSN deep learning model using training MRI; and (2) apply the test MRI to generate segmented pancreas volume.

feature maps, consequently retaining high-frequency details to improve pancreatic boundary delineation, and reducing the total number of trainable parameters in the decoders. Unlike other models that have been fine-tuned from pre-trained CNNs using a large number of natural images [3,13], this network is trained from scratch using exclusively pancreas datasets. Since this organ accounts for ~1% in a scan, there is a need to weight the loss differently based on the true class: Median frequency balancing [14] is utilised, in which the weight assigned to a class in the loss function is the ratio of the median of class frequencies computed on the entire training set divided by the class frequency. The HSSN also employs data augmentation of random reflections and translations to reduce overfitting [15], and further address problems caused by high shape variability.

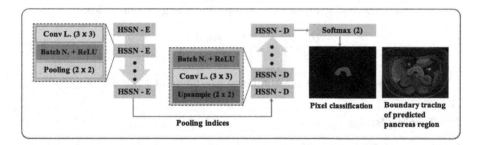

**Fig. 2.** Overview of HSSN model. An encoder stage (5 blocks of HSSN-E) downsamples the MRI input through convolution, batch normalisation and ReLU. A decoder stage (5 blocks of HSSN-D) upsamples its input using the transferred pooling indices from its corresponding encoder to generate sparse feature maps. From here, convolution is performed with a trainable filter of weights to density the feature map. Resulting decoder output feature maps are fed to soft-max classifier for 2-channel pixel-wise classification of the input image as "pancreas" or "non-pancreas".

**Integrated Hausdorff-Sine Loss Function:** A novel loss function is proposed for training the segmentation neural network. The optimisation of the modified Hausdorff distance and a sinusoidal functionality serves to reduce the boundary matching error and "enhance" a resulting pixel-wise pancreas prediction. Let $T_H$ and $Y_H$ represent the ground-truth and network boundary predictions respectively, where $T_H, Y_H \subset \mathbb{R}^n$ such that $|T_H|, |Y_H| < \infty$. Furthermore, $t_j$ and $y_j \in \{0,1\}$ are indexed pixel values in $T_H$ and $Y_H$ respectively, and can be viewed as boundary points. The Euclidean distance between a point $t_j$ and set of points, $Y_H$ is $s(t_j, Y_H) = \min\limits_{y_j \in Y_H} \|t_j - y_j\|$, and the distance between a point $y_j$ and set of points, $T_H$ is $s(y_j, T_H) = \min\limits_{t_j \in T_H} \|y_j - t_j\|$. If $\varepsilon_Y = \frac{1}{|Y_H|} \sum\limits_{y_j \in Y_H} s(t_j, Y_H)$ and $\varepsilon_T = \frac{1}{|T_H|} \sum\limits_{t_j \in T_H} s(y_j, T_H)$, the modified Hausdorff distance loss, $L_{mhd}$ is:

$$L_{mhd} = \max\{\varepsilon_Y,\ \varepsilon_T\} \tag{1}$$

Thus, computing the gradient yields:

$$\frac{\partial L_{mhd}}{\partial Y_H} = \begin{cases} \frac{\partial}{\partial Y_H}(\varepsilon_Y) & \text{if } \varepsilon_Y > \varepsilon_T \\ \frac{\partial}{\partial Y_H}(\varepsilon_T) & \text{if } \varepsilon_T < \varepsilon_Y \\ \text{undefined} & \text{if } \varepsilon_Y = \varepsilon_T \end{cases} \tag{2}$$

An additional sinusoidal component increases non-linearity during network training and, empirically evaluated, raises the true positive predictions. If $T$ and $Y$ represent the ground-truth and network predictions, the loss $L_{sine}$ is defined:

$$L_{sine} = -\frac{1}{|Y|} \sum_{i=1}^{nC} \sin(T_i) \log_2(Y_i) \tag{3}$$

where $nC = 2$ is the number of classes (e.g., $Y_1$ refers to "pancreas" and $Y_2$ refers to "non-pancreas"). From here, computing the gradient yields:

$$\frac{\partial L_{sine}}{\partial Y_i} = -\frac{1}{|Y|} \frac{\sin(T_i)}{Y_i \log_{10}(2)} \tag{4}$$

The model is updated via the combined gradients of $L_{sine}$ and $L_{mhd}$.

## 2.2   Testing Stage

**(A) Targeted Pancreas Binary Mask:** The trained HSSN model performs pixel-wise prediction on each slice in a test MRI volume to generate a resulting volumetric binary mask (VBM). Columns (a) and (b) in Fig. 3 displays three sample input slices in three different image volumes, and the corresponding positive pancreas region (white mask) as predicted by the HSSN model. The red contouring in each image in column (b) is the ground-truth.

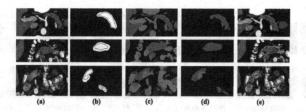

**Fig. 3.** Visualising proposed approach.

**(B) Achieve Dense Contouring:** The test MRI volume undergoes non-local means for denoising, after which a learned intensity model incorporates a sigmoid function to exhaustively differentiate pancreatic tissue against background classes. Every $s_i$-th slice transforms to $C(s_i) = 1/(1 + \exp\left[g(c-s_i)\right])$, where $g$ controls the actual contrast, and $c$ is the cut-off value representing the (normalised) greyscale value about which $g$ is changed [12,16]. The VBM is applied to the enhanced image volume and processed through a 3D unsupervised energy-minimisation method via continuous max-flow [17], revealing detailed contouring as highlighted in Fig. 3, column (c). The accurate HSSN predictions reduce the level of non-pancreatic tissue carried into the max-flow segmentation stage, as shown in Fig. 3, column (d), eliminating the need for post-processing.

## 3    Experimental Results and Analysis

### 3.1    Datasets and Evaluation

Two expert-led annotated pancreas datasets are utilised. MRI-A and MRI-B contain 180 and 120 abdominal MRI scans (T2-weighted, fat suppressed), which have been obtained using a Philips Intera 1.5T and a Siemens Trio 3T scanner, respectively. Every MRI-A scan has 50 slices, each of size $384 \times 384$ with spacing 2 mm, and 0.9766 mm pixel interval in the axial and sagittal direction. Every MRI-B scan has 80 slices, each of size $320 \times 260$ with 1.6 mm spacing, and 1.1875 mm pixel interval in the axial and sagittal direction. The proposed approach is evaluated using the Dice Similarity Coefficient (DSC), precision (PC), recall (RC) and the Hausdorff distance (HSD) representing the maximum boundary deviation between the segmentation and ground-truth.

### 3.2    Network Implementation

The training and testing data are randomly split into 160 and 20 (MRI-A) and 100 and 20 (MRI-B). The HSSN model employs stochastic gradient descent with parameters momentum (0.9), initial learning rate (0.001), maximum epochs (300) and mini-batch size (10). The mean time for model training is $\sim$11 h and the testing phase is $\sim$7.5 min per MRI volume using an i7-59-30k-CPU at 3.50 Ghz. Future work can potentially reduce these run-times by a factor of 10 via multiple GeForce Titan X GPUs.

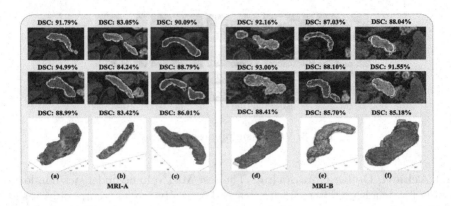

**Fig. 4.** Segmentation results in six different MRI scans (volumes). Every column corresponds to a single MRI volume. From left, first row displays sample MRI axial slices with segmentation outcome (green) against ground-truth (red), and computed DSC. Second row displays 3D reconstruction of entire pancreas with computed DSC. (Color figure online)

**Fig. 5.** Box plots of DSC and JI.

## 3.3    Analysis of Proposed Approach

Figure 4 displays the final segmentation results in six MRI scans, equally split between MRI-A and MRI-B. Columns (a, b, c) are part of MRI-A, yet there is high variation between intensity and contrast in the original axial MRI slices. Columns (d, e, f) corresponds to exemplars from MRI-B. As reflected in Fig. 5, 85% of MRI-A compared to 95% in MRI-B segmentations score above 80% in DSC, demonstrating the robust performance of the approach with respect to poor image quality, intensity distribution and spatial dimensions.

**Hausdorff-Sine Loss:** Figure 6 compares the segmentation results (in DSC) using Hausdorff-Sine and the loss functions, Hausdorff, Cross-entropy, Dice [18] and Jaccard [19] in the probability range [0.05,0.95]. The cross-entropy penalises true positive predictions, forcing the "optimum" probability to approximately 0.5. Although the Dice loss minimises the class distribution distance, squaring the weights in the backpropagation stage causes instability and a higher rate of false negative predictions. Similarly, the Jaccard loss suffers from low true positive predictions. Empirically tested, the Hausdorff loss minimises the maximum deviation between a prediction and desired outcome; however, the addition of a sinusoidal component increases non-linearity during training, and thus Hausdorff-Sine achieves improved true positive predictions across differing

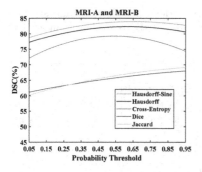

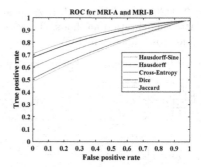

**Fig. 6.** DSC across threshold ranges [0.05, 0.95] via multiple loss functions.

**Fig. 7.** Averaged ROC curves via multiple loss functions.

thresholds while delivering strong discrimination of true negatives. The ROC curves in Fig. 7 highlight the inferior performance of other loss functions in the extremely unbalanced segmentation, whereas Hausdorff-Sine generally improves the true positive accuracy results.

**Phase B of Testing Stage:** Integrating the second phase (B) produces contextual boundary information that is essential for accurate segmentation in biomedical imaging. Figure 3, column (b) and column (e) visibly highlights the differences in segmentation boundary delineation against the ground-truth before and after this phase. Thus, the mean HSD metric confirms less deviation from the ground-truth (see Tables 1 and 2) by approximately 1 mm, and furthermore, the mean DSC raises by approximately 4% in both MRI-A and MRI-B.

**Table 1.** Deep learning model performance using state-of-the-art loss functions versus the integrated novel Hausdorff and Hausdorff-Sine loss. Datasets MRI-A and MRI-B are evaluated in 9-fold and 6-fold cross-validation (FCV), respectively. DSC, PC, RC and HSD are presented as mean ± standard deviation.

| MRI-A: Train/Test (160/20) 9-FCV | | | | MRI-B: Train/Test (100/20) 6-FCV | | | |
|---|---|---|---|---|---|---|---|
| Loss | DSC(%) | PC(%) | RC(%) | HSD(mm) | Loss | DSC(%) | PC(%) | RC(%) | HSD(mm) |
| CE | 77.9±3.6 | 88.4±6.18 | 95.6±2.26 | 12.4±5.5 | CE | 79.9±4.33 | 92.6±6.89 | 96.3±2.76 | 10.5±3.34 |
| Dice | 63.5±9.1 | 63.8±20.0 | 86.8±10.5 | 16.8±5.3 | Dice | 67.1±12.8 | 77.2±15.1 | 85.2±16.8 | 21.4±12.3 |
| Jac | 63.2±9.6 | 62.5±19.8 | 87.1±10.0 | 17.0±5.4 | Jac | 68.6±6.96 | 68.3±16.9 | 88.5±8.34 | 17.9±7.58 |
| Haus | 78.4±6.1 | 89.5±9.11 | 96.2±4.06 | 12.7±4.9 | Haus | 81.0±4.25 | 94.8±3.84 | 98.3±2.28 | 10.2±4.17 |
| Haus-Sin | 79.7±4.0 | 93.2±7.46 | 97.2±2.67 | 11.2±3.6 | Haus-Sin | 82.1±2.99 | 97.7±2.50 | 99.1±0.78 | 10.0±6.63 |

**Comparison with the State-of-the-Art:** Table 2 highlights the proposed approach outperforming state-of-the-art methods [8,10–12] in terms of accuracy and statistical stability despite employing non-organ optimised protocol data.

**Table 2.** DSC, PC, RC and HSD as mean ± standard deviation [lowest, highest] for automatic segmentation methods. Datasets MRI-A and MRI-B are evaluated in 9-fold and 6-fold cross-validation (FCV), respectively.

| MRI-A: Train/Test (160/20) 9-FCV | | | |
|---|---|---|---|
| Method | DSC(%) | PC(%) | RC(%) | HSD (mm) |
| U-Net [10] | 66.8±8.8 [42.3, 77.3] | 71.3±4.4 [62.9, 80.5] | 85.1±4.8 [76.9, 88.16] | 16.9±5.8 [8.22, 24.1] |
| Cascaded-CNN [8] | 52.7±6.9 [34.4, 60.7] | 64.0±4.1 [50.4, 68.0] | 75.2±4.6 [68.1, 78.25] | 21.5±9.3 [15.7, 38.6] |
| Dense V-Net [11] | 73.6±6.1 [49.6, 78.8] | 86.1±3.3 [78.5, 88.5] | 94.6±3.4 [82.8, 96.37] | 14.4±7.2 [6.63, 20.5] |
| Geo-Desc [12] | 78.2 ±5.8 [67.1, 86.3] | 85.3±9.7 [70.8, 98.9] | 93.9±9.5 [52.5, 99.13] | 13.8±4.4 [6.11, 18.4] |
| **Proposed** | **84.1±4.6 [72.1, 89.6]** | **95.5±6.3 [71.7, 99.7]** | **97.6±3.0 [89.9, 100.0]** | **10.6±3.7 [6.184, 18.4]** |
| MRI-B: Train/Test (100/20) 6-FCV | | | |
| Method | DSC(%) | PC(%) | RC(%) | HSD (mm) |
| U-Net [10] | 72.8±6.0 [58.9, 80.8] | 83.8±3.1 [74.2, 87.46] | 94.6±3.5 [82.8, 95.72] | 14.0±8.1 [6.82, 21.7] |
| Cascaded-CNN [8] | 54.8±5.1 [44.4, 65.7] | 64.3±3.5 [59.5, 67.91] | 76.2±3.7 [69.9, 79.64] | 22.3±8.6 [16.0, 37.5] |
| Dense V-Net [11] | 74.0±5.3 [65.1, 80.3] | 85.4±3.1 [78.5, 89.74] | 93.0±3.8 [84.9, 96.35] | 16.7±7.0 [8.46, 19.8] |
| Geo-Desc [12] | 81.2±5.0 [72.6, 85.8] | 84.7±5.8 [73.1, 93.64] | 84.6±8.2 [69.2, 97.28] | 14.7±4.1 [8.13, 17.6] |
| **Proposed** | **85.7±2.3 [79.9, 90.3]** | **96.1±3.6 [86.7, 100.0]** | **99.3±0.7 [99.9, 100.0]** | **9.08±2.0 [4.87, 14.8]** |

## 4    Conclusion

This paper presents a novel approach for automatic pancreas segmentation in MRI volumes generated from different scanner protocols. Combined with the proposed Hausdorff-Sine loss, an encoder-decoder network reinforces pancreatic boundary detection in MRI slices, outperforming the rate of true positive predictions compared to multiple loss functions. In the later stage, a 3D hybrid energy-minimisation algorithm addresses the intensity consistency problem that is often the case when segmenting image volumes on a 2D basis. The proposed approach generates quantitative accuracy results that surpass reported state-of-the-art methods, and moreover, preserve detailed contouring.

## References

1. Macauley, M., Percival, K., Thelwall, P.E., Hollingsworth, K.G., Taylor, R.: Altered volume, morphology and composition of the pancreas in type 2 diabetes. PLoS ONE **10**(5), 1–14 (2015)
2. Omeri, A., et al.: Contour variations of the body and tail of the pancreas: evaluation with MDCT. J. Radiol. **35**(6), 310–318 (2017)
3. Cai, J., Lu, L., Zhang, Z., Xing, F., Yang, L., Yin, Q.: Pancreas segmentation in MRI using graph-based decision fusion on convolutional neural networks. In: Ourselin, S., Joskowicz, L., Sabuncu, M.R., Unal, G., Wells, W. (eds.) MICCAI 2016. LNCS, vol. 9901, pp. 442–450. Springer, Cham (2016). https://doi.org/10.1007/978-3-319-46723-8_51
4. Okada, T., et al.: Abdominal multi-organ segmentation of CT images based on hierarchical spatial modeling of organ interrelations. In: Yoshida, H., Sakas, G., Linguraru, M.G. (eds.) ABD-MICCAI 2011. LNCS, vol. 7029, pp. 173–180. Springer, Heidelberg (2012). https://doi.org/10.1007/978-3-642-28557-8_22
5. Shimizu, A., Kimoto, T., Kobatake, H., Nawano, S., Shinozaki, K.: Automated pancreas segmentation from three-dimensional contrast-enhanced computed tomography. Int. J. Comput. Assist. Radiol. Surg. **5**(1), 85–98 (2010)
6. Okada, T., Linguraru, M.G., Hori, M., Summers, R., Tomiyama, N., Sato, Y.: Abdominal multi-organ segmentation from CT images using conditional shape-location and unsupervised intensity priors. Med. Image Anal. **26**, 1–18 (2015)

7. Cai, J., Lu, L., Xie, Y., Xing, F., Yang, L.: Improving deep pancreas segmentation in CT and MRI images via recurrent neural contextual learning and direct loss function. CoRR, abs/1707.04912 (2017)
8. Farag, A., Lu, L., Roth, H.R., Liu, J., Turkbey, E., Summers, R.M.: A bottom-up approach for pancreas segmentation using cascaded superpixels and (deep) image patch labeling. IEEE Trans. Image **26**(1), 386–399 (2017)
9. Badrinarayanan, V., Kendall, A., Cipolla, R.: SegNet: a deep convolutional encoder-decoder architecture for image segmentation. arXiv:1511.00561 (2015)
10. Ronneberger, O., Fischer, P., Brox, T.: U-net: convolutional networks for biomedical image segmentation. In: Navab, N., Hornegger, J., Wells, W.M., Frangi, A.F. (eds.) MICCAI 2015. LNCS, vol. 9351, pp. 234–241. Springer, Cham (2015). https://doi.org/10.1007/978-3-319-24574-4_28
11. Gibson, E., et al.: Automatic multi-organ segmentation on abdominal CT with dense V-Networks. IEEE Trans. Med. Imaging **37**, 1822–1834 (2018)
12. Asaturyan, H., Gligorievski, A., Villarini, B.: Morphological and multi-level geometrical descriptor analysis in CT and MRI volumes for automatic pancreas segmentation. Comput. Med. Imaging Graph. **75**, 1–13 (2019)
13. Xie, S., Tu, Z.: Holistically-nested edge detection. In: Proceedings of the IEEE ICCV, pp. 1395–1403 (2015)
14. Eigen, D., Fergus, R.: Predicting depth, surface normals and semantic labels with a common multi-scale convolutional architecture. In: Proceedings of the IEEE International Conference on Computer Vision, pp. 2650–2658 (2015)
15. Perez, L., Wang, J.: The effectiveness of data augmentation in image classification using deep learning. arXiv:1712.04621 (2017)
16. Asaturyan, H., Villarini, B.: Hierarchical framework for automatic pancreas segmentation in MRI using continuous max-flow and min-cuts approach. In: Campilho, A., Karray, F., ter Haar Romeny, B. (eds.) ICIAR 2018. LNCS, vol. 10882, pp. 562–570. Springer, Cham (2018). https://doi.org/10.1007/978-3-319-93000-8_64
17. Yuan, J., Bae, E., Tai, X.-C.: A study on continuous max-flow and min-cut approaches. In: Proceedings of the IEEE Computer Society Conference on Computer Vision and Pattern Recognition, pp. 2217–2224 (2010)
18. Milletari, F., Navab, N., Ahmadi, S.A.: V-Net: fully convolutional neural networks for volumetric medical image segmentation. In: Fourth Fourth International Conference on 3D Vision, pp. 565–571 (2016)
19. Rahman, M.A., Wang, Y.: Optimizing intersection-over-union in deep neural networks for image segmentation. In: Bebis, G., et al. (eds.) ISVC 2016. LNCS, vol. 10072, pp. 234–244. Springer, Cham (2016). https://doi.org/10.1007/978-3-319-50835-1_22

# WSI-Net: Branch-Based and Hierarchy-Aware Network for Segmentation and Classification of Breast Histopathological Whole-Slide Images

Haomiao Ni[1], Hong Liu[1(✉)], Kuansong Wang[2,3], Xiangdong Wang[1], Xunjian Zhou[2,3], and Yueliang Qian[1]

[1] Beijing Key Laboratory of Mobile Computing and Pervasive Device, Institute of Computing Technology, Chinese Academy of Sciences, Beijing 100190, China
hliu@ict.ac.cn

[2] Department of Pathology, Xiangya Hospital, Central South University, Changsha, Hunan, China

[3] Department of Pathology, School of Basic Medical Sciences, Central South University, Changsha, Hunan, China

**Abstract.** This paper proposes a novel network WSI-Net for segmentation and classification of gigapixel breast whole-slide images (WSIs). WSI-Net can segment patches from the WSI into three types, including non-malignant, ductal carcinoma in situ, and invasive ductal carcinoma. It adds a parallel classification branch on the top of the low layer of a semantic segmentation model DeepLab. This branch can fast identify and discard those non-malignant patches in advance and thus the high layer of DeepLab can only focus on the remaining possible cancerous inputs. This strategy can accelerate inference and robustly improve segmentation performance. For training WSI-Net, a *hierarchy-aware loss* function is proposed to combine pixel-level and patch-level loss, which can capture the pathology hierarchical relationships between pixels in each patch. By aggregating patch segmentation results from WSI-Net, we generate a segmentation map for the WSI and extract its morphological features for WSI-level classification. Experimental results show that our WSI-Net can be *fast, robust* and *effective* on our benchmark dataset.

## 1 Introduction

Traditional diagnosis of breast cancer requires a careful microscopic examination of stained tissue slides, which is time-consuming and error-prone [2]. Due to the

**Electronic supplementary material** The online version of this chapter (https://doi.org/10.1007/978-3-030-32692-0_5) contains supplementary material, which is available to authorized users.

H.-I. Suk et al. (Eds.): MLMI 2019, LNCS 11861, pp. 36–44, 2019.
https://doi.org/10.1007/978-3-030-32692-0_5

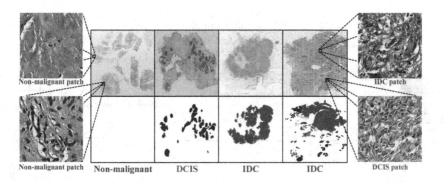

**Fig. 1.** Examples of non-malignant, DCIS and IDC slides and their sampled patches. The first row includes the original WSIs and the second row shows their pixel-wise labeled images. Non-malignant, DCIS, and IDC pixels are white, blue and red, respectively. Note that the IDC slide can contain DCIS areas. (Color figure online)

advances in slide scanning technology [1], now pathologists can review whole-slide images (WSIs) by computers to identify tumor regions. WSI is stored in a multi-resolution pyramid structure and the number of pixels at the highest 40× magnification can exceed 10 billion.

Recently, automatic breast cancer detection in WSIs has been well explored [1,7]. However, little work exists in classifying WSIs into non-malignant, ductal carcinoma in situ (DCIS) and invasive ductal carcinoma (IDC), where DCIS and IDC are the most typical preinvasive and invasive lesions, respectively. This problem is difficult due to the morphological diversity of non-malignant regions and the visual similarity between DCIS and IDC areas, as shown in Fig. 1.

To deal with this problem, we focus on segmenting DCIS and IDC areas in breast WSIs and classifying WSIs into non-malignant, DCIS, and IDC. To our best knowledge, Bejnordi et al. [2] firstly applied deep learning to this task. Due to the massive size of WSI, they first divided the slide into multiple smaller patches. Then they employed a convolutional neural network (CNN) to extract cellular-level features and a fully convolutional network (FCN) with larger input size to increase context information. Their system achieved a three class accuracy of 81.3% on their own dataset, which contained 221 WSIs. However, they simply adopted semantic segmentation architectures used in natural images such as FCN, which may not be completely suitable for our histopathological WSI task.

Typically, breast WSIs include lots of non-malignant regions (Fig. 1), which are needless to be pixel-wise segmented because they are similar to those background areas in natural images. But general segmentation networks execute pixel-level prediction for all the WSI patches, which is quite inefficient. Also, it is commonly hard to define a single label for the image or patch containing multiple instances. So most segmentation models only consider the pixel-level loss. In our task, doctors assign the WSI a slide-level label according to its worst abnormality condition [2], i.e., a slide containing IDC and DCIS will be labeled

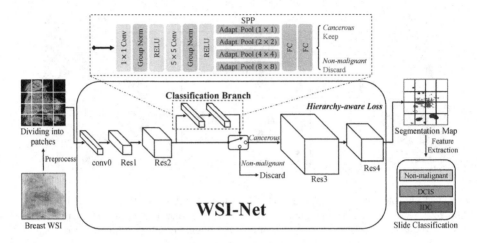

**Fig. 2.** The overview of our proposed framework.

as IDC, since IDC is more serious than DCIS. Using this kind of pathology knowledge, we can also assign a patch-level label for each sampled patch. Thus, the patch-level loss can be combined with our task. Based on these observations, we improve a natural image segmentation model, DeepLab [3]. We summarize our main contributions and the related improvements on DeepLab as follows.

Firstly, we propose a network WSI-Net to segment the pixels of patches from WSIs into non-malignant, DCIS, and IDC. It adds a parallel classification branch on the low layer of DeepLab, which can fast identify and remove many non-malignant patches in advance and thus the high layer of DeepLab can only focus on those remaining possible cancerous inputs. This is similar to doctors' diagnosis process, where they ignore normal regions and only care about those potential cancer areas. Besides accelerating inference, our classification branch is robust and it can also enhance the segmentation performance of DeepLab.

Secondly, we propose a *hierarchy-aware loss* to train our WSI-Net. It combines the standard pixel-level loss with the patch-level loss, where patch label is generated by pathology hierarchical relationships between pixels in the patch.

Finally, we introduce an effective framework to classify breast WSIs into non-malignant, DCIS and IDC. Our WSI-Net performs dense prediction for each patch sampled from the WSI. We then aggregate their segmentation results to produce a segmentation map for the WSI. Morphological features are further extracted from this map for WSI-level classification. Experiments show that our method can be *fast*, *robust* and *effective* for WSI segmentation and classification.

## 2  Proposed Framework

Figure 2 shows the overview of our framework. When testing, we first preprocess the WSI by adopting OTSU [9] to binarize the WSI and remove its non-tissue areas. We later divide it into multiple patches with overlap at 40×. Then we feed them into WSI-Net to perform pixel-wise prediction. WSI-Net includes a baseline segmentation model DeepLab [3] (1 conv layer *conv0* plus 4 ResNet blocks *Res1-4*) and an extra classification branch. We add this branch between Res2 and Res3 to control whether the input feature maps will be removed or propagated forward to the high layer of DeepLab during testing. The details of the branch are also shown in Fig. 2. Considering computational constraints, we abandon the multi-scale input processing and bilinear interpolation operations used in the initial DeepLab [3]. So this generates segmentation outputs with the 1/8 side of input patches. We aggregate these outputs to generate a segmentation map for the WSI, which has the same size as the WSI at 5×. When performing aggregation, we simply adopt the majority voting to handle boundary prediction inconsistency of adjacent patches. We extract 18 morphological features from the WSI segmentation map and finally leverage random forest to classify it into non-malignant, DCIS, and IDC. For training WSI-Net, we propose a hierarchy-aware loss. More training details are in Sect. 3. The details of our branch, hierarchy-aware loss, and slide-level feature extraction are described as follows.

**Classification Branch.** The classification branch has been adopted by many state-of-the-art methods, such as Mask R-CNN [4] and Y-Net [8]. Mask R-CNN adopted the branch for instance segmentation. Y-Net utilized the branch to generate a discriminative map, which was combined with the segmentation result to enhance performance. Similarly, we also adopt the classification branch in our WSI-Net (Fig. 2). But different from the above methods, during inference, our branch can fast classify input feature maps into non-malignant and cancerous at the low layer of the DeepLab. Then it will remove those non-malignant inputs and only keep those possible cancerous ones for the subsequent time-consuming pixel-level segmentation operations. This is also similar to doctors' diagnosis process, where they only focus on those possible cancer regions while ignoring other non-malignant areas.

Figure 2 shows the details of our branch. We first employ $1 \times 1$ convolution to reduce the channel number of input feature maps to keep the branch simple and thus help acceleration. For fewer parameters, we only adopt two convolutional layers and two FC layers. Considering the possible small batch size when training, we utilize the Group Normalization (GN) [11] instead of Batch Normalization(BN) [6]. We also replace the standard pooling layer with spatial pyramid pooling (SPP) [5] to make our branch adapt to arbitrary-sized inputs like DeepLab. Here SPP includes four adaptive pooling layers to capture multi-scale information. Note that our branch can leverage the low layer of DeepLab to extract features and perform binary classification.

When testing, our branch discards those inputs with probabilities of being cancerous lower than a preset threshold $t$ ($0 < t \leq 0.5$). Experiments in Sect. 3 will illustrate that segmentation performance changes little under different $t$, which validates the robustness of our branch. When jointly training branch and DeepLab, we employ Eq. 1 to combine branch loss, $loss_{branch}$, and DeepLab segmentation loss (pixel-to-pixel loss), $loss_{pixel}$, where $\alpha$ is the balancing parameter. Both $loss_{branch}$ and $loss_{pixel}$ employ cross entropy criteria. When calculating

$loss_{branch}$, we label a patch as cancerous if it contains DCIS or IDC pixels.

$$loss = loss_{pixel} + \alpha \cdot loss_{branch} \tag{1}$$

**Hierarchy-Aware Loss.** It is usually hard to define a single label for the image or patch containing multiple instances. So most segmentation models only consider the pixel-level loss, $loss_{pixel}$. However, in our task, pathologists assign the WSI a slide-level label based on its worst abnormality condition. According to this pathology definition, we can also infer a patch-level label for each input patch from its segmentation result. Specially, we first define the hierarchical relationships between different pixels as follows: $pixel_{IDC} > pixel_{DCIS} > pixel_{Non\text{-}malignant}$. We then assign the label of the patch according to the highest hierarchy of its pixels, i.e., a patch including IDC, DCIS and non-malignant pixels will be labeled as IDC. Therefore, for each input patch, we can infer the true patch label and the predicted patch label using its pixel-wise annotation and segmentation result and further calculate $loss_{patch}$. This $loss_{patch}$ can model the global pathology interdependency between pixels in the patch and also provide an extra constraint for the segmentation model. So we propose a hierarchy-aware loss to combine this $loss_{patch}$ and $loss_{pixel}$, as Eq. 2 shows. Here $\beta$ is the balancing parameter. Note that both $loss_{pixel}$ and $loss_{patch}$ are directly calculated from the pixel-level segmentation result and they both adopt cross entropy criteria.

$$\text{hierarchy-aware loss} = loss_{pixel} + \beta \cdot loss_{patch} \tag{2}$$

Finally, WSI-Net uses the Eq. 3 to combine our classification branch and hierarchy-aware loss. Note that $loss_{branch}$ is only related to branch binary classification and irrelevant to DeepLab segmentation results while $loss_{patch}$ is relevant to three-class classification and determined by segmentation results like $loss_{pixel}$.

$$loss = loss_{pixel} + \beta \cdot loss_{patch} + \alpha \cdot loss_{branch} \tag{3}$$

**Slide-Level Feature Extraction.** We extract 18 features from the WSI segmentation map. Assuming that $R_c$ is the set of regions predicted to be class $c$ in a WSI, and the maximum region and minimum area in $R_c$ is $R_c^{max}$ and $R_c^{min}$, our features include the area, eccentricity, and extent of $R_c^{max}$, the area of $R_c^{min}$, the percentage of $R_c$ over all the cancerous areas, and the percentage of $R_c$ over all the tissue areas, where $c$ is DCIS or IDC. So this creates 12 features. We also consider the average area and total area of $R_c$, where $c$ is DCIS, IDC or cancerous (DCIS+IDC). This generates the last 6 features.

## 3    Experimental Evaluation

We evaluate our methods on a WSI dataset, which contains 300 breast WSIs from the pathology archive of Xiangya Hospital. All the slides were pixel-wise annotated and reviewed by three pathologists. We split this dataset into training, validation, and testing sets, which contain 150, 50, and 100 WSIs respectively. The training set includes 60 non-malignant, 45 DCIS, and 45 IDC. The validation set contains 20 non-malignant, 15 DCIS, and 15 IDC. The test set has 40 non-malignant, 30 DCIS and 30 IDC. Some slide examples are also shown in Fig. 1. The average size of a WSI at 40× is over 45,000 pixels by 40,000 pixels, which is similar to 1800 images with the size of 1000 × 1000 pixels.

We evaluate segmentation performance by four metrics based on the mean region intersection over union (mIoU) [3] as Eq. 4 shows. Here $n_{ij}$ is the number of pixels of class $i$ predicted to be class $j$, where there are $n_c$ classes. The first metric mIoU considers all the three classes. To finer measure cancer segmentation results, we also adopt Cancer-mIoU that just considers IDC and DCIS lesions, and DCIS-IoU and IDC-IoU that are only calculated on DCIS and IDC regions, respectively. We also compute WSI-level classification accuracy WSI-Acc to measure slide classification results. To estimate results more accurately, we report their 95% confidence intervals using the bootstrap approach in [7].

We design several experiments to measure WSI segmentation and classification performance. 1. We apply hierarchy-aware loss to DeepLab (represented as DeepLab-HA) and evaluate its performance. 2. We combine DeepLab with classification branch (BranchNet) and test it with different branch thresholds $t$ (BranchNet-$t$). 3. We incorporate hierarchy-aware loss and our branch into WSI-Net and test it with different branch thresholds $t$ (WSI-Net-$t$). Besides DeepLab, we also list other two baseline methods, Inception V3 [7] and U-Net [10] in Table 1. DeepLab surpasses these two models evidently. The reason may be its deeper architecture, ResNet-101, which has more powerful feature representation ability. But using this very deep network also increases the processing time. So We accelerate it by adding our branch.

$$\text{mIoU} = (1/n_c) \sum_i n_{ii} / \left( \sum_j n_{ij} + \sum_j n_{ji} - n_{ii} \right) \tag{4}$$

**Implement Details.** When training DeepLab, to capture a large context, we sample patches with the size of 1280 × 1280 pixels using an overlap step of 640 at 40×. This generates 60K cancerous patches (patches including DCIS and/or IDC pixels) and 160K non-malignant patches. Note that DeepLab performs three-class segmentation. Then we train DeepLab using a batch size of 4 from a pretrained model available online [3]. Some typical data augmentation techniques are adopted, including color jittering, rotation, and flip. The initial learning rate is $2.5 \times 10^{-4}$ and the poly learning rate policy [3] with the power of 0.9 is employed. We iterate training for 10 epochs and find the optimal model with the validation set. When testing, to reduce the inference times, we extract patches as large as 2048 × 2048 (determined by the capacity of GPU memory) from the WSI with an overlap step of 192 and test with two GTX 1080 Ti GPUs using a batch size of 2.

When training DeepLab-HA, we empirically set $\beta$ in Eq. 2 to be 7/3, i.e., $\text{loss}_{patch} : \text{loss}_{pixel}$ is 7:3. This helps the model penalize patch-level errors more and guide it to focus more on the hierarchical relationships between pixels.

For training BranchNet-$t$ (DeepLab + Branch), to find the optimal position for adding our branch, we analyze the architecture of DeepLab. DeepLab can be regarded as a stack of ResNet blocks, which includes Res1, Res2, Res3, and Res4 according to the authors' codes [3]. We calculate the ratio of running time of each module and obtain $Res1 : Res2 : Res3 : Res4 = 9 : 10 : 70 : 11$. So we add the branch before Res3 for considerable acceleration and also helping our branch leverage more low layers of DeepLab (conv0, Res1, and Res2) to extract features and perform binary classification between cancerous and non-malignant inputs. When training, we first train DeepLab for 1 epoch from pretrained model and fix it. Then we train the branch for 25 epochs. We later jointly train the branch and DeepLab for 9 epochs, where parameter $\alpha$ in Eq. 1 is empirically set as $7/3$ to ensure the high performance of branch. When testing, we preset a threshold $t$ and our branch will remove those inputs whose predictions are lower than $t$.

When training WSI-Net-$t$ (DeepLab-HA + Branch), We still set both $\alpha$ and $\beta$ in Eq. 3 to be $7/3$. The other implement details are the same as BranchNet-$t$.

**Evaluation of Hierarchy-Aware Loss.** As Table 1 shows, DeepLab-HA exceeds DeepLab on the primitive scores[1] of all the four segmentation metrics. This demonstrates that the combination with patch-level loss can facilitate WSI pixel-level segmentation. For WSI classification, our morphological feature extraction focuses more on the *global* structure of tumors in WSIs, which results in the similar WSI-Acc for DeepLab and DeepLab-HA. These WSI features also pay more attention to the maximum and minimum cancer regions of the WSI, which may ignore DeepLab-HA's segmentation improvement for some middle-sized cancer areas. Our 95% confidence intervals also show similar results.

**Table 1.** Evaluation results of proposed methods (95% confidence intervals). KP (Kept Patches) and T (Time) are used to measure our classification branch.

| Methods | mIoU (%) | Cancer-mIoU (%) | DCIS-IoU (%) | IDC-IoU (%) | WSI-Acc (%) | KP (%) | T(s) |
|---|---|---|---|---|---|---|---|
| Inception [7] | 60.92 (55.57, 65.82) | 44.50 (36.38, 51.57) | 30.96 (22.35, 39.40) | 58.05 (44.72, 67.97) | 52 (42, 62) | - | - |
| U-Net [10] | 61.70 (56.56, 66.46) | 45.92 (38.22, 52.55) | 36.19 (27.70, 43.92) | 55.64 (43.22, 65.85) | 57 (47, 66) | - | - |
| DeepLab [3] | 68.69 (64.27, 72.52) | 55.12 (48.53, 60.62) | 42.77 (35.24, 49.67) | 67.47 (56.74, **76.21**) | 80 (72, 88) | 100 | 341 |
| DeepLab-HA | **70.39 (65.99, 74.50)** | **57.51 (51.18, 63.42)** | **47.46 (37.01, 56.59)** | **67.56 (57.85**, 75.57) | 80 (72, 87) | 100 | 349 |
| BranchNet-0.0 | 71.86 (67.26, **76.28**) | 59.83 (53.10, **65.99**) | 52.23 (**43.98, 59.41**) | 67.43 (57.10, 76.92) | 82 (74, 89) | 100 | 342 |
| BranchNet-0.1 | **71.93 (67.54**, 76.20) | **59.92 (53.54**, 65.94) | **52.29** (43.52, 59.16) | 67.55 (57.55, 76.49) | 83 (75, 90) | 34.70 | 186 |
| BranchNet-0.2 | 71.83 (66.98, 76.22) | 59.76 (52.63, 65.89) | 51.84 (42.84, 59.08) | 67.68 (57.63, 76.95) | 84 (77, 91) | 27.69 | 179 |
| BranchNet-0.3 | 71.84 (67.30, 76.24) | 59.75 (52.93, 65.95) | 51.52 (42.53, 58.70) | 67.97 (58.10, **77.46**) | **87 (80, 93)** | 23.77 | 161 |
| BranchNet-0.4 | 71.50 (66.73, 75.93) | 59.22 (52.30, 65.32) | 50.38 (40.98, 57.18) | 68.06 (58.09, 76.97) | 86 (79, **93**) | 21.19 | 156 |
| BranchNet-0.5 | 70.73 (65.96, 75.15) | 58.06 (51.07, 64.32) | 47.94 (38.86, 55.29) | **68.18 (58.36**, 77.45) | 84 (77, 91) | **19.34** | 146 |
| WSI-Net-0.0 | 72.34 (68.05, 76.60) | 60.52 (54.28, 66.44) | 53.44 (44.80, 60.34) | 67.60 (57.75, 76.50) | 80 (72, 88) | 100.0 | 351 |
| WSI-Net-0.1 | 72.57 (68.20, 76.71) | 60.86 (54.52, 66.68) | 54.04 (45.42, 61.00) | 67.68 (58.25, 76.46) | 81 (73, 88) | 33.89 | 203 |
| WSI-Net-0.2 | 72.74 (68.09, 76.78) | 61.09 (54.36, 66.73) | 54.29 (45.76, 61.23) | 67.88 (58.26, 76.67) | 82 (74, 89) | 27.62 | 175 |
| WSI-Net-0.3 | **72.94 (68.59, 77.06)** | **61.36 (54.84**, 67.04) | **54.51 (45.92, 61.43)** | 68.22 (**58.97**, 76.90) | 82 (74, 89) | 24.19 | 167 |
| WSI-Net-0.4 | 72.85 (68.20, 76.93) | 61.20 (54.40, **67.05**) | 53.98 (45.25, 61.04) | 68.41 (58.37, **77.53**) | **85 (78, 92)** | 21.54 | 153 |
| WSI-Net-0.5 | 72.70 (68.34, 76.64) | 60.95 (54.61, 66.56) | 53.31 (45.22, 59.73) | **68.59 (58.45**, 77.16) | 82 (74, 89) | **19.58** | 149 |

**Evaluation of Classification Branch.** When testing, the branch abandons those patches with probabilities of being cancer lower than $t$. So the branch of

---

[1] "Primitive score" means the result on the initial test dataset without resampling.

BranchNet-0.0 still keeps all the inputs and thus the percentage of inputs kept by branch (Kept Patches, KP) is 100% in Table 1. As $t$ increases, our branch will require inputs to have higher probabilities and thus the percentage of KP and the average WSI inference time T decrease, as Table 1 shows. When $t$ changes from 0.1 to 0.5, our branch removes 65.3%−80.7% inputs and accelerates DeepLab by reducing the average test time by 45.5%−57.2%.

The comparison of DeepLab with BranchNet-0.0 also illustrates that the joint training of branch and DeepLab can improve both segmentation and classification performance, which increases primitive scores of mIoU, Cancer-mIoU, DCIS-IoU, and WSI-Acc by 3.17%, 4.71%, 9.46%, and 2%, respectively. The reason may be that the joint training will enable the low layer of DeepLab to learn better representation since the training of branch also involves their optimization. Table 1 also shows the robustness of our branch in most segmentation metrics. As $t$ varies, the changes in primitive scores of mIoU, Cancer-mIoU, and IDC-IoU are within 1.2%, 1.86%, and 0.75%, respectively. Compared with DeepLab, except IDC-IoU, primitive scores of all the other metrics of BranchNet-$t$ are improved regardless of the change of $t$. This shows the effectiveness of employing our branch to imitate the doctors' diagnosis process, where they ignore normal regions and only concentrate on the remaining possible cancer areas. Overall, our classification branch can *accelerate* and *improve* DeepLab while keeping segmentation *robustness*. Our 95% confidence intervals also show similar results.

**Evaluation of WSI-Net.** As Table 1 shows, all the WSI-Net-$t$ methods surpass BranchNet-$t$ on the primitive scores of mIoU, Cancer-mIoU and DCIS-IoU. This shows again the benefits of our hierarchy-aware loss, which can fuse pathology hierarchical relationships with our model. Table 1 also shows the advantages of using our classification branch. WSI-Net obviously reduces the WSI inference time of DeepLab-HA while improving its performance. With $t$ varying, the changes in primitive scores of all the segmentation metrics are also small.

Though WSI-Net-$t$ models show a better WSI segmentation performance, their WSI-Acc results are slightly lower than BranchNet-$t$ in general. For analysis, we choose BranchNet-0.3 and WSI-Net-0.4, which have the best *primitive* WSI-Acc (87% and 85%) among BranchNet-$t$ and WSI-Net-$t$. Table 2 shows that WSI-Net-0.4 actually performed the *same* well as BranchNet-0.3 in the classification of non-malignant and DCIS slides. But it misclassified two more IDC slides. However, though BranchNet-0.3 classifies these two slides correctly, this is just because it predicts slightly more pixels accurately. So actually both BranchNet-0.3 and WSI-Net-0.4 segment these two slides similarly badly, which shows that in fact our models fail to be generalized to these slides. This problem can be resolved by adding more WSIs for training. The figures of segmentation results in our supplementary materials will help to demonstrate this point.

**Table 2.** The number of correctly classified WSIs for each class in our methods.

| Methods | Non-malignant | DCIS | IDC |
|---|---|---|---|
| BranchNet-0.3 | 35 | 29 | 23 |
| WSI-Net-0.4 | 35 | 29 | 21 |

## 4  Conclusion

This paper proposes an efficient framework for breast WSI segmentation and classification. We introduce a novel network WSI-Net to combine our classification branch and hierarchy-aware loss for *fast*, *robust*, and *effective* semantic segmentation of breast cancer. Our WSI-Net has achieved better results on both lesion segmentation and slide classification than the existing networks on our WSI dataset. The future work is to further generalize our improvements to other deep segmentation models and optimize and evaluate them on more WSIs.

## References

1. Bejnordi, B.E., et al.: Diagnostic assessment of deep learning algorithms for detection of lymph node metastases in women with breast cancer. Jama **318**(22), 2199–2210 (2017)
2. Bejnordi, B.E., et al.: Context-aware stacked convolutional neural networks for classification of breast carcinomas in whole-slide histopathology images. J. Med. Imaging **4**(4), 044504 (2017)
3. Chen, L.C., Papandreou, G., Kokkinos, I., Murphy, K., Yuille, A.L.: DeepLab: semantic image segmentation with deep convolutional nets, atrous convolution, and fully connected CRFs. IEEE Trans. Pattern Anal. Mach. Intell. **40**(4), 834–848 (2018)
4. He, K., Gkioxari, G., Dollár, P., Girshick, R.: Mask R-CNN. In: 2017 IEEE International Conference on Computer Vision (ICCV), pp. 2980–2988. IEEE (2017)
5. He, K., Zhang, X., Ren, S., Sun, J.: Spatial pyramid pooling in deep convolutional networks for visual recognition. In: Fleet, D., Pajdla, T., Schiele, B., Tuytelaars, T. (eds.) ECCV 2014. LNCS, vol. 8691, pp. 346–361. Springer, Cham (2014). https://doi.org/10.1007/978-3-319-10578-9_23
6. Ioffe, S., Szegedy, C.: Batch normalization: accelerating deep network training by reducing internal covariate shift. arXiv preprint arXiv:1502.03167 (2015)
7. Liu, Y., et al.: Detecting cancer metastases on gigapixel pathology images. arXiv preprint arXiv:1703.02442 (2017)
8. Mehta, S., Mercan, E., Bartlett, J., Weave, D., Elmore, J.G., Shapiro, L.: Y-net: joint segmentation and classification for diagnosis of breast biopsy images. arXiv preprint arXiv:1806.01313 (2018)
9. Otsu, N.: A threshold selection method from gray-level histograms. IEEE Trans. Syst. Man Cybern. **9**(1), 62–66 (1979)
10. Ronneberger, O., Fischer, P., Brox, T.: U-net: convolutional networks for biomedical image segmentation. In: Navab, N., Hornegger, J., Wells, W.M., Frangi, A.F. (eds.) MICCAI 2015. LNCS, vol. 9351, pp. 234–241. Springer, Cham (2015). https://doi.org/10.1007/978-3-319-24574-4_28
11. Wu, Y., He, K.: Group normalization. arXiv preprint arXiv:1803.08494 (2018)

# Lesion Detection with Deep Aggregated 3D Contextual Feature and Auxiliary Information

Han Zhang[(✉)] and Albert C. S. Chung

The Hong Kong University of Science and Technology, Kowloon, Hong Kong
hanzhang@ust.hk, achung@cse.ust.hk

**Abstract.** Detecting different kinds of lesions in computed tomography (CT) scans at the same time is a difficult but important task for a computer-aided diagnosis (CADx) system. Compared to single-lesion detection methods, our lesion detection method considers additional intra-class differences. In this work, we present a CT image analysis framework for lesion detection. Our model is developed based on a dense region-based fully convolutional network (Dense R-FCN) model using 3D context and is equipped with a dense auxiliary loss (DAL) scheme for end-to-end learning. It fuses shallow, medium, and deep features to meet the needs of detecting lesions of various sizes. Owing to its fully-connected structure, it is called Dense R-FCN. Meanwhile, the DAL supervises the intermediate hidden layers in order to maximize the use of the shallow layer information, which benefits the detection results, especially for small lesions. Experiment results on the DeepLesion dataset corroborate the efficacy of our method.

## 1 Introduction

Most computer-aided diagnosis (CADx) systems are limited to diagnosing only one kind of diseases such as the method presented in [12], which performs both the segmentation and classification of breast tumors at the same time. At the time of diagnosis, the most obvious difference between the current CADx systems and clinicians is that clinicians are able to locate different types of lesions simultaneously. For example, some patients with liver cancer will also be suffering lymph node metastasis. For these patients, clinicians will outline both types of lesions simultaneously during diagnosis. They would then combine the characteristics and morphology of the two types of lesions to give more comprehensive and accurate diagnoses and cancer staging. From this perspective, our model is able to fully imitate a clinician's diagnosis. Unlike mammograms, which only capture the mammary glands, computed tomography (CT) images encapsulate a large amount of tissues and organs which may include multiple lesions: in the lungs, liver, kidneys, and so on, and enlarged lymph nodes in the chest, abdomen, and pelvis. Therefore, clinicians need to pay more attention to each organ and the surrounding tissue which will increase clinicians' workloads

© Springer Nature Switzerland AG 2019
H.-I. Suk et al. (Eds.): MLMI 2019, LNCS 11861, pp. 45–53, 2019.
https://doi.org/10.1007/978-3-030-32692-0_6

who would normally only check the mammary glands in a mammogram. For this reason, our lesion-based detection system can help clinicians better than other single-lesion detection methods. Clinicians may have more pressing needs for this kind of lesion detection systems which can help to effectively reduce the rate of missed diagnoses.

It is well known that a faster region-based convolutional neural network (faster RCNN) [8] has been a very effective model for object detection in the past several years, and is also widely used in medical image detection tasks. Other than the faster RCNN based methods, there are also some methods which rely on 3D convolutional networks (ConvNets). In [5], Dou et al. proposed a 3D ConvNets comprising two parts: candidate screening and false positive reduction for pulmonary nodule detection. Nevertheless, these methods either require manual intervention or need multi-stage training. Moreover, the four-step training strategy in the faster RCNN implementation is more cumbersome than an end-to-end training strategy. The 3D ConvNets also need 3D annotations and is hard to pre-train using the ImageNet [4]. To solve these problems, Yan et al. [10] proposed the 3D Context enhanced (3DCE) Region-based ConvNets. Through delivering the neighboring CT image slices into the 2D detection network, it incorporates crucial 3D context information to extract the feature maps rather than only using one CT slice. These feature maps are then concatenated together to perform the final prediction. However, it only focuses on deep features and results in the disappearance of the shallow information. However, the shallow information plays a critical role in the detection of lesions, especially small lesions. In order to overcome these drawbacks, our work proposes some improvements.

In this paper, we propose an end-to-end ConvNets based model with dense auxiliary losses (DALs) to perform the detection of lesions on the DeepLesion database. This model is developed based on a 3DCE region-based fully convolutional network (R-FCN) [3] model with VGG-16 [9] as the feature extractor. To facilitate the integrity of the training process of the deep network as well as boosting its performance, we extract all-level features and add DALs in each level. Owing to its fully-connected structure, we name it Dense 3DCE R-FCN. To evaluate the proposed method, we have performed extensive experiments on a publicly available lesion dataset, i.e., DeepLesion [11]. The results presented in Sect. 3 demonstrate the efficacy of DAL and the Dense 3DCE R-FCN scheme.

## 2 Method

### 2.1 Motivation

In the DeepLesion dataset, all lesions are labeled with a short diameter and a long diameter by the radiologists. A long diameter ranges from 0.42 to 342.5 mm and a short diameter is 0.21 to 212.4 mm [11]. The largest lesion is nearly 1000 times larger than the smallest lesion. For a lesion detection task, the large variation in the lesion size is a very difficult problem and may cause more false positives (FPs). Also the feature extractor continuously convolves and pools the images, we then obtain low resolution feature maps after the Conv5 block as shown in

Fig. 1 which contain global information which is more discriminative for large lesion detection, however it will increase the difficulty of detecting small lesions. Also due to the depth of the network, it is easy to cause gradient vanishing and model degradation.

In order to address the problems mentioned above, we propose two modifications: (1) Extracting multi-level and multi-resolution feature maps to promote the network suitable for both small and large lesion detections. (2) Adding DAL pathways to force the model to learn more discriminate features in the shallow layers which will benefit the detection of small lesions. These improvements can help us in the following three aspects. First, making better use of the shallow layer information can accelerate the process of gradient descent. Second, features on different levels (shallow features, medium features, deep features) provide their own irreplaceable information. Third, regularizing the deep network by deeply supervising the hidden layers in the early stages can better overcome overfitting. Therefore, we propose the Dense 3DCE R-FCN with DAL method used in lesion detection tasks to address these problems.

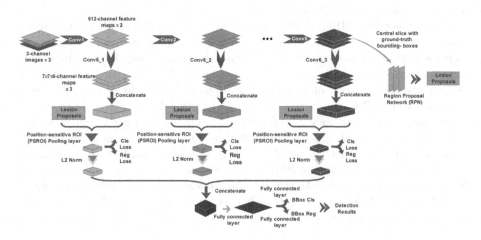

**Fig. 1.** Architecture of the Dense 3D context enhanced R-FCN model with Dense auxiliary losses. Several pathways are omitted.

## 2.2 Dense 3DCE R-FCN

Different from the most widely-used faster R-CNN, the based framework we have adopted is the R-FCN [3]. Better than a faster R-CNN, R-FCN can fuse the location information of the object target through a position-sensitive region of interest (PSROI) pooling layer [3]. The 3DCE R-FCN [10] improved the original R-FCN through adding three additional layers, including one fully connected (FC) layer, one ReLU activation layer and two FC layers for final prediction. Also, the 4th and 5th pooling layers in VGG-16 are deleted to avoid the resolution of the feature maps becoming too small. Moreover, according to the CT imaging principle, the 3D organs and tissues are transformed to many 2D image slices. Therefore, the 3D context is valuable and necessary especially in lesion detection tasks. It can help to observe the entire image roughly and the multi-resolution features provide more fine-grained details, which are complementary by nature. With regard to this, the 3D context is used to enhance the R-FCN network. Rather than using 3D volume as the input, the 3DCE network combines the 3D context information at the feature map level, so that 2D annotations as well as the 2D pre-trained weights are also available. As shown in Fig. 1, first, every three image is aggregated to form one 3-channel image, then the $i$ 3-channel images (one sample) are exploited as the input of the feature extraction network (we show the case of $i = 3$ in Fig. 1). During the training time, the central image provides the ground truth information and the other two slices offer knowledge of 3D context. In all experiments, we set $i = 3$ to obtain a fair comparison. The number of the filters is $(64, 128, 256, 512, 512)$ for each convolution block from Conv1 to Conv5. After Conv5, only the feature maps extracted from the central slice which includes the bounding box information can be passed to the region proposal network (RPN) [8] subnetwork.

Extending to the 3DCE R-FCN model, we extract various scale feature maps from Conv1 to Conv5 as shown in Fig. 1. These feature maps incorporate image features that are deep but with rich semantic information, intermediate but complementary, and shallow but in high resolution [6]. All feature maps will be delivered to the next convolution layer for dimension reduction, in which we use $j$ to control the 2D feature map number and empirically set it to 6. Then, using a reshape operation to concatenate the feature maps together to generate 3D information. After that, one $(7 \times 7)$ PSROI pooling layer is applied. Inspired by [1], in order to normalize the amplitude of differently scaled feature maps, a L2 norm layer is followed by the PSROI pooling layer. Therefore, all-level 3DCE feature maps are obtained. At last, another concatenate layer helps to combine the all-level 3DCE feature maps together, three FC layers are added to get the final classification and regression results.

## 2.3 Dense Auxiliary Loss

As shown in Fig. 1, we employ DALs after each pooled 3D context feature maps. Rather than only having the classification and regression losses at the output layer, the DALs can further provide the integrated optimization via direct supervision to the earlier hidden layers (Conv1$-$Conv5) through the "auxiliary loss" [7]. Furthermore, it speeds up the network's convergence by adding these pathways. It also propagates the supervision back to the hidden layers. The network aims to minimize the optimization objective as follows:

$$\mathcal{L}(p, l, t, t^u) = \mathcal{L}_{cls}(p, l) + \alpha[l = 1]\mathcal{L}_{reg}(t, t^u), \tag{1}$$

$$\mathcal{L}_{cls}(p, l) = \sum_{d \in D} -log(p_{l_d}), \text{and} \tag{2}$$

$$\mathcal{L}_{reg}(t, t^u) = \sum_{d \epsilon D} \sum_{i \epsilon \{x,y,w,h\}} L_1^{smooth}(t_{i_d}^u - t_{i_d}). \tag{3}$$

where the loss includes two components: the classification loss ($\mathcal{L}_{cls}$) and the regression loss ($\mathcal{L}_{reg}$). $l$ donates the true class label, $l \epsilon 0, 1$ because there are only two labels for the regions of interest (ROIs): 1 for lesions and 0 for non-lesions. $p$ is per ROI's discrete probability distribution over 2 classes: $p = (0, 1)$, getting through a fully-connected layer to perform the softmax computation. $t$ donates the bounding box regression targets, $t = (t_x, t_y, t_w, t_h)$, where $x, y, w$ and $h$ denote the box's center coordinates and its width and height. $t^u$ includes 4 items: translational amount $(t_x^u, t_y^u)$ and scale factor $(t_w^u, t_h^u)$ as predicted bounding-box regression targets. Meanwhile, $\alpha$ is a constant that controls the relative importance of the classification loss and the regression loss. We set $\alpha = 10$ in the experiments. $[l = 1]$ is an indicator function which aims to ignore the regression loss of the background ROIs thorough setting the value to 1 if $l = 1$ and 0 otherwise. $-log(p_{l_d})$ denotes the cross-entropy loss of the true class in the $d$-th supervision pathway, while $d$ has the same meaning in $t_{i_d}^u$ and $t_{i_d}$. Meanwhile, $D$ is a set that contains the indices of the layers directly connected to DAL paths. $L_1^{smooth}$ is a robust loss and the same as in [8].

## 3   Experiments

### 3.1   Dataset

The proposed method was evaluated on a publicly available dataset, i.e., DeepLesion [11], which provides 32,120 axial slices from 10,594 CT studies of 4,427 patients. There are 1–3 lesions in each image with accompanying bounding boxes and size measurements, adding up to 32,735 lesions in total. The original resolution size of most CT scans is $512 \times 512$, while just 0.12% of them are $768 \times 768$ or $1024 \times 1024$. In order to test the efficacy of our method on small lesions, we also selected lesions with an area less than 1% of the largest lesion to form a small lesion dataset. We also test our methods on both the small lesion dataset and the original DeepLesion dataset. In pre-processing, we used intensity windowing ($-1024$–3071 HU) that covers the intensity range of various organs and tissue such as soft tissue, lungs, and the bones to rescale the image so that its range becomes [0, 255] with the format as floating-point numbers. The black frame is also removed. Meanwhile, to make each pixel the same corresponding length, we rescaled every image slice. Meanwhile, we made the intervals of all volumes the same using interpolation along the z-axis. The data split we used is given by the DeepLesion dataset, 70% for training, 15% for testing and 15% for validation. It is easy to make a comparison between methods by using the official data split.

### 3.2   Implementation Details

The proposed method was implemented with MXNet [2] 1.5.0 on a PC with one NVIDIA 2080 GPU. For the optimizer of the model, we used the stochastic gradient descent (SGD) method with a momentum of 0.9, with an initial learning rate of 0.01 and multiplied by 0.1 after the 4th, 5th and 6th epochs. In all experiments, the model was trained for 7 epochs. The convolutional blocks (Conv1 to Conv5) were also initialized with a pre-trained model using ImageNet [4] database. Three ratios (1:1, 1:2, 2:1) and five scales (16, 24, 32, 48, 96) were used to generate anchors. During training, only batch size $= 1$ and $i = 3$ were available because of the limited GPU memory.

## 3.3   Results

In order to evaluate the performance of our method, the free-response receiver operating characteristic (FROC) curves on the test set are shown in Fig. 2 for an obvious performance comparison of different models. The Dense 3DCE R-FCN + DAL has the best performance among all competitive models on both the original DeepLeison dataset as well as the selected small leison dataset using the same data split. Note that for the predicted bounding boxes, if its intersection over union (IoU) with the ground-truth bounding box is larger than 0.5, it is predicted to be correct, and negative otherwise.

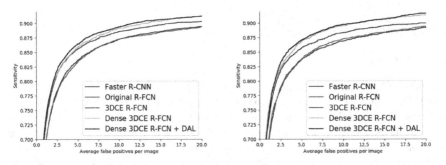

**Fig. 2.** FROC curves of multiple methods on the official data split of the original DeepLesion dataset (left) and the selected small lesion dataset (right).

For quantitative comparison, we utilized the widely-used sensitivity at 6 different values (0.5, 1, 2, 4, 8, 16) of FPs per image to calculate the fraction of correctly localized lesions. A series of experiments were conducted on the original DeepLesion dataset and the selected small lesion dataset using the official data split to investigate the effectiveness of the proposed Dense 3DCE R-FCN + DAL scheme. Results are listed in Tables 1 and 2 respectively. It can be observed that the Dense 3DCE R-FCN + DAL model achieves the best sensitivity for most FPs values on the original DeepLeison dataset. Dense 3DCE R-FCN + DAL outperforms the 3DCE R-FCN model with a convincing merge (88.52% vs 87.66% when FPs per image = 8) which indicates the necessity of the dense structure of 3DCE R-FCN as well as the DAL pathways. Meanwhile Dense 3DCE R-FCN also has good performance on the selected small lesion dataset. Compared to 3DCE R-FCN, the Dense 3DCE R-FCN improves the sensitivity by 0.77% - 2.13% at different FPs values per image, indicating that the shallow layer and medium layer information promotes the detection of lesions, especially the small lesions. Furthermore, with the auxiliary of DALs, the sensitivity further increases from 84.47% to 85.10% (4 FPs per image) on the original DeepLesion dataset, which we attribute to the DAL scheme. Due to it forcing the network to learn features based on a larger area, even if it is the whole CT slice, the network has lower sensitivity in local patterns, and this benefits the large lesion detection process.

**Table 1.** Detection results and inference time on the original DeeepLesion dataset. Sensitivity (%) at various FPs per image is used as the evaluation metric. *IT* denotes the inference time.

| FPs per image | 0.5 | 1 | 2 | 4 | 8 | 16 | IT (ms) |
|---|---|---|---|---|---|---|---|
| Faster R-CNN | 56.19 | 67.81 | 75.98 | 82.13 | 86.14 | 88.76 | **207** |
| Original R-FCN | 56.45 | 67.55 | 76.02 | 81.72 | 86.22 | 88.58 | 214 |
| 3DCE R-FCN [10] | 60.25 | 71.01 | 78.99 | 84.39 | 87.66 | 89.90 | 232 |
| Dense 3DCE R-FCN (ours) | **61.28** | **72.17** | 79.36 | 84.47 | 88.09 | 90.57 | 234 |
| Dense 3DCE R-FCN+DAL (ours) | 60.61 | 71.52 | **79.78** | **85.10** | **88.52** | **90.68** | 243 |

**Table 2.** Detection results and inference time on the selected small lesion dataset. Sensitivity (%) at various FPs per image is used as the evaluation metric. *IT* denotes the inference time.

| FPs per image | 0.5 | 1 | 2 | 4 | 8 | 16 | IT (ms) |
|---|---|---|---|---|---|---|---|
| Faster R-CNN | 58.93 | 68.46 | 76.69 | 82.27 | 85.98 | 88.52 | **200** |
| Original R-FCN | 57.89 | 68.69 | 76.60 | 82.12 | 86.28 | 88.61 | 222 |
| 3DCE R-FCN [10] | 62.70 | 72.20 | 79.85 | 84.51 | 87.43 | 89.67 | 239 |
| Dense 3DCE R-FCN (ours) | **64.21** | **74.33** | 80.70 | 85.28 | 88.76 | **90.88** | 238 |
| Dense 3DCE R-FCN+DAL (ours) | 63.32 | 72.79 | **80.94** | **85.93** | **88.88** | 90.82 | 235 |

We also use the official data spilt of the DeepLesion dataset to test two existing baseline methods including faster R-CNN and original R-FCN. As listed in Tables 1 and 2, our method (Dense 3DCE R-FCN + DAL) outperforms the faster R-CNN and original R-FCN with a large margin on both the original DeepLesion dataset and the selected small lesion dataset. Besides, our model is easy to deploy with end-to-end training. Detection results of several test images with different lesion scales have been demonstrated in Fig. 3.

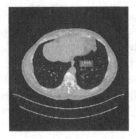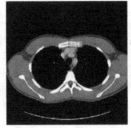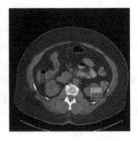

**Fig. 3.** Qualitative results using Dense 3DCE R-FCN+DAL framework on different image scales. Predictions with score >0.9 are shown. Green and yellow bounding boxes are respectively ground truth and automatic detection results. (Color figure online)

## 4  Conclusion

In this paper, we have improved the 3D context enhanced (3DCE) to Dense 3DCE, which leverages not only 3D contextual features but also shallow and medium layer features from volumetric data when performing lesion detection. We have also proposed the dense auxiliary loss (DAL) scheme, via adding the DAL pathways, with which the auxiliary classifiers can solve the supervision problem at the early hidden layers of the network through forcing the model to learn more discriminative features from them. We seamlessly integrate these two schemes into one model and have carried out extensive experiments on the publicly available DeepLesion dataset. The experiment results demonstrate that our framework can boost the accuracy with a convincing improvement as compared with the baseline methods and show the particular benefits in detecting small lesions.

## References

1. Bell, S., Lawrence Zitnick, C., Bala, K., et al.: Inside-outside net: detecting objects in context with skip pooling and recurrent neural networks. In: Proceedings of the IEEE Conference on Computer Vision and Pattern Recognition, pp. 2874–2883 (2016)
2. Chen, T., Li, M., Li, Y., et al.: MXNet: a flexible and efficient machine learning library for heterogeneous distributed systems. arXiv preprint arXiv:1512.01274 (2015)
3. Dai, J., Li, Y., He, K., et al.: R-FCN: object detection via region-based fully convolutional networks. In: Advances in Neural Information Processing Systems, pp. 379–387 (2016)
4. Deng, J., Dong, W., Socher, R., et al.: ImageNet: a large-scale hierarchical image database. In: 2009 IEEE Conference on Computer Vision and Pattern Recognition, pp. 248–255. IEEE (2009)
5. Dou, Q., Chen, H., Jin, Y., Lin, H., Qin, J., Heng, P.-A.: Automated pulmonary nodule detection via 3D convnets with online sample filtering and hybrid-loss residual learning. In: Descoteaux, M., Maier-Hein, L., Franz, A., Jannin, P., Collins,

D.L., Duchesne, S. (eds.) MICCAI 2017. LNCS, vol. 10435, pp. 630–638. Springer, Cham (2017). https://doi.org/10.1007/978-3-319-66179-7_72

6. Kong, T., Yao, A., Chen, Y., et al.: HyperNet: towards accurate region proposal generation and joint object detection. In: Proceedings of the IEEE Conference on Computer Vision and Pattern Recognition, pp. 845–853 (2016)

7. Lee, C.Y., Xie, S., Gallagher, P., et al.: Deeply-supervised nets. In: Artificial Intelligence and Statistics, pp. 562–570 (2015)

8. Ren, S., He, K., Girshick, R., et al.: Faster R-CNN: towards real-time object detection with region proposal networks. In: Advances in Neural Information Processing Systems, pp. 91–99 (2015)

9. Simonyan, K., Zisserman, A.: Very deep convolutional networks for large-scale image recognition. arXiv preprint arXiv:1409.1556 (2014)

10. Yan, K., Bagheri, M., Summers, R.M.: 3D context enhanced region-based convolutional neural network for end-to-end lesion detection. In: Frangi, A.F., Schnabel, J.A., Davatzikos, C., Alberola-López, C., Fichtinger, G. (eds.) MICCAI 2018. LNCS, vol. 11070, pp. 511–519. Springer, Cham (2018). https://doi.org/10.1007/978-3-030-00928-1_58

11. Yan, K., Wang, X., Lu, L., et al.: Deeplesion: automated mining of large-scale lesion annotations and universal lesion detection with deep learning. J. Med. Imaging 5(3), 036501 (2018)

12. Zhang, R., Zhang, H., Chung, A.C.S.: A unified mammogram analysis method via hybrid deep supervision. In: Stoyanov, D., et al. (eds.) RAMBO/BIA/TIA -2018. LNCS, vol. 11040, pp. 107–115. Springer, Cham (2018). https://doi.org/10.1007/978-3-030-00946-5_12

# MSAFusionNet: Multiple Subspace Attention Based Deep Multi-modal Fusion Network

Sen Zhang[1], Changzheng Zhang[1], Lanjun Wang[2], Cixing Li[1], Dandan Tu[1],
Rui Luo[3], Guojun Qi[3], and Jiebo Luo[4(✉)]

[1] Huawei, Shenzhen, China
[2] Huawei Canada, Markham, Canada
[3] Futurewei, Bellevue, USA
[4] University of Rochester, Rochester, USA
jluo@rochester.edu

**Abstract.** It is common for doctors to simultaneously consider multimodal information in diagnosis. However, how to use multi-modal medical images effectively has not been fully studied in the field of deep learning within such a context. In this paper, we address the task of end-to-end segmentation based on multi-modal data and propose a novel deep learning framework, multiple subspace attention-based deep multi-modal fusion network (referred to as MSAFusionNet hereon-forth). More specifically, MSAFusionNet consists of three main components: (1) a multiple subspace attention model that contains inter-attention modules and generalized squeeze-and-excitation modules, (2) a multi-modal fusion network which leverages CNN-LSTM layers to integrate sequential multimodal input images, and (3) a densely-dilated U-Net as the encoder-decoder backbone for image segmentation. Experiments on ISLES 2018 data set have shown that MSAFusionNet achieves the state-of-the-art segmentation accuracy.

**Keywords:** Deep learning · Multi-modal learning · Segmentation

## 1 Introduction

In the field of biomedical imaging and computer-aided diagnosis, image acquisition and analysis with more than one modality have been a common practice for years as different modalities contain abundant information that can be complementary to each other. Taking the multi-modal imaging segmentation task with ISLES (Ischemic Stroke Lesion Segmentation) 2018 data set [1] as an example, each modality reveals a unique type of biological information about changes on the stroke-induced tissue. In particular, CBV, CBF and MTT images are defined by blood characteristics, and raw CT images mainly reveal tissue contrast which may be of less significance in the task of identifying lesion regions. Therefore,

---

S. Zhang and C. Zhang—Equal contribution. This work is done when Sen Zhang is an intern at Huawei.

the combination of complementary information enables comprehensive analysis and accurate segmentation.

In recent years, deep learning methodologies, especially convolutional neural networks (CNNs) have achieved state-of-the-art accuracy in medical image segmentation. With the rapidly increasing amount of multi-modal image data, CNN approaches have already been applied to multi-modal segmentation tasks [2–6]. However, the question of how to use multi-modal data effectively is still not sufficiently investigated.

Most of the CNN-based segmentation approaches use multi-modal images by fusing different modalities together. Some of these methods, known as early fusion, integrate multi-modal information from original images or low-level features. For instance, the early fusion in one study [3] learns information from MRI TI, MRI T2, and FA images. These images from different modalities are concatenated together as the input of CNN models. This method does not take complex correlations between modalities into consideration. The other methods follow the late fusion strategy, using independent network architectures for each modality and then combining the high-level feature maps. The late fusion strategy shows better performance in [4], but also significantly increases the complexity of the network and makes the network more prone to over-fitting. Besides early fusion and late fusion strategies, a recent study from Tseng et al. [6] presents a novel framework which combines four modalities of MRI for brain tumor segmentation. The network first extracts low-level feature maps for each modality through multi-modal encoders and then uses a cross-modality convolution block to fuse feature maps together. Moreover, motivated by the concept of dense connection, [2] proposes a hyper-dense connected CNN which trains each modality in one path and densely connects all the paths. In summary, previous methods treat all modalities equally. However, it is a fact that different modalities have unequal contributions toward an accurate prediction.

Inspired by the success of the attention mechanism [7] and the LSTM structure [12], we propose MSAFusionNet, a multiple subspace attention method for fusion of multiple modalities. This architecture is designed to effectively leverage implicit correlations between different modalities. It utilizes our proposed inter-attention and generalized squeeze-excitation modules to generate attention weights and modify the output feature map by the importance. The network also integrates a U-Net architecture [9] and a densely-dilated convolution module [10] whose effectiveness have been proved in medical and general image segmentation tasks.

In this study, we address on four major contributions:

- We propose MSAFusionNet to analyze multi-modal image data and achieve the state-of-the-art segmentation accuracy on ISLES 2018.
- We design a multiple subspace attention model to generate more representative fused feature maps.
- We construct a multi-modal fusion network which leverages CNN-LSTMs for sequential multi-modal data.
- We apply a densely-dilated U-Net backbone for the medical image segmentation task.

It is also worth noting that the proposed multiple subspace attention model can be easily embedded with other networks and the multi-modal fusion network

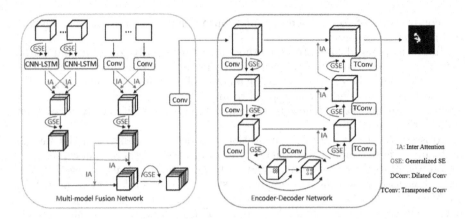

**Fig. 1.** The overall framework of the proposed MSAFusionNet.

is also compatible with any segmentation network backbone. We believe these two points can promote the development of more effective methods.

## 2   Methods

### 2.1   Overview

MSAFusionNet, as shown in Fig. 1, consists of two major parts: a multi-modal fusion network (MFN) and an encoder-decoder network (EDN). MFN is designed to fuse multiple modalities. It accepts input data in two kinds of formats: an image and a sequence of images. In this study, according to ISLES 2018 data set, we consider the input as 2D images and 3D volumes each of which is a sequence of 2D images. This framework can be easily extended to include 3D images and 4D volumes by replacing 2D convolution operators with 3D convolution operators in the network. EDN is built upon a modified U-Net structure. A dense dilation convolution block is used to replace the original bottom layer. Moreover, we also leverage a convolution layer to feed the output feature map from MFN into EDN. As a result, two networks can be trained jointly in an end-to-end manner.

More specifically, MSAFusionNet leverages a novel multiple subspace attention (MSA) model which contains two types of modules: inter-attention (IA) modules and generalized squeeze-and-excitation (GSE) modules. The details of the MSA model will be introduced in Sect. 2.2. In general, MSA in MFN is to fully utilize information between and within modalities. Meanwhile, in EDN, MSA facilitates to extract more representative features and works as connections between encoders and decoders.

### 2.2   Multiple Subspace Attention (MSA)

As introduced, IA and GES are two modules in the MSA. IA is an attention mechanism to embed a subspace with an auxiliary gating signal, and GSE focuses on identifying the importance of a single dimension in a subspace.

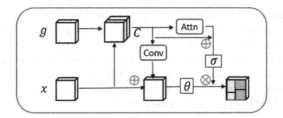

**Fig. 2.** The inter-attention module.

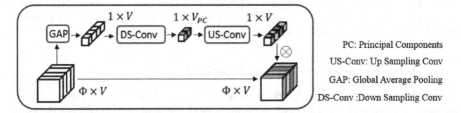

PC: Principal Components

US-Conv: Up Sampling Conv

GAP: Global Average Pooling

DS-Conv :Down Sampling Conv

**Fig. 3.** The generalized squeeze-and-excitation module.

**Inter-Attention Module.** Given a signal from one modality, information from other modalities can serve as helpful auxiliaries with appropriate gating mechanisms. Moreover, feature maps at different scales can also augment each other. As a result, we propose IA to facilitate information among multiple input modalities and multiple feature maps with different scales.

As shown in Fig. 2, an IA module first concatenates a gating signal $g$ with a feature map $x$ into a concatenated feature map $C$. Then, $C$ is analyzed by two convolution paths. One path serves as a gate function, which learns a gating attention map with a range of $[0, 1]$ via a convolution module with $G$ layers to impose different attentions on $C$. The other path directly uses a convolution module with $L$ layers to extract high-level joint features, and then adds it to the input low-level features to maintain the original information. The output of the IA module is an element-by-element product of the gating attention map and the feature map. The IA module, denoted as $\mathcal{IA}(.,.)$, given by:

$$\mathcal{IA}(x, g) = \theta(\mathcal{F}^{(L)}(C) + x) \otimes \sigma(\mathcal{F}^{(G)}(C) + C) \tag{1}$$

where $C$ is the concatenation of $x$ and $g$. $\mathcal{F}^{(G)}(.)$ and $\mathcal{F}^{(L)}(.)$ denote convolution modules with $G$ layers and $L$ layers, respectively. $\theta$ is an activation function such as ReLU or ELU, and $\sigma$ is a sigmoid function to maintain the range of the gating attention map.

**Generalized Squeeze-and-Excitation Module.** The squeeze-and-excitation unit has been proved successful for many studies by putting more attentions on channels with more semantic information [13]. In this study, we extend it to a generalized squeeze-and-excitation (GSE) module that can learn the importance of each element along any axis.

The input of a GSE module is a parameter space with a size of $\Phi \times V$, where $V$ is the dimension to be applied on the attention, and $\Phi$ represents the remaining dimensions. As shown in Fig. 3, global average pooling, denoted as $\mathcal{GAP}(.)$, is first applied to obtain local statistics along the attention dimension. Next, two cascaded dense connected convolution layers add the ability to learn the underlying principal components in a subspace with a dimension of $V$. The generated attention weighted vector is used to gate the original signal via an element-wise multiplication along the attention dimension. As a result, the GSE module, denoted as $\mathcal{GSE}(.)$, is described as:

$$\mathcal{GSE}(x) = x \otimes \sigma(W_{us} \cdot \theta(W_{ds} \cdot \mathcal{GAP}(x) + b_{ds}) + b_{us}) \tag{2}$$

where $W_{us}$ and $W_{ds}$ are the weights of the upsampling and downsampling convolution layers, respectively. $b_{us}$ and $b_{ds}$ are the corresponding biases. $\theta$ is a ReLU function and $\sigma$ is a sigmoid function.

### 2.3 Multi-modal Fusion Network (MFN)

Given that the input data $X$ contains a set of modalities in the format of 2D images, denoted as $\mathbb{P}$, and a set of modalities in the format of 3D volumes denoted as $\mathbb{Q}$. We first focus on generating a feature map of one modality $i$ from the 2D modality set $\mathbb{P}$ by an IA module, which is given by:

$$Y_s^{(i)} = \mathcal{IA}(\mathcal{P}_s(X_{2D}^{(i)}), \mathcal{R}_s(\{\mathcal{P}_s(X_{2D}^{(k)})|k \neq i, k \in \mathbb{P}\})) \tag{3}$$

where $\mathcal{P}_s(.)$ is a convolution unit with two layers and $\mathcal{R}_s(.)$ is a channel reduction function applied on the concatenated feature map of the modalities in $\mathbb{P}$ other than $i$. Followed by the similar approach, an IA module is applied to obtain a feature map of one modality $j$ from the 3D modality set $\mathbb{Q}$, given by:

$$Y_d^{(j)} = \mathcal{IA}(\mathcal{P}_d(X_{3D}^{(j)}), \mathcal{R}_d(\{\mathcal{P}_d(X_{3D}^{(l)})|l \neq j, l \in \mathbb{Q}\})) \tag{4}$$

where $\mathcal{P}_d(.)$ represents a 3D convolution unit which has two CNN-LSTM layers in our design, and $\mathcal{R}_d(.)$ is a channel reduce function which works in the same manner as $\mathcal{R}_s(.)$.

We concatenate $\{Y_s^{(i)}| i \in \mathbb{P}\}$ into $Y_s$, and $\{Y_d^{(j)}| j \in \mathbb{Q}\}$ into $Y_d$. $Y_s$ and $Y_d$ then are processed by GSE modules to adaptively calibrate attention-wise feature responses. They are further merged by IA modules using each other as the gating signal. Finally, a GSE module is applied to the concatenated IA results to generate the final combined feature map $Y$. The entire procedure is:

$$Y = \mathcal{GSE}(\mathcal{IA}(\mathcal{GSE}(Y_s), \mathcal{GSE}(Y_d)), \mathcal{IA}(\mathcal{GSE}(Y_d), \mathcal{GSE}(Y_s))) \tag{5}$$

### 2.4 Encoder-Decoder Network (EDN)

**U-Net with Dense Dilation Module.** We adopt U-Net which is commonly suggested as the encoder-decoder backbone for small medical data sets [9]. More specifically, we use a deep U-Net structure with five blocks, which have 16, 32, 64, 128, and 256 filters in the convolution layers of each block, respectively. In each block, there are two convolution layers with the same kernel size of $3 \times 3$, and a dropout layer between these two convolution layers. The transitions between the blocks are implemented by a $2 \times 2$ max pooling layer in the encoder and a transpose convolution layer with $2 \times 2$ strides in the decoder. All convolutions are followed by a batch normalization layer to facilitate the learning process.

Different from the traditional U-Net structure [9], we replace the bottom block with a dense dilation module [11]. The dilation rates are set to $\{1, 2, 3, 4\}$ to achieve larger receptive fields. This design is suitable for cases such as ISLES 2018 data set, which has a large range of lesion sizes. The enlarged receptive field can help large lesions, e.g. those nearly cover the whole image, reveal clearer boundaries.

**MSA in EDN.** As mentioned in Sect. 2.2, IA and GSE modules can be regarded as attentions on multiple subspaces with different dimensions, given an auxiliary gating signal or not. These two modules can be used in the encoder-decoder structure as well. We apply IA and GES in EDN as follows. First, before each transition, a GSE module is used to modify the interest on different feature maps along the channels. Second, an IA module is used in the connection between the encoder and the decoder at every scale. We gate the features from the encoder with the feature map from the decoder. This design reduces the dependence on potential unnecessary areas of the encoder features, where more effective connections is better to leverage the information contained in the network.

## 2.5 Loss Function

For ISLES 2018 segmentation task, the network is jointly trained with a hybrid loss function consisting of contributions from both cross-entropy loss and DICE coefficient loss, given by:

$$L = \frac{1}{|\mathbb{K}|} \sum_{i \in \mathbb{K}} (\omega_i L_{DICE}^{(i)} + \lambda L_{CE}^{(i)}), \quad \omega_i = \frac{|\mathbb{K}|}{S^{(i)} \times M} \tag{6}$$

$$L_{DICE}^{(i)} = 2 \frac{|Z^{(i)} \cap G^{(i)}|}{|Z^{(i)}| + |G^{(i)}|} \tag{7}$$

$$L_{CE}^{(i)} = \frac{1}{|\Omega^{(i)}|} \sum_{j \in \Omega^{(i)}} [-g_j^{(i)} log(z_j^{(i)}) - (1 - g_j^{(i)}) log(1 - z_j^{(i)})] \tag{8}$$

where $M$ is the number of scans, $\mathbb{K}$ denotes the slice set from all scans, $S^{(i)}$ is the number of slices in the corresponding scan which the $i$-th slice in $\mathbb{K}$ belongs, $\omega_i$ is the weight of the $i$-th slice, and $\lambda$ is a relax parameter set to 0.5 in the following experiments. $\Omega^{(i)}$ is the voxel set of the $i$-th slice, $Z^{(i)} = \{z_j^{(i)} | j \in \Omega^{(i)}\}$ and $G^{(i)} = \{g_j^{(i)} | j \in \Omega^{(i)}\}$ are the predicted mask and the ground truth mask of the $i$-th slice, respectively. It is noted that we use $\omega_i$ to adjust the importance of each slice based on the number of slices in the corresponding scan. The reason for adding $\omega_i$ is that the number of slices in one scan varies in ISLES 2018 data set. Since many scans with only two slices may limit the power of 3D convolution operators, we have to train the network in the slice level but not the scan level. Meanwhile, we understand that the stereoscopic accuracy of the prediction on a scan really matters. As a result, we design a weight $\omega_i$ to balance the scans with a large number of slices and those with only two slices.

# 3   Experiments on the ISLES Data Set

## 3.1   Data Set and Pre-processing

We evaluate the performance of the proposed MSAFusionNet on ISLES 2018 data set, with six modalities as inputs, namely, CT, CBV, CBF, MTT, Tmax and 4DPWI. The first five modalities are 2D images, while 4DPWI is a 3D volume. There are 63 patients and 94 scans for training because the stroke lesion volumes in some patients are split into two scans. The slice number per scan has a wide range of $[2, 22]$. Standard normalization is applied to each modality. Data augmentation approaches, including random horizontal/vertical flip, width/height shift, zoom, and rotation, are adopted to reduce over-fitting caused by the small data size.

## 3.2   Training and Evaluation

The network is implemented with Tensorflow. The Adam optimizer is used with an initial learning rate of 0.0003. The learning rate is reduced by a factor of 0.1 if the loss does not improve for 30 consecutive epochs. The batch size is set to four slices per GPU and the training is stopped after 120 epochs. In the evaluation, we first leverage a series of ablation studies to show the effectiveness of each component in the proposed MSAFusionNet and then evaluate the performance of the entire MSAFusionNet by comparing with other methods from ISLES 2018 leader board.

The settings of ablation studies are shown in Table 1. The baseline does not have MSA in either MFN or EDN. In addition, the baseline ignores the sequential property of 4DPWI and applies CNNs separately on each image from 4DPWI. Compared with the baseline, No-MSA-FusionNet replaces CNNs with CNN-LSTM layers for 4DPWI, but without MSA. Sub-MSA-FusionNet adds MSA in EDN, and MSAFusionNet incorporates the complete design in Fig. 1.

In this experiment, we use DICE to evaluate the performance. Table 1 shows that the MSA module can improve the performance significantly no matter applied in the fusion network or in the encoder-decoder backbone individually. It is also clear that the full MSAFusionNet outperforms other experiment settings. For the modality with sequential data, the CNN-LSTM layers bring marginal improvements over convolutions only. All the improvements are also shown in Fig. 4[1]. The segmentation results produced by the full MSAFusionNet are much closer to the ground-truth than any produced by any incomplete MSAFusionNet.

Moreover, we compare MSAFusionNet with the state-of-the-art methods on the testing leader board of ISLES 2018[2]. As shown in Table 2, our method achieves the best AVD (Absolute Volume Difference) score, which is the most important criterion for lesion volumetry studies, with other scores comparable to the top methods[3].

---

[1] Normalization is applied to improve the contrast.

[2] https://www.smir.ch/ISLES/Start2018#resultsTesting [Accessed March 25, 2019].

[3] No details are available of these methods.

**Table 1.** The results of ablation studies.

|  | CNN-LSTM | MSA(EDN) | MSA(MFN) | DICE |
|---|---|---|---|---|
| Baseline |  |  |  | 0.43608 |
| No-MSA-FusionNet | ✓ |  |  | 0.43982 |
| Sub-MSA-FusionNet | ✓ | ✓ |  | 0.47461 |
| MSAFusionNet | ✓ | ✓ | ✓ | 0.50544 |

**Table 2.** The results on the ISLES 2018 testing leader board.

|  | DICE | AVD | Precision | Recall |
|---|---|---|---|---|
| SenseTime Inc | **0.51 ± 0.31** | 10.24 ± 9.94 | 0.55 ± 0.36 | 0.55 ± 0.34 |
| Beijing Univ. of Tech | 0.49 ± 0.31 | 10.08 ± 10.58 | 0.56 ± 0.37 | 0.53 ± 0.33 |
| VICOROB, Univ. of Girona | 0.49 ± 0.31 | 12.18 ± 11.08 | 0.51 ± 0.36 | **0.57 ± 0.35** |
| **MSAFusionNet** | 0.49 ± 0.32 | **9.81 ± 9.36** | 0.53 ± 0.35 | 0.54 ± 0.35 |
| Youtu Lab, Tencent Inc | 0.48 ± 0.33 | 10.59 ± 13.16 | **0.59 ± 0.38** | 0.46 ± 0.33 |
| Malong Inc | 0.47 ± 0.31 | 11.14 ± 12.74 | 0.56 ± 0.37 | 0.49 ± 0.33 |

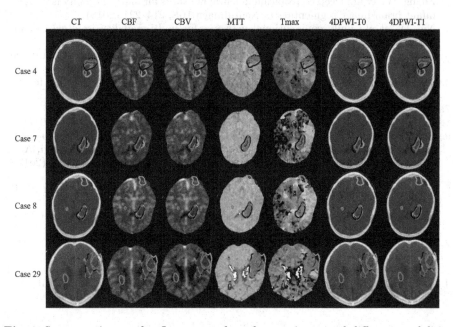

**Fig. 4.** Segmentation results. Images are from four patients, and different modalities are shown. Particularly, we list time points T0 and T1 of 4DPWI due to the page limit. We compare the results from MSAFusionNet (blue) with the ground-truth (solid red), as well as the results from ablation studies: Sub-MSA-FusionNet (purple), No-MSA-FusionNet (yellow) and the baseline (green). (Color figure online)

# 4    Conclusion and Future Work

In this paper, we present a novel framework called MSAFusionNet that can effectively integrate multi-modal medical image data. We demonstrate its competitive performance on ISLES 2018 segmentation challenge. We believe its application is beyond ISLES 2018 because the proposed multiple subspace attention model can be easily embedded with other networks and the multi-modal fusion network is also compatible with any segmentation network backbone. In the future, we will identify and use additional multi-modal image data set to further validate and improve our framework. It would also be interesting to extend the current framework to handle multi-modal fusion over time [14].

# References

1. ISLES 2018 Challenge. http://www.isles-challenge.org/
2. Dolz, J., et al.: HyperDense-Net: a hyper-densely connected CNN for multi-modal image segmentation. IEEE TMI **38**, 1116–1126 (2018)
3. Zhang, W., et al.: Deep convolutional neural networks for multi-modality isointense infant brain image segmentation. NeuroImage **108**, 214–224 (2015)
4. Nie, D., et al.: Fully convolutional networks for multi-modality isointense infant brain image segmentation. In: ISBI (2016)
5. Guo, Z., et al.: Medical image segmentation based on multi-modal convolutional neural network: study on image fusion schemes. In: ISBI (2018)
6. Tseng, K.L., et al.: Joint sequence learning and cross-modality convolution for 3D biomedical segmentation. In: CVPR (2017)
7. Vaswani, A., et al.: Attention is all you need. In: NIPS (2017)
8. Huang, G., et al.: Densely connected convolutional networks. In: CVPR (2017)
9. Ronneberger, O., Fischer, P., Brox, T.: U-net: convolutional networks for biomedical image segmentation. In: Navab, N., Hornegger, J., Wells, W.M., Frangi, A.F. (eds.) MICCAI 2015. LNCS, vol. 9351, pp. 234–241. Springer, Cham (2015). https://doi.org/10.1007/978-3-319-24574-4_28
10. Yu, F., et al.: Multi-scale context aggregation by dilated convolutions. In: ICLR (2016)
11. Yang, M., et al.: DenseASPP for semantic segmentation in street scenes. In: CVPR (2018)
12. Srivastava, N., et al.: Unsupervised learning of video representations using LSTMs. In: ICML (2015)
13. Hu, J., et al.: Squeeze-and-excitation network. In: CVPR (2018)
14. Yang, X., et al.: Deep multimodal representation learning from temporal data. In: CVPR (2017)

# DCCL: A Benchmark for Cervical Cytology Analysis

Changzheng Zhang[1], Dong Liu[4], Lanjun Wang[2], Yaoxin Li[1], Xiaoshi Chen[1],
Rui Luo[3], Shuanlong Che[4], Hehua Liang[4], Yinghua Li[4], Si Liu[4], Dandan Tu[1],
Guojun Qi[3], Pifu Luo[4(✉)], and Jiebo Luo[5(✉)]

[1] Huawei, Shenzhen, China
[2] Huawei Canada, Markham, Canada
[3] Futurewei, Bellevue, USA
[4] KingMed Diagnostics Co., Ltd., Guangzhou, China
gz-luopf@kingmed.com.cn
[5] University of Rochester, Rochester, USA
jluo@rochester.edu

**Abstract.** Medical imaging analysis has witnessed impressive progress
in recent years thanks to the development of large-scale labeled datasets.
However, in many fields, including cervical cytology, a large well-
annotated benchmark dataset remains missing. In this paper, we introduce by far the largest cervical cytology dataset, called Deep Cervical
Cytological Lesions (referred to as DCCL). DCCL contains 14,432 image
patches with around $1,200 \times 2,000$ pixels cropped from 1,167 whole slide
images collected from four medical centers and scanned by one of the
three kinds of digital slide scanners. Besides patch level labels, cell level
labels are provided, with 27,972 lesion cells labeled based on The 2014
Bethesda System and the bounding box by six board-certified pathologists with eight years of experience on the average. We also use deep
learning models to generate the baseline performance for lesion cell detection and cell type classification on DCCL. We believe this dataset can
serve as a valuable resource and platform for researchers to develop new
algorithms and pipelines for advanced cervical cancer diagnosis and prevention.

**Keywords:** Cervical cancer screening · Liquid-based cytology · Deep
learning

## 1 Introduction

Cervical cancer is one of the most common cancers among women and ranks
fourth in terms of incidence and mortality, with approximately 570,000 cases
and 311,000 deaths in 2018 worldwide. Moreover, in many developing countries,
this disease has been even more commonly diagnosed but has the highest death

---

C. Zhang and D. Liu—Equal contribution.

© Springer Nature Switzerland AG 2019
H.-I. Suk et al. (Eds.): MLMI 2019, LNCS 11861, pp. 63–72, 2019.
https://doi.org/10.1007/978-3-030-32692-0_8

rate among cancers [3]. Nevertheless, cervical cancer is preventable and can be cured in the early stage as it can be largely detected by cytological screening combined with human papillomavirus virus (HPV) testing. When the patients are infected by HPV, the cervical epithelial cells result in different morphological changes, together with loss of maturity of the squamous epithelial cells and abnormal proliferation. The process is called dysplasia and manifests as loss polarity of the squamous cells, nuclear enlargement, coarse and hyperchromatic nuclei, as well as nuclear condensation. These phenomenons always indicate a higher probability of progressing to cervical cancer.

The application of liquid-based cytology test has greatly improved the diagnosis rate of precancerous and cancerous lesions at the cell level and has become one of the most important methods for cervical cancer diagnosis and prevention. Based on The 2014 Bethesda System for Reporting Cervical Cytology (2014 TBS) [12], the precancerous squamous intraepithelial lesions include four types with an increasing level of severity: atypical squamous cells of undetermined significance (ASC-US), low squamous intraepithelial lesion (LSIL), atypical squamous cell-cannot exclude HSIL (ASC-H) and high squamous intraepithelial lesion (HSIL); while cancerous lesions include mainly two types: squamous cell carcinoma (SCC) and adenocarcinoma (AdC). However, challenges exist when assessing cytology tests. First, it is time-consuming to examine a gigapixel pathological slide that contains thousands of cervical cells. The extremely low ratio of pathologists to patients has become a bottleneck of cervical cancer screening, especially in developing countries. Second, the diagnosis of precancerous and cancerous lesions is highly uncertain, subject to the experiences of pathologists.

To tackle the challenges, it would be highly valuable to develop automatic cervical cytology analysis models. Based on existing cervical cytology datasets [1, 8], several works have been done for lesion cell classification [8,19,20], as well as cytoplasm and nuclei segmentation [16]. Nevertheless, current cervical cytology datasets typically contain a few thousand lesion cells. To facilitate future cervical cytology analysis, we introduce by-far the largest and densely labeled cervical digital pathology dataset, namely DCCL.

The contributions of this work are summarized as follows:

- We introduce a large-scale cervical cytology dataset called DCCL. To the best of our knowledge, this is the largest cervical cytology dataset. We crop a total of 14,432 image patches from 1,167 whole slides. The number of slides is ten times larger than the previous benchmark datasets [13,18].
- We release 27,972 lesion cell bounding boxes ranging from low-grade precancerous lesions to cancerous lesions, and 6,420 semi-supervised labeled negative cell samples (model results). The overall number of cells is three times larger than the previous benchmark datasets [8,13,18].
- We provide benchmark performance on lesion cell classification and detection by leveraging widely used deep neural network models.
- We visualize the lesion cell similarity map to facilitate the understanding of inter-class and intra-class relationships via t-SNE.

## 2   Related Work

We roughly divide current datasets for cervical cytology analysis into two groups based on their target usages: (i) for lesion cell classification, and (ii) for cytoplasmic and nuclei segmentation.

**Lesion Cell Classification.** The most well-known dataset is Papanicolaou (Pap) smear based Herlev Dataset [2,8] collected by microscopes and digital cameras. In Herlev, a cell image is categorized into four types: NILM (negative for intraepithelial lesion or malignancy), LSIL, HSIL and SCC based on Bethesda standard [2]. Besides, there are CerviSCAN dataset results from CerviSCAN project [18] for low-cost cervical cancer screening, and HEMLBC Dataset [19] relies on liquid-based cytology. Details of these datasets are shown in Table 3.

We observe that the performance of recent lesion classification algorithms become saturated with these datasets [4,20]. However, those classifiers cannot achieve comparable performance in practice, because the existing datasets have limited variations on lesion types, cell morphological structures, and background clutters. Thus, a challenging dataset is required to facilitate future cervical cytology analysis for clinical applications.

**Cytoplasm and Nuclei Segmentation.** For cytoplasm segmentation, Shenzhen University (SZU) Dataset [16] consists of 21 cervical cytology images in seven clumps with 6.1 cells per clump on the average. For nuclei segmentation, in ISBI 2015 challenge [1], there are eight cervical cytology images, each of which has 20–60 Pap stained cervical cells.

A recent study leverages the above two to formulate the segmentation problem with a graphical model, which can take more geometric information into account and generate an accurate prediction [16]. However, due to the small size, these datasets have not been used to design any deep learning model.

## 3   DCCL

### 3.1   Collection Methodology

There are 1,167 specimens of cervical cytology from participants whose ages are in the range of 32 to 67. The specimens are prepared by Thinprep methods stained with Papanicolaou stain, which were collected by four provincial medical centers from 2016 to 2018. The gathered slides to generate DCCL include 933 positive patients and 234 normal cases. The slide labels are from pathology reports. All of the slides are scanned evenly by one of three kinds of digital slide scanners (Nanozoomer2.0HT, KFBIO KF-RPO-400, and AperioAT2) all with 200× zoom and in 24-bit color.

We cut each slide image in grids, where rectangular areas are around 1200 × 2000 pixels (with a physical size of 1011.6 μm × 606.96 μm). Generally, a slide is converted to 700–800 patches. In detail, DCCL is composed of 14,432 image patches without cell-free, out-of-focus, blur, fade or any bubble inside. It includes 9,930 positive image patches which have precancerous and/or cancerous lesions and 4,502 negative image patches which are from normal cases. The details about the slide distribution and patch distribution are shown in Table 1. It is noted that: (i) all of the data used in our study are strictly anonymized; (ii) the types of slides, as well as patches, are from the diagnosis of pathologists; (iii) "unlabeled" and "labeled" in Table 1 indicates whether a patch is labeled manually on the cell level, the process of which is to be explained in Sect. 3.2.

**Table 1.** Statistics on slides and patches by types

| | Train | | | Val | | | Test | | | Total | | | Ratio | | |
|---|---|---|---|---|---|---|---|---|---|---|---|---|---|---|---|
| | Slide | Patch | | Slide | Patch | | Slide | Patch | | Slide | Patch | | Slide | Patch | |
| | | Unlabeled | Labeled | | Unlabeled | Labeled | | Unlabeled | Labeled | | Unlabeled | Labeled | | Unlabeled | Labeled |
| NILM | 117 | 2301 | 0 | 46 | 812 | 0 | 71 | 1389 | 0 | 234 | 4502 | 0 | 20% | 31% | 0% |
| ASC-US | 67 | 0 | 203 | 27 | 0 | 61 | 41 | 0 | 105 | 135 | 0 | 369 | 12% | 0% | 3% |
| ASC-H | 84 | 1227 | 295 | 34 | 264 | 278 | 51 | 493 | 389 | 169 | 1984 | 962 | 14% | 14% | 7% |
| LSIL | 197 | 3 | 1683 | 79 | 9 | 579 | 119 | 12 | 884 | 395 | 24 | 3146 | 34% | 0% | 22% |
| HSIL | 90 | 988 | 466 | 36 | 48 | 210 | 55 | 40 | 253 | 181 | 1076 | 929 | 16% | 7% | 6% |
| SCC | 14 | 406 | 154 | 5 | 158 | 42 | 8 | 152 | 111 | 27 | 716 | 307 | 2% | 5% | 2% |
| AdC | 13 | 130 | 115 | 5 | 45 | 23 | 8 | 81 | 23 | 26 | 256 | 161 | 2% | 2% | 1% |
| Total | 582 | 5055 | 2916 | 232 | 524 | 1193 | 353 | 778 | 1765 | 1167 | 8558 | 5874 | 100% | 59% | 41% |

## 3.2   Image Annotation

We extract 5,874 patches from DCCL to label manually, and the rest are unlabeled. The details of the labeled data distribution and unlabeled data distribution, as well as the patch distribution on training, validation and testing sets, are shown in Table 1. It is noted that DCCL contains unlabeled patches, because they may help to promote semi-supervised and unsupervised learning, even transfer learning for intelligent cervical cytology analysis.

In each patch, a lesion cell is annotated with its type based on 2014 TBS [12] along with a bounding box. There are 27,972 lesion cells labeled manually, including ASC-US, LSIL, ASC-H, HSIL, SCC and AdC, a total of six types of lesion cells. The details of the labeled lesion cells are in Table 2 and some examples are shown in Fig. 1. There are six board-certified pathologists participated in the annotation task. In the initial blind reading phase, each patch is annotated by two pathologists independently to mark all suspicious lesion cells. Next, every pair of two bounding boxes with consistent lesion type from different readers are merged by average if the Intersection over Union (IoU) is larger than 0.3. That is to say, we skip the bounding boxes marked by only one pathologist to keep high quality, and the merged bounding box together with its lesion type is the final annotation on a cell.

Nevertheless, if DCCL only contains lesion cell bounding boxes, the analysis result may have a bias on positive samples. Hence, DCCL also considers negative cells by leveraging those 4,502 negative patches where none lesion cell exists. However, it would introduce large data bias to add all negative cells in the dataset because they are in a huge amount and easy to be distinguished from lesion cells. In order to be beneficial for cervical cytology analysis algorithms, what we need are hard cases which are negative cells but easy to be recognized as positives, such as NILMs in Fig. 1. With these hard negative cells, the community

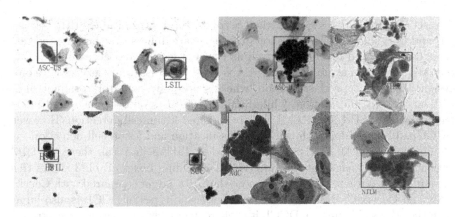

**Fig. 1.** Examples of cells

can focus on some inherent challenges of cervical cytology recognition, such as intra-class variance (e.g., parts of LSIL cells have a sharply defined perinuclear cavity, but the rests do not have) and inter-class similarity (e.g., both HSIL and SCC have high nuclear to cytoplasmic ratios).

In the study, we leverage the widely used detection methods trained with labeled positive patches and regard those bounding boxes on negative patches with high false positive probabilities to be hard negatives. In detail, Faster R-CNN and RetinaNet are trained on 5,874 labeled positive patches, respectively. We test them on 4,502 negative patches and get 6,420 bounding boxes whose average positive probability obtained by two methods is over 0.2. The distribution of the generated hard negatives (a.k.a. NILM) is also shown in Table 2.

**Table 2.** Statistics on training/validation/test sets by types

|        | Train | Val  | Test  | Total |       | Ratio |      |
|--------|-------|------|-------|-------|-------|-------|------|
| NILM   | 2588  | 1540 | 2292  | 6420  | 6420  | 19%   | 19%  |
| ASC-US | 2471  | 838  | 1378  | 4687  | 27972 | 14%   | 81%  |
| ASC-H  | 1147  | 543  | 591   | 2281  |       | 7%    |      |
| LSIL   | 1739  | 356  | 595   | 2690  |       | 8%    |      |
| HSIL   | 5890  | 1807 | 3482  | 11179 |       | 33%   |      |
| SCC    | 3006  | 1225 | 2731  | 6962  |       | 20%   |      |
| AGC    | 122   | 20   | 31    | 173   |       | 1%    |      |
| Total  | 16963 | 6329 | 11100 | 34392 | 34392 | 100%  | 100% |

### 3.3  Dataset Statistics

We analyze the properties of DCCL by comparing with other widely used datasets, including CerviSCAN [18], Herlev Dataset [8], ISBI 2015 Challenge

Dataset [1], HEMLBC [19], Shenzhen Second People's Hospital (SSPH) Dataset [11] and Cervix93 [13]. Table 3 shows that they are different in the targeted task type, data size and diversity, as well as types of lesions and accessibility. Take the task type as an example, CerviSCAN, Herlev Dataset and Cervix93 are only designed for cell type classification, where samples are cut from original slides without context information, while ISBI 2015 focuses on cytoplasm and nuclei segmentation; SSPH and HEMLBC are targeted lesion cell detection. However, DCCL can be used for both cell type classification and lesion cell detection.

The volume of DCCL is also illustrated in Table 3. In total, there are 1,167 patients, 14,432 image patches and 34,392 bounding boxes. Table 3 shows that the number of patients of DCCL is more than 10× larger compared with CerviS-CAN and Cervix93. Besides, the number of lesion types of DCCL is also larger than the others. To sum up, DCCL is challenging due to diversities on geographical data sources, types of digital slides scanners, patient ages, types of lesion cells and background clutters. More importantly, all of these diverse factors are essential to building a robust and reliable clinical application system. Furthermore, it is noted that DCCL will be open upon the acceptance of this paper.

**Table 3.** Properties of cervical cytology datasets.

| Dataset | Num. of Patients | Num. of labelled patch | Num. of labelled cells | Num. of lesion cell types | Cell Classifi-cation | Cell Detec-tion | Cell Seg-mentation | Open |
|---|---|---|---|---|---|---|---|---|
| CerviSCAN [18] | 82 | >900 | 12043 | 3 | ✓ | ✗ | ✗ | ✓ |
| ISBI 2015 [1] | – | 961 | – | – | ✗ | ✗ | ✓ | ✓ |
| SSPH [11] | 500 | 5721 | 10307 | 5 | ✓ | ✓ | ✗ | ✗ |
| Herlev [8] | – | – | 917 | 3 | ✓ | ✗ | ✗ | ✓ |
| HEMLBC [19] | 200 | – | 2370 | 4 | ✓ | ✓ | ✓ | ✗ |
| Cervix93 [13] | 93 | – | 2705 | 2 | ✓ | ✗ | ✗ | ✓ |
| **DCCL** | **1167** | **14432** | **34392** | **6** | ✓ | ✓ | ✗ | ✓ |

## 4   Experiments Results

### 4.1   Lesion Cell Detection

**Baseline Detection Model.** Our baseline detectors are Faster R-CNN [14] and RetinaNet [10] that represent two-stage algorithms and one-stage algorithms, respectively. Both of them are based on a ResNet-50 [6] backbone network. More detailed implementations are referred to Appendix 6.1.

**Evaluation Metrics.** We follow the evaluation metric used for Pascal VOC [5] and MS COCO [9], which is mean average precision (mAP). Since DCCL cell detection is a much more challenging task, the performance of the trained detectors in our experiments is evaluated at lower IoU values: mAP@0.1:0.2:0.5.

**Results.** Table 4 illustrates the results for fine-grained cell detection based on Faster R-CNN and RetinaNet. In the experiments, we extract positive cell anchors as positive anchors, while two types of negative anchors: negative cell anchors and background anchors (without any cells). We observer that negative cell anchors and positive cell anchors tend to have some smaller variations. However, the percentage of negative cell anchors are extremely low as compared with the percentage of background anchors, which makes the model hard to distinguish them from positive cell anchors, even using the focal loss function in RetinaNet, and causes high false positive detection. As a result, Table 4 shows mAP@0.5, mAP@0.3, and mAP@0.1 do not present a huge boosting with IoU values decreasing, which indicates DCCL is a challenging benchmark.

Table 4 also illustrates the results for coarse-grained cell detection, in which Faster R-CNN and RetinaNet output two classes of lesion cells and negative cells, as well as the corresponding bounding boxes. The same reason for low mAPs is that methods both generate a large number of false positives.

To improve low mAPs in Table 4, a potential method is to attach a false positive reduction module after the lesion cell detection module, which has been proved to be feasible in LUNA2016 challenge [15]. How to combine these two models would be our future work.

**Table 4.** Detection evaluation on DCCL

| Method | Metrics | Fine-grained cell | | | | | | | Coarse-grained cell |
|---|---|---|---|---|---|---|---|---|---|
| | | mAP | ASCUS | LSIL | ASCH | HSIL | SCC | AGC | mAP |
| Faster R-CNN | mAP@0.1 | 21.16 | 25.91 | 27.08 | 17.46 | 16.68 | 14.03 | 25.81 | 26.16 |
| | mAP@0.3 | 19.8 | 24.3 | 24.95 | 16.58 | 14.09 | 13.1 | 25.81 | 22.18 |
| | mAP@0.5 | 17.1 | 21.01 | 20.46 | 14.1 | 10.73 | 10.41 | 25.71 | 19.35 |
| Retina-Net | mAP@0.1 | 19.61 | 23.41 | 25.79 | 14.11 | 16.64 | 15.09 | 22.64 | 24.01 |
| | mAP@0.3 | 18.37 | 21.98 | 23.48 | 13.22 | 14.01 | 14.89 | 22.64 | 21.85 |
| | mAP@0.5 | 15.93 | 18.71 | 19.89 | 11.86 | 10.08 | 12.67 | 22.39 | 18.07 |

## 4.2  Cell Type Classification

**Baseline Classification Model.** In order to improve cell type classification, we include six lesion cell types plus the negative cell types to conduct deep learning based classification experiments.

The experiments are conducted on three different CNN architectures: Inception-v3 [17], ResNet-101 [6] and DenseNet-121 [7]. According to 2014 TBS, determining the type of a cell depends on multiple factors. Besides the properties of an individual cell (e.g., cell size, nuclear size, nuclear to cytoplasmic ratio, irregularity of cytoplasm, chromatin and nuclear, etc.), the contextual factors by comparing the cell with the other cells in the same slide also play an important role. Thus, we set up a series of experiments on DenseNet-121 to explore local, context as well as geometric information, where "local" only includes the bounding box area of cytologic, "context" indicates a dilated area around the bounding box, and "deform" indicates the network considers an extra deformable layer to model geometric transformations of cells. The other detailed implementations are referred to Appendix 6.2.

**Table 5.** Classification results on test set with different training mode

| Model | Local/context information | Accuracy | F-score | Precision | Recall |
|---|---|---|---|---|---|
| ResNet-101 | Local | 86.92% | 48.32% | 48.70% | 47.94% |
| Inception-v3 | Local | 87.38% | 50.89% | 50.30% | 51.50% |
| DenseNet-121 | Local | 87.87% | 52.22% | 51.40% | 53.07% |
| | Local+Deform | 87.73% | 54.51% | 54.35% | 54.66% |
| | Context | 87.90% | 53.66% | 51.02% | 56.59% |
| | Context+Deform | 88.52% | 57.33% | 53.78% | 61.39% |
| | Local+Deform+Context+Deform | 88.84% | 59.96% | 58.88% | 61.08% |

**Evaluation Metrics.** We follow the evaluation metrics in [2], including both accuracy and F-score. Precision and recall are also included for reference.

**Results.** As shown in Table 5, for models trained based on local information, we observe that DenseNet-121 [7] obtains the best result compared with Inception-v3 [17] and ResNet-101 [6]. Meanwhile, by leveraging the context information, DenseNet-121 only enhances the accuracy and F-score by 0.13% and 1.44%, respectively. By adding the deformable layer on "local" and "context", F-scores increase 2.31% and 3.67% comparing with no deformable layer, respectively. Moreover, the "Local+Deform" and "Context+Deform" ensemble can achieve the F-score as high as 59.96%. These results suggest the context and geometric information provide useful clues to improve cell type classification.

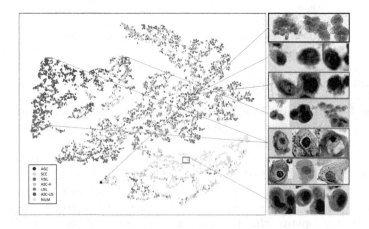

**Fig. 2.** t-SNE visualization of the lesion cell embeddings

Moreover, lesion cell clusters are visualized via t-SNE in Fig. 2 by deriving test set feature embeddings based on DenseNet-121 with "Context+Deform" training mode. This figure shows that the cells at adjacent lesion levels tend to have similar visual appearances, thus are hard to be distinguished: e.g. NILM vs. ASC-US, ASC-US vs. LISL, and HSIL vs. SCC. This is predictable given the progression of a cell lesion is gradual without clear boundaries. A better approach to analyzing fine-grained cervical cytology remains an open problem for future research.

## 5 Conclusions

In this paper, we present a new benchmark dataset to enable cervical cytology analysis for future research and clinical studies on cervical cancer screening. The presented DCCL is highlighted with three distinguishing features. First, compared with the existing cervical cytology datasets, DCCL has a larger scale with diverse fine-grained types of lesion cells. Second, it provides full annotations on six types of lesion cells, ranging from low-grade precancerous lesions to cancerous lesions. A large volume of hard negative cell bounding boxes is also provided. Finally, the baseline lesion cell classification and detection results on DCCL are reported. This dataset presents inherent challenges for cervical cytology recognition, such as intra-class variance (e.g., parts of LSIL cells have a sharply defined perinuclear cavity, but the rests do not have) and inter-class similarity (e.g., both HSIL and SCC have high nuclear-to-cytoplasmic ratios), which are ubiquitous in real clinical studies. These labels on fine-grained types of cell lesions play a crucial role in the screening and diagnosis of cervical cancer. The dataset will be released upon the acceptance of this paper.

## References

1. https://cs.adelaide.edu.au/simcarneiro/isbi15_challenge/
2. Bora, K., et al.: Pap smear image classification using convolutional neural network. In: 10th ICVGIP, p. 55. ACM (2016)
3. Bray, F., et al.: Global cancer statistics 2018: GLOBOCAN estimates of incidence and mortality worldwide for 36 cancers in 185 countries. CA: Cancer J. Clin. **68**(6), 394–424 (2018)
4. Chen, Y.F., et al.: Semi-automatic segmentation and classification of pap smear cells. IEEE J. Biomed. Health Inform. **18**, 94–108 (2014)
5. Everingham, M., et al.: The pascal visual object classes (VOC) challenge. IJCV **88**(2), 303–338 (2010)
6. He, K., et al.: Deep residual learning for image recognition. In: CVPR (2016)
7. Huang, G., et al.: Densely connected convolutional networks. In: CVPR (2017)
8. Jantzen, J., et al.: Pap-smear benchmark data for pattern classification. NiSIS (2005)
9. Lin, T.-Y., et al.: Microsoft COCO: common objects in context. In: Fleet, D., Pajdla, T., Schiele, B., Tuytelaars, T. (eds.) ECCV 2014. LNCS, vol. 8693, pp. 740–755. Springer, Cham (2014). https://doi.org/10.1007/978-3-319-10602-1_48
10. Lin, T.-Y., et al.: Focal loss for dense object detection. In: CVPR (2017)
11. Meiquan, X., et al.: Cervical cytology intelligent diagnosis based on object detection technology (2018)
12. Nayar, R., et al.: The Pap Test and Bethesda 2014. Acta Cytologica (2015)

13. Phoulady, H.A., et al.: A new cervical cytology dataset for nucleus detection and image classification (Cervix93) and methods for cervical nucleus detection. arXiv preprint arXiv:1811.09651 (2018)
14. Ren, S., et al.: Faster R-CNN: towards real-time object detection with region proposal networks (2015)
15. Setio, A.A.A., et al.: Validation, comparison, and combination of algorithms for automatic detection of pulmonary nodules in computed tomography images: the luna16 challenge. Med. Image Anal. **42**, 1–13 (2017)
16. Song, Y., et al.: Automated segmentation of overlapping cytoplasm in cervical smear images via contour fragments. In: AAAI 2018 (2018)
17. Szegedy, C., et al.: Rethinking the inception architecture for computer vision. In: CVPR (2016)
18. Tucker, J.: CERVISCAN: an image analysis system for experiments in automatic cervical smear prescreening. Comput. Biomed. Res. **9**(2), 93–107 (1976)
19. Zhang, L., et al.: Automation-assisted cervical cancer screening in manual liquid-based cytology with hematoxylin and eosin staining. Cytometry Part A **85**, 214–230 (2014)
20. Zhang, L., et al.: DeepPap: deep convolutional networks for cervical cell classification. IEEE J. Biomed. Health Inform. **21**, 1633–1643 (2017)

# Smartphone-Supported Malaria Diagnosis Based on Deep Learning

Feng Yang[1,2(✉)] [iD], Hang Yu[2], Kamolrat Silamut[3],
Richard J. Maude[3], Stefan Jaeger[2] [iD], and Sameer Antani[2]

[1] School of Computer and Information Technology, Beijing Jiaotong University,
Beijing 100044, China
feng.yang2@nih.gov
[2] National Library of Medicine, National Institute of Health, Bethesda,
MD 20894, USA
stefan.jaeger@nih.gov
[3] Mahidol-Oxford Tropical Medicine Research Unit, Mahidol University,
Bangkok 10400, Thailand

**Abstract.** Malaria remains a major burden on global health, causing about half a million deaths every year. The objective of this work is to develop a fast, automated, smartphone-supported malaria diagnostic system. Our proposed system is the first system using both image processing and deep learning methods on a smartphone to detect malaria parasites in thick blood smears. The underlying detection algorithm is based on an iterative method for parasite candidate screening and a convolutional neural network model (CNN) for feature extraction and classification. The system runs on Android phones and can process blood smear images taken by the smartphone camera when attached to the eyepiece of a microscope. We tested the system on 50 normal patients and 150 abnormal patients. The accuracies of the system on patch-level and patient-level are 97% and 78%, respectively. AUC values on patch-level and patient-level are, respectively, 98% and 85%. Our system could aid in malaria diagnosis in resource-limited regions, without depending on extensive diagnostic expertise or expensive diagnostic equipment.

**Keywords:** Mobile health · Computer-aided diagnosis · Malaria · Deep learning · Image analysis

## 1 Introduction

Malaria remains a major burden on global health, causing millions of deaths every year in more than 90 countries and territories. According to the World Health Organization's (WHO) malaria report in 2018, about 219 million malaria cases were detected worldwide in 2017, causing approximately 435,000 deaths [1]. Malaria is caused by Plasmodium parasites that are transmitted though the bites of infected female Anopheles mosquitoes. An estimated 9 out of 10 malaria deaths occur in sub-Saharan Africa; most deaths occur among children, where a child dies almost every minute from the disease [1]. Microscopy examination of stained thick and thin blood smears is currently considered as the gold standard for malaria diagnosis [2, 3]. Thick blood

© Springer Nature Switzerland AG 2019
H.-I. Suk et al. (Eds.): MLMI 2019, LNCS 11861, pp. 73–80, 2019.
https://doi.org/10.1007/978-3-030-32692-0_9

smears are used to detect the presence of malaria parasites in a drop of blood, whereas thin blood smears allow differentiating parasite species and development stages. Microscopy examination is low-cost and widely available, but is time-consuming. Moreover, the effectiveness of microscopy diagnosis depends on a parasitologists' expertise [4]. In situations with poor quality control, inaccurate results can lead to misdiagnosis or inappropriate treatment [4]. Thus, a fast and efficient automated diagnosis system is essential to malaria control.

The development of small camera-equipped microscopic devices, such as smartphones, has offered a new way for malaria diagnosis in resource-poor areas, using image processing and machine learning techniques [5]. Previous work has focused on the design and development of mobile devices for capturing images to replace current microscopes [6–12], also in combination with image processing [13–17]. However, so far, most of the work has concentrated on thin blood smears, and only the system in [16] is developed for parasite detection in thick blood smears.

In this paper, we propose a fast, low-cost, automated system for diagnosing malaria in thick smears. In fact, our system is the first system that can process thick blood smears on smartphones using image processing and deep learning methods. We implemented the system as a smartphone application (app), which runs on Android phones and which can detect parasites in a thick blood smear image within ten seconds. Our system aims to aid in clinical diagnosis of malaria in resource limited areas by trying to solve pending issues such as accessibility, cost, rapidness, and accuracy. Compared to the work in [16], we apply deep learning techniques for parasite detection and achieve more accurate results on more patients, including both normal and abnormal patients.

The paper structure will be as follows: Sect. 2 describes the image processing and analysis methods for our proposed system; Sect. 3 presents our smartphone tool for automated malaria diagnosis; Sect. 4 shows the experimental results on 200 patients; and Sect. 5 concludes the paper with the discussion and conclusion.

## 2   Image Processing and Deep Learning Methods

For our automated malaria diagnosis in thick smear images, we split the problem into two sub-problems: white blood cell (WBC) detection and parasite detection. We first detect WBCs and remove them from the image so that they do not distract our subsequent parasite counting method. This also provides the WBC count, which is an essential part of the standard protocol for diagnosing malaria in thick smears. The second stage, parasite detection, consists of a screening step using image-processing methods and a classification step using deep learning methods. Figure 1 shows the flowchart of our automated malaria diagnosis system.

**Fig. 1.** Flowchart of our automated malaria diagnosis system.

## 2.1    WBC Detection

Based on a histogram analysis of thick blood smears, we assume that both the nuclei of parasites and WBCs have lower intensities than the background due to their staining. To avoid confusing WBCs with parasites, we first filter out WBCs before performing parasite candidate screening. For WBC detection, we first convert a thick smear RGB image into a grayscale image. Then, we threshold the grayscale image using Otsu's method [18]. After this, we apply morphological operations to separate out WBCs. We can count potentially touching WBCs as separate cells by considering the typical expected size of a white blood cell. Before we screen for parasites in the next stage, we set all pixels of detected WBCs to zero.

## 2.2    Parasite Detection

Parasite detection in thick blood smear images involves parasite candidate screening and classification. We identify parasite candidates using our proposed Iterative Global Minimum Screening (IGMS) method and perform classification by a customized Convolutional Neural Network (CNN) classifier.

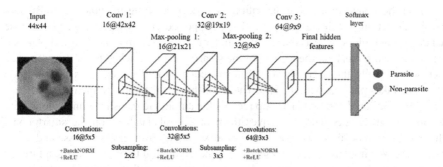

**Fig. 2.** Architecture of the customized CNN model for parasite classification. The numbers below the green dotted line represent the convolutional kernel sizes and the sizes of the max-pooling regions. The hidden layers include three fully-connected layers and two dropout layers with a dropout ratio of 0.5. The output softmax layer computes the probabilities of the input patch being either a parasite or non-parasite. (Color figure online)

IGMS identifies parasite candidates by localizing the minimum non-zero intensity pixel values in a grayscale image. If only one pixel is localized, a circular region centered at this pixel location with a pre-defined radius of 22 pixels, which is the average parasite radius, is cropped from the original RGB image and is considered a parasite candidate. If several pixels with the same minimum intensity are localized, a circular candidate region is extracted for each of them when its distance to at least one of the other pixels is larger than 22. Once a parasite candidate is selected, the intensity values inside this region of the grayscale image will be replaced by zeros to guarantee the convergence of the IGMS method. To further reduce the runtime of parasite candidate screening, the original thick blood smear image is downsampled by a factor of two in each dimension for localizing minimum intensities, while the candidates are always cropped from the original RGB image. The IGMS screening procedure stops when the number of parasite candidates reaches a given number. In our experiments, we identify 400 parasite candidates for each image to cover the true parasites as much as possible, while still providing an acceptable runtime. Using this number, experiments on our dataset of 200 patients show that we can achieve a sensitivity above 97% on image level and patient-level. Each parasite candidate is a $44 \times 44 \times 3$ RGB image patch, with pixels outside the circular region set to zero.

Once the parasite candidates are identified, we use a CNN model to classify them either as true parasites or background. In this work, we customize a CNN model consisting of three convolutional layers, three batch normalization layers, three max-pooling layers, two fully-connected layers and a softmax classification layer as shown in Fig. 2. The batch normalization layer is used to allow a higher learning rate and to be less sensitive to the initialization parameters, followed by a rectified linear unit (ReLU) as the activation function.

## 3   Smartphone Tool

Based on the image processing algorithms and deep learning methods for WBC and parasite detection, we develop a smartphone-supported automated system to diagnose malaria in thick blood smear images. We implement the system as an Android platform app. When using this app, the camera of the smartphone is attached to the eyepiece of a microscope, while the user adjusts the microscope to find target fields in the blood smear and takes pictures with the app. The algorithms in the app will then process these images directly on the phone. The app records the automatic parasite counts, along with patient and smear metadata, and saves them in a local database on the smartphone, where they can be used to monitor disease severity, drug effectiveness, and other parameters. We implemented an embedded camera function to preview and capture the image seen through the microscope. A user will operate with the optical zoom of the microscope to bring the image into focus and enlarge the image. The app does provide the option to adjust white balance and the option to adjust the color of the image among different lighting conditions. Once the image is taken, the app presents the captured image to the user for review. When the user accepts the image, the app processes the image, counts and records the infected cells and parasites, and displays the results in the user interface. Typically, users will take several images until they have acquired enough data to meet the requirements of their protocols, which usually involves counting a minimum number of white blood cells. The app will aggregate the parasite counts across all images. We implemented the algorithms for WBC and parasite detection using the OpenCV4Android SDK library.

After the image acquisition and processing stage, the app will go through a series of input masks for the user to fill in the information associated with the current patient and smear. This information is saved in the local database of the app, which we built with the SQLite API provided by Android. The app offers a user interface to the database where the user can view the data and images of previous smears, allowing hospital staff to monitor the condition of patients.

Since malaria is a disease that is widespread in different areas around the world, the app aims to support several languages to accommodate users in different countries. With English being the default language, the app, currently, also supports Thai and simplified Chinese. We are working on adding support for other languages. This app, called *NLM Malaria Screener*, is available in the Google Play™ store (https://play. google.com/store). Figure 3 shows our smartphone-supported automated malaria diagnosis system and a screenshot with detected parasites in a thick blood smear image.

**Fig. 3.** Automated malaria diagnosis via smartphone.

## 4 Experimental Setup and Results

We acquired Giemsa-stained thick blood smear images from 150 patients infected with *P. falciparum* and from 50 normal patients at Chittagong Medical College Hospital, Bangladesh. The images were acquired using an Android smartphone and its camera. They were captured with 100x magnification in RGB color space with a 3024 × 4032 pixel resolution. An expert microscopist manually annotated each image at the Mahidol-Oxford Tropical Medicine Research Unit (MORU), Bangkok, Thailand. We archived all images and their annotations at the U.S. National Library of Medicine (IRB#12972). In this work, we use 2967 thick blood smear images from all 200 patients, including 1819 images from the 150 patients infected with parasites. We evaluate the performance of our automated malaria diagnosis system with five-fold cross evaluation, splitting the dataset into training sets and test sets on patient-level. To achieve a better performance, we use a balanced training set with an equal number of positive and negative patches. We do so by cropping the positive patches from the manually annotated images while generating the negative patches based on IGMS.

### 4.1 Patch-Level Five-Fold Cross Evaluation

We perform the five-fold training, validation, and testing of our customized CNN classifier on an Intel(R) Xeon(R) CPU E3-1245 (Dual CPU, 3.5 GHz, 16 GB). Table 1 shows the mean performance of our automated malaria diagnosis system across five folds, using a threshold of 0.7 for the CNN classifier, in terms of accuracy, F-score, AUC, sensitivity, specificity, precision, and negative predictive value, which are 96.89%, 81.80%, 98.48%, 90.82%, 97.43%, 74.84% and 99.17%, respectively. The left-hand side of Fig. 4 shows the corresponding ROC curves. Note that the performance on patient-level is generally lower because computing the parasitemia for a patient involves classifying multiple parasite candidate patches.

**Table 1.** Patch classification performance on five folds for 200 patients.

|  | Accuracy | F-score | AUC | Sensitivity | Specificity | Precision | Neg_pred |
|---|---|---|---|---|---|---|---|
| Mean | 96.89% | 81.80% | 98.48% | 90.82% | 97.43% | 74.84% | 99.17% |

Note: Neg_pred is the negative predictive value.

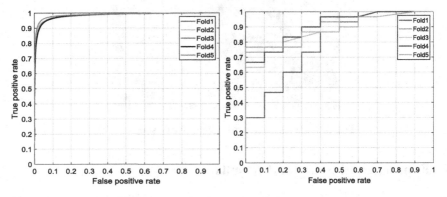

**Fig. 4.** ROC curves of five-fold cross evaluation on patch-level (left: AUC = 98.48 ± 0.15%) and on patient-level (right: AUC = 84.90% ± 4.21%).

### 4.2   Patient-Level Five-Fold Cross Evaluation

For each run of our patient-level cross evaluation, we train on a set of 90 infected patients and 30 normal patients, validate on a set of 30 infected patients and 10 normal patients, and test on a set of 30 infected patients and 10 normal patients. The image set for each patient contains on average 12 images.

For the five-fold cross evaluation on patient-level, we obtain an average AUC value of 84.90% with a standard deviation of 4.21%. The right-hand side of Fig. 4 shows the ROC curve for the evaluation on patient-level. The average accuracy, precision, sensitivity, and specificity values we obtain on patient-level are 78.00%, 90.42%, 79.33%, and 74.00%, respectively. For a specificity of 80%, the average accuracy, precision, and sensitivity values on patient-level are 77.50%, 91.90%, and 76.67%, respectively.

## 5   Discussion and Conclusion

We present the first smartphone-based system exploiting deep learning for detecting malaria parasites in thick blood smear images. The idea is to develop a fast, low-cost, automated, smartphone-supported tool to diagnose malaria in resource-limited malaria-prone regions, using image pre-processing and deep learning methods. For five-fold cross evaluation on patch-level and patient-level we achieve average AUC values of 98.48% and 84.90%, respectively, and average accuracy values of 96.89% and 78.00%, respectively. The input patch size of the CNN model can influence the experimental results. We have evaluated the CNN classifier performance using three different patch sizes, $36 \times 36$, $44 \times 44$, and $52 \times 52$, and obtained the best performance with an input size of $44 \times 44$. When testing on a Samsung Galaxy S6 with an Exynos 7 Octa 7420 Processor and Android 7.0, our system can diagnose a thick blood smear image within ten seconds, proving that we can run powerful deep learning methods for malaria screening on a resource-limited mobile platform.

We have also applied object detection networks, such as faster-RCNN [19] and YOLO [20], to detect parasites in thick blood smears. However, these object detection networks need to be adapted to work well for very small objects like parasites, with an average size of $44 \times 44$ pixels in an image of $4032 \times 3024$ pixels, otherwise they would result in many more false negatives compared to our customized CNN classifier.

In conclusion, we have developed a fast and low-cost diagnostic application for smartphones that can be used in resource-limited regions without the need for specific malaria expertise. Future work will use multi-scale information to improve the classification performance and will test the stability of our app under diverse slide preparation methods and protocols.

**Acknowledgment.** We would like to thank Dr. Md. A. Hossain for supporting our data acquisition at Chittagong Medical Hospital, Bangladesh. This research is supported by the Intramural Research Program of the National Institutes of Health, National Library of Medicine, and Lister Hill National Center for Biomedical Communications. Mahidol-Oxford Tropical Medicine Research Unit is funded by the Wellcome Trust of Great Britain. This research is also supported by the National Basic Research Program of China under No. 61671049 and the National Key R&D Plan of China under No. 2017YFB1400100.

# References

1. WHO: World malaria report 2018 (2018)
2. WHO: Guidelines for the treatment of malaria. 3rd edn. World Health Organization (2015)
3. Makhija, K.S., Maloney, S., Norton, R.: The utility of serial blood film testing for the diagnosis of malaria. Pathology **47**(1), 68–70 (2015)
4. WHO: Malaria micropscopy quality assurance manual. World Health Organization (2016)
5. Poostchi, M., Silamut, K., Maude, R.J., Jaeger, S., Thoma, G.: Image analysis and machine learning for detecting malaria. Transl. Res. **194**, 36–55 (2018)
6. Breslauer, D.N., Maamari, R.N., Switz, N.A., Lam, W.A., Fletcher, D.A.: Mobile phone based clinical microscopy for global health applications. PLoS ONE **4**(7), 1–7 (2009)
7. Tuijn, C.J., Li, J.: Data and image transfer using mobile phones to strengthen microscopy-based diagnostic services in low and middle income country laboratories. PLoS One **6**(12), e28348 (2011)
8. Skandarajah, A., Reber, C.D., Switz, N.A., Fletcher, D.A.: Quantitative imaging with a mobile phone microscope. PLoS One **9**(5), e96906 (2014)
9. Pirnstill, C.W., Coté, G.L.: Malaria diagnosis using a mobile phone polarized microscope. Sci. Rep. **5**, 1–13 (2015)

10. Coulibaly, J.T., et al.: Evaluation of malaria diagnoses using a handheld light microscope in a community-based setting in rural Côte d'Ivoire. Am. J. Trop. Med. Hyg. **95**(4), 831–834 (2016)
11. Kaewkamnerd, S., Uthaipibull, C., Intarapanich, A., Pannarut, M., Chaotheing, S., Tongsima, S.: An automatic device for detection and classification of malaria parasite species in thick blood film. BMC Bioinform. **13**(Suppl 17), S18 (2012)
12. Quinn, J.A., Nakasi, R., Mugagga, P.K.B., Byanyima, P., Lubega, W., Andama, A.: Deep convolutional neural networks for microscopy-based point of care diagnostics. In: International Conference on Machine Learning for Health Care, Los Angeles, CA, pp. 1–12 (2016)
13. Cesario, M., Lundon, M., Luz, S., Masoodian, M., Rogers, B.: Mobile support for diagnosis of communicable diseases in remote locations. In: 13th International Conference of the NZ Chapter of the ACM's Special Interest Group on Human-Computer Interaction – CHINZ 2012, Dunedin, New Zealand, pp. 25–28 (2012)
14. Dallet, C., Kareem, S., Kale, I.: Real time blood image processing application for malaria diagnosis using mobile phones. In: IEEE International Symposium on Circuits and Systems, Melbourne VIC, Australia, pp. 2405–2408 (2014)
15. Rosado, L., Da Costa, J.M.C., Elias, D., Cardoso, J.S.: Automated detection of malaria parasites on thick blood smears via mobile devices. Procedia Comput. Sci. **90**, 138–144 (2016)
16. Rosado, L., Correia da Costa, J.M., Elias, D., Cardoso, J.S.: Mobile-based analysis of malaria-infected thin blood smears: automated species and life cycle stage determination. Sensors **17**(10), 2167 (2017)
17. Eysenbach, G., Ofli, F., Chen, S., Kevin, G., Oliveira, A.D.: The malaria system microapp: a new, mobile device-based tool for malaria diagnosis. JMIR Res. Protoc. **6**(4), e70 (2017)
18. Otsu, N.: A threshold selection method from gray-level histograms. IEEE Trans. Syst. Man Cybern. **9**(1), 62–66 (1979)
19. Ren, S., He, K., Girshick, R., Sun, J.: Faster R-CNN: towards real-time object detection with region proposal networks. IEEE Trans. Pattern Anal. Mach. Intell. **39**(6), 1137–1149 (2017)
20. Redmon, J., Divvala, S., Girshick, R., Farhadi, A.: You only look once: unified, real-time object detection. https://arxiv.org/pdf/1506.02640.pdf. Accessed 01 Apr 2019

# Children's Neuroblastoma Segmentation Using Morphological Features

Shengyang Li[1], Xiaoyun Zhang[1](✉), Xiaoxia Wang[2], Yumin Zhong[2](✉),
Xiaofen Yao[2], Ya Zhang[1], and Yanfeng Wang[1]

[1] Cooperative Medianet Innovation Center, Shanghai Jiao Tong University,
Shanghai, China
xiaoyun.zhang@sjtu.edu.cn
[2] Shanghai Children's Medical Center, Shanghai, China
zhongyumin@scmc.com.cn

**Abstract.** Neuroblastoma (NB) is a common type of cancer in children that can develop in the neck, chest, or abdomen. It causes about 15% of cancer deaths in children. However, the automatic segmentation of NB on CT images has been addressed weakly, mostly because children's CT images have much lower contrast than adults, especially those aged less than one year. Furthermore, neuroblastomas can develop in different body parts and are usually in variable size and irregular shape, which also add to the difficulties of NB segmentation. In view of these issues, we propose a morphological constrained end-to-end NB segmentation approach by taking the sizes and shapes of tumors in consideration for more accurate boundaries. The morphological features of neuroblastomas are predicted as an auxiliary task while performing segmentation and used as additional supervision for the segmentation prediction. We collect 248 CT scans from distinct patients with manually-annotated labels to establish a dataset for NB segmentation. Our method is evaluated on this dataset as well as the public Brats2018, and experimental results shows that the morphological constraints can improve the performance of medical image segmentation networks.

**Keywords:** Neuroblastoma · Morphological constraint · Segmentation

## 1 Introduction

Neuroblastoma is a type of embryonal tumors, originating from primitive neuroblasts of the embryonic neural crest. It can occur anywhere within the sympathetic nervous system including abdomen, chest, pelvis and neck. It is the most common extracranial malignant solid tumor in children, about 15% of cancer deaths in children are due to neuroblastoma. However, automatic neuroblastoma segmentation in CT images of children has been addressed rarely duo to its high difficulty.

Lately, convolutional neural networks (CNNs) have attracted a great deal of attention for medical image segmentation [2–6]. However, for the distinctiveness

H.-I. Suk et al. (Eds.): MLMI 2019, LNCS 11861, pp. 81–88, 2019.
https://doi.org/10.1007/978-3-030-32692-0_10

of neuroblastoma, applying such approaches to NB segmentation faces considerable challenges. Firstly, tumors of NB have poor contrast with respect to adjacent tissues or organs, especially for children aged only a few months, while the pixels within tumors are usually not in uniform values. Secondly, the location, size and shape of NB vary among patients, which also add to the difficulties of segmentation. Some typical CT images of neuroblastoma patients are shown in Fig. 1.

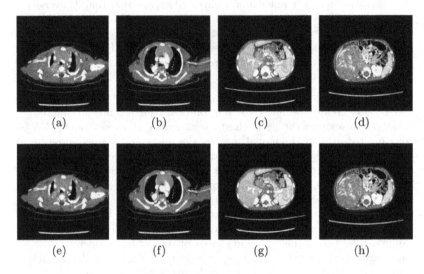

**Fig. 1.** Neuroblastoma (NB) in different patients. (a–d) are the original CT images, (a, b) show a mass in neck and chest respectively, while (c, d) show masses in abdomen. (e–h) show the masses (red contours) delineated by radiologists based in original CT images (a–d). The tumors have very poor contrast and their size, shape and location are greatly variable in these four patients. (Color figure online)

Considering the wide variation of size and shape of neuroblastoma, we expect additional information such as perimeter and area of NB may help improve its segmentation. Therefore, in this paper, we propose an end-to-end NB segmentation architecture embedded with mathematical morphological features, which takes the sizes and shapes of tumors in consideration as additional constraints. Morphological features of neuroblastomas are predicted as an auxiliary task based on feature maps from backbone segmentation network. Perimeter and area are then computed by dilation operation for the binary ground-truth labels and gray-scale probability mask, respectively, where the computation should be derivable for back propagation. Finally, a morphological constrained loss is specifically designed which leads to more accurate segmentation boundary. In addition, depthwise separable convolutions [7,8] rather than trivial convolutions are also employed to improve the backbone performance with small training data set.

CT scans from 248 patients with NB are collected and annotated by experts from Shanghai Children's Medical Center. Our method is evaluated on this NB dataset as well as BraTS2018, and the experimental results shows that the morphological constraints can improve the segmentation performance in dice coefficient from 76.5% of U-net to 79.2% of the proposed DS-Unet in the NB dataset. Experiment result on BraTS2018 also validates the efficiency of our method. To the best of our knowledge, this is the first CNN-based method that addresses automatic neuroblastoma segmentation for children on CT images.

## 2  Proposed Network Architecture

Our proposed Depthwise Separable Unet (DS-Unet) is as shown in Fig. 2. With U-net as the backbone, a morphological feature extraction path is embedded into the architecture. The feature map from the last layer in the U-net encoding path is fed as input for morphological feature extraction. It is firstly compressed on both spatial dimension and channel dimension, in order to reduce the parameters of feature extraction layers and prevent the network from overfitting. Then, two fully connected layers is followed to extract the morphological features of the perimeter and area of neuroblastoma. Finally, an additional loss using these morphological features is designed to constrain the prediction mask of U-net, which leads to more accurate segmentation boundary.

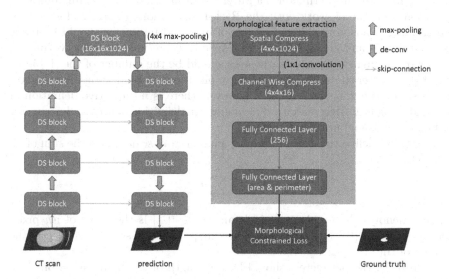

**Fig. 2.** The architecture of proposed DS-Unet. The morphological extraction path predicts the perimeter and the area of neuroblastoma while the decode path output the probability mask. A morphological constrained loss is designed for end-to-end training.

And, depthwise separable convolutions are utilized in the backbone U-net, which decouple the spatial and depthwise information to relieve overfitting problem. Specifically, DS-block with two depthwise separable layers [7,8] are employed to extract contextual features, and batch normalization (BN) is also implemented. Therefore, the layers in a DS-block are organized as BN-relu-SepConv-BN-relu-SepConv, where SepConv is the depthwise separable convolution and relu is the rectified linear unit.

# 3   Morphological Constraints

In this section, morphological features are first defined and extracted respectively for binary and gray-scale images. Then, a specific loss function is defined which takes both the pixelwise mask and the global morphological features in consideration.

## 3.1   Morphological Features

Image segmentation models usually take binary maps as ground-truth labels and output a probability mask. The probability masks hold continuous pixel values and can be regarded as gray-scale images. The measures of area and perimeter are important and useful features to describe a binary map, so it is considerable to use them to supervise the segmentation models. As for the probability mask of the network, it is intuitive to use a threshold to quantify it to a binary map, then calculate its area and perimeter. However, quantification is a non-differentiable operation and cannot work with the Back-Propagation Algorithm for end-to-end training. Thus derivable definitions of area and perimeter should be made on binary maps and gray-scale images respectively to build the supervision.

For binary maps, intuitively, the area should be the number of the '1's in it, and the perimeter should be the number of pixels on the boundaries between '0's and '1's. For the gray-scale images, however, there is no intuitive definition of area and perimeter. Here we introduce a uniform definition of area and perimeter on binary maps and gray-scale images.

Firstly, we define the area of a binary map or gray-scale image the sum of all its pixels:

$$A(x) = \sum_{i=1}^{n} x_i \tag{1}$$

where $n$ denotes the number of pixels and $x_i \in [0,1]$ is the value of $ith$ pixel. Specifically, $x_i \in \{0,1\}$ when $x$ is a binary map, in this case $A(x)$ is exactly the number of the '1's in $x$.

Intuitively, the perimeters should be the length of the boundaries, but it is difficult to make a definition of boundaries on gray-scale images. To avoid this problem, we use morphological tools here to define the perimeter. Morphologically, we define perimeter the difference of the area of its dilation and itself, or the area of its morphological edge, as shown below:

$$P(x) = \sum_{i=1}^{n} (dil(x)_i - x_i) = \sum_{i=1}^{n} dil(x)_i - \sum_{i=1}^{n} x_i = A(dil(x)) - A(x) \tag{2}$$

where $dil(x)$ stands for the morphological gray-scale dilation [9] or binary dilation of image $x$ and $A(x)$ means the area of $x$ defined in Eq. (1). The structuring element used in dilation is a square of size $3 \times 3$. In this paper, the gray-scale dilation operation is performed by replacing every pixel with the max value in its neighborhood.

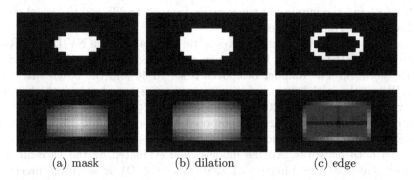

(a) mask                (b) dilation                (c) edge

**Fig. 3.** Illustration of dilation and morphological edge of binary map (first row) and gray-scale image (second row). The resolution of those two images are $8 \times 16$. Here the morphological edge of a binary or gray-scale map is defined as the difference of its dilation and itself. As the definition in Eqs. (1) and (2), the area of the two masks are both 24 and the perimeter of them are both 28.

Figure 3 shows the dilation and morphological edge of a binary map and a gray-scale image.

### 3.2 Morphological Constrained Loss Function

Firstly, we employ the morphological feature extraction path to predict the ground-truth area and perimeter. Secondly, we use the predicted morphological feature to guide segmentation task by minimizing the gap between the predicted feature and the feature calculated from the probability mask. Considering that the ratio between the predicted and calculated values matters more than the absolute value, we organize the constraint in logarithmic form:

$$C_m = \lambda_1 ln^2(A_{gt}/A_{pmf}) + \lambda_2 ln^2(P_{gt}/P_{pmf}) \\ + \lambda_3 ln^2(A_{ppm}/A_{pmf}) + \lambda_4 ln^2(P_{ppm}/P_{pmf}) \tag{3}$$

In Eq. (3), $A$ means area and $P$ means perimeter, the subscripts $gt$, $ppm$, $pmf$ denotes the ground truth, the calculated and the predicated morphological feature respectively. In our experiment, we set all the $\lambda$ parameters in Eq. (3) to 0.1 for the best performance.

The proposed overall morphological constrained loss function $L$ is defined as the sum of $L_{bce}$ (the binary cross entropy loss) and the morphology constraint $C_m$ in Eq. (3).

$$L = L_{bce} + C_m \tag{4}$$

## 4    Experiments and Results

Our experimental dataset consists of 248 CT scans from NB patients, each with a manually-annotated label map by experts from Shanghai Children's Medical Center. The dataset is divides into three parts: training set (179 patients), validation set (20 patients) and testing set (49 patients). The intra slices image size is $512 \times 512$ and the number of slices varies from 67 to 395 and the voxel size is $0.49 \times 0.49 \times 1.24\,\text{mm}^3$ on average.

Our approach is implemented in Keras [10] and trained on a NVIDIA GeForce GTX1080Ti GPU for about 10 h. Images are resized to $256 \times 256$ before feed into the network. The number of epochs is set to 40 and the batch size is set to 16. We set the initialization of learning rate to 1e-3, and reduce the learning rate by 10 times in the last 20 and 10 epochs respectively.

In this section, we compare the proposed architecture named DS-Unet with the well-known U-Net [4] and evaluate the effect of using morphological constraint on both networks. All the models were evaluated by the Dice Similarity Coefficient (DSC) and mean surface distance (MSD). In addition, precision, recall and the mean relative error of the area and perimeters calculated from predicted mask are also reported. Evaluations are performed on both our own neuroblastoma dataset and the BraTS2018 brain tumor segmentation dataset [11, 12].

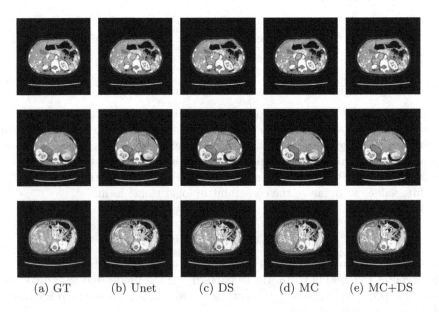

(a) GT        (b) Unet        (c) DS        (d) MC        (e) MC+DS

**Fig. 4.** The results on the task of neuroblastoma segmentation. Form left to right, The red contours stand for the ground-truth and the blue contours for predictions of models. Here, MC and DS mean morphological constraints and depthwise convolutions. (Color figure online)

Figure 4 shows the results of different models on the task of neuroblastoma segmentation. As shown in the figure, morphological constraints help networks to make predictions whose sizes and shapes are close to the ground truth. With morphological constraints, models are able to provides more accurate boundaries. Besides, the depthwise separable convolutions also contribute to the improvement of performance.

We employ U-net on our neuroblastoma dataset as the baseline method. As discussed in Sect. 3, the constraints introduce new paths to propagate gradients in the networks and helps them to converge quicker and better. The comparison in Table 1 suggests that our morphological constrained loss make considerable contribution to the improvement of the performance. Network with morphological constraints and depthwise convolutions with advanced constraints achieve the best performance among all the models.

**Table 1.** Comparison of different networks and constraints. Here, MC and DS mean morphological constraints and depthwise convolutions. Area and perimeter are reported in the form of root mean square error(RMSE).

| Method | Baseline | Proposed | | |
|---|---|---|---|---|
| | | DS | MC | MC+DS |
| DSC(%) | $76.5 \pm 7.9$ | $77.4 \pm 8.5$ | $78.3 \pm 4.4$ | **79.2** ±4.4 |
| MSD(mm) | $3.17 \pm 5.21$ | $3.11 \pm 5.54$ | $2.78 \pm 3.98$ | **2.68** ±4.11 |
| Precision | $0.85 \pm 0.20$ | $0.85 \pm 0.19$ | **0.87** ±0.17 | $0.86 \pm 0.17$ |
| Recall | $0.75 \pm 0.22$ | $0.75 \pm 0.24$ | $0.74 \pm 0.22$ | **0.76** ±0.20 |
| RMSE(area) | 84 | 139 | 78 | **67** |
| RMSE(perimeter) | 55.8 | 55.4 | 56.4 | **54.7** |

**Table 2.** Results on BraTS2018 dataset. We use the validation set to evaluate our model. Here are the results on the whole tumor segmentation subtask.

| Constraint | Average dice | Max dice | Min dice | RMSE(area) | RMSE(perimeter) |
|---|---|---|---|---|---|
| N | 0.819 | 0.922 | 0.433 | 120 | 75 |
| MC | 0.831 | 0.945 | 0.429 | 79 | 56 |

To illustrate the generalizability of the proposed method, we also test on the BraTS2018 dataset for brain tumor segmentation. Table 2 show the results on BraTS2018 validation set. On the task of brain tumor segmentation, the morphological constraints can also improve the performance, which shows the generality of our proposed method in the area of medical image segmentation.

# 5   Conclusions

In this paper, we proposed a new end-to-end mathematical morphology based medical image segmentation approach to segment neuroblastoma on CT images. We develop the well-defined morphological features and use morphological constraints for the accurate segmentation of medical images, and the result of experiments proves its superiority. Besides, depthwise separable convolutions are also used in our model. We collect 248 CT scans from distinct patients with manually-annotated labels and establish a dataset for NB segmentation. Experiments on our neuroblastoma datasets and the BraTS2018 dataset demonstrated the advantage and considerable competence of our morphological constraints in the medical image segmentation tasks.

# References

1. Litjens, G., et al.: A survey on deep learning in medical image analysis. Med. Image Anal. **42**, 60–88 (2017)
2. Ciresan, D., Ciusti, A., Schmidhuber, J.: Deep neural networks segment neural membrane in electron microscopy image. In: Advance in Neural Information Processing System, pp. 2843–2851 (2012)
3. Brosch, T., Yoo, Y., Tang, L.Y.W., Li, D.K.B., Traboulsee, A., Tam, R.: Deep convolutional encoder networks for multiple sclerosis lesion segmentation. In: Navab, N., Hornegger, J., Wells, W.M., Frangi, A.F. (eds.) MICCAI 2015. LNCS, vol. 9351, pp. 3–11. Springer, Cham (2015). https://doi.org/10.1007/978-3-319-24574-4_1
4. Ronneberger, O., Fischer, P., Brox, T.: U-Net: convolutional networks for biomedical image segmentation. In: Navab, N., Hornegger, J., Wells, W.M., Frangi, A.F. (eds.) MICCAI 2015. LNCS, vol. 9351, pp. 234–241. Springer, Cham (2015). https://doi.org/10.1007/978-3-319-24574-4_28
5. Hao, C., Xiaojuan, Q., Lequan, Y., Pheng-Ann, H.: DCAN: deep contour-aware networks for accurate gland segmentation. In: IEEE Computer Vision Pattern Recognition, pp. 2487–2496 (2016)
6. Milletari, F., Navab, N., Ahmadi, S.: V-net: fully convolutional neural networks for volumetric medical image segmentation. In: International Conference on 3D Vision, pp. 565–571 (2016)
7. Howard, A., et al.: Mobilenets: efficient convolutional neural networks for mobile vision applications. arXiv preprint arXiv:1704.04861 (2017)
8. Chollet, F., et al.: Xception: deep learning with depthwise separable convolutions. In: CVPR, pp. 1251–1258 (2017)
9. Sternberg, S.R.: Grayscale morphology. Comput. Vis. Graph. Image Process. **35**(3), 333–355 (1986)
10. Keras: Deep learning library for theano and tensorflow (2015). http://keras.io
11. Menze, B.H., et al.: The multimodal brain tumor image segmentation benchmark (BRATS). IEEE Trans. Med. Imaging **34**(10), 1993–2024 (2015)
12. Bakas, S., et al.: Advancing the cancer genome atlas glioma MRI collections with expert segmentation labels and radiomic features. Sci. Data **4**, 170117 (2017)

# GFD Faster R-CNN: Gabor Fractal DenseNet Faster R-CNN for Automatic Detection of Esophageal Abnormalities in Endoscopic Images

Noha Ghatwary[1,2]($\boxtimes$), Massoud Zolgharni[3], and Xujiong Ye[1]

[1] School of Computer Science, University of Lincoln, Lincoln LN6 7TS, UK
nghatwary@lincoln.ac.uk, noha.ghatwary@aast.edu
[2] Computer Engineering Department, Arab Academy for Science and Technology,
Alexandria, Egypt
[3] School of Computing and Engineering, University of West London, London, UK

**Abstract.** Esophageal cancer is ranked as the sixth most fatal cancer type. Most esophageal cancers are believed to arise from overlooked abnormalities in the esophagus tube. The early detection of these abnormalities is considered challenging due to their different appearance and random location throughout the esophagus tube. In this paper, a novel Gabor Fractal DenseNet Faster R-CNN (*GFD Faster R-CNN*) is proposed which is a two-input network adapted from the Faster R-CNN to address the challenges of esophageal abnormality detection. First, a Gabor Fractal (GF) image is generated using various Gabor filter responses considering different orientations and scales, obtained from the original endoscopic image that strengthens the fractal texture information within the image. Secondly, we incorporate Densely Connected Convolutional Network (DenseNet) as the backbone network to extract features from both original endoscopic image and the generated GF image separately; the DenseNet provides a reduction in the trained parameters while supporting the network accuracy and enables a maximum flow of information. Features extracted from the GF and endoscopic images are fused through bilinear fusion before ROI pooling stage in Faster R-CNN, providing a rich feature representation that boosts the performance of final detection. The proposed architecture was trained and tested on two different datasets independently: Kvasir (*1000 images*) and MICCAI'15 (*100 images*). Extensive experiments have been carried out to evaluate the performance of the model, with a recall of 0.927 and precision of 0.942 for Kvasir dataset, and a recall of 0.97 and precision of 0.92 for MICCAI'15 dataset, demonstrating a high detection performance compared to the state-of-the-art.

**Keywords:** Gabor Fractal · DenseNet · Faster R-CNN · Esophagitis · EAC

© Springer Nature Switzerland AG 2019
H.-I. Suk et al. (Eds.): MLMI 2019, LNCS 11861, pp. 89–97, 2019.
https://doi.org/10.1007/978-3-030-32692-0_11

# 1  Introduction

Esophageal cancer (EC) is an aggressive type of cancer that often remains asymptomatic until late stages. There are two types of esophageal cancer: Esophageal Adenocarcinoma (EAC) and Squamous Cell Carcinoma (SCC). EC has low survival rate of only 19% on a 5-year plan [1]. Most instances of EC arise from the untreated/undetected precancerous abnormalities such as Barrett's Esophagus (BE) and Esophagitis. The early detection and treatment for any abnormalities will help to prevent the development of the cells into cancerous stages. Furthermore, the detection of early EC stages is considered important as advanced stages require invasive treatment with low prognosis. The High-Definition White Light Endoscopy (HD-WLE) is considered the primary tool for detection. Studies show that early cancer stages are usually overlooked and require an experienced gastroenterologist to locate precancerous abnormalities.

Recently, Convolution Neural Networks (CNN's) have attracted a huge amount of attention to the analysis of medical imaging. However, only a few CNN methods for esophageal abnormality detection from endoscopic images have been proposed in the literature. Those methods focused on finding EAC regions and mainly relied on CNN *Transfer Learning*. Mendel et al. [2] used the deep residual network (ResNet) through transfer learning to extract features from endoscopic images to detect EAC regions. First, the parameters of the ImageNet were initialized to a 50-layer ResNet architecture. Then CNN features were extracted from non-overlapping patches from the image resulted in a sensitivity of 0.94 and a specificity of 0.88. Later, Reil et al. [3], suggested an automatic EAC detection using CNN transfer learning with conventional classifiers (*Support Vector Machine (SVM) & Random Forest*). Different CNN architectures (*AlexNet, VGG, GoogleNet*) were trained with ImageNet parameters and evaluated using both classifiers. The best performance showed a value of 0.92 area-under-the-curve (AUC) with AlexNet-SVM. (*Our approach shows improved performances using the same dataset, which will be discussed in Sect.* 3)

There exists various object detection methods that rely on region-based CNN features for final detection, including Regional-Based Convolutional Neural Network (R-CNN) [4], Fast R-CNN [5] and Faster R-CNN [6]. The Faster R-CNN is considered one of the leading deep learning detection methods that generates proposals based on the extracted CNN features. Lately, there are several CNN architectures that extract features to deal with classification and detection problems. Huang et al. [7] proposed an architecture called Densely Connected Convolution Neural Network (DenseNet) that showed superior performance in image classification. The advantage of using the DenseNet is that it guarantees a maximum flow of information between layers in the network, it also encourages feature reuse and alleviates the vanishing gradient problem.

In this paper, we introduce a novel Gabor Fractal DenseNet Faster R-CNN (GFD Faster R-CNN) to automatically detect abnormal esophagus regions from endoscopic images. A Gabor Fractal (GF) image is generated from the responses of different Gabor filters. Features are extracted from both original endoscopic image and the generated GF image using the DenseNet as a backbone CNN, which are then fused using the bilinear fusion for the final stage detection in the Faster R-CNN. To the best of our knowledge, this is the first end-to-end training framework to address the challenges of automatic abnormalities detection in the esophagus from endoscopic images.

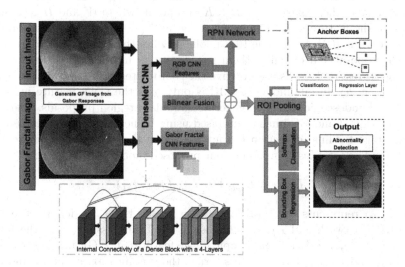

**Fig. 1.** The proposed GFD Faster R-CNN framework. The GF image is first produced by extracting different Gabor filter responses from the endoscopic image. Proposals are generated through the RPN stage using anchor boxes and CNN features of the endoscopic image only. Features from the two images are fused using bilinear fusion before ROI pooling stage for final detection of abnormality location. The DenseNet is used as a backbone CNN to learn features. (Color figure online)

## 2   Method: GFD Faster R-CNN

A novel GFD Faster R-CNN model is proposed to automatically detect esophageal abnormalities. The main framework of the model is presented in Fig. 1. As shown, first, we generate a Gabor Fractal (GF) image from the original endoscopic image which is later used as a second input in our model. Then we introduce the DenseNet to learn features from both images independently. The CNN features of the endoscopic image are used by RPN stage to obtain candidate region proposals. Later, the features from both images are combined together through bilinear fusion presenting a pairwise interaction between the two feature maps, so providing informative feature representation. Finally, the fused features are used in the ROI pooling stage for the final abnormality detection.

**Faster R-CNN.** The baseline of the proposed model is the Faster R-CNN [6]. It is composed of two stages: *Region Proposal Network (RPN)* and *Region-of-Interest (ROI) pooling layer.* The RPN is responsible to generate a list of region proposals that might be an abnormality. The RPN relies on *anchor boxes* to produce $K$ proposals for each location (as shown in Fig. 1 (*blue dotted box*)). For each image, there exist $(W \times H \times K)$ proposals where $W$ and $H$ represent the size of the feature map. The input of the ROI pooling is dependent on the output from the RPN layer. The ROI pooling unifies the size of the feature map for each proposal and classifies them using softmax into abnormal or normal, while the regression layer is used to give the coordinates of the output bounding box $(c_x, c_y, w, h)$. In our model, the RPN only uses the CNN feature maps of the original endoscopic image to generate candidate region proposals. Features from the original and GF images are fused using bilinear fusion before the ROI pooling stage for final detection output (based on the proposals generated by the RPN). The total loss function of our proposed model is defined as:

$$L_{total} = L_{rpn} + L_{fusion}(f_{rgb}, f_{gf}) \tag{1}$$

where $L_{total}$ represents the total loss of the model, the $L_{rpn}$ denotes the loss of the RPN network and $L_{fusion}$ the loss of the ROI classifier from the fused features map ( $f_{rgb}$: original endoscopic image features, $f_{gf}$: GF image features). Both $L_{rpn}$ and $L_{fusion}$ have two loss terms: the classification accuracy and the regression loss of the bound box coordinates of the predicted output. The loss functions for each stage was measured as the default setting for the Faster R-CNN as described in [6].

**DenseNet.** We adopt the DenseNet [7] as the backbone network in our proposed method. There are two main components that form the DenseNet: *Dense_Block* and *Transition_Layer.* The **Dense_Block** is composed of $L$ layers, where each layer is connected to all proceeding layers within the same *dense_block* (as shown in the bottom (*yellow dotted box*) of Fig. 1). The output of a *dense_block* can be represented as $x_l$ showing:

$$x_l = H_l([x_1, x_2, ..., x_{l-1}]) \tag{2}$$

where, (.) represents the concatenation between the layers. $H_l$ is the composite function of three operations: *Batch Normaliation* (BN), Rectified Linear Unit (ReLu) and $(3 \times 3)$ *Convolution Layer* (Conv). The increase of the size of the feature map from each layer is controlled by a factor **Growth_Rate** $(G)$. This variable helps to adjust the amount of new information added by each layer and prevents the network from getting too big. The output from $x_l$ from each dense_block is forwarded to the next dense_block through a **Transition_Layer**. The *transition_layer* is composed of a BN, $(1 \times 1)$ Conv and $(2 \times 2)$ Average Pooling. Our proposed CNN DenseNet includes five denseblocks each having an equal number of internal layers $L = 4$ and growth rate $G = 16$.

**Gabor Fractal (GF) Image.** In our model, we propose a Gabor Fractal (GF) image by generating different Gabor filter responses from the original endoscopic image. The use of Gabor features has shown a remarkable effect in detection methods and proved its ability to improve the representation of deep features [8]. The Gabor responses are generated by adopting a set of filters with various orientations and scales defined as:

$$f(x, y, \theta_k, \lambda) = \exp\left[-\frac{1}{2}\left\{\frac{A_{\theta_k}^2}{\sigma_x^2} + \frac{B_{\theta_k}^2}{\sigma_y^2}\right\}\right] \exp\left\{i\frac{2\pi A}{\lambda}\right\} \qquad (3)$$

where, $A = xcos(\theta_k) + ysin(\theta_k)$, $B = -xsin(\theta_k) + ycos(\theta_k)$ and $i$ provides the central frequency of the sinusoidal plane wave at an orientation $\theta_k$ and wavelength $\lambda$. The orientation of $\theta_k = \frac{\pi(k-1)}{n}$ where $k = 1, 2, 3.., n$ and $n$ represents the numbers of orientations. Finally, the $\sigma_x$ and $\sigma_y$ represent the standard deviations of the Gaussian envelope along the $x$ and $y$ axis. The response of the Gabor filter is produced by convolving each filter with the input image by:

$$G_f = I(x, y) \otimes f(x, y, \theta_k, \lambda) \qquad (4)$$

where, $I$ is the input image and $\otimes$ symbolize the convolution operation with the filters generated in different orientations and scales defined in Eq. 3. All the generated filters $G_f$ are used to produce the GF image as follows:

$$GF_{img}(x, y) = Max(\forall G_{f_i}(x, y)) \qquad \{i = 1, 2, ..., N\} \qquad (5)$$

where, $Max$ is the maximum pixel value at each location $(x, y)$ for all the generated $(N)$ number of Gabor filter responses (Eq. 4). Figure 2 demonstrates different examples of the endoscopic images and their corresponding generated GF images. As shown, the GF image emphasizes the hidden fractal features in the image which complements the feature representation extracted through CNN. The GF image is used as a second input in our model as illustrated in Fig. 1. In our model, we set 16 orientations with $\theta = (0, \frac{\pi}{16}, \frac{\pi}{8}, \frac{3\pi}{16}, \frac{\pi}{4}, \frac{5\pi}{16}, \frac{3\pi}{8}, \frac{7\pi}{16}, \frac{9\pi}{16}, \frac{5\pi}{8}, \frac{11\pi}{16}, \frac{3\pi}{4}, \frac{13\pi}{16}, \frac{7\pi}{8}, \frac{15\pi}{16}, \pi)$ & frequency 0.5 Hz.

**Feature Map Fusion.** In the last stage before the ROI pooling, the CNN features produced from both the original endoscope and Gabor Fractal images are combined through *Bilinear Fusion* to improve the final detection performance. The *Bilinear Fusion* [9] computes a matrix from the outer product of each location from both feature maps followed by global average pooling as defined in the following equation:

$$F_{bil} = \sum_{i=1}^{H} \sum_{j=1}^{W} F_{i,j}^{rgbT} \odot F_{i,j}^{gf} \qquad (6)$$

where, $F^{rgb}$ is the feature map from the original endoscopic image, $F^{gf}$ is the feature map from gabor fractal image, $T$ is transpose, $H, W$ represent the height and width of the feature map and $i, j$ represent the location within feature map.

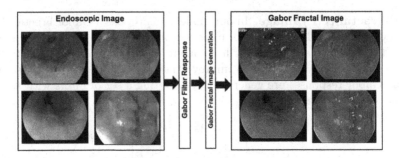

**Fig. 2.** Examples of the GF output images. The Gabor filter response are extracted from different orientations and scales to generate the GF image. (Color figure online)

## 3   Experimental Setup and Results

**Materials.** This study includes two different datasets of esophageal endoscopic images. The first dataset is from 39 patients of 100 HD-WLE images (50 non-cancerous barrett's and 50 EAC) provided by **MICCAI'15** Endovis Subchallenge [10]. Each patient held from one to eight images with resolution of 1600×1200 per image. In this dataset, the EAC regions were delineated by 5 experts in the field, taking the intersection between them (know as sweet-spot) as the ground-truth for training and testing phase. The second dataset is composed of 1000 endoscopic images provided by **Kvisar** open access [11] which has Esophagitis abnormality. The resolution of each image varied from 720×576 to 1920×1072 and the images were annotated by experts in the field.

**Implementation Details and Evaluation Metrics.** The GFD Faster R-CNN is implemented using Keras library and trained end-to-end on a Geforce GTX1080 Ti with 11 GB on GPU memory. The weights are initialized randomly with a gaussian distribution ($\mu = 0$, $\sigma = 0.01$). The initial learning rate is set to ($1e - 4$) and trained for 500 epochs with 1000 iterations. The original endoscopic image is resized so that the shorter length is equal to 600 pixels (for both datasets). To evaluate the performance of the GFD Faster R-CNN, the standard evaluation measures are adopted: *Recall, Precision & F-measure*. The predicting bounding-box is considered as a true positive if it overlaps with the ground-truth by more than 50% and false positive otherwise even if it is in the correct area. To illustrate the effectiveness of the GF feature fusion, we compare our model with the Faster R-CNN with only using the original endoscopic image features extracted by DenseNet. Additionally, to evaluate the impact of using the DenseNet as the backbone network, the results are also compared with Faster R-CNN model using the VGG'16 (state-of-the-art Faster R-CNN) with and without fusing the GF features.

**Esophagitis Detection Performance and Discussion (*Kvasir dataset*).** The Kvasir data was divided randomly into 50% training, 10% validation and

40% testing. Table 1 yields a quantitative comparison of the detection performance in finding ***Esophagitis*** abnormalities with other Faster R-CNN networks. As shown, our proposed GFD Faster R-CNN outperformed against the
other detection networks with a recall of 0.927, precision of 0.942 and F-measure
of 0.934. Moreover, the impact of GF features fusion with features from original
image is assessed. As shown in Table 1, when fusing the features, the performance
of correctly detecting Esophagitis regions has improved the recall from 0.879 to
0.927 (using DenseNet) and from 0.836 to 0.892 (using the VGG'16). Moreover,
the precision was enhanced from 0.884 to 0.942 (using DenseNet) and from 0.861
to 0.901 (using the VGG'16). The high recall and precision performances demonstrate that the fusion of the features provided rich feature representation that
led to an improvement in the final detection stage. Furthermore, the detection
results when using the DenseNet as the backbone network for feature extraction
surpass the results when using the VGG'16. As illustrated, learning features
using the DenseNet architecture increased the recall from 0.892 to 0.927 and
the precision from 0.901 to 0.942 when fusing the GF features. Additionally, the
results of the recall increased from 0.836 to 0.879 and the precision from 0.861
to 0.884 without considering the GF features. These results indicate the effectiveness of using the DenseNet as a backbone in providing a maximum flow of
information that enhances the final detection results.

**Table 1.** Comparison of the GFD Faster R-CNN with other detection networks
with/without GF features, using different backbones in detecting Esophagitis.

| Methods | Recall | Precision | F-Measure |
|---|---|---|---|
| GFD Faster R-CNN | **0.927** | **0.942** | **0.934** |
| DenseNet Faster R-CNN | 0.879 | 0.884 | 0.882 |
| VGG'16 GF Faster R-CNN | 0.892 | 0.901 | 0.896 |
| VGG'16 Faster R-CNN | 0.836 | 0.861 | 0.848 |

**EAC Detection Performance and Discussion (*MICCAI'15 dataset*).**
For the MICCAI dataset, due to the limited dataset, data augmentation is
applied to increase the size of the training set by performing different geometric
transformations. The model was evaluated using this dataset based on a Leave-
One-Patient-Out cross-validation (LOPO-CV) to detect **EAC** regions. Table 2
compares our performance with the state-of-the-art method Mendel *et al.* [2]
and the standard Faster R-CNN networks. The proposed GFD Faster R-CNN
obtained a recall of 0.97, a precision of 0.92 and F-measure of 0.94. Our method
surpassed the state-of-the-art results in [2] on the same dataset with the same
validation method in terms of all performance measures. This illustrates that
our method is more efficient than patch-based CNN approach as suggested by
[2]. Furthermore, by fusing the GF features, the results of detection are significantly improved when using different CNN backbone networks, increasing the

**Table 2.** Comparison of the GFD Faster R-CNN with other networks with/without GF features, different backbone networks and method by Mendel et al. [2] to detect EAC.

| Methods | Recall | Precision | F-Measure |
|---|---|---|---|
| GFD Faster R-CNN | **0.97** | **0.92** | **0.94** |
| DenseNet Faster R-CNN | 0.90 | 0.88 | 0.89 |
| VGG'16 GF Faster R-CNN | 0.93 | 0.88 | 0.90 |
| VGG'16 Faster R-CNN | 0.88 | 0.86 | 0.87 |
| Mendel et al. [2] | 0.94 | 0.88 | 0.91 |

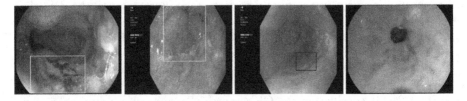

**Fig. 3.** Esophagitis detection from the **Kvasir dataset**. Bounding boxes (BB) are shown in *yellow* for true positives, *blue* for false positive and *no BB* show missed regions. (Color figure online)

recall from 0.90 to 0.97 and precision from 0.88 to 0.92 with the DenseNet and the recall from 0.88 to 0.93 and precision from 0.88 to 0.92 with VGG'16. Additionally, it can be observed that using the DenseNet as a CNN feature extractor enhances the performance of the final detection.

Moreover, Figs. 3 and 4 illustrate qualitative samples of the detection results by the proposed model. The figures show samples of correct detection (**yellow Boxes**), false detection (**blue boxes**) and missed regions (**no prediction**).

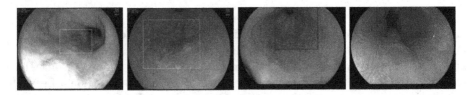

**Fig. 4.** EAC detection from **MICCAI'15 dataset**. Bounding boxes (BB) are shown in *yellow* for true positives, *blue* for false positive and *no BB* show missed regions. (Color figure online)

# 4 Conclusion and Future Work

In this paper, we propose a novel GFD Faster R-CNN network that automatically detects esophageal abnormalities from endoscopic images. A significant effort has been made to adapt the Faster R-CNN to address the challenges of esophageal abnormalities detection which includes the generation of GF image and employing the DenseNet to learn discriminative features from both endoscope and GF images. The GF image is produced by maximizing each pixel value based on different Gabor filter responses of the endoscopic image, resulting in an enhanced image that highlights the hidden fractal details. The ROI pooling layer was adjusted to perform the final detection based on the bilinear fused features obtained from the original endoscopic and GF images which improved the output performance. The model was trained and evaluated on two different datasets. The results demonstrate the effectiveness of the proposed detection model in finding different abnormalities. In future work, more studies will be conducted to consider automatic detection from esophagus videos with more types of abnormalities.

# References

1. Cancer.Net. https://www.cancer.net/cancer-types/esophageal-cancer/statistics
2. Mendel, R., Ebigbo, A., Probst, A., Messmann, H., Palm, C.: Barrett's esophagus analysis using convolutional neural networks. Bildverarbeitung für die Medizin 2017. I, pp. 80–85. Springer, Heidelberg (2017). https://doi.org/10.1007/978-3-662-54345-0_23
3. Van Riel, S., Van Der Sommen, F., Zinger, S., Schoon, E.J., de With, P.H.: Automatic detection of early esophageal cancer with CNNS using transfer learning. In: IEEE ICIP, pp. 1383–1387 (2018)
4. Girshick, R., Donahue, J., Darrell, T., Malik, J.: Region-based convolutional networks for accurate object detection and segmentation. IEEE Trans. Pattern Anal. Mach. Intell. **38**(1), 142–158 (2016)
5. Girshick R.: Fast R-CNN. In: ICCV 2015, pp. 1440–1448. IEEE (2015)
6. Ren, S., He, K., Girshick, R., Sun, J.: Faster R-CNN: towards real-time object detection with region proposal networks. IEEE Trans. Pattern Anal. Mach. Intell. **39**(6), 1137–1149 (2017)
7. Huang, G., Liu, Z., Van Der Maaten, L., Weinberger, K.Q.: Densely connected convolutional networks. In: CVPR 2017, pp. 4700–4708, IEEE (2017)
8. Shangzhen, L., Chen, C., Zhang, B., Han, J., Liu, J.: Gabor convolutional networks. IEEE Trans. Image Process. **27**(9), 4357–4366 (2018). https://doi.org/10.1109/TIP.2018.2835143
9. Feichtenhofer, C., Pinz, A., Zisserman, A.: Convolutional two-stream network fusion for video action recognition. In: CVPR 2016, pp. 1933–1941. IEEE (2016)
10. Sub-Challenge Early Barrett's cancer detection. https://endovissub-barrett.grand-challenge.org
11. Pogorelov, K., et al.: KVASIR: a multi-class image dataset for computer aided gastrointestinal disease detection. In: The 8th ACM on Multimedia Systems Conference, pp. 164–169. ACM (2017)

# Deep Active Lesion Segmentation

Ali Hatamizadeh[1(✉)], Assaf Hoogi[2], Debleena Sengupta[1], Wuyue Lu[1],
Brian Wilcox[2], Daniel Rubin[2], and Demetri Terzopoulos[1]

[1] Computer Science Department, University of California, Los Angeles, CA, USA
ahatamiz@cs.ucla.edu
[2] Department of Biomedical Data Science, Stanford University, Stanford, CA, USA

**Abstract.** Lesion segmentation is an important problem in computer-assisted diagnosis that remains challenging due to the prevalence of low contrast, irregular boundaries that are unamenable to shape priors. We introduce Deep Active Lesion Segmentation (DALS), a fully automated segmentation framework that leverages the powerful nonlinear feature extraction abilities of fully Convolutional Neural Networks (CNNs) and the precise boundary delineation abilities of Active Contour Models (ACMs). Our DALS framework benefits from an improved level-set ACM formulation with a per-pixel-parameterized energy functional and a novel multiscale encoder-decoder CNN that learns an initialization probability map along with parameter maps for the ACM. We evaluate our lesion segmentation model on a new Multiorgan Lesion Segmentation (MLS) dataset that contains images of various organs, including brain, liver, and lung, across different imaging modalities—MR and CT. Our results demonstrate favorable performance compared to competing methods, especially for small training datasets.

**Keywords:** Lesion segmentation · Active contour model · Level sets · Deep learning

## 1 Introduction

Active Contour Models (ACMs) [6] have been extensively applied to computer vision tasks such as image segmentation, especially for medical image analysis. ACMs leverage parametric ("snake") or implicit (level-set) formulations in which the contour evolves by minimizing an associated energy functional, typically using a gradient descent procedure. In the level-set formulation, this amounts to solving a partial differential equation (PDE) to evolve object boundaries that are able to handle large shape variations, topological changes, and intensity inhomogeneities. Alternative approaches to image segmentation that are based on deep learning have recently been gaining in popularity. Fully Convolutional Neural Networks (CNNs) can perform well in segmenting images within datasets

A. Hatamizadeh and A. Hoogi—Co-primary authorship.
D. Rubin and D. Terzopoulos—Co-senior authorship.

© Springer Nature Switzerland AG 2019
H.-I. Suk et al. (Eds.): MLMI 2019, LNCS 11861, pp. 98–105, 2019.
https://doi.org/10.1007/978-3-030-32692-0_12

(1) Brain MR     (2) Liver MR     (3) Liver CT     (4) Lung CT

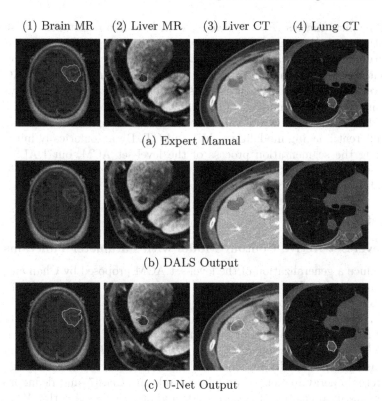

(a) Expert Manual

(b) DALS Output

(c) U-Net Output

**Fig. 1.** Segmentation comparison of (a) medical expert manual with (b) our DALS and (c) U-Net [9], in (1) Brain MR, (2) Liver MR, (3) Liver CT, and (4) Lung CT images.

on which they have been trained [2,5,9], but they may lack robustness when cross-validated on other datasets. Moreover, in medical image segmentation, CNNs tend to be less precise in boundary delineation than ACMs.

In recent years, some researchers have sought to combine ACMs and deep learning approaches. Hu et al. [4] proposed a model in which the network learns a level-set function for salient objects; however, they predefined a fixed weighting parameter $\lambda$ with no expectation of optimality over all cases in the analyzed set of images. Marcos et al. [8] combined CNNs and parametric ACMs for the segmentation of buildings in aerial images; however, their method requires manual contour initialization, fails to precisely delineate the boundary of complex shapes, and segments only single instances, all of which limit its applicability to lesion segmentation due to the irregular shapes of lesion boundaries and widespread cases of multiple lesions (e.g., liver lesions).

We introduce a fully automatic framework for medical image segmentation that combines the strengths of CNNs and level-set ACMs to overcome their respective weaknesses. We apply our proposed Deep Active Lesion Segmentation (DALS) framework to the challenging problem of lesion segmentation in MR and CT medical images (Fig. 1), dealing with lesions of substantially different sizes within a single framework. In particular, our proposed encoder-decoder architecture learns to localize the lesion and generates an initial attention map along with associated parameter maps, thus instantiating a level-set ACM in which every location on the contour has local parameter values. We evaluate our lesion segmentation model on a new Multiorgan Lesion Segmentation (MLS) dataset that contains images of various organs, including brain, liver, and lung, across different imaging modalities—MR and CT. By automatically initializing and tuning the segmentation process of the level-set ACM, our DALS yields significantly more accurate boundaries in comparison to conventional CNNs and can reliably segment lesions of various sizes.

## 2   Method

### 2.1   Level-Set Active Contour Model with Parameter Functions

We introduce a generalization of the level-set ACM proposed by Chan and Vese [1]. Given an image $I(x,y)$, let $C(t) = \{(x,y)|\phi(x,y,t) = 0\}$ be a closed time-varying contour represented in $\Omega \in R^2$ by the zero level set of the signed distance map $\phi(x,y,t)$. We select regions within a square window of size $s$ with a characteristic function $W_s$. The interior and exterior regions of $C$ are specified by the smoothed Heaviside function $H_\epsilon^I(\phi)$ and $H_\epsilon^E(\phi) = 1 - H_\epsilon^I(\phi)$, and the narrow band near $C$ is specified by the smoothed Dirac function $\delta_\epsilon(\phi)$. Assuming a uniform internal energy model [1], we follow Lankton $et\ al.$ [7] and define $m_1$ and $m_2$ as the mean intensities of $I(x,y)$ inside and outside $C$ and within $W_s$. Then, the energy functional associated with $C$ can be written as

$$E(\phi) = \int_\Omega \delta_\epsilon(\phi(x,y,t)) \left( \mu |\nabla \phi(x,y,t)| + \int_\Omega W_s F(\phi(u,v,t))\,du\,dv \right) dx\,dy,$$
(1)

where $\mu$ penalizes the length of $C$ (we set $\mu = 0.1$) and the energy density is

$$F(\phi) = \lambda_1(u,v)(I(u,v) - m_1(x,y))^2 H_\epsilon^I(\phi)$$
$$+ \lambda_2(u,v)(I(u,v) - m_2(x,y))^2 H_\epsilon^E(\phi).$$
(2)

Note that to afford greater control over $C$, in (2) we have generalized the scalar parameter constants $\lambda_1$ and $\lambda_2$ used in [1] to $parameter\ functions$ $\lambda_1(x,y)$ and $\lambda_2(x,y)$ over the image domain. Given an initial distance map $\phi(x,y,0)$ and parameter maps $\lambda_1(x,y)$ and $\lambda_2(x,y)$, the contour is evolved by numerically time-integrating, within a narrow band around $C$ for computational efficiency, the finite difference discretized Euler-Lagrange PDE for $\phi(x,y,t)$ (refer to [1] and [7] for the details).

### 2.2   CNN Backbone

Our encoder-decoder is a fully convolutional architecture (Fig. 2) that is tailored and trained to estimate a probability map from which the initial distance function $\phi(x,y,0)$ of the level-set ACM and the functions $\lambda_1(x,y)$ and $\lambda_2(x,y)$ are

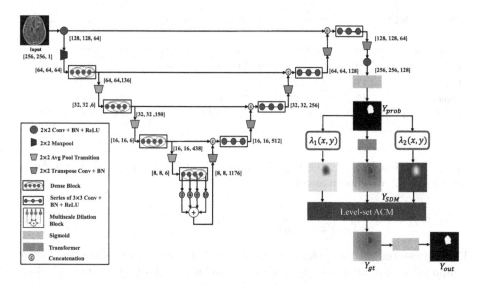

**Fig. 2.** The proposed DALS architecture. DALS is a fully automatic framework without the need for human supervision. The CNN initializes and guides the ACM by its learning local weighted parameters.

computed. In each dense block of the encoder, a composite function of batch normalization, convolution, and ReLU is applied to the concatenation of all the feature maps $[x_0, x_1, \ldots, x_{l-1}]$ from layers 0 to $l-1$ with the feature maps produced by the current block. This concatenated result is passed through a transition layer before being fed to successive dense blocks. The last dense block in the encoder is fed into a custom multiscale dilation block with 4 parallel convolutional layers with dilation rates of 2, 4, 8, and 16. Before being passed to the decoder, the output of the dilated convolutions are then concatenated to create a multiscale representation of the input image thanks to the enlarged receptive field of its dilated convolutions. This, along with dense connectivity, assists in capturing local and global context for highly accurate lesion localization.

## 2.3 The DALS Framework

Our DALS framework is illustrated in Fig. 2. The boundaries of the segmentation map generated by the encoder-decoder are fine-tuned by the level-set ACM that takes advantage of information in the CNN maps to set the per-pixel parameters and initialize the contour.

The input image is fed into the encoder-decoder, which localizes the lesion and, after $1 \times 1$ convolutional and sigmoid layers, produces the initial segmentation probability map $Y_{prob}(x, y)$, which specifies the probability that any point $(x, y)$ lies in the interior of the lesion. The Transformer converts $Y_{prob}$ to a Signed Distance Map (SDM) $\phi(x, y, 0)$ that initializes the level-set ACM. Map $Y_{prob}$ is also utilized to estimate the parameter functions $\lambda_1(x, y)$ and $\lambda_2(x, y)$ in the

**Table 1.** MLS dataset statistics. GC: Global Contrast; GH: Global Heterogeneity.

| Organ | Modality | # Samples | Mean$_{GC}$ | Var$_{GC}$ | Mean$_{GH}$ | Var$_{GH}$ | Lesion radius (pixels) |
|-------|----------|-----------|---------|--------|---------|--------|------------------------|
| Brain | MRI | 369 | 0.56 | 0.029 | 0.907 | 0.003 | $17.42 \pm 9.516$ |
| Lung | CT | 87 | 0.315 | 0.002 | 0.901 | 0.004 | $15.15 \pm 5.777$ |
| Liver | CT | 112 | 0.825 | 0.072 | 0.838 | 0.002 | $20.483 \pm 10.37$ |
| Liver | MRI | 164 | 0.448 | 0.041 | 0.891 | 0.003 | $5.459 \pm 2.027$ |

energy functional (1). Extending the approach of Hoogi et al. [3], the $\lambda$ functions in Fig. 2 are chosen as follows:

$$\lambda_1(x,y) = \exp\left(\frac{2 - Y_{prob}(x,y)}{1 + Y_{prob}(x,y)}\right); \quad \lambda_2(x,y) = \exp\left(\frac{1 + Y_{prob}(x,y)}{2 - Y_{prob}(x,y)}\right). \quad (3)$$

The exponential amplifies the range of values that the functions can take. These computations are performed for each point on the zero level-set contour $C$. During training, $Y_{prob}$ and the ground truth map $Y_{gt}(x,y)$ are fed into a Dice loss function and the error is back-propagated accordingly. During inference, a forward pass through the encoder-decoder and level-set ACM results in a final SDM, which is converted back into a probability map by a sigmoid layer, thus producing the final segmentation map $Y_{out}(x,y)$.

*Implementation Details:* DALS is implemented in Tensorflow. We trained it on an NVIDIA Titan XP GPU and an Intel® Core™ i7-7700K CPU @ 4.20 GHz. All the input images were first normalized and resized to a predefined size of 256× 256 pixels. The size of the mini-batches is set to 4, and the Adam optimization algorithm was used with an initial learning rate of 0.001 that decays by a factor of 10 every 10 epochs. The entire inference time for DALS takes 1.5 s. All model performances were evaluated by using the Dice coefficient, Hausdorff distance, and BoundF.

## 3   Multiorgan Lesion Segmentation (MLS) Dataset

As shown in Table 1, the MLS dataset includes images of highly diverse lesions in terms of size and spatial characteristics such as contrast and homogeneity. The liver component of the dataset consists of 112 contrast-enhanced CT images of liver lesions (43 hemangiomas, 45 cysts, and 24 metastases) with a mean lesion radius of $20.483 \pm 10.37$ pixels and 164 liver lesions from 3 T gadoxetic acid enhanced MRI scans (one or more LI-RADS (LR), LR-3, or LR-4 lesions) with a mean lesion radius of $5.459 \pm 2.027$ pixels. The brain component consists of 369 preoperative and pretherapy perfusion MR images with a mean lesion radius of $17.42 \pm 9.516$ pixels. The lung component consists of 87 CT images with a mean lesion radius of $15.15 \pm 5.777$ pixels. For each component of the MLS dataset, we used 85% of its images for training, 10% for testing, and 5% for validation.

**Table 2.** Segmentation metrics for model evaluations. Box and whisker plots are shown in Fig. 3. CI denotes the confidence interval.

| Dataset: | Brain MR | | | | | Lung CT | | | | |
|---|---|---|---|---|---|---|---|---|---|---|
| Model | Dice | CI | Hausdorff | CI | BoundF | Dice | CI | Hausdorff | CI | BoundF |
| U-Net | 0.776 ± 0.214 | 0.090 | 2.988 ± 1.238 | 0.521 | 0.826 | 0.817 ± 0.098 | 0.0803 | 2.289 ± 0.650 | 0.53 | 0.898 |
| CNN Backbone | 0.824 ± 0.193 | 0.078 | 2.755 ± 1.216 | 0.49 | 0.891 | 0.822 ± 0.115 | 0.0944 | 2.254 ± 0.762 | 0.6218 | 0.900 |
| Level-set | 0.796 ± 0.095 | 0.038 | 2.927 ± 0.992 | 0.400 | 0.841 | 0.789 ± 0.078 | 0.064 | 3.27 ± 0.553 | 0.4514 | 0.879 |
| DALS | **0.888 ± 0.0755** | **0.03** | **2.322 ± 0.824** | **0.332** | **0.944** | **0.869 ± 0.113** | **0.092** | **2.095 ± 0.623** | **0.508** | **0.937** |

| Dataset: | Liver MR | | | | | Liver CT | | | | |
|---|---|---|---|---|---|---|---|---|---|---|
| Model | Dice | CI | Hausdorff | CI | BoundF | Dice | CI | Hausdorff | CI | BoundF |
| U-Net | 0.769 ± 0.162 | 0.093 | 1.645 ± 0.598 | 0.343 | 0.92 | 0.698 ± 0.149 | 0.133 | 4.422 ± 0.969 | 0.866 | 0.662 |
| CNN Backbone | 0.805 ± 0.193 | 0.11 | 1.347 ± 0.671 | 0.385 | 0.939 | 0.801 ± 0.178 | 0.159 | 3.813 ± 1.791 | 1.6 | 0.697 |
| Level-set | 0.739 ± 0.102 | 0.056 | 2.227 ± 0.576 | 0.317 | 0.954 | 0.765 ± 0.039 | 0.034 | 3.153 ± 0.825 | 0.737 | 0.761 |
| DALS | **0.894 ± 0.0654** | **0.036** | **1.298 ± 0.434** | **0.239** | **0.987** | **0.846 ± 0.090** | **0.0806** | **3.113 ± 0.747** | **0.667** | **0.773** |

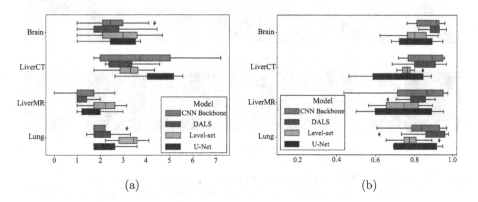

(a)                                            (b)

**Fig. 3.** Box and whisker plots of: (a) Dice score; (b) Hausdorff distance.

## 4 Results and Discussion

*Algorithm Comparison:* We have quantitatively compared our DALS against U-Net [9] and manually-initialized level-set ACM with scalar $\lambda$ parameter constants as well as its backbone CNN. The evaluation metrics for each organ are reported in Table 2 and box and whisker plots are shown in Fig. 3. Our DALS achieves superior accuracies under all metrics and in all datasets. Furthermore, we evaluated the statistical significance of our method by applying a Wilcoxon paired test on the calculated Dice results. Our DALS performed significantly better than the U-Net ($p < 0.001$), the manually-initialized ACM ($p < 0.001$), and DALS's backbone CNN on its own ($p < 0.005$).

*Boundary Delineation:* As shown in Fig. 4, the DALS segmentation contours conform appropriately to the irregular shapes of the lesion boundaries, since the learned parameter maps, $\lambda_1(x, y)$ and $\lambda_2(x, y)$, provide the flexibility needed to accommodate the irregularities. In most cases, the DALS has also successfully avoided local minima and converged onto the true lesion boundaries, thus

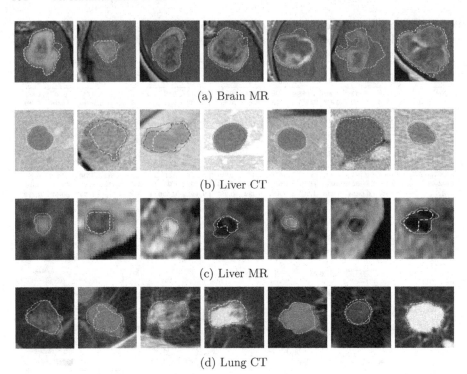

(a) Brain MR

(b) Liver CT

(c) Liver MR

(d) Lung CT

**Fig. 4.** Comparison of the output segmentation of our DALS (red) against the U-Net [9] (yellow) and manual "ground truth" (green) segmentations on images of Brain MR, Liver CT, Liver MR, and Lung CT on the MLS test set. (Color figure online)

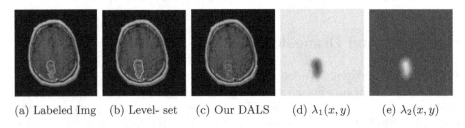

(a) Labeled Img    (b) Level- set    (c) Our DALS    (d) $\lambda_1(x, y)$    (e) $\lambda_2(x, y)$

**Fig. 5.** (a) Labeled image. (b) Level-set (analogous to scalar $\lambda$ parameter constants). (c) DALS output. (d), (e) Learned parameter maps $\lambda_1(x, y)$ and $\lambda_2(x, y)$.

enhancing segmentation accuracy. DALS performs well for different image characteristics, including low contrast lesions, heterogeneous lesions, and noise.

*Parameter Functions and Backbone CNN:* The contribution of the parameter functions was validated by comparing the DALS against a manually initialized level-set ACM with scalar parameters constants as well as with DALS's backbone CNN on its own. As shown in Fig. 5, the encoder-decoder has predicted the $\lambda_1(x, y)$ and $\lambda_2(x, y)$ feature maps to guide the contour evolution. The learned maps serve as an attention mechanism that provides additional degrees of freedom for the contour to adjust itself precisely to regions of interest. The segmentation outputs of our DALS and the manual level-set ACM in Fig. 5 demonstrate the benefits of using parameter functions to accommodate significant boundary complexities. Moreover, our DALS outperformed the manually-initialized ACM and its backbone CNN in all metrics across all evaluations on every organ.

## 5    Conclusion

We have presented Deep Active Lesion Segmentation (DALS), a novel framework that combines the capabilities of the CNN and the level-set ACM to yield a robust, fully automatic medical image segmentation method that produces more accurate and detailed boundaries compared to competing state-of-the-art methods. The DALS framework includes an encoder-decoder that feeds a level-set ACM with per-pixel parameter functions. We evaluated our framework in the challenging task of lesion segmentation with a new dataset, MLS, which includes a variety of images of lesions of various sizes and textures in different organs acquired through multiple imaging modalities. Our results affirm the effectiveness our DALS framework.

## References

1. Chan, T.F., Vese, L.A.: Active contours without edges. IEEE Trans. Image Process. **10**(2), 266–277 (2001)
2. Hatamizadeh, A., Hosseini, H., Liu, Z., Schwartz, S.D., Terzopoulos, D.: Deep dilated convolutional nets for the automatic segmentation of retinal vessels. arXiv preprint arXiv:1905.12120 (2019)
3. Hoogi, A., Subramaniam, A., Veerapaneni, R., Rubin, D.L.: Adaptive estimation of active contour parameters using convolutional neural networks and texture analysis. IEEE Trans. Med. Imaging **36**(3), 781–791 (2017)
4. Hu, P., Shuai, B., Liu, J., Wang, G.: Deep level sets for salient object detection. In: Proceedings IEEE Conference on Computer Vision and Pattern Recognition (2017)
5. Imran, A.-A.-Z., Hatamizadeh, A., Ananth, S.P., Ding, X., Terzopoulos, D., Tajbakhsh, N.: Automatic segmentation of pulmonary lobes using a progressive dense V-network. In: Stoyanov, D., et al. (eds.) DLMIA/ML-CDS -2018. LNCS, vol. 11045, pp. 282–290. Springer, Cham (2018). https://doi.org/10.1007/978-3-030-00889-5_32
6. Kass, M., Witkin, A., Terzopoulos, D.: Snakes: active contour models. Int. J. Comput. Vis. **1**(4), 321–331 (1988)
7. Lankton, S., Tannenbaum, A.: Localizing region-based active contours. IEEE Trans. Image Process. **17**(11), 2029–2039 (2008)
8. Marcos, D., et al.: Learning deep structured active contours end-to-end. In: Proceedings of IEEE Conference on Computer Vision and Pattern Recognition (CVPR), pp. 8877–8885 (2018)
9. Ronneberger, O., Fischer, P., Brox, T.: U-Net: convolutional networks for biomedical image segmentation. In: Navab, N., Hornegger, J., Wells, W.M., Frangi, A.F. (eds.) MICCAI 2015. LNCS, vol. 9351, pp. 234–241. Springer, Cham (2015). https://doi.org/10.1007/978-3-319-24574-4_28

# Infant Brain Deformable Registration Using Global and Local Label-Driven Deep Regression Learning

Shunbo Hu[1,2(✉)], Lintao Zhang[1,2], Guoqiang Li[1,2], Mingtao Liu[1,2], Deqian Fu[1,2], and Wenyin Zhang[1,2]

[1] School of Information Science and Engineering, Linyi University, Linyi, Shandong, China
hushunbo@lyu.edu.cn
[2] Linda Institute, Shandong Provincial Key Laboratory of Network Based Intelligent Computing, Linyi University, Linyi, Shandong, China

**Abstract.** Accurate image registration is important for quantifying dynamic brain development in the first year of life. However, it is challenging to deformable registration of infant brain magnetic resonance (MR) images because: (1) there are large *anatomical and appearance variations* in these longitudinal images; (2) there is a *one-to-many correspondence* in appearance between global anatomical regions and local small therein regions. In this paper, we apply a deformable registration scheme based on the global and local label-driven learning with convolution neural networks (CNN). Two to-be-registered patches are fed into an U-Net-like regression network. Then a dense displacement field (DDF) is obtained by optimizing the loss function between many pairs of label patches. Global and local label patch pairs are only leveraged to drive registration during training stage. During inference, the resulting 3D DDF is obtained by inputting two new MR images to the trained network. The highlight is that the global tissues, i.e. white matter (GM), gray matter (GM), cerebrospinal fluid (CSF), and the local hippocampi are well aligned at the same time without any priori ground-truth deformation. Especially for the local hippocampi, their Dice ratios between two aligned images are highly improved. Experiment results are given based on intra-subject and inter-subject registration of infant brain MR images between different time points, yielding higher accuracy in both global and local tissues compared with state-of-the-art registration methods.

**Keywords:** Infant brain MR images · Deformable registration · Label-driven learning

## 1 Introduction

Infant brain deformable registration is very important for studying early brain development, diagnosing developmental disorders, and building population atlases. Magnetic resonance imaging (MRI) is a noninvasive technique to acquire high-contrast soft-tissue information. Hence, MRI has been widely used in neuroimaging studies of

H.-I. Suk et al. (Eds.): MLMI 2019, LNCS 11861, pp. 106–114, 2019.
https://doi.org/10.1007/978-3-030-32692-0_13

infant brain. Unfortunately, there are dynamic and non-linear *anatomical and appearance variations* in infant brain MR images for the reason of fast brain growth and mature myelin [1]. In addition, local tissues are often a part of global tissues, and they have similar appearance in MRI. In Fig. 1, The hippocampi are mainly located in GM region, and they possess strong statistical correlation with other parts of GM. Hence, the global GM tissue alignment doesn't mean the local hippocampal tissue alignment, which is a *one-to-many correspondence* problem. In short, deformable image registration of infant brain MR images becomes difficult for two problems: *anatomical and appearance variations* and *one-to-many correspondences*.

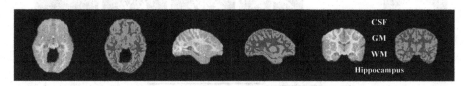

**Fig. 1.** The slices of infant brain MR images and four labels: CSF, GM, WM and hippocampus.

By maintaining the voxel-to-voxel spatial correspondence of image deformable registration, unsupervised [2, 3] or weakly-supervised [4] deep learning methods were applied to image registration without any ground-truth deformation supervision, which were mainly based on CNN. Cao et al. employed the contextual cues to train the voxel correspondence at patch center, and then applied thin-plate spline to obtain DDF [2]. Balakrishnan et al. proposed VoxelMorph to get DDF by optimizing the total loss function with summing cross-correlation similarity and deformation regularization [3]. Hu YP et al. stated that these image-similarity-driven unsupervised learning would inherit the key shortcomings (e.g. modal-dependent) of classical intensity-based image registration algorithms, so they proposed a label-driven weakly-supervised registration framework. They took Dice similarity loss function of anatomical labels to optimize the DDF between two unlabeled images during training stage, and applied two new unlabeled images to acquire DDF during inference [4]. Generative adversarial networks (GAN) were also used to assess the quality of image alignment [5].

Motivated by these studies, we apply a global and local label-driven deformable registration scheme for infant brain MR images. The major contributions are summarized as follows:

(1) Both global tissues and local tissues are well aligned at the same time. During training, not only the global labels, i.e. WM, GM and CSF, but also local labels are utilized. This overcomes the *one-to-many* problem and establishes the voxel correspondence of global tissues as well as local tissues. Furthermore, because of the local tissue alignment, the deformation folding in the neighborhood global regions will be alleviated.

(2) The local tissue alignment is subject-independent and time-point-independent. The registration (dis)similarity between local tissues is incorporated as a part of the total loss function, and DDF of the local tissue is also trained during the training phase. Therefore, regardless of intra-subject registration or inter-subject

registration of infant brain MR images, local small tissue regions will be well aligned for any time-point-pair.

(3) As far as we know, this is the first time that the deformable registration based on global and local label-driven deep regression learning has been used in the research of infant brain MR image alignment, which helps to address the huge appearance and morphological differences in infant brain MR images without any ground-truth deformation.

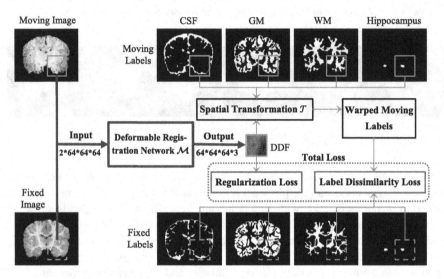

**Fig. 2.** The framework of the proposed deformable image registration scheme that is based on global and local label-driven deep regression learning.

In addition, we use DDF regularization, multi-strides and surface-discarding to increase the accuracy and the smoothness of DDF, and data augmentations and shuffle orders to increase the generalization ability.

## 2   Methods

In this work, we apply a deep regression architecture to model the infant brain deformable registration network $\mathcal{M} : \left(I_m^A, I_m^B\right) \Rightarrow \phi_m$ for the $m$-th patch pair, $m = 1, 2, \cdots, M$. The 3D patch pair $\left(I_m^A, I_m^B\right)$ is extracted from the moving image $A$ and the fixed image $B$, which have been affinely aligned in preprocessing. $\phi_m$ is the DDF indicating the voxel dense correspondence, which is the output of the registration network $\mathcal{M}$ by minimizing the total loss function (including regularization loss and label dissimilarity loss) between all the label patch pairs, i.e., the warped moving label patch $l_{mn}^W$ and the fixed label patch $l_{mn}^B$, $(n = 1, 2, \cdots, N)$. $N$ is the total label number.

Since there are large appearance variations between moving and fixed MR images at two time points, we calculate a multi-scale modality-independent Dice similarity between their corresponding label patches. According to the total loss function, the network $\mathcal{M}$ is trained under the weakly-supervision of global and local labels.

After the registration network is trained, we apply it during inference. By feeding a pair of new MR images' patches into the network, DDF between them is obtained without any label. As seen in Fig. 2, only the blue paths are needed during inference.

## 2.1 Loss Function Using Global and Local Labels

To train $\mathcal{M}$, the total loss function of the $m$-th pair of label patch is defined as:

$$E = \frac{1}{|\{i\}|} \sum_i E_G\left(l_{mi}^W, l_{mi}^B\right) + \frac{1}{N_1} \sum_j \alpha_j E_L\left(l_{mj}^W, l_{mj}^B\right) + \beta E_R(\phi_m), \tag{1}$$

where $i$ is a sequence number of global label, $j$ is the local label sequence number after $\{i\}$, and $|\{i\}| + |\{j\}| = N$. $E_G$ measures the global dissimilarity between the $i$-th warped moving label patch $l_{mi}^W$ and the corresponding fixed one $l_{mi}^B$. $E_L$ represents the local dissimilarity between two local label patches, i.e. $l_{mj}^W$ and $l_{mj}^B$. $l_m^W = T\left(\phi_m, l_m^A\right)$, is the warped label patch by transforming the moving label patch $l_m^A$ with DDF $\phi_m$. $\alpha_j = 1$ if the voxel number of local label $j$ locating in patch $m$ is larger than a predefined threshold, otherwise, $\alpha_j = 0$. $N_1 = \max\left(1, \sum_j \alpha_j\right)$. $\beta$ is a hyper-parameter of regularization, which controls the smoothness of DDF. We choose $\beta = 0.5$ if $\sum_j \alpha_j = 0$, otherwise $\beta = 1$. Therefore, we utilize all possible global labels and the local labels that mainly locate in the chosen patches.

The multi-scale dissimilarity loss function $E_G$ is defined as the following:

$$E_G(l_{mi}^W, l_{mi}^B) = 1 - \frac{1}{N_2}\sum_\sigma \delta_{Dice}\left(\mathcal{G}_\sigma(l_{mi}^W), \mathcal{G}_\sigma(l_{mi}^B)\right), \tag{2}$$

where $N_2$ is the number of scales, and is set to 6 in this work, with scale set $\{0,1,2,4,8,16\}$. $\sigma$ is the isotropic standard deviation of a 3D Gaussian filter kernel. The kernel can be given as follows:

$$\mathcal{G}_\sigma(x) = \frac{1}{(\sqrt{2\pi}\sigma)^3}e^{-\frac{|x|^2}{2\sigma^2}}, \tag{3}$$

where $|x|$ means the distance to the kernel center. $E_L$ is similar to (2) except that it is defined between two local labels.

$\delta_{Dice}$ measures the Dice similarity between two labels, which is defined as:

$$\delta_{Dice}\left(\mathcal{G}_\sigma(l_{mi}^W), \mathcal{G}_\sigma(l_{mi}^B)\right) = \frac{2|\mathcal{G}_\sigma(l_{mi}^W) \cap \mathcal{G}_\sigma(l_{mi}^B)|}{|\mathcal{G}_\sigma(l_{mi}^W)| + |\mathcal{G}_\sigma(l_{mi}^B)|}. \tag{4}$$

Additionally, DDF should be smooth to preserve a topology correspondence. A regularization term of bending energy is used as the following discrete form:

$$E_R(\phi) = \frac{1}{|V|} \sum \left[ \left(\frac{\partial^2 \phi}{\partial x^2}\right)^2 + \left(\frac{\partial^2 \phi}{\partial y^2}\right)^2 + \left(\frac{\partial^2 \phi}{\partial z^2}\right)^2 + 2\left(\frac{\partial^2 \phi}{\partial xy}\right)^2 + 2\left(\frac{\partial^2 \phi}{\partial yz}\right)^2 + 2\left(\frac{\partial^2 \phi}{\partial xz}\right)^2 \right],$$

(5)

where $|V|$ represents the number of voxels in a patch.

## 2.2   Deformable Registration Network

The detailed architecture of the infant brain MR deformable registration network is shown in Fig. 3. The inputs are a pair of patches extracted from two infant brain MR images at different time points, each patch with the size of $64 \times 64 \times 64$. The output DDF patch is $64 \times 64 \times 64 \times 3$, which is located in the same position as the input patch.

The network is densely connected by four up-sampling Resnet blocks and four down-sampling Resnet blocks. Four summation skip layers are used to shortcut the entire network and to alleviate gradient vanishing problem. The output DDF is calculated by summation at five resolution levels. Four of them are obtained by trilinear interpolation after convoluting feature data with a bias term from the three end layers of up-sampling blocks and $s_m$ layer. The remaining part of DDF is obtained by convoluting from the end layer of the last Resnet block without trilinear interpolation.

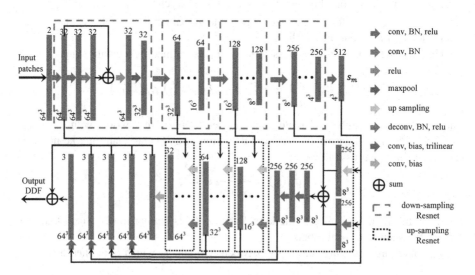

**Fig. 3.** Detailed architecture of patch-based deformable registration network.

## 2.3    Calculation of the Whole DDF During Inference

During inference, the total DDF is determined by averaging the output DDF $\phi_m$ from the network $\mathcal{M}$. The total DDF at location $\boldsymbol{u}$, $\phi_{total}(\boldsymbol{u})$, is obtained by the following:

$$\phi_{total}(\boldsymbol{u}) = \frac{1}{N_3} \sum_{\{m|\boldsymbol{u} \in P_m\}} \phi_m(\boldsymbol{u}), \tag{6}$$

where $N_3 = |\{m|\boldsymbol{u} \in P_m\}|$ is the number of patches covering location $\boldsymbol{u}$. $N_3$ has relation to the stride value and the position of patch $P_m$. We choose patches in stride 32 during training, and 4 during inference. At the same time, in order to further improve the smoothness of DDF and enclose sufficient neighborhood information, surface-discarding is used. For example, the patch size of DDF is $64 \times 64 \times 64 \times 3$ during training, during inference we only utilize the middle part of the patch with the size of $58 \times 58 \times 58 \times 3$, by discarding 3-voxel-width surfaces in each face of the patch.

Two DDFs' coronal slices and their detailed grids are shown in Fig. 4, which describes the intra-subject registration deformations from 2-week-old to 12-month-old MR images. The DDF on the left doesn't use the local hippocampal labels, while the right utilizes those labels. From Fig. 4, we conclude that there are two advantages when global and local labels' information is incorporated together to optimize DDF. Firstly, there is better anti-folding performance, which is illustrated in two regions pointing by two green arrows. This indicates that the correct local alignment may give smooth regularization to the global neighborhood deformations. Secondly, as is shown by the yellow arrows, there is better local transformation alignment. This is significant when we analyze the development of local tissues, lesions or tumors.

**Fig. 4.** The DDF calculated without (left) or with (right) local hippocampal label.

## 3    Experimental Results

The experimental dataset included infant brain MR images of 24 subjects, where each subject had T1-weighted MR images at 2-week-old, 3-, 6-, 9- and 12-month-old, with a resolution $1 \times 1 \times 1$ mm$^3$. In preprocessing, FLIRT [6] linear registration of other time point to 12-month-old was performed. The corresponding segmentation labels, i.e. WM, GM and hippocampus, were obtained by iBEAT toolbox [7] and experts' manual refinement. Next, all images were cropped to the same size as $160 \times 192 \times 128$. Finally, data augmentations were leveraged by applying a random affine transformation to each image and label before training.

For intra-subject registration, we used 22 subjects for training, 1 subject for validation and 1 subject for inference; for inter-subject registration, 21 subjects for training, 1 subject for validation, 1 subject for inference and 1 subject for the fixed images. The network was trained on a 12 GB Nvidia TitanX GPU with 10000 iterations. In each iteration, a pair of randomly augmented MR images were produced and further sampled to 60 patches. Hence, during training, the total different patch pairs of MR images were $10000 \times 60 = 600000$. In each cycling, the orders of subjects and patches were shuffled. It took $\sim 72$ h using an Adam optimizer starting at a learning rate $10^{-5}$ with a minibatch size of 4 during training, and only $\sim 11$ s to calculate the total DDF during inference with the same stride.

## 3.1  Registration Results

Dice ratios of WM, GM and hippocampus are applied to evaluate the registration performance. In Table 1, we list intra/inter-subject registration results from 2-week, 3-, 6- and 9-month-old to 12-month-old by Demons [8], Label-reg [4] with global labels (LRG) and our method, respectively.

In Table 1, for global GM and WM labels, our registration scheme has the similar large Dice ratios as LRG method, and higher Dice ratios than Demons in most cases. For the local hippocampal label, our registration method achieves the best results among three registration methods in all cases. For example, the mean Dice ratios of hippocampus increase about 90%, 44%, 27% and 23% for registration from 2-week-old, 3-, 6- and 9-month-old images to 12-month-old images by intra-subject registration in comparison with Demons, and 81%, 54%, 43% and 39% with inter-subject

**Table 1.** Dice ratios of three labels using three registration methods

| Registration | Labels | Methods | 2 week to 12-month | 3-Month to 12-Month | 6-Month to 12-Month | 9-month to 12-month |
|---|---|---|---|---|---|---|
| Intra-subject | GM | Demons | 0.611 ± 0.017 | 0.668 ± 0.030 | 0.823 ± 0.013 | **0.879** ± 0.010 |
| | | LRG | 0.837 ± 0.012 | **0.828** ± 0.021 | **0.871** ± 0.006 | 0.876 ± 0.007 |
| | | Our | **0.849** ± 0.009 | 0.796 ± 0.017 | 0.867 ± 0.005 | 0.876 ± 0.005 |
| | WM | Demons | 0.703 ± 0.008 | 0.695 ± 0.039 | 0.746 ± 0.038 | 0.834 ± 0.043 |
| | | LRG | 0.834 ± 0.014 | **0.804** ± 0.070 | 0.855 ± 0.006 | **0.869** ± 0.006 |
| | | Our | **0.835** ± 0.010 | **0.804** ± 0.049 | **0.859** ± 0.006 | 0.864 ± 0.006 |
| | Hippocampus | Demons | 0.447 ± 0.090 | 0.589 ± 0.064 | 0.664 ± 0.077 | 0.708 ± 0.035 |
| | | LRG | 0.467 ± 0.173 | 0.637 ± 0.066 | 0.631 ± 0.112 | 0.735 ± 0.046 |
| | | Our | **0.850** ± 0.015 | **0.851** ± 0.012 | **0.842** ± 0.010 | **0.870** ± 0.019 |
| Inter-subject | GM | Demons | 0.600 ± 0.016 | 0.639 ± 0.038 | 0.746 ± 0.033 | 0.793 ± 0.032 |
| | | LRG | **0.770** ± 0.023 | **0.759** ± 0.020 | **0.810** ± 0.022 | **0.814** ± 0.027 |
| | | our | 0.759 ± 0.027 | 0.726 ± 0.025 | 0.772 ± 0.030 | 0.788 ± 0.032 |
| | WM | Demons | **0.727** ± 0.012 | **0.714** ± 0.035 | 0.695 ± 0.017 | 0.689 ± 0.042 |
| | | LRG | 0.725 ± 0.035 | 0.687 ± 0.041 | **0.752** ± 0.034 | **0.760** ± 0.037 |
| | | Our | 0.716 ± 0.038 | 0.663 ± 0.045 | 0.732 ± 0.036 | 0.740 ± 0.039 |
| | Hippocampus | Demons | 0.465 ± 0.104 | 0.552 ± 0.058 | 0.597 ± 0.071 | 0.612 ± 0.059 |
| | | LRG | 0.402 ± 0.175 | 0.522 ± 0.080 | 0.541 ± 0.092 | 0.652 ± 0.055 |
| | | Our | **0.843** ± 0.020 | **0.850** ± 0.010 | **0.856** ± 0.011 | **0.851** ± 0.007 |

registration, respectively. Compared with LRG method, the hippocampal Dice ratios in our method also increase a lot. We can conclude: (1) the registration of local tissue, hippocampus, is subject-independent and time-point-independent, and both intra-subject and inter-subject registration can achieve good alignment performance for every time-point pair; (2) for global tissues (i.e., WM and GM), our scheme has achieved good registration results as LRG, and better than Demons in most cases.

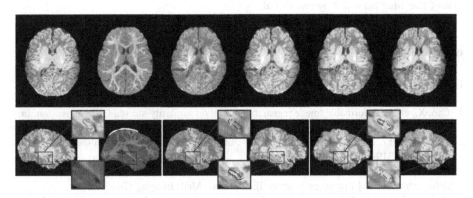

**Fig. 5.** Visualization of inter-subject registration from 2-week to 12-month. Slices come from 3D images. Columns from left to right are from moving image, fixed image, warped images by Demons, MI, LRG and our method, with the moving or warped (green), fixed (red), overlap (yellow) hippocampal contours. Our method obtains the largest yellow overlap hippocampal contours. (Color figure online)

Qualitative comparisons are provided in Fig. 5, which visualizes the same axial or sagittal slices from 2-week-old to 12-month-old MR images during inter-subject registration. From the tissues pointing by the pink arrows in the top row, we can see that our registration method outperforms Demons and mutual information (MI) [9] methods. In the bottom, the registration of hippocampus is emphasized. The yellow edges are the overlap between the hippocampal contour (green) in warped images and that (red) in the fixed image. Obviously, our method obtains the largest yellow overlap contours, which shows the best registration performance for the local hippocampus.

## 4   Conclusion

In this work, we have proposed a novel patch-based deformable registration method for infant brain MR images, which incorporates global and local labels' information to train DDF via U-Net-like regression network. Then during inference, the total DDF between two new whole longitudinal infant brain MR images are calculated by averaging the network outputs for denser pairwise patches. Our registration scheme can overcome problems of large *anatomical and appearance variations* and *one-to-many correspondences* without any ground-truth deformation or transformation. Experiment results are reported by intra-subject and inter-subject registration among different time-point infant brain MR image pairs, and show promising registration performance not only for global tissues but also for local tissues.

**Acknowledgments.** This work was supported in part by NSFC 61771230, 61773244, Shandong Provincial Natural Science Foundation ZR2016FM40, ZR2019PF005, and Shandong Key R&D Program Project 2019GGX101006, 2019GNC106027. And we also thanks for the open source code of Label-reg published by Hu Y et al.

# References

1. Wang, L., Nie, D., Li, G., et al.: Benchmark on automatic 6-month-old infant brain segmentation algorithms: the iSeg-2017 challenge. IEEE Trans. Med. Imaging (2019)
2. Cao, X., et al.: Deformable image registration based on similarity-steered CNN regression. In: Descoteaux, M., Maier-Hein, L., Franz, A., Jannin, P., Collins, D.L., Duchesne, S. (eds.) MICCAI 2017. LNCS, vol. 10433, pp. 300–308. Springer, Cham (2017). https://doi.org/10.1007/978-3-319-66182-7_35
3. Balakrishnan, G., Zhao, A., Sabuncu, M.R., et al.: VoxelMorph: a learning framework for deformable medical image registration. IEEE Trans. Med. Imaging (2019)
4. Hu, Y., Modat, M., Gibson, E., et al.: Weakly-supervised convolutional neural networks for multimodal image registration. Med. Image Anal. 49, 1–13 (2018)
5. Haskins, G., Kruger, U., Yan, P.: Deep learning in medical image registration: a survey. arXiv preprint arXiv:1903.02026 (2019)
6. Jenkinson, M., Smith, S.: A global optimisation method for robust affine registration of brain images. Med. Image Anal. 5(2), 143–156 (2001)
7. Dai, Y., Shi, F., Wang, L., et al.: iBEAT: a toolbox for infant brain magnetic resonance image processing. Neuroinformatics 11(2), 211–225 (2013)
8. Vercauteren, T., Pennec, X., Perchant, A., et al.: Diffeomorphic demons: efficient non-parametric image registration. Neuroimage 45, S61–S72 (2009)
9. Maes, F., Collignon, A., Vandermeulen, D., et al.: Multimodality image registration by maximization of mutual information. IEEE Trans. Med. Imaging 16(2), 187–198 (1997)

# A Relation Hashing Network Embedded with Prior Features for Skin Lesion Classification

Wenbo Zheng[1,3], Chao Gou[2(✉)], and Lan Yan[3,4]

[1] School of Software Engineering, Xi'an Jiaotong University, Xi'an, China
[2] School of Intelligent Systems Engineering, Sun Yat-sen University,
Guangzhou, China
gouchao@mail.sysu.edu.cn
[3] The State Key Laboratory for Management and Control of Complex Systems,
Institute of Automation, Chinese Academy of Sciences, Beijing, China
[4] School of Artificial Intelligence, University of Chinese Academy of Sciences,
Beijing, China

**Abstract.** Deep neural networks have become an effective tool for solving end-to-end classification problems and are suitable for many diagnostic settings. However, the success of such deep models often depends on a large number of training samples with annotations. Moreover, deep networks do not leverage the power of domain knowledge which is usually essential for diagnostic decision. Here we propose a novel relation hashing network via meta-learning to address the problem of skin lesion classification with prior features. In particular, we present a deep relation network to capture and memorize the relation among different samples. To employ the prior domain knowledge, we construct the hybrid-prior feature representation via joint meta-learning based on handcrafted models and deep-learned features. In order to utilize the fast and efficient computation of representation learning, we further create a hashing hybrid-prior feature representation by incorporating deep hashing into hybrid-prior representation learning, and then integrating it into our proposed network. Final recognition is obtained from our hashing relation network by learning to compare among the hashing hybrid-prior features of samples. Experimental results on ISIC Skin 2017 dataset demonstrate that our hashing relation network can achieve the state-of-the-art performance for the task of skin lesion classification.

**Keywords:** Skin lesion classification · Meta-learning · Prior feature · Deep-hashing

## 1 Introduction

Skin cancer is one of the most prevalent types of cancer, with 5 million cases occurring annually [6]. As a result, there is a growing need for accurate and

© Springer Nature Switzerland AG 2019
H.-I. Suk et al. (Eds.): MLMI 2019, LNCS 11861, pp. 115–123, 2019.
https://doi.org/10.1007/978-3-030-32692-0_14

scalable decision support systems for skin diseases. To assist doctors in making correct diagnoses, decision support systems can be trained on dermoscopic images. Classifying skin lesions in dermoscopy images is a significant computer-aided diagnosis task.

Up to now, mainstream algorithms of skin lesion classification are mainly divided into six categories: instance-based methods, decision-tree-based methods, Bayesian-learning-based methods, artificial-neural-network-based methods, support-vector-machine-based methods, and ensemble methods [5]. Recently, deep-learning-based methods, particularly those based on deep convolutional neural networks, have achieved significantly improved performance [5]. However, there are two main challenges for skin lesion classification using deep learning:

(1) The lack of training samples limits the success of deep-learning-based methods in this task, as small data sets typically exist in most medical imaging studies.
(2) Inter-class similarities and intra-class variations influence the accuracy of the classification of samples from skin lesions. As an example, some samples from different categories have similar visual similarities in their shape and color.

To tackle the problem of limited training data, we utilize the principle of meta-learning [10] which promises to be able to generalize well with a limited amount of training data. Hence, we further introduce a deep network to capture the relation among skin lesions via meta-learning. To address the second challenge, inspired by hybrid-augmented intelligence [9], considering that hand-crafted features are approximations of the visual content designed by human experts using mathematical and statistical formulations and according to prior knowledge of the visual regions of interest [3], we propose to embed handcrafted models as prior domain knowledge into the network model to form hybrid-prior features. Moreover, in order to compute fast and efficiently, we employ the deep hashing approach to encode hybrid-prior features and then get hashing hybrid-prior features by mapping high-dimensional representations to compact binary codes.

Therefore, in this paper, we propose a novel relational hashing network via meta-learning to address the problem of skin lesion classification. We propose an effective feature fusion approach to combine the extracted feature using the network with the handcrafted feature as prior knowledge for getting the better results of feature-based representative learning. Further, we utilize the deep hashing approach to encode this fusion feature. We build the two-branch relation network via meta-learning. First, we introduce the embedding approach to perform feature fusion representation learning. Then, to compute fast and efficiently, we incorporate the deep hashing approach into the feature representation of our network. Finally, we design a relation model to capture and memorize the relation among different samples for final classification. We conduct experiments on ISIC Skin 2017 dataset [2]. Experimental results show that the proposed algorithm performs better than similar works.

In short, the main contributions of this work are in four-fold.

(1) We present a relation network with meta-learning to compare the features of different samples. It allows to capture and memorize the relation among different skin lesion samples which is critical for skin lesion classification.
(2) In order to learn inductive prior knowledge for relation network, we further propose to embed handcrafted features into the relation network to enhance the classification performance.
(3) We incorporate the deep hashing approach into the proposed network for the fast and efficient computation of feature learning.
(4) Our network is effective, and experimental results show this method leads to better classification performance than other state-of-the-art algorithms.

## 2 Prior Features Embedding Relation Hashing Network

### 2.1 Problem Setup and Network Architecture

Deep convolutional neural networks have achieved the state-of-the-art skin lesion classification performance in the case of enough training data. However, it is costly to annotate a amount of skin lesion samples [1]. In contrast, human being is able to learn new concepts and skills faster and more efficiently. Is it possible to quickly design a machine learning model with similar properties by training a small number of samples? This is the problem that meta-learning aims to solve [8]. Hence, we consider the problem of skin lesion classification as meta-learning based classifier, which consists of two phases: meta-training and meta-testing. In meta-training, our training data $\mathcal{D}_{\text{meta-train}} = \{(x_i, y_i)\}^n_{i=1}$ from a set of classes $\mathcal{C}_{train}$ are used for training a classifier, where $x_i$ is a skin lesion sample, $y_i \in \mathcal{C}_{train}$ is the corresponding label, and $n$ is the number of training samples. In meta-testing, a support set of $v$ labeled examples $\mathcal{D}_{\text{support}} = \{(x_j, y_j)\}^v_{j=1}$ from a set of new classes $\mathcal{C}_{test}$ is given, where $x_j$ is a skin lesion sample for testing, and $y_j \in \mathcal{C}_{test}$ is the corresponding label. The goal is to predict the labels of a query set $\mathcal{D}_{\text{query}} = \{(x_j)\}^{v+q}_{j=v+1}$, where $q$ is the number of queries. This split strategy of training and support set aims to simulate the support and query set that will be encountered at test time. Further, we use the meta-learning on the training set to transfer the extracted knowledge to on the support set. It aims to perform the network's learning on the support set better and classify the query set more successfully.

Our proposed network architecture shown in Fig. 1 consists of three parts. The first part deals with traditional convolution [4], residual block [11], pooling and activation neurons for input images; the second part processes additional handcrafted feature representations of the same image, as the process of the approximate visual content of prior knowledge of the same image. These two sub-networks are finally linked together to produce a full-fledged image description so that the second part will regularize the first part during learning. At this point, our hybrid-prior feature is extracted from the fusion layer. The third part consists of three fully connected layers, the front being the fusion layer. In our model, we introduce a hashing layer [7] in place of the last standard fully connected layer to learn a binary code. At this point, our hashing hybrid-prior

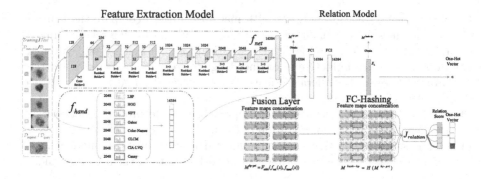

**Fig. 1.** Our hashing relation network

feature is extracted from the last hashing layer. It allows that feature extraction and deep hashing learning are integrated into a deep unified architecture. The learned hashing hybrid-prior features are expected to predict the skin lesion samples' labels well.

## 2.2 Model Learning

**Meta-Learning Based Classifier:** As illustrated in Fig. 1, our matching network consists of two branches: a feature extraction model and a relation model during the training of our network. We define the function $f_{net}$ represents feature extraction function using only network, the function $f_{hand}$ represents feature extraction function using handcrafted feature descriptors, the function $C$ represents feature concatenation function, and the function $F_{n\&h}$ represents feature fusion function. Moreover, considering to efficient computation during feature learning, we define the deep hashing function $H$ to encode feature maps.

Suppose sample $x_j \in \mathcal{D}_{\text{support}}$ and sample $x_i \in \mathcal{D}_{\text{meta-train}}$, the concatenated hashing feature map $M^{hash-hp}{}_{i,j}$ of the training and testing sets is used as the relation model $J_{relation}(\cdot)$ to get a scalar in range of 0 to 1 representing the similarity between $x_i$ and $x_j$, which is called relation score. Suppose we have one labeled sample for each of $n$ unique classes, our model can generate $n$ relation scores $Judge_{i,j}$ for the relation between one support input $x_j$ and training sample set examples $x_i$:

$$
\begin{aligned}
M^{hy-pri}{}_i &= F_{n\&h}(f_{net}(x_i), f_{hand}(x_i)), M^{hy-pri}{}_j = F_{n\&h}(f_{net}(x_j), f_{hand}(x_j)), \\
M^{hy-pri}{}_{i,j} &= C(M^{hy-pri}{}_i, M^{hy-pri}{}_j), \\
M^{hash-hp}{}_i &= H(M^{hy-pri}{}_i), M^{hash-hp}{}_j = H(M^{hy-pri}{}_j), \\
M^{hash-hp}{}_{i,j} &= C(M^{hash-hp}{}_i, M^{hash-hp}{}_j), \\
Judge_{i,j} &= J_{relation}(M^{hash-hp}{}_{i,j}), i = 1, 2, \cdots, n
\end{aligned}
\tag{1}
$$

Furthermore, we can element-wise sum over our feature extraction model outputs of all samples from each training class to form this class's feature map.

And this pooled class-level feature map is concatenated with the feature map of the test image as above.

**Objective Function:** We use mean square error (MSE) loss to train our model, regressing the relation score $Judge_{i,j}$ to the ground truth: matched pairs have similarity 1 and the mismatched pair have similarity 0. Inspired by the work [7] of Su et al., we add a penalty term $||M^{hy-pri}{}_{i,j} - \text{sgn}(M^{hy-pri}{}_{i,j})||_p^{p}$, in which $|| \cdot ||_p^{p}$ is entry-wise matrix norm, in the objective function to make it as close to zero as possible.

$$Loss = \arg\min \sum_{i=1}^{n} \sum_{j=1}^{m} \left(Judge_{i,j} - (y_i == y_j)\right)^2 + \beta \times ||M^{hy-pri}{}_{i,j} - \text{sgn}(M^{hy-pri}{}_{i,j})||_p^{p}$$

(2)

where $\beta$ is a parameter. Note that we set $\beta = 0.1 \times \frac{1}{E_L \times D}$ where $E_L$ is the length of the hashing code and $D$ is the input size in our work.

In the test stage, given the support set $\mathcal{D}_{\text{support}}$ never seen during training, our model can rapidly predict the class label for an unlabelled image from the query set $\mathcal{D}_{\text{query}}$ through meta-learning mechanism.

## 3    Experimental Results

All experiments are conducted using a 4-core PC with an 12 GB NVIDIA TITAN XP GPU, 16 GB of RAM, and Ubuntu 16.

**Dateset.** The ISIC Skin 2017 dataset contains 2000 training, 150 validation and 600 test dermoscopy images. Similarly, each skin lesion is paired with a standard gold diagnosis, i.e., melanoma, nevus and seborrheic keratosis. This dataset contains two binary classifications sub-tasks melanoma classifications (i.e., melanoma vs. others) and seborrheic keratosis classification (i.e., seborrheic keratosis vs. others). Similar to ARLCNN [11], we also collect 1320 additional dermoscopy images from the ISIC Archive to enlarge the training dataset.

**Implementation.** Since our model takes $224 \times 224 \times 3$ images as input, all dermoscopy images should be shrunk to this size before they can be fed into our model. We apply data augmentation (DA), including the random rotation and horizontal and vertical flips, to the training data, aiming to enlarge the dataset and hence alleviate the overfitting of our model. In our experiment, we randomly select 200 images from 3320 training images to conduct the training set, use 150 validation images to conduct the support set, and 600 test images to conduct the query set. Note that we randomly choose 10 times following the above strategy for comparison.

**Settings.** We use the Adam optimizer with a batch size of 32, for training where the learning rate was set to 0.00001 and momentums were set to 0.5 and 0.999. We set the length $E_L$ of the hashing code to 64.

**Quantitative Evaluation.** To quantitatively compare our model with others, we used the classification accuracy (Acc), average precision (AP), area under the receiver operating characteristic curve (AUC), sensitivity, specificity and average AUC as performance metrics. In order to quantitative analysis our model more clearly, we used average Acc, average AUC and inference time per image as performance metrics in the discussion sub-section.

**Table 1.** Performance of our model and baseline methods with or without DA

| Methods | DA? | Melanoma Classification | | | | | Seborrheic Keratosis Classification | | | | | Average AUC |
| | | AUC | AP | Acc | Sensitivity | Specificity | AUC | AP | Acc | Sensitivity | Specificity | |
|---|---|---|---|---|---|---|---|---|---|---|---|---|
| *Ours* | × | *0.883* | *0.810* | *0.890* | *0.732* | *0.901* | *0.961* | *0.843* | *0.885* | *0.912* | *0.907* | *0.926* |
| Ours | √ | **0.912** | **0.834** | **0.906** | **0.743** | **0.907** | **0.979** | **0.886** | **0.937** | **0.926** | **0.917** | **0.943** |
| *Resnet-14* | × | *0.650* | *0.313* | *0.739* | *0.503* | *0.792* | *0.738* | *0.414* | *0.752* | *0.733* | *0.605* | *0.733* |
| *VGG-16* | × | *0.633* | *0.412* | *0.727* | *0.386* | *0.891* | *0.793* | *0.476* | *0.732* | *0.312* | *0.854* | *0.789* |
| *VGG-19* | × | *0.675* | *0.534* | *0.829* | *0.357* | *0.893* | *0.826* | *0.542* | *0.833* | *0.613* | *0.884* | *0.796* |
| *Resnet-50* | × | *0.774* | *0.610* | *0.850* | *0.690* | *0.845* | *0.866* | *0.623* | *0.851* | *0.832* | *0.818* | *0.887* |
| Resnet-14 | √ | 0.732 | 0.307 | 0.748 | 0.538 | 0.799 | 0.820 | 0.464 | 0.711 | 0.800 | 0.696 | 0.750 |
| VGG-16 | √ | 0.715 | 0.390 | 0.732 | 0.402 | 0.812 | 0.875 | 0.693 | 0.877 | 0.322 | 0.899 | 0.811 |
| VGG-19 | √ | 0.757 | 0.469 | 0.832 | 0.308 | 0.905 | 0.908 | 0.538 | 0.890 | 0.678 | 0.912 | 0.816 |
| Resnet-50 | √ | 0.856 | 0.590 | 0.853 | 0.632 | 0.888 | 0.948 | 0.794 | 0.842 | 0.867 | 0.837 | 0.902 |

### 3.1   Comparing to Baseline Methods

**Baseline.** We compare against various state-of-the-art baselines for skin lesion classification, including Resnet-14, Resnet-50, VGG-16 and VGG-19.

**Performance With and Without Data Augmentation.** Table 1 shows AP, Acc, AUC, sensitivity, specificity and average AUC of baseline methods and our model on the test set with or without DA in melanoma classification and seborrheic keratosis classification. It shows that our model performs steadily better than baseline methods in term of four evaluation metrics no matter using or not using DA. It demonstrates that the introduced deep meta-learning strategy makes a significant contribution to the higher performance of our model, compared with baselines without meta-learning.

### 3.2   Comparing to the State-of-the-Art Records

Table 2 shows the performance comparison of our model to the ARLCNN [11], SDL [12,13], and six top ranking results in the ISIC 2017 challenge leaderboard. It shows that our model achieves better performance over the state-of-the-art methods in melanoma classification and seborrheic keratosis classification, in term of AP, Acc, AUC and average AUC. Even though #2 achieves the highest AUC and specificity in seborrheic keratosis classification, this solution has an extremely low sensitivity. According to the ranking rule of the challenge which is the average AUC of melanoma classification and seborrheic keratosis classification, our method achieves an average AUC of 0.943 in two sub-tasks, which is higher than the top-ranking performance listed in the leaderboard and is, to the best of our knowledge, the best skin lesion classification performance on the ISIC Skin 2017 dataset. Meanwhile, we also compare our model to the one presented in #5 without external data. In this scenario, our model attained an average AUC of 0.926, which is noticeably higher than #5.

**Table 2.** Performance of our model to the ARLCNN [11], SDL [12,13], and six top ranking results in the leaderboard

| Methods | External data | Melanoma Classification | | | | | Seborrheic Keratosis Classification | | | | | Average AUC |
|---|---|---|---|---|---|---|---|---|---|---|---|---|
| | | AUC | AP | Acc | Sensitivity | Specificity | AUC | AP | Acc | Sensitivity | Specificity | |
| *Ours* | 0 | *0.883* | *0.810* | *0.890* | *0.732* | *0.901* | *0.961* | *0.843* | *0.885* | *0.912* | *0.907* | *0.926* |
| *Ours* | 1320 | **0.912** | **0.834** | **0.906** | **0.743** | 0.907 | **0.979** | **0.886** | **0.937** | 0.926 | 0.911 | **0.943** |
| ARLCNN [11] | 1320 | 0.875 | - | 0.850 | 0.658 | 0.896 | 0.958 | - | 0.868 | 0.878 | 0.867 | 0.917 |
| SDL [12,13] | 1320 | 0.868 | 0.689 | 0.872 | - | - | 0.955 | 0.818 | 0.917 | - | - | 0.912 |
| #1 | 1444 | 0.868 | 0.710 | 0.828 | 0.735 | 0.851 | 0.953 | 0.786 | 0.803 | **0.978** | 0.773 | 0.911 |
| #2 | 900 | 0.856 | 0.747 | 0.823 | 0.103 | 0.998 | 0.965 | 0.839 | 0.875 | 0.178 | **0.998** | 0.910 |
| #3 | 7544 | 0.874 | 0.715 | 0.872 | 0.547 | 0.95 | 0.943 | 0.790 | 0.895 | 0.356 | 0.99 | 0.908 |
| #4 | 1600 | 0.870 | 0.732 | 0.858 | 0.427 | 0.963 | 0.921 | 0.770 | 0.918 | 0.589 | 0.976 | 0.896 |
| #5 | 0 | 0.830 | 0.665 | 0.830 | 0.436 | **0.925** | 0.942 | 0.808 | 0.917 | 0.7 | **0.995** | 0.886 |
| #6 | 1341 | 0.836 | 0.703 | 0.845 | 0.35 | **0.965** | 0.935 | 0.771 | 0.913 | 0.556 | 0.976 | 0.886 |

### 3.3   Discussion

**Hashing Coding with Different Length.** The length $E_L$ of the hashing code is important in our model. Figure 2(a) shows the variation of the performances of our model with different values of $E_L$. It reveals that, as $E_L$ increases, the average AUC and average Acc of our model monotonically increases when $E_L$ is more than 64 and the extent of this monotonically increase is few. However, the inference time per image is growing rapidly when $E_L$ is more than 64.

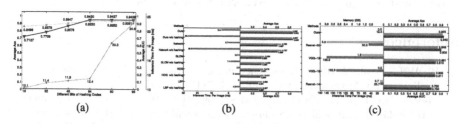

(a)                                    (b)                                    (c)

**Fig. 2.** Discussion results. (a) Performance of our model under different bits of hashing codes; (b) Performances on the ablation experiment. "w/o" means without; (c) The average AUC, average Acc, inference time cost and memory cost of our model and baseline methods

**Ablation Study.** In order to verify the reasonableness and effectiveness of our hybrid-prior features and hashing hybrid-prior features, we design the Ablation experiment. We use the LBP, HOG, GLCM, and the only network features, and compared them with our model with and without hashing. From Fig. 2(b), our model outperforms others with or without hashing, in term of average AUC and average Acc. This suggests that the design of hybrid-prior features is reasonable. The method of using only network features are less effective than using our hybrid-prior features. It shows the design of our hybrid-prior features is effective. Although average AUC and average Acc of the various methods has been slightly reduced after hash coding, the inference time per image of various methods has a cliff-like reduction. This shows that using the strategy of deep hashing can achieve the fast and efficient computation of representation learning. In general, it is reasonableness and effectiveness that our design of our hashing hybrid-prior features.

**Average AUC and Average Acc vs. Inference Time Cost and Memory Cost.** The average AUC and average Acc versus inference time-cost and memory-cost of our model and baseline methods are plotted in Fig. 2(c). It is clear that the average AUC and average Acc of our model are higher than others. Meanwhile, inference time-cost of our model is less than others and memory-cost of our model is least as same as VGG-16. Therefore, taking the computational and spatial complexity into consideration, we suggest using our model to achieve skin lesion classification.

## 4    Conclusion and Future Work

In this paper, we propose a relational hashing network embedded with prior domain knowledge to address the skin lesion classification. Our model uses the strategy of meta-learning, learning inductive priors and deep hashing to compare the features of different samples. Our results on the ISIC Skin 2017 dataset show that our model achieves the state-of-the-art performance in the skin lesion classification task. In future research, we consider the investigation of the meta-learning and domain knowledge-driven skin lesion classification.

## References

1. Bi, W.L., et al.: Artificial intelligence in cancer imaging: clinical challenges and applications. CA: Cancer J. Clin. **69**(2), 127–157 (2019)
2. Codella, N.C.F., et al.: Skin lesion analysis toward melanoma detection: a challenge at the 2017 International Symposium on Biomedical Imaging (ISBI), Hosted by the International Skin Imaging Collaboration (ISIC). arXiv e-prints arXiv:1710.05006, October 2017
3. Cruz-Roa, A., et al.: High-throughput adaptive sampling for whole-slide histopathology image analysis (HASHI) via convolutional neural networks: application to invasive breast cancer detection. PLOS One **13**(5), 1–23 (2018)
4. Esteva, A., et al.: Dermatologist-level classification of skin cancer with deep neural networks. Nature **542**, 115 (2017)
5. Oliveira, R.B., Papa, J.P., Pereira, A.S., Tavares, J.M.R.S.: Computational methods for pigmented skin lesion classification in images: review and future trends. Neural Comput. Appl. **29**(3), 613–636 (2018)

6. Siegel, R.L., Miller, K.D., Jemal, A.: Cancer statistics. CA: Cancer J. Clin. **69**(1), 7–34 (2019)
7. Su, S., Zhang, C., Han, K., Tian, Y.: Greedy hash: towards fast optimization for accurate hash coding in CNN. In: Bengio, S., Wallach, H., Larochelle, H., Grauman, K., Cesa-Bianchi, N., Garnett, R. (eds.) Advances in Neural Information Processing Systems, vol. 31, pp. 798–807. Curran Associates, Inc. (2018)
8. Sung, F., Yang, Y., Zhang, L., Xiang, T., Torr, P.H., Hospedales, T.M.: Learning to compare: relation network for few-shot learning. In: CVPR (2018)
9. Ullman, S.: Using neuroscience to develop artificial intelligence. Science **363**(6428), 692–693 (2019)
10. Wang, J.X., et al.: Prefrontal cortex as a meta-reinforcement learning system. Nat. Neurosci. **21**(6), 860–868 (2018)
11. Zhang, J., Xie, Y., Xia, Y., Shen, C.: Attention residual learning for skin lesion classification. IEEE Trans. Med. Imaging (2019, in press)
12. Zhang, J., Xie, Y., Wu, Q., Xia, Y.: Skin lesion classification in dermoscopy images using synergic deep learning. In: Frangi, A.F., Schnabel, J.A., Davatzikos, C., Alberola-López, C., Fichtinger, G. (eds.) MICCAI 2018. LNCS, vol. 11071, pp. 12–20. Springer, Cham (2018). https://doi.org/10.1007/978-3-030-00934-2_2
13. Zhang, J., Xie, Y., Wu, Q., Xia, Y.: Medical image classification using synergic deep learning. Med. Image Anal. **54**, 10–19 (2019)

# End-to-End Adversarial Shape Learning for Abdomen Organ Deep Segmentation

Jinzheng Cai[1(✉)], Yingda Xia[2], Dong Yang[2], Daguang Xu[2], Lin Yang[1], and Holger Roth[2]

[1] University of Florida, Gainesville, USA
caijinzhengcn@gmail.com
[2] NVIDIA, Bethesda, USA
hroth@nvidia.com

**Abstract.** Automatic segmentation of abdomen organs using medical imaging has many potential applications in clinical workflows. Recently, the state-of-the-art performance for organ segmentation has been achieved by deep learning models, *i.e.*, convolutional neural network (CNN). However, it is challenging to train the conventional CNN-based segmentation models that aware of the shape and topology of organs. In this work, we tackle this problem by introducing a novel end-to-end shape learning architecture – organ point-network. It takes deep learning features as inputs and generates organ shape representations as points that located on organ surface. We later present a novel adversarial shape learning objective function to optimize the point-network to capture shape information better. We train the point-network together with a CNN-based segmentation model in a multi-task fashion so that the shared network parameters can benefit from both shape learning and segmentation tasks. We demonstrate our method with three challenging abdomen organs including liver, spleen, and pancreas. The point-network generates surface points with fine-grained details and it is found critical for improving organ segmentation. Consequently, the deep segmentation model is improved by the introduced shape learning as significantly better Dice scores are observed for spleen and pancreas segmentation.

**Keywords:** 3D segmentation · Abdomen organ · Shape learning · Surface point generation · Adversarial learning

## 1 Introduction

Automatic organ segmentation becomes an important technique providing supports for routine clinical diagnoses and treatment plannings. Organ segmentation in medical images, *e.g.*, computed tomography (CT) and magnetic resonance imaging (MRI), is usually formulated as a voxel-wise classification problem. Recently, deep learning methods (*e.g.*, fully convolutional network (FCN) based segmentation [2,6,7]) have been reported as powerful baselines to various

© Springer Nature Switzerland AG 2019
H.-I. Suk et al. (Eds.): MLMI 2019, LNCS 11861, pp. 124–132, 2019.
https://doi.org/10.1007/978-3-030-32692-0_15

segmentation tasks, where the deep learning methods can perform reliably on the majority cases. However, segmentation error often occur near the organ surface largely due to low image quality, vague organ boundaries, and large organ shape variation. Although several attempts [1,9] have been reported in the literature, it is still challenging for deep learning models to produce segmented results with smooth and realistic shapes as it would require strong global reasoning ability to model relations between all image voxels.

We propose a shape learning network – organ point-network to improve the segmentation performance of FCN-based methods. The organ point-network takes deep learning features as its inputs and the deep learning features are extracted from raw 3D medical images by 3D convolutional neural network layers. The point-network outputs shape representations of target organs, where the shape representations are defined as sets of points locating on organ surface. The idea of point-network is inspired by a point set generator that proposed by Fan *et al.* [3]. In [3], the point generator is built with 2D convolutional neural network layers. It takes 2D images and segmentation masks as its inputs and outputs sets of points as 3D reconstructions of target objects. To obtain 3D reconstruction from 2D images, it requires to introduce moderate level of uncertainty. Thus, the point generator in [3] uses only coarse-scale features from the top network layer. Therefore, it generates points that lacks of fine-grained shape details. Differently, the 3D organ segmentation setup requires our organ point-network to process 3D information and to use only the deep features due to the lack of available segmentation masks. Besides, the organ point-network needs to reconstruct organ accurately with recovering as may shape details as possible, otherwise, the segmentation model could be significantly distracted by the inaccurate shape information under the multi-task learning context.

In this work, we introduce shape learning to improve 3D FCN-based organ segmentation. We summarize our contributions as, (1) we evaluate the multi-task learning mechanism, which jointly optimizes the segmentation task with the shape learning task and improves the segmentation results; (2) we propose a novel organ point-network and an effective adversarial learning strategy for accurate organ reconstruction; (3) we demonstrate our method with extensive experiments and report significant segmentation improvements.

## 2 Method

### 2.1 Multi-task Learning

In our multi-task learning setup, the proposed organ point-network is jointly optimized with FCN-base segmentation model. Figure 1 shows the pipeline of the proposed multi-task learning. The pipeline consists of a 3D FCN backbone, a segmentation loss branch, and a shape learning branch. Specifically, the 3D FCN backbone is built with 3D convolutional layers and it extracts deep features from 3D CT inputs. Resolution of the deep features ranges from coarse to fine, where the coarse-scale feature contains more high-level representations and less

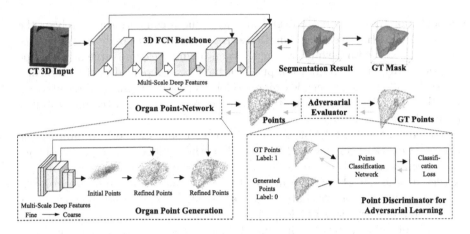

**Fig. 1.** Pipeline of the proposed multi-task learning.

image details, while the fine-scale feature has more image details but less high-level representations. In the pipeline, the segmentation loss branch takes the fine-scale feature into a Sigmoid activation layer and outputs the segmentation results. The shape learning branch contains the proposed organ point-network and adversarial evaluator. It takes the multi-scale deep features and outputs organ surface points.

## 2.2   Organ Point-Network

We design the organ point-network to take multi-scale deep features as its inputs. It first initializes points using the coarsest-scale feature and then finetunes the location of each point using the fine-scale features to factor in local shape information. Figure 2 shows the network configuration of the proposed organ point-network. To name the network components, we denote the coarse-scale feature input as $X_C$, and the fine-scale feature input as $X_F$. We formulate the points initialization procedure as a mapping function $\mathcal{F}_i(\cdot; \theta_i)$, where $\theta_{init}$ is the set of network parameters. Similarly, we define the first and second points refinement procedures as $\mathcal{F}_{r1}(\cdot; \theta_{r1})$, and $\mathcal{F}_{r2}(\cdot; \theta_{r2})$, respectively. We propose a "feature index" network layer and refer to it as $\mathcal{M}_{FI}(\cdot)$. For presentation clarity, we omit the standard network components, such as ReLU, Sigmoid activation, Batch-Normalization, and element-wise summation layers. The point set is presented as a $N_P$ by 3 matrix, where $N_P$ presents the number of points and 3 is the dimension. The point size $N_P$ is fixed along the initial and refined point sets.

The points $P \in R^{N_P \times 3}$ is initialized as

$$P = \mathcal{F}_i(X_C; \theta_i), \tag{1}$$

where the coarse-scale feature $X_C$ is from the top layer of the 3D FCN backbone. As passed through multiple 3D convolution and spatial pooling layers, each voxel

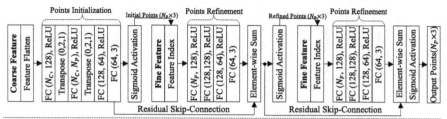

**Fig. 2.** Architecture configuration of the proposed organ point-network.

in $X_C$ should represent the aggregated information of a sub-region from the input image. In other words, the coarse-scale feature $X_C$ contains high-level image representations of the image but lacks of local details. Thus, points in $P$ present only a rough shape of the target organ lacking of details. Figure 1 shows an example of the initial points.

Later, the point-network refines each point in $P$ using the fine-scaled feature and this procedure is referred as "points refinement" in Fig. 2. A "feature index" layer $M_{FI}(\cdot)$ is defined to extract point-wise local feature,

$$f_i = M_{FI}(X_F, p_i), \qquad (2)$$

where $p_i \in R^{1\times3}$ is the i-th point in $P$, and $f_i$ is the indexed local feature. The three coordinates in $p_i$ are normalized values in the range $[0,1]$. Thus, $M_{FI}$ first scale the three coordinates in $p_i$ with the width, height, and depth of $X_F$, respectively. Then, $M_{FI}$ extracts the $3\times3\times3$ sub-region in $X_F$ that centered at the scaled $p_i$ location. The extracted $3\times3\times3$ sub-region contains local image information at position $p_i$ and it is vectorized as $f_i$. Like standard pooling layers, the "feature index" layer processes only indexing operations and no network parameter need to be learned, thus the point-network with "feature index" layers can be trained end-to-end.

Given the fact that the indexed feature $f_i$ contains only local image information, learning of local point movement would be inherently easier than predicting the global coordinate. Thus to refine point $p_i$, we formulate the refinement as a residual learning

$$p_i = p_i + \mathcal{F}_{r1}(f_i; \theta_{r1}). \qquad (3)$$

It is implemented via a "Skip-Connection" between the points initialization module and the points refinement module (see Fig. 2). Thus, the "points refinement" is a combination of Eqs. 2 and 3 and its matrix form is

$$P = P + \mathcal{F}_{r1}(M_{FI}(X_F, P); \theta_{r1}). \qquad (4)$$

Practically, some of the initial points would locate close to the actual organ surface while the others could be far away. Therefore, a second "points refinement" is required in the point-network to secure the convergence. In the same spirit of the first refinement, we formulate the second refinement as

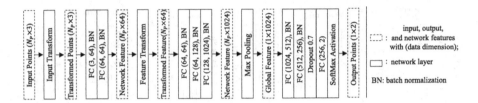

**Fig. 3.** Architecture configuration of the points classification network.

$$P = P + \mathcal{F}_{r2}(M_{FI}(X_F, P); \theta_{r2}). \tag{5}$$

There is a "Skip-Connection" between the first and second refinements.

### 2.3 Adversarial Evaluator

In this section, we discuss point-based training objectives to train the proposed point-network. In [3], Fan *et al.* uses Chamfer distance (CD), Earth Mover's distance (EMD) for shape learning. These objectives first find one-versus-one point correspondence between the predicted points $P$ and the ground-truth points $P_{gt}$ (where $P_{gt} \in R^{N_p \times 3}$). Then, difference between the paired predicted point and ground-truth point is calculated and the mean difference of the $N_P$ point pairs is used as prediction error that back-propagated to update the network parameters. Due to the calculation of mean differences, these objectives are not sensitive to outliers which lie far away from the organ surface. Thus, we further propose a novel adversarial learning (AL) loss that works complementary to the CD and EMD metrics to remove the outlier points. During model training, the proposed adversarial loss can be jointly optimized with CD, and EMD losses.

In the adversarial evaluator, a point set classifier is trained to differentiate the generated points $P$ and ground truth points $P_{gt}$. The classifier would project the points onto the manifold of the target anatomy. Figure 3 shows the architecture configuration of the points classification network. The classifier takes $N_P$ by 3 points matrix as input and outputs its tag of the input point set. In the classifier, we use "transformation" layers proposed in [5], so that the learned representation by the point set is invariant to geometric transformations. We define the classifier as $\mathcal{D}(\cdot; \theta_D)$, and labels for the generated points $P$ and ground truth points $P_{gt}$ are 0 and 1, respectively. Then, the loss function for adversarial learning is,

$$\mathcal{L}_{AL} = H(\mathcal{D}(P; \theta_D), 0) + H(\mathcal{D}(\hat{P}_{gt}; \theta_D), 1), \tag{6}$$

where $H(\cdot, \cdot)$ is the cross entropy loss function, and $\hat{P}_{gt}$ are the ground truth points $P_{gt}$ with randomly added noise that generated from a specified range (*i.e.* $[-0.005, 0.005]$ in our experiments). The noise is applied to balance the classifier's convergence speed over $P$ and $P_{gt}$.

**Table 1.** Evaluation of generated points with EMD, which is shown as mean $\pm$ sd.

| Method | | Liver | Spleen | Pancreas |
|---|---|---|---|---|
| Two-Branch | | $1.66 \pm 1.19$ | $4.3 \pm 1.4$ | $9.7 \pm 6.8$ |
| Point-Network | w/o Adversarial-Loss | $0.72 \pm 0.44$ | $5.2 \pm 2.4$ | $9.1 \pm 7.7$ |
| | with Adversarial-Loss | $\mathbf{0.69 \pm 0.39}$ | $\mathbf{3.8 \pm 1.9}$ | $\mathbf{8.4 \pm 7.4}$ |

## 3    Experiments and Analyses

**Data Preparation:** To demonstrate the proposed shape learning method, we test three abdomen organs, including liver, pancreas, and spleen. These datasets are publicly available from a organ segmentation competition[1] and contain 131, 281, and 41 voxel-wise annotated CT volumes for liver, pancreas, and spleen, respectively. For each organ, we randomly separate the images into 50%, 25%, and 25% for training, validating, and testing. To evaluate the effectiveness of the proposed organ point-network, the target organ in each CT volume is center cropped to preserve the whole organ shape information. To include sufficient image background, 20-voxel padding is added to each direction of the cropped volume. Based on the sizes of organs, liver and pancreas volumes are down-sampled to $128 \times 128 \times 128$ and spleen volumes are down-sampled $32 \times 128 \times 128$. Using the original image resolution for training and testing may obtain better performance, however, we fit the segmentation model, point-network, and points classifier into a single GPU for computation stability, and we mainly focus on the segmentation improvements from the proposed 3D shape learning.

To generate ground truth points $P_{gt}$, we fuse the organ and lesion annotations to generate the outer organ surface, on which ground truth surface points are generated using the marching cubes algorithm and farthest point sampling [3]. The size of the point set $N_P$ is empirically set to 2048 in all experiments. The using of $P$ to reconstruct segmentation mask has its own challenges and is out the scope of this paper. Here, we focus on comparing results from segmentation networks that are trained with and without point set generation.

**Implementation Details:** We use 3D U-Net [2] as the universal backbone for all segmentation models. It consists of totally 3 times symmetric down-sampling and up-sampling, which are performed by stride 2 max-poling and nearest up-sampling, respectively. Based on the multi-scale features extracted by the 3D U-Net, we construct the proposed organ point-network and point classifier with the architectures as shown in Figs. 2 and 3, respectively. Network parameters are initialized with Xavier and trained with Adam optimizer. We set the learning rate as 5e-4. The batch-size is fixed to 1 due to the limitation of GPU memory. Since models may converge differently, we train each model with sufficient number of epochs until it gains no performance improvement on the validation set. We then

---

[1] http://medicaldecathlon.com.

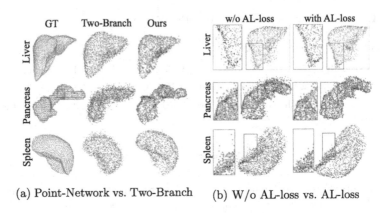

(a) Point-Network vs. Two-Branch    (b) W/o AL-loss vs. AL-loss

**Fig. 4.** Visualization of generated points.

select the model checkpoint with the best validation performance to report the testing result. All the experiments have been conducted on a NVIDIA TITAN X GPU.

We consider the 3D U-Net as a strong 3D FCN backbone. Using 100% images, the best solution [4] reported in the segmentation competition has reported 95.2% Dice scores for liver segmentation. In our experiments, only 50% of the images is applied for model training and the rest is used for validating and testing. However, the 3D U-Net still achieves 94.1% Dice score.

Firstly, we evaluate the proposed point-network and adversarial learning (AL) loss with quantitative and qualitative analyses. A state-of-the-art point generator – Two-Branch [3] is choose to be the baseline. The Two-Branch model is designed to map 2D images into points using only the global image information. We modify its 2D convolutional network layers with 3D convolutions so that it can process 3D CT volumes. We follow that same setting in [3] and normalize coordinates of each point cloud into the range of (0,1) and measure the difference between generated and ground truth points with Earth Mover's distance (EMD). In Table 1, we present quantitative assessment of different point generation methods. We also present visual examples in Fig. 4. The Two-Branch model performs as a strong baseline outperforming the proposed Point-Network (without AL-loss) for spleen shape learning. However, for organs with more complex surfaces, it is observed that the "point refinement" in point-network has improved the generated points with lots of details. The point-network reduces the mean EMD score for liver from 1.66 to 0.72, and for pancreas from 9.7 to 9.1. Figure 4a shows the ground-truth, Two-Branch generated points, and point-network generated points. Comparing point-networks trained with and without AL-loss, we observe systematical improvements. The AL-loss have reduced mean EMD scores for liver, pancreas, and spleen by 4%, 7% and 27%. As shown in Fig. 4b, AL-loss has significantly reduced the number of outlier points.

In the second experiment, we evaluate segmentation results with Dice using the original CT spacing and report Hausdorff distance (HD), and Average dis-

**Table 2.** Evaluation of organ segmentation with Dice similarity (DICE), Hausdorff distance (HD), and average distance (AVGD) which are shown in the form of mean ± sd. We use **bold** to indicate experiment sets where 3D U-Net is outperformed and ***italic bold*** to indicate improvements with statistical significance.

| Metric | Organ | 3D U-Net | Two-Branch | Ours |
|---|---|---|---|---|
| Dice | Liver | $0.941 \pm 0.034$ | $0.925 \pm 0.050$ | **$0.944 \pm 0.034$** |
| | Spleen | $0.955 \pm 0.014$ | $0.934 \pm 0.043$ | ***$0.960 \pm 0.007$*** |
| | Pancreas | $0.732 \pm 0.120$ | ***$0.734 \pm 0.139$*** | ***$0.743 \pm 0.122$*** |
| HD [voxels] | Liver | $35.862 \pm 17.960$ | $39.041 \pm 20.061$ | **$31.365 \pm 15.576$** |
| | Spleen | $6.889 \pm 1.998$ | $7.482 \pm 3.454$ | **$6.632 \pm 2.543$** |
| | Pancreas | $25.406 \pm 17.953$ | **$22.653 \pm 13.109$** | **$22.723 \pm 12.536$** |
| AVGD [voxels] | Liver | $0.325 \pm 0.436$ | $0.453 \pm 0.506$ | **$0.273 \pm 0.322$** |
| | Spleen | $0.061 \pm 0.033$ | $0.101 \pm 0.078$ | **$0.051 \pm 0.016$** |
| | Pancreas | $1.080 \pm 1.050$ | **$1.074 \pm 1.104$** | ***$0.997 \pm 0.991$*** |

tance (AVGD) [8] in voxel. We compare 3D U-Nets trained with and without point generators, which should introduce shape learning to affect the segmentation performance. Quantitative result shown in Table 2 demonstrate that 3D U-Net can be improved by its attached point generators. The proposed Point-network has significantly[2] improved the Dice scores of spleen and pancreas segmentation. However, we also observe performance degradation when the Two-Branch is applied for liver and spleen segmentation. Based on this observation, we argue that accurate shape learning is critical for improving the segmentation performance, otherwise, it will bring unwanted performance loss. Compared with Two-Branch model, the proposed Point-network generator performs much more stable and robustly improves the 3D U-Net on the three organs in terms of all evaluation metrics.

## 4   Conclusion

In this paper, we presented a multi-task deep learning model for shape learning and abdomen organ segmentation. Under the multi-task context, the proposed shape learning model – point-network uses multi-scale deep learning features from the segmentation model to generate organ surface points with fine-grained details. A novel adversarial learning strategy is introduces to improve the generated points with less outliers. The shape learning then improves the intermediate network layers of the segmentation model and improves organ segmentation. The effectiveness of the proposed method has been demonstrated by experiments of three challenging abdominal organs including liver, spleen, and pancreas.

---

[2] P-value $< 0.05$ in Wilcoxon Signed rank test.

# References

1. Cai, J., Lu, L., Xie, Y., Xing, F., Yang, L.: Improving deep pancreas segmentation in CT and MRI images via recurrent neural contextual learning and direct loss function. CoRR abs/1707.04912 (2017). http://arxiv.org/abs/1707.04912
2. Çiçek, Ö., Abdulkadir, A., Lienkamp, S.S., Brox, T., Ronneberger, O.: 3D U-net: learning dense volumetric segmentation from sparse annotation. In: Ourselin, S., Joskowicz, L., Sabuncu, M.R., Unal, G., Wells, W. (eds.) MICCAI 2016. LNCS, vol. 9901, pp. 424–432. Springer, Cham (2016). https://doi.org/10.1007/978-3-319-46723-8_49
3. Fan, H., Su, H., Guibas, L.J.: A point set generation network for 3D object reconstruction from a single image. In: IEEE CVPR, pp. 2463–2471 (2017)
4. Isensee, F., et al.: nnU-Net: self-adapting framework for U-Net-based medical image segmentation. CoRR abs/1809.10486 (2018)
5. Qi, C.R., Su, H., Mo, K., Guibas, L.J.: PointNet: deep learning on point sets for 3D classification and segmentation. In: IEEE CVPR, pp. 77–85 (2017)
6. Ronneberger, O., Fischer, P., Brox, T.: U-Net: convolutional networks for biomedical image segmentation. In: Navab, N., Hornegger, J., Wells, W.M., Frangi, A.F. (eds.) MICCAI 2015. LNCS, vol. 9351, pp. 234–241. Springer, Cham (2015). https://doi.org/10.1007/978-3-319-24574-4_28
7. Roth, H.R., et al.: Spatial aggregation of holistically-nested convolutional neural networks for automated pancreas localization and segmentation. Med. Image Anal. **45**, 94–107 (2018)
8. Taha, A.A., Hanbury, A.: Metrics for evaluating 3D medical image segmentation: analysis, selection, and tool. BMC Med. Imaging **15**(1), 29 (2015)
9. Yang, D., et al.: Automatic liver segmentation using an adversarial image-to-image network. In: Descoteaux, M., Maier-Hein, L., Franz, A., Jannin, P., Collins, D.L., Duchesne, S. (eds.) MICCAI 2017. LNCS, vol. 10435, pp. 507–515. Springer, Cham (2017). https://doi.org/10.1007/978-3-319-66179-7_58

# Privacy-Preserving Federated Brain Tumour Segmentation

Wenqi Li[1]([✉]), Fausto Milletarì[1], Daguang Xu[1], Nicola Rieke[1], Jonny Hancox[1],
Wentao Zhu[1], Maximilian Baust[1], Yan Cheng[1], Sébastien Ourselin[2],
M. Jorge Cardoso[2], and Andrew Feng[1]

[1] NVIDIA, Santa Clara, CA 95051, USA
wenqil@nvidia.com
[2] Biomedical Engineering and Imaging Sciences, King's College London, London, UK

**Abstract.** Due to medical data privacy regulations, it is often infeasible
to collect and share patient data in a centralised data lake. This poses
challenges for training machine learning algorithms, such as deep convolutional networks, which often require large numbers of diverse training examples. Federated learning sidesteps this difficulty by bringing
code to the patient data owners and only sharing intermediate model
training updates among them. Although a high-accuracy model could be
achieved by appropriately aggregating these model updates, the model
shared could indirectly leak the local training examples. In this paper,
we investigate the feasibility of applying differential-privacy techniques
to protect the patient data in a federated learning setup. We implement
and evaluate practical federated learning systems for brain tumour segmentation on the BraTS dataset. The experimental results show that
there is a trade-off between model performance and privacy protection
costs.

## 1 Introduction

Deep Neural Networks (DNN) have shown promising results in various medical
applications, but highly depend on the amount and the diversity of training
data [10]. In the context of medical imaging, this is particularly challenging
since the required training data may not be available in a single institution due
to the low incidence rate of some pathologies and limited numbers of patients.
At the same time, it is often infeasible to collect and share patient data in a
centralised data lake due to medical data privacy regulations.

One recent method that tackles this problem is Federated Learning (FL) [6,8]:
it allows collaborative and decentralised training of DNNs without sharing the
patient data. Each node trains its own local model and, periodically, submits
it to a parameter server. The server accumulates and aggregates the individual contributions to yield a global model, which is then shared with all nodes.
It should be noted that the training data remains private to each node and is
never shared during the learning process. Only the model's trainable weights or

© Springer Nature Switzerland AG 2019
H.-I. Suk et al. (Eds.): MLMI 2019, LNCS 11861, pp. 133–141, 2019.
https://doi.org/10.1007/978-3-030-32692-0_16

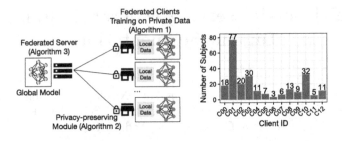

**Fig. 1.** Left: illustration of the federated learning system; right: distribution of the training subjects ($N = 242$) across the participating federated clients ($K = 13$) studied in this paper.

updates are shared, thus keeping patient data private. Consequently, FL succinctly sidesteps many of the data security challenges by leaving the data where they are and enables multi-institutional collaboration.

Although FL can provide a high level of security in terms of privacy, it is still vulnerable to misuse such as reconstructions of the training examples by model inversion. One effective countermeasure is to inject noise to each node's training process, distort the updates and limit the granularity of information shared among them [1,9]. However, existing privacy-preserving research only focuses on general machine learning benchmarks such as MNIST, and uses vanilla stochastic gradient descent algorithms.

In this work, we implement and evaluate practical federated learning systems for brain tumour segmentation. Throughout a series of experiments on the BraTS 2018 data, we demonstrate the feasibility of privacy-preserving techniques. Our primary contributions are: (1) implement and evaluate, to the best of our knowledge, the first privacy-preserving federated learning system for medical image analysis; (2) compare and contrast various aspects of federated averaging algorithms for handling momentum-based optimisation and imbalanced training nodes; (3) empirically study the sparse vector technique for a strong differential privacy guarantee.

## 2   Method

We study FL systems based on a client-server architecture (illustrated in Fig. 1 (left)) implementing the federated averaging algorithm [6]. In this configuration, a centralised server maintains a global DNN model and coordinates clients' local stochastic gradient descent (SGD) updates. This section presents the client-side model training procedure, the server-side model aggregation procedure, and the privacy-preserving module deployed on the client-side.

### 2.1   Client-Side Model Training

We assume each federated client has a fixed local dataset and reasonable computational resources to run mini-batch SGD updates. The clients also share

---

**Algorithm 1.** Federated learning: client-side training at federated round $t$.

**Require:** local training data $\mathcal{D} = \{x_i, y_i\}_{i=1}^{N_c}$, num_local_epochs
**Require:** learning rate $\eta$, decay rates $\beta_1, \beta_2$, small constant $\epsilon$
**Require:** loss function $\ell$ defined on training pairs $(x, y)$ parameterised by $W$
1: **procedure** LOCAL_TRAINING(global model $W^{(t)}$)
2:     Set initial local model: $W^{(0,t)} \leftarrow W^{(t)}$
3:     Initialise momentum terms: $m^{(0)} \leftarrow 0$, $v^{(0)} \leftarrow 0$
4:     Compute number of local iterations: $N^{(local)} \leftarrow N_c \cdot$ num_local_epochs
5:     **for** $l \leftarrow 1 \cdots N^{(local)}$ **do**            ▷ *Training with Adam optimiser*
6:         Sample a training batch: $\mathcal{B}^{(l)} \sim \mathcal{D}$
7:         Compute gradient: $g^{(l)} \leftarrow \nabla\ell(\mathcal{B}^{(l)}; W^{(l-1,t)})$
8:         Compute 1st moment: $m^{(l)} \leftarrow \beta_1 \cdot m^{(l-1)} + (1 - \beta_1) \cdot g^{(l)}$
9:         Compute 2nd moment: $v^{(l)} \leftarrow \beta_2 \cdot v^{(l-1)} + (1 - \beta_2) \cdot g^{(l)} \cdot g^{(l)}$
10:        Compute bias-corrected learning rate: $\eta^{(l)} \leftarrow \eta \cdot \sqrt{1 - \beta_2^l}/(1 - \beta_1^l)$
11:        Update local model: $W^{(l,t)} \leftarrow W^{(l-1,t)} - \eta^{(l)} \cdot m^{(l)}/(\sqrt{v^{(l)}} + \epsilon)$
12:    **end for**
13:    Compute federated gradient: $\Delta W^{(t)} \leftarrow W^{(l,t)} - W^{(0,t)}$
14:    $\Delta \hat{W}^{(t)} \leftarrow$ PRIVACY_PRESERVING($\Delta W^{(t)}$)
15:    **return** $\Delta \hat{W}^{(t)}$ and $N^{(local)}$            ▷ *Upload to server*
16: **end procedure**

---

the same DNN structure and loss functions. The proposed training procedure is listed in Algorithm 1. At federated round $t$, the local model is initialised by reading global model parameters $W^{(t)}$ from the server, and is updated to $W^{(l,t)}$ by running multiple iterations of SGD. After a fixed number of iterations $N^{(local)}$, the model difference $\Delta W^{(t)}$ is shared with the aggregation server.

DNNs for medical image are often trained with a momentum-based SGD. Introducing the momentum terms takes the previous SGD steps into account when computing the current one. It can help accelerate the training and reduce oscillation. We explore the choices of design for handling these terms in FL. In the proposed Algorithm 1 (exemplified with Adam optimiser [4]), we re-initialise each client's momentums at the beginning of each federated round (denoted as m.restart). Since local model parameters are initialised from the global ones, which aggregated information from other clients, the restarting operation effectively clears the clients' local states that could interfere the training process. This is empirically compared with (a) clients maintaining a set of local momentum variables without sharing; denoted as baseline m. (b) treating the momentum variables as a part of the model, i.e., the variables are updated locally and aggregated by the server (denoted as m.aggregation). Although m.aggregation is theoretically plausible [11], it requires the momentums to be released to the server. This increases both communication overheads and data security risks.

## 2.2    Client-Side Privacy-Preserving Module

The client-side is designed to have full control over which data to share and local training data never leave the client's site. Still, model inversion attacks

---

**Algorithm 2.** Federated learning: client-side differential privacy module.

---

**Require:** privacy budgets for gradient query, threshold, and answer $\varepsilon_1, \varepsilon_2, \varepsilon_3$
**Require:** sensitivity $s$, gradient bound and threshold $\gamma, \tau$, proportion to release $Q$
**Require:** number of local training iterations $N^{(local)}$
1: **procedure** PRIVACY_PRESERVING($\Delta W$)
2:     Normalise by iterations: $\Delta W \leftarrow \Delta W / N^{(local)}$
3:     Compute number of parameters to share: $q \leftarrow Q \cdot size(\Delta W)$
4:     Track parameters to release: $\Delta \hat{W} \leftarrow empty\ set$
5:     Compute a noisy threshold: $\hat{h} \leftarrow h + Lap(\frac{s}{\varepsilon_2})$
6:     **while** $size(\Delta \hat{W}) < q$ **do**
7:         Randomly draw a gradient component $w_i$ from $\Delta W$
8:         **if** $abs(clip(w_i, \gamma)) + Lap(\frac{2qs}{\varepsilon_1}) \geq \hat{h}$ **then**
9:             Compute a noisy answer: $w_i \leftarrow clip(w_i + Lap(\frac{qs}{\varepsilon_3}), \gamma)$
10:             Release the answer: append $w_i$ to $\Delta \hat{W}$
11:         **end if**
12:     **end while**
13:     Undo normalisation: $\Delta \hat{W} \leftarrow \Delta \hat{W} * N^{(local)}$
14:     **return** $\Delta \hat{W}$
15: **end procedure**

---

such as [3] can potentially extract sensitive patient data from the update $\Delta W_k^{(t)}$ or the model $W^{(t)}$ during federated training. We adopt a selective parameter update [9] and the sparse vector technique (SVT) [5] to provide strong protection against indirect data leakage.

**Selective Parameter Sharing.** The full model at the end of a client-side training process might have over-fitted and memorised local training examples. Sharing this model poses risks of revealing the training data. Selective parameter sharing methods limit the amount of information that a client shares. This is achieved by (1) only uploading a fraction of $\Delta W_k^{(t)}$: component $w_i$ of $\Delta W_k^{(t)}$ will be shared iif $abs(w_i)$ is greater than a threshold $\tau_k^{(t)}$; (2) further replacing $\Delta W_k^{(t)}$ by clipping the values to a fixed range $[-\gamma, \gamma]$. Here $abs(x)$ denotes the absolute value of $x$; $\tau_k^{(t)}$ is chosen by computing the percentile of $abs(\Delta W_k^{(t)})$; $\gamma$ is independent of specific training data and can be chosen via a small publicly available validation set before training. Gradient clipping is also applied, which is a widely-used method, acting as a model regulariser to prevent over-fitting.

**Differential Privacy Module.** The selective parameter sharing can be further improved by having a strong differential privacy guarantee using SVT. The procedure of selecting and sharing distorted components of $w_i$ is described in Algorithm 2. Intuitively, instead of simply thresholding $abs(\Delta W_k^{(t)})$ and sharing its components $w_i$, every sharing $w_i$ is controlled by the Laplacian mechanism. This is implemented by first comparing a clipped and noisy version of $abs(w_i)$ with a noisy threshold $\tau^{(t)} + Lap(s/\varepsilon_2)$ (Line 8, Algorithm 2), and then only sharing a noisy answer $clip(w_i + Lap(qs/\varepsilon_3), \gamma)$, if the thresholding condition is satisfied. Here $Lap(x)$ denotes a random variable sampled from the Laplace dis-

---

**Algorithm 3.** Federated learning: server-side aggregation of $T$ rounds.

**Require:** num_federated_rounds
1: **procedure** AGGREGATING
2:     Initialise global model: $W^{(0)}$
3:     **for** $t \leftarrow 1 \cdots T$ **do**
4:         **for** *client* $k \leftarrow 1 \cdots K$ **do**                ▷ *Run in parallel*
5:            Send $W^{(t-1)}$ to client $k$
6:            Receive $(\Delta W_k^{(t-1)}, N_k^{(local)})$ from client's LOCAL_TRAINING($W^{(t-1)}$)
7:         **end for**
8:         $W^{(t)} \leftarrow W^{(t-1)} + \frac{1}{\sum_k N_k^{(local)}} \sum_k (N_k^{(local)} \cdot \Delta W_k^{(t-1)})$
9:     **end for**
10:    **return** $W^{(t)}$
11: **end procedure**

---

tribution parameterised by $x$; $clip(x, \gamma)$ denotes clipping of $x$ to be in the range of $[-\gamma, \gamma]$; $s$ denotes the sensitivity of the federated gradient which is bounded by $\gamma$ in this case [9]. The selection procedure is repeated until $q$ fraction of $\Delta W_k^{(t)}$ is released. This procedure satisfies $(\varepsilon_1 + \varepsilon_2 + \varepsilon_3)$-differential privacy [5].

### 2.3 Server-Side Model Aggregation

The server distributes a global model and receives synchronised updates from all clients at each federated round (Algorithm 3). Different clients may have different numbers of local iterations at round $t$, thus the contributions from the clients could be SGD updates at different training speeds. It is important to require an $N^{(local)}$ from the clients, and weight the contributions when aggregating them (Line 8, Algorithm 3). In the case of partial model sharing, utilising the sparse property of $\Delta W_k^{(t)}$ to reduce the communication overheads is left for future work.

## 3 Experiments

This section describes the experimental setup, including the common hyperparameters used for each FL system.

**Data Preparation.** The BraTS 2018 dataset [2] contains multi-parametric pre-operative MRI scans of 285 subjects with brain tumours. Each subject was scanned with four modalities, i.e. (1) T1-weighted, (2) T1-weighted with contrast enhancement, (3) T2-weighted, and (4) T2 fluid-attenuated inversion recovery (T2-FLAIR). Each subject was associated with voxel-level annotations of "whole tumour", "tumour core", and "enhancing tumour". For details of the imaging and annotation protocols, we refer the readers to Bakas et al. [2]. The dataset was previously used for benchmarking machine learning algorithms and is publicly available. We use it to evaluate the FL algorithms on the multi-modal and multi-class segmentation task. For the client-side local training, we adapted the state-of-the-art training pipeline originally designed for data-centralised training [7] and implemented as a part of the NVIDIA Clara Train SDK[1].

To test the generalisation ability across the subjects, we randomly split the dataset into a model training set ($N = 242$ subjects) and a held-out test set ($N = 43$ subjects). The scans were collected from thirteen institutions with different equipment and imaging protocols, and thus heterogeneous image feature distributions. To make our federated setup realistic, we further stratified the training set into thirteen disjoint subsets, according to where the image data were originated and assigned each to a federated client. The setup is challenging for FL algorithms, because (1) each client only processes data from a single institution, which potentially suffers from more severe domain-shift and over-fitting issues compared with a data-centralised training; (2) it reflects the highly imbalanced nature of the dataset (shown in Fig. 1).

**Federated Model Setup.** The evaluation of the FL procedures is perpendicular to the choice of convolutional network architectures. Without loss of generality, we chose the segmentation backbone of [7] as the underlying federated model and used the same set of local training hyperparameters for all experiments: the input image window size of the network was $224 \times 224 \times 128$ voxels, and spatial dropout ratio of the first convolutional layer was 0.2. Similarly to [7], we minimised a soft Dice loss using Adam [4] with a learning rate of $10^{-4}$, batch size of 1, $\beta_1$ of 0.9, $\beta_2$ of 0.999, and $\ell_2$ weight decay coefficient of $10^{-5}$. For all federated training, we set the number of federated rounds to 300 with two local epochs per federated round. A local epoch is defined as every client "sees" its local training examples exactly once. At the beginning of each epoch, data were shuffled locally for each client. For a comparison of model convergences, we also train a data-centralised baseline for 600 epochs.

In terms of computational costs, the segmentation model has about $1.2 \times 10^6$ parameters; a training iteration with an NVIDIA Tesla V100 GPU took 0.85 s.

**Evaluation Metrics.** We measure the segmentation performance of the models on the held-out test set using mean-class Dice score averaged over the three types of tumour regions and all testing subjects. For the FL systems, we report the performance of the global model shared among the federated clients.

**Privacy-Preserving Setup.** The selective parameter updates module has two system parameters: fraction of the model $q$ and the gradient clipping value $\gamma$. We report model performance by varying both. For differential privacy, we fixed $\gamma$ to $10^{-4}$, the sensitivity $s$ to $2\gamma$, and $\varepsilon_2$ to $(2qs)^{\frac{2}{3}}\varepsilon_1$ according to [5]. The model performance by varying $q$, $\varepsilon_1$, and $\varepsilon_3$ are reported in the next section.

## 4    Results

**Federated vs. Data-Centralised Training.** The FL systems are compared with the data-centralised training in Fig. 2 (left). The proposed FL procedure

---

[1] https://devblogs.nvidia.com/annotate-adapt-model-medical-imaging-clara-train-sdk/.

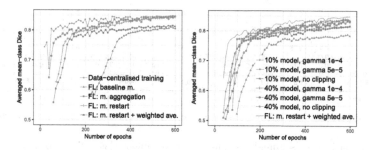

**Fig. 2.** Comparison of segmentation performance on the test set with (left): FL vs. non-FL training, and (right): partial model sharing.

can achieve a comparable segmentation performance without sharing clients' data. In terms of training time, the data-centralised model converged at about 300 training epochs, FL training at about 600. In our experiments, an epoch of data-centralised training ($N = 242$) with an NVIDIA Tesla V100 GPU takes $0.85$ s $\times 242 = 205.70$ s per epoch. The FL training time was determined by the slowest client ($N = 77$), which takes $0.85$ s $\times 77 = 65.45$ s plus small overheads for client-server communication.

**Momentum Restarting and Weighted Averaging.** Figure 2 (left) also compares variants of the FL procedure. For the treatment of momentum variables, restarting them at each federated round outperforms all the other variants. This suggests (1) each client maintaining an independent set of momentum variables slows down the convergence of the federated model; (2) averaging the momentum variables across clients improved the convergence speed over `baseline m.`, but still gave a worse global model than the data-centralised model. On the server-side, weighted averaging of the model parameters outperforms the simple model averaging (i.e. $W^{(t+1)} \leftarrow \sum_k W_k^{(t+1)}/K$). This suggests that the weighted version can handle imbalanced numbers of iterations across the clients.

**Partial Model Sharing.** Figure 2 (right) compares partial model sharing by varying the fraction of the model to share and the gradient clipping values. The figure suggests that sharing larger proportions of models can achieve better performance. Partial model sharing does not affect the model convergence speed and the performance decrease can be almost negligible when only 40% of the full model is shared among the clients. Clipping of the gradient can, sometimes, improve the model performance. However, the value needs to be carefully tuned.

**Differential Privacy Module.** The model performances by varying differential privacy (DP) parameters are shown in Fig. 3. As expected, there is a trade-off between DP protection and model performance. Sharing 10% model showed better performance than sharing 40% under the same DP setup. This is due to the fact that the overall privacy costs $\varepsilon$ are jointly defined by the amount of noise added and the number of parameters shared during training. By fixing the

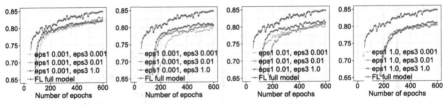

(a) 10% model sharing  (b) 40% model sharing  (c) 40% model sharing  (d) 40% model sharing

**Fig. 3.** Comparison of segmentation models (ave. mean-class Dice score) by varying the privacy parameters: percentage of partial models, $\varepsilon_1$, and $\varepsilon_3$.

per-parameter DP costs, sharing fewer variables has less overall DP costs and thus better model performance.

## 5    Conclusion

We propose a federated learning system for brain tumour segmentation. We studied various practical aspects of the federated model sharing with an emphasis on preserving patient data privacy. While a strong differential privacy guarantee is provided, the privacy cost allocation is conservative. In the future, we will explore differentially private SGD (e.g. [1]) for medical image analysis tasks.

**Acknowledgements.** We thank Rong Ou at NVIDIA for the helpful discussions.

The research was supported by the Wellcome/EPSRC Centre for Medical Engineering (WT203148/Z/16/Z), the Wellcome Flagship Programme (WT213038/Z/18/Z), the UKRI funded London Medical Imaging and AI centre for Value-based Healthcare, and the NIHR Biomedical Research Centre based at Guy's and St Thomas' NHS Foundation Trust and King's College London. The views expressed are those of the authors and not necessarily those of the NHS, the NIHR or the Department of Health.

## References

1. Abadi, M., et al.: Deep learning with differential privacy. In: SIGSAC Conference on Computer and Communications Security, pp. 308–318 (2016)
2. Bakas, S., et al.: Identifying the best machine learning algorithms for brain tumor segmentation, progression assessment, and overall survival prediction in the BRATS challenge. arXiv preprint arXiv:1811.02629 (2018)
3. Hitaj, B., Ateniese, G., Perez-Cruz, F.: Deep models under the GAN: information leakage from collaborative deep learning. In: SIGSAC Conference on Computer and Communications Security, pp. 603–618 (2017)
4. Kingma, D.P., Ba, J.: Adam: a method for stochastic optimization. arXiv preprint arXiv:1412.6980 (2014)
5. Lyu, M., Su, D., Li, N.: Understanding the sparse vector technique for differential privacy. Proc. VLDB Endow. **10**(6), 637–648 (2017)
6. McMahan, B., et al.: Communication efficient learning of deep networks from decentralized data. In: Artificial Intelligence and Statistics, pp. 1273–1282 (2017)

7. Myronenko, A.: 3D MRI brain tumor segmentation using autoencoder regularization. In: Crimi, A., Bakas, S., Kuijf, H., Keyvan, F., Reyes, M., van Walsum, T. (eds.) BrainLes 2018. LNCS, vol. 11384, pp. 311–320. Springer, Cham (2019). https://doi.org/10.1007/978-3-030-11726-9_28

8. Sheller, M.J., Reina, G.A., Edwards, B., Martin, J., Bakas, S.: Multi-institutional deep learning modeling without sharing patient data: a feasibility study on brain tumor segmentation. In: Crimi, A., Bakas, S., Kuijf, H., Keyvan, F., Reyes, M., van Walsum, T. (eds.) BrainLes 2018. LNCS, vol. 11383, pp. 92–104. Springer, Cham (2019). https://doi.org/10.1007/978-3-030-11723-8_9

9. Shokri, R., Shmatikov, V.: Privacy-preserving deep learning. In: SIGSAC Conference on Computer and Communications Security, pp. 1310–1321 (2015)

10. Sun, C., Shrivastava, A., Singh, S., Gupta, A.: Revisiting unreasonable effectiveness of data in deep learning era. In: ICCV (2017)

11. Yu, H., Jin, R., Yang, S.: On the linear speedup analysis of communication efficient momentum SGD for distributed non-convex optimization. In: ICML (2019)

# Residual Attention Generative Adversarial Networks for Nuclei Detection on Routine Colon Cancer Histology Images

Junwei Li, Wei Shao, Zhongnian Li, Weida Li, and Daoqiang Zhang$^{(\boxtimes)}$

College of Computer Science and Technology,
MIIT Key Laboratory of Pattern Analysis and Machine Intelligence,
Nanjing University of Aeronautics and Astronautics, Nanjing 211106, China
dqzhang@nuaa.edu.cn

**Abstract.** The automatic detection of nuclei in pathological images plays an important role in diagnosis and prognosis of cancers. Most nuclei detection algorithms are based on the assumption that the nuclei center should have larger responses than their surroundings in the probability map of the pathological image, which in turn transforms the detection or localization problem into finding the local maxima on the probability map. However, all the existing studies used regression algorithms to determine the probability map, which neglect to take the spatial contiguity within the probability map into consideration. In order to capture the higher-order consistency within the generated probability map, we propose an approach called Residual Attention Generative Adversarial Network (*i.e.*, RAGAN) for nuclei detection. Specifically, the objective function of the RAGAN model combines a detection term with an adversarial term. The adversarial term adopts a generator called Residual Attention U-Net (*i.e.*, RAU-Net) to produce the probability maps that cannot be distinguished by the ground-truth. Based on the adversarial model, we can simultaneously estimate the probabilities of many pixels with high-order consistency, by which we can derive a more accurate probability map. We evaluate our method on a public colorectal adenocarcinoma images dataset with 29756 nuclei. Experimental results show that our method can achieve the F1 Score of 0.847 (with a Precision of 0.859 and a Recall of 0.836) for nuclei detection, which is superior to the conventional methods.

## 1 Introduction

Pathological images could confer important cell-level information of tumors, and thus are considered to be the golden standards for the diagnosis, staging, and prognosis for cancers [10]. From the derived pathological images, the problem of nuclei detection is a prerequisite for analyzing morphological properties of cells. Manual detection, although feasible, requires an excessive amount of effort

© Springer Nature Switzerland AG 2019
H.-I. Suk et al. (Eds.): MLMI 2019, LNCS 11861, pp. 142–150, 2019.
https://doi.org/10.1007/978-3-030-32692-0_17

due to the large size of the histopathological images, and is likely to suffer from human errors. Hence, finding an automatic way to complete nuclei detection task has become a new focus in computational biology.

Generally, nuclei detection for pathological images can be roughly divided into two categories, e.g., the classification based methods and the probability map based approaches. One the one hand, the classification based methods aim at building supervised algorithms to distinguish nuclei and non-nuclei patches. For instance, Vink *et al.* [7] firstly constructed a large morphological feature set from the image patches, and then applied a modified AdaBoosting classifier to detect nuclei. In addition, since deep learning techniques have emerged as a powerful tool to solve many problems of computer vision, Xu *et al.* [10] explored a stacked sparse auto-encoder algorithm to learn high-level features for each sliding window patch, followed by a softmax classifier to detect nuclei in the pathological images. Other works include [1] trained a CNN classifier to classify mitotic and non-mitotic cells in breast cancer histopathological images.

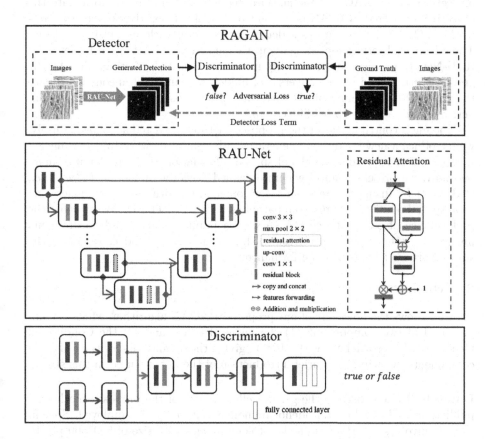

**Fig. 1.** Framework of the proposed RAGAN, which consisted of a nuclei detector and a Conditional Generative Adversarial Networks.

On the other hand, since the classification based methods usually have difficulty in capturing the structured information exhibited in the sliding window patches, many researchers have used the probability map to encode every pixel's proximity to the nucleus, by which we could detect the centers of the nuclei by finding the position of the maximum response in the probability map. Specifically, Sirinukunwattana *et al.* [6] proposed a spatially constrained convolutional Neural Network (SC-CNN) to perform nucleus detection on colorectal adenocarcinomas. Xie *et al.* [9] presented a novel structured regression model based on a proposed fully residual convolutional neural network for cell detection. All the results suggest that the incorporation of probability map can improve the accuracy for nuclei detection.

Even though much progress has been achieved, all the existing methods used the regression algorithm to generate the probability maps of pathological images, which overlook spatial contiguity within the probability map. To address this issue, we explore an approach called Residual Attention Generative Adversarial Network (*i.e.*, RAGAN) for nuclei detection. Specifically, we formulate the objective function of RAGAN based on Conditional Generative Adversarial Networks (CGAN) that integrates a detection loss term with an adversarial term. The adversarial term adopts a generator called Residual Attention U-Net (*i.e.*, RAU-Net) to produce the probability maps that cannot be distinguished by the ground-truth. Based on the adversarial model, we can simultaneously estimate the probabilities of many pixels with high-order consistency, by which we can derive a more accurate probability map.

The main contributions of the proposed method are listed as follows. Firstly, we introduce a new conditional generative adversarial network to detect nuclei, which aims at exploring the global spatial information of the probability map. Secondly, we present a novel generator called Residual Attention U-Net (*i.e.*, RAU-Net) by fusing the residual attention module with U-Net for generating local spatial relation features from pathological images. Thirdly, We evaluate the performance of our proposed RAGAN on a public colorectal adenocarcinoma images dataset. Experimental results show that our method can achieve the state-of-art nuclei detection performance.

## 2   Method

Figure 1 shows the flowchart of our proposed RAGAN algorithm, which is compromised of two components: (1) the nuclei detector and (2) the Conditional Generative Adversarial Networks. Before giving the detailed descriptions of these components, we will give a brief introduction of the dataset used in this study.

**Dataset:** To demonstrate the general effectiveness of the proposed method, a publicly available colorectal adenocarcinomas dataset [6] is employed. Specifically, it involves 100 H&E stained histology images with size of 500*500 pixels. The H&E stained histology images were cropped from non-overlapping areas of 10 whole-slide images from 9 patients. For detection purposes, there are 29756 nuclei were marked at the center within the dataset.

**Probability Map for Pathological Images:** Suppose we have $l$ pathological images $X = \{x_1, x_2, \ldots, x_l\}$ in the training set with their corresponding probability maps represented as $Y = \{y_1, y_2, \ldots, y_l\}$. Here, $x_i \in Z^{m \times n \times 3}$, $y_i \in R^{m \times n}$, and $m, n$ correspond to the height and width for each image, respectively. We define the probability for each pixel (*i.e.*, $y_i^{a,b}$) as follows:

$$
y_i^{a,b} = \begin{cases} \dfrac{1}{1 + \frac{\min\{d_i^1, d_i^2, \ldots, d_i^{k_i}\}}{2}} & \min\{d_i^1, d_i^2, \ldots, d_i^{k_i}\} < r, \\ 0 & otherwise, \end{cases} \tag{1}
$$

where $d_i^j$ denotes the Euclidean distance from the pixel with coordinates $(a, b)$ to the center of $j$th nucleus in $x_i$, $k_i$ is the number of nuclei in $x_i$ and $r$ is a distance threshold, which is set as 4. It is worth noting that the probability map defined by Eq. (1) has a high peak in the vicinity of the center of each nucleus and flat elsewhere. Accordingly, the identification of nuclei can be transformed into locating maxima in the probability map of pathological images.

**Conditional Generative Adversarial Networks:** In order to estimate the probability map of each pathological image, the existing studies in [6,9] used regression algorithms to determine the probability of each pixel, which overlook the spatial contiguity within the probability map. In order to capture the higher-order consistency within the probability map, we generate it under the conditional generative adversarial network (*i.e.*, CGAN). Specifically, CGAN can capture the global spatial information in the probability map. In comparison with regression based methods that assess the output of each pixel independently, CGAN can jointly estimate the probability map of many pixels by considering their inner-correlation. We show the objective function of the CGAN as follows:

$$
\min_G \max_D L_c(G, D) = \log D(x, y) + \log(1 - D(x, G(x))) \tag{2}
$$

where $G$ and $D$ represent the generator and the discriminator, respectively. In Eq. (2), we directly input the pathological image $x$ to the generator $G$ for producing the probability map that cannot be distinguished with the ground-truth $y$ via discriminator $D$, and thus can correct higher-order inconsistencies between ground truth and generated probability maps.

**Residual Attention Generative Adversarial Networks (RAGAN) for Nuclei Detection:** Our proposed RAGAN is under the CGAN framework (shown in Eq. (2)). Specifically, the generator of RAGAN (*i.e.*, RAU-Net) is the combination of U-Net [5] and the Residual Attention Network [2], and we show the framework of RAU-Net in Fig. 1. Here, we use the U-Net as prototype generator, which utilizes the skip connection to join the up-sampling and down-sampling information of the images. For the input pathological images, we also adopt the attention mechanism that can orient the perception of the deep neural network on the important regions of images [8]. That is to say, the incorporation of attention mechanism can help to capture the characteristics of the nuclear regions more accurately. Last but not least, residual network shows excellent performance for image recognition by increasing considerable networks depth [3]. Therefore, we integrate residual attention module into the high layers of U-Net that makes the generator produce probability map with more local spatial information. As to discriminator, it is compromised of 8 convolutional layers and 7 max-pooling layers for model training, we show its architecture in Fig. 1.

In addition, since the area of nuclei regions is much smaller than the background regions for histology images, we introduce a cost-sensitive regression term to calculate the loss between the generated and ground-truth probability map, which is shown in Eq. (3).

$$L_{pixel} = \frac{1}{N} \sum_{i=1}^{N} \sum_{j=0}^{1} [I(c_i = j)] \omega_{1-j} (t_i^j + \log \sum_{k=0}^{1} \exp(t_i^k)) \tag{3}$$

where $N$ is the number of pixels in a pathological image, and $I(\cdot)$ is a indicate function. We divide each pixel $p_i$ into $M = 2$ categories according to its value $v_i$ on the probability map. Namely, if $v_i < 0.15$, $p_i$ belongs to the background category $(c_i = 0)$, otherwise $p_i$ is in the nuclear area $(c_i = 1)$. In addition, $t_i^j$ represents the estimated probability that pixel $p_i$ belongs to category $j$, and the weight $\omega_0, \omega_1$ can be calculated by the ratio between the number of background pixels or nuclear pixels and $N$, respectively.

Based on generative adversarial network (GAN), the objective function of RAGAN is formulated by integrating a detection loss term with an adversarial term. Therefore, the objective function of our method is:

$$\min_{G} \max_{D} L_{ra}(G, D) = L_c(G, D) + \alpha L_{pixel}(G) \tag{4}$$

where $G$ denotes the generator of RAGAN, $D$ denotes the discriminator of RAGAN, $L_c(G, D)$ denotes the conditional generative adversarial loss, $L_{pixel}(G)$ indicates the detection and $\alpha$ is the weight of detection loss.

The way to optimize the maximum and minimum objective function for RAGAN is to train $G$ and $D$ alternately and iteratively. When optimizing the $G$, the parameters of $D$ is fixed and solve the minimization problem. When optimizing the $D$, the parameters of $G$ is fixed and solve the maximization problem. The optimization procedure proceeds until the loss of RAGAN converges.

## 3    Experimental Results

**Experimental Settings:** To evaluate the performance of RAGAN, we follow the partition strategy introduced in [6] as they selected half pathological images for training and whereas the anther half is for performance evaluation. For parameter settings, we tune the parameter $\alpha$ from $\{50, 100, 200\}$. The proposed RAGAN algorithm is implemented on pytorch with the python environment on a NVIDIA GeForce GTX 1080 Ti with 11 GB GPU memory, we used

ADAM with momentum for parameter optimization and set the initial learning rate as 0.0001.

**Quantitative Comparisons of Different Methods:** In this section, we compare our method with the following nuclei detection methods by the measurements of Precision, Recall and F1-Score. For RAGAN and all the comparative methods, the detection of a cell is correct when its detected position is within the radius of 6 pixels from the annotated center of the nucleus, and the results are shown in Table 1.

- LIPSyM [4], CRImage [11]: Detecting nuclei based on the morphological features that are extracted from pathological images.
- SSAE [10]: Consist of two auto-encoder layers followed by a softmax classifier, which is trained to distinguish between nuclear and non-nuclear patches
- SC-CNN [6], SR-CNN [9]: Two probability map based methods, which use the regression algorithm under deep learning frameworks to generate probability maps.
- UGAN: A variant of RAGAN, which neglect to take the residual attention module in the generator of RAGAN.

**Table 1.** Comparative results for nucleus detection

| Method | Precision | Recall | F1 Score |
|---|---|---|---|
| LIPSyM [4] | 0.725 | 0.517 | 0.604 |
| CRImage [11] | 0.657 | 0.461 | 0.542 |
| SSAE [10] | 0.617 | 0.644 | 0.630 |
| SR-CNN [9] | 0.783 | 0.804 | 0.793 |
| SC-CNN (M = 1) [6] | 0.758 | 0.827 | 0.791 |
| SC-CNN (M = 2) [6] | 0.781 | 0.823 | 0.802 |
| UGAN | **0.863** | 0.809 | 0.835 |
| RAGAN | 0.859 | **0.836** | **0.847** |

As can be seen from Table 1, firstly, the detection power of the morphological feature based methods (*i.e.*, LIPSyM [4], CRImage [11]) is inferior to the other deep learning based algorithms. This is because the deep model can better represent the pathological images than the hand-crafted features. Secondly, the proposed RAGAN and its variant UGAN can achieve superior detection performance to the comparative methods. Since the generation of probability maps based on CGAN can better capture their high-level consistency. Finally, we find that the proposed RAGAN could provide better detection performance (with F1 Score of 0.847) than UGAN (with F1 Score of 0.835), which shows the advantages of incorporating residual attention module to generate probability maps for nuclei detection.

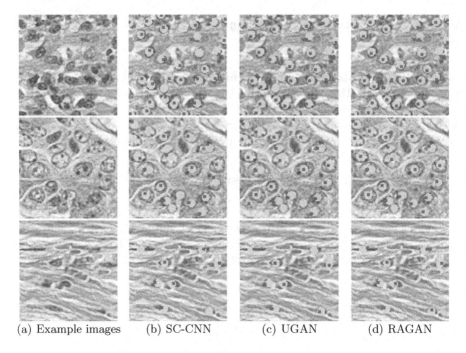

(a) Example images     (b) SC-CNN     (c) UGAN     (d) RAGAN

**Fig. 2.** Sample results on nuclei detection (a) Input pathological images (b) Detection results by SC-CNN method. (c) Detection results by UGAN method. (d) Detection results for the proposed RAGAN method. Here, the detected nuclei are marked by red dots and the ground truth areas are shown as yellow circles. (Color figure online)

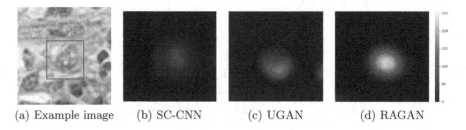

(a) Example image     (b) SC-CNN     (c) UGAN     (d) RAGAN

**Fig. 3.** (a) An example image with ground truth area (the ground truth areas are shown as yellow dots.) (b) Probability map of the example image with the red box generated by SC-CNN method. (c) Probability map of the example image with the red box generated by UGAN method. (d) Probability map of the example image with the red box generated by the proposed RAGAN method. (Color figure online)

**Qualitative Comparisons of Different Methods:** In order to evaluate the quality of the detection results, we also visualize some typical results in Fig. 2 where the detected nuclei are marked by red dots and the ground truth areas are shown as yellow circles. As can be seen from Fig. 2, our method can successfully detect the cells with large shape variation. The main reason lies in that the proposed RAGAN could estimate the probability map of each nuclei with high-order consistency (sample results are shown in Fig. 3). Therefore, our proposed method can more accurately capture the local maxima on the probability map related to the positions of nuclei.

## 4    Conclusion

In this paper, we propose a novel framework, *i.e.*, RAGAN, to detect nuclei from pathological images. To the best of our knowledge, the RAGAN algorithm is among the first to unitize the generative adversarial network that can generate high-order consistent probability map for nuclei detection, and the experimental results on a colorectal adenocarcinoma demonstrate the effectiveness of the proposed method. In future, we plan to test our method on the pathological images of other types of cancers, through which we could make diagnostic and prognostic assessments on cancer patients.

**Acknowledgement.** This work was supported by the National Natural Science Foundation of China (Nos. 61876082, 61861130366, 61703301) and the Royal Society-Academy of Medical Sciences Newton Advanced Fellowship (No. NAF\R1\180371).

## References

1. Cireşan, D.C., Giusti, A., Gambardella, L.M., Schmidhuber, J.: Mitosis detection in breast cancer histology images with deep neural networks. In: Mori, K., Sakuma, I., Sato, Y., Barillot, C., Navab, N. (eds.) MICCAI 2013. LNCS, vol. 8150, pp. 411–418. Springer, Heidelberg (2013). https://doi.org/10.1007/978-3-642-40763-5_51
2. Fei, W., Jiang, M.: Residual attention network for image classification. In: IEEE Conference on Computer Vision and Pattern Recognition, pp. 6450–6458 (2017)
3. He, K., Zhang, X.: Deep residual learning for image recognition. In: IEEE Conference on Computer Vision and Pattern Recognition, pp. 770–778 (2015)
4. Kuse, M., Kalasannavar, V.: Local isotropic phase symmetry measure for detection of beta cells and lymphocytes. J. Pathol. Inform. **2**(2), S2 (2011)
5. Ronneberger, O., Fischer, P., Brox, T.: U-Net: convolutional networks for biomedical image segmentation. In: Navab, N., Hornegger, J., Wells, W.M., Frangi, A.F. (eds.) MICCAI 2015. LNCS, vol. 9351, pp. 234–241. Springer, Cham (2015). https://doi.org/10.1007/978-3-319-24574-4_28
6. Sirinukunwattana, K., Raza, S.: Locality sensitive deep learning for detection and classification of nuclei in routine colon cancer histology images. IEEE Trans. Med. Imaging **35**(5), 1196–1206 (2016)
7. Vink, J., Leeuwen, V.: Efficient nucleus detector in histopathology images. J. Microsc. **249**, 124–135 (2013)
8. Walther, D., Itti, L., Riesenhuber, M., Poggio, T., Koch, C.: Attentional selection for object recognition—a gentle way. In: Bülthoff, H.H., Wallraven, C., Lee, S.-W., Poggio, T.A. (eds.) BMCV 2002. LNCS, vol. 2525, pp. 472–479. Springer, Heidelberg (2002). https://doi.org/10.1007/3-540-36181-2_47

9. Xie, Y., Xing, F., Kong, X., Su, H., Yang, L.: Beyond classification: structured regression for robust cell detection using convolutional neural network. In: Navab, N., Hornegger, J., Wells, W.M., Frangi, A.F. (eds.) MICCAI 2015. LNCS, vol. 9351, pp. 358–365. Springer, Cham (2015). https://doi.org/10.1007/978-3-319-24574-4_43
10. Xu, J., Xiang, L.: Stacked sparse autoencoder (SSAE) for nuclei detection on breast cancer histopathology images. IEEE Trans. Med. Imaging **35**(1), 119–130 (2016)
11. Yuan, Y., Failmezger, H.: Quantitative image analysis of cellular heterogeneity in breast tumors complements genomic profiling. Sci. Transl. Med. **4**(157), 157ra143 (2012)

# Semi-supervised Multi-task Learning with Chest X-Ray Images

Abdullah-Al-Zubaer Imran$^{(\boxtimes)}$ and Demetri Terzopoulos

Computer Science Department, University of California, Los Angeles, CA, USA
aimran@cs.ucla.edu

**Abstract.** Discriminative models that require full supervision are inefficacious in the medical imaging domain when large labeled datasets are unavailable. By contrast, generative modeling—i.e., learning data generation and classification—facilitates semi-supervised training with limited labeled data. Moreover, generative modeling can be advantageous in accomplishing multiple objectives for better generalization. We propose a novel multi-task learning model for jointly learning a classifier and a segmentor, from chest X-ray images, through semi-supervised learning. In addition, we propose a new loss function that combines absolute KL divergence with Tversky loss (KLTV) to yield faster convergence and better segmentation performance. Based on our experimental results using a novel segmentation model, an Adversarial Pyramid Progressive Attention U-Net (APPAU-Net), we hypothesize that KLTV can be more effective for generalizing multi-tasking models while being competitive in segmentation-only tasks.

**Keywords:** Semi-supervised · Multi-tasking · Generative modeling · Classification · Segmentation · KL-Tversky loss · Chest X-ray

## 1 Introduction

The effective supervised training of deep neural networks normally requires large pools of labeled data. In medical imaging, however, datasets tend to be limited in size due to privacy issues, and labeled data is scarce since manual annotation requires tedious, time-consuming effort by medical experts, making it not only expensive, but also susceptible to subjectivity, human error, and variance across different experts. Although some large labeled datasets are available, they can be seriously imbalanced by over-representation of common problems and under-representation of rare problems.

The success of discriminative models such as regular CNNs for classification or segmentation, depends on large labeled training datasets to make predictions about future unobserved examples. Generative modeling has recently received much attention with the advent of deep generative models, such as GANs. Since they can learn real data distributions, they are becoming increasingly popular given the abundance of unlabeled data.

© Springer Nature Switzerland AG 2019
H.-I. Suk et al. (Eds.): MLMI 2019, LNCS 11861, pp. 151–159, 2019.
https://doi.org/10.1007/978-3-030-32692-0_18

Via generative modeling, we can perform multi-task learning in a semi-supervised manner, without large labeled datasets. In practice, we train a deep learning model to perform a single task (classification, segmentation, detection, etc.) by fine-tuning parameters until its performance no longer improves. The same model can subsequently be enabled to perform better in other tasks. In fact, the domain-specific features from the related tasks are leveraged to improve the generalization of the model through multi-task learning [1]. Hence, one objective regularizes another to accomplish multiple tasks within a common model.

We introduce a novel generative modeling approach to joint segmentation and classification from limited labeled data, in a semi-supervised manner, and apply it to chest X-ray imagery. Our technical contributions are twofold: (1) a novel multi-task learning model for semi-supervised classification and segmentation from small labeled medical image datasets and (2) a new loss function combining absolute KL divergence and Tversky loss (KLTV) for semantic segmentation.

## 1.1 Related Work

Several single-task classification and segmentation models are available in the chest X-ray literature. Based on the popular segnet architecture, Mittal *et al.* [2] proposed a fully convolutional encoder-decoder with skip connections for lung segmentation in chest X-ray images. Adversarial training of an FCN followed by a CRF has been applied to non-overfitting mammogram segmentation [3]. Adversarial learning has been utilized for segmentation (semantic-aware generative adversarial nets [4], structure correcting adversarial nets [5], etc.) as well as in disease classification from chest X-ray images (semi-supervised domain adaptation [6], attention-guided CNN [7], semi-supervised multi-adversarial encoder [8]).

Unlike the above models, our model jointly performs both classification and segmentation. Several prior efforts address multi-task learning with CNNs and generative modeling. Rezaei *et al.* [9] proposed a GAN model combining a set of auto-encoders with an LSTM unit and an FCN as discriminator for semantic segmentation and disease prediction. Girard *et al.* [10] used a U-Net-like architecture coupled with graph propagation to jointly segment and classify retinal vessels. Mehat *et al.* [11] proposed a Y-Net, with parallel discriminative and convolutional modularity, for the joint segmentation and classification of breast biopsy images. Another multi-tasking model was proposed by Yang *et al.* [12] for skin lesion segmentation and melanoma-seborrheic keratosis classification, using GoogleNet extended to three branches for segmentation and two classification predictions. Khosravan *et al.* [13] used a semi-supervised multi-task model for the joint learning of false positive reduction and nodule segmentation from 3D CT. Ours is the first model to pursue a multi-task learning approach to the analysis of chest X-ray images.

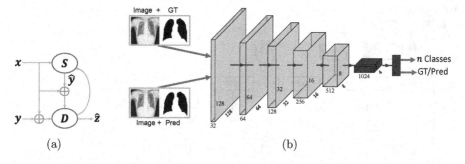

(a)                                                         (b)

**Fig. 1.** (a) Basic structure of the proposed APPAU-Net model. The segmentor $S$ predicts segmentation $\hat{y}$ from a given image $x$. The discriminator $D$ predicts the class label $\hat{z}$ from image-real label pair $(x, y)$; $z = 0, \ldots, n$ are real disease classes and $z = n + 1$ denotes the predicted class; (b) Detailed architecture of the Discriminator $D$ (as a CNN) network of the APPAU-Net model.

## 2   Model Description

### 2.1   Adversarial Pyramid Progressive Attention U-Net

Our proposed APPAU-Net model consists of two major building blocks, a segmentor $S$ and a discriminator $D$ (Fig. 1). $S$ primarily performs segmentation prediction $\hat{y}$ from a given image $x$. $S$ consists of a pyramid encoder and a progressive attention-gated decoder modifying a U-Net. The $S$ network, which is illustrated in Fig. 2, receives the image input $x$ at different scales in different stages of the encoder [14]. This pyramidal input allows the model to access class details at different scales. Moreover, while lowering resolution, the model can keep track of the ROIs, avoiding the possibility of losing them after the subsequent convolutions. The pyramid input to the encoder network enables the model to learn more locally-aware features crucial to semantic segmentation.

Following [15], with deep-supervision, APPAU-Net generates side-outputs at different resolutions from the decoder. The side-outputs are progressively added to the next side-outputs before reaching the final segmentation at the original image resolution. Combining pyramid inputs and progressive side-outputs helps the model perform better in segmenting small ROIs. The side-output segmentation maps $\hat{y}_i$ are compared to the ground truth mask to calculate the side-losses of varying weights (higher resolutions are usually assigned higher weights). Therefore, the final segmentation loss is calculated as

$$L_{seg_{(x,y)}} = \sum_{i=1}^{4} w_i L_{(y_i, \hat{y}_i)}. \tag{1}$$

However, generating segmentation maps (side-outputs) at different stages of the decoder might lead to loss of spatial detail. In cases with substantial shape variability of the ROIs, this eventually incurs larger false positives. To

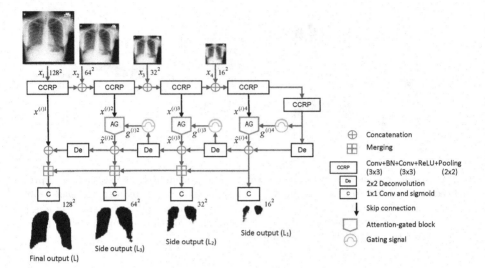

**Fig. 2.** Architecture of the segmentor or PPAU-Net in our APPAU-Net model. The encoder takes inputs at different scales and progressively adds the side-outputs from the attention-gated decoder. The discriminator takes image-label or image-predicted label pairs and classifies the images.

tackle this problem, we adapt soft-attention gates that help draw relevant spatial features from the low-level feature maps of the pyramid encoder [16]. Feature maps are then propagated to the high-level features to generate side-outputs at different stages of the decoder. Attention-gated (AG) modules produce attention coefficients $\alpha \in [0, 1]$ at each pixel $i$ that scale input feature maps $x^{(i)l}$ at layer $l$ to semantically relevant features $\hat{x}^{(i)l}$. A gating signal from coarser resolution, serves to determine the focus regions through the computation of intermediate maps, as follows:

$$G_{\text{attn}}^l = \psi^T(\sigma(w_x^T x^{(i)l} + w_g^T g^{(i)l} + b_g)) + b_\psi. \qquad (2)$$

The linear attention coefficients are computed by element-wise summation and a $1 \times 1$ linear transformation. The parameters are $w_x$, $w_g$, $b_g$, and $b_\psi$. The intermediate maps are then transformed using ReLU $\sigma_1$ and sigmoid $\sigma_2$ activations. Finally, after element-wise multiplication of the feature map $x^{(i)l}$ (via skip) and nonlinear transformation, $\hat{x}^{(i)l}$ is generated at each decoder stage.

The attention coefficients $\alpha_i$ retain the relevant features by scaling the low level query signal $x^{(i)l}$ through an element-wise product. These pruned features are then concatenated with upsampled output maps at different stages of the decoder. A $1 \times 1$ convolution and sigmoid activation is applied on each output map in the decoder to generate the side-outputs at different resolutions. With deep supervision and gating from the pyramid encoder, the model becomes semantically more discriminative.

## 2.2  Loss Functions

The two building blocks of our APPAU-Net model have different objectives.

*Segmentor Loss:* As in the semi-supervised learning-scheme, the segmentor's objective is just based on the labeled samples. We employ Tversky loss, a generalization of Dice loss that weighs false negatives higher than false positives in order to balance precision and recall. The segmentor's objective includes a segmentation loss and an adversarial loss, where the segmentor wants the discriminator $D$ to maximize the likelihood for the predicted segmentation generated by the segmentor. We combine an absolute KL divergence with a Tversky loss, proposing the new loss function

$$L_S = L_{S_{seg(y,\hat{y})}} + cL_{S_{adv(x,\hat{y})}}, \tag{3}$$

where $L_{S_{seg(y,\hat{y})}} = aL_{S_{KL}} + bL_{S_{TV}}$, with $L_{S_{KL}} = \sum_i^{m^2} |(y_{pl}(i) - \hat{y}_{pl}^{(i)}) \log(y_{pl}^{(i)}/\hat{y}_{pl}^{(i)})|$, and

$$L_{S_{TV}} = 1 - \frac{\sum_i^{m^2} y_{pl}^{(i)} \hat{y}_{pl}^{(i)} + \epsilon}{\sum_i^{m^2} y_{pl}^{(i)} \hat{y}_{pl}^{(i)} + \alpha \sum_i^{m^2} y_{p\bar{l}}^{(i)} \hat{y}_{pl}^{(i)} + \beta \sum_i^{m^2} y_{pl}^{(i)} \hat{y}_{p\bar{l}(i)} + \epsilon}, \tag{4}$$

where $\hat{y}_{pl}(i)$ is the prediction probability that pixel $i$ is assigned label $l$ (one of the ROI labels) and $\hat{y}_{p\bar{l}}(i)$ is the probability that the pixel $i$ is assigned the non-ROI (background) label. Similarly, $y_{pl}(i)$ and $y_{p\bar{l}}(i)$ denote the pixel-wise mapping labels in the ground-truth masks. Hyper parameters $a$, $b$, $\alpha$, and $\beta$ can be tuned to weigh the KL-divergence against the Tversky loss (first pair) and weigh FPs against FNs. Small constant $\epsilon$ avoids division by zero. The second term in the segmentor's objective is an adversarial loss, where the segmentor wants the discriminator to maximize likelihood for the paired data $x$ and predicted segmentation $\hat{y}$. Therefore, the segmentor's adversarial loss is

$$L_{S_{adv(x,\hat{y})}} = -\mathbb{E}_{x,\hat{y}\sim S} \log[1 - p(z = n + 1|(x,\hat{y})]. \tag{5}$$

Since the main objective of the segmentor is to generate the segmentation map, $L_{S_{adv}}$ is usually weighed using a small number $c$.

*Discriminator Loss:* The discriminator is trained on multiple objectives—adversary on the segmentor's output and classification of the images into one of the real classes. Since the model is trained on both labeled and unlabeled training data, the loss function of the discriminator $D$ includes both supervised and unsupervised losses. When the model receives image-label pairs $(x, y)$, it is just the standard supervised learning loss

$$L_{D_{sup}} = -\mathbb{E}_{x,y,z\sim p_{data}} \log[p(z = i|x, y; i < n + 1)]. \tag{6}$$

**Table 1.** Segmentation-only performance comparison of different models in four different data setups.

| Dataset | Model | DS | JS | SSIM | F1 | HD | SN | SP | PR | RC |
|---|---|---|---|---|---|---|---|---|---|---|
| MCX | U-Net-TV | 0.991 | 0.983 | 0.950 | 0.966 | 2.968 | 0.965 | 0.989 | 0.968 | 0.965 |
| | U-Net-KLTV | 0.990 | 0.980 | 0.947 | 0.962 | 3.009 | 0.966 | 0.985 | 0.958 | 0.966 |
| | Attention U-Net-TV | 0.984 | 0.968 | 0.922 | 0.937 | 3.768 | 0.915 | 0.987 | 0.960 | 0.915 |
| | Attention U-Net-KLTV | 0.990 | 0.980 | 0.941 | 0.960 | 3.063 | 0.957 | 0.987 | 0.962 | 0.957 |
| | PPAU-Net-TV | 0.988 | 0.978 | 0.966 | 0.958 | 3.143 | 0.967 | 0.982 | 0.949 | 0.967 |
| | PPAU-Net-KLTV | **0.992** | 0.983 | 0.949 | 0.989 | **2.690** | 0.989 | 0.958 | 0.989 | 0.976 |
| SCX | U-Net-TV | 0.964 | 0.931 | 0.860 | 0.955 | 4.181 | 0.975 | 0.799 | 0.936 | 0.975 |
| | U-Net-KLTV | 0.960 | 0.923 | 0.850 | 0.950 | 4.023 | 0.963 | 0.803 | 0.936 | 0.963 |
| | Attention U-Net-TV | 0.958 | 0.919 | 0.842 | 0.948 | 4.562 | 0.983 | 0.725 | 0.915 | 0.983 |
| | Attention U-Net-KLTV | **0.965** | 0.933 | 0.862 | 0.955 | **3.684** | 0.946 | 0.894 | 0.964 | 0.946 |
| | PPAU-Net-TV | 0.954 | 0.913 | 0.838 | 0.944 | 4.523 | 0.983 | 0.700 | 0.908 | 0.983 |
| | PPAU-Net-KLTV | 0.964 | 0.930 | 0.858 | 0.954 | 3.855 | 0.961 | 0.836 | 0.946 | 0.961 |
| JCX | U-Net-TV | 0.989 | 0.979 | 0.937 | 0.985 | 2.804 | 0.990 | 0.956 | 0.981 | 0.990 |
| | U-Net-KLTV | **0.990** | 0.980 | 0.939 | 0.986 | **2.553** | 0.980 | 0.988 | 0.995 | 0.977 |
| | Attention U-Net-TV | 0.988 | 0.977 | 0.929 | 0.983 | 2.882 | 0.993 | 0.940 | 0.974 | 0.993 |
| | Attention U-Net-KLTV | 0.989 | 0.977 | 0.932 | 0.984 | 2.781 | 0.981 | 0.970 | 0.986 | 0.981 |
| | PPAU-Net-TV | **0.990** | 0.981 | 0.941 | 0.987 | 2.768 | 0.992 | 0.958 | 0.981 | 0.992 |
| | PPAU-Net-KLTV | **0.990** | 0.979 | 0.937 | 0.985 | 2.751 | 0.987 | 0.959 | 0.982 | 0.987 |
| CCX | U-Net-TV | **0.978** | 0.958 | 0.907 | 0.968 | **3.322** | 0.974 | 0.928 | 0.962 | 0.974 |
| | U-Net-KLTV | 0.969 | 0.939 | 0.874 | 0.953 | 3.502 | 0.946 | 0.926 | 0.960 | 0.946 |
| | AttnU-Net-TV | 0.970 | 0.941 | 0.878 | 0.956 | 3.643 | 0.972 | 0.883 | 0.940 | 0.972 |
| | AttnU-Net-KLTV | 0.971 | 0.943 | 0.877 | 0.956 | 3.481 | 0.944 | 0.941 | 0.968 | 0.944 |
| | PPAU-Net-TV | 0.969 | 0.940 | 0.875 | 0.955 | 3.807 | 0.978 | 0.870 | 0.934 | 0.978 |
| | PPAU-Net-KLTV | 0.967 | 0.936 | 0.868 | 0.951 | 3.472 | 0.939 | 0.932 | 0.963 | 0.939 |

When it receives unlabeled data $(x, y)$ or $(x, \hat{y})$ from two different sources, the unsupervised loss combines the original adversarial losses for image-real label and image-prediction pairs:

$$L_{D_{label}} = -\mathbb{E}_{x,y \sim p_{data}} \log[1 - p(z = n + 1|x, y)] \tag{7}$$

and

$$L_{D_{pred}} = -\mathbb{E}_{(x,\hat{y}) \sim S} \log[p(z = n + 1|x, \hat{y})]. \tag{8}$$

## 3   Experiments and Results

*Dataset and Implementation Details:* For the supervised segmentation, we used our PPAU-Net model and KLTV as the loss function. We compared against all the preliminary segmentation models and TV loss. Then we performed semi-supervised multi-tasking for semi-supervised disease classification and lung segmentation from chest X-ray images. We used three chest X-ray datasets: the Montgomery County chest X-ray set (MCX) comprising 138 images, the Shenzhen chest X-ray set (SCX) comprising 527 images [17], and the JSRT dataset

(JCX) comprising 247 images [18]. In addition, we created another dataset (CCX) comprising 912 images, by combining prior datasets. Each dataset was split into train and test sets in a 75:25 ratio and 10% of the train set was used for model selection. Except for CCX, all the datasets were used for binary classification (normal/abnormal), while CCX was used for 3-class classification (normal, nodule, tuberculosis). The X-ray images were normalized and resized to $128 \times 128$ pixels. For multi-tasking, we used the Adam optimizer with momentum 0.9 and learning rates $1.0^{-5}$ ($S$) and $1.0^{-4}$ ($D$). Each model was trained using a batch size of 16. All the convolutional layers were followed by batch-normalization, except for the convolutions that generate side-outputs. We performed dropout at a rate of 0.4 in the discriminator. Each model was evaluated after training for 300 epochs. For the classification, along with the overall accuracy, we reported the class-wise F1 scores. For the segmentation, we used the following performance metrics: Dice similarity (DS), Average Hausdorff distance (HD), Jaccard index (JI), Sensitivity (SN), Specificity (SP), F1 score, Structural Similarity Measure (SSIM), Precision (PR), and Recall (RE) scores.

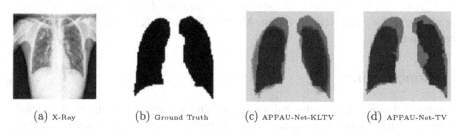

(a) X-Ray        (b) Ground Truth        (c) APPAU-Net-KLTV        (d) APPAU-Net-TV

**Fig. 3.** Visual comparison of the lung segmentation by the APPAU-Net model with TV loss (d) and KLTV loss (c). The predicted lung mask with TV and KLTV losses are overlaid with the ground truth mask.

*Segmentation-Only:* At first, we evaluated the performance of our PPAU-Net model for the segmentation-only task, and compared with the baseline models incrementally. Table 1 reports the performance measures of different models with varying choices of loss (TV and KLTV), showing that our model is competitive.

*Semi-supervised Multi-task Learning:* In the semi-supervised setting, we applied our new APPAU-Net model. Along with TV loss, we used cross-entropy with TV (XETV) loss and the proposed KLTV loss. 10% labeled and 90% unlabeled training data were used for every dataset. Table 2 shows that for all four datasets the APPAU-Net model with the new KLTV loss consistently outperformed the APPAU-Net model with TV and XETV losses in both overlap and distance measures, and suggests that the model with KLTV loss generalizes better in multi-task learning. While both TV and XETV losses tend to lose some accuracy because of the additional classification task, KLTV still achieves good

**Table 2.** Performance evaluation of the APPAU-Net model for semi-supervised multi-tasking in different data settings.

| Dataset | Model | Classification | | | Segmentation | | | | | | | | |
|---------|-------|-----|-----|-----|-----|-----|------|-----|-------|-----|-----|-----|-----|
| | | Acc | PR | RE | DS | JI | SSIM | F1 | HD | SN | SP | PR | RE |
| MCX | APPAU-Net-TV | **0.571** | 0.690 | 0.290 | 0.956 | 0.916 | 0.815 | 0.814 | 4.514 | 0.800 | 0.988 | 0.953 | 0.800 |
| | APPAU-Net-XETV | 0.514 | 0.620 | 0.280 | 0.929 | 0.868 | 0.788 | 0.778 | 4.554 | 0.903 | 0.856 | 0.684 | 0.903 |
| | APPAU-Net-KLTV | 0.543 | 0.680 | 0.200 | **0.974** | 0.950 | 0.880 | 0.898 | **3.914** | 0.857 | 0.944 | 0.944 | 0.857 |
| JCX | APPAU-Net-TV | **0.758** | 0.000 | 0.860 | 0.972 | 0.945 | 0.864 | 0.963 | 3.755 | 0.996 | 0.831 | 0.929 | 0.996 |
| | APPAU-Net-XETV | **0.758** | 0.000 | 0.860 | 0.975 | 0.952 | 0.878 | 0.966 | 3.489 | 0.995 | 0.857 | 0.939 | 0.994 |
| | APPAU-Net-KLTV | **0.758** | 0.000 | 0.860 | **0.976** | 0.953 | 0.885 | 0.966 | **3.351** | 0.975 | 0.904 | 0.958 | 0.975 |
| SCX | APPAU-Net-TV | 0.477 | 0.580 | 0.300 | 0.883 | 0.790 | 0.713 | 0.877 | 6.601 | 0.999 | 0.162 | 0.782 | 0.992 |
| | APPAU-Net-XETV | **0.553** | 0.670 | 0.290 | 0.889 | 0.800 | 0.720 | 0.882 | 6.372 | 0.997 | 0.205 | 0.791 | 0.997 |
| | APPAU-Net-KLTV | 0.508 | 0.530 | 0.490 | **0.921** | 0.853 | 0.746 | 0.910 | **4.368** | 0.992 | 0.434 | 0.841 | 0.992 |
| CCX | APPAU-Net-TV | **0.776** | 0.800 | 0.780 | 0.874 | 0.777 | 0.682 | 0.845 | 5.375 | 0.936 | 0.576 | 0.770 | 0.959 |
| | APPAU-Net-XETV | 0.732 | 0.81 | 0.70 | 0.923 | 0.862 | 0.768 | 0.890 | 4.692 | 0.974 | 0.632 | 0.823 | 0.954 |
| | APPAU-Net-KLTV | 0.750 | 0.770 | 0.750 | **0.926** | 0.863 | 0.780 | 0.903 | **4.669** | 0.979 | 0.645 | 0.838 | 0.953 |

accuracy, comparable to fully-supervised segmentation models in Table 1 and LF-segnet [2]. Figure 3 shows the segmented lungs by different models, confirming the superior performance of our APPAU-Net with KLTV loss compared to the TV loss.

## 4    Conclusions

Generative modeling provides unique advantages for learning from small labeled datasets. With adversarial training, we can perform multi-task learning to concurrently accomplish multiple objectives. We proposed and demonstrated in different settings the performance of a novel semi-supervised multi-task learning model for joint classification and segmentation from a limited number of labeled chest X-ray images. Our experimental results confirm that our APPAU-Net model even against the single-task learning of fully supervised models.

## References

1. Caruana, R.: Multitask learning: a knowledge-based source of inductive bias. In: International Conference on Machine Learning (1993)
2. Mittal, A., Hooda, R., Sofat, S.: LF-SegNet: a fully convolutional encoder-decoder network for segmenting lung fields from chest radiographs. WPC **101**, 511–529 (2018)
3. Zhu, W., Xiang, X., Tran, T.D., Hager, G.D., Xie, X.: Adversarial deep structured nets for mass segmentation from mammograms. In: ISBI (2018)
4. Chen, C., Dou, Q., et al.: Semantic-aware generative adversarial nets for unsupervised domain adaptation in chest X-ray segment. arXiv:1806.00600 (2018)
5. Dai, W., Dong, N., Wang, Z., Liang, X., Zhang, H., Xing, E.P.: SCAN: structure correcting adversarial network for organ segmentation in chest X-rays. In: Stoyanov, D., et al. (eds.) DLMIA/ML-CDS -2018. LNCS, vol. 11045, pp. 263–273. Springer, Cham (2018). https://doi.org/10.1007/978-3-030-00889-5_30

6. Madani, A., et al.: Semi-supervised learning with GANs for chest X-ray classification with ability of data domain adaptation. In: Proceedings of ISBI (2018)
7. Guan, Q., Huang, Y., et al.: Diagnose like a radiologist: attention guided convolutional net for thorax disease classification. arXiv:1801.09927 (2018)
8. Imran, A.A.Z., Terzopoulos, D.: Multi-adversarial variational autoencoder networks. arXiv preprint arXiv:1906.06430 (2019)
9. Rezaei, M., Yang, H., et al.: Multi-task generative adversarial network for handling imbalanced clinical data. CoRR (2018)
10. Girard, F., Kavalec, C., Cheriet, F.: Joint segmentation and classification of retinal arteries/veins from fundus images. AI Med. **94**, 96–109 (2019)
11. Mehta, S., Mercan, E., Bartlett, J., Weaver, D., Elmore, J.G., Shapiro, L.: Y-Net: joint segmentation and classification for diagnosis of breast biopsy images. In: Frangi, A.F., Schnabel, J.A., Davatzikos, C., Alberola-López, C., Fichtinger, G. (eds.) MICCAI 2018. LNCS, vol. 11071, pp. 893–901. Springer, Cham (2018). https://doi.org/10.1007/978-3-030-00934-2_99
12. Yang, X., Zeng, Z., Yeo, S.Y., et al.: A novel multi-task deep learning model for skin lesion segmentation and classification. arXiv:1703.01025 (2017)
13. Khosravan, N., Bagci, U.: Semi-supervised multi-task learning for lung cancer diagnosis. In: EMBC (2018)
14. Fu, H., Cheng, J., Xu, Y., et al.: Joint optic disc and cup segmentation based on multi-label deep network and polar transformation. IEEE TMI **37**, 1597–1605 (2018)
15. Imran, A.-A.-Z., Hatamizadeh, A., Ananth, S.P., Ding, X., Terzopoulos, D., Tajbakhsh, N.: Automatic segmentation of pulmonary lobes using a progressive dense V-network. In: Stoyanov, D., et al. (eds.) DLMIA/ML-CDS 2018. LNCS, vol. 11045, pp. 282–290. Springer, Cham (2018). https://doi.org/10.1007/978-3-030-00889-5_32
16. Oktay, O., Schlemper, J., Folgoc, L.L., et al.: Attention U-net: learning where to look for the pancreas. arXiv:1804.03999 (2018)
17. Jaeger, S., Candemir, S., et al.: Two public chest X-ray datasets for computer-aided screening of pulmonary diseases. Quant. Imaging Med. Surg. **4**, 475 (2014)
18. Shiraishi, J., Katsuragawa, S., et al.: Development of a digital image database for chest radiographs with and without a lung nodule. J. Roentgenol. **174**, 71–74 (2000)

# Novel Bi-directional Images Synthesis Based on WGAN-GP with GMM-Based Noise Generation

Wei Huang[1], Mingyuan Luo[1], Xi Liu[1], Peng Zhang[2], Huijun Ding[3], and Dong Ni[3(✉)]

[1] School of Information Engineering, Nanchang University, Nanchang, China
[2] School of Computer Science, Northwestern Polytechnical University, Xi'an, China
[3] Guangdong Provincial Key Laboratory of Biomedical Measurements and Ultrasound Imaging, School of Biomedical Engineering, Health Science Center, Shenzhen University, Shenzhen, China
nidong@szu.edu.cn

**Abstract.** A novel WGAN-GP-based model is proposed in this study to fulfill bi-directional synthesis of medical images for the first time. GMM-based noise generated from the Glow model is newly incorporated into the WGAN-GP-based model to better reflect the characteristics of heterogeneity commonly seen in medical images, which is beneficial to produce high-quality synthesized medical images. Both the conventional "down-sampling"-like synthesis and the more challenging "up-sampling"-like synthesis are realized through the newly introduced model, which is thoroughly evaluated with comparisons towards several popular deep learning-based models both qualitatively and quantitatively. The superiority of the new model is substantiated based on a series of rigorous experiments using a multi-modal MRI database composed of 355 real demented patients in this study, from the statistical perspective.

**Keywords:** Medical images synthesis · Generative adversarial network · Dementia diseases diagnosis

## 1 Introduction

It is widely acknowledged that, medical images synthesis receives more and more popularity in recent year because of the rapid development of deep learning techniques. Various imaging modalities, including T1/T2/DTI MRI image [1,2], PET images [3], cardiac ultrasound images [4], retinal images [5], etc., have been successfully synthesized via various deep learning models. Medical images synthesis is also widely known to be valuable, since adequate high-quality medical images data that may become challenging to be acquired through actual scanning (i.e., because of various reasons including high acquisition costs, patient concerns, etc.) can be produced, alternatively. Hence, the notorious problem of

© Springer Nature Switzerland AG 2019
H.-I. Suk et al. (Eds.): MLMI 2019, LNCS 11861, pp. 160–168, 2019.
https://doi.org/10.1007/978-3-030-32692-0_19

overfitting in the training of sophisticated deep learning models is likely to be largely alleviated and their generalization capabilities can be boosted, therein.

In this study, an important functional MRI modality in dementia diseases diagnosis, i.e., the arterial spin labeling (ASL) [6], is emphasized for the synthesis purpose. A novel WGAN-GP model with GMM-based noise generated by the Glow model (i.e., "WGAN-GP+Glow") is proposed for the first time to fulfill the above-mentioned synthesis task. It is widely acknowledged that, GAN (i.e., generative adversarial networks) [7] becomes quite popular in contemporary deep learning studies. The basic idea of GAN is to generate "pseudo-but-real" data through a generator and to differentiate the very synthesized data from real data through a discriminator. The quality of the synthesized data is regarded to be high, when the discriminator cannot fulfill its classification mission. Also, because neither the Jensen-Shannon divergence nor the Kullback-Leibler divergence mainly incorporated in the original GAN model can reasonably reflect the actual difference between distributions of synthesized data and real data, the Wasserstein distance is then incorporated to replace the above two conventional divergences, and related GAN derivatives (e.g., WGAN [8], WGAN-GP [9]) are proposed, therein. For WGAN-GP, it utilizes the gradient penalty to conveniently fulfill the well-known Lipschitz constraint for avoiding the vanishing gradient problem, which is more favored than WGAN in most recent studies. Therefore, WGAN-GP is also incorporated in the new "WGAN-GP+Glow" model of this study.

The problem of only adopting WGAN-GP for realizing medical images synthesis is that, the noise in the generator of WGAN-GP only follows a simple Gaussian distribution for producing synthesized images. It is quite challenging, as the characteristics of heterogeneity commonly seen in medical images cannot be simply reflected by only one Gaussian distribution. In this study, GMM-based (i.e., Gaussian mixture model) noise is generated using the Glow model [10], and the generated GMM-based noise is then fed into WGAN-GP to complete the new "WGAN-GP+Glow" model. Moreover, the new "WGAN-GP+Glow" model has been investigated for bi-directional synthesis between ASL images and structural MRI in this study. It is necessary to point out that, the spatial resolution of ASL images is often not as high as that of structural MRI. Hence, synthesizing ASL images from structural MRI is described as a "downsampling" process, while synthesizing structural MRI from ASL images is considered as an "upsampling" process, to the contrary. Generally speaking, the "upsampling" synthesis is more challenging than the conventional "downsampling" synthesis, since the input information is less. In this study, the superiority of the new "WGAN-GP+Glow" model will be comprehensively verified through both the conventional "downsampling" synthesis and the more challenging "upsampling" synthesis.

## 2    Methodology

In this section, technical details of the new "WGAN-GP+Glow" model for realizing bi-directional images synthesis are elaborated. In Subsect. 2.1, details about generating GMM-based noise via the Glow model are described. In Subsect. 2.2, bi-directional images synthesis via WGAN-GP with GMM-based noise is emphasized.

## 2.1   GMM-Based Noise Generation via the Glow Model

Given an image set $X$, $x \in X$ denotes one image following the probability distribution $P_X$. Also, provided the latent feature set of $X$ as $Z$, and $z \in Z$ represents the latent feature of image $x$ following the prior probability distribution $P_Z$. The formula of $P_X$ can be explicitly represented as Eq. 1.

$$P_X(x) = \int P_Z(z)P(x|z)dz \tag{1}$$

Meanwhile, a pair of bi-jection functions $(f, g) = \{f : X \to Z, g = f^{-1}\}$ can be defined (i.e., $-1$ indicates the inverse function). Suppose $P(x|z)$ follows the Dirac distribution $\delta(x - g(z))$, Eq. 2 can be obtained to reveal the fact that image $x$ can be reconstructed and represented based on the latent feature $z$.

$$\begin{cases} x = g(z) & \text{(i.e., } x \text{ reconstructed from } z) \\ z = f(x) & \text{(i.e., } z \text{ as the latent representation of } x) \end{cases} \tag{2}$$

Therefore, Eq. 1 can be re-written as Eq. 3, in which $\frac{\partial f(x)}{\partial x}$ denotes the Jacobian determinant of $x$ with respect to $f(x)$ (i.e., detailed derivations are omitted here).

$$P_X(x) = \int P_Z(z)\delta(x - g(z))dz = P_Z(f(x)) \left| det(\frac{\partial f(x)}{\partial x}) \right| \tag{3}$$

In order to avoid the potential underflow problem in Eq. 3, it needs to be revised via the logarithm form in Eq. 4.

$$logP_X(x) = logP_Z(f(x)) + log \left| det(\frac{\partial f(x)}{\partial x}) \right| \tag{4}$$

Furthermore, to obtain the optimal $f$, the classic idea of MLE (i.e., maximum likelihood estimation) can be incorporated based on $\mathbb{E}_{x \sim P_X}(logP_X(x))$ in Eq. 5.

$$\max_f \mathbb{E}_{x \sim P_X}(logP_X(x)) = \max_f \mathbb{E}_{x \sim P_X}(logP_Z(f(x)) + log \left| det(\frac{\partial f(x)}{\partial x}) \right|) \tag{5}$$

which suggests that the optimal $f$ needs to satisfy the invertible characteristics (i.e., bi-jective characteristics). Meanwhile, the Jacobian determinant in Eq. 5 is convenient to be calculated as well.

It is necessary to point out that, the majority of contemporary "flow-based" generative models, including Glow [10], NICE [11], RealNVP [12], etc., all represent $f$ by stacking multiple simple bi-jections. Therefore, within each individual bi-jection, the input $x$ can be decomposed into two parts: $x = [x_1, x_2]_{1 \times 1}$ (i.e.,

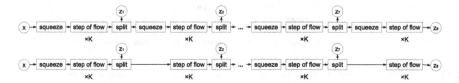

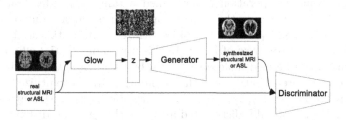

**Fig. 1.** Model structures of the original Glow (i.e., the top row) and the utilized Glow in the novel "WGAN-GP+Glow" model (i.e., the bottom row).

**Fig. 2.** The flowchart of the new "WGAN-GP+Glow" model to fulfill bi-directional synthesis between structural MRI and ASL images.

$[\cdot]_{1\times1}$ represents the concatenation operation after refreshing the order of elements in $x$ using the $1 \times 1$ convolution [10]). Equation 6 can be introduced, therein.

$$\begin{cases} y_1 = x_1 \\ y_2 = s(x_1) \bigotimes x_2 + t(x_1) \end{cases} \tag{6}$$

in which, $y = [y_1, y_2]$ indicates the output (i.e., $[\cdot]$ also denotes the concatenation operation); $s$ and $t$ stand for scaling and translation operations; $\bigotimes$ represents the element-wised multiplication. The Jacobian matrix of the affine transformation of $y$ can be represented via a triangular matrix in Eq. 7.

$$\left(\frac{\partial y}{\partial x}\right) = \left(\begin{matrix} \mathbb{I} & \mathbb{O} \\ \left(\frac{\partial s}{\partial x_1} \bigotimes x_2 + \frac{\partial t}{\partial x_1}\right) & s \end{matrix}\right) \tag{7}$$

Fortunately, the determinant of Eq. 7 can be simply represented as the product of elements in $s$. Therefore, a flow can be generated using multiple simple bijections $h_i$ that are successively connected as shown in Eq. 8.

$$x = h_0 \leftrightarrow h_1 \leftrightarrow h_2 \leftrightarrow \cdots \leftrightarrow h_{N-1} \leftrightarrow h_N = z \tag{8}$$

Hence, the logarithm form of the Jacobian determinant in Eq. 4 can be derived based on Eq. 8, whose outcome is described in Eq. 9.

$$\log\left|det(\frac{\partial z}{\partial x})\right| = \log\left|det(\frac{\partial h_n}{\partial h_0})\right| = \sum_{i=0}^{n-1} \log\left|det(\frac{\partial h(i+1)}{\partial h_i})\right| \tag{9}$$

For the model structure of the original Glow, it utilizes a flow of length $K$ as the main structure as illustrated on the left of Fig. 1. It is necessary to point

**Fig. 3.** Model structures of the discriminator (i.e., the top row) and the generator (i.e., the bottom row) in the new "WGAN-GP+Glow" model.

out that, the squeeze operation is performed within each individual block of the original Glow. However, the squeeze operation is carried out only within every other block (i.e., $Z_1, Z_3, Z_5, Z_7$) of the utilized Glow in this study, which is illustrated at the bottom row of Fig. 1. In this way, more spatial affinity can be retained within synthesized images generated by the revised Glow of this study.

Moreover, the latent feature $z$ of the final output from the utilized Glow can be concatenated as $z = [z_1, z_2, \cdots, z_8]$. Provided $P_{z_i}$ as the distribution that $z_i$ follows (i.e., $P_{z_i}$ is normally distributed and $z_i$ is the gaussian-distributed noise in this study), the distribution that $z$ follows should be the weighted sum of each $P_{z_i}$ that follows the GMM-based distribution. The above idea can be represented in Eq. 10 after adding a translation transformation to each individual $P_{z_i}$.

$$P_Z(z) = \sum_{i=1}^{K} \phi_i P_{z_i} \left( \begin{pmatrix} \mathbb{I} & d_i \\ \mathbb{O} & 1 \end{pmatrix} \begin{pmatrix} z_i \\ 1 \end{pmatrix} \right) \tag{10}$$

where, $K$ and $\phi_i$ are the number of Gaussian distributions and the normalized weight of $P_{z_i}$ (i.e., regarding $\sum_{i=1}^{K} \phi_i = 1$), respectively; $\begin{pmatrix} \mathbb{I} & d_i \\ \mathbb{O} & 1 \end{pmatrix}$ is the translation transformation matrix of $Z_i$.

### 2.2    WGAN-GP Images Synthesis with GMM-Based Noise via Glow

The flowchart of the new "WGAN-GP+Glow" model to fulfill bi-directional synthesis between structural MRI and ASL images in this study is illustrated in Fig. 2. To be specific, $Z$ represents the GMM-based noise generated by Glow, and it will then be fed into the generator of WGAN-GP during either way of the bi-directional synthesis. After that, the discriminator of WGAN-GP will try to differentiate the synthesized image from the corresponding real one. Moreover, detailed structures of the generator and the discriminator of WGAN-GP are displayed in Fig. 3, in which the number of neurons in each FC layer is annotated. It can be observed that, essential sub-structures of "FC+leakyReLu" are mainly adopted. The reason to incorporate the leaky ReLu function (i.e., $f(x) = \max(\alpha x, x)$, $\alpha \in [0, 1]$), rather than other activation functions is that, it is more effective in dealing with the "dying ReLu" problem that always outputs the same value for any input. For the generator, BN (i.e., batch normalization) is incorporated in each sub-structure of "FC+BN+leakyReLu", in order to avoid potential problems of vanishing/exploding gradients. Furthermore, it is also helpful to speed up the training of the whole new model.

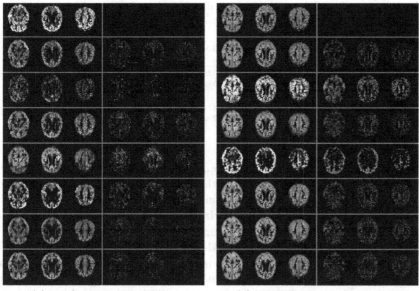

(a) synthesized ASL images        (b) synthesized structural MRI

**Fig. 4.** Synthesized images and corresponding difference images obtained by all compared models based on an example patient in this study. In each subplot, Rows 1: Golden standard (real images obtained via actual scanning), 2: WGAN-GP+Glow, 3: Glow, 4: WGAN-GP, 5: LSGAN, 6: CycleGAN, 7: ResNet-19, 8: CNN-7; Columns I: Real/Synthesized images, II: Corresponding difference images.

The objective function to be optimized in the training of the new "WGAN-GP+Glow" model can be described as Eq. 11.

$$\min_{G} \max_{D} \mathbb{E}_{z \sim \mathbb{P}_Z}[D(G(z))] - \mathbb{E}_{x \sim \mathbb{P}_R}[D(x)] + \gamma \mathbb{E}_{\hat{x} \sim \hat{\mathbb{P}}}[(\|\nabla_{\hat{x}} D(\hat{x})\|_2 - 1)^2] \quad (11)$$

in which, the 1st, 2nd and 3rd term of RHS (i.e., the right hand side) in Eq. 11 denote the generator's loss, the discriminator's loss, and the gradient penalty, respectively; $D$ and $G$ represent the discriminator and the generator, separately; $z$ denotes the noise following the GMM distribution $\mathbb{P}_z$; $x$ represents the target data following the data distribution $\mathbb{P}_R$; $\hat{x} = \epsilon x + (1 - \epsilon)G(z)$, in which $\epsilon$ is randomly chosen between $[0, 1]$; $\gamma$ is the weight of the gradient penalty. The training of the new "WGAN-GP+Glow" model is then carried out via the popular Adam optimization algorithm.

## 3   Experimental Analyses

The dataset of this study was constructed from an on-going demented population-based study. There are totally 355 real patients in this dataset, including 38 AD (i.e., Alzheimer's disease) patients, 185 MCI (i.e., mild cognitive

**Table 1.** Accuracies of dementia diseases diagnosis based on synthesized structural MRI or synthesized ASL images using diverse diagnosis tools.

| | WGAN-GP+Glow | Glow | WGAN-GP | LSGAN | CycleGAN | CNN-7 | ResNet-19 | Real |
|---|---|---|---|---|---|---|---|---|
| Synthesized structural MRI | 66.96% ± 4.98% | 63.35% ± 2.77% | 61.20% ± 2.72% | 62.02% ± 3.05% | 64.09% ± 3.99% | 64.01% ± 3.12% | 64.70% ± 2.79% | 68.65% ± 2.34% |
| Synthesized ASL | 65.75% ± 4.65% | 64.18% ± 5.79% | 64.85% ± 3.99% | 64.34% ± 3.62% | 63.21% ± 5.15% | 63.36% ± 3.94% | 64.04% ± 4.98% | 67.35% ± 1.39% |

impairments) patients, and 132 NCI (i.e., non-cognitive impairments) patients as normal controls. The average age of these patients is 70.56 ± 7.20 years old, and informed consents were obtained from all patients for conducting this study. High-resolution MPRAGE (i.e., magnetization prepared rapid acquisition gradient echo) T1-weighted MRI images were acquired as structural MRI using a SIEMENS 3T TIM Trio MR scanner. Meanwhile, the pseudo-continuous ASL scanning was applied for acquiring ASL images from each individual patient as well. Acquisition parameters mainly include: labeling duration = 1500 ms, postlabeling delay = 1500 ms, TR/TE = 4000/9.1 ms, ASL voxel size = $3 \times 3 \times 5$ mm$^3$, etc. Spatial resolutions of MRI images in this study are $64 \times 64 \times 21$. After obtaining raw MRI data, a series of pre-processes are essential to be applied, including motion correction, brain extraction (i.e., skull removal), intra-modality registration (i.e., using the first slice as the reference) separately within ASL and structural MRI images, inter-registration between ASL and structural MRI, etc. These pre-processes are realized by the well-known SPM toolbox.

A series of rigorous experiments are carried out in this study. Both qualitative and quantitative evaluations are fulfilled to reveal the superiority of the new model in bi-directional synthesis between ASL images and structural MRI. The new model has been compared with several popular GAN-based and non-GAN-based synthesis models, including Glow, WGAN-GP, LSGAN, CycleGAN, ResNet-19 and CNN-7. Figure 4 illustrates synthesized ASL/synthesized structural MRI images and their corresponding difference images. It is necessary to point out that, difference images are produced as the direct absolute difference between synthesized images and their golden standards that are real images obtained via actual scanning. It can be observed from Fig. 4 that, the ideal case belongs to Row 1 as there is no difference after subtracting the golden standard from itself. For Rows 2–8, it is clear that the new "WGAN-GP+Glow" model is capable to provide the least difference after comprehensively taking both synthesized ASL images and synthesized structural MRI outcomes into consideration.

Another more detailed quantitative experiment is carried out to differentiate progressions of dementia diseases (i.e., AD, MCI, and NCI) using synthesized ASL or synthesized structural MRI images obtained from all compared deep learning-based models. Five deep learning-based/shallow learning-based diagnosis tools are implemented and the diagnosis accuracy in Table 1 is calculated as the average based on all diagnosis outcomes obtained from the 5-fold cross validation. It can be summarized that, besides adopting real structural

MRI (i.e., 68.65% ± 2.34%) or real ASL images (i.e., 67.35% ± 1.39%), the new "WGAN-GP+Glow" model can provide the highest accuracies based on synthesized structural MRI (i.e., 66.96% ± 4.98%) or synthesized ASL images (i.e., 65.75% ± 4.65%), among all compared models. Hence, the superiority of synthesized structural MRI/ASL images via the new "WGAN-GP+Glow" model can be quantitatively substantiated based on the dementia diagnosis test from the statistical point of view.

## 4    Conclusions

In this study, a novel "WGAN-GP+Glow" model is proposed to realize bidirectional synthesis between structural MRI and ASL images for the first time. GMM-based noise generated from Glow is incorporated into WGAN-GP to better reflect the characteristics of heterogeneity, which is commonly seen in medical images. Both the conventional "down-sampling" synthesis (i.e., from structural MRI to ASL images) and the more challenging "up-sampling" synthesis (i.e., from ASL images to structural MRI) are realized through the new model, which is thoroughly evaluated with comprehensive comparisons towards several popular GAN-based and conventional non-GAN-based deep learning models, both qualitatively and quantitatively. The superiority of the new model can be suggested therein. Future efforts will be emphasized on investigating more sophisticated GAN models to enrich details of synthesis outcomes in medical images.

**Acknowledgements.** This work was jointly supported by the grant 61862043 approved by National Natural Science Foundation of China, and the key grant 20181ACB20006 approved by Natural Science Foundation of Jiangxi Province.

## References

1. Cordier, N., Delingette, H., Le, M., Ayache, N.: Extended modality propagation: image synthesis of pathological cases. IEEE-TMI **35**(12), 2598–2608 (2016)
2. Huang, Y., et al.: Cross-modality image synthesis via weakly coupled and geometry co-regularized joint dictionary learning. IEEE-TMI **37**(3), 815–827 (2018)
3. Polycarpou, I., et al.: Synthesis of realistic simultaneous positron emission tomography and magnetic resonance imaging data. IEEE-TMI **37**(3), 703–711 (2018)
4. Zhou, Y., Giffard-Roisin, S., De Craene, M., et al.: A framework for the generation of realistic synthetic cardiac ultrasound and magnetic resonance imaging sequences from the same virtual patients. IEEE-TMI **37**(3), 741–754 (2018)
5. Costa, P., Galdran, A., Meyer, M., et al.: End-to-end adversarial retinal image synthesis. IEEE-TMI **37**(3), 781–791 (2018)
6. Huang, W., et al.: Arterial spin labeling images synthesis from sMRI using unbalanced deep discriminant learning. IEEE-TMI (2019). https://doi.org/10.1109/TMI.2019.2906677
7. Goodfellow, I., Pouget-Abadie, J., Mirza, M., et al.: Generative adversarial networks. In: NIPS, Montreal, pp. 2672–2680 (2014)
8. Arjovsky, M., Chintala, S., Bottou, L.: Wasserstein GAN. arXiv arXiv:1701.07875 (2017)

9. Gulrajani, I., Ahmed, F., Arjovsky, M., Dumoulin, V., Courville, A.: Improved training of Wasserstein GANs. arXiv arXiv:1704.00028 (2017)
10. Kingma, D., Dhariwal, P.: Glow: generative flow with invertible 1x1 convolutions. In: NIPS, Vancouver, pp. 10236–10245 (2018)
11. Dinh, L., Krueger, D., Bengio, Y.: NICE: non-linear independent components estimation. In: ICLR, San Diego (2015)
12. Dinh, L., Sohl-Dickstein, J., Bengio, S.: Density estimation using Real NVP. In ICLR, Toulon (2017)

# Pseudo-labeled Bootstrapping and Multi-stage Transfer Learning for the Classification and Localization of Dysplasia in Barrett's Esophagus

Joost van der Putten[1][✉], Jeroen de Groof[2], Fons van der Sommen[1], Maarten Struyvenberg[2], Svitlana Zinger[1], Wouter Curvers[3], Erik Schoon[3], Jacques Bergman[2], and Peter H. N. de With[1]

[1] Eindhoven University of Technology, Eindhoven, The Netherlands
j.a.v.d.putten@tue.nl
[2] Amsterdam University Medical Center, Amsterdam, The Netherlands
[3] Catharina Hospital, Eindhoven, The Netherlands

**Abstract.** Patients suffering from Barrett's Esophagus (BE) are at an increased risk of developing esophageal adenocarcinoma and early detection is crucial for a good prognosis. To aid the endoscopists with the early detection for this preliminary stage of esophageal cancer, this work concentrates on improving the state of the art for the computer-aided classification and localization of dysplastic lesions in BE. To this end, we employ a large-scale endoscopic data set, consisting of $494,355$ images, to pre-train several instances of the proposed GastroNet architecture, after which several data sets that are increasingly closer to the target domain are used in a multi-stage transfer learning strategy. Finally, ensembling is used to evaluate the results on a prospectively gathered external test set. Results from the performed experiments show that the proposed model improves on the state-of-the-art on all measured metrics. More specifically, compared to the best performing state-of-the-art model, the specificity is improved by more than 20% while preserving sensitivity at a high level, thereby reducing the false positive rate substantially. Our algorithm also significantly outperforms state-of-the-art on the localization metrics, where the intersection of all experts is correctly indicated in approximately 92% of the cases.

**Keywords:** Convolutional neural network · Semi-supervised learning · Transfer learning · Barrett's Esophagus

## 1 Introduction

Patients suffering from Barrett's Esophagus (BE) are at an increased risk of developing dysplasia and, consequently, Esophageal AdenoCarcinoma (EAC). For this reason, BE patients regularly undergo endoscopic surveillance, and

© Springer Nature Switzerland AG 2019
H.-I. Suk et al. (Eds.): MLMI 2019, LNCS 11861, pp. 169–177, 2019.
https://doi.org/10.1007/978-3-030-32692-0_20

four-quadrant biopsies are taken at 2-cm intervals for subsequent histopathological examination. However, endoscopic detection of early neoplastic lesions or high-grade dysplasia is rather difficult, since the appearance of these lesions are often quite subtle. Moreover, progression to early neoplasia in BE is rare and surveillance endoscopies are usually performed in community hospitals. For these reasons, general endoscopists are only infrequently exposed to these types of lesions and are thus unfamiliar with their endoscopic appearance [1]. As a result, early neoplastic lesions are easily missed by non-expert endoscopists. Recently, *Computer Aided Detection* (CAD) has increasingly become a field of interest in endoscopy [6]. It has the potential to improve endoscopic practice by assisting general endoscopists with locating dysplastic lesions in BE at an early stage, for which local endoscopic treatment is still an option.

Recent work by De Groof *et al.* [5], improved on earlier work with a clinically inspired approach, using BE-specific Gabor and color features. Van der Putten *et al.* [10], and Ebigbo *et al.* [4] both employ a patch-based approach for the detection and localization of dysplasia in BE using deep learning. While these methods show great promise for automated lesion detection in Barrett's Esophagus, all above-mentioned studies lack an external test set and work with a limited sample size. In this paper, a prospectively gathered external test set is employed to compare the performance of our deep learning model with current state-of-the-art algorithms.

Training large neural networks from scratch generally requires many samples. Unfortunately, obtaining a large quantity of high-quality labeled BE data is difficult, due to a number of reasons: (1) the relative rarity of dysplasia in BE and (2) high cost and strict privacy laws associated with labeling medical images. A very popular method to overcome this problem is the use of transfer learning. Using pre-trained networks has shown improved performance for many computer vision problems, particularly when small data sets are involved [9]. While transfer learning leads to increased performance in many cases, natural images are used because obtaining a large labeled data set is easier in that domain. In this work, we propose to use an endoscopy data set that has a number of images in the same order of magnitude as ImageNet, but is much closer to the target domain compared to natural images. As a tradeoff, only a small amount of images have labels which requires the use of a semi-supervised learning approach, in order to produce a network with sufficiently diverse and relevant features.

The contribution of our work is threefold: (1) we improve on state-of-the-art results on an external prospectively gathered test set. The results are compared to both deep learning state-of-the-art for dysplasia detection in BE, as well as a traditional machine learning approach, showing a much higher specificity in combination with a high sensitivity. (2) Pseudo-labeled bootstrapping Ensemble (PLBE) is proposed as a novel method to generate multiple relevant and diverse pre-trained networks, which are used to create an ensemble of models to improve model performance from a large set of unsupervised data. (3) We propose GastroNet, a multi-task learning architecture, pre-trained on nearly half a million endoscopic samples, capable of seamlessly incorporating image class labels in addition to expert delineations, to train a classification/localization algorithm.

# 2    Methods

## 2.1    Data Sets

In this work, we employ 4 separate data sets. (1) The pre-training set contains $494,355$ endoscopic images of a wide variety of gastro-intestinal organs. From this set, $3,743$ of the images were labeled by gastro-intestinal experts into: colon (n = 679), duodenum (n = 339), stomach (n = 876), esophasus (n = 1,305) or other (n = 544). This set is used for pre-training with the PLB algorithm, as described in Sect. 2.4. (2) The training set consists of *retrospectively* collected White Light Endoscopy (WLE) overview images of Barrett's neoplasia (n = 690) and non-dysplastic BE (NDBE; n = 557) with coarse annotations. (3) The fine-tuning set consists of *prospectively* collected overview images of Barrett neoplasia (n = 129) and NDBE (n = 168). (4) The test set consists of 40 *prospectively* collected WLE overview images of Barrett neoplasia and 40 WLE NDBE images from 80 patient not included in the other data sets. All NDBE images were reviewed by experts for absence of neoplasia. All neoplastic images were delineated by multiple experts, where the area with $\geq 1$ expert delineation served as ground truth for training and validation. The first 3 sets are used in the multi-stage transfer learning methodology described in Sect. 2.3.

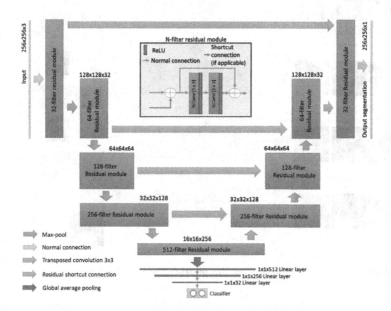

**Fig. 1.** Block diagram of the GastroNet architecture

## 2.2    GastroNet

In order to train a model with both segmentations and image labels, we propose GastroNet. The model is similar to the standard U-net model with some key differences. (1) The skip connections are made fully residual instead of concatenations like in the standard U-Net model, which reduces the number of trainable parameters in the decoder. (2) A fully connected feature layer and a classification layer are added at the bridge of the encoder-decoder network. This allows multi-task learning to calculate a classification loss in addition to a segmentation loss from the learned low-dimensional features in the U-net bridge. The dual classification/segmentation-loss approach enables the use of the expert segmentation masks for directly training a classification algorithm instead of training separate classification and segmentation networks, or classifying separate patches of the original image [4,10]. Additionally, this approach allows for pre-training with a larger similar data set without ground-truth segmentations prior to employing a transfer learning strategy on a smaller data set with expert delineations. A block diagram of the network architecture is shown in Fig. 1.

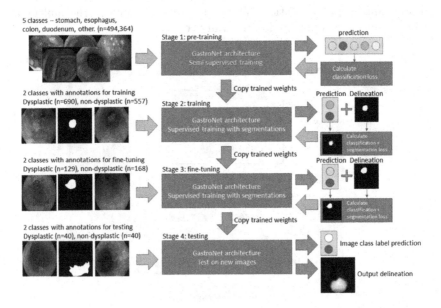

**Fig. 2.** Schematic overview of the multi-stage transfer learning process.

## 2.3    Multi-stage Transfer Learning

Recently, transfer learning techniques have been applied successfully in many real-world applications [9]. Transfer learning is particularly effective in domains where image and ground-truth acquisition is expensive, *e.g.* cancer detection.

Many image classification algorithms that use transfer learning employ a network pre-trained on the ImageNet data set as a starting point for training [12]. Using weights pre-trained with natural images such as those in the ImageNet data set, leads to better results compared to training from scratch with small data sets. However, the main reason for using the natural image domain is accessability and inexpensive labeling and not because pre-training with natural images is optimal. It is a likely assumption that data sets which are closely related to the target domain are preferred for transfer learning when the order of magnitude of images is comparable. In this work, a large pre-training set with endoscopic images (Sect. 2.1) is employed as an alternative to ImageNet. Since the images in the pre-training data set are much more representative of the target domain (test set), the learned features are likely to be more representative for both domains.

To further fine-tune the final algorithm, we employ two additional data sets (training set, fine-tuning set). Both data sets contain WLE overview images of Barrett's neoplasia as well as non-dysplastic BE. However, the data is captured with different brands of endoscopes and the training data set contains more retrospectively collected images with coarser annotations compared to the fine-tuning set, which is more finely delineated and collected prospectively. After pre-training with the first set, the algorithm is first further refined with the training set and subsequently with the fine-tuning data set. With each step, the total training time and learning rate is reduced (see Sect. 2.5), since the network parameters get closer to the target domain with each step. An overview of the multi-stage transfer learning methodology is shown in Fig. 2.

### 2.4 Pseudo-labeled Bootstrapping Ensemble

Most images in the pre-training data set have no label. From the $498,107$ endoscopic images, only $3,743$ are labelled. In order to obtain descriptive features suitable for transfer learning with a small amount of labels, we propose a new semi-supervised learning approach. Pseudo-Labeled Bootstrap Ensembling (PLBE) is a combination of the original pseudo-labeling algorithm [7] and bootstrapping [8] to create a diverse ensemble of models. *Ensembling* is an effective way to increase model performance both for problems with little data [3] as well as complex problems with a large amount of images such as the ILSVRC ImageNet challenge, where an ensemble of models won the challenge in 2017. Ensembles are particularly effective when the used models are diverse [2]. This diversity concept is also one of the reasons why Random Forests have been so successful in the past.

In this work, we propose to leverage the size of the pre-training set by splitting the data in multiple subsets to obtain a diverse ensemble of models. The key to this solution is that we obtain a variety of initializations, correlated to the target domain. The hypothesis is that the aggregated predictions of the individual models outperform a single pre-trained network. The proposed pseudo-labeled bootstrap ensemble is implemented as follows:

**Table 1.** Results of the performed experiments. For the localization metrics, only true positive samples were evaluated.

| | Accuracy | Sensitivity | Specificity | Sos Flag | Sws Flag |
|---|---|---|---|---|---|
| Van der Sommen *et al.* [5] | $76.2_{(61/80)}$ | $92.5_{(37/40)}$ | $60.0_{(24/40)}$ | $89.2_{(33/37)}$ | $73.0_{(27/37)}$ |
| Ebigbo *et al.* [4] | $68.8_{(55/80)}$ | $77.5_{(31/40)}$ | $60.0_{(24/40)}$ | $64.5_{(20/31)}$ | $22.3_{(7/31)}$ |
| Ours (no pre-training) | $62.5_{(50/80)}$ | $60.0_{(24/40)}$ | $65.0_{(26/40)}$ | $79.2_{(19/24)}$ | $66.7_{(16/24)}$ |
| Ours (no ensemble) | $81.2_{(65/80)}$ | $87.5_{(35/40)}$ | $75.0_{(30/40)}$ | $91.4_{(32/35)}$ | $80.0_{(28/35)}$ |
| Ours (with ensemble) | $\mathbf{87.5}_{(70/80)}$ | $\mathbf{92.5}_{(37/40)}$ | $\mathbf{82.5}_{(33/40)}$ | $\mathbf{97.3}_{(36/37)}$ | $\mathbf{91.9}_{(34/37)}$ |

1. Create a base classification model from supervised samples.
2. Predict pseudo labels of the entire data set.
3. Train on all supervised + pseudo-labeled samples until convergence.
4. Take $N$ random subsets of entire pre-training set and take a percentage $p$ of the samples with the highest class probabilities.
5. Retrain $N$ models with the different pseudo-labeled subsets + labeled samples, until convergence.

This approach results in $N$ models which have all been trained with the entire pre-training data set. However, each model is still diverse as a different subset of all the data of the pre-training set is subsequently used to fine-tune the models. In our experiments, we chose $N = 5$ where each subset consisted of $50,000$ randomly selected samples from the unlabeled images and percentage $p = 10\%$. After obtaining 5 diverse models, the multi-stage transfer learning approach, described in Sect. 2.3, is employed for each of these models, resulting in 5 test predictions. The development of the PLBE algorithm is still ongoing and further experiments and comparisons about the performance are outside the scope of this paper.

## 2.5 Training Details

The algorithm was trained using Adam and AMS-grad with a weight decay of $10^{-5}$. A cyclic cosine learning-rate scheduler [11] was used to control the learning rate. Binary cross-entropy and Dice loss were used for the classification and segmentation loss, respectively. Additionally, batch normalization was used to regularize the network. The model was further regularized with data augmentation. Images were randomly rotated with $\theta \in \{0, 90, 180, 270\}$ degrees and randomly flipped along the $x$- and $y$-axis with probability 0.5. Additionally, random permutations were made to the color, contrast and brightness of the images. Furthermore, images were randomly sheared by up to $8°$ and randomly translated by up to $10\%$ of image width. Lastly, during training with the pre-training and training data sets, random crops of various sizes were taken from the original images without resizing, to preserve consistency in feature size.

# 3   Results

The results from the performed experiments for the task of Barrett's cancer classification on the prospective test set are shown in Table 1. The employed classification metrics are defined by the standard definitions for a binary classification problem, where a positive sample indicates dysplasia. The localization metrics were first introduced in [5], where *Sos Flag* and *Sws Flag* are the percentage of true positive images where the region with the highest score in the predicted segmentation touches the union and intersection of all experts, respectively. The first two rows of reported results were obtained by implementing the algorithms by Van der Sommen *et al.* and Ebigo *et al.*. The third row contains results for our architecture without pre-training and ensembling. For these three algorithms, the *Fine-tuning* set was used to train the algorithms and the *test* set was subsequently applied to generate the scores. Standard algorithm settings were employed.

While the sensitivity of the handcrafted feature approach by Van der Sommen *et al.* is comparable to our best model, the specificity and localization metrics are significantly lower. The deep learning approach by Ebigbo *et al.* was not able to generalize to this data set and performed considerably worse, even compared to a handcrafted feature approach. Our experiment where no pre-training or ensembling was used (row three) was also unable to effectively classify the test images into the proper category. However, by applying the proposed PLBE algorithm, fine-tuning, and ensembling, the classification and localization performance is drastically improved by more than 10% when compared to state-of-the-art.

# 4   Discussion and Conclusion

Visual detection of early neoplastic lesions or high-grade dysplasia is difficult in patients suffering from Barrett's Esophagus. This leads to many early-stage cancers going unnoticed during endoscopic inspection, thereby greatly affecting the life expectancy of patients. For this reason, a CAD algorithm which assists general endoscopists with locating dysplastic lesions on time is crucial. To this end, we propose a multi-stage deep learning approach which leverages a large related data set to create a diverse ensemble of models capable of classifying and localizing dysplasia in Barrett's Esophagus images with high accuracy.

The proposed algorithm significantly outperforms state-of-the-art deep learning as well as a handcrafted feature approach on all metrics. The handcrafted feature approach by Van der Sommen *et al.* generalizes well to the test set employed in this study, since the reported results are similar to the scores reported in their work [5]. In contrast, the algorithm by Ebigbo *et al.* fails to generalize to this data set. This could be caused by several factors: (1) The used network architecture is significantly larger (ResNet101) compared to our network (Similar in size to ResNet18). Larger networks are harder to train, especially when there is a limited amount of data. (2) Ebigbo *et al.* use a patch-based approach (224×224), however, the resolution of the images in this data set is smaller, which may negatively effect their scores. Additionally, the class of the extracted patch can be difficult to establish in ambiguous regions. (3) The reported results [4] were optimized by setting the dysplasia decision threshold based on the test set, which may have led to overfitting on their data. This suspicion is reinforced as Ebigbo *et al.* set different thresholds for different experiments. (4) This work employs an external test set to evaluate the results instead of cross-fold validation.

The results of our experiments show that the multi-stage transfer learning strategy in combination with ensembling leads to a better classifier for the detection of dysplasia. As of now, only the pseudo-labeled bootstrapping method has been used to pre-train the GastroNet architecture. However, a variety of unsupervised and semi-supervised learning algorithms have been proposed in the literature. In future work, a larger variety of algorithms will be evaluated to find a mapping from endoscopic images to an "endoscopy feature space" best suited for classification and segmentation in a variety of endoscopic data sets.

In this paper, we have proposed a method for the classification and localization of dysplastic lesions in Barrett's Esophagus. We employ a large-scale endoscopic data set, consisting of 494, 355 images, to pre-train several instances of the GastroNet architecture, subsequently, multi-stage transfer learning and ensembling is used to evaluate the results on an external test set. We compare our results against state-of-the-art algorithms and report a significant increase in performance on all measured metrics. More specifically, compared to the best performing state-of-the-art model, the specificity is improved by more than 20% points with equal sensitivity, thereby reducing the false positive rate significantly. Our algorithm also significantly outperforms state-of-the-art on the localization metrics, where the intersection of expert predictions is correctly indicated in approximately 92% of the cases.

# References

1. Boerwinkel, D.F., Swager, A.F., Curvers, W.L., et al.: The clinical consequences of advanced imaging techniques in Barrett's esophagus. Gastroenterology **146**(3), 622–629 (2014)
2. Brown, G., Wyatt, J., Harris, R., et al.: Diversity creation methods: a survey and categorisation. Inf. Fusion **6**(1), 5–20 (2005)
3. Dietterich, T.G.: Ensemble methods in machine learning. In: Kittler, J., Roli, F. (eds.) MCS 2000. LNCS, vol. 1857, pp. 1–15. Springer, Heidelberg (2000). https://doi.org/10.1007/3-540-45014-9_1
4. Ebigbo, A., Mendel, R., Probst, A., et al.: Computer-aided diagnosis using deep learning in the evaluation of oesophageal adenocarcinoma. Gut **68**, 1143–1145 (2018). p. gutjnl
5. de Groof, J., van der Sommen, F., van der Putten, J., et al.: The Argos project: the development of a computer-aided detection system to improve detection of Barrett's neoplasia on white light endoscopy. UEGJ
6. Iakovidis, D.K., Maroulis, D.E., Karkanis, S.A.: An intelligent system for automatic detection of gastrointestinal adenomas in video endoscopy. Comput. Biol. Med. **36**(10), 1084–1103 (2006)

7. Lee, D.H.: Pseudo-label: the simple and efficient semi-supervised learning method for deep neural networks. In: Workshop on Challenges in Representation Learning, ICML, vol. 3, p. 2 (2013)

8. Mooney, C.Z., Duval, R.D., Duvall, R.: Bootstrapping: A Nonparametric Approach to Statistical Inference. Sage, Thousand Oaks (1993). No. 94–95

9. Pan, S.J., Yang, Q., et al.: A survey on transfer learning. IEEE Trans. Knowl. Data Eng. **22**(10), 1345–1359 (2010)

10. van der Putten, J., Wildebour, R., de Groof, J., et al.: Deep learning biopsy marking of early neoplasia in Barrett's esophagus by combining WLE and BLI modalities. In: Biomedical Imaging (ISBI 2019). IEEE (2019)

11. Smith, L.N.: Cyclical learning rates for training neural networks. In: 2017 IEEE Winter Conference on Applications of Computer Vision, pp. 464–472. IEEE (2017)

12. Urban, G., Tripathi, P., Alkayali, T., et al.: Deep learning localizes and identifies polyps in real time with 96% accuracy in screening colonoscopy. Gastroenterology **155**, 1069–1078 (2018)

# Anatomy-Aware Self-supervised Fetal MRI Synthesis from Unpaired Ultrasound Images

Jianbo Jiao[1]([✉]), Ana I. L. Namburete[1], Aris T. Papageorghiou[2], and J. Alison Noble[1]

[1] Department of Engineering Science, University of Oxford, Oxford, UK
jianbo.jiao@eng.ox.ac.uk
[2] Nuffield Department of Women's and Reproductive Health, University of Oxford, Oxford, UK

**Abstract.** Fetal brain magnetic resonance imaging (MRI) offers exquisite images of the developing brain but is not suitable for anomaly screening. For this ultrasound (US) is employed. While expert sonographers are adept at reading US images, MR images are much easier for non-experts to interpret. Hence in this paper we seek to produce images with MRI-like appearance directly from clinical US images. Our own clinical motivation is to seek a way to communicate US findings to patients or clinical professionals unfamiliar with US, but in medical image analysis such a capability is potentially useful, for instance, for US-MRI registration or fusion. Our model is self-supervised and end-to-end trainable. Specifically, based on an assumption that the US and MRI data share a similar anatomical latent space, we first utilise an extractor to determine shared latent features, which are then used for data synthesis. Since paired data was unavailable for our study (and rare in practice), we propose to enforce the distributions to be similar instead of employing pixel-wise constraints, by adversarial learning in both the image domain and latent space. Furthermore, we propose an adversarial structural constraint to regularise the anatomical structures between the two modalities during the synthesis. A cross-modal attention scheme is proposed to leverage non-local spatial correlations. The feasibility of the approach to produce realistic looking MR images is demonstrated quantitatively and with a qualitative evaluation compared to real fetal MR images.

## 1 Introduction

Ultrasound (US) imaging is widely employed in image-based diagnosis, as it is portable, real-time, and safe for body tissue. Obstetric US is the most commonly used clinical imaging technique to monitor fetal development. Clinicians use fetal brain US imaging (fetal neurosonography) to detect abnormalities in the fetal brain and growth restriction. However, fetal neurosonography suffers from acoustic shadows and occlusions caused by the fetal skull. MRI is unaffected

© Springer Nature Switzerland AG 2019
H.-I. Suk et al. (Eds.): MLMI 2019, LNCS 11861, pp. 178–186, 2019.
https://doi.org/10.1007/978-3-030-32692-0_21

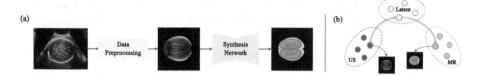

**Fig. 1.** (a) Overview of the proposed framework. Images from left to right: original US, pre-processed US, and the synthesised MR; (b) assumption of the shared latent space. (Color figure online)

by the presence of bone and typically provides good and more complete spatial detail of the full anatomy [13]. On the other hand, MRI is time-consuming and costly, making it unsuitable for fetal anomaly screening, but it is often used for routine fetal brain imaging in the second and third trimester [2]. Therefore, we seek to generate MR images of fetal brains directly from clinical US images.

Medical image synthesis has received growing interest in recent years. Most prior work has focused on the synthesis of MR/CT (computed tomography) images [11,17,19] or retinal images [4]. Some works simulate US for image alignment [8,9]. Prior to the deep learning era, medical image synthesis was primarily based on segmentation and atlases. Taking MR-to-CT image synthesis as an example, in segmentation-based approaches [1,5], different tissue classes are segmented for the MR image, followed by an intensity-filling step to generate the corresponding CT image. Atlas-based methods [3,16] first register an MR atlas to the input MRI, and then apply the transformation to synthesise the corresponding CT image from a CT atlas. However, these methods highly depend on the accuracy of segmentation and registration. With the popularity of deep learning techniques, recent convolutional neural network (CNN) based methods have achieved promising results for image synthesis. Some works [11,14,19] have directly learned the mapping from MR to CT via a CNN architecture, assuming a large number of MR-CT data pairs. To overcome a paired data requirement, other approaches [17,18] have utilised a CycleGAN architecture [20] for image-to-image translation. Although they do not need perfectly registered data, previous methods have either needed weakly paired data (from the same subject) or supervision from other auxiliary tasks (segmentation). In addition, the aforementioned works do not consider synthesis from US images, which is much more challenging than anatomical imaging (CT/MR) due to its more complex image formation process.

In this paper, we propose an anatomy-aware framework for US-to-MR image synthesis. An overview of the proposed framework is shown in Fig. 1. Based on an assumption that US and MR modalities share a common latent representation, we design an anatomically constrained learning approach to model the mapping from US to MR images, that is achieved via an adversarial learning architecture. To the best of our knowledge, this is the first attempt to synthesise MR images from unpaired US images in a self-supervised manner. The proposed method is evaluated both qualitatively and quantitatively, which demonstrate that, even with highly-imbalanced data, neurologically-realistic images can be achieved.

## 2    Method

Given a fetal neurosonography image, our work aims to generate the corresponding MRI-like image. In this section, we present the proposed framework for US-to-MR image synthesis. Specifically, the US image is first pre-processed [10] to provide spatially normalised data. Then we employ an original data-driven learning-based approach to synthesise the corresponding MR image from the US input. The design of the proposed anatomy-aware synthesis framework is shown in Fig. 2. Given a source US image, the corresponding MR image is synthesised with reference to the real MR image domain. As our available US and MR data is unpaired, constraints on both pixel-level (*rec. loss*) and feature-level (*dis. loss*) are proposed to ensure anatomical consistency during the synthesis. Referring to Fig. 2 during inference/test, only blocks A, B, C and Attention are used. Next, we describe the key steps in the proposed framework in detail.

### 2.1    Anatomy-Aware Synthesis

Paired fetal brain US and MR data is uncommon in clinical practice, and in our case was not available. Therefore, directly learning the mapping from US to MR using conventional deep learning based methods is not applicable to our task. As a result, we propose to model the task as a synthesis framework by enforcing the synthesised MR images to lie in a similar data distribution to real MR images. However, a valid and important constraint is that clinically important anatomical structures should be correctly mapped between the two modalities. Thus we specifically design anatomy-aware constraints to guarantee that the synthesis process is anatomically consistent.

**Anatomical Feature Extraction:** It is rare to have clinical MR and US of the same fetus at the same gestational age, and even if available, the data is not simultaneously co-registered as has often been assumed in other medical image analysis work [11,19]. This makes the modelling of the mapping quite difficult. Without the availability of paired data, we assume the US and MR images share a similar anatomical latent space (Fig. 1(b)). Based on this assumption, we propose to extract the underlying anatomical features and synthesise the corresponding MR domain data from it, instead of from the original image domain. Specifically, we utilise an autoencoder (encoder-A → decoder-B) to extract the latent features, as shown in the bottom-left part of the framework (Fig. 2). Assume $\{x_U^i\}_{i=1}^n$ the set of $n$ original US images where $x_U^i \in \mathcal{X}_U$ is the $i^{th}$ image, the extracted anatomical feature $y^i$ can be formulated as $y^i = F(x_U^i)$ where $F()$ is the extractor.

**Bi-directional Latent Space Consistency:** The extracted anatomical features are fed into a decoder-C to generate a synthesised MR image. Since there is

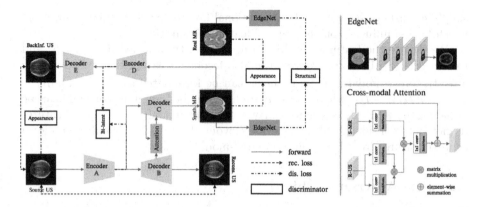

**Fig. 2.** Architecture of the proposed anatomy-aware synthesis framework (the blue block in Fig. 1(a)). Detailed structures of the *Cross-modal Attention* and *EdgeNet* modules are shown on the right side. The locker symbol indicates a frozen layer. (Color figure online)

no pixel-level supervision available for *Synth. MR*, we propose to add a backward-inference path (encoder-D → decoder-E) in the reverse direction that reconstructs the original US image. At the end of the encoder for this reverse path, the encoded feature in the latent space can be extracted. Denoting this encoded feature as $y_b^i$, we propose a bi-directional latent space consistency constraint, based on the anatomical-feature-sharing assumption. This constraint enforces $y^i$ and $y_b^i$ to be similar in latent feature distribution, by a discriminator (*Bi-latent* block in Fig. 2) accompanied with adversarial learning.

**Structural Consistency:** The anatomical feature extraction module encodes the main structure of the US image. However, for the MR domain data the image structure is quite different in appearance than in the US domain. To synthesise realistic MR images, we propose to constrain the structures of the *Synth. MR* and the *Real MR* to be similar. Due to the unpaired nature of our task, we enforce the structures to lie in a similar distribution. Specifically, we extract the edges of the *Synth. MR* and *Real MR* by an EdgeNet and measure edge similarity by a structural discriminator (*Structural* block in Fig. 2). The detailed structure of the EdgeNet is illustrated in Fig. 2 top-right, which consists of four $3 \times 3$ convolutional layers with parameters fixed.

### 2.2    Cross-Modal Attention

As described to this point, MR image synthesis is mainly guided by the latent features $y^i$ from the end of encoder-A. To provide cross-modal guidance, we propose a cross-modal attention scheme between the US decoder-B and the MR decoder-C, shown as the *Attention* (red) block in Fig. 2. To this end, the US features are reformulated as self-attention guidance for MR image generation, and the guidance is implicitly provided at the feature level. This attention scheme simply consists of several $1 \times 1$ convolutional layers with a residual connection, which has no influence on the original feature dimension.

We denote the features (R-US in Fig. 2) from the US decoder-B as $f_U$ and the features (S-MR in Fig. 2) from the MR decoder-C as $f_M$, the revised feature after the cross-modal attention scheme can be formulated as: $\widetilde{f}_M = \eta(\delta(f_U)^T \cdot \phi(f_U) \cdot g(f_M)) + f_M$, where $\eta, \delta, \phi, g$ are linear embedding functions and can be implemented by $1 \times 1$ convolutions. By using cross-modal attention, the features do not only consider local information (favoured by CNNs) but also non-local context features from both self- and cross-modal guidance.

## 2.3   Joint Adversarial Objective

Here we formally define the objective functions for model training. As mentioned before and illustrated in Fig. 2, there are two objectives: a pixel-level reconstruction objective and a distribution similarity objective. The pixel-level reconstruction is achieved by an L1-norm, while the distribution similarity is achieved by the discriminator in adversarial learning [7].

For the forward direction (US-to-MR), we denote the reconstructed US as $\hat{x}_U \in \hat{\mathcal{X}}_U$, the latent feature as $y \in \mathcal{Y}$, the synthesised MR and real MR as $\hat{x}_M \in \hat{\mathcal{X}}_M$ and $x_M \in \mathcal{X}_M$ respectively. The forward objective is defined as:

$$\{\min \mathcal{L}_f \mid \mathcal{L}_f = \lambda \mathcal{L}_{lat} + \mathcal{L}_{app} + \mathcal{L}_{stru}\}, \tag{1}$$

$$\mathcal{L}_{lat} = \mathbb{E}_{x_U \in \mathcal{X}_U} \|G_U(F(x_U)) - x_U\|_1, \tag{2}$$

$$\mathcal{L}_{app} = \mathbb{E}_{x_M \in \mathcal{X}_M}(D_{app}(x_M)) + \mathbb{E}_{y \in \mathcal{Y}} \log(1 - D_{app}(G_M(y))), \tag{3}$$

$$\mathcal{L}_{stru} = \mathbb{E}_{x_M \in \mathcal{X}_M}(D_{stru}(E(x_M))) + \mathbb{E}_{y \in \mathcal{Y}} \log(1 - D_{app}(E(G_M(y)))). \tag{4}$$

Here $G_U$ is the decoder-B used to generate the reconstructed US, $G_M$ is the decoder-C to synthesise the MR, and $\hat{x}_U = G_U(F(x_U))$, $\hat{x}_M = G_M(y)$. $D_{app}$ and $D_{stru}$ are the discriminators (by four *conv* layers) to measure appearance and structure similarity respectively. $E$ represents the EdgeNet. $\lambda$ is a weighting parameter to balance the objective terms and is empirically set to 10.

For the reverse (backward-inference) path, the back-inferred US from the *Synth. MR* is denoted as $\widetilde{x}_U \in \widetilde{\mathcal{X}}_U$ and the back-inferred feature at the end of encoder-D as $y^{back} \in \mathcal{Y}^{back}$, the reverse objective is defined as:

$$\{\min \mathcal{L}_r \mid \mathcal{L}_r = \lambda \mathcal{L}_{proj} + \mathcal{L}_{app}^{back} + \mathcal{L}_{bi}\}, \tag{5}$$

$$\mathcal{L}_{proj} = \mathbb{E}_{\widetilde{x}_U \in \widetilde{\mathcal{X}}_U, x_U \in \mathcal{X}_U} \|\widetilde{x}_U - x_U\|_1, \tag{6}$$

$$\mathcal{L}_{app}^{back} = \mathbb{E}_{x_U \in \mathcal{X}_U}(D_{app}^{back}(x_U)) + \mathbb{E}_{y^{back} \in \mathcal{Y}^{back}} \log(1 - D_{app}^{back}(G_{BU}(y^{back}))), \tag{7}$$

$$\mathcal{L}_{bi} = \mathbb{E}_{y \in \mathcal{Y}}(D_{bi}(y)) + \mathbb{E}_{y^{back} \in \mathcal{Y}^{back}} \log(1 - D_{bi}(y^{back})). \tag{8}$$

Here $G_{BU}$ is the decoder-E used to back project the US and $\tilde{x}_U = G_{BU}(y^{back})$. $D_{app}^{back}$ and $D_{bi}$ are the discriminators to measure the backward-inference similarity and bi-directional latent space similarity, respectively. Then the final training model loss based on the above joint adversarial objective functions is:

$$\mathcal{L} = \mathcal{L}_f + \mathcal{L}_r. \tag{9}$$

# 3 Experiments

## 3.1 Data and Implementation Details

We evaluated the proposed synthesis framework on a dataset consisting of healthy fetal brain US and MR volume data. The fetal US data was obtained from a multi-centre, ethnically diverse dataset [12] of 3D ultrasound scans collected from normal pregnancies. We obtained the MR data from the CRL fetal brain atlas [6] database and data scanned at Hammersmith hospital. As proof of principle, we selected US and MR data at the gestational age of 23 weeks. In total, we used 107 US volumes and 2 MR volumes, from which approximately 36,000 2D slices were extracted for US and 600 slices for MR. We used 80% of the total data as the training and validation set, and the remaining 20% for testing. Our model was implemented by simple *conv*, *up-conv*, and *max-pooling* layers. Skip connections were added between each encoder-decoder pair to preserve structural information. An Nvidia Titan V GPU was utilised for model training. The complete model was trained end-to-end. The testing phase only takes an US scan as input without any discriminators and the reverse path.

## 3.2 Evaluation Metrics

Since we are not using US-MR paired data, traditional evaluation metrics like PSNR (Peak Signal-to-Noise Ratio) and SSIM (Structural Similarity) cannot be applied. Therefore, we evaluated the quality of the synthesised MRI using two alternative metrics: (1) the Mean Opinion Score (MOS) and (2) a Jacobian-based registration metric. The MOS is expressed in a rating range between 1 and 5, in which 5 indicates *excellent* while 1 *bad*. The MOS test was performed by two groups (2 medical experts and 11 beginners) with 80 samples shown to each participant. For the registration-based objective score, we performed a deformable registration (FFD [15]) between the synthesised MR and the real MR at a similar imaging plane, and then computed the average Jacobian of the deformation (normalised to [0, 1]) required to achieve this. We assume a high-quality synthesised MRI will have a lower Jacobian for the registration.

## 3.3 Results

We present synthesised MR results and image synthesis quality evaluations. In the testing phase, all the discriminators were removed, leaving only the anatomical feature extractor and the synthesis decoder, which took the test US image as

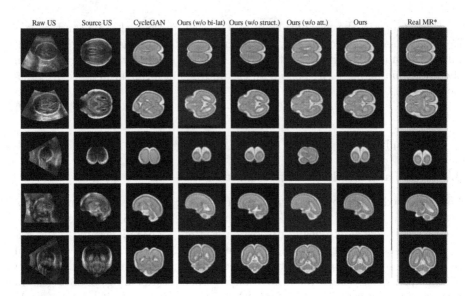

**Fig. 3.** Qualitative performance on the US-to-MR image synthesis. Each row shows an example sample. From left to right are the original raw US, pre-processed US, synthesised MR by CycleGAN [20] and Ours (with its counterparts), and the reference real MR. *Note that the last column is **NOT** the exact corresponding MR images.

**Table 1.** Quantitative evaluation on our synthesised MR images for MOS test (on both experts and beginners) and deformation score, with the comparison to several possible solutions. MOS the higher the better while deformation the lower the better.

| Method | | AE | GAN | CycleGAN | Ours (w/o bi-lat) | Ours (w/o struct.) | Ours (w/o att.) | Ours | Real |
|---|---|---|---|---|---|---|---|---|---|
| MOS↑ | Expert | 1.00 | 2.05 | 2.50 | 3.05 | 3.45 | 3.30 | **3.90** | 4.35 |
| | Beginner | 1.01 | 2.75 | 3.42 | 3.69 | 3.87 | 3.65 | **4.08** | 4.23 |
| Deformation↓ | | 0.97 | 0.78 | 0.66 | 0.55 | 0.65 | 0.47 | **0.46** | 0.00 |

input. Several synthesised MR results with the corresponding US input samples are shown in Fig. 3. Note that the last column shows a real MR example for comparison (**not** in direct correspondence to the synthesised one). From the results, we observe that the visual appearance of the synthetic MR images is very similar to the real ones, and is visually superior to the results from CycleGAN [20]. In addition, anatomical structures are well preserved between the source US and the synthetic MR image in each case.

Quantitative results are reported in Table 1. We compare our method with the vanilla autoencoder (*AE*), GAN [7], and CycleGAN [20]. We also performed an ablation study by removing the bi-directional latent consistency (*w/o bi-lat*) module, removing the structural consistency module (*w/o struct.*), or removing the cross-modal attention module (*w/o att.*). The results in Table 1 suggest that the proposed method performs better than the other possible solutions, and also supports the inclusion of each proposed term in our model.

# 4   Conclusion

In this paper, we have presented to our knowledge the first attempt to synthesise MRI-like fetal brain data from unpaired US data, by a new anatomy-aware self-supervised framework. Specifically, we first extract shared features between the two imaging modalities and then synthesise the target MRI by a group of anatomy-aware constraints. A cross-modal attention scheme was introduced to incorporate non-local guidance across the different modalities. Experimental results demonstrated the proposed framework effectiveness both qualitatively and quantitatively, with comparison to alternative architectures. We believe the proposed method may be useful within analysis tasks such as US-MR alignment and for communicating US findings to paediatricians and patients. While we made the first step for US-to-MR synthesis in 2D in this paper, the extension to 3D synthesis would be an interesting direction to explore in future work.

**Acknowledgments.** We thank Andrew Zisserman for many helpful discussions, the volunteers for assessing images, NVIDIA Corporation for a GPU donation, and acknowledge the ERC (ERC-ADG-2015 694581), the EPSRC (EP/M013774/1, EP/R013853/1), the Royal Academy of Engineering Research Fellowship programme and the NIHR Biomedical Research Centre funding scheme.

# References

1. Berker, Y., et al.: MRI-based attenuation correction for hybrid PET/MRI systems: a 4-class tissue segmentation technique using a combined ultrashort-echo-time/Dixon MRI sequence. J. Nuclear Med. **53**, 796–804 (2012)
2. Bulas, D., Egloff, A.: Benefits and risks of MRI in pregnancy. In: Seminars in Perinatology (2013)
3. Catana, C., et al.: Towards implementing an MR-based PET attenuation correction method for neurological studies on the MR-PET brain prototype. J. Nuclear Med. **51**, 1431–1438 (2010)
4. Costa, P., et al.: End-to-end adversarial retinal image synthesis. IEEE TMI **37**, 781–791 (2018)
5. Delpon, G., et al.: Comparison of automated atlas-based segmentation software for postoperative prostate cancer radiotherapy. Front. Oncol. **6**, 178 (2016)
6. Gholipour, A., et al.: Construction of a deformable spatiotemporal MRI atlas of the fetal brain: evaluation of similarity metrics and deformation models. In: Golland, P., Hata, N., Barillot, C., Hornegger, J., Howe, R. (eds.) MICCAI 2014. LNCS, vol. 8674, pp. 292–299. Springer, Cham (2014). https://doi.org/10.1007/978-3-319-10470-6_37
7. Goodfellow, I., et al.: Generative adversarial nets. In: NeurIPS (2014)
8. King, A.P., et al.: Registering preprocedure volumetric images with intraprocedure 3-D ultrasound using an ultrasound imaging model. IEEE TMI **29**, 924–937 (2010)
9. Kuklisova-Murgasova, M., et al.: Registration of 3D fetal neurosonography and MRI. MedIA **17**, 1137–1150 (2013)
10. Namburete, A.I., et al.: Fully-automated alignment of 3D fetal brain ultrasound to a canonical reference space using multi-task learning. MedIA **46**, 1–14 (2018)

11. Nie, D., et al.: Medical image synthesis with context-aware generative adversarial networks. In: Descoteaux, M., Maier-Hein, L., Franz, A., Jannin, P., Collins, D.L., Duchesne, S. (eds.) MICCAI 2017. LNCS, vol. 10435, pp. 417–425. Springer, Cham (2017). https://doi.org/10.1007/978-3-319-66179-7_48

12. Papageorghiou, A.T., et al.: International standards for fetal growth based on serial ultrasound measurements: the Fetal Growth Longitudinal Study of the INTERGROWTH-21st Project. Lancet **384**, 869–879 (2014)

13. Pugash, D., et al.: Prenatal ultrasound and fetal MRI: the comparative value of each modality in prenatal diagnosis. Eur. J. Radiol. **68**, 214–226 (2008)

14. Roy, S., Butman, J.A., Pham, D.L.: Synthesizing CT from ultrashort echo-time MR images via convolutional neural networks. In: Tsaftaris, S.A., Gooya, A., Frangi, A.F., Prince, J.L. (eds.) SASHIMI 2017. LNCS, vol. 10557, pp. 24–32. Springer, Cham (2017). https://doi.org/10.1007/978-3-319-68127-6_3

15. Rueckert, D., et al.: Nonrigid registration using free-form deformations: application to breast MR images. IEEE TMI **18**, 712–721 (1999)

16. Sjölund, J., et al.: Generating patient specific pseudo-CT of the head from MR using atlas-based regression. Phys. Med. Biol. **60**, 825 (2015)

17. Yang, H., et al.: Unpaired brain MR-to-CT synthesis using a structure-constrained CycleGAN. In: Stoyanov, D., et al. (eds.) DLMIA/ML-CDS 2018. LNCS, vol. 11045, pp. 174–182. Springer, Cham (2018). https://doi.org/10.1007/978-3-030-00889-5_20

18. Zhang, Z., et al.: Translating and segmenting multimodal medical volumes with cycle-and shape-consistency generative adversarial network. In: CVPR (2018)

19. Zhao, Y., et al.: Towards MR-only radiotherapy treatment planning: synthetic CT generation using multi-view deep convolutional neural networks. In: Frangi, A.F., Schnabel, J.A., Davatzikos, C., Alberola-López, C., Fichtinger, G. (eds.) MICCAI 2018. LNCS, vol. 11070, pp. 286–294. Springer, Cham (2018). https://doi.org/10.1007/978-3-030-00928-1_33

20. Zhu, J.Y., et al.: Unpaired image-to-image translation using cycle-consistent adversarial networks. In: ICCV (2017)

# End-to-End Boundary Aware Networks for Medical Image Segmentation

Ali Hatamizadeh[1,2], Demetri Terzopoulos[1], and Andriy Myronenko[2(✉)]

[1] Computer Science Department, University of California, Los Angeles, CA, USA
[2] NVIDIA, Santa Clara, CA, USA
amyronenko@nvidia.com

**Abstract.** Fully convolutional neural networks (CNNs) have proven to be effective at representing and classifying textural information, thus transforming image intensity into output class masks that achieve semantic image segmentation. In medical image analysis, however, expert manual segmentation often relies on the boundaries of anatomical structures of interest. We propose boundary aware CNNs for medical image segmentation. Our networks are designed to account for organ boundary information, both by providing a special network edge branch and edge-aware loss terms, and they are trainable end-to-end. We validate their effectiveness on the task of brain tumor segmentation using the BraTS 2018 dataset. Our experiments reveal that our approach yields more accurate segmentation results, which makes it promising for more extensive application to medical image segmentation.

**Keywords:** Medical image segmentation · Semantic segmentation · Convolutional neural networks · Deep learning

## 1 Introduction

Deep learning approaches to semantic image segmentation have achieved state-of-the-art performance in medical image analysis [4,5,8,9]. With the advent of convolutional neural networks (CNNs), the earliest segmentation methods attempted to classify every pixel based on a corresponding image patch, which often resulted in slow inference times. Fully convolutional neural networks [9], can segment the whole image at once, but the underlying assumption remained—instead of a patch, the corresponding image region (receptive field) centered on the pixel is used for the final pixel segmentation. Since convolutions are spatially invariant, segmentation networks can operate on any image size and infer dense pixel-wise segmentation.

Geirhos et al. [3] empirically demonstrated that, unlike the human visual system, common CNN architectures are biased towards recognizing image textures, not object shape representations. In medical image analysis, however, expert manual segmentation usually relies on boundary and organ shape identification. For instance, a radiologist segmenting a liver from CT images would usually trace

© Springer Nature Switzerland AG 2019
H.-I. Suk et al. (Eds.): MLMI 2019, LNCS 11861, pp. 187–194, 2019.
https://doi.org/10.1007/978-3-030-32692-0_22

liver edges first, from which the internal segmentation mask is easily deduced. This observation motivates us to devise segmentation networks that prioritize the representation of edge information in anatomical structures by leveraging an additional edge module whose training is supervised by edge-aware loss functions.

Recently, several authors have pursued deep learning approaches for object edge prediction. Yu et al. [11] proposed a multilabel semantic boundary detection network to improve a wide variety of vision tasks by predicting edges directly, including a new skip-layer architecture in which category-wise edge activations at the top convolution layer share and are fused with the same set of bottom layer features, along with a multilabel loss function to supervise the fused activations. Subsequently, Yu et al. [12] showed that label misalignment can cause considerably degraded edge learning quality, and addressed this issue by proposing a simultaneous edge alignment and learning framework. Acuna et al. [1] predicted object edges by identifying pixels that belong to class boundaries, proposing a new layer and a loss that enforces the detector to predict a maximum response along the normal direction at an edge, while also regularizing its direction. Takikawa et al. [10] proposed gated-shape CNNs for semantic segmentation of natural images in which such gates are employed to remove the noise from higher-level activations and process the relevant boundary-related information separately. Aiming to learn semantic boundaries, Hu et al. [6] presented a framework that aggregates different tasks of object detection, semantic segmentation, and instance edge detection into a single holistic network with multiple branches, demonstrating significant improvements over conventional approaches through end-to-end training.

In the present paper, we introduce an encoder-decoder architecture that leverages a special interconnected edge layer module that is supervised by edge-aware losses in order to preserve boundary information and emphasize it during training. By explicitly accounting for the edges, we encourage the network to internalize edge importance during training. Our method utilizes edge information only to assist training for semantic segmentation, not for the main purpose of predicting edges directly. This strategy enables a structured regularization mechanism for our network during training and results in more accurate and robust segmentation performance during inference. We validate the effectiveness of our network on the task of brain tumor segmentation using the BraTS 2018 dataset [2].

## 2   Methods

### 2.1   Architecture

Our network comprises a main encoder-decoder stream for semantic segmentation as well as a shape stream that processes the feature maps at the boundary level (Fig. 1). In the encoder portion of the main stream, every resolution level includes two residual blocks whose outputs are fed to the corresponding resolution of the shape stream. A $1 \times 1$ convolution is applied to each input to the shape stream and the result is fed into an attention layer that is discussed in the next section. The outputs of the first two attention layers are fed into connection residual blocks. The output of the last attention layer is concatenated with the output of the encoder in the main stream and fed into a dilated spatial pyramid pooling layer. Losses that contribute to tuning the weights of the model come from the output of the shape stream that is resized to the original image size, as well as the output of the main stream.

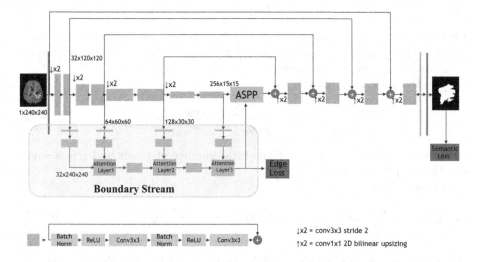

**Fig. 1.** Our 2D fully convolutional architecture. We use dilated spatial pyramid pooling to effectively aggregate the outputs of different stages.

## 2.2   Attention Layer

Each attention layer receives inputs from the previous attention layer as well as the main stream at the corresponding resolution. Let $s_l$ and $m_l$ denote the attention layer and main stream layer inputs at resolution $l$. We first concatenate $s_l$ and $m_l$ and apply a $1 \times 1$ convolution layer $C_{1 \times 1}$ followed by a sigmoid function $\sigma$ to obtain an attention map

$$\alpha_l = \sigma\big(C_{1 \times 1}(s_l \,\|\, m_l)\big). \tag{1}$$

An element-wise multiplication is then performed with the input to the attention layer to obtain the output of the attention layer, denoted as

$$o_l = s_l \odot \alpha_l. \tag{2}$$

## 2.3   Boundary Aware Segmentation

Our network jointly learns the semantics and boundaries by supervising the output of the main stream as well as the edge stream. We use the generalized Dice loss on predicted outputs of the main stream and the shape stream. Additionally, we add a weighted binary cross entropy loss to the shape stream loss in order to deal with the large imbalance between the boundary and non-boundary pixels. The overall loss function of our network is

$$L_{\text{total}} = \lambda_1 L_{\text{Dice}}(y_{\text{pred}}, y_{\text{true}}) + \lambda_2 L_{\text{Dice}}(s_{\text{pred}}, s_{\text{true}}) + \lambda_3 L_{\text{Edge}}(s_{\text{pred}}, s_{\text{true}}), \quad (3)$$

where $y_{\text{pred}}$ and $y_{\text{true}}$ denote the pixel-wise semantic predictions of the main stream while $s_{\text{pred}}$ and $s_{\text{true}}$ denote the boundary predictions of the shape stream; $s_{\text{true}}$ can be obtained by computing the spatial gradient of $y_{\text{true}}$.

The Dice loss [7] in (3) is

$$L_{\text{Dice}} = 1 - \frac{2 \sum y_{\text{true}} y_{\text{pred}}}{\sum y_{\text{true}}^2 + \sum y_{\text{pred}}^2 + \epsilon}, \quad (4)$$

where summation is carried over the total number of pixels and $\epsilon$ is a small constant to prevent division by zero.

The edge loss in (3) is

$$L_{\text{Edge}} = -\beta \sum_{j \in y_+} \log P(y_{\text{pred},j} = 1 | x; \theta) - (1 - \beta) \sum_{j \in y_-} \log P(y_{\text{pred},j} = 0 | x; \theta), \quad (5)$$

where $x$, $\theta$, $y_-$, and $y_+$ denote the input image, CNN parameters, and edge and non-edge pixel sets, respectively, $\beta$ is the ratio of non-edge pixels over the entire number of pixels, and $P(y_{\text{pred},j})$ denotes the probability of the predicated class at pixel $j$.

## 3   Experiments

### 3.1   Datasets

In our experiments, we used the BraTS 2018 [2], which provides multimodal 3D brain MRIs and ground truth brain tumor segmentations annotated by physicians, consisting of 4 MRI modalities per case (T1, T1c, T2, and FLAIR). Annotations include 3 tumor subregions—the enhancing tumor, the peritumoral edema, and the necrotic and non-enhancing tumor core. The annotations were combined into 3 nested subregions—whole tumor (WT), tumor core (TC), and enhancing tumor (ET). The data were collected from 19 institutions, using various MRI scanners. For simplicity, we use only a single input MRI modality (T1c) and aim to segment a single tumor region—TC, which includes the main tumor components (necrotic core, enhancing, and non-enhancing tumor regions). Furthermore, even though the original data is 3D ($240 \times 240 \times 155$), we operate on 2D slices for simplicity. We have extracted several axial slices centered around the tumor region from each 3D volume, and combined them into a new 2D dataset.

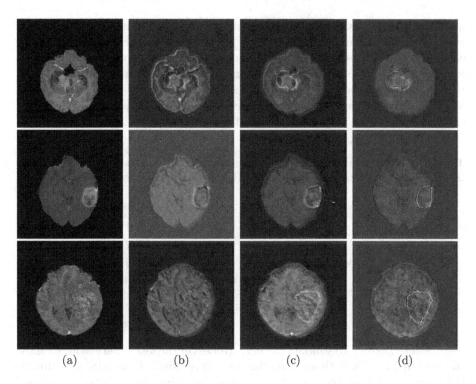

(a)                    (b)                    (c)                    (d)

**Fig. 2.** (a) Input image. Outputs of: (b) Attention Layer 1. (c) Attention Layer 2. (d) Attention Layer 3. The boundary emphasis becomes more prominent in the subsequent attention layers.

### 3.2 Implementation Details

We have implemented our model in Tensorflow. The brain input images were resized to predefined sizes of $240 \times 240$ and normalized to the intensity range $[0, 1]$. The model was trained on NVIDIA Titan RTX and an Intel Core i7-7800X CPU @ 3.50 GHz $\times$ 12 with a batch size of 8 for all models. We used $\lambda_1 = 1.0$, $\lambda_2 = 0.5$, and $\lambda_3 = 0.1$ in (3). The Adam optimization algorithm was used with initial learning rate of $\alpha_0 = 1.0^{-3}$ and further decreased according to

$$\alpha = \alpha_0 \left(1 - e/N_e\right)^{0.9}, \tag{6}$$

where $e$ denotes the current epoch and $N_e$ the total number of epochs, following [8]. We have evaluated the performance of our model by using the Dice score, Jaccard index, and Hausdorff distance.

## 4 Results and Discussion

*Boundary Stream:* Figure 2 demonstrates the output of each of the attention layers in our dedicated boundary stream. In essence, each attention layer progressively localizes the tumor and refines the boundaries. The first attention layer has learned rough estimate of the boundaries around the tumor and localized it, whereas the second and third layers have learned more fine-grained details of the edges and boundaries, refining the localization. Moreover, since our architecture leverages a dilated spatial pyramid pooling to merge the learned feature maps of the regular segmentation stream and the boundary stream, multiscale regional and boundary information have been preserved and fused properly, which has enabled our network to capture the small structural details of the tumor.

**Table 1.** Performance evaluations of different models. We validate the contribution of the edge loss by measuring performance with and without this layer

| Model | Dice score | Jaccard index | Hausdorff distance |
|---|---|---|---|
| U-Net [9] | $0.731 \pm 0.230$ | $0.805 \pm 0.130$ | $3.861 \pm 1.342$ |
| V-Net [7] | $0.769 \pm 0.270$ | $0.837 \pm 0.140$ | $3.667 \pm 1.329$ |
| Ours (no edge loss) | $0.768 \pm 0.236$ | $0.832 \pm 0.136$ | $3.443 \pm 1.218$ |
| Ours | $\mathbf{0.822 \pm 0.176}$ | $\mathbf{0.861 \pm 0.112}$ | $\mathbf{3.406 \pm 1.196}$ |

*Edge-Aware Losses:* To validate the effectiveness of the loss supervision, we have trained our network without enforcing the supervision of the edge loss during the learning process, but with the same architecture. Table 1 shows that our network performs very similarly to V-Net [7] without edge supervision, since ours employs similar residual blocks as V-Net in its main encoder-decoder, and its boundary stream does not seem to contribute to the learning of useful features for segmentation. In essence, the boundary stream also impacts the down-stream layers of the encoder by emphasizing edges during training.

*Comparison to Competing Methods:* We have compared the performance of our model against the most popular deep learning-based semantic segmentation networks, U-Net [9] and V-Net [7] (Fig. 3). Our model outperforms both by a considerable margin in all evaluation metrics. In particular, U-Net performs poorly in most cases due to the high false positive of its segmentation predictions, as well as the imprecision of its boundaries. The powerful residual block in the V-Net architecture seems to alleviate these issues to some extent, but V-Net also fails to produce high-quality boundary predictions. The emphasis of learning useful edge-related information during the training of our network appears to effectively regularize the network such that boundary accuracy is improved.

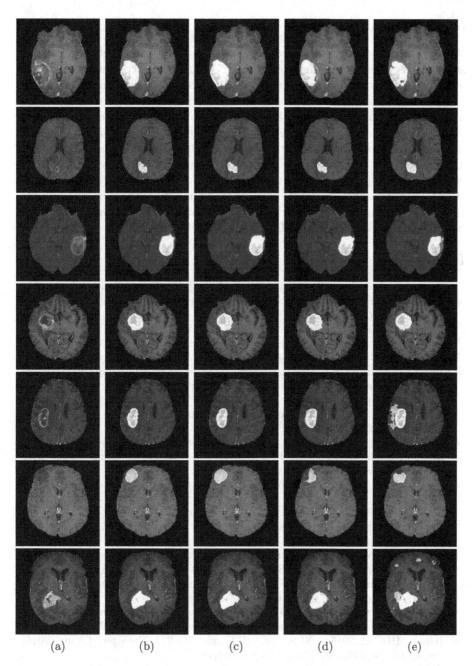

(a)      (b)      (c)      (d)      (e)

**Fig. 3.** (a) Input images. (b) Labels. (c) Ours. (d) V-Net. (e) U-Net.

# 5   Conclusion

We have proposed an end-to-end-trainable boundary aware network for joint semantic segmentation of medical images. Our network explicitly accounts for object edge information by using a dedicated shape stream that processes the feature maps at the boundary level and fuses the multiscale contextual information of the boundaries with the encoder output of the regular segmentation stream. Additionally, edge-aware loss functions emphasize learning of the edge information during training by tuning the weights of the downstream encoder and regularizing the network to prioritize boundaries. We have validated the effectiveness of our approach on the task of brain tumor segmentation using the BraTS 2018 dataset. Our results indicate that our network produces more accurate segmentation outputs with fine-grained boundaries in comparison to the popular segmentation networks U-Net and V-Net.

# References

1. Acuna, D., Kar, A., Fidler, S.: Devil is in the edges: Learning semantic boundaries from noisy annotations. In: The IEEE Conference on Computer Vision and Pattern Recognition (CVPR) (2019)
2. Bakas, S., et al.: Advancing the cancer genome atlas glioma MRI collections with expert segmentation labels and radiomic features. Sci. Data **4**, 170117 (2017)
3. Geirhos, R., Rubisch, P., Michaelis, C., Bethge, M., Wichmann, F.A., Brendel, W.: ImageNet-trained CNNs are biased towards texture; increasing shape bias improves accuracy and robustness. In: International Conference on Learning Representations (ICLR) (2019)
4. Hatamizadeh, A., et al.: Deep active lesion segmentation. arXiv preprint arXiv:1908.06933 (2019)
5. Hatamizadeh, A., Hosseini, H., Liu, Z., Schwartz, S.D., Terzopoulos, D.: Deep dilated convolutional nets for the automatic segmentation of retinal vessels. arXiv preprint arXiv:1905.12120 (2019)
6. Hu, Y., Zou, Y., Feng, J.: Panoptic edge detection. https://arxiv.org/abs/1906.00590 (2019)
7. Milletari, F., Navab, N., Ahmadi, S.A.: V-net: fully convolutional neural networks for volumetric medical image segmentation. In: Fourth International Conference on 3D Vision (3DV) (2016)
8. Myronenko, A.: 3D MRI brain tumor segmentation using autoencoder regularization. In: Crimi, A., Bakas, S., Kuijf, H., Keyvan, F., Reyes, M., van Walsum, T. (eds.) BrainLes 2018. LNCS, vol. 11384, pp. 311–320. Springer, Cham (2019). https://doi.org/10.1007/978-3-030-11726-9_28
9. Ronneberger, O., Fischer, P., Brox, T.: U-net: convolutional networks for biomedical image segmentation. In: Navab, N., Hornegger, J., Wells, W.M., Frangi, A.F. (eds.) MICCAI 2015. LNCS, vol. 9351, pp. 234–241. Springer, Cham (2015). https://doi.org/10.1007/978-3-319-24574-4_28
10. Takikawa, T., Acuna, D., Jampani, V., Fidler, S.: Gated-SCNN: gated shape CNNs for semantic segmentation. arXiv preprint arXiv:1907.05740 (2019)
11. Yu, Z., Feng, C., Liu, M., Ramalingam, S.: CASENet: deep category-aware semantic edge detection. In: CVPR (2017)
12. Yu, Z., et al.: Simultaneous edge alignment and learning. In: Ferrari, V., Hebert, M., Sminchisescu, C., Weiss, Y. (eds.) ECCV 2018. LNCS, vol. 11207, pp. 400–417. Springer, Cham (2018). https://doi.org/10.1007/978-3-030-01219-9_24

# Automatic Rodent Brain MRI Lesion Segmentation with Fully Convolutional Networks

Juan Miguel Valverde[1]($\boxtimes$)(iD), Artem Shatillo[2]($\boxtimes$), Riccardo De Feo[3]($\boxtimes$)(iD),
Olli Gröhn[1]($\boxtimes$), Alejandra Sierra[1]($\boxtimes$)(iD), and Jussi Tohka[1]($\boxtimes$)(iD)

[1] AI Virtanen Institute for Molecular Sciences, University of Eastern Finland,
Kuopio, Finland
{juanmiguel.valverde,olli.grohn,alejandra.sierralopez,jussi.tohka}@uef.fi
[2] Charles River Discovery Services, Kuopio, Finland
artem.shatillo@crl.com
[3] Centro Fermi - Museo Storico della Fisica e Centro Studi e Ricerche Enrico Fermi,
Rome, Italy
riccardo.defeo@uniroma1.it

**Abstract.** Manual segmentation of rodent brain lesions from magnetic resonance images (MRIs) is an arduous, time-consuming and subjective task that is highly important in pre-clinical research. Several automatic methods have been developed for different human brain MRI segmentation, but little research has targeted automatic rodent lesion segmentation. The existing tools for performing automatic lesion segmentation in rodents are constrained by strict assumptions about the data. Deep learning has been successfully used for medical image segmentation. However, there has not been any deep learning approach specifically designed for tackling rodent brain lesion segmentation. In this work, we propose a novel Fully Convolutional Network (FCN), RatLesNet, for the aforementioned task. Our dataset consists of 131 T2-weighted rat brain scans from 4 different studies in which ischemic stroke was induced by transient middle cerebral artery occlusion. We compare our method with two other 3D FCNs originally developed for anatomical segmentation (VoxResNet and 3D-U-Net) with 5-fold cross-validation on a single study and a generalization test, where the training was done on a single study and testing on three remaining studies. The labels generated by our method were quantitatively and qualitatively better than the predictions of the compared methods. The average Dice coefficient achieved in the 5-fold cross-validation experiment with the proposed approach was 0.88, between 3.7% and 38% higher than the compared architectures. The presented architecture also outperformed the other FCNs at generalizing on different studies, achieving the average Dice coefficient of 0.79.

**Keywords:** Lesion segmentation · Deep learning · Rat brain · Magnetic resonance imaging

© Springer Nature Switzerland AG 2019
H.-I. Suk et al. (Eds.): MLMI 2019, LNCS 11861, pp. 195–202, 2019.
https://doi.org/10.1007/978-3-030-32692-0_23

# 1   Introduction

Medical image segmentation constitutes a bottleneck in research due to the time required to delineate regions of interest (ROI). In particular, pre-clinical studies involving animals can potentially produce 3D images in the order of hundreds, i.e., several animals with varied characteristics such as age, gender and strain at different time-points may be needed for a certain study.

Rodent brain lesion segmentation is a challenging problem subject to inter- and intra-operator variability. There are multiple factors that influence segmentation quality such as the characteristics of the lesion, the scan parameters and the annotators' knowledge and experience. Despite that, manual segmentation remains the de facto gold standard, decreasing the reproducibility of research.

Convolutional neural networks (CNNs) and, in particular, U-Net-like architectures [16] have recently become a popular choice for anatomical segmentation. There are numerous methods specifically designed for human brains to parcellate anatomical structures [3,17], tumors [8] and lesions [14]. On contrary, animal brain segmentation algorithms based on CNNs are still infrequent [6]. As one example, Roy et al. showed that the same CNN can be used for extraction of human and mouse brains (i.e., skull-stripping) [18].

Recently, few automatic approaches were developed to tackle rodent brain lesion segmentation, including statistical models [2], thresholding [4] and level-sets [13]. However, these methods rely on strict assumptions such as the distribution of the data, or they are limited to use a single image modality. To the best of the authors' knowledge, CNNs have not yet been proposed for segmenting rat brain lesions.

In this work, we present RatLesNet, a 3D Fully Convolutional Network (FCN) to automatically segment rat brain lesions. Our dataset consists of a total of 131 Magnetic Resonance (MR) T2-weighted rat brain scans from 4 different studies with their corresponding lesion segmentation. Brain scans were acquired at different time-points after the lesions were caused by ischemic stroke induced by an occlusion of transient middle cerebral artery. Unlike other studies in which the segmentation algorithms rely on additional steps [2,4,13], RatLesNet uses unprocessed MR-images that are not skull-stripped nor corrected for bias-field inhomogeneity. As well, we do not post-process the final predictions by filling holes or discarding small isolated clusters of voxels.

We compare RatLesNet with two other 3D FCNs performing internal five-fold cross-validation in one study of the dataset, and by training on volumes from that study to assess their generalization capability on the remaining 3 studies.

# 2   Materials and Methods

**Material:** The dataset consists of 131 MR brain scans of different adult male Wistar rats weighting between 250–300 g. The data, provided by Charles River Laboratories[1], are derived from four different studies: 03AUG2015 (21 scans),

---

[1] https://www.criver.com/.

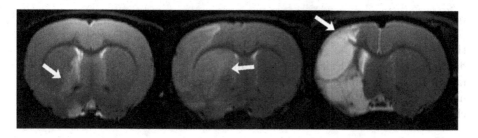

**Fig. 1.** Representative lesion progression of a rat at 2 h, 24 h and 35 days after MCA occlusion. The arrows point to the lesion, which appear hyperintense in T2-weighted images on the right hemisphere.

03MAY2016 (45 scans), 02NOV2016 (48 scans) and 02OCT2017 (17 scans). Transient (120 min) focal cerebral ischemia was produced by middle cerebral artery occlusion (tMCAO) in the right hemisphere of the brain [12]. MR data acquisitions were performed at different time-points in a horizontal 7 T magnet, more specifically at 2 h (12 animals from 02NOV2016 study), 24 h (12 animals from 02NOV2016 and all animals from 03MAY2016 and 02OCT2017) and 35 days (all animals from 03AUG2015 except 1) after the occlusion. 02NOV2016 and 03AUG2015 studies included 24 and 1 sham animals, respectively, that underwent through identical procedures, including anesthesia regime, but without the actual tMCAO occlusion. All animal experiments are carried out according to the National Institute of Health (NIH) guidelines for the care and use of laboratory animals, and approved by the National Animal Experiment Board, Finland. Multi-slice multi-echo sequence was used with the following parameters; TR = 2.5 s, 12 echo times (10–120 ms in 10 ms steps) and 4 averages. Eighteen (18) coronal slices of thickness 1 mm were acquired using a field-of-view of $30 \times 30$ mm$^2$ producing $256 \times 256$ imaging matrices.

The T2-weighted MR images and their corresponding lesion segmentation were provided in form of NIfTI files. We chose a single study (02NOV2016) and performed an independent lesion segmentation to approximate inter-rate variability. The Dice coefficient [7] between our independent manual segmentation and the one provided was 0.73.

**Network Architecture:** RatLesNet's architecture (Fig. 2) is composed by three types of blocks: (1) Dense blocks, (2) 3D convolutions with filter size of 1 followed by an activation function and (3) Max-pooling/Unpooling operations. Dense blocks encapsulate two 3D convolutions with filter size of 3 and ReLU activation functions concatenated with the outputs of the previous layers within the same block in a ResNet [9] fashion. The number of channels increasing within the block (i.e. growth rate) is 18 and, unlike the original Dense blocks [10], these do not include a transition layer at the end. Due to the consequent widening of layers along the network, the external 3D convolutional layers with filter size of 1 are of special importance for adjusting the number of channels, similarly to traditional bottleneck layers. Max-pooling and unpooling layers are used to reduce and recover the spatial dimensions of the volumes, respectively. Max-pooling has a window size and stride of 2, and unpooling reuses the indices of the values from the max-pooling operation to place the new values back to their original location [15]. Finally, the input and output volumes of the network have identical spatial dimensions, and their number of channels correspond to the number of medical imaging modalities (here 1 that is T2) and the number of classes (here 2: lesion and non-lesion), respectively.

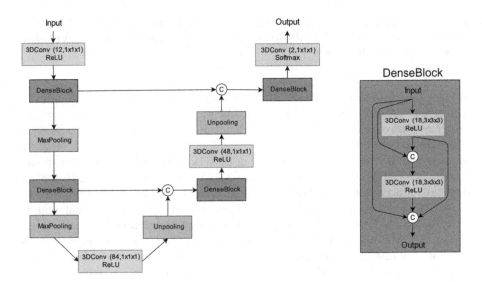

**Fig. 2.** Overview of the network architecture.

**Training:** The network was trained on entire T2-weighted images with a resolution of $256 \times 256 \times 18$ voxels and a mini-batch size of 1. Image intensities in each volume were standardized by subtracting their mean and dividing them by their standard deviation. Cross-entropy loss function was minimized using Adam [11] with a starting learning rate of $10^{-5}$. Training lasted for a maximum of 1000 epochs or until the validation loss increased 5 consecutive times.

## 3   Experiments and Results

**Cross-Validation.** Five-fold cross-validation was performed on the scans of the study that was segmented independently (02NOV2016) to assess the performance of the proposed RatLesNet method. Additionally, RatLesNet was compared to 3D U-Net [5] and VoxResNet [3], two 3D fully convolutional networks originally designed for anatomical segmentation. Both architectures were implemented according to the original design resulting in 19M parameters (3D U-Net) and 1.5M parameters (VoxResNet). In contrast, our RatLesNet implementation has only 0.37M parameters, reducing the possibility of overfitting. The models that provided the reported results were trained with the best performing learning rate found.

**Table 1.** Average 5-fold cross-validation Dice scores and standard deviation from 02NOV2016 dataset with and without sham animals (no brain lesion). The column Inter-operator refers to differences between the two independent manual segmentations by different operators.

| Time-point | Shams | 3D U-Net | VoxResNet | RatLesNet | Inter-operator |
|---|---|---|---|---|---|
| 2 h | Yes | $0.57 \pm 0.42$ | $0.80 \pm 0.23$ | $0.84 \pm 0.19$ | $0.84 \pm 0.19$ |
|  | No | $0.17 \pm 0.13$ | $0.60 \pm 0.16$ | $0.67 \pm 0.12$ | $0.67 \pm 0.12$ |
| 24 h | Yes | $0.7 \pm 0.35$ | $0.89 \pm 0.18$ | $0.92 \pm 0.11$ | $0.90 \pm 0.12$ |
|  | No | $0.43 \pm 0.13$ | $0.79 \pm 0.2$ | $0.85 \pm 0.11$ | $0.79 \pm 0.08$ |
| Average | Yes | $0.64 \pm 0.39$ | $0.85 \pm 0.21$ | $0.88 \pm 0.16$ | $0.87 \pm 0.16$ |
|  | No | $0.30 \pm 0.26$ | $0.70 \pm 0.20$ | $0.76 \pm 0.14$ | $0.73 \pm 0.12$ |

Our RatLesNet provided better quantitative and qualitative results than 3D U-Net [5] and VoxResNet [3]. Table 1 compares the mean Dice coefficients and their variability across the implemented networks. As brain lesion's appearance varies depending on the time passed since the lesion was caused (see Fig. 1), Dice coefficients were averaged separately. Furthermore, due to the incorporation of sham animals (rats without lesion), two averages are provided: one that includes all animals and one that excludes rats without lesion. The methods recognized well the brains with no lesions and therefore the average Dice coefficients and their standard deviations were higher when shams were included. Due to the pronounced class imbalance, the network tends to classify voxels as non-lesion. On average, the number of lesion voxels in our independent segmentation in 2 h and 24 h time-points were 6060 (0.51% of all voxels) and 21333 (1.81% of all voxels), respectively. Additionally, 2h scans are more troublesome to segment because the lesion is considerably smaller and some affected areas resemble healthy tissue.

The segmentations generated with RatLesNet have higher Dice coefficients than inter-operator variability. Furthermore, predictions did not only achieve greater Dice coefficients than the other 3D networks, but also the quality of the final segmentations was noticeably better in visual inspection: Fig. 3 depicts the predicted lesion in the same slice of the brain generated by the three different architectures, together with the original MR image and its ground truth. 3D U-Net's segmentation shows that the architecture did not learn to generalize properly since it classifies large areas of unequivocal healthy tissue as lesion. The borders of VoxResNet's prediction were comparatively crispier than the borders of the segmentation produced by our architecture. RatLesNet generated consistent boundaries such as the gap between the two affected areas at the bottom of the slice and the exclusion of the vein in the left side of the cortical

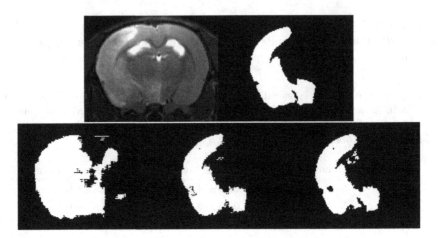

**Fig. 3.** Top: A slice of a T2-weighted rat brain image with lesion and its segmentation. Bottom: segmentations generated by 3D U-Net, VoxResNet and our architecture in the cross-validation test.

region. The consistency in the boundaries also increased the size of holes within the segmented lesion and the size of clustered lesion voxels outside the affected area.

**Generalization Capability.** 3D U-Net, VoxResNet and the proposed architecture were trained on the scans from 02NOV2016 study (including sham animals) and tested on the scans from the remaining 3 studies to compare their generalization capabilities. Table 2 summarizes the results. Our approach produced markedly larger Dice coefficients than VoxResNet and 3D U-Net in 03MAY2016 and 02OCT2017 studies. On the other hand, VoxResNet architecture produced the largest Dice coefficients in 03AUG2015 study. With 03MAY2016 and 02OCT2017 studies, the Dice coefficients of our network were markedly larger than the Dice coefficient between two independent manual segmentations (0.73) of 02NOV2016 study.

**Table 2.** Average Dice scores and standard deviation. The model was trained on the 02NOV2016 study.

| Study | 3D U-Net | VoxResNet | RatLesNet |
|---|---|---|---|
| 03AUG2015 (D35) | $0.64 \pm 0.27$ | $0.71 \pm 0.23$ | $0.68 \pm 0.26$ |
| 03MAY2016 (24 h) | $0.62 \pm 0.18$ | $0.77 \pm 0.12$ | $0.82 \pm 0.05$ |
| 02OCT2017 (24 h) | $0.60 \pm 0.18$ | $0.78 \pm 0.07$ | $0.84 \pm 0.04$ |
| Average | $0.62 \pm 0.21$ | $0.76 \pm 0.15$ | $0.79 \pm 0.15$ |

**Computation Time:** The network was implemented in Tensorflow [1] and it was run on a Ubuntu 16.04 with an Intel Xeon W-2125 CPU @ 4.00 GHz processor, 64 GB of memory and an NVidia GeForce GTX 1080 Ti with 11 GB of memory. Training lasted for approximately 6 h and inference time was about half a second per scan.

# 4 Conclusion

We have presented RatLesNet, the first FCN specifically designed for rat brain lesion segmentation. Our approach does not rely on corrections on the MR images or post-processing operations, and utilizes the entire 3D volume to explicitly use spatial information in three dimensions. In addition, the architecture of our RatLesNet is agnostic to the number of modalities and MR sequences presented in the input channels, so its generalization to multimodal data is technically straightforward. Five-fold cross-validation showed that our approach is more accurate than two other 3D FCNs designed for anatomical segmentation, and the boundaries consistency of the predicted segmentations is higher. Furthermore, the generalization capabilities of the architectures was assessed with data from three additional studies, and our approach provided with markedly larger Dice coefficients in two of the three studies. Its performance on the third study was slightly worse than the performance of VoxResNet.

Future work will expand the dataset increasing the variability of the lesion's appearance by including brain scans at different time-points after the lesion is caused. Additional study is also needed to understand if the underperformance of the other two networks is caused by the comparatively large number of parameters as they are more prone to overfit the data.

**Acknowledgments.** J.M.V.'s work was funded from the European Union's Horizon 2020 Framework Programme (Marie Skłodowska Curie grant agreement #740264 (GENOMMED)) and R.D.F.'s work was funded from Marie Skłodowska Curie grant agreement #691110 (MICROBRADAM). We also acknowledge the Academy of Finland grants (#275453 to A.S. and #316258 to J.T.).

# References

1. Abadi, M., et al.: TensorFlow: a system for large-scale machine learning. In: 12th USENIX Symposium on Operating Systems Design and Implementation (OSDI 2016), pp. 265–283 (2016)
2. Arnaud, A., Forbes, F., Coquery, N., Collomb, N., Lemasson, B., Barbier, E.L.: Fully automatic lesion localization and characterization: application to brain tumors using multiparametric quantitative MRI data. IEEE Trans. Med. Imaging **37**(7), 1678–1689 (2018)
3. Chen, H., Dou, Q., Yu, L., Qin, J., Heng, P.A.: VoxResNet: deep voxelwise residual networks for brain segmentation from 3D MR images. NeuroImage **170**, 446–455 (2018)

4. Choi, C.H., et al.: A novel voxel-wise lesion segmentation technique on 3.0-T diffusion MRI of hyperacute focal cerebral ischemia at 1 h after permanent MCAO in rats. J. Cereb. Blood Flow Metab. **38**(8), 1371–1383 (2018)
5. Çiçek, Ö., Abdulkadir, A., Lienkamp, S.S., Brox, T., Ronneberger, O.: 3D U-net: learning dense volumetric segmentation from sparse annotation. In: Ourselin, S., Joskowicz, L., Sabuncu, M.R., Unal, G., Wells, W. (eds.) MICCAI 2016. LNCS, vol. 9901, pp. 424–432. Springer, Cham (2016). https://doi.org/10.1007/978-3-319-46723-8_49
6. De Feo, R., Giove, F.: Towards an efficient segmentation of small rodents brain: a short critical review. J. Neurosci. Methods **323**, 82–89 (2019)
7. Dice, L.R.: Measures of the amount of ecologic association between species. Ecology **26**(3), 297–302 (1945)
8. Havaei, M., et al.: Brain tumor segmentation with deep neural networks. Med. Image Anal. **35**, 18–31 (2017)
9. He, K., Zhang, X., Ren, S., Sun, J.: Deep residual learning for image recognition. In: Proceedings of the IEEE Conference on Computer Vision and Pattern Recognition, pp. 770–778 (2016)
10. Huang, G., Liu, Z., Van Der Maaten, L., Weinberger, K.Q.: Densely connected convolutional networks. In: Proceedings of the IEEE Conference on Computer Vision and Pattern Recognition, pp. 4700–4708 (2017)
11. Kingma, D.P., Ba, J.: Adam: a method for stochastic optimization. arXiv preprint arXiv:1412.6980 (2014)
12. Koizumi, J., Yoshida, Y., Nakazawa, T., Ooneda, G.: Experimental studies of ischemic brain edema. 1. A new experimental model of cerebral embolism in rats in which recirculation can be introduced in the ischemic area. Jpn. J. stroke **8**, 1–8 (1986)
13. Mulder, I.A., et al.: Automated ischemic lesion segmentation in MRI mouse brain data after transient middle cerebral artery occlusion. Front. Neuroinform. **11**, 3 (2017)
14. Myronenko, A.: 3D MRI brain tumor segmentation using autoencoder regularization. In: Crimi, A., Bakas, S., Kuijf, H., Keyvan, F., Reyes, M., van Walsum, T. (eds.) BrainLes 2018. LNCS, vol. 11384, pp. 311–320. Springer, Cham (2019). https://doi.org/10.1007/978-3-030-11726-9_28
15. Noh, H., Hong, S., Han, B.: Learning deconvolution network for semantic segmentation. In: Proceedings of the IEEE International Conference on Computer Vision, pp. 1520–1528 (2015)
16. Ronneberger, O., Fischer, P., Brox, T.: U-net: convolutional networks for biomedical image segmentation. In: Navab, N., Hornegger, J., Wells, W.M., Frangi, A.F. (eds.) MICCAI 2015. LNCS, vol. 9351, pp. 234–241. Springer, Cham (2015). https://doi.org/10.1007/978-3-319-24574-4_28
17. Roy, A.G., Conjeti, S., Navab, N., Wachinger, C., Initiative, A.D.N., et al.: Quick-NAT: a fully convolutional network for quick and accurate segmentation of neuroanatomy. NeuroImage **186**, 713–727 (2019)
18. Roy, S., et al.: A deep learning framework for brain extraction in humans and animals with traumatic brain injury. In: 2018 IEEE 15th International Symposium on Biomedical Imaging (ISBI 2018), pp. 687–691. IEEE (2018)

# Morphological Simplification of Brain MR Images by Deep Learning for Facilitating Deformable Registration

Dongming Wei[1,2], Sahar Ahmad[2], Zhengwang Wu[2], Xiaohuan Cao[3], Xuhua Ren[1], Gang Li[2], Dinggang Shen[2(✉)], and Qian Wang[1(✉)]

[1] Institute for Medical Imaging Technology, School of Biomedical Engineering, Shanghai Jiao Tong University, Shanghai 200030, China
`wang.qian@sjtu.edu.cn`
[2] Department of Radiology and Biomedical Research Imaging Center (BRIC), University of North Carolina at Chapel Hill, Chapel Hill, NC 27599, USA
`dgshen@med.unc.edu`
[3] Shanghai United Imaging Intelligence Co., Ltd., Shanghai, China

**Abstract.** Brain MR image registration is challenging due to the large inter-subject anatomical variation. Especially, the highly convoluted brain cortex makes it difficult to accurately align the corresponding structures of the underlying images. In this paper, we propose a novel deep learning strategy to simplify the image registration task. Specifically, we train a morphological simplification network (MS-Net), which can generate a *simplified* image with fewer anatomical details given a *complex* input image. With this trained MS-Net, we can reduce the complexity of both the fixed and the moving images and iteratively derive their respective trajectories of gradually *simplified* images. The generated images at the ends of the two trajectories are so simple that they are very similar in appearance and morphology and thus easy to register. In this way, these two trajectories can act as a bridge to link the fixed and the moving images and guide their registration. Our experiments show that the proposed method can achieve more accurate registration results than state-of-the-art methods. Moreover, the proposed method can be generalized to the unseen dataset without the need for re-training or domain adaptation.

**Keywords:** Deformable registration · Brain MRI · Deep learning · Morphology

## 1 Introduction

Deformable image registration plays an important role in medical image analysis as it establishes anatomical correspondences across images. The goal of deformable registration is to find a deformation field by optimizing the cost function that maximizes the similarity between the fixed and the moving images

© Springer Nature Switzerland AG 2019
H.-I. Suk et al. (Eds.): MLMI 2019, LNCS 11861, pp. 203–211, 2019.
https://doi.org/10.1007/978-3-030-32692-0_24

while regularizing the deformation. The regularization ensures that the anatomical topology is preserved and the computed deformation field is smooth. Existing diffeomorphic methods, *e.g.,* Diffeomorphic Demons [1], LDDMM [2] and SyN [3], have drawn much attention, as they can achieve promising registration accuracy while preserving smoothness of the estimated deformation fields.

A manifold is often adopted to describe the distribution of many subjects, while the deformation field that aligns a pair of images can be designated as a pathway linking the two subjects on the manifold. However, it might be difficult to directly estimate the deformation pathway between two images with large variation and thus distributed faraway on the manifold. To this end, some methods have proposed to utilize the intermediate images, which can decompose the deformation pathway between the fixed and the moving images into several segments [4]. The final deformation field could then be easily estimated by concatenating multiple deformation fields, each of which corresponds to a segment.

However, it is non-trivial to build the image manifold and seek for intermediate guidance especially for brain MR images. The imaging data is high-dimensional, indicating a huge number of intermediate images is required to model the complex distribution of the image population. Meanwhile, a global image similarity metric is needed to create the manifold, while the metric is challenging to design and cannot describe the local anatomical variation effectively [5]. Some researchers also proposed to use high-order features and sophisticated constraints derived from brain tissue segmentation (*i.e.,* gray matter (GM) and white matter (WM)) [6,7]. Recently, Zhang *et al.* used the smoothed cortical surfaces with reduced complexity to guide the volumetric registration [8]. However, it is difficult to get an accurate tissue segmentation and the reconstructed cortical surface.

Recently, deep learning has been applied to medical image registration [9]. For example, deformable image registration via the deep neural network [10] can directly predict the deformation fields given the input images. Here, the image similarity metric and the regularization constraint are jointly used to train the network. Although deep learning has shown tremendous success in deformable image registration, it ignores the issue of large anatomical variation.

In this paper, we propose a novel deep learning strategy to simplify the brain MR image registration. Specifically, we train a morphological simplification network (MS-Net) to reduce the anatomical complexity (*i.e.,* the cortical folding pattern). By calling MS-Net iteratively, each image derives its individual trajectory, which consists of a series of images with gradually reducing anatomical complexity. As the two trajectories approach to the end, the two images are *simplified* to an extent that they appear similar with each other. The two *simplified* images with reduced anatomical complexity are thus easier to register than the original fixed and moving images. By composing multiple deformable registration tasks along the two trajectories, the moving image can be reliably registered to the fixed image. The results show that our proposed method achieves higher accuracy than the existing methods for brain MR image registration. Also, the

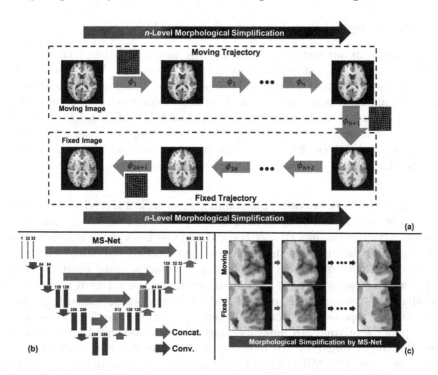

**Fig. 1.** (a) Overview of our proposed method; (b) The architecture of MS-Net; (c) Zoomed-in views of the fixed, moving and morphologically simplified images by MS-Net.

proposed network works well on the unseen dataset because of its generalization capability.

## 2   Methods

We propose to simplify the brain MR image registration task by deep learning. The pipeline of our method is shown in Fig. 1(a). In particular, we train the MS-Net to reduce the anatomical complexity and generate the trajectories for the fixed and the moving images, respectively. This iterative reduction in morphological details results in two *simplified* images that appear similar at the ends of their respective trajectories, thereby allowing the two images to be registered easily. In this way, we can use the fixed/moving trajectories to link the input fixed/moving images, and decompose the original complex registration problem into simplified ones (*i.e.*, finding $\{\phi_i | i = 1, \ldots, 2n+1\}$ along the two trajectories, as shown in Fig. 1(a)).

## 2.1 Morphological Simplification Network (MS-Net)

The main idea of our method is to reduce the anatomical complexity of brain MR images in order to simplify the image registration task. We propose to use deep learning to reduce the structural complexity in the intensity space directly, which is significantly different from Zhang *et al.* [8] relying on tissue segmentation and cortical surface reconstruction. The proposed 3D MS-Net follows the U-Net [11] architecture (see Fig. 1(b)) to iteratively map a *complex* brain MR image to a *simplified* one. Examples of the *complex* fixed/moving images and the corresponding *simplified* images generated by MS-Net are presented in Fig. 1(c).

**Training Data Preparation:** The training data consists of original MR images and the corresponding *simplified* images. We get the *simplified* MR images by: (1) reconstructing the inner/outer cortical surfaces from the segmented tissue maps; (2) applying umbrella smoothing on the reconstructed surfaces and converting the smoothed surfaces into tissue segmentation maps by the strategy in [12], which ensures that the segmented tissues are not shrinked after surface smoothing; (3) registering the original and the corresponding (smoothed) tissue segmentation maps using diffeomorphic Demons [1] to get the deformation field; (4) warping the original MR intensity images with the aforementioned deformation fields to get *simplified* MR intensity images. The above steps are repeated iteratively to generate MR images of fewer and fewer morphological details. The two corresponding images, before and after each smoothing operation, compose of a *complex-simple* pair for training the MS-Net. Specifically, $n$ *complex-simple* pairs $\{(I_s^{i-1}, I_s^i)|i = 1, \ldots, n\}$ can be prepared from subject $s$, where $I_s^0$ represents the original intensity MR image of the subject.

**Network Implementation:** We train MS-Net in a patch-wise manner, by extracting spatially corresponding 3D patch pairs of the size $2 \times 16 \times 16 \times 16$ from the *complex-simplified* training image pairs. The probability for a patch to be sampled is determined by the intensity gradient at the patch center [13]. In this way, our training samples are non-uniformly distributed in the image space for covering more information about the morphological details and their simplification. The MS-Net is trained on an Nvidia Titan X GPU by Keras. We use Adam optimizer with 0.001 as the initial learning rate.

## 2.2 Trajectory Guided Registration

We train the MS-Net as detailed in Sect. 2.1 and use it in an iterative fashion, where the current output of the MS-Net is the input to the MS-Net in the next iteration. It thus generates two trajectories of gradually *simplified* MR images for both the fixed and the moving images, respectively. Then, the trajectory guided registration is implemented by: (1) registering (using diffeomorphic Demons) the current moving image $\{I_m^0(\phi_0 \circ \ldots \circ \phi_k)|k = 0, \ldots, 2n\}$ with its corresponding *simplified* image $\{I_m^{k+1}|k = 0, \ldots, n - 1\}$ or $\{I_f^{2n-k}|k = n, \ldots, 2n\}$ to obtain the deformation field $\phi_{k+1}$, where $\phi_o$ represents the identity transformation; (2) warping the moving image to obtain $I_m^0(\phi_0 \circ \ldots \circ \phi_k \circ \phi_{k+1})$. The above two steps are iteratively executed from $k = 0$ to $k = 2n + 1$. The *simplified* fixed image $I_f^n$ and the moving image $I_m^0(\phi_0 \circ \ldots \circ \phi_n)$ at the ends of the trajectories are registered together to bridge the link between the fixed and moving trajectories. Specifically, $\phi_{n+1}$ is easier to be recovered than the direct deformation field between the original fixed and moving images. Subtle anatomical structural difference is encoded into $\{\phi_i | i = 1, \ldots, n, n+2, \ldots, 2n+1\}$, and thus only large-scale shape variation need to be registered at the ends of trajectories. Thus, the final deformation field that warps the original moving image to the fixed image is estimated by composing the intermediate deformation fields along the two trajectories as follows:

$$\phi = \phi_0 \circ \phi_1 \circ \ldots \circ \phi_{2n+1} \tag{1}$$

## 3   Experiments and Results

We used two public datasets, *i.e.*, NIREP NA0 [14] and LONI LPBA40 [15] to evaluate our proposed registration method. The NIREP NA0 dataset consists of 16 3D brain MR images, each of which is annotated into 32 regions of interest (ROIs). LONI LPBA40 dataset consists of 40 young adult brain MR images with 54 ROIs. After pre-processing and affine registration, all the images of the two datasets were resampled to the same resolution $(1 \times 1 \times 1 \text{ mm}^3)$. The images were then registered using the proposed method, as well as two state-of-the-art registration methods, *i.e.*, diffeomorphic Demons [1] and SyN [3], for comparison. To quantitatively evaluate the registration performance, we computed Dice similarity coefficient (DSC) and average symmetric surface distance (ASSD) over the ROIs. These two metrics are widely used for registration evaluation, as a higher DSC (or lower ASSD) usually indicates better registration quality.

The MS-Net was trained with the NIREP dataset using the leave-two-out strategy, *i.e.*, 14 subjects were selected for training with $14000 \times 14 \times 10 = 2156000$ patch pairs. Note that each patch pair had the same smoothness step when preparing the training data. Specifically, given subject $s$, $\{I_s^i | i = 1, \ldots, 10\}$ was generated by the method described in Sect. 2.1. Therefore, 14000 patch pairs were collected from each image pair of $\{(I_s^{i-1}, I_s^i) | i = 1, \ldots, 10\}$. In the inference stage, the MS-Net can generate any length trajectory iteratively given a certain input image. We particularly applied the MS-Net for 7 times to simplify the brain complexity gradually. The trajectories can then guide the registration of the fixed and the moving images as described in Sect. 2.2.

### 3.1   Evaluation over NIREP Dataset

From 16 subjects in NIREP, we ran the registration task for $16 \times 15 = 240$ times by cross-validation. Two subjects were selected as the registration pair each time, and MS-Net was trained by the remaining 14 subjects. The overall DSC results on all 32 ROIs were $70.1 \pm 5.2\%$ for our method, $66.3 \pm 6.6\%$ for

**Table 1.** Mean ± std of DSC and ASSD for GM and WM based on 16 subjects from NIREP and 40 subjects from LONI after registration by Demons, SyN and the proposed method.

|  |  | DSC (%) | | ASSD (mm) | |
|---|---|---|---|---|---|
|  |  | GM | WM | GM | WM |
| NIREP | Demons | 81.7 ± 1.0 | 84.2 ± 0.8 | 0.43 ± 0.06 | 0.53 ± 0.09 |
|  | SyN | 81.6 ± 2.3 | 83.9 ± 2.1 | 0.40 ± 0.08 | 0.53 ± 0.12 |
|  | Proposed | **87.1 ± 0.9** | **89.6 ± 0.7** | **0.30 ± 0.05** | **0.41 ± 0.09** |
| LONI | Demons | 76.5 ± 1.9 | 82.6 ± 0.8 | 0.42 ± 0.04 | 0.50 ± 0.09 |
|  | SyN | 77.7 ± 1.9 | 84.2 ± 0.9 | 0.38 ± 0.04 | 0.45 ± 0.09 |
|  | Proposed | **82.0 ± 1.5** | **87.9 ± 0.6** | **0.33 ± 0.04** | **0.41 ± 0.09** |

diffeomorphic Demons, and $66.3 \pm 7.1\%$ for SyN. The statistical significance using $t$-test indicates that for 31/32 ROIs, our method performs better than the other two methods with $p < 0.05$. The detailed results on individual ROIs are presented in Fig. 2. We also evaluated the metrics over GM and WM tissues, where our method performed better as well (cf. Table 1).

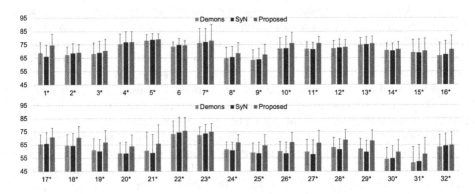

**Fig. 2.** The mean and standard deviation of DSC (%) for 32 ROIs over 16 subjects from NIREP dataset after registration by Demons, SyN and the proposed method. Asterisk (*) indicates statistically significant improvement ($p < 0.05$) of our method over the two compared method.

## 3.2    Evaluation over LONI Dataset

To demonstrate that our method can be generalized to unseen datasets, we further used the LONI LPBA40 dataset for evaluating the registration performance. Particularly, $40 \times 39$ pairs of the fixed and moving images were drawn from the dataset, while the pre-trained MS-Net on NIREP dataset was directly used for

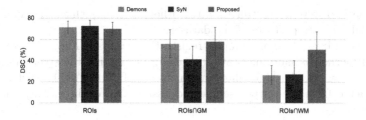

**Fig. 3.** Mean DSC with standard deviation over 54 ROIs of LONI dataset (40 × 39 registration pairs) after registration by Demons, SyN and proposed method.

image simplification. We evaluated the same metrics (*i.e.*, DSC and ASSD) as presented in Table 1. Our method outperformed the other two methods over WM/GM tissues.

Note that the ROIs in LONI dataset do not follow the same segmentation protocol with NIREP. While the LONI ROIs contain a small amount of WM volumes, we refined the ROIs to focus on the registration quality near the highly convoluted cortical areas [14]. Specifically, we separated each ROI into the intersections with GM (ROI ∩ GM) and WM (ROI ∩ WM), respectively. The results show significant improvement of our method as demonstrated in Fig. 3. For example, for ROIs ∩ GM, the average DSC for our method is $58.2 \pm 13.0$, compared to $55.9 \pm 13.3$ (Demons) and $41.5 \pm 12.1$ (SyN). Note that the overall DSC scores

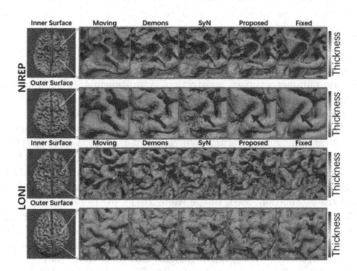

**Fig. 4.** Inner (*first* and *third rows*) and outer (*second* and *fourth rows*) cortical surfaces of the two datasets obtained by registration using Demons, SyN and the proposed method. Red arrows indicate that the proposed method can better align the cortical structures. (Color figure online)

for our method were not better than the other methods, which was mainly due to the ROI labeling protocol of the dataset.

The visual inspection of exemplar registration results in Fig. 4 shows that the proposed method is more accurate, especially in aligning the structures of the cerebral cortex (cf. the highlighted red arrows in Fig. 4). All the surfaces were reconstructed from the warped segmented tissue maps of the moving images.

## 4 Conclusion

In this paper, we proposed a novel method to guide and facilitate the deformable registration by the trajectories that contain a series of images with gradually reduced morphological complexity. The MS-Net generates a trajectory of the subject-specific intermediate images in the intensity space, which acts as the guidance for inter-subject registration, without performing non-trivial pre-processing like tissue segmentation or anatomical parcellation. Moreover, the simplification within the trajectory is applied to the morphological complexity, while the image size/resolution is not reduced. Therefore, our method significantly differs from the classical multi-resolution multi-scale registration schemes. As our method can be easily applied to different datasets, in future we will use it for different applications such as voxel-based morphometric analysis.

**Acknowledgement.** This work was partially supported by the National Key Research and Development Program of China (2018YFC0116400) and STCSM (19QC1400600).

## References

1. Vercauteren, T., Pennec, X., Perchant, A., Ayache, N.: Diffeomorphic demons: efficient non-parametric image registration. NeuroImage **45**(1), S61–S72 (2009)
2. Beg, M.F., et al.: Computing large deformation metric mappings via geodesic flows of diffeomorphisms. Int. J. Comput. Vis. **61**(2), 139–157 (2005)
3. Avants, B.B., et al.: A reproducible evaluation of ANTs similarity metric performance in brain image registration. Neuroimage **54**(3), 2033–2044 (2011)
4. Hamm, J., Ye, D.H., Verma, R., Davatzikos, C.: GRAM: a framework for geodesic registration on anatomical manifolds. Med. Image Anal. **14**(5), 633–642 (2010)
5. Wang, Q., et al.: Predict brain MR image registration via sparse learning of appearance and transformation. Med. Image Anal. **20**(1), 61–75 (2015)
6. Shen, D., Davatzikos, C.: HAMMER: hierarchical attribute matching mechanism for elastic registration. IEEE Trans. Med. Imaging **21**(11), 1421–1439 (2002)
7. Joshi, A.A., et al.: Surface-constrained volumetric brain registration using harmonic mappings. IEEE Trans. Med. Imaging **26**, 1657–1668 (2007)
8. Zhang, J., Wang, Q., Wu, G., Shen, D.: Cross-manifold guidance in deformable registration of brain MR images. In: Zheng, G., Liao, H., Jannin, P., Cattin, P., Lee, S.-L. (eds.) MIAR 2016. LNCS, vol. 9805, pp. 415–424. Springer, Cham (2016). https://doi.org/10.1007/978-3-319-43775-0_38
9. Haskins, G., Uwe, K., Yan, P.: Deep learning in medical image registration: a survey. arXiv:1903.02026 (2019)

10. Balakrishnan, G., et al.: An unsupervised learning model for deformable medical image registration. In: CVPR, pp. 9252–9260 (2018)
11. Ronneberger, O., Fischer, P., Brox, T.: U-Net: convolutional networks for biomedical image segmentation. In: Navab, N., Hornegger, J., Wells, W.M., Frangi, A.F. (eds.) MICCAI 2015. LNCS, vol. 9351, pp. 234–241. Springer, Cham (2015). https://doi.org/10.1007/978-3-319-24574-4_28
12. Taubin, G.: Curve and surface smoothing without shrinkage. In: ICCV, pp. 852–857 (1995)
13. Cao, X., et al.: Deformable image registration using a cue-aware deep regression network. IEEE Trans. Biomed. Eng. 65(9), 1900–1911 (2018)
14. Christensen, G.E., et al.: Introduction to the non-rigid image registration evaluation project (NIREP). In: Pluim, J.P.W., Likar, B., Gerritsen, F.A. (eds.) WBIR 2006. LNCS, vol. 4057, pp. 128–135. Springer, Heidelberg (2006). https://doi.org/10.1007/11784012_16
15. Shattuck, D.W., et al.: Construction of a 3D probabilistic atlas of human cortical structures. Neuroimage 39(3), 1064–1080 (2008)

# Joint Shape Representation
# and Classification for Detecting PDAC

Fengze Liu[1](✉), Lingxi Xie[1], Yingda Xia[1], Elliot Fishman[2], and Alan Yuille[1]

[1] The Johns Hopkins University, Baltimore, MD 21218, USA
fliu23@jhu.edu
[2] The Johns Hopkins University School of Medicine, Baltimore, MD 21287, USA

**Abstract.** We aim to detect pancreatic ductal adenocarcinoma (PDAC) in abdominal CT scans, which sheds light on early diagnosis of pancreatic cancer. This is a 3D volume classification task with little training data. We propose a two-stage framework, which first segments the pancreas into a binary mask, then compresses the mask into a shape vector and performs abnormality classification. Shape representation and classification are performed in a *joint* manner, both to exploit the knowledge that PDAC often changes the **shape** of the pancreas and to prevent overfitting. Experiments are performed on 300 normal scans and 136 PDAC cases. We achieve a specificity of 90.2% (false alarm occurs on less than 1/10 normal cases) at a sensitivity of 80.2% (less than 1/5 PDAC cases are not detected), which show promise for clinical applications.

## 1 Introduction

Pancreatic cancer is a major killer causing hundreds of thousands of deaths globally every year. It often starts with a small set of localized cells multiplying themselves out of control and invading other parts of the body. The five-year survival rate of the patient can reach 20% [6] if the cancer is detected at an early stage, but quickly drops to 5% if it is discovered late and the cancerous cells have spread to other organs [10]. Therefore, early diagnosis of pancreatic cancer can mean the difference between life and death for the patients.

This paper deals with PDAC, the major type of pancreatic cancer accounting for about 85% of the cases [10], and attempts to detect it by checking abdominal CT scans. The pancreas, even in a healthy state, is difficult to segment from a CT volume [9], partly because its 3D shape is irregular [12]. The segmentation, particularly for the cancer lesion area, becomes even more challenging when the pancreas is abnormal, *e.g.*, cystic [13]. In recent years, with the development of deep learning frameworks [3], researchers were able to construct effective deep encoder-decoder networks [4] for organ segmentation [8] or shape representation [1], boosting the accuracy of conventional models for a wide range of medical imaging analysis tasks.

The goal of this paper is to discriminate abnormal pancreases from normal ones[1]. This is a classification task, but directly training a volumetric classifier

---

[1] Throughout this paper, an *abnormal* pancreas is defined as one suffering from PDAC.

© Springer Nature Switzerland AG 2019
H.-I. Suk et al. (Eds.): MLMI 2019, LNCS 11861, pp. 212–220, 2019.
https://doi.org/10.1007/978-3-030-32692-0_25

may suffer from over-fitting due to limited training data. Inspired by the fact that PDAC often changes the pancreas shape, we set shape representation as an intermediate goal, so as to constrain the learning space and regularize the model. Our framework contains two stages. First, we train an encoder-decoder network [11] for voxel-wise pancreas segmentation from CT scans[2]. Second, we use a joint shape representation and classification network to predicts if the patient suffers from PDAC. The weights of the shape representation module are initialized using an auto-encoder [1,2], and then jointly optimized with the classifier. Joint optimization improves classification accuracy at the testing stage.

The radiologists in our team collected and annotated a dataset with 436 CT scans, including 300 normal cases and 136 PDAC cases. Our approach achieves a sensitivity of 80.2% at a specificity of 90.2%, *i.e.*, finding 4/5 of abnormal cases with false alarms on only 1/10 of the normal cases. Some detected PDAC cases contain tiny tumors, which are easily missed by segmentation algorithms and even some professional radiologists. According to the radiologists, our approach can provide auxiliary cues for clinical purposes.

## 2   Detecting PDAC in Abdominal CT Scans

### 2.1   The Overall Framework

A CT-scanned image, $\mathbf{X}$, is a $W \times H \times L$ matrix, where $W$, $H$ and $D$ are the width, height and length of the cube, respectively. Each element in the cube indicates the Hounsfield unit (HU) at the specified position. Each volume is annotated with a binary pancreas mask $\mathbf{S}^\star$ which shares the same dimensionality with $\mathbf{X}$. Our goal is to design a discriminative function $p(\mathbf{X}) \in \{0,1\}$, with 1 indicating that this person suffers PDAC and 0 otherwise.

Our idea is to decompose the function into two stages. The first stage is a segmentation model $\mathbf{f}(\cdot)$ for voxel-wise pancreas segmentation, *i.e.*, where $\mathbf{S} = \mathbf{f}(\mathbf{X})$. The second stage is a mask classifier $c(\cdot)$ which assigns a binary label to the mask $\mathbf{S}$. To make use of shape information, $c(\cdot)$ is further decomposed into a shape encoder $\mathbf{g}(\cdot)$ which produces a compact vector $\mathbf{v} = \mathbf{g}(\mathbf{S})$ to depict the shape properties of the binary mask $\mathbf{S}$, and a shape classifier $h(\cdot)$ which determines if the shape vector $\mathbf{v}$ corresponds to a pancreas suffering from PDAC.

Therefore, the overall framework, shown in Fig. 1, can be written as:

$$p(\mathbf{X}) = c \circ \mathbf{f}(\mathbf{X}) = h \circ \mathbf{g} \circ \mathbf{f}(\mathbf{X}). \tag{1}$$

We can of course design an alternative function, *e.g.*, a 3D classifier which works on CT image data directly, but our stage-wise model makes use of the prior knowledge from the radiologists, *i.e.*, PDAC often changes the shape of the pancreas. This sets up an intermediate goal of optimization and shrinks the search space of our model, which is especially helpful in preventing over-fitting

---

[2] To make our approach generalized, we do not assume the tumors are annotated in the training set, and so we do not perform tumor segmentation.

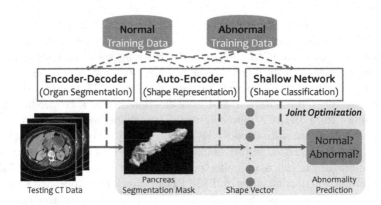

**Fig. 1.** The overall framework of our approach (best viewed in color).

given limited training data. In addition, this also enables us to interpret our prediction. We will show in experiments that, without such prior knowledge, the classifier produces unstable results and less satisfying prediction accuracy.

## 2.2    Pancreas Segmentation by Encoder-Decoder Networks

Our approach starts with an encoder-decoder network for pancreas segmentation. There are typically two choices, which differ from each other in the way of processing volumetric data. The first one applies 2D segmentation networks [8,9] from orthogonal planes, while the other one trains a 3D network directly [5] in a patch-based manner. Either method requires cutting volumetric data into 2D slices or 3D patches at both training and testing stages. As a result, the segmentation function $S = f(X)$ cannot be optimized together with the subsequent modules, namely shape representation and classification.

In practice, we apply a recent 2D segmentation approach named RSTN (Recurrent Saliency Transformation Network) [11] for pancreas segmentation. It trains three models from the *coronal*, *sagittal* and *axial* planes, respectively. In our own dataset, RSTN works very well, providing an average DSC (Dice Similarity Coefficient) of over 87% for normal pancreas segmentation, and over 70% for abnormal pancreas segmentation. We make two comments here. First, the segmentation accuracy of 87% almost reaches the agreement between two individual annotations by different radiologists. Second, the abnormal pancreases are often more difficult to segment, as their appearance and geometry properties can be changed by PDAC. However, as shown later, such imperfections in segmentation only cause little accuracy drop in abnormality classification.

## 2.3    Joint Shape Representation and Classification

Based on pancreas segmentation $S = f(X)$, it remains to determine the abnormality of this pancreas. We achieve this by first compressing the segmentation

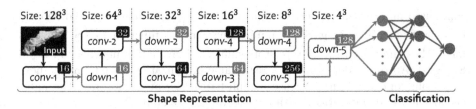

**Fig. 2.** Shape representation and classification network (best viewed in color). Each rectangle is a layer, with the number at the upper-right corner indicating the number of channels. Each convolution (*conv*) layer contains a set of $3 \times 3 \times 3$ kernels, and each down-sampling (*down*) layer uses $2 \times 2 \times 2$ convolution with a stride of 2. Batch normalization and ReLU activation are used after all these layers. The last layer in shape representation (the green neurons) is the low-dimensional shape vector, followed by a 2-layer fully-connected network for classification.

mask into a low-dimensional vector $\mathbf{v} = \mathbf{g}\,(\mathbf{S})$ to compress $\mathbf{v}$, and then applying a classifier $h\,(\cdot)$ on top of $\mathbf{v}$.

The shape representation network $\mathbf{g}\,(\cdot)$ involves down-sampling the segmentation mask gradually. Following [1], this is implemented by a series of 3D convolutional layers. The detailed network configuration is shown in Fig. 2. Regarding the dimensionality of the shape vectors (*i.e.*, the number of output neurons), a high-dimensional representation carries more information, but also risks overfitting under limited training data. We analyze this parameter in experiments. Essentially, both segmentation and shape representation networks perform image down-sampling. The former starts with the raw input image and thus requires complicated and expensive computations. The latter, however, is much simpler, with the network much shallower, which processes the entire volume at once. This makes it possible to be optimized together with the classifier.

In the final step, we implement $h\,(\cdot)$ as a 2-layer fully-connected network. The simplicity of $h\,(\cdot)$ aligns with our motivation, *i.e.*, the vector $\mathbf{v}$ carries discriminative shape information which is easy to classify. Being a differentiable module, it can the optimized with the shape representation network in a joint manner (details are elaborated below), which brings consistent accuracy gain.

The training process starts by sampling a segmentation mask $\mathbf{S}$ from training data. We first perform slight rotation ($0°$ or $\pm 10°$ along three axes individually, 27 possibilities) as data augmentation, and rescale the region within the minimal bounding box into $128 \times 128 \times 128$. Note that direct optimization on $h \circ \mathbf{g}\,(\cdot)$ cannot guarantee that $\mathbf{g}\,(\cdot)$ learns shape information. In addition, direct optimization can lead to over-fitting with limited training data, even after data augmentation (see experiments). Hence, we use a two-step method for gradual optimization.

In the first step, we deal with $\mathbf{g}\,(\cdot)$ by concatenating this module with a decoder network $\tilde{\mathbf{g}}\,(\cdot)$, which performs reverse operations (all convolutions are replaced by deconvolutions) to restore the compressed vector into the original image. This framework, named an auto-encoder [1,2], can be trained in a weakly-supervised manner, *i.e.*, given an input mask **S**, we can minimize the difference between **S** and $\tilde{\mathbf{S}} = \tilde{\mathbf{g}} \circ \mathbf{g}(\mathbf{S})$ by minimizing the loss function $\mathcal{L}_S\left(\mathbf{S}, \tilde{\mathbf{S}}\right)$. This forces the compressed vector **v** to store sufficient information in order to restore $\mathbf{S} = \tilde{\mathbf{g}}(\cdot)$. Auto-encoder provides a reasonable initialization for $\mathbf{g}(\cdot)$ in the next step (joint optimization). We use a mini-batch size of 1 and train the auto-encoder for 40,000 iterations with a fix learning rate of $10^{-6}$.

The second step optimizes $\mathbf{g}(\cdot)$ and $h(\cdot)$ jointly. We use the cross-entropy loss $\mathcal{L}_C(y, p) = y \ln p + \eta \cdot (1 - y) \ln (1 - p)$ where $y$ is the ground-truth and $p = h \circ \mathbf{g}(\mathbf{S})$ is the predicted confidence. $\eta$ performs class-balancing to avoid model bias. The mini-batch size is still set to be 1, and we perform a total of 40,000 iterations. We start with a learning rate of 0.0005, and divide it by 10 after 20,000 and 30,000 iterations. To maximally preserve stability, we freeze all weights of $\mathbf{g}(\cdot)$ in the first 5,000 iterations, so that the 2-layer network $h(\cdot)$, initialized as scratch, is reasonably trained before being optimized together with $\mathbf{g}(\cdot)$.

Last but not least, there is an alternative way of jointly optimizing $\mathbf{g}(\cdot)$ and $h(\cdot)$, *i.e.*, applying a discriminative auto-encoder [7], which preserves the shape restoration loss in the second step and optimizes $\mathcal{L}_S\left(\mathbf{S}, \tilde{\mathbf{S}}\right) + \lambda \cdot \mathcal{L}_C(y, p)$. We do not use this strategy because our ultimate goal is classification – shape representation is an important cue, but we do not hope the constraints in shape restoration harms classification accuracy. In experiments, we find that a discriminative auto-encoder produces less stable classification accuracy.

## 3 Experiments

### 3.1 Dataset and Settings

To the best of our knowledge, there are no publicly available datasets for PDAC diagnosis. We collect a dataset with the help of the radiologists in our team. There are 300 normal CT scans and 136 biopsy-proven abnormal (PDAC) cases, and all of them were scanned by the same machine. The pancreas annotation was done by four expert in abdominal anatomy and each case was checked by a experienced board certified Abdominal Radiologist. The spatial resolution of our data is relatively high, *i.e.*, the physical distance between the neighboring voxels is 0.5 mm in the long axis, and varies from 0.5 mm to 1.0 mm in the other two axes. We do not use data scanned from other types of machines (*e.g.*, the NIH dataset [9]) to avoid dataset bias, *i.e.*, the classifier works by simply checking the spatial resolution or other meta-information of the scan.

We use 100 normal cases for training the RSTN [11] and auto-encoder [1] for pancreas segmentation and shape representation, respectively. The remaining 200 normal and 136 abnormal scans are first segmented using the RSTN then compressed by the auto-encoder. These examples are randomly split into 4 folds, each of which has 50 normal and 34 abnormal cases. We perform cross-validation, *i.e.*, training a classifier on three folds and testing it on the remaining one. We report the sensitivity and specificity of different models.

## 3.2  Quantitative Results

Results are summarized in Table 1. To compare with the joint training strategy, we provide two other competitors, namely a support vector machine (SVM) and the individually-optimized 2-layer network (equivalent to freezing the parameters in the auto-encoder throughout the entire training process). We observe consistent accuracy gains brought by the proposed approach over both competitors, in particular the 2-layer network optimized individually. This stresses the importance and effectiveness of joint optimization. Regarding other options, we find that the classification accuracy of our approach either drops or becomes unstable if we (i) train the entire network from scratch; (ii) preserve the shape restoration loss with classification loss; or (iii) do not freeze the weights of the auto-encoder in the early training sections.

**Table 1.** The sensitivity (sens., %) and specificity (spec., %) reported by different approaches and dimensionalities of shape. We denote the models optimized individually and jointly by (I) and (J), respectively. All these numbers are the average over 5 individual runs. 2LN (J) with 1,024-dimensional vectors has the best average performance.

| Dimension | SVM | | 2LN (I) | | 2LN (J) | |
|---|---|---|---|---|---|---|
| | Sens. | Spec. | Sens. | Spec. | Sens. | Spec. |
| 128 | $73.4 \pm 3.1$ | $87.8 \pm 2.9$ | $77.5 \pm 2.2$ | $87.6 \pm 1.5$ | $79.3 \pm 1.0$ | $89.9 \pm 1.0$ |
| 256 | $75.0 \pm 1.9$ | $87.6 \pm 3.2$ | $78.2 \pm 1.6$ | $89.1 \pm 1.2$ | $79.0 \pm 0.4$ | $90.5 \pm 0.8$ |
| 512 | $78.1 \pm 1.9$ | $89.5 \pm 1.0$ | $80.7 \pm 1.5$ | $88.3 \pm 1.0$ | $79.0 \pm 0.8$ | $\mathbf{90.9 \pm 0.9}$ |
| 1,024 | $75.0 \pm 0.0$ | $89.0 \pm 0.0$ | $78.8 \pm 0.7$ | $90.5 \pm 0.6$ | $\mathbf{80.2 \pm 0.5}$ | $90.2 \pm 0.2$ |

In clinics, an important issue to consider is the tradeoff between sensitivity and specificity. A higher sensitivity implies that more abnormal cases are detected, but also brings the price of a lower specificity. Our approach, by simply tuning the classification threshold, can satisfy different requirements. The ROC curves of different models are shown in Fig. 3. Using our best model (1,024-dimensional shape vector with joint optimization), we can achieve a sensitivity of 95% at a specificity of 53.8%, or a specificity of 95% at a sensitivity of 67.9%.

## 3.3  Qualitative Analysis

We first investigate the relationship between pancreas segmentation quality and classification accuracy. Trained on a standalone set of 100 normal cases, RSTN reports average DSCs of 86.66% and 71.45% on the 200 testing normal and 136 abnormal cases, respectively. The radiologists randomly checked around 20 cases, and verified that our segmentation results, especially on the normal pancreases, have achieved the level of being used for diagnosis. We also use the ground-truth segmentation masks of these 200 + 136 pancreases in classification. With 1,024-dimensional shape vectors, the sensitivity and specificity of the SVM classifier are improved by 9.0% and 2.0%, and these numbers for the 2-layer network are 5.6% and 0.6%, respectively. This indicates that the imperfection of abnormal pancreas segmentation mainly causes drops in sensitivity. But, built on top of automatic segmentation, our framework can be applied to a wide range of scenarios where the manual annotation is not available.

Next, we consider the accuracy of shape representation, or more specifically, the similarity between the restored segmentation mask and the original one. It is obvious that a higher dimension in shape representation stores richer information and thus produces more accurate restoration. However, as shown in Table 1, we do not observe significant gain brought by high dimensionalities. This verifies our assumption, $i.e.$, the classifier does not require accurate shape reconstruction. This also explains the advantage of joint optimization, in which the classifier can capture discriminative information from shape representation, and the shape model can also adjust itself to help classification.

We visualize several successful and failure examples in Fig. 3. Our approach is able to detect some cases with tiny tumors which are easily missed even by the radiologists[3]. On the other hand, our approach is likely to fail when the pancreas segmentation is less accurate, leading to a strange pancreas shape which is not seen in training data and thus confuses the classifier. One false-negative and one false-positive cases are shown in Fig. 3.

Finally, we point out that there is an alternative to our approach, which directly trains segmentation/detection networks to find the tumors in these PDAC cases. In comparison, our approach has two advantages. First, we do not require the tumors to be annotated in the training data, which is an extremely challenging task. Second, our approach can detect some PDAC cases with very small tumors (which largely changed the shape of the pancreas) that are missed by segmentation. We train a tumor segmentation network individually, and find that more than half of the false negative can be recovered by our approach. This suggests that shape representation serves as an auxiliary cue. However, a clear drawback of our approach is not being able to find the exact position of the lesion area. In all, our approach provides an important cue (shape), and it can be integrated with other cues in the future towards more accurate diagnosis, $e.g.$, when voxel-wise tumor annotations are available, we can incorporate pancreas/tumor segmentation into our joint optimization framework.

---

[3] The early diagnosis of PDAC is difficult and can be uncertain from CT scans. In our case, the radiologists proved these PDAC cases with biopsy checks. They can easily miss some of these cases if they were not told their abnormality beforehand.

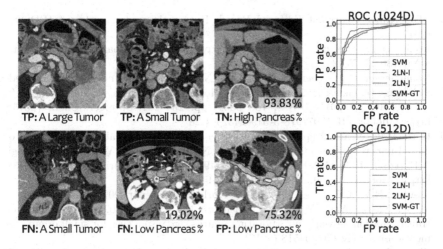

**Fig. 3.** Left: classification results by our approach. Right: the ROC curves. Red and blue contours mark the labeled pancreas and tumor, and blue regions indicate the predicted pancreas. TP, TN, FP, FN: for {true,false}-{positive,negative}, respectively. (Color figure online)

## 4 Conclusions

Our approach is motivated by knowledge from surgical morphology, which claims that the PDAC can be discovered by observing the shape change of the pancreas. We first use an encoder-decoder network to obtain pancreas segmentation, and design a joint framework for shape representation and classification. We initialize shape representation using an auto-encoder, and optimize it with the classifier in a joint manner.

In experiments, our approach achieved a sensitivity of 80.2% with a specificity of 90.2%. It even detected several challenging cases which are easily missed by the radiologists. Given a larger amount of training data, we can expect even higher performance. Our future research directions also involve adding other cues (*e.g.*, tumor segmentation) and training the entire framework in a joint manner.

## References

1. Brock, A., Lim, T., Ritchie, J.M., Weston, N.: Generative and discriminative voxel modeling with convolutional neural networks. arXiv:1608.04236 (2016)
2. Hinton, G.E., Salakhutdinov, R.R.: Reducing the dimensionality of data with neural networks. Science **313**(5786), 504–507 (2006)
3. Krizhevsky, A., Sutskever, I., Hinton, G.E.: ImageNet classification with deep convolutional neural networks. In: NIPS (2012)
4. Long, J., Shelhamer, E., Darrell, T.: Fully convolutional networks for semantic segmentation. In: CVPR (2015)
5. Milletari, F., Navab, N., Ahmadi, S.A.: V-Net: fully convolutional neural networks for volumetric medical image segmentation. In: 3DV (2016)

6. PDQ Adult Treatment Editorial Board: Pancreatic cancer treatment (PDQ®) (2017)
7. Rolfe, J.T., LeCun, Y.: Discriminative recurrent sparse auto-encoders. arXiv:1301.3775 (2013)
8. Ronneberger, O., Fischer, P., Brox, T.: U-Net: convolutional networks for biomedical image segmentation. In: Navab, N., Hornegger, J., Wells, W.M., Frangi, A.F. (eds.) MICCAI 2015. LNCS, vol. 9351, pp. 234–241. Springer, Cham (2015). https://doi.org/10.1007/978-3-319-24574-4_28
9. Roth, H.R., et al.: DeepOrgan: multi-level deep convolutional networks for automated pancreas segmentation. In: Navab, N., Hornegger, J., Wells, W.M., Frangi, A.F. (eds.) MICCAI 2015. LNCS, vol. 9349, pp. 556–564. Springer, Cham (2015). https://doi.org/10.1007/978-3-319-24553-9_68
10. Stewart, B.W.K.P., Wild, C.P., et al.: World cancer report 2014. Health (2017)
11. Yu, Q., Xie, L., Wang, Y., Zhou, Y., Fishman, E.K., Yuille, A.L.: Recurrent saliency transformation network: incorporating multi-stage visual cues for small organ segmentation. arXiv:1709.04518 (2017)
12. Zhang, L., Lu, L., Summers, R.M., Kebebew, E., Yao, J.: Personalized pancreatic tumor growth prediction via group learning. In: Descoteaux, M., Maier-Hein, L., Franz, A., Jannin, P., Collins, D.L., Duchesne, S. (eds.) MICCAI 2017. LNCS, vol. 10434, pp. 424–432. Springer, Cham (2017). https://doi.org/10.1007/978-3-319-66185-8_48
13. Zhou, Y., Xie, L., Fishman, E.K., Yuille, A.L.: Deep supervision for pancreatic cyst segmentation in abdominal CT scans. In: Descoteaux, M., Maier-Hein, L., Franz, A., Jannin, P., Collins, D.L., Duchesne, S. (eds.) MICCAI 2017. LNCS, vol. 10435, pp. 222–230. Springer, Cham (2017). https://doi.org/10.1007/978-3-319-66179-7_26

# Fusionnet: Incorporating Shape and Texture for Abnormality Detection in 3D Abdominal CT Scans

Fengze Liu[1(✉)], Yuyin Zhou[1], Elliot Fishman[2], and Alan Yuille[1]

[1] The Johns Hopkins University, Baltimore, MD 21218, USA
fliu23@jhu.edu
[2] The Johns Hopkins University School of Medicine, Baltimore, MD 21287, USA

**Abstract.** Automatic abnormality detection in abdominal CT scans can help doctors improve the accuracy and efficiency in diagnosis. In this paper we aim at detecting pancreatic ductal adenocarcinoma (PDAC), the most common pancreatic cancer. Taking the fact that the existence of tumor can affect both the shape and the texture of pancreas, we design a system to extract the shape and texture feature at the same time for detecting PDAC. In this paper we propose a two-stage method for this 3D classification task. First, we segment the pancreas into a binary mask. Second, a FusionNet is proposed to take both the binary mask and CT image as input and perform a binary classification. The optimal architecture of the FusionNet is obtained by searching a pre-defined functional space. We show that the classification results using either shape or texture information are complementary, and by fusing them with the optimized architecture, the performance improves by a large margin. Our method achieves a specificity of 97% and a sensitivity of 92% on 200 normal scans and 136 scans with PDAC.

## 1 Introduction

Pancreatic cancer is one of the most dangerous type of cancer. In 2019, about 56770 people will be diagnosed with pancreatic cancer, and pancreatic cancer accounts for about 3% of all cancers in the US and about 7% of all cancer deaths [1]. The 5-year relative survival rate for all stages of pancreatic cancer is only about 9%, while it can rise to 34% if the cancer is detected in an early stage. However, even experienced doctors may miss an early stage cancer because it is small and hard to observe. So developing an reliable automatic system to assist doctors to diagnosis can help decrease the missing rate of patients with early stage of cancer.

This paper is aimed at discriminating normal cases from cases with pancreatic ductal adenocarcinoma (PDAC), the major type of pancreatic cancer accounting for about 85% of the cases, by checking into the abdominal 3D CT scans. With the development of deep learning in recent years [4], researchers have made significant progress in automatically segmenting organs like pancreas

© Springer Nature Switzerland AG 2019
H.-I. Suk et al. (Eds.): MLMI 2019, LNCS 11861, pp. 221–229, 2019.
https://doi.org/10.1007/978-3-030-32692-0_26

from CT scans [7,14,15], which is already a hard task due to the irregular shape of pancreas [12]. Even though, segmenting the lesion region is an even more challenging task due to the large variation in shape, size and location of the lesion [13]. And the full annotation for the lesion region requires more expertise and time to obtain. So instead of directly segmenting the lesion region, detecting the patients with PDAC can already help the diagnosis and, more importantly, is more feasible when the annotation is limited.

We choose to utilize the segmentation mask and CT image for pancreatic abnormality detection, since the segmentation mask can represent the shape while the CT image represents the texture, which are both important for abnormality detection. However we find that the classification results of using only shape and only texture information are quite complementary, which motivates us to combine them in a unified system and thereby can improve the classification outcome. In the natural image domain, how to effectively combine different information has been explored in several different works. [3] proposes a fusion network incorporating depth to improve the segmentation. [8] calculates the normal, depth and silhouette from a single image for better 3D reconstruction. Other works like [9] build different networks for different views of the same data and present co-training strategy to enable the models to incorporate different views.

In this paper we develop a two-stage method for this problem. Firstly, a recent state-of-the-art segmentation network [11] is used to segment the pancreas and then tested on all the data to get the prediction mask for pancreas. Secondly, the CT image is fed into a deep discriminator together with the prediction mask. The discriminator is employed to extract information from both the image and segmentation mask for abnormality classification. We optimize the architecture of the discriminator by searching from a functional space, which includes functions with different fusion strategies. Unlike [16] that needs full annotation for the lesion, our method only requires annotation masks for the pancreas region on cases without PDAC in the first stage, and image-level labels indicating abnormality in the second stage. Other works like [2,5] make use of the information from either the prediction mask or CT image for classification. We show in the experiments that these two kinds of information are complementary to each other and the combination can improve the classification result by a large margin.

We test our framework on 200 normal and 136 abnormal (with PDAC) CT scans. We report a 92% sensitivity and 97% specificity, *i.e.* missing 11 out of 136 abnormal cases with 6 false alarms out of 200 normal cases. Compared with using only single branch, our method improves the result by more than 5% in specificity and 10% in sensitivity.

## 2 Fusion Network for Detecting PDAC

### 2.1 The Overall Framework

The CT scan $\mathbf{X} \in \mathcal{X}$ is a volume of size $L \times W \times H$, where $L$,$W$,$H$ represents the length, width and height of the volume respectively. Typically, a CT scan is of size $512 \times 512 \times H$, where $H$ is the number of slices along the axial axis. Each element in the volume indicates the Hounsfield Unit (HU) at a certain position. Our goal is to learn a discriminative function $f(\mathbf{X}) \in \{0, 1\}$, where 1 indicates PDAC and 0 otherwise.

Directly learning the function $f(\cdot)$ is feasible but not optimal. Because the high dimensionality and rich texture information in the CT image can easily make the model overfit, especially when the number of training data is limited. [5] introduces a constraint by segmenting the pancreas first and learn $f(g(\mathbf{X}))$, where $g(\cdot)$ is a segmentation function to get a binary mask of pancreas $\mathbf{S}$. However this will result in loss of texture information since $g(\mathbf{X})$ is only a binary mask. In order to fully exploit both shape and texture information we consider learning

$$f(g(\mathbf{X}), \mathbf{X}),$$

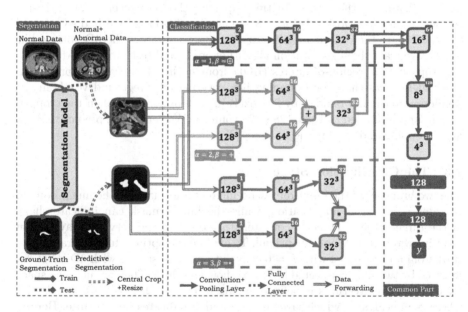

**Fig. 1.** The pipeline of our framework. In stage 1, a segmentation network is trained using the normal data. Then the segmentation network is tested on both normal and abnormal data. The 3D mask and image are cropped and scaled as the input of second stage. At the right side, we show the examples of fusion model using different $\alpha, \beta$. Note that these three models share the same architecture after layer 3 because $\alpha <= 3$ in the examples but they do not share the weights. Each convolution layer uses a set of $3 \times 3 \times 3$ kernels, and each pooling layer uses $2 \times 2 \times 2$ kernels with a stride of 2. Batch normalization and ReLU activation are used after all these layers.

which takes both the segmentation mask and image as input. The major problem here is how to design the function $f(\cdot)$ so that it can well extract shape information from $g(\mathbf{X})$ and texture information from $\mathbf{X}$ and combine them for the classification task. Our idea is to define a functional space representing a set of different fusion strategies and the optimal architecture is obtained by searching that functional space. Given a normal CT dataset $\mathcal{X}_1 = \{(\mathbf{X}, \mathbf{Y})\}$, where the annotation for pancreas $\mathbf{Y}$ is available, and $\mathcal{X}_2 = \{(\mathbf{X}, z)\}$ which contains both normal and abnormal cases with only image-level label $\mathbf{z}$ indicating the abnormality, we split our framework into two stages. First we train a segmentation function $g(\cdot)$ on $\mathcal{X}_1$ and test it on $\mathcal{X}_2$, then the prediction masks together with CT images on $\mathcal{X}_2$ become the input for the second stage to train a classification function $f(\cdot)$. We will introduce each stage in detail in the following sections.

## 2.2   The Segmentation Stage

This stage is necessary in the framework for getting the segmentation mask which will provide shape information in the second stage. Since the focus in this paper is how to combine $g(\mathbf{X})$ and $\mathbf{X}$ in $f(\cdot)$, and also the two stages are executed separately, so the form of $g(\cdot)$ is out of range of this study and will be investigated in the future. In this paper we choose a recent stat-of-the-art segmentation framework [11] for $g$. Since $g(\cdot)$ is a 2D-based method so we need to concatenate the output of different slices to reconstruct the 3D volume like in [10]. We train the segmentation algorithm on $\mathcal{X}_1$ and test it on $\mathcal{X}_2$. After that, we crop out the region-of-interest(ROI) from both CT image and prediction mask, defined as the cube bounding box covering all foreground voxels in the prediction mask and padded by 20 voxels in each dimension. Then the cropped regions are resampled to $128 \times 128 \times 128$ volumes. We denote the predictive mask after cropping and resampling as $\hat{\mathbf{S}} = \mathbf{g}(\mathbf{X})$.

## 2.3   The Classification Stage

The two branches of the input represent different information. The image domain contains rich texture information, while the binary mask can indicate shape of the target object. Directly concatenating them in the very first layer is an intuitive way but may not be optimal. To explore the optimal fusion strategy, we start from a base model with $L = 6$ convolution layers similar with 3D VNet [6], followed by two fully connected layers, as shown in Fig. 1. Then a functional space for different architectures is defined as $\{(\alpha, \beta) | \alpha \in \{1, 2, ..., L\}, \beta \in \{+, *, \oplus\}\}$, where $\alpha$ indicates at which layer to fuse and $\beta$ indicates how to fuse. Here $\oplus$ represents concatenation. See also in Fig. 1 for specific examples for different combination of $\alpha, \beta$. We formulate each fusion function in the functional space $f_{\alpha\beta}(\cdot)$ as following.

$$f_{\alpha\beta}(\mathbf{S}, \mathbf{X}; w) = f_{\alpha:L}(\beta(f_{1:\alpha}(\mathbf{S}; w_{1:\alpha}^1), f_{1:\alpha}(\mathbf{X}; w_{1:\alpha}^2)); w_{\alpha:L}).$$

Here $f_{1:\alpha}(\cdot)$ is the first $\alpha$ convolution layers of the base model while $f_{\alpha:L}(\cdot)$ is the remaining layers. $w = \{w_{1:\alpha}^1, w_{1:\alpha}^2, w_{\alpha:L}\}$ is the parameters to learn. The feature maps of two branches after the first $\alpha$ layers are fused using operation $\beta(\cdot)$ as $\beta(f_{1:\alpha}(\mathbf{S}; w_{1:\alpha}^1), f_{1:\alpha}(\mathbf{X}; w_{1:\alpha}^2))$, and then fed into $f_{\alpha:L}(\cdot)$. The idea of this design is to alleviate the effect of changing the model structure but only focus on finding the best way to combine two different input.

Once given $\alpha, \beta$, we learn $w$ by optimizing a weighted cross-entropy loss

$$L = -\lambda \log p^z - (1 - \lambda) \log(1 - p)^{1-z},$$

where $p = f_{\alpha\beta}(\hat{S}, X; w)$. The output of $f_{\alpha\beta}(\cdot)$ is activated by a sigmoid function so that $p \in [0, 1]$. $z \in \{0, 1\}$ is the label for a CT scan indicating whether this study suffers from PDAC. We set $\lambda = 0.7$ for balancing the class difference during training.

## 3   Experiments

In this section we test our two-stage framework on our dataset containing 3D abdominal CT scans with both patients with and without PDAC. We compare our method with other method using single source input and also show the result of different fusion architectures. We report the sensitivity (SEN), specificity (SPEC), ROC AUC Score (AUC) and F1 Score (F1) to evaluate the classification model.

### 3.1   Dataset and Settings

We collect the dataset with the help of the radiologists. There are 300 normal cases and 136 biopsy proven PDAC cases. 100 out of 300 normal cases have voxel-wise annotations for pancreas (denoted as set $\mathcal{X}_1$), and the remaining 200 normal cases as well as the 136 PDAC cases only have image-level labels, *i.e.*, abnormal/normal (denoted as set $\mathcal{X}_2$). In the first stage, we train the segmentation network on $\mathcal{X}_1$ and test it on $\mathcal{X}_2$. In the second stage, $\mathcal{X}_2$ is randomly split into four folds for cross-validation, where each fold contains 50 normal and 34 abnormal cases and the fusion network is trained on three of the folds and tested on the remaining one.

For the first stage, we follow the instruction of [11] to train a segmentation network. For the second stage, we apply grid search on $\alpha$ and $\beta$, *i.e.* we choose for every pair of $(\alpha, \beta) \in \{(\alpha, \beta) | \alpha \in \{1, 2, ...L\}, \beta \in \{+, *, \oplus\}\}$. In our case, $L = 6$, so there are $3L = 18$ different architectures in total in the search space. After setting $\alpha$ and $\beta$, for training $f_{\alpha\beta}(\cdot)$, we use stochastic gradient descent(SGD) with batch size of 4. The learning rate is set to 0.01 with exponential decay rate 0.9997. We also perform data augmentation on both the CT image and prediction mask by slightly rotating $0°, \pm10°$ along three axes individually (27 possibilities) to prevent from overfitting, since the number of training data is very limited. For each pair of $\alpha, \beta$, the model is trained for 10,000 iterations, which takes about 1.5 h on a NVIDIA TITAN RTX(24GB) GPU.

## 3.2  Primary Results

We compare our method with [5] which utilizes the feature from pre-trained auto-encoder for classification (AE+Mask). We also compare with the base model using either the CT image (Image) or prediction mask (Mask) as input. Our fusion model has the same network structure with the base model after the fusing point for fair comparison. The best result is achieved when fusing the two branches in third layer with multiplication operation. The result is summarized in Table 1. The ROC curves of different models are shown in Fig. 2. Image+Mask GT indicates the strategy that if either one of the two methods (Image and Mask) correctly classifies the case, then we treat this case as correctly classified. This can be the upper bound of merging because it fuses the result based on the ground-truth label. The large improvement in the upper bound result shows that the information provided by the CT image and prediction mask for abnormality detection are quite complementary to each other, which proves the necessity of combining them together. Naive Fusion is done by taking the average of output

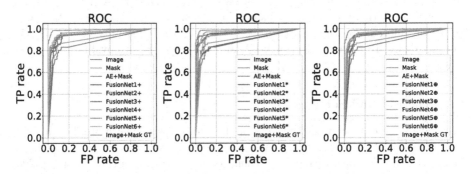

**Fig. 2.** ROC curves for comparison of different fusion strategies. **Left**: fused by +. **Mid**: fused by ∗. **Right**: fused by ⊕. The Image, Mask and AE+Mask are the baseline methods without fusing. The Image+Mask GT is the pseudo upper bound of the fusing.

**Table 1.** Comparison between our method and baseline methods on the sensitivity (SEN), specificity (SPEC), area under the curve (AUC) and F1 score (F1). FusionNet3* achieves the best result, indicating the best way to fuse is to multiply two branches in the third layer.

|                    | SEN   | SPEC  | AUC   | F1    |
| ------------------ | ----- | ----- | ----- | ----- |
| AE+Mask [5]        | 77.94 | 91.00 | 89.04 | 81.54 |
| Mask               | 82.35 | 91.50 | 92.94 | 84.53 |
| Image              | 83.09 | 92.00 | 95.95 | 85.28 |
| Naive Fusion       | 83.09 | 95.50 | 97.17 | 87.60 |
| FusionNet3*(Ours)  | **92.65** | **97.00** | **97.72** | **94.03** |
| Mask+Image GT      | 94.12 | 97.50 | 99.53 | 95.17 |

from Mask and Image and only shows limited improvement. This fact further validates the efficacy of our proposed FusionNet.

### 3.3   Analysis and Discussion

*Single Branch Comparison:* From Table 1 we can see the comparison among Image, Mask and AE+Mask which all use only one branch of information. Using only the image works the best, which indicates the importance of texture for detecting PDAC. For the other two methods using only shape information, directly training a discriminator achieves better results, showing that the constraint of auto-encoder can harm the classification performance.

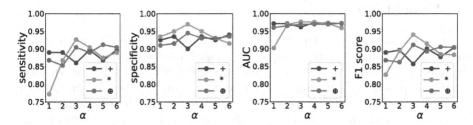

**Fig. 3.** Comparison on the sensitivity, specificity, AUC and F1 score between different fusion architectures.

**Table 2.** Comparison between different fusion architectures on the F1 scores, number of parameters and floating-point operations (FLOPs). As $\alpha$ increases, the two branches fuse at more latter layer, so the parameters number also increases. However the best performance is achieved when $\alpha = 3$.

| $\alpha$ | | 1 | 2 | 3 | 4 | 5 | 6 |
|---|---|---|---|---|---|---|---|
| $\beta = +$ | F1 | 88.97 | 89.63 | 85.71 | 90.04 | 87.73 | 90.37 |
| | # Para | 3.99M | 3.99M | 4.01M | 4.10M | 4.45M | 5.86M |
| | FLOPs | 7.99M | 7.99M | 8.04M | 8.21M | 8.92M | 11.74M |
| $\beta = *$ | F1 | 82.68 | 89.39 | 94.03 | 91.45 | 88.48 | 88.32 |
| | # Para | 3.99M | 3.99M | 4.01M | 4.10M | 4.45M | 5.86M |
| | FLOPs | 7.99M | 7.99M | 8.04M | 8.21M | 8.92M | 11.74M |
| $\beta = \oplus$ | F1 | 86.76 | 86.25 | 91.11 | 89.30 | 90.51 | 90.44 |
| | # Para | 3.99M | 4.01M | 4.07M | 4.32M | 5.34M | 7.96M |
| | FLOPs | 7.99M | 8.02M | 8.15M | 8.66M | 10.69M | 15.94M |

*Fusion Comparison:* The result of fusing at different layers with different operations is as shown in Table 2 and Fig. 3. First of all, almost all the fusion models can perform better than the single branch model, which proves the advantages of fusing shape and texture. Table 2 shows the number of parameters and floating-point operations for each model to show how the size of model affects the classification result. We can see as $\alpha$ increases, the size of model increases, but the classification result does not always improve correspondingly. For the + fusion operation, the performance is better when fusing at the earlier or later layers of the network. For the $*$ and $\oplus$ operation, however, fusing at the middle layer of the network shows better performance. The best result is obtained when fusing at the third layer with $*$ operation.

## 4    Conclusion

In this paper we propose a FusionNet which combines shape and texture information from the segmentation mask and CT image for detecting PDAC. Compared with using only single source of information, using both shape and texture information improves the performance by a large margin. We also explore the best network structure for fusing these two branches together by searching from a functional space, which is to multiply the feature map of two branches in the middle of the network. We report a 92% sensitivity and a 97% specificity by doing 4-fold cross-validation on 200 normal patients and 138 patients with PDAC.

## References

1. Seer cancer statistics review 1975–2015. National Cancer Institute. Bethesda, MD
2. Chen, X., Chen, Y., Ma, C., Liu, X., Tang, X.: Classification of pancreatic tumors based on MRI images using 3D convolutional neural networks. In: ISICDM (2018)
3. Hazirbas, C., Ma, L., Domokos, C., Cremers, D.: FuseNet: incorporating depth into semantic segmentation via fusion-based CNN architecture. In: Lai, S.-H., Lepetit, V., Nishino, K., Sato, Y. (eds.) ACCV 2016. LNCS, vol. 10111, pp. 213–228. Springer, Cham (2017). https://doi.org/10.1007/978-3-319-54181-5_14
4. Krizhevsky, A., Sutskever, I., Hinton, G.E.: ImageNet classification with deep convolutional neural networks. In: NIPS (2012)
5. Liu, F., Xie, L., Xia, Y., Fishman, E.K., Yuille, A.L.: Joint shape representation and classification for detecting PDAC. ArXiv (2018)
6. Milletari, F., Navab, N., Ahmadi, S.A.: V-Net: fully convolutional neural networks for volumetric medical image segmentation, pp. 565–571, October 2016
7. Roth, H.R., et al.: DeepOrgan: multi-level deep convolutional networks for automated pancreas segmentation. In: Navab, N., Hornegger, J., Wells, W.M., Frangi, A.F. (eds.) MICCAI 2015. LNCS, vol. 9349, pp. 556–564. Springer, Cham (2015). https://doi.org/10.1007/978-3-319-24553-9_68
8. Wu, J., Wang, Y., Xue, T., Sun, X., Freeman, W.T., Tenenbaum, J.B.: MarrNet: 3D shape reconstruction via 2.5D sketches. In: Advances in Neural Information Processing Systems (2017)
9. Xia, Y., et al.: 3D semi-supervised learning with uncertainty-aware multi-view co-training. arXiv

10. Xia, Y., Xie, L., Liu, F., Zhu, Z., Fishman, E.K., Yuille, A.L.: Bridging the gap between 2D and 3D organ segmentation with volumetric fusion Net. In: Frangi, A.F., Schnabel, J.A., Davatzikos, C., Alberola-López, C., Fichtinger, G. (eds.) MICCAI 2018. LNCS, vol. 11073, pp. 445–453. Springer, Cham (2018). https://doi.org/10.1007/978-3-030-00937-3_51
11. Yu, Q., Xie, L., Wang, Y., Zhou, Y., Fishman, E.K., Yuille, A.L.: Recurrent saliency transformation network: incorporating multi-stage visual cues for small organ segmentation. In: CVPR (2018)
12. Zhang, L., Lu, L., Summers, R.M., Kebebew, E., Yao, J.: Personalized pancreatic tumor growth prediction via group learning. In: Descoteaux, M., Maier-Hein, L., Franz, A., Jannin, P., Collins, D.L., Duchesne, S. (eds.) MICCAI 2017. LNCS, vol. 10434, pp. 424–432. Springer, Cham (2017). https://doi.org/10.1007/978-3-319-66185-8_48
13. Zhou, Y., Xie, L., Fishman, E.K., Yuille, A.L.: Deep supervision for pancreatic cyst segmentation in abdominal CT scans. In: Descoteaux, M., Maier-Hein, L., Franz, A., Jannin, P., Collins, D.L., Duchesne, S. (eds.) MICCAI 2017. LNCS, vol. 10435, pp. 222–230. Springer, Cham (2017). https://doi.org/10.1007/978-3-319-66179-7_26
14. Zhou, Y., Xie, L., Shen, W., Wang, Y., Fishman, E.K., Yuille, A.L.: A fixed-point model for pancreas segmentation in abdominal CT scans. In: Descoteaux, M., Maier-Hein, L., Franz, A., Jannin, P., Collins, D.L., Duchesne, S. (eds.) MICCAI 2017. LNCS, vol. 10433, pp. 693–701. Springer, Cham (2017). https://doi.org/10.1007/978-3-319-66182-7_79
15. Zhu, Z., Xia, Y., Shen, W., Fishman, E., Yuille, A.: A 3D coarse-to-fine framework for volumetric medical image segmentation. In: 2018 International Conference on 3D Vision (3DV) (2018)
16. Zhu, Z., Xia, Y., Xie, L., Fishman, E.K., Yuille, A.L.: Multi-scale coarse-to-fine segmentation for screening pancreatic ductal adenocarcinoma. ArXiv (2018)

# Ultrasound Liver Fibrosis Diagnosis Using Multi-indicator Guided Deep Neural Networks

Jiali Liu[1,2], Wenxuan Wang[1,2], Tianyao Guan[2], Ningbo Zhao[3],
Xiaoguang Han[1,2], and Zhen Li[1,2($\boxtimes$)]

[1] Shenzhen Research Institute of Big Data, Shenzhen, Guangdong, China
[2] Chinese University of Hong Kong, Shenzhen, Shenzhen, Guangdong, China
lizhen@cuhk.edu.cn
[3] The Third Peoples Hospital of Shenzhen, Shenzhen, China

**Abstract.** Accurate analysis of the fibrosis stage plays very important roles in follow-up of patients with chronic hepatitis B infection. In this paper, a deep learning framework is presented for automatically liver fibrosis prediction. On contrary of previous works, our approach can take use of the information provided by multiple ultrasound images. An indicator-guided learning mechanism is further proposed to ease the training of the proposed model. This follows the workflow of clinical diagnosis and make the prediction procedure interpretable. To support the training, a dataset is well-collected which contains the ultrasound videos/images, indicators and labels of 229 patients. As demonstrated in the experimental results, our proposed model shows its effectiveness by achieving the state-of-the-art performance, specifically, the accuracy is **65.6%** (**20%** higher than previous best).

**Keywords:** Multi-indicator · Liver fibrosis diagnosis · Ultrasound

## 1 Introduction

It was estimated that about 248 million people worldwide were chronic HBV infections in 2010 [1]. Most people with HBV infection would develop to cirrhosis or hepatocellular carcinoma. As reported, the number of deaths from cirrhosis and or hepatocellular carcinoma caused by HBV increased by 33% between 1990 and 2013 [2]. An accurate analysis of the fibrosis stage is thus very important during follow-up of patients with chronic hepatitis B infection. The development of fibrosis is not only a major prognostic factor, but often used to determine whether a patient needs antiviral therapy. Although liver biopsy is considered of the gold standard, it has many shortcomings. The most important thing is that the false negative result for diagnosing cirrhosis can reach 20% to 30% due to sampling errors [3]. As a result, patients will usually miss the optimal

---

J. Liu and W. Wang—Equal contribution.

© Springer Nature Switzerland AG 2019
H.-I. Suk et al. (Eds.): MLMI 2019, LNCS 11861, pp. 230–237, 2019.
https://doi.org/10.1007/978-3-030-32692-0_27

treatment time. In addition, biopsy is invasive and expensive [4], which brings great pain and a heavy financial burden to the patient. There is also a risk of serious complications (0.4%) and may even result in death (0.03%). Therefore, various non-invasive methods have been developed to replace the role of liver biopsy in fibrosis staging [5], such as measuring related biomarkers and observing their morphological changes by ultrasound or magnetic resonance. Considering ultrasonic examination is non-radiation, cheap and easy-to-access in practice, this paper focuses on designing algorithms for automatic liver fibrosis diagnosis using ultrasound images.

Previously, many works have utilized conventional machine learning methods for this task. The work of [6] developed a method for textured feature modeling, which is then applied to classify liver disease. Yeh et al. [7] proposed to classify the liver fibrosis status using the features extracted by gray level concurrence and non-separable wavelet transform. Advanced deep learning approaches, such as convolutional neural networks (CNN), show high superiority than conventional learning methods on the feature modeling [8]. They are also successfully applied in some applications of medical image analysis. For example, the work of [9] trained a VGG model for skin cancer diagnosis using the photos captured with a daily camera.

The deep learning method has been also utilized in [10] for the same task studied in our paper. Its algorithm for liver fibrosis diagnosis is formulated as a classification task that takes only one ultrasound image (usually liver parenchyma echo) as input. However, this method does not resemble the practical clinician's process, which usually utilizes multiple ultrasound images for diagnosis. Due to insufficient input information, it tends to result in low prediction accuracy.

The clinical workflow of liver fibrosis is consisting of two primary steps: Firstly, the doctors usually scan 10 ultrasound images for different body locations and then predict a set of indicators. Secondly, they conduct the diagnosis by observing both the indicators and the scanned images. Our approach is designed following this procedure from two aspects: (1) A multi-stream feature modeling module is developed to extract features from the 10 images in parallel, which are then concatenated for further liver fibrosis classification. This is implemented by a VGG model with weights sharing. (2) We innovatively involve the multi-indicator labels as extra supervisions and form an indicator-guided learning scheme. The indicators are connected with their corresponding feature streams based on the clinical guidelines. These strategies not only efficiently improve the prediction accuracy but also make the automatic diagnosis interpretable. To support the training, a dataset is carefully collected, which contains the samples of 229 patients. For each patient, 8 ultrasound videos and 10 ultrasound images are scanned, the results of 13 indicators and the final diagnosis are also collected.

To this end, the contributions of this paper can be concluded as:

- An novel algorithm for automatic liver fibrosis diagnosis is proposed, which well-follows the clinical workflow and achieves the state-of-the-art performance.

- A dataset is carefully-prepared, including the ultrasound videos/images and the results of both 13 indicators and the final diagnosis.
- A novel indicator-guided multi-stream deep neural network is designed which efficiently ease the training procedure and also makes the model interpretable.

## 2   Dataset Construction

According to the radiologists' routine diagnostic procedure, by only exploiting one ultrasound image containing liver echo information provides insufficient information for the liver fibrosis diagnosis. Thus, we designed a protocol to collect ultrasound dataset with multiple ultrasound images and videos, aiming at promoting the development of automatic diagnosis of liver fibrosis.

### 2.1   Clinical Workflow

The diagnosis process for radiologists is very instructive. Specifically, radiologists first saved 10 indicators images for each patient. Then 8 videos are also saved for supplemented temporal information. We follow the same process to collect our own dataset.

The concrete diagnosis process is described below. First, place the ultrasound probe on the left side of the xiphoid and obtain a clear image of the left hepatic angle by vertical section scanning. Second, move to the place below the right costal margin, we will see right liver and hepatic vein. Third, move to the place below the left costal margin, and there are spleen. Then, we will place the probe on right intercostal space, and obtain the image of portal vein. And we can obtain the image of liver parenchyma concatenated with the image of spleen. Based on domain knowledge, liver parenchyma echo should be distinguished with spleen parenchyma echo. Except the image of liver capsule is obtained through convex array probe, the others are obtained by linear array probe.

### 2.2   Dataset Details

**Patients.** Since our research focuses on liver disease caused by hepatitis B, patients collected in our dataset are primarily infected with hepatitis B. Besides, those who have received liver surgery, gallbladder surgery, or spleen surgery are further excluded as information of these organ will affect liver fibrosis diagnosis. In total, we collect the samples for 229 patients from a hospital.

**Indicators.** Before conducting final diagnosis, the clinical doctors usually predict a set of indicators by observing the statuses of 10 ultrasound images in different body locations. We call these images as indicator images (illustrated in Fig. 1). Due to the lack of authoritative ultrasound diagnosis guideline for liver fibrosis, we investigate relevant medical literature [11] and consult with experienced radiologists, concluding 13 indicators, i.e., left hepatic angle, right liver slant diameter, gallbladder wall morphology, gallbladder wall thickness, spleen size, spleen thickness, spleen Length, liver parenchyma echo, liver capsule morphology, portal vein diameter, portal vein blood flow direction, hepatic vein diameter and hepatic vein morphology. Each indicator is of multiple statues, making the indicator prediction can be formulated as a classification task. For example, on the basis of indicator 1, left hepatic angle of a patient can have two categories, i.e., acute or blunt. The classification labels of those indicators are given by experienced radiologists.

**Indicator Images.** The ultrasound images containing the indicators information are called indicator images. In consistent with practical clinical procedure, we also collect 10 indicator images for each patient for 13 indicators judgement. Note that, the 10 indicator images and the 13 indicators have a many-to-many mapping. This is given by experience radiologists and is very helpful for our model design. For example, indicator image1 contains information about indicator 1, i.e., left hepatic angle.

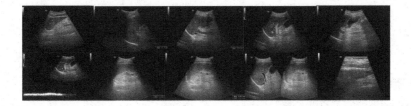

**Fig. 1.** Indicator images

**Ultrasound Videos.** In order to supplement the temporal coherence information of indicators that the radiologists may use during the diagnosis, each patient collected 8 ultrasound videos and each video lasted 5 s. For example, the video_4 corresponding indicator_6 which is the liver capsule morphology.

**Diagnoses.** Diagnosis is given based on the information of all indicators. All patients were divided into 4 categories by experienced radiologists, which are normal, coarseness of liver parenchyma echo, liver brosis and liver cirrhosis.

**Dataset Summary.** All the dataset summaries are listed in Table 1, which consists of distribution of diagnoses and indicators for 229 patients.

## 3    Methodology

### 3.1    Multi-stream Feature Extraction

As illustrated in Fig. 2, 10 indicator images are fed into 10 VGG models (a vanilla VGG-16 without last two fully connected layers) in parallel, which achieves a

**Table 1.** Data summary

| Label | Diagnoses | Indicator_1 (Left hepatic angle) | Indicator_2 (Liver size) | Indicator_3 (Right liver slant) | Indicator_4 (Liver parenchyma echo) | Indicator_5 (Spleen size) | Indicator_6 (Liver capsule form) |
|---|---|---|---|---|---|---|---|
| 0 | 38 (Normal) | 149 (Acute) | 180 (Normal) | 124 (Less than 130mm) | 138 (coarseness of liver parenchyma echo) | 174 (Mild swelling) | 122 (Smooth) |
| 1 | 73 (Coarseness of liver parenchyma echo) | 80 (Blunt) | 49 (Zoom out) | 105 (Larger than 130mm) | 12 (Asymmetry) | 22 (Moderate swelling) | 63 (Wavy) |
| 2 | 58 (Liver Fibrosis) | - | - | - | 58 (Patch) | 19 (Severe swelling) | 44 (Jagged) |
| 3 | 60 (Liver Cirrhosis) | - | - | - | - | - | - |

| Label | Indicator_7 (Portal vein diameter) | Indicator_8 (Portal vein flow direction) | Indicator_9 (Hepatic vein morphology) | Indicator_10 (Spleen thickness) | Indicator_11 (Spleen length) | Indicator_12 (Gallbladder wall thickness) | Indicator_13 (Gallbladder wall morphology) |
|---|---|---|---|---|---|---|---|
| 0 | 146 (Less than 12mm) | 224 (Into the liver) | 185 (Stiffness) | 160 (Less than 40mm) | 167 (Less than 120mm) | 214 (Less than 3mm) | 49 (Smooth) |
| 1 | 83 (Larger than 12mm) | 5 (Out the liver) | 44 (Slim) | 55 (Larger than 40mm) | 48 (Less than 120mm) | 8 (Larger than 3mm) | 173 (Rough) |

4096-D feature vector for each indicator image. To reduce the model complexity and enhance feature learning between different indicator images, we exploit shared weights for 10 parallel VGG models. Such weight-sharing strategy means the same weights are leveraged for the forward and the total losses are accumulated from 10 parallel paths for the backward, which can avoid over-fitting problem effectively.

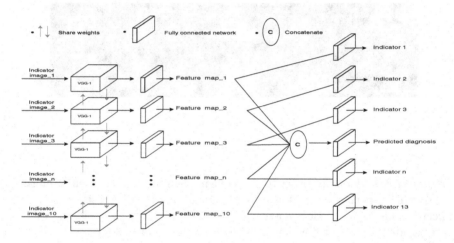

**Fig. 2.** Multi-indicator guided deep neural networks for ultrasound liver fibrosis diagnosis with weight-sharing.

### 3.2 Indicator-Guided Learning

As the whole pipeline shown in Fig. 2, then the feature map of one indicator image extracted in multi-stream feature extraction module is divided to two streams. One is fed to a fully connected layer to predict corresponding indicator label. The other one is concatenated with other 9 indicator image's feature maps as the patient level feature to predict diagnosis label through another fully connected layer.

**Loss Functions.** We design two losses to train our model, i.e., Indicator Loss and Diagnosis Loss. Indicator Loss and Diagnosis Loss are the cross-entropy losses between predicted labels and their ground truth labels. We use the following weighted sum of $n$ Indicator Loss and Diagnosis Loss as our Total Loss for joint learning.

$$Total\_Loss = Diagnosis\_Loss + \sum_{i=0}^{n} \lambda_i * Indicator\_Loss_i$$

### 3.3 Training Strategy

In order to get good performance, we utilize several training strategies as follows.

**Pre-training Using Ultrasound Videos.** Vanilla VGG is a pre-trained model on ImageNet dataset consisting of nature images, so it cannot be used as feature extractor for ultrasound images directly. Thus, we first fine-tune the VGG model based on the large amount of frames extracted from ultrasound videos, detailed setting is presented in Sect. 4.1.

**3-Stage Optimization.** In training stage, our model aims to predict indicator label and diagnosis label, which is known as a multi-task learning task. To accelerate model training, we utilize a 3-stage-training strategy. In the first stage, we focus on learning indicators, i.e., we fix the parameters of diagnosis prediction layers and only use Indicator Loss to update our model. Corresponding to the first stage, we fix the parameters of indicator prediction layers and use Diagnosis Loss to update our model. In final stage, we use the joint Total Loss as introduced above to optimize the whole model.

## 4 Experiments

### 4.1 Implementation Details

Our model is implemented in Pytorch[1]. We use video frames to pre-train our model. Each video is sampled one frame per second. And the label of each frame is assigned the same as the corresponding video. Based on the pre-trained model, we further fine-tune our model using indicator images. In each batch, 10 indicator images from one patient as inputs are fed into the model, and the patient's diagnosis label and indicator labels work as supervision. We use Momentum SGD with weight decay as optimization method. The initial learning rate is $2 \times 10^{-3}$ and momentum is set as 0.9. We trained our model by 50 epochs with non-decreasing model policy. For data augmentation, we use random resize crop and random flip. And we set $\lambda = 0.1$ experimentally.

---

[1] https://pytorch.org/.

**Table 2.** Experimental results

| Methods | Accuracy |
|---|---|
| [10] | 45.6% |
| **Ours** | **65.6%** |
| Without 3-stage | 59.5% |
| Without indicator | 56.2% |
| Without weight sharing | 55.0% |
| Without pre-train | 40.6% |

### 4.2 Comparison Against State-of-the-Arts

To the best of our knowledge, only [10] designs a deep learning framework for the liver fibrosis diagnosis using ultrasound images. Thus, we reproduce their method and compare with our methods on our large dataset. As the results presented in Table 2, Our method outperforms [10] by a large margin.

### 4.3 Ablation Studies

To discover the vital elements or components of our model, we conduct an ablation study by removing or reap lacing some components. The detailed experimental results are also shown in Table 2.

**w/o Indicator Guidance.** In order to evaluate the effect of indicator guidance, we simplify our model by removing the indicator supervision and just use diagnosis labels for the training. The results show that our model can get better performance with an extra supervision of indicator labels.

**w/o Video Pre-training.** Without using ultrasound data to pre-train VGG, the diagnosis accuracy decreases dramatically, which shows the effectiveness of pre-training.

**w/o Weights Sharing.** Rather than using a shared weight VGG to extract feature from 10 kinds of indicator images, we use 10 different VGG models. The results show that weight sharing is a good way to reduce over-fitting, which is essential for small dataset.

**w/o 3-Stage Optimization.** Rather than using three stages training strategy, we compare results training with only one stage, which exploits the combined Diagnosis Loss and Indicator Loss to train the whole model jointly. The results show that one stage learning is not stable to get the optimal solution.

## 5   Conclusion

In this paper, a deep learning framework is presented for automatically liver fibrosis prediction. Our approach can take using the information provided by multiple ultrasound images. An indicator-guided learning mechanism is further proposed to ease the training of the proposed network through weight-sharing. This follows the workflow of clinical diagnosis and make the prediction procedure interpretable. Besides, a dataset is well-collected which contains the ultrasound videos/images, indicators and labels of 229 patients. Our proposed model shows its effectiveness by achieving the state-of-the-art performance. In the future, how to fully encode the information from ultrasound video instead of selected frames and how to fuse video and indicator images information better may be two possible research directions.

# References

1. Schweitzer, A., Horn, J., Mikolajczyk, R.T., Krause, G., Ott, J.J.: Estimations of worldwide prevalence of chronic hepatitis B virus infection: a systematic review of data published between 1965 and 2013. The Lancet **386**(10003), 1546–1555 (2015)
2. Stanaway, J.D., et al.: The global burden of viral hepatitis from 1990 to 2013: findings from the global burden of disease study 2013. The Lancet **388**(10049), 1081–1088 (2016)
3. Denzer, U., Arnoldy, A., Kanzler, S., Galle, P.R., Dienes, H.P., Lohse, A.W.: Prospective randomized comparison of minilaparoscopy and percutaneous liver biopsy: diagnosis of cirrhosis and complications. J. Clin. Gastroenterol. **41**(1), 103–110 (2007)
4. Wong, J.B., Koff, R.S.: Watchful waiting with periodic liver biopsy versus immediate empirical therapy for histologically mild chronic hepatitis C: a cost-effectiveness analysis. Ann. Intern. Med. **133**(9), 665–675 (2000)
5. Dohan, A., Guerrache, Y., Boudiaf, M., Gavini, J.-P., Kaci, R., Soyer, P.: Transjugular liver biopsy: indications, technique and results. Diagn. Intervent. Imaging **95**(1), 11–15 (2014)
6. Mojsilovic, A., Popovic, M., Markovic, S., Krstic, M.: Characterization of visually similar diffuse diseases from B-scan liver images using nonseparable wavelet transform. IEEE Trans. Med. Imaging **17**(4), 541–549 (1998)
7. Yeh, W.-C., Huang, S.-W., Li, P.-C.: Liver fibrosis grade classification with B-mode ultrasound. Ultrasound Med. Biol. **29**(9), 1229–1235 (2003)
8. Simonyan, K., Zisserman, A.: Very deep convolutional networks for large-scale image recognition. arXiv preprint arXiv:1409.1556 (2014)
9. Esteva, A., et al.: Dermatologist-level classification of skin cancer with deep neural networks. Nature **542**(7639), 115 (2017)
10. Meng, D., Zhang, L., Cao, G., Cao, W., Zhang, G., Bing, H.: Liver fibrosis classification based on transfer learning and fcnet for ultrasound images. IEEE Access **5**, 5804–5810 (2017)
11. Crespo, G., et al.: ARFI, FibroScan® elf, and their combinations in the assessment of liver fibrosis: a prospective study. J. Hepatol. **57**(2), 281–287 (2012)

# Weakly Supervised Segmentation
## by a Deep Geodesic Prior

Aliasghar Mortazi[1,2,3](✉), Naji Khosravan[1], Drew A. Torigian[2], Sila Kurugol[3], and Ulas Bagci[1]

[1] Center for Research in Computer Vision (CRCV),
School of Computer Science, University of Central Florida,
Orlando, FL, USA
a.mortazi@knights.ucf.edu

[2] Medical Image Processing Group (MIPG), Department of Radiology,
University of Pennsylvania, Philadelphia, PA, USA

[3] Computational Radiology Laboratory (CRL), Department of Radiology,
Boston Children's Hospital and Harvard Medical School, Boston, MA, USA

**Abstract.** The performance of the state-of-the-art image segmentation methods heavily relies on the high-quality annotations, which are not easily affordable, particularly for medical data. To alleviate this limitation, in this study, we propose a weakly supervised image segmentation method based on *a deep geodesic prior*. We hypothesize that integration of this prior information can reduce the adverse effects of weak labels in segmentation accuracy. Our proposed algorithm is based on a prior information, extracted from an auto-encoder, trained to map objects' geodesic maps to their corresponding binary maps. The obtained information is then used as an extra term in the loss function of the segmentor. In order to show efficacy of the proposed strategy, we have experimented segmentation of cardiac substructures with clean and two levels of noisy labels (L1, L2). Our experiments showed that the proposed algorithm boosted the performance of baseline deep learning-based segmentation for both clean and noisy labels by 4.4%, 4.6%(L1), and 6.3%(L2) in dice score, respectively. We also showed that the proposed method was more robust in the presence of high-level noise due to the existence of shape priors.

**Keywords:** Medical image segmentation · Deep learning · Shape prior · Weakly supervised · Geodesic prior

## 1 Introduction

Driven by deep learning, artificial intelligence (AI) has attracted a widespread interest towards solving many challenging clinical problems. In medical AI applications, image segmentation is one of the mostly affected field from deep learning

A. Mortazi—This work was done partially during internship at Boston Children's Hospital under the supervision of Dr. Kurugol and was supported partially by Crohns and Colitis Foundation of Americas (CCFA) Career Development Award and AGA-Boston Scientific Technology and Innovation Award.

© Springer Nature Switzerland AG 2019
H.-I. Suk et al. (Eds.): MLMI 2019, LNCS 11861, pp. 238–246, 2019.
https://doi.org/10.1007/978-3-030-32692-0_28

as it is often the first step for many image analysis tasks (shape analysis, volume measurements, and computer aided diagnosis). Since manual measurements are very expensive, time consuming, and prone to inter- and intra-observer variations, having an automated, accurate, and efficient segmentation tool is the ultimate goal in many medical systems. In the deep learning era, numerous works have been published, showing feasibility of deep learning in segmentation of radiology images. However, most of these works focus on new network architectures adopted to the medical problem, and they rarely consider the fundamental challenge of the medical AI: availability of precisely annotated data.

In this work, we propose a weakly-supervised segmentation method coupled with a deep geodesic prior to solve 3D medical image segmentation problem in a robust manner. This prior is mainly introduced to improve the performance of segmentation networks, more specifically when the annotations are noisy (i.e., not excellent). We argue that our proposed method is a significant step toward using inexpert and noisy annotations to train deep models for image segmentation without sacrificing the accuracy. The deep geodesic prior is specifically designed to put more attention in constructing accurate edges from weak labels. Although the proposed strategy is generic and can theoretically be applied to any medical image segmentation problem, herein we focus on cardiac MRI analysis due to its clinical significance and challenging nature of the MR imaging [1].

**Related Works:** One of the most successful deep-learning based segmentation methods is based on an encoder-decoder style architecture, called *SegNet*, proposed by [2]. Among many other architectures, U-Net [10] has became the most popular due to its properties such as efficient flow of low-level features through skip connections from decoder to encoder. To decrease the highly occupied parameter space of U-Net architecture(s), new network architectures were also presented: for instance, segmentation capsules (SegCaps) [7], densely-connected network [4] and Tiramisu [5] have shown drastic decrease in parameter space, while maintaining relatively good accuracy compared to baseline U-Nets.

The literature for integrating shape priors into image segmentation is vast, mostly from pre-deep learning era. A mainstream approach is to construct a shape prior from a set of training samples represented implicitly by signed distance functions [6,8]. In the deep learning era, Zotti et al. [12] used image registration to align shape priors and created atlas(es) to guide segmentation. Simply, authors have used this atlas for adding an extra loss term to the segmentation network. Modeling a prior (in shape or appearance) from medical images is still a challenging task due to highly diverse appearance, shape, and size of the anatomical objects. The first attempt to model shape prior with deep features was done by training an auto-encoder (AE) for creating features from the binary labels [9]. The AE was trained to reconstruct the binary input images in its output with a fully-connected layer as a bottleneck to capture the shape features. Then, these shape features were integrated into the segmentation network through an appropriate loss term. While the work in [9] is promising, it is not entirely clear whether the local anatomical variations are captured in detail.

We hypothesize that, if modeled correctly, prior information can lead to a more robust segmentation even when the labels are noisy (i.e., labels annotated by non-experts). To test this hypothesis, we propose a novel method for learning the prior from the geodesic maps of multiple objects. Then, an AE-like network is used to generate the original binary images from their corresponding geodesic maps. Finally, the features from the trained AE are used as a prior to be integrated into the segmentor for better guidance and performance improvement.

## 2  Method

Our framework consists of two main components: (1) the segmentation network (or *segmentor* in short), and (2) the geodesic prior learning network. While our segmentation network assigns a class label to each pixel of the input image, our second network (AE) learns a prior from geodesic maps, generated for each object of interest (for multiple objects). We anticipate (and show later in the results section) that incorporating a well-designed prior into the segmentation network improves its performance, especially in the presence of inaccurate labels.

The overview of our approach is illustrated in Fig. 1. The segmentation network ($Net_{seg}$) (Fig. 1(a)) is an encoder-decoder architecture with 3D kernel convolutions. We utilize skip connections in the form of dense connection throughout this network [4]. For the prior learning network (AE), noisy annotations (or binary ground truths) are used to generate geodesic maps (Fig. 1(c)). Then, the geodesic auto-encoder (GAE) is designed to generate binary ground truths from geodesic maps. Once trained, GAE can be used to calculate two sets of bottleneck features: features resulted from feeding the geodesic map to GAE, and features resulted from feeding the corresponding $Net_{seg}$'s output probability map to GAE. Finally, the distance between these two feature vectors are used to form an extra term in the loss function of the $Net_{seg}$ (Fig. 1).

We define the segmentation network as a function, mapping a gray-scale 3D input image $I_i(I_i \in R^3)$ into a probability map $P_i$, ($i \in \{1, 2, \ldots, N\}$), $N$ being number of 3D images:

$$P_i = Net_{seg}(I_i, \theta_{seg}), \tag{1}$$

where $\theta_{seg}$ are the parameters of $Net_{Seg}$, trained to minimize $\mathcal{L}_{tot}$ defined in Eq. 3. A geodesic map, on the other hand, is generated from ground truth binary images $B_i$ as $G_i = F_{geo}(B_i)$ and then a GAE network ($Net_{gae}$) is trained to generate binary image from this corresponding geodesic map (explained in Sect. 2.2). The GAE consists of an encoder, a fully connected (FC) layer, and a decoder. The encoder and FC layers are the feature extraction ($Enc_{gae}$) parts, mapping the input geodesic map to the feature vector $Feat_{gae} = Enc_{gae}(G_i)$ of length $L_{feat}$. The decoder ($Dec_{gae}$) reconstructs the corresponding binary image(s) from the $Feat_{gae}$. Hence, the geodesic network can be formulated as:

$$\hat{B}_i = Net_{gae}(G_i, \theta_{gae}) = Dec_{gae}(Enc_{gae}(G_i, \theta_{enc}), \theta_{dec}), \tag{2}$$

where $\theta_{gae}$ are the parameters of $Net_{gae}$, trained to minimize the binary map reconstruction loss $\mathcal{L}_{recon}$ in $Net_{gae}$. $\mathcal{L}_{recon}$ is a cross-entropy loss between ground-truth and $Net_{gae}$'s output and $\theta_{gae} = \theta_{enc} \cup \theta_{dec}$. Since $Net_{gae}$ is

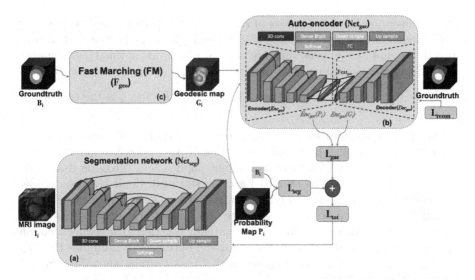

**Fig. 1.** The proposed framework has two main components: (1) segmentation network: assigns a class label to each pixel, and, (2) *AE* which learns a prior from geodesic maps. Green arrows show the flow of training of the segmentor and red arrows show the flow of training of GAE. Note that in test phase only segmentor is used. Also, the in our method the noisy annotations are used for whole training process. (Color figure online)

designed to learn the relation between geodesic maps and their corresponding binary maps, $Feat_{gae}$ contains high-level features inferred from shapes and texture of the objects of interests. This encoded knowledge can be used as an extra term of supervision for better training of $Net_{seg}$. For each training sample $i$, we calculate a loss function $\mathcal{L}_{gae}(Enc_{gae}(P_i), Enc_{gae}(G_i))$ to be back-propagated into the segmentation network along with loss of the segmentor itself. The total loss function of the segmentator is then represented as:

$$\mathcal{L}_{tot} = \sum_i \mathcal{L}_{seg}(P_i, B_i) + \mathcal{L}_{gae}(Enc_{gae}(P_i), Enc_{gae}(G_i)). \tag{3}$$

We first train $\theta_{gae}$ with $\mathcal{L}_{recon}$. Once trained, $\theta_{seg}$ is updated with the loss function $\mathcal{L}_{tot}$, while $\theta_{gae}$ are fixed.

### 2.1 Network Architecture for Segmentation

We extend fully convolutional dense nets, called *Tiramisu* [5], from 2D to fully 3D. The details of the adapted network are shown in Fig. 1(a). The encoder and decoder include four dense blocks, each. Within dense blocks, there are four 3D convolution layers followed by a *Batch Normalization* (BN) layer with *Leaky*

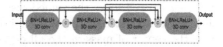

**Fig. 2.** Dense Block (DB) content. $C$: concatenation operation, $BN$: Batch normalization, $LReLu$: Leaky ReLu activation, and *3D conv*: 3D convolution with a $3 \times 3 \times 3$ filter.

*ReLu* nonlinear activation. The size of the convolution kernels are set to $3 \times 3 \times 3$ in all convolution layers (Fig. 2). The number of filters in the first convolution layer and the *growth rate* are set to *16* for an optimal performance after extensive explorations. The number of output filters in a dense block is

$$N_f(\mathbf{X}_l) = N_f( \mathop{\|}_{l'=0}^{l'=l-1} N_f(\mathbf{X}_{l'})), \text{ where } l = \{1, 2, \ldots, L\} \text{ and } \| \text{ is the concatenation.}$$

The encoder includes four 3D max pooling operations as transition layers after each dense block. The pooling operation is set to downsample the input size by 2 in *x-y* plane. Downsampling is not applied to $z$ direction due to its low resolution (but could be applied for other settings). Similarly, the decoder includes four up-samplers (using bilinear interpolation) as transition layers. Each up-sampler is designed to double the size of its input. Finally, the last layer contains a convolution layer following by a *softmax* function to introduce a notion of probability map in the output. We use *Adam* optimizer to minimize the $\mathcal{L}_{tot}$ in $Net_{seg}$. $\mathcal{L}_{seg}$ and $\mathcal{L}_{gae}$ are designed with *Cross Entropy* and *Mean Square Error* functions, respectively.

## 2.2    Learning a Geodesic Prior

Most existing literature related to prior incorporation into segmentation utilize *accurate* binary labels for extracting shape information [9,12]. Unlike the mainstream studies, we propose to use geodesic maps to increase robustness of the priors when dealing with *noisy* labels, which has never been done before. This approach can particularly be beneficial when the object has complex boundary information to be delineated. In this study, geodesic maps are generated from labels, regardless of being noisy or clean. We expect the proposed geodesic map to capture more information then conventional shape priors.

For each object in our images, we compute an independent geodesic distance map from its binary map $B_i$ by using the Fast Marching (FM) approach [11]. FM is a numerical method to solve boundary value problems of the Eikonal as:

$$\begin{cases} F(x)|\Delta T(x)| = 1, & \forall x \notin S, \\ F(x) = 0, & \forall x \in S, \end{cases} \tag{4}$$

describing the evolution of a contour as a function of time, $T(x)$, with the speed of $F(x)$ in the normal direction at a point $x$ on the propagating surface starting from the zero-level $S$. With a specified speed, $F(x)$, the time when the contour crosses point $x$ can be computed by solving Eq. 4. In this setting, the special case of $F(x) = 1$ gives the signed distance of every point $x$ from $S$. In our case, since we have multiple objects (i.e., 3 objects: LV, RV, Myocardium), we defined $S$ as the center of mass of the all closed objects. In our experimental setup, we have also an object with non-Jordan surface (i.e., Myocardium, having donuts shape). In order to include such objects in the geodesic computation, we simply define the the skeleton of the shape and the distances of all the points within each object are computed from their zero line contours $S$. These maps (obtained from each object) are combined in $n$-channels (i.e., 3 in our experiments: LV, RV, Mayo) and fed into the auto-encoder as described below.

The proposed AE architecture ($Net_{gae}$), for learning prior information, is illustrated in Fig. 1(b). This architecture is very similar to the segmentor with a FC layer in the middle (instead of a convolution layer) to generate deep geodesic features. Also, in order to increase the robustness of these features, there is no skip connections from encoder to decoder. Both encoder and decoders include four DBs and the filters size in each convolution layer was set to $3 \times 3 \times 3$. The growth rate for the encoder part is set to 16 (empirically) as in the segmentor and $Adam$ optimizer is used to minimize $\mathcal{L}_{recons}$ (*Cross Entropy* loss).

# 3    Experiments and Results

To show the robustness of our algorithm and its performance on noisy labels, we ran all the experiments on both expert as well as two levels of noise in the labels (L1 and L2). We reported Dice Index (DI) and Hausdorff distance (HD) in Table 1. Also, in cases where we were dealing with noisy labels, there was an upper bound for the performance of the networks. This upper bound was due to lack of information in the presence of noise. To have a sense of this upper bound, for the sake of a more extensive and fair comparison, DI and HD of generated noisy labels with respect to clean ground truths are reported in this table (*Upper boundary* columns). Higher DI and lower HD indicate a superior segmentation performance. While training of the networks were done using weak/noisy labels, validation was performed on expert/accurate labels.

**Data set:** We used the cine MR cardiac data set from Automated Cardiac Diagnosis Challenge (ACDC) MICCAI challenge 2017 [3]. The images in this data set were obtained from two MRI scanners of different magnetic strengths (1.5 T and 3.0 T). Cine MR images were acquired in breath-hold with a retrospective or prospective gating and with a SSFP sequence which LV was covered by series of short axis slices with a thickness of 5 mm. The spatial resolution of the images goes from 1.37 to 1.68 mm$^2$/pixel and 28 to 40 images cover completely or partially the cardiac cycle. Out of 150 cine MR images, we used 100 for training and validation (including expert annotation for LV, Myo, and RV at ES and ED), and the remaining 50 for testing (with online evaluation). Subject categories (5) are the following: 30 normal subjects, 30 with myo infarction, 30 with dilated cardiomyopathy, 30 with hypertrophic cardiomyopathy, and 30 with abnormal right ventricle which make the segmentation task challenging over different cases.

**Generating Noisy Labels:** The current annotations at ES and ED in ACDC dataset are considered as expert annotations (as clearly defined by the challenge organizers). Usually, the inexpert annotations include some under-segmentation and/or over-segmentation. This is due to lack of

**Fig. 3.** Generating noisy labels. Binary images went through a two-step process of adding pepper noise and filling inside object which makes the boundaries inaccurate.

naive annotator's knowledge in finding the edges. Thus, in order to mimic such inexpert annotations (weak labels), we manipulated the ground truths as follows: first we obtained the outer shell of each object by applying *erosion* to the binary image and then calculate the difference between the original binary image and eroded one. Then, salt-pepper noises were added to each object's binary shell randomly and *filling* was applied to the shell. This process effected *only* edges of the objects without changing the background, resulting in a shape with distorted boundaries. Finally, eroded binary edges was added to the distorted shell. A sample of weak labels vs. expert labels is shown in Fig. 3. Participating radiologists confirmed the weak labels through visual evaluations.

**Baseline Models for Comparisons:** We have conducted several baseline architectures in order to show the strength of our proposed method. First, the segmentor was trained only with $\mathcal{L}_{seg}$ and without using prior information with both of the inexpert and expert annotations. Also, in order to illustrate the advantage of using the geodesic maps instead of binary maps in modeling shape information, the segmentation network was trained with the prior information obtained from binary AE (*segmentation + binary labels shape*). In this baseline, the AE was trained to reconstruct binary map in its output from its corresponding binary input map (instead of geodesic in our method). The results of this baseline (*Binary Prior*) and our proposed method (*Geodesic Prior*) for inexpert and expert annotations are reported in Table 1.

**Table 1.** DI and HD are reported for both expert and inexpert labels.

| Labels | | Expert labels | | | Inexpert labels (L1) | | | | Inexpert labels (L2) | | | |
|---|---|---|---|---|---|---|---|---|---|---|---|---|
| Methods | | Seg Net. | Binary Prior | Geodesic Prior | Seg Net. | Binary Prior | Geodesic Prior | Upper boundary | Seg Net. | Binary Prior | Geodesic Prior | Upper boundary |
| DI | LV | 0.854 | 0.879 | **0.885** | 0.831 | 0.867 | **0.878** | 0.880 | 0.811 | 0.856 | **0.873** | 0.869 |
| | RV | 0.803 | **0.851** | 0.847 | 0.791 | 0.828 | **0.836** | 0.835 | 0.762 | 0.811 | **0.831** | 0.824 |
| | MYO | 0.771 | 0.816 | **0.826** | 0.762 | 0.798 | **0.810** | 0.812 | 0.751 | 0.780 | **0.809** | 0.801 |
| | Ave. | 0.809 | 0.849 | **0.853** | 0.795 | 0.831 | **0.841** | 0.842 | 0.775 | 0.816 | **0.838** | 0.831 |
| HD (mm) | LV | 14.79 | **10.08** | 10.14 | 15.87 | 12.57 | **11.73** | 11.75 | 14.89 | 13.03 | **11.65** | 11.81 |
| | RV | 17.77 | 13.77 | **13.45** | 18.89 | 17.01 | **15.14** | 15.15 | 17.57 | 17.53 | **15.44** | 15.76 |
| | MYO | 16.53 | 12.58 | **12.04** | 16.91 | 13.95 | **12.73** | 12.70 | 16.47 | 15.12 | **12.88** | 13.12 |
| | Ave | 16.36 | 12.14 | **11.88** | 17.22 | 14.51 | **13.20** | 13.20 | 15.64 | 15.23 | **13.32** | 13.56 |

**Implementation Details:** As a pre-processing step, we applied the anisotropic filtering to reduce noise from MRI, histogram matching to standardize MRI intensities, and all images were resized to $200 \times 200 \times 10$ by using B-spline interpolation. First the *GAE* was trained (early-stopping) and then the deep geodesic features ($Feat_{gae}$) were extracted from training data. Then, during training of $Net_{seg}$ the output probability maps of the $Net_{seg}$ were passed though $Enc_{gae}$ and then the loss ($\mathcal{L}_{gae}$) between two feature vector was calculated and back-propagated though the $Net_{seg}$. Finally, Conditional Random Field is used for post-processing. We used 80 MR images for training, the 20 images were used as validation, and the 50 images were used for test (with online evaluation). Also, we have used NVIDIA Quadro P6000 GPU for training the networks.

# 4 Conclusion

In this study, we propose a novel framework incorporating a deep geodesic prior information into the segmentation framework. Our AE network is capable of learning high-level features from generated geodesic maps for multiple objects. We show that our proposed approach outperforms the state-of-the-art methods both on clean and noisy labels with several key advantages. First, incorporating prior information improves segmentation results even with imperfect ground truths. Second, more specifically, shape prior is shown to be useful both in Euclidean and Geodesic distance based evaluations, and geodesic priors are shown to be more accurate than the former. Furthermore, the proposed network is capable of performing fully 3D image segmentation unlike most 2D methods in the literature, and can handle multiple objects too. One may argue to obtain inexpert annotations directly from inexpert annotators for more realistic evaluations, but the regulations for medical imaging data sharing in general (and ACDC challenge in particular) didn't allow to get such annotations. Our future work will comprehensively test our hypothesis for different components of our present study such as different clinical imaging problem, large number of inexpert annotators, and inspecting the results based on object type and size.

# References

1. Cardiovascular Diseases (CVDs) (2007). http://www.who.int/mediacentre/fact sheets/fs317/en/. Accessed 30 June 2017
2. Badrinarayanan, V., Kendall, A., Cipolla, R.: SegNet: a deep convolutional encoder-decoder architecture for image segmentation. arXiv preprint arXiv:1511.00561 (2015)
3. Bernard, O., et al.: Deep learning techniques for automatic mri cardiac multi-structures segmentation and diagnosis: is the problem solved? IEEE Trans. Med. Imaging **37**(11), 2514–2525 (2018)
4. Huang, G., Liu, Z., Van Der Maaten, L., Weinberger, K.Q.: Densely connected convolutional networks. In: CVPR, vol. 1, p. 3 (2017)
5. Jégou, S., Drozdzal, M., Vazquez, D., Romero, A., Bengio, Y.: The one hundred layers Tiramisu: fully convolutional DenseNets for semantic segmentation. In: 2017 IEEE Conference on Computer Vision and Pattern Recognition Workshops (CVPRW), pp. 1175–1183. IEEE (2017)
6. Kurugol, S., Ozay, N., Dy, J.G., Sharp, G.C., Brooks, D.H.: Locally deformable shape model to improve 3D level set based esophagus segmentation. In: 2010 20th International Conference on Pattern Recognition (ICPR). IEEE (2010)
7. LaLonde, R., Bagci, U.: Capsules for object segmentation. In: MIDL Conference, ArXiv preprint arXiv:1804.04241 (2018)
8. Lim, P.H., Bagci, U., Bai, L.: A new prior shape model for level set segmentation. In: San Martin, C., Kim, S.-W. (eds.) CIARP 2011. LNCS, vol. 7042, pp. 125–132. Springer, Heidelberg (2011). https://doi.org/10.1007/978-3-642-25085-9_14
9. Oktay, O., et al.: Anatomically constrained neural networks (ACNNs): application to cardiac image enhancement and segmentation. IEEE Trans. Med. Imaging **37**(2), 384–395 (2018)

10. Ronneberger, O., Fischer, P., Brox, T.: U-Net: convolutional networks for biomedical image segmentation. In: Navab, N., Hornegger, J., Wells, W.M., Frangi, A.F. (eds.) MICCAI 2015. LNCS, vol. 9351, pp. 234–241. Springer, Cham (2015). https://doi.org/10.1007/978-3-319-24574-4_28

11. Telea, A.: An image inpainting technique based on the fast marching method. J. Graph. Tools **9**(1), 23–34 (2004)

12. Zotti, C., Luo, Z., Lalande, A., Jodoin, P.M.: Convolutional neural network with shape prior applied to cardiac MRI segmentation. IEEE J. Biomed. Health Inform. **23**, 1119–1128 (2018)

# Correspondence-Steered Volumetric Descriptor Learning Using Deep Functional Maps

Diya Sun[1], Yuru Pei[1(✉)], Yungeng Zhang[1], Yuke Guo[2], Gengyu Ma[3], Tianmin Xu[4], and Hongbin Zha[1]

[1] Key Laboratory of Machine Perception (MOE),
Department of Machine Intelligence, Peking University,
Beijing, China
Peiyuru@cis.pku.edu.cn
[2] Luoyang Institute of Science and Technology, Luoyang, China
[3] uSens Inc., San Jose, USA
[4] School of Stomatology, Peking University, Beijing, China

**Abstract.** In this paper, we consider the dense correspondence of volumetric images and propose a convolutional network-based descriptor learning framework using the functional map representation. Our main observation is that the correspondence-steered descriptor learning improves dense volumetric mapping compared with the hand-crafted descriptors. We present an unsupervised way to find the optimal network parameters by aligning volumetric probe functions and the enforcement of invertible coupled maps. The proposed framework takes the one-channel volume as input and outputs the multi-channel volumetric descriptors using the cascaded convolutional operators, which are faster than the conventional descriptor computations. We follow the deep functional map framework and represent the dense correspondence by the low-dimensional spectral mapping for the functional transfer and dense correspondence using the linear algebra. We demonstrate that by using the correspondence-steered deep descriptor learning, the quality of both the dense correspondence and attribute transfer are improved in the extensive experiments.

## 1 Introduction

Dense correspondence of 3D volumetric images is one of the key issues in medical image analysis with applications in fields ranging from statistical shape analysis [9] and the morphology evaluation due to treatments and aging to a wide variety of others. The volumetric matching algorithm is desirable to enable the attribute transfer in such application of atlas-based label propagation [7]. In the past several decades, there is a collection of hand-crafted features developed for image matching, including the histogram of intensity and oriented gradient [4,11], the self-similarity-context-based descriptor [6], the scale-invariant feature

© Springer Nature Switzerland AG 2019
H.-I. Suk et al. (Eds.): MLMI 2019, LNCS 11861, pp. 247–255, 2019.
https://doi.org/10.1007/978-3-030-32692-0_29

transform [2], and the multi-dimensional modality independent neighbourhood descriptor (MIND)[5]. The contextual features defined by a surrounding cube have the modality-independent property [5,6]. The spherical intensity integral is used to describe textural appearances of voxels [11]. However, the orientation determination and histogram estimation in the gradient domain is a non-trivial task and often computationally intensive.

The discriminative feature descriptor specific to the dense correspondence is desirable. The supervised classification and regression forests [7] perform feature selection and have been used for voxel-wise correspondence. However, the additional regularization is required for a smooth map. Instead of solving correspondence in the spatial domain, the functional maps [10] have shown potentials for dense correspondence of 2D/3D manifolds by solving the low-dimensional spectral matching [9,13,14]. Recently, the supervised deep functional maps have been used for 2D manifold correspondence [8]. However, the above systems rely on hand-crafted descriptors agnostic to the correspondence task, as well as prior paired landmarks for model learning.

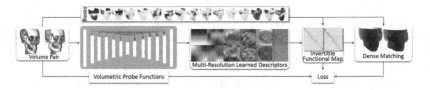

**Fig. 1.** Flowchart of our system (with sampled bases and learned descriptors plotted).

In this work, we argue that the more accurate correspondence can be achieved by virtue of the task-steered deep descriptor learning. We present an end-to-end descriptor learning network when given the one-channel volumetric images. The output multi-channel features are projected to the reduced functional space to solve the dense correspondence. We learn the network parameters, i.e., the convolutional kernels, in an unsupervised way by finding descriptors appropriate for the semantic matching of volumetric images and satisfying the invertibility of coupled maps. We follow the functional map representation and solve the low-dimensional spectral mapping. The spectral mapping enables the transfer of volumetric attributes, such as the segmentation maps and landmarks, without solving the one-to-one matching in the spatial domain. The network is learned from a corpus of volumetric images and enables the generalization to novel volumes. We demonstrate the improvements in both the dense correspondence and attribute transfer using the learned descriptors. In the online testing, the end-to-end convolutional network realizes efficient descriptor extraction.

## 2   Volumetric Descriptor Learning

Instead of using prior hand-crafted descriptors agnostic to the correspondence task, we present a convolutional network-based descriptor learning framework with the functional map representation. The goal is to identify the volumetric descriptors to solve the nonrigid mapping between pairs of volumetric images. Given a training dataset $V = \{V_i | i = 1, \dots, M\}$, we learn the optimal network parameters $\Theta$, such as the convolutional kernels, and construct a mapping function from the input 1-channel intensity volume to the output $q$-channel descriptor functions $h_\Theta : V \rightarrow \mathbb{R}^q$. Unlike the existing deep functional map techniques [8], we present an unsupervised way to train the network by aligning volumetric probe functions in a reduced functional space.

**Functional Map.** The technique of the functional maps enables finding correspondences of 2D manifolds, including natural images and 3D surface meshes [9,10,13], as well as 3D volumes [14]. Suppose we have two volumes $V_i$ and $V_j$ consisting of $N_i$ and $N_j$ voxels. The steps are as follows: 1. Construct the bases functions of both $V_i$ and $V_j$, such as the eigendecomposition of discretized Laplace Beltrami operator. The first $k_i(k_i \ll N_i)$ and $k_j(k_j \ll N_j)$ bases functions related to the low frequencies are kept as columns in the matrices $\Phi_i$ and $\Phi_j$ respectively. 2. Embed $q$ descriptor functions of $V_i$ and $V_j$ using the orthogonal bases $\Phi_i$ and $\Phi_j$, and record the coefficients as columns of matrices $F_i$ and $F_j$ with the dimensions of $k_i \times q$ and $k_j \times q$. 3. Find the optimal $k_i \times k_j$-dimensional functional map $C_{ij}$ by aligning descriptor functions.

$$C_{ij} = \arg \min_C \|CF_i - F_j\|_F^2 + \alpha\|\Psi_j C - C\Psi_i\|_F^2. \tag{1}$$

The first term is used to align the feature space of $V_i$ and $V_j$. The second term is the operator commutativity constraint, where $\Psi_i$ and $\Psi_j$ denote the Laplace-Beltrami operators of $V_i$ and $V_j$ expressed in the bases. We measure the matrix distance using the Frobenius norm $\|\cdot\|_F$. The constant $\alpha$ is set to 1. The functional map is solved by the least squared method as [14]. The main advantage of the functional map is to avoid solving the $N_i \times N_j$-dimensional dense matching matrix. Instead, the small functional map $C_{ij}$ is enough to recover the dense correspondence represented as a soft permutation matrix $P = \Phi_i C_{ij} \Phi_j^\dagger$, with an entry indicating the matching probability. $\dagger$ denotes the Moore-Penrose pseudo-inverse. The column normalization with the nearest neighbor searching is used to find the dense matching [10].

## 2.1 Loss Function

As shown in Fig. 1, when given a volume pair $(V_i, V_j)$, the network produces the descriptor functions $F_i = h_\Theta(V_i)$ and $F_j = h_\Theta(V_j)$ using existing network parameters $\Theta$, which are then used to estimate the functional map $C_{ij}$ (Eq. 1) and the dense permutation matching matrix $P_{ij}$. We consider the loss function

$$\mathcal{L}(\Theta) = \sum_{(V_i, V_j) \in V} \|H_i P_{ij} - H_j\|_F^2 + \gamma_1 \|C_{ij} C_{ij}^T - I\|_F^2, \tag{2}$$

where the first term is used to align the pre-defined appearance-related volumetric probe functions $H$ when given the soft matching matrix $P$. Considering the entry of $P_{ij}$ as the matching probability of one voxel pair, $H_i P_{ij}$ can be viewed as a weighted combination of the nearest neighboring probe functions. Without loss of generality, we decompose each volume into 30k supervoxels by the SLIC algorithm [1]. We use 720 probe functions for each volume [14], where the first 120 are the intensity histogram of supervoxels. There are 400 context-related probe functions as the Chi-squared distance from sampled surrounding supervoxels, as well as 200 geodesic distance functions. $H_i \in \mathbb{R}^{720 \times N_i}$ and $H_j \in \mathbb{R}^{720 \times N_j}$. $N_i$ and $N_j$ denote the number of supervoxels of $V_i$ and $V_j$ respectively.

In the second term, we enforce the orthogonality of the functional maps, and $C_{ij} C_{ij}^T = I$. Given the orthonormal functional map, the pairwise permutation matrix is also orthonormal, and $P_{ij} P_{ij}^T = (\Phi_i C_{ij} \Phi_j^\dagger)(\Phi_j^{\dagger T} C_{ij}^T \Phi_i^T) = \Phi_i C_{ij} C_{ij}^T \Phi_i^T = I$, where $\Phi_i$ and $\Phi_j$ are the orthogonal bases.

**Invertibility.** Instead of considering the unidirectional mapping $C_{ij} : V_i \rightarrow V_j$, we enforce the invertibility of the coupled functional maps and the permutation matching matrices for the one-to-one mapping. Given an arbitrary volume pair $(V_i, V_j)$, we require that the dense matching matrices $P_{ij}$ and $P_{ji}$ be invertible. It is straightforward that when the functional map satisfies the invertibility property with $C_{ij} C_{ji} = I$, the corresponding permutation matrix $P$ has the invertibility property. $P_{ij} P_{ji} = \Phi_i C_{ij} \Phi_j^\dagger (\Phi_j C_{ji} \Phi_i^\dagger) = I$. We rewrite the loss function (Eq. 2) to enforce the pairwise invertible matching.

$$
\mathcal{L}(\Theta) = \sum_{(V_i, V_j) \in \mathcal{V}} \left\{ \left[ \| H_i P_{ij} - H_j \|_F^2 + \| H_j P_{ji} - H_i \|_F^2 \right] + \right.
$$
$$
\left. \gamma_1 \left[ \| C_{ij} C_{ij}^T - I \|_F^2 + \| C_{ji} C_{ji}^T - I \|_F^2 \right] + \gamma_2 \left[ \| C_{ij} C_{ji} - I \|_F^2 + \| C_{ji} C_{ij} - I \|_F^2 \right] \right\}.
$$
$$
\tag{3}
$$

The constant coefficients are used to balance the alignment of the volumetric probe functions, the orthonormal, and the invertible regularizations of the functional maps. In our experiments, $\gamma_1$ and $\gamma_2$ are both set to 0.5.

**Functional Transfer.** Given the learned descriptors, we solve the functional map $C$ (Eq. 1). The real-valued attribute function $f$ defined on the reference volume $V_r$, such as that associated with the segmentation maps, is transferred to the corresponding function $g$ on the novel volume $V_t$, and $g = \Phi_t C \Phi_r^\dagger f$. The functional transfer is determined by the map $C$ in the low-dimensional embedding space, which satisfies the optimal descriptor alignments.

## 2.2    Architecture

The network is built upon the symmetric 3D U-net [3] with long-jump residual connections. Both the encoder and decoder are composed of six $3 \times 3 \times 3$ convolutional layers. In the encoder, we use the instance normalization and Leaky ReLU. A $2 \times 2 \times 2$ pooling follows each convolution layer. In the decoder, we use the convolution layer with a fractional stride of $1/2$ to up-sample the descriptor volumes to the same resolution as the input. We concatenate the multi-resolution feature volumes obtained in the decoder as the output descriptor functions. There are totally 1992 feature volumes, consisting of 512, 512, 512, 256, 128, 64, 8 feature volumes with the resolution of $2^3$, $4^3$, $8^3$, $16^3$, $32^3$, $64^3$, and $128^3$ respectively. In our experiments, we demonstrate that a small portion of feature volumes are enough to establish the dense volumetric correspondence.

**Training Details.** Instead of learning the network from scratch, we use a two-stage pre-training procedure. To begin with, we initialize the encoder using the convolutional autoencoder (CAE) [12] based representation learning. Second, we fine-tune the network using a set of synthetic data. We construct synthetic data by the B-spline-based nonrigid deformation. We randomly perturb the displacement vectors at the control grid under a normal distribution with zero mean and a variance of 8 mm. The dense displacement field obtained by the cubic interpolation is required to have positive determinants of the Jacobian matrix to avoid structural folding. We perform the supervoxel-decomposition on the synthetic volumes in the same manner as the reference and set the dense matching to an identity matrix, and $P_{ij} = I$. The network parameters are fine-tuned by minimizing $\|P_{ij} - I\|_F^2$ in the pre-training. We implement the network using the open-source PyTorch on a PC with an NVIDIA GTX TITAN X GPU. The training is by the ADAM optimizer. The learning rate is set to 1e−4 with the momentums of 0.5 and 0.999. The mini-batch contains two volumes to evaluate the correspondence-related loss. The training takes 60 h after 30 epochs. The online descriptor computation takes 1.2s.

## 3   Experiments

**Dataset.** We evaluate the proposed method on the clinical 3D CBCT images. The training dataset consists of 390 CBCT images with a resolution of 128 × 128 × 128. The voxel size is of $1.5^3$ mm$^3$. We randomly sample 10 k volume pairs from the dataset to train the network. The testing dataset consists of 20 clinical CBCT images. In our system, we only consider the foreground volumes (without air) consisting of 14k supervoxels. We also generate a synthetic dataset with ground-truth correspondence for evaluations. The synthetic testing dataset consists of 20 volumes produced by the B-spline-based deformation in the same way as those used in the pre-training.

**Results.** We quantitatively evaluate the proposed volumetric descriptor learning method in the attribute transfer scenarios using the Dice similarity coefficient (DSC) and the average Hausdorff distance (AHD). We compare with the state-of-the-art volumetric correspondence methods, including the regression (Reg) and classification (Cla) forests with feature selection of the hand-crafted descriptors [7], the functional maps using the hand-crafted appearance descriptors (HC) [14] and the MIND [5], and the representation learning using the CAE [12]. We report the performance of the proposed descriptor learning network VDN with the orthonormal regularization (Eq. 2) using 200 spectral bases and the VDN$_{inv}$ with the additional invertible constraint (Eq. 3).

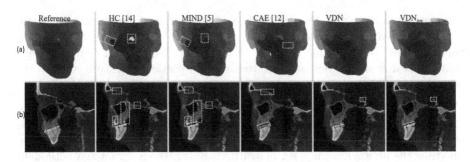

**Fig. 2.** (a) Dense correspondence of clinical data using the descriptors of the HC [14], the MIND [5], the CAE [12], and the proposed VDN and VDN$_{inv}$. (b) Segmentation map transfers of anatomical structures. (Red-maxilla, green-mandible, cyan-frontal bone, magenta-sphenoid, beige-occipital bone, and brown-temporal bone.) (Color figure online)

Table 1 shows the matching accuracy $e_m = \frac{n_m}{n}$ of seven anatomical structures using the deep learning-based volumetric descriptors, including the CAE [12], the proposed VDN, and the VDN$_{inv}$. $n$ denotes the total number of testing supervoxels, and $n_m$ the number of supervoxels with the matching identical to the ground truth or within the 1-ring neighbors (bracketed). Compared with the CAE-based deep representation learning [12], the proposed method improves the matching accuracy by the task-specific learning of descriptors. Note that the learned descriptors with the invertible constraints also help to improve the correspondence by enforcing the one-to-one mapping.

**Table 1.** The matching accuracy of anatomical structures by the deep learning-based volumetric descriptors on the synthetic dataset. The matching accuracy within one-ring neighbors is shown in brackets.

| $e_m$ | Mandible | Maxilla | Zygoma | Frontal | Sphenoid | Occipital | Temporal |
|---|---|---|---|---|---|---|---|
| VDN | 0.69(.97) | 0.73(.98) | 0.81(.98) | 0.74(.92) | **0.89(.97)** | 0.82(.98) | **0.85(.98)** |
| VDN$_{inv}$ | **0.72(.98)** | **0.76(.99)** | **0.89(1.0)** | **0.82(.95)** | 0.84(.96) | **0.88(1.0)** | **0.85(.99)** |
| CAE [12] | 0.47(.80) | 0.43(.92) | 0.45(.76) | 0.29(.61) | 0.56(.85) | 0.33(.67) | 0.41(.81) |

Figure 2(a) shows the dense correspondence using the descriptors of the HC [14], the MIND [5], the deep learning-based CAE [12], and the proposed VDN and the VDN$_{inv}$. The corresponding supervoxels are assigned the same color, and errors white blocked. Note that the proposed VDN and the VDN$_{inv}$ are helpful to realize the smooth and accurate correspondence. Given the dense correspondence, we transfer the segmentation map from the annotated reference volume to novel ones. Figure 2(b) shows a qualitative example of real-valued functional transfers of anatomical structures. Compared with the hand-crafted descriptors using the predefined filters, such as the MIND, the proposed approach improves the functional transfer performance. We quantitatively evaluate the transfer on the clinical dataset by the DSC and the AHD as shown in Fig. 3(a,b), where the proposed VDN and the $VDN_{inv}$ outperform others with the DSCs of 0.89 and 0.91 vs. 0.83, 0.84 and 0.83 using the MIND [5], the HC [14], the deep learning-based CAE [12] in the mandible segmentation. The proposed method also outperforms the random forest-based descriptor selection [7] as shown in Fig. 3(c).

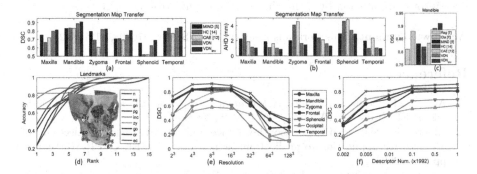

**Fig. 3.** (a) The DSC and (b) the AHD of segmentation map transfer of clinical data. (c) The DSC of the mandible segmentation map transfer. (d) The landmark transfer accuracy. (e) The segmentation accuracy with multi-resolution descriptor functions and (f) increasing numbers of descriptor functions.

We perform the landmark transfer using the functional maps, where the landmark is defined by a delta function with 1 for the landmark and 0 otherwise. Figure 3(d) shows the transfer accuracies of nine landmarks of the skull on the clinical data. We use top-ranked supervoxels to measure matching accuracies. More than 90% of supervoxels have real matches in top 8 ranked supervoxels.

Figure 3(e) shows the segmentation transfer errors of seven anatomical structures using descriptor functions from different layers in the decoder. In our experiments, the performances related to the feature volumes with the resolution of $4^3$, $8^3$, and $16^3$ are better than others. The low-resolution feature volumes focus on the global structural information, while the relatively small number of high-resolution feature volumes emphasize local structural details. The combination of feature volumes from different layers takes advantage of both the global and local structural information. We also compare the segmentation performances using different numbers of descriptor functions as shown in Fig. 3(f). In our experiments, the transfer accuracy increases with the numbers of descriptor functions and reaches a plateau with approx. 200 ($0.1 \times 1992$) descriptors.

## 4   Conclusion

In this paper, we propose a convolutional network-based descriptor learning framework for the dense volumetric correspondence. We follow the functional map representation and present an unsupervised way to train the network by the alignment of volumetric probe functions and the enforcement of invertible coupled maps. We perform the function transfer using low-dimensional spectral mapping without the conversion to the one-to-one voxel-wise mapping. The proposed method is applied to the clinical and synthetic CBCT images. One main observation is that by using the correspondence-steered descriptors, both the dense volumetric correspondence and attribute transfer performances are improved. The proposed system realizes efficient multi-channel volumetric descriptor computation by using the cascaded convolutional operators.

**Acknowledgement.** This work was supported by NSFC 61876008, 61272342.

# References

1. Achanta, R., et al.: SLIC superpixels compared to state-of-the-art superpixel methods. IEEE Trans. PAMI **34**(11), 2274–2282 (2012)
2. Allaire, S., et al.: Full orientation invariance and improved feature selectivity of 3D sift with application to medical image analysis. In: IEEE CVPR Workshops, pp. 1–8 (2008)
3. Çiçek, Ö., Abdulkadir, A., Lienkamp, S.S., Brox, T., Ronneberger, O.: 3D U-Net: learning dense volumetric segmentation from sparse annotation. In: Ourselin, S., Joskowicz, L., Sabuncu, M.R., Unal, G., Wells, W. (eds.) MICCAI 2016. LNCS, vol. 9901, pp. 424–432. Springer, Cham (2016). https://doi.org/10.1007/978-3-319-46723-8_49
4. Daenzer, S., et al.: VolHOG: a volumetric object recognition approach based on bivariate histograms of oriented gradients for vertebra detection in cervical spine MRI. Med. Phys. **41**(8Part1), 082305 (2014)
5. Heinrich, M.P., et al.: MIND: modality independent neighbourhood descriptor for multi-modal deformable registration. Med. Image Anal. **16**(7), 1423–1435 (2012)
6. Heinrich, M.P., Jenkinson, M., Papież, B.W., Brady, S.M., Schnabel, J.A.: Towards realtime multimodal fusion for image-guided interventions using self-similarities. In: Mori, K., Sakuma, I., Sato, Y., Barillot, C., Navab, N. (eds.) MICCAI 2013. LNCS, vol. 8149, pp. 187–194. Springer, Heidelberg (2013). https://doi.org/10.1007/978-3-642-40811-3_24
7. Kanavati, F., et al.: Supervoxel classification forests for estimating pairwise image correspondences. Pattern Recogn. **63**, 561–569 (2017)
8. Litany, O., Remez, T., Rodolà, E., Bronstein, A., Bronstein, M.: Deep functional maps: structured prediction for dense shape correspondence. In: ICCV 2017, pp. 5659–5667 (2017)
9. Lombaert, H., Arcaro, M., Ayache, N.: Brain transfer: spectral analysis of cortical surfaces and functional maps. In: Ourselin, S., Alexander, D.C., Westin, C.-F., Cardoso, M.J. (eds.) IPMI 2015. LNCS, vol. 9123, pp. 474–487. Springer, Cham (2015). https://doi.org/10.1007/978-3-319-19992-4_37
10. Ovsjanikov, M., Ben-Chen, M., Solomon, J., Butscher, A., Guibas, L.: Functional maps: a flexible representation of maps between shapes. ACM Trans. Graph. **31**(4), 30 (2012)
11. Pei, Y., Ma, G., Chen, G., Zhang, X., Xu, T., Zha, H.: Superimposition of cone-beam computed tomography images by joint embedding. IEEE Trans. BME **64**(6), 1218–1227 (2017)

12. Vincent, P., Larochelle, H., Lajoie, I., Bengio, Y., Manzagol, P.A.: Stacked denoising autoencoders: learning useful representations in a deep network with a local denoising criterion. J. Mach. Learn. Res. **11**(12), 3371–3408 (2010)
13. Wang, F., Huang, Q., Guibas, L.J.: Image co-segmentation via consistent functional maps. In: ICCV, pp. 849–856 (2013)
14. Zhang, Y., Pei, Y., Guo, Y., Ma, G., Xu, T., Zha, H.: Consistent correspondence of cone-beam CT images using volume functional maps. In: Frangi, A.F., Schnabel, J.A., Davatzikos, C., Alberola-López, C., Fichtinger, G. (eds.) MICCAI 2018. LNCS, vol. 11070, pp. 801–809. Springer, Cham (2018). https://doi.org/10.1007/978-3-030-00928-1_90

# Sturm: Sparse Tubal-Regularized Multilinear Regression for fMRI

Wenwen Li[1,4(✉)], Jian Lou[2], Shuo Zhou[1], and Haiping Lu[1,3]

[1] Department of Computer Science, The University of Sheffield, Sheffield S1 4DP, UK
{wenwen.li,szhou20,h.lu}@sheffield.ac.uk
[2] Department of Computer Science, Emory University, Atlanta 30322, USA
jian.lou@emory.edu
[3] Sheffield Institute for Translational Neuroscience, Sheffield S10 2HQ, UK
[4] Centre for Clinical Brain Sciences, The University of Edinburgh,
Edinburgh EH16 4SB, UK
wenwen.li@ed.ac.uk

**Abstract.** While functional magnetic resonance imaging (fMRI) is important for healthcare/neuroscience applications, it is challenging to classify or interpret due to its multi-dimensional structure, high dimensionality, and small number of samples available. Recent sparse multilinear regression methods based on tensor are emerging as promising solutions for fMRI. Particularly, the newly proposed tensor singular value decomposition (t-SVD) sheds light on new directions. In this work, we study t-SVD for sparse multilinear regression and propose a **S**parse **tu**bal-**r**egularized **m**ultilinear regression (**Sturm**) method for fMRI. Specifically, the Sturm model performs multilinear regression with two regularization terms: a tubal tensor nuclear norm based on t-SVD and a standard $\ell_1$ norm. An optimization algorithm under the alternating direction method of multipliers framework is derived for solving the Sturm model. We then perform experiments on four classification problems, including both resting-state fMRI for disease diagnosis and task-based fMRI for neural decoding. The results show the superior performance of Sturm in classifying fMRI using just a small number of voxels.

## 1 Introduction

Brain diseases affect millions of people worldwide and impose significant challenges to healthcare systems. Functional magnetic resonance imaging (fMRI) is a key brain imaging technique for diagnosis, monitoring and treatment of brain diseases. Beyond healthcare, fMRI is also an indispensable tool in neuroscience studies [5].

Facing the challenging "large $p$ (brain voxels) small $n$ (samples)" problem in brain imaging, sparse learning models [9,11] are found to be attractive on

---

W. Li and J. Lou—These authors contributed equally to this work.

H.-I. Suk et al. (Eds.): MLMI 2019, LNCS 11861, pp. 256–264, 2019.
https://doi.org/10.1007/978-3-030-32692-0_30

fMRI data because they can reveal the direct dependency of a response (e.g., diagnosis outcome or brain states) on a small portion of features i.e., brain voxels. Recently, tensor-based sparse multilinear regression methods are emerging as a promising direction, where *tensor* refers to multidimensional array. For example, a 3D fMRI volume can be seen as a 3D tensor or a third-order tensor.

Tensor-based sparse multilinear regression models relate a feature tensor with a univariate response via a coefficient tensor, generalizing Lasso-based models [4] to tensor data. Regularization that promotes sparsity and *low rankness* is also generalized to the coefficient tensor. For example, the regularized multilinear regression and selection (Remurs) model [12] incorporates a sparse regularization term, via an $\ell_1$ norm, and a *Tucker rank*-minimization term [13], via a summation of the nuclear norms (SNN) of unfolded matrices with application to task-based fMRI data. A new Tubal Tensor Nuclear Norm (TNN) [14] has recently been proposed based on the *tubal rank*, which originates from the tensor singular value decomposition (t-SVD) [6]. In this work, we study sparse multilinear regression under the t-SVD framework for fMRI classification. The success of TNN was limited to *unsupervised* learning settings such as completion/recovery and robust PCA [2]. To our knowledge, TNN has not been studied in a *supervised* setting yet, such as multilinear regression for predicting a response based on a set of tensor-structural samples. Moreover, the targeted fMRI classification tasks have the challenge of small sample size (relative to the feature dimension).

Our contributions are twofold: (1) We propose a **S**parse **tu**bal-**r**egularized **m**ultilinear regression (**Sturm**) method that incorporates TNN regularization and a sparsity regularization on the coefficient tensor; (2) We evaluate Sturm and related methods on *both* resting-state and task-based fMRI classification problems, instead of only one of them as in previous work [3].

## 2    Method

**Notations.** We use lowercase, bold lowercase, bold uppercase, calligraphic uppercase letters to denote scalar, vector, matrix, and tensor, respectively. A third-order tensor $\mathcal{A} \in \mathbb{R}^{I_1 \times I_2 \times I_3}$ is addressed by three indices $\{i_n\}$, $n = 1, 2, 3$. Each $i_n$ usually addresses the $n$th mode of $\mathcal{A}$. For example, in a 3D fMRI volume, $I_1, I_2$ and $I_3$ could indicate the sagittal, coronal and axial dimension, respectively.

### 2.1    Tubal Rank and Tubal Tensor Nuclear Norm (TNN)

*Tubal rank* is derived from the t-SVD as illustrated in Fig. 1, where $\mathcal{U} \in \mathbb{R}^{I_1 \times I_1 \times I_3}$, $\mathcal{V} \in \mathbb{R}^{I_2 \times I_2 \times I_3}$ are orthogonal tensors, and $\mathcal{S} \in \mathbb{R}^{I_1 \times I_2 \times I_3}$ is an *f-diagonal* tensor. The number of nonzero singular tubes (along the diagonal direction) of $\mathcal{S}$ is defined as the tubal rank.

t-SVD can be computed efficiently via the discrete Fourier transfer (DFT). Denote the Fourier transformed tensor $\mathcal{A}$ as $\mathcal{A}_{\mathcal{F}}$, $\mathcal{A}_{\mathcal{F}} = \text{fft}(\mathcal{A}, [\,], 3)$. As a convex relaxation for the tubal rank, the TNN of $\mathcal{A} \in \mathbb{R}^{I_1 \times I_2 \times I_3}$ is defined as $\|\mathcal{A}\|_{TNN} = \frac{1}{I_3} \sum_{i_3=1}^{I_3} \|\mathbf{A}_{\mathcal{F}}^{(i_3)}\|_*$, where $\| \cdot \|_*$ denotes the matrix nuclear norm. More about t-SVD and TNN can be found in [14].

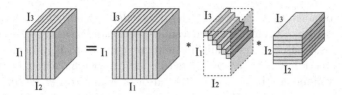

**Fig. 1.** Illustration of t-SVD $\mathcal{A} = \mathcal{U} * \mathcal{S} * \mathcal{V}^\top$, $*$ means tensor product [6], assuming $I_1 > I_2$. $\mathcal{U}$ and $\mathcal{V}$ are orthogonal tensors. $\mathcal{S}$ is an f-diagonal tensor. Tubal rank is the number of nonzero singular tubes of $\mathcal{S}$. In this example, the tubal rank is 6.

## 2.2   The Sturm Model

**Regularized Multilinear Regression Model.** This approach trains a model from $M$ pairs of feature tensor and associated response label, $(\mathcal{X}_m \in \mathbb{R}^{I_1 \times I_2 \times I_3}, y_m)$ with $m = 1, ..., M$, to relate them via a *coefficient tensor* $\mathcal{W} \in \mathbb{R}^{I_1 \times I_2 \times I_3}$ as

$$\min_{\mathcal{W}} \frac{1}{M} \sum_{m=1}^{M} L(\langle \mathcal{X}_m, \mathcal{W} \rangle, y_m) + \lambda \Omega(\mathcal{W}), \tag{1}$$

where $L(\cdot)$ is a loss function, $\Omega(\cdot)$ is a regularization term, $\lambda$ is a balancing hyperparameter, and $\langle \mathcal{X}, \mathcal{W} \rangle$ denotes the inner product (a.k.a. the scalar product) of two tensors of the same size:

$$\langle \mathcal{X}, \mathcal{W} \rangle := \sum_{i_1} \sum_{i_2} \sum_{i_3} \mathcal{X}(i_1, i_2, i_3) \cdot \mathcal{W}(i_1, i_2, i_3). \tag{2}$$

**The State-of-the-Art Model.** The Remurs [12] model has been successfully applied to task-based fMRI data. It uses a conventional least square loss function and assumes $\mathcal{W}$ to be both sparse and low rank. The sparsity of $\mathcal{W}$ is regularized by an $\ell_1$ norm and the low rank by an SNN norm. However, the SNN requires unfolding $\mathcal{W}$ into matrices, susceptible to losing some higher-order structural information. Moreover, it has been pointed out in [10] that SNN is not a tight convex relaxation of its target rank.

**A New Model.** The limitation of SNN motivates us to propose a **S**parse **tu**bal-**r**egularized **m**ultilinear regression (**Sturm**) model which replaces SNN in Remurs with TNN. This leads to the following objective function

$$\min_{\mathcal{W}} \frac{1}{2} \sum_{m=1}^{M} (y_m - \langle \mathcal{X}_m, \mathcal{W} \rangle)^2 + \tau \|\mathcal{W}\|_{TNN} + \gamma \|\mathcal{W}\|_1, \tag{3}$$

where $\tau$ and $\gamma$ are hyperparameters, and $\|\mathcal{W}\|_1$ is the $\ell_1$ norm of tensor $\mathcal{W}$, defined as $\|\mathcal{W}\|_1 = \sum_{i_1} \sum_{i_2} \sum_{i_3} |\mathcal{W}(i_1, i_2, i_3)|$, which is equivalent to the $\ell_1$ norm of its vectorized representation $\mathbf{w}$. Here, the TNN regularization term $\|\mathcal{W}\|_{TNN}$ enforces low tubal rank in $\mathcal{W}$.

**Optimization Algorithm for Sturm.** ADMM [1] is a standard solver for Problem (3). Thus, we derive an ADMM algorithm to optimize the Sturm objective function. We begin with introducing two auxiliary variables, $\mathcal{A}$ and $\mathcal{B}$ to disentangle the TNN and $\ell_1$-norm regularization:

$$\min_{\mathcal{W}} \frac{1}{2} \sum_{m=1}^{M} (y_m - \langle \mathcal{X}_m, \mathcal{A} \rangle)^2 + \tau \|\mathcal{B}\|_{TNN} + \gamma \|\mathcal{W}\|_1, \, s.t. \, \mathcal{A} = \mathcal{W} \text{ and } \mathcal{B} = \mathcal{W}. \quad (4)$$

Then, we introduce two Lagrangian dual variables $\mathcal{P}$ (for $\mathcal{A}$) and $\mathcal{Q}$ (for $\mathcal{B}$). With a Lagrangian constant $\rho$, the augmented Lagrangian becomes,

$$L_\rho(\mathcal{A}, \mathcal{B}, \mathcal{W}, \mathcal{P}, \mathcal{Q}) = \frac{1}{2} \sum_{m=1}^{M} (y_m - \langle \mathcal{X}_m, \mathcal{A} \rangle)^2 + \tau \|\mathcal{B}\|_{TNN} + \gamma \|\mathcal{W}\|_1$$
$$+ \left\langle \mathcal{P}, \mathcal{A} - \mathcal{W} \right\rangle + \frac{\rho}{2} \|\mathcal{A} - \mathcal{W}\|_F^2 + \left\langle \mathcal{Q}, \mathcal{B} - \mathcal{W} \right\rangle + \frac{\rho}{2} \|\mathcal{B} - \mathcal{W}\|_F^2. \quad (5)$$

where $\| \cdot \|_F$ is the Frobenius norm defined as $\|\mathcal{T}\|_F = \sqrt{\langle \mathcal{T}, \mathcal{T} \rangle}$ using Eq. (2). We further introduce two scaled dual variables $\mathcal{P}' = \frac{1}{\rho} \mathcal{P}$ and $\mathcal{Q}' = \frac{1}{\rho} \mathcal{Q}$ only for notational convenience. Next, we derive the update from iteration $k$ to $k+1$ by minimizing one variable with all the other variables fixed.

**Updating $\mathcal{A}^{k+1}$:**

$$\mathcal{A}^{k+1} = \arg\min_{\mathcal{A}} \frac{1}{2} \sum_{m=1}^{M} (y_m - \langle \mathcal{X}_m, \mathcal{A} \rangle)^2 + \frac{\rho}{2} \|\mathcal{A} - \mathcal{W}^k + \mathcal{P}'^k\|_F. \quad (6)$$

This can be rewritten as a linear-quadratic objective function by vectorizing all the tensors. Specifically, let $\mathbf{a} = \text{vec}(\mathcal{A})$, $\mathbf{w}^k = \text{vec}(\mathcal{W}^k)$, $\mathbf{p}'^k = \text{vec}(\mathcal{P}'^k)$, $\mathbf{y} = [y_1 \cdots y_M]^\top$, $\mathbf{x}_m = \text{vec}(\mathcal{X}_m)$, and $\mathbf{X} = [\mathbf{x}_1 \cdots \mathbf{x}_M]^\top$. Then we get an equivalent objective function with the following solution:

$$\mathbf{a}^{k+1} = (\mathbf{X}^\top \mathbf{X} + \rho \mathbf{I})^{-1} (\mathbf{X}^\top \mathbf{y} + \rho(\mathbf{w}^k - \mathbf{p}'^k)), \quad (7)$$

where $\mathbf{I}$ is an identity matrix. $\mathcal{A}^{k+1}$ is obtained by folding (reshaping) $\mathbf{a}^{k+1}$ into a third-order tensor, denoted as $\mathcal{A}^{k+1} = \text{tensor}_3(\mathbf{a}^{k+1})$.

**Updating $\mathcal{B}^{k+1}$:**

$$\mathcal{B}^{k+1} = \arg\min_{\mathcal{B}} \tau \|\mathcal{B}\|_{TNN} + \frac{\rho}{2} \|\mathcal{B} - \mathcal{W}^k + \mathcal{Q}'^k\|_F^2 = \text{prox}_{\frac{\tau}{\rho} \|\cdot\|_{TNN}} (\mathcal{W}^k - \mathcal{Q}'^k). \quad (8)$$

The proximal operator for the TNN at tensor $\mathcal{T}$ with parameter $\mu$ is denoted by $\text{prox}_{\mu \|\cdot\|_{TNN}}(\mathcal{T})$ and defined as
$\text{prox}_{\mu \|\cdot\|_{TNN}}(\mathcal{T}) := \arg\min_{\mathcal{W}} \mu \|\mathcal{W}\|_{TNN} + \frac{1}{2} \|\mathcal{W} - \mathcal{T}\|_F^2$. More details of the TNN proximal operator can be found in [14].

**Updating $\mathcal{W}^{k+1}$:**

$$\mathcal{W}^{k+1} = \text{prox}_{\frac{\gamma}{2\rho} \|\cdot\|_1} (\mathcal{A}^{k+1} + \mathcal{P}'^k + \mathcal{B}^{k+1} + \mathcal{Q}'^k)/2. \quad (9)$$

It can be solved by calling the proximal operator of the $\ell_1$ norm with parameter $\frac{\gamma}{2\rho}$, which is simply the element-wise soft-thresholding, i.e., $\text{prox}_{\mu\|\cdot\|_1}(\mathcal{T}) = sign(\mathcal{T})(|\mathcal{T}| - \mu)_+$.

**Updating $\mathcal{P}^{k+1}$ and $\mathcal{Q}^{k+1}$:**

$$\mathcal{P}'^{k+1} = \mathcal{P}'^k + \mathcal{A}^{k+1} - \mathcal{W}^{k+1}, \text{ and } \mathcal{Q}'^{k+1} = \mathcal{Q}'^k + \mathcal{B}^{k+1} - \mathcal{W}^{k+1}. \quad (10)$$

**Optimization Algorithm Analysis.** *Sturm* is an instance of the ADMM algorithm applied to linear constraint convex optimization problem, which is guaranteed to converge with a $\frac{1}{\epsilon}$ convergence rate [1].

## 3  Experiments and Discussion

### 3.1  Classification Problems and Datasets

**Resting-State fMRI for Disease Diagnosis.** We use two freely available datasets. *Rest 1 – ABIDE$_{NYU\&UM}$*: the two largest subsets NYU and UM from the Autism Brain Imaging Data Exchange (ABIDE)[1], which consists of 101 patients with autism spectrum disorder (ASD) and 131 healthy control subjects. *Rest 2 – ADHD-200$_{NYU}$*: the NYU subset from the Attention Deficit Hyperactivity Disorder (ADHD) 200 dataset[2] with 118 ADHD patients and 98 healthy controls. The 4D raw fMRI data is reduced to 3D by either taking the average or the amplitude of low frequency fluctuation of voxel values along the time dimension. We perform experiments on both and report the best results.

**Task-Based fMRI for Neural Decoding.** We consider four datasets from the OpenfMRI[3] in two binary classification problems. *Task 1 – Balloon vs Mixed Gamble*, two gamble-related datasets with 64 subjects in total; and *Task 2 – Simon vs Flanker*, two recognition and response related tasks with overall 94 subjects. The OpenfMRI data is processed with a standard template following [8] to obtain the 3D statistical parametric maps (SPMs) for each brain condition.

### 3.2  Algorithms and Evaluation Settings

**Algorithms.** Sturm and Sturm + SVM (support vector machine) are compared against the following four algorithms and three additional algorithms combining with SVM.

- *SVM*: a linear SVM is chosen for both speed and accuracy consideration.
- *Lasso* [4]: a linear regression method with the $\ell_1$ norm regularization.
- *Elastic Net (ENet)* [15]: a linear regression method with $\ell_1$ and $\ell_2$ norm.
- *Remurs* [12]: a multilinear regression model with $\ell_1$ norm and Tucker rank-based SNN regularization.

---

[1] http://fcon_1000.projects.nitrc.org/indi/abide.
[2] http://neurobureau.projects.nitrc.org/ADHD200/Data.html.
[3] https://legacy.openfmri.org.

SVM, Lasso, and ENet take vectorized fMRI data as input while Remurs directly takes 3D fMRI tensors as input. In addition, Lasso, ENet, Remurs, and Sturm can also be used for feature selection. Hence, we can use the selected voxels from each of the above algorithm as input to SVM for classification i.e., Lasso + SVM, ENet + SVM, Remurs + SVM and Sturm + SVM.

**Model Hyper-parameter Tuning.** For Sturm, we follow the Remurs default setting [12] to set $\rho$ to 1 and use the same set $\{10^{-3}, 5 \times 10^{-3}, 10^{-2}, \ldots, 5 \times 10^2, 10^3\}$ for $\tau$ and $\gamma$, additionally scaling the first term in Eq. (3) by a factor $\alpha = \sqrt{(\max(I_1, I_2) \times I_3)}$ to better balance the scales of the loss function and regularization terms [7]. Ten-fold cross validation is applied for tuning hyper-parameters in all the algorithms.

**Image Resizing.** To improve computational efficiency and reduce the small sample size problem (and overfitting), the input 3D tensors are further re-sized into three different sizes with a factor $\beta$, choosing from $\{0.3, 0.5, 0.7\}$. The best accuracy from all three sizes is reported for each algorithm in this paper.

**Feature Selection.** In Lasso + SVM, ENet + SVM, Remurs + SVM, and Sturm + SVM, we rank the selected features by their associated absolute values of $\mathcal{W}$ in the descending order and feed the top $\eta\%$ of the features to SVM. We study five values of $\eta$: $\{1, 5, 10, 50, 100\}$ and report the best accuracy for each algorithm.

**Evaluation Metric and Method.** The classification accuracy is our primary evaluation metric, and we also examine the sparsity of the obtained solutions for all algorithms except SVM. The sparsity is calculated as the ratio of the number of zeros in the output coefficient tensor $\mathcal{W}$ to its size $I_1 \times I_2 \times I_3$. In general, higher sparsity implies better interpretability [4].

**Table 1.** Classification accuracy (mean ± standard deviation in %). Rest 1 and Rest 2 denote two disease diagnosis problems on ABIDE$_{NYU\&UM}$ and ADHD-200, respectively. Task 1 and Task 2 denote two neural decoding problems on OpenfMRI datasets for Balloon vs Mixed gamble and Simon vs Flanker, respectively. The best accuracy among all of the compared algorithms for each column is highlighted in **bold** and the second best is underlined.

| Method | Rest 1 | Rest 2 | Task 1 | Task 2 | Average | | |
|---|---|---|---|---|---|---|---|
| | | | | | Rest | Task | All |
| SVM | 60.78 ± 0.09 | 63.97 ± 0.09 | 87.38 ± 0.12 | 82.56 ± 0.17 | 62.38 | 84.97 | 73.67 |
| Lasso | 61.16 ± 0.08 | 64.84 ± 0.11 | 87.38 ± 0.12 | 85.22 ± 0.07 | 63.00 | 86.30 | 74.65 |
| ENet | 61.21 ± 0.10 | 64.38 ± 0.10 | 81.19 ± 0.15 | 82.56 ± 0.17 | 62.80 | 81.87 | 72.34 |
| Remurs | 60.72 ± 0.08 | 62.13 ± 0.09 | 87.14 ± 0.13 | 84.67 ± 0.15 | 61.43 | 85.90 | 73.67 |
| Sturm | 62.05 ± 0.11 | 63.47 ± 0.07 | **89.10 ± 0.09** | **86.89 ± 0.16** | 62.76 | **88.00** | **75.38** |
| Lasso + SVM | 63.37 ± 0.08 | 62.56 ± 0.09 | 74.05 ± 0.20 | 72.11 ± 0.16 | 62.97 | 73.08 | 68.02 |
| ENet + SVM | 64.20 ± 0.07 | 61.61 ± 0.08 | 76.43 ± 0.14 | 72.00 ± 0.14 | 62.91 | 74.21 | 68.56 |
| Remurs + SVM | **64.67 ± 0.10** | 60.23 ± 0.10 | 81.19 ± 0.12 | 83.56 ± 0.19 | 62.45 | 82.37 | 72.41 |
| Sturm+ SVM | 64.66 ± 0.12 | **66.24 ± 0.06** | 78.10 ± 0.22 | 82.44 ± 0.16 | **65.45** | 80.27 | 72.86 |

**Table 2.** Sparsity (mean ± standard deviation) for respective results in Table 1 with the **best** and <u>second best</u> highlighted.

| Method | Rest 1 | Rest 2 | Task 1 | Task 2 | Average | | |
|---|---|---|---|---|---|---|---|
| | | | | | Rest | Task | All |
| Lasso | 0.52 ± 0.09 | 0.23 ± 0.32 | 0.74 ± 0.12 | 0.73 ± 0.01 | 0.38 | 0.73 | 0.55 |
| ENet | 0.60 ± 0.01 | 0.01 ± 0.01 | **0.96 ± 0.05** | **0.95 ± 0.03** | 0.31 | **0.96** | 0.63 |
| Remurs | 0.69 ± 0.03 | 0.73 ± 0.17 | 0.81 ± 0.08 | <u>0.81 ± 0.07</u> | 0.71 | <u>0.81</u> | <u>0.76</u> |
| Sturm | <u>0.86 ± 0.18</u> | <u>0.86 ± 0.24</u> | 0.72 ± 0.24 | 0.60 ± 0.15 | <u>0.86</u> | 0.66 | <u>0.76</u> |
| Lasso + SVM | 0.57 ± 0.05 | 0.19 ± 0.40 | 0.77 ± 0.10 | 0.75 ± 0.06 | 0.38 | 0.76 | 0.57 |
| ENet + SVM | 0.58 ± 0.09 | 0.02 ± 0.01 | **0.96 ± 0.04** | **0.95 ± 0.04** | 0.30 | **0.96** | 0.63 |
| Remurs + SVM | 0.70 ± 0.13 | 0.74 ± 0.17 | 0.80 ± 0.04 | 0.79 ± 0.13 | 0.72 | 0.79 | 0.76 |
| Sturm + SVM | **0.87 ± 0.07** | **0.99 ± 0.01** | <u>0.85 ± 0.14</u> | 0.56 ± 0.11 | **0.93** | 0.71 | **0.82** |

### 3.3    Result Discussion and Visualization

**Classification Accuracy.** Table 1 shows the classification accuracy for all algorithms. Over the two resting-state problems, Sturm + SVM has the highest accuracy of 65.45%, and Lasso is the second-best (63.00%). Whereas, on these two task-based problems, Sturm has outperformed all other algorithms in accuracy, with 88.00% accuracy. Lasso is again the second-best in accuracy (86.30%). One interesting observation is that on task-based classification problems, Sturm + SVM has significant drop in accuracy compared with Sturm alone, and Lasso + SVM, ENet + SVM and Remurs + SVM all have lower accuracy compared to without SVM. Overall, Sturm still achieves the highest accuracy.

**Model Sparsity.** Table 2 presents the respective sparsity values except SVM, which uses all features so the sparsity is zero. Over the two resting-state classification problems, Sturm + SVM and Sturm are the top two algorithms with sparsity of 0.93 and 0.86, respectively. Noticeably, Lasso & ENet fail to select a sparse solution via cross validation on Rest 2. Over the two task-based problems, both ENet and ENet + SVM have the best sparsity (0.96). However, both of them have much lower accuracy than Sturm and Remurs. Over all the problems, Sturm + SVM obtains the most sparse model with the overall sparsity of 0.82, meanwhile, Sturm and Remurs have almost identical sparsity of 0.76.

**Weight Map Visualization.** Take Task Simon vs Flanker as an example. The selected voxels on two brain slices from the top 5% (4514 voxels, ranked by the absolute weights) of the full-brain voxels are visualized in Fig. 2 using the best performing parameters in cross-validation of Lasso, ENet, Remurs and Sturm. Figure 2 clearly shows that Sturm and Remurs select more spatially connected voxels than Lasso or ENet does, resulting in more robust and easier interpreted models for further analysis. Both Sturm and Remurs choose voxels from highly consistent regions, while Sturm produces weight maps with slightly higher visual contrast than Remurs does.

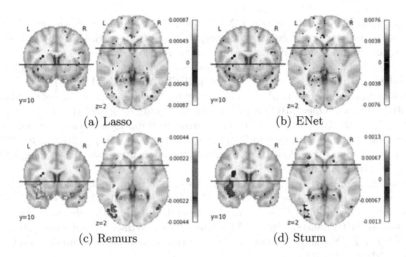

(a) Lasso    (b) ENet

(c) Remurs    (d) Sturm

**Fig. 2.** Weight maps on Task Simon vs Flanker. Sturm and Remurs select clear regions which are easier for further analysis than Lasso and ENet.

## 4    Conclusion

The proposed multilinear regression model (*Sturm*) performs regression with regularization on the tubal tensor nuclear norm (TNN), demonstrates the superior overall performance of Sturm (and Sturm + SVM, in some cases) over other methods in terms of accuracy, sparsity and weight maps. Thus, it is promising to use TNN and tubal rank regularization in a supervised setting for fMRI.

**Acknowledgement.** This work was supported by the grant from the UK Engineering and Physical Sciences Research Council (EP/R014507/1).

## References

1. Boyd, S., Parikh, N., Chu, E., Peleato, B., Eckstein, J.: Distributed optimization and statistical learning via the alternating direction method of multipliers. Found. Trends® Mach. Learn. **3**(1), 1–122 (2011)
2. Candès, E.J., Li, X., Ma, Y., Wright, J.: Robust principal component analysis? J. ACM (JACM) **58**(3), 11 (2011)
3. Eickenberg, M., Dohmatob, E., Thirion, B., Varoquaux, G.: Grouping total variation and sparsity: statistical learning with segmenting penalties. In: Navab, N., Hornegger, J., Wells, W.M., Frangi, A.F. (eds.) MICCAI 2015. LNCS, vol. 9349, pp. 685–693. Springer, Cham (2015). https://doi.org/10.1007/978-3-319-24553-9_84
4. Hastie, T., Tibshirani, R., Wainwright, M.: Statistical Learning with Sparsity: The Lasso and Generalizations. CRC Press, Boca Raton (2015)
5. Huettel, S.A., Song, A.W., McCarthy, G.: Functional Magnetic Resonance Imaging, vol. 1. Sinauer Associates, Sunderland (2004)

6. Kilmer, M.E., Braman, K., Hao, N., Hoover, R.C.: Third-order tensors as operators on matrices: a theoretical and computational framework with applications in imaging. SIAM J. Matrix Anal. Appl. **34**(1), 148–172 (2013)
7. Lu, C., Feng, J., Liu, W., Lin, Z., Yan, S.: Tensor robust principal component analysis with a new tensor nuclear norm. IEEE Trans. PAMI (2019)
8. Poldrack, R.A., Barch, D.M., Mitchell, J., et al.: Toward open sharing of task-based fMRI data: the OpenfMRI project. Front. Neuroinf. **7**, 12 (2013)
9. Rao, N., Cox, C., Nowak, R., et al.: Sparse overlapping sets lasso for multitask learning and its application to fMRI analysis. In: NeurIPS, pp. 2202–2210 (2013)
10. Romera-Paredes, B., Pontil, M.: A new convex relaxation for tensor completion. In: NeurIPS, pp. 2967–2975 (2013)
11. Ryali, S., Supekar, K., Abrams, D.A., Menon, V.: Sparse logistic regression for whole-brain classification of fmri data. NeuroImage **51**(2), 752–764 (2010)
12. Song, X., Lu, H.: Multilinear regression for embedded feature selection with application to fMRI analysis. In: AAAI Conference on Artificial Intelligence (2017)
13. Tucker, L.R.: Some mathematical notes on three-mode factor analysis. Psychometrika **31**(3), 279–311 (1966)
14. Zhang, Z., Aeron, S.: Exact tensor completion using t-SVD. IEEE Trans. Sig. Process. **65**(6), 1511–1526 (2017)
15. Zou, H., Hastie, T.: Regularization and variable selection via the elastic net. J. Roy. Stat. Soc.: Ser. B (Stat. Methodol.) **67**(2), 301–320 (2005)

# Improving Whole-Brain Neural Decoding of fMRI with Domain Adaptation

Shuo Zhou[1]([⊠]), Christopher R. Cox[2], and Haiping Lu[1,3]

[1] Department of Computer Science, University of Sheffield, Sheffield, UK
{szhou20,h.lu}@sheffield.ac.uk
[2] Department of Psychology, Louisiana State University, Baton Rouge, USA
chriscoxs@lsu.edu
[3] Sheffield Institute for Translational Neuroscience, Sheffield, UK

**Abstract.** In neural decoding, there has been a growing interest in *machine learning* on functional magnetic resonance imaging (fMRI). However, the size discrepancy between the *whole-brain* feature space and the training set poses serious challenges. Simply increasing the number of training examples is infeasible and costly. In this paper, we propose a *domain adaptation framework for whole-brain fMRI* (DawfMRI) to improve whole-brain neural decoding on *target* data leveraging *source* data. DawfMRI consists of two steps: (1) source and target *feature adaptation*, and (2) source and target *classifier adaptation*. We evaluate its four possible variations, using a collection of fMRI datasets from OpenfMRI. The results demonstrated that appropriate choices of source domain can help improve neural decoding accuracy for challenging classification tasks. The best-case improvement is 10.47% (from 77.26% to 87.73%). Moreover, visualising and interpreting voxel weights revealed that the adaptation can provide additional insights into neural decoding.

## 1 Introduction

Functional magnetic resonance imaging (fMRI) [8] is a medical imaging technique that can measure the neural activity associated with multiple cognitive behaviours. Distinguishing functional brain activities can be framed as classification problems and solved with machine learning techniques, e.g., classifying cognitive tasks [3,4]. However, an individual fMRI dataset provides only a few training examples, which is relatively small for machine learning compared to the feature (voxel) space, typically less than one hundred examples per brain state. This size discrepancy makes accurate prediction a challenging problem.

Traditionally, this challenge is dealt with by pre-selecting voxels that belong to regions of interest (ROIs) based on prior work and established knowledge of domain experts [12], or by performing a "searchlight" analysis [6]. While making the problem computationally more tractable, it may ignore a significant portion of information, and miss potentially valid and superior solutions in the first place.

© Springer Nature Switzerland AG 2019
H.-I. Suk et al. (Eds.): MLMI 2019, LNCS 11861, pp. 265–273, 2019.
https://doi.org/10.1007/978-3-030-32692-0_31

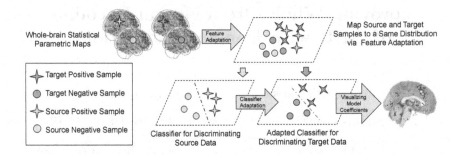

**Fig. 1.** DawfMRI framework consists of two steps: feature adaptation, and classifier adaptation. Learnt model can be visualised for cognitive interpretation.

Recently, *domain adaptation* has been used in several neural decoding studies [7,15] for tackling the small sample problems. Domain adaptation is an emerging machine learning scheme for improving the classification performance in a classification problem by utilising the knowledge learnt from different but related data [10]. The effectiveness of domain adaptation has been shown in varied domains such as computer vision and natural language processing. The mainstream domain adaptation methods can be divided into two categories: *feature-based* and *classifier-based* adaptation [10,11,14]. In domain adaptation terminology, the data to be classified are called the *target domain data*, while the data to be leveraged are called the *source domain data*.

Domain adaptation techniques and growing public data repositories enable analysing fMRI data from different datasets. However, the existing state-of-the-art domain adaptation methods have not been well for neural decoding.

**Contributions:** This paper proposes a *Domain adaptation framework for whole-brain fMRI* (DawfMRI) to improve the performance in a *target domain* classification problem leveraging *source domain* data. It consists of two steps: (1) *feature adaptation*, and (2) *classifier adaptation*. Under this framework, we employed one state-of-the-art realisation of each step and evaluated all four possible variations. We designed experiments systematically using a collection of tasks from the OpenfMRI[1] project. Results demonstrated domain adaptation is a promising way of improving neural decoding. Visualising the decoding model coefficients revealed additional insights obtained via domain adaptation.

## 2    Methodology

Figure 1 depicts the proposed domain adaptation framework for whole-brain fMRI (DawfMRI). This framework consists of two steps: feature adaptation, and classifier adaptation, for informing machine learning models about the domain difference in both feature extraction and prediction making stages. To study DawfMRI systematically, we employ one state-of-the-art method for each step:

---

[1] Now known as OpenNeuro. We will use the name OpenfMRI in the rest of this paper.

transfer component analysis (TCA) [9] for feature adaptation, and cross-domain SVM (CDSVM) [5] for classifier adaptation.

**Feature Adaptation by TCA.** This step aims to extract common features across domains. TCA is an approach that targets on the problem where there is a distribution mismatch between target and source domains, which is measured by the Maximum mean discrepancy (MMD) [2]. Given source domain data $\mathbf{X}_s \in \mathbb{R}^{D \times n_s}$, target domain data $\mathbf{X}_t \in \mathbb{R}^{D \times n_t}$, where $n_s$ and $n_t$ denote the number of samples of $\mathbf{X}_s$ and $\mathbf{X}_t$ respectively, and $D$ denotes the input feature dimension, MMD between the two domains is $\| \frac{1}{n_s} \sum_{i=1}^{n_s} \phi(\mathbf{x}_{s_i}) - \frac{1}{n_t} \sum_{i=1}^{n_t} \phi(\mathbf{x}_{t_i}) \|_{\mathcal{H}}^2$, where $\mathcal{H}$ denotes a reproducing kernel Hilbert space (RKHS) [1], $\mathbf{x}_{s_i}$ and $\mathbf{x}_{t_j}$ are the $i$th and $j$th sample of $\mathbf{X}_s$ and $\mathbf{X}_t$, respectively. The empirical MMD can be computed by $\mathrm{tr}(\mathbf{KL})$, where $\mathrm{tr}(\cdot)$ is a trace function, $\mathbf{K} \in \mathbb{R}^{n \times n} = k(\mathbf{X}, \mathbf{X})$, $\mathbf{X} = [\mathbf{X}_s, \mathbf{X}_t] \in \mathbb{R}^{D \times n}$, $k(\cdot, \cdot)$ denotes a kernel function (e.g., linear, Gaussian, or polynomial), $n = n_s + n_t$, and $\mathbf{L} \in \mathbb{R}^{n \times n}$ is a matrix where $L_{i,j} = \frac{1}{n_s^2}$, if $\mathbf{x}_i, \mathbf{x}_j \in \mathbf{X}_s$, $L_{i,j} = \frac{1}{n_t^2}$ if $\mathbf{x}_i, \mathbf{x}_j \in \mathbf{X}_t$, and $L_{i,j} = -\frac{1}{n_s n_t}$ otherwise.

The objective of TCA is learning a mapping matrix $\mathbf{U} \in \mathbb{R}^{n \times d}$ to map the samples from kernel space to a $d$-dimensional space ($d \ll n_s + n_t$) with a minimal difference in distribution. The MMD of the learnt space is $\mathrm{tr}((\mathbf{KUU}^\top \mathbf{K})\mathbf{L}) = \mathrm{tr}(\mathbf{U}^\top \mathbf{KLKU})$. Additionally, covariance matrix is used to preserve the variance of input data. Then the overall objective becomes

$$\min_{\mathbf{U}} \; \mathrm{tr}(\mathbf{U}^\top \mathbf{KLKU}) + \lambda \cdot \mathrm{tr}(\mathbf{U}^\top \mathbf{U})$$
$$\text{s.t. } \mathbf{U}^\top \mathbf{KHKU} = \mathbf{I}_d, \quad \lambda > 0, \tag{1}$$

where $\mathbf{I}_d \in \mathbb{R}^{d \times d}$ is an identity matrix, $\mathbf{H} = \mathbf{I} - \frac{1}{n}\mathbf{1}\mathbf{1}^\top \in \mathbb{R}^{n \times n}$ is a centering matrix, $\lambda$ is a hyperparameter parameter for regularisation. Problem (1) can be optimised by the method of Lagrange multipliers and eigendecomposition. The solution is the $d$ smallest eigenvectors of $(\mathbf{KLK} + \lambda \mathbf{I})(\mathbf{KHK})^{-1}$.

**Classifier Adaptation by CDSVM.** This step aims to learn a generalised decoding model for target samples by leveraging the source samples. CDSVM learns a decision function $f(\mathbf{x}) = \mathbf{w}^\top \mathbf{x}$ with limited target training samples by utilising the support vectors from a standard SVM fitted on source domain samples. The objective function of CDSVM is

$$\min_{\mathbf{w}} \frac{1}{2}\|\mathbf{w}\|^2 + C\sum_{i=1}^{M}\xi_i + C\sum_{j=1}^{K}\bar{\xi}_j \sum_{\mathbf{x}_i \in \mathbf{D}_l^t} \exp(-\beta\|\mathbf{v}_j^s - \mathbf{x}_i\|_2^2)$$
$$\text{s.t. } \; y_i f(\mathbf{x}_i) \geq 1 - \xi_i, \quad \xi_i \geq 0, \quad \forall(\mathbf{x}_i, y_i) \in \mathbf{D}_l^t,$$
$$y_j^s f(\mathbf{v}_j^s) \geq 1 - \bar{\xi}_j, \quad \bar{\xi}_j \geq 0, \quad \forall(\mathbf{v}_j^s, y_j^s) \in \mathbf{V}^s, \tag{2}$$

where $\mathbf{V}^s = [\mathbf{v}_1^s, \mathbf{v}_2^s, \dots \mathbf{v}_K^s]^\top \in \mathbb{R}^{K \times d}$ is a matrix of source support vectors. $\mathbf{D}_l^t \in \mathbb{R}^{M \times d}$ represents the labelled target training samples. $\xi_i$ and $\bar{\xi}_j$ are slack variables for the $i$th target training sample and $j$th source support vector respectively. $C$ is a hyperparameter controlling the SVM soft margin. $\beta$ is a hyperparameter controlling the influence of the source support vectors. Larger value of $\beta$ leads to less influence of source support vectors, and vice versa.

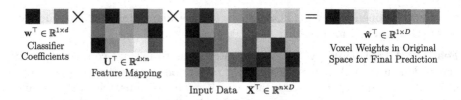

**Fig. 2.** Mapping classifier coefficients **w** to voxel weights **ŵ**.

**Table 1.** List of OpenfMRI datasets used in the experiments (ACN denotes accession number. $N_{sample}$ denotes the number of samples for each dataset. Abbr denotes abbreviations, which are used in the rest of this paper for easy reference).

| ACN | $N_{sample}$ | Task & contrast description | Abbr |
|---|---|---|---|
| ds001 | 32 | Balloon analog risk task: Parametric pump effect vs. control | BART |
| ds002 | 34 | Probabilistic classification: Task vs. baseline | CT1 |
| ds002 | 34 | Deterministic classification: Feedback vs. baseline | CT2 |
| ds002 | 34 | Mixed event-related probe: Task vs. baseline | CT3 |
| ds003 | 13 | Rhyme judgement: Task vs. baseline | RJT |
| ds005 | 32 | Mixed-gambles task: Parametric gain response | MGT |
| ds007 | 40 | Stop signal task: Letter classification vs. baseline | SST1 |
| ds007 | 38 | Stop signal task: Letter naming vs. baseline | SST2 |
| ds007 | 39 | Stop signal task: Pseudoword naming vs. baseline | SST3 |
| ds101 | 42 | Simon task: Incorrect vs. correct | ST |
| ds102 | 52 | Flanker task: Incongruent vs. congruent | FT |

**Visualising Model Coefficients for Interpretation.** The final classifier coefficients (or weights) indicate the significance of the corresponding features for a classification problem. Visualising them in the brain voxel space can help us gain insights into which areas contribute more to prediction performance. To achieve this, we chose a linear kernel for each DawfMRI step and developed a method to map the classifier coefficients back to voxel weights in the original brain voxel space for interpretation, as shown in Fig. 2.

## 3    Experiments

**Datesets and Preprocessing.** Eleven datasets[2] from OpenfMRI were used in the experiments. Table 1 lists the details of the selected datasets. Each dataset is from a cognitive experiment. Each sample was preprocessed with the protocol in [13] to obtain the Z-score statistical parametric map (SPM) of size $91 \times 109 \times 91$, which is then reduced to a vector of size $211,106$ containing only the voxels within the brains. The contrasts associated with each task represent differences between the primary tasks and baseline conditions. We conducted our experiments using the single contrast per task. The contrasts used are also reported in Table 1.

---

[2] https://legacy.openfmri.org or https://openneuro.org.

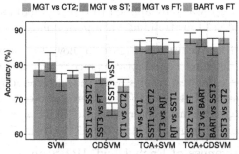

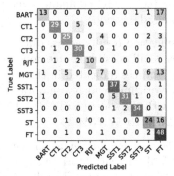

(a) Multi-class classification confusion matrix for linear SVM performance on the whole-brain SPMs.

(b) Classification accuracy of four DawfMRI variations (x-axis) on the four target domains (coloured bars). Error bars indicate the standard derivations. Adaptation algorithms use the best source domains, as indicated in the bars.

**Fig. 3.** Four most challenging pairs in 3a were selected as target domains to perform domain adaptation. The obtained results are shown in 3b. (Color figure online)

**Target Domain Setup.** We consider the most basic scenario that a pair of cognitive tasks as a classification problem. We anticipate the classification problems with lower prediction accuracy have higher potential of improvement via domain adaptation. Thus, we performed multi-class classification via a linear SVM to identify the most confusing domains resulting a confusion matrix in Fig. 3a, where each entry $(i, j)$ is the number of observations actually in task $i$, but predicted to be in task $j$. Consequently, four most confusing pairs of tasks are identified as target domains: (1) BART vs FT, (2) MGT vs CT2, (3) MGT vs ST, (4) MGT vs ST, and (5) MGT vs FT.

**Source Domain Setup and Class Labels.** For one target domain, the remaining nine tasks are combined pairwise to give 36 unique pairs, each of which is a candidate source domain. Tasks of each pair are labelled 1 (positive) and $-1$ (negative). We studied both cases of matching source labels with target labels, i.e., 1 with 1 and $-1$ with $-1$, or 1 with $-1$ and $-1$ with 1.

**Algorithm setup.** We evaluated four possible variations of the DawfMRI framework: (1) SVM, (2) CDSVM, (3) TCA+SVM, (4) TCA+CDSVM.

For TCA+SVM, a SVM was fit to the both source and target training samples after performing TCA. For CDSVM and TCA+CDSVM, a SVM was fit to the source samples, and then the source support vectors were used as additional input for training CDSVM on the target samples. A linear kernel was used for TCA, SVM, and CDSVM for easy interpretation. We fixed the regularisation penalty $\lambda = 1$ and output dimension $d = 100$ for TCA. The hyper-parameters $C$ for SVM and CDSVM, and $\beta$ for CDSVM, were optimised on regular grids of log scale in $[10^{-3}, 10^3]$, with a step size of one in exponent.

**Evaluation Methods.** We performed $10 \times 10$-fold cross-validation (CV) evaluation. All training samples were sampled uniformly at random for cross validation. CV was only applied to target domain samples. Source domain samples were all used for training when performing domain adaptation.

**Decoding Accuracy.** Figure 3b shows the classification results across different target domains. For adaptation algorithms, we tested all possible source domains to report the best results, with the corresponding sources indicated in the bars. In general, TCA+ CDSVM outperformed other algorithms, which also obtained the largest accuracy improvement (BART vs FT with the source SST2 vs CT2). This improves over SVM by **10.47%** (**from 77.26% to 87.73%**).

**Effectiveness of Each DawfMRI Step.** For *feature adaptation*, as shown in Fig. 3b, TCA+SVM consistently outperformed SVM with appropriate sources. This indicates that TCA can extract common features across domain with lower dimension from whole-brain SPMs. For *classifier adaptation*, CDSVM can improve the accuracy when combined with TCA. However, SVM outperformed CDSVM consistently. This indicates that the effectiveness of CDSVM tends to be related to the distribution distances between domains.

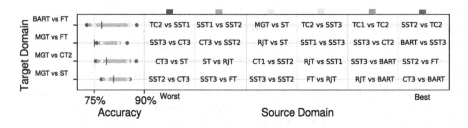

**Fig. 4.** Adaptation effectiveness of TCA+CDSVM (colored dots) over SVM (black vertical bars) across all four target domains. Target domains (y axis) are sorted w.r.t. the maximum accuracy improvement. The worst three and best three source domains are listed from left to right. (Color figure online)

**Sensitivity to Source Domain.** Figure 4 summarises the *adaptation effectiveness* of different source domains over the four different target domains, which are sorted by the largest accuracy improvements of TCA+CDSVM over SVM. The accuracy were improved on 123 out of 144 possible target and source combinations. However, the improvement varies across different source domains. It shows that the effectiveness of domain adaptation was significantly affected by the source domain. We also observed that SVM outperformed TCA+CDSVM in some cases, which is called "negative transfer" [10].

## 4    Discussion: Model Overlapping Study

It is also important to understand why a model performs well and which brain networks are particularly important in cognitive neuroscience. Exploring what information tends to emerge through domain adaptation can help to answer this question. Therefore, we carried out a study to examine where the important

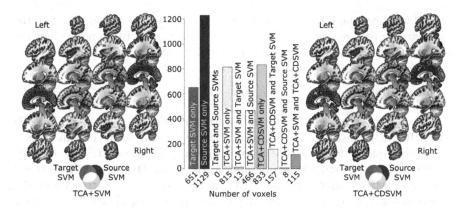

**Fig. 5.** Visualisation of the voxels with top 1% weight magnitude and occurring in clusters of at least 20 voxels in the four models: target SVM, source SVM, TCA+SVM (left), and TCA+CDSVM (right). Numbers of distinct and overlapped voxels identified by the models are shown in the middle bars.

voxels are in the brain, and how much the voxel sets in the target domain, source domain, and adapted models overlap.

We studied the case of a balanced classification problem, which is MGT vs CT2. SST2 vs FT is used as source, which showed the biggest improvement in classification accuracy for the selected target problem.

Figure 5 shows the voxels with the top 1% weight magnitude in the four models (target SVM, source SVM, TCA+SVM, and TCA+CDSVM) and occurring in clusters of at least 20 voxels. The target and source domain SVMs place their important voxels in completely different areas. Not only is there no overlap, but the supra-threshold voxels in each model are sampled from different lobes of the brain: the target domain SVM is associated primarily with supra-threshold voxels in the frontal lobes, while the source domain SVM is associated primarily with supra-threshold voxels in the occipital lobe and sensory motor cortex. The distribution of coefficients is different between source and target models, but adaptation can be very effective.

TCA+SVM has substantial overlap with the source SVM, and nearly no overlap with the target SVM. This substantial overlap, however, is only about 1/3 of the supra-threshold voxels in the TCA+SVM model. The remaining 2/3 are completely distinct from either the target or source models, indicating that information from the source domain has revealed a different dimension along to which to dissociate the tasks in the target domain than was apparent in the target data in isolation.

This general pattern is echoed in TCA+CDSVM, except that in this case there is virtually no overlap with the source domain and there is instead modest overlap with the target domain. Again, the adaptation model is largely associated with supra-threshold voxels that do not overlap with either the target or source

SVMs. Thus, the adaptation procedure has provided additional insights into the classification problem, showing the exploited information to be more than the simple sum of information from the target and source domain models.

## 5 Conclusion

In this paper, we proposed a domain adaptation framework for whole-brain fMRI (DawfMRI) that consists of two key steps: feature adaptation and classifier adaptation. We employed two state-of-the-art algorithms, TCA and CDSVM, for each step of DawfMRI. We studied four different variations of DawfMRI on task-based whole-brain fMRI from eleven OpenfMRI datasets. Results show that DawfMRI can significantly improve the performance for challenging binary classification problems. Finally, we interpreted how the models provide additional insights.

**Acknowledgement.** This work was supported by grants from the UK Engineering and Physical Sciences Research Council (EP/R014507/1) and Medical Research Council 515 (MR/J004146/1), and the European Research Council (GAP: 670428 - BRAIN2MIND NEUROCOMP).

## References

1. Berlinet, A., Thomas-Agnan, C.: Reproducing Kernel Hilbert Spaces in Probability and Statistics. Springer, Boston (2011). https://doi.org/10.1007/978-1-4419-9096-9
2. Borgwardt, K.M., Gretton, A., Rasch, M.J., Kriegel, H.P., Schölkopf, B., Smola, A.J.: Integrating structured biological data by kernel maximum mean discrepancy. Bioinformatics **22**(14), e49–e57 (2006)
3. Cheng, W., et al.: Voxel-based, brain-wide association study of aberrant functional connectivity in schizophrenia implicates thalamocortical circuitry. NPJ Schizophrenia **1**, 15016 (2015)
4. Gheiratmand, M., et al.: Learning stable and predictive network-based patterns of schizophrenia and its clinical symptoms. NPJ Schizophrenia **3**(1), 22 (2017)
5. Jiang, W., Zavesky, E., Chang, S.F., Loui, A.: Cross-domain learning methods for high-level visual concept classification. In: ICIP, pp. 161–164. IEEE (2008)
6. Kriegeskorte, N., Goebel, R., Bandettini, P.: Information-based functional brain mapping. PNAS **103**(10), 3863–3868 (2006)
7. Mensch, A., Mairal, J., Bzdok, D., Thirion, B., Varoquaux, G.: Learning neural representations of human cognition across many fMRI studies. In: NeurIPS, pp. 5883–5893 (2017)
8. Ogawa, S., Lee, T.M., Kay, A.R., Tank, D.W.: Brain magnetic resonance imaging with contrast dependent on blood oxygenation. PNAS **87**(24), 9868–9872 (1990)
9. Pan, S.J., Tsang, I.W., Kwok, J.T., Yang, Q.: Domain adaptation via transfer component analysis. IEEE Trans. Neural Netw. **22**(2), 199–210 (2011)
10. Pan, S.J., Yang, Q.: A survey on transfer learning. TKDE **22**(10), 1345–1359 (2010)
11. Patel, V.M., Gopalan, R., Li, R., Chellappa, R.: Visual domain adaptation: a survey of recent advances. IEEE Sig. Process. Mag. **32**(3), 53–69 (2015)
12. Poldrack, R.A.: Region of interest analysis for fMRI. Soc. Cogn. Affect. Neurosci. **2**(1), 67–70 (2007)

13. Poldrack, R.A., et al.: Toward open sharing of task-based fMRI data: the OpenfMRI project. Front. Neuroinform. **7**, 12 (2013)
14. Weiss, K., Khoshgoftaar, T.M., Wang, D.: A survey of transfer learning. J. Big Data **3**(1), 9 (2016)
15. Zhang, H., Chen, P.H., Ramadge, P.: Transfer learning on fMRI datasets. In: AISTATS, pp. 595–603. PMLR (2018)

# Automatic Couinaud Segmentation from CT Volumes on Liver Using GLC-UNet

Jiang Tian$^{(\boxtimes)}$, Li Liu, Zhongchao Shi, and Feiyu Xu

AI Lab, Lenovo Research, Beijing, China
{tianjiang1,liuli16,shizc2,fxu}@lenovo.com

**Abstract.** Automatically generating Couinaud segments on liver, a prerequisite for modern surgery of the liver, from computed tomography (CT) volumes is a challenge for the computer-aided diagnosis (CAD). In this paper, we propose a novel global and local contexts UNet (GLC-UNet) for Couinaud segmentation. In this framework, intra-slice features and 3D contexts are effectively probed and jointly optimized for accurate liver and Couinaud segmentation using attention mechanism. We comprehensively evaluate our system performance (98.51% in terms of Dice per case on liver segmentation, and 92.46% on Couinaud segmentation) on the Medical Segmentation Decathlon dataset (task 8, hepatic vessels and tumor) from MICCAI 2018 with our annotated 43, 205 CT slices on liver and Couinaud segmentation. (https://github.com/GLCUnet/dataset).

## 1 Introduction

Liver cancer is one of the most common cancer diseases and the fourth leading cause of cancer death in the world.[1] "A good knowledge of the anatomy is a prerequisite for modern surgery of the liver." [5] The Couinaud segmentation (detailed definition in Sect. 1 in the Supplementary) is currently the most widely used system to describe functional liver anatomy [8]. It is the preferred anatomy classification system since it divides the liver into eight independent functional units allowing resection of segments without damaging other segments. The system uses the vascular supply in the liver to separate the functional units [9].

In the clinical diagnosis, partitioning sub-regions in Couinaud segmentation is with 3D surfaces. As shown in Fig. 4, partitioning of green and red regions is obtained by a line containing the inferior vena cava (IVC) and the major branch

---

[1] http://www.who.int/news-room/fact-sheets/detail/cancer.

**Electronic supplementary material** The online version of this chapter (https://doi.org/10.1007/978-3-030-32692-0_32) contains supplementary material, which is available to authorized users.

H.-I. Suk et al. (Eds.): MLMI 2019, LNCS 11861, pp. 274–282, 2019.
https://doi.org/10.1007/978-3-030-32692-0_32

of the right hepatic vein (RHV) (shifts from slice to slice). Couinaud segmentation of a CT volume is consequently on a slice-by-slice basis. It is worth noting that the caudate lobe of liver, a very important sub-region (light blue region in Fig. 4, missing in traditional method [10]), is partitioned using a curve. The hepatic artery and portal vein inflow to and hepatic vein drainage of the liver have many anatomic variations. More specifically, there may be an early bifurcation, early trifurcation or even multiple hepatic veins running in the hepatic fissure. Meanwhile, the liver is a common site of primary or secondary tumor development. Their heterogeneous and diffusive shape will make the situation even worse. Consequently, it is difficult to deduce segmental anatomy of the liver. Since the treatment planning enters "segment era", accurate measurement of each segment is a prerequisite for modern surgery of the liver.

In the clinical diagnosis, it is necessary to probe the spatial information far along the $z$-axis to make Couinaud segmentation, which is time-consuming. Therefore, fully automatic methods are highly demanded. Recently, fully convolutional neural networks (FCNs) [1,3,7] have achieved great success on a broad array of computer vision problems. Many researchers advance this stream using deep learning methods in the liver and tumor segmentation problem [2]. However, 2D FCN based methods ignore the contexts along the $z$-axis, which would lead to limited segmentation accuracy. Meanwhile, a 3D FCN, where convolutions in regular 2D FCN are replaced by 3D convolutions with volumetric data input, may probe the 3D contexts. However, the high memory consumption limits the depth of the network to capture long-range context.

To address the aforementioned problem, in this paper, we propose a framework, GLC-UNet, where 3D contexts are effectively probed using attention mechanism for accurate Couinaud segmentation. Meanwhile, experienced doctors usually observe the hepatic hilum and the second hepatic hilum first to obtain a holistic overview of hepatic vessels, which serves as a "skeleton" to constrain the Couinaud segmentation of each slice. Inspired by this fact, in this paper, the proposed framework utilizes this "skeleton" as the global context in Couinaud segmentation. The global context is a sampling of the CT volume[2] around the hepatic hilum and the second hepatic hilum, which are highly correlated with the slices which contain the right and left branch of portal veins (the RPV and the LPV). Incorporating such clinical domain knowledge into network design boosts the performance. Furthermore, we apply this system to a publicly available liver CT dataset. We make annotation on both liver and Couinaud segments of this dataset. Finally, we conduct comprehensive experiments to analyze the effectiveness of our proposed GLC-UNet.

## 2    Couinaud Segmentation Using GLC-UNet

Given a CT volume, a GLC-UNet is first utilized to obtain segmentation of the liver, which serves as the region of interest for Couinaud segmentation. Next, the RPV and the LPV are detected. The slices contain these two veins are baseline

---

[2] A set of CT slices selected from the CT volume.

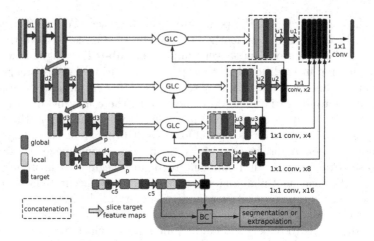

**Fig. 1.** Overall illustration of the proposed GLC-UNet. In the contracting path, except the bottom level, the global, local, and target feature maps are transferred into two directions, one to GLC and the other to the following convolutional layers. On the bottom level, only the feature maps of the target slice is transferred into the expanding path. In the expanding path, feature maps from GLC are transferred to the following upsampling layer. Meanwhile, feature maps from different layers are fused ($1 \times 1$ convolution followed by bilinear resize) before the final prediction. In the end, the features, from all the branches, are combined into a single tensor via concatenation. The segmentation or extrapolation classification in the shaded area is for Couinaud segmentation only. Operation d1 denotes concatenation of 3 different convolutional layers: "$6 \times 6, 12, a2$", "$6 \times 6, 12, a2$", and "$3 \times 3, 24, c$. Note that "$6 \times 6, 12, a2$" corresponds to atrous convolutional layer (rate $= 2$) with kernel size of $6 \times 6$ and 12 features, and "$3 \times 3, 24, c$" stands for regular convolutional layer with kernel size of $3 \times 3$ and 24 features. Detailed operations parameters are listed in Sect. 2 in the Supplementary. GLC model is shown in Fig. 2, and Fig. 3 illustrates the corresponding binary classification used in Couinaud segmentation.

for global context for Couinaud segmentation. Finally, another multi-task GLC-UNet is used to obtain Couinaud segmentation of liver.

**GLC-UNet with Multi-scale Information.** As shown in Fig. 1, the proposed GLC-UNet efficiently probes intra-slice and inter-slice features. The inter-slice feature extraction consists of two parts. One is the global context, and the other is the local context. A context at the input level is defined as a set of CT slices selected from a CT volume. Denote by $\mathbf{G}$ the input global context. We have the corresponding global context feature maps at level $t$ for the $i$-th slice in $\mathbf{G}$ as $\mathbf{G}_{ti}$ (similarly for the input local context $\mathbf{L}$ and the corresponding $\mathbf{L}_{ti}$). It is worth noting that convolutional and pooling operations in the contracting path independently applied on each input in this set. For intra-slice feature, the idea is to provide the model with multi-scale information. To do that, we add a series of atrous convolutions with different dilation rates. These rates are designed to capture long-range in-plane context.

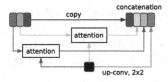

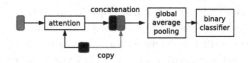

**Fig. 2.** GLC architecture.    **Fig. 3.** Segmentation or extrapolation.

In the contracting path, the feature maps are transferred into two directions, one to GLC and the other to the following convolutional layers. The global context, local context, and the target slice are combined using attention mechanisms as shown in Fig. 2, which distill the visual features by concatenating the global and the local contexts, the target slice's feature maps, and the upsampled feature maps. On the bottom level, only the feature map of the target slice is transferred into the expanding path to generate intra-slice features. In the expanding path, feature maps from GLC are transferred to the following upsampling layer. Meanwhile, feature maps from different levels are fused before the final prediction. In the end, the features, from all the branches, are combined into a single tensor via concatenation.

**Global and Local Contexts Composition.** Let $(S_1, \ldots, S_\Psi)$ be the set of slices in a CT volume, and $tar$ be the index along $z$-axis of the target slice.

For a specific CT volume, in Couinaud segmentation, the global context (a set of slices) is the same for all slices to be segmented in this CT volume. It is driven by liver anatomy specifically. Throughout the paper, we will denote by $\Pi$ the total number of the global context slices, and by $zt$ the top index of the slice with liver region. We have $\mathbf{G}$, the input global context, as follows.

$$ze = (zl + zt)/2, \tag{1}$$

$$zb = min(ze - (\Pi - 1), zr), \tag{2}$$

$$step = (ze - zb)/(\Pi - 1), \tag{3}$$

$$\mathbf{G} = (S_{zb}, S_{zb+step}, \ldots, S_{ze-step}, S_{ze}), \tag{4}$$

where $zl$ and $zr$ are the corresponding coordinates along $z$-axis of the LPV and the RPV, respectively. These coordinates are obtained via detection of the RPV and the LPV via a faster R-CNN network.

In clinical, a radiologist usually observes a couple of adjacent slices to segment liver. Therefore, for liver segmentation, $\mathbf{G}$ is obtained as follows.

$$\mathbf{G} = (S_{tar-4}, S_{tar-2}, S_{tar+2}, S_{tar+4}), \tag{5}$$

where the range along $z$-axis is empirically set to $\pm 4$.

Adjacent slices, $\mathbf{L} = (S_{tar-1}, S_{tar+1})$, are employed to provide local context, which serves as a smoothing factor both for liver and Couinaud segmentation.

**GLC Model.** As shown in Fig. 2, information extracted from coarse level is used in GLC to disambiguate irrelevant and noisy responses in skip connections, and to guide the global and local contexts composition. It is performed right before the concatenation operation to merge only relevant activations.

The global context feature maps $\mathbf{G}_t = \sum_{i=1}^{\Pi} \alpha_{ti} \mathbf{G}_{ti}$ is dynamic maps that represent the relevant part of features at level $t$, where $\alpha_{ti}$ is a scalar weighting of feature maps $\mathbf{G}_{ti}$ at level $t$, defined as follows.

$$\alpha_{ti} = exp(e_{ti}) / \sum_{k=1}^{\Pi} exp(e_{tk}), \qquad e_{ti} = f_{att}(\mathbf{a}_{ti}, \mathbf{h}_{t+1}). \qquad (6)$$

$f_{att}$ is a function that determines the amount of attention allocated to feature maps $\mathbf{G}_{ti}$, conditioned on the target feature maps $\mathbf{H}_{t+1}$ from coarser level. This function is implemented as a multilayer perceptron as $f_{att} = \mathbf{w}^T tanh(U\mathbf{h}_{t+1} + W\mathbf{a}_{ti} + \mathbf{b})$. Note that by construction $\sum_{i=1}^{\Pi} \alpha_{ti} = 1$. Feature vectors $\mathbf{a}_{ti}$ and $\mathbf{h}_{t+1}$, reduced from three dimensional tensors, are obtained using global average pooling (GAP) as $\mathbf{a}_{ti} = GAP(\mathbf{G}_{ti})$ and $\mathbf{h}_{t+1} = GAP(\mathbf{H}_{t+1})$.

Similarly, the local context feature maps are obtained as $\mathbf{L}_t = \sum_{i=1}^{2} \beta_{ti} \mathbf{L}_{ti}$, where $\beta_{ti}$ is a scalar weighting of feature maps $\mathbf{L}_{ti}$ at level $t$. Skip-connection brings feature maps $\mathbf{H}_t$ in the encoder to the decoder of the same level. Feature maps $\mathbf{D}_t$ generated on the same level of the expanding path are merged through concatenation to combine global and local contexts as $\mathbf{Z}_t = [\mathbf{H}_t, \mathbf{L}_t, \mathbf{G}_t, \mathbf{D}_t]$.

**Segmentation or Extrapolation.** There are a couple of slices with no visible vascular information in the upper and the lower part of a liver. In this situation, an experienced radiologist extrapolates the Couinaud segments from the nearest slice with acceptable visual feature. Consequently, for each slice to be processed, GLC-UNet has to first decide whether segmentation should proceed or come to an extrapolation.

Feature vector $\mathbf{v}$ is obtained by concatenating feature vectors (in Fig. 3) from the global context feature maps and the target one as $\mathbf{v} = [GAP(\mathbf{G}_t), GAP(\mathbf{H}_t)]$, where $\mathbf{G}_t = \sum_{i=1}^{\Pi} \alpha_{ti} \mathbf{G}_{ti}$, $\alpha_{ti}$ is a scalar weighting of feature maps $\mathbf{G}_{ti}$ at level $t$ defined in Section **GLC Model**. However, the amount of attention allocated to feature maps $\mathbf{G}_{ti}$ is conditioned on the feature maps $\mathbf{H}_t$ from the same level. A linear projection from $\mathbf{v}$ and a logistic classifier produce a distribution over $[SEG = 0, EXT = 1]$ as $p(ext|\mathbf{v}) \propto exp(G_{ext}\mathbf{v} + B_{ext})$, where $G_{ext}$ and $B_{ext}$ are parameters to be learned. If $p(ext|\mathbf{v})$ is greater than predefined threshold (e.g. 0.5), then GLC-UNet will stop producing segmentation and make extrapolation.

## 3   Experiments

We use a publicly available dataset of MICCAI 2018 Medical Segmentation Decathlon (task 8) [4]. Both training and testing datasets have no annotated ground truth segmentation masks for liver and Couinaud segments. For liver, we annotate 443 CT volumes in total ($31,668$ slices). For Couinaud segments, we annotate 193 sampled CT volumes in total ($11,537$ slices). To be consistent, we use the same 193 CT volumes for both liver and Couinaud segmentation.

We randomly select 50 cases for testing. Training is conducted on the remaining 143 ones. By default, the number of input global context slices $\Pi$ for Couinaud segmentation is set to 10 in the experiments considering both performance and model complexity.

**Comparison with Other Methods.** We compare the proposed GLC-UNet with UNet [3], UNet 2.5D, UNet 3D, and UNet with convolutional LSTM [6] both on liver and Couinaud segmentation. For the latter one, in order to make fair comparison, we only use slices with Couinaud segments annotation. The input for UNet 2.5D, UNet 3D, and UNet with convolutional LSTM are 7 consecutive slices. UNet and UNet 2.5D are in their canonical configurations. Both methods are inherently not designed to capture long-range 3D context effectively. Due to GPU memory limit, in Couinaud segmentation, it is not possible to feed 13 slices (input for GLC-UNet, NVIDIA Tesla P100) into UNet 3D, and UNet with convolutional LSTM. Meanwhile, two different experiments, one with ground truth liver mask and another based on predicted mask, are conducted.

We evaluate the performance on the Dice per case score over all of the CT volumes. The results are given in Table 1. The comparison on Couinaud Dice per case score indicates not only that model using inter-slice context improves over the baseline model (UNet) with only intra-slice features, but also that the richer the context information, the bigger the performance difference compared with the baseline model. It suggests that our framework provides better alignment from Couinaud segments to provided vascular features, and global context becomes particular necessary. In order to assess how the results of GLC-UNet will generalize to the whole dataset (193 CT volumes in total), we perform a 4-fold cross validation. The dataset is divided into four parts randomly. Three-fourths are utilized for training and one-fourth for validation. The last row in Table 1 demonstrates that GLC-UNet achieves good performance consistently.

**Table 1.** Dice per case scores on liver segmentation and Couinaud segmentation. All values (mean ± std) are reported as percentage (%).

| Method | Couinaud segmentation | | Liver segmentation |
|---|---|---|---|
| | Ground truth liver | Predicted liver | |
| GLC-UNet | 95.10 ± 3.06 | 92.80 ± 3.08 | 98.18 ± 0.85 |
| UNet | 91.31 ± 3.67 | 83.86 ± 5.44 | 95.33 ± 2.78 |
| UNet 2.5D | 92.41 ± 3.30 | 89.04 ± 4.30 | 97.61 ± 1.59 |
| UNet 3D | 92.92 ± 3.46 | 88.93 ± 4.44 | 96.97 ± 1.65 |
| UNet with convolutional LSTM | 93.26 ± 3.12 | 90.06 ± 4.01 | 97.73 ± 1.73 |
| GLC-UNet (cross validation) | 94.51 ± 3.62 | 92.46 ± 3.84 | 98.51 ± 0.74 |

**Effectiveness of Multi-scale Intra-slice Information** One advantage in the proposed method is that we provide the model with multi-scale intra-slice information, which consists of atrous convolutions with different dilation rates and a $3 \times 3$ convolution. Here, we analyze the behaviors of GLC-UNet with and without atrous convolutions. Both two experiments are conducted under the same experimental settings. As shown in Table 2 (Methods 1 and 2), it is clearly observed that with the atrous convolution model, GLC-UNet achieves better Dice per case score, which shows the importance of utilizing the atrous convolution to capture long-range in-plane context.

**Table 2.** Dice per case scores for Couinaud segmentation by ablation study of our methods on the dataset. All values (mean $\pm$ std) are reported as percentage (%).

| # | Method | Dice per case | # | Method | Dice per case |
|---|--------|---------------|---|--------|---------------|
| 1 | GLC-UNet | $95.10 \pm 3.06$ | 2 | without atrous convolution | $94.49 \pm 3.09$ |
| 3 | $\Pi = 3$ | $94.25 \pm 3.10$ | 4 | without $3 \times 3$ convolution | $94.53 \pm 3.11$ |
| 5 | $\Pi = 5$ | $94.58 \pm 3.64$ | 6 | without resized features | $94.53 \pm 3.20$ |
| 7 | $\Pi = 7$ | $94.97 \pm 2.98$ | 8 | $3 \times 3$ convolution in decoder | $94.75 \pm 2.87$ |

Method 4 in Table 2 demonstrates that the $3 \times 3$ convolution in in the contracting path can help the network achieve better performance by extracting abundant vascular information, which plays an important role in achieving the promising results. Combining feature maps from different levels just before the final prediction makes local predictions respect global structure, which is confirmed by the result in Method 6 in Table 2. Meanwhile, as shown in Method 8 in Table 2, Couinaud segments are global information, small convolutional kernel ($3 \times 3$) in the expanding path will degrade the performance.

**Effectiveness of Inter-slice Information.** In the clinical diagnosis, an experienced radiologist usually observes and makes Couinaud segmentation according to many slices along the $z$-axis. Here, we analyze the behaviors of GLC-UNet with different number of global context slices. Other experimental settings are the same for all experiments. As shown in Table 2 (Methods 3, 5 and 7), increasing the number of global context slices $\Pi$ can generally lead to performance improvements. This is due to the fact that more slices increase the possibility of sampling important landmark veins, which in turn leads to better performance.

**Couinaud Segmentation Results.** Among $1,272$ slices (from the testing dataset) with liver region for segmentation, 67 ones are predicted as extrapolation. In comparison, among 877 slices with liver region for extrapolation, 63 ones are predicted as segmentation. Misclassification usually occurs in the transition area (from extrapolation to segmentation or vice versa). The Couinaud segments on the slices in Fig. 4 marked with red circles are extrapolated from the nearest slice with acceptable visual feature.

As far as performance of locating the slices which contain the LPV and the RPV is concerned, the recall rate is 79%. If we set the threshold to $\pm 1$ slice, which means that the LPV and the RPV are located at adjacent slices of the

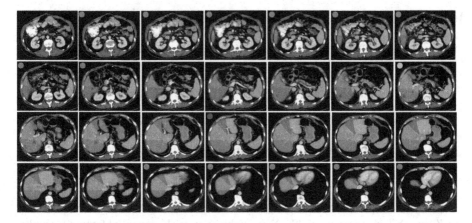

**Fig. 4.** An example of generating Couinaud segmentation (more results are available in Sect. 4 in the Supplementary). Segments I to VIII are marked with different colors. Slices marked with red circle are from extrapolation. RPV is on the slice with green circle, and LPV is on the one with blue circle. (Color figure online)

target, the rate will be 96%. As shown in Fig. 4, the last slice in the second row and the first one in the third row are almost indistinguishable to be marked as the slice which contains the RPV.

**Experiment on Other Dataset.** We perform an 8-fold cross validation on the training dataset of the task 09 (spleen segmentation) in Medical Segmentation Decathlon [4] to validate the effectiveness of GLC-UNet. The same GLC-UNet as the one used in the liver segmentation in the paper is utilized here. The Dice score is 95.4%. It shows that the design is generalizable for other organ segmentation tasks, and has been validated by spleen segmentation.

## 4 Conclusion

This paper investigates automatically generating Couinaud segmentation, which is the preferred anatomy classification system in clinical, on liver from CT volumes. We propose a novel convolutional encoder-decoder network for 2D slice segmentation where 3D contexts are efficiently probed using attention mechanism. Finally, extensive experiments on the Medical Segmentation Decathlon dataset from MICCAI 2018 with our annotated 43,205 CT slices on liver and Couinaud segmentation demonstrate the effectiveness of our proposed GLC-UNet.

# References

1. Long, J., Shelhamer, E., Darrell, T.: Fully convolutional networks for semantic segmentation. In: CVPR (2015)
2. Sun, C., et al.: Automatic segmentation of liver tumors from multiphase contrast-enhanced ct images based on FCNs. AI Med. **83**, 58–66 (2017)
3. Ronneberger, O., Fischer, P., Brox, T.: U-Net: convolutional networks for biomedical image segmentation. In: Navab, N., Hornegger, J., Wells, W.M., Frangi, A.F. (eds.) MICCAI 2015. LNCS, vol. 9351, pp. 234–241. Springer, Cham (2015). https://doi.org/10.1007/978-3-319-24574-4_28
4. MICCAI 2018 Medical Segmentation Decathlon. http://medicaldecathlon.com/
5. Rutkauskas, S., Gedrimas, V., Pundzius, J., Barauskas, G., Basevicius, A.: Clinical and anatomical basis for the classification of the structural parts of liver. Medicina-Lithuania **42**(2), 98–106 (2006)
6. Zhang, Y., et al.: SequentialSegNet: combination with sequential feature for multi-organ segmentation. In: ICPR (2018)
7. Milletari, F., Navab, N., Ahmadi, S.-A.: V-Net: fully convolutional neural networks for volumetric medical image segmentation. In: 3DV (2016)
8. Lowe, M.C., D'Angelica, M.I.: Anatomy of hepatic resectional surgery. Surg. Clin. North Am. **96**(2), 183–195 (2016)
9. Jarnagin, W.R., Belghiti, J., Blumgart, L.H.: Blumgart's Surgery of the Liver, Biliary Tract, and Pancreas. Elsevier, Amsterdam (2012)
10. Oliveira, D.A.B., Feitosa, R.Q., Correia, M.M.: Automatic couinaud liver and veins segmentation from CT images. In: BIOSIGNALS (2008)

# Biomedical Image Segmentation by Retina-Like Sequential Attention Mechanism Using only a Few Training Images

Shohei Hayashi, Bisser Raytchev[(✉)], Toru Tamaki, and Kazufumi Kaneda

Department of Information Engineering, Hiroshima University,
Higashihiroshima, Japan
bisser@hiroshima-u.ac.jp

**Abstract.** In this paper we propose a novel deep learning-based algorithm for biomedical image segmentation which uses a sequential attention mechanism able to shift the focus of attention across the image in a
selective way, allowing subareas which are more difficult to classify to be
processed at increased resolution. The spatial distribution of class information in each subarea is learned using a retina-like representation where
resolution decreases with distance from the center of attention. The final
segmentation is achieved by averaging class predictions over overlapping
subareas, utilizing the power of ensemble learning to increase segmentation accuracy. Experimental results for semantic segmentation task for
which only a few training images are available show that a CNN using
the proposed method outperforms both a patch-based classification CNN
and a fully convolutional-based method.

**Keywords:** Image segmentation · Attention · Retina · iPS cells

## 1 Introduction

Recently deep learning methods [2], which automatically extract hierarchical features capturing complex nonlinear relationships in the data, have managed to
successfully replace most task-specific hand-crafted features. This has resulted in
a significant improvement in performance on a variety of biomedical image analysis tasks, like object detection, recognition and segmentation (see e.g. [10] for
a recent survey of the field and representative methods used in different applications), and currently Convolutional Neural Network (CNN) based methods
define the state-of-the-art in this area.

In this paper we concentrate on biomedical image *segmentation*. For segmentation, where each pixel needs to be classified into its corresponding class,
initially *patch-wise training/classification* was used [1]. In patch-based methods,
local patches of pre-determined size are extracted from the images, typically
using a CNN as pixel-wise classifier. During training, the patch is used as an

© Springer Nature Switzerland AG 2019
H.-I. Suk et al. (Eds.): MLMI 2019, LNCS 11861, pp. 283–291, 2019.
https://doi.org/10.1007/978-3-030-32692-0_33

input to the network and it is assigned as a label the class of the pixel at the *center* of the patch (available from ground-truth data provided by a human expert). During the test phase, a patch is fed into the trained net and the output layer of the net provides the probabilities for each class. More recently, Fully Convolutional Networks (FCN) [8], which replace the fully connected layers with convolutional ones, have replaced the patch-wise approach by providing a more efficient way to train CNNs end-to-end, pixels-to-pixels, and methods stemming from this approach presently define the state-of-the-art in biomedical image segmentation, exemplified by conv-deconv-based methods like U-Net [7].

Although fully convolutional methods have shown state-of-the-art performance on many segmentation tasks, they typically need to be trained on large datasets to achieve good accuracy. In many biomedical image segmentation tasks, however, only a few training images are available – either data simply being not available, or providing pixel-level ground truth by experts being too costly to obtain. Here we are motivated by a similar problem (Sect. 3), where less than 50 images are available for training. On the other hand, *patch-wise methods* need only local patches, a huge number of which can be extracted even from a small number of training images. They however suffer from the following problem. While fully convolutional methods learn a map from pixel areas (multiple input image values) to pixel areas (multiple classes of all the pixels in the area), patch-wise methods learn a map from pixel areas (input image values) to a single pixel (class of the pixel in the center of the patch). As illustrated in Fig. 1 [i], this wastes the rich information about the topology of the class structure inside the patch for many of the samples which contain more than a single class, and these would typically be the most interesting/difficult samples [4]. Instead of trying to represent in a suitable way and learn the complex class topology, it just substitutes it by a single class (the class of the pixel in the center of the patch).

Regarding fully convolutional methods, they treat all locations in the images in the same way, which is in contrast with how human visual perception works. It is known that humans employ attentional mechanisms to focus selectively on *subareas of interest* and construct a global scene-representation by combining the information from different local subareas [6].

Based on the above observations, we propose a new method, which takes a middle ground between fully convolutional and patch-wise learning and combines the benefits of both of these strategies. As shown in Fig. 1, as in the patch-wise approach we consider subareas of the whole image at a time, which provides us with sufficient number of training samples, even if only a few ground-truth labeled images are available. However, as illustrated in Fig. 1 [ii], the class information is organized as in the retina [3]: the spatial resolution is highest in the central area (corresponding to the *fovea*), and it diminishes as we go to the periphery of the subarea. We propose a *sequential attention mechanism* which shifts the focus of attention in such a way that areas of the image which are difficult to classify (i.e. the classification uncertainty is higher) are considered in much more detail than areas which are easy to classify. Since the focus of

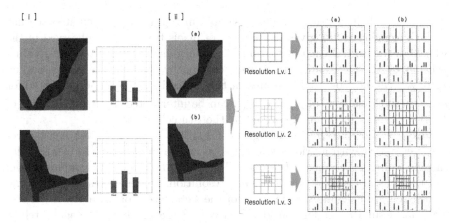

**Fig. 1.** [i] Local patch containing pixels belonging to 3 classes shown in different color. On the right is normalized histogram showing the empirical distribution of the classes inside the patch, which can be interpreted as probabilities. A standard patch-wise method learns only the class of the pixel at the center, ignoring completely class topology. [ii] The proposed method learns the structure of the spatial distribution of the class topology in a local subarea represented similarly to the retina - the resolution is highest in the center and decreases progressively in the periphery. As attention shifts inside the image, the information of overlapping subareas is combined to produce the final segmented image (details explained in the text). Figure best viewed in color. (Color figure online)

attention moves the subarea under investigation much slower over difficult areas (i.e. with much smaller step), this results in many *overlapping subareas* in these regions. The final segmentation is achieved by averaging the class predictions over the overlapping subareas. In this way, the power of *ensemble learning* [5] is utilized by incorporating information from all overlapping subareas in the neighborhood (each of which provides slightly different views of the scene) to further improve accuracy.

This is the basic idea of the method proposed in the paper, and details how to implement it in a CNN will be given in the next section. Experimental results are reported in Sect. 3, indicating that a significant improvement in segmentation accuracy can be achieved by the proposed method compared to both patch-based and fully convolutional-based methods.

## 2   Method

We represent a subarea $\mathcal{S}$ extracted from an input image (centered at the current focus of attention) as a tensor of size $d \times d \times c$, where $d$ is the size of the subarea in pixels and $c$ stands for the color channels if color images are used (as typically done, and $c = 3$ for RGB images). As shown in Fig. 1 [ii], we can represent the class information corresponding to this subarea as grids of different resolution, where each cell in a grid contains a sample histogram $h^{(i)}$ calculated so that the $k$-th element of $h^{(i)}$ gives the number of pixels from class $k$ observed in the $i$-th cell of the grid. If each histogram $h^{(i)}$ is normalized to sum to 1 by dividing each bin by the total number of pixels covered by the cell, the corresponding vector $p^{(i)}$ can now be used to represent the probability mass function ($pmf$) for cell $i$: the $k$-th element of $p^{(i)}$, i.e. $p_k^{(i)}$, can be interpreted as the probability of observing class $k$ in the area covered by the $i$-th cell of the grid.

Next, we show how retina-like grids of different resolution levels can be created. Let's start with a grid of size $4 \times 4$, as shown in the top row of Fig. 1 [ii]. This we will call *Resolution Level* 1 and denote it as $r = 1$. At resolution level 1 all the cells in the grid have the same resolution, i.e. the $pmf$s corresponding to each cell are calculated from areas of the same size. For example, if the size of the local subarea under consideration is $d = 128$ pixels (i.e. image patch of size $128 \times 128$ pixels), each cell in the grid at resolution level $r = 1$ would correspond to an image area of size $32 \times 32$ pixels from which a probability mass function $p^{(i)}$ would be calculated, as explained above. Next, we can create a grid at *Resolution Level* 2 ($r = 2$) by dividing in half the four cells in the center of the grid, so that they form an inner $4 \times 4$ grid, whose resolution is double. We can continue this process of dividing the innermost 4 cells into 2 to obtain still higher resolution levels. It is easy to see that the number of cells $N$ in a grid obtained at resolution level $r$ is $N = 16 + 12(r - 1)$. Of course, it is not necessary the initial grid at $r = 1$ to be of size $4 \times 4$, but choosing this number makes the process of creating different resolution levels especially simple, since in this case the innermost cells are always 4 ($2 \times 2$).

In our method, we train a CNN to learn the map between a local subarea image given as input to the network, and the corresponding $pmf$s $p^{(i)}$ used as target values. We use the cross-entropy between the $pmf$s of the targets $p^{(i)}$ and the corresponding output unit activations $y^{(i)}$ as loss function $L$:

$$L = -\sum_n \sum_i \sum_k p_{k,n}^{(i)} \log y_{k,n}^{(i)}(S_n; \boldsymbol{w}), \qquad (1)$$

where $n$ indexes the training subarea image patches ($S_n$ being the $n$-th training subarea image patch), $i$ indexing the cells in the corresponding resolution grid, and $k$ the classes. Here, $\boldsymbol{w}$ represents the weights of the network, to be found by minimizing the loss function. To form probabilities, the network output units corresponding to each cell are passed through the *soft-max* activation function.

Finally, we describe the sequential attention mechanism we utilize, whose purpose is to move the focus of attention across the image in such a way that those parts which are difficult to classify (i.e. classification uncertainty is high) are observed at the highest possible resolution, and the retina-like grid of $pmf$s moves with smaller steps across such areas. To evaluate the classification uncertainty of the grid over the present subarea $S$, we use the following function,

$$H(S) = -\frac{1}{N} \sum_{i \in S} \sum_k p_k^{(i)} \log p_k^{(i)}, \qquad (2)$$

which represents the average entropy obtained from the posterior $pmf$s $p^{(i)}$ for each cell (indexed by $i$) inside the grid, and $k$ indexes the classes. Using $H(S)$ as a measure of classification uncertainty, the position of the next location where to move the *focus of attention* (horizontal shift in pixels) is given by

$$f(H(S)) = d\exp\{-(H(S))^2/2\sigma^2\}. \tag{3}$$

The whole process is illustrated in Fig. 2. We start at the upper left corner of the input image, with a subarea of size $d \times d$ pixels (the yellow patch (a) in the figure). The classification uncertainty for that subarea is calculated using Eq. 2, and the step size in pixels to move in the horizontal direction is calculated by Eq. 3. As illustrated in the graph in the center of Fig. 2, since in this case the classification uncertainty is 0 (all pixels in the subarea belong to the same class), the focus of attention moves $d$ pixels to the right, i.e. in this extreme case there is no overlap between the current and next subareas. For the subarea (b) shown in green, the situation is very different. In this case the classification uncertainty is very high, and the focus of attention would move only slightly to the right, allowing the image around this area to be assessed at the highest resolution. This would result in very high level of overlap between neighboring subareas, as shown in the heat map on the right (where intensity is proportional to the level of overlap). This process is repeated until the right corner of the image is reached. Then the focus of attention is moved 10 pixels in the vertical direction to scan the next row and everything is repeated until the whole image is processed.

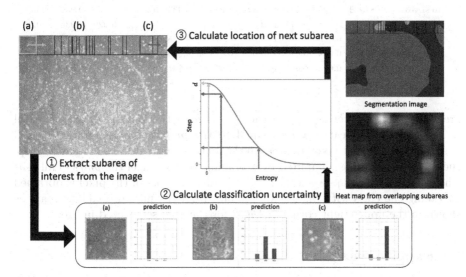

**Fig. 2.** Overview of the sequential attention mechanism (see text for details). (Color figure online)

While the above attention mechanism moves the focus of attention across the image, the posterior class $pmf$s from the grids corresponding to each subarea

**Table 1.** Experimental results for different values $d$ of the size of the local subareas

| $d$ | Method | Jaccard index | Dice | TPR | TNR | Accuracy |
|---|---|---|---|---|---|---|
| 96 | patch-center | 0.811 ± 0.039 | 0.879 ± 0.034 | 0.877 ± 0.039 | 0.922 ± 0.014 | 0.932 ± 0.016 |
| | ResLv-1 | 0.798 ± 0.046 | 0.868 ± 0.040 | 0.866 ± 0.042 | 0.914 ± 0.016 | 0.928 ± 0.015 |
| | ResLv-2 | 0.811 ± 0.037 | 0.879 ± 0.031 | 0.878 ± 0.035 | 0.919 ± 0.020 | 0.931 ± 0.015 |
| | ResLv-3 | 0.819 ± 0.034 | 0.884 ± 0.029 | 0.883 ± 0.035 | 0.923 ± 0.012 | 0.936 ± 0.010 |
| | ResLv-4 | 0.820 ± 0.033 | 0.884 ± 0.029 | 0.881 ± 0.036 | 0.926 ± 0.013 | 0.936 ± 0.012 |
| | UNet-patch | 0.788 ± 0.051 | 0.861 ± 0.047 | 0.859 ± 0.045 | 0.916 ± 0.013 | 0.922 ± 0.011 |
| 128 | patch-center | 0.811 ± 0.029 | 0.878 ± 0.026 | 0.873 ± 0.028 | 0.917 ± 0.012 | 0.931 ± 0.012 |
| | ResLv-1 | 0.812 ± 0.038 | 0.878 ± 0.032 | 0.874 ± 0.033 | 0.918 ± 0.020 | 0.935 ± 0.012 |
| | ResLv-2 | 0.815 ± 0.039 | 0.881 ± 0.032 | 0.878 ± 0.034 | 0.923 ± 0.015 | 0.934 ± 0.014 |
| | ResLv-3 | 0.816 ± 0.030 | 0.881 ± 0.029 | 0.879 ± 0.033 | 0.920 ± 0.011 | 0.935 ± 0.008 |
| | ResLv-4 | 0.818 ± 0.034 | 0.821 ± 0.031 | 0.881 ± 0.031 | 0.921 ± 0.017 | 0.936 ± 0.011 |
| | ResLv-5 | 0.826 ± 0.032 | 0.891 ± 0.030 | 0.890 ± 0.032 | 0.924 ± 0.018 | 0.936 ± 0.009 |
| | UNet-patch | 0.810 ± 0.035 | 0.879 ± 0.030 | 0.873 ± 0.034 | 0.921 ± 0.014 | 0.933 ± 0.012 |
| 192 | patch-center | 0.778 ± 0.029 | 0.856 ± 0.025 | 0.849 ± 0.020 | 0.899 ± 0.017 | 0.917 ± 0.017 |
| | ResLv-1 | 0.810 ± 0.037 | 0.876 ± 0.030 | 0.872 ± 0.031 | 0.914 ± 0.021 | 0.933 ± 0.016 |
| | ResLv-2 | 0.817 ± 0.041 | 0.880 ± 0.038 | 0.879 ± 0.041 | 0.922 ± 0.017 | 0.936 ± 0.011 |
| | ResLv-3 | 0.821 ± 0.032 | 0.885 ± 0.030 | 0.883 ± 0.032 | 0.926 ± 0.010 | 0.935 ± 0.011 |
| | ResLv-4 | **0.832 ± 0.036** | **0.894 ± 0.030** | **0.890 ± 0.034** | **0.926 ± 0.015** | **0.940 ± 0.012** |
| | ResLv-5 | 0.825 ± 0.032 | 0.887 ± 0.030 | 0.883 ± 0.032 | 0.925 ± 0.015 | 0.938 ± 0.012 |
| | UNet-patch | 0.809 ± 0.036 | 0.878 ± 0.029 | 0.870 ± 0.034 | 0.920 ± 0.015 | 0.933 ± 0.015 |
| 256 | patch-center | 0.732 ± 0.038 | 0.822 ± 0.037 | 0.813 ± 0.039 | 0.862 ± 0.023 | 0.897 ± 0.019 |
| | ResLv-1 | 0.804 ± 0.039 | 0.871 ± 0.035 | 0.866 ± 0.036 | 0.910 ± 0.018 | 0.931 ± 0.012 |
| | ResLv-2 | 0.810 ± 0.038 | 0.877 ± 0.037 | 0.870 ± 0.040 | 0.918 ± 0.018 | 0.932 ± 0.012 |
| | ResLv-3 | 0.819 ± 0.029 | 0.882 ± 0.028 | 0.879 ± 0.034 | 0.922 ± 0.016 | 0.937 ± 0.010 |
| | ResLv-4 | 0.814 ± 0.033 | 0.877 ± 0.030 | 0.871 ± 0.031 | 0.917 ± 0.020 | 0.936 ± 0.011 |
| | ResLv-5 | 0.815 ± 0.038 | 0.880 ± 0.034 | 0.876 ± 0.035 | 0.919 ± 0.016 | 0.934 ± 0.012 |
| | UNet-patch | 0.811 ± 0.034 | 0.879 ± 0.028 | 0.874 ± 0.030 | 0.921 ± 0.014 | 0.933 ± 0.012 |
| | UNet-image | 0.806 ± 0.033 | 0.877 ± 0.029 | 0.874 ± 0.031 | 0.919 ± 0.013 | 0.928 ± 0.008 |

are stored in a *probability map* of the same size as the image, i.e. to each pixel in the image is allocated a *pmf* equal to the *pmf* of the cell from the grid positioned above that pixel. In areas in the image where several subareas overlap, the probability map is computed by averaging for each pixel the *pmf*s of all cells which partially overlap over that pixel. Finally, the class of the pixel is obtained by taking the class with highest probability from the final probability map, as shown in the upper right corner of Fig. 2 for the final segmented image.

## 3   Experiments

In this section we evaluate the proposed method in comparison with a standard patch-wise classification-based CNN [1] and the fully convolutional-based U-Net [7] on the dataset described below. Additionally we implemented a U-Net version, called *UNet-patch*, which applies U-Net to local patches rather than to a whole

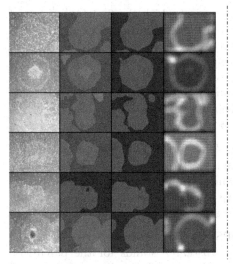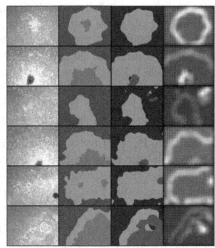

**Fig. 3.** Segmentation results for several images from the iPS dataset, obtained by the proposed method (3rd column), using ResLv-4 with subarea size of $d = 192$. First column shows the original images and second column the ground truth segmentation provided by an expert (red corresponds to class Good, green to Bad and blue to Background). The last column shows the corresponding heat map, where areas in which there was high overlap over neighboring subareas are shown with high intensity values. (Color figure online)

image. The original U-Net method which takes as input the whole image we will call *UNet-image*.

**Dataset:** Our dataset consists of 59 images showing colonies of undifferentiated and differentiated iPS cells obtained through phase-contrast microscopy. Induced pluripotent stem (iPS) cells [9], for whose discovery S. Yamanaka received the Nobel prize in Physiology and Medicine in 2012, contain great promise for regenerative medicine. Still, in order to fulfill their promise a steady supply of iPS cells obtained through harvesting of individual cell colonies is needed and automating the detection of abnormalities arising during the cultivation process is crucial. Thus, our task is to segment the input images into three categories: Good (undifferentiated), Bad (differentiated) and Background (BGD, the culture medium). Several representative images together with ground-truth provided by experts can be seen in Fig. 3. All images in this dataset are of size 1600 × 1200 pixels. Several images contained a few locations where even the experts were not sure what the corresponding class was. Such ambiguous regions are shown in pink and these areas were not used during training and not evaluated during test.

**Network Architecture and Hyperparameters:** We used a network architecture based on the VGG-16 CNN net, apart from the following differences. There are 13 convolutional layers in VGG-16, while we used 10 here. Also, in

VGG-16 there are 3 fully-convolutional layers of which the first two consist of 4096 units, while those had 1024 units in our implementation. The learning rate was set to 0.0001 and for the optimization procedure we used ADAM. Batch size was 16, training for 20 epochs (U-Net-patch for 15 epochs and U-Net-image for 200 epochs). For the implementation of the CNNs we used TensorFlow and Keras. Four different sizes for the local subareas were tried: $d = 96, 128, 192, 256$ and resolution level was changed between $r = 1$ to $r = 5$. The width of the Gaussian in Eq. 3 was empirically set to $\sigma = 0.4$ for all experimental results.

**Evaluation Procedure and Criteria:** The quality of the obtained segmentation results for each method were evaluated by 5-fold cross-validation using the following criteria: Jaccard index (the most challenging one), Dice coefficient, True Positive Rate (TPR), True Negative Rate (TNR) and Accuracy. For each score the average and standard deviation are reported.

**Results:** The results obtained on the iPS cell colonies dataset for each of the methods are given in Table 1, where, *patch-center* stands for the patch-wise classification method, and results for resolution levels from $r = 1$ to $r = 5$ are given for the proposed method. As can be seen from the results, the proposed method outperforms both patch-wise classification and the U-Net-based methods. Figure 3 gives some examples of segmentation on images from the iPS dataset, showing that very good accuracy of segmentation can be achieved by the proposed method. The heat maps given in the last column demonstrate that the proposed attentional mechanism is able to focus the high-resolution parts of the retina-like grid on the boundaries between the classes which seem to be most difficult to classify, resulting in increased accuracy of segmentation.

# 4    Conclusion

In this paper we have shown that the combined power of (1) a sequential attention mechanism controlling the shift of the focus of attention, (2) local retina-like representation of the spatial distribution of class information and (3) ensemble learning can lead to increased segmentation accuracy in biomedical segmentation tasks. We expect that the proposed method can be especially useful for datasets for which only a few training images are available.

# References

1. Cireşan, D.C., Giusti, A., Gambardella, L.M., Schmidhuber, J.: Deep neural networks segment neuronal membranes in electron microscopy images. In: NIPS, pp. 2843–2851 (2012)
2. Goodfellow, I., Bengio, Y., Courville, A.: Deep Learning. MIT Press, Cambridge (2016)
3. Kandel, E.R., Schwarz, J., Jessell, T.M., Siegelbaum, S.A., Hudspeth, A.J.: Principles of Neural Science, 5edn. McGraw-Hill, New York (2013)

4. Kontschieder, P., Bulo, S.R., Bischof, H., Pelillo, M.: Structured class-labels in random forests for semantic image labeling. In: Proceedings of ICCV 2012, pp. 2190–2197 (2012)
5. Kuncheva, L.: Combining Pattern Classifiers, 2edn. Wiley, Hoboken (2014)
6. Rensink, R.A.: The dynamic representation of scenes. Vis. Cogn. **7**(1–3), 17–42 (2000)
7. Ronneberger, O., Fischer, P., Brox, T.: U-Net: convolutional networks for biomedical image segmentation. In: Navab, N., Hornegger, J., Wells, W.M., Frangi, A.F. (eds.) MICCAI 2015. LNCS, vol. 9351, pp. 234–241. Springer, Cham (2015). https://doi.org/10.1007/978-3-319-24574-4_28
8. Shelhamer, E., Long, J., Darrell, T.: Fully convolutional networks for semantic segmentation. IEEE Trans. Pattern Anal. Mach. Intell. **39**(4), 640–651 (2017)
9. Takahashi, K., et al.: Induction of pluripotent stem cells from adult human fibroblasts by defined factors. Cell **131**(5), 861–871 (2007)
10. Zhou, S.K., Greenspan, H., Shen, D. (eds.): Deep Learning for Medical Image Analysis. Academic Press, Cambridge (2017)

# Conv-MCD: A Plug-and-Play Multi-task Module for Medical Image Segmentation

Balamurali Murugesan[1,2](✉) ⓘ, Kaushik Sarveswaran[2] ⓘ,
Sharath M. Shankaranarayana[3] ⓘ, Keerthi Ram[2], Jayaraj Joseph[2],
and Mohanasankar Sivaprakasam[1,2]

[1] Indian Institute of Technology Madras (IITM), Chennai, India
balamurali@htic.iitm.ac.in
[2] Healthcare Technology Innovation Centre (HTIC), IITM, Chennai, India
[3] Zasti India, Chennai, India

**Abstract.** For the task of medical image segmentation, fully convolutional network (FCN) based architectures have been extensively used with various modifications. A rising trend in these architectures is to employ joint-learning of the target region with an auxiliary task, a method commonly known as multi-task learning. These approaches help impose smoothness and shape priors, which vanilla FCN approaches do not necessarily incorporate. In this paper, we propose a novel plug-and-play module, which we term as Conv-MCD, which exploits structural information in two ways - (i) using the contour map and (ii) using the distance map, both of which can be obtained from ground truth segmentation maps with no additional annotation costs. The key benefit of our module is the ease of its addition to any state-of-the-art architecture, resulting in a significant improvement in performance with a minimal increase in parameters. To substantiate the above claim, we conduct extensive experiments using 4 state-of-the-art architectures across various evaluation metrics, and report a significant increase in performance in relation to the base networks. In addition to the aforementioned experiments, we also perform ablative studies and visualization of feature maps to further elucidate our approach.

**Keywords:** Multi-task learning · Segmentation · Deep learning

## 1 Introduction

Segmentation is the process of extracting a particular region in an image and it is an essential task in medical image analysis. The extraction of these regions is challenging due to shape variations and fuzzy boundaries. Recently, deep learning networks like UNet [7] having encoder-decoder architecture with cross-entropy loss are used for medical image segmentation and have shown promising

B. Murugesan—Code and supplementary https://github.com/Bala93/Multi-task-deep-network.

H.-I. Suk et al. (Eds.): MLMI 2019, LNCS 11861, pp. 292–300, 2019.
https://doi.org/10.1007/978-3-030-32692-0_34

results. The two major drawbacks associated with these approaches are: (1) encoder-decoder networks suffer from structural information loss due to down-sampling operations performed via max-pooling layers, and (2) cross-entropy loss is prone to foreground-background class imbalance problem. In many medical image applications, we will also be interested in multiple object instance segmentation. Also, the extracted region of interest will be used for diagnosis and surgery purposes, creating the need for outlier reduction. In this paper, we propose a module design which incorporates structural information as auxiliary tasks, inspired from the multi-task learning work [2]. The module helps any state-of-the-art architecture handle structural information loss, reduce outliers, alleviate class imbalance and improve multi-instance object segmentation. We also show that learning a main task along with its related tasks will enable the model to generalize better on the original task because of its ability to learn common sub-features.

Recently, multiple works have used multi-task learning to handle the structure information loss. Of these, DCAN [4] and DMTN [9] are of our interest. The commonality between DCAN and DMTN is their single encoder and two decoders architecture. The two decoders are used to learn multiple tasks at a time. In the case of DCAN, the mask is learned along with contour. Similarly, with DMTN, the mask is learned along with the distance map. The network DCAN provides additional information about the structure and shape through a parallel decoder to handle the information loss, but suffers from issues related to class imbalance similar to that of UNet. Both these class imbalance and structural information loss problems are overcome by the joint classification and regression based network DMTN. The mask predicted with this network also has reduced outliers compared to DCAN. But the network DMTN has difficulty in handling multi-instance object segmentation, wherein if one object is relatively small compared to the other object, it considers the small object as an outlier and removes it, which was not the case with UNet and DCAN. While the idea of learning contour and distance as a parallel task to the mask as done by DCAN and DMTN is appreciable, the main disadvantage stems from the architecture design. The task of extending the dual-decoder design to other popular architectures can be done in the following ways: (1) adding the auxiliary decoder part of DCAN or DMTN as a parallel decoder branch to the other base networks. (2) duplicating the already existing decoder block of base networks for some auxiliary task. Both these techniques increase the parameter count, memory usage and time consumption. The key contributions of our paper are as follows:

- We propose a novel module Conv-MCD (**M**ask prediction, **C**ontour extraction and **D**istance Map estimation). The module consists of three parallel convolutional filters to learn the three related tasks simultaneously. The proposed module handles class imbalance, reduces outliers, alleviates structural information loss and it works well with multi-instance object segmentation.
- The proposed module can be added to any state-of-the-art base network with minimal effort. In this paper, we have added our module to some of them and compared it with the base networks. We observed that the networks with

our module showed better results compared to the base networks. The same has been achieved with minimal increase in time, memory and number of parameters.

– To validate the performance improvement achieved from including our module, we conducted ablative studies, feature map visualization and validation error curve comparison. These studies showed that learning a major task in parallel with two related tasks reduces overfitting and enables the network to generalize well.

## 2    Methodology

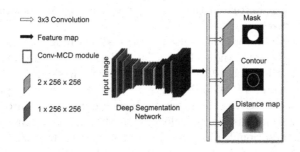

**Fig. 1.** Sample block diagram illustrating the proposed module Conv-MCD. Proposed module could be included at the end of a typical deep segmentation network.

### 2.1    Proposed Module

The proposed module Conv-MCD (Fig. 1) takes the feature maps from the deep learning networks as input and outputs mask, contour and distance map. This module helps the network to learn the multiple related tasks in parallel, enabling the network to generalize well. Mask prediction and contour extraction are classification tasks while the distance map estimation is a regression task. All these outputs are obtained by parallel convolution layers. The parameters of the filters are: kernel size is 3 × 3 with stride 1 and padding 1, the number of channels of the kernel is decided by the number of output channels of the feature maps. The number of filters for classification task is 2, which denotes the number of classes considered. Similarly, the number of filters for regression is 1. To show the effectiveness of the module with multi-task learning, we have considered only the binary classification problem. The same idea can be easily extended to multiple classes with appropriate change in module parameters.

### 2.2    Capturing Structural Information

We harness the structural information that is implicitly present in ground truth segmentation masks, which can be achieved in two ways:

**Contour Extraction.** For obtaining the contour map C, we first extract the boundaries of connected components based on the ground truth segmentation maps which are subsequently dilated using a disk filter of radius 5. We empirically found that setting a radius of 5 was optimal for an image of size 256 × 256.

**Distance Map Estimation.** Using distance map alleviates the pixel-wise class imbalances which arise in the segmentation maps. We explore three kinds of distance maps and show that their choice is also an important factor in model performance. The distance maps D1 and D2 are obtained by applying euclidean distance transforms to mask and contour respectively. Distance map D3 is obtained by applying signed distance transform to the contour.

### 2.3 Loss Function

The loss function consists of three components - Negative Log Likelihood (NLL) loss for mask and contour, Mean Square Error (MSE) loss for the distance. The total loss is given by

$$\mathcal{L}_{total} = \lambda_1 \mathcal{L}_{mask} + \lambda_2 \mathcal{L}_{contour} + \lambda_3 \mathcal{L}_{distance} \tag{1}$$

where $\lambda_1, \lambda_2, \lambda_3$ are scaling factors.

The individual losses are formulated below:

$$\mathcal{L}_{mask} = \sum_{x \in \Omega} log \, p_{mask}(\boldsymbol{x}; l_{mask}(\boldsymbol{x})) \tag{2}$$

$$\mathcal{L}_{contour} = \sum_{x \in \Omega} log \, p_{contour}(\boldsymbol{x}; l_{contour}(\boldsymbol{x})) \tag{3}$$

$$\mathcal{L}_{distance} = \sum_{x \in \Omega} (\hat{D}(\boldsymbol{x}) - D(\boldsymbol{x}))^2 \tag{4}$$

$\mathcal{L}_{mask}, \mathcal{L}_{contour}$ denotes the pixel-wise classification error. $\boldsymbol{x}$ is the pixel position in image space $\Omega$. $p_{mask}(\boldsymbol{x}; l_{mask})$ and $p_{contour}(\boldsymbol{x}; l_{contour})$ denotes the predicted probability for true label $l_{mask}$ and $l_{contour}$ after softmax activation function. $\mathcal{L}_{distance}$ denotes the pixel-wise mean square error. $\hat{D}(\boldsymbol{x})$ is the estimated distance map after sigmoid activation function while $D(\boldsymbol{x})$ is the ground-truth distance map.

## 3   Experiments and Results

### 3.1   Dataset

**Polyp Segmentation**: We use Polyp segmentation dataset from MICCAI 2018 Gastrointestinal Image ANAlysis (GIANA) [10]. We deemed this dataset to be ideal for our experiments since it exhibits the following characteristics: (1)

large variations in shape (2) multi-instance object occurrences (3) foreground-background imbalance (4) difficulty in extracting the boundary of smooth, blobby objects. The dataset consists of 912 images with ground truth masks. The dataset is randomly split into 70% for training and 30% for testing. The images are center cropped and resized to 256 × 256.

## 3.2 Implementation Details

Models are trained for 150 epochs using Adam optimizer, with a learning rate of 1e-4 and batch size 4 in all the reported experiments, for consistent comparison. The train and validation loss plots can be found in supplementary material.

## 3.3 Evaluation Metrics

The predicted and ground truth masks are evaluated using the following metrics: (1) **Segmentation evaluation**: Jaccard index and Dice similarity score are the most commonly used evaluation metrics for segmentation. (2) **Shape Similarity**: The shape similarity is measured by using the Hausdorff Distance (HD) between the shape of segmented object and that of the ground truth object. (3) **Segmentation around boundaries**: We evaluate the segmentation accuracy around the boundary with the method adopted in [6]. Specifically, we count the relative number of misclassified pixels within a narrow band ("trimap") surrounding actual object boundaries, obtained from the accurate ground truth images. (4) **Boundary smoothness**: We extract the boundaries from the predicted mask and compare it with the ground truth boundaries using the maximum F-score (MF) as done in [5].

## 3.4 Results and Discussion

Some notations used in this section are Encoder (Enc), Decoder (Dec), Mask (M), Contour (C), Distance (D) and our proposed module (Conv-MCD). The results of the network (1Enc 1Dec Conv-MCD) with the proposed module are compared with the following combinations of networks and loss functions: (1) A network (1Enc 1Dec M) [7] with a single encoder and a decoder having NLL as loss function for mask estimation. (2) A network (1Enc 2Dec MC) [4] with a single encoder and two decoders having NLL as loss function for both mask and contour estimation. (3) A network (1Enc 2Dec MD) [9] with a single encoder and two decoders having NLL as loss function for mask and MSE as loss function for distance map estimation. From Table 1, it can be seen that the network 1Enc 1Dec Conv-MCD gives better segmentation, shape and boundary metrics compared to 1Enc 1Dec M, 1Enc 2Dec MC and 1Enc 2Dec MD with parameters and running time quite close to 1Enc 1Dec M. This brings the best of both worlds: better performance with lesser time and memory consumption. The graph in Fig. 2b shows the network with our module is better than other networks at all trimap widths. From the figure, it can also be seen that 1Enc 2Dec MC and

1Enc 2Dec MD is better than 1Enc 1Dec M across all trimap widths. A similar observation can be found in the Table 1, where 1Enc 1Dec MC and 1Enc 2Dec MD shows better metrics compared to 1Enc 1Dec M. This shows that contour and distance maps act as regularizers to the mask prediction.[1]

**Table 1.** Comparison of 1Enc 1Dec Conv-MCD (ours) with [4,7,9]

| Architecture | Dice | Jaccard | HD | MF | Time (ms) | # parameters |
|---|---|---|---|---|---|---|
| 1Enc 1Dec M [7] | 0.8125 | 0.7323 | 24.13 | 0.6144 | 1.3131 | 7844256 |
| 1Enc 2Dec MC [4] | 0.8151 | 0.7391 | 22.74 | 0.616 | 1.8677 | 10978272 |
| 1Enc 2Dec MD [9] | 0.8283 | 0.7482 | 22.68 | 0.5681 | 1.8531 | 10977984 |
| 1Enc 1Dec Conv-MC (Ours) | 0.8149 | 0.7389 | 22.86 | 0.6083 | 1.3384 | 7844832 |
| 1Enc 1Dec Conv-MD (Ours) | 0.8286 | 0.7489 | 22.54 | 0.5844 | 1.3235 | 7844544 |
| 1Enc 1Dec Conv-MCD (Ours) | **0.8426** | **0.7692** | **22.27** | **0.6552** | 1.3501 | 7845120 |

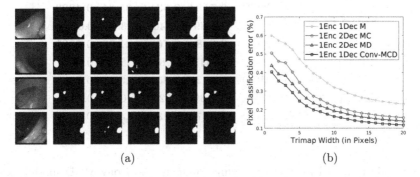

(a)                                           (b)

**Fig. 2.** Left (a): Four sample cases, from left to right: Image, Ground truth, 1Enc 1Dec M, 1Enc 2Dec MC, 1Enc 2Dec MD and 1Enc 1Dec Conv-MCD. Right (b): Pixel classification error vs trimap width for 1Enc 1Dec M, 1Enc 2Dec MC, 1Enc 2Dec MD and 1Enc 1Dec Conv-MCD.

The qualitative comparison of the network 1Enc 1Dec Conv-MCD with other networks is displayed in Fig. 2a. From first two rows of Fig. 2a, it can be seen that the mask predictions by networks 1Enc 1Dec Conv-MCD and 1Enc 2Dec MD have smooth boundaries without outliers. The third row of the same figure depicts the case where 1Enc 2Dec MD fails, owing to its inability to segment multi-instance objects. The fourth row of the figure displays the case where 1Enc 1Dec Conv-MCD works better than the other networks.

---

[1] To validate the generalisability of our proposed approach, we further test it against the baseline models on the ORIGA cup segmentation dataset. The quantitative results and observations on the same can be found in the supplementary material.

Our proposed module is helpful in improving the performances of state-of-the-art segmentation networks. Adding our module to the segmentation networks is relatively simpler and is independent of the architecture design. Table 2 shows the performance of various state-of-the-art networks across different metrics, with and without our module. The networks used for comparison are UNet [7], UNet16 (UNet with VGG16 [8] pre-trained encoder), SegNet [1] and LinkNet34 [3]. It is evident that networks with our module gave improved results across all evaluation metrics. The qualitative comparison of these networks is shown in Fig. 3a. From the figure, it can be observed that networks with our module were able to capture the shape, handle outliers better than networks without the module. In Fig. 3b, it is shown that adding our module to the networks shows lower pixel classification error for different trimap widths compared to the base network.

**Table 2.** Comparison of evaluation metrics for various state-of-the-art networks

| Architecture | Module type | Dice | Jaccard | HD | MF |
|---|---|---|---|---|---|
| SegNet | - | 0.6515 | 0.5497 | 41.31 | 0.4127 |
| | Conv-MCD | **0.7194** | **0.6314** | **35.61** | **0.4923** |
| UNet | - | 0.8249 | 0.7468 | 23.27 | 0.6144 |
| | Conv-MCD | **0.838** | **0.7652** | **21.05** | **0.6161** |
| UNet16 | - | 0.8441 | 0.7676 | 15.24 | 0.7514 |
| | Conv-MCD | **0.9124** | **0.8559** | **13.17** | **0.7753** |
| LinkNet34 | - | 0.8835 | 0.8206 | 16.02 | 0.7358 |
| | Conv-MCD | **0.8979** | **0.8383** | **14.28** | **0.7474** |

The selection of the type of distance map in the Conv-MCD module also affects model performance. We conducted experiments using 1Enc 1Dec Conv-MCD with different distance maps and found that D2 and D3 perform better than D1. Overall, 1Enc 1Dec Conv-MCD performs better than 1Enc 1Dec M for all types of distance maps. The results reported in this paper are from the best performing distance map. The comparison of distance map types can be found in the supplementary material.

To validate the effect of our module to the network performance, we conducted the following studies. In the first study, we plotted the validation loss values of the mask obtained from 1Enc 1Dec Conv-MCD and 1Enc 1Dec M against the number of epochs. The plot clearly showed that learning the additional tasks together did not allow the network to overfit, thus enabling the network to generalize better. As a second study, the feature maps extracted from the last layer of the network before the module are visualized. By visualization, it was found that while mask and contour had a direct representation, distance map could be represented by a linear combination of some feature maps. These feature representations demonstrate that a single decoder with our module will

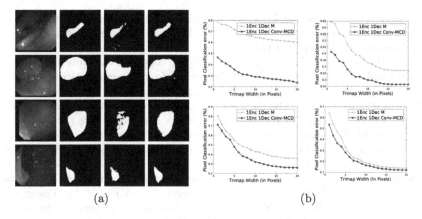

(a)                                           (b)

**Fig. 3.** Left (a): From row 1 to 4: SegNet, UNet, UNet16 and LinkNet34. In each row from left to right: Image, Ground Truth, network without our module Conv-MCD, network with our module Conv-MCD. Right (b): Row-wise order: Pixel classification error vs trimap width for SegNet, UNet, UNet16 and LinkNet34. In the graph, green line represents the base network and black line represents network with our module Conv-MCD. (Color figure online)

be sufficient instead of parallel decoders. The feature maps and the validation graphs can be found in supplementary material. The third one is an ablative study, where we compared our module with modules having a single auxiliary task, namely Conv-MC and Conv-MD. We observed that the network 1Enc 1Dec with Conv-MCD gives better results compared to Conv-MC and Conv-MD. This phenomenon can be attributed to increase in the number of related tasks [2]. Quantitative results are available in Table 1.

## 4   Conclusion

In this paper, we have proposed a novel plug-and-play module Conv-MCD. The module was specifically designed for medical images. It handles class imbalance, reduces outliers, alleviates structural information loss and works well with multi-instance object segmentation. Also, Conv-MCD can be added to any deep segmentation network, resulting in a significant improvement in performance with minimal increase in parameters.

## References

1. Badrinarayanan, V., Kendall, A., Cipolla, R.: Segnet: a deep convolutional encoder-decoder architecture for image segmentation. IEEE Trans. Pattern Anal. Mach. Intell. **39**, 2481–2495 (2016)
2. Caruana, R.: Multitask learning: a knowledge-based source of inductive bias. In: ICML (1993)

3. Chaurasia, A., Culurciello, E.: Linknet: exploiting encoder representations for efficient semantic segmentation. In: 2017 IEEE Visual Communications and Image Processing (VCIP), pp. 1–4 (2017)
4. Chen, H., Qi, X., Yu, L., Heng, P.: DCAN: deep contour-aware networks for accurate gland segmentation. In: 2016 IEEE Conference on Computer Vision and Pattern Recognition (CVPR), pp. 2487–2496 (2016)
5. Csurka, G., Larlus, D.: What is a good evaluation measure for semantic segmentation? In: Proceedings of the British Machine Vision Conference (2013)
6. Krähenbühl, P., Koltun, V.: Efficient inference in fully connected CRFs with Gaussian edge potentials. In: Advances in Neural Information Processing Systems, vol. 24, pp. 109–117 (2011)
7. Ronneberger, O., Fischer, P., Brox, T.: U-net: convolutional networks for biomedical image segmentation. In: Navab, N., Hornegger, J., Wells, W.M., Frangi, A.F. (eds.) MICCAI 2015. LNCS, vol. 9351, pp. 234–241. Springer, Cham (2015). https://doi.org/10.1007/978-3-319-24574-4_28
8. Simonyan, K., Zisserman, A.: Very deep convolutional networks for large-scale image recognition. In: 3rd International Conference on Learning Representations, ICLR (2015)
9. Tan, C., Zhao, L., Yan, Z., et al.: Deep multi-task and task-specific feature learning network for robust shape preserved organ segmentation. In: 2018 IEEE 15th International Symposium on Biomedical Imaging (ISBI 2018), pp. 1221–1224 (2018)
10. Vázquez, D., Bernal, J., Sánchez, F.J., et al.: A benchmark for endoluminal scene segmentation of colonoscopy images. J. Healthcare Eng. **2017**, 9 (2017)

# Detecting Abnormalities in Resting-State Dynamics: An Unsupervised Learning Approach

Meenakshi Khosla[1]([✉]), Keith Jamison[2,3], Amy Kuceyeski[2,3], and Mert R. Sabuncu[1,4]

[1] School of Electrical and Computer Engineering, Cornell University, Ithaca, USA
mk2299@cornell.edu
[2] Radiology, Weill Cornell Medical College, New York, USA
[3] Brain and Mind Research Institute, Weill Cornell Medical College, New York, USA
[4] Nancy E. and Peter C. Meinig School of Biomedical Engineering, Cornell University, Ithaca, USA

**Abstract.** Resting-state functional MRI (rs-fMRI) is a rich imaging modality that captures spontaneous brain activity patterns, revealing clues about the connectomic organization of the human brain. While many rs-fMRI studies have focused on static measures of functional connectivity, there has been a recent surge in examining the temporal patterns in these data. In this paper, we explore two strategies for capturing the normal variability in resting-state activity across a healthy population: (a) an autoencoder approach on the rs-fMRI sequence, and (b) a next frame prediction strategy. We show that both approaches can learn useful representations of rs-fMRI data and demonstrate their novel application for abnormality detection in the context of discriminating autism patients from healthy controls.

## 1 Introduction

Resting-state fMRI captures intrinsic neural activity, in the absence of external stimuli and task requirements. Much of the research in this direction has aimed at identifying connectivity based biomarkers, restricting the analysis to so-called "static" functional connectivity measures that quantify the *average* degree of synchrony between brain regions. For e.g., machine learning based strategies have been used with static connectivity measures to parcellate the brain into functional networks, and extract individual-level predictions about cognitive state or clinical condition [2]. In recent years, there has been a surge in the study of the temporal dynamics of rs-fMRI data, offering a complementary perspective on the functional connectome and how it is altered in disease, development, and aging [14]. However, to our knowledge, there has been a dearth of machine learning applications to dynamic rs-fMRI analysis.

Thanks to large-scale datasets, modern machine learning methods have fueled significant progress in computer vision. Compared to natural vision applications,

© Springer Nature Switzerland AG 2019
H.-I. Suk et al. (Eds.): MLMI 2019, LNCS 11861, pp. 301–309, 2019.
https://doi.org/10.1007/978-3-030-32692-0_35

however, medical imaging poses a unique set of challenges. Data, particularly labeled data, are often scarce in medical imaging applications. This makes data-hungry methods such as supervised CNNs possibly less useful. One potential approach to tackle the limited sample size issue is to exploit unsupervised or semi-supervised learning strategies that don't depend on large amounts of labeled training data. In this paper, we explore the use of unsupervised end-to-end learning for capturing rs-fMRI dynamics and demonstrate that the representations our models learn can be useful for detecting abnormal patterns in data.

**Related Work:** Machine learning methods are increasingly used to compute individual-level predictions from rs-fMRI data, e.g. about disease [2]. The conventional approach of supervised learning relies on labeled training data and uses hand-crafted features such as the static correlation between pairs of regions. Such features fail to capture the dynamics of resting-state activity as it relates to behavior or disease. Moreover, emerging data suggest that learning models that exploit the full-resolution 4-dimensional fMRI data can potentially reveal more discriminative resting-state biomarkers [7]. In this work, we are motivated by this observation and our goal is to move away from hand-crafted features and take full advantage of the spatio-temporal structure of rs-fMRI.

Unsupervised approaches such as clustering of static connectivity measures have been previously used for disease classification and discovery of novel disease sub-types [16]. Similarly, autoencoders have been used in pre-training to improve generalization capabilities of supervised learning algorithms, as in [13]. An alternative application of unsupervised learning is outlier detection. Here, the goal is to identify data points that deviate markedly from normal samples. For example, autoencoder models have been popular for outlier detection in video [4]. In recent years, predictive modeling has also been shown to be a powerful framework in unsupervised feature learning of video representations [12]. In this approach, a model is trained to predict future frames of a video sequence. These models learn useful internal representations of the data that can in turn be used for anomaly detection or downstream object recognition or classification tasks [8].

In the present paper, we propose a novel unsupervised approach that learns rs-fMRI representations on voxel-level time-course data captured via a convolutional RNN model, in an end-to-end learning fashion. Models are trained to predict the next frame in an rs-fMRI sequence or to reconstruct the entire sequence. We apply our approach to the novel problem of outlier detection in rs-fMRI, and demonstrate its utility in discriminating autism patients from healthy controls.

## 2    Methodology

In this section, we describe the autoencoder and prediction models considered in the study. As we demonstrate empirically, the models learn to accurately reconstruct or predict "normal" resting-state activity in healthy subjects, but yield higher reconstruction/prediction errors in patients.

## 2.1 Network Building Blocks

*Convolutional Networks:* CNNs have achieved unprecedented levels of performance across many vision tasks [6]. The main ingredients of CNNs include convolutional layers that serve as feature extractors, and pooling/un-pooling layers that perform down/up-sampling in resolution. In this paper, we employ encoder-decoder style networks since we are reconstructing/predicting structured image data, i.e., rs-fMRI frames. Encoder-decoder networks are widely deployed in image segmentation and generation tasks, as in [10]. The encoding part computes a cascade of increasingly high-level representations from the images, whereas the decoding part reconstructs pixel-level features from these representations.

*Convolutional-LSTM Networks:* Recurrent neural networks (RNNs), e.g., LSTMs [5], offer state-of-the-art results in many domains with sequential data, such as speech or natural language processing. Conv-LSTM cells, an extension of LSTM units, integrate convolutional layers with LSTM modules and allow the temporal propagation of high-level spatial features captured by convolutional layers. Conv-LSTM cells have shown remarkable performance in sequence forecasting problems [11]. This stems from their ability to simultaneously capture rich spatial and temporal structures in the data.

## 2.2 Next Frame Prediction Model

Given a sequence of rs-fMRI frames, we trained a model to predict the next frame in the sequence. To improve the localization accuracy of predicted frames and capture spatio-temporal correlations at multiple resolutions, we incorporate skip connections with Conv-LSTM modules in our architecture. This U-Net style architecture [10] is shown in Fig. 1. The input to the model is a 2D rs-fMRI sequence of $T$ axial slices. In the encoding layers, we used 3D convolutions and max pooling, where the first two dimensions are the spatial coordinates on the axial cross-section and the third dimension is time. We compared our prediction model with several baselines, including: (a) simply using the last frame of the input sequence as a prediction of the next frame; (b) a non-learning based extrapolation model that fits separate cubic splines at each pixel on the input sequence; and (c) a non-recurrent 2-D U-Net model that excludes the Conv-LSTM modules from the proposed architecture and treats the temporal component of the input as T channels. We also considered (d) an interpolation scheme that interpolated with cubic splines between the $T$ frames of the input sequence that precede the predicted frame *and* the frame *after* the predicted frame. This interpolation method is different than the other methods as it is not a forecasting model, yet we found it useful to assess the performance of the other methods.

## 2.3 Autoencoder Model

The autoencoder is an unsupervised learning approach that encodes the input into a lower dimensional representation, which is then decoded into a reconstruction of the input. The model is trained to minimize a distance function between

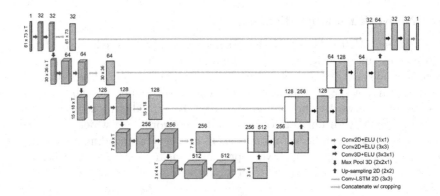

**Fig. 1.** Next frame prediction model. Each cuboid represents a 3D (2 spatial dimensions + time) feature map with number of features indicated on top. Flat boxes represent 2D feature maps, with number of channels on top. Input is an axial fMRI slice with T sequential frames. Conv-LSTM cell returns the last output of the output sequence.

the reconstruction and input, such as the squared $L_2$ distance. The architecture of our reconstruction model is the same as the prediction model above, with two important differences. First, there are no skip connections, which are indicated as a "concatenate with crop" operation, to avoid the trivial solution of copying input to the output. The second difference is that, in the decoder layers and the output we have $T$ frames, instead of a single frame. So in the visualization of this architecture, those would be represented with cuboids and 3D convolution/up-sampling operations. Further, we retained Conv-LSTM unit in the bottleneck to capture temporal dependencies between the frames of a rs-fMRI sequence.

## 3   Experiments

### 3.1   Data

We conducted our experiments on data from the Autism Brain Imaging Data Exchange (ABIDE) study [9]. Because of difference in TRs and other imaging parameters across sites, we restricted our experiments to the acquisition site with the largest sample size, namely NYU. We only used data that passed quality assessments by all functional raters and retained enough time-points after motion scrubbing for band-pass filtering. We randomly selected two thirds of the healthy group (54 subjects) for training/validating the reconstruction & imputation models. A validation split of 10% was used during training to monitor convergence of these models. The remaining one-third group comprising 28 healthy controls was used as test data to evaluate predictions/reconstruction performance for comparison against ASD patients (N = 67).

Rs-fMRI preprocessing included slice timing correction, motion correction, global mean intensity normalization, standardization of functional data to MNI space, global signal regression, motion scrubbing (volume censoring) and band-pass filtering. We note that band-pass filtering was performed after motion scrubbing to avoid any motion contamination. Individual rs-fMRI scans were normalized between 0 to 1 by min-max scaling each-individual voxel's time series. Finally, we applied a binary gray matter mask to all 3D volumes [15].

## 3.2 Implementation Details

During training, we identified non-overlapping contiguous segments of $(T + 1)$ frames for each subject in the training set. For each such segment, we extracted all axial slices and trained a unified model to predict the next frame, i.e, for a given architecture a single model was trained for all subjects and axial slices, comprising 16,560 training instances. Squared loss was optimized with Adam and a learning rate 1e-4. We implemented our code using Keras, with a Tensor-Flow back-end. The network was trained for 150 epochs with a batch size of 32. Validation curves were monitored to ensure convergence. We used same training paradigm for the non-recurrent baseline U-Net model. In our experiments, we tried different values for $T$ and observed diminishing returns beyond $T = 20$ in the performance of the next frame prediction models. The overall pattern in comparing the accuracy of different models was the same. Thus, in the remainder we fix $T = 20$. We note that, while not necessary, we fixed $T = 20$ for the autoencoder models too, which ensured training was done on identical datasets for these different approaches. Once the models were trained, we used them to compute predictions or reconstructions on independent data, which included both controls and ASD patients. For each test subject, we computed the mean squared error (between reconstruction/prediction and ground truth frames) as a single metric. Note that we averaged over all frames and pixels in an rs-fMRI scan. We hypothesized that this metric would be different between patients and controls, demonstrating that it could be used as an outlier detector. We also analyzed the voxel-level squared errors and conducted a statistical comparison between patients and controls to reveal the anatomical distribution of the differences.

## 4    Results

### 4.1    Next Frame Prediction and Reconstruction Errors

We first demonstrate that the next frame in rs-fMRI sequence can be accurately predicted. Table 1 shows the performance of the different methods we implemented. We list both MSE and the mean Pearson's correlation between predicted and ground truth frames, computed within the gray matter mask on healthy test subjects. We observe that the proposed recurrent U-Net architecture achieves the best prediction performance, even exceeding the cubic-spline based interpolator, which was given both the preceding 20 frames and the frame *after* the predicted frame. The recurrent LSTM modules that capture the temporal dynamics also enabled a significant boost in quality, as can be noted by comparing the performance of the U-Net and proposed architecture. Finally, the U-Net models outperformed the non-learning based methods of extrapolation, suggesting that accounting for both the spatial and temporal structure in the data yielded better results.

Table 2 shows the mean reconstruction errors of the autoencoder on healthy test subjects for various input sequence lengths at test time. We note that the performance is worse than next-frame prediction because of the absence of skip connections. Reconstruction quality degraded with fewer frames suggesting that the autoencoder is not reconstructing frames independently and is indeed exploiting the long-term temporal dependencies between frames. For outlier detection, we thus used the temporal window T = 20 as it gives the best reconstruction performance and captures longer dynamics.

**Table 1.** Next frame prediction performance on healthy test subjects for different models. *Interpolation model had access to the frame after the predicted frame.

| Imputation models | Mean squared error | Pearson's correlation |
|---|---|---|
| Last observation copy | 0.01969 | 0.7558 |
| Extrapolation | 0.01203 | 0.8938 |
| Interpolation* | 0.00065 | 0.9939 |
| Non-recurrent U-Net | 0.00026 | 0.9967 |
| Proposed recurrent U-Net | 0.00007 | 0.9990 |

**Table 2.** Reconstruction performance of the proposed recurrent autoencoder on healthy test subjects for different input sequence lengths.

| Recurrent autoencoder: sequence length | Mean squared error | Pearson's correlation |
|---|---|---|
| T = 10 frames | 0.0625 | 0.354 |
| T = 15 frames | 0.0475 | 0.503 |
| T = 20 frames | 0.0437 | 0.550 |

## 4.2   Outlier Detection: Discriminating Patients and Controls

We were interested in examining whether the next frame prediction and reconstruction models can be used to detect outlier subjects. To test this, we computed mean squared error on all test subjects, including healthy controls and ASD patients. Figure 2 shows these error values for the proposed next frame prediction and autoencoder models. Both models yield error values that are statistically significantly different between the two clinical groups. Further, AUC values obtained with autoencoder and imputation models, as shown in Table 3, are on par with recent supervised ASD v/s control classification results [1].

We also note that the non-recurrent U-Net benchmark achieves a weaker separation between the two clinical groups. This indicates that the conv-LSTM

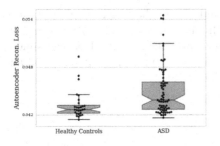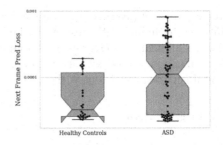

**Fig. 2.** Whisker plots showing reconstruction and prediction errors (mean squared error) for ASD patients and controls, with proposed recurrent models trained on T = 20 consecutive frames. Points are individual subjects. The ends of the box are upper and lower quartiles, the median is marked by a horizontal line inside the box.

**Table 3.** Area under the ROC curve for discriminating ASD vs Controls. P-values of the unpaired t-test comparing means of the two clinical groups are shown in brackets.

| Model | AUC (p-value) |
|---|---|
| Recurrent autoencoder | 69.6 (0.00466) |
| U-Net imputation | 62.5 (0.00293) |
| Recurrent U-Net imputation | 65.9 (0.00151) |

layers enhance diagnostic sensitivity presumably because they are more equipped to exploit spatiotemporal structure in extracting representations. Importantly, we observed no correlation between frame-wise displacement values (a widely used metric to quantify subject motion) and the prediction/reconstruction errors- neither at the frame-level (Pearson's correlation $-0.0161/0.0218$, p = $0.0739/0.0251$, computed on non-motion scrubbed frames only) nor at the individual level (Pearson's correlation $0.0033/0.1730$, p = $0.9744/0.0936$).

Finally, we were interested in exploring the anatomical differences in errors between the two clinical groups. We thus conducted a t-test of the regional

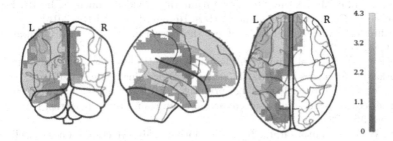

**Fig. 3.** Statistical significance of the difference in regional reconstruction error of the recurrent autoencoder between controls and ASD patients. FDR with $q = 0.05$ was implemented for multiple testing correction. $- \log_{10}$ p values are shown.

prediction error (averaged within the boundaries of the widely used AAL atlas [15]) on the model with best AUC, i.e. the autoencoder. As can be seen from Fig. 3, significant differences were mainly constrained to the left hemisphere, particularly localizing within the language network, involving the temporal and frontal cortices, consistent with prior literature [3].

## 5   Discussion

We considered a novel unsupervised learning strategy to analyze rs-fMRI data, where we train recurrent models to reconstruct rs-fMRI clips or to predict the next frame in a sequence. Results indicate that the proposed recurrent U-Net architecture produces very accurate predictions that yield a correlation greater than 0.99 with ground truth. Furthermore, this performance is better than an interpolation approach that had access to the frame after the predicted frame. Next, we demonstrated the utility of the proposed models in detecting outliers in rs-fMRI. Our results indicate that next frame prediction error or reconstruction error can be used to discriminate patients from controls, achieving a classification performance close to state-of-the-art results obtained with supervised methods. There are several directions we will be exploring with this technique. For example, we are interested in using the next frame prediction model to assess the quality of individual frames, particularly in the context of motion and other artifacts. Another possible application could be to use this model to impute frames that have been discarded for motion scrubbing. Finally, we believe unsupervised models can offer novel insights into the dynamics of resting state fluctuations.

## References

1. Abraham, et al.: Deriving reproducible biomarkers from multi-site resting-state data: an autism-based example. NeuroImage **147**, 736–745 (2017)
2. Khosla, et al.: Machine learning in resting-state fMRI analysis. arXiv preprint arXiv:1812.11477 (2018)
3. Eyler, L.T., et al.: A failure of left temporal cortex to specialize for language is an early emerging and fundamental property of autism. Brain **135**(3), 949–960 (2012)
4. Hasan, M., et al.: Learning temporal regularity in video sequences. In: IEEE Conference on Computer Vision and Pattern Recognition (CVPR) (2016)
5. Hochreiter, S., Schmidhuber, J.: Long short-term memory. Neural Comput. **9**(8), 1735–1780 (1997)
6. Krizhevsky, A., et al.: Imagenet classification with deep convolutional neural networks. In: Advances in Neural Information Processing Systems (2012)
7. Liu, et al.: Chronnectome fingerprinting: identifying individuals & predicting higher cognitive function using dynamic brain connectivity patterns. Hum. Brain Mapp. **39**, 902–915 (2018)
8. Liu, W., et al.: Future frame prediction for anomaly detection - a new baseline. In: 2018 IEEE/CVF Conference on Computer Vision and Pattern Recognition (2018)
9. Di Martino, A., et al.: The autism brain imaging data exchange: towards a large-scale evaluation of intrinsic brain architecture in autism. Mol. Psychiatry **19**, 659 (2014)

10. Ronneberger, O., Fischer, P., Brox, T.: U-Net: convolutional networks for biomedical image segmentation. In: Navab, N., Hornegger, J., Wells, W.M., Frangi, A.F. (eds.) MICCAI 2015. LNCS, vol. 9351, pp. 234–241. Springer, Cham (2015). https://doi.org/10.1007/978-3-319-24574-4_28
11. Shi, X., et al.: Convolutional LSTM network: a machine learning approach for precipitation nowcasting. In: NIPS (2015)
12. Srivastava, N., Mansimov, E., Salakhutdinov, R.R.: Unsupervised learning of video representations using LSTMs. In: ICML (2015)
13. Suk, H.-I., Lee, S.-W., Shen, D.: A hybrid of deep network and hidden Markov model for MCI identification with resting-state fMRI. In: Navab, N., Hornegger, J., Wells, W.M., Frangi, A.F. (eds.) MICCAI 2015. LNCS, vol. 9349, pp. 573–580. Springer, Cham (2015). https://doi.org/10.1007/978-3-319-24553-9_70
14. Tian, L., et al.: Changes in dynamic functional connections with aging. Neuroimage **172**, 31–39 (2018)
15. Tzourio-Mazoyer, N., et al.: Automated anatomical labeling of activations in SPM using a macroscopic anatomical parcellation of the MNI MRI single-subject brain. NeuroImage **15**(1), 273–289 (2002)
16. Zeng, L.L., et al.: Unsupervised classification of major depression using functional connectivity MRI. Hum. Brain Mapp. **35**(4), 1630–1641 (2014)

# Distanced LSTM: Time-Distanced Gates in Long Short-Term Memory Models for Lung Cancer Detection

Riqiang Gao[1], Yuankai Huo[1(✉)], Shunxing Bao[1], Yucheng Tang[1],
Sanja L. Antic[2], Emily S. Epstein[2], Aneri B. Balar[2], Steve Deppen[2],
Alexis B. Paulson[2], Kim L. Sandler[2], Pierre P. Massion[2],
and Bennett A. Landman[1]

[1] Vanderbilt University, Nashville, TN 37235, USA
yuankai.huo@vanderbilt.edu
[2] Vanderbilt University Medical Center, Nashville, TN 37235, USA

**Abstract.** The field of lung nodule detection and cancer prediction has been rapidly developing with the support of large public data archives. Previous studies have largely focused cross-sectional (single) CT data. Herein, we consider longitudinal data. The Long Short-Term Memory (LSTM) model addresses learning with regularly spaced time points (i.e., equal temporal intervals). However, clinical imaging follows patient needs with often heterogeneous, irregular acquisitions. To model both regular and irregular longitudinal samples, we generalize the LSTM model with the Distanced LSTM (DLSTM) for temporally varied acquisitions. The DLSTM includes a Temporal Emphasis Model (TEM) that enables learning across regularly and irregularly sampled intervals. Briefly, (1) the temporal intervals between longitudinal scans are modeled explicitly, (2) temporally adjustable forget and input gates are introduced for irregular temporal sampling; and (3) the latest longitudinal scan has an additional emphasis term. We evaluate the DLSTM framework in three datasets including simulated data, 1794 National Lung Screening Trial (NLST) scans, and 1420 clinically acquired data with heterogeneous and irregular temporal accession. The experiments on the first two datasets demonstrate that our method achieves competitive performance on both simulated and regularly sampled datasets (e.g. improve LSTM from 0.6785 to 0.7085 on F1 score in NLST). In external validation of clinically and irregularly acquired data, the benchmarks achieved 0.8350 (CNN feature) and 0.8380 (LSTM) on area under the ROC curve (AUC) score, while the proposed DLSTM achieves 0.8905.

**Keywords:** Lung cancer · Longitudinal · LSTM · Time distance · TEM

## 1 Introduction

Early detection of lung cancer from clinically acquired computed tomography (CT) scans are essential for lung cancer diagnosis [1]. Lung cancer detection is a binary classification (cancer or non-cancer) task from the machine learning perspective. Convolutional neural network (CNN) methods have been widely used in lung cancer

© Springer Nature Switzerland AG 2019
H.-I. Suk et al. (Eds.): MLMI 2019, LNCS 11861, pp. 310–318, 2019.
https://doi.org/10.1007/978-3-030-32692-0_36

detection, which typically consist of two steps: nodule detection and classification. Nodule detection detects the pulmonary nodules from a CT scan with coordinates and region of interest (e.g., [2]), while the classification assigns the nodules to be either benign or malignant categories [3], and the whole CT scan is classified as cancer when containing at least one malignant nodule. One prevalent method was proposed by Liao et al. [3], which won the Kaggle DSB2017 challenge. In this method, the pipeline was deployed on detecting top five confidence nodule regions to classify whole CT scan. The Liao et al. network focuses on a single CT scan, rather than multiple longitudinal scans.

In clinical practice, longitudinal CT scans may contain temporal relevant diagnostic information. To learn from the longitudinal scans, recurrent neural networks (RNN) have been introduced to medical image analysis when longitudinal (sequential) imaging data are available (e.g., [4]). Long Short-Term Memory (LSTM) [5] is one of the most prevalent variants of RNN, which is capable of learning both long-term and short-term dependencies between features using three gates (i.e., forget, input, and output gates). Many variants of LSTM have been proposed [6–8]. For instance, convolutional LSTM [6] is designed to deal with spatial temporal variations in images [9, 10].

In canonical LSTM, the temporal intervals between consecutive scans are equal. However, this rarely occurs in clinical practice. Temporal intervals have been modeled in LSTM for recommendation system in finance [8] and abnormality detection on 2D chest X-ray [11]. However, no previous studies have been conducted to model global temporal variations. The previous methods [8, 11] modeled the relative local time intervals between consecutive scans. However, for lung cancer detection, the last scan is typically the most informative. Therefore, we propose a new Temporal Emphasis Model (TEM) to model the global time interval between previous time points to the last scan as a global multiplicative function to input gate and forget gate, rather than a new gate as [8] or an additive term as [11].

Our contributions are: (1) this is the first study that models the time distance from last point for LSTM in lung cancer detection; (2) the novel DLSTM framework is proposed to model the temporal distance with adaptive forget gate and input gate; (3) a toy dataset called "Tumor-CIFAR" is released to simulate dummy benign and malignant cancer on natural images. 1794 subjects from the widely used National Lung Screening Trial (NLST) [12] and 1420 subjects from two institutional cohorts are used to evaluate the methods.

## 2 Theory and Method

**Distanced LSTM** - LSTM is the most widely used RNN networks in classification or prediction upon sequential data. Standard LSTM employ three gates (i.e., forget gate $f_t$, input gate $i_t$, and output gate $o_t$) to maintain internal states (i.e., hidden state $H_t$ and cell state $C_t$). The forget gate controls the amount of information used for the current state from the previous time steps. To incorporate the "distance attribute" to LSTM, we multiply a Temporal Emphasis Model (TEM) $D(d_t, a, c)$ as a multiplicative function to the forget gate and the input gate with learnable parameters (Fig. 1).

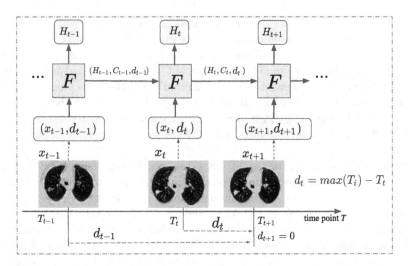

**Fig. 1.** The framework of DLSTM (three "steps" in the example). $x_t$ is the input data at time point $t$, and $d_t$ is the time distance from the time point $t$ to the latest time point. "$F$" represents the learnable DLSTM component (convolutional version in this paper). $H_t$ and $C_t$ are the hidden state and cell state, respectively. The input data, $x_t$, could be 1D, 2D, or 3D.

Briefly, our DLSTM is defined by following the terms and variables in [6]:

$$\begin{aligned}
i_t &= D(d_t, a, c) \cdot \sigma(W_{xi} * X_t + W_{hi} * H_{t-1} + W_{ci} \circ C_{t-1} + b_i) \\
f_t &= D(d_{t-1}, a, c) \cdot \sigma\big(W_{xf} * X_t + W_{hf} * H_{t-1} + W_{cf} \circ C_{t-1} + b_f\big) \\
C_t &= f_t \circ C_{t-1} + i_t \circ tanh(W_{xc} * X_t + W_{hc} * H_{t-1} + b_i) \\
o_t &= \sigma(W_{xo} * X_t + W_{ho} * H_{t-1} + W_{co} \circ C_t + b_o) \\
H_t &= o_t \circ tanh(C_t)
\end{aligned} \tag{1}$$

where $x_t$ is the input data of time point $t$, $d_t$ is the global time distance from any $x_t$ to the latest scan, $W$ and $b$ are the learnable parameters, and "$*$" and "$\circ$" denotes the convolution operator and Hadamard product respectively. Different from canonical LSTM, the TEM function is introduced in the proposed DLSTM as

$$D(d_t, a, c) = a \cdot e^{-c \cdot d_t} \tag{2}$$

where $a$ and $c$ are positive learnable parameters. Different from tLSTM [11], which introduced an additive term to model local relative time interval between scans, the proposed DLSTM introduces the TEM function as a global multiplicative function to model the time interval (distance) from each scan to the last scan. Using TEM in Eq. (1), both the forget gate $f_t$ and input gate $i_t$ are weakened if the input scan is far from the last scan. Note the "LSTM" represents the convolutional version in this paper.

## 3  Experiment Design and Results

We include both simulation (Tumor-CIFAR) and empirical validations (NLST and clinical data from two in-house projects, see Table 1) to validate the baseline methods and the proposed method. Firstly, to test if our algorithm can handle the time-interval distances effectively, we introduce the synthetic dataset: Tumor-CIFAR.

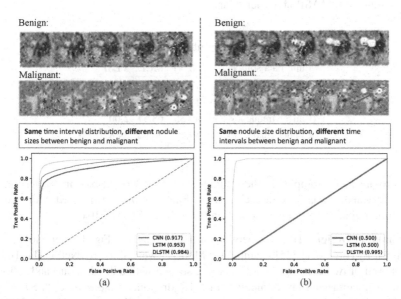

**Fig. 2.** The receiver operating characteristic (ROC) curves of Tumor-CIFAR. The left panels simulate the situation that the images are sampled with the same interval distribution, while the right panels are sampled with the same size distribution. The upper panels show the examples of images in Tumor-CIFAR. The noise (white and black dots) are added, while the dummy nodules are shown as white blobs (some are indicated by red arrows). The lower panels show the Area Under the Curve of ROC (AUC) values of different methods. (Color figure online)

In Tumor-CIFAR, we show the test results with a training/validation/test split (Fig. 2). We perform three different validations on lung datasets: (1) cross-validation on NLST with longitudinal data (Table 2); (2) cross-validation on clinical data with both cross-sectional and longitudinal scans (Table 3); and (3) external-validation on longitudinal scans (train and validation on NLST and test result on clinical data, Table 4).

### 3.1  Simulation: Tumor-CIFAR

**Data.** Based on [13], the growth speed of malignant nodules is approximate three times faster compared with benign ones. To incorporate temporal variations in the simulation, we add dummy nodules on CIFAR10 [14] with different growth rate for benign and malignant nodules (malignant nodules grow three times faster than benign ones).

Two cases are simulated: image samples with the same "interval distribution" (Fig. 2a), or with the same nodule "size distribution" (Fig. 2b). The same interval distribution indicates intervals follow the same Gaussian distribution. The same nodule size distribution represents the growth rate of nodules follow the same Gaussian distribution (simulation code, detail descriptions and more image examples are publicly available at https://github.com/MASILab/tumor-cifar).

**Table 1.** Demographic distribution in our experiments

| Lung data source | NLST | MCL | VLSP |
|---|---|---|---|
| Total subject | 1794 | 567 | 853 |
| Longitudinal subject | 1794 | 105 | 370 |
| Cancer frequency (%) | 40.35 | 68.57 | 2.00 |
| Gender (male, %) | 59.59 | 58.92 | 54.87 |

There are 5,000 samples in the training set and 1,000 samples in the testing set. Cancer prevalence was 50% in each dataset. Each sample is simulated with five different time points. The training/validation/test split is 40k/10k/10k.

**Experimental Design.** The base network structure (CNN in Fig. 1) is employed from the official PyTorch 0.41 [15] example for MNIST (we call it "ToyNet"). The ToyNet is composed of two convolutional layers (the second with a 2D dropout) and followed by two fully connected layers along with a 1D dropout in the middle. "LSTM" and "DLSTM" in Fig. 2 represents a 2D convolutional LSTM component and 2D convolutional of our proposed DLSTM component is stacked in the beginning of the "ToyNet", respectively. The maximum training epoch number is 100. The initial learning rate set to 0.01 and is multiplied by 0.4 at $50^{th}$, $70^{th}$ and $80^{th}$ epoch.

**Results.** For the same time interval distribution (Fig. 2a), the LSTM achieves higher performance compared with baseline CNN method, while the DLSTM works even better. This task is relatively easy since the malignant nodules clearly grow faster compared benign nodules. However, if we control the sampling strategy to guarantee the same nodule size for corresponding samples (Fig. 2b), the task becomes challenging if the time intervals are not modeled in the network design since the nodules are now having the same size. In this case, the CNN and LSTM only achieve 0.5 AUC values, while our DLSTM is able to almost perfectly capture the temporal variations with an AUC value of 0.995.

## 3.2 Empirical Validation on CT

**Data.** The National Lung Screening Trial (NLST) [12] is a large-scale randomized controlled trial for early diagnosis of lung cancer study with low-dose CT screening exams publicly available. We obtain a subset (1794 subjects) from NLST, which contains all longitudinal scans with "follow-up confirmed lung cancer", as well as a random subset of all "follow-up confirmed not lung cancer" scans (Table 1). One in-house dataset combines two clinical lung sets Molecular Characterization Laboratories (MCL, https://mcl.nci.nih.gov) and Vanderbilt Lung Screening Program (VLSP, https://www.vumc.org/radiology/lung) which is also evaluated by our algorithm. These data are used in de-identified form under internal review board supervision.

**Experimental Design.** The DLSTM can be trained in an end-to-end network (simulation experiments in Sect. 3.1) or as lightweight post-processing manner. In this section, we evaluate the proposed DLSTM as a post processing network for the imaging features extracted from Liao et al. [3]. We compare the DLSTM with a recently proposed benchmark tLSTM [11], which models the relative time interval as an additive term. Five highest risk regions (possible nodules) for each scan are detected by [3], and the feature dimension for each region is 64, then the scan-level feature is achieved by concatenating region features as $5 \times 64$ inputs. For a fair comparison, the same features are provided to the networks Multi-channel CNN (MC-CNN), LSTM, tLSTM, and DLSTM, with 1D convolutional layer of 5 kernel size. MC-CNN concatenates multi-scan features in the "channel" dimension. The maximum training epoch number is 100, the initial learning rate is set to 0.01 and multiplied by 0.4 at the $50^{th}$, $70^{th}$, and $80^{th}$ epoch. Since most of the longitudinal lung CT scans contain two time points, we evaluate the MC-CNN, LSTM, tLSTM and DLSTM with two time points ("2 steps") in this study (the last two points are picked if the patient with more than two scans).

The "Ori CNN" in Tables 2, 3 and 4 represents the results obtained by open source code and trained model of [3]. If there is on special explanation, our results are reported at subject-level rather than scan-level, and the "Ori CNN" reports the performance of the latest scan of patients.

**Preprocessing.** Our preprocessing follows Liao et al. [3]. We resample the 3D volume to $1 \times 1 \times 1$ mm isotropic resolution. The lung CT scan is segmented using (https://github.com/lfz/DSB2017) from the original CT volume and the non-lung regions are zero-padded to Hounsfield unit score of 170. Then, the 3D volumes are resized to $128 \times 128 \times 128$ to use pre-trained model for extracting image features.

**Results: Cross-validation on Longitudinal Scans.** Table 2 shows the five-fold cross-validation results on 1794 longitudinal subjects from the NLST dataset. All the training and validation data are longitudinal (with "2 steps").

**Table 4.** Experimental results on cross-dataset test (external-validation)

| Method | Accuracy | AUC | F1 | Recall | Precision |
|---|---|---|---|---|---|
| Train and Test both on longitudinal subjects | | | | | |
| Ori CNN (all scans) | 0.8342 | 0.8350 | 0.5253 | 0.4577 | 0.6266 |
| Ori CNN [3] | 0.8758 | 0.8510 | 0.5931 | 0.5513 | **0.6418** |
| MC-CNN | 0.8589 | 0.7654 | 0.5621 | 0.5513 | 0.5733 |
| LSTM [5, 6] | 0.8589 | 0.8380 | 0.5732 | 0.5769 | 0.5692 |
| tLSTM [11] | 0.8673 | 0.8869 | 0.6631 | **0.7949** | 0.5688 |
| DLSTM(ours) | **0.8863** | **0.8905** | **0.6824** | 0.7436 | 0.6304 |

**Results: Cross-validation on Combining Cross-sectional and Longitudinal Scans.**
More than half of the patients only have cross-sectional CT (single time point) scans
from clinical projects (see Table 1). Therefore, we evaluate the proposed method as
well as the baseline methods on the entire clinical cohorts with both longitudinal and
cross-sectional testing with cross-validation on all 1420 subjects by duplicating scans
for subjects with only one scan to 2 steps. Table 3 indicates the five-fold cross-
validation results on the clinical data. As for tLSTM [11] and the proposed DLSTM,
we set the time interval and time distance to be zero for cross-sectional scans,
respectively.

**Results: External-validation on Longitudinal Scans.** We directly apply the trained
models from NLST to the in-house subjects as external validation, without any further
parameter tuning (Table 4). Note that the longitudinal data are regularly sampled in
NLST while the clinical datasets are irregularly acquired. The final predicted cancer
probability is the average of five models trained on five-folds of NLST. The "Ori CNN
(all scans)" in Table 4 represents the scan-level results of all scans from longitudinal
subjects.

**Analyses:** In both public dataset NLST and our private datasets, the proposed DLSTM
achieves competitive results in accuracy, AUC, F1, recall and precision. For example,
the proposed DLSTM improves the conventional LSTM on F1 score from 0.6785 to
0.7085 (Table 2, NLST dataset), and from 0.7417 to 0.7611 (Table 3, clinical datasets).
External validation experiments indicate the generalization ability of the proposed
method.

**Table 2.** Experimental results on NLST dataset (%, average (std) of cross-validation)

| Method | Accuracy | AUC | F1 | Recall | Precision |
|---|---|---|---|---|---|
| Ori CNN [3] | 71.94(2.07) | 74.18(2.11) | 52.18(2.83) | 38.07(2.63) | 83.24(4.24) |
| MC-CNN | 73.26(3.10) | 77.96(0.98) | 59.39(3.70) | 47.91(4.87) | 78.62(3.09) |
| LSTM [5, 6] | 77.05(1.46) | 80.84(1.20) | 67.85(2.41) | 59.92(4.43) | 78.68(3.32) |
| tLSTM [11] | 77.37(2.97) | 80.80(1.45) | 67.47(3.58) | 58.65(5.12) | 79.81(3.34) |
| DLSTM(ours) | **78.96(1.57)** | **82.55(1.31)** | **70.85(1.82)** | **61.61(2.01)** | **83.38(4.34)** |

\* The AUC represents Area Under the Curve of receiver operating characteristic,
and best result is shown in **bold** (also used in the following).

**Table 3.** Experimental results on clinical datasets (%, average (std) of cross-validation)

| Method | Accuracy | AUC | F1 | Recall | Precision |
|---|---|---|---|---|---|
| Ori CNN [3] | 84.80(2.43) | 89.00(1.65) | 70.29(4.26) | 63.46(3.51) | 78.83(5.70) |
| MC-CNN | 84.51(1.29) | 90.85(1.13) | 70.55(1.29) | 62.85(1.53) | 80.84(4.42) |
| LSTM [5, 6] | 86.27(1.29) | 90.27(1.15) | 74.17(2.47) | 69.73(2.62) | 79.56(5.69) |
| tLSTM [11] | 86.42(1.48) | 91.06(1.48) | 74.36(1.99) | 68.55(1.55) | **81.49(5.28)** |
| DLSTM(ours) | **86.97(1.45)** | **91.17(1.53)** | **76.11(2.68)** | **72.71(2.38)** | 80.04(5.18) |

In the external validation, (1) the latest scans achieve higher performance compare with longitudinal scans, which indicates that emphasis on latest longitudinal scan in our DLSTM is meaningful. (2) the algorithms with time information (tLSTM and the proposed DLSTM) outperform those methods without temporal emphasis when the test dataset is irregularly sampled.

# 4 Conclusion and Discussion

In this paper, we propose a novel DLSTM method to model the global temporal intervals between longitudinal CT scans for lung cancer detection. Our method has been validated using both simulations on Tumor-CIFAR, empirical validations on 1794 NLST and 1420 clinically subjects. From cross-validation and external-validation, the proposed DLSTM method achieves generally superior performance compared with baseline methods. Meanwhile, the Tumor-CIFAR dataset is publicly available.

**Acknowledgments.** This research was supported by NSF CAREER 1452485, 5R21 EY024036, R01 EB017230. This study was supported in part by a UO1 CA196405 to Massion. This study was in part using the resources of the Advanced Computing Center for Research and Education (ACCRE) at Vanderbilt University, Nashville, TN. This project was supported in part by the National Center for Research Resources, Grant UL1 RR024975-01, and is now at the National Center for Advancing Translational Sciences, Grant 2 UL1 TR000445-06. We gratefully acknowledge the support of NVIDIA Corporation with the donation of the Titan X Pascal GPU used for this research. The de-identified imaging dataset(s) used for the analysis described were obtained from ImageVU, a research resource supported by the VICTR CTSA award (ULTR000445 from NCATS/NIH), Vanderbilt University Medical Center institutional funding and Patient-Centered Outcomes Research Institute (PCORI; contract CDRN-1306-04869). This research was also supported by SPORE in Lung grant (P50 CA058187), University of Colorado SPORE program, and the Vanderbilt-Ingram Cancer Center.

# References

1. Gould, M.K., et al.: Evaluation of patients with pulmonary nodules: when is it lung cancer?: ACCP Evid.-Based Clin. Practice Guidelines **132**, 108S–130S (2007)
2. Van Ginneken, B., et al.: Comparing and combining algorithms for computer-aided detection of pulmonary nodules in computed tomography scans: the ANODE09 study, vol. 14, pp. 707–722 (2010)
3. Liao, F., Liang, M., Li, Z., Hu, X., Song, S.: Evaluate the malignancy of pulmonary nodules using the 3-D deep leaky noisy-or network. IEEE Trans. Neural Netw. Learn. Syst. (2019)
4. Xu, Y., et al.: Deep learning predicts lung cancer treatment response from serial medical imaging. Clin. Cancer Res. **25**, 3266–3275 (2019)
5. Hochreiter, S., Schmidhuber, J.: Long short-term memory. Neural Comput. **9**, 1735–1780 (1997)
6. Xingjian, S., Chen, Z., Wang, H., Yeung, D.-Y., Wong, W.-K., Woo, W.-C.: Convolutional LSTM network: a machine learning approach for precipitation nowcasting. In: Advances in Neural Information Processing Systems, pp. 802–810 (2015)

7. Neil, D., Pfeiffer, M., Liu, S.-C.: Phased LSTM: accelerating recurrent network training for long or event-based sequences. In: Advances in Neural Information Processing Systems, pp. 3882–3890 (2016)
8. Zhu, Y., et al.: What to do next: modeling user behaviours by time-LSTM. In: IJCAI, pp. 3602–3608 (2017)
9. Finn, C., Goodfellow, I., Levine, S.: Unsupervised learning for physical interaction through video prediction. In: Advances in Neural Information Processing Systems, pp. 64–72 (2016)
10. Lotter, W., Kreiman, G., Cox, D.: Deep predictive coding networks for video prediction and unsupervised learning (2016)
11. Santeramo, R., Withey, S., Montana, G.: Longitudinal detection of radiological abnormalities with time-modulated LSTM. In: Stoyanov, D., Taylor, Z., et al. (eds.) DLMIA/ML-CDS -2018. LNCS, vol. 11045, pp. 326–333. Springer, Cham (2018). https://doi.org/10.1007/978-3-030-00889-5_37
12. National Lung Screening Trial Research Team: The national lung screening trial: overview and study design. Radiology **258**, 243–253 (2011)
13. Duhaylongsod, F.G., Lowe, V.J., Patz Jr., E.F., Vaughn, A.L., Coleman, R.E., Wolfe, W.G.: Lung tumor growth correlates with glucose metabolism measured by fluoride-18 fluorodeoxyglucose positron emission tomography. Ann. Thoracic Surg. **60**, 1348–1352 (1995)
14. Krizhevsky, A., Hinton, G.: Learning multiple layers of features from tiny images. Citeseer (2009)
15. Paszke, A., et al.: Automatic differentiation in pytorch (2017)

# Dense-Residual Attention Network
# for Skin Lesion Segmentation

Lei Song[1], Jianzhe Lin[2], Z. Jane Wang[2], and Haoqian Wang[1,3(✉)]

[1] Department of Automation, Graduate School at Shenzhen, Tsinghua University,
Shenzhen 518055, China
wanghaoqian@tsinghua.edu.cn
[2] Department of Electrical and Computer Engineering,
University of British Columbia, Vancouver, BC V6T 1Z4, Canada
[3] Shenzhen Institute of Future Media Technology, Shenzhen 518071, China

**Abstract.** In this paper, we propose a dense-residual attention network
for skin lesion segmentation. The proposed network is end-to-end and
doesn't need any post-processing operations or pretrained weights to
fine-tune. Specifically, we propose the dense-residual block in our network to deal with the problem of fixed receptive field and meanwhile
ease the gradient vanishing problem (as often occurred in convolution
neural networks). Moreover, an attention gate is designed to enhance
the network discriminative ability and ensure the efficiency of feature
learning. During the network training, we introduce a novel loss function based on the jaccard distance to tackle the class imbalance issue
in medical datasets. The proposed network achieves the state-of-the-art
performance on the benchmark ISIC 2017 Challenge dataset without any
external training samples. Experimental results show the effectiveness of
our dense-residual attention network.

**Keywords:** Skin lesion segmentation · Dense-residual block ·
Attention gate · Convolution neural networks

## 1 Introduction

Skin lesion is the most deadly cancer and has become prevalent over the past
years. It is estimated that about 100000 new cases and 7000 deaths will happen
in the US in 2019 [7]. Skin lesion diagnosis is time-consuming and difficult due
to high visual similarity between non-lesion and lesion, obscure boundary and
artifacts in dermoscopy images. Accurate segmentation is often a fundamental
step of skin lesion diagnosis. Therefore developing an accurate method for skin
lesion segmentation is of great importance.

This work is supported by the Guangdong Provincial Science and Technology
Project (2017B010110005), the Shenzhen Science and Technology Project under Grant
(JCYJ20170817161916238, GGFW2017040714161462).

Recently, deep learning, especially convolution neural network, gets success in many computer vision areas like classification, detection and registration. In the medical image segmentation domain, Ronneberger et al. [6] presented a UNet model that consists of one contracting path and one expanding path to segment neuronal structure. Depending on its excellent feature extraction ability, UNet became the most popular network in medical image segmentation. And many researchers made some improvements based on that and led a series of UNet variations. Among these methods, Oktay et al. [5] proposed an Attention UNet for pancreas segmentation, which was the first attempt to integrate the attention mechanism into UNet to improve the model accuracy. Venkatesh et al. [8] added skip connections in UNet to preserve the lost information in the encoder stage. Recurrent convolution network based on UNet was presented by Alom et al. [1] for feature accumulation.

However, the above methods share three potential concerns generally. First, these networks have a fixed receptive field. Most of them simply stack convolution filters to extract features at a local level and ignore the relationship between different pixels. Taking skin lesion segmentation as an example, the convolution filter just cares about whether each pixel belongs to lesion or non-lesion rather than exploring the most important context information, and hence could cause unreasonable predictions. Second, the network discriminative ability can be improved. These methods usually treat the features from the whole image region equally, which is against our intuitive understanding, especially for medical images. For instance, each skin image may only contain a small lesion area while the majority part is normal that contributes very limited to the model. Third, these networks often apply the cross entropy as loss function in training and may result in a lower performance. The reason is that the cross entropy loss function doesn't consider the severe class imbalance issue in medical domain.

To address above-mentioned concerns, we propose a dense-residual attention network for skin lesion segmentation. More specifically, we propose the dense-residual block to deal with the problem of fixed receptive field and using this block as the basic module of our network. Furthermore, an attention gate is designed to enhance the network discriminative ability, mainly by focusing on the useful part and suppressing the irrelevant area. Finally, a novel loss function based on the jaccard distance is introduced to solve the class imbalance issue in medical datasets and improve the segmentation performance. We evaluate our network extensively on the ISIC 2017 Challenge dataset. Experimental results show that our proposed network is accurate and effective.

## 2   Method

The architecture of our proposed dense-residual attention network is shown in Fig. 1. The proposed network takes the original dermoscopy images as input and outputs the predicted mask for skin lesion without any post-processing operations. The network is an encoder-decoder structure in general, where the feature map decreases gradually in the encoder stage to extract context information and increases in the decoder stage to obtain details about the skin lesion. In order to make full use of abundant hierarchical features, we propose the dense-residual block (DRB) and apply it in both stages separately. The skip connection between the encoder and decoder stage is then used to combine the context and details information. On that basis, an attention gate is designed to learn the features adaptively.

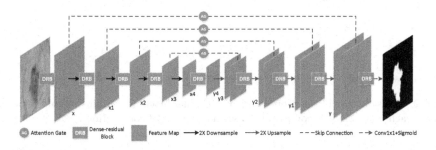

**Fig. 1.** The architecture of the proposed dense-residual attention network.

As shown in Fig. 1, the encoder stage consists of four dense-residual blocks and four 2× downsample operations, and the decoder stage contains four dense-residual blocks and four 2× upsample operations. When an image is fed into the network, it will be processed by a DRB firstly to get its feature map, and then pass by 2× downsample and DRB in sequence until the feature map size equals to 1/16 of original size. We denote these feature map as $x$, $x_1$, $x_2$, $x_3$, $x_4$, respectively. After obtaining feature map $x_4$, we apply DRB on it and get feature map $y_4$ that is the beginning of the decoder stage. Similar to the encoder stage, the feature map $y_4$ will pass by four 2× upsample and four DRB to recover corresponding resolution, and we denote these feature map as $y_4$, $y_3$, $y_2$, $y_1$, $y$, respectively. It is worthy mentioning that we concatenate the feature map in the decoder stage with the feature map passed by attention gate in the encoder stage, which brings about the accumulation of different level features. In the last layer, we use convolution 1 × 1 to adjust the feature map channels to 1 and add the sigmoid function that projects the pixel value into range of 0 to 1 for mask generation. More details about the DRB and attention gate are given in following subsection.

## 2.1   Dense-Residual Block (DRB)

We present the dense-residual block in Fig. 2. It is composed of one convolution 1 × 1 and many inner blocks, which are combined in a residual way. The convolution 1 × 1 used here adjusts the number of feature map that fed into the inner block and controls input information. Each inner block stacks a series of convolution 3 × 3, BN, Relu in sequence and connects with the input densely. These dense connections are added into the output of intermediate layers for strengthening the intermediate supervision. As a result, the inner block eases the gradient vanishing problem caused by too many layers. On the other hand, the input can be accessed by all subsequent layers through skip connection, which realizes feature fusion among all levels. Such a multi-level feature fusion solves the problem of fixed receptive field to some degree.

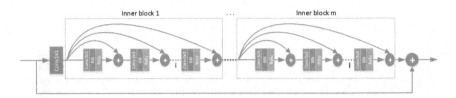

**Fig. 2.** The structure of the proposed dense-residual block. It contains $m$ inner blocks, where each inner block is composed of $i$ stacking series of convolution $3 \times 3$, BN, Relu.

The dense-residual block extracts the features from all levels with no need to change the feature map size. Relying on this unique characteristic, it can be easily integrated into existing convolution neural networks to improve the model performance. Notably, the number of inner blocks and the number of stacking series in each inner block should be changed according to specific tasks. For our experiments, we set the inner blocks as 3 and the stacking series as 2. We then use DRB as the basic module of our proposed network.

## 2.2    Attention Gate (AG)

We propose the attention gate to enhance network discriminative ability and its specific structure is shown in Fig. 3. Inspired by self-attention mechanism [10], our attention gate can focus on salient features like lesion area by itself without any external refer signal. The proposed attention gate mainly includes three steps. First, produce the key and the value for each feature map $(n, h, w)$. Second, compute the similarity between the key and the value, and then obtain corresponding attention probability. Third, calculate the weighted summation according to attention probability and output final attention map.

The feature map $(n, h, w)$ passes by a series of convolution to get the key (feature map $(n1, h, w)$). In our experiment, it is the stack of DRB, 2× downsample and 2× upsample. Concretely, the feature map $x_k$ is in pair with $y_k$, where $k$ equals to 1–4. We set the original feature map $(n, h, w)$ as the value. After obtaining the key and the value, we adjust their size to the universal $(n2, h, w)$ by one convolution $1 \times 1$ and BN. Then making the summation and Relu activation to enhance the nonlinearity. Another convolution $1 \times 1$ and BN are used to adjust size to $(1, h, w)$. The attention probability will be gained after a sigmoid projection on the resized feature map. Finally, we compute the weighted summation between the input feature map $(n, h, w)$ and the attention probability.

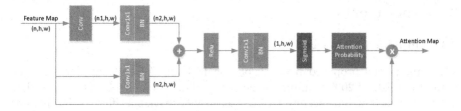

**Fig. 3.** The illustration of the proposed attention gate, where $(n, h, w)$ denotes the channel, height and width of the feature map, respectively.

The attention probability of salient area are usually higher than those in normal area. Therefore, the attention gate makes the network pay more attention to salient features and suppress the irrelevant area in feature map. The real useful features of the encoder stage like context information are passed to the decoder stage in attention way, which avoids the influence of too much unrelated information in medical images. In this way, the network discriminative ability gets improved.

### 2.3 Loss Function

During the network training, we propose a novel loss function based on the jaccard distance to tackle the class imbalance issue. Generally the pixels in lesion area are much less than in unrelated background area for medical images. If we only use cross entropy loss function in training, the network would barely learn the useful features or fully concentrate on the background area. To address this concern, our proposed loss function is defined as:

$$
L = -\frac{\alpha}{m^2} \sum_{1 \leq i,j \leq m} \left[ y_{ij}^* \cdot \log y_{ij} + \left(1 - y_{ij}^*\right) \log \left(1 - y_{ij}\right) \right] + \beta \cdot \left[ 1 - \frac{y_{ij}^* \cdot y_{ij}}{\left(y_{ij}^* + y_{ij} - y_{ij}^* \cdot y_{ij}\right)} \right].
\tag{1}
$$

where $y_{ij}^*$ is the label of pixel $(i, j)$ in given image $m \times m$, and $y_{ij}$ is the predicted value in the same position. $\alpha$, $\beta$ are the linear scale factor that control the effect of their own part. In our experiment, we set both $\alpha$ and $\beta$ equal to 0.5.

The jaccard distance measures the dissimilarity between two sets and its complimentary jaccard index is an evaluation metric for medical image segmentation. Here we introduce the jaccard distance (the right item in Eq. (1)) in our loss function. It serves as a regularization term to improve the segmentation performance. Meanwhile, the original cross entropy part (the left item in Eq. (1)) ensures the reliability of classification results in pixel-wise prediction process. The proposed loss function makes the network devoted to output results that are more similar to the ground truth, which alleviates the impact of the lesion-background imbalance.

# 3 Experiments

## 3.1 Implementation Details

We evaluate the proposed network on the ISIC 2017 Challenge dataset. The dataset consists of 2000 training images, 150 validation and 600 test images. The metrics we used include accuracy (AC), sensitivity (SE), specificity (SP), jaccard index (JA), dice coefficient (DI) according to official challenge requirements. We compute these metrics for each test image and report the average as the final result. These metrics are defined as follows:

$$AC = \frac{TP + TN}{TP + FP + TN + FN} \tag{2}$$

$$SE = \frac{TP}{TP + FN} \tag{3}$$

$$SP = \frac{TN}{TN + FP} \tag{4}$$

$$JA = \frac{TP}{TP + FN + FP} \tag{5}$$

$$DI = \frac{2 \cdot TP}{2 \cdot TP + FN + FP} \tag{6}$$

where $TP$, $TN$, $FP$, $FN$ are the number of true positive, true negative, false positive and false negative samples respectively. In our experiments, a lesion pixel is marked as true positive if prediction is a lesion, otherwise it is marked as false negative. A non-lesion pixel is marked as true negative if prediction is a non-lesion, otherwise marked as false positive.

All experiments are implemented on PyTorch library. Adam stochastic optimizer [3] is employed to train the network, where we set the initial learning rate as 0.0002, the momentum1 as 0.5 and momentum2 as 0.999. We train all models for 150 epochs from scratch. Concretely, we firstly train the model for 50 epochs with the initial learning rate, and then train for 100 epochs in a decayed learning rate. The learning rate decreases 1/100 in per decay epoch.

The original input size ranges from 540 × 722 to 4499 × 6748, to train the network in batches efficiently, we resize images proportionally to keep the aspect ratio whose width equals to 128. If the resized height is smaller than 128, we then pad the periphery with zero, otherwise it is center cropped to 128 × 128. This operation avoids the distortion caused by aspect ratio change effectively. Moreover, we perform data augmentation like flipping images horizontally and vertically, randomly changing the brightness, contrast and saturation of the image and image normalization. The model is trained on a single NVIDIA GTX 1080TI GPU.

## 3.2    Ablation Study

We investigate the effect of different part in our proposed network in Table 1. We firstly remove the DRB, attention gate, and replace the proposed loss function by traditional cross entropy as our benchmark. Then we add these components on the benchmark separately. To be more specific, we alternatively add DRB, or attention gate, or the proposed loss function, and we denoted these operations as with DRB, with AG, with proposed loss respectively. Finally, we integrate all these components together and report the results on the ISIC 2017 Test dataset. To make a fair comparison, all the networks are trained under the same condition as implementation details described.

**Table 1.** Ablation study of the dense-residual attention network. The higher value represents a better performance for the five used metrics.

| Model | Accuracy | Sensitivity | Specificity | Jaccard index | Dice coefficient |
| --- | --- | --- | --- | --- | --- |
| Benchmark | 0.949 | 0.809 | 0.988 | 0.711 | 0.801 |
| with DRB | 0.954 | 0.856 | 0.983 | 0.733 | 0.825 |
| with AG | 0.950 | 0.815 | **0.989** | 0.726 | 0.817 |
| with Proposed Loss | 0.950 | 0.821 | 0.986 | 0.715 | 0.809 |
| with All | **0.958** | **0.869** | 0.982 | **0.765** | **0.856** |

From the Table 1, we can see that the benchmark network yields the performance of AC 0.949, SE 0.809, SP 0.988, JA 0.711, DI 0.801. When we add DRB, the segmentation performance improved significantly, where SE increases nearly five percent and JA, DI increase two percent. The attention gate also improves the performance, resulting in a rise on all metrics compared with the benchmark, especially with the highest SP. In addition, if we replace the cross entropy with our proposed loss function, it leads an increase in SE from 0.809 to 0.821, which reveals the superiority in handling on class imbalance issue for medical images (lesion pixels are extremely less than non-lesion pixels in skin lesion segmentation). The performance can be further improved with all part integration, achieving the highest for AC, SE, JA and DI. Overall, our proposed DRB, attention gate and loss function improve the model performance effectively and the proposed network composed of these parts achieves the promising results for skin lesion segmentation.

## 3.3    Comparison with Other Methods

We compare our results with the state-of-the-art methods on the ISIC 2017 Test dataset in Table 2. It is noted that our network outperforms other methods without any post-processing operations or pretrained weights. In terms of AC and SP, we get approximately two and one percent gain separately. As for SE, a significant performance improvement is noted, exceeding nearly four percent than state-of-the-art methods, while JA and DI are equivalent to that of the compared best method. The experimental results validate the effectiveness of our proposed dense-residual attention network for skin lesion segmentation. Some visualization results are shown in Fig. 4.

**Table 2.** Comparison with state-of-the-art methods on the ISIC 2017 Test dataset.

| Method | Accuracy | Sensitivity | Specificity | Jaccard index | Dice coefficient |
|---|---|---|---|---|---|
| Ours | **0.958** | **0.869** | **0.982** | **0.765** | **0.856** |
| Venkatesh [8] | 0.936 | 0.830 | 0.976 | 0.764 | 0.856 |
| Yuan [9] | 0.934 | 0.825 | 0.975 | 0.765 | 0.849 |
| Berseth [2] | 0.932 | 0.820 | 0.978 | 0.762 | 0.847 |
| Menegola [4] | 0.931 | 0.817 | 0.970 | 0.754 | 0.839 |

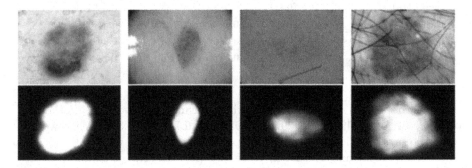

**Fig. 4.** Some image examples and corresponding outputs from the proposed network, where the first row is the original dermoscopy image and the second row is the segmentation result.

## 4   Conclusion

In this paper, we propose a dense-residual attention network that takes dermoscopy images with arbitrary size as input and outputs the predicted mask for skin lesion. The proposed network is end-to-end and doesn't need any post-processing operations or pretrained weights. Specifically, we propose the dense-residual block to deal with the problem of fixed receptive field and vanishing gradient in training (as often occurred in convolution neural networks). We also propose the attention gate to enhance the network discriminative ability and ensure the feature learning efficiency. Moreover, a novel loss function is introduced to mitigate the impact of pixel-level imbalance in skin lesion segmentation. We integrate these ideas together and propose a dense-residual attention network. The experimental results on ISIC 2017 Challenge dataset show the effectiveness of our proposed network. Further investigations including dilated convolution and group normalization will be explored in the future.

# References

1. Alom, M.Z., Hasan, M., Yakopcic, C., Taha, T.M., Asari, V.K.: Recurrent residual convolutional neural network based on U-Net (R2u-Net) for medical image segmentation. arXiv preprint arXiv:1802.06955 (2018)
2. Berseth, M.: Isic 2017-skin lesion analysis towards melanoma detection. arXiv preprint arXiv:1703.00523 (2017)
3. Kingma, D.P., Ba, J.: Adam: A method for stochastic optimization. arXiv preprint arXiv:1412.6980 (2014)
4. Menegola, A., Tavares, J., Fornaciali, M., Li, L.T., Avila, S., Valle, E.: Recod titans at ISIC challenge 2017. arXiv preprint arXiv:1703.04819 (2017)
5. Oktay, O., et al.: Attention U-Net: learning where to look for the pancreas. arXiv preprint arXiv:1804.03999 (2018)
6. Ronneberger, O., Fischer, P., Brox, T.: U-Net: convolutional networks for biomedical image segmentation. In: Navab, N., Hornegger, J., Wells, W.M., Frangi, A.F. (eds.) MICCAI 2015. LNCS, vol. 9351, pp. 234–241. Springer, Cham (2015). https://doi.org/10.1007/978-3-319-24574-4_28
7. Siegel, R.L., Miller, K.D., Jemal, A.: Cancer statistics, 2019. CA: Cancer J. Clin. **69**, 7–34 (2019)
8. Venkatesh, G.M., Naresh, Y.G., Little, S., O'Connor, N.E.: A deep residual architecture for skin lesion segmentation. In: Stoyanov, D., et al. (eds.) CARE/CLIP/OR 2.0/ISIC -2018. LNCS, vol. 11041, pp. 277–284. Springer, Cham (2018). https://doi.org/10.1007/978-3-030-01201-4_30
9. Yuan, Y., Lo, Y.C.: Improving dermoscopic image segmentation with enhanced convolutional-deconvolutional networks. IEEE J. Biomed. Health Inform. **23**, 519–526 (2017)
10. Zhang, H., Goodfellow, I., Metaxas, D., Odena, A.: Self-attention generative adversarial networks. arXiv preprint arXiv:1805.08318 (2018)

# Confounder-Aware Visualization of ConvNets

Qingyu Zhao[1]([✉]), Ehsan Adeli[1], Adolf Pfefferbaum[1,2], Edith V. Sullivan[1], and Kilian M. Pohl[1,2]

[1] School of Medicine, Stanford University, Stanford, USA
qingyuz@stanford.edu
[2] Center of Health Sciences, SRI International, Menlo Park, USA

**Abstract.** With recent advances in deep learning, neuroimaging studies increasingly rely on convolutional networks (ConvNets) to predict diagnosis based on MR images. To gain a better understanding of how a disease impacts the brain, the studies visualize the salience maps of the ConvNet highlighting voxels within the brain majorly contributing to the prediction. However, these salience maps are generally confounded, i.e., some salient regions are more predictive of confounding variables (such as age) than the diagnosis. To avoid such misinterpretation, we propose in this paper an approach that aims to visualize confounder-free saliency maps that only highlight voxels predictive of the diagnosis. The approach incorporates univariate statistical tests to identify confounding effects within the intermediate features learned by ConvNet. The influence from the subset of confounded features is then removed by a novel partial back-propagation procedure. We use this two-step approach to visualize confounder-free saliency maps extracted from synthetic and two real datasets. These experiments reveal the potential of our visualization in producing unbiased model-interpretation.

## 1 Introduction

The development of deep-learning technologies in medicine is advancing rapidly [1]. Leveraging labeled big data and enhanced computational power, deep convolutional neural networks have been applied in many neuroscience studies to accurately classify patients with brain diseases from normal controls based on their MR images [1,2]. State-of-the-art saliency visualization techniques are used to interpret the trained model and to visualize specific brain regions that significantly contribute to the classification [2]. The resulting saliency map therefore provides fine-grained insights into how the disease may impact the human brain.

Despite the promises of deep learning, there are formidable obstacles and pitfalls [1,3]. One of the most critical challenges is the algorithmic bias introduced by the model towards confounding factors in the study [4]. A confounding factor

---

Q. Zhao and E. Adeli—Equal contribution.
Source code: github.com/QingyuZhao/Confounder-Aware-CNN-Visualization.git.

© Springer Nature Switzerland AG 2019
H.-I. Suk et al. (Eds.): MLMI 2019, LNCS 11861, pp. 328–336, 2019.
https://doi.org/10.1007/978-3-030-32692-0_38

(or confounder) correlates with both the dependent variable (group label) and independent variable (MR image) causing spurious association. For instance, if the age distribution of the disease group is different from that of the normal controls, age might become a potential confounder because one cannot differentiate whether the trained model characterizes neurodegeneration caused by the disease or by normal aging.

Since the end-to-end training scheme disfavors any additional intervention, controlling for confounding effects in deep learning is inherently difficult. This often leads to misinterpretation of the trained model during visualization: while some salient regions correspond to true impact of the disease, others are potentially linked to the confounders. In this paper, we present an approach that identifies confounding effects within a trained ConvNet and removes them to produce confounder-free visualization of the model. The central idea is first to detect confounding effects in each intermediate feature via univariate statistical testing. Then, the influence of confounded features is removed from the saliency map by a novel "partial back-propagation" operation, which can be intuitively explained by a chain-rule derivation on voxelwise saliency scores. This operation is efficiently implemented with a model refactorization trick. We apply our visualization procedure to interpret ConvNet classifiers trained on a synthetic dataset with known confounding effects and on two real datasets, i.e., MRIs of 345 adults for analyzing Human Immunodeficiency Virus (HIV) effects on the brain and MRIs of 674 adolescents for analyzing sexual dimorphism. In all three experiments, our visualization shows the potential in producing unbiased saliency maps compared to traditional visualization techniques.

## 2   Confounder-Aware Saliency Visualization

We base our approach on the saliency visualization proposed in [5]. Given an MR image $\mathcal{I}$ and a trained ConvNet model, saliency visualization produces a voxelwise saliency map specific to $\mathcal{I}$ indicating important regions that strongly impact the classification decision. Without loss of generality, we assume a ConvNet model is trained for a binary classification task (pipeline generalizable to multi-group classification and regression), where the prediction output is a continuous score $s \in [0, 1]$. Then, the saliency value at voxel $v$ is computed as the partial derivative $|\partial s / \partial \mathcal{I}_v|$. Intuitively, it quantifies how the prediction changes with respect to a small change in the intensity value at voxel $v$. Computationally, this quantity can be computed efficiently using back-propagation.

As discussed, when the ConvNet is confounded, some salient regions may actually contribute to the prediction of confounding variables rather than the group label. To address this issue, we propose a two-step approach to remove confounding effects from the saliency map enabling an unbiased interpretation of a trained ConvNet. To do this, we assume that a typical ConvNet architecture is composed of an encoder and a predictor. The encoder contains convolutional layers (including their variants and related operations such as pooling, batch normalization and ReLU) that extract a fixed-length feature vector $\boldsymbol{f}_i \in \mathbb{R}^M = [f_i^1, ..., f_i^M]$ from the $i^{th}$ training image. The predictor, usually a fully connected network, takes the $M$ features as input and produces a prediction score $s_i$ for image $i$. To disentangle confounding effects from the saliency map, we propose in Sect. 2.1 to first test each of the $M$ features separately for confounding effects using a general linear model (GLM). Next, the influence from the subset of features with significant confounding effects can be removed from the saliency map by performing a novel partial back-propagation procedure based on an intuitive chain-rule derivation (Sect. 2.2).

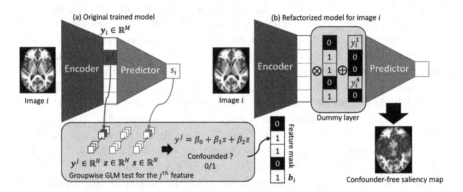

**Fig. 1.** Our confounder-aware visualization is composed two steps: (a) A GLM test is performed on each individual feature collected over all training images to detect confounding effects. (b) For each image, the model is refactorized to fix the value of confounded features, thereby enabling a partial back-propagation to derive a confounder-free saliency map.

## 2.1   Univariate Test for Identifying Confounding Effects

This section introduces a way to test for the presence of confounding effect within a specific feature. Let $\boldsymbol{f}^j = [f_1^j, ..., f_N^j]$ denote the $j^{th}$ feature derived from all $N$ training images. Likewise, denote $\boldsymbol{s} = [s_1, ..., s_N]$ as the $N$ prediction scores and $\boldsymbol{z} = [z_1, ..., z_N]$ as a confounding variable (e.g., age of the $N$ subjects). In this work, we use GLM [6] to perform a group-level statistical test for detecting whether the relationship between $\boldsymbol{s}$ and $\boldsymbol{f}^j$ is confounded by $\boldsymbol{z}$. Specifically, GLM decomposes the variance in $\boldsymbol{f}^j$ into variance explained by $\boldsymbol{s}$ and variance explained by $\boldsymbol{z}$. The model reads

$$\boldsymbol{f}^j = \beta_0 + \beta_1 \boldsymbol{s} + \beta_2 \boldsymbol{z}. \tag{1}$$

We claim feature $\boldsymbol{f}^j$ is confounded by $\boldsymbol{z}$ if the null hypothesis that linear coefficient $\beta_2$ is zero can be rejected (e.g., $p < 0.05$ by $t$-test). In other words, when the variance in $\boldsymbol{f}^j$ is partially explained by $\boldsymbol{z}$, $\boldsymbol{f}^j$ potentially contributes to the prediction of the confounder rather than the key variable of interest. This analysis can be extended to handle multiple confounding variables, where all confounders are included in the GLM as independent covariates. Then, $\boldsymbol{f}^j$ is confounded when the $p$-value for at least one confounder is significant. Note, this model is a specific instance of the mediation model [7], a popular model for confounding analysis. However, our model makes fewer assumptions so that it is more sensitive in detecting confounding effects than the mediation model. We also emphasize that such confounding analysis can only be performed on the feature-level instead of voxel-level. Unlike features encoding geometric patterns that are commensurate within a group, voxel intensities are only meaningful within a neighborhood but variant across MRIs. As such, removing confounding effects based on feature-analysis is prevalent in traditional feature-based models (non-deep-learning models) [8,9].

Repeating the above analysis for all $M$ features, we generate a binary mask $\boldsymbol{b} \in [0,1]^M = [b^1, ..., b^M]$, where $b^j = 0$ indicates the presence of confounding effect in the $j^{th}$ feature and $b_j = 1$ otherwise.

## 2.2   Visualization via Partial Back-Propagation

To generate a saliency map unbiased towards the subset of confounded features, we further investigate the voxelwise partial derivative. Based on the chain-rule,

$$\frac{\partial s_i}{\partial \mathcal{I}_v} = \frac{\partial s_i(f_i^1, ..., f_i^M)}{\partial \mathcal{I}_v} = \sum_{j=1}^{M} \frac{\partial s_i}{\partial f_i^j} \frac{\partial f_i^j}{\partial \mathcal{I}_v}. \tag{2}$$

Equation (2) factorizes the voxelwise partial derivative with respect to the $M$ features, where each $\partial s_i / \partial f_i^j$ quantifies the impact of the $j^{th}$ feature on the prediction. Therefore, to derive a confounder-free saliency map, we set this impact to zero for the confounded features. In doing so, the saliency score can be computed as

$$\sum_{j=1}^{M} b^j \frac{\partial s_i}{\partial f_i^j} \frac{\partial f_i^j}{\partial \mathcal{I}_v}. \tag{3}$$

Computationally, this corresponds to a partial back-propagation procedure, where the gradient is only back-propagated through the un-confounded features.

**The Refactorization Trick.** We show that performing the partial back-propagation for a training image $\mathcal{I}$ can be implemented by refactorizing the trained ConvNet model and then applying the original visualization pipeline of full back-propagation. As enforcing a zero $\partial f_i^j / \partial \mathcal{I}_v$ is equivalent to fixing $f_i^j$ to a constant value independent of the input image, we design a dummy layer $\mathcal{L}$ between the encoder and the predictor that performs $\mathcal{L}(\boldsymbol{x}) = \boldsymbol{x} \otimes \boldsymbol{b}_i \oplus ((1 - \boldsymbol{b}_i) \otimes \boldsymbol{y}_i)$, where $\otimes$ and $\oplus$ denote element-wise operators, and $\boldsymbol{y}_i$ is a constant feature vector for image $i$ pre-computed by the trained ConvNet. As shown in Fig. 1b, the dummy layer fixes the value of confounded features while keeping un-confounded features dependent on the input image. As such, the partial back-propagation of Eq. (3) can by simply computed by running the full back-propagation on the refactorized model. Note, model refactorization is performed for each MR image independently to yield subject-specific saliency maps.

## 3  Experiments

We first performed synthetic experiments, in which image data were imputed by known confounding effects so that we could test whether the proposed approach can successfully remove those effects during visualization. Next, we applied the approach to two real datasets to visualize (1) the impact of HIV on brain structures while controlling for aging effects; (2) sexual dimorphism during adolescence while controlling for 'puberty stage'.

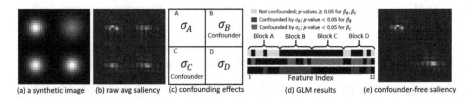

(a) a synthetic image     (b) raw avg saliency     (c) confounding effects          (d) GLM results          (e) confounder-free saliency

**Fig. 2.** Synthetic experiments: (a) Each synthetic image contains 4 Gaussians that are created differently between the two groups; (b) Average saliency map produced by the original visualization pipeline; (c) Widths of the two off-diagonal Gaussians are considered as confounders; (d) GLM identifies selective features, mainly in Blocks B and C, as confounded; (e) Removing the confounded features in the visualization leads to a confounder-free saliency map. (Color figure online)

### 3.1  Synthetic Data

We first generated a synthetic dataset containing two groups. Each group consisted of 512 2D images (dimension: $32 \times 32$ pixels). Each image was generated by 4 Gaussians (Fig. 2a), the width of which was controlled by the standard deviation $\sigma$. For each image of Group 1, we sampled $\sigma$ from the uniform distribution $\mathcal{U}(2,6)$. Images of Group 2 generally had wider distributions as we sampled from $\mathcal{U}(4,8)$ instead. To predict group labels from the synthetic images, we constructed a simple ConvNet with the encoder consisting of 3 stacks of $2*2$ convolution/ReLu/max-pooling layers and producing 32 intermediate features. The fully-connected predictor had one hidden layer of dimension 16 with tanh as the non-linear activation function. We trained the network for binary classification on the entire synthetic dataset as the focus here was to interpret the trained model as opposed to measuring classification accuracy. With the trained ConvNet, we first applied the original visualization pipeline to each image and averaged the resulting subject-specific saliency maps. The average saliency map shown in Fig. 2b indicates that all 4 Gaussians contributed to the classification.

Next, we viewed the width of the two off-diagonal Gaussians, i.e., the standard deviations $\sigma_B$ of Block B and $\sigma_C$ of Block C as confounders. Based on Eq. 1, we then tested the presence of confounding effects in each of the 32 intermediate features with the following GLM: $f^j = \beta_0 + \beta_1 s + \beta_B \sigma_B + \beta_C \sigma_C$. The results revealed that all features extracted from Blocks B and C were detected as confounded ($p < 0.05$ for either $\beta_B$ or $\beta_C$), while only features from Blocks A and D were identified as unconfounded ($p \geq 0.05$ for both $\beta_B$ and $\beta_C$). We can see that our conservative test was sensitive in detecting confounding effects (no false negative but several false positives), thereby potentially removing some features representing true group difference. Such trade-off can be controlled by the $p$-value threshold used in the GLM tests. Finally, using the binary mask (yellow mask in Fig. 2d) for partial back-propagation, we produced a confounder-free average saliency map (Fig. 2e) that successfully removed the confounding effects.

## 3.2   Visualizing HIV Effects

The second experiment examined the impact of HIV on the human brain. The classification was performed on the T1-weighted MRI data of 223 control subjects (CTRL) and 122 HIV patients [8]. Participants ranged in age between 18–86 years, and there was a significant age difference between CTRL and HIV subjects (CTRL: $45 \pm 17$, HIV: $51 \pm 8.3$, $p < 0.001$ by two-sample $t$-test). As HIV has been frequently suggested to accelerate brain aging [10], age is therefore a confounder that needs to be controlled for when interpreting the saliency map associated with the trained classifier.

**Preprocessing and Classification.** The MR images were first preprocessed by denoising, bias field correction, skull striping, affine registration to the SRI24 template (which accounts for differences in head size), and re-scaling to a $64 \times 64 \times 64$ volume [8]. Even though the present study focused on the visualization technique, we measured the classification accuracy as a sanity check via 5-fold cross validation. To ensure the classifier can reasonably learn the group difference between HIV and CTRL subjects, the training dataset was augmented by random shifting (within one-voxel distance), rotation (within one degree) in all 3 directions, and left-right flipping. Note, the flipping was based on the assumption that HIV infection affects the brain bilaterally [8]. The data augmentation resulted in a balanced training set of 1024 CTRLs and 1024 HIVs.

As the flipping removed left-right orientation, the ConvNet was built on half of the 3D volume containing one hemisphere. The encoder contained 4 stacks of $2*2*2$ 3D convolution/ReLu/batch-normalization/max-pooling layers yielding 4096 intermediate features. The fully-connected predictor had 2 hidden layers of dimension (64, 32) with tanh as the non-linear activation function. An L2-regularization ($\lambda = 0.1$) was applied to all fully-connected layers. Based on this ConvNet architecture, we achieved 73% normalized accuracy for HIV/CTRL classification, which was comparable to other recent studies on this dataset [8].

**Model Visualization.** To visualize the HIV effect, we re-trained the ConvNet on a dataset of 1024 CTRLs and 1024 HIVs augmented from the entire dataset of 345 MRIs. We first visualized the average saliency map produced by the original visualization pipeline. Since the ConvNet operated on only one hemisphere, we mirrored the resulting average saliency map to the other hemisphere to create bilaterally symmetric display and overlaid it on the SRI24 T1 atlas (Fig. 3a). For comparison, we then visualized the confounder-free saliency map produced by our approach. Specifically, we tested each of the 4096 features with $f^j = \beta_0 + \beta_1 s + \beta_2 age$, and 804 were identified to be confounded by age. Figure 3b shows the saliency map after removing aging effects, and Fig. 3c shows that saliency at the posterior ventricle (red regions) was attenuated by our approach indicating those regions contained aging effects instead of HIV effects. This finding is consistent with current concept that the ventricular volume significantly increases with age [11].

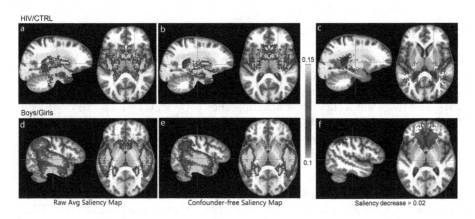

**Fig. 3.** Visualization of ConvNets trained for HIV/CTRL classification (top row) and sexual dimorphism (bottom row). (Color figure online)

### 3.3 Visualizing Sexual Dimorphism

The third experiment aimed to improve understanding of sexual dimorphism in brain development that emerges during adolescence. The classification was performed on the baseline T1 MR images of 334 boys and 340 girls (age 12–21) from the National Consortium on Alcohol and NeuroDevelopment in Adolescence (NCANDA) [12]. All subjects met the no-to-low alcohol drinking criteria of the study, and there was no significant age-difference between boys and girls ($p > 0.5$ two-sample $t$-test). As puberty stage [12] of girls was significantly higher than boys during adolescence, the pubertal development score (PDS: boys $2.86 \pm 0.7$, girls $3.41 \pm 0.6$, $p < 0.001$ by two-sample $t$-test) was a potential confounder of the study.

All experimental setups complied with the previous HIV study. As the first attempt of predicting sex on the NCANDA data, we achieved 89.5% normalized accuracy based on a 5-fold cross-validation. The original saliency map produced for the ConvNet trained on the entire augmented dataset is shown in Fig. 3d.

After testing and removing PDS effects, the confounder-free saliency map is shown in Fig. 3e. Consistent with existing adolescence literature, sex difference was mainly found in the temporal lobe [13]. Figure 3f indicates PDS effects mainly existed in the frontal and inferior parietal region. Another interesting observation is in the caudate, which has been frequently reported as proportionately larger in female participants across different ages [7]. As shown in our results, the saliency at the caudate region attenuated after removing confounding effects, suggesting a potential compounding effect of PDS in that region.

## 4    Discussion and Conclusion

In this paper, we introduced a novel approach for confounder-free visualization and interpretation of a trained ConvNet. By performing partial back-propagation with respect to a set of unconfounded intermediate features, the approach disentangled true group difference from confounding effects and produced unbiased saliency maps. We successfully illustrated its usage on a synthetic dataset with ground-truth confounding effects and two real neuroimaging datasets. Because our approach is a type of post-hoc analyses with respect to a trained model, further extension could potentially integrate similar confounder-control procedures during model-training time to fully explore unbiased group differences within a dataset.

**Acknowledgements..** This research was supported in part by NIH grants AA017347, AA005965, AA010723, AA021697, AA013521, AA026762 and MH113406.

## References

1. Topol, E.J.: High-performance medicine: the convergence of human and artificial intelligence. Nat. Med. **25**(1), 44–56 (2019)
2. Esmaeilzadeh, S., Belivanis, D.I., Pohl, K.M., Adeli, E.: End-to-end Alzheimer's disease diagnosis and biomarker identification. In: Shi, Y., Suk, H.-I., Liu, M. (eds.) MLMI 2018. LNCS, vol. 11046, pp. 337–345. Springer, Cham (2018). https://doi.org/10.1007/978-3-030-00919-9_39
3. He, J., Baxter, S.L., Xu, J., Zhou, X., Zhang, K.: The practical implementation of artificial intelligence technologies in medicine. Nat. Med. **25**(1), 30–36 (2019)
4. Pourhoseingholi, M.A., Baghestani, A.R., Vahedi, M.: How to control confounding effects by statistical analysis. Gastroenterol. Hepatol. Bed Bench **5**(2), 79–83 (2012)
5. Simonyan, K., et al.: Deep inside convolutional networks: Visualising image classification models and saliency maps. CoRR abs/1312.6034 (2013)
6. Dobson, A.J.: An Introduction to Generalized Linear Models. Chapman and Hall, New York (1990)
7. MacKinnon, D.P.: Introduction to Statistical Mediation Analysis. Erlbaum, New York (2008)
8. Adeli, E., et al.: Chained regularization for identifying brain patterns specific to HIV infection. Neuroimage **183**, 425–437 (2018)

9. Park, S.H., et al.: Alcohol use effects on adolescent brain development revealed by simultaneously removing confounding factors, identifying morphometric patterns, and classifying individuals. Sci. Rep. **8**(1), 1–14 (2018)
10. Cole, J., et al.: Increased brain-predicted aging in treated HIV disease. Neurology **88**(14), 1349–1357 (2017)
11. Kaye, J.A., et al.: The significance of age-related enlargement of the cerebral ventricles in healthy men and women measured by quantitative computed X-ray tomography. J. Am. Geriatr. Soc. **40**(3), 225–31 (1992)
12. Brown, S., Brumback, T., Tomlinson, K., et al.: The national consortium on alcohol and neurodevelopment in adolescence (NCANDA): a multisite study of adolescent development and substance use. J. Stud. Alcohol Drugs **76**(6), 895–908 (2015)
13. Sowell, E.R., Trauner, D.A., Gamst, A., Jernigan, T.L.: Development of cortical and subcortical brain structures in childhood and adolescence: a structural MRI study. Dev. Med. Child Neurol. **44**(1), 4–16 (2002)

# Detecting Lesion Bounding Ellipses
# with Gaussian Proposal Networks

Yi Li[✉]🆔

GreyBird Ventures LLC, 31 Pond View Lane, Concord, MA 01742, USA
yil8@uci.edu

**Abstract.** Lesions characterized by computed tomography (CT) scans, are arguably often elliptical objects. However, current lesion detection systems are predominantly adopted from the popular Region Proposal Networks (RPNs) [9] that only propose bounding boxes without fully leveraging the elliptical geometry of lesions. In this paper, we present Gaussian Proposal Networks (GPNs), a novel extension to RPNs, to detect lesion bounding ellipses. Instead of directly regressing the rotation angle of the ellipse as the common practice, GPN represents bounding ellipses as 2D Gaussian distributions on the image plane and minimizes the Kullback-Leibler (KL) divergence between the proposed Gaussian and the ground truth Gaussian for object localization. Experiments on the DeepLesion [13] dataset show that GPN significantly outperforms RPN for lesion bounding ellipse detection thanks to lower localization error.

**Keywords:** Lesion detection · Bounding ellipses · Deep learning

## 1 Introduction

Current state-of-the-art object detection systems are predominantly based on deep neural networks that learn to propose object regions which are usually represented by bounding boxes [1,5,9]. Region Proposal Networks (RPNs), first introduced in Faster R-CNN [9], simultaneously predicts the objectness and region bounds at every predefined anchor location on a grid of feature map. When object regions are annotated as bounding boxes, the region bounds in RPN are defined by the two center coordinates, the width and the height of the object region with respect to the corresponding anchor. In this case, regressing the region bounds is directly optimize the overlap between the proposed bounding box and the ground truth bounding box.

---

This work was partially performed at Baidu Research.

---

**Electronic supplementary material** The online version of this chapter (https://doi.org/10.1007/978-3-030-32692-0_39) contains supplementary material, which is available to authorized users.

© Springer Nature Switzerland AG 2019
H.-I. Suk et al. (Eds.): MLMI 2019, LNCS 11861, pp. 337–344, 2019.
https://doi.org/10.1007/978-3-030-32692-0_39

Lesions characterized by computed tomography (CT) scans are often elliptical and additional geometry information about the lesion regions may be
annotated besides bounding boxes. For example, the large-scale medical imaging dataset DeepLesion [13] recently released from NIH is annotated with the
response evaluation criteria in solid tumors (RECIST) diameters. Each RECIST-
diameter annotation consists of two axies, the first one measures the longest
diameter of the lesion and the second one measures the longest diameter perpendicular to the first axis. Therefore, the RECIST diameters closely represent
the major and minor axes of a bounding ellipse of the lesion.

Extensions for bounding ellipse detection based on the RPN framework have
been introduced to predict the rotation angle of the object [4,7]. However, it is
not trivial to directly optimizing the overlap between the proposed ellipse and
the ground truth ellipse using the rotation angle. Most of the methods directly
use an ellipse regressor to minimize the difference between the proposed angle
and the ground truth angle, e.g. in the co/tangent domain [4,7], as an additional
term in the regression loss for localization. We argue that directly regressing the
rotation angle is not optimal for bounding ellipse localization, when the essential
goal is to optimize the overlap between the proposed ellipse and the ground truth
ellipse. The rotation angle affects the overlap between the two ellipses differently,
depending on whether the ratio of the major axis to the minor axis, i.e. the aspect
ratio, is significantly larger than 1. Supplementary Fig. 1 shows two illustrative
examples.

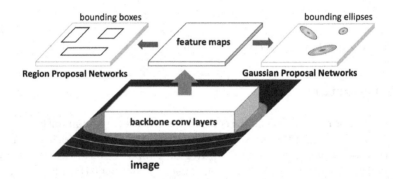

**Fig. 1.** Comparison between Region Proposal Networks and Gaussian Proposal Networks. Instead of proposing bounding boxes, Gaussian Proposal Networks propose
bounding ellipses as 2D Gaussian distributions on the image plane and use a single KL
divergence loss for object localization.

In this work, we present Gaussian Proposal Networks (GPNs) that learn
to propose bounding ellipses as 2D Gaussian distributions on the image plane.
Figure 1 shows an illustrative comparison between GPN and RPN. Unlike most
of the extensions to the RPN framework that introduce an additional term to
directly regress the rotation angle for object localization, GPN minimizes the

Kullback-Leibler (KL) divergence between the proposed Gaussian distribution and the ground truth Gaussian distribution as one single loss for localization. KL divergence directly measures the overlap of one distribution with respect to a reference distribution. When the two distributions are Gaussian, KL divergence has analytical form and is differentiable. Therefore, GPN can be readily implemented with standard automatic differentiation packages [8] and trained with back-propagation algorithm. We also show that when the rotation angle is 0, the KL divergence loss approximately incarnates the regression loss used in the RPN framework for bounding box localization. We experiment the efficacy of GPN for detecting lesion bounding ellipses on the DeepLesion [13] dataset. Compared to RPN with the additional regression loss to predict the rotation angle, GPN achieves significantly higher free-response receiver operating characteristics across two different experimental settings. Error analysis shows that GPN achieves significantly lower localization error compared to RPN. Further analysis on the distribution of predicted rotation angles from GPN supports our conjecture that it may not be necessary to regress the rotation angle when the ground truth bounding ellipse has similar lengths of major and minor axes.

## 2  Related Work

The design of GPN generally follows the principles of RPN [9]. RPN has a fully convolutional backbone network that processes the input image and generates a feature map grid. The feature vector of each position on the feature map is further processed with a $3 \times 3$ convolutional layer and then associated with potentially multiple anchors of various scales and aspect ratios. The ground truth regions of interest (RoIs) are then assigned to anchors that meet certain overlapping criteria, e.g. intersection over union (IoU) greater than 0.7. Finally, two separate $1 \times 1$ convolutional layers are used to predict the objectness scores and the bounding box offsets of the RoIs with respect to the anchors. RPN is jointly trained with one classification loss and multiple smoothed L1 regression losses for localization.

Compared to classical RPN, GPN proposes bounding ellipses as 2D Gaussian distributions and minimizes a single KL divergence loss between two Gaussian distributions for localization. GPN could be applied with the same extensions that apply to RPN, such as training with multi-scale feature maps [5], online hard negative mining [10] and focal loss [6]. However, in the Faster R-CNN two-stage detector, a second R-CNN classifier [9] is appended to RPN through a RoI pooling layer [3] and classifies each RoI into object categories or background. Performing RoI pooling with bounding ellipses is nontrivial and is beyond the scope of this paper. Thus, GPN currently only applies to one-stage detectors.

Bounding ellipse annotation has been widely used in human faces detection [4,7]. We discuss the differences and connections between GPN and other bounding ellipse detectors with more details in the Supplementary.

# 3  Gaussian Proposal Networks (GPNs)

This section describes the mathematical overview of GPN. The exact details of derivation and implementation of GPN is given in the Supplementary.

The equation of an ellipse in a 2D coordinate system without rotation is given by

$$\frac{(x - \mu_x)^2}{\sigma_x^2} + \frac{(y - \mu_y)^2}{\sigma_y^2} = 1, \tag{1}$$

where we denote $\mu_x, \mu_y$ as the center coordinates of the ellipse, and $\sigma_x, \sigma_y$ as the lengths of semi-axes along $x$ and $y$ axes.

The probability density function of a 2D Gaussian distribution is given by

$$f(\mathbf{x}|\boldsymbol{\mu}, \boldsymbol{\Sigma}) = \frac{\exp(-\frac{1}{2}(\mathbf{x} - \boldsymbol{\mu})^\mathsf{T}\boldsymbol{\Sigma}^{-1}(\mathbf{x} - \boldsymbol{\mu}))}{2\pi|\boldsymbol{\Sigma}|^{\frac{1}{2}}}, \tag{2}$$

where $\mathbf{x}$ is the vector representation of coordinates $(x, y)$, $\boldsymbol{\mu}$ is the mean, $\boldsymbol{\Sigma}$ is the covariance matrix and $|\boldsymbol{\Sigma}|$ is the determinant of the covariance matrix.

When the major axis of the ellipse is rotated by an angle $\theta$ with respect to the $x$ axis, we use a rotation matrix $R(\theta)$ to transform the coordinate system. Therefore, we can use a 2D Gaussian distribution in the $(x, y)$ coordinate system parameterized by

$$\boldsymbol{\mu} = \begin{bmatrix} \mu_x \\ \mu_y \end{bmatrix}, \boldsymbol{\Sigma}^{-1} = R^\mathsf{T}(\theta) \begin{bmatrix} \frac{1}{\sigma_l^2} & 0 \\ 0 & \frac{1}{\sigma_s^2} \end{bmatrix} R(\theta), \tag{3}$$

to represent the ellipse centered at $(\mu_x, \mu_y)$, with semi-major and semi-minor axes of lengths $(\sigma_l, \sigma_s)$, and a rotation angle of $\theta$ between its major axis and the $x$ axis, where $\theta \in [-\frac{\pi}{2}, \frac{\pi}{2}]$. The goal of GPN is to propose bounding ellipses such that their parameters, $(\mu_x, \mu_y, \sigma_l, \sigma_s, \theta)$, match the ground truth ellipses through the criteria of KL divergence.

The KL divergence between a proposed 2D Gaussian distribution $\mathcal{N}_p$ and a target 2D Gaussian distribution $\mathcal{N}_t$ is given by [2]

$$D_{\mathrm{KL}}(\mathcal{N}_t||\mathcal{N}_p) = \frac{1}{2}\left[\mathrm{tr}(\boldsymbol{\Sigma}_p^{-1}\boldsymbol{\Sigma}_t) + (\boldsymbol{\mu}_p - \boldsymbol{\mu}_t)^\mathsf{T}\boldsymbol{\Sigma}_p^{-1}(\boldsymbol{\mu}_p - \boldsymbol{\mu}_t) + \ln\frac{|\boldsymbol{\Sigma}_p|}{|\boldsymbol{\Sigma}_t|} - 2\right], \tag{4}$$

where $\mathrm{tr}(\mathbf{X})$ is the trace of matrix $\mathbf{X}$.

Assuming $\mathcal{N}_p$ and $\mathcal{N}_t$ are parameterized by $(\mu_{x_p}, \mu_{y_p}, \sigma_{l_p}, \sigma_{s_p}, \theta_p)$ and $(\mu_{x_t}, \mu_{y_t}, \sigma_{l_t}, \sigma_{s_t}, \theta_t)$ following Eq. 3, we can derive each term in Eq. 4 as

$$\mathrm{tr}(\boldsymbol{\Sigma}_p^{-1}\boldsymbol{\Sigma}_t) = \cos^2\!\varDelta\theta\,\frac{\sigma_{l_t}^2}{\sigma_{l_p}^2} + \cos^2\!\varDelta\theta\,\frac{\sigma_{s_t}^2}{\sigma_{s_p}^2} + \sin^2\!\varDelta\theta\,\frac{\sigma_{l_t}^2}{\sigma_{s_p}^2} + \sin^2\!\varDelta\theta\,\frac{\sigma_{s_t}^2}{\sigma_{l_p}^2}, \tag{5}$$

$$(\boldsymbol{\mu}_p - \boldsymbol{\mu}_t)^\mathsf{T}\boldsymbol{\Sigma}_p^{-1}(\boldsymbol{\mu}_p - \boldsymbol{\mu}_t) = \frac{(\cos\theta_p\varDelta x + \sin\theta_p\varDelta y)^2}{\sigma_{l_p}^2} + \frac{(\cos\theta_p\varDelta y - \sin\theta_p\varDelta x)^2}{\sigma_{s_p}^2}, \tag{6}$$

$$\ln\frac{|\boldsymbol{\Sigma}_p|}{|\boldsymbol{\Sigma}_t|} = \ln\frac{\sigma_{l_p}^2}{\sigma_{l_t}^2} + \ln\frac{\sigma_{s_p}^2}{\sigma_{s_t}^2}, \tag{7}$$

where we define

$$\Delta\theta = \theta_p - \theta_t, \Delta x = \mu_{x_p} - \mu_{x_t}, \Delta y = \mu_{y_p} - \mu_{y_t}. \tag{8}$$

The general form of KL divergence looks rather complex. However, if we omit the rotation angle, i.e. assuming $\theta_p$ and $\theta_t$ are always 0, then $\sigma_l$ and $\sigma_s$ are actually the half width and the half height of the bounding box that tightly surrounds the bounding ellipse. We show the KL divergence loss approximately incarnates the regression loss in the RPN framework when the rotation angle is 0 in the Supplementary. GPN is open sourced at https://github.com/baidu-research/GPN.

## 4   Experiments

We present comprehensive evaluation of GPN for detecting lesion bounding ellipses on the DeepLesion dataset [13]. We first introduce some details about the DeepLesion dataset in Sect. 4.1, and experiments setup in Sect. 4.2. Next, we show GPN significantly outperforms RPN for bounding ellipse detection across two different settings in Sect. 4.3. Finally, we present a comprehensive error analysis in Sect. 4.4.

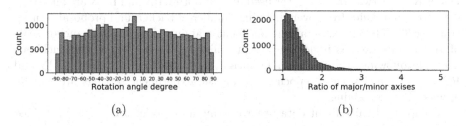

(a)                                        (b)

**Fig. 2.** (a) The distribution of the rotation angles between the lesion's major axis and the x axis in degree, (b) the distribution of lesions' aspect ratios.

### 4.1   DeepLesion Dataset

DeepLesion is a large-scale medical imaging dataset recently released from NIH [13]. It contains 32,735 lesions in 32,120 CT slice images from 4,427 unique patients. More than 99% of the slice images are $512 \times 512$ pixels. Each lesion is annotated with two response evaluation criteria in solid tumors (RECIST) diameters. The first one measures the longest diameter of the lesion and the second one measures the longest diameter perpendicular to the first diameter, so they closely represent the major and minor axes of a bounding ellipse, and we use this notion thereafter. We note this assumption may be inaccurate when the center of the minor axis is not aligned with the center of the major axis. However, we found that for more than 90% of the RECIST-diameter annotations, the center of the minor axis is within the middle 20% range of the major axis, so we think the assumption approximately holds. DeepLesion has a wide range of rotation angles and aspect ratios, therefore it is particularly challenge for bounding ellipse detection and localization. Figure 2a shows the distribution of the rotation angles between the lesion's major axis and the x-axis. Figure 2b shows the distribution of lesions' aspect ratios.

## 4.2  Experiments Setup

We follow the practices from [12] to convert the raw slice images with pixel value in Hounsfield Unit (HU) into $512 \times 512$ three channel images with pixel values between 0 and 255. We use the official split from DeepLesion for training (70%), validation (15%), and test (15%). We compute intersection over union (IoU) between ellipses by rasterizing ellipses first and then counting the pixel overlaps.

We use RPN as our baseline to evaluate lesion bounding ellipses detection, since it shares the same model structure as GPN, except using different regression loss for bounding ellipses localization. Specifically, we use RPN to predict lesion bounding ellipses by regressing the offsets of their centroid coordinates, long and short axes, and the tangent of the rotation angle following [4] with respect to the corresponding anchor. We use a single-scale feature map of stride 8 and five anchor scales, i.e. $(16, 24, 32, 48, 96)$, following [12]. Compared to the Faster R-CNN two-stage detector used in [12], both GPN and RPN are one-stage detectors that suffer from overwhelming number of background proposals during training [6]. Therefore, we also experiment training with just one anchor scale of 16 to mitigate this issue. We use pretrained VGG-16 [11] as the backbone network following [12] and a single anchor aspect ratio of 1:1. Both GPN and RPN are trained with 20 epochs, and all the experiment settings are equally applied during training.

Complete details about data preprocessing and model training are provided in the Supplementary.

## 4.3  Performances for Bounding Ellipse Detection

GPN consistently outperforms RPN using both 1 anchor scale and 5 anchor scales by a significant margin. Figure 3a and Supplementary Table 1 show the overall performances of GPN and RPN on the test set of DeepLesion across both settings measured by the free-response receiver operating characteristic (FROC). FROC measures the detection sensitivity with different average false positives per image. We consider a proposed bounding ellipse is correct if its IoU with the ground truth ellipse is greater than or equal to 0.5. Note that, IoU between ellipses is a very stringent criteria, especially when the ellipse aspect ratio is significantly larger than one, as demonstrated in Supplementary Fig. 1 a.

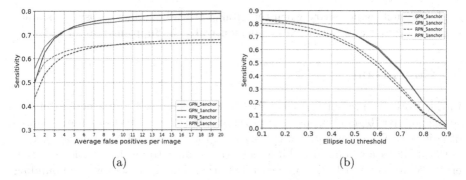

(a)                                                      (b)

**Fig. 3.** (a) FROC curves of GPN and RPN on the test set of DeepLesion at 0.5 ellipse IoU threshold. (b) Detection sensitivities of GPN and RPN on the test set of DeepLesion with different ellipse IoU thresholds at 4 false positives per image.

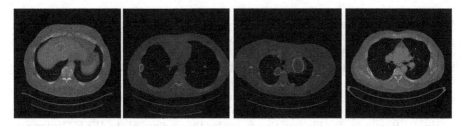

**Fig. 4.** Selected examples of proposed bounding ellipses from GPN-5anchor (cyan) and RPN-5anchor (magenta) compared to the ground truth (orange) on the test set of DeepLesion. Only the top 3 proposed ellipses with the highest classification scores from each model are selected for each image. (Color figure online)

We also find one anchor scale training improve the performances of GPN when the average false positives per image is less than or equal to 3.

Figure 4 shows a few examples of proposed bounding ellipses from GPN-5anchor and RPN-5anchor compared to the ground truth on the test set of DeepLesion. We can see that GPN detects ellipses of various sizes, rotation angles and aspect ratios with more accurate overlaps than RPN.

### 4.4   Error Analysis

GPN achieves significant lower localization error compared to RPN. Figure 3b shows the detection sensitivities of GPN and RPN with different ellipse IoU thresholds at 4 false positives per image. We can see that, when the IoU threshold is small, both GPN and RPN have comparable detection sensitivities since it is dominated by proposals vs background classification accuracy. As the IoU threshold increases, the performance of RPN decreases significantly faster than GPN, suggesting its localization error is significantly higher than GPN.

We also investigate the rotation angle error of GPN and RPN in the Supplementary. The results support our conjecture that directly regressing the rotation angle may not be necessary when the ground truth bounding ellipse has similar lengths of major and minor axes as demonstrated in Supplementary Fig. 1b.

## 5   Conclusion

In this work, we present Gaussian Proposal Networks (GPNs), a new extension to the popular Region Proposal Networks (RPNs) [9], to detect bounding ellipses of lesions on CT scans. On the DeepLesion [13] dataset, GPN significantly outperforms RPN for bounding ellipse detection thanks to much lower localization error. We also expect GPN to be useful in other detection tasks where bounding ellipse annotations are available.

## References

1. Dai, J., Li, Y., He, K., Sun, J.: R-FCN: object detection via region-based fully convolutional networks. In: Advances in Neural Information Processing Systems, pp. 379–387 (2016)
2. Duchi, J.: Derivations for linear algebra and optimization. Berkeley, California 3 (2007)
3. Girshick, R.: Fast R-CNN. In: Proceedings of the IEEE International Conference on Computer Vision, pp. 1440–1448 (2015)
4. Hu, P., Ramanan, D.: Finding tiny faces. In: Proceedings of the IEEE Conference on Computer Vision and Pattern Recognition, pp. 1522–1530 (2017)
5. Lin, T.Y., Dollár, P., Girshick, R., He, K., Hariharan, B., Belongie, S.: Feature pyramid networks for object detection. In: Proceedings of the IEEE Conference on Computer Vision and Pattern Recognition, pp. 936–944 (2017)
6. Lin, T.Y., Goyal, P., Girshick, R., He, K., Dollár, P.: Focal loss for dense object detection. IEEE Trans. Pattern Anal. Mach. Intell. **39**, 2999–3007 (2018)
7. Liu, L., Pan, Z., Lei, B.: Learning a rotation invariant detector with rotatable bounding box. arXiv preprint arXiv:1711.09405 (2017)
8. Paszke, A., et al.: Automatic differentiation in pytorch (2017)
9. Ren, S., He, K., Girshick, R., Sun, J.: Faster R-CNN: towards real-time object detection with region proposal networks. In: Advances in Neural Information Processing Systems, pp. 91–99 (2015)
10. Shrivastava, A., Gupta, A., Girshick, R.: Training region-based object detectors with online hard example mining. In: Proceedings of the IEEE Conference on Computer Vision and Pattern Recognition, pp. 761–769 (2016)
11. Simonyan, K., Zisserman, A.: Very deep convolutional networks for large-scale image recognition. arXiv preprint arXiv:1409.1556 (2014)
12. Yan, K., Bagheri, M., Summers, R.M.: 3D context enhanced region-based convolutional neural network for end-to-end lesion detection. In: Frangi, A.F., Schnabel, J.A., Davatzikos, C., Alberola-López, C., Fichtinger, G. (eds.) MICCAI 2018. LNCS, vol. 11070, pp. 511–519. Springer, Cham (2018). https://doi.org/10.1007/978-3-030-00928-1_58
13. Yan, K., Wang, X., Lu, L., Summers, R.M.: Deeplesion: automated mining of large-scale lesion annotations and universal lesion detection with deep learning. J. Med. Imaging **5**(3), 036501 (2018)

# Modelling Airway Geometry as Stock Market Data Using Bayesian Changepoint Detection

Kin Quan[1](✉), Ryutaro Tanno[1], Michael Duong[2], Arjun Nair[3],
Rebecca Shipley[4], Mark Jones[5], Christopher Brereton[5], John Hurst[6],
David Hawkes[1], and Joseph Jacob[1]

[1] Centre for Medical Image Computing, University College London, London, UK
kin.quan.10@ucl.ac.uk
[2] Statistical Science, University College London, London, UK
[3] Department of Radiology, University College Hospital, London, UK
[4] Mechanical Engineering, University College London, London, UK
[5] NIHR Biomedical Research Centre, University of Southampton, Southampton, UK
[6] UCL Respiratory, University College London, London, UK

**Abstract.** Numerous lung diseases, such as idiopathic pulmonary fibrosis (IPF), exhibit dilation of the airways. Accurate measurement of dilatation enables assessment of the progression of disease. Unfortunately the combination of image noise and airway bifurcations causes high variability in the profiles of cross-sectional areas, rendering the identification of affected regions very difficult. Here we introduce a noise-robust method for automatically detecting the location of progressive airway dilatation given two profiles of the same airway acquired at different time points. We propose a probabilistic model of abrupt relative variations between profiles and perform inference via Reversible Jump Markov Chain Monte Carlo sampling. We demonstrate the efficacy of the proposed method on two datasets; (i) images of healthy airways with simulated dilatation; (ii) pairs of real images of IPF-affected airways acquired at 1 year intervals. Our model is able to detect the starting location of airway dilatation with an accuracy of 2.5 mm on simulated data. The experiments on the IPF dataset display reasonable agreement with radiologists. We can compute a relative change in airway volume that may be useful for quantifying IPF disease progression.

## 1 Introduction

Monitoring the progression of airway dilatation in chest CT scans have proven effective as predictors of outcome in idiopathic pulmonary fibrosis (IPF). However, analysis of CT airway images are restricted to crude visual inspection and categorical scores [8]. Computerised quantification of change in airway dilatation is limited to computing the difference in cross-sectional area (CSA) on a signal point at each generational branch [9]. Introducing contiguous CSA changes along

© Springer Nature Switzerland AG 2019
H.-I. Suk et al. (Eds.): MLMI 2019, LNCS 11861, pp. 345–354, 2019.
https://doi.org/10.1007/978-3-030-32692-0_40

the airway track (e.g. in Fig. 1) would enable analysis of subtle dilatation. However one would have to distinguish a dilatation from various sources of noise including: (i) Biases and precision from computing CSA such as from centreline generation [13] and lumen identification [6]. (ii) Artefactual measurements such as in bifurcation regions [15]. (iii) Normal biological variations [2].

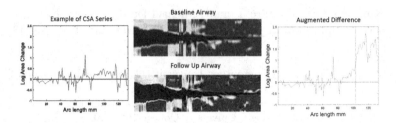

**Fig. 1.** Example of a healthy contiguous CSA change (left) along an airway track between longitudinal scans (middle). In addition, an augmented diseased CSA change from the same airway track (right). The red line corresponds to our ground truth as the starting point of dilatation α. (Colour figure online)

We introduce a novel application of Bayesian Changepoint Detection (BCPD) for airway quantification in CT. Specifically, to automatically identify the location of airway dilatation of the same airway across longitudinal CT scans in the presence of measurement noise. The BCPD model, typically used in stock market data analysis [12], aims to capture abrupt variations in the underlying distributions of a given signal or a time series. Our method processes a series of CSA changes between baseline and follow-up CT scans, and generates the posterior distribution over multiple possible points of abnormal variations, whose mode is taken as the final prediction. The hypothesis being the initial perturbation of an airway track that can lead to a cascade of events that pushes the overall measure beyond the normal statistical fluctuations seen in a stable system. BCPD models the 1D signals as a distribution of points thus taking account normal biological functions and measurement error. Furthermore, we set the sampling algorithm to choose the number of changepoints thus taking account spurious measurements along the 1D signal. We test the efficacy of the method on (1) CT images of healthy airways with simulated dilatation, and (2) pairs of real images of IPF-affected airways acquired after approximately 1 year. For the simulated datasets, we measured the detection accuracy with respect to the commonly used threshold and maximum likelihood based methods [10]. For the longitudinal IPF dataset we compare the predictions of our model to radiologist interpretation based on two different protocols.

## 2    Method

First we construct a 1D signal of CSA change across longitudinal scans (Sect. 2.1). Secondly, we propose a Bayesian Changepoint model to find locations of abrupt airway dilatation (Sects. 2.2 and 2.3). Finally, we determine the point $t$ of dilatation (Sect. 2.4).

## 2.1 Airway Pre-processing

For each airway track, we compute a series of CSA measurements [15]. Following interactive identification of the airway, the method outputs a 1D function of CSA along the airway arclength at baseline $f_B(x)$ and at follow-up $f_F(x)$ from the carina to the most distal point of the airway (e.g. on Fig. 4). Starting at the carina we resample along the centreline at 1 mm intervals using cubic interpolation. We align using the first 50 points on both signals $g_B, g_F$ and apply the transformation $f_F(x - a)$ where $a = \text{argmin}_{a \in [-5,5]} \left\| \log \left( \frac{g_B(x)}{g_F(x-a)} \right) \right\|_2$. We consider the series difference defined as $\boldsymbol{y} = \log(f_F) - \log(f_B)$ (e.g. of $\boldsymbol{y}$ on Fig. 1).

## 2.2 Bayesian Changepoint Model

We hypothesise that at the start of dilatation, the series $\boldsymbol{y}$ undergoes an abrupt variation, which we refer to as a changepoint. More formally, given signal $\boldsymbol{y} = (y_1, \ldots, y_n)$ of length $n$, we define a changepoint $\tau$ as the location where there exists a change in parameters $\theta$ in the underlying distribution $F$. In other words, at changepoint $1 < \tau < n$, the observations $\boldsymbol{y}$ can be separated at $\tau$ such that $(y_1, \ldots, y_\tau) \sim F(\theta_1)$ and $(y_{\tau+1}, \ldots, y_n) \sim F(\theta_2)$ where $\theta_1 \neq \theta_2$. This definition can be naturally extended to the scenario with $M$ changepoints; we denote the changepoint location vector by $\tau = (\tau_1, \ldots, \tau_k)$, with parameters $\theta = (\theta_1, \ldots, \theta_{k+1})$ for each respective segment. For ease of notation, we also denote $\tau_0 = 1$ and $\tau_{k+1} = n$. Assuming statistical independence between segments, the likelihood factorises as: $p(\boldsymbol{y}|\tau, \theta, M) = \prod_{l=1}^{k+1} F(y_{\tau_{l-1}:\tau_l}|\theta_l)$, where $y_{\tau_{l-1}:\tau_l} = (y_{\tau_{l-1}}, \ldots, y_{\tau_l})$. We also specify prior distributions on the number of changepoints $p(M; \delta)$, the locations of the changepoints $p(\tau|M; \gamma)$, and the parameters of the corresponding segments $p(\theta|M; \beta)$ where $\beta$, $\gamma$ and $\delta$ represent the hyper-parameters.

Given the likelihood and the prior distributions above, we require an estimate of the posterior distribution over the locations of changepoints $p(\tau|\boldsymbol{y})$. As discussed in Sect. 1, our signal $\boldsymbol{y}$ is subjected to anatomical and acquisition noise. To overcome these variations in CSA, we choose the likelihood $F$ as the Student t-distribution [14]. Thus, we denote degrees of freedom $\nu$, mean $\mu$, variance $\sigma^2$ and parameter $\theta = (\mu, \sigma^2, \nu)$.

## 2.3 Reversible Jump MCMC for Posterior Inference

Posterior inference with our model possesses two challenges. Firstly, without the conjugacy assumption, computing the posterior distribution is intractable. In our case, the Student's t distribution is not an exponential family and therefore cannot have a conjugate prior. Thus the posterior is not available in a closed form. Secondly, the dimensionality of the posterior distribution over the change-points $\tau$ is given by $M$ and varies during inference. To combat the first problem, we use the Metropolis-Hasting (MH) algorithm [1], a variant of Markov Chain Monte Carlo (MCMC) methods that can sample from the posterior, with or without conjugacy. Given that the number of changepoints $M$ is known, MH can be used to sample from the posterior distributions over the changepoints $\tau$ and segment parameters $\theta$. To address varying posterior dimensionality $M$, we extend the above sampling scheme to the Reversible Jump MCMC framework [5]. Taken altogether, the method is capable of traversing the full posterior distributions for $M, \tau, \theta$ and we refer to this as the Reversible Jump Metropolis Hasting (RJMH) algorithm.

**Overview of RJMH:** The RJMH proceeds by randomly executing one of four possible moves, denoted as $\Upsilon_i$ at each iteration: (i) resample parameters $\theta$, $\Upsilon_\theta$; (ii) move an existing changepoint, $\Upsilon_\tau$; (iii) add a new changepoint, $\Upsilon_{M \to M+1}$; (iv) delete an existing changepoint, $\Upsilon_{M+1 \to M}$. We also define the maximum number of changepoints $k_{max}$ and at the boundary cases for $k$, we impose restrictions such that $\Upsilon_{M \to M+1}, \Upsilon_{M+1 \to M}$ are skipped for $k = 0, k_{max}$ respectively. Each move updates the appropriate subset of parameters $\theta, \tau$ by sampling from the corresponding distributions $q(\theta_{new}|\theta_{old})$ and $q(\tau_{new}|\tau_{old})$, and is only executed if it passes the associated acceptance criteria $\alpha$.

**MH Steps:** For $\Upsilon_\theta$, we set $q(\theta_{new}|\theta_{old}) = (\mu_{old}, \sigma^2_{old}, \nu_{old}) + N(0, \epsilon)$. This step resamples parameters of each segment by proposing Gaussian perturbations around the current values of parameters for all segments. For $\Upsilon_\tau$, we set $q(\tau_{new}|\tau_{old}) = \tau_{old} + (-1)^b \text{Poi}(\lambda)$ where b~Binary[0,1]. This step selects a changepoint $\tau$ at random and shifts it with a Poisson perturbation. The segments neighbouring this new changepoint location have parameters $\theta$ resampled as in move $\Upsilon_\theta$ using the current segment parameters.

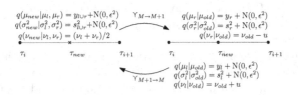

**Fig. 2.** A schematic diagram describing the proposals moves $\Upsilon_{M \to M+1}, \Upsilon_{M+1 \to M}$. Note that $u$~$N(0, \epsilon^2)$ and $y_i, s_i^2$ are the mean and variance respectively of data within the coloured segment. (Colour figure online)

**RJ Steps:** For $\Upsilon_{M \to M+1}$, we proposed random new changepoints over our data, $\tau_{new}$~$U[1, n-1]$. The proposed $\tau_{new}$ split an existing segment into a new left segment $\theta_l = (\mu_l, \sigma_l^2, \nu_l)$ and new right segment $\theta_r = (\mu_r, \sigma_r^2, \nu_r)$. Our proposal for $\mu_i, \sigma_i^2$ are defined by a Gaussian perturbation on empirical values of the respective $i = l, r$ segments (Fig. 2). The proposal for $\nu_i$, is Gaussian perturbation of the previous update $\nu_{old}$. Due to dependence of the $\nu_i$ proposal, a Jacobian term is introduced $|J_{M \to M+1}| = 2$. For $\Upsilon_{M+1 \to M}$, we remove a changepoint $\tau_{new}$. As before, proposals for $\mu_{new}, \sigma^2_{new}$ are defined using empirical values of the segments and Gaussian perturbation (Fig. 2). The proposal for $\nu_{new}$ is the mean of the previous $\nu_l, \nu_r$. The move introduces Jacobian term $|J_{M+1 \to M}| = 0.5$.

**Implementation:** We follow the same RJMH algorithm as defined in the literature [3,4]. The priors were set as $\mu \sim N(0,1)$, $\sigma^2 \sim$ Scaled-Inv-$\chi^2(5, 0.4^2)$, $\nu \sim U[2, 100]$ and $M \sim \text{Bin}(n - 1, \frac{0.5}{n-1})$, where $\mu, \sigma^2, \nu$ were chosen to be non-informative and within plausible ranges. The expectation for $M$ was sufficiently low to avoid detecting changepoints in noise. Finally, we set burn-in for 25% of the total iteration count and only storing the $5^{\text{th}}$ iteration, after the burn-in period to avoid auto-correlation.

### 2.4   Locating Change in Airway Dilatation

For airways affected by IPF, dilatation starts and progresses from the distal point of the airway [7]. Topologically, we can assume each airway undergoes a signal changepoint from which dilatation starts. To locate such a unique changepoint, we consider the posterior over of the changepoint $p(\tau|\boldsymbol{y})$, and perform the following post-processing steps. On each $\boldsymbol{y}$, the proximal region is surrounded by cartilage [16]. The end of cartilage causes an anatomical changepoint independent of disease state. We eliminate it by discounting the most proximal peak on $p(\tau|\boldsymbol{y})$. We then selected the highest peak on the modified posterior $p(\tau|\boldsymbol{y})$ as the starting point of dilatation denoted as $t$.

## 3   Evaluation and Results

We evaluated our proposed method with two experiments: (i) Simulated dilatations from healthy airways to assess accuracy. (ii) Airways affected by IPF to assess clinical utility. The image properties are displayed on Table 1.

**Table 1.** Table of the image properties of voxel size, number of airways used and the time interval between scans. Voxel size is in the form (x,y,z), units: mm. The airways were selected by a trained radiologist R1. All patients in Experiment 1 do not have IPF. Abbreviation: BL - Baseline Scan, FU - Follow-up Scan, M - Months, D - Days.

| Experiment | Patient | BL Voxel size | FU Voxel size | Airway | Time between scans |
|---|---|---|---|---|---|
| 1 | 1 | 0.67, 0.67, 1.00 | 0.56, 0.56, 1.00 | 6 | 9M 6D |
| 1 | 2 | 0.63, 0.63, 1.00 | 0.78, 0.78, 1.00 | 7 | 35M 6D |
| 1 | 3 | 0.72, 0.72, 1.00 | 0.72, 0.72, 1.00 | 1 | 5M 22D |
| 2 | 4 | 0.72, 0.72, 1.00 | 0.64, 0.64, 1.00 | 3 | 12M 5D |
| 2 | 5 | 0.67, 0.67, 1.00 | 0.87, 0.87, 1.00 | 1 | 10M 24D |

## 3.1   Disease Simulation

To quantitatively assess accuracy, a ground truth is required. To this end, we applied our changepoint detection algorithm on augmented healthy airway series to simulate the airway dilatation caused by IPF. A trained radiologist (R1) selected 14 pairs of healthy airways in both baseline and follow-up scans. The image properties are displayed on Table 1. They were acquired from different scanners and used different reconstruction kernels. The airways were preprocessed as described in Sect. 2.1 to produce a function of CSA change along the length of the airway.

We modelled the change in dilatation with a logistic function $l = M/(1 + e^{-\lambda(x-\alpha)})$, where $M$ is magnitude of dilatation and $\alpha$ as the point of dilatation. The parameters $\alpha$ are set such that the dilatation starts 10–40 mm from the distal point and we set $M$ to range from 0.5–3. Finally we set $\lambda = 0.5$ mm$^{-1}$, in order to create an abnormal increase in CSA. To simulate the dilatation on the airway; the logistic function was added to the logarithmic CSA change of the airways, as shown on Fig. 1. We applied our proposed method to every permutation of $M$ and $\alpha$ on each of the 14 healthy airways.

The proposed method was compared against two conventional methods. First, a basic thresholding method. We smoothed and thresholded the point at which $y$ reached above the upper quartile from the right hand side. Secondly, we implemented the method based on Lavielle [10] and implemented in a Matlab inbuilt function; findchangepts[1]. In summary we consider $K$ changepoint and these changepoints $y_i$, minimize the function: $J(K) = \sum_{r=0}^{K-1} \sum_{i=k_r}^{k_{r+1}-1} \Delta(y_i, y_{k_r:k_{r+1}-1}) + \beta K$, where $\beta$ is modified such that the function finds less than $K$ changepoints. We found $\Delta = y_i - \text{mean}(y_{k_r:k_{r+1}-1})$ gives the most accurate results. The method [10] assumes the data $y$ is Gaussian distributed. To replicate the post processing in Sect. 2.4, we consider $K = 2$ possible changepoints and minimum distance of 20 mm. This takes into account the changepoint caused by the support cartilage. The most peripheral point was chosen as the point of dilatation.

Figure 3 shows the accuracy for each method as a heatmap. Each entry on the heatmap corresponds to the median average of all displacements over 14 airway pairs. A positive displacement corresponds to an overestimation of the ground truth towards the distal point. When the magnitude of dilation is larger than $M > 0.75$, our proposed method achieves consistently higher accuracy than Lavielle [10]. The accuracy gain in the peripheral regions of the airways at $\alpha = 10$–30 mm from the distal point are the most clinically relevant in IPF as parenchymal damage begins in the lung periphery and progresses proximally [7]. Furthermore, on the same peripheral regions $\alpha = 10$–30 mm, the baseline method showed systematic bias in accuracy towards the central airways. This was due to the baseline method being influenced by outliers from the longer expanses of normal airway regions. The proposed method uses the t-distribution

---

[1] https://www.mathworks.com/help/signal/ref/findchangepts.html last accessed on August 16, 2019.

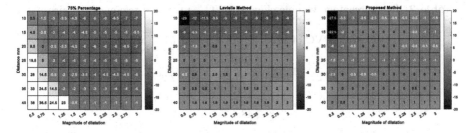

**Fig. 3.** Heatmap showing the accuracy of each method in mm. (Left). Thresholding method. (Middle). Method from Lavielle [10]. (Right). Our proposed method. The colour scale is the same on all of the heatmaps. (Colour figure online)

as the likelihood thus making it robust to possible outliers within the data [14]. The proposed method suffers from poor accuracy below magnitudes of dilatation $M = 0.75$. However, in physical terms a dilatation of $M = 0.75$ corresponds to a percentage increase in CSA of $e^{0.75} - 1 \approx 112\%$. This is within the range of normal change of the airways [2].

## 3.2  Application to Airways Affected by IPF

To show clinically utility, we acquired 4 airway pairs from 2 patients (Table 1). All airways were judged by the radiologist R1 to be dilated as a consequence of IPF on baseline and to have visually worsened on follow-up imaging.

We compared the performance of our method against two trained thoracic radiologists R1, R2. To assessed the reproducibility of manual labelling, each radiologist labelled the same airway twice through two different protocols. First, the radiologists interrogated axial CT images. Using 2 separate workstations and the airway centreline, the radiologists identified the point on the centreline (on the follow-up scan) where the airway demonstrated definitive worsened dilatation. Second, the radiologist compared the aligned reconstructed cross-sectional planes on baseline and follow-up scans (e.g. Fig. 4). The radiologist then selected the slice where the airway had worsened when evaluated against the baseline.

The results (Fig. 4) indicate that the predictions for Airway 1, 3 and 4 are within the range of the radiologists' labels. In the case of Airway 2 our method overestimates compared to radiologists' predictions. The posterior distribution contains another equally probable peak that underestimates the radiologists' labels (see the second highest peak at 70 mm), potentially indicating a more proximal point of dilatation. To test this, we delineated the boundary of the lumen on the reconstructed cross sectional slices at baseline in the neighbourhood of this peak, and Fig. 4 shows the initial few slices (62–64 mm). When the delineated boundary from baseline was superimposed on the follow-up scan, the boundary is contained inside the follow-up lumen. This result indicates that the starting point of dilatation is more proximal than the labels from the radiologists.

**Table 2.** The percentage volume change (PVC %) for each region of the airway.

| Airway | PVC of $V_{c \to d}$ | PVC of $V_{t \to d}$ | PVC of $V_{c \to t}$ |
|--------|---------|----------|---------|
| 1 | 2.6% | 32.9% | 1.1% |
| 2 | 3.2% | 129.7% | 2.2% |
| 3 | 2.6% | 47.4 % | -0.3% |
| 4 | 7.4% | 48.4 % | 7.1% |

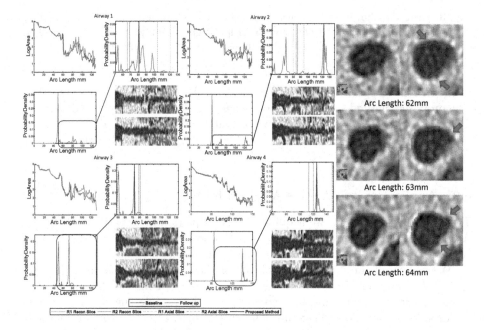

**Fig. 4.** Left: The log CSA and posterior distribution $p(\tau|y)$ for each of the four airway pairs. In the magnified region (black) we compared the labels from our proposed method with the radiologist. The top and bottom reconstructed airway corresponds to the baseline and follow up scans respectively. Right: A row of three consecutive reconstructed slices in Airway 2, arc length of 62–64 mm, baseline (left) and follow-up (right). The boundary delineation (red) from the baseline are superimposed on the follow-up scan. The blue arrows indicate pixels from the lumen outside the boundary (Colour figure online).

**Volumetric Analysis:** By computing the starting point $t$ of dilatation of the airways, we can compute airway volume changes in diseased and healthy regions of the airway track by integrating CSA measurements along arclength $f_F, f_B$. We used the trapezium rule to find 3 volumetric regions: (i) the entire airway track, $V_{c \to d}$, (ii) carina to $t$, $V_{c \to t}$, (iii) $t$ to the distal point $V_{t \to d}$. Table 2, shows the results of the percentage volume change. The volume change in $V_{t \to d}$ had greater sensitivity for selecting progressive airway dilatation in IPF than the volume change in the entire airway $V_{c \to d}$.

# 4   Discussion and Conclusion

In this paper, we propose a novel application of the BCPD in detecting airway dilatation caused by progression of IPF. The model uses a series of CSA changes between longitudinal scans with presence of normal biological variation and precision errors in measuring CSA. Experiments on simulated data show our model can detect the starting location of airway dilatation with superior accuracy to competing methods. The results display reasonable agreement with radiologists. One case indicated a more plausible location of dilatation, potentially missed by the experts. There is a clinical need for head to head comparisons for the effectiveness of drugs in treating IPF [11]. Identifying a change in airway dilatation over time could become a sensitive measure of IPF worsening, providing an important secondary endpoint in drug trials. As future work, we believe the technology can be be applied to other progressive diseases that results in a cascade of events leading to spread of pathology, such as the growth of plaque and aneurysms in major blood vessels.

# References

1. Chib, S., et al.: Understanding the metropolis-hastings algorithm. Am. Stat. **49**(4), 327–335 (1995)
2. Gazourian, L., et al.: Quantitative computed tomography assessment of bronchiolitis obliterans syndrome after lung transplantation. Clin. Transplant. **31**(5), e12943 (2017)
3. Gelman, A., et al.: Bayesian Data Analysis. CRC Press, Boca Raton (2014)
4. Green, P.J.: Reversible jump Markov chain monte carlo computation and Bayesian model determination. Biometrika **82**(4), 711–732 (1995)
5. Green, P.J., et al.: Reversible jump MCMC. Genetics **155**(3), 1391–1403 (2009)
6. Gu, S., et al.: Computerized identification of airway wall in CT examinations using a 3D active surface evolution approach. Med. Image Anal. **17**(3), 283–96 (2013)
7. Jacob, J., et al.: HRCT of fibrosing lung disease. Respirology **20**(6), 859–872 (2015)
8. Jacob, J., et al.: Serial automated quantitative CT analysis in idiopathic pulmonary fibrosis: functional correlations and comparison with changes in visual CT scores. Eur. Radiol. **28**(3), 1318–1327 (2018)
9. Konietzke, P., et al.: Quantitative CT detects changes in airway dimensions and air-trapping after bronchial thermoplasty for severe asthma. Eur. J. Radiol. **107**, 33–38 (2018)
10. Lavielle, M.: Using penalized contrasts for the change-point problem. Signal Process. **85**(8), 1501–1510 (2005)
11. Lederer, D., et al.: Idiopathic pulmonary fibrosis. New Engl. J. Med. **378**(19), 1811–1823 (2018)
12. Mikosch, T., et al.: Changes of structure in financial time series and the GARCH model. REVSTAT Stat. J. **2**(1), 41–73 (2004)

13. Palágyi, K., et al.: Quantitative analysis of pulmonary airway tree structures. Comput. Biol. Med. **36**(9), 974–96 (2006)
14. Prince, S.J.D.: Computer Vision: Models, Learning, and Inference. Cambridge University Press, Cambridge (2012)
15. Quan, K., et al.: Tapering analysis of airways with bronchiectasis. In: Proceedings of SPIE (2018)
16. Weibel, E.R.: Morphometry of the Human Lung. Springer-Verlag, Heidelberg (1963). https://doi.org/10.1007/978-3-642-87553-3

# Unsupervised Lesion Detection with Locally Gaussian Approximation

Xiaoran Chen[1]($\boxtimes$), Nick Pawlowski[2], Ben Glocker[2], and Ender Konukoglu[1]

[1] Computer Vision Laboratory, ETH Zurich, Zurich, Switzerland
chenx@vision.ee.ethz.ch
[2] Biomedical Image Analysis Group, Imperial College London, London, UK

**Abstract.** Generative models have recently been applied to unsupervised lesion detection, where a distribution of normal data, i.e. the normative distribution, is learned and lesions are detected as out-of-distribution regions. However, directly calculating the probability for the lesion region using the normative distribution is intractable. In this work, we address this issue by approximating the normative distribution with local Gaussian approximation and evaluating the probability of test samples in an iterative manner. We show that the local Gaussian approximator can be applied to several auto-encoding models to perform image restoration and unsupervised lesion detection. The proposed method is evaluated on the BraTS Challenge dataset, where the proposed method shows improved detection and achieves state-of-the-art results.

## 1 Introduction

Automated lesion detection has been an active topic in medical imaging research. Conventionally, lesions are detected by visual inspection based on intensity characteristics in medical scans, such as Computed Tomography (CT) and Magnetic Resonance Images (MRI).

Algorithmic approaches have emerged as viable automatic alternatives to visual inspection, where lesion detection is often formulated as a classification or segmentation problem. Early approaches are based on supervised classification [1,2]. More recently, impressive performance has been achieved by deep learning-based methods in supervised [3] and weakly supervised [4] settings. Despite the success, methods with supervision require laborious image acquisition for annotated labels. On the other hand, those methods are lesion-specific as they learn a mapping between images and labels and may be limited in applications such as pre-screening for a large range of abnormalities. In contrast, unsupervised methods are not specific to lesions in the training data and enable critical applications such as automatic screening for radiological assessment.

The principle behind unsupervised detection is to learn a normative distribution of images from healthy individuals [5]. Lesions can then be detected as out-of-distribution areas in the images. Compared to supervised methods, unsupervised detection is arguably more difficult as the model cannot encode any lesion

H.-I. Suk et al. (Eds.): MLMI 2019, LNCS 11861, pp. 355–363, 2019.
https://doi.org/10.1007/978-3-030-32692-0_41

specific characteristics. Earlier attempts model the normative distribution either by assuming the expected tissue composition or via atlas registration [6–8]. More recent methods use deep learning models to estimate the normative distributions, for example, via Generative Adversarial Nets (GANs) [9] and Variational Auto-Encoders (VAEs) [10]. AnoGAN [5] uses GANs to model the normative distribution. Given an image with abnormalities, it estimates a "pseudo-normal" version of the image by determining the closest image the GAN can generate. Abnormal pixels are then detected using the absolute differences between the original and generated pseudo-normal images. VAE-based methods take a similar approach where pseudo-normal images are estimated by reconstructing the image with an encoder-decoder model trained only on healthy images. Lesions are then detected as regions with high reconstruction errors [11–13]. An advantage of VAEs is the explicit estimation of the normative distribution.

However, the generation of pseudo-normal images in previous works relies on mapping the image to the latent space and back, assuming the healthy regions would not change during this operation. This assumption may not hold as the mapping to the latent space may drift away from the ideal point due to the abnormality, leading to false positive detection caused by reconstruction errors in healthy regions. We also seek the "pseudo-normal" images to detect the lesions, but with a probabilistic formulation. To find the pseudo-healthy images more accurately, we use the image with lesion as an observation and the normative distribution as its prior distribution. The corresponding "pseudo-normal" image is then obtained by maximizing the probability of the observation in the normative distribution. However the normative distribution estimated by models such as VAE cannot be explicitly accessed, we propose a locally Gaussian approximation method to perform likelihood maximization with the normative distribution.

Likelihood maximization is performed with the local Gaussian approximator accessing the prior distribution by approximating its gradients. The most related work to ours is You et al. [14], where they perform Maximum-a-Posteriori to obtain "pseudo-normal" images and the normative distribution is approximated with the Evidence Lower Bound (ELBO) of GMVAE, which can be inaccurate and cannot be applied to models that do not optimize the ELBO. Unlike [14], our approximation constructs local Gaussian approximations to the prior for each gradient ascent step rather than taking derivatives of the ELBO. We investigate two variations for constructing the proposed approximator. We evaluate the detection performance on BraTS dataset and achieve state-of-the-art performance.

## 2    Methods

Define a latent space model with $z \in \mathbb{R}^d$ and $X \in \mathbb{R}^{m \times n}$. The latent space model can estimate $P(X) = \int P(X|z)P(z)dz$ with mapping $z = f(X)$ and $X = g(z)$. Direct computation of $P(X)$ is often very difficult. Depending on the purpose, such direct computation is not always required. Specifically, for the propose of maximum likelihood estimation (MLE), one calculates the gradients of $P(X)$

instead of $P(X)$ itself. We describe a local Gaussian approximation method to provide gradients for MLE with an indirect $P(X)$ as a prior distribution.

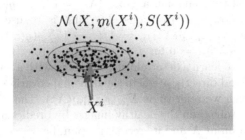

$$\mathcal{N}(X; m(X^i), S(X^i))$$

**Fig. 1.** Gaussian approximation illustration where grey shaded region represents the normative distribution for healthy images modelled by a VAE. The red arrow represents the derivative of the $(\log P(X))_{X^i}$, which is intractable to compute, while the blue arrow represents gradient computed using the proposed approach that locally approximates the image prior with a Gaussian close to $X^i$ and uses its derivative.

### 2.1 Local Gaussian Approximation for Likelihood Estimation

To compute the gradients from $P(X)$, we assume that $P(X)$ locally follows a Gaussian distribution, $P_{local}(X) \sim \mathcal{N}(X; \mu_{local}, \Sigma_{local})$, where estimate $\mu_{local}$ and $\Sigma_{local}$ can be easily estimated using the latent space model and MLE can be performed in an iterative manner until convergence.

For likelihood maximization, we start with the observation $X^0$ and perform gradient ascent with gradients computed from the approximated local Gaussian parameterized by $\mu_{local,X|z}$ and $\Sigma_{local,X|z}$ at each iteration $i$ to obtain $X^i$ (Eq. 1).

$$(\nabla \log P(X))_{X^i} \approx (\nabla \log \mathcal{N}(X; \mu_{local}(X^i), \Sigma_{local}(X^i)))_{X^i}, \qquad (1)$$
$$X^{i+1} = X^i + \eta \nabla \log P(X))_{X^i}$$

where $\mu_{local}(X^i)$ and $\Sigma_{local}(X^i)$ are the mean and covariance matrix of the approximation, respectively. The principal behind this approximation is pictorially depicted in Fig. 1. The role of $(\nabla \log P(X))_{X^i}$ is to direct the gradient ascent towards the image prior, which is depicted as the gray cloud in the figure with darker areas illustrating higher probability regions in the prior. At $X^i$, instead of taking the derivative of $\log P(X)$, which is intractable, the approach approximates the local region of the prior close to $X^i$ with a local Gaussian distribution and uses its derivative, which is much easier to compute.

Assuming the mean and covariance are obtained, the local Gaussian approximation produces gradients w.r.t to $X$ as $(\nabla \log P(X))_{X_i} \approx -\Sigma_{local}(X^i)^{-1}(X^i - \mu_{local}(X^i))$.

We observe in this equation that while the gradient direction tries to move $X$ towards $\mu_{local}(X^i)$, $\Sigma_{local}(X^i)$ provides additional knowledge on the expected variation in pixel intensities of healthy images at that local region of the prior. Next, we provide technical details on the estimation of $\mu_{local}(X^i)$ and $\Sigma_{local}(X^i)$.

For computational reasons $\Sigma_{local}(X^i)$ is modeled as a diagonal matrix. We compute the mean of the Gaussian as $\mu_{local}(X^i) = 1/L \sum_l g(z^l)$, $z^l \sim Q(z|X^i)$ For $\Sigma_{local}(X^i)$ we provide two options. The first is to use the sample variance at every pixel as $\Sigma_{local}(X^i)_{jj} = 1/(L-1) \sum_l (g(z^l)_j - \mu_{local}(X^i)_j)^2$, $z^l \sim Q(z|X^i)$, $\Sigma_{local}(X^i)_{jk} = 0$ for $j \neq k$. which we refer to as $\Sigma_{local,est}(X^i)$. The second option is to learn a deterministic mapping with a neural network that takes the image $X^i$ and directly predicts the diagonal covariance matrix as illustrated in Fig. 2, which we refer to as $\Sigma_{local,neural}(X^i)$. The network predicting $\Sigma_{local,neural}$ can be trained on the healthy images by predicting the expected $\ell_2$ loss between a given input $X$ and its reconstruction, i.e. $\mathbb{E}_{z \sim Q(z|X)}[(g(z) - X)^2]$.

## 2.2   Unsupervised Detection with Probabilistic Image Restoration

One of the task that our approximation can applied to is unsupervised lesion detection. To perform unsupervised detection, we learn the prior distribution $P(X)$ for normal samples and perform image restoration using the local Gaussian approximation to maximize the likelihood of test samples. The lesions can then be revealed by the absolute difference between the test image and its restoration.

Auto-Encoder (VAE) is a typical model to estimate the prior distribution from the healthy images without lesions. For detailed explanation of VAEs, we refer readers to [10]. Note that the proposed local Gaussian approximation is not limited to combination with VAE but can also be used together with other latent space models that model $P(X)$, e.g. Adversarial Auto-encoder (AAE) [15]. Here we use VAE as an example to demonstrate the unsupervised detection work-flow.

VAEs assume that the image distribution can be modelled with a lower-dimensional latent variable model as $P(X) = \int P(X \mid z)P(z)dz$, where $P(z)$ stands for the pre-specified prior distribution in the latent space and $P(X|z)$ is modeled with a *decoding* network as $P(X|z) = \mathcal{N}(X; \mu(z), \sigma(z)\mathbf{I})$. VAEs build an *encoding* network to approximate the true posterior $P(z|X) \approx Q(z|X) = \mathcal{N}(z; \mu_z, \sigma_z\mathbf{I})$. Overall, VAEs encode an image $X$ in the latent space and then reconstruct it with information encoded in the latent space. With networks for $Q(z|X)$ and $P(X|z)$ defined, the evidence lower bound (ELBO) can be derived as $\mathbb{E}_{z \sim Q(z|X)}[\log P(X \mid z)] - KL[Q(z \mid X)||P(z)]$ and used as a lower bound for $\log P(X)$ and is maximized to train VAE as a surrogate of $\log P(X)$.

An abnormal image $Y$ is seen as a healthy image $X$ with "errors" $\delta$, $Y = X + \delta$, where $\delta$ corresponds to the lesion. To detect $\delta$, $X$ is restored from $Y$ by maximizing $\log P(X|Y) \propto \log[P(Y|X)P(X)]$ with respect to $X$ using gradient ascent with steps defined as,

$$L(X) = \log P(Y|X) + \log P(X), \ X^{i+1} = X^i + \eta(\nabla L)_{X^i} \text{ and } X^0 = Y, \quad (2)$$

where $\eta$ is the step size, superscripts denote iterations and the subscript denotes where gradient is evaluated. $\log P(Y|X)$ integrates modelling assumptions on the

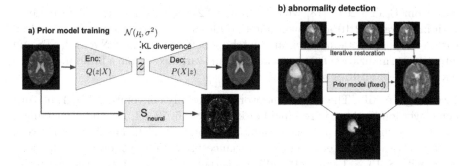

**Fig. 2.** Unsupervised lesion detection work-flow. (a) Learning prior normative distribution, the network takes healthy images as input and outputs reconstructed images and predicted variance, (b) likelihood maximization via local Gaussian approximation for test images using the prior distribution learned in (a).

abnormality. The restoration given in Eq. 2 iteratively computes the gradient at each $X^i$,

$$(\nabla L)_{X^i} = (\nabla \log P(X))_{X^i} + (\nabla \log P(Y|X))_{X^i}. \tag{3}$$

Define a generic cost $\lambda R(Y, X)$ to calculate $\log P(Y|X)$, we obtain the final gradient ascent step with the proposed approximation,

$$X^{i+1} = X^i + \eta \left[ -\Sigma_{local}(X^i)^{-1}(X^i - \mu_{local}(X^i)) + \lambda (\nabla R(Y, X))_{X^i} \right], \tag{4}$$

with $X^0 = Y$ and for $i = 0, \ldots, \texttt{max\_iter}$. Here, $\lambda$ controls the relative strength of $R$ and is selected on the training data. We select the suitable $\lambda$ by restoring healthy images and quantifying the similarity between the restored and original images with Structural Similarity (SSIM). Specifically, we choose the smallest $\lambda$ to obtain SSIM of at least 0.95. The final detection, i.e. an abnormality map, is computed at the end of the restoration as $\delta^* = |Y - X^{\texttt{max\_iter}}|$.

### 2.3   One-Class Segmentation with Allowed False Positive Rate

To obtain the lesion segmentation, a threshold on $\delta^*$ is required. Using the same approach as in [16], we select the minimum $\tau$ that produces a false positive rate (FPR) of at most $x\%$ on the training data by assuming all detection is false positives as training images are lesion-free. The segmented lesion are defined as the set of pixels $\{r | \delta^*(r) > \tau\}$. Here, $x\%$ is a user-defined parameter.

## 3   Experiments

**Datasets and Pre-processing.** We train and evaluate the proposed method on publicly available datasets: (1) Healthy individuals from the Cam-CAN study [17] which contains T2-weighted brain MRI of 652 subjects of age 18–87. All subjects have been confirmed to be normal by radiological assessment; (2) Abnormal data from BraTS 2018 [18] which contains T2-weighted images of 285 patients with high-grade (210) and low-grade (75) gliomas. All images are pre-processed with N4 bias correction, histogram matching between Cam-CAN and BraTS and intensity normalization to zero mean and unit variance within a brain mask, with background intensities set to $-3.5$.

**Training details.** The encoder network of the fully convolutional VAE has one `conv` layer followed by six residual blocks with 8, 16, 32, 64, 128 and 256 channels and $3 \times 3$ kernels, with a latent variable $z$ size of $2 \times 2 \times 256$. The decoder network is symmetrical to the encoder. The variance prediction network has four `conv` layers with 8, 16, 8, 1 channels and $3 \times 3$ kernels without reducing the image size in hidden layers. We use `LeakyRelu` activation for hidden layers and `identity` activation for output layers. The network is trained on $128 \times 128$ images with a batch size of 64 using the Adam optimizer and a learning rate of $2 \times 10^{-5}$ for 193k iterations on one GPU Titan X for approximately 18 h. Abnormal images are restored with $\lambda$ selected as in Sect. 2.3 using `Adam` and a learning rate of $5 \times 10^{-3}$ for 800 iterations.

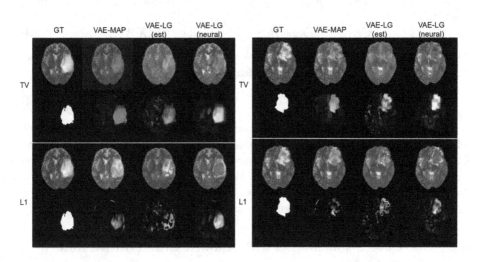

**Fig. 3.** Restoration of low-grade (left) and high-grade (right) gliomas. Abnormal images are restored using VAE-MAP, VAE-LG(est), VAE-LG(neural) (column 2–4) with TV- and L1-norms. Restoration results (top) and the corresponding absolute error maps $\delta$ (bottom) are shown along with the abnormal images (top) and reference segmentation (bottom) in the column GT.

## 3.1   Results

We evaluate VAE and AAE with the proposed approximation, which we refer to as VAE-LG and AAE-LG, specifically VAE-LG(est) with estimated variance $\Sigma_{local,est}$ and VAE-LG(neural) with predicted variance $\Sigma_{local,neural}$, AAE-LG(neural) with predicted variance $\Sigma_{local,neural}$. We compare to the state-of-the-art method, VAE-MAP [14] as well as auto-encoding methods without image restoration as in [19].

When restored with the same constraint, local Gaussian approximation successfully restored the lesion area into a healthy-looking region compared to MAP as shown in Fig. 3. For each method, restoration with TV-norm gave better visual results than with L1-norm. The advantage of TV may be attributed to the intensity characteristics of the gliomas. The best restoration was achieved by VAE-LG(neural). In contrast, the other methods either only restore the lesion partially (VAE-LG (est)) or naively lower the intensity values without restoring normal structures (VAE-MAP). This confirms the effectiveness of the proposed variance prediction network which preserves high-frequency details for meaningful restoration.

We quantify detection performance by Area-Under-Curve of ROC (AUC) and Dice computed at thresholds corresponding to different FPR limits in Table 1. The results are consistent with the visual inspection. VAE-LG(neural) achieves the highest AUC of 0.828 with TV-norm, followed by a slightly lower AUC of 0.824 for VAE-LG(neural) with L1-norm. VAE-LG(neural) with TV norm reaches the highest Dice at all thresholds except for 5%fpr outperforming the other methods by a large margin. Notably, our detection methods using the predicted variance achieve high Dice at low FPR limits, such as .1%fpr, where the other methods are ineffective. VAE-LG(neural) with TV norm achieved +0.220, +0.142 and +0.190 improvement over VAE-MAP with TV norm, VAE-LG(est) with TV norm and GMVAE-MAP with TV norm at .1%fpr. The high AUC and low Dice for GMVAE-MAP with TV norm at low FPR limits indicate that it is difficult to identify the threshold of this method using the training set. Comparison between GMVAE-MAP and VAE-MAP indicates that a more complex prior distribution brings improvement in the detection while neither are effective at low FPR limits, such as .1%fpr and .5%fpr. We also combine the proposed local Gaussian approximation with AAE as AAE-LG(neural). AAE-LG(neural) gives similar results to VAE-LG(neural).

**Table 1.** Performance comparison of Dice for different thresholds and AUC. Best results are in bold. Run-time is reported per iteration. *na*: evaluation not available.

| Methods | Constraints | .1%fpr | .5%fpr | 1%fpr | 5%fpr | AUC | Runtime (s) |
|---|---|---|---|---|---|---|---|
| GMM [7] | / | na | *na* | *na* | *na* | 0.800 | / |
| AnoGAN [5] | / | $0.000 \pm 0.000$ | $0.006 \pm 0.006$ | $0.020 \pm 0.020$ | $0.100 \pm 0.060$ | 0.670 | / |
| VAE [19] | / | $0.000 \pm 0.000$ | $0.030 \pm 0.030$ | $0.090 \pm 0.060$ | $0.200 \pm 0.140$ | 0.690 | / |
| AAE [19] | / | $0.000 \pm 0.000$ | $0.011 \pm 0.011$ | $0.030 \pm 0.030$ | $0.180 \pm 0.140$ | 0.700 | / |
| VAE-MAP [14] | TV | $0.039 \pm 0.076$ | $0.286 \pm 0.222$ | $0.341 \pm 0.221$ | $0.365 \pm 0.187$ | 0.805 | 0.177 |
| GMVAE-MAP [14] | TV | $0.069 \pm 0.084$ | $0.195 \pm 0.109$ | $0.218 \pm 0.208$ | $\mathbf{0.455 \pm 0.225}$ | 0.827 | 0.170 |
| VAE-LG(est) | L1 | $0.063 \pm 0.025$ | $0.213 \pm 0.183$ | $0.269 \pm 0.208$ | $0.347 \pm 0.216$ | 0.772 | 0.127 |
| VAE-LG(neural) | L1 | $0.133 \pm 0.143$ | $0.309 \pm 0.288$ | $0.360 \pm 0.276$ | $0.315 \pm 0.224$ | 0.824 | **0.096** |
| VAE-LG(est) | TV | $0.117 \pm 0.101$ | $0.236 \pm 0.155$ | $0.296 \pm 0.195$ | $0.362 \pm 0.203$ | 0.782 | 0.125 |
| VAE-LG(neural) | TV | $\mathbf{0.259 \pm 0.246}$ | $\mathbf{0.407 \pm 0.252}$ | $\mathbf{0.448 \pm 0.209}$ | $0.303 \pm 0.123$ | **0.828** | 0.098 |
| AAE-LG (neural) | TV | $0.220 \pm 0.207$ | $0.395 \pm 0.244$ | $0.418 \pm 0.210$ | $0.302 \pm 0.156$ | 0.821 | 0.097 |

# 4    Conclusion

We have presented an unsupervised detection method with prior distribution learning and local Gaussian approximation with estimated pixel-wise variance. By restoring abnormal images, abnormalities are detected as the absolute difference resulted from the restoration. With restoration visualization and quantitative evaluation, we compared with previous works and observed significant improvement of detection accuracy with reduced false positives.

# References

1. Zikic, D., et al.: Decision forests for tissue-specific segmentation of high-grade gliomas in multi-channel MR. In: Ayache, N., Delingette, H., Golland, P., Mori, K. (eds.) MICCAI 2012. LNCS, vol. 7512, pp. 369–376. Springer, Heidelberg (2012). https://doi.org/10.1007/978-3-642-33454-2_46
2. Cocosco, C.A., Zijdenbos, A.P., Evans, A.C.: A fully automatic and robust brain MRI tissue classification method. MedIA **7**(4), 513–527 (2003)
3. Kamnitsas, K., et al.: Efficient multi-scale 3D CNN with fully connected CRF for accurate brain lesion segmentation. MedIA **36**, 61–78 (2017)
4. Andermatt, S., Horváth, A., Pezold, S., Cattin, P.: Pathology segmentation using distributional differences to images of healthy origin. arXiv:1805.10344 (2018)
5. Schlegl, T., Seeböck, P., Waldstein, S.M., Schmidt-Erfurth, U., Langs, G.: Unsupervised anomaly detection with generative adversarial networks to guide marker discovery. In: Niethammer, M., et al. (eds.) IPMI 2017. LNCS, vol. 10265, pp. 146–157. Springer, Cham (2017). https://doi.org/10.1007/978-3-319-59050-9_12
6. Prastawa, M., Bullitt, E., Ho, S., Gerig, G.: A brain tumor segmentation framework based on outlier detection. MedIA **8**(3), 275–283 (2004)
7. Van Leemput, K., Maes, F., Vandermeulen, D., Colchester, A., Suetens, P.: Automated segmentation of multiple sclerosis lesions by model outlier detection. IEEE TMI **20**(8), 677–688 (2001)
8. Zeng, K., Erus, G., Sotiras, A., Shinohara, R.T., Davatzikos, C.: Abnormality detection via iterative deformable registration and basis-pursuit decomposition. IEEE TMI **35**(8), 1937–1951 (2016)
9. Goodfellow, I., et al.: Generative adversarial nets. In: NIPS (2014)
10. Kingma, D.P., Welling, M.: Auto-encoding variational bayes. In: ICLR (2014)
11. Alaverdyan, Z., Jung, J., Bouet, R., Lartizien, C.: Regularized siamese neural network for unsupervised outlier detection on brain multiparametric magnetic resonance imaging: application to epilepsy lesion screening. In: MIDL (2018)
12. Baur, C., Wiestler, B., Albarqouni, S., Navab, N.: Deep autoencoding models for unsupervised anomaly segmentation in brain MR images. In: Crimi, A., Bakas, S., Kuijf, H., Keyvan, F., Reyes, M., van Walsum, T. (eds.) BrainLes 2018. LNCS, vol. 11383, pp. 161–169. Springer, Cham (2019). https://doi.org/10.1007/978-3-030-11723-8_16
13. Zimmerer, D., Kohl, S.A.A., Petersen, J., Isensee, F., Maier-Hein, K.H.: Context-encoding variational autoencoder for unsupervised anomaly detection. arXiv:1812.05941 (2018)
14. You, S., Tezcan, K., Chen, X., Konukoglu, E.: Unsupervised Lesion Detection via Image Restoration with a Normative Prior. In: MIDL (2019)

15. Makhzani, A., Shlens, J., Jaitly, N., Goodfellow, I., Frey, B.: Adversarial autoencoders. arXiv preprint arXiv:1511.05644 (2015)
16. Konukoglu, E., Glocker, B., Initiative, A.D.N., et al.: Reconstructing subject-specific effect maps. NeuroImage **181**, 521–538 (2018)
17. Taylor, J.R., et al.: The cambridge centre for ageing and neuroscience (cam-CAN) data repository: structural and functional MRI, MEG, and cognitive data from a cross-sectional adult lifespan sample. NeuroImage **144**, 262–269 (2017)
18. Bakas, S., et al.: Advancing the cancer genome atlas glioma MRI collections with expert segmentation labels and radiomic features. Sci. Data **4**, 170117 (2017)
19. Chen, X., Pawlowski, N., Rajchl, M., Glocker, B., Konukoglu, E.: Deep Generative Models in the Real-World: An Open Challenge from Medical Imaging. arXiv:1806.05452 (2018)

# A Hybrid Multi-atrous and Multi-scale Network for Liver Lesion Detection

Yanan Wei[1](✉), Xuan Jiang[1], Kun Liu[2], Cheng Zhong[1], Zhongchao Shi[1], Jianjun Leng[2], and Feiyu Xu[1]

[1] AI Lab, Lenovo Research, Beijing, China
{weiyn1,jiangxuan2,zhongcheng3,shizc2,fxu}@lenovo.com
[2] Peking University Shougang Hospital, Beijing, China
{liukun,leng}@pkusurgery.org

**Abstract.** Liver lesion detection on abdominal computed tomography (CT) is a challenging topic because of its large variance. Current detection methods based on a 2D convolutional neural network (CNN) are limited by the inconsistent view of lesions. One obvious observation is that it can easily lead to a discontinuity problem since it ignores the information between CT slices. To solve this problem, we propose a novel hybrid multi-atrous and multi-scale network (HMMNet). Our network treats the liver lesion detection in a 3D setting as finding a 3D cubic bounding box of a liver lesion. In our work, a multi-atrous 3D convolutional network (MA3DNet) is designed as the backbone. It comes with different dilation rate along z-axis to tackle the various resolutions in z-axis for different CT volumes. In addition, multi-scale features are extracted in a component, called feature extractor, to cover the volume and appearance diversities of liver lesions in a transversal plane. Finally, the features from our backbone and feature extractor are combined to offer the sizing and position measures of liver lesions. These information are frequently referred in a diagnostic report. Compared with other state-of-the-art 2D and 3D convolutional detection models, our HMMNet achieves the top-notch detection performance on the public Liver Tumor Segmentation Challenge (LiTS) dataset, where the F-score are 54.8% and 34.2% on average with the intersection-over-union (IoU) of 0.5 and 0.75 respectively. We also notice that our HMMNet model can be directly applied to the public Medical Segmentation Decathlon dataset without fine-tuning. This further illustrates the generalization capability of our proposed method.

## 1 Introduction

Liver cancer as the sixth most frequent cancer in the world brings the second most common cause of cancer death[1]. Abdominal computed tomography (CT) is a widely used modality for liver lesion diagnosis and treatment. However, manually reading CTs for lesion location and size estimation is time-consuming

---

[1] http://www.who.int/mediacentre/factsheets/fs297/en.

© Springer Nature Switzerland AG 2019
H.-I. Suk et al. (Eds.): MLMI 2019, LNCS 11861, pp. 364–372, 2019.
https://doi.org/10.1007/978-3-030-32692-0_42

and strongly depends on radiologists' experience. It becomes urgent to develop an automatic liver lesion detection approach to improve both the efficiency and effectiveness for diagnosis. Recognizing liver lesions is an inherently difficult task due to the variety of their size, shape and position. Both medical and radiographic knowledge are required for an accurate detection. The recent evolution of deep neural networks (DNNs) [1] with strong computing power provides us a promising way.

Mainstream regular image detection approaches under a 2D setting [2–5] can be directly employed on each CT slice for liver lesion detection. However, it ignores the information between slices which leads to several serious problems. An immediate noticeable problem, as shown in Fig. 1, is the spatial discontinuity between slices, in which the failure of detection on $(i + 4)^{th}$ slice splits a lesion component into two and thus brings a measurement error to the diagnostic report.

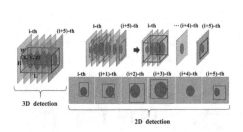

Fig. 1. The problem of 2D detection.

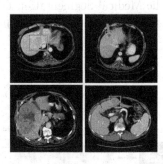

Fig. 2. Examples of liver lesion in CT slices.

3D approach is a promising way to reduce the discontinuity problem. More importantly, 3D approach can offer the sizing and position measures frequently referred in a diagnostic report. Recently, 3D approaches have been applied in lung nodule detection [6–8]. In these tasks, a lung nodule is modeled as a sphere under a solid-colored background and a detector estimates the center and radius of the sphere. Different from lung nodule detection task, a liver lesion detection is more complicated. The background of a liver lesion consists of hepatic parenchyma and blood vessels, which is much more diverse compared with that of a lung nodule. Also, some kinds of hepatic lesions are infiltrating and their boundaries are obscure. Moreover, the shape and scale of liver tumors vary significantly which makes it almost impossible to model them as spheres. The examples of liver lesion are shown in Fig. 2. The liver lesion distinguishes itself from lung nodules and prevents us from directly applying 3D lung nodule detection approaches to a liver lesion detection task.

In this paper, we define a liver lesion detection task as finding a 3D cubic bounding box for each liver lesion. It helps us to avoid the discontinuity problem occurring on 2D object detections due to the neglect of the intra-slice correlation.

A 3D bounding box also provides a consistent view for any possible follow-up processes such as liver lesion segmentation and classification in which the correct alignment of detected regions is critical to offer relative spatial information. Our main contributions can be summarized as follows:

- We define liver lesion detection task as finding a 3D cubic bounding box for each liver lesion, which helps us to avoid the discontinuity problem occurring on a series of 2D object detections.
- To alleviate the diverse resolution along z-axis (ranging from 0.69 mm to 5 mm), we propose a novel multi-atrous 3D convolutional network as the backbone with different dilation rates in z-axis.
- We apply the multi-scale strategy to extract comprehensive intra-slice features to tackle the large variance in both size and appearance.
- Our proposed HMMNet outperforms other widely-used detection models on the public LiTS dataset, and our model can be directly applied to the public Medical Segmentation Decathlon dataset without fine-tuning which illustrates its generalization capability.

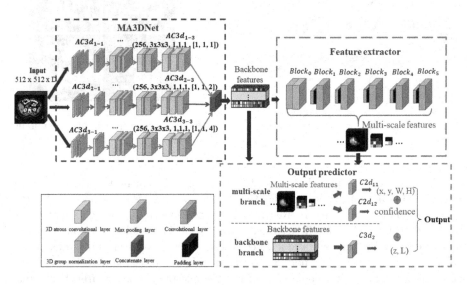

**Fig. 3.** The architecture of HMMNet. $C2d_i(k, s \times s, c)$ means the $i$-th 2D convolutional layer with $k$ filters of size $s \times s$ and the stride is $c$ pixels. The definition of $C3d_j(m, n \times n \times n, d_1, d_2, d_3)$ is similar to $C2d_i(k, s \times s, c)$ but is 3D convolution. $AC3d_{i-j}(m, n \times n \times n, d_1, d_2, d_3, [r_1, r_2, r_3])$ denotes the $j$-th atrous 3D convolutional layer in branch $i$ with $m$ output filters of size $n \times n \times n$. The strides are $d_1, d_2$ and $d_3$, the dilation rates in x, y and z directions are $r_1, r_2$ and $r_3$ respectively.

# 2    Our Approach

Figure 3 shows the architecture of our HMMNet net. HMMNet is composed by three parts: MA3DNet, multi-scale feature extractor and output predictor. The input of the model is $D$ consecutive slices of a CT volume of size $512 \times 512 \times N$ ($D < N$). The output is the estimated 3D bounding boxes and their confidence of lesions.

## 2.1    MA3DNet

A multi-atrous 3D convolutional network, namely MA3DNet, is designed as the backbone of our HMMNet. The MA3DNet which benefits from the VGG-16 network [9] includes three 3D atrous convolutional [10] branches to handle varying spacing problem of CT volumes, since the majority of variation in space is along z-axis ranging from 0.69 mm to 5 mm. Based on our pre-knowledge of the thickness of CT volumes from radiologists, multiple dilation rates (1, 2 and 4) are adopted in z-axis for 3D convolutional kernels. Also group normalization layers [11] are extended to 3D to adopt to our scenarios accordingly.

## 2.2    Multi-scale Feature Extractor

The multi-scale feature extractor is designed to help our model to identify lesions in various scales and shapes especially to improve the recall rate of small lesions. It contains six groups of convolutional blocks ($Block_i$, $i \in [0, 5]$) shown in Fig. 3. For $Block_1$ to $Block_5$, it includes two convolutional layers with the kernel sizes of $1 \times 1$ and $3 \times 3$ and their strides are 1 and 2 respectively. Between them, we pad zeros to each side of the features so that the shape of the block's output feature is $2^{(6-i)} \times 2^{(6-i)}$. Combining the features from the 3D convolutional layer $C3d_1$ in $Block_0$, we collect features in six scales, which then serve as one of the inputs to our output predictor.

## 2.3    Output Predictor

The output predictor accepts two features as its input, the multi-scale features from feature extractor and the backbone features from our MA3DNet. The two features are then processed via two branches, called multi-scale branch and backbone branch. In multi-scale branch, $C2d_{11}$ is applied on features from $Block_0$ to $Block_4$ and followed by a reshape operation to predict locations of lesions in a transversal plane. And the confidence estimation of lesion is also applied in multi-scale branch because the transversal plane in CTs is much more dense and includes more information. For each anchor, we predict 6 boxes with the aspect ratios of $[1, \frac{1}{2}, 2, \frac{1}{3}, 3]$. In backbone branch, backbone features keep the continuity between slices. So we exploit it to predict $z$ and $L$ by a convolution ($C3d_2$) and a reshape operation.

## 3   Experiments

The effectiveness and generalization capability of our proposed method are evaluated based on 2 public datasets, the Liver Tumor Segmentation Challenge (LiTS) dataset[2] and the hepatic vessels and tumour dataset of Medical Segmentation Decathlon[3].

### 3.1   Setting

In our experiments, all CT volumes and annotations in 2 datasets are rotated to a standard orientation, liver left with backbone bottom. This is a regular angle for radiologists to view abdominal CTs. The HU values of CT images are clipped to $[-75, 175]$. We calculate the 2D bounding box for each lesion in each slice as the ground bounding box for 2D detection algorithms. For our 3D detection approach, we calculate a 3D connected component for each lesion and generate its corresponding 3D bounding cube as the ground truth.

We compare our HMMNet with state-of-the-art 2D detection approaches YOLO-V3 [3], R-FCN [4], Mask R-CNN [5]. We also compare with a 3D Net, which is a general 3D detection model composed by a 3D VGG backbone without special design for intra-slice correlation. Specifically, the 3D Net is formed by keeping only one branch unchanged with no dilation in MA3DNet of our HMMNet. The parameter initialization of the backbone of the 3D Net follows the same way as of our HMMNet. R-FCN and Mask R-CNN use ResNet-50 [12] as the backbone. YOLO-V3 uses Darknet-53 as the backbone. All backbone nets are pre-trained on the ImageNet classification task[4].

The MA3DNet of our model is initialized from the first 4 layers of the VGG-16 model pre-trained on ImageNet. We duplicate a $3 \times 3$ convolutional kernel in VGG-16 three times to construct the $3 \times 3 \times 3$ kernel for our dilated 3D convolutions in each branch. In our experiment, we group $D = 8$ consecutive slices on lesion regions as the input. Our loss function is constructed by an identification (background and foreground) and a localization loss respectively. We set a weighting factor $\frac{10}{9}$ for the localization loss to signify the importance of the lesion position. Our model is trained by an Adam optimizer [13] with an initial learning rate $10^{-6}$.

**Table 1.** The average discontinuity over three detection confidences.

| | IoU $= 0.25$, k $= 1$ | IoU $= 0.25$, k $= 3$ | IoU $= 0.5$, k $= 1$ | IoU $= 0.5$, k $= 3$ | IoU $= 0.75$, k $= 1$ | IoU $= 0.75$, k $= 3$ |
|---|---|---|---|---|---|---|
| YOLO-V3 | 0.116 | 0.102 | 0.114 | 0.102 | 0.108 | 0.102 |
| R-FCN | 0.111 | 0.103 | 0.109 | 0.103 | 0.106 | 0.104 |
| Mask R-CNN | 0.112 | 0.102 | 0.109 | 0.101 | 0.107 | 0.102 |

---

[2] https://competitions.codalab.org/competitions/17094.
[3] http://medicaldecathlon.com/.
[4] http://www.image-net.org.

## 3.2   Experiments on LiTS

LiTS dataset contains 201 CT scans for training and testing. And the sizes of the training CT volumes are $512 \times 512 \times N$ ($74 \leq N \leq 987$). The spacing of voxels in z-axis varies from 0.69 mm to 5 mm. Since the testing set does not offer annotations of liver or lesion, we only use the training set in our experiments. The metrics are evaluated through a 5-fold cross validation where 104 scans are for model training and 26 scans are for performance evaluation.

$$\text{Discontinuity}_k = \frac{1}{Num_{all}} \sum_{i=1}^{Num_{all}} \left( \frac{Num_{k-missing,i}}{Num_i} \right), \tag{1}$$

**Discontinuity.** To evaluate how severe the discontinuity problem is in 2D detection methods, a metric, $\text{Discontinuity}_k$, is designed in Eq. 1. Particularly, a k-missing is a group of k consecutive slices for a lesion component which is ignored by a detector. $\frac{Num_{k-missing,i}}{Num_i}$ is the proportion of the k-missings for $i$-th lesion. For completeness, we define this proportion is 0 if nothing or only one lesion slice is detected since these cases do not involve the concept of continuity. A larger $\text{Discontinuity}_k$ indicates the detector is more likely to miss a sequence of k slices in a lesion component in the detection results.

During the process of detection, if the number of missing slices is more than 3, the missing slices are usually hard to call back by post-processing methods, especially when the lesion is inconspicuous in these slices. Therefore we evaluate the average $\text{Discontinuity}_k$ over three detection confidences ($C = 0.5$, $0.7$, $0.9$), with $k = 1, 3$ for trivial and severe discontinuity under different intersection-over-unions (IoUs) in Table 1. We find that even in these severe situations, at least 10% discontinuity occurs in all 2D approaches. To avoid detection failures, a 3D approach is worth considering.

**Table 2.** Precision, recall and F-score abbreviated by Pre, Rec and F under certain thresholds of IoU and C.

|      |     | YOLO-V3 | | | R-FCN | | | Mask R-CNN | | | 3D Net | | | HMMNet | | |
|------|-----|------|------|------|------|------|------|------|------|------|------|------|------|------|------|------|
| IoU  | C   | Pre  | Rec  | F    | Rre  | Rec  | F    | Pre  | Rec  | F    | Pre  | Rec  | F    | Pre  | Rec  | F    |
| 0.25 | 0.5 | 49.1 | 68.9 | 57.3 | 73.5 | 47.2 | 57.4 | 19.4 | 72.4 | 30.6 | 60.2 | 56.0 | 58.0 | 61.4 | 58.0 | **59.6** |
|      | 0.7 | 67.3 | 61.4 | 64.2 | **68.9** | 50.7 | 58.4 | 25.8 | 69.7 | 37.6 | 64.0 | 55.2 | 59.2 | 65.2 | 56.5 | 60.5 |
|      | 0.9 | 84.8 | 43.5 | 57.5 | 77.7 | 43.8 | 56.0 | 38.5 | 64.1 | 48.1 | 65.3 | 49.7 | 56.4 | 66.6 | 50.7 | **57.6** |
| 0.5  | 0.5 | 35.5 | 56.7 | 43.6 | 60.4 | 43.7 | 50.7 | 14.9 | 62.7 | 24.0 | 46.7 | 54.2 | 50.1 | 47.0 | 56.3 | **51.2** |
|      | 0.7 | 67.3 | 50.4 | 57.6 | 63.3 | 42.1 | 50.5 | 20.3 | 60.6 | 30.4 | 60.2 | 51.3 | 55.4 | 62.4 | 54.0 | **57.9** |
|      | 0.9 | 84.8 | 35.7 | 50.2 | 67.9 | 39.6 | 50.0 | 31.4 | 56.4 | 40.3 | 63.9 | 46.0 | 53.5 | 65.4 | 48.3 | **55.5** |
| 0.75 | 0.5 | 16.5 | 28.3 | 20.8 | 35.6 | 26.6 | 30.4 | 8.3  | 37.9 | 13.6 | 30.0 | 34.3 | 32.0 | 32.2 | 36.0 | **34.0** |
|      | 0.7 | 24.0 | 25.2 | 24.5 | 38.2 | 26.1 | 31.0 | 20.6 | 37.1 | 26.4 | 35.5 | 30.0 | 32.5 | 36.7 | 31.1 | **33.7** |
|      | 0.9 | 32.3 | 18.2 | 23.2 | 41.9 | 25.2 | 31.4 | 29.4 | 35.1 | 31.9 | 40.2 | 29.2 | 33.8 | 40.6 | 30.5 | **34.8** |

**Main Results.** Precision and recall [14] are two measures of the performance for both 2D and 3D methods in our experiments. F-score provides a quantitative measure for the trade-off between the two which is also evaluated in our experiments.

Table 2 shows the precision, recall and F-score of all approaches on LiTS dataset. On IoU $= 0.25$, our HMMNet presents the same competitive ability with YOLO-V3 and outperforms R-FCN, Mask R-CNN and 3D Net. When IoU $= 0.5$, the precision of our model shows a growing trend and with the highest F-score, our approach performs better than all other approaches. Especially when C $= 0.9$, our HMMNet presents 2.0%, 5.3%, 5.5% and 15.2% increases of F-score compared with 3D Net, YOLO-V3, R-FCN and Mask R-CNN. With IoU $= 0.75$, our model has obvious advantages over other approaches. These results indicate that our HMMNet gives more accurate prediction of bounding boxes which benefits from the multi-scale design. An average increase 1.7% of recall rate between our HMMNet and 3D Net verifies the efficiency of our MA3DNet which can effectively capture the spatial correlations of intra- and inter-CT slices.

### 3.3  Experiments on Decathlon

In order to verify the generalization capability of our HMMNet, the hepatic vessels and tumor dataset of Medical Segmentation Decathlon is evaluated in this section. The slice spacing along z-axis varies from 0.8 to 8 mm. All CTs with lesion annotations from LiTS dateset are used for training, and the Decathlon dataset is solely for testing.

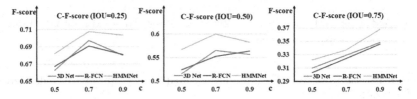

**Fig. 4.** The C and F-score curves of all approaches under certain IoU (0.25, 0.5, 0.75).

Figure 4 shows that our HMMNet outperforms other approaches on the Decathlon dataset. It should be mentioned that only R-FCN which ranks the top among all other 2D approaches is included in Fig. 4. Without considering the variation of liver lesions along z-axis, 3D Net gives unsatisfied predictions which are no better than R-FCN. Figure 5 shows a comparison of the subjective results for our HMMNet, 3D Net and R-FCN. Ignoring the inter-slice spatial correlation, R-FCN suffers frequent detection failure and misalignment between slices. Without considering the variation of liver lesions along z-axis, detection failure also occurs in 3D Net. However, by exploring various intra-slice and inter-slice spatial correlations, our HMMNet alleviates the missing detection and shows the generalization capability across datasets.

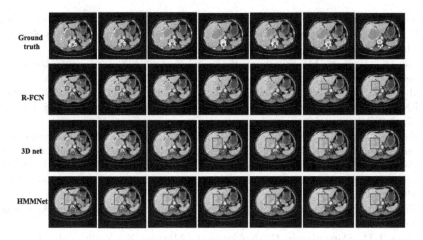

**Fig. 5.** Subjective results of lesion detection.

# 4 Conclusion

In this paper, we proposed a novel HMMNet for liver lesion detection on abdominal CT volumes. Different from the lung nodule detection with fixed diameter annotation, liver lesions inherently are more complex in both shape and scale. To effectively extract the liver lesion features, a MA3DNet is designed to deal with the diversity of resolutions in z-axis for different CT volumes, and a multi-scale strategy is applied in the feature extractor to tackle the various volumes and appearances of liver lesions. In addition, by exploring the information between multiple CT slices, HMMNet is capable of solving the discontinuity problem which commonly exists in the state-of-the-art 2D CNN detection models. Experimental results on 2 public databases show the effectiveness and generalization capability of our proposed HMMNet.

# References

1. Shen, D., Wu, G., Suk, H.I.: Deep learning in medical image analysis. Annu. Rev. Biomed. Eng. **19**(1), 221–248 (2017). annurev-bioeng-071516-044442
2. Liu, W., et al.: SSD: Single shot multibox detector. In: European Conference on Computer Vision, pp. 21–37 (2016)
3. Redmon, J., Farhadi, A.: Yolov3: an incremental improvement. arXiv preprint arXiv:1804.02767 (2018)
4. Dai, J., Li, Y., He, K., Sun, J.: R-FCN: Object detection via region-based fully convolutional networks. In: Advances in Neural Information Processing Systems, pp. 379–387 (2016)
5. He, K., Gkioxari, G., Dollar, P., Girshick, R.: Mask R-CNN. In: 2017 IEEE International Conference on Computer Vision (ICCV), pp. 2980–2988 (2017)
6. Dou, Q., Chen, H., Jin, Y., Lin, H., Qin, J., Heng, P.-A.: Automated pulmonary nodule detection via 3D ConvNets with online sample filtering and hybrid-loss

residual learning. In: Descoteaux, M., Maier-Hein, L., Franz, A., Jannin, P., Collins, D.L., Duchesne, S. (eds.) MICCAI 2017. LNCS, vol. 10435, pp. 630–638. Springer, Cham (2017). https://doi.org/10.1007/978-3-319-66179-7_72

7. Yan, K., Bagheri, M., Summers, R.M.: 3D context enhanced region-based convolutional neural network for end-to-end lesion detection. In: Frangi, A.F., Schnabel, J.A., Davatzikos, C., Alberola-López, C., Fichtinger, G. (eds.) MICCAI 2018. LNCS, vol. 11070, pp. 511–519. Springer, Cham (2018). https://doi.org/10.1007/978-3-030-00928-1_58

8. Zhu, W., Vang, Y.S., Huang, Y., Xie, X.: DeepEM: Deep 3D ConvNets with EM for weakly supervised pulmonary nodule detection. In: Frangi, A.F., Schnabel, J.A., Davatzikos, C., Alberola-López, C., Fichtinger, G. (eds.) MICCAI 2018. LNCS, vol. 11071, pp. 812–820. Springer, Cham (2018). https://doi.org/10.1007/978-3-030-00934-2_90

9. Simonyan, K., Zisserman, A.: Very deep convolutional networks for large-scale image recognition. arXiv preprint arXiv:1409.1556 (2014)

10. Chen, L.C., Papandreou, G., Kokkinos, I., Murphy, K., Yuille, A.L.: DeepLab: semantic image segmentation with deep convolutional nets, atrous convolution, and fully connected CRFS. IEEE Trans. Pattern Anal. Mach. Intell. 40(4), 834–848 (2016)

11. Wu, Y., He, K.: Group normalization. In: Ferrari, V., Hebert, M., Sminchisescu, C., Weiss, Y. (eds.) ECCV 2018. LNCS, vol. 11217, pp. 3–19. Springer, Cham (2018). https://doi.org/10.1007/978-3-030-01261-8_1

12. He, K., Zhang, X., Ren, S., Sun, J.: Deep residual learning for image recognition. In: Proceedings of the IEEE Conference on Computer Vision and Pattern Recognition, pp. 770–778 (2016)

13. Kingma, D.P., Ba, J.: Adam: a method for stochastic optimization. arXiv preprint arXiv:1412.6980 (2014)

14. Wiedemann, C., Heipke, C., Mayer, H., Jamet, O.: Empirical evaluation of automatically extracted road axes. In: Empirical Evaluation Techniques in Computer Vision, pp. 172–187 (1998)

# BOLD fMRI-Based Brain Perfusion Prediction Using Deep Dilated Wide Activation Networks

Danfeng Xie[1,2], Yiran Li[1], HanLu Yang[1,2], Donghui Song[3], Yuanqi Shang[3], Qiu Ge[3], Li Bai[1], and Ze Wang[2(✉)]

[1] Temple University, Philadelphia, PA 19131, USA
[2] University of Maryland School of Medicine, Baltimore, MD 21201, USA
ze.wang@som.umaryland.edu
[3] Hangzhou Normal University, Hangzhou 311121, China

**Abstract.** Arterial spin labeling (ASL) perfusion MRI and blood-oxygen-level-dependent (BOLD) fMRI provide complementary information for assessing brain functions. ASL is quantitative, insensitive to low-frequency drift but has lower signal-to-noise-ratio (SNR) and lower temporal resolution than BOLD. However, there still lacks a way to fuse the benefits provided by both of them. When only one modality is available, it is also desirable to have a technique that can extract the other modality from the one being acquired. The purpose of this study was to develop such a technique that can combine the advantages of BOLD fMRI and ASL MRI, i.e., to quantify cerebral blood flow (CBF) like ASL MRI but with high SNR and temporal resolution as in BOLD fMRI. We pursued this goal using a new deep learning-based algorithm to extract CBF directly from BOLD fMRI. Using a relatively large dataset containing dual-echo ASL and BOLD images, we built a wide residual learning based convolutional neural network to predict CBF from BOLD fMRI. We dubbed this technique as a BOA-Net (BOLD to ASL networks). Our testing results demonstrated that ASL CBF can be reliably predicted from BOLD fMRI with comparable image quality and higher SNR. We also evaluated BOA-Net with different deep learning networks.

**Keywords:** Arterial spin labeling · BOLD fMRI · Deep learning · Dilated convolution · Wide activation · Residual learning

## 1 Introduction

Human brain function can be assessed non-invasively using two MR techniques with a whole brain coverage and relatively high spatial resolution. One is the blood-oxygen-level-dependent fMRI [10]; the other is arterial spin labeling (ASL) perfusion MRI [2]. BOLD fMRI is more widely used, offering high temporal and spatial resolution, but only provides relative values. It is sensitive to low-frequency drift and suffers from the susceptibility gradient-induced artifacts.

© Springer Nature Switzerland AG 2019
H.-I. Suk et al. (Eds.): MLMI 2019, LNCS 11861, pp. 373–381, 2019.
https://doi.org/10.1007/978-3-030-32692-0_43

By contrast, ASL MRI measures cerebral blood flow (CBF) in a physical unit of ml/100 g/min. The quantitative nature of ASL MRI makes it insensitive to low-frequency drift. Measuring signal from the capillary bed, ASL MRI is potentially more accurate for localizing functional activation than BOLD fMRI which is often mainly contributed by oxygen level change in venous vessels rather than the activation site. However, ASL MRI has lower signal-to-noise-ratio (SNR), lower temporal resolution, and has only seen increasing visibility in recent years. An important but still open question is how to fuse the benefits provided by the two complementary functional imaging modalities. Since many finished and ongoing large size fMRI projects only had or have BOLD fMRI, a related question is whether we can reliably extract CBF signal from BOLD fMRI. Solving both questions requires understanding the elusive relationship between these two imaging modalities.

Theoretically, ASL MRI works by magnetically labeling the arterial blood water as an endogenous tracer using radio-frequency (RF) pulses [2]. The perfusion-weighted MR image is acquired after the labeled spins reach the imaging place. To remove the background signal, a control image is also acquired using the same ASL imaging sequence but with modulations to avoid labeling the arterial blood so the background signal under the influence of RF pulses is the same as that in the spin labeling condition. The perfusion-weighted signal is subsequently extracted from the difference between the label (L) image and the control (C) and converted into a quantitative CBF measure using an appropriate compartment model [1]. Due to the limitation of the longitudinal relaxation rate (T1) of blood water and the post-labeling transmit process a small portion of tissue water can be labeled, resulting in a low SNR [15]. Thus, ASL often acquires many pairs of L/C images to improve SNR of the mean perfusion map. Practically, 10–50 L/C pairs are allowed in a typical 3–6 min scan, which can only provide minor to moderate SNR improvement by averaging across the limited number of measurements. The interleaved labeling and non-labeling procedure reduces the temporal resolution of ASL MRI by half compared to the regular dynamic MR imaging. The relatively long labeling and post-labeling delay time before data acquisition further reduces the temporal resolution of ASL MRI. Ideally, these drawbacks can be avoided instantly if CBF can be extracted from BOLD fMRI. From a technical point of view, ASL MRI can be acquired with many different imaging sequences. That is why the gradient-echo weighted BOLD imaging sequence is still widely used to acquire ASL MRI data. It is then theoretically reasonable to hypothesize that CBF can be extracted from the BOLD fMRI. The challenge is then to find an appropriate model for the unknown BOLD-CBF relationship.

A canonical BOLD-CBF model has been proposed in [4], but requires data acquired under gas-challenging. The underlying assumption of no change of cerebral metabolic rate of oxygen by gas-challenging may also be inaccurate. Without extra experiments, there isn't an analytic way to extract quantitative CBF from BOLD fMRI. Alternatively, a learning-based approach might be able to solve this problem. Over the years, machine learning especially deep machine learning has been increasingly used to achieve astonishing success for modeling various highly complex data relationship [7].

Deep learning (DL) is motivated by the hierarchical learning in the visual system [3]. The most widely used deep neural networks consist of multiple layers of receptive field constrained local filters which are trained layer by layer by error backpropagations [6] and are often called convolutional neural networks (CNN). The local feature extraction, hierarchical abstraction, step-wise backpropagation of CNN and the introduction of several training strategies such as weight dropout, batch-normalization, skip connection, and residual learning etc make CNN high flexible and capable for modeling any nonlinear function buried in a large data. Because medical imaging processing is often hindered by some unknown nonlinear processes or transforms, DL may provide a potentially versatile tool for medical imaging processing as increasingly demonstrated in a variety of applications, including image segmentation [11] and image reconstructions [13] etc. Specific to ASL MRI, DL has been adopted to improve SNR of ASL CBF maps [5,16]. Most related to this study is that Xie et al. [17] piloted a pairwise label to control image prediction using CNN. Since the ASL MRI used in the so-called super-ASL network was acquired with the gradient-echo weighted BOLD fMRI sequence, it suggests the feasibility of directly extracting CBF from BOLD fMRI.

The purpose of this study was mainly to build and validate a DL-based BOLD-ASL relationship learning model to predict CBF signal directly from BOLD fMRI. We dubbed the network as the BOA-Net. Different from the super-ASL work, we used current ASL MRI and BOLD fMRI acquired with a dual-echo ASL MRI sequence [12] so the network doesn't need to consider the physiological difference or signal drift-induced difference between the BOLD fMRI and ASL CBF. Another contribution is that we introduced a new CNN architecture based on dilated convolution [19] and wide activation residual block [20].

## 2   Methods

### 2.1   Problem Formulation

Denote the CBF image generated by $i$-th L/C pair by $y_i$ and the BOLD image (the 2nd echo) after the $i$-th C image by $x_i$. Given same brain structure and transitory acquisition time, we want to build a parametric regression model $f_\Theta$ that learns the mapping $f_\Theta(x_i) \to y_i$, where $i = 1, 2, ..., N$, and $N$ is the total number of one subject's CBF maps. $\Theta$ are the parameters of the model and are adjusted through the training process. The model, typically a CNN, can be learned by minimizing the loss function: $\sum_i L(f_\Theta(x_i), y_i)$, where the loss function can be either the mean square error or mean absolute error between input and reference.

As we don't have gold standard CBF maps as the training references, using the low SNR ASL CBF images as the training references may result in an inaccurate BOA-Net. Interestingly, a recent study [8] showed that the inaccurate model training concern due to the use of noisy reference is not necessarily true. Inspired by their work, we proposed a noisy reference-based BOA-Net. Instead of using the L2 norm as the loss function, we chose the L1 norm to reduce sensitivity to outliers which are common to ASL MRI [9].

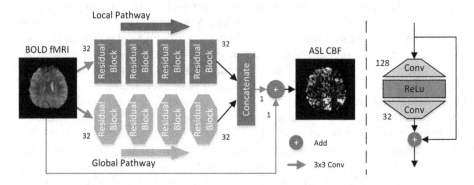

**Fig. 1.** A schematic illustration of the proposed DWAN network (left) and wide activation residual block (right). All residual blocks in DWAN are made with wide activation residual blocks. The numbers in the figure represent the number of feature maps in corresponding position.

## 2.2    Network Architecture

Figure 1 demonstrates the architecture of DWAN used in BOA-Net and the wide activation residual block. The two-path DilatedNet [5] were used to extract both local and global contextual features. The wide activation residual blocks were adapted to expand data features and pass more information through the network [20]. In DWAN, each pathway contains 4 wide activation residual blocks. Inside each wide activation residual block, the first convolution layer expands the number of input feature maps by a factor of 4. After a ReLU layer, the following convolution layer shrinks the number of feature maps back to input size. The difference between local pathway and global pathway is that, the first convolution layer of the 4 wide activation residual blocks in the global pathway used a dilation rate of 2, 4, 8 and 16 respectively. The convolution kernel size was $3 \times 3$. A $3 \times 3$ convolution link [20] from the input layer to the output layer implements the residual learning of DWAN.

## 2.3    Data Preparation and Model Training

ASL and BOLD fMRI data were acquired with the dual-echo ASL sequence [12] from 50 young healthy subjects at Hangzhou Normal University with signed informed written consent forms. The experiment and the form were applied by local IRB. Imaging parameters were: labeling time/delay time/TR/TE1/TE2 = 1.4 s/1.5 s/4.5 s/11.7 msec/68 msec, 90 acquisitions (90 BOLD images and 45 C/L image pairs), FOV = 22 cm, matrix = $64 \times 64$, 16 slices with a thickness of 5 mm plus 1 mm gap. We used ASLtbx [14] to prepro-cess ASL images with the procedures in [9].

The BOA-Net was trained with data from 23 subjects' CBF maps (input and reference). 4 different subjects were used for validation samples. The remaining 23 subjects' CBF maps were used as test samples. For each subject, we extracted slices from 7 to 11 of 3D ASL CBF maps. The number of total 2D CBF maps extracted for training and validation were $27 \times 5 \times 45 = 6075$. The 2D CBF maps were $64 \times 64$ pixels. U-Net [18] and DilatedNet [5], two popular CNN structure widely used in medical imaging, were implemented as a comparison to our DWAN-based BOA-Net.

We also compare the effects of training with smoothing CBFs versus non-smoothing CBFs. The CBFs that were generated from the L/C pairs with Gaus-sian smoothing were called smoothing CBFs. The CBFs that were generated from the L/C pairs without Gaussian smoothing were called non-smoothing CBFs. the suffix 'sm' and 'nsm' were added to the name of each model to rep-resent that the model was trained using the smoothed or non-smoothed CBFs, respectively. We use Peak signal-to-noise ratio (PSNR) and structure similarity index (SSIM) to quantitatively compare the performance of DWAN with U-Net and DilatedNet. When calculating PSNR and SSIM, all the predicted results were compared with genuine mean CBF maps from smoothed ASL data.

All networks were implemented using the Keras and Tensorflow platform. The network was trained using adaptive moment estimation (ADAM) algorithm with basic learning rate of 0.001. All the models were trained with batches, each containing 64 training samples. All experiments were performed on a PC with Intel(R) Core(TM) i7-5820k CPU @3.30 GHz and a Nvidia GeForce Titan Xp GPU.

We used SNR to measure the image quality of ASL CBF. The SNR was calculated by using the mean signal of a grey matter (GM) region-of-interest (ROI) divided by the standard deviation of a white matter (WM) ROI in slice 9. Similarity of mean CBF from the outputs of BOA-Net to genuine mean CBF maps from ASL data, was evaluated by the correlation coefficient between the CBF values of all testing subjects ($n = 23$). This process was performed at each voxel for BOA-Net_sm and BOA-Net_nsm separately. The correlation coefficient maps were thresholded by $r > 0.3$ for the purpose of comparison and display.

## 3   Results

Figure 2 shows the results of BOLD-based CBF prediction for one representative subject. As compared to the genuine mean CBF map from the acquired ASL MRI, the CBF map produced by BOA-Net showed substantially improved qual-ity in terms of suppressed noise and better perfusion contrast between tissues. Moreover, BOA-Net recovered CBF signals in the air-brain boundaries. Signal loss in the genuine mean CBF in the prefrontal region was caused by the signal loss in BOLD images.

Figure 3 shows box plot of the SNR and spatial correlation BOA-Net_sm and BOA-Net_nsm. the average SNR of genuine mean CBF maps from non-smoothed

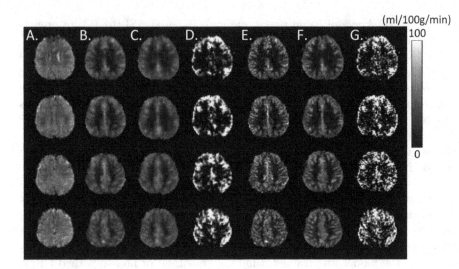

**Fig. 2.** From left to right: A. BOLD fMRI (input to BOA-Net_sm and BOA-Net_nsm); B. Mean CBF maps from 45 smoothed L/C pairs; C. Mean CBF maps from the output of BOA-Net_sm; D. CBF map from one smoothed L/C pair (reference for BOA-Net_sm). E. Mean CBF maps from 45 non-smoothed L/C pairs; F. Mean CBF maps from the outputs of BOA-Net_nsm; G. CBF map from one non-smoothed L/C pair (reference for BOA-Net_nsm). From top to bottom: slice 8, 9, 10, 11.

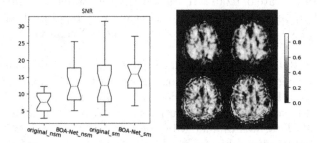

**Fig. 3.** The notched box plot of the SNR (left) and correlation coefficient maps between genuine mean CBF and output of BOA-Net (right). Original_nsm and original_sm represent the genuine mean CBF maps from non-smoothed and smoothed ASL data. BOA-Net_nsm and BOA-Net_sm represent mean CBF maps from outputs of BOA-Net_nsm and BOA-Net_sm. The correlation coefficient maps between genuine mean CBF and output of BOA-Net_sm is shown in the top row. The correlation coefficient maps between genuine mean CBF and output of BOA-Net_nsm is shown in the bottom row. Only 2 axial slices were shown. Correlation coefficients less than 0.3 were thresholded to be 0.

and smoothed ASL data were 6.96 and 12.64 respectively. The average SNR of mean CBF maps from outputs of BOA-Net_nsm and BOA-Net_sm were 12.26 and 15.11. BOA-Net_sm improved SNR by 19.54% compared with mean CBF maps of smoothed ASL while BOA-Net_nsm achieved a 76.15% SNR improvement compared with the mean CBF maps of non-smoothed ASL. Correlation coefficient at each voxel was calculated between the genuine mean CBF map and network output. Figure 3 shows outputs of BOA-Net_sm and BOA-Net_nsm strongly correlated to the genuine mean CBF, proving that both networks can predict individual subjects' CBF patterns correctly.

**Table 1.** The average PSNR and SSIM from different CNN architectures used in BOA-Net_sm and BOA-Net_nsm

|       | BOA-Net_sm |  |  | BOA-Net_nsm |  |  |
|-------|------------|--------------|----------|-------------|---------------|------------|
| Model | U-Net_sm | DilatedNet_sm | DWAN_sm | U-Net_nsm | DilatedNet_nsm | DWAN_nsm |
| PSNR | 24.15 | 24.10 | **24.58** | 21.88 | 21.51 | **22.49** |
| SSIM | 0.884 | 0.892 | **0.895** | 0.856 | 0.841 | **0.865** |

Table 1 shows the PSNR and SSIM of mean CBF maps predicted from different models. DWAN achieved highest PSNR and SSIM in both BOA-Net_sm and BOA-Net_nsm categories. Figure 4 demonstrates the visual comparison of mean CBF maps predicted from BOLD fMRI using different CNN architectures. DWAN suppressed more noises than DilatedNet while recovered more details than U-Net. Moreover, DWAN_nsm has better perfusion contrast than DWAN_sm while DWAN_sm recover more signals in air-brain boundaries.

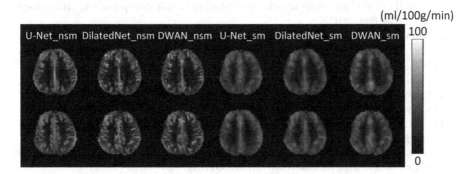

**Fig. 4.** Two representative slices of the mean CBF maps produced by different processing methods. The three columns on the left side are mean CBF maps of outputs of U-Net_nsm, DilatedNet_nsm, and DWAN_nsm respectively. The three columns on the right side are mean CBF maps of outputs of U-Net_sm, DilatedNet_sm, and DWAN_sm

## 4   Discussion and Conclusion

To our knowledge, this study represents the first effort to extract quantitative CBF from BOLD fMRI. Comparing with genuine mean CBF from ASL data, the BOA-Net can provide CBF measurement with higher SNR, higher temporal resolution, both inherited from BOLD fMRI (higher SNR is also contributed by DL denoising). For existing dataset without ASL MRI acquired, this provides a unique opportunity to generate a new functional imaging modality. For future studies, it offers an opportunity to avoid ASL MRI scan though that will need more evaluations especially in diseased populations. Even if ASL MRI scan is still needed, its scan time can be substantially shortened and the reduced SNR can be compensated by CBF estimated from BOA-Net. Because this study was only tested on dual-echo MRI sequences, future work will also aim at extending our work on different datasets.

**Acknowledgements.** This work was supported by NIH/NIA grant: R01AG060054-01A1.

# References

1. Alsop, D.C., et al.: Recommended implementation of arterial spin-labeled perfusion MRI for clinical applications. Magn. Reson. Med. **73**(1), 102–116 (2015)
2. Detre, J.A., et al.: Perfusion imaging. Magn. Reson. Med. **23**(1), 37–45 (1992)
3. Fukushima, K., et al.: Neocognitron: a neural network model for a mechanism of visual pattern recognition. IEEE Trans. Syst. Man Cybern. **5**, 826–834 (1983)
4. Hoge, R.D., et al.: Linear coupling between cerebral blood flow and oxygen consumption in activated human cortex. Proc. Natl. Acad. Sci. **96**(16), 9403–9408 (1999)
5. Kim, K.H., et al.: Improving arterial spin labeling by using deep learning. Radiology **287**(2), 658–666 (2017)
6. Krizhevsky, A., et al.: ImageNet classification with deep convolutional neural networks. In: Advances in Neural Information Processing Systems, pp. 1097–1105 (2012)
7. LeCun, Y., Bengio, Y., Hinton, G.: Deep learning. Nature **521**(7553), 436 (2015)
8. Lehtinen, J., et al.: Noise2Noise: learning image restoration without clean data. arXiv preprint arXiv:1803.04189 (2018)
9. Li, Y., et al.: Priors-guided slice-wise adaptive outlier cleaning for arterial spin labeling perfusion MRI. J. Neurosci. Methods **307**, 248–253 (2018)
10. Ogawa, S., et al.: Brain magnetic resonance imaging with contrast dependent on blood oxygenation. Proc. Natl. Acad. Sci. **87**(24), 9868–9872 (1990)
11. Shen, D., Wu, G., Suk, H.I.: Deep learning in medical image analysis. Annu. Rev. Biomed. Eng. **19**, 221–248 (2017)
12. Shin, D.D., et al.: Pseudocontinuous arterial spin labeling with optimized tagging efficiency. Magn. Reson. Med. **68**(4), 1135–1144 (2012)
13. Wang, S., et al.: Accelerating magnetic resonance imaging via deep learning. In: 2016 IEEE 13th International Symposium on Biomedical Imaging (ISBI), pp. 514–517. IEEE (2016)
14. Wang, Z., et al.: Empirical optimization of ASL data analysis using an asl data processing toolbox: ASLtbx. Magn. Reson. Imaging **26**(2), 261–269 (2008)
15. Wong, E.: Potential and pitfalls of arterial spin labeling based perfusion imaging techniques for MRI. In: Moonen, C.T.W., Bandettini, P.A. (eds.) Functional MRI, pp. 63–69. Springer, Heidelberg (1999)

16. Xie, D., et al.: Denoising arterial spin labeling cerebral blood flow images using deep learning. arXiv preprint arXiv:1801.09672 (2018)
17. Xie, D., et al.: Super-ASL: Improving SNR and temporal resolution of ASL MRI using deep learning. In: 2018 ISMRM Workshop on Machine Learning (2018)
18. Xu, J., et al.: 200x low-dose pet reconstruction using deep learning. arXiv preprint arXiv:1712.04119 (2017)
19. Yu, F., Koltun, V.: Multi-scale context aggregation by dilated convolutions. arXiv preprint arXiv:1511.07122 (2015)
20. Yu, J., et al.: Wide activation for efficient and accurate image super-resolution. arXiv preprint arXiv:1808.08718 (2018)

# Jointly Discriminative and Generative Recurrent Neural Networks for Learning from fMRI

Nicha C. Dvornek[1,2(✉)], Xiaoxiao Li[2], Juntang Zhuang[2],
and James S. Duncan[1,2,3,4]

[1] Department of Radiology & Biomedical Imaging, Yale School of Medicine,
New Haven, CT, USA
nicha.dvornek@yale.edu
[2] Department of Biomedical Engineering, Yale University, New Haven, CT, USA
[3] Department of Electrical Engineering, Yale University, New Haven, CT, USA
[4] Department of Statistics and Data Science, Yale University, New Haven, CT, USA

**Abstract.** Recurrent neural networks (RNNs) were designed for dealing with time-series data and have recently been used for creating predictive models from functional magnetic resonance imaging (fMRI) data. However, gathering large fMRI datasets for learning is a difficult task. Furthermore, network interpretability is unclear. To address these issues, we utilize multitask learning and design a novel RNN-based model that learns to discriminate between classes while simultaneously learning to generate the fMRI time-series data. Employing the long short-term memory (LSTM) structure, we develop a discriminative model based on the hidden state and a generative model based on the cell state. The addition of the generative model constrains the network to learn functional communities represented by the LSTM nodes that are both consistent with the data generation as well as useful for the classification task. We apply our approach to the classification of subjects with autism vs. healthy controls using several datasets from the Autism Brain Imaging Data Exchange. Experiments show that our jointly discriminative and generative model improves classification learning while also producing robust and meaningful functional communities for better model understanding.

## 1  Introduction

Functional magnetic resonance imaging (fMRI) has become an important tool for investigating neurological disorders and diseases. In addition, machine learning has begun to play a large role, in which classification models are learned and interpreted to discover potential fMRI biomarkers for disease. Traditional approaches for building classification models from resting-state fMRI first parcellate the brain into a number of regions of interest (ROIs) and use functional connectivity between the ROIs as inputs to a classification algorithm [1]. Recently

---

This work was supported by NIH grants R01MH100028 and R01NS035193.

H.-I. Suk et al. (Eds.): MLMI 2019, LNCS 11861, pp. 382–390, 2019.
https://doi.org/10.1007/978-3-030-32692-0_44

with the advent of deep learning, temporal inputs based on the time-series data combined with recurrent neural network (RNN) models have been explored for predicting from fMRI [7,9,14]. Such RNN models are attractive for processing fMRI as they were designed for dealing with sequential data. However, the large sample sizes required for effective deep learning are difficult to gather for fMRI data, particularly for many different patient populations or types of studies.

One way to handle the limited data problem is to apply multitask learning [4]. The idea in multitask learning is that shared information across related tasks is jointly learned in order to improve the learning of each individual task. For a classification task based on fMRI data, e.g., distinguish subjects with a given disease from healthy individuals, the amount of labeled data is often limited. Thus, we propose to apply multitask learning to improve the learning of a target discriminative task by jointly learning an auxiliary generative model for the fMRI data, which does not require any annotation. Moreover, simultaneous learning of the generative model will assist in interpreting the discriminative model.

Specifically, we propose to jointly learn a discriminative task while also learning to generate the input fMRI time-series by using an RNN with long short-term memory (LSTM). Generative RNN models have been extensively used in natural language processing, e.g., for text generation [8], but application to the medical imaging field has been limited. Furthermore, multitask learning with discriminative and generative components have been combined in many different neural network architectures, notably generative adversarial networks, but such a joint learning approach utilizing the RNN framework has only begun to be explored and under the context of adversarial training for a target generative task [2].

In this paper, we design a novel RNN-based model with LSTM to simultaneously learn a discriminative and generative task by utilizing the state information in a shared LSTM layer. Using fMRI ROI time-series as inputs, we interpret the LSTM block as modeling the coordination of functional activity in the brain and the nodes of the LSTM as representing functional communities, i.e., groupings of the input brain ROIs that work together to both generate the fMRI time-series and perform the discriminative task. We apply the proposed network for classification of ASD vs. healthy controls, validating on multiple datasets from the Autism Brain Imaging Data Exchange (ABIDE) I dataset. Compared to several recent methods, we achieve some of the highest accuracy reported on single-site ABIDE data. Finally, we evaluate the generative results by analyzing the robustness of the extracted functional communities and validate influential communities for classification in the context of ASD.

## 2 Methods

### 2.1 Network Architecture

**LSTM Block for Communities.** The LSTM module was designed to learn long-term dependencies in sequential data [10]. An LSTM cell is composed of 4 neural network layers with $K$ nodes that modulate two state vectors, the hidden state $h_t \in \mathbb{R}^K$ and the cell state $c_t \in \mathbb{R}^K$. The state vectors are updated using input from the current time point $x_t \in \mathbb{R}^R$ and state information from the previous time point $h_{t-1}$ and $c_{t-1}$:

$$g_t = \sigma\left(W_g x_t + U_g h_{t-1} + b_g\right), \text{with } g \in \{i, f, o\} \tag{1}$$

$$\tilde{c}_t = \tanh\left(W_c x_t + U_c h_{t-1} + b_c\right) \tag{2}$$

$$c_t = i_t * \tilde{c}_t + f_t * c_{t-1}, \quad h_t = o_t * \tanh\left(c_t\right) \tag{3}$$

where for layer $l \in \{i, f, o, c\}$, $W_l$ are the weights for the input, $U_l$ are the weights for the hidden state, and $b_l$ are the bias parameters.

The proposed network first takes the fMRI ROI time-series as inputs to an LSTM layer (Fig. 1, blue path). The purpose of this layer is to discover meaningful groupings of the ROIs, i.e. functional communities, that are important for both generating and classifying the input data. The LSTM block acts as a model for the interaction between $R$ individual ROIs and $K$ functional communities formed by the brain network to generate community activity. The activity generated by each functional community $k$ is then represented by the hidden state $h_t(k)$ and cell state $c_t(k)$, which will serve as inputs to the rest of the network.

Standard community detection methods for fMRI perform clustering based on functional connectivity, where highly positively correlated ROIs are grouped into a community. In our approach, we propose defining a functional community by the interactions modeled in the LSTM and the generated ROI data (see Sect. 2.2). To ensure that ROIs within a community have positive ties as in standard approaches, we constrain the input weights $W_l$ to be non-negative.

**Discriminative Path.** The discriminative portion of the network aims to classify subjects with ASD vs. typical controls (Fig. 1, orange path). The architecture is similar to the network in [7]. The difference is our approach first processes the input time-series through an LSTM layer that learns to represent functional communities of the ROI data. The *hidden state* of the LSTM cell at each time point is then fed to another LSTM layer, followed by a shared 1-node dense layer, mean pooling layer, and sigmoid activation to give the probability of ASD.

**Generative Path.** The generative portion of the network looks to generate the data at the next time point $x_{T+1}$ of an input time-series with length $T$ (Fig. 1, green path). The input is first processed by the same LSTM layer for functional communities as in the discriminative network. The final *cell state* $c_T$ of the LSTM cell is then passed to a dense layer with $R$ nodes to produce the predicted ROI values for the next time point $\widehat{x_{T+1}} = W_d c_T + b_d$. To enforce that communities exert a positive influence on their members, we constrain $W_d$ to be non-negative.

**Model Training.** The discriminative and generative paths are tied together during training with the loss function $L = L_G\left(x_{T+1}, \widehat{x_{T+1}}\right) + \lambda L_D\left(y, \hat{y}\right)$, where $L_G$ is the loss for the generative model, $L_D$ is the loss for the discriminative model, $y \in \{0, 1\}$ is the true label (1 denoting ASD), $\hat{y}$ is the predicted probability of ASD, and $\lambda$ is a hyperparameter to balance the two losses. For regularization, we include dropout layers before the shared dense layer and mean pooling layer in the discriminative network and before the dense layer in the generative network.

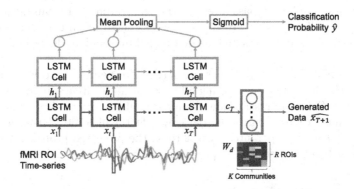

**Fig. 1.** Architecture of our jointly discriminative and generative RNN: LSTM for functional communities (blue), discriminative path (orange), and generative path (green). (Color figure online)

## 2.2   Extraction of Functional Communities

As described above, we propose interpreting each node of the first LSTM block as representing a functional community, where community activity is summarized by state vectors $h_t$ and $c_t$. Since it is difficult to analyze the interactions between ROIs and communities via all the layers of the LSTM block, we propose defining the communities based on their influence on each individual ROI. Recall that the generative path uses the cell state $c_T$ as input to a dense layer to generate the next ROI values $\widehat{x_{T+1}} = W_d c_T + b_d$. From a graph structure perspective, a community is defined by densely connected nodes, i.e. each member of a community is strongly influenced by that community, but also the community is strongly influenced by its members. Thus, we will use the weights $W_d \in \mathbb{R}^{R \times K}$ to denote the membership between individual ROIs and their functional communities. Row $r$ of $W_d$ represents the influence of each community on ROI $r$, while column $k$ of $W_d$ represents the influence of each ROI on community $k$. To provide hard membership assignments, we perform k-means clustering with 2 clusters on the membership weights in column $k$ of $W_d$ and assign the extracted ROIs in the cluster with larger weights to community $k$ (Fig. 1, lower right).

## 3   Experiments

### 3.1   Data

We used resting-state fMRI data from the four ABIDE I [6] sites with the largest sample sizes: New York University (NY), University of Michigan (UM),

University of Utah School of Medicine (US), and University of California, Los Angeles (UC). We selected preprocessed data from the Preprocessed Connectomes Project [5] using the Connectome Computation System pipeline, global signal regression and band-pass filtering, and the Automated Anatomical Labeling (AAL) parcellation with 116 ROIs. The extracted mean time-series of each ROI was standardized (subtracted mean, divided by standard deviation) for each subject.

Since the number of subjects per site is small for neural network training, we augmented the datasets by extracting all possible consecutive subsequences with length $T = 30$ (i.e., 1 min. scantime) from each subject, producing inputs of size $30 \times 116$. Thus, we augmented the data by a factor of ~150–250 for a total of ~14000–38000 samples per site. At test time, the predicted probability of ASD for a given subject was set to the proportion of subsequences labeled as ASD.

## 3.2 Experimental Methods

Models for classification of ASD vs. control were trained for each individual ABIDE site. We implemented the following LSTM-based networks which all take the ROI time-series data as input: the proposed joint discriminative/generative LSTM network (LSTM-DG); the same network but using the hidden state for both data generation and class discrimination (LSTM-H); the same network but with no generative constraint, i.e. only the discriminative loss (LSTM-D); and a single layer discriminative LSTM network as proposed in [7] (LSTM-S). Models were implemented in Keras, with 50 nodes for the first LSTM (for functional communities) and 20 nodes for the second LSTM. Optimization was performed using the Adam optimizer, with binary cross-entropy for $L_D$, mean squared error for $L_G$, a batch size of 32, and early stopping based on validation loss and a patience of 10 epochs. For joint discriminative/generative networks, we set $\lambda = 0.1$ so that $L_G$ and $L_D$ are on similar scales. We also implemented a traditional learning pipeline for resting-state fMRI (FC-SVM) [1]: the functional connectivity based on Pearson correlation was input to a linear support vector machine with L2 regularization, using nested cross-validation to choose the penalty hyperparameter. All implemented models were trained and tested on the augmented datasets. In addition, we compared published results for the same ABIDE datasets and AAL atlas, including another time-series modeling approach using hidden markov models (HMM) [11] and another neural network approach based on stacked autoencoders and deep transfer learning (DTL) [13].

To assess our implemented models, we used 10-fold cross-validation (CV), keeping all data from the same subject within the same partition (training, validation, or test). We measured model classification performance by computing the accuracy (ACC), true positive rate (TPR), true negative rate (TNR), and area under the receiver operating characteristic curve (AUC). Paired one-tailed t-tests were used to compare model performance over all folds and datasets.

For the generative results, with no ground truth for functional communities, we instead evaluated the robustness of extracted communities and compared a tensor decomposition approach for finding overlapping communities. For each sample, we calculated the correlation matrix of the $R$ ROI time-series, then generated a tensor $\mathbf{T}$ with dimension $R \times R \times S$, where $S$ is the number of samples. We then used non-negative PARAFAC [3] to decompose $\mathbf{T} \approx \sum_{k=1}^{K} a_k \circ b_k \circ c_k$, where $K$ is the number of communities, $a_k = b_k \in \mathbb{R}^R$ contains the membership weight of each ROI to community $k$, $c_k \in \mathbb{R}^S$ contains the membership weight of each sample to community $k$, and $\circ$ is the vector outer product. Similar to our approach, we set $K = 50$ communities and use k-means clustering to assign hard ROI memberships to each community. Then for each approach, we computed the correlation of the membership weights and the Dice similarity coefficient (DSC) of hard membership assignments between community $k$ in fold 1 and all communities in fold $f \neq 1$. The robustness of community $k$ in fold 1 compared to fold $f$ was measured as the maximum correlation/DSC computed in fold $f$. We then assessed overall community robustness between fold 1 and $f$ using the average correlation/DSC over all communities.

We also performed validation of the functional communities in the context of the ASD classification task using Neurosynth [15], which correlates over 14000 fMRI studies with 1300 descriptors. The influence of a community for classification was denoted by the sum of absolute weights across all nodes in the second LSTM block for the discriminative task. A binary mask of the extracted ROIs for an important discriminative community was then input to Neurosynth to assess neurocognitive processes associated with ASD classification.

### 3.3  Classification Results

Classification results for each ABIDE site are in Tables 1 and 2. Our LSTM-DG model produced the highest accuracy for 3 of the 4 sites and second highest for US, in which the LSTM-H variation of our model (generative path from hidden state) performed best. Furthermore, LSTM-DG produced the highest or nearly highest AUC for each site. Overall, our LSTM-DG consistently outperformed all non-generative implemented models (ACC $p < 0.05$) and showed potential for improved classification compared to LSTM-H (ACC $p = 0.08$). Moreover, LSTM-DG was the only method to significantly outperform LSTM-S (ACC $p = 0.04$, TNR $p = 0.04$), the original LSTM model for fMRI classification. The results demonstrate the effectiveness of our proposed LSTM-DG method to improve classification by jointly learning the generative fMRI time-series model.

### 3.4  Learned Functional Communities

Results for extracted communities by tensor-based community detection (CD, blue) and the proposed LSTM approach (orange) are plotted in Fig. 2. Our LSTM method produced consistently smaller communities with more uniform size compared to CD, with an average of 11 ROIs compared to 16. Furthermore, our LSTM approach consistently generated communities with higher correlation of membership weights and higher DSC of hard community assignments across CV folds for all sites, with a 15% increase in average correlation and 11% increase in average DSC. Thus, our proposed network produced smaller and more robust

**Table 1.** NY and UM classification results

| Model | NY (184 subjects, 42.3% ASD) | | | | UM (143 subjects, 46.2% ASD) | | | |
|---|---|---|---|---|---|---|---|---|
| | Mean (Std) ACC (%) | Mean (Std) TPR (%) | Mean (Std) TNR (%) | AUC | Mean (Std) ACC (%) | Mean (Std) TPR (%) | Mean (Std) TNR (%) | AUC |
| LSTM-S [7] | 69.5 (11.0) | 52.4 (26.5) | 83.1 (12.0) | 0.720 | 69.8 (11.4) | 56.7 (24.2) | 74.0 (25.3) | 0.740 |
| FC-SVM [1] | 70.7 (8.2) | 54.8 (21.5) | 83.2 (11.8) | 0.783 | 69.2 (12.0) | 46.7 (18.9) | 89.8 (12.8) | 0.713 |
| HMM [11] | 70.6 (6.6) | 61.6 | 66.7 | 0.712 | 73.4 (10.5) | 68.5 | 76.9 | 0.738 |
| DTL [13] | – | – | – | – | 67.2 | 68.9 | 67.6 | 0.67 |
| LSTM-D | 70.7 (11.0) | 48.9 (27.1) | 86.7 (16.1) | 0.746 | 67.0 (12.0) | 52.9 (22.2) | 78.6 (25.6) | 0.738 |
| LSTM-H | 68.0 (7.7) | 52.0 (19.8) | 80.1 (10.1) | 0.779 | 69.2 (11.4) | 57.9 (14.5) | 78.7 (18.1) | 0.777 |
| **LSTM-DG** | **72.2 (14.7)** | **57.4 (25.5)** | **84.1 (12.2)** | **0.772** | **74.8 (10.0)** | **60.8 (12.8)** | **85.6 (14.5)** | **0.774** |

**Table 2.** US and UC classification results

| Model | US (101 subjects, 57.4% ASD) | | | | UC (99 subjects, 54.6% ASD) | | | |
|---|---|---|---|---|---|---|---|---|
| | Mean (Std) ACC (%) | Mean (Std) TPR (%) | Mean (Std) TNR (%) | AUC | Mean (Std) ACC (%) | Mean (Std) TPR (%) | Mean (Std) TNR (%) | AUC |
| LSTM-S [7] | 67.5 (15.4) | 79.8 (25.3) | 56.2 (41.8) | 0.659 | 62.7 (14.8) | 74.4 (31.5) | 51.5 (32.5) | 0.691 |
| FC-SVM [1] | 67.3 (13.5) | 86.2 (13.6) | 43.5 (27.6) | 0.721 | 61.7 (18.0) | 73.3 (20.6) | 47.7 (31.7) | 0.624 |
| DTL [13] | 70.4 | 72.5 | 67.0 | 0.73 | 62.3 | 55.9 | 68.0 | 0.60 |
| LSTM-D | 64.7 (17.8) | 75.3 (32.2) | 61.8 (39.6) | 0.682 | 63.6 (8.8) | 71.8 (27.3) | 51.3 (30.5) | 0.662 |
| LSTM-H | 76.4 (13.9) | 85.6 (18.0) | 65.8 (22.2) | 0.757 | 61.6 (11.4) | 66.6 (14.5) | 54.7 (18.1) | 0.705 |
| **LSTM-DG** | **73.2 (14.7)** | **82.8 (25.5)** | **61.8 (12.2)** | **0.746** | **67.4 (10.0)** | **67.5 (12.8)** | **62.2 (14.5)** | **0.715** |

functional communities than CD, giving our model the potential for more reliable interpretation of further analyses on the functional communities.

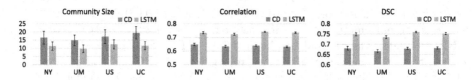

**Fig. 2.** Size (left) and robustness of extracted functional communities across CV folds measured by correlation of membership weights (middle) and DSC of hard assignments (right). CD = tensor-based community detection, LSTM = proposed network.

The top 3 influential communities for the ASD classification of the largest dataset (NY) were extracted from the best CV fold and analyzed in Neurosynth. ASD is characterized by impaired social skills and communication; thus, we expect to find communities related to associated neurological functions. The top extracted community (Fig. 3, yellow) includes the temporal lobe and ventromedial prefrontal cortex, which are associated with social and language processes.

The second community (Fig. 3, green) includes the ventromedial prefrontal cortex, hippocampus, and amygdala, which are associated with memory. The third community (Fig. 3, pink), containing the ventromedial prefrontal cortex and ventral striatum, is involved in reward processing and decision making. Dysfunction of all these brain regions and processes in ASD have previously been shown [12].

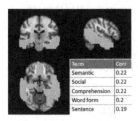 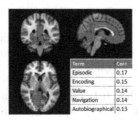 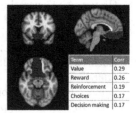

| Term | Corr |
|------|------|
| Semantic | 0.22 |
| Social | 0.22 |
| Comprehension | 0.22 |
| Word form | 0.2 |
| Sentence | 0.19 |

| Term | Corr |
|------|------|
| Episodic | 0.17 |
| Encoding | 0.15 |
| Value | 0.14 |
| Navigation | 0.14 |
| Autobiographical | 0.13 |

| Term | Corr |
|------|------|
| Value | 0.29 |
| Reward | 0.26 |
| Reinforcement | 0.19 |
| Choices | 0.17 |
| Decision making | 0.17 |

**Fig. 3.** Top 3 influential communities for ASD classification of the NY dataset and the top associated neurocognitive terms from Neurosynth. (Color figure online)

## 4  Conclusions

We have presented a novel RNN-based network for jointly learning a discriminative task and a generative model for fMRI time-series data. We achieved higher ASD classification performance on several datasets, demonstrating the advantage of joint learning. Finally, we showed that functional communities defined by the LSTM nodes provide robust representations of brain activity and facilitate interpretation of the ASD classification model. Understanding functional network organization will offer insights into brain disease as well as healthy cognition.

## References

1. Abraham, A., et al.: Deriving reproducible biomarkers from multi-site resting-state data: an autism-based example. Neuroimage **147**, 736–745 (2017)
2. Adate, A., Tripathy, B.: S-LSTM-GAN: shared recurrent neural networks with adversarial training. In: 2nd International Conference on Data Engineering and Communication Technology (2019)
3. Carroll, J., Chang, J.: Analysis of individual differences in multidimensional scaling via an n-way generalization of eckart-young decomposition. Psychometrika **35**, 283–319 (1970)
4. Caruana, R.: Mach. Learn. **28**, 41 (1997). https://doi.org/10.1023/A:1007379606734
5. Craddock, C., et al.: The neuro bureau preprocessing initiative: open sharing of preprocessed neuroimaging data and derivatives. In: Neuroinformatics (2013)

6. Di Martino, A., et al.: The autism brain imaging data exchange: towards a large-scale evaluation of the intrinsic brain architecture in autism. Mol. Psychiatry **16**, 659 (2014)
7. Dvornek, N.C., Ventola, P., Pelphrey, K.A., Duncan, J.S.: Identifying autism from resting-state fMRI using long short-term memory networks. In: Wang, Q., Shi, Y., Suk, H.-I., Suzuki, K. (eds.) MLMI 2017. LNCS, vol. 10541, pp. 362–370. Springer, Cham (2017). https://doi.org/10.1007/978-3-319-67389-9_42
8. Graves, A.: Generating sequences with recurrent neural networks (2014). https://arxiv.org/abs/1308.0850
9. Güçlü, U., van Gerven, M.A.J.: Modeling the dynamics of human brain activity with recurrent neural networks. Front. Comput. Neurosci. **11**, 7 (2017)
10. Hochreiter, S., Schmidhuber, J.: Long short-term memory. In: Neural Computation (1997)
11. Jun, E., Kang, E., Choi, J., Suk, H.I.: Modeling regional dynamics in low-frequency fluctuation and its application to autism spectrum disorder diagnosis. NeuroImage **184**, 669–686 (2019)
12. Kaiser, M., et al.: Neural signatures of autism. Proc. Natl. Acad. Sci. USA **107**, 21223–21228 (2010)
13. Li, H., Parikh, N.A., He, L.: A novel transfer learning approach to enhance deep neural network classification of brain functional connectomes. Front. Neurosci. **12**, 491 (2018)
14. Li, H., Fan, Y.: Brain decoding from functional MRI using long short-term memory recurrent neural networks. In: Frangi, A.F., Schnabel, J.A., Davatzikos, C., Alberola-López, C., Fichtinger, G. (eds.) MICCAI 2018. LNCS, vol. 11072, pp. 320–328. Springer, Cham (2018). https://doi.org/10.1007/978-3-030-00931-1_37
15. Yarkoni, T., Poldrack, R.A., Nichols, T.E., Van Essen, D.C., Wager, T.D.: Large-scale automated synthesis of human functional neuroimaging data. Nature Methods (2011). www.neurosynth.org

# Unsupervised Conditional Consensus Adversarial Network for Brain Disease Identification with Structural MRI

Jing Zhang[1,2], Mingxia Liu[2(✉)], Yongsheng Pan[2,3], and Dinggang Shen[2(✉)]

[1] Department of Mathematics, Zhejiang A & F University, Hangzhou 311300, China
[2] Department of Radiology and BRIC,
University of North Carolina at Chapel Hill, Chapel Hill, NC 27599, USA
{mxliu,dgshen}@med.unc.edu
[3] School of Computer Science and Engineering,
Northwestern Polytechnical University, Xi'an 710072, China

**Abstract.** Effective utilization of multi-domain data for brain disease identification has recently attracted increasing attention since a large number of subjects from multiple domains could be beneficial for investigating the pathological changes of disease-affected brains. Previous machine learning methods often suffer from inter-domain data heterogeneity caused by different scanning parameters. Although several deep learning methods have been developed, they usually assume that the source classifier can be directly transferred to the target (i.e., to-be-analyzed) domain upon the learned domain-invariant features, thus ignoring the shift in data distributions across different domains. Also, most of them rely on fully-labeled data in both target and source domains for model training, while labeled target data are generally unavailable. To this end, we present an Unsupervised Conditional consensus Adversarial Network (UCAN) for deep domain adaptation, which can learn the disease classifier from the labeled source domain and adapt to a different target domain (without any label information). The UCAN model contains three major components: (1) a *feature extraction module* for learning discriminate representations from the input MRI, (2) a *cycle feature adaptation module* to assist feature and classifier adaptation between the source and target domains, and (3) a *classification module* for disease identification. Experimental results on 1,506 subjects from ADNI1 (with 1.5 T structural MRI) and ADNI2 (with 3.0 T structural MRI) have demonstrated the effectiveness of the proposed UCAN method in brain disease identification, compared with state-of-the-art approaches.

## 1 Introduction

Alzheimer's disease (AD) is a slow fatal neurodegenerative disease affecting people over the age of 65 years. Thus, the identification and analysis of AD and its prodromal phase, *i.e.*, mild cognitive impairment (MCI), are essential for early treatment and possible delays in disease progression. Significant advances in neuroimaging have provided opportunities to study brain-related diseases, bringing

© Springer Nature Switzerland AG 2019
H.-I. Suk et al. (Eds.): MLMI 2019, LNCS 11861, pp. 391–399, 2019.
https://doi.org/10.1007/978-3-030-32692-0_45

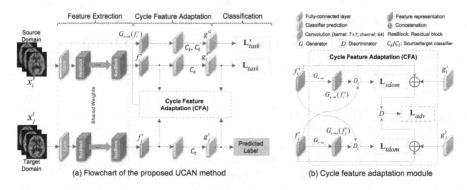

**Fig. 1.** Illustration of the proposed Unsupervised Conditional consensus Adversarial Network (UCAN), including (1) a *feature extraction* module with a convolutional (Conv) layer and four type of residual blocks as the backbone, (2) a *cycle feature adaptation* (CFA) module to harmonize learned features and classifiers of the source and target domains, and (3) a *classification* module. The input are a pair of images, *i.e.*, $x_i^s$ from the labeled source domain and $x_j^t$ from the unlabeled target domain (with learned features as $f_i^s$ and $f_j^t$, respectively). Here, $g^G = C_s(G_{s\to t}(f_i^s)) + C_t(G_{s\to t}(f_i^s))$.

improvements in early detection of AD and MCI. Structural magnetic resonance imaging (MRI) is widely used in AD studies because it provides an excellent spatial resolution and a non-invasive method to study a patient's brain. MRI-based methods help predict the progression of MCI to AD, by describing brain atrophy and change in the size of brain tissues explicitly [1,2].

Conventional MRI-based methods often suffer from inter-domain data heterogeneity caused by different scanning parameters, because models learned on source domains are directly applied to problems in the to-be-analyzed target domain [3–5]. For example, Cheng *et al.* [3] proposed the sharing domain transfer learning method for MCI conversion prediction, which directly use the source domain to be auxiliary for the target domain to select a subset of common features. Several deep learning methods have been recently developed to alleviate the issue of domain shift [6–10]. For example, Motiian *et al.* [6] provided a unified framework to learn an embedding subspace for addressing the problem of supervised domain adaptation. A deep domain confusion network [7] was developed to map data from both domains into a common feature space to reduce the domain shift, measured by the maximum mean discrepancy (MMD). This method was further extended to a deep adaptation network (DAN) via a multi-layer multi-kernel selection technique [8] and a joint adaptation network (JAN) [9] for natural image classification. Long *et al.* [10] presented a conditional adversarial domain adaptation network (CDAN) by integrating adversarial learning and domain adaptation to a unified framework.

However, existing methods typically suffer from two limitations. (1) They are usually based on the assumption that the source classifier and target classifier can be shared directly. Unfortunately, such an assumption is too strong and could not always hold in practical applications. (2) Many of them are supervised, relying on fully-labeled data in both target and source domains, and hence, they cannot be applied to general problems, where there are labeled data in the source domain and unlabeled data in the target domain.

As shown in Fig. 1, we propose an Unsupervised Conditional consensus Adversarial Network (UCAN) for brain disease identification, where classifiers learned from labeled source domain can be robustly adapt to a different target domain (without any label information). Three major components are included: (1) a *feature extraction module* for learning discriminate representations from the input MRI, (2) a *cycle feature adaptation module* to harmonize learned MRI features and classifiers of the source and target domains, and (3) a *classification module*. Experimental results on two public datasets with structural MRIs (acquired using different scanning parameters) suggest the efficacy of our method in both tasks of AD/MCI identification and MCI conversion prediction.

## 2 Materials and Method

### 2.1 Subjects and Structural MR Image Pre-processing

Two datasets from the ADNI database [11] were employed in this work, including ADNI1 and ADNI2. Since several subjects participated in both ADNI1 and ADNI2, we remove these subjects from ADNI2 to ensure that these two datasets are independent. Subjects in these datasets were divided into four categories: (1) AD, (2) cognitively normal (CN), (3) progressive MCI (pMCI) that would progress to AD within 36 months after baseline, and (4) static MCI (sMCI) that would not progress to AD. The baseline ADNI1 dataset consists of 1.5 T T1-weighted MR images acquired from a total of 785 subjects, including 231 NC, 246 sMCI, 103 pMCI, and 205 AD subjects. The baseline ADNI2 dataset includes 3.0 T T1-weighted sMRI data acquired from 721 subjects, including 205 NC, 312 sMCI, 42 pMCI, and 162 AD subjects. A standard pipeline was used to pre-process structural MR images, including (1) anterior commissure (AC)-posterior commissure (PC) alignment; (2) skull stripping; (3) intensity correction; (4) cerebellum removal; (5) linear alignment to the Colin27 template [12]; (6) re-sampling all MR images to have the same size of $142 \times 142 \times 178 \, \text{mm}^3$ (with a spatial resolution of $1 \times 1 \times 1 \, \text{mm}^3$) corresponding to the coronal-plane view, sagittal-plane view, and axial-plane view, respectively; and (7) intensity inhomogeneity correction using the N3 algorithm [13].

### 2.2 Unsupervised Conditional Consensus Adversarial Network

We now present our conditional consensus adversarial domain adaptation framework (see Fig. 1). We consider the problem of unsupervised adaptation in this work. Denote $x_i^s$ (with its label $y_i^s$) and $x_j^t$ (without label) as the $i$-th and the $j$-th subjects from the source and target domains, respectively. Given $n_s$ subjects from the source domain and $n_t$ subjects from the target domain, we represent the labeled source domain as $\mathcal{D}_s = \{(x_i^s, y_i^s)\}_{i=1}^{n_s}$ and the unlabeled target domain as $\mathcal{D}_t = \{x_j^t\}_{j=1}^{n_t}$. The goal is to learn a model that can correctly predict the label of subjects from the target domain, based on labeled source data.

**Feature Extraction Module:** Each input image is first fed into a convolution (Conv) layer with the kernel/filter size of $7 \times 7$ and the channel size of 64 (stride: 2), followed by a max pooling with $3 \times 3$ filter (stride: 2). Then, we use the ResNet-50 model [14] to extract MRI features of images from both the source and target domains, including four types of residual blocks (with each block containing 3 Conv layers). The numbers of blocks are 3, 4, 6, and 3 for four types of residual blocks, respectively. And the different parameters (*i.e.*, [*filters*, *channels*]) for these four types of blocks are listed below:

$$
\begin{bmatrix} 1 \times 1, & 64 \\ 3 \times 3, & 64 \\ 1 \times 1, & 256 \end{bmatrix}, \begin{bmatrix} 1 \times 1, & 128 \\ 3 \times 3, & 128 \\ 1 \times 1, & 512 \end{bmatrix}, \begin{bmatrix} 1 \times 1, & 256 \\ 3 \times 3, & 256 \\ 1 \times 1, & 1024 \end{bmatrix}, \begin{bmatrix} 1 \times 1, & 512 \\ 3 \times 3, & 512 \\ 1 \times 1, & 2048 \end{bmatrix}.
$$

**Cycle Feature Adaptation Module:** Using learned features (*i.e.*, $f_i^s$ for $x_i^s$ and $f_j^t$ for $x_j^t$) via the feature extraction module, we further perform domain adaptation to harmonize data from the source and target domains. Let $C_s$ and $C_t$ be the task-specific classification models trained on the source and target domains, respectively. We can begin by simply learning a source classifier $C_s$ with the cross-entropy loss as follows

$$
\mathcal{L}_{task}(C_s, x_i^s, y_i^s) = \mathbb{E}_{(x_i^s, y_i^s) \sim \mathcal{D}^s} \frac{1}{n_s} \sum_{i=1}^{n_s} L(C_s(x_i^s), y_i^s), \tag{1}
$$

where $L(\cdot, \cdot)$ is the cross-entropy function.

As shown in Fig. 1 (b), our proposed cycle feature adaptation module has a symmetric network design, based on which we augment the cycle generative adversarial structure to promote the efficacy of feature adaptation. By directly mapping the source feature (*e.g.*, $f_i^s$) to the target domain via a generator $G_{s \to t}$ and mapping the target feature (*e.g.*, $f_j^t$) to the source domain via a generator $G_{t \to s}$, we aim to remove the low-level differences between features from two domains, ensuring that our learned model is well-conditioned on target domain alignment. We assume that having cycles in both directions helps perform *global domain alignment* by learning features in the adaptation process, and employ the following source domain loss $\mathcal{L}_{sdom}$ and the target domain loss $\mathcal{L}_{tdom}$:

$$
\mathcal{L}_{sdom}(D_s, f_i^s, f_j^t) = -\mathbb{E}_{x_i^s \sim \mathcal{D}^s} \log D_s(f_i^s) - \mathbb{E}_{x_j^t \sim \mathcal{D}^t} \log(1 - D_s(G_{t \to s}(f_j^t))), \tag{2}
$$

$$
\mathcal{L}_{tdom}(D_t, f_i^s, f_j^t) = -\mathbb{E}_{x_j^t \sim \mathcal{D}^t} \log D_t(f_j^t) - \mathbb{E}_{x_i^s \sim \mathcal{D}^s} \log(1 - D_t(G_{s \to t}(f_i^s))), \tag{3}
$$

where $D_s$ and $D_t$ denote the discriminators corresponding to the source and target domains, respectively. And $G_{s \to t}$ denotes the generator to map source features to the target domain, while $G_{t \to s}$ is the generator to map target features to the source domain.

To distinguish features from different domains, we first concatenate the feature representation (*e.g.*, $f_i^s$) and classifier prediction (*e.g.*, $g_i^s$) from each domain.

Such a concatenation operation could capture the inherent relationship of task-specific features and classifier prediction results, formulated as follows:

$$h_i^s = f_i^s \oplus g_i^s, \quad h_j^t = f_j^t \oplus g_j^t.$$

We then employ the above inherent relationship between features and classifier prediction as discriminative representation conditioning on the adversarial learning, encouraging the distributions of source data and target data to be similar. Thus, the adversarial loss based on the discriminative representations (*e.g.*, $h_i^s$ and $h_j^t$) of the source and target domains can be formulated as follows:

$$\mathcal{L}_{adv}(D, h_i^s, h_j^t) = -\mathbb{E}_{x_i^s \sim \mathcal{D}^s} \log D(h_i^s) - \mathbb{E}_{x_j^t \sim \mathcal{D}^t} \log(1 - D(h_j^t)), \quad (4)$$

where $D$ is the discriminator to tell the domain labels (*e.g.*, source or target domain) of the input paired images based on $h_i^s$ and $h_j^t$.

**Classification Module:** Since data in the target domain are unlabeled, we propose to employ the generated feature representation (via the generator $G_{s \rightarrow t}$) and its label in the source domain to improve the robustness of the target classifier. Given a feature vector $f_i^s$, we denote $g^G = C_s(G_{s \rightarrow t}(f_i^s)) + C_t(G_{s \rightarrow t}(f_i^s))$ as the prediction for our generated feature $G_{s \rightarrow t}(f_i^s)$, and such predictions are achieved by the source classifier $C_s$ and the target classifier $C_t$. Then, we develop a task-specific loss to assist the classification tasks in both the source and target domains, which is formulated as follows:

$$\mathcal{L}'_{task}(C_s, C_t, G_{s \rightarrow t}(f_i^s), y_i^s)$$
$$= \mathbb{E}_{(G_{s \rightarrow t}(f_i^s), y_i^s) \sim \mathcal{D}^s} \frac{1}{n_s} \sum_{i=1}^{n_s} \left( L(C_s(G_{s \rightarrow t}(f_i^s)), y_i^s) + L(C_t(G_{s \rightarrow t}(f_i^s)), y_i^s) \right), \quad (5)$$

through which we can explicitly learn the target classifier $C_t$, even though there are no labeled data in the target domain.

By combining Eqs. (1)–(5), we obtain the objective function of our UCAN model as follows:

$$\min_{C_s, C_t} \min_{G_{t \rightarrow s}, G_{s \rightarrow t}} \min_{D_s, D_t, D} \mathcal{L}_{total}(C_s, C_t, x_i^s, y_i^s, x_j^t, G_{t \rightarrow s}, G_{s \rightarrow t}, D_s, D_t, D)$$
$$= \mathcal{L}_{task}(C_s, x_i^s, y_i^s) + \mathcal{L}'_{task}(C_s, C_t, G_{s \rightarrow t}(f_i^s), y_i^s) \quad (6)$$
$$+ \mathcal{L}_{sdom}(D_s, f_i^s, f_j^t) + \mathcal{L}_{tdom}(D_t, f_i^s, f_j^t)$$
$$+ \mathcal{L}_{adv}(D, h_i^s, h_j^t).$$

**Implementation:** The proposed network is implemented in PyTorch. Specifically, in the *training* stage, we first pre-train the feature extraction module using ResNet-50 [14] on ImageNet (with the Pytorch source code provided in https://github.com/KaimingHe/deep-residual-networks), and then train the entire network in an end-to-end manner for 500 epochs. The Adam solver is used with a

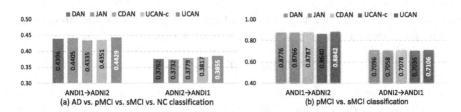

**Fig. 2.** Results of five different methods in both tasks of (a) disease identification and (b) MCI conversion prediction.

batch size of 36 and a learning rate of $3 \times 10^{-3}$. In the *testing* stage, we feed the testing MRI into the bottom part of the trained UCAN model (only the target domain) to predict its class label. For each 3D structural MR image, we extract its slices from three views (*i.e.*, coronal-plane, sagittal-plane and axial-plane views), followed by feeding slides of each view to the proposed network. Finally, the results based on slides of three views for each subject are fused using the majority voting strategy to get the final result. Each slice is re-sized to $256 \times 256$ with zero-filling before being fed into our network. Besides, we apply both horizontal and vertical flip to MRI slides for data augmentation.

## 3   Experiment

**Experimental Setup:** The proposed UCAN method was compared with three state-of-the-art methods for deep domain adaptation using structural MR images, including (1) Deep Adaptation Network (**DAN**) [8], and (2) Joint Adaptation Network (**JAN**) [9], and (3) Conditional Domain Adaptation Network (**CDAN**) [10]. To evaluate the efficacy of the proposed cycle feature adaptation (CFA) module (see Fig. 1), we further compare our UCAN with its variant without using the CFA module (called **UCAN-c**). Except for the CFA module, UCAN-c and UCAN share the same network architecture. For a fair comparison, both DAN and JAN methods employ the suggested network architecture and parameters provided by the authors (see https://github.com/thuml/Xlearn), while CDAN uses the same settings provided by the respective paper (see https://github.com/thuml/CDAN). Two groups of experiments were performed, including (1) brain disease identification (*i.e.*, AD vs. pMCI vs. sMCI vs. NC classification), and (2) MCI conversion prediction (*i.e.*, pMCI vs. sMCI classification). To validate the robustness of a specific method, a two-fold cross-validation was used in the experiments. In the $1^{st}$ fold (*i.e.*, "ADNI1→ADNI2"), we treated ADNI1 as the source domain and ADNI2 as the target domain. In the $2^{nd}$ fold (*i.e.*, "ADNI2→ADNI1"), we regarded ADNI2 as the source domain and ADNI1 as the target domain. The classification accuracy was employed as the evaluation metric in the task of pMCI vs. sMCI classification, while the averaged accuracy among four categories was used in the task of brain disease identification.

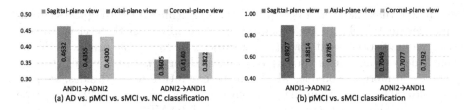

**Fig. 3.** Results of the proposed UCAN model using MRI slices from three different views in (a) disease identification and (b) MCI conversion prediction.

**Results of Disease Identification:** Figure 2(a) reports the results achieved by five different methods in the task of brain disease identification (*i.e.*, AD vs. pMCI vs. sMCI vs. NC classification), from which one may have the following observations. *First*, our UCAN method achieved the best performance in two-fold cross-validation, compared with three deep learning methods (*i.e.*, DAN, JAN, and CDAN). *Second*, our UCAN consistently outperforms its degenerated variant (*i.e.*, UCAN-c). For instance, using ADNI1 as the source domain (*i.e.*, "ADNI1→ADNI2"), the average accuracy of four-category classification achieved by UCAN is 0.4429 for subjects in the target ADNI2 domain, while UCAN-c only yields an average accuracy of 0.4351. This clearly suggests the effectiveness of our proposed cycle feature adaptation module to alleviate the data distribution shift among source and target domains. *Besides*, the overall performance achieved by five methods in the $2^{nd}$ fold (*i.e.*, "ADNI2→ADNI1") is worse than that of different methods in the $1^{st}$ fold (*i.e.*, "ADNI1→ADNI2"). The possible reason is that ADNI2 is a relatively unbalanced dataset (*e.g.*, the number of pMCI subjects is largely less than the other three categories, compared with ADNI1. In such a case, models trained on ADNI2 are less robust than those trained on the balanced ADNI1 dataset.

**Results of Disease Progression Prediction:** We also report the results of five methods in MCI conversation prediction (*i.e.*, pMCI vs. sMCI classification) in Fig. 2(b). From this figure, a similar trend can be found as that in the task of brain disease identification. That is, our UCAN method is consistently superior to the four competing methods in both folds. The underlying reason is being that our method can capture the relationship between feature representations and classifier predictions as complementary information in the training process. Considering that the domain adaptation between the source and target domains in the task of pMCI vs. sMCI classification is a severe data unbalanced problem, these results further demonstrate the robustness of the proposed UCAN method.

**Discussion and Future Work:** In the current work, the input data of UCAN are 2D image slices extracted from three views (*i.e.*, sagittal-plane, axial-plane, and coronal-plane views). We now investigate the influence of different views on the performance of our method, with results reported in Fig. 3. From Fig. 3, one can observe that the overall best performance is achieved by using the sagittal-plane view in $1^{st}$ fold. In the experiments, we equally treat three views to generate the prediction result for a testing subject, by fusing the results of UCAN using slides of three views via majority voting. Using a weighted voting strategy seems to be more reasonable, which will be our future work. Besides, we plan to employ 3D (rather than 2D) convolution in the proposed network to take advantage of the global structure information of 3D MRIs.

## 4 Conclusion

We present an unsupervised conditional consensus adversarial network (UCAN) for deep domain adaptation, which can learn the disease classifier from the labeled source domain and adapt to a different target domain. Specifically, we first design a feature extraction module to learn representations from input MRI, followed by a cycle feature adaptation module to harmonize features and classifiers of the source and target domains. Experimental results on 1,506 subjects suggest the efficacy of the proposed method.

## References

1. Liu, M., Zhang, D., Shen, D.: Relationship induced multi-template learning for diagnosis of Alzheimer's disease and mild cognitive impairment. IEEE Trans. Med. Imaging **35**(6), 1463–1474 (2016)
2. Lian, C., et al.: Multi-channel multi-scale fully convolutional network for 3D perivascular spaces segmentation in 7T MR images. Med. Image Anal. **46**, 106–117 (2018)
3. Cheng, B., Liu, M., Zhang, D., Munsell, B.C., Shen, D.: Domain transfer learning for MCI conversion prediction. IEEE Trans. Biomed. Eng. **62**(7), 1805–1817 (2015)
4. Lian, C., Liu, M., Zhang, J., Shen, D.: Hierarchical fully convolutional network for joint atrophy localization and Alzheimer's disease diagnosis using structural MRI. IEEE Trans. Pattern Anal. Mach. Intell. (2018)
5. Zhu, Y., et al.: MRI-based prostate cancer detection with high-level representation and hierarchical classification. Med. Phys. **44**(3), 1028–1039 (2017)
6. Motiian, S., Piccirilli, M., Adjeroh, D.A., Doretto, G.: Unified deep supervised domain adaptation and generalization. CoRR. abs/1709.10190 (2017)
7. Tzeng, E., Hoffman, J., Zhang, N., Saenko, K., Darrell, T.: Deep domain confusion: maximizing for domain invariance. arXiv preprint arXiv:1412.3474 (2014)
8. Long, M., Cao, Y., Cao, Z., Wang, J., Jordan, M.I.: Transferable representation learning with deep adaptation networks. IEEE Trans. Pattern Anal. Mach. Intell. (2018)
9. Long, M., Zhu, H., Wang, J., Jordan, M.I.: Deep transfer learning with joint adaptation networks. In: ICML, pp. 2208–2217 (2017)
10. Long, M., Cao, Z., Wang, J., Jordan, M.I.: Conditional adversarial domain adaptation. In: NIPS, pp. 1640–1650 (2018)
11. Jack, C., Bernstein, M., Fox, N., et al.: The Alzheimer's disease neuroimaging initiative (ADNI): MRI methods. J. Magn. Reson. Imaging **27**(4), 685–691 (2008)

12. Holmes, C.J., Hoge, R., Collins, L., Woods, R., Toga, A.W., Evans, A.C.: Enhancement of MR images using registration for signal averaging. J. Comput. Assist. Tomogr. **22**(2), 324–333 (1998)
13. Sled, J.G., Zijdenbos, A.P., Evans, A.C.: A nonparametric method for automatic correction of intensity nonuniformity in MRI data. IEEE Trans. Med. Imaging **17**(1), 87–97 (1998)
14. He, K., Zhang, X., Ren, S., Sun, J.: Deep residual learning for image recognition. In: CVPR, pp. 770–778 (2016)

# A Maximum Entropy Deep Reinforcement Learning Neural Tracker

Shafa Balaram$^{(\boxtimes)}$, Kai Arulkumaran, Tianhong Dai,
and Anil Anthony Bharath

Department of Bioengineering, Imperial College London,
London SW7 2AZ, UK
{shafa.balaram15,kailash.arulkumaran13,tianhong.dai15,
a.bharath}@imperial.ac.uk

**Abstract.** Tracking of anatomical structures has multiple applications in the field of biomedical imaging, including screening, diagnosing and monitoring the evolution of pathologies. Semi-automated tracking of elongated structures has been previously formulated as a problem suitable for deep reinforcement learning (DRL), but it remains a challenge. We introduce a maximum entropy continuous-action DRL neural tracker capable of training from scratch in a complex environment in the presence of high noise levels, Gaussian blurring and detractors. The trained model is evaluated on two-photon microscopy images of mouse cortex. At the expense of slightly worse robustness compared to a previously applied DRL tracker, we reach significantly higher accuracy, approaching the performance of the standard hand-engineered algorithm used for neuron tracing. The higher sample efficiency of our maximum entropy DRL tracker indicates its potential of being applied directly to small biomedical datasets.

**Keywords:** Tracking · Tracing · Neuron · Axon · Reinforcement learning · Maximum entropy

## 1 Introduction

In the field of image analysis, tracking can be defined as the process of locating an object through time and/or space [17], introducing an ordering in the observation points. While segmentation can be a precursor, tracking is used to provide additional information about structures. Additionally, tracking is often used to address partial loss of visibility of the structure caused by apparent gaps, low contrast or occlusion, a common problem in video analysis [20], through inference. In addition, morphological attributes of spatial structures, such as branching patterns [5], can be obtained about biological structures, which can aid the detection and treatment of ophthalmologic and cardiovascular pathologies [10].

**Electronic supplementary material** The online version of this chapter (https://doi.org/10.1007/978-3-030-32692-0_46) contains supplementary material, which is available to authorized users.

Hand-engineered trackers have been applied to obtain measurements about thin, elongated structures in biomedical imaging [5,17]. To address the dependence of trackers on specific biomedical datasets, Dai et al. [4] extended prior work on the application of deep reinforcement learning (DRL) to tracking in biomedical images [23], performing subpixel neural tracking while coping with a limited number of labelled images [3] through the use of a synthetic dataset, eventually performing zero-shot transfer learning on axonal images from two-photon imaging of mouse cortex.

In order to improve the sample efficiency, and hence applicability, of the DRL neural tracker to other biomedical datasets, we opt for the off-policy soft actor-critic (SAC) algorithm [8]. SAC also uses a maximum entropy formulation of reinforcement learning (RL), which leads to better exploration. In comparison to Dai et al. [4], our tracker could be trained and validated on artificially-simulated images modelled with a higher degree of complexity and detractors, including background structure mimicking cell debris and high noise levels.

We show that not only does SAC benefit from vastly improved sample efficiency, but it also achieves far greater accuracy than Dai et al.'s tracker—approaching that of the standard hand-engineered algorithm used [14]—with only a slight drop in robustness. Furthermore, we show that the ability to train on more complex synthetic environments increases the tracker's generalisation to real data. Together, this makes our approach more appealing for application to other biomedical image datasets.

## 2    Background

### 2.1    Tracking

Segmentation was used in previous two-photon axon image analysis by Li et al. [11] as a prior step to improve their neuron tracing algorithm. However, by combining both techniques, the performance of the tracking algorithm becomes dependent on the accuracy of the segmentation process. Instead, our semi-automatic tracking algorithm employs a local exploration strategy, where a seed starting point of each neuron is specified explicitly. This is similar to the Vaa3D algorithm [14], an ImageJ plugin which is currently the standard for neuron tracing. Through the availability of seed points, the algorithm can adapt locally to changing image quality and contrast conditions, which becomes important in neuron images with non-uniform backgrounds, such as varying noise levels, inhomogeneous microscopic blurring and presence of cell debris [19].

### 2.2    Maximum Entropy Reinforcement Learning

RL is a branch of machine learning which provides a mathematical framework for an agent to learn independently by interacting with its environment with the aim of maximising its return (sum of rewards) [21]. In conventional RL, the environment produces a state $s_t$ at every timestep $t$ after which the agent samples an action $\mathbf{a}_t$ from a policy $\pi$, a probability distribution which maps states to actions. Consequently, the agent receives a successor state $\mathbf{s}_{t+1}$ from the environment together with a scalar reward $r_{t+1}$ as feedback to the decision taken. This closed loop mechanism ends when a terminal state is reached.

In our scenario, a trained agent should be able to trace the centreline of neurons in the presence of varying imaging conditions and detractors by learning an optimal sequence of decisions related to displacements in a 2D Cartesian coordinate system. Previously, Dai et al. [4] used the on-policy proximal policy optimisation (PPO) algorithm [18], which utilises an actor-critic (policy $\pi$ and state value function $V(\mathbf{s}_t)$) setup [21], where both the policy and state value function are parameterised by neural networks. In contrast, we use the off-policy maximum entropy SAC algorithm [8].

SAC is also an actor-critic algorithm, but utilises two (soft) state-action value functions $Q(\mathbf{s}_t, \mathbf{a}_t)$ in place of the single state value function [9]. Unlike on-policy algorithms, off-policy algorithms can learn from past trajectories, improving their sample efficiency over on-policy algorithms. Then, the RL formulation used by SAC has been extended with a maximum entropy term to improve exploration and robustness [7,24]. The objective is to learn an optimal stochastic policy $\pi^*$ which maximises both the expected discounted return and its expected entropy [8]. Finally, SAC uses a temperature parameter which determines the relative influence of the reward and entropy terms on the policy and thus balances the exploration-exploitation trade-off [8]. The most significant change we made to apply this to microscopy images was to use a different neural network architecture that makes use of privileged information during training [15].

### 2.3   Deep Reinforcement Learning in Biomedical Imaging

Deep neural networks have been used successfully as function approximators of the policy and the state-action value function in multiple applications, including real-world visual navigation tasks where RL agents can learn directly from raw pixel values [2]. Their applications in biomedical imaging include landmark detection [6], view planning [1] and vascular centreline tracing [23], which all make use of deep Q-network algorithm [12], constraining them to using discrete action spaces. In order to predict the centreline observation points to subpixel accuracy, a continuous action space is required. This issue was addressed by Dai et al. [4] through the use of PPO.

Biomedical datasets manually-labelled by experts can be both limited and expensive to acquire. With a small dataset of 20 annotated microscopy images available [3], Dai et al. [4] simulated synthetic images of single neurons based on two-dimensional splines for training and tuning of hyperparameters during validation. Since they had access to the ground truth locations of synthetic centrelines during training, they used an asymmetric actor-critic architecture which improves value function learning [15]. This is achieved by providing the critic (value) network with extra information only during training, i.e. the binary maps containing the neuron centrelines. The trained tracker was then tested directly on microscopy data—which can be considered transductive or "zero-shot" transfer

[13]. Similarly, we also employ the asymmetric actor-critic architecture, whereby the two soft-Q functions (critics) of SAC are each provided with the binary ground truth maps.

# 3 Entropy-Based Deep Reinforcement Learning for Tracking

We now define the key entities of RL in the context of tracking neural centrelines.

**Environment:** Owing to the availability of only 20 greyscale expert-annotated axonal mouse cortex images [3], we simulate artificial images of single neurons "on the fly" in a pseudo-random manner with controlled degrees of complexity during training. We introduce a few modifications to the images generated by Dai *et al.* [4] in terms of the cosinusoidal axon intensity profiles and presence of detractors with the aim of imitating the complex natural environment of neurons (refer to Subsect. 4.1 for further details). Figure 1 shows examples of synthetic (both ours and Dai *et al.*'s [4]) and microscopy images for visual comparison; matching the rough structure of the real data appears to be enough for some generalisation to real data. The terminal state definition is described in the supplementary material.

**State Space:** Our state space is the same as that of Dai *et al.* [4]. We refer the reader to the supplementary material for further details.

**Action Space:** Actions in a continuous control space are sampled by the agent directly from its stochastic policy. We parameterise the policy as a Gaussian "squashed" by a tanh function; the actions are then floating point numbers $\in (-1, 1)$, and represent subpixel displacements in the image's coordinate system without requiring any further processing.

**Reward Function:** The reward function has to be defined in such a way so as to achieve the aim of tracing the neural centreline with subpixel accuracy. We use a simplified version of the original reward function formulated by Dai *et al.* [4] and include a full description in the supplementary material.

**Agent:** The agent's policy and two soft Q-functions are modelled using convolutional neural networks, as shown in Fig. 2 of the supplementary material along with their input states. The actor network outputs the parameters of two independent Gaussian distributions, namely the means $\mu$ and logarithm of the standard deviations $\log \sigma$. We constrain $\log \sigma \in [-20, 2]$ to prevent highly deterministic or stochastic policies. The support for the distributions is bounded with a tanh squashing function and the sampled actions represent displacements in the $x - y$ coordinate system of the images. The two critic networks each output a scalar soft Q-function, $Q(\mathbf{s}_t, \mathbf{a}_t)$. We provide more explanation behind the choice of this SAC variant [9] as well as the final training algorithm for subpixel neural tracking in the supplementary material.

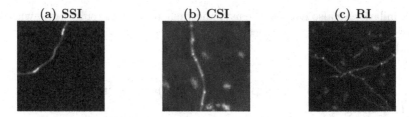

**Fig. 1.** Comparison of synthetic and microscopy datasets: (a) a simple artificially-simulated image (SSI) used during training by Dai *et al.* [4] with relatively low levels of background noise, no blurring and no cells, (b) a complex synthetic image (CSI) used in our training, generated with Gaussian blurring, "cell debris" and higher levels of background noise, and (c) a real image (RI) obtained from the somatosensory cortex of a mouse using two-photon microscopy [3].

## 4    Experiments

### 4.1    Datasets and Performance Evaluation

There are two different datasets used throughout our experiments: the synthetic and microscopy images of neurons (see Fig. 1 for examples). For reasons discussed in Sect. 2.1, the starting points of the neurons of each dataset are provided to all trackers as seed points.

**Synthetic Dataset.** We first train and validate our tracker on synthetic single-neuron images. The ability to train the agent in the synthetic dataset is also an implicit part of performance evaluation. We increase the complexity of images simulated by Dai *et al.* [4] in several ways. We choose cosine intensity profiles for axons to imitate regions in different stages of synaptic transmission. Highly-illuminated blob-like structures are also present to simulate synaptic boutons. We add background image structure mimicking cell debris as well as Gaussian and Poisson noise as detractors from the centreline to be tracked. Finally, a common artefact in real datasets is an out-of-focus microscope, which we try to capture using the Gaussian blurring operation.

**Microscopy Dataset.** We evaluate the performance of our best performing maximum-entropy DRL trained tracker on a mouse cortical axon dataset [3][1]. There are 20 greyscale images, maximum-intensity projected from 3D stacks, with their corresponding binary ground truth images annotated by an expert.

**Metrics.** In order to quantify and compare the performance of our tracker, two measures are used: the root mean squared error (RMSE) and coverage [4]. The RMSE quantifies the perpendicular error between the predicted and target

---

[1] Dataset available at: https://www.zenodo.org/record/1182487#.XP2UBS2ZMxc.

centrelines and thus, represents the accuracy of the tracker. To measure the robustness of the tracker, we utilise the coverage, which is the proportion of the neuron tracked by predicted points that lie within a margin of 3 pixels of the target centreline.

## 4.2 Training and Validation

We tune the original SAC model's hyperparameters on a held-out synthetic dataset of 20 images for a 10:1 training/validation split. During the validation process, we investigated whether the absence of detractors, such as cells and boutons, in the environment has an impact on the agent's transfer learning ability. In addition, we looked into whether adding a local response normalisation layer [16] after each ReLU activation function of the feature learning stage could tackle the lower contrast of the microscopy dataset and improve generalisation to the real data. Finally, for each variant mentioned, we considered automatic entropy tuning [9]. We observed that models trained in the absence of detractors (simulated boutons or cell debris) performed worse on the microscopy dataset (details in the supplementary material), indicating the importance of being able to train DRL agents on more challenging image data. In contrast, we were unable to train a PPO tracker [4] on this more complex synthetic image data. Our best performing model is the original SAC trained for $3.5 \times 10^5$ timesteps using a fixed temperature parameter $\alpha$ of 1.0 in the presence of all detractors. Its training requires approximately 2000 synthetic images and takes around 5h on K80 GPUs. We refer the reader to the supplementary material for the variance across 5 random seeds during training. Our code is available at https://bitbucket.org/bicv/maximum-entropy-drl-tracker.

## 4.3 Testing

Our best SAC model was tested on the microscopy dataset, without further tuning of parameters or hyperparameters. As in Dai et al. [4], we take into consideration the higher resolution of the microscopy images by extracting larger windows of sizes $15 \times 15$ pixels and $31 \times 31$ pixels before downscaling all views to $11 \times 11$ pixels. We increase the maximum episode length from 200 to 350 to

**Table 1.** Test performance of 20 microscopy images: mean and ±1 standard deviation of the root mean squared error (RMSE) in pixels and coverage of the SAC and PPO DRL trackers, and the Vaa3D algorithm. Note that although the maximum-entropy DRL tracker is less robust than the PPO DRL tracker, its accuracy approaches that of the Vaa3D algorithm.

| SAC | | PPO | | Vaa3D | |
|---|---|---|---|---|---|
| RMSE | Coverage | RMSE | Coverage | RMSE | Coverage |
| $4.36 \pm 3.63$ | $0.808 \pm 0.242$ | $27.62 \pm 27.96$ | $0.841 \pm 0.130$ | $1.75 \pm 1.73$ | $0.923 \pm 0.089$ |

account for the larger dimensions of the microscopy images. The starting point of each axon is provided to the agent separately in multi-axon images.

Table 1 compares the performance of our best-performing tracker against Dai et al.'s PPO tracker [4] and the Vaa3D algorithm [14]. The RMSE and coverage values of the individual microscopy images are shown in the supplementary material. Despite the slightly lower robustness of our maximum entropy tracker in comparison to PPO, it achieves much higher accuracy, approaching that of the Vaa3D algorithm.

## 5    Conclusion

We proposed a maximum entropy DRL tracker trained in a complex environment simulated to mimic an axon microscopy dataset. Our training algorithm combines the state-of-the-art SAC algorithm [9] with the asymmetric actor-critic architecture [15]. Our improvements on prior work [4] include the requirement for only a small training dataset owing to the high sample efficiency of the chosen off-policy training algorithm. We also demonstrate the ability to track neural centrelines to subpixel accuracy in the presence of background image structure mimicking cell debris and higher noise levels. Finally, while our maximum entropy DRL tracker is less robust with its slightly lower coverage value, it has an accuracy 6-fold higher than the PPO tracker, with its RMSE approaching that of the standard algorithm for neuron tracing [14].

The maximum entropy DRL tracker can be combined with active contour methods to track boundaries of other structures, such as walls of blood vessels, after redefining the reward function based on the nature of the structure of interest. Furthermore, the need for a smaller labelled dataset of only 2000 images increases the likelihood of training the tracker directly on biomedical datasets in cases where artificial models cannot be built easily. Future work could include training in synthetic multi-axon images and accounting for branching of neurons, potentially by combining the network with an automatic junction detection algorithm [22], or extending to subvoxel tracking through extending the environment to 3D, and introducing highly anisotropic spatial sampling into the environment—a common challenge in confocal imaging.

## References

1. Alansary, A., et al.: Automatic view planning with multi-scale deep reinforcement learning agents. In: Frangi, A.F., Schnabel, J.A., Davatzikos, C., Alberola-López, C., Fichtinger, G. (eds.) MICCAI 2018. LNCS, vol. 11070, pp. 277–285. Springer, Cham (2018). https://doi.org/10.1007/978-3-030-00928-1_32
2. Arulkumaran, K., Deisenroth, M.P., Brundage, M., Bharath, A.A.: Deep reinforcement learning: a brief survey. IEEE Signal Process. Mag. 34(6), 26–38 (2017)
3. Bass, C., Helkkula, P., De Paola, V., Clopath, C., Bharath, A.A.: Detection of axonal synapses in 3D two-photon images. PLoS ONE 12(9), 1–18 (2017)

4. Dai, T., et al.: Deep reinforcement learning for subpixel neural tracking. In: Proceedings of the International Conference on Medical Imaging with Deep Learning, pp. 130–150 (2019)
5. Fraz, M.M., et al.: Blood vessel segmentation methodologies in retinal images-a survey. Comput. Methods Programs Biomed. 108(1), 407–433 (2012)
6. Ghesu, F.C., et al.: Multi-scale deep reinforcement learning for real-time 3D-landmark detection in CT scans. IEEE Trans. Pattern Anal. Mach. Intell. 41(1), 176–189 (2017)
7. Haarnoja, T., Tang, H., Abbeel, P., Levine, S.: Reinforcement learning with deep energy-based policies. In: Proceedings of the 34th International Conference on Machine Learning, vol. 70, pp. 1352–1361. JMLR.org (2017)
8. Haarnoja, T., Zhou, A., Abbeel, P., Levine, S.: Soft actor-critic: off-policy maximum entropy deep reinforcement learning with a stochastic actor. arXiv preprint arXiv:1801.01290 (2018)
9. Haarnoja, T., et al.: Soft actor-critic algorithms and applications. arXiv preprint arXiv:1812.05905 (2018)
10. Kanski, J.J., Bowling, B.: Clinical Ophthalmology: A Systematic Approach. Elsevier Health Sciences, Edinburgh (2011)
11. Li, R., Zeng, T., Peng, H., Ji, S.: Deep learning segmentation of optical microscopy images improves 3-D neuron reconstruction. IEEE Trans. Med. Imaging 36(7), 1533–1541 (2017)
12. Mnih, V., et al.: Human-level control through deep reinforcement learning. Nature 518(7540), 529 (2015)
13. Pan, S.J., Yang, Q.: A survey on transfer learning. IEEE Trans. Knowl. Data Eng. 22(10), 1345–1359 (2009)
14. Peng, H., Ruan, Z., Long, F., Simpson, J.H., Myers, E.W.: V3D enables real-time 3D visualization and quantitative analysis of large-scale biological image data sets. Nat. Biotechnol. 28(4), 348 (2010)
15. Pinto, L., Andrychowicz, M., Welinder, P., Zaremba, W., Abbeel, P.: Asymmetric actor critic for image-based robot learning. arXiv preprint arXiv:1710.06542 (2017)
16. Pinto, N., Cox, D.D., DiCarlo, J.J.: Why is real-world visual object recognition hard? PLoS Comput. Biol. 4(1), e27 (2008)
17. Poulin, P., et al.: Learn to track: deep learning for tractography. In: Descoteaux, M., Maier-Hein, L., Franz, A., Jannin, P., Collins, D.L., Duchesne, S. (eds.) MICCAI 2017. LNCS, vol. 10433, pp. 540–547. Springer, Cham (2017). https://doi.org/10.1007/978-3-319-66182-7_62
18. Schulman, J., Wolski, F., Dhariwal, P., Radford, A., Klimov, O.: Proximal policy optimization algorithms. arXiv preprint arXiv:1707.06347 (2017)
19. Skibbe, H., et al.: PAT-probabilistic axon tracking for densely labeled neurons in large 3-D micrographs. IEEE Trans. Med. Imaging 38(1), 69–78 (2018)
20. Smeulders, A.W., Chu, D.M., Cucchiara, R., Calderara, S., Dehghan, A., Shah, M.: Visual tracking: an experimental survey. IEEE Trans. Pattern Anal. Mach. Intell. 36(7), 1442–1468 (2013)
21. Sutton, R.S., Barto, A.G.: Reinforcement Learning: An Introduction. MIT Press Ltd., Cambridge (2018). https://mitpress.mit.edu/books/reinforcement-learning-second-edition
22. Uslu, F., Bharath, A.A.: A multi-task network to detect junctions in retinal vasculature. In: Frangi, A.F., Schnabel, J.A., Davatzikos, C., Alberola-López, C., Fichtinger, G. (eds.) MICCAI 2018. LNCS, vol. 11071, pp. 92–100. Springer, Cham (2018). https://doi.org/10.1007/978-3-030-00934-2_11

23. Zhang, P., Wang, F., Zheng, Y.: Deep reinforcement learning for vessel centerline tracing in multi-modality 3D volumes. In: Frangi, A.F., Schnabel, J.A., Davatzikos, C., Alberola-López, C., Fichtinger, G. (eds.) MICCAI 2018. LNCS, vol. 11073, pp. 755–763. Springer, Cham (2018). https://doi.org/10.1007/978-3-030-00937-3_86

24. Ziebart, B.: Modeling purposeful adaptive behavior with the principle of maximum causal entropy (2010). http://search.proquest.com/docview/845728212/

# Weakly Supervised Confidence Learning for Brain MR Image Dense Parcellation

Bin Xiao[1,2], Xiaoqing Cheng[3], Qingfeng Li[4], Qian Wang[2],
Lichi Zhang[2], Dongming Wei[2], Yiqiang Zhan[1], Xiang Sean Zhou[1],
Zhong Xue[1], Guangming Lu[3], and Feng Shi[1(✉)]

[1] Shanghai United Imaging Intelligence Co., Ltd., Shanghai, China
feng.shi@united-imaging.com
[2] School of Biomedical Engineering, Med-X Research Institute,
Shanghai Jiao Tong University, Shanghai, China
[3] Department of Medical Imaging, Jinling Hospital,
Nanjing University School of Medicine, Nanjing, China
[4] School of Biomedical Engineering, Southern Medical University,
Guangdong, China

**Abstract.** Automatic dense parcellation of brain MR image, which labels hundreds of regions of interest (ROIs), plays an important role for neuroimage analysis. Specifically, the brain image parcellation using deep learning technology has been widely recognized for its effective performance, but it remains limited in actual application due to its high demand for sufficient training data and intensive memory allocation of GPU resources. Due to the high cost of manual segmentation, it is usually not feasible to provide large dataset for training the network. On the other hand, it is relatively easy to transfer labeling information to many new unlabeled datasets and thus augment the training data. However, the augmented data can only be considered as weakly labeled for training. Therefore, in this paper, we propose a cascaded weakly super- vised confidence integration network (CINet). The main contributions of our method are two-folds. First, we propose the image registration-based data argumentation method, and evaluate the confidence of the labeling information for each augmented image. The augmented data, as well as the original yet small training dataset, contribute to the modeling of the CINet jointly for segmentation. Second, we propose the random crop strategy to handle the large amount of feature channels in the network, which are needed to label hundreds of neural ROIs. The demanding requirement to GPU memory is thus relieved, while better accuracy can also be achieved. In experiments, we use 37 manually labeled subjects and augment 96 images with weak labels for training. The testing result in overall Dice score over 112 brain regions reaches 75%, which is higher than using the original training data only.

**Keywords:** MRI · Brain segmentation · CNN · Weakly supervised

© Springer Nature Switzerland AG 2019
H.-I. Suk et al. (Eds.): MLMI 2019, LNCS 11861, pp. 409–416, 2019.
https://doi.org/10.1007/978-3-030-32692-0_47

# 1 Introduction

Whole brain segmentation toward structural MRI is of great significance for both brain researches and clinical applications. As the topic has been investigated for long time, there are several ways to implement whole brain segmentation, which can be generally grouped as follows:

(1) Registration-based method [2, 4]. One can label a brain image in two steps, by first registering the atlas image, as well as its label map, to the target image precisely, and then derive the segmentation result for the target by fusing the warped label maps (e.g., through voting). However, the registration-based methods may suffer from large structural variation and registration errors;

(2) Patch-based method [5]. Atlas images are first roughly registered to the target image (e.g., by affine registration). Then, sophisticated patch-based label fusion algorithms are adopted to evaluate the patch-wise similarity between the target image and the atlases. If patches have similar intensity appearance in a spatially non-local area, they should have similar labels. Though the non- local label fusion has shown its superior accuracy and alleviated the demanding requirement to precise registration, the process could be very time-consuming due to the patch-by-patch processing;

(3) Learning-based method. Supervised machine learning has long been ap- plied to solve brain image segmentation. The fully convolution neural network (FCN) [7] in particular has become state-of-the-art solution in many problems of medical image segmentation. We can directly learn a network from the atlas data set, in which every atlas comes with its labels for supervision. At the same time, the inference upon a target image is very fast by the FCN framework.

However, it is challenging if we are trying to automatically label the whole brain into a large number of small ROIs (e.g. >100 labels corresponding to different neural structural and functional areas) by FCN. The limited GPU memory has restricted the number of the channels in the later convolutional layers of the network, thus making it hard for the network to handle hundreds of ROIs simultaneously. Meanwhile, with many ROIs to label, it is more difficult to prepare sufficient training data, which obviously hurts the generalization capability of the trained network.

In this paper, we propose a cascaded weakly supervised confidence integration network (CINet) to address the problem of the limited GPU memory and limited training data. Specifically, we design the registration-based data augmentation method as well as the confidence evaluation mechanism upon the augmented data. The augmented images, with their evaluated confidences, can act as weak supervision and help optimize the network in addition to the original training dataset. Besides, we extend the V-Net [8] framework by the novel random crop strategy, such that hundreds of ROIs can be simultaneously handled in both training and testing. We apply our method to whole brain parcellation, and achieve superior performance in segmenting brain MR images.

## 2  Method

In this section, we present the proposed data augmentation method and the details of CINet. Particularly we propose a registration-based approach to augment the training data with weak labels in Sect. 2.1. The confidence evaluation toward the weak labeling information of the augmented images is provided in Sect. 2.2. Then, we introduce CINet and apply it to brain image segmentation in Sect. 2.3.

### 2.1  Augmentation Toward Weakly Labeled Images

An important factor that limits the accuracy of the trained segmentation network is the insufficient number of high-quality training data. Concerning the difficulty to generate many high-quality experts labeling, we propose to argument the limited number of initial training data. Although the augmented images own weak labels only, the segmentation network can benefit from incorporating more training images, i.e., by combing the augmented images with the initial high-quality training data.

The augmentation toward the weakly labeled data is attained through conventional registration-based segmentation, which can only label the ROIs roughly for an unlabeled image. Specifically, given an arbitrary image that is unlabeled, we first use SyN [1] to register the well labeled images (i.e., from the initial training dataset) and warp their label maps accordingly. Then, for label fusion, we adopt majority voting weighted by local patch-to-patch similarity. In our implementation, the patch size is set to 5*5*5.

Since the above registration and label fusion process introduces high errors, the new image can only be considered as weakly labeled. For convenience, the weakly labeled images form a dataset $\{(F_1, W_1), (F_2, W_2), \cdots, (F_s, W_s)\}$, as $F_i$ has its weak label map as $W_i$. Since the unlabeled image can be arbitrarily selected, theoretically we can acquire unlimited number of augmented images and their weak labels in the way above.

### 2.2  Confidence of the Weakly Labeled Data

In order to make proper use of the weakly labeled images in $\{(F_1, W_1), (F_2, W_2), \cdots, (F_s, W_s)\}$, we train a confidence network to predict the confidence that measures the quality of the label at each point of $F_j$. The role of the confidence network is illustrated in Fig. 1. The confidence network is trained by using the initial training data set, which is designated by $\{(M_1, L_1), (M_2, L_2), \cdots, (M_k, L_k)\}$. For a certain image $M_i$, we can apply the protocol in Sect. 2.1, and generate its corresponding weak label (i.e., $L_i'$) by using other training images in the dataset. Then, $M_i$ and $L_i'$ are input to the

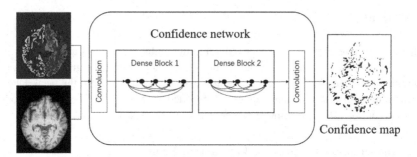

**Fig. 1.** The architecture of the confidence network. The unlabeled image and its weak label map (left) are input to the network, while the errors between the weak labels and the real labels (right) supervise the training of the network. In inference, the output of the network can be regarded as confidence measure to the weak labels of the input image.

confidence network, which aims to predict the errors in $L_i'$ by referring to the supervision of $L_i$. That is, for location x in the image space, the output of the confidence network is 1 if $L_i'(x) = L_i(x)$, or 0 if $L_i'(x) \neq L_i(x)$. The architecture of the confidence network, which has two dense.

Blocks, is shown in Fig. 1. The exemplar inputs and output of the network are also shown in Fig. 1.

Once the training of the confidence network is completed, it can be used to evaluate the weakly labeled data in Sect. 2.1. We apply it to the weakly labeled dataset and obtain the confidence map $C_i$ for each $W_i$. At each position, $C_i$ gives $W_i$ a confidence flag. If it is equal to 1, it means that the label in Wi can be used as a correct label for network training. If it is equal to 0, it means that the label in $W_i$ is wrong which should not participate in the training process of the network. Thus, we have the set of $\{(F_1, W_1, C_1), (F_2, W_2, C_2), \cdots, (F_s, W_s, C_s)\}$, which will be used to train CINet in the next.

## 2.3   Confidence Integration Network (CINet) and Loss Function

Besides the insufficient number of high-quality training data problem, the net- work training also suffers from large memory consumption of GPU memory. The root of the problem lies in one-hot encoding. For example, if the image size is 208*208*160, which we use in this paper, the output of the network with 112 brain regions would be 208*208*160*113. This will take up to 20G GPU memory. To tackle the above dilemma, previous studies follow region-based method [6] which train more than one network to track different part of the brain. As a result, the whole process will become quite complex. Another way to track that problem is that train the network on a random patch of the image and test it on the whole brain image. However, the segmentation accuracy will accept a decrease as the field of view (FOV) at the test stage is different from that at the training stage. Therefore, it seems that there must always be an inevitably trade-off between GPU memory consumption and input image size.

Here we made three changes on the basic framework of V-Net to track that con-tradictions: (1) Decompose V-Net into two sub-networks as describe in Fig. 2. At any time, point in the training stage, only intermediate variables associated with one of the sub-networks are stored in the GPU memory. This can be easily implemented with the help of technology checkpoint provided by Pytorch; (2) Replace all the convolution operation in the second sub-network by 1*1*1 convolution. This allows the FOV to remain unchanged at this stage; (3) In the training stage, we randomly crop a patch from the output of the first sub-network as the input of the second sub-network. Naturally, the corresponding image patch in the ground truth was used to calculate the loss of the network. In the test stage, the crop operation will be ignored. We name this strategy Random crop mechanism.

It is clearly that, we can freely change the memory occupied by subnetwork 2 according to the GPU memory we have and the FOV of the whole network will make no difference between training and testing stage. Meanwhile, the proposed network can process the entire brain image in one network instead of training multiple networks in different part of the brain as SLANT [6].

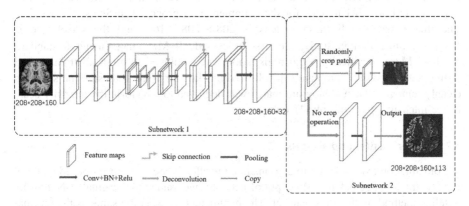

**Fig. 2.** Illustration of the two-stage process in CINet. We use part of the V-Net as the Sub-network 1 of our CINet. The input image size is 208*208*160. After Subnetwork 1 (V-Net alike), the feature map has a resolution of 208*208*160*32. In the training stage, Subnetwork 2 use a patch randomly cropped from that feature map to optimize the network parameter. While in the test stage, the Subnetwork 2 use the whole feature map to predict the label map without crop operation. The label map has 113 channels as we have 112 regions of interest and background.

For atlas data set $\{(M_1, L_1), (M_2, L_2), \cdots, (M_k, L_k)\}$ and the weakly labeled data set $\{(F_1, W_1, C_1), (F_2, W_2, C_2), \cdots, (F_s, W_s, C_s)\}$, we use two different loss function in the training stage. With atlas data set $\{(M_1, L_1), (M_2, L_2), \cdots, (M_k, L_k)\}$, we use cross-entropy as loss. For $\{(F_1, W_1, C_1), (F_2, W_2, C_2), \cdots, (F_s, W_s, C_s)\}$, we use confidence map $C_i$ as masks by setting a threshold (i.e., $\gamma$) to select parts of the image to enhance the performance of the segmentation network. Thus, our proposed loss can be defined by:

$$Loss = \sum_{x} [C(x) > \gamma] \times CrossEntrpy(CINet(F), W)(x)$$

Here, we named the modified model CINet which trained on the confidence integration data set in Sect. 2.2. The framework of CINet is outlined in Fig. 2.

## 3    Materials and Experiments

### 3.1    Materials

Our brain data set consisted of 67 brain T1 MRI images from clinical partner hospital. We randomly chose 37 as training set, 10 subjects as validation set and the remaining 20 subjects as test set. All 67 subjects were processed by FreeSurfer first and manually-corrected by an experienced doctor. Each subject has 112 brain areas. Besides, we have also acquired 96 MRI images for data augmentation proposed in Sects. 2.1 and 2.2. The image size of all these images is $208 \times 208 \times 160$, and the voxel size is $1 \times 1 \times 1\,mm^3$. In this study, we first processed all MR image using a standard pipeline. More specifically, rigid registration was employed to align all training and testing data to colin27 template [3], followed by skull stripping to ensure the skull are cleanly removed. Then Histogram match was deployed to transform the intensity-scale to the intensity space of colin27 cohort.

### 3.2    Experimental and Results

We did ablation experimental to demonstrate the effectiveness of our proposed method. First, with an image patch as the input of network, we trained the original V-Net as the baseline method on the atlas data set. The parameters were set the same as the original V-Net. Next, we trained our CINet on the same atlas data set which have 37 brain images (CINet-37). By using extra weakly labeled data set which obtained by Sect. 2.1, we first trained the CINet on it and fine-tuning the network on the atlas data set. Finally, we coalesced confidence map provide in Sect. 2.2 and augmented data in Sect. 2.3 to train our network where VNet was modified to fulfill GPU memory limitation (CINet-37+96C).

We used Pytroch to implement all the experiments. For all networks, we used the same hyper-parameter with batch size = 4, input resolution = 208*208*160 (96*96*96 for the original V-Net), input channel = 1, output channel = 113, optimizer = Adam, max iteration = 1000. The learning rate for segmentation network and confidence network are initialized to 0.001. Every 100 epoch, the learning rate automatically decreased 50%. Two GPUs with 32 GB are utilized to train the networks. After training each network, we use the atlas image set to fine-tuning the segmentation network.

**Table 1.** Segmentation result in terms of Dice, evaluated on the test data set. We report the mean (standard deviation) Dice coefficient across all 112 brain labels on all test subjects.

| Dataset | Model | | | |
|---|---|---|---|---|
| | VNet | CINet | CINet- 37 +96 W | CINet- 37 +96C |
| Atlas data set | √ | √ | √ | √ |
| Weakly labeled data set | | | √ | √ |
| Confidence map | | | | √ |
| Dice | 0.690 ± 0.021 | 0.700 ± 0.022 | 0.738 ± 0.019 | 0.750 ± 0.015 |

We evaluated the accuracy of each segmentation experimental in terms of Dice score. The quantitative result has been showed in Table 1. The mean Dice coefficient of the original V-Net trained by patch-based method only achieve 0.69. Meanwhile, the proposed CINet got a dice = 0.70 which prove training the net- work with the whole brain image can improve segmentation accuracy. In our opinion, this is because our CINet is not bothered by FOV inconsistency during training and testing. Consistent with the conclusion of [9], the weakly labeled data set bring 3.7% improvements on the test data set. This shows that although the data obtained by data augmentation has the components of the incorrect labeling, these data still bring diversity to the training samples and improve the generalization performance of the model. Further, the effectiveness of confidence map was confirmed by the final result obtained by CINet-37

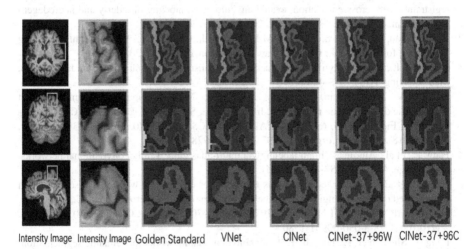

Intensity Image  Intensity Image  Golden Standard    VNet          CINet        CINet-37+96W  CINet-37+96C

**Fig. 3.** Visual comparison of labeling results by VNet, CINet, CINet-37+96 W, and CINet-37 +96C. The proposed method CINet-37+96C produces the most accurate labels for the regions inside the box. We can observe that the segmentation result is better from vnet to CINet-37+96C, and CInet is better than Vnet as it overcomes the problem of inconsistency of field of view in the training and testing phases. At the same time, thanks to the weakly labeled data, the generalization ability of CINet-37+96 W and CINet-37+96C to the unknown data is gradually improved, and better segmentation results are obtained.

+96C which is the best result of all the method. It is easy to explain because the confidence map reduces the misleading information of incorrectly labeled training for the net- work. Figure 3 shows a visual comparison of different labeling results with VNet, CINet, CINet-37+96 W, and CINet-37+96C.

## 4   Conclusion and Discussion

In this study, we develop the CINet to reduce the consumption of GPU memory which enable us to train a neural network on the whole brain space. Because of this advantage, we can greatly improve the speed of segmentation algorithm, and make it possible to explore more complex network structure. For the same network, results from 96 extra weakly annotated data acquired automatically helps us achieved better performance than the results from atlas image set. We demonstrate that our method reduces the cost of labeling and achieves segmentation accuracy close to all data with accurate labeling by automatic data argumentation.

**Acknowledgement.** This research was supported by the grants from the National Key Research and Development Program of China (No. 2018YFC0116400).

## References

1. Avants, B.B., Epstein, C.L., Grossman, M., Gee, J.C.: Symmetric diffeomorphic image registration with cross-correlation: evaluating automated labeling of elderly and neurodegenerative brain. Med. Image Anal. **12**(1), 26–41 (2008)
2. Balakrishnan, G., Zhao, A., Sabuncu, M.R., Guttag, J., Dalca, A.V.: Voxelmorph: A learning framework for deformable medical image registration **PP**(99), 1 (2018)
3. Collins, D.L., et al.: Design and construction of a realistic digital brain phantom. IEEE Trans. Med. Imaging **17**(3), 463–468 (1998)
4. Dalca, A.V., Balakrishnan, G., Guttag, J., Sabuncu, M.R.: Unsupervised learning for fast probabilistic diffeomorphic registration. In: Frangi, A., Schnabel, J., Davatzikos, C., Alberola-López, C., Fichtinger, G. (eds.) MICCAI 2018. LNCS, vol. 11070, pp. 729–738. Springer, Cham (2018). https://doi.org/10.1007/978-3-030-00928-1_82
5. Fang, L., et al.: Automatic brain labeling via multi-atlas guided fully convolutional networks. Med. Image Anal. **51**, 157–168 (2019)
6. Huo, Y., et al.: Spatially localized atlas network tiles enables 3D whole brain segmentation from limited data. In: Frangi, A., Schnabel, J., Davatzikos, C., Alberola-López, C., Fichtinger, G. (eds.) MICCAI 2018. LNCS, vol. 11072, pp. 698–705. Springer, Cham (2018). https://doi.org/10.1007/978-3-030-00931-1_80
7. Long, J., Shelhamer, E., Darrell, T.: Fully convolutional networks for semantic segmentation. In: Proceedings of the IEEE Conference on Computer Vision and Pattern Recognition, pp. 3431–3440 (2015)
8. Milletari, F., Navab, N., Ahmadi, S.A.: V-net: fully convolutional neural networks for volumetric medical image segmentation. In: Fourth International Conference on 3D Vision (2016)
9. Zlateski, A., Jaroensri, R., Sharma, P., Durand, F.: On the importance of label quality for semantic segmentation. In: Proceedings of the IEEE Conference on Computer Vision and Pattern Recognition, pp. 1479–1487 (2018)

# Select, Attend, and Transfer: Light, Learnable Skip Connections

Saeid Asgari Taghanaki[1,2]([⊠]), Aicha Bentaieb[1], Anmol Sharma[1],
S. Kevin Zhou[2], Yefeng Zheng[2], Bogdan Georgescu[2], Puneet Sharma[2],
Zhoubing Xu[2], Dorin Comaniciu[2], and Ghassan Hamarneh[1]

[1] Medical Image Analysis Lab, School of Computing Science,
Simon Fraser University, Burnaby, Canada
sasgarit@sfu.ca
[2] Medical Imaging Technologies, Siemens Healthineers, Princeton, NJ, USA

**Abstract.** Skip connections in deep networks have improved both segmentation and classification performance by facilitating the training of deeper network architectures and reducing the risks for vanishing gradients. The skip connections equip encoder-decoder like networks with richer feature representations, but at the cost of higher memory usage, computation, and possibly resulting in transferring non-discriminative feature maps. In this paper, we focus on improving the skip connections used in segmentation networks. We propose light, learnable skip connections which learn to first select the most discriminative channels, and then aggregate the selected ones as single channel attending to the most discriminative regions of input. We evaluate the proposed method on 3 different 2D and volumetric datasets and demonstrate that the proposed skip connections can outperform the traditional heavy skip connections of 4 different models in terms of segmentation accuracy (2% Dice), memory usage (at least 50%), and the number of network parameters (up to 70%).

**Keywords:** Deep neural networks · Skip connections · Image segmentation

## 1 Introduction

Recent works in image segmentation has shown that stacking tens of convolutional layers generally perform better than shallower networks [7], due to their ability to learn more complex nonlinear functions. However, they are difficult to train because of the high number of parameters and gradient vanishing. One of the recent key ideas to effectuate the training process and handle gradient vanishing is to introduce skip connections between subsequent layers in the network, which has been shown to improve some of the encoder-decoder segmentation networks (e.g., 2D U-Net [19], 3D U-Net [2], 3D V-Net [18], and The One Hundred

© Springer Nature Switzerland AG 2019
H.-I. Suk et al. (Eds.): MLMI 2019, LNCS 11861, pp. 417–425, 2019.
https://doi.org/10.1007/978-3-030-32692-0_48

Layers Tiramisu (DensNet) [12]). Skip connections help in the training process by recovering spatial information lost during down-sampling, as well as reducing the risks of vanishing gradients [11]. However, direct transfer of feature maps from previous layers to subsequent layers may also lead to redundant and non-discriminatory feature maps being transferred. Also, as the transferred feature maps are concatenated to the feature maps in subsequent layers, the memory usage increases many folds.

**Complexity Reduction.** Recently, there have been several efforts to reduce the training and runtime computations of deep classification networks [9,16]. A few other works have attempted to simplify the structure of deep networks, e.g., by tensor factorization [13], channel/network pruning [23] or applying sparsity to connections [6]. However, the non-structured connectivity and irregular memory access, which is caused by sparsity regularization and connection pruning methods, adversely impacts practical speedup [23]. On the other hand, tensor factorization is not compatible with the recently designed networks, e.g., GoogleNet and ResNet, and many such methods may even end up with more computations than the original architectures [8].

**Gates and Attention.** Attention can be viewed as using information transferred from several subsequent layers/feature maps to localize the most discriminative (or salient) part of the input signal. Srivastava et al. [21] modified ResNet in a way to control the flow of information through a connection; their proposed gates control the level of contribution between unmodified input and activations to a consecutive layer. Hu et al. [10] proposed a selection mechanism where feature maps are first aggregated using global average pooling and reduced to a single channel descriptor, then an activation gate is used to highlight the most discriminative features. Recently, Wang et al. [22] added an attention module to ResNet for image classification. Their proposed attention module consists of several encoding-decoding layers, which although helped in improving image classification accuracy, also increased the computational complexity of the model by an order of magnitude [22]. Lin et al., adopted one step fusion without *filtering* the channels. Xiao et al. [1] added an non-learnable extra branch, called hourglass residual units, to the original residual connections.

In this paper, we propose a modification of the traditional skip connections, using a novel *select-attend-transfer gate*, which *explicitly* enforces learnability and aims at simultaneously improving segmentation accuracy and reducing memory usage and network parameters (Fig. 1). We focus on skip connections in encoder-decoder architectures (i.e. as opposed to skip connections in residual networks) designed for segmentation tasks. Our proposed *select-attend-transfer gate* favours sparse feature representations and uses this property to select and attend to the most discriminative feature channels and spatial regions within a skip connection. Specifically, we first learn to identify the most discriminative feature maps in a skip connection, using a set of trainable weights under sparsity constraint. Then, we reduce the feature maps to a single channel using a convolutional filter followed by an attention layer to identify salient spatial locations within the produced feature map. This compact representation forms the final feature map of the skip connection.

## 2    The Select-Attend-Transfer (SAT) Gate

**Notation:** We define $f$ as an input feature map of size $H \times W \times D \times C$ where $H$, $W$, $D$, and $C$ refer to the height, width, and depth of the volumetric data, and number of channels, respectively. The notation in the paper is defined for 3D (volumetric) input images but the method can be easily adapted to 2D images by removing an extra dimension and applying 2D convolutions instead of 3D. An overview of the proposed SAT gate is shown in Fig. 1. It consists of the following modules: (1) Select: re-weighting the channels of the input feature maps $f$, using a learned weight vector with sparsity constraints, to encourage sparse feature map representations, that is, only those channels with non-zero weights are selected; (2) Attend: discovering the most salient spatial locations within the final feature map; and (3) Transfer: transferring the output of the gate into subsequent layers via a skip connection.

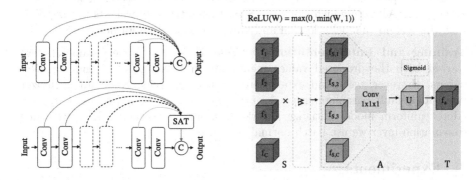

**Fig. 1.** The proposed select-attend-transfer (SAT) gate placed in a dense block for a volumetric 3D data. The different shades of green colour show the result of applying the proposed soft channel selection, i.e., some channels can be totally turned off (grey) or partially turned on. (Color figure online)

**Selection via Sparsification.** We weight the channels of an input feature map $f$ by using a scalar weight vector $W$ trained along with all other network parameters. The weight vector is defined such that we encourage sparse feature maps, resulting in completely/partially turning off or on feature maps. Instead of relying on complex loss functions, we clip negative weights to zero and positives to at most one using a truncated ReLU function. Each channel of the feature map block $f$ is multiplied by $W$ as $f_{s,c} = f_c * trelu(W_c)$, where $W_c$ is a scalar weight value associated with the input feature map channel $f_c$; $trelu(.)$ is the truncated ReLU function. The output $f_s$ is of size $H \times W \times D \times C$ and is a sparse representation of $f$. Zero weights turn off corresponding feature maps completely, whereas positive weights fully/partially turn on features maps; i.e., implementing the soft feature map selection.

**Attention via Filtering.** The output $f_s$ is further filtered to identify the most discriminative linear combination of feature channels $C$. For this, we employ a convolution filter $K$ of size $1 \times 1 \times 1 \times C$ ($1 \times 1 \times C$ for 2D data), which learns how best to aggregate the different channels of the feature map $f_s$. The output (i.e. $U$) of this feature selection step reduces $f_s$ to $K \star f_s$ of size $H \times W \times D \times 1$. where $\star$ is the convolution operation. To identify salient spatial locations within the $U$, we introduce an attention gate $f_a = \sigma(U)$ composed of a sigmoid activation function ($\sigma$). Using the sigmoid as an activation function allows us to identify multiple discriminative spatial locations (as opposed softmax which identifies one single location) within the feature map $U$. The computed $f_a$ forms a compact summary of the input feature map $f$.

**Transfer via Skip Connection.** The computed $f_a$ is transferred to subsequent layers via a skip connection.

**Special Examples.** There are two special cases of the proposed SAT gate. One is the ST gate which skips the A part, that is, only channel selection but no attention is performed. The signal $f_s$ is directly fed to subsequent layers. The other is the AT gate which skips the S part by setting all weights to one. This way, there is no channel selection and only attention is performed.

**Training and Implementation Details.** To set the hyperparameters, we started with the proposed values mentioned in U-Net, V-Net, and DensNet papers. However, we found experimentally that applying Adadelta optimizer (with its default parameters: $\eta = 1$, $\rho = 0.95$, $\epsilon = 1e - 8$, and $decay = 0$) with Glorot uniform model initializer, works best for all the networks. After each convolution layer we use batch normalization.

## 3  Experiments

In this section, we evaluate the performance of the proposed method on three commonly used fully convolutional segmentation networks which leverage skip connections: U-Net (both 2D and 3D), V-Net (both 2D and 3D), and the DensNet network (both 2D and 3D). We test the proposed method on three datasets (Fig. 2) including (i) a magnetic resonance imaging (MRI) dataset; (ii) a skin lesion dataset; and (iii) a computed tomography (CT) dataset. To analyze the performance of the proposed method, we performed the following experiments: (a) We tested the performance of the proposed method, in terms of segmentation accuracy, on datasets i and ii. (b) We applied the proposed SAT gate to the recently introduced method deep image to image network (DI2IN) [24] for liver segmentation method (Sect. 3.2). (c) We quantitatively and qualitatively analyzed the proposed skip connections in terms of the amount of data transferred and we visualized the outputs of both channel selection and attention layers. We also compared the proposed method vs. the original networks in terms of memory usage and number of parameters (Sect. 3.2)

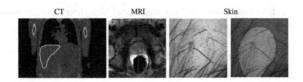

**Fig. 2.** Three samples of the used datasets. The liver (contoured in red) in CT scan, the prostate in an MRI scan, a sample skin images containing lesions highlighted in red from left to right. (Color figure online)

## 3.1 Volumetric and 2D Binary Segmentation

**Volumetric CT Liver Segmentation:** In this experiment, the goal is to segment the liver from CT images. We used more than 2000 CT scans (to the best of our knowledge this is the largest CT dataset used in the literature so far) of different resolutions collected internally and from The Cancer Imaging Archive (TCIA) QIN-HEADNECK dataset [4], which were resampled to isotropic voxels of size $2 \times 2 \times 2$ (mm). We picked 61 volumes of whole dataset for testing and trained the networks on the remaining volumes.

**Volumetric MRI Prostate Segmentation:** In this experiment, we test the proposed method on a volumetric MRI prostate dataset of 1029 MRI volumes of different resolutions which were collected internally and from TCIA ProstateX dataset [5] that were resampled to isotropic voxels of size $2 \times 2 \times 2$ (mm). We used 770 images for training and 258 images for testing.

**2D RGB Skin Lesion Segmentation:** For this experiment, we used the 2D RGB skin lesion dataset from the 2017 IEEE ISBI International Skin Imaging Collaboration (ISIC) Challenge [3]. We train on a dataset of 2000 images and test on a different set of 150 images. As reported in Table 1, overall, equipping U-Net and V-Net with SAT improved Dice results for all 4 (2 modalities times 2 networks) experiments. Specifically: (i) For the MRI dataset, the SAT gate improves U-Net performance by 1.15% (0.87 to 0.88) in Dice. Using SAT with V-Net improved Dice results by 2.4% (0.85 to 0.87). Note that, although for V-Net (MRI data) the Dice improvement is small, instead of transferring all the channels, the proposed method transfers only one attention map, which reduces memory usage to a high extent. (ii) For the skin dataset, equipping U-Net with SAT improved Dice by 2.53% (0.79 to 0.81), and similarly V-Net with SAT resulted in 2.5% (0.81 to 0.83) improvement in terms of Dice.

To select the winner in Table 1, we consider different criteria: accuracy, number of parameters, and memory usage. We argue that the winner is SAT as with SAT we are able to reduce memory and # params without sacrificing accuracy. When there is no attention, i.e. only ST, multiple channels are transferred which implies higher memory usage and # params, and our results show that, even then, there is no clear gain in accuracy compared to AT and SAT. That said, ST does outperform standard models (i.e. U-Net, V-Net, and DensNet). When there is attention but no multiple channel selection, i.e. only AT, although we

**Table 1.** U-Net and V-Net results of prostate and skin lesion segmentation. N is the total number of channels C before skip connection.

| Data | Model | Method | # C | Dice |
|------|-------|--------|-----|------|
| MRI | 3D U-Net [2] | ORIG | $C = N$ | $0.87 \pm 0.05$ |
|  |  | AT | $C = 1$ | $0.88 \pm 0.05$ |
|  |  | ST | $C \leqslant N$ | $0.88 \pm 0.05$ |
|  |  | **SAT** | **$C = 1$** | **$0.88 \pm 0.05$** |
|  | 3D V-Net [18] | ORIG | $C = N$ | $0.85 \pm 0.05$ |
|  |  | AT | $C = 1$ | $0.86 \pm 0.05$ |
|  |  | ST | $C \leqslant N$ | $0.86 \pm 0.05$ |
|  |  | **SAT** | **$C = 1$** | **$0.87 \pm 0.04$** |
| Skin | 2D U-Net [19] | ORIG | $C = N$ | $0.79 \pm 0.001$ |
|  |  | AT | $C = 1$ | $0.79 \pm 0.001$ |
|  |  | ST | $C \leqslant N$ | $0.79 \pm 0.001$ |
|  |  | **SAT** | **$C = 1$** | **$0.81 \pm 0.001$** |
|  | 2D V-Net | ORIG | $C = N$ | $0.81 \pm 0.001$ |
|  |  | AT | $C = 1$ | $0.82 \pm 0.002$ |
|  |  | ST | $C \leqslant N$ | $0.82 \pm 0.001$ |
|  |  | **SAT** | **$C = 1$** | **$0.83 \pm 0.001$** |

manage to reduce memory and # params, the results show erroneous segmentations and lower Dice (Table 1). So, the main competition is between the AT and SAT as both transfer a single channel resulting in reduction in # params and memory usage. However, looking at the quantitative results in Table 1, SAT outperforms AT in terms of Dice in 3 out of 4 cases. Also, looking at the qualitative results in Fig. 3, SAT wins as AT tends to attend to several wrong areas for different datasets. As reported by Gao et al. [11], DenseNet outperforms Highway Networks [21], Network in Network [17], ResNet [7], FractalNet [14], Deeply Supervised Nets [15], and "Striving for simplicity: The all convolutional net" [20], all of which attempted to optimize the data flow and number of parameters in deep networks. We tested the proposed SAT gate on the segmentation version of the winner model i.e. The One Hundred Layers Tiramisu network [12] (i.e. DensNet). Note that we apply the proposed SAT gate to more skip connections in this network i.e. both long skip connections between the encoder and decoder and the long skip connections inside of each dense block (Fig. 1). While our proposed SAT gate reduces the number of parameters in DensNet by ~70%, it improves Dice results by 3.7% ($0.79 \pm 0.12$ to $0.82 \pm 0.07$) for MRI and by 2.5% ($0.79 \pm 0.002$ to $0.81 \pm 0.001$) for Skin.

As the next experiment, we applied our proposed SAT gate to the DI2IN [24] method for liver segmentation from CT images and achieved the same performance as the original DI2IN network i.e. Dice score of 0.96 while reducing the number of the *whole* network parameters by 12% by applying SAT to *only* skip connections and reducing number of channels for each skip connection to only *one* channel.

## 3.2    Quantitative and Qualitative Analysis of the Proposed Skip Connections

In this section, we visualize the outputs of both the channel selection and attention layers. As shown in Fig. 3, after applying the selection step, some of the less discriminative channels are completely turned off by the proposed channel selection. As can be seen in both Fig. 3, a model with only attention layer (i.e., only AT) tends to attend to several areas of the image; including both where the object is present and absent (note the red colour visible over the whole image). However, applying channel selection (i.e., ST) before the attention layer curtails the model from attending to less discriminative regions. We also quantitatively analyzed the proposed learnable skip connections in terms of percentage of channels "turned off" (i.e., channels i for which $w_i$ is zero in the channel selection layer). For U-Net, $55.7 \pm 5$ and $66.7 \pm 7$ and for V-Net, $57.0 \pm 12.9$ and $54.5 \pm 6.9$ percentage of channels were off for MRI and skin datasets, respectively. After applying SAT, the number of parameters of *only* the skip connections is reduced by 28%, 50%, and 70% for U-Net, V-Net, and DensNet networks. Since transferring only one channel (instead of N channels) as the output of the SAT gate, reduces the needed number of convolution kernel parameters in the other side of skip connections, we further report the total number of parameters before and after applying the proposed method (i.e., SAT).

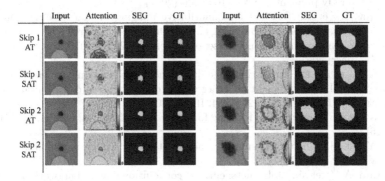

**Fig. 3.** Attention maps, segmentation, and ground truth for 2 skip connections of 2D U-Net for only attention (AT) and channel selection + attention (SAT) for skin images.

Further note that the proposed method reduces the number of convolution operations after each concatenation to almost 50% as demonstrated next. As an example, after an original skip connection that carries 256 channels and concatenates them with another 256 channels on the other side of the network, the consequent convolution layer right after the concatenation will need

512 ( $= 256 + 256$ ) convolution operations. However, as the proposed skip connections carry only one channel, for the same example, only 257 ( $= 1 + 256$ ) convolutions are needed.

# 4   Conclusions

We proposed a novel architecture for skip connections in fully convolutional segmentation networks. Our proposed skip connection involves a channel selection step followed by an attention gate. Equipping popular segmentation networks with the proposed skip connections allowed us to reduce computations and network parameters (the proposed method transfer only one unique feature channel instead of many), improve the segmentation results (it attends to the most discriminative channels and regions within the feature maps of a skip connection) and consistently obtain more accurate segmentation results.

# References

1. Chu, X., et al.: Multi-context attention for human pose estimation. arXiv preprint arXiv:1702.07432 **1**(2) (2017)
2. Çiçek, Ö., Abdulkadir, A., Lienkamp, S.S., Brox, T., Ronneberger, O.: 3D U-Net: learning dense volumetric segmentation from sparse annotation. In: Ourselin, S., Joskowicz, L., Sabuncu, M.R., Unal, G., Wells, W. (eds.) MICCAI 2016. LNCS, vol. 9901, pp. 424–432. Springer, Cham (2016). https://doi.org/10.1007/978-3-319-46723-8_49
3. Codella, N.C., et al.: Skin lesion analysis toward melanoma detection: ISBI, hosted by ISIC. arXiv preprint arXiv:1710.05006 (2017)
4. Fedorov, A., et al.: DICOM for quantitative imaging biomarker development: a standards based approach to sharing clinical data and structured PET/CT analysis results in head and neck cancer research. PeerJ **4**, e2057 (2016). https://doi.org/10.7717/peerj.2057
5. Geert, L., et al.: Prostatex challenge data. The cancer imaging archive (2017)
6. Han, S., et al.: EIE: efficient inference engine on compressed deep neural network. In: ISCA, ACM/IEEE, pp. 243–254. IEEE (2016)
7. He, K., et al.: Deep residual learning for image recognition. In: CVPR, pp. 770–778 (2016)
8. He, Y., et al.: Channel pruning for accelerating very deep neural networks. In: ICCV, vol. 2, p. 6 (2017)
9. Howard, A.G., et al.: Mobilenets: efficient convolutional neural networks for mobile vision applications. arXiv preprint arXiv:1704.04861 (2017)
10. Hu, J., et al.: Squeeze-and-excitation networks. arXiv preprint arXiv:1709.01507 (2017)
11. Huang, G., et al.: Densely connected convolutional networks. In: CVPR (2017)
12. Jégou, S., et al.: The one hundred layers tiramisu: Fully convolutional densenets for semantic segmentation. In: CVPRW (2017)
13. Kim, Y.D.: Compression of deep convolutional neural networks for fast and low power mobile applications. arXiv preprint arXiv:1511.06530 (2015)
14. Larsson, G., et al.: Fractalnet: ultra-deep neural networks without residuals. arXiv preprint arXiv:1605.07648 (2016)

15. Lee, C.Y., et al.: Deeply-supervised nets. In: AIS, pp. 562–570 (2015)
16. Leroux, S., et al.: IamNN: iterative and adaptive mobile neural network for efficient image classification. arXiv preprint arXiv:1804.10123 (2018)
17. Lin, M., et al.: Network in network. arXiv preprint arXiv:1312.4400 (2013)
18. Milletari, F., et al.: V-net: fully convolutional neural networks for volumetric medical image segmentation. In: 3DV, 2016, pp. 565–571. IEEE (2016)
19. Ronneberger, O., Fischer, P., Brox, T.: U-Net: Convolutional networks for biomedical image segmentation. In: Navab, N., Hornegger, J., Wells, W.M., Frangi, A.F. (eds.) MICCAI 2015. LNCS, vol. 9351, pp. 234–241. Springer, Cham (2015). https://doi.org/10.1007/978-3-319-24574-4_28
20. Springenberg, J.T., et al.: Striving for simplicity: the all convolutional net. arXiv preprint arXiv:1412.6806 (2014)
21. Srivastava, R.K., et al.: Highway networks. arXiv preprint arXiv:1505.00387 (2015)
22. Wang, F., et al.: Residual attention network for image classification. arXiv preprint arXiv:1704.06904 (2017)
23. Wen, W., et al.: Learning structured sparsity in deep neural networks. In: NIPS, pp. 2074–2082 (2016)
24. Yang, D., et al.: Automatic liver segmentation using an adversarial image-to-image network. In: Descoteaux, M., Maier-Hein, L., Franz, A., Jannin, P., Collins, D.L., Duchesne, S. (eds.) MICCAI 2017. LNCS, vol. 10435, pp. 507–515. Springer, Cham (2017). https://doi.org/10.1007/978-3-319-66179-7_58

# Learning-Based Bone Quality Classification Method for Spinal Metastasis

Shiqi Peng[1], Bolin Lai[1], Guangyu Yao[2], Xiaoyun Zhang[1], Ya Zhang[1(✉)],
Yan-Feng Wang[1], and Hui Zhao[2]

[1] Cooperative Medianet Innovation Center,
Shanghai Jiao Tong University, Shanghai 200240, People's Republic of China
{pengshiqi,xiaoyun.zhang,ya_zhang,wangyanfeng}@sjtu.edu.cn,
lai.b.bryan@gmail.com
[2] Shanghai Jiao Tong University Affiliated Sixth People's Hospital,
Shanghai 200233, People's Republic of China
ygy504187803@126.com, zhao-hui@sjtu.edu.cn

**Abstract.** Spinal metastasis is the most common disease in bone metastasis and may cause pain, instability and neurological injuries. Early detection of spinal metastasis is critical for accurate staging and optimal treatment. The diagnosis is usually facilitated with Computed Tomography (CT) scans, which requires considerable efforts from well-trained radiologists. In this paper, we explore a learning-based automatic bone quality classification method for spinal metastasis based on CT images. We simultaneously take the posterolateral spine involvement classification task into account, and employ multi-task learning (MTL) technique to improve the performance. MTL acts as a form of inductive bias which helps the model generalize better on each task by sharing representations between related tasks. Based on the prior knowledge that the mixed type can be viewed as both blastic and lytic, we model the task of bone quality classification as two binary classification sub-tasks, *i.e.*, whether blastic and whether lytic, and leverage a multiple layer perceptron to combine their predictions. In order to make the model more robust and generalize better, self-paced learning is adopted to gradually involve from easy to more complex samples into the training process. The proposed learning-based method is evaluated on a proprietary spinal metastasis CT dataset. At slice level, our method significantly outperforms an 121-layer DenseNet classifier in sensitivities by $+12.54\%$, $+7.23\%$ and $+29.06\%$ for blastic, mixed and lytic lesions, respectively, meanwhile $+12.33\%$, $+23.21\%$ and $+34.25\%$ at vertebrae level.

**Keywords:** Spinal metastasis · Bone quality classification · Multi-task learning · Self-paced learning

© Springer Nature Switzerland AG 2019
H.-I. Suk et al. (Eds.): MLMI 2019, LNCS 11861, pp. 426–434, 2019.
https://doi.org/10.1007/978-3-030-32692-0_49

# 1   Introduction

Metastasis is the spread of cancer from one part of the body to another. Approximately two-thirds of patients with cancer will develop bone metastasis. The spine is the most common site of bone metastasis. A spinal metastasis may cause pain, instability and neurological injuries. Thus, the early diagnosis of spinal metastasis is crucial to change the patients' prognosis and improve the clinical outcome.

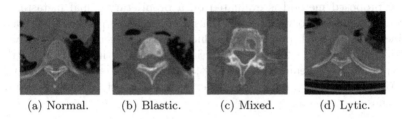

(a) Normal.        (b) Blastic.        (c) Mixed.        (d) Lytic.

**Fig. 1.** Typical examples for bone quality of spinal metastasis.

In 2017, the Spinal Instability Neoplastic Score (SINS) [2] was developed for assessing patients with spinal neoplasia. It acts as a prognostic tool for surgical decision making. Among the six components in the SINS system, both bone quality and posterolateral involvement of spinal elements can be diagnosed from the axial view. Thus we are motivated to leverage Multi-task Learning (MTL) technique to address these two issues simultaneously. Recently, more and more MTL methods are applied to the field of medical imaging. A multi-task residual fully convolutional network was proposed for the pelvic Magnetic Resonance Image (MRI) segmentation task, employing three regression tasks to provide more information for helping optimize the segmentation task [1]. A multi-task convolutional neural network was utilized to automatically predict radiological scores in spinal MRIs [5]. MTL can be viewed as a form of inductive transfer. Inductive transfer can help improve a model by introducing an inductive bias, which causes a model to prefer some hypotheses over others and generally leads to solutions that generalize better.

In the SINS system, metastatic bone quality is divided into three types (blastic, mixed and lytic, as shown in Fig. 1). Different types indicate different clinical outcomes and therapies. Previous work on bone lesion quality classification was primarily a binary classification of benign and malignant [7]. To the best of our knowledge, we are the first to use deep neural networks to achieve automatic four-category bone quality classification. However, satisfactory results for this problem can not be achieved by simply using a deep neural network because (1) training data is limited, (2) the classification cues are fine-grained and (3) it is hard to learn the decision boundaries between categories. We then target to address these three issues. We handle this problem from 2D axial slices. Thus hundreds of training images can be collected from each patient. For an axial image, we adopt a threshold extraction method introduced in [3] to increase

SNR based on HU values and concentrate on the bone areas instead of soft tissues. Then we model the task of bone quality classification as two binary classification sub-tasks, *i.e.*, whether blastic and whether lytic. In order to make the model more robust and generalize better, self-paced learning [6] is adopted to gradually involve from easy to more complex samples into the learning process. Finally, the predictions of sub-tasks are combined to obtain the four-category predictions, and the slice predictions are merged to get the vertebrae predictions by a voting method.

The proposed method is evaluated on a proprietary spinal metastasis CT dataset. A four-category 121-layer DenseNet classifier [4] is selected as our baseline. At slice level, our method achieves an improvement in sensitivity of +12.54%, +7.23% and +29.06% for blastic, mixed and lytic lesions, respectively, meanwhile an improvement of +12.33%, +23.21% and +34.25% at vertebrae level. More importantly, our method is expected to assist radiologists in practical diagnosis.

# 2 Proposed Method

## 2.1 Framework

The framework of our proposed learning-based method is depicted in Fig. 2. Two tasks, bone quality classification and posterolateral involvement classification, are learned at the same time. Based on the prior knowledge that the mixed type can be viewed as both blastic and lytic, we model the task of bone quality classification as two sub-tasks, whether blastic and whether lytic. Similarly, the labels of training data can also be decomposed in the same way.

Now we implicitly have three tasks to learn and MTL is suitable for such situation. The premise of using MTL is that the tasks should be relevant so that they can be learned jointly. In our case, all these tasks have to extract features from the axial view which can be shared with each other. Hence these tasks are strongly relevant and MTL technique is appropriate. In order to make more use of the low-level features, DenseNet is selected as feature extractor for its dense skip connections. For each task, we use four dense blocks with $6, 12, 24, 16$ dense layers respectively. And the growth rate is 32. Between each two adjacent dense blocks, a transition layer is employed for feature map downsampling.

After obtaining the logits of two sub-tasks of bone quality, and passing them through two softmax layers, we can get the probabilities of an image being blastic and lytic respectively. For the final diagnosis, we have to combine these two predictions together. The general approach is to use a threshold to obtain the binary predictions and combine them. However, this approach causes information loss due to the thresholding operation. We are expected to get the final prediction directly from the logits. In order to learn such a mapping function, we concatenate the logits from two sub-tasks and then pass them through a multiple layer perceptron with two linear layers and tanh activation function. Passing the embedded vectors through a softmax layer, the final probabilities for four categories can be obtained.

**Feature Sharing:** The feature sharing operation is performed at the end of each dense block. Feature sharing can be formulated as $[\tilde{x}_A, \tilde{x}_B] = f([x_A, x_B])$, where function $f$ is the feature sharing method, $A$ and $B$ are two relevant tasks, $x$ and $\tilde{x}$ are input and output features respectively. In the context of deep learning, shared representation is typically done with either *hard sharing* or *soft sharing* of hidden layers. Hard sharing is the most commonly used approach, which is generally applied by sharing the hidden layers between all tasks while keeping several task-specific output layers. On the other hand in soft sharing, each task has its own model with its own parameters. The distance between the feature maps of the models is then regularized in order to encourage the feature maps to be similar. In Sect. 3.4, we compare the performances of these two different kinds of shared representations and the experimental results demonstrate that hard sharing is the better choice for our problem.

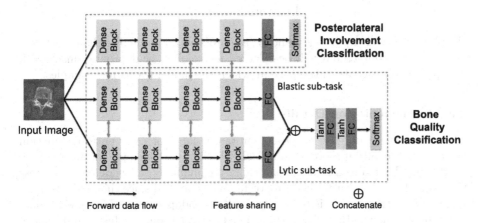

Fig. 2. The proposed multi-task learning framework.

**Loss Function:** The overall loss can be defined as

$$\mathcal{L}_{overall} = \lambda_1 * \mathcal{L}_{Blastic} + \lambda_2 * \mathcal{L}_{Lytic} + \lambda_3 * \mathcal{L}_{BQ} + \mathcal{L}_{PI} \tag{1}$$

where $\lambda_1$, $\lambda_2$ and $\lambda_3$ weight the relative contributions, $BQ$ and $PI$ denote for bone quality and posterolateral involvement respectively. All four loss function are cross entropy loss with the form $\mathcal{L} = -\sum_{i=1}^{n} y_i \log \hat{y}_i$, where $y_i$ is the ground truth and $\hat{y}_i$ is the prediction. In the experiments, we value the bone quality classification task more therefore $\lambda_1$, $\lambda_2$ and $\lambda_3$ are all set to be 2.

## 2.2 Self-paced Learning

During the training process, there exist many complex training examples disturbing the model optimization, such as sacral images and mislabeled samples.

To address this issue, we leverage self-paced learning (SPL) to gradually learn from easy to complex examples.

Formally, given a training set $\mathcal{D} = \{(\mathbf{x}_i, y_i)\}_{i=1}^n$. Let $f(\cdot, \mathbf{w})$ denote the learned model and $\mathbf{w}$ be the model parameters. $L(y_i, f(\mathbf{x}_i, \mathbf{w}))$ is the loss function of $i$-th sample. The objective is to jointly learn the model parameter $\mathbf{w}$ and the latent weight variable $\mathbf{v} = [v_1, v_2, \ldots, v_n]^T$ by minimizing:

$$\min_{\mathbf{w}, \mathbf{v} \in [0,1]^n} \mathbb{E}(\mathbf{w}, \mathbf{v}; \lambda) = \sum_{i=1}^n v_i L(y_i, f(\mathbf{x}_i, \mathbf{w})) - \lambda \sum_{i=1}^n v_i, \tag{2}$$

where $\lambda$ is a penalty parameter that controls the learning pace. With the fixed $\mathbf{w}$, the global optimum $\mathbf{v}^* = [v_1^*, v_2^*, \ldots, v_n^*]^T$ can be calculated by:

$$v_i^* = \begin{cases} 1, & L(y_i, f(\mathbf{x}_i, \mathbf{w})) < \lambda, \\ 0, & \text{otherwise.} \end{cases} \tag{3}$$

When alternatively updating $\mathbf{v}$ and $\mathbf{w}$, a sample with loss smaller than $\lambda$ is taken as an "easy" sample, and will be selected in training, or otherwise unselected. The parameter $\lambda$ controls the pace at which the model learns new samples.

### 2.3   Implementation Details

The usually used one-hot encoding for target label of cross entropy function encourages the output scores dramatically distinctive, which potentially leads to overfitting. Therefore the label smoothing technique [8] is leveraged to address this issue. Besides, transfer learning technique is applied since the model is quite large but the training set is relatively small. We adopt weights for convolutional layers pre-trained on ImageNet, which help the model converge faster and achieve better results. In order to reduce the numerical instability and generalize better, the learning rate warmup strategy [9] is also taken into consideration. These methods are analyzed in detail in Sect. 3.4.

## 3   Experimental Results

### 3.1   Dataset

We evaluate the proposed method on a proprietary spinal metastasis dataset. This dataset contains 800 CT scans come from patients with metastasis. The scans are reconstructed to in-plane resolution between 0.234 mm and 2.0 mm, and slice thickness between 0.314 mm and 5.0 mm. These CT scans cover four kinds of the spine, including cervical, thoracic, lumbar and sacral vertebraes. The reference labels are jointly annotated by three senior radiologists. Sub-sampling is used for data imbalance problem. The slices of each category for training are 9875(normal), 9256(blastic), 5846(mixed) and 7164(lytic) respectively, while 24133, 698, 642 and 607 for testing.

## 3.2   Metrics

We use sensitivity(SE) and specificity(SP) as metrics to evaluate the classification performances. For the bone quality classification, four categories are denoted as subscript N(normal), B(blastic), M(mixed) and L(lytic) in Tables 1, 3 and 4. For the auxiliary posterolateral involvement classification, three categories are denoted as subscript N(normal), U(unilateral) and B(Bilateral) in Table 2.

## 3.3   Experiments

All the experiments are implemented in PyTorch[1]. SGD optimizer is used to optimize parameters with a learning rate and momentum of 0.001 and 0.9, respectively. We train the model for 50 epochs on an NVIDIA 1080 Ti GPU with 12 GB memory. All the experiments are repeated five times and the averaged results are reported thus random errors are reduced.

In general, the vertebraes only take up a relatively small part of the CT image. Therefore the classification cues are fine-grained and it is hard for model to concentrate on the bone areas. Based on the prior knowledge that the HU values of bones are relatively high than soft tissues, we adopt a threshold extraction method introduced in [3] to extract the area of bone and crop the image from $512 \times 512$ to $224 \times 224$.

**Table 1.** Bone quality classification results at slice level.

|                   | $SE_N$ | $SP_N$ | $SE_B$ | $SP_B$ | $SE_M$ | $SP_M$ | $SE_L$ | $SP_L$ |
|-------------------|--------|--------|--------|--------|--------|--------|--------|--------|
| **Single-task**   | **94.65** | 76.77 | 71.56 | **97.31** | 38.91 | 98.50 | 41.15 | **97.16** |
| **Soft-sharing**  | 85.18 | 86.09 | 79.03 | 93.49 | 38.36 | 98.28 | 58.66 | 92.11 |
| **Hard-sharing-1** | 85.03 | 85.44 | 76.50 | 94.26 | 36.81 | 98.23 | 51.65 | 91.17 |
| **Hard-sharing-2** | 92.48 | 87.13 | 80.00 | 96.53 | 41.80 | 98.68 | 65.02 | 95.78 |
| **Hard-sharing-PI** | 92.63 | **89.42** | 80.23 | 96.69 | 41.67 | 98.80 | 66.84 | 95.51 |
| **Hard-sharing-MLP** | 93.66 | 85.70 | 81.23 | 96.84 | 44.03 | **98.94** | 66.88 | 96.57 |
| **Final model**   | 92.43 | 88.88 | **84.10** | 96.08 | **46.14** | 98.93 | **70.21** | 96.15 |

**Table 2.** Posterolateral involvement classification results at slice level.

|                  | $SE_N$ | $SP_N$ | $SE_U$ | $SP_U$ | $SE_B$ | $SP_B$ |
|------------------|--------|--------|--------|--------|--------|--------|
| **Single task**  | **97.26** | 59.43 | 31.63 | **98.42** | 49.61 | **97.88** |
| **MTL (ours)**   | 96.98 | **63.85** | **39.32** | 98.28 | **53.63** | 97.84 |

---

[1] https://pytorch.org/.

## 3.4   Ablation Studies

**Feature Sharing Method:** We first discuss the feature sharing method for the blastic and lytic classification tasks. The forementioned soft feature sharing method and hard feature sharing method are investigated. The **single task** four-category classification is selected as baseline. For soft sharing, we leverage the $\ell_2$ norm to regularize the feature maps after each dense block to be similar (denoted as **Soft-sharing**). In this situation, the overall loss function is defined as

$$\mathcal{L}_{soft} = \mathcal{L}_{Blastic} + \mathcal{L}_{Lytic} + \sum_{i=1}^{4}\lambda_i\|f^i_{Blastic} - f^i_{Lytic}\|^2_F \qquad (4)$$

where $f^i$ is the feature map of $i$th dense block, $\|\cdot\|_F$ is the Frobenius Norm and $\lambda_i$ are the weights. For hard sharing, we compare the effect of sharing three dense blocks (denoted as **Hard-sharing-1**) and sharing four dense blocks (denoted as **Hard-sharing-2**). The results in Table 1 shows that hard sharing all four dense blocks is the best shared representation for our tasks.

**Posterolateral Involvement:** We then explore the contribution of taking posterolateral involvement (PI) into account. The same hard sharing approach is adopted for PI and bone quality task. The experimental results for bone quality classification with PI is shown in Table 1 denoted as **Hard-sharing-PI**. Compared with the results without it (**Hard-sharing-2**), $SP_N$, $SE_B$ and $SE_L$ are all improved, while $SE_M$ remains basically unchanged.

As for the PI task, experimental results are displayed in Table 2. The multi-task learning method is compared with the single task learning method by a 121-layer DenseNet classifier. It can be observed that $SP_N$, $SE_U$ and $SE_B$ have been greatly improved while other metrics have remained basically unchanged. The above results show that joint learning bone quality and PI classification allows each task to generalize better.

**Bone Quality:** As for the label combination of the sub-tasks in bone quality classification, we investigate the performance improvement brought by MLP. Based on the hard sharing method, we adopt a two-layer perceptron with 10 hidden units and tanh activation function. The sensitivies of three kinds of lesions are all promoted in Table 1 (denoted as **Hard-sharing-MLP**).

**Table 3.** Bone quality classification results with learning methods at slice level. SPL, LS and LRS denote self-paced learning, label smoothing and LR scheduler, respectively.

| SPL | LS | LRS | $SE_N$ | $SP_N$ | $SE_B$ | $SP_B$ | $SE_M$ | $SP_M$ | $SE_L$ | $SP_L$ |
|---|---|---|---|---|---|---|---|---|---|---|
| | | | 92.48 | 87.13 | 80.00 | **96.53** | 41.80 | 98.68 | 65.02 | 95.78 |
| ✓ | | | 91.73 | 88.49 | 81.86 | 96.18 | 41.75 | 98.83 | 66.93 | 95.26 |
| ✓ | ✓ | | 91.87 | **89.14** | 82.26 | 96.45 | 44.24 | 98.80 | **68.74** | 95.22 |
| ✓ | ✓ | ✓ | **92.84** | 87.22 | **84.11** | 95.93 | **48.37** | **99.12** | 66.31 | **96.59** |

**Table 4.** Bone quality classification results at vertebrae level.

|  | $SE_N$ | $SP_N$ | $SE_B$ | $SP_B$ | $SE_M$ | $SP_M$ | $SE_L$ | $SP_L$ |
|---|---|---|---|---|---|---|---|---|
| **Single task** | **96.71** | 72.89 | 70.77 | **97.49** | 36.23 | **97.86** | 38.39 | **97.71** |
| **MTL (ours)** | 88.47 | **87.71** | **83.10** | 95.47 | **59.44** | 97.52 | **72.64** | 94.02 |

**SPL and Implementations:** We then analyze the effect of self-paced learning (SPL) and other implementations in Table 3. LR scheduler contains learning rate warmup and cosine decay strategy. It is observed that these three modules can help the model generalization to a certain degree. When adding the LR scheduler to the previous model, $SE_B$ and $SE_M$ are improved while $SE_L$ is decreased, which can be considered as a tradeoff between mixed type and lytic type.

### 3.5    Final Results

Finally, we combine all the components above to obtain the final model (denoted as **Final-model** in Table 1), which achieves the best performance on the $SE_B$, $SE_M$ and $SE_L$ outperforms baseline method by +12.54%, +7.23% and +29.06%, respectively. Figure 3 depicts the confusion matrices of the experiment for slices and vertebraes. Table 4 shows the results for vertebrae predictions. The vertebraes are detected by an extra detection model. For each detected vertebrae, we use a voting method to obtain the vertebrae prediction from the slice predictions. If the maximum slice number of a kind of lesion is greater than a threshold, then the predict label of this vertebrae is determined as this kind of lesion. Otherwise the vertebrae is determined as normal. The proposed method achieves an improvement on $SP_N$, $SE_B$, $SE_M$ and $SE_L$ by +14.82%, +12.33%, +23.21% and +34.25%, respectively. These improvements allow our approach to help doctors with laborious work in practice.

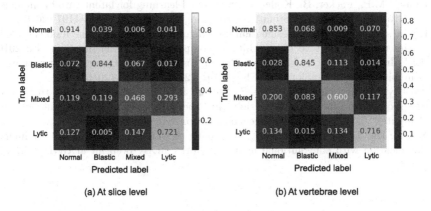

(a) At slice level                     (b) At vertebrae level

**Fig. 3.** Confusion matrices for bone quality at slice level and vertebrae level.

## 4 Conclusion

In this paper, we have explored an automatic learning-based method to classify the bone quality and posterolateral involvement of spinal metastasis. Multi-task learning helps both tasks generalize better by sharing representations. Besides, we model the task of bone quality classification as two sub-tasks and leverage a multiple layer perceptron to combine their predictions. Furthermore, in order to make the model more robust and generalize better, we adopt self-paced learning to gradually involve from easy to more complex samples into the training process. Adequate experiments on our proprietary dataset prove that the proposed method is effective. In the future, our method is expected to assist radiologists in practical diagnosis.

## References

1. Feng, Z., Nie, D., Wang, L., Shen, D.: Semi-supervised learning for pelvic MR image segmentation based on multi-task residual fully convolutional networks. In: 2018 IEEE 15th International Symposium on Biomedical Imaging (ISBI 2018), pp. 885–888. IEEE (2018)
2. Fox, S., Spiess, M., Hnenny, L., Fourney, D.R.: Spinal instability neoplastic score (SINS): reliability among spine fellows and resident physicians in orthopedic surgery and neurosurgery. Glob. Spine J. **7**(8), 744–748 (2017)
3. Guan, H., et al.: Deep dual-view network with smooth loss for spinal metastases classification. In: 2018 IEEE Visual Communications and Image Processing (VCIP), pp. 1–4. IEEE (2019)
4. Huang, G., Liu, Z., Van Der Maaten, L., Weinberger, K.Q.: Densely connected convolutional networks. In: Proceedings of the IEEE Conference on Computer Vision and Pattern Recognition, pp. 4700–4708 (2017)
5. Jamaludin, A., Kadir, T., Zisserman, A.: SpineNet: automatically pinpointing classification evidence in spinal MRIs. In: Ourselin, S., Joskowicz, L., Sabuncu, M.R., Unal, G., Wells, W. (eds.) MICCAI 2016. LNCS, vol. 9901, pp. 166–175. Springer, Cham (2016). https://doi.org/10.1007/978-3-319-46723-8_20
6. Kumar, M.P., Packer, B., Koller, D.: Self-paced learning for latent variable models. In: Advances in Neural Information Processing Systems, pp. 1189–1197 (2010)
7. Kumar, R., Suhas, M.: Classification of benign and malignant bone lesions on CT images using support vector machine: a comparison of kernel functions. In: 2016 IEEE International Conference on Recent Trends in Electronics, Information & Communication Technology (RTEICT), pp. 821–824. IEEE (2016)
8. Szegedy, C., Vanhoucke, V., Ioffe, S., Shlens, J., Wojna, Z.: Rethinking the inception architecture for computer vision. In: Proceedings of the IEEE Conference on Computer Vision and Pattern Recognition, pp. 2818–2826 (2016)
9. Xie, J., He, T., Zhang, Z., Zhang, H., Zhang, Z., Li, M.: Bag of tricks for image classification with convolutional neural networks. arXiv preprint arXiv:1812.01187 (2018)

# Automated Segmentation of Skin Lesion Based on Pyramid Attention Network

Huan Wang, Guotai Wang[✉], Ze Sheng, and Shaoting Zhang

University of Electronic Science and Technology of China, Chengdu, China
guotai.wang@uestc.edu.cn

**Abstract.** Automatic segmentation of skin lesion in dermatoscope images is important for clinic diagnosis and assessment of melanoma. However, due to the large variations of scale, shape and appearance of the lesion area, accurate and automatic segmentation of skin lesion is faced with great challenges. In this paper, we first introduce the pyramid attention module for global multi-scale features aggregation. The module selectively integrates different multi-scale features associated with lesion by optimizing the features of each scale and suppressing the irrelevant noise. Based on this module, we propose an automatic framework for skin lesion segmentation. In addition, the widely used loss function based on dice coefficient is independent of the relative size of the segmented target, which leads to the insufficient attention of the network to small-scale samples. Therefore, we propose a new loss function based on scale-attention to effectively balance the weight of attention of the network to samples with different scales and improve the segmentation accuracy of small-scale samples. The robustness of the proposed method was evaluated on two public databases: ISIC 2017 and 2018 for skin lesion analysis towards melanoma detection challenge and it could prove that the proposed method could considerably improve the performance of skin lesion segmentation and achieve the state-of-the-art results on ISIC 2017.

**Keywords:** Skin lesion segmentation · Attention · Pyramid module

## 1 Introduction

Skin cancer is one of the most common cancers in the world. Early detection and treatment of skin cancer can significantly improve the survival rate of patients [1]. Dermoscopy, a non-invasive dermatology imaging method, can help dermatologists to diagnose malignant melanoma at an early stage. However, it is still a time-consuming work for even professional dermatologists to diagnose the lesion in the skin from a large number of dermoscopic images. Therefore, the development of automatic segmentation system for skin lesion can greatly improve doctors' work efficiency and diagnostic accuracy.

In recent years, full convolutional network (FCN) has achieved great success in the field of medical image segmentation [2–4]. Many scholars have proposed FCN-based skin lesion segmentation methods and achieved good performance [5, 6]. However, the lesion area of the skin often presents complex morphology, multi-scale changes and

© Springer Nature Switzerland AG 2019
H.-I. Suk et al. (Eds.): MLMI 2019, LNCS 11861, pp. 435–443, 2019.
https://doi.org/10.1007/978-3-030-32692-0_50

fuzzy boundaries. Additionally, the image quality is corrupted by body hair and blood vessels, so it is still a great challenge to learn the global multi-scale context information for accurate segmentation.

Existing methods used in FCN to capture multi-scale information can be roughly divided into three categories. The first type creates an image pyramid at multiple scales [7]. The image is down-sampled and processed at different resolutions. The second type uses an encoder-decoder network to combine multi-scale context layer by layer through skip connection [3]. The third type is to build the spatial pyramid module and learn features at different scales through multiple parallel convolution branches [5, 8].

However, different branches of the pyramid module have different importance for recognizing the segmentation target, some of which may be less discriminative. Additionally, traditional pyramid modules simply concatenate all output features of different branches, so they may ignore the differences of the features in different branches, resulting in some errors in judgment. Besides, for the segmentation of target samples with different scales, context information at different scales is required. Therefore, it is necessary to enhance some scale features adaptively in the network and suppress irrelative scale features. Based on the above motivation, we introduce a pyramid attention module (PAM), which could aggregate the optimal multi-scale context features in a data-driven and learnable way to identify objects with different scales so as to enhance the multi-scale learning ability of the network. Especially, the attention mechanism that PAM uses can recalibrate the features in terms of both space and channel to enhance the most relative features and suppress the irrelative noise. Finally, we introduce a new skin lesion segmentation network by combining PAM with an encoder-decoder structure.

For the loss function to train CNNs for segmentation such as Dice loss [9], the fewer misclassified pixels are, the smaller the loss will be. The sensitivity of the change of the loss function is independent of the relative size of the segmented target, but the context information of small-scale targets is more difficult to be learnt by the network, so the loss function is adverse to the segmentation of small-scale targets. In order to improve the attention weight of small-scale targets, a new scale-attention-based loss function is proposed to make the network pay more attention to the segmentation of small-scale objects by adjusting the attention weight of samples with different scales.

To sum up, this paper mainly contains the following three contributions. Firstly, a new pyramid attention module which can improve the ability of networks to learn multi-scale features is proposed. Taking advantage of this module, we propose a new framework for automatic skin lesion segmentation. Finally, we propose a new loss function based on scale attention to improve the segmentation accuracy of small-scale objects. The proposed method was applied to ISIC 2017 and 2018 skin lesion segmentation dataset with state-of-the-art performance achieved.

## 2    Method

### 2.1    Method Overview

The proposed pyramid attention network (PA-Net) for the automatic segmentation of skin lesion is shown in Fig. 1. It consists of an encoder network, a corresponding decoder network and PAM. The encoder network converts the input image into a set of feature maps with high-level semantic information. PAM is responsible for adaptively learning task-related global multi-scale information from the input feature maps. The decoder network is to recover the original resolution from the feature maps with multi-scale information and output segmentation results. Each convolution module consists of a 3 × 3 convolution layer, a group normalization layer [10] and a rectified linear unit (ReLU) layer. In addition, PA-Net contains three down-samplings and three up-samplings, and the final segmentation probability map is obtained through Sigmoid function. PAM in PA-Net aims to focus on the optimal multi-scale information, spatial region and channel features in a data-driven, and learnable manner, to accurately learn complex contextual information in the lesion area. Finally, we introduce a scale-attention-based loss function to improve the ability of PA-Net to learn small-scale samples, which will be detailed in Sect. 2.3.

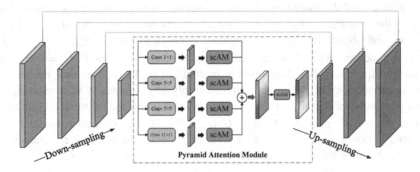

**Fig. 1.** Illustration of the architecture of our proposed PA-Net.

## 2.2 Pyramid Attention Module

Each feature map in FCN is only to encode the corresponding scale information and the output feature maps of the encoder network cannot effectively integrate the context information at different scales. Therefore, after obtaining the high-level semantic features from the encoder network, PAM extracts the context information at different scales from the input features by using four convolution branches with different convolution kernel sizes. Inspired by literature [11], PAM firstly adopts a parallel spatial and channel attention module (scAM) to adaptively optimize multi-scale information, spatial features and channel features in different branches, so as to enhance the target-related feature information in the feature maps in different branches. Subsequently, we concatenate these multi-scale features into a set of feature maps, and a use 3 × 3 convolution layer to fuse information across multiple scales and reduce channel dimensions. Moreover, PAM uses residual connection [12] to directly combine the original output features of encoder network with multi-scale features so as to make full use of the scale information in the original features. In addition, PAM uses a series of scAM to adaptively optimize multi-scale features and to focus on the multi-scale information required by the current task. Finally, the mixed multi-scale features are used as the input of the decoder network, as shown in Fig. 1.

Here, we detail the scAM used in PAM. As shown in Fig. 2, we extract the global context information of the input feature maps along space and channel respectively, and generate the feature recalibration vector to increase the weight of target-related regions and channels. Specifically, we assume that the input feature $U = [u_1, u_2, u_3, \ldots, u_c]$ has $c$ channels and the $i$-th channel is denoted as $u_i \in R^{H \times W}$. Then, a feature transformation is used to aggregate the global information of feature $U$ along the channel direction and generate a projection map in space $s = F_{tr}(U)$, where $F_{tr}(\cdot)$ denotes $1 \times 1$ convolution with output channel 1. Subsequently, the spatial recalibration map $\tilde{s} = \sigma(s)$, $\tilde{s} \in R^{H \times W}$ is obtained through a Sigmoid function. On the other hand, the global spatial information of feature $U$ is aggregated through a global average pooling layer, and the channel-wise statistics vector $z = Avgpool(U)$ is generated. Then encodes the interdependence among channels in feature $U$ by using two $1 \times 1$ convolution, and obtains the channel recalibration vector $\tilde{z} = \sigma(F'_{tr}(z)), z \in R^{1 \times 1 \times c}$ by a Sigmoid function. After that, the calibrated features $\tilde{U}_s = \tilde{s} \otimes U, \tilde{U}_z = \tilde{z} \otimes U$ are obtained respectively by element-wise multiplication. Here, we also introduce a residual connection [12] to improve the feasibility of optimization with retaining the original information. Finally we use the residual connection and reformat the calibrated features $\tilde{U}_s$ and $\tilde{U}_z$ as $\tilde{U}_s = (1 + \tilde{s}) \otimes U, \tilde{U}_z = (1 + \tilde{z}) \otimes U$, then concatenate $\tilde{U}_s, \tilde{U}_z$ and send it into a $3 \times 3$ convolution layer to integrate the respective feature information and reduce the channel dimensions.

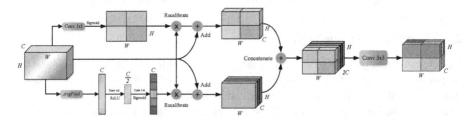

**Fig. 2.** Architecture of spatial and channel attention module (scAM).

## 2.3   Scale-Attention Loss Function

FCN-based medical image segmentation methods mostly adopt dice loss [9] for training. Since the change in dice loss is independent of the relative size of the segmented targets, the network may fail to pay enough attention to small-scale samples. To solve this problem, we propose a scale-attention loss function (SA-Loss) which gives different attention weights to the segmentation targets with different scales so as to make the network pay more attention to the segmentation accuracy of small-scale samples. The scale-attention loss function is thus defined as:

$$L_{SA} = \frac{1}{N} \sum_{n=1}^{N} \left(1 + (\beta - \frac{\sum G_n}{T_n})\right)^{\gamma} (1 - Dice_n) \text{ with } Dice_n = \frac{2(\sum (P_n G_n))}{\sum G_n + \sum P_n} \quad (1)$$

Where $N$ is the batch size, and $n$ represents each individual training sample. $P_n$ and $G_n$ are the predicted probability map and the ground truth binary label for sample $n$, respectively. $T_n$ is the number of pixels in sample $n$. $\beta$ is the scale-attention parameter with a range of [0, 1]. The value of $\beta$ determines whether the loss gives an enough attention to samples. When the ratio between $\sum G_n$ and $T_n$ is less than $\beta$, the loss will pay more attention to that sample, and the smaller the ratio is, the greater the attention weight will be given to the sample. At the same time, it will suppress the attention to large-scale samples. However, no matter what the value of $\beta$ is, the loss will always give more attention weight to small-scale samples than large-scale samples. Therefore, we introduce another modulating factor $\gamma$ with a range of [0, 5], which is used to control the relative size of loss's attention weight among samples with different scales. When $\gamma$ is greater than 1, the weight gap of loss will increase as the increase of $\gamma$. When $\gamma$ is less than 1, loss will narrow the weight as $\gamma$ decreases. Finally, when $\gamma = 0$, the weight is consistent. By adjusting $\beta$ and $\gamma$, the SA-Loss can be adapted to different datasets.

## 3 Experiments

### 3.1 Data and Experimental Setups

To verify the robustness of the proposed method, it was evaluated on two public benchmark datasets of dermoscopy images for skin lesion analysis: ISIC 2017[1] and ISIC 2018[2]. The ISIC 2017 dataset consist of 2750 dermoscopic images from multiple clinical centers around the world, where 2000, 150 and 600 images were used for training, validation and testing respectively. In the ISIC 2018 dataset, because the challenge is over and marked test data cannot be obtained, we used 2,594 dermoscopy images from the training dataset, and randomly divided them into 1700 for training, 144 for validation and 750 for testing.

Our PA-Net was implemented using Pytorch on a Linux system with an Nvidia 1080Ti GPU. During training, we used the Adam optimizer with a learning rate of $1 \times 10^{-4}$ and the batch size of 6, with a learning rate reduction of 0.1 times after every 15 epochs. In each experiment, we saved the model that performed best on the validation set during training as the final testing model. We used data augmentation

---

[1] https://challenge2017.isic-archive.com/.

[2] https://challenge2018.isic-archive.com/.

including random copping and flipping to improve the model's robustness. Before the training, we re-scaled all images to $256 \times 192$ pixels and normalized the pixel values of each RGB channel to between 0 and 1. Besides the original RGB channels, we added an additional grayscale channel.

In order to verify the feasibility of the proposed module and network, we conducted ablation studies on the two datasets, and compared PA-Net with Unet [3] and Res-Unet. Res-Unet was a modified Unet where each convolution block was replaced by the bottleneck building block used in the ResNet [12]. Dice coefficient, jaccard index and accuracy were used to quantitative evaluation of the segmentation performance, and the settings of all the compared methods are consistent.

### 3.2 Results and Discussion

We first trained Unet for skin lesion segmentation from ISIC 2017 dataset using different configurations of SA-Loss. We also compared SA-Loss with dice loss. The results are shown in Table 1. For SA-Loss, we evaluated different combinations of $\beta$ and $\gamma$. When $\gamma = 1$ and 2, the performance of SA-Loss with $\beta > 0$ is better than that of dice loss, which proves the effectiveness of SA-Loss. In general, the larger the $\beta$ is, the better the network is likely to perform. This is because with the increase of $\beta$, the loss's attention weight on small-scale samples increases, while the suppression on large-scale samples is also weakened. This also indicates that there may be some hard samples in large-scale samples, which need additional attention from the network. When $\gamma = 0.5$, with the increase of $\beta$, the difference of attention weight among samples will decrease, but the importance of attention to every sample will increase accordingly, and thus the performance of SA-Loss will first decrease and then increase. Additionally, the value of $\gamma$ will greatly affect the performance of SA-Loss. The smaller $\gamma$ is, the less influence of $\beta$ on SA-Loss will be. When $\gamma$ is relatively large, with the change of $\beta$, the performance of SA-Loss will fluctuate greatly. In this experiment, when $\gamma = 1$ and $\beta = 0.8$, SA-Loss has the best performance, and its jaccard index increases by 2.4% compared with dice loss. However, the increase of loss will affect the stability of network training. In the following experiments, SA-Loss with $\gamma = 1$ and $\beta = 0.5$ is used.

**Table 1.** Performance of Unet trained by SA-Loss with different parameters on ISIC 2017.

|  | Dice Loss | Parameters | $\beta = 0.1$ | $\beta = 0.2$ | $\beta = 0.3$ | $\beta = 0.4$ | $\beta = 0.5$ | $\beta = 0.6$ | $\beta = 0.7$ | $\beta = 0.8$ | $\beta = 0.9$ |
|---|---|---|---|---|---|---|---|---|---|---|---|
| Dice | 0.824 | $\gamma = 0.5$ | 0.840 | 0.837 | 0.837 | 0.832 | 0.832 | 0.839 | 0.838 | **0.841** | **0.841** |
| Jaccard | 0.734 | | 0.752 | 0.750 | 0.750 | 0.745 | 0.743 | 0.750 | 0.749 | 0.753 | **0.754** |
| Dice | – | $\gamma = 1.0$ | 0.828 | 0.837 | 0.842 | 0.839 | 0.843 | 0.838 | 0.843 | **0.844** | **0.844** |
| Jaccard | – | | 0.738 | 0.748 | 0.755 | 0.753 | 0.756 | 0.752 | 0.757 | **0.758** | 0.756 |
| Dice | – | $\gamma = 2.0$ | 0.817 | 0.831 | 0.834 | 0.834 | 0.838 | **0.839** | **0.839** | **0.839** | 0.834 |
| Jaccard | – | | 0.726 | 0.741 | 0.745 | 0.745 | 0.750 | **0.752** | 0.751 | 0.751 | 0.747 |

**Table 2.** Quantitative evaluation of different methods for skin lesion segmentation on ISIC 2017 and ISIC 2018 datasets (P denotes pyramid module, PA denotes pyramid attention module, L denotes SA-loss and G denotes group normalization).

ISIC 2017

| Method | Yuan et al. [13] | Unet | Res-Unet | PA-Net (No P) | PA-Net (With P) | PA-Net (With PA) | PA-Net (With PA-L) | PA-Net (With PA-L-G) |
|---|---|---|---|---|---|---|---|---|
| Dice | 0.849 | 0.824 | 0.827 | 0.781 | 0.828 | 0.841 | 0.849 | **0.858** |
| Jaccard | 0.765 | 0.734 | 0.737 | 0.683 | 0.740 | 0.756 | 0.765 | **0.776** |
| Accuracy | 0.934 | 0.926 | 0.929 | 0.913 | 0.926 | 0.931 | 0.933 | **0.936** |
| ISIC 2018 | | | | | | | | |
| Dice | – | 0.876 | 0.874 | 0.830 | 0.876 | 0.886 | 0.893 | **0.898** |
| Jaccard | – | 0.804 | 0.801 | 0.743 | 0.805 | 0.818 | 0.826 | **0.832** |
| Accuracy | – | 0.952 | 0.951 | 0.938 | 0.952 | 0.955 | 0.956 | **0.960** |
| Parameters | – | $1.9\times10^6$ | $2.0\times10^6$ | $0.3\times10^6$ | $1.4\times10^6$ | $2.0\times10^6$ | $2.0\times10^6$ | $2.0\times10^6$ |

Table 2 shows the evaluation results of different variants of the proposed method (without pyramid module, with pyramid module, with PAM, with PAM and SA-Loss and PA-Net) on ISIC 2017 dataset and ISIC 2018 dataset respectively. It also shows the performance of Unet, Res-Unet and the score of the ISIC 2017 challenge winner [13]. It can be seen that the pyramid module can effectively improve network's performance, indicating that it can effectively learn multi-scale features. The use of PAM increases the jaccard index by 1.6% on ISIC 2017 dataset and by 1.3% on ISIC 2018 dataset, indicating that PAM has better performance than pyramid module. Additionally, SA-Loss further improves the network segmentation result. Finally, we found that replacing the batch normalization layer with group normalization layer could effectively improve the performance of network in the skin lesion segmentation. PA-Net integrated with PAM and SA-Loss has the best performance among all methods. It's jaccard index on ISIC 2017 and ISIC 2018 datasets increases 4.2% and 2.8% over Unet's respectively, and is 1.1% higher than the ISIC 2017 challenge winner. And the number of PAM parameters is close to that of Unet, which indicate that our method leads to a large improvement of segmentation accuracy with a marginal increase of the amount of parameters.

The qualitative segmentation results of two examples (A, B) from ISIC 2017 dataset are shown in Fig. 3. In the first case, the lesion margin is fuzzy, so Unet incorrectly predict a portion of normal skin as lesion area. The pyramid module improves this situation. PAM and SA-Loss further obtain more accurate segmentation results. The background area of the second example is very close to the lesion area, so Unet is unable to accurately identify the location of the lesion area, resulting in a poor segmentation, and the pyramid module alone fails to improve the segmentation accuracy. In contrast, PAM effectively improves the segmentation result for this sample, which indicates that better segmentation can be achieved by gradually focusing attention on the segmentation targets through the attention mechanism. In addition, we visualized the spatial recalibration maps in PAM. It can be clearly seen that the scAM enhances or suppresses the features of different branches in different degrees, so as to obtain the optimal multi-scale features adaptively.

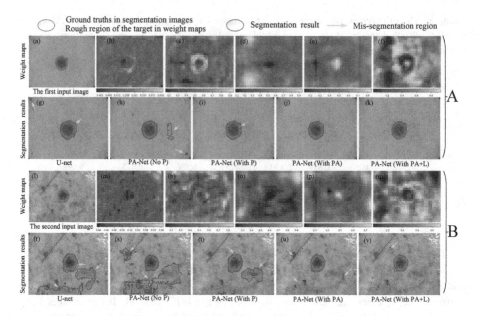

**Fig. 3.** Qualitative segmentation results of two different examples (A, B) on ISIC 2017. Each example contains different segmentation results and the visualization of PAM spatial weight (recalibration) maps. The photos (b-e, m-p) are visualizations of spatial weight maps of different parallel scAMs, and the last photos (f, q) are the visualization of serial scAM.

## 4   Conclusion

In this paper, we propose a pyramid attention module, which can adaptively aggregate the optimal global multi-scale information and improve the ability to learn multi-scale features. Additionally, the scale-attention loss function is introduced, which can improve the segmentation accuracy of small-scale samples by applying different attention weight to samples with different scales. Based on these two methods, we propose a pyramid attention network for automatic segmentation of skin lesion. The effectiveness and adaptability of the proposed method have been extensively evaluated on ISIC 2017 dataset and ISIC 2018 dataset, and very competitive performance has been achieved.

## References

1. Kardynal, A., Olszewska, M.: Modern non-invasive diagnostic techniques in the detection of early cutaneous melanoma. J. Dermatol. Case Rep. **8**(1), 1–8 (2014)
2. Long, J., Shelhamer, E., Darrell, T.: Fully convolutional networks for semantic segmentation. In: CVPR, pp. 3431–3440 (2015)
3. Ronneberger, O., Fischer, P., Brox, T.: U-Net: convolutional networks for biomedical image segmentation. In: Navab, N., Hornegger, J., Wells, W., Frangi, A. (eds.) MICCAI 2015.

LNCS, vol. 9351, pp. 234–241. Springer, Cham (2015). https://doi.org/10.1007/978-3-319-24574-4_28

4. Wang, H., Gu, R., Li, Z.: Automated segmentation of intervertebral disc using fully dilated separable deep neural networks. In: CSI, pp. 66–76 (2018)

5. Sarker, M.M.K., et al.: SLSDeep: skin lesion segmentation based on dilated residual and pyramid pooling networks. In: Frangi, A., Schnabel, J., Davatzikos, C., Alberola-López, C., Fichtinger, G. (eds.) MICCAI 2018. LNCS, vol. 11071, pp. 21–29. Springer, Cham (2018). https://doi.org/10.1007/978-3-030-00934-2_3

6. Mirikharaji, Z., Hamarneh, G.: Star shape prior in fully convolutional networks for skin lesion segmentation. In: Frangi, A., Schnabel, J., Davatzikos, C., Alberola-López, C., Fichtinger, G. (eds.) MICCAI 2018. LNCS, vol. 11073, pp. 737–745. Springer, Cham (2018). https://doi.org/10.1007/978-3-030-00937-3_84

7. Farabet, C., Couprie, C., Najman, L., LeCun, Y.: Learning hierarchical features for scene labeling. IEEE Trans. PAMI **35**(8), 1915–1929 (2013)

8. Zhao, H., Shi, J., Qi, X., Wang, X., Jia, J.: Pyramid scene parsing network. In: CVPR, pp. 2881–2890 (2017)

9. Milletari, F., Navab, N., Ahmadi, S.A.: V-net: fully convolutional neural networks for volumetric medical image segmentation. In: 3DV, pp. 565–571 (2016)

10. Wu, Y., He, K.: Group normalization. In: Ferrari, V., Hebert, M., Sminchisescu, C., Weiss, Y. (eds.) ECCV 2018. LNCS, vol. 11217, pp. 3–19. Springer, Cham (2018). https://doi.org/10.1007/978-3-030-01261-8_1

11. Roy, A.G., Navab, N., Wachinger, C.: Concurrent spatial and channel 'squeeze & excitation' in fully convolutional networks. In: Frangi, A., Schnabel, J., Davatzikos, C., Alberola-López, C., Fichtinger, G., et al. (eds.) MICCAI 2018. LNCS, vol. 11070, pp. 421–429. Springer, Cham (2018). https://doi.org/10.1007/978-3-030-00928-1_48

12. He, K., Zhang, X., Ren, S., Sun, J.: Deep residual learning for image recognition. In: CVPR, pp. 770–778 (2016)

13. Yuan, Y.: Automatic skin lesion segmentation with fully convolutional-deconvolutional networks. arXiv preprint arXiv:1803.08494 (2017)

# Relu Cascade of Feature Pyramid Networks for CT Pulmonary Nodule Detection

Guangrui Mu[1,2], Yanbo Chen[1], Dijia Wu[1], Yiqiang Zhan[1],
Xiang Sean Zhou[1], and Yaozong Gao[1(✉)]

[1] Shanghai United Imaging Intelligence Co., Ltd., Shanghai, China
yaozong.gao@united-imaging.com
[2] School of Biomedical Engineering, Southern Medical University, Guangzhou,
China

**Abstract.** Screening of pulmonary nodules in computed tomography (CT) is important for early detection and treatment of lung cancer. Many existing works utilize faster RCNN (regions with convolutional neural network or region proposal network) for this task. However, their performance is often limited, especially for detecting small pulmonary nodules (<4 mm). In this work, we propose a new cascade paradigm called "Relu cascade" to detect pulmonary nodules. The training of "Relu cascade" is similar to the conventional cascade learning approach. First, a detection network is trained using limited positive annotations (nodules) and randomly sampled negative samples (background). Then, a second detection network is trained with the same amount of positives and false positives produced by the first network. By repeating this process, multiple detection networks can be trained with subsequent detection networks tuned specifically to eliminate the false positives produced by previous detection networks. The novelty of "Relu cascade" lies in the way of chaining these networks into a cascade. Different from the conventional cascade learning, each level filters out false positive detections independently in the testing phase, which is prone to overfitting as later levels are very specific to a small amount of negative samples. In "Relu cascade", nodule likelihoods at all previous levels are aggregated, based on which false positives are identified and filtered out. Experimental results on 606 CT scans of different patients show that "Relu cascade" greatly improves the detection performance of conventional cascade learning.

**Keywords:** Deep learning · Feature pyramid network · Pulmonary nodule detection · Cascade learning · Ensemble learning

## 1 Introduction

Lung cancer is one of the common cancers and the leading causes of cancer-related death worldwide. Clinical trials [1] show that early screening of pulmonary nodules for high-risk subjects would allow detecting lung cancer at early stages, thus greatly reducing death rates caused by lung cancer. Low-dose CT scan is an effective and recommended way for pulmonary nodule screening. However, reading hundreds of slice images per CT scan is time-consuming, radiologists under labor-intensive work

© Springer Nature Switzerland AG 2019
H.-I. Suk et al. (Eds.): MLMI 2019, LNCS 11861, pp. 444–452, 2019.
https://doi.org/10.1007/978-3-030-32692-0_51

only spend very limited time on each scan, which will result in missed detections of pulmonary nodules, and hence decreasing the efficacy of CT pulmonary nodule screening. Therefore, it is highly desirable to develop a computer-aided approach to automatically discovering pulmonary nodules in clinical CT scans.

CT pulmonary nodule detection is technically challenging because (1) nodule sizes vary to a great extent, *i.e.*, 3 mm to 3 cm; and (2) the appearance of nodules is inconsistent, as shown in Fig. 1. Most existing computer aided detection (CAD) systems for pulmonary nodules consist of two stages [2]: (1) candidate generation; and (2) false positive (FP) reduction. In the first stage, a detection network (*e.g.*, faster RCNN [3]) is often applied to find all nodules in lung fields while filtering out as many background positions (negatives) as possible. In order to keep a high sensitivity, detection precision is often compromised, and many false positives are generated in the first stage. In the second stage, a binary classifier (*e.g.*, CNN) is trained to separate these false positive detections produced in the first stage.

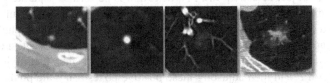

**Fig. 1.** Different density types of pulmonary nodules in CT scans. From left to right: solid nodule, calcific nodule, ground glass opacifications (GGO) and mixed GGO.

In this work, we formulate CT pulmonary nodule detection as a cascade learning problem. Instead of using a two-stage approach, we train multiple stages of detection networks in a cascade fashion and chain them into an ensemble model to gradually separate background from pulmonary nodules. Compared to existing pulmonary nodule detection systems, our work has two major contributions. First, we use detection networks *not only* in the first stage *but also* in the subsequent stages, as we empirically found that a binary CNN classifier is prone to overfitting in FP reduction. Second, a feature pyramid network [4] is used as the backbone detection network because it performs detection on multi-scale feature maps, which can better handle the large size variation of pulmonary nodules than faster RCNN [3] that performs detection on a single-scale feature map. In addition, we propose a new cascade paradigm called "Relu cascade". At each cascade level, we use a Relu strategy to aggregate the judgements from all previous cascade levels before filtering false positives. Validated on a large internal CT dataset, the Relu strategy greatly improves the detection performance of pulmonary nodules compared to the conventional cascade that filters false positives independently at each level in the inference phase.

## 2 Method

### 2.1 3D Feature Pyramid Network for Pulmonary Nodule Detection

The sizes of pulmonary nodules vary greatly from 3 mm to 3 cm. Conventional deep learning approaches, *e.g.*, faster RCNN [3], are not suitable for detecting objects with large scale variations, because they detect objects at a single scale. For example, the faster RCNN uses the interleaving of convolutions and down-sampling to extract context information, and detects objects on the final coarse feature maps. Using such methods for pulmonary nodule detection will inevitably miss small nodules. To detect nodules of all sizes, detection has to be performed on various scales. To this end, we extend feature pyramid network (FPN) [4] for 3D pulmonary nodule detection. We derive our FPN network architecture from the popular segmentation network, V-Net [5], as shown in Fig. 2. The difference is that the top level in the ascending path of V-Net is removed, as this level contains very fine-grained features, which is generally unnecessary for object detection. In FPN, detection is performed separately on feature maps of four different scales by attaching a detection head onto each feature map. The detection head consists of two convolution layers at each scale, and it outputs an anchor likelihood map $P$ and an anchor regression map $R$. The nodule detection process follows the conventional region proposal network [3] by first identifying positive anchor boxes on $P$ and then adjusting these positive boxes using the predicted anchor regression maps $R$. Finally, redundant bounding boxes are suppressed using non-maximum suppression.

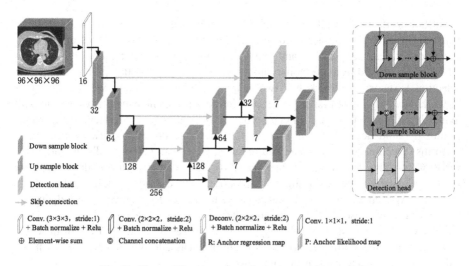

**Fig. 2.** The architecture of our feature pyramid network.

**Training Loss of FPN:** The training loss of FPN is the summation of losses of all four different scales. The loss at a single scale is given as:

$$Loss(P, R) = \lambda L_{cls}(P, P^*) + L_{reg}(R, R^*),  \quad (1)$$

where $L_{cls}$ and $L_{reg}$ are anchor classification and regression losses, respectively, and $\lambda$ is a balancing weight between them. Conventionally, the classification loss is measured over all anchor boxes. However, considering that the positive and negative anchor boxes are highly imbalanced ($1:10^6$) in this task, we use online hard negative example mining (OHEM) to pick the top $K$ hard negative anchors in a min-batch, and then use focal loss [6] to measure classification losses for all positive anchors and the top $K$ hard negative anchors. Mathematically, the classification loss is defined as,

$$L_{cls}(P, P^*) = - \sum_i^{N_{pos}} \alpha(1 - p_i)^\gamma log p_i - \sum_i^{N_{neg}} 1_{i \in TopK}(1 - \alpha)p_i^\gamma log p_i,  \quad (2)$$

where $N_{pos}$ and $N_{neg}$ are the numbers of positive and negative anchors, $p_i$ is the classification likelihood of the $i$-th anchor, $1_{i \in TopK}$ is an indicator function to pick only the top $K$ hard negative anchors into loss calculation. $\gamma$ and $\alpha$ are parameters of focal loss, respectively. We set $K = 5000 N_{pos}$, $\alpha = 0.9$, $\gamma = 2$ in our experiments.

The regression loss $L_{reg}$ follows the definition of faster RCNN:

$$L_{reg}(R, R^*) = \sum_i 1_{l_i=1} L1_{smooth}\left(r_i - r_i^*\right),  \quad (3)$$

where $1_{l_i=1}$ is an indicator function to pick only the positive anchors, $L1_{smooth}$ is the smooth $L1$ loss, $r_i^*$ is a 6-tuple $(\Delta x^*, \Delta y^*, \Delta z^*, \Delta w^*, \Delta h^*, \Delta d^*)$ defined for the $i$-th positive anchor box, and $r_i$ is the same 6-tuple predicted by the network. The definitions of $\Delta^*$ values are given below:

$$\Delta x = \frac{x^* - x_a}{w_a}, \Delta y = \frac{y^* - y_a}{h_a}, \Delta z = \frac{z^* - z_a}{d_a}, \Delta w = log\left(\frac{w^*}{w_a}\right), \Delta h = log\left(\frac{h^*}{h_a}\right), \Delta d$$
$$= log\left(\frac{d^*}{d_a}\right),  \quad (4)$$

where $x_a, y_a, z_a, w_a, h_a$ and $d_a$ are the 3D box center and size of the positive anchor box, $x^*, y^*, z^*, w^*, h^*$, and $d^*$ are the 3D box center and size of the ground-truth box that has the largest overlap ratio with the positive anchor box.

## 2.2  Relu Cascade of FPNs for Pulmonary Nodule Detection

Compared to the background (negatives), the number of pulmonary nodules (positives) per CT scan is very limited, *e.g.*, 2–3 per scan. Given the imbalanced positive and negative training dataset, it is difficult for a single detection network (essentially a classifier) to clearly separate massive background positions from limited nodule positions. A classic solution to this imbalanced problem is cascade learning [7], which trains multiple classifiers one by one to gradually filter massive negatives from limited positives.

When combined with FPNs, the workflow is shown in Fig. 3. Specifically, a first FPN is trained with *positive patches* sampled around all nodule locations and *random negative patches* sampled from the background. Then, the trained FPN forms a cascade with one level. It is applied to all training images and a likelihood threshold is determined by choosing a maximum value that correctly classifies all positive anchor boxes (100% sensitivity). Doing so clearly produces many false positive detections. In the next round, negative patches are randomly sampled only from these false positive locations, and a second FPN is trained aiming to reduce these false positives. By chaining two FPNs together, the second FPN can filter out negatives that the first FPN fails to do (*i.e.*, false positives). The same process continues until all false positives are eliminated or a specific number of FPNs is obtained.

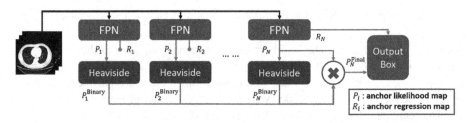

**Fig. 3.** The paradigm of conventional cascade with feature pyramid networks (FPNs). (Color figure online)

The drawback of the conventional cascade in the inference can be illustrated in Fig. 3, where Heaviside = Heaviside$(P_i - T_i)$, $P_i$ and $T_i$ are the anchor likelihood map and threshold at level $i$, respectively, the circled red cross is an element-wise product operator. As we can see, each level in the conventional cascade filters out negatives based on its own judgement without referring to peer levels. As long as one level classifies a sample as negative, the sample location is filtered out. This strategy can be very risky as FPNs trained in the later cascade are more specific and easier to overfit the training data than FPNs in the beginning cascade levels. The reason is because the negative training samples that later FPNs trained with are extracted from false positives left by the previous cascade levels. As the level of cascade increases, the number of false positives decreases. The latter FPNs are exposed to limited negative samples, thus very sensitive and prone to overfitting.

To address this problem, we propose a new cascade called "Relu cascade" as shown in Fig. 4. The training process is the same with the conventional cascade. The difference lies in the inference stage, where Relu cascade introduces two operators to aggregate the judgements from all previous cascade levels before filtering out negatives.

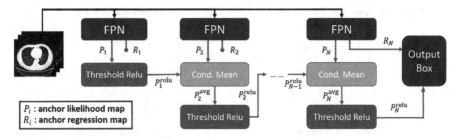

**Fig. 4.** The paradigm of Relu cascade with feature pyramid networks (FPNs).

(1) **Threshold Relu** operator is defined as $P_i^{relu} = max(0, P_i^{avg} - T_i) + 1_{P_i^{avg} \geq T_i} * T_i$, where $P_i^{avg}$, $P_i^{relu}$ and $T_i$ are the input anchor likelihood map, output anchor likelihood map, and likelihood threshold at cascade level $i$, respectively.

(2) **Conditional mean** operator is defined as:

$$P_i^{avg} = \begin{cases} \left(P_{i-1}^{relu} + P_i\right)/2, & if \ P_{i-1}^{relu} > 0 \\ 0, & if \ P_{i-1}^{relu} = 0 \end{cases} \quad (5)$$

Unlike the conventional cascade (Fig. 3) that uses Heaviside function for binary judgement, our Relu cascade (Fig. 4) uses an "threshold Relu" operator to filter out negative samples while still preserving anchor likelihoods estimated by previous cascade levels. The preserved anchor likelihoods are treated as prior information. The conditional mean operator then combines this prior with the current likelihood estimation to derive more reliable anchor likelihoods. Since each cascade level in Relu cascade utilizes *not only* its own judgement *but also* considers the judgements from previous levels, the overfitting problem of conventional cascade can be largely relieved, and the detection performance can be further boosted.

## 3  Results

**Dataset and Parameter Setting:** Our experimental data consists of 2595 CT scans from 2595 patients. The in-plane resolution is 0.6–0.8 mm, and the slice thickness is 5 mm. Pulmonary nodules at each CT scan were first annotated as 3D bounding boxes by a senior radiologist using our internal tool. The annotations were then reviewed and confirmed by another senior radiologist with more than 20 years' experience. The distribution of pulmonary nodule sizes is shown in Fig. 5 (right). We can see that the majority of pulmonary nodule sizes in our dataset is less than 4 mm (47.7%), which poses a great challenge for automatic nodule detection algorithms.

In the experiments, we randomly split the dataset into two parts: (1) training set of 1989 CT scans with 2932 pulmonary nodules; (2) testing set of 606 CT scans with 1076 pulmonary nodules. All CT scans are first resampled to the same spatial resolution (*i.e.*, 0.7 mm × 0.7 mm × 1.0 mm) before any processing step. During training, due to the limitation of GPU memory, we sample random 3D patches from CT

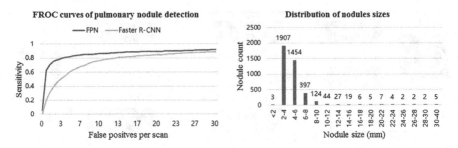

**Fig. 5.** Left: quantitative comparison of FROC curves of faster RCNN and FPN. Right: the distribution of nodule sizes in our dataset (nodule size is defined as the average of the largest major axis and the vertical maximum minor axis measurement in-plane).

scans to train FPNs. The 3D patch size is $96 \times 96 \times 96$. $\lambda$ in the FPN loss is 1000. We evaluate the detection performance of different algorithms using two metrics: (1) average precision (AP) of precision-recall (PR) curve; (2) free-response ROC curve (FROC).

**Impact of Multi-scale Feature Maps:** We first evaluated the importance of multi-scale feature maps in pulmonary nodule detection by comparing faster RCNN and FPN. Faster RCNN utilizes only the coarsest feature maps for pulmonary nodule detection. It tends to miss small pulmonary nodules. By detecting pulmonary nodules at various scales of feature maps, FPN outperforms faster RCNN by a large margin (0.12 increase in AP) as shown in both Fig. 5 (left) and Table 1, which justifies the importance of multi-scale feature maps.

**Table 1.** Quantitative comparison of average precisions of different algorithms.

| Method | Faster RCNN | FPN | FPN cascade | FPN Relu cascade |
|---|---|---|---|---|
| Average precision | 0.523 | 0.642 | 0.699 | 0.741 |

**Evaluation of Different Loss Functions:** We evaluated the detection performance of different loss functions under the FPN framework. The loss functions under comparison are: (1) weighted cross entropy loss, (2) focal loss, (3) cross entropy loss with online hard negative example mining (cross entropy + OHEM), and (4) focal loss with OHEM (focal loss + OHEM). The best performance of each loss function is reported in Fig. 6. Focal loss with OHEM achieves the best detection performance. Without OHEM, the number of negatives is way too many than the number of positives in a min-batch, which limits training efficacy. With OHEM, the detection performance of focal loss is slightly better than that of cross entropy as shown in Fig. 6 (right). Besides, we found that the convergence is accelerated using focal loss compared with cross entropy loss.

**Evaluation of Cascade Learning:** We evaluated the performance gain using cascade learning in Tables 1, 2 and Fig. 7. As we can see from Table 2, cascade learning improves the detection performance gradually by adding more FPNs. In the

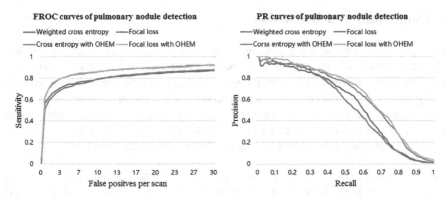

**Fig. 6.** The quantitative comparison of FPN detection performance using different loss functions. Left: FROC curve; Right: PR curve.

**Table 2.** The detection performance at different cascade levels and using different cascades

| Average precision | Stage 1 | Stage 2 | Stage 3 | Stage 4 | Stage 5 |
|---|---|---|---|---|---|
| Conventional cascade | 0.642 | 0.678 | 0.680 | 0.696 | 0.699 |
| Relu cascade | 0.642 | 0.694 | 0.712 | 0.732 | 0.741 |

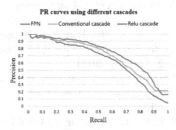

**Fig. 7.** PR curves without cascade (FPN), with conventional cascade, and with Relu cascade.

experiments, we trained up to 5 FPNs considering the performance gain in the expense of inference time increase. Comparing with the conventional cascade, Relu cascade is clearly better at all cascade levels, which justifies the effectiveness of aggregating judgements from previous cascade levels in Relu cascade.

**Inference Time and GPU Memory Cost:** We use pytorch to implement the training part of our algorithm, and build the inference part from scratch using CUDNN. This allows us to fully optimize the inference speed and GPU memory cost of the entire algorithm. After optimization, the runtime of our algorithm is 6 to 12 s using a Geforce Titan Xp graphics card. The runtime GPU memory cost is about 3 to 5 gigabytes depending on the size of lung fields.

## 4   Conclusion and Discussion

In this paper, we propose a new paradigm of cascade using Relu cascade. We combine this strategy with feature pyramid networks (FPNs) for pulmonary nodule detection. We show that, compared with faster RCNN, FPN improves the detection performance greatly in our dataset that contains many small pulmonary nodules. Using our proposed Relu cascade, the detection performance of cascade can be further boosted. The methodology proposed in this paper is very general, and we will validate its performance in other computer-aided detection problems in the near future.

**Acknowledgement.** This work was partially supported by the Shanghai Municipal Commission of Economy and Informatization (2017RGZN01026) and the National Key Research and Development Program of China (2018YFC0116400).

## References

1. National Lung Screening Trial Research Team: The national lung screening trial: overview and study design. Radiology **258**, 243–253 (2011)
2. Shen, W., et al.: Multi-crop convolutional neural networks for lung nodule malignancy suspiciousness classification. Pattern Recognit. **61**, 663–673 (2017)
3. Ren, S., He, K., Girshick, R., Sun, J.: Faster R-CNN: towards real-time object detection with region proposal networks. In: Advances in Neural Information Processing Systems, pp. 91–99 (2015)
4. Lin, T.-Y., Dollár, P., Girshick, R., He, K., Hariharan, B., Belongie, S.: Feature pyramid networks for object detection. In: Proceedings of the IEEE Conference on Computer Vision and Pattern Recognition, pp. 2117–2125 (2017)
5. Milletari, F., Navab, N., Ahmadi, S.-A.: V-net: fully convolutional neural networks for volumetric medical image segmentation. In: 2016 Fourth International Conference on 3D Vision (3DV), pp. 565–571. IEEE (2016)
6. Lin, T.-Y., Goyal, P., Girshick, R., He, K., Dollár, P.: Focal loss for dense object detection. In: Proceedings of the IEEE International Conference on Computer Vision, pp. 2980–2988 (2017)
7. Viola, P., Jones, M.: Rapid object detection using a boosted cascade of simple features. CVPR. **1**, 511–518 (2001)

# Joint Localization of Optic Disc and Fovea in Ultra-widefield Fundus Images

Zhuoya Yang[1,2,3], Xirong Li[1,2,3(✉)] (iD), Xixi He[3], Dayong Ding[3],
Yanting Wang[4], Fangfang Dai[4], and Xuemin Jin[4]

[1] MOE Key Lab of DEKE, Renmin University of China, Beijing, China
[2] AI and Media Computing Lab, School of Information, Renmin University of China,
Beijing, China
xirong@ruc.edu.cn
[3] Vistel AI Lab, Visionary Intelligence Ltd., Beijing, China
[4] Henan Provincal Peoples' Hospital, Zhengzhou, China

**Abstract.** Automated localization of optic disc and fovea is important
for computer-aided retinal disease screening and diagnosis. Compared
to previous works, this paper makes two novelties. First, we study the
localization problem in the new context of ultra-widefield (UWF) fundus
images, which has not been considered before. Second, we propose a
spatially constrained Faster R-CNN for the task. Extensive experiments
on a set of 2,182 UWF fundus images acquired from a local eye center
justify the viability of the proposed model. For more than 99% of the test
images, the improved Faster R-CNN localizes the fovea within one optic
disc diameter to the ground truth, meanwhile detecting the optic disc
with a high IoU of 0.82. The new model works reasonably well even in
challenging cases where the fovea is occluded due to severe retinopathy
or surgical treatments.

**Keywords:** Object localization · UWF fundus image · Faster R-CNN

## 1 Introduction

This paper studies joint localization of the optic disc (OD) and the fovea in
ultra-widefield (UWF) fundus images. Localizing the OD is a prerequisite for
computer-aided diagnosis of optic nerve diseases such as glaucoma, the progression of which is assessed by the optic cup-to-disc ratio. The fovea is responsible
for sharp central vision, so any retinal lesions observed in its surrounding area
shall be taken seriously. Automated localization of the two objects is thus crucial
for fundus image analysis.

Existing works on localizing either the OD [6,10], the fovea [4], or their combination [1,7,8] deal with normal fundus images. Different from normal fundus

This work was supported by NSFC (No. 61672523), the Fundamental Research Funds
for the Central Universities and the Research Funds of Renmin University of China
(No. 18XNLG19).

H.-I. Suk et al. (Eds.): MLMI 2019, LNCS 11861, pp. 453–460, 2019.
https://doi.org/10.1007/978-3-030-32692-0_52

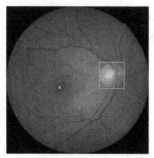

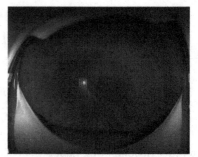

(a) Normal, 45° field of view          (b) Ultra-Widefield, 200° field of view

**Fig. 1.** Two types of fundus images. (a) A normal fundus image captures up to 15% of the retina, showing main structures such as optic disc (green bounding box), fovea (yellow cross) and vessel. (b) A UWF fundus image, which reaches the far peripheral retina and covers approximately 82% of the retina. (Color figure online)

photography, a UWF fundus image provides a much larger field of view. It covers more retinal surface, as shown in Fig. 1(b), and thus peripheral retinal lesions can be spotted. Despite the increasing use of UWF fundus images in varied clinical scenarios [2,3], automated localization of both OD and fovea in a UWF fundus image has not been touched, to the best of our knowledge.

In a fundus image, the OD is an oval bright object at the nasal side of the fovea. Meanwhile, the fovea is a small pit located at the center of the darkest area known as macula, see Fig. 1. As the visual appearance of the two objects seems to be vivid, a natural idea is to use a present-day object detection network, *e.g.,* Faster R-CNN [9]. Although there have been few CNN-based solutions for OD and fovea localization in normal fundus images [1], we see no attempt for exploiting any deep object detection network.

Different from objects in natural photos, the OD and the fovea are spatially correlated. Using the optic disc diameter (DD) as a unit, the horizontal distance between the OD and the fovea is around 2.5 DD, with the latter located slightly below the former. For normal fundus images, some initial efforts have been made to leverage such spatial constraints, implemented either as a two-step approach [7] or as post-processing to refine the localization [8]. How to supervise an object detection network with the spatial constraints remains open.

The contributions of this paper are as follows:

- We present the first study on joint localization of both OD and fovea in UWF fundus images.
- We propose *spatially constrained* Faster R-CNN that effectively leverage the spatial constraints between the OD and the fovea.
- We provide an extensive evaluation, justifying the effectiveness of the proposed solutions on a real-world dataset.

**Table 1. State-of-the-art for fovea and OD localization in fundus images.** This paper goes one step further w.r.t. the target domain and the localization technique.

| Fundus image | Target | Paper | Localization method |
|---|---|---|---|
| Normal | OD | Zou et al. [10] | Intensity-based ROIs proposal + Vessel-based verification |
|  |  | Meng et al. [6] | Sliding window + Patch-based CNN classification |
|  | Fovea | Gegundez et al. [4] | OD & Vessel-based ROIs proposal + Contour finding |
|  | OD & Fovea | Niemeijer et al. [7] | KNN based regression |
|  |  | Qureshi et al. [8] | Ensemble of multiple low-level OD/fovea detectors |
|  |  | Al-Bander et al. [1] | Two-step CNN based regression |
| UWF | OD & Fovea | This work | Proposed spatially constrained Faster R-CNN |

## 2   Related Work

Good efforts have been made for automated localization of the OD [6,10], the fovea [4], and both [1,7,8]. However, all target at normal fundus images, as we summarize in Table 1.

For OD localization, Zou et al. [10] generate regions of interest (ROIs) by simple intensity thresholding, and subsequently identify the OD by vessel-based verification. Meng et al. [6] train a patch-based convolutional neural network (CNN) to locate the OD, using sliding window to generate proposals. It predicts only the OD center, without precise boundary.

For fovea localization, Gegundez et al. [4] assume the availability of the OD and the vascular tree. A pixel within the fovea region is estimated, which is set to be 2.5 optic disc diameters (DD) away from the OD center. The orientation of the vasculature is used to determine if the pixel is on the OD's left or right side. Then, contour finding is performed on a 2DD×2DD sub-image centered on the pixel to localize the fovea.

For joint localization, Niemeijer et al. [7] develop a regression model. For each pixel in a given image, its distance to the (unknown) OD center is predicted based on intensity and vascular features. The pixel with the smallest distance is chosen as the OD center. In a similar vein, the fovea is localized, with the search area enforced to be 2DD away from the detected OD center. Qureshi et al. [8] take an ensemble approach to locate OD (fovea) by combining several low-level OD (fovea) detectors. Among the multiple OD and fovea candidates, the pair that best match spatial constraint is selected. More recently, Al-Bander et al. [1] build three CNN based regression models. One CNN is used to predict the initial centers of the OD and the fovea. With a sub-image cropped around the predicted OD center as input, the second CNN is used to re-predict the OD center. In a similar way, the third CNN is used to re-predict the fovea center.

Note that the majority of the previous efforts rely heavily on intensity and vascular features [4,7,8,10]. However, such features are unreliable due to varied factors including changes in imaging conditions, retinal disorders and surgical treatments on the eye. The few CNN based attempts are cumbersome, as they require either pixel-by-pixel classification [6] or a triplet of CNNs [1]. Spatial constraints between the two objects are largely unexplored.

# 3    Spatially-Constrained Joint Localization

We aim to automatically localize both OD and fovea in a given UWF fundus image. The task differs from conventional object detection in the following two aspects. First, there is only one OD and one fovea. Second, due to the physiological structure of the retina, constraints on spatial locations of the two objects exit. We hypothesize that such constraints are helpful for localizing the two objects, especially the fovea, in challenging cases where UWF images are presented with severe retinopathy. In order to exploit the spatial constraints, we propose two strategies, one is an OD-guided two-step approach and the other is to directly incorporate the constraints into the loss function of Faster R-CNN, and consequently achieve a simultaneous localization in one forward computation.

## 3.1    Strategy 1. OD-guided Fovea Localization

The OD in a fundus image appears as a bright area where blood vessels converge. Such a visual pattern is unique and relatively stable, making the object more easily to be localized than the fovea. This observation motivates us to localize the OD first, and accordingly use it as a guidance to localize the fovea. We term this strategy OD-guided fovea localization. Note that the OD-guided strategy conceptually resembles [7] to some extent, as both works use the OD to narrow down the search space for fovea localization. Nonetheless, our module is end-to-end and requires no vascular information, making the overall solution simplified.

We first train a Faster R-CNN for OD localization. While the OD is known to be placed to the nasal side of the fovea, no laterality information is available in our study. So at each side, a squared candidate area is heuristically estimated, with its location and size relatively determined in the unit of the DD. The region is cropped and fed into another Faster R-CNN trained for fovea localization. OD-guided fovea localization implements the spatial constraints by enforcing the object detection network to search for the fovea in the two sub-images.

This strategy is effective for reducing false alarms in the peripheral area of the retina. However, both the training and the execution of the fovea localization network remain independent of the OD. Moreover, two Faster R-CNNs are required. To overcome these downsides, we consider another strategy as follows.

## 3.2    Strategy 2. Spatially-Constrained Loss

We train the Faster R-CNN network with a new loss which takes into account the spatial constraints between the OD and the fovea. In order to make the paper more self-contained, we describe briefly how Faster R-CNN works in this new context. As an end-to-end object detection network, Faster R-CNN is composed of a Region Proposal Network (RPN) for ROI generation and a Fast R-CNN [5] for ROI refinement and classification. Given a UWF fundus image, the RPN generates many bounding-box proposals and classifies them either as foreground or as background. Proposals classified as foreground, after bounding-box regression and non-maximum suppression, are preserved as candidate ROIs. The Fast

R-CNN then classifies these ROIs into one of the three classes, *i.e.*, OD, fovea and background. In order to get a reliable set of ROIs to represent the OD, we let OD-ROIs consist of ROIs predicted as OD with scores larger than 0.5. In a similar vein we obtain fovea-ROIs. For better localization, these chosen OD-ROIs and fovea-ROIs are further fed into a bounding-box regression subnetwork.

With the OD-ROIs and fovea-ROIs identified, we exploit the spatial constraint in two aspects, one is distance-based and the other is direction-based. Let $d(OD, fovea)$ be the Euclidean distance between the averaged center of OD-ROIs and fovea-ROIs. We define a distance-based loss $loss_d$ as

$$loss_d := \max(0, d_{min} - d(OD, fovea)) + \max(0, d(OD, fovea) - d_{max}), \quad (1)$$

where $d_{min}$ and $d_{max}$ are the 2nd and the 98th percentiles of the OD-fovea distances calculated using the ground truth of our training data. Whenever the distance is smaller than $d_{min}$ or larger than $d_{max}$, a loss occurs.

To consider the direction-based constraint, we compute the angle between the averaged center of OD-ROIs and that of fovea-ROIs, denoted by $\theta(OD, fovea)$. The value is positive if the fovea is below the OD, and negative otherwise. Note that in a well-positioned fundus image, the fovea shall be placed slightly below the OD. However, minor rotations might occur in practice. We therefore consider the upper bound only, defining a direction-based loss $loss_\theta$ as

$$loss_\theta := \max(0, abs(\theta(OD, fovea)) - \theta_{max}), \quad (2)$$

where the upper bound $\theta_{max}$ is the 98th percentile of the angles, computed using the same ground truth as used for obtaining $d_{min}$ and $d_{max}$.

By adding the above two losses to the original loss of Faster R-CNN (denoted as $loss_{fr}$), we obtain the new spatially-constrained loss $loss_{sc}$ as

$$Loss_{sc} := loss_{fr} + \lambda_1 \cdot loss_d + \lambda_2 \cdot loss_\theta, \quad (3)$$

where $\lambda_1$ and $\lambda_2$ are two positive weights controlling the influence of the distance-based and direction-based losses, respectively. Based on a hold-out validation set, we empirically set $\lambda_1 = 0.002$ and $\lambda_2 = 0.1$.

## 4   Evaluation

### 4.1   Experimental Setup

**Data.** As no public dataset is available, we acquire 2,182 UWF images from our collaborating eye center, with manually labeled bounding boxes of the OD and the coordinate of the fovea. The dataset is divided at random into three disjoint subsets for training, validation and test, respectively, with a ratio of 4:1:1.5. To avoid over-fitting, the data split is based on patients s so images from a specific patient appear only in one subset.

**Implementation.** Original images are downsized from $3900 \times 3072$, to $762 \times 600$. We implement Faster R-CNN with VGGNet-16 as their backbone. Per model, the top-ranked OD-ROI is used as the final OD region, while the center of the top-ranked fovea-ROI is used as the predicted coordinate of the fovea.

**Evaluation Criteria.** As the OD is an area and the fovea is a point to be localized, we use Intersection over Union (IoU) for OD and the Euclidean distance between the center of predicted box and the center of ground true for fovea. Overall performance is obtained by averaging scores of all test images.

**Table 2. Performance of different models for optic disc/fovea localization.** The operator $[\![\cdot]\!]$ computes accuracy, *i.e.*, the rate of test images satisfying a given criterion. Per test image, DD is the vertical disc diameter of the ground truth. The proposed spatially constrained Faster R-CNN models achieve the best joint localization.

| Model | Optic Disc (OD) | | Fovea | | | | |
|---|---|---|---|---|---|---|---|
| | IoU | $[\![IoU \geq 0.5]\!]$ | Distance | Std. | $[\![< \frac{1}{5}DD]\!]$ | $[\![< \frac{1}{4}DD]\!]$ | $[\![< DD]\!]$ |
| *Baselines:* | | | | | | | |
| OD Faster R-CNN | **0.8445** | **0.9980** | – | – | – | – | – |
| Fovea Faster R-CNN | – | – | 35.90 | 140.15 | 0.8039 | 0.8495 | 0.9841 |
| Joint Faster R-CNN | 0.8131 | 0.9881 | 31.24 | 92.59 | 0.8039 | 0.8475 | 0.9841 |
| *Spatially Constrained:* | | | | | | | |
| OD-guided | **0.8445** | **0.9980** | 27.25 | 82.55 | 0.8019 | 0.8514 | 0.9881 |
| $loss_{sc}$ | 0.8174 | 0.9960 | **25.29** | **52.47** | **0.8059** | **0.8594** | **0.9920** |

### 4.2 Experiment 1. Joint Localization Versus Separate Localization

The first uncertainty we need to address is the necessity of joint localization. We train two Faster R-CNN models separately, one for the OD and the other for the fovea. We then train another model that localizes the two objects simultaneously.

The performance of the three models is reported in the top part of Table 2. Comparing with the two individual models, Joint Faster R-CNN performs worse than the OD model for OD localization, while providing more precise fovea localization than the fovea model. Note that IoU exceeding 0.80 is sufficient, as shown in Fig. 2. So we focus our discussion on fovea localization.

Joint Faster R-CNN obtains a noticeably smaller standard deviation for fovea localization. The result justifies the necessity of joint localization, and also suggests the spatial relations between the OD and the fovea are implicitly modeled.

### 4.3 Experiment 2. Spatially-Constrained Joint Localization

With Joint Faster R-CNN as our baseline, we now evaluate the two proposed strategies for spatially-constrained joint localization. Recall that the OD-guided strategy uses the OD model in its first step, so the strategy scores the same IoU as the baseline in Table 2. Both strategies give better fovea localization than the baseline, suggesting the importance of explicitly modeling the spatial constraints. Moreover, Faster R-CNN trained with the proposed loss gives the best fovea localization with the smallest deviation ($25.29 \pm 52.47$). For more than

99% of the test images, the fovea is localized within one DD to the ground truth. We further conduct an ablation study concerning distinct spatial constraints, *i.e.*, distance-based, direction-based and their combination. As shown in Table 3, the joint loss is the best.

Some qualitative results are provided in Fig. 2. From Fig. 2(a) to (e), while the baseline incorrectly predicts the fovea on the opposite side, our improved Faster R-CNN localizes the fovea on the correct side. For Fig. 2(f) where the macular

**Table 3. The influence of distinct spatial constraints,** *i.e.*, distance-based ($d_{min}$ and $d_{max}$ in Eq. 1), direction-based ($\theta_{max}$ in Eq. 2) and their combination, on fovea localization. Faster R-CNN trained with the joint loss (the last row) performs the best.

| $d_{min}$ | $d_{max}$ | $\theta_{max}$ | Distance | Std. |
|:---:|:---:|:---:|:---:|:---:|
| ✓ | ✗ | ✗ | 27.04 | 75.29 |
| ✓ | ✓ | ✗ | 25.75 | 62.76 |
| ✓ | ✓ | ✓ | **25.29** | **52.47** |

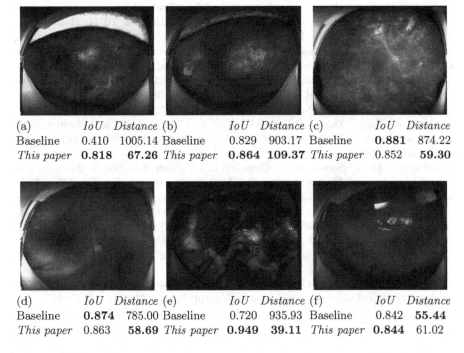

(a)          *IoU   Distance* (b)          *IoU   Distance* (c)          *IoU   Distance*
Baseline     0.410   1005.14 Baseline     0.829   903.17 Baseline     **0.881**   874.22
*This paper* **0.818**   **67.26** *This paper* **0.864**   **109.37** *This paper* 0.852   **59.30**

(d)          *IoU   Distance* (e)          *IoU   Distance* (f)          *IoU   Distance*
Baseline     **0.874**   785.00 Baseline     0.720   935.93 Baseline     0.842   **55.44**
*This paper* 0.863   **58.69** *This paper* **0.949**   **39.11** *This paper* **0.844**   61.02

**Fig. 2. Some localization results** by the baseline (Joint Faster R-CNN) and the improved Faster R-CNN. OD and fovea are indicated by bounding boxes and crosses, respectively. Ground truth/baseline/our results are shown in green/purple/yellow. Below each image are IoU of the detected OD and distance of the predicted fovea to the ground truth. Better numbers are shown in bold font. Best viewed digitally in close-up. (Color figure online)

area appears to be filled with silicone oil, the baseline gives a better localization. At the cost of slightly dropping the performance of OD localization, the new Faster R-CNN noticeably improves fovea localization.

## 5  Conclusions

For joint localization of OD and fovea in UWF fundus images, we recommend to train Faster R-CNN with the proposed joint loss. As experiments on a set of 2,182 real-world images show, for more than 99% of the test images, the improved Faster R-CNN localizes the fovea within one DD to the ground truth, meanwhile localizing the OD with a high IoU of 0.82.

## References

1. Al-Bander, B., Al-Nuaimy, W., Williams, B., Zheng, Y.: Multiscale sequential convolutional neural networks for simultaneous detection of fovea and optic disc. Biomed. Sig. Process. Control **40**, 91–101 (2018)
2. Assil, K.K., Batra, V.N.: The role of ultra-widefield retinal imaging as a standard assessment tool in the cataract practice. Am. J. Ophthalmol. **10**(1), 31–34 (2017)
3. Falavarjani, K.G., Wang, K., Khadamy, J., Sadda, S.R.: Ultra-wide-field imaging in diabetic retinopathy; an overview. J. Curr. Ophthalmol. **28**(2), 57–60 (2016)
4. Gegundez-Arias, M.E., Marin, D., Bravo, J.M., Suero, A.: Locating the fovea center position in digital fundus images using thresholding and feature extraction techniques. Comput. Med. Imaging Graph. **37**(5–6), 386–393 (2013)
5. Girshick, R.: Fast R-CNN. In: Proceedings of ICCV (2015)
6. Meng, X., Xi, X., Yang, L., Zhang, G., Yin, Y., Chen, X.: Fast and effective optic disk localization based on convolutional neural network. Neurocomputing **312**, 285–295 (2018)
7. Niemeijer, M., Abrámoff, M.D., Ginnekena, B.V.: Fast detection of the optic disc and fovea in color fundus photographs. Med. Image Anal. **13**(6), 859–870 (2009)
8. Qureshi, R.J., Kovacs, L., Harangi, B., Nagy, B., Peto, T., Hajdu, A.: Combining algorithms for automatic detection of optic disc and macula in fundus images. Comput. Vis. Image Underst. **116**(1), 138–145 (2012)
9. Ren, S., He, K., Girshick, R., Sun, J.: Faster R-CNN: towards real-time object detection with region proposal networks. IEEE Trans. Pattern Anal. Mach. Intell. **39**(6), 1137–1149 (2017)
10. Zou, B., Chen, C., Zhu, C., Duan, X., Chen, Z.: Classified optic disc localization algorithm based on verification model. Comput. Graph. **70**, 281–287 (2017)

# Multi-scale Attentional Network for Multi-focal Segmentation of Active Bleed After Pelvic Fractures

Yuyin Zhou[1(✉)], David Dreizin[2], Yingwei Li[1], Zhishuai Zhang[1], Yan Wang[1], and Alan Yuille[1]

[1] The Johns Hopkins University, Baltimore, USA
zhouyuyiner@gmail.com
[2] University of Maryland & R. Adams Cowley Shock Trauma Center, Baltimore, USA

**Abstract.** Trauma is the worldwide leading cause of death and disability in those younger than 45 years, and pelvic fractures are a major source of morbidity and mortality. Automated segmentation of multiple foci of arterial bleeding from abdominopelvic trauma CT could provide rapid objective measurements of the total extent of active bleeding, potentially augmenting outcome prediction at the point of care, while improving patient triage, allocation of appropriate resources, and time to definitive intervention. In spite of the importance of active bleeding in the quick tempo of trauma care, the task is still quite challenging due to the variable contrast, intensity, location, size, shape, and multiplicity of bleeding foci. Existing work presents a heuristic rule-based segmentation technique which requires multiple stages and cannot be efficiently optimized end-to-end. To this end, we present, Multi-Scale Attentional Network (MSAN), the first yet reliable end-to-end network, for automated segmentation of active hemorrhage from contrast-enhanced trauma CT scans. MSAN consists of the following components: (1) an encoder which fully integrates the global contextual information from holistic 2D slices; (2) a multi-scale strategy applied both in the training stage and the inference stage to handle the challenges induced by variation of target sizes; (3) an attentional module to further refine the deep features, leading to better segmentation quality; and (4) a multi-view mechanism to leverage the 3D information. MSAN reports a significant improvement of more than 7% compared to prior arts in terms of DSC.

## 1 Introduction

High-energy pelvic fractures, which are usually related to motor vehicle accidents, falls from height, or crush injury, are the second leading cause of death from acute physical trauma after brain injury. The mortality rate of pelvic fractures ranges from 5%−15%, overall, increasing from 36% to 54% in those with hemorrhagic shock [12]. With the widespread availability of CT in trauma bays, the majority of patients with severe pelvic trauma admitted to level I trauma

© Springer Nature Switzerland AG 2019
H.-I. Suk et al. (Eds.): MLMI 2019, LNCS 11861, pp. 461–469, 2019.
https://doi.org/10.1007/978-3-030-32692-0_53

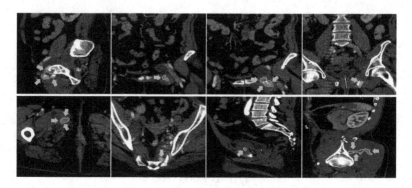

**Fig. 1.** Visual examples of pelvic CT scans from axial/coronal/saggital views. Red contour denotes the boundaries of the active hemorrhage, where we can observe large variations of shape and textures. (Color figure online)

centers currently undergo an examination with contrast-enhanced trauma CT, in part to assess for foci of active bleeding, manifesting as contrast extravasation [3]. The size of foci of contrast extravasation from bleeding vessels correlates with the need for blood transfusion, angiographic or surgical hemostatic intervention, and mortality, but reliable measurements of contrast extravasation volume cannot be derived at the point of care using manual, semi-automated, or shorthand diameter-based methods. Fully automated methods are necessary for real-time point-of-care decision making, treatment planning, and prognostication (Fig. 1).

In this paper, we focus on volumetric segmentation of foci of active bleeding (i.e. contrast extravasation) after pelvic fractures. This task is of vital importance yet challenging for the following reasons: (1) hemorrhage gray levels vary from patient to patient, depending on a variety of factors (*e.g.*, the rate of bleeding, the timing of the scan, and the patient's physiologic state after trauma), (2) hemorrhage boundaries are often very poorly defined and highly irregular; and (3) the intensity levels are inconsistent throughout the region of a hemorrhagic focus. Prior works have utilized semi-automated threshold- or region growing-based methods using post-processing software [5]. However, these techniques are too time-consuming for clinical use in the trauma radiology setting. To overcome this difficulty, a method [4] was previously proposed to first utilize spatial contextual information from artery and bone to detect the hemorrhage, and then employ a rule-based strategy to refine the segmentation results. This heuristic approach requires multiple stages which cannot be efficiently optimized end-to-end. Moreover, this method cannot properly handle other challenges such as variation of target sizes and ambiguous boundaries.

Recently, the emerge of deep learning has largely advanced the field of computer aided diagnosis (CAD). Riding on the success of convolutional neural networks, *e.g.*, fully convolutional networks [9], researchers have achieved accurate segmentation on many medical image analysis tasks [10,11,15,16]. Existing coarse-to-fine methods [14,15], which propose to refine segmentation results through explicit cropping of a single region of interest (ROI) are more suitable for single connected structures such as the pancreas or liver, while sites of active bleeding are frequently discontinuous and multi-focal and occur in widely disparate vascular territories. Herein, we present a multi-scale attentional network (MSAN), for segmenting active bleed after pelvic features, the first yet reliable framework, for segmenting active bleed after pelvic features. Specifically, our framework is able to (1) fully exploit contextual information from holistic 2D slices via using an encoder which is capable of extracting the global contextual information across different levels of image features; (2) efficiently handle the variation of active hemorrhage sizes by adopting multi-scale strategies during the training phase and the testing phase; (3) deal with the ambiguous boundaries by utilizing an attentional mechanism to better enhance the discrimination between trauma region and non-trauma region; (4) utilize the aggregation of multiple views (*i.e.*, Coronal, Sagittal and Axial views) to further leverage the 3D information. To assess the effectiveness of our framework, we collect a dataset of 65 patients with pelvic fractures and active hemorrhage with widely varying degrees of severity. For each case, every pixel/voxel of active hemorrhage was manually labeled by an experienced radiologist. Unlike the previously described heuristic method which used crude and not widely adopted measurements of accuracy such as missegmented area [4], we employed the Dice-Sørensen coefficient (DSC) for evaluation based on pixel/voxel-wise predictions. Experimental results demonstrate the superiority of our framework compared with a series of 2D/3D state-of-the-art deep learning algorithms.

## 2    Multi-scale Attentional Network

### 2.1    Overall Framework

We denote a 3D CT-scanned image as $\mathbf{X}$ with size $W \times H \times L$, where each element of $\mathbf{X}$ indicated the Housefield Unit (HU) of a voxel. The corresponding binary ground-truth segmentation mask is denoted as $\mathbf{Y}$ where $y_i = 1$ indicates a foreground voxel. Consider a segmentation model $M : \mathbf{Z} = \mathbf{f}(\mathbf{X}; \Theta)$, where $M$ is parameterized by $\Theta$, our goal is to predict a binary output volume $\mathbf{Z}$ of the same dimension as $\mathbf{X}$. We denote $\mathcal{Y}$ and $\mathcal{Z}$ as the set of foreground voxels in the ground-truth and prediction, *i.e.*, $\mathcal{Y} = \{i \mid y_i = 1\}$ and $\mathcal{Z} = \{i \mid z_i = 1\}$. The accuracy of segmentation is evaluated by the Dice-Sørensen coefficient (DSC): $\mathrm{DSC}(\mathcal{Y}, \mathcal{Z}) = \frac{2 \times |\mathcal{Y} \cap \mathcal{Z}|}{|\mathcal{Y}| + |\mathcal{Z}|}$. This metric falls in the range of $[0, 1]$, and $\mathrm{DSC} = 1$ implies a perfect segmentation.

Following [11,14,15], 3 sets of images, *i.e.*, $\mathbf{X}_{C,w}$ ($w = 1, 2, \dots, W$), $\mathbf{X}_{S,h}$ ($h = 1, 2, \dots, H$) and $\mathbf{X}_{A,l}$ ($l = 1, 2, \dots, L$) are obtained along three axes. The subscripts C, S and A stand for "coronal", "sagittal" and "axial", respectively. We train an individual model $M$ for each of the three viewpoints. Without loss of generality, we consider a 2D slice along the *axial* view, denoted by $\mathbf{X}_{A,l}$. Our goal is to infer a binary segmentation mask $\mathbf{Z}_{A,l}$ of the same dimensionality. In the context of deep networks [1,9], it is achieved by computing a *probability map*

$\mathbf{P}_{A,l} = \mathbf{f}[\mathbf{X}_{A,l}; \theta]$, where $\mathbf{f}[\cdot; \theta]$ is the architecture as in Fig. 2(a). This network contains an encoder (Sect. 2.2) to extract different levels of features for distilling global context and an attentional module (Sect. 2.3) as further refinement.

Specifically, we apply Atrous Spatial Pyramid Pooling (ASPP) [1] at the end of the backbone model to extract high-level features with enriched global context. Meanwhile, the low-level features extracted from earlier layers which contain local information are fed to an attentional module to distill more useful information. The refined low-level features are then concatenated with high-level features extracted by ASPP and fed to the final classifier layer, which outputs probabilities $\mathbf{P}_{A,l}$, $\mathbf{P}_{C,l}$ and $\mathbf{P}_{S,l}$ which are then binarized into $\mathbf{Z}_{A,l}$, $\mathbf{Z}_{C,l}$ and $\mathbf{Z}_{S,l}$ respectively. The final segmentation outcome can be fused from the three views via majority voting [14,15]. Multi-scale processing [1,8] is used in both the training stage and the inference stage to further enhance the segmentation accuracy, especially for small targets. As illustrated in Fig. 2, different rescaled version of the original image are fed to the network during training. During the testing stage, to produce the final segmentation mask, the output from different scales are fused by taking at each position the average response. If the average probability is larger than a certain threshold $\rho$ it is regarded as foreground otherwise it is regarded as background.

## 2.2   Encoder Backbone Architecture

Atrous Convolution has been widely applied in computer vision problems, which can efficiently allow for larger receptive field via controlling atrous rates. Given an input feature map $x$, atrous convolution is applied over $x$ as follows:

$$y[i] = \sum_k x[i + r \cdot k] w[k], \tag{1}$$

where $i$ and $w$ denote the spatial location and the convolution filter, respectively. $r$ stands for the atrous rate.

Atrous Spatial Pyramid Pooling (ASPP) is originated from Spatial Pyramid Pooling [7]. The main difference is that ASPP uses atrous convolution which allows for larger field-of-view during training and thus can efficiently integrate global contextual information. As a strong contextual aggregation module [1], ASPP is applied (see Fig. 2(a)) so that the contextual information from artery and bone can be better exploited. In our experiment, we set the atrous rates to be $\{12, 24, 36\}$, respectively.

## 2.3   Attentional Module

We adapt the non-local block [13] as the attentional module in our framework. Specifically, it first computes an attention map $y$ of an input feature map $x$ by taking a weighted average of features in all spatial locations $\mathcal{L}$:

$$y_i = \frac{1}{\mathcal{C}(x)} \sum_{\forall j \in \mathcal{L}} f(x_i, x_j) \cdot x_j, \tag{2}$$

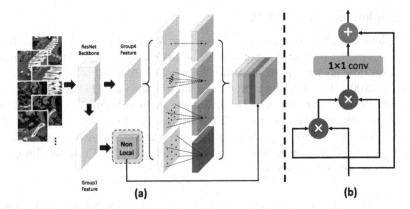

**Fig. 2.** (a) The network architecture structure of MSAN. Low-level features are refined by an attentional module. Meanwhile ASPP is applied at the end of the backbone model to extract high-level features with enriched global context. (b) Our implementation of the attentional module, where we use nonlocal means [13] as the main operation.

where i and j are spatial indices. A pairwise function $f(x_i, x_j)$ is used to compute the spatial attention coefficients between each i and all j. And these coefficients are applied as the weighting of the input feature to better prune out irrelevant background features and thereby distinguish salient image regions. $\mathcal{C}(x)$ is a normalization function. We use the dot product version in [13] by setting $f(x_i, x_j) = x_i^\mathrm{T} x_j$ and $\mathcal{C}(x) = N$, where $N$ is the number of pixels in $x$.

Following [13], the attention map $y$ is then processed by a $1 \times 1$ convolutional layer and added to the input feature map $x$ to obtain the final output $z$, *i.e.*, $z = wy + x$, where $w$ is the weight of the convolutional layer. An illustration our attentional module can be found in Fig. 2(b).

## 3   Experiments

### 3.1   Dataset and Evaluation

We have collected 65 studies were routinely acquired with 64 section or higher MDCT scanners in the trauma bay in either the late arterial or portal venous phase of enhancement. We use 45 cases for training and evaluate the segmentation performance on the rest 20 cases. Note that [4] was studied on only 12 cases, which, to the best of our knowledge, was the first and only curated dataset with manual ground truth label masks. Therefore our dataset can be considered as a valid set for evaluation. The metric we use is DSC, which measures the similarity between the prediction voxel set $\mathcal{Z}$ and the ground-truth set $\mathcal{Y}$, with the mathematical form of $\mathrm{DSC}(\mathcal{Z}, \mathcal{Y}) = \frac{2 \times |\mathcal{Z} \cap \mathcal{Y}|}{|\mathcal{Z}| + |\mathcal{Y}|}$.

## 3.2    Implementation Details

Our implementations are based on Tensorflow. We used two standard architectures, *i.e.*, ResNet-50 and ResNet-101 [6] as backbone models. All our segmentation experiments were performed on the whole pelvic CT scan and were run on Tesla V100 GPU. For data pre-processing, following [11], we simply truncated the raw intensity values to be within the range of $[-80, 320]$ HU and then normalized each raw CT case to $[0, 255.0]$. Random rotation of $[0, 15]$ is used as online data augmentation. A *poly* learning policy is applied with an initial learning rate of 0.05 with a decay power of 0.9. We follow [11,14,15] to use ImageNet pretrained model for initialization.

**Table 1.** DSC comparison of active bleed segmentation. ResNet101-MSAN-3-scale achieves the best performance of 59.89%, surpassing the prior art by more than 7%.

| Model | scale = 1.0 | scale = 1.25 | scale = 1.5 | scale = 1.75 | Avg. dice |
|---|---|---|---|---|---|
| ResNet50-single-scale | | – | – | – | 35.96% |
| ResNet50-single-scale | – | | – | – | 48.14% |
| ResNet50-single-scale | – | – | | – | 47.71% |
| ResNet50-single-scale | – | – | – | | 46.29% |
| ResNet50-2-scale | – | | | – | 52.75% |
| ResNet50-MSAN-2-scale | – | | | – | 54.31% |
| ResNet50-3-scale | – | | | | 54.40% |
| ResNet50-MSAN-3-scale | – | | | | 55.61% |
| ResNet101-single-scale | | – | – | – | 37.53% |
| ResNet101-single-scale | – | | – | – | 46.38% |
| ResNet101-single-scale | – | – | | – | 52.67% |
| ResNet101-single-scale | – | – | – | | 54.56% |
| ResNet101-2-scale | – | | | – | 54.98% |
| ResNet101-MSAN-2-scale | – | | | – | 55.70% |
| ResNet101-3-scale | – | | | | 58.72% |
| ResNet101-MSAN-3-scale | – | | | | **59.89%** |
| Zhou *et al.* [15] | – | – | – | – | 50.15% |
| Yu *et al.* [14] | – | – | – | – | 52.12% |
| 3D-UNet [2] | – | – | – | – | 40.81% |

## 3.3    Results and Discussions

All results are summarized in Table 1, where we list thorough comparisons under different configuration of network architecture (*i.e.*, ResNet50 and ResNet101 [6]) and scales (*i.e.*, $scales = \{1.0, 1.25, 1.5, 1.75\}$). Note that we use larger scales ($\geq 1.0$) since our goal is to segment small targets. Under different settings, our method consistently outperforms others, indicating the effectiveness of MSAN.

*Efficacy of Multi-scale Processing.* As shown in Table 1, larger scales generally lead to better results. For instance, using ResNet50 as the backbone model, the performance under *scale* = 1.0 is ~10% lower than that under other larger scales. ResNet101-single-scale yields the best result of 54.56% under *scale* = 1.75, which is more than 17% better than using the scale of 1.0. These facts all indicate the efficacy of utilizing larger scales. Another observation is that the integration of more scales also leads to better segmentation quality than using just one scale. Using either ResNet50 or ResNet101 as the backbone, 3-scales always yield better results than 2-scales/single-scale, which shows that the learned knowledge from these different scales is complementary to each other. Therefore combining the information from these different scales can be beneficial for handling targets with a large variety of sizes, such as active bleed in our study.

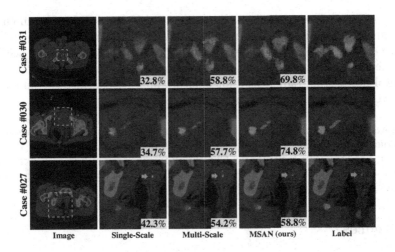

**Fig. 3.** Qualitative comparison of different methods. from left to right: original CT image, predictions of single-scale method (*scale* = 1.50), multi-scale method (*scale* = {1.25, 1.50, 1.75}), MSAN and the manual label. (Best viewed in color)

*Efficacy of the Attentional Module.* Meanwhile, we also witness additional benefit from the attentional module. For instance, ResNet50-MSAN-3-scale observes an improvement of 1.17% compared with ResNet101-3-scale; ResNet101-MSAN-2-scale) observes an improvement of 0.72% compared with ResNet101-2-scale. A similar improvement can be also witnessed for ResNet-50. Three qualitative examples are shown in Fig. 3, where MSAN consistently outperforms other existing methods. For case 027, our MSAN successfully removes the outlier (indicated by the orange arrows) which is detected as false positives by other methods. This further justifies that the usage of attentional mechanisms can indeed refine the results and diminish non-trauma outliers.

Overall, our proposed MSAN observes a significant performance gain under different settings, which shows the generality and soundness of our approach. Additionally, we also compare our method with other state-of-art 3D segmentation methods including [14,15] and [2]. Our method outperforms all these methods significantly (*p-values* for testing significant difference satisfy $p < 0.0001$), which further demonstrates the effectiveness of our approach. In order to further validate the generality and stability of MSAN, we directly test on a newly collected additional 15 cases without any retraining. Our method obtains an average DSC of 50.19%, whereas prior arts report 44.15% [14], 35.14% [15] and 27.32% [2]. MSAN significantly outperforms these methods.

## 4　Conclusions

In this paper, we present Multi-Scale Attentional Network (MSAN), an end-to-end framework for automated segmentation of active hemorrhage from pelvic CT scans. Our proposed MSAN substantially improves the segmentation accuracy by more than 7% compared with prior arts. We note this framework can be practical in assisting radiologists for clinical applications, since the annotation in 3D volumes requires massive labor from radiologists.

**Acknowledgements.** This work was supported by NIBIB (National Institute of Biomedical Imaging and Bioengineering)/NIH under award number K08EB027141, University of Maryland Institute for Clinical and Translational Research Accelerated Translational Incubator Pilot (ATIP) award and Radiologic Society of North America (RSNA) Research Scholar Award #1605.

## References

1. Chen, L., Papandreou, G., Kokkinos, I., Murphy, K., Yuille, A.: Semantic image segmentation with deep convolutional nets and fully connected CRFs. In: International Conference on Learning Representations (2015)
2. Çiçek, Ö., Abdulkadir, A., Lienkamp, S.S., Brox, T., Ronneberger, O.: 3D U-Net: learning dense volumetric segmentation from sparse annotation. In: Ourselin, S., Joskowicz, L., Sabuncu, M.R., Unal, G., Wells, W. (eds.) MICCAI 2016. LNCS, vol. 9901, pp. 424–432. Springer, Cham (2016). https://doi.org/10.1007/978-3-319-46723-8_49
3. Cullinane, D.C., et al.: Eastern association for the surgery of trauma practice management guidelines for hemorrhage in pelvic fracture-update and systematic review. J. Trauma Acute Care Surg. **71**(6), 1850–1868 (2011)
4. Davuluri, P., et al.: Hemorrhage detection and segmentation in traumatic pelvic injuries. Comput. Math. Methods Med. **2012**(2012)
5. Dreizin, D., et al.: CT prediction model for major arterial injury after blunt pelvic ring disruption. Radiology **287**(3), 1061–1069 (2018)
6. He, K., Zhang, X., Ren, S., Sun, J.: Deep residual learning for image recognition. In: CVPR (2016)

7. He, K., Zhang, X., Ren, S., Sun, J.: Spatial pyramid pooling in deep convolutional networks for visual recognition. IEEE Trans. Pattern Anal. Mach. Intell. **37**(9), 1904–1916 (2015)
8. Kamnitsas, K., et al.: Efficient multi-scale 3D CNN with fully connected CRF for accurate brain lesion segmentation. arXiv (2016)
9. Long, J., Shelhamer, E., Darrell, T.: Fully convolutional networks for semantic segmentation. In: CVPR (2015)
10. Ronneberger, O., Fischer, P., Brox, T.: U-Net: convolutional networks for biomedical image segmentation. In: Navab, N., Hornegger, J., Wells, W.M., Frangi, A.F. (eds.) MICCAI 2015. LNCS, vol. 9351, pp. 234–241. Springer, Cham (2015). https://doi.org/10.1007/978-3-319-24574-4_28
11. Roth, H.R., Lu, L., Farag, A., Sohn, A., Summers, R.M.: Spatial aggregation of holistically-nested networks for automated pancreas segmentation. In: Ourselin, S., Joskowicz, L., Sabuncu, M.R., Unal, G., Wells, W. (eds.) MICCAI 2016. LNCS, vol. 9901, pp. 451–459. Springer, Cham (2016). https://doi.org/10.1007/978-3-319-46723-8_52
12. Sathy, A.K., et al.: The effect of pelvic fracture on mortality after trauma: an analysis of 63,000 trauma patients. JBJS **91**(12), 2803–2810 (2009)
13. Wang, X., Girshick, R., Gupta, A., He, K.: Non-local neural networks. In: CVPR (2018)
14. Yu, Q., Xie, L., Wang, Y., Zhou, Y., Fishman, E.K., Yuille, A.L.: Recurrent saliency transformation network: incorporating multi-stage visual cues for small organ segmentation. In: CVPR, pp. 8280–8289 (2018)
15. Zhou, Y., Xie, L., Shen, W., Wang, Y., Fishman, E.K., Yuille, A.L.: A fixed-point model for pancreas segmentation in abdominal CT scans. In: Descoteaux, M., Maier-Hein, L., Franz, A., Jannin, P., Collins, D.L., Duchesne, S. (eds.) MICCAI 2017. LNCS, vol. 10433, pp. 693–701. Springer, Cham (2017). https://doi.org/10.1007/978-3-319-66182-7_79
16. Zhu, W., et al.: AnatomyNet: deep learning for fast and fully automated whole-volume segmentation of head and neck anatomy. Med. Phys. **46**(2), 576–589 (2019)

# Lesion Detection by Efficiently Bridging 3D Context

Zhishuai Zhang[1]([✉]), Yuyin Zhou[1], Wei Shen[1], Elliot Fishman[2],
and Alan Yuille[1]

[1] The Johns Hopkins University, Baltimore, MD 21218, USA
zhshuai.zhang@gmail.com
[2] The Johns Hopkins University School of Medicine, Baltimore, MD 21287, USA

**Abstract.** Lesion detection in CT (computed tomography) scan images
is an important yet challenging task due to the low contrast of soft tissues
and similar appearance between lesion and the background. Exploiting
3D context information has been studied extensively to improve detection accuracy. However, previous methods either use a 3D CNN which
usually requires a sliding window strategy to inference and only acts on
local patches; or simply concatenate feature maps of independent 2D
CNNs to obtain 3D context information, which is less effective to capture 3D knowledge. To address these issues, we design a hybrid detector
to combine benefits from both of the above methods. We propose to
build several light-weighted 3D CNNs as subnets to bridge 2D CNNs'
intermediate features, so that 2D CNNs are connected with each other
which interchange 3D context information while feed-forwarding. Comprehensive experiments in DeepLesion dataset show that our method can
combine 3D knowledge effectively and provide higher quality backbone
features. Our detector surpasses the current state-of-the-art by a large
margin with comparable speed and GPU memory consumption.

## 1 Introduction

Lesion detection is an essential task for clinical applications such as computer-
aided diagnosis. With the emergence of modern CNNs, object detection in
2D natural images has been developed quickly and achieves promising performance [1,5–7]. However, it is still unclear how to adapt these algorithms into
CT scans effectively. The main gap is how to efficiently involve 3D context information into these detectors. This problem has attracted many research attentions [2,4,10], due to its importance for the success of lesion detection.

Current solutions come in two folds. One uses fully 3D connected CNNs,
which can directly exploit 3D knowledge, for detection and classification. However, due to GPU memory limit, it can only be performed on small patches in
a sliding-window fashion [4] or on small-patch candidates generated by a 2D
detector [2], leading to high time complexity. It is also unable to make use of
ImageNet pretraining, thus only achieves inferior lesion detection accuracy as

© Springer Nature Switzerland AG 2019
H.-I. Suk et al. (Eds.): MLMI 2019, LNCS 11861, pp. 470–478, 2019.
https://doi.org/10.1007/978-3-030-32692-0_54

reported in [10]. To alleviate the issues of 3D CNNs, other studies are exploring how to combine 2D CNN features from consecutive CT slices for classification and regression, so as to better utilize the 3D context information. [10] followed R-FCN [1] which used a Region Proposal Network (RPN) to predict suspicious regions and a Region Classification Network (RCN) to further classify and regress those suspicious regions. [10] proposed to concatenate backbone feature maps from neighboring CT slices to feed into RCN, in order to gather 3D information in the RCN subnet. Under this pipeline, a backbone network can take the whole CT scans as input which can be trained in an end-to-end manner, from ImageNet pretrained weights. However, the backbone networks are still independent 2D CNNs, and no 3D information can be aggregated until the final backbone features are computed. Another problem is that the central CT slice and the contextual CT slices share the same 2D CNN weights, which may be less optimal since we expect to distill different and complementary knowledge from those different slices.

We propose a hybrid detector combining advantages of fully 3D connected CNN detectors (strong knowledge of 3D context) [2,4] and 2D CNN concatenated detectors (efficiency and ability to use ImageNet pretrained weights) [10]. Similar to [10], we use 2D CNNs for CT slices at different axial locations as our backbone. However, as discussed before, this is less optimal since these isolated 2D CNNs cannot extract and exploit 3D context information. To address this problem, we propose light-weighted 3D CNN subnets named 3D Fusion Modules (3DFMs) to bridge those 2D CNNs, allowing information flow from different slices. These subnets connect the internal layers of 2D CNNs, so that each 2D CNN can distill knowledge from its neighbor 2D CNNs, to exploit 3D information and focus on different knowledge. The main difference between [10] and our method is that in [10], the 3D context information is not exploited in the layers before the RCN, and the RCN cannot fully utilize 3D context since the its input features only have high-level semantics without low-level details, and the RCN has a very shallow structure which is incapable of learning rich 3D information; on the contrary, in our method, the 3D information is exploited gradually throughout our backbone CNNs, and 3DFMs learn 3D information at low-level, mid-level and high-level layers. Our design breaks the isolation among 2D CNNs, and enables them to distill different knowledge from different input slices, thus the backbone provides stronger features with richer 3D context encoded.

3DFMs introduce few parameters and small computation overhead, while greatly improving the detection accuracy. Experiments on DeepLesion [11] show our hybrid detector significantly improves the sensitivities at every false positive (FP) rate and on every lesion type. With 27 CT scan slices as input, hybrid detector improves the average sensitivities by 1.4 and the sensitivity at $\frac{1}{8}$ FP per image by 2.7. Our method surpasses [10] and achieves a new state-of-the-art.

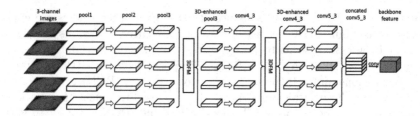

**Fig. 1.** Backbone of our hybrid lesion detector. Different rows illustrate different 2D CNNs for the corresponding images. The ground-truth boxes are labelled in the central image (with red boundary) and other 3-channel images (with yellow boundary) are served as 3D context. The central `conv5_3` feature (marked in green) is used in RPN and the fused feature (marked in blue) is used in RCN. Best view in color. (Color figure online)

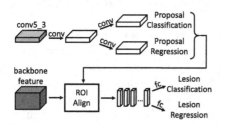

**Fig. 2.** RPN (in the top row) and RCN (in the bottom row) sub-networks.

**Fig. 3.** 3D Fusion Module. $K$ is 5 in this example. See Subsect. 2.2 for details.

## 2 Approach

### 2.1 Overview Pipeline of Our Detector

The backbone of our detector is shown in Fig. 1. Following [10], to make use of ImageNet pretrained weights, we combine 3 adjacent CT slices into a 3-channel image like a natural image, to feed to VGG16 [9], which serves as the backbone 2D CNN of our detector. When considering more 3D context, we combine context slices into 3-channel images and feed them to different VGG16 branches. Each VGG16 branch takes a 3-channel image as input, and generates a `conv5_3` feature map as output. The `conv5_3` feature from the central slice (marked in green) is used in the Region Proposal Network (RPN) to generate proposals, and the concatenation of `conv5_3` features from all slices (marked in blue) is used in the Region Classification Network (RCN) to classify and regress proposals. However, unlike [10], where 2D CNNs feed-forward isolatedly, we use a novel and efficient 3D Fusion Module (3DFM) to bridge internal features from different 2D CNNs to build a hybrid backbone. The hybrid detector backbone can better exploit 3D context and make different 2D CNNs to learn different patterns, while utilizing ImageNet pretrained weights. Details of 3DFM are discussed in Subsect 2.2.

Given the backbone of our hybrid lesion detector, we follow [7] to employ an RPN and an RCN to generate and classify proposals. As Fig. 2 shows, we use the conv5_3 feature of the central branch (marked in green) to generate proposals, and use ROIAlign [3] to generate features from the concatenated feature of different branches (marked in blue), for each proposal. Finally, those features are used to classify and regress the proposals, and generate lesion detection results.

## 2.2 3D Fusion Module

3D context has been shown to be extremely important to detect objects in CT scan images [2,4,10]. However, existing methods to utilize 3D information are either memory expensive and only able to process small 3D patches, or inefficient which naively concatenate features from different slices. In this paper, we propose an efficient and computation cheap 3D Fusion Module (3DFM), as shown in Fig. 3, to combine 3D context information in the backbone 2D CNNs.

3DFM takes internal features ($A_i \in \mathbb{R}^{C \times H \times W}$, $C$, $H$ and $W$ are the channel, height and width of the feature map) from the backbone CNNs as inputs, as shown in the first column in Fig. 3. Given $K$ input images, there will be $K$ intermediate features, and each of them is generated from a 3-channel CT image as shown in Fig. 1. We first concatenate them to build a 4D tensor $\mathbf{A} \in \mathbb{R}^{K \times C \times H \times W}$, and transpose it make the channel to be the first dimension ($\mathbf{B} \in \mathbb{R}^{C \times K \times H \times W}$), as shown in the second column in Fig. 3. A 3D convolution is used to gather 3D context information to generate a 3D fused feature map $\mathbf{C} \in \mathbb{R}^{C \times K \times H \times W}$. The kernel size is $3 \times 1 \times 1$ corresponding to the $K$, $H$ and $W$ dimensions, so we are utilizing the context along the axial direction by convolving across neighbor slices. We use $3 \times 1 \times 1$ instead of $3 \times 3 \times 3$ because the context along the other two directions is already considered in the 2D convolutions in the backbone CNN, and thus we only need to consider the axial direction to reduce computation/memory overhead. Finally $\mathbf{C}$ is transposed backed to $K \times C \times H \times W$ as $\mathbf{D}$, and the sum of $\mathbf{A}$ and $\mathbf{D}$ (noted as $\mathbf{E}$) is split to K feature maps with shape $C \times H \times W$, which are used in the backbone 2D CNNs for future processing.

3DFM is flexible and can be inserted anywhere in the backbone CNNs to fuse the 3D information. In our detector, we insert 3DFMs in a sparse manner: only at the pool3 and conv4_3 layers in VGG16, as in Fig. 1. These 3DFMs will combine those independent 2D VGG16 branches into a sparsely bridged 3D CNN, which will serve as the backbone CNN of our detector. Extensive experiments show our design is light-weighted and takes very little computation/memory overhead, while effectively exploiting 3D context knowledge and improving the accuracy significantly.

## 3 Experiments

### 3.1 Implementation Details

Our hybrid detector is implemented with Tensorflow. We use VGG16 as our backbone CNN, and remove the pool4 layer to keep the output resolution to be

**Table 1.** Performance (%) on the official `test` split for DeepLesion dataset. $0.125, 0.25, \cdots, 16$ represent the number of FPs per image.

| Settings | 0.125 | 0.25 | 0.5 | 1 | 2 | 4 | 8 | 16 | AVG@$\frac{1}{8}$:8 |
|---|---|---|---|---|---|---|---|---|---|
| Baseline - 3 slices | 31.52 | 43.95 | 57.19 | 68.51 | 77.47 | 83.59 | 87.77 | 90.66 | 64.28 |
| 3DCE [10] - 9 slices | - | - | 59.32 | 70.68 | 79.09 | 84.34 | 87.81 | 89.62 | - |
| Baseline - 9 slices | 35.48 | 48.84 | 62.42 | 73.06 | 80.73 | 85.82 | 89.22 | 91.21 | 67.94 |
| Hybrid - 9 slices | 38.25 | 50.66 | 62.97 | 73.20 | 80.66 | 85.80 | 89.04 | 91.21 | 68.65 |
| Baseline - 15 slices | 37.53 | 51.23 | 63.97 | 74.53 | 81.39 | 86.15 | 89.37 | 91.28 | 69.17 |
| Hybrid - 15 slices | 40.33 | 53.01 | 65.26 | 75.78 | 82.44 | 86.84 | 89.76 | **91.69** | 70.49 |
| Baseline - 21 slices | 38.81 | 52.32 | 64.93 | 75.25 | 82.19 | 86.61 | 89.44 | 91.25 | 69.93 |
| Hybrid - 21 slices | 40.74 | 53.80 | 66.06 | 75.66 | 82.60 | 86.88 | 89.79 | 91.62 | 70.79 |
| 3DCE [10] - 27 slices | - | - | 62.48 | 73.37 | 80.70 | 85.65 | 89.09 | 91.06 | - |
| Baseline - 27 slices | 38.43 | 52.09 | 65.03 | 75.10 | 81.88 | 86.05 | 89.10 | 91.05 | 69.67 |
| Hybrid - 27 slices | **41.12** | **53.83** | **66.32** | **76.27** | **82.89** | **87.01** | **89.84** | 91.69 | **71.04** |

$\frac{1}{8}$ of the input image. We take the same CT scan image preprocessing as in [10], which rescales the CT intensity to 0–255, resizes the images and clips the black border. We use the horizontal flip data augmentation which is very common for object detection. For each sample, we take adjacent 3, 9, 15, 21 or 27 CT slices to generate 1, 3, 5, 7 or 9 input images with 3 channels each, to evaluate the efficacy of hybrid detector at different 3D context richness levels, and to make a fair comparison with the state-of-the-art 3DCE [10]. For the training, we use a batch size of 2, and train the hybrid detector for 120k iterations. The initial learning rate is $10^{-3}$ and is reduced to $10^{-4}$ after the first 90k iterations. We take the official `train`/`test` subsets to train and report accuracy. Comprehensive experiments and ablation studies are reported in the following subsections.

## 3.2  Experimental Results

To evaluate the efficacy of our method, we conduct extensive experiments on DeepLesion [11]. Following the metric used in LUNA challenge [8], we compute the sensitivity at 7 pre-defined false positive (FP) per image rates: $\frac{1}{8}$, $\frac{1}{4}$, $\frac{1}{2}$, 1, 2, 4 and 8 FPs per sample, as well as the average sensitivity at these 7 pre-defined FP rates. We also compute the sensitivity at the FP per image rate of 16, to compare with the 3DCE [10]. For all our baselines and hybrid detectors, we train and evaluate for four times, and report the average performance, to alleviate the randomness caused by initialization and training data shuffling.

The results on the official `test` set are shown in Table 1. We also compare with 3DCE which is the current state-of-the-art and already surpasses fully 3D connected detectors. 'Baseline' in the table is a Faster-RCNN [7] based detector with feature concatenation after the backbone CNN, and 'Hybrid' is 'Baseline' equipped with 3DFMs illustrated in Fig. 3. We also plot the free-response receiver operating characteristic curves for our baseline and hybrid detectors in Fig. 4. In the table and figure, we find that our hybrid detector with 3DFM is very effective in improving the detection quality. The sensitivity consistently goes up at all FP rate levels significantly with 27 slices as input, especially in the high precision case (*i.e.* fewer FPs per image). Our hybrid detector surpasses 3DCE greatly with the same `train/test` sets and achieves a new state-of-the-art.

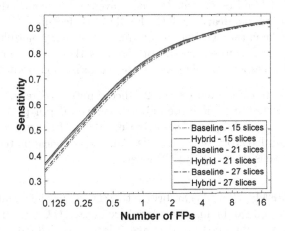

**Fig. 4.** FROCs of Baseline and Baseline+3DFM (Hybrid). Best view in color. (Color figure online)

**Table 2.** Performance on the official `test` split for DeepLesion dataset.

| Settings | AVG@$\frac{1}{8}$:8 | Runtime (s) | FPS | Inference GPU memory (GB) |
|---|---|---|---|---|
| Baseline - 9 slices | 67.94 | 246 | 19.58 | 0.455 |
| Hybrid - 9 slices | 68.65 | 256 | 18.82 | 0.459 |
| Baseline - 15 slices | 69.17 | 345 | 13.96 | 0.693 |
| Hybrid - 15 slices | 70.49 | 369 | 13.05 | 0.696 |
| Baseline - 21 slices | 69.93 | 452 | 10.66 | 0.930 |
| Hybrid - 21 slices | 70.79 | 479 | 10.06 | 0.934 |
| Baseline - 27 slices | 69.67 | 564 | 8.54 | 1.167 |
| Hybrid - 27 slices | 71.04 | 608 | 7.92 | 1.171 |

### 3.3   Ablation Studies

**Inference Speed and Memory Overhead.** Our 3D Fusion Modules (3DFM) efficiently combine 3D context information in the backbone. To quantitatively evaluate the computation/memory overhead, we run all our baselines and detectors on a machine with a single nVIDIA Titan Xp GPU. We report the total runtime for the official `test` set (4817 samples) and the max GPU memory consumed for inference. Results are shown in Table 2. Our 3DFMs introduce very small computation overhead and negligible GPU memory overhead. This verifies the efficiency of our method, which may be applied to more complex datasets.

**Architecture of 3DFM.** In this subsection, we compare our 3D Fusion Module with some other potential architectures combining 3D context information:

- Without Skip Connection: the 3D context information bridging module is the same as 3DFM (see Fig. 3), but does not have the skip connection to combine the original backbone features with the 3D fused features.
- Without 3D Conv: the 3D context information bridging module concatenates the $K$ backbone features with size of $C \times H \times W$ to a thicker tensor $KC \times H \times W$, and takes a $1 \times 1$ 2D Conv to fuse information from different slices.

All experiments are conducted on the 27-slice inputs, and results are shown in Table 3. Both architectures described above achieve inferior performance: without skip connection, it has lower sensitivities at high FP levels even compared with our baseline detector; and using 2D Conv on a concatenated feature map leads to inferior sensitivities at all FP levels.

**Number of 3DFMs.** 3DFMs can bridge the 3D context information in the 2D CNN backbones, and can be inserted anywhere in the 2D CNNs. In our detector, we insert 3DFMs at the `pool3` and `conv4_3` layers in VGG16 as in Fig. 1. We also conduct diagnostic experiments by 1) inserting 3DFM at only `conv4_3` layer and 2) inserting 3DFMs at `pool2`, `pool3` and `conv4_3` layers. Results are shown in '3DFM@4' and '3DFM@234' of Table 3. Compared with '3DFM@4', adding another 3DFM at `pool3` significantly improve the performance from 70.62 to 71.04. However, adding an extra 3DFM at `pool2` will only give a marginal performance gain. For simplicity, we use only two 3DFMs in our final detector.

**Table 3.** Ablation of 3DFM architecture.

| Setting | 0.125 | 0.25 | 0.5 | 1 | 2 | 4 | 8 | 16 | AVG@$\frac{1}{8}$:8 |
|---|---|---|---|---|---|---|---|---|---|
| Baseline | 38.43 | 52.09 | 65.03 | 75.10 | 81.88 | 86.06 | 89.10 | 91.05 | 69.67 |
| Hybrid (Ours) | 41.12 | 53.83 | 66.32 | 76.27 | 82.89 | 87.01 | 89.84 | 91.69 | 71.04 |
| W/O Skip Connection | 42.10 | 54.22 | 66.29 | 75.15 | 81.79 | 86.11 | 88.93 | 90.78 | 70.66 |
| W/O 3D Conv | 39.96 | 53.46 | 65.66 | 75.36 | 81.96 | 86.72 | 89.71 | 91.56 | 70.40 |
| 3DFM@4 | 40.56 | 53.37 | 65.62 | 75.91 | 82.49 | 86.77 | 89.56 | 91.57 | 70.62 |
| 3DFM@234 | 40.87 | 54.27 | 66.45 | 76.35 | 82.90 | 87.18 | 90.15 | 92.00 | 71.17 |

**Table 4.** Sensitivities of different types of lesion at 4 false positive per image. Our detector outperforms baseline on all 8 types.

| Type | BN | AB | ME | LV | LU | KD | ST | PV |
|---|---|---|---|---|---|---|---|---|
| Baseline | 72.69 | 84.07 | 87.27 | 90.04 | 89.70 | 85.73 | 76.99 | 83.50 |
| Hybrid (Ours) | **73.84** | **84.63** | **88.43** | **91.14** | **90.50** | **86.16** | **77.91** | **85.64** |

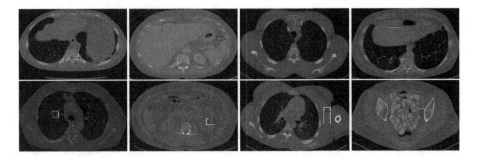

**Fig. 5.** Detection examples of eight types. Yellow and blue boxes are for ground-truth and detection result. All examples are detected by our hybrid detector while missed by our baseline detector. (Color figure online)

### 3.4 Analysis on Different Lesion Types

We test our hybrid detector on different lesion types in DeepLesion [11]. There are 8 types of lesion labelled in the dataset, and the abbreviations are in the parentheses: bone (BN), abdomen (AB), mediastinum (ME), liver (LV), lung (LU), kidney (KD), soft tissue (ST) and pelvis (PV). In Table 4, we evaluate the sensitivities of our baseline detector and our hybrid detector equipped with 3DFM, at 4 FPs per image (27 slices). The results further confirms that our hybrid detector can improve the detection quality under all 8 lesion types, thus it is very general with consistent gains. We also show some qualitative results in Fig. 5, where our baseline detector fails to detect the lesion, but the 3DFM equipped hybrid detector detects them with scores greater than 0.9 at 4 FP per image threshold. We observe that our detector is able to find difficult lesions such as small or low-contrast lesions.

## 4  Conclusions

We propose a hybrid detector which bridges 3D context information in 2D CNN backbones. Based on a baseline detector which takes adjacent CT scan images independently with the same 2D CNN, we enhance the backbone feature quality by fusing 3D context knowledge via 3DFMs. Extensive experiments have been conducted to show the efficacy of our hybrid detector, which improves the sensitivity at all false positive levels. The improvement is consistent under different settings (*e.g.*, number of input slices and lesion types). Qualitative analysis also suggests that our method outperforms the baseline method and remains valid even for some extremely difficult cases. Our approach surpasses existing methods and thus establishes a new state-of-the-art. The superior performance demonstrates its potential usage for different clinical applications.

**Acknowledgements.** This work was supported by the Lustgarten Foundation for Pancreatic Cancer Research and NSFC No. 61672336.

# References

1. Dai, J., Li, Y., He, K., Sun, J.: R-FCN: object detection via region-based fully convolutional networks. In: NIPS, pp. 379–387 (2016)
2. Ding, J., Li, A., Hu, Z., Wang, L.: Accurate pulmonary nodule detection in computed tomography images using deep convolutional neural networks. In: Descoteaux, M., Maier-Hein, L., Franz, A., Jannin, P., Collins, D.L., Duchesne, S. (eds.) MICCAI 2017. LNCS, vol. 10435, pp. 559–567. Springer, Cham (2017). https://doi.org/10.1007/978-3-319-66179-7_64
3. He, K., Gkioxari, G., Dollár, P., Girshick, R.: Mask R-CNN. In: ICCV, pp. 2961–2969 (2017)
4. Liao, F., Liang, M., Li, Z., Hu, X., Song, S.: Evaluate the malignancy of pulmonary nodules using the 3D deep leaky noisy-or network. arXiv preprint arXiv:1711.08324 (2017)
5. Liu, W., Anguelov, D., Erhan, D., Szegedy, C., Reed, S., Fu, C.-Y., Berg, A.C.: SSD: single shot multibox detector. In: Leibe, B., Matas, J., Sebe, N., Welling, M. (eds.) ECCV 2016. LNCS, vol. 9905, pp. 21–37. Springer, Cham (2016). https://doi.org/10.1007/978-3-319-46448-0_2
6. Redmon, J., Divvala, S., Girshick, R., Farhadi, A.: You only look once: unified, real-time object detection. In: CVPR, pp. 779–788 (2016)
7. Ren, S., He, K., Girshick, R., Sun, J.: Faster R-CNN: towards real-time object detection with region proposal networks. In: NIPS, pp. 91–99 (2015)
8. Setio, A.A.A., et al.: Validation, comparison, and combination of algorithms for automatic detection of pulmonary nodules in computed tomography images: the luna16 challenge. Med. Image Anal. 42, 1–13 (2017)
9. Simonyan, K., Zisserman, A.: Very deep convolutional networks for large-scale image recognition. arXiv preprint arXiv:1409.1556 (2014)
10. Yan, K., Bagheri, M., Summers, R.M.: 3D context enhanced region-based convolutional neural network for end-to-end lesion detection. In: Frangi, A.F., Schnabel, J.A., Davatzikos, C., Alberola-López, C., Fichtinger, G. (eds.) MICCAI 2018. LNCS, vol. 11070, pp. 511–519. Springer, Cham (2018). https://doi.org/10.1007/978-3-030-00928-1_58
11. Yan, K., et al.: Deep lesion graphs in the wild: relationship learning and organization of significant radiology image findings in a diverse large-scale lesion database. In: CVPR, pp. 9261–9270 (2018)

# Communal Domain Learning for Registration in Drifted Image Spaces

Awais Mansoor[1,2](✉) and Marius George Linguraru[1]

[1] The Sheikh Zayed Institute for Pediatric Surgical Innovation,
Children's National Health System, Washington DC, USA
awais.mansoor@gmail.com
[2] Digital Technology and Innovation, Siemens Healthineers, Princeton, NJ, USA

**Abstract.** Designing a registration framework for images that do not share the same probability distribution is a major challenge in modern image analytics yet trivial task for the human visual system (HVS). Discrepancies in probability distributions, also known as *drifts*, can occur due to various reasons including, but not limited to differences in sequences and modalities (e.g., MRI T1-T2 and MRI-CT registration), or acquisition settings (e.g., multisite, inter-subject, or intra-subject registrations). The popular assumption about the working of HVS is that it exploits a communal feature subspace exists between the registering images or fields-of-view that encompasses key drift-invariant features. Mimicking the approach that is potentially adopted by the HVS, herein, we present a representation learning technique of this invariant communal subspace that is shared by registering domains. The proposed communal domain learning (CDL) framework uses a set of hierarchical nonlinear transforms to learn the communal subspace that minimizes the probability differences and maximizes the amount of shared information between the registering domains. Similarity metric and parameter optimization calculations for registration are subsequently performed in the drift-minimized learned communal subspace. This generic registration framework is applied to register multisequence (MR: T1, T2) and multimodal (MR, CT) images. Results demonstrated generic applicability, consistent performance, and statistically significant improvement for both multi-sequence and multi-modal data using the proposed approach ($p$-value$< 0.001$; Wilcoxon rank sum test) over baseline methods.

**Keywords:** Image registration · Multimodal images · Multisequence images · Domain adaptation

## 1 Introduction

Image registration is a fundamental operation in image-based analytics involving fusion of information, quantitative comparison, or spatial normalization. A

**Electronic supplementary material** The online version of this chapter (https:// doi.org/10.1007/978-3-030-32692-0_55) contains supplementary material, which is available to authorized users.

H.-I. Suk et al. (Eds.): MLMI 2019, LNCS 11861, pp. 479–488, 2019.
https://doi.org/10.1007/978-3-030-32692-0_55

typical registration pipeline consists of the following three major components. A **transformation model** $(\mathbf{T}_\mu)$ that defines the geometric relationship between the registering images. Depending upon the parameter vector $\mu$, the transformation model can be rigid, affine, or nonrigid (deformable). A **similarity metric or cost function** (C) measuring the degree of alignment between the $d$-dimensional image belonging to the target domain $(\mathbf{x}_t \in \mathbb{R}^d)$ and the transformed image belonging to the source domain $(\mathbf{T}_\mu \mathbf{x}_s \in \mathbb{R}^d)$. The source and the target domains can be identical or different. Then an **optimizer** iteratively improves $\mu$ based on C. Specifically, at a $k^{\text{th}}$ iteration, the current vector $\mu_k$ is updated by taking a step in the search direction $\mathbf{d}_k \mu_{k+1} = \mu_k - a_k \mathbf{d}_k$, where $a_k$ is the scalar step size. A typical registration task involves finding the optimal transformation parameters that maximizes the degree of similarity across the registering images: $\hat{\mu} = \arg \max_\mu \mathrm{C}\left(\mathbf{T}_\mu \mathbf{x}_s, \mathbf{x}_t\right)$.

**State-of-the-Art Methods.** The registration of images belonging to domains with substantial discrepancy, also known as *drift*, remains challenging. Drift in medical images generally occurs due to changes in either the field-of-view (e.g., 2D-3D), modalities or sequences (e.g., CT-MRI, T1-T2 MRI), or acquisition settings (e.g., data acquired with different protocols). Typical approaches to handle drifts use either information theoretic similarity metrics such as mutual information or normalized cross correlation that maximize the transferability of knowledge between domains [1]. In addition, significant research effort has been invested in devising methods for the effective representations of registering domains, more recently using the deep learning approaches [2–4]. These representation transformation approaches known as *domain adaptation* or *transfer learning* methods range from simplistic techniques such as intensity standardization to more sophisticated feature mapping approaches [5]. Commonly used domain adaptation methods estimate a representation transformation of one registering domain to imitate the second one as accurately as possible. The principal hypothesis behind these approaches is that by reducing the drift that exists between the two images through transformation, the task of the similarity metric can be made easier, thus resulting in a more accurate registration. However, depending upon the extent of drift, the predictability of one domain from another can be very limited even theoretically[1] which is the major bottleneck in the performance of these methods.

**Our Contributions.** The human visual system (HVS) is able to recognize objects despite tremendous variation in their appearance resulting from variation in view, size, lighting, etc. This ability known as "invariant" object recognitions central to visual perception, yet its computational underpinnings are not well understood. One prominent theory behind the cognitive neuroscience of visual object recognition suggests that a drift invariant communal space could be created by the HVS instead of mapping information between spaces [6].

---

[1] For maximum mutual information and therefore perfect predictability:

$$I(\mathbf{x}_s; \mathbf{x}_t) = H(\mathbf{x}_s) - \cancelto{0}{H(\mathbf{x}_s|\mathbf{x}_t)} = H(\mathbf{x}_t) - \cancelto{0}{H(\mathbf{x}_t|\mathbf{x}_s)},$$ where $I$ and $H$ denotes mutual information and entropy respectively.

Mimicking the HVS, instead of learning to imitate one domain from another through domain adaptation, in this work, we propose learning the communal feature subspace between domains. As demonstrated in the next section, a communal subspace $\mathbb{W}$ between registering domains that captures images with the same field-of-view can be guaranteed to exist, at least theoretically. Our paper introduces an approach to estimate $\mathbb{W}$ using training instances from the registering domains, what we call communal domain learning (CDL). Specifically, CDL estimates the $\mathbb{W}$ between source and target domains that consecutively: (I) maximizes the amount of shared information between the source and the target domains; and (II) minimizes the probability differences between the two domains. Subsequently, the similarity metric and transform parameters for the registration are performed in the estimated communal subspace $\widehat{\mathbb{W}}$. We demonstrated the efficacy of the generically applicable CDL on the registration of multisequence (MR: T1, T2) and multimodal (MR, CT) brain images.

## 2  Methods

The flow diagram of the proposed registration framework is presented in Fig. 1. The core of the framework is the CDL network: a multi-layered fully connected neural network. CDL learns the communal domain $\mathbb{W}$ between source and target domains through a set of hierarchical nonlinear transformations. During training, CDL takes as input perfectly aligned (through manual inspection, details are explained in the Experiments section) pairs of source and target instances (i.e., $\mathbf{T}_\mu = \mathbb{1}$). Let $\mathbf{x} = \{(\mathbf{x}_{s_i}, \mathbf{x}_{t_i}) | i = 1, \ldots, N\}$ be the scalar-valued training pair and $N$ is the total number of training tensor pairs. There are $M + 1$ layers in the CDL network and $p^{(m)}$ denotes the number of units in the $m^{\text{th}}$ layer. The output of the network at the $m^{\text{th}}$ layer is:

$$\mathbf{h}^{(m)} = \phi\left(\mathbf{W}^{(m)}\mathbf{h}^{(m-1)} + \mathbf{b}^{(m)}\right) = \phi\left(\mathbf{z}^{(m)}\right), \tag{1}$$

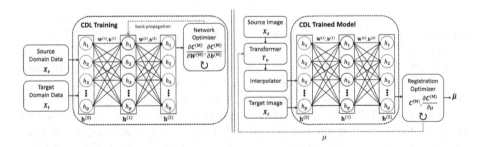

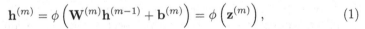

**Fig. 1.** The proposed registration framework with communal domain learning (CDL) network. (*Left*) The CDL network training module. The input to the network are aligned source and target image pairs, output is the learned network parameters $\mathbf{W}^{(m)}$ and $\mathbf{b}^{(m)}$, $1 \le m \le 2$. (*Right*) The proposed registration framework using the trained CDL network for similarity calculation of registration hypothesis.

where $\mathbf{W}^{(m)} \in \mathbb{R}^{p^{(m)} \times p^{(m-1)}}$ is the weight matrix and $\mathbf{b}^{(m)} \in \mathbb{R}^{p^{(m)}}$ is the bias vector for the $m^{\text{th}}$ layer. $\phi$ is the nonlinear activation function and $\mathbf{h}^{(m)}$ : $\mathbb{R}^{p^{(m-1)}} \rightarrow \mathbb{R}^{p^{(m)}}$ is the nonlinear mapping defined over the Hilbert space $\Omega_{\mathbf{h}^{(m)}}$. For the first layer, $\mathbf{h}^{(0)} = \mathbf{x}$ and $p^{(0)} = d$. $d = 3$ for volumetric images.

## 2.1    Communal Domain Learning

**Proposition 1.** *For sets $\mathbf{x}_s$ and $\mathbf{x}_t$ defined over two separate vector domains $\mathbb{V}_s$ and $\mathbb{V}_t$, respectively, then $\exists \mathbb{W} : \mathbb{W} \subseteq \mathbb{V}_s$ and $\mathbb{W} \subseteq \mathbb{V}_t$ if and only if $\mathbb{V}_s \not\perp \mathbb{V}_t$, where $\mathbb{W}$ is a non-empty subset of vector domains $\mathbb{V}_s$ and $\mathbb{V}_t$.*

In other words, Proposition 1. suggests that as long as the two domains ($\mathbb{V}_s$ and $\mathbb{V}_t$) are imaging the same field-of-view, a communal domain ($\mathbb{W}$) possessing drift invariant features can be theoretically guaranteed to exist between them. To learn the communal domain $\mathbb{W}$, it is desired to adjust the CDL network parameters ($\theta = \{\mathbf{W}, \mathbf{b}\}$) that satisfy the constraints I and II, described in the previous section, at the output of the network. Henceforth, the cost function C at the top layer, $M$, is formulated as the following optimization problem:

$$\max_{\mathbf{h}^{(M)}} \mathrm{C}\left(\mathbf{h}_t^{(M)}, \mathbf{h}_s^{(M)}\right) = I(\mathbf{h}_t^{(M)}; \mathbf{h}_s^{(M)}) - \alpha D(\mathbf{h}_t^{(M)}, \mathbf{h}_s^{(M)}) - \beta \sum_{m=1}^{M}(\|\mathbf{W}^{(m)}\|_F^2 + \|\mathbf{b}^{(m)}\|_2^2), \quad (2)$$

where $\alpha > 0$ and $\beta > 0$ are the regularization parameters, $I(\mathbf{h}_t^{(m)}; \mathbf{h}_s^{(m)})$ and $D(\mathbf{h}_t^{(m)}, \mathbf{h}_s^{(m)})$ denote the mutual information and the distribution difference distance at the $m^{\text{th}}$ layer respectively. $\|\mathbf{Z}\|_F$ is the Frobenius norm of the matrix $\mathbf{Z}$. The typical cost function for registration ($\hat{\mu} = \arg \max_\mu \mathrm{C}\left(\mathbf{T}_\mu \mathbf{x}_s, \mathbf{x}_t\right)$) and (2) are equivalent owing to the way the registration framework is set up Fig. 1. The *back-propagation* algorithm for training the neural network requires computing the derivatives of (2) with respect to network parameters $\theta$ while the registration optimizer requires the derivative with respect to transformation model parameters $\mu$.

**Mutual Information.** Empirical determination of $I(\mathbf{h}_t^{(M)}; \mathbf{h}_s^{(M)})$ in (2) requires the estimation of the joint and marginal distributions of the source and target domains. Methods such as the *Parzen*-window [5] are generally used; however, these window-based methods are computationally complex. Instead, we used a parametric modeling approach in CDL. Specifically, Katyal et al. [7] demonstrated that the joint and marginal distributions of voxel intensities from multi-sequence/multi-modal MR/CT images that share the same field-of-view, is Gaussian distributed[2]. Moreover, through Taylor series expansion that the set of hierarchical transformations presented in Eq. (1) when applied to Gaussian data preserve its Gaussianity (proof is provided in the supplementary

---

[2] Optimal parametric models are expected to be dependent on source and target domains and is the topic of our future research.

material). Subsequently, for Gaussian distributed $\mathbf{h}_s^{(m)}$ and $\mathbf{h}_t^{(m)}$, their mutual information is a monotonic function of cross-correlation that is lower-bounded by: $I\left(\mathbf{h}_s^{(m)}; \mathbf{h}_t^{(m)}\right) \geq -\frac{1}{2}\left(1 - Corr(\mathbf{h}_t^{(m)}, \mathbf{h}_s^{(m)})\right)$. Equality in the equation is achieved, if joint Gaussianity is also assumed [8]. Henceforth,

$$I(\mathbf{h}_t^{(m)}, \mathbf{h}_s^{(m)}) = -\frac{1}{2}\left(1 - \frac{\sum_{i=1}^{N} \mathbf{h}_{ti}^{(m)} \mathbf{h}_{si}^{(m)}}{N\sigma_t^{(m)}\sigma_s^{(m)}} + \frac{\overline{\mathbf{h}_t^{(m)}} \cdot \overline{\mathbf{h}_s^{(m)}}}{\sigma_t^{(m)}\sigma_s^{(m)}}\right), \qquad (3)$$

where overbar indicates the expected value. $\sigma_s^{(m)}$ and $\sigma_t^{(m)}$ denote the standard deviation of source and target domain data, respectively. Subsequently, the gradients of mutual information with respect to network parameters $\mathbf{W}^{(m)}$ and $\mathbf{b}^{(m)}$ are computed as follows:

$$\frac{\partial}{\partial \mathbf{W}^{(m)}} I(\mathbf{h}_t^{(m)}, \mathbf{h}_s^{(m)}) = \left(N\sigma_{\mathbf{h}_t}^{(m)}\sigma_{\mathbf{h}_s}^{(m)}\right)^{-1} \sum_{i=1}^{N}\left(\mathbf{L}_{ti}^{(m)}\mathbf{h}_{ti}^{(m-1)} + \mathbf{L}_{si}^{(m)}\mathbf{h}_{si}^{(m-1)}\right), \qquad (4)$$

$$\frac{\partial}{\partial \mathbf{b}^{(m)}} I(\mathbf{h}_t^{(m)}, \mathbf{h}_s^{(m)}) = \left(N\sigma_{\mathbf{h}_t}^{(m)}\sigma_{\mathbf{h}_s}^{(m)}\right)^{-1} \sum_{i=1}^{N}\left(\mathbf{L}_{ti}^{(m)} + \mathbf{L}_{si}^{(m)}\right), \qquad (5)$$

The updating equations in (4) and (5) for back propagation are calculated as:

$$\begin{aligned}
\mathbf{L}_{ti}^{(M)} &= \phi'(\mathbf{z}_{ti}^{(M)}) \odot \phi(\mathbf{z}_{si}^{(M)}), & \mathbf{L}_{si}^{(M)} &= \phi'(\mathbf{z}_{si}^{(M)}) \odot \phi(\mathbf{z}_{ti}^{(M)}), \\
\mathbf{L}_{ti}^{(m)} &= \left(\mathbf{W}^{(m+1)^T}\mathbf{L}_{ti}^{(m+1)}\right), & \mathbf{L}_{si}^{(m)} &= \left(\mathbf{W}^{(m+1)^T}\mathbf{L}_{si}^{(m+1)}\right),
\end{aligned}$$

where $\odot$ denotes the element-wise multiplication.

**Distribution Difference.** To estimate the distribution differences between two domains, we apply the maximum mean discrepancy (MMD) criteria [9]. MMD is a statistical measure that estimates the dependence of two random variables. Henceforth, the distribution difference distance at the $m^{\text{th}}$ layer is defined as:

$$D\left(\mathbf{h}_t^{(m)}, \mathbf{h}_s^{(m)}\right) = \|\frac{1}{N}\sum_{i=1}^{N}\left(\mathbf{h}_{ti}^{(m)} - \mathbf{h}_{si}^{(m)}\right)\|_2^2. \qquad (6)$$

Similar to mutual information, the partial derivatives of $D\left(\mathbf{h}_t^{(m)}, \mathbf{h}_s^{(m)}\right)$ with respect to network parameters are:

$$\frac{\partial}{\partial \mathbf{W}^{(m)}} D\left(\mathbf{h}_t^{(m)}, \mathbf{h}_s^{(m)}\right) = \frac{2}{N}\sum_{i=1}^{N}(\mathbf{L}_{ti}^{(m)}\mathbf{h}_{ti}^{(m-1)^T} + \mathbf{L}_{si}^{(m)}\mathbf{h}_{si}^{(m-1)^T}), \qquad (7)$$

$$\frac{\partial}{\partial \mathbf{b}^{(m)}} D\left(\mathbf{h}_t^{(m)}, \mathbf{h}_s^{(m)}\right) = \frac{2}{N}\sum_{i=1}^{N}(\mathbf{L}_{ti}^{(m)} + \mathbf{L}_{si}^{(m)}), \qquad (8)$$

Please note that although the same symbols are used to denote losses as (4) and (5), they are defined differently below. Subsequently, the updating equations in (7) and (8) for the back propagation framework are:

$$\mathbf{L}_{ti}^{(M)} = \frac{1}{N} \sum_{j=1}^{N} \left( \mathbf{h}_{tj}^{(M)} - \mathbf{h}_{sj}^{(M)} \right) \odot \phi' \left( \mathbf{z}_{ti}^{(M)} \right), \qquad \mathbf{L}_{ti}^{(m)} = \left( \mathbf{W}^{(m+1)^T} \mathbf{L}_{ti}^{(m+1)} \right),$$

$$\mathbf{L}_{si}^{(M)} = \frac{1}{N} \sum_{j=1}^{N} \left( \mathbf{h}_{sj}^{(M)} - \mathbf{h}_{tj}^{(M)} \right) \odot \phi' \left( \mathbf{z}_{si}^{(M)} \right), \qquad \mathbf{L}_{si}^{(m)} = \left( \mathbf{W}^{(m+1)^T} \mathbf{L}_{si}^{(m+1)} \right).$$

Algorithm 1 summarizes the training of the CDL network (Fig. 1(*Left*)). The final form of the gradients of the cost function in (2) with respect to $\mathbf{W}^{(m)}$ and $\mathbf{b}^{(m)}$ are also provided in (9) and (10), respectively, in Algorithm 1.

---

**Algorithm 1.** Training of Communal Domain Learning (CDL) Network.

---

    **Input**   : Pair-wise training data ($\mathbf{x}$). Free parameters $\alpha$, $\beta$; learning rate $\lambda$; convergence error $\varepsilon$, and maximum number of iterations $K$.

    **Output:** Weights $\{\mathbf{W}^{(m)}\}_{m=1}^{M}$ and biases $\{\mathbf{b}^{(m)}\}_{m=1}^{M}$ after convergence.

 1  **for** $k = 1, \ldots, T$ **do**
 2     Perform forward-propagation;
 3     Compute mutual information (3) and maximum mean discrepancy (6);
 4     **for** $m = M-1, \ldots, 1$ **do**
 5         Calculate

$$\frac{\partial}{\partial \mathbf{W}^{(m)}} \mathcal{C} = -\frac{1}{2} \left( N \sigma_{\mathbf{h}_t}^{(m)} \sigma_{\mathbf{h}_s}^{(m)} \right)^{-1} \sum_{i=1}^{N} \left( \mathbf{L}_{ti}^{(m)} \mathbf{h}_{ti}^{(m-1)} + \mathbf{L}_{si}^{(m)} \mathbf{h}_{si}^{(m-1)} \right) - \frac{2\alpha}{N} \sum_{i=1}^{N} (\mathbf{L}_{ti}^{(m)} \mathbf{h}_{ti}^{(m-1)^T}$$
$$+ \mathbf{L}_{si}^{(m)} \mathbf{h}_{si}^{(m-1)^T}) - 2\beta \mathbf{W}^{(m)} \tag{9}$$

$$\frac{\partial}{\partial \mathbf{b}^{(m)}} \mathcal{C} = -\frac{1}{2} \left( N \sigma_{\mathbf{h}_t}^{(m)} \sigma_{\mathbf{h}_s}^{(m)} \right)^{-1} \sum_{i=1}^{N} \left( \mathbf{L}_{ti}^{(m)} + \mathbf{L}_{si}^{(m)} \right) - \frac{2\alpha}{N} \sum_{i=1}^{N} (\mathbf{L}_{ti}^{(m)} + \mathbf{L}_{si}^{(m)}) - 2\beta \mathbf{b}^{(m)} \tag{10}$$

        using back-propagation.
 6     **end**
 7     **for** $m = 1, \ldots, M$ **do**
 8         $\mathbf{W}^{(m)} \leftarrow \mathbf{W}^{(m)} - \lambda \frac{\partial}{\partial \mathbf{W}^{(m)}} \mathcal{C}$; // Iteratively update weights.
 9         $\mathbf{b}^{(m)} \leftarrow \mathbf{b}^{(m)} - \lambda \frac{\partial}{\partial \mathbf{b}^{(m)}} \mathcal{C}$; // Iteratively update biases.
10     **end**
11     $\lambda \leftarrow 0.95 \times \lambda$; // Reduce the learning rate.
12     Calculate $\mathcal{C}_k$;
13     **if** $(|\mathcal{C}_k - \mathcal{C}_{k-1}| < \varepsilon) \vee (k \geq K)$ **then**
14         **return** $\{\mathbf{W}^{(m)}\}_{m=1}^{M}$ and $\{\mathbf{b}^{(m)}\}_{m=1}^{M}$; // Network optimization.
15     **end**
16 **end**

---

## 2.2 Registration Parameter Estimation

The registration framework searches for the optimal transformation model parameters in the communal subset domain by performing a constrained hypothesis search within the valid parameter space [5]. Although several constrained hypothesis strategies have been adopted in the literature [5], the commonality is the expression for search direction $\mathbf{d}_k \propto \partial C / \partial \mu_k$. Therefore, differentiating C at the output of the network with respect to the parameter vector at the $k^{\text{th}}$ iteration yields the search direction:

$$\mathbf{d}_k = \mathbf{h}_t^{(M)} \phi'\left(\mathbf{z}_s^{(M)}\right) \mathbf{W}^{(M)} \frac{\partial}{\partial \mu_k} \mathbf{T}_\mu - 2\alpha \left(\mathbf{h}_t^{(M)} - \mathbf{h}_{s,\mu}^{(M)}\right) \phi'\left(\mathbf{z}_s^{(M)}\right) \mathbf{W}^{(M)} \frac{\partial}{\partial \mu_k} \mathbf{T}_\mu,$$
(11)

where $\mathbf{z}_s^{(m)} = \mathbf{W}^{(m)} \mathbf{h}_{s,\mu}^{(m-1)} + \mathbf{b}^{(m)}$. The optimization strategy ($\mu_{k+1} = \mu_k - a_k \mathbf{d}_k$) is subsequently used to iteratively estimate the parameter vector $\mu$ until convergence, i.e.,

$$\max_\mu C = I(\mathbf{h}_t^{(M)}; \mathbf{h}_{s,\mu}^{(M)}) - \alpha D(\mathbf{h}_t^{(M)}, \mathbf{h}_{s,\mu}^{(M)}) - \beta \sum_{m=1}^{M} (\|\mathbf{W}^{(m)}\|_F^2 + \|\mathbf{b}^{(m)}\|_2^2), \quad (12)$$

Since the transformed source image ($\mathbf{T}_\mu \mathbf{x}_s$) is also evaluated at non-voxel positions, $B$-spline interpolation to estimate values at voxel locations.

## 3 Experiments

**Data. [MRI]** We used publicly available T1-T2 volumes from IXI dataset (http://brain-development.org/ixi-dataset) for training. A total of 30 T1-T2 pairs from the dataset were used: 20 pairs for training and the rest for validation. The MIPAV application (https://mipav.cit.nih.gov) was used for adjustments in alignment followed by expert inspection for training. For testing, we used 53 T1-T2 pairs acquired at our institution. Spatial resolution in the test data ranges from $0.4\,\text{mm} \times 0.4\,\text{mm} \times 0.6\,\text{mm}$ for T1 and $0.43\,\text{mm} \times 0.43\,\text{mm} \times (1.2\,\text{mm}–4.0\,\text{mm})$ for T2.

**[CT].** A total of 20 MR (T1)-CT pairs were acquired for training and 12 for validation. Testing was performed on separate 10 pairs. Spatial resolution was $0.4\,\text{mm} \times 0.4\,\text{mm} \times 0.6\,\text{mm}$ for T1 scans and $0.48\,\text{mm} \times 0.48\,\text{mm} \times (0.62\,\text{mm}–4.0\,\text{mm})$ for CT.

**Baseline Method.** The baseline method used for comparison purposes is mutual information (MI), the standard metric for multimodal registration. MI-based registration tend to perform better when image domains are restricted to the object of interest [10]. Therefore, we used a fixed intensity threshold of 0.01 for masking the background; we denote this variant by MI+M. Furthermore, to restrict to the whole brain region, brain extraction tool (BET) [11] was used to obtain the whole brain mask; this variant is denoted by MI+B. Unfortunately, we could not compare our approach with other learning-based metrics [2–4,10] as their implementation was not available.

**Miscellaneous Implementation Details.** We used Theano with Keras wrapper, Nvidia Titan X GPU, CUDA 7.5, and CuDNN 4.0 for network training. Sigmoid activation, $\lambda = 0.2$, $\alpha = 0.1$, and $\beta = 10$ were used in CDL network. The registration pipeline for every framework consists of regular step gradient decent (max 500 iterations, step size $a_k = 0.2/k$). 75 histogram bins were adopted for MI, MI+M, and MI+B variants.

## 3.1  Performance

**Registration Accuracy.** Statistically significant improvement in the registration performance was observed for both multi-sequence and multi-modal data using the proposed approach ($p$-value$<$ 0.001; Wilcoxon rank sum test) (Table 1). Masking had negligible effect on the performance of the proposed method.

**Plausibility of Cost Function and Search Direction.** To investigate the gain of registering in the communal domain, we monitor the behavior of C and its

**Table 1.** Quantitative comparison (Dice score and Hausdorff distance-HD) of multisequence/multimodal affine registration. Please note that the boundaries of whole brain are not clearly imaged in CT hence results for whole brain are not listed for multi-sequence registration.

| | | | Mask | | | |
|---|---|---|---|---|---|---|
| | | | Background subtracted | | Whole brain | |
| | Method | | Dice score | HD (mm) | Dice score | HD (mm) |
| Multisequence | MI | None | 0.80 ± 0.05 | 122.41 ± 37.16 | 0.76 ± 0.54 | 87.41 ± 25.33 |
| | | MI+M | 0.86 ± 0.17 | 107.78 ± 29.21 | 0.80 ± 0.27 | 76.15 ± 18.91 |
| | | MI+B | N/A | N/A | 0.82 ± 0.21 | 58.11 ± 16.77 |
| Registration (T1-T2) | **Proposed** | None | **0.93 ± 0.18** | **91.77 ± 18.12** | **0.86 ± 0.19** | **55.95 ± 19.09** |
| Multimodal | MI | None | 0.83 ± 0.11 | 108.33 ± 11.21 | N/A | N/A |
| | | MI+M | 0.89 ± 0.21 | 98.79 ± 30.11 | N/A | N/A |
| Registration (T1-CT) | **Proposed** | None | **0.96 ± 0.26** | **82.21 ± 31.18** | N/A | N/A |

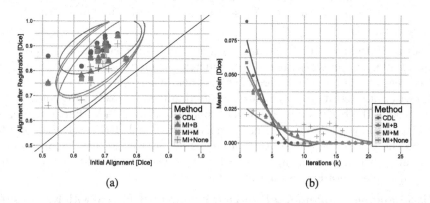

(a)                                           (b)

**Fig. 2.** Quantitative performance evaluation of our framework, (a) Dice score gain through registration for the validation data. Each data point represents a registration run; higher is the centroid of the cluster, the greater is the overall improvement. Diagonal line denotes the identity transform ($\mathbf{T}_\mu = \mathbb{1}$). (b) Mean gain in the Dice score per iteration.

derivative in determining the optimal search direction. We randomly perturbed a rotation parameter of the transformation for one image per pair using the 10 aligned validation pairs. Figure 2(a) presents the scatter plots of initial and final Dice scores for each registration pair. The scatter plot demonstrates superior performance of the proposed method for all registering pairs. Figure 2(b) shows the average gain in Dice score in each iteration. Along with Fig. 2(a), the plot also demonstrates faster convergence.

## 4  Conclusion

We introduced a framework for the registration of images that do not share the same probability distribution. Unlike the conventional approaches that aim at reducing the appearance gap between two domains, the proposed approach learns the communal subset domain. Our approach aims to emulates the human visual system for object recognition in the presence of substantial appearance variation. Unlike previous approaches that focus on addressing a specific aspect of registration through learning (e.g., similarity metric, optimization), our framework presents a complete registration pipeline based on learning. Experimental results have demonstrated higher registration accuracy and potential of generic applicability.

## References

1. Sotiras, A., Davatzikos, C., Paragios, N.: Deformable medical image registration: a survey. IEEE Trans. Med. Imaging **32**(7), 1153 (2013)
2. de Vos, B.D., Berendsen, F.F., Viergever, M.A., Sokooti, H., Staring, M., Išgum, I.: A deep learning framework for unsupervised affine and deformable image registration. Med. Image Anal. **52**, 128–143 (2019)
3. Cao, X., Yang, J., Wang, L., Xue, Z., Wang, Q., Shen, D.: Deep learning based inter-modality image registration supervised by intra-modality similarity. In: Shi, Y., Suk, H.-I., Liu, M. (eds.) MLMI 2018. LNCS, vol. 11046, pp. 55–63. Springer, Cham (2018). https://doi.org/10.1007/978-3-030-00919-9_7
4. Zheng, J., Miao, S., Wang, Z.J., Liao, R.: Pairwise domain adaptation module for cnn-based 2-D/3-D registration. J. Med. Imaging **5**(2), 021204 (2018)
5. Klein, S., Staring, M., Pluim, J.P.: Evaluation of optimization methods for nonrigid medical image registration using mutual information and B-splines. IEEE Trans. Image Process. **16**(12), 2879–2890 (2007)
6. Zoccolan, D., Oertelt, N., DiCarlo, J.J., Cox, D.D.: A rodent model for the study of invariant visual object recognition. Proc. Natl. Acad. Sci. **106**(21), 8748–8753 (2009)
7. Katyal, R., Paneri, S., Kuse, M.: Gaussian intensity model with neighborhood cues for fluid-tissue categorization of multisequence MR brain images. In: Proceedings of the MICCAI Grand Challenge on MR Brain Image Segmentation (2013)
8. Kleeman, R.: Information theory and dynamical system predictability. Entropy **13**(3), 612–649 (2011)
9. Gretton, A., Borgwardt, K.M., Rasch, M., Schölkopf, B., Smola, A.J.: A kernel method for the two-sample-problem. In: Advances in Neural Information Processing Systems, pp. 513–520 (2006)

10. Simonovsky, M., Gutiérrez-Becker, B., Mateus, D., Navab, N., Komodakis, N.: A deep metric for multimodal registration. In: Ourselin, S., Joskowicz, L., Sabuncu, M.R., Unal, G., Wells, W. (eds.) MICCAI 2016. LNCS, vol. 9902, pp. 10–18. Springer, Cham (2016). https://doi.org/10.1007/978-3-319-46726-9_2
11. Jenkinson, M., Pechaud, M., Smith, S.: BET2: MR-based estimation of brain, skull and scalp surfaces. In: Eleventh Annual Meeting of the Organization for Human Brain Mapping, vol. 17, p. 167, Toronto (2005)

# Conv2Warp: An Unsupervised Deformable Image Registration with Continuous Convolution and Warping

Sharib Ali$^{(\boxtimes)}$ and Jens Rittscher

Department of Engineering Science, Institute of Biomedical Engineering,
University of Oxford, Oxford, UK
{sharib.ali,jens.rittscher}@eng.ox.ac.uk

**Abstract.** Recent successes in deep learning based deformable image registration (DIR) methods have demonstrated that complex deformation can be learnt directly from data while reducing computation time when compared to traditional methods. However, the reliance on fully linear convolutional layers imposes a uniform sampling of pixel/voxel locations which ultimately limits their performance. To address this problem, we propose a novel approach of learning a continuous warp of the source image. Here, the required deformation vector fields are obtained from a concatenated linear and non-linear convolution layers and a learnable bicubic Catmull-Rom spline resampler. This allows to compute smooth deformation field and more accurate alignment compared to using only linear convolutions and linear resampling. In addition, the continuous warping technique penalizes disagreements that are due to topological changes. Our experiments demonstrate that this approach manages to capture large non-linear deformations and minimizes the propagation of interpolation errors. While improving accuracy the method is computationally efficient. We present comparative results on a range of public 4D CT lung (POPI) and brain datasets (CUMC12, MGH10).

## 1 Introduction

Image registration is required in many medical imaging applications - from multimodal data fusion to inter- and intra-patient comparisons. Rigid or affine registration methods can be used to align source image to its target image by computing a simple transformation matrix, i.e., optimization of only few parameters. However, such an alignment does not model changes due to organ deformation, patient weight loss, or tumour shrinkage. In order to tackle these changes non-rigid or deformable image registration (DIR) methods are advised. Traditional DIR methods are usually mathematically complex to model and therefore

**Electronic supplementary material** The online version of this chapter (https://doi.org/10.1007/978-3-030-32692-0_56) contains supplementary material, which is available to authorized users.

© Springer Nature Switzerland AG 2019
H.-I. Suk et al. (Eds.): MLMI 2019, LNCS 11861, pp. 489–497, 2019.
https://doi.org/10.1007/978-3-030-32692-0_56

require the optimization of a very larger number of parameters which makes them computationally expensive. Recently, deep learning based methods have shown tremendous success in tackling such complex problems in image registration. This is mainly due to two reasons: (1) By learning the model parameters of the neural network through optimizing a loss function directly from the data a wide range of image features are considered. (2) These methods make very efficient use of hardware acceleration as a result they require significantly less time than traditional methods.

Recently, supervised as well as unsupervised learning techniques for medical image registration have been proposed. Supervised techniques [6] rely on ground truth deformation vector fields (DVFs) computed by traditional methods. Here, a neural network is only used as a regressor for approximating traditional methods. This restricts their learning process and such training requires a large number of DVFs which are both time consuming to generate and carries the risk of mitigating unreliable deformations. On the other hand, unsupervised techniques [1,7,10] can learn to predict DVFs without requiring ground truth deformations. Linear convolutional neural networks (ConvNets) were used in [1,7,10]. Guha et al. [1] and Li et al. [7] used linear sampling techniques for upscaling the obtained DVFs. We argue that such models do not approximate complex and non-linear local deformations with a sufficient accuracy. These methods were evaluated on brain datasets where local deformations are limited. While, [10] proposed to use a B-spline as transformation model and interpolation method for the predicted DVFs and presented results on more complex cardiac cine MRI and lung datasets. However, in [10] only linear ConvNets were used. Despite of good local support, B-splines can lead to larger interpolation errors as they do not pass through data points (see Suppl. Mat. Sect. 1 for details).

With this paper, we introduce an unsupervised approach for deformable image registration that is capable of learning complex deformations and is able to compute smooth, accurate and plausible DVFs. We propose to: (1) Relax the fixed geometric constrain imposed by traditional convolutional filters by adding a series of deformable convolutional filters [3] combined with linear convolutional filters which allows to capture complex features. (2) Apply a learnt bicubic Catmull-Rom spline resampler to minimize error in DVF resampling, (3) Aggregate large deformations using a multiple scale warping strategy. (4) Finally, to impose further smoothness of the DVF using a $L_2$-norm regularization. We show that interpolation technique influence the learning phenomena. We also illustrate deformable convolutions as presented in this work through experiments. We have evaluated our model on publicly available lung CT and brain MRI datasets.

## 2   Method

As motivated, we now introduce the key elements to our Conv2Warp model (each highlighted in Fig. 1), and describe our constrained loss function.

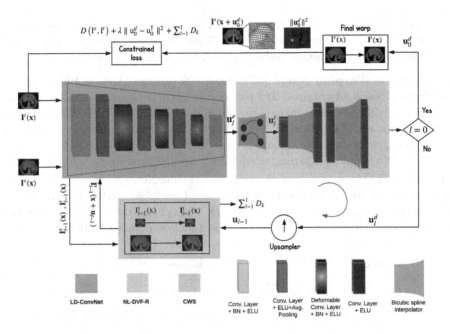

**Fig. 1. Conv2Warp model.** Three main components are presented as colored blocks: Blue: linear and deformable convolution network (LD-ConvNet), Green: non-linear DVF resampler network (NL-DVF-R) and Orange: continuous warping stage (CWS). (Color figure online)

***Linear and Deformable Convolutional Network (LD-ConvNet).*** LD-ConvNet (blue block in Fig. 1) consists of 5 linear convolutions and 3 deformable convolution layers. Each convolution layer is combined with a batch normalization and ELU activation function. After the second convolution layer an average pooling layer with downsampling factor of 0.5 is applied. Throughout we use a sequential ConvNet of (input, output) channels as follows: $(2, 64)$, $(64, 64)$, $(64, 64)$, $(64, 32)$, $(32, 32)$, $(32, 16)$, $(16, 16)$, $(16, 2)$ with kernel size 3 and stride 1. Two images $I^s$ (*source*) and $I^t$ (*target*) are concatenated first and set as an input to the first layer of the Conv2Warp model.

***Non-linear DVF Resampler (NL-DVF-R).*** NL-DVF-R (green block in Fig. 1) consists of a sequential bicubic Catmull-Rom spline resampler and convolutional filter for resampling the obtained DVF from the LD-ConvNet. Since, this is integrated in our learning model, complex non-linear deformations learnt by the LD-ConvNet are guaranteed to have smooth deformation fields and the interpolation error is minimal.

Catmull-Rom spline consist of 4 basis functions with local support and are $C_1$ continuous and differentiable (see Suppl. Mat. Sect. 1). These properties makes them smoother compared to standard linear interpolation techniques. Qualitative comparison of Catmull-Rom spline with linear resampling technique is provided in Fig. 2 of Suppl. Mat.

Comparison of Catmull-Rom spline with other spline-based resamplers (including B-spline) is presented in Fig. 2. It can be observed that Catmull-Rom spline has the lowest training losses for both lung and brain datasets.

***Continuous Warping Stage (CWS).*** CWS (orange block in Fig. 1) warps the deformation field obtained at $l$ pyramid levels in a continuous fashion. Here $l = 4$ for our 2D case with image size $256 \times 256$ and $l = 2$ for our 3D case with patch volume size $64 \times 64 \times 64$. Note that $l$ pyramids are constructed prior to feeding images into the LD-ConvNet.

The CWS employs warping of the next level source image $I^s_{l-1}$ with the computed DVF from previous coarse level LD-ConvNet, i.e., $\mathbf{u}_{l-1} = \mathbf{u}_l^{d\uparrow}$. This process is repeated until the final level, i.e., $l = 0$. At each level the losses $D\left(I^s_l, I^t_l\right)$ between the warped image $I^s_{l-1}\left(\mathbf{x} + \mathbf{u}_{l-1}\right)$ and the target are summed and transferred to the final constrained loss function detailed in the Sect. 2.

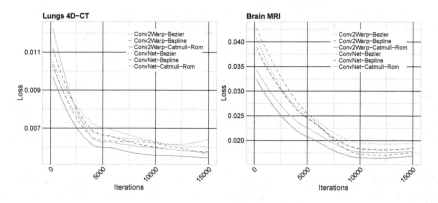

**Fig. 2. Training losses:** Effect of interpolation methods on linear convolution model (ConvNet) and our proposed non-linear Conv2Warp model. Conv2warp has better convergence than the linear model for every interpolation technique, while the best with the Catmull-Rom spline interpolation.

***Loss Function.*** A multi-modal normalized cross-correlation (NCC) metric is used as data term $D$ in our loss function. We propose to use a derived sum-of-squared difference (SSD) which guarantees maximization of NCC metric [4] and is written as $D\left(I^s, I^t\right) = \frac{1}{2N} \sum \left( \frac{|I^s(\mathbf{x}) - \mu^s|}{\sqrt{\sigma_s^2 + \epsilon^2}} - \frac{|I^t(\mathbf{x}) - \mu^t|}{\sqrt{\sigma_t^2 + \epsilon^2}} \right)^2$, with mean $\mu$, standard deviation $\sigma$, the total number of pixels $N$ and $\epsilon = 10^{-3}$ (used to avoid division by zero). For obtaining a smooth deformation vector field we apply an $L_2$-norm of the difference between the computed $\mathbf{u}_0^d$ from the NL-DVF-R block and $\mathbf{u}_0^\uparrow$ which is the previous upsampled input DVF to CWS block (see Fig. 1). Losses computed during $l$ pyramid levels in our CWS block $\sum_{l-1}^{1} D_k$ are aggregated to the final loss. The resulting equation for the backward propagation is: $\mathcal{L} = D\left(I^s, I^t\right) + \lambda \left[\|\mathbf{u}_0^d - \mathbf{u}_0^\uparrow\|^2\right]_0^{0.25} + \sum_{l-1}^1 D_k$, where $\lambda$ is the trade-off between the regularization and the data-term. In our experiments it is set to 0.001. We restrict the regularization to the interval $[0, 0.25]$ to prevent over smoothing problem during training. Omitting this constraints results in failures which are documented in Fig. 2 of Suppl. Mat. (see plot for Conv2Warp-FullReg). The loss saturates after 6000 iterations. However, regularised models with the interval continue to minimise the loss function. Our constrained loss is optimized using Adam optimizer with learning rate $10^{-3}$.

## 3   Experiments and Results

### 3.1   Datasets and Training

**4D CT.** DIR-LAB [2] thoracic image dataset for DIR that includes inspiratory and expiratory breath-hold CT image pairs were used for training. Although large permutations are possible, only breathing cycles 00–50, 10–80 and 30–90 were considered from 10 different sets (a total of 120 volumes). As a consequence we avoid an imbalance in the training dataset as most of the breathing cycles did not present strong deformations. For testing the POPI [9] lung dataset was used. The provided segmentation for air, body and lungs were used for evaluation.

**MRI.** The LBPA40 [8] dataset were used to train the model. We performed a random combination of these brain pairs and used nearly 300 volumes for our training. We have used MGH10 and CUMC12 [5] datasets for which masks are available for evaluation. 300 epochs with batch size of 4 were used for training performed on a 16GB NVIDIA Tesla P100 for nearly 48 h.

**Table 1. Evaluation on lung 4D CT dataset (POPI [9]).** Dice(Jaccard) coefficients for 7 different volume pairs with larger inhalation and exhalation cycles. Grid-parameter search was done for all methods and only best performance is reported.

| 4D-CT | Methods | | | | | |
|---|---|---|---|---|---|---|
| | Pre-align. | Demons | ANTS-SyN | SE | ConvNet | Conv2Warp |
| 00–50 | 0.83(0.76) | 0.87(0.83) | 0.87(0.82) | **0.89(0.85)** | 0.87(0.82) | **0.89**(0.83) |
| 00–70 | 0.86(0.79) | 0.90(0.85) | 0.89(0.84) | **0.92(0.88)** | 0.90(0.84) | 0.91(0.85) |
| 10–50 | 0.82(0.75) | 0.86(0.82) | 0.86(0.81) | **0.88(0.85)** | 0.87(0.81) | **0.88**(0.83) |
| 10–70 | 0.85(0.78) | 0.88(0.83) | 0.87(0.82) | 0.88(0.84) | 0.89(0.83) | **0.90(0.84)** |
| 20–50 | 0.84(0.77) | 0.87(0.83) | 0.86(0.82) | **0.91(0.86)** | 0.87(0.81) | 0.89(0.85) |
| 20–70 | 0.86(0.79) | 0.89(0.84) | 0.88(0.83) | 0.88(**0.84**) | 0.89(0.83) | **0.90(0.84)** |
| 30–50 | 0.87(0.82) | 0.90(0.86) | 0.89(0.85) | **0.91(0.87)** | 0.88(0.83) | 0.90(0.86) |
| Mean | 0.84(0.78) | 0.88(0.83) | 0.87(0.82) | **0.90(0.85)** | 0.88(0.82) | **0.90(0.84)** |
| $\bar{t}$ (in s.) | - | 23.51 | 216.45 | 416.78 | **2.94** | **2.94** |

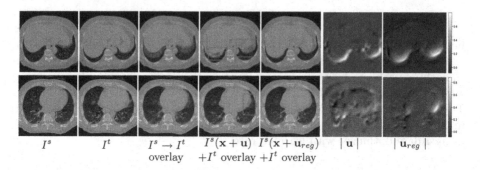

$I^s$          $I^t$          $I^s \to I^t$   $I^s(\mathbf{x} + \mathbf{u})$   $I^s(\mathbf{x} + \mathbf{u}_{reg})$   $|\mathbf{u}|$   $|\mathbf{u}_{reg}|$
                          overlay   $+I^t$ overlay   $+I^t$ overlay

**Fig. 3. Visual validation of proposed Conv2warp method** without ($\lambda = 0$) and with regularization ($\lambda = 0.001$) in our loss function on POPI dataset. Overlay images represents source or warped images in magenta and target image in green. Red rectangles in overlay images with $I^s(\mathbf{x} + \mathbf{u})$ show unrestricted flow of pixels when no regularization is used. Smoother deformation fields are obtained with regularized Conv2warp. Brighter pixels in magnitude images on left represent large displacements. (Color figure online)

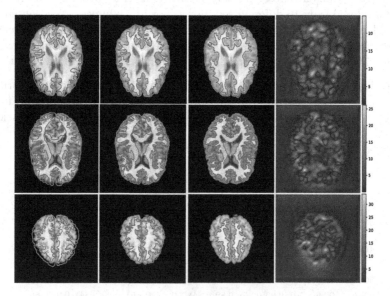

**Fig. 4. Visual validation of proposed Conv2Warp method on brain dataset.** $1^{st}$ column: Target image with source mask, $2^{nd}$ column: target image with deformed (transformed) mask, $3^{rd}$ column: Target image with target mask, and last column: magnitude of predicted deformation field. Grey matter (GM) and white-matter (WM) areas are marked by green and magenta borders and yellow borders, respectively. (Color figure online)

**Table 2. Evaluation on T1-weighted MRI datasets.** Mean Dice and Jaccard coefficients for two datasets with the state-of-the-art DIR methods and Conv2Warp (checkpoints trained on LBPA40 dataset) are shown. Only rigid registration was performed for pre-alignment prior to applying deformable registration.

| Methods | Dataset | | | | Avg. |
|---|---|---|---|---|---|
| | MGH10 | | CUMC12 | | Time |
| | $\mu_{dice}$ | $\mu_{jaccard}$ | $\mu_{dice}$ | $\mu_{jaccard}$ | $\bar{t}$ |
| Rigid | $0.92 \pm 0.011$ | $0.86 \pm 0.019$ | $0.90 \pm 0.030$ | $0.82 \pm 0.050$ | - |
| SimpleElastix (SE) | **0.95 ± 0.003** | **0.90 ± 0.005** | $0.95 \pm$ **0.002** | $0.91 \pm$ **0.002** | 1008.2 |
| ANTS (SyN-CC) | $0.94 \pm 0.007$ | **0.90 ± 0.011** | $0.95 \pm 0.010$ | $0.90 \pm 0.017$ | 246.4 |
| ConvNet | $0.93 \pm 0.008$ | $0.88 \pm 0.014$ | $0.95 \pm 0.007$ | $0.91 \pm 0.012$ | **2.9** |
| Conv2Warp | **0.95 ± 0.007** | **0.90 ± 0.012** | **0.97± 0.005** | **0.93 ± 0.008** | **2.9** |

## 3.2 Registration of 4D CT Data

Conv2Warp has been evaluated by comparing it to the DIR state-of-the-methods. We also provide results where we restrict the convolution blocks in the Conv2Warp model to linear convolution only (ConvNet). For both these architectures, we will compare them only for Catmull-Rom spline based interpolation as it outperformed other spline techniques in our experiments. Seven pairs of different breathing cycles of 4D-CT data [9], each with 141 slices, where improvement of DIR methods compared to pre-alignment were significant are shown in Table 1. While the accuracy of our method measured by Dice (.90) and Jaccaard coefficient (.84) is similar to the rigorous simpleElastix (SE[1]), the run time is reduced by a factor of 141. Conv2Warp outperforms all other state-of-the art methods and ConvNet for almost all considered pairs. The test time on CPU is nearly 2.94 s which is multiple-folds lower than conventional DIR methods. Our model is light weight with inference time on a GPU of less than 1 s.

## 3.3 Registration of T1 MRI Data

T1-weighted MRI scans for 9 volume pairs of MGH10 and 11 volume pairs of CUMC12 [5] where each image from different volumes were registered to the first volume data were also used for evaluation. The weights trained on LBPA [8] dataset were used in this case. In Table 2 Conv2Warp have $\mu_{dice}$ (mean dice) and $\mu_{jaccard}$ (mean Jaccard) of 0.95 and 0.90, respectively for MGH10 dataset (same as for SE), and 0.97 and 0.93, respectively for CUMC12 dataset (higher than SE). Conv2Warp has higher $\mu_{dice}$ and $\mu_{jaccard}$ for both datasets compared to ANTS (SyN-CC) and ConvNet. When compared with speed Conv2Warp is computationally the fastest among all other conventional DIR methods.

---

[1] http://simpleelastix.github.io.

### 3.4 Visual Validation

In Fig. 3 Conv2Warp without ($\lambda = 0$) regularization and with ($\lambda = 0.001$) regularization are shown in 4th and 5th columns respectively and their corresponding DVF magnitudes in 6th and 7th columns, respectively. It can be observed that the unconstrained loss function results in some unrealistic deformations (red rectangular regions in 4th column) while a more realistic deformations are visible for the constrained loss proposed in Conv2Warp (5th column). A smooth deformation can be seen in the magnitude image of the DVF | $\mathbf{u}_{reg}$ | (7th column). Colour overlay images show a large improvement in the alignment of source images $I^s$ with the target images $I^t$ (3rd column) with Conv2Warp method (5th column). Figure 4 shows the results on T1 MRI test datasets which were first rigidly aligned to MNIspace and then co-registered using Conv2Warp. It can be observed that Conv2Warp handles different magnitudes of non-linear deformations.

## 4    Conclusion

We have proposed a novel end-to-end convolutional neural network that consists of a sequential linear and deformable convolutions along with a learnt non-linear sampler. To handle wide range of non-linear deformations between source and target data pairs deformations are concurred by the continuous warping strategy. Our experimental results demonstrate that our proposed model outperforms most of the traditional methods and has very low computational complexity. When compared to the existing linear deep learning models such as ConvNets, Conv2Warp produces more accurate deformation fields. Additional details and evaluations are available in the supplementary material.

**Acknowledgments.** SA is supported by the NIHR Oxford BRC and JR by EPSRC EP/M013774/1 Seebibyte.

## References

1. Balakrishnan, G., Zhao, A., Sabuncu, M.R., Guttag, J., Dalca, A.V.: Voxelmorph: a learning framework for deformable medical image registration. IEEE Trans. Med. Imaging **38**(8), 1788–1800 (2019)
2. Castillo, R., Castillo, E., Guerra, R., Johnson, V., McPhail, T., Garg, A., Guerrero, T.: Phys. Med. Biol. **54**(7), 1849–1870 (2009)
3. Dai, J., Qi, H., Xiong, Y., Li, Y., Zhang, G., Hu, H., Wei, Y.: Deformable convolutional networks. In: 2017 IEEE International Conference on Computer Vision (ICCV), pp. 764–773 (2017)
4. Drulea, M., Nedevschi, S.: Motion Estimation Using the Correlation Transform. IEEE Transactions on Image Processing **22**(8), 3260–3270 (2013)
5. Klein, A., Andersson, J., Ardekan, B.A., et al.: Evaluation of 14 nonlinear deformation algorithms applied to human brain MRI registration. NeuroImage **46**(3), 786–802 (2009)

6. Krebs, J., Mansi, T., Delingette, H., Zhang, L., Ghesu, F.C., Miao, S., Maier, A.K., Ayache, N., Liao, R., Kamen, A.: Robust non-rigid registration through agent-based action learning. In: Medical Image Computing and Computer Assisted Intervention (MICCAI). pp. 344–352. Springer (2017)

7. Li, H., Fan, Y.: Non-rigid image registration using self-supervised fully convolutional networks without training data. In: 2018 IEEE 15th International Symposium on Biomedical Imaging (ISBI). pp. 1075–1078 (2018)

8. Shattuck, D.W., Mirza, M., Adisetiyo, V., Hojatkashani, C., Salamon, G., Narr, K.L., Poldrack, R.A., Bilder, R.M., Toga, A.W.: Construction of a 3d probabilistic atlas of human cortical structures. NeuroImage 39(3), 1064–1080 (2008)

9. Vandemeulebroucke, J., Rit, S., Kybic, J., Clarysse, P., Sarrut, D.: Spatiotemporal motion estimation for respiratory-correlated imaging of the lungs. Medical Physiscs 38(1), 166–178 (2011)

10. de Vos, B.D., Berendsen, F.F., Viergever, M.A., Sokooti, H., Staring, M., Isgum, I.: A deep learning framework for unsupervised affine and deformable image registration. Medical Image Analysis 52, 128–143 (2019)

# Semantic Filtering Through Deep Source Separation on Microscopy Images

Avelino Javer[1,2（✉）] and Jens Rittscher[1,2]

[1] Institute of Biomedical Engineering, Department of Engineering Science,
University of Oxford, Oxford, UK
avelino.javer@eng.ox.ac.uk
[2] Big Data Institute, University of Oxford, Oxford, UK

**Abstract.** By their very nature microscopy images of cells and tissues consist of a limited number of object types or components. In contrast to most natural scenes, the composition is known *a priori*. Decomposing biological images into semantically meaningful objects and layers is the aim of this paper. Building on recent approaches to image de-noising we present a framework that achieves state-of-the-art segmentation results requiring little or no manual annotations. Here, synthetic images generated by adding cell crops are sufficient to train the model. Extensive experiments on cellular images, a histology data set, and small animal videos demonstrate that our approach generalizes to a broad range of experimental settings. As the proposed methodology does not require densely labelled training images and is capable of resolving the partially overlapping objects it holds the promise of being of use in a number of different applications.

**Keywords:** Microscopy image analysis · Semantic segmentation ·
Data augmentation · Deep learning

## 1 Introduction

In contrast to natural images, the scene composition in microscopy images is typically known. The image acquisition is done in a controlled environment where the objects of interest are highlighted by physical methods such as optical contrast, staining or fluorescence labelling. At the same time, noise, low contrast and diverse imaging artifacts can make image analysis challenging. It is not uncommon to deal with overcrowded scenes or objects with complex morphology. Additionally, many typical assumptions of natural scenes do not apply to histological images, *i.e.* objects can be rotated in any direction, they can be out of plane or have different appearance depending on the sample preparation.

**Electronic supplementary material** The online version of this chapter (https://doi.org/10.1007/978-3-030-32692-0_57) contains supplementary material, which is available to authorized users.

© Springer Nature Switzerland AG 2019
H.-I. Suk et al. (Eds.): MLMI 2019, LNCS 11861, pp. 498–506, 2019.
https://doi.org/10.1007/978-3-030-32692-0_57

Deep learning has been successfully adopted for microscopy image analysis, in particular for segmentation and localization tasks [7,8], however its adoption is limited by the need for large manually annotated datasets. The annotation of microscopy images is demanding due to the large number of individuals and the heterogeneity of their shapes. Additionally, the object identification in microscopy data typically requires a level of expertise that cannot be easily outsourced. Deep learning has enabled a number of new approaches to image denoising and restoration, a type of inverse problem that aims to recover an image $x$ from its degraded version $f(x)$. The general training procedure requires the collection of hundredths of pairs of noisy and cleaned images. The acquisition of clean targets typically requires altering the imaging conditions during acquisition [9] making it quite demanding or in some situations nonfeasible. This limitation was partially solved, with Noise2Noise [3], where Lehtinen et al. demonstrated that it is possible to train a denoising network without the need of clean targets if noisy pairs of the same scene are given. The basic idea is that if we train a network using pairs of noisy images such as $(s + n, s + n')$ where $s$ is the same signal, and $n$ and $n'$ are the independently drawn noise, the network converges to a representation that cancels out the noise component. Nonetheless, the image restoration methods do not include any semantic information, i.e. they are not capable of separating the signal coming from the objects of interest from the signal of other objects.

In this paper, we expand on the idea of Noise2Noise to filter semantically meaningful information on microscopy images. We show that we can train a network to remove objects on training pairs where the objects change position and the scene remains static. This approach can be used to learn to identify moving objects from videos without any manual labelling. Additionally, we demonstrate that if we train a network on pairs of images where the signal from the objects of interest remains the same while the rest of the scene changes, the network learns to only retain the objects of interest. The most challenging part of this second approach is to get the required training data. For this, we use the fact that the composition of certain microscopy images is known a priori to synthesize the training set using a very simple method. We show that even if the synthetic images are far from realistic, a network trained on them is capable of producing high quality outputs. Contrary to the pixel-labelled images typically used in semantic segmentation, our semantic filtering has the advantage of retaining textural information and of resolving overlapping objects from different classes. Additionally its training does not need dense image annotations, but rather requires representative exemplars that can be extracted with traditional image segmentation methods.

In Sect. 2, we present how we expand the Noise2Noise idea to semantically filter microscopy images and describe our synthetic image generation model. In Sect. 3 we apply our methodology to different experimental settings. In Sect. 3.1 we use videos from C. elegans wild isolates to remove the animals from the background by training directly raw video data. In Sect. 3.2 we use data from fluorescent microglia cells to demonstrate that our approach is capable of removing out of focus objects while retaining complex cell morphologies. We then apply our method on two public datasets taken from the Broad Bioimage Benchmark Collection [5]: BBBC026 [6] (Sect. 3.3) where we demonstrate that our method can resolve overlapped shapes, and BBBC042 [8] (Sect. 3.4) where we show the same ideas can be applied to histological images. We provide a quantitative evaluation of the results.

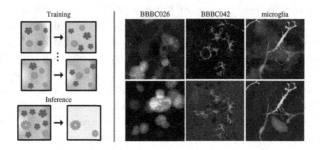

**Fig. 1.** Illustration of the training procedure. Left, the method consists in try to make a network learn the mapping between pairs of images where the only thing in common is the target objects. Once trained, the network is then capable of outputing only the signal from the objects of interest and smoothing out the rest. Right, examples of synthetic training pairs for the different datasets. For illustration purposes the fixed parts between pair of images that correspond to the target objects are coloured in green. (Color figure online)

## 2  Method

We are interested in extracting data from biological samples which contain one or more entities and are set up to study phenotypical differences within a specific class or interactions between them. The object categories are referred to as $\mathcal{O}_i$. For the purpose of this paper, two objects categories are considered among all $\mathcal{O}_i$, the target category $\mathcal{O}_t$ and the rest $\mathcal{O}_u$. We will denote the background signal with $b$ and the image layer formed only by sparsely located objects from $\mathcal{O}_i$ with $\ell^i$. Therefore an image can be modeled as $x = f(\ell^t, \ell^u, b)$. The task of interest is, given $x$, to extract the layer $\ell^t$ that contains only the pixel intensities coming from the objects of interest.

### 2.1  Training Model

The major insight in Lehtinen *et al.* [3] is that when a neural network is used to map one images to another, the learned representation is an average of all the plausible explanations for a given training data. In some cases, this can lead to unwanted artifacts like blurry edges. Nonetheless, if the network is trained on pairs of images with different noise realizations (Noise2Noise), *e.g.* same scene

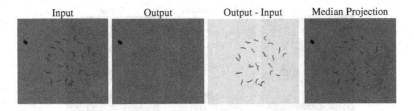

**Fig. 2.** Using consecutive frames of movies of moving objects makes possible to train a model to remove the objects in static images. The output can be subtracted from input to recover the target objects. By comparison, the median projection along the video will fail to remove all the worms in cases where the animals motility is impaired.

with different Gaussian noise, the learned representation is capable of cancel out the noise just as well as if it had been trained using cleaned targets.

Expanding on this idea, we can use pairs of images where the layer $\ell^t$ remains the same, while we change a combination of the layers $\ell^u$ and $b$. If the objects in $\ell^u$ are randomly located, the network learns to smooth the background objects out while enhancing the target objects. Conversely, we can learn to remove $\ell^t$ if we train on pairs where $\ell^u$ and $b$ remains static while $\ell^t$ changes between images. As we will see in Sect. 3.1 this later case occurs naturally on videos with moving targets and a fixed camera. For the rest of the experiments we rely on synthetic image pairs generated as explained below. For simplicity, in all our experiments we used a U-Net architecture with the same architecture as the one used by Lehtinen *et al.* [3]. However, it is worth to remark that the approach is not limited to a specific network architecture (Fig. 2).

### 2.2 Synthetic Image Generation

We use a simple model to create synthetic images where we assume that the image formation is additive $x = \ell^t + \ell^u + b$. Additionally, we assume that it is possible to obtain sample crops of isolated individuals $o_k^i \in \mathcal{O}_i$ and patches of the background $b$ where any pixel belonging to any $\mathcal{O}_i$ has been set to zero. We can then create $\ell^t$ and $\ell^u$ by randomly placing $o_k^i$ from their respective classes, and $b$ from the patches. Partial overlaps between the objects is allowed (up to 50–90% of the placed object) but we observed that complete overlaps can be detrimental leading to artifacts. Each crop is augmented using random rotations, flips, and resizes, as well as multiplying by a random constant and substracting a random constant. Additionally, the zero parts of the patch background are replaced by a random constant.

The required crops can be extracted using traditional segmentation algorithms plus a manual or automatic filtering of representative examples. The main requirement is that the crops are exemplars of a given class. Examples of the generated training pairs are shown in Fig. 1, and examples of the input crops are shown Fig. S1.

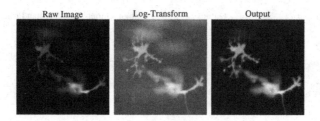

**Fig. 3.** The signal from the out of focus cells is removed while preserving the complex morphology of the microglia cells.

## 3    Applications

### 3.1    Learning Morphology from Moving Objects

Videos taken using a static camera where only the objects of interest are moving are a natural realization of the data required to train our semantic filtering model. In this case, we can use pairs of frames separated by a fixed time lag to train a network capable of removing the target objects on single frames. This occurs because the equivalent of minimizing the L1 loss on pairs of samples with random noise is the median [3]. The network effectively learns to calculate the equivalent of a median projection over a video. Therefore, as long as the median projection over a video at a given time lag results in a cleaned background, we can used those frames in our training set. The trained network output can be then subtracted from the original image in order to recover the pixels corresponding to the target objects.

We tested this approach on the set of videos of *C. elegans* wild isolates [2]. We used 279 videos for training and 32 for testing. From each video we extracted five 2048 × 2048 frames spaced every three minutes. We trained the model on patches of 256 × 256 pixels on pairs of consecutive frames. To validate the results we used as ground truth the original segmentation [2]. The localization scores are precision (P) 0.995, recall (R) 0.999, F1-score (F1) 0.997, while the mean IoU for the whole image is 0.850.

It is worth noting that in the training set our model is rather unnecessary, it will be much easier to calculate the median projection over each video. However, in cases were the motility of the worms is limited during inference, like in the case of mutations or drugs, the median projection will contain pixel that correspond to worms. We shown an example of this in Sect. 3.1 on a video of the strain *unc-51* that has a mutation that severely impairs the worms mobility.

### 3.2    Removing Out of Focus Cells on Microglia Cultures

The dataset consist of images of a co-culture of microglia cells and neurons. The only fluorescent cells in the images are the microglia, however, the intensity of the cell processes is much dimmer than their bodies. In order to resolve better the cell morphology we first took the log-transform of the raw images. This creates the problem of increasing the signal coming from out of focus cells. Our model is capable of cleaning the out of focus cells while retaining almost completely the cell morphology. Example of the model outputs are presented in Fig. 3.

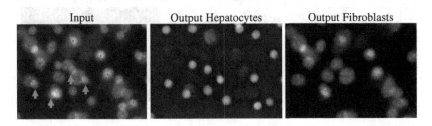

**Fig. 4.** The model is capable of resolve overlapping cells on co-cultures of hepatocyte and fibroblasts. We display the outputs of two different models trained using either the hepatocytes or the fibroblast as the target class. The dots in the input image show the dataset annotations, fibroblast in red and hepatocytes in cyan. In this region there are four heavily overlap hepatocytes (green arrows) that were resolved by our model but are not labeled as such in the dataset. (Color figure online)

### 3.3 Segmentation of Co-cultures in Microscopy Fluorescence Images

The BBBC026 [6] dataset consists of images of co-cultures of hepatocytes and fibroblast taken using epifluorescence. The dataset has five hand-annotated ground truth images where each cell is labeled either as hepatocyte, fibroblast or debris. The annotations consist of a single pixel inside each object coloured according to its class. We used this information to extract the crops needed for our image synthesis model. We train our model using 5-fold cross validation, training with four images and using the remaining one for testing. We repeat the procedure two separate times using either the hepatocytes or the fibroblasts as the target class. The real ground truth for our method would be images with only the hepatocytes or fibroblast in separate channels. Since we do not have this data we decide to validate our results with the localization results reported in the dataset source paper [6]. Our results are for the hepatocytes ($P = 0.81$, $R = 0.92$, $F1 = 0.86$) compared with ($P = 0.94$, $R = 0.70$, $F1 = 0.80$), and for the fibroblasts ($P = 0.95$, $R = 0.96$, $F1 = 0.95$) compared with ($P = 0.86$, $R = 0.98$, $F1 = 0.92$). For both classes, we obtain a moderate increase in the F1-score. Interestingly, we observe that in the case of hepatocytes, the decrease of precision can be explained by apparent false positives created by overlapped cells that were not labelled in the original dataset but our network was capable of resolving (Fig. 4).

Finally, to further corroborate our results we use the unlabelled images in the BBBC026. This images were taken using two different hepatocytes concentrations while keeping the same number of fibroblasts. Compared to the results reported in Logan *et al.* we observe a smaller p-value among the two samples

$(3.1 \cdot 10^{-6}$ vs $3.3 \cdot 10^{-6})$, and a larger Z-factor (0.28 vs 0.16) that indicates a higher statistical power to identify between different hepatocytes concentrations.

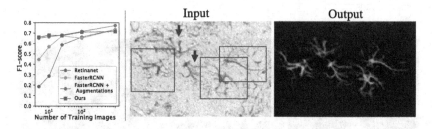

**Fig. 5.** Performance on histological images of astrocytes cells (BBBC042). Left, our model has a performance close to the state of the art models on object detection, and shows only a small reduction of performance as the number of training images is reduced. Right, the output of our model highlights the cell morphology and could help an expert annotator to localize missing targets. In the displayed region, there are only three labeled cell (red boxes), however our model predicts two extra structures (blue arrows) that show a similar morphology to the cells. (Color figure online)

### 3.4   Segmentation on Histological Images

The BBBC042 [8] dataset consists of histological images from different rat brain regions stained with antibodies specific to astrocytes. The dataset is particularly challenging since the images have low contrast, diverse cell morphology and a large number of stained non-specific structures. The dataset consists of 1118 images with the location of around 15000 astrocytes marked by their bounding box. We use 1000 images for training, 50 for validation and the rest for testing. To adapt this set into our image synthesis model, we first convert each RGB image to gray scale and calculate its complement so the background is dark and the foreground bright.

We validate the quality of our results using the localization task. The network outputs are binarized using Otsu thresholding and the bounding box calculate for each connected component removing any blob with less that 300 pixels. The assignment to the true labels is done as described by Suleymanova *et al.* [8]. We compare our results with the state of the art object detection models: FasterRCNN [1] and Retinanet [4]. We trained FasterRCNN using random crops, and horizontal and vertical flips as augmentations, however the augmentations create instability in the training for Retinanet. The results are: semantic filtering $(P = 0.66, R = 0.78, 0.72)$, FasterRCNN with augmentations $(P = 0.73, R = 0.82, F1 = 0.77)$, FasterRCNN without augmentations $(P = 0.80, R = 0.68, F1 = 0.73)$ and Retinanet $(P = 0.81, R = 0.67, F1 = 0.74)$. Additionally, we test how the performance our model changes as less training data is used. The results are shown in Fig. 5 Right. When using 100 or less images, our model performance is the same as the top model, FasterRCNN with augmentations.

The lower performance of our model when using all data could be explained by the likely presence of real cells in the background. As reported in the dataset paper [8], it is common that experts do not coincide in their annotations. The authors report F1 scores between 0.77–0.82 between data labelled by two different experimenters. As consequence it is likely that the dataset labels have an important number of false negatives. Since our network is not directly trained on the cell localization but rather in cleaning the background from the signal, noisy labels will affect our segmentation mask and therefore our ability to detect cells accurately. At the same time, this can be a one major advantage of our model with respect to a network designed to only output the bounding boxes, since the network output will return a clearer outlook of the cell morphology. This output can be used to highlight to the annotator possible missing cells (Fig. 5 left).

# 4 Conclusions

Simplifying the training data acquisition is of great importance for real world settings such as high-content imaging. Our experiments demonstrate that the proposed approach can be applied to time-lapse data completely eliminating the need for any annotation. Additionally, as a result of decomposing the image into separate layers we can effectively study cells with very complex morphology without ever providing accurate dense annotations. Our work demonstrates that synthetically generated images are sufficient for training semantically meaningful mappings. We consider that our work is of significance for a number of concrete applications in cell and tissue imaging. Going forward we will explore the application of our image synthesis paradigm in combination of different network architectures for specific tasks such as instance segmentation or pose detection.

**Acknowledgments.** We thank Serena Ding for providing the video of *C. elegans unc-51*, and Francesca Nicholls and Sally Cowley for providing the microglia data. This work was supported by the EPSRC SeeBiByte Programme EP/M013774/1. Computations used the Oxford Biomedical Research Computing (BMRC) facility.

# References

1. Girshick, R.: Fast R-CNN. In: Proceedings of the IEEE International Conference on Computer Vision, pp. 1440–1448 (2015)
2. Javer, A., et al.: An open-source platform for analyzing and sharing worm-behavior data. Nat. Methods **15**(9), 645 (2018)
3. Lehtinen, J., et al.: Noise2Noise: learning image restoration without clean data. In: PMLR, pp. 2965–2974 (2018)
4. Lin, T.Y., Goyal, P., Girshick, R., He, K., Dollár, P.: Focal loss for dense object detection. In: Proceedings of the IEEE International Conference on Computer Vision, pp. 2980–2988 (2017)
5. Ljosa, V., Sokolnicki, K.L., Carpenter, A.E.: Annotated high-throughput microscopy image sets for validation. Nat. Methods **9**(7), 637 (2012)

6. Logan, D.J., Shan, J., Bhatia, S.N., Carpenter, A.E.: Quantifying co-cultured cell phenotypes in high-throughput using pixel-based classification. Methods **96**, 6–11 (2016)
7. Ronneberger, O., Fischer, P., Brox, T.: U-Net: convolutional networks for biomedical image segmentation. In: Navab, N., Hornegger, J., Wells, W.M., Frangi, A.F. (eds.) MICCAI 2015. LNCS, vol. 9351, pp. 234–241. Springer, Cham (2015). https://doi.org/10.1007/978-3-319-24574-4_28
8. Suleymanova, I., et al.: A deep convolutional neural network approach for astrocyte detection. Sci. Rep. **8** (2018)
9. Weigert, M., et al.: Content-aware image restoration: pushing the limits of fluorescence microscopy. Nat. Methods **15**(12), 1090 (2018)

# Adaptive Functional Connectivity Network Using Parallel Hierarchical BiLSTM for MCI Diagnosis

Yiqiao Jiang[1], Huifang Huang[1(✉)], Jingyu Liu[2], Chong-Yaw Wee[3], and Yang Li[2(✉)]

[1] School of Computer and Information Technology, Beijing Jiaotong University, Beijing, China
huifangbj@hotmail.com
[2] School of Automation Sciences and Electrical Engineering, Beihang University, Beijing, China
liyang@buaa.edu.cn
[3] Department of Biomedical Engineering, National University of Singapore, Singapore, Singapore

**Abstract.** Most of the existing dynamic functional connectivity (dFC) analytical methods compute the correlation between pairs of time courses with the sliding window. However, there is no clear indication on the standard window characteristics (length and shape) that best suit for all analyses, and it cannot pinpoint to compute the dynamic correlation of brain region for each time point. Besides, most of the current studies that utilize the dFC for MCI identification mainly relied on the local clustering coefficient for extracting dynamic features and the support vector machine (SVM) as a classifier. In this paper, we propose a novel adaptive dFC inference method and a deep learning classifier for MCI identification. Specifically, a group-constrained structure detection algorithm is first designed to identify the refined topology of the effective connectivity network, in which the individual information is preserved via different connectivity values. Second, based on the identified topology structure, the adaptive dFC network is then constructed by using the Kalman Filter algorithm to estimate the brain region connectivity strength for each time point. Finally, the adaptive dFC network is validated in MCI identification using a new Parallel Hierarchical Bidirectional Long Short-Term Memory (PH-BiLSTM) network, which extracts as much brain status change information as possible from both the past and future information. The results show that the proposed method achieves relatively high classification accuracy.

## 1 Introduction

Brain connectivity network derived from functional magnetic resonance imaging (fMRI) data has been prevalently used to identify the individuals with mild cognitive impairment (MCI)/Alzheimer's disease (AD) from the normal controls (NCs) [1]. To capture the time-varying information of brain networks, dynamic functional connectivity (dFC) was proposed to characterize the time-resolved connectome [2]. The

© Springer Nature Switzerland AG 2019
H.-I. Suk et al. (Eds.): MLMI 2019, LNCS 11861, pp. 507–515, 2019.
https://doi.org/10.1007/978-3-030-32692-0_58

simplest yet most commonly used analytical strategy of investigating the dFC is to segment the time courses from spatial locations (brain voxels or regions) using a set of temporal windows [3]. The sliding window correlation (SWC) straightforwardly investigates the temporal evolution of functional connectivity (FC). However, the SWC technique with a fixed window length limits the analysis to the frequency range that below the window period, while the ideal window length remains under debate [4]. Besides, most of the current dFC studies are based on detecting discrete major "brain status" via spatial clustering, which may ignore rich spatiotemporal dynamics contained in such brain regions [5].

To deal with nonstationary properties of fMRI time series, and to assess the interaction of FC in the frequency domain, in this paper, we propose a novel adaptive dFC network modeling method to extract dynamic features. This method is able to compute the dynamic correlation between brain regions of interest (ROIs) for each time point. Then further to improve the performance of MCI diagnosis, a parallel hierarchical bidirectional Long Short-Term Memory (PH-BiLSTM) classifier is applied on these dFC networks for identifying MCI. Specifically, the effective network topological structure is first detected via a group-constrained structure detection algorithm, which can accurately filter out insignificant or spurious connections [6]. Thus, it increases the noise resistibility and the robustness of the modeling, which helps to characterize the model more accurately. Second, based on the detected structure, an adaptive dFC network algorithm based on Kalman Filter is employed to estimate the strength of the effective connectivity networks. This algorithm updates the model correlation coefficient recursively at each time point and is based on transients instead of peaks in the fMRI signal. Then some topological features are further extracted to characterize the effective connectivity networks. Following the feature extraction, a PH-BiLSTM is designed as the classifier to identify MCI. LSTM only exploits the historical context, while BiLSTM can solve the sequential modelling task better than LSTM [5]. Therefore, we develop a new PH-BiLSTM networks consisting of two parallel hierarchical BiLSTM networks to learn time-varying functional information. In this method, the bidirectional connection concatenates the positive time direction (forward state) and the negative time direction (backward state), and meanwhile each of the BiLSTM with fully connected layer (H-BiLSTM) adaptively detect dynamic functional state transitions in a data-driven way without any explicit model assumptions. Finally the outputs of two H-BiLSTM networks are combined via a final fully connected layer. The proposed method adaptively detects change points that split the resting-state fMRI (rs-fMRI) data into segments with significantly different functional connectivity patterns. Experimental results have demonstrated that the proposed method could obtain high detection accuracy.

## 2   Method

The proposed framework for diagnosing MCI essentially involves data preprocessing, network topology detection, adaptive dFC construction, feature extraction and classification, as graphically shown in Fig. 1. Procedures of the proposed framework are summarized as follows: (1) detect the topology of effective connectivity networks via group-constrained structure detection algorithm; (2) apply an adaptive recursive Kalman Filter algorithm to dynamically estimate the effective connectivity strength; (3) split the dataset into training data and testing data, and extract topological features from adaptive dFC networks with the optimal parameters; (4) train a PH-BiLSTM model, and employ it to identify MCI.

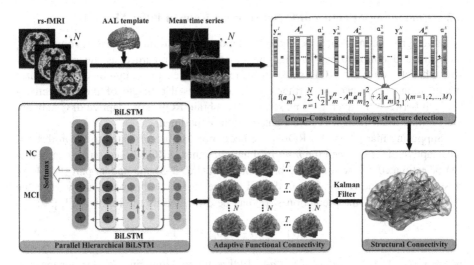

**Fig. 1.** Overview of the proposed method for MCI diagnosis.

## 2.1 Group-Constrained Network Topology Detection

Suppose there are $N$ training subjects and each of them has $M(M = 90)$ ROIs, we denote the regional mean time series of the $m$-th ROI signal for the $n$-th subject as $y_m^n$, and $y_m^n = [y_m^n(1); y_m^n(2); \ldots; y_m^n(T)]$ with $T$ being the number of time points of the time series. For filtering out the spurious connections, a group-constrained structure detection algorithm is used to identify the topological structure of the effective connectivity networks. The sparse brain functional connectivity modeling of the $m$-th ROI for the $n$-th subject can be considered to minimize the object loss function as

$$f(\alpha_m) = \sum_{n=1}^{N} \left( \frac{1}{2} \|y_m^n - A_m^n \alpha_m^n\|_2^2 + \lambda \|\alpha_m\|_{2,1} \right) (m = 1, 2, \ldots, M) \qquad (1)$$

where $A_m^n = [y_1^n, \ldots, y_{m-1}^n, y_{m+1}^n, \ldots, y_M^n]$ is the data matrix of the $m$-th ROI (consisting of all time series except for the $m$-th ROI), and $\alpha_m^n = [\alpha_1^n; \ldots; \alpha_{m-1}^n; \alpha_{m+1}^n; \ldots; \alpha_M^n]$ is the weight vector that quantifies the degree of influence of other ROIs on the $m$-th ROI. Inspired by associated works [6], $\alpha_m = [\alpha_m^1, \alpha_m^2, \ldots, \alpha_m^N]$ is the weight matrix, and the coefficients in $\alpha_m$ are treated as the indicators indicating whether the $m$-th ROI is connected to the other eighty-nine ROIs. $\|\alpha_m\|_{2,1}$ is the summation of $l_2$-norms. The regularization parameter $\lambda$ forces certain coefficients to be zero, adaptively choosing a subset of features with non-zero coefficients and controlling the 'sparsity' of the model. We use the SLEP toolbox to solve the objective function in Eq. (1). The non-zero coefficients in $\alpha_m$ indicate the corresponding ROIs are correlated with the $m$-th ROI, and vice versa. In our experiment, the correlation threshold is set at 0.01 to eliminate the weak correlation, and thus we get $L$ pairs of correlative ROIs.

## 2.2    Computing Adaptive dFC Network via Kalman Filter Method

Although group-constrained method can filter out insignificant or spurious connections, the estimated non-zero coefficients cannot be directly regarded as the connectivity strength between brain ROIs since they are biased due to group-constrained sparse penalization [7]. Hence, to further obtain an unbiased estimate of the connectivity strength between the average time series of two brain ROIs. An adaptive dFC network via Kalman filter method is investigated in our experiment.

Supposing that $Q(Q<M)$ ROIs have been found to be correlated to the $m$-th ROI, the adaptive dFCs between the $m$-th ROI and the other $Q$ ROIs based on Kalman Filter can be estimated by the following prediction part (Eq. 2–3) and update part (Eq. 4–5). Assume $y_m^n(t)$ is the value of the $m$-th ROI at time $t$ for the $n$-th subject, and $\hat{y}_m^n(t)$ is the prediction of $y_m^n(t)$, the prediction $\hat{y}_m^n(t)$ can be estimated by the following Eq. 2:

$$\hat{y}_m^n(t) = y_q^n(t-1)\theta_{m,q}^n(t-1) \tag{2}$$

where $y_q^n(t-1)$ is the value of the $q$-th ROI at the previous time $(t-1)$ for the $n$-th subject, and $\theta_{m,q}^n(t-1)$ denotes the adaptive correlation coefficient between the $m$-th ROI and $q$-th ROI at time $(t-1)$ for the $n$-th subject. $\theta_{m,q}^n(t)$ at the current time $t$ can be calculated by $\theta_{m,q}^n(t-1)$ at the previous time $(t-1)$ plus the product of the Kalman gain $K_{m,q}^n(t)$ and the prediction error of the $m$-th ROI at time $t$, and can be formalized as follows:

$$\theta_{m,q}^n(t) = \theta_{m,q}^n(t-1) + K_{m,q}^n(t)\left(y_m^n(t) - \hat{y}_m^n(t)\right) \tag{3}$$

The gain, $K_{m,q}^n(t)$ (Eq. 4), which changes over time, and determines how much the current prediction error affects the update of the correlation coefficient, can be defined and updated as follows:

$$K_{m,q}^n(t) = \frac{p_{m,q}^n(t-1)}{1+y_q^n(t-1)p_{m,q}^n(t-1)y_q^n(t-1)}y_q^n(t-1) \tag{4}$$

$$p_{m,q}^n(t) = p_{m,q}^n(t-1) - K_{m,q}^n(t)y_q^n(t-1)p_{m,q}^n(t-1) + R_1 \tag{5}$$

where $p_{m,q}^n(t)$ is a residual that indicates the difference between the residual at the previous time $(t-1)$ and $y_q^n(t-1)$. The parameter $R_1$ represents the variance of adaptive correlation coefficient, and affects the update of the adaptive correlation coefficient. The initial values of $p_{m,q}^n(0)$ and $\theta_{m,q}^n(0)$ are set to values near zero.

Accordingly, we can establish $T$ adaptive dFC networks $\theta_l^n(t)$, $(n = 1, 2, \ldots, N; t = 1, 2, \ldots, T; l = 1, 2, \ldots, L)$ for the $n$-th subject that measure the correlation between the average time series of two ROIs, and capture the temporal variation of the connection strength for $L$ pairs of correlative ROIs.

### 2.3    Parallel Hierarchical BiLSTM Structure

BiLSTM is a modification to the conventional LSTM to process sequences of observations from both directions, starting from the first input observation to the last, and starting from the last observation back to the first [8]. However, this is insufficient for functional connectivity-based diagnosis, since the connectivity strength of each brain region for each subject may continuously different across time. Indeed, the more BiLSTM networks we utilize, the more features we can capture to better identify MCI patients. However, as investigated in [5], the deeper model generated by stacking two BiLSTM networks did not improve the final performance, and meanwhile, deeper or wider network means a larger number of parameters, which makes the enlarged network more prone to overfitting, Thus, we design a parallel hierarchical BiLSTM (PH-BiLSTM) to extract effective long short-term dependency features (Fig. 2). First, adaptive dFC networks $\left(\theta_l^n(t) \in \mathbb{R}^{N \times T \times L}\right)$ serve as the inputs of two fully connected networks, where the more complicated are the nonlinear transformations and the more abstract is the information extracted from this fully connected layer. Then the outputs enter into respective H-BiLSTM network, and finally the outputs of two H-BiLSTM networks are combined via a final fully connected layer. Additionally, each of fully connected layers involves the batch normalization and rectified linear unit (ReLu) activation function. The whole PH-BiLSTM network we proposed is shown in Fig. 2. For brief description, we denote a process of a LSTM cell as $\mathcal{H}$, and BiLSTM first computes the forward hidden sequence output $\overrightarrow{h}_t$, and the backward hidden sequence output $\overleftarrow{h}_t$ respectively (Eq. 6–7). Then $\overrightarrow{h}$ and $\overleftarrow{h}_t$ are used to generate the output $y_t$ that is formed by concatenating these two hidden states, and then updating the final output layer. The associated formulas are as follows:

$$\overrightarrow{h}_t = \mathcal{H}\left( W_{\theta h} \theta_t + W_{hh} \overrightarrow{h}_{t+1} + b_{h} \right) \tag{6}$$

$$\overleftarrow{h}_t = \mathcal{H}\left( W_{\theta h} \theta_t + W_{hh} \overleftarrow{h}_{t+1} + b_{h} \right) \tag{7}$$

$$y_t = \left[ \overrightarrow{h}_t, \overleftarrow{h}_t \right] \tag{8}$$

where $W_{\theta h}$ and $W_{\theta h}$ are the weight matrices for the input vector $\theta_t$. $W_{hh}$ and $W_{hh}$ are the weight matrices for the hidden state, and $b_{h}$ and $b_{h}$ denote the bias vectors.

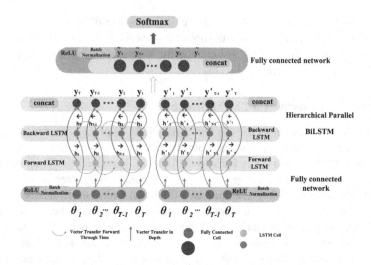

**Fig. 2.** PH-BiLSTM network architecture. The outputs of two parallel bidirectional LSTM are combined into a final fully connected layer.

## 3   Results and Discussion

### 3.1   Data Acquisition and Preprocessing

The present study involved 73 participants (36 MCI patients and 37 healthy controls) selected from the Alzheimer's Disease Neuroimaging Initiative (ADNI) dataset (http://adni.loni.usc.edu/). Data acquisition was performed using a 3 T Siemens scanner with the following parameters: flip angle = $90°$; matrix size = $64 \times 64$; voxel thickness = 3.4 mm; 197 volumes; 48 slices; TR = 3000 ms and TE = 30 ms. Specifically, we used only the last 180 volumes of the acquired R-fMRI series for the following preprocessing steps to ensure magnetization equilibrium. Please refer to [1] for more details.

### 3.2   Parameter Optimization and Training Strategy

As the parameter's sparsity level $\lambda$ and covariance $R_1$ have a great impact on the construction of adaptive dFC network, the identification of suitable network model parameters is crucial to achieve a good classification performance. The larger the parameter $\lambda$ is, the sparser the structural networks are. We set $\lambda = 0.01$ in our experiment to construct effective topological networks, resulting in $L(L = 161)$ pairs of correlative ROIs. As shown in Fig. 3, the classification accuracy can be improved with different $R_1$ values at fixed $\lambda$, and the highest accuracy of 87.67% can be reached when the parameter $R_1$ equals 0.5. The PH-BiLSTM model was trained and evaluated using Tensorflow. Data was split into 80% for training and 20% for testing (i.e., 5-fold cross-validation). Each of fully connected layer uses 64 neurons and ReLu activation function, and the LSTM module hidden size is 64. The network weights were learned using the Adam optimizer (Adaptive Moment Estimation) with an initial learning rate of

$10e - 4$, and we employed an exponential decay to decrease the learning rate, with the decay step 100 and decay rate 0.95. Training was stopped when the training loss stopped decreasing for the last 100 epochs or when the maximum epochs has been reached. Batch normalization was used to accelerate the neural network training. To improve the generalization performance of the model and to overcome the overfitting problem, the model was trained for minimizing the weighted cross-entropy loss function. Meanwhile, the dropout with a probability of 0.9 was adopted, and $l_2$ ($l_2 = 0.0015$) regularization was used to optimize network correctly.

### 3.3    Classification Performance

**Overview of Classification Performance.** As dFC is novel in this field, the disease diagnosis studies using dFC are quite limited. We compared our adaptive dFC against the traditional dFC based on SWC. We also compared various BiLSTM classifiers to validate the effectiveness of the proposed PH-BiLSTM for MCI diagnosis. In this study, several evaluation metrics such as the accuracy (ACC), sensitivity (SEN), and specificity (SPE) were adopted to evaluate the classification performance. The performance comparison results are summarized in Table 1, and the normalized confusion matrix for PH-BiLSTM is shown Fig. 4. The diagonal elements are ratios that indicate the predicted label is equal to the true label, which demonstrates that our method is effective.

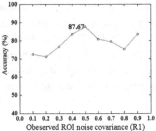
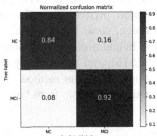

**Fig. 3.** Influence of parameter R1 to the accuracy.

**Fig. 4.** Confusion matrix for PH-BiLSTM.

**Efficacy of Adaptive FC via Kalman Filter.** In the traditional SWC method, using a rectangle window with different window lengths can yield substantially different results. As for the selection of window size $S$, we compared the MCI classification accuracies of different window sizes (($S = 20, 30, 40, 50, 60, 70$) points). As a result, the window size $S = 40$ yielded the best classification accuracy, which was thus adopted for the subsequent analysis in our experiment. The SWC method using a window size of 40 points and a step size of 2 points (6 s) resulted in 71 segments of BOLD signals. For each subject and each scan, 71 FC matrices were obtained, and correspondingly only $L$ pairs of correlative ROIs produced by the previous group-constrained model were preserved to reflect the dFC. A comparison between SWC with

BiLSTM and adaptive dFC with BiLSTM demonstrates that our adaptive dFC approach significantly improves the classification accuracy from 53.24% to 81.81%. Another comparison between SWC with PH-BiLSTM and adaptive dFC with PH-BiLSTM approaches shows that the classification accuracy is improved from 57.18% to 87.67%. The results indicate that the incorporation of the dependent information of datum points into connectivity network construction can indeed boost the performance of clinical identification of MCI.

**Table 1.** Performance comparison of different methods in MCI/NC classification.

| Method | ACC% | SEN% | SPE% | F1% | AUC% |
|---|---|---|---|---|---|
| SWC with BiLSTM | 53.24 | 52.50 | 53.93 | 50.73 | 51.30 |
| SWC with PH-BiLSTM | 57.18 | 47.50 | 66.43 | 51.87 | 55.71 |
| Adaptive dFC with BiLSTM | 81.81 | 85.71 | 78.21 | 82.53 | 87.91 |
| Adaptive dFC with H-BiLSTM | 71.46 | 69.28 | 73.57 | 70.38 | 78.24 |
| **Adaptive dFC with PH-BiLSTM** | **87.67** | **91.18** | **84.61** | **87.21** | **92.24** |

**Classification Performance of PH-BiLSTM.** To validate the advantage of PH-BiLSTM, we tested two other BiLSTM based architectures (BiLSTM and H-BiLSTM), and all these models use the same parameters. As shown in Table 1, we find that (1) H-BiLSTM performs worse than BiLSTM when using adaptive dFC, and (2) PH-BiLSTM outperforms BiLSTM and H-BiLSTM. H-BiLSTM does not increase the classification performance. The proposed PH-BiLSTM improves the classification performance, since it can capture more long time-dependent dFC networks characteristics. In addition, we compared the traditional SWC with PH-BiLSTM to the one with BiLSTM, and the accuracy of the former is increased by 4%. The experimental results suggest that our method can effectively extract as much change information of brain status as possible from both past and future information for each time step.

## 4   Conclusion

In summary, we explore an adaptive dFC network-based classification framework for MCI identification, and achieve superior classification performance. Experimental results illustrate that the adaptive dFC can effectively detect dynamic functional state transitions in a data-driven way without any explicit model assumptions. In addition, the comparison of the classification performance successfully validates the feasibility of the PH-BiLSTM classifier toward the automated diagnosis of MCI patients using the effective correlation coefficients as input pattern. The combination of the novel adaptive dFC network inference method and the PH-BiLSTM classifier can be useful for providing an interpretable and robust framework to the clinical diagnosis of cognitive impairment. Ultimately, the proposed method can effectively improve the diagnosis performance of MCI and benefit the development of computer-aided diagnosis tools in the clinical and pre-clinical practice.

# References

1. Li, Y., et al.: Novel effective connectivity inference using ultra-group constrained orthogonal forward regression and elastic multilayer perceptron classifier for MCI identification. IEEE Trans. Med. Imaging **38**, 1227–1239 (2018)
2. Calhoun, V.D.: The chronnectome: time-varying connectivity networks as the next frontier in fMRI data discovery. Neuron **84**(2), 262–274 (2014)
3. Preti, M.G.: The dynamic functional connectome: state-of-the-art and perspectives. Neuroimage **160**, 41–54 (2017)
4. Laumann, T.O., et al.: On the stability of BOLD fMRI correlations. Cerebral Cortex **27**(10), 4719–4732 (2017). https://doi.org/10.1093/cercor/bhw265
5. Yan, W., Zhang, H., Sui, J., Shen, D.: Deep chronnectome learning via full bidirectional long short-term memory networks for MCI diagnosis. In: Frangi, A.F., Schnabel, J.A., Davatzikos, C., Alberola-López, C., Fichtinger, G. (eds.) MICCAI 2018. LNCS, vol. 11072, pp. 249–257. Springer, Cham (2018). https://doi.org/10.1007/978-3-030-00931-1_29
6. Wee, C.Y.: Group-constrained sparse fMRI connectivity modeling for mild cognitive impairment identification. Brain Struct. Funct. **219**(2), 641–656 (2014)
7. Li, Y.: Multimodal hyper-connectivity of functional networks using functionally-weighted LASSO for MCI classification. Med. Image Anal. **52**, 80–96 (2019)
8. Elsheikh, A., et al.: Bidirectional handshaking LSTM for remaining useful life prediction. Neurocomputing **323**, 148–156 (2018)

# Multi-template Based Auto-Weighted Adaptive Structural Learning for ASD Diagnosis

Fanglin Huang[1], Peng Yang[1], Shan Huang[1], Le Ou-Yang[2],
Tianfu Wang[1(✉)], and Baiying Lei[1(✉)]

[1] National-Regional Key Technology Engineering Laboratory for Medical
Ultrasound, Guangdong Key Laboratory for Biomedical Measurements
and Ultrasound Imaging, School of Biomedical Engineering,
Health Science Center, Shenzhen University, Shenzhen 518060, China
{tfwang, leiby}@szu.edu.cn

[2] Guangdong Key Laboratory of Intelligent Information Processing
and Shenzhen Key Laboratory of Media Security, College of Information
Engineering, Shenzhen University, Shenzhen 518060, China

**Abstract.** Autism spectrum disorder (ASD) is a group of neurodevelopmental disorder and its diagnosis is still a challenging issue. To handle it, we propose a novel multi-template ensemble classification framework for ASD diagnosis. Specifically, based on different templates, we construct multiple functional connectivity brain networks for each subject using resting-state functional magnetic resonance imaging (rs-fMRI) data and extract features representations from these networks. Then, our auto-weighted adaptive structural learning model can learn the shared similarity matrix by an adaptive process while selecting informative features. In addition, our method can automatically allot optimal weight for each template without extra weights and parameters. Further, an ensemble classification strategy is adopted to get the final diagnosis results. Our extensive experiments conducted on the Autism Brain Imaging Data Exchange (ABIDE) database demonstrate that our method can improve ASD diagnosis performance. Additionally, our method can detect the ASD-related biomarkers for further medical analysis.

**Keywords:** Autism spectrum disorder · Multi-template · Adaptive structure learning · Auto-weighted

## 1 Introduction

Autism spectrum disorder (ASD) is a broad range of mental disability, which can lead to serious social, communication and behavioral challenges [1]. According to the latest news released by Centers for Disease Control and Prevention, about 1 in 59 children were diagnosed as ASD. Therefore, constructing an effective ASD diagnosis model has become a hot topic. As more and more evidence shows that ASD is associated with disruptions in functional organization of the brain [2], functional connectivity network (FCN) constructed from rs-fMRI has become a commonly-used tool for ASD identification. Therefore, we utilize FCN to explore abundant brain functional connectivity

© Springer Nature Switzerland AG 2019
H.-I. Suk et al. (Eds.): MLMI 2019, LNCS 11861, pp. 516–524, 2019.
https://doi.org/10.1007/978-3-030-32692-0_59

information among brain regions and consider these information as the feature representations of each subject.

For the identification of ASD, most current methods utilize only single brain template [3, 4]. However, researches suggested feature representations derived from a single template may not be sufficient to reveal population differences between patients and normal controls (NC) [5]. Meanwhile, the multi-template based methods that extract multiple sets of feature representations for each subject can decrease the negative impacts of registration errors and provide complementary information for diagnosis [6]. For example, Jin *et al.* [7] proposed to parcellate a brain template with 90 cerebral regions of interest (ROIs) into multiple different number of sub-ROIs, and then combined feature representations from these sub-ROIs together into one multi-kernel support vector machine classification scheme to get better ASD classification results. Hence, developing a new multi-template diagnosis method is highly desirable.

Regarding ASD recognition, most of the current approaches simply connect or average multiple sets of feature representations obtained from multiple templates [6, 8], and then conduct feature selection algorithms on them directly. They neglect the underlying data distribution information of multi-template space. On the other hand, previous studies considering structure information often exist the following disadvantages: first, most of them constructed similarity matrix and selected features separately. Hence, the similarity matrix is often derived from the raw data with lots of noise, which produces an inaccurate similarity matrix and thus further disrupts the local neighboring structure. Moreover, most acquired similarity matrixes are not in the ideal state, where the number of connected component in it is the same as the number of class label. Additionally, those approaches often combine different templates via extra weight parameters, leading to model selection becoming difficult.

To tackle the above issues, we propose a novel auto-weighted adaptive structure learning based multi- template ensemble classification method (ASL-E). Figure 1 shows the overview of proposed method. Our method is mainly composed of three parts: FCNs construction, ASL model construction, and ensemble classification. The promising diagnosis performance achieved on the public Autism Brain Imaging Data Exchange (ABIDE) database implies our method is feasible for the diagnosis of ASD. Our main contribution is summarized as below (1) Based on multiple templates, we construct multiple FCNs for each subject and extract feature from them. (2) We develop an auto-weighted adaptive structure learning based model, which can select the most discriminative features by considering the structural information of each template space. (3) We get the final diagnosis results by an ensemble strategy.

## 2  Proposed Method

### 2.1  Auto-Weighted Adaptive Structural Learning

**Multi-task Sparse Learning.** Suppose that there are $M$ supervised learning tasks, i.e., $M$ templates. Let $\mathbf{X}^m = \left[\mathbf{x}_1^m, \mathbf{x}_2^m, \ldots, \mathbf{x}_N^m\right]^T \in \mathbb{R}^{N \times d}$ denote the feature matrix corresponding to the $m$-th task, where $\mathbf{x}_i^m \in \mathbb{R}^d$ denotes the feature vector of the $i$-th subject in the $m$-th task, $N$ denotes the total number of training subjects. Let $\mathbf{y} = [y_1, y_2, \ldots, y_N]^T \in \mathbb{R}^N$ denote the label vector, where $y_i \in \{-1, +1\}$, i.e., NC or patient. Hence, the linear multi-task learning model is formulated as follows by using $\mathbf{w}^m \in \mathbb{R}^d$ to parameterize a linear discriminant function for $m$-th task:

$$\min_{\mathbf{w}} \sum_{m=1}^{M} \frac{1}{2} \|\mathbf{y} - \mathbf{X}^m \mathbf{w}^m\|_2^2 + \gamma \|\mathbf{W}\|_1 \qquad (1)$$

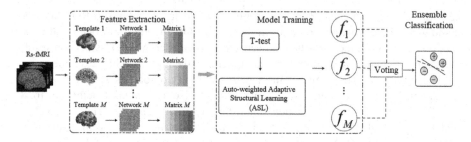

**Fig. 1.** Overview of the proposed ASD diagnostic framework.

where $\mathbf{W} = [\mathbf{w}^1, \mathbf{w}^2, \ldots, \mathbf{w}^M] \in \mathbb{R}^{d \times M}$ is the weight matrix. Here, $\|\mathbf{W}\|_1$ is alied to fces some entries of $\mathbf{W}$ to be zero to select informative features specific to different templates space. The sparsity control parameter $\gamma$ is applied to balance the relative contributions of the two terms in Eq. (4). It is worth note that, since the number of ROIs corresponding to different templates is different, the feature of each sample derived from different templates are also different. Accordingly, $\ell_{2,1}$-norm rularizer, which guides the joint selection of the common feature across different template, is not appropriate in our experiment.

**Auto-Weighted Adaptive Structural Learning.** We denote $\mathbf{S} \in \mathbb{R}^{N \times N}$ as similarity mrix, and $s_{ij}$ as the $(i\,j)$-entry in $\mathbf{S}$. Suppose that each subject $\mathbf{x}_i$ is linked by all other subjects with probability $s_{ij}$. Such probability can be considered as the similarity between them. Since closer subjects are likely to have greater probability to link, $s_{ij}$ is inversely proportional to the distance between subject $\mathbf{x}_i$ and subject $\mathbf{x}_j$. Therefore, $\mathbf{S}$ can be obtained by addressing

$$\min_{\mathbf{S}} \sum_{i=1}^{N} \sum_{j=1}^{N} \|\mathbf{x}_i - \mathbf{x}_i\|_2^2 s_{ij} + \alpha \|\mathbf{S}\|_F^2, \ s.t. \forall i, \mathbf{s}_i^T \mathbf{1} = 1, 0 \le s_{ij} \le 1. \qquad (2)$$

where the above regularizer is used to avoid the trivial solution, $\alpha$ is the corresponding turning parameter.

However, the number of connected components of $\mathbf{S}$ determined by Eq. (2) is one, not equal to the number of label categories [9]. To address this issue, we denote $\mathbf{L}_s$ $\left(\mathbf{L}_s = \mathbf{D} - (\mathbf{S}^T + \mathbf{S})/2\right)$ as Laplacian matrix, where $\mathbf{D}$ $\left(d_{ii} = \sum_j (s_{ij} + s_{ji})/2\right)$ is the corresponding degree matrix. It can be proved that if $rank(\mathbf{L}_s) = n - c$, $\mathbf{S}$ will contain exact $c$ connected components [10]. So, we add a rank constraint to Eq. (2) as follows:

$$\min_{\mathbf{S}} \sum_{i=1}^{N} \sum_{j=1}^{N} \|\mathbf{x}_i - \mathbf{x}_i\|_2^2 s_{ij} + \alpha \|\mathbf{S}\|_F^2, \ s.t. \forall i, \mathbf{s}_i^T \mathbf{1} = 1, 0 \le s_{ij} \le 1, rank(\mathbf{L}_s) = n - c. \tag{3}$$

where $c$ represents the number of label categories. It allocates adaptive neighbors to each subject, which implies that $\mathbf{S}$ is updated until it involves the appropriate number of connected components.

We assume that although the feature representations are collected based on different templates, they come from the same samples, so the intrinsic distribution should be identical. Accordingly, the shared similarity matrix can be determined by solving

$$\min_{\mathbf{S},\mu_m} \sum_m^M (\mu_m)^{\varphi} \sum_{i=1}^{N} \sum_{j=1}^{N} \|\mathbf{x}_i - \mathbf{x}_i\|_2^2 s_{ij} + \alpha \|\mathbf{S}\|_F^2,$$
$$s.t. \forall i, \mathbf{s}_i^T \mathbf{1} = 1, 0 \le s_{ij} \le 1, rank(\mathbf{L}_s) = n - c, 0 \le \mu_m \le 1, \mu_m^T \mathbf{1} = 1. \tag{4}$$

where $\mu_m (m = 1, 2, \ldots, M)$ is the weight corresponding to the $m$-th template, $\varphi$ is the non-negative scalar imposed to keep weights distribution smooth.

If two subjects are very similar in high-dimensional feature space, the distance between them should be small in the label space. To maintain this relationship between samples, we proposed a new regularization item.

$$\min_{\mathbf{W},\mathbf{S},\mu_m} \sum_m^M (\mu_m)^{\varphi} \sum_{i=1}^{N} \sum_{j=1}^{N} \left\| (\mathbf{w}^m)^T \left( \mathbf{x}_i^m - \mathbf{x}_j^m \right) \right\|_2^2 s_{ij} + \alpha \|\mathbf{S}\|_F^2,$$
$$s.t. \forall i, \mathbf{s}_i^T \mathbf{1} = 1, 0 \le s_{ij} \le 1, rank(\mathbf{L}_s) = n - c, 0 \le \mu_m \le 1, \mu_m^T \mathbf{1} = 1. \tag{5}$$

It preserves the local neighboring structures of the original data during mapping by incorporating the above regularization terms.

By combining the above regularization terms and multi-task learning model, we get the following objective function.

$$\min_{\mathbf{W},\mathbf{S},\mu_m} \frac{1}{2} \sum_{m=1}^{M} \|\mathbf{y} - \mathbf{X}^m \mathbf{w}^m\|_2^2 + \gamma \|\mathbf{W}\|_{1,1} +$$
$$\beta \sum_{m=1}^{M} (\mu_m)^{\varphi} \sum_{i=1}^{N} \sum_{j=1}^{N} \left\| (\mathbf{w}^m)^T \left( \mathbf{x}_i^m - \mathbf{x}_j^m \right) \right\|_2^2 s_{ij} + \alpha \|\mathbf{S}\|_F^2, \tag{6}$$
$$s.t. \forall i, \mathbf{s}_i^T \mathbf{1} = 1, 0 \le s_{ij} \le 1, rank(\mathbf{L}_s) = n - c, 0 \le \mu_m \le 1, \mu_m^T \mathbf{1} = 1.$$

where $\beta$ denotes the positive parameter.

To remove the undesirable parameter $\varphi$, we propose the auto-weighted multi-template learning method with adaptive neighbors as follows

$$\min_{\mathbf{W},\mathbf{S}} \frac{1}{2} \sum_{m=1}^{M} \|\mathbf{y} - \mathbf{X}^m \mathbf{w}^m\|_2^2 + \gamma \|\mathbf{W}\|_{1,1} + \beta \sum_{m=1}^{M} \sqrt{\sum_{i=1}^{N} \sum_{j=1}^{N} \left\| (\mathbf{w}^m)^T \left( \mathbf{x}_i^m - \mathbf{x}_j^m \right) \right\|_2^2 s_{ij}} + \alpha \|\mathbf{S}\|_F^2, \tag{7}$$
$$s.t. \forall i, \mathbf{s}_i^T \mathbf{1} = 1, 0 \le s_{ij} \le 1, rank(\mathbf{L}_s) = n - c.$$

To facilitate optimization of Eq. (7), we compute the derivatives of the square root, and obtain the following formulations

$$\min_{\mathbf{W},\mathbf{S}} \frac{1}{2} \sum_{m=1}^{M} \|\mathbf{y} - \mathbf{X}^m \mathbf{w}^m\|_2^2 + \gamma \|\mathbf{W}\|_{1,1} + \beta \sum_{m=1}^{M} \mu_m \sum_{i=1}^{N} \sum_{j=1}^{N} \left\| (\mathbf{w}^m)^T \left( \mathbf{x}_i^m - \mathbf{x}_j^m \right) \right\|_2^2 s_{ij} + \alpha \|\mathbf{S}\|_F^2, \quad (8)$$
$$s.t. \forall i, \mathbf{s}_i^T \mathbf{1} = 1, 0 \le s_{ij} \le 1, rank(\mathbf{L}_s) = n - c.$$

and

$$\mu_m = 1/2 \sqrt{ \sum_{i=1}^{N} \sum_{j=1}^{N} \left\| (\mathbf{w}^m)^T \left( \mathbf{x}_i^m - \mathbf{x}_j^m \right) \right\|_2^2 s_{ij} } \quad (9)$$

From that, we find, unlike other methods, our method can learn optimal weights for each template automatically without additive parameters as previous methods do [11].

## 2.2   Ensemble Classification

To better make use of multiple sets of informative features selected from multiple different templates space, we utilize an ensemble classification strategy. Specifically, after feature selection via ASL model, we get $M$ subsets of feature with respect to the $M$ task (i.e., templates). Then, we can construct $M$ classifiers separately via linear mapping function $\mathbf{y} = \mathbf{X}^m \mathbf{w}^m$. Next, we apply the majority voting strategy to balance the outputs of $M$ classifiers to get the class label of each testing subject.

# 3   Experiments

## 3.1   Subjects

We select to assess the results of our method using rs-fMRI scans downloaded from two imaging centers in the ABIDE database, i.e., the University of Michigan: sample 1 (UM_1) center and the New York University (NYU) Langone Medical Center. In UM_1 center, there is totally 82 subjects (46 NC and 36 ASD), while NYU center involves totally 171 subjects (98 NC and 73 ASD), respectively. Our experiments involve male and female subjects with ages ranging from 6 to 40 years old.

## 3.2   Experimental Setting

In our paper, we utilize the upper triangular entries of the functional connectivity matrices as feature vectors. Such strategy has achieved extensive successes in rs-fMRI-based identification applications [12]. We further adopt $t$-test strategy to reduce feature dimensionality before model training, which can greatly reduce the subsequent computational burden. We use 10-fold cross-validation to assess the diagnosis performance of our method. Then, we repeat the processing ten times and report the average of the results to avoid the biased result resulted from the fold selection. For the sake of fairness, we set all parameters in the same range, i.e., $\{10^{-3}, \ldots, 10^3\}$. To quantitatively estimate the results, we adopt the metrics of accuracy (ACC), sensitivity (SEN), specificity (SPE), positive predictive value (PPV), negative predictive value (NPV), and area under the receiver operating characteristic curve (AUC).

We compare our method with CSVC to show the effectiveness of feature selection. In addition, one of the main contributions in this work is to incorporate the local manifold structure of each template space in an auto-weighted adaptive learning manner. To this end, we adopt the following three comparison strategies: (1) we set our proposed ASL-E method with $\alpha = 0$, $\beta = 0$, such that the manifold regularization is disabled (denoted as LeaL). (2) we obtain the similarity matrix via a binary weighting method (denoted as Binary) [7]. (3) Similarly, the similarity matrix is obtained by Heat kernel weighting (denoted as Heat) [5]. We also compare our method with a popular multi-task learning algorithm, LogisticLasso in MALSAR1.1 package (denoted as LogL) [13]. To show the effectiveness of multi-template, we run our proposed method on different sets of feature derived from different single template (Automatic Anatomical Labeling (AAL), Dosenbach 160 (Dos160), Craddock 200 (CC200)).

### 3.3 Comparisons with State-of-the-Art Methods

Figure 2 shows the overall classification performance of the competing methods on two imaging centers. We can observe that our proposed ASL-E algorithm can achieve the mean classification accuracies of 76.25% and 77.29% on NYU and UM_1, respectively, which are better than its rivals on the same centers. Comparing ASL-E with CSVC, we observe that the feature selection helps improve classification results. Different from other methods, ASL-E integrates local manifold structure in an adaptive process and obtains better results. The results suggest the superiority of joint feature selection and adaptive structure learning. LeaL and LogL neglect the subject-subject relation exists in each template space. In addition, Binary and Heat incorporate the local structure information without considering the optimal neighbor assignment of its similarity matrix. ASL-E performs both local structure learning and feature selection simultaneously, and thus outperforms its rivals accordingly.

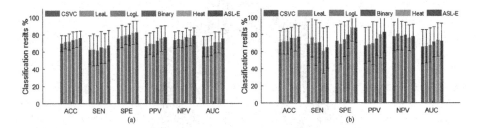

**Fig. 2.** Comparison of classification results achieved by different methods. (a) NYU center and (b) UM_1 center.

### 3.4 Comparisons with Different Templates

From Fig. 3(a), we can find method based on the combined features achieve consistently higher accuracy on all centers. It implies that different template can provide the complementary information needed to classify the images accurately. Figure 3(b) shows the box plots. We find the classification results are large divergent while utilizing different template. The reason is that the disease-related features obtained from a certain template may be more informative than those achieved by other templates.

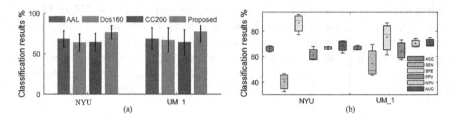

**Fig. 3.** Classification results achieved on two imaging centers with respect to different template. (a) The comparison of classification accuracy. (b) Distributions of ACC, SEN, SPE, PPV, NPV, and AUC based on three different single templates.

### 3.5 Disease-Related Features

We reveal the disease-related features selected by our ASL-E method to identify the ASD patients from NC. Figure 4 visualizes top 30 commonly selected discriminative features shared by two imaging centers. We observe from Fig. 4 that the features promoting accurate ASD diagnosis not only exist in in the left or right hemisphere, but across the two hemispheres [14]. Besides, the feature weights of right hemispheres are smaller than left hemispheres. Furthermore, the selected features involve multiple cortical regions and subcortical structures, such as the calcarine sulcus, temporal lobes and occipital lobes, which have been proved to be associated with ASD [15, 16].

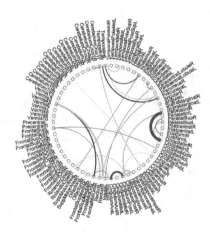

**Fig. 4.** Common discriminative features selected by ASL-E from two imaging centers.

# 4 Conclusion

This paper develops a multi-template ensemble classification framework for ASD diagnosis. Particularly, to learn the local neighbor structure exists in multiple templates, we impose the relationship between subjects as a regularization term into our multi-task sparse learning model. Meanwhile, we learn the optimal similarity matrix shared across different template. Our experiment results show that the performance of our method is superior to other existing methods, which is potential for diagnosis.

**Acknowledgment.** This work was supported partly by National Natural Science Foundation of China (Nos. 61871274, 61801305 and 81571758), National Natural Science Foundation of Guangdong Province (No. 2017A030313377), Guangdong Pearl River Talents Plan (2016 ZT06S220), Shenzhen Peacock Plan (Nos. KQTD2016053112051497 and KQTD2015033016 104926), and Shenzhen Key Basic Research Project (Nos. JCYJ2017 0413152804728, JCYJ20180507184647636, JCYJ20170818142347251 and JCYJ20170818094109846).

# References

1. Lord, C., Cook, E.H., Leventhal, B.L., Amaral, D.G.: Autism spectrum disorders. Neuron **28**, 355–363 (2000)
2. Shi, F., Wang, L., Peng, Z., Wee, C.-Y., Shen, D.: Altered modular organization of structural cortical networks in children with autism. PLoS ONE **8**, e63131 (2013)
3. Wang, M., Zhang, D., Huang, J., Yap, P., Shen, D., Liu, M.: Identifying autism spectrum disorder with multi-site fMRI via low-rank domain adaptation. IEEE Trans. Med. Imaging (2019)
4. Huang, H., Liu, X., Jin, Y., Lee, S.W., Wee, C.Y., Shen, D.: Enhancing the representation of functional connectivity networks by fusing multi - view information for autism spectrum disorder diagnosis. Hum. Brain Mapp. **40**(3), 833–854 (2018)
5. Liu, M., Zhang, D., Shen, D.: Relationship induced multi-template learning for diagnosis of Alzheimer's disease and mild cognitive impairment. IEEE Trans. Med. Imaging **35**, 1463–1474 (2016)
6. Min, R., Wu, G., Cheng, J., Wang, Q., Shen, D., Alzheimer's Disease Neuroimaging Initiative: Multi - atlas based representations for Alzheimer's disease diagnosis. Hum. Brain Mapp. **35**, 5052–5070 (2014)
7. Jie, B., Zhang, D., Cheng, B., Shen, D., Alzheimer's Disease Neuroimaging Initiative: Manifold regularized multitask feature learning for multimodality disease classification. Hum. Brain Mapp. **36**, 489–507 (2015)
8. Leporé, N., et al.: Multi-atlas tensor-based morphometry and its application to a genetic study of 92 twins. In: Proceedings MICCAI Workshop, New York, USA, pp. 48–55 (2008)
9. Nie, F., Cai, G., Li, X.: Multi-view clustering and semi-supervised classification with adaptive neighbours. In: Proceedings AAAI, San Francisco, California, USA, pp. 2408–2414 (2017)
10. Nie, F., Zhu, W., Li, X.: Unsupervised feature selection with structured graph optimization. In: Proceedings AAAI, Phoenix, Arizona, USA, pp. 1302–1308 (2016)
11. Lei, B., et al.: Neuroimaging retrieval via adaptive ensemble manifold learning for brain disease diagnosis. IEEE Biomed. Health Inform. **23**(4), 1661–1673 (2018)

12. Abraham, A., et al.: Deriving reproducible biomarkers from multi-site resting-state data: an autism-based example. NeuroImage **147**, 736–745 (2017)
13. Zhou, J., Chen, J., Ye, J.: MALSAR: Multi-task learning via structural regularization. Arizona State University, vol. 21 (2011)
14. Wang, J., Wang, Q., Zhang, H., Chen, J., Wang, S., Shen, D.: Sparse multiview task-centralized ensemble learning for ASD diagnosis based on age-and sex-related functional connectivity patterns. IEEE Trans. Cybern. **49**(8), 3141–3154 (2018)
15. Johnson, M.H., et al.: The emergence of the social brain network: evidence from typical and atypical development. Dev. Psychopathol. **17**, 599–619 (2005)
16. Redcay, E.: The superior temporal sulcus performs a common function for social and speech perception: implications for the emergence of autism. Neurosci. Biobehav. Rev. **32**, 123–142 (2008)

# Learn to Step-wise Focus on Targets for Biomedical Image Segmentation

Siyuan Wei[(⊠)] and Li Wang

Key Laboratory of Urban Run Emergency Security Simulation Technology,
School of Economics and Management, Beihang University, Beijing, China
{wsybuaa,wl2008}@buaa.edu.cn

**Abstract.** Current segmentation networks based on the encoder-decoder architecture have tried recovering spatial information by stacking convolution blocks in the decoder. Unconventionally, we consider that iteratively exploiting spatial attention from high stage to refine lower stage features can form an attention-driven mechanism to step-wise recover detailed features. In this paper, we rethink image segmentation from a novel perspective: a process of step-wise focusing on targets. We develop a lightweight Focus Module (FM) and present a powerful transplantable Step-wise Focus Network (SFN) for biomedical image segmentation. FM extracts high-level spatial attention and combines it with low-level features by our proposed focus learning to generate revised features. Our SFN extends U-Net encoder sub-network and employs just FMs to construct a focus path in order to consistently refine features. We evaluate SFNs in comparison with U-Net and other state-of-art methods on multiple biomedical image segmentation benchmarks. While using 30% floating-point operations and 60% parameters of U-Net, SFNs achieve great performances without any postprocessing.

## 1 Introduction

Image segmentation is a fundamental task in biomedical image analysis, which demands pixel-wise labeling with high accuracy. However, manually labeling is error-prone with consuming much time. With the objective of precise and automatic segmentation, deep convolutional neural networks (CNNs) have been broadly applied to biomedical image segmentation. Since the fully convolutional network (FCN) [3], the encoder-decoder architecture has proved to be quite effective for dense prediction. Lots of great works based on FCN have obtained excellent results on various benchmarks. In the encoder-decoder architecture, the encoder gradually downsamples to hierarchically encode semantic features, and the decoder upsamples feature maps to produce precise results. Among them, U-Net [6] performs greatly in biomedical image segmentation task.

For a better performance, FCN and U-Net both use skip connections between the encoder and decoder subnetworks to combine deep semantic features and shallow detailed features. Based on U-Net, numerous works proposed different powerful methods to enhance models' representational powers. The UNet++ [14] designed nested dense skip pathways to reduce the semantic gap between the encoder's and

© Springer Nature Switzerland AG 2019
H.-I. Suk et al. (Eds.): MLMI 2019, LNCS 11861, pp. 525–532, 2019.
https://doi.org/10.1007/978-3-030-32692-0_60

decoder's feature maps. Deep supervision methods with additional labels [13] have been proposed to help networks obtain better results in retinal vessel segmentation. Furthermore, recent works [2, 5, 12] utilize attention mechanism to assist models to learn the attention distribution on the channel or spatial domain.

Although methods based on U-Net have achieved satisfactory performances, there is lack of more effective and interpretable methods to guide feature refinement than stacking convolutional blocks to constructing a decoder. Given that attention mechanism helps selectively reinforce features, there could be a better way to guide feature refinement in an attention-driven manner.

In this paper, we rethink biomedical image segmentation task from a novel perspective: a process of step-wise focusing on targets from rough location to accurate contour. Inspired by attention mechanism, we consider that iteratively exploiting high-level spatial attention to refine low-level features helps form an attention-driven mechanism of step-wise refining features.

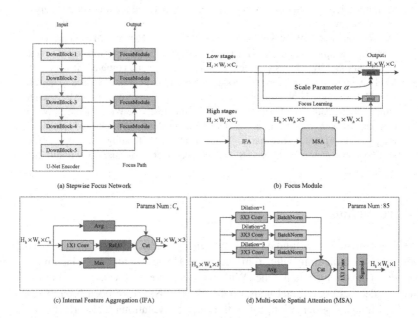

**Fig. 1.** An overview of Step-wise Focus Network (SFN). (a) SFN based on the U-Net encoder. (b) Components of Focus Module. (c) Internal Feature Aggregation Operations. (d) Multi-scale Spatial Attention Operations. The green line and red line respectively represent max-pooling operation and bilinear interpolation up-sample operation. (Color figure online)

Driven by this assumption, we propose a lightweight but effective Focus Module (FM) as depicted in Fig. 1(b). FM extracts the high-level spatial attention to generate a single channel mask and then utilize it to refine low-level features by our proposed focus learning mechanism. Based on FM, we present our step-wise focus network (SFN), a novel, powerful and elegant architecture of high interpretability, which involves two parts: an encoder and a focus path.

We extensively evaluate SFN in comparison with U-Net and other state-of-art methods on multiple biomedical image segmentation benchmarks: cell nuclei segmentation, optic disc and cup segmentation in eye fundus, vessels segmentation in retinal fundus images. Our SFN has achieved great performances including less computation costs, smaller capacity, and better accuracy without any postprocessing.

## 2 Method

### 2.1 Focus Module

Previous attention mechanism methods in computer vision tasks have tried using another branch to get attention weights [2, 11] in order to selectively recalibrate feature maps from the main branch, which may increase occupied GPU memory, extra parameters and computation overhead. In contrast, we would like to construct a lightweight architectural unit to combine high-level attention and low-level features. Based on this idea, we propose Focus Module and Focus Learning Mechanism inspired by attention mechanism and residual connection [1]. In 2-D image segmentation task, given high stage and low stage feature maps, $X_h \in \mathbb{R}^{H_h \times W_h \times C_h}, X_l \in \mathbb{R}^{H_l \times W_l \times C_l}$, as inputs, our focus module works in the following three steps:

**Internal Feature Aggregation.** In order to avoid information loss while extracting spatial attention, we adopt a simple way to generate a spatial descriptor with internal information aggregated. Concretely speaking, we utilize three paralleled branches: one branch uses a $1 \times 1$ convolution with ReLU function followed to compress the feature maps' channels to one, and the other two branches utilize average-operation and max-operation respectively along the channel axis to extract the internal information of $X_h$. Then the three results are concatenated along the channel to produce the results $X_s$. All above operations shown in Fig. 1(c) can be summarized as follows:

$$X_s = I(X_h) = \text{Concat}[\delta(W_\theta X_h); Avg(X_h); Max(X_h)], \tag{1}$$

where $\delta$ stands for the ReLU function, $W_\theta$ are weights of $1 \times 1$ convolution filter.

**Extract Multi-scale Spatial Attention.** To extract multi-scale spatial attention embedded in $X_S$ a lightweight feature pyramid unit is employed in this step. In our suggested design as shown in Fig. 1(d), three dilated convolution branches with dilation rates of 1, 2 and 3 are paralleled with a channel-axis average operation. It's worth noting that using larger dilated convolution kernel here may interfuse irrelevant long-ranged information especially when the segmented targets are small-scale and close-set. Finally, the result is compressed to 1 channel by $1 \times 1$ convolution and normalized by sigmoid function. Formally, the focus module generates a spatial attention mask $X_m$ as the following equation shows:

$$X_m = M(X_s) = \sigma(W_c Concat[W_1 X_s; W_2 X_s; W_3 X_s; Avg(X_s)]) \tag{2}$$

Where $W_c$ are weights of $1 \times 1$ convolution, $W_1$, $W_2$, $W_3$ are weights of three dilated convolution and $\sigma$ denotes the sigmoid function. The bilinear interpolation up-sample operation on the spatial mask $X_m$ is omitted in the above equation. We choose a feature pyramid module rather than n × n convolution for it has more stable performances in our experiments. Due to the limitation of pages, related ablation study is not shown in this paper.

**Focus Learning.** The mask $X_m$ softly weights spatial attention extracted from high stage. Since the mask is produced from the high-stage feature map, it has deeper semantic features but worse spatial information. Simply using skip connection or multiplication cannot guide feature fusing effectively between the mask $X_m$ and the low stage feature map $X_l$. Therefore, we propose focus learning mechanism to effectively combine the high stage single channel attention mask and low-level feature maps. Specifically, the mask, $X_m \in \mathbb{R}^{H' \times W' \times 1}$, is element-wise multiplied with the low-stage feature map $X_l = [x_l^1, x_l^2, \ldots, x_l^{c'}]$ along the channel axis. Then we perform an element-wise sum operation with $X_l$ inspired by residual connection. During above operations, a scale parameter $\alpha$ that can be learned is used to balance the influence of $X_m$. Consequently, all operations by focus learning can be summarized as the following equation:

$$H(X_m, X_l) = (1 + \alpha X_m) \otimes X_l, \tag{3}$$

where $\otimes$ denotes the element-wise multiplication along the channel axis.

## 2.2 Step-wise Focus Network

Our proposed Step-wise Focus Network (SFN) consists of two part: an encoder and a focus path. As illustrated in Fig. 1(a), SFN employs U-Net encoder sub-network to encode semantic features from 5 stages and integrate a focus path constructed by 4 focus modules. Compared to the normal decoder design, our SFN introduces an attention-driven feature refinement mechanism in a bottom-up manner, which can be applied to other base architectures. Specifically, the deepest focus module combines spatial attention extracted from the high stage with low stage features to generate a revised feature map, which will be fed into the next focus module as the high stage input. Each time the spatial attention and low stage features are combined by focus learning mechanism, SFN learns to focus on targets with one step forward. By iteratively utilizing focus modules, the spatial information is consistently recalibrated along the focus path. We call this process the attention-driven feature refinement mechanism.

## 3 Experiments

We extensively evaluate our SFN in multiple biomedical image segmentation tasks including 3 datasets. More details about datasets and experiments are shown in Sect. 3.1. To prove the merits and high transportability of SFN, we compare SFNs that extends different base architectures as encoder with the baseline model U-Net on the task of cell nuclei segmentation. Furthermore, we conduct extensive experiments on the other two benchmarks to exhibit SFN's broad effectiveness.

## 3.1    Datasets

**Data Science Bowl 2018 (DSB 2018).** The dataset contains 670 segmented nuclei images (536/134 for training/testing) of different cell types, which were acquired under various conditions and vary in magnification, resolution and imaging modality.

**DRIVE [10].** The DRIVE dataset contains 40 retinal images (20/20 for training/testing). For the test cases, two manual segmentations are provided. We use the one that is normally used as golden standard to test models. We extract the green channel of original image as model input.

**Drishti-GS [9, 10].** It consists of 101 eye fundus images (50/51 for training/testing). The optic disc and cup in all the images have been marked by 4 experienced eye experts. We use pixel-wise annotations that is confirmed by at least 3 experts as evaluation standard.

## 3.2    Implementation Details

We use the original U-Net (output channels of stages in the encoder are 32, 64, 128, 256, 512) to compare with the SFNs that extend U-Net' encoder and other base architectures. We have also designed Res18-SFN and Mobile-SFN that extend MobileNetV2 [7] and ResNet18 [1] separately. The strides of convolution layers in ResNet-18 and MobileNetV2 are adjusted to guarantee the unified output stride of 16. A focus path that consists of 4 focus modules is deployed in each SFN architecture. The focus path in Res18-SFN accepts the initial convolution block and 4 residual building blocks' outputs. The focus path in Mobile-SFN connects with the last five inverted residual building blocks.

Adam optimizer are used to train all models and cross-entropy is employed as loss function on all tasks. Normal data augmentation methods (affine transformation, random scale, axial flip, random crop) are applied to pre-process images. Pixel intensity in each image is rescaled to the range of [0, 1]. All models are trained on 1 NVIDIA Tesla K80 GPU. During evaluation, we feed images with batch size of 1 into models to calculate the Intersection over Union (IoU), Dice Score (DSC) and pixel-wise accuracy.

## 3.3    Results

**Results on Cell Nuclei Segmentation.** Experiment results in Table 1 have shown that our SFN achieves a great balance between performances and device limitation. Compared with U-Net, our SFN almost obtains an equal IoU score to U-Net while using 60% parameters, 30% floating-point operations. Furthermore, SFN has the same efficient usage of GPU memory as U-Net architecture. We have also tested SFNs bases on other models. The evaluation results of Res18-SFN and Mobile-SFN have indicated the highly transplantable and powerful architecture of SFN. Due to expanding operations in inverted residual bottlenecks, SFN based on MobileNetV2 has a higher GPU memory occupation than others. By selecting lightweight MobileNetV2 to distill inherent semantic information from different stages, we can build the same high-performance SFN models as U-Net on mobile devices.

**Table 1.** Segmentation results, parameter number, giga floating-point operations (GFLOPS), max occupied GPU memory of models trained on cell nuclei segmentation task. Results of all models are computed for input tensor of size 128 × 128 × 3.

| Architectures | Params | GFLOPS | GPU memory | IoU |
|---|---|---|---|---|
| U-Net SFN | 7.85M | 6.99 | **26.60M** | **0.870** |
| | 4.72M | **2.15** | **26.60M** | 0.859 |
| Res18-SFN | 11.18M | 2.24 | 31.33M | 0.857 |
| Mobile-SFN | **1.81M** | 1.67 | 45.57M | **0.870** |

**Table 2.** Segmentation results for SFN, U-Net and another method recently reported on extensive benchmarks. "—" means the result is not reported.

| Dataset | Methods | IoU | DSC | Accuracy |
|---|---|---|---|---|
| DRIVE | Yishuo et al. [13] | — | — | 0.950 |
| | U-Net | **0.690** | **0.816** | **0.968** |
| | SFNet | 0.670 | 0.801 | 0.964 |
| Drishti-GS Optic Disc | Zilly et al. [15] | 0.910 | **0.970** | — |
| | U-Net | 0.916 | 0.953 | 0.996 |
| | SFNet | **0.931** | 0.963 | **0.997** |
| Drishti-GS Optic Cup | Zilly et al. [15] | **0.850** | 0.870 | — |
| | U-Net | 0.759 | 0.854 | 0.994 |
| | SFNet | 0.807 | **0.888** | **0.996** |

**Results on Extensive Benchmarks.** Table 2 compares SFN predication scores with U-Net and another recently reported method on three extensive datasets. On DRIVE dataset, although U-Net performs better than SFN, SFN obtains higher pixel-wise accuracy than deep supervised methods in [13]. On Drishti-GS, SFN is competitive with U-Net, yielding improvement of 1.5 and 4.8 points in IoU on optic disk and cup segmentation. All above results have indicated that SFN architecture has achieve great performance on biomedical image segmentation tasks that differ in organ, shape and tissue. Figure 2 shows a visual comparison between input image, ground truth and predication results of SFN on all segmentation tasks involved.

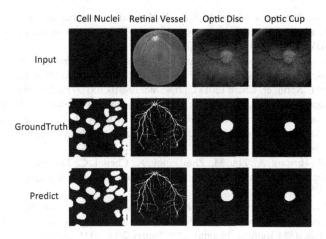

**Fig. 2.** Visual Comparison between input image, ground truth and results predicted by SFN.

# 4    Conclusion

We propose SFN that learns to step-wise focus on targets for biomedical image segmentation. SFN simulates human visual perception by integrating the encoder with an attention-driven focus path, which contains 4 focus modules to step-wise refine spatial information. Our experiments on multiple biomedical image segmentation benchmarks show that SFN achieves great performance that are competitive with U-Net and other great methods, while only need using 60% parameters, 30% floating-point operations and the equal occupied GPU memory compared with U-Net. Further evaluation of SFNs that are based on ResNet and MobileNetV2 has proved its high transportability and representational power. In the future, we will investigate a more powerful architecture with attention-driven feature refinement mechanism applied.

**Acknowledgements.** This work was supported in part by the National Key R&D Program of China (No. 2018YFC0807500), in part by the National Key Research and Development Plan (Grant No. 2017YFF0209604).

# References

1. He, K., Zhang, X., Ren, S., Sun, J.: Deep residual learning for image recognition. In: Proceedings of the IEEE Conference on Computer Vision and Pattern Recognition, pp. 770–778 (2016)
2. Hu, J., Shen, L., Sun, G.: Squeeze-and-excitation networks. In: Proceedings of the IEEE Conference on Computer Vision and Pattern Recognition, pp. 7132–7141 (2018)
3. Long, J., Shelhamer, E., Darrell, T.: Fully convolutional networks for semantic segmentation. In: Proceedings of the IEEE Conference on Computer Vision and Pattern Recognition, pp. 3431–3440 (2015)

4. Milletari, F., Navab, N., Ahmadi, S.A.: V-Net: fully convolutional neural networks for volumetric medical image segmentation. In: 2016 Fourth International Conference on 3D Vision (3DV), pp. 565–571. IEEE (2016)

5. Qin, Y., et al.: Autofocus layer for semantic segmentation. In: Frangi, A.F., Schnabel, J.A., Davatzikos, C., Alberola-López, C., Fichtinger, G. (eds.) MICCAI 2018. LNCS, vol. 11072, pp. 603–611. Springer, Cham (2018). https://doi.org/10.1007/978-3-030-00931-1_69

6. Ronneberger, O., Fischer, P., Brox, T.: U-Net: convolutional networks for biomedical image segmentation. In: Navab, N., Hornegger, J., Wells, William M., Frangi, Alejandro F. (eds.) MICCAI 2015. LNCS, vol. 9351, pp. 234–241. Springer, Cham (2015). https://doi.org/10.1007/978-3-319-24574-4_28

7. Sandler, M., Howard, A., Zhu, M., Zhmoginov, A., Chen, L.C.: Inverted residuals and linear bottlenecks: Mobile networks for classification. Detection and Segmentation. arXiv 1801 (2018)

8. Sivaswamy, J., Krishnadas, S., Chakravarty, A., Joshi, G., Tabish, A.S., et al.: A comprehensive retinal image dataset for the assessment of glaucoma from the optic nerve head analysis. JSM Biomed. Imaging Data Papers 2(1), 1004 (2015)

9. Sivaswamy, J., Krishnadas, S., Joshi, G.D., Jain, M., Tabish, A.U.S.: Drishti-GS: retinal image dataset for optic nerve head (ONH) segmentation. In: 2014 IEEE 11th International Symposium on Biomedical Imaging (ISBI), pp. 53–56. IEEE (2014)

10. Staal, J., Abràmoff, M.D., Niemeijer, M., Viergever, M.A., Van Ginneken, B.: Ridge-based vessel segmentation in color images of the retina. IEEE Trans. Med. Imaging 23(4), 501–509 (2004)

11. Wang, F., et al.: Residual attention network for image classification. In: Proceedings of the IEEE Conference on Computer Vision and Pattern Recognition, pp. 3156–3164 (2017)

12. Wang, Y., et al.: Deep attentional features for prostate segmentation in ultrasound. In: Frangi, Alejandro F., Schnabel, J.A., Davatzikos, C., Alberola-López, C., Fichtinger, G. (eds.) MICCAI 2018. LNCS, vol. 11073, pp. 523–530. Springer, Cham (2018). https://doi.org/10.1007/978-3-030-00937-3_60

13. Zhang, Y., Chung, A.C.S.: Deep supervision with additional labels for retinal vessel segmentation task. In: Frangi, Alejandro F., Schnabel, Julia A., Davatzikos, C., Alberola-López, C., Fichtinger, G. (eds.) MICCAI 2018. LNCS, vol. 11071, pp. 83–91. Springer, Cham (2018). https://doi.org/10.1007/978-3-030-00934-2_10

14. Zhou, Z., Rahman Siddiquee, M.M., Tajbakhsh, N., Liang, J.: UNet++: a nested U-Net architecture for medical image segmentation. In: Stoyanov, D., et al. (eds.) DLMIA/ML-CDS - 2018. LNCS, vol. 11045, pp. 3–11. Springer, Cham (2018). https://doi.org/10.1007/978-3-030-00889-5_1

15. Zilly, J., Buhmann, J.M., Mahapatra, D.: Glaucoma detection using entropy sampling and ensemble learning for automatic optic cup and disc segmentation. Comput. Med. Imaging Graph. 55, 28–41 (2017)

# Renal Cell Carcinoma Staging with Learnable Image Histogram-Based Deep Neural Network

Mohammad Arafat Hussain[1](✉), Ghassan Hamarneh[2], and Rafeef Garbi[1]

[1] BiSICL, University of British Columbia, Vancouver, BC, Canada
{arafat,rafeef}@ece.ubc.ca
[2] Medical Image Analysis Lab, Simon Fraser University, Burnaby, BC, Canada
hamarneh@sfu.ca

**Abstract.** Renal cell carcinoma (RCC) is the seventh most common cancer worldwide, accounting for an estimated 140,000 global deaths annually. An important RCC prognostic predictor is its 'stage' for which the tumor-node-metastasis (TNM) staging system is used. Although TNM staging is performed by radiologists via pre-surgery volumetric medical image analysis, a recent study suggested that such staging may be performed by studying the image features of the RCC from computed tomography (CT) data. Currently TNM staging mostly relies on laborious manual processes based on visual inspection of 2D CT image slices that are time-consuming and subjective; a recent study reported about ~25% misclassification in their patient pools. Recently, we proposed a learnable image histogram based deep neural network approach (ImHist-Net) for RCC grading, which is capable of learning textural features directly from the CT images. In this paper, using a similar architecture, we perform the stage low (I/II) and high (III/IV) classification for RCC in CT scans. Validated on a clinical CT dataset of 159 patients from the TCIA database, our method classified RCC low and high stages with about 83% accuracy.

## 1 Introduction

Renal cell carcinoma (RCC) is the 7th most common cancer in men and 10th most common cancer in women [1] accounting for an estimated 140,000 global deaths annually [2]. The natural growth pattern varies across RCC, which has led to the development of different prognostic models for the assessment of patient-wise risk [3]. Clinical RCC staging is vital for proper treatment planning and thus considered one of the important prognostic predictors of cancer specific survival [4].

The American Joint Committee on Cancer (AJCC)/Union for International Cancer Control (UICC) specifies the criteria for tumor-node-metastasis (TNM) staging of each cancer depending on the primary tumor size (TX, T0-4); number and location of lymph node involvement (NX, N1-2); and metastatic nature, i.e.

© Springer Nature Switzerland AG 2019
H.-I. Suk et al. (Eds.): MLMI 2019, LNCS 11861, pp. 533–540, 2019.
https://doi.org/10.1007/978-3-030-32692-0_61

tumor spreading to other organs (M0-1) [3,5]. Clinical guidelines require clinicians to assign TNM stages prior to initiating any treatment [5]. AJCC TNM is currently a manual process that includes two separate staging processes, performed before treatment planning and during/after surgery, to reflect the time-sensitive staging mechanism [3]. Clinical staging is performed prior to treatment by expert radiologists via physical examination, CT image measurements, and tumor biopsies. Clinically determined TNM stages (e.g. T or M) are designated with prefix 'c' (i.e. cT and cM). Pathological staging on the other hand is based on the resected tumor pathology results either during or after surgery [5], and designated with prefix 'p' (i.e. pT and pM). Radiologists also use the TNM description to assign an overall 'Anatomical stage' from 1 to 4 using the Roman numerals I, II, III, and IV [3], see Table 1. Accurate clinical staging of RCC is vital for appropriate management decisions [6]. Partial nephrectomy (PN), also known as nephron-sparing surgery, is typically preferred for T1 and T2 tumors [3]. After studying 7,138 patients with T1 kidney cancer, Tan et al. [7] suggested that treatment with PN was associated with improved survival. In a similar study on pT2 tumor patients, Janssen et al. [4] showed that patients having PN had a significantly longer overall survival. Radical nephrectomy (RN), which refers to complete removal of kidney with/without the removal of the adrenal gland and neighboring lymph node, is generally reserved for T3 and T4 tumors [6].

**Table 1.** Staging of RCC (AJCC TNM classification of tumors).

| Stage I | T1 (Tumor $\leq 7\,$cm) | N0 | M0 |
|---|---|---|---|
| Stage II | T2 (Tumor $>7\,$cm but limited to kidney) | N0 | M0 |
| Stage III | T1-2, T3 (Tumour extends up to Gerota's fascia) | N1, Any | M0 |
| Stage IV | T4, Any (Tumour invades beyond Gerota's fascia) | Any | M0-1 |

The pre-surgery clinical tumor staging often suffers from misclassification errors. For example, in a recent study, Bradley et al. [6] reported 23 disagreement cases between cT and pT stages of 90 patients. The study further reported that 5 patients were miscassified with cT3 but later down-staged to pT2, while 6 patients were misclassified with cT2 but later up-staged to pT3 for the same patient cohort (~12%). In another study on 1,250 patients who underwent nephrectomy, Shah et al. [8] reported 11% (140 patients) upstaging of tumors from cT1 to pT3. In addition, there was tumor recurrence in 44 patients (31.4% of the pT3 upstaged cases), where most of these patients initially had PN. These alarming findings suggest that PN is associated with better survival in low stage tumors (T1 and T2), while RN is associated with reduce recurrence in high stage (T3 and T4) tumors. However, high stage tumors (T3-4) are often misclassified as low stage (T1-2) in the clinical staging phase. In addition, we see in the rows 1–3 of Table 1 that the tumor criterion is not well defined for stages T1, T2, and T3. In contrast, anatomical stages I–IV defines better discrimination among tumor stages (see Table 1).

For accurate staging of RCC before treatment planning, contrast-enhanced abdominal CT is considered essential [3]. Although tumor staging is believed to be dependent on the tumor size, by studying the pT stages of 94 kidney samples, Bradley et al. [6] argued that stages > T3 does not always correlate with tumor size and suggested to use CT image features to improve tumor staging.

Supervised deep learning using convolutional neural networks (CNN) have gained popularity for automatic feature learning and classification. However, the learned features of a classical CNN tend to ignore diffuse textural features that are often important for applications such as our tumor staging problem. Very recently, we proposed ImHistNet, a deep neural network for end to end texture-based image classification [9]. In [9] we showed ImHistNet to be capable of learning complex and subtle task-specific textural features directly from images completely avoiding any pre-segmentation of the RCC as the learnable image histogram can stratify tumor and background textures well.

In this paper, we propose automatic low stage (I–II) and high stage (III–IV) RCC classification using ImHistNet. We demonstrate that RCC stages can be determined from the CT textural features of the tumor. Our approach learns a histogram directly from the CT data and deploys it to extract representative discriminant textural tumor features to correlate to RCC stages.

## 2  Materials and Methods

### 2.1  Data

We used CT scans of 159 patients from the TCIA database [10]. These patients were diagnosed with clear cell RCC, of which 95 were staged low (I–II) and 66 were staged high (III–IV). The images in this database have variations in CT scanner models, contrast administration, field of view, and spatial resolution. The in-plane pixel size ranged from 0.29 to 1.87 mm and the slice thickness ranged from 1.5 to 7.5 mm. We divided the dataset for training/validation/testing as 77/3/15 and 48/3/15 for stage low and stage high, respectively. Note that typical tumor radiomic analysis comprises [11]: (i) 3D imaging, (ii) tumor detection and/or segmentation, (iii) tumor phenotype quantification, and (iv) data integration (i.e. phenotype + genotype + clinical + cproteomic) and analysis. Our approach falls under step-iii. The input data to our method are thus 2D image patches of size 64 × 64 pixels, taken from kidney+RCC (i.e. both mutually inclusively present) bounding boxes. We do not require any fine pre-segmentation of the RCC rather only assume a kidney+RCC bounding box, generated in step-ii. Given data imbalance where samples for stage high are fewer than for stage low, we allowed more overlap among adjacent patches for the stage low dataset. The amount of overlap is calculated to balance the samples from both cohorts.

## 2.2 Learnable Image Histogram for RCC Stage Classification

**Learnable Image Histogram:** Our learnable image histogram (LIH) [9] strat-
ifies the pixel values in an image $x$ into different learnable and possibly overlapping intervals (bins of width $w_b$) with learnable means (bin centers $\beta_b$). The
feature value $h_b(x) : b \in \mathcal{B} \to \mathcal{R}$, corresponding to the pixels in $x$ that falls in
the $b^{th}$ bin, is estimated as:

$$h_b(x) = \Phi\{H_b(x)\} = \Phi\{\max(0, 1 - |x - \beta_b| \times \widetilde{w}_b)\}, \tag{1}$$

where $\mathcal{B}$ is the set of all bins, $\Phi$ is a global pooling operator, $H_b(x)$ is a piece-wise
linear basis function that accumulates positive votes from the pixels in $x$ that
fall in the $b^{th}$ bin of interval $[\beta_b - w_b/2, \beta_b + w_b/2]$, and $\widetilde{w}_b$ is the learnable weight
related to the width $w_b$ of the $b^{th}$ bin: $\widetilde{w}_b = 2/w_b$. Any pixel may vote for multiple
bins with different $H_b(x)$ since there could be an overlap between adjacent bins in
our learnable histogram. The final $|\mathcal{B}| \times 1$ feature values from the learned image
histogram are obtained using a global pooling $\Phi$ over each $H_b(x)$ separately.
This pooling can be a 'non-zero elements count' (NZEC), which matches the
convention of a traditional histogram, or can be an 'average' or 'max' pooling,
depending on the task-specific requirement. The linear basis function $H_b(x)$ of
the LIH is piece-wise differentiable and can back-propagate (BP) errors to update
$\beta_b$ and $\widetilde{w}_b$ during training. Readers are referred to the original manuscript on
the ImHistNet [9] for details.

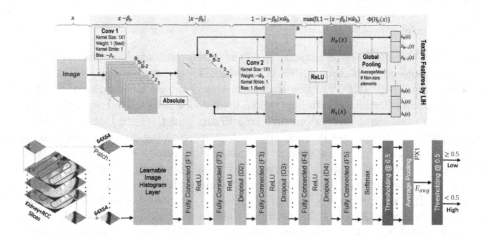

**Fig. 1.** Multiple instance decisions aggregated ImHistNet for stage classification.

**Design of LIH using CNN Layers:** The LIH is implemented using CNN
layers as illustrated in Fig. 1. The input of LIH is a 2D image, and the output
is a $|\mathcal{B}| \times 1$ histogram feature vector. The operation $x - \beta_b$ for a bin centered at
$\beta_b$ is equivalent to convolving the input by a $1 \times 1$ kernel with fixed weight of 1

(i.e. with no updating by BP) and a learnable bias term $\beta_b$ ('Conv 1' in Fig. 1). A total of $B = |\mathcal{B}|$ number of similar convolution kernels are used for a set of $\mathcal{B}$ bins. Then an absolute value layer produces $|x - \beta_b|$. This is followed by a set of convolutions ('Conv 2' in Fig. 1) with a total of $B$ separate (non-shared across channels) learnable $1 \times 1$ kernels and a fixed bias of 1 (i.e. no updating by BP) to model the operation of $1 - |x - \beta_b| \times \widetilde{w}_b$. We use the rectified linear unit (ReLU) to model the $\max(0, \cdot)$ operator in Eq. 1. The final $|\mathcal{B}| \times 1$ feature values $h_b(x)$ are obtained by global pooling over each feature map $H_b(x)$ separately.

**ImHistNet Classifier Architecture:** The classification network comprises ten layers: the LIH layer, five (F1–F5) fully connected layers (FCLs), one softmax layer, one average pooling (AP) layer, and two thresholding layers (see Fig. 1). The first seven layers contain trainable weights. The input is a $128 \times 128$ pixel image patch extracted from the kidney+RCC slices. During training, randomly shuffled image patches are individually fed to the network. The LIH layer learns the variables $\beta_b$ and $\widetilde{w}_b$ to extract representative textural features from image patches. In implementing the proposed ImHistNet, we chose $B = 128$ and 'average' pooling at $H_b(x)$. We set subsequent FCL (F1–F5) size to $4096 \times 1$. The number of FCLs plays a vital role as the overall depth of the model has been shown to be important for good performance [12]. Empirically, we achieved good performance with five FCL layers. Layers 8, 9 and 10 of the ImHistNet are used during the testing phase and do not contain any trainable weights.

**Training:** We trained our network by minimizing the multinomial logistic loss between the ground truth and predicted labels (1: stage low, and 0: stage high). We employed a Dropout unit (Dx) that drops 20%, 30%, and 40% of units in F2, F3 and F4 layers, respectively (Fig. 1) and used a weight decay of 0.005. The base learning rate was set to 0.001 and was decreased by a factor of 0.1 to 0.0001 over 250,000 iterations with a batch of 128 patches. Training was performed on a workstation with Intel 4.0 GHz Core-i7 processor, an Nvidia GeForce Titan Xp GPU with 12 GB of VRAM, and 32 GB of RAM.

**RCC Stage Classification:** After training ImHistNet (layers 1 to 7) by estimating errors at layer 7 (i.e. Softmax layer), we used the full configuration (from layer 1 to 10) in the testing phase. Although we used patches from only RCC-containing kidney slices during training and validation, not all the RCC cross-sections contained discriminant features for proper grade identification. Thus our trained network may miss-classify the interrogated image patch. To reduce such misclassification, we adopt a multiple instance decision aggregation procedure similar to our work in [13]. In this approach, we feed randomly shuffled single image patches as inputs to the model during training. During inference, we feed all candidate image patches of a particular kidney to the trained network and accumulate the patch-wise binary classification labels (0 or 1) at layer 8 (the thresholding layer). We then feed these labels into a $P \times 1$ average pooling layer, where $P$ is the total number of patches of an interrogated kidney. Finally, we feed the estimated average ($E_{avg}$) from layer 9 to the second thresholding layer

(layer 10), where $E_{avg} \geq 0.5$ indicates the stage 'low', and stage 'high' otherwise (see Fig. 1).

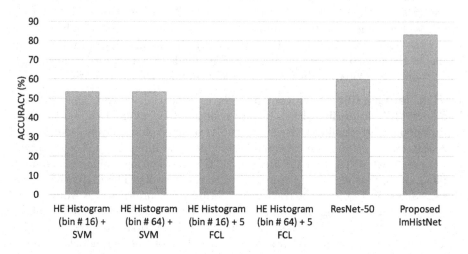

**Fig. 2.** Automatic RCC stage classification performance comparison. Acronyms used - HE: hand engineered, SVM: support vector machines.

## 3   Results and Discussion

We compared our RCC stage classification performance in terms of accuracy (%) to a wide range of methods in Fig. 2. To our knowledge, there is no automatic and/or machine learning-based approach for RCC stage classification. Therefore, we compare the RCC staging performance of different methods by implementing those in our own capacity. Note that for all our implementations, we trained models with shuffled single image patches, and used multiple instance decision aggregation per kidney during inference. We fixed our patch size to $128 \times 128$ pixels across all contrasted methods except ResNet-50.

First, in order to compare performance to that of traditional hand-engineered (HE) feature based machine learning approaches, we evaluated an SVM employing a conventional image histogram of 16 and 64 bins. Figure 2 shows a resulting poor performance at 53% accuracy. Next, to contrast the performance of SVM against DNN, we fed the conventional histogram (16 and 64 bins) features to a DNN of 5 FCL with weight sizes $(4096 \times 1)$-$(4096 \times 1)$-$(4096 \times 1)$-$(4096 \times 1)$-$(2 \times 1)$. We chose this FCL configuration for fairer comparisons since our ImHist-Net contains the same. Figure 2 shows that the FCL with conventional histogram performed the worst achieving a 50% accuracy. Next, we used ResNet-50 with transfer learning in order to test the performance of high performing modern CNN (see Fig. 2). We used full kidney+RCC slices of size $224 \times 224$ pixels as input. As mentioned in Sect. 1, a classical CNN typically fails to capture textural features, which is evident from our results where ResNet-50 performed poorly in learning the textural features of RCC, resulting in 60% accuracy. Finally, we show the performance of our proposed method in Fig. 2 where ImHistNet achieved the highest accuracy (83%) among all contrasted methods.

## 4  Conclusions

We proposed a powerful automatic RCC stage classification method that uses a learnable image histogram based deep neural network framework we recently proposed for tumor grading. Our approach learns a histogram directly from the image data and deploys it to extract representative discriminant textural image features. We also used multiple instance decision aggregation to further robustify binary classification. Our proposed ImHistNet outperformed competing approaches for this task including SVM classification, deep learning with hand crafted traditional histogram features, as well as currently top performing deep CNNs. ImHistNet appears to be very well-suited for radiomic studies, where learned textural features using the learnable image histogram can aid in improving diagnosis accuracy.

**Acknowledgement.** We thank NVIDIA Corporatoin for supporting our research through their GPU Grant Program by donating the GeForce Titan Xp.

## References

1. Siegel, R.L., Miller, K.D., Jemal, A.: Cancer statistics, 2016. CA: Cancer J. Clin. **66**(1), 7–30 (2016)
2. Ding, J., et al.: CT-based radiomic model predicts high grade of clear cell renal cell carcinoma. Eur. J. Radiol. **103**, 51–56 (2018)
3. Escudier, B., et al.: Renal cell carcinoma: ESMO clinical practice guidelines for diagnosis, treatment and follow-up. Ann. Oncol. **27**(suppl 5), v58–v68 (2016)
4. Janssen, M., et al.: Survival outcomes in patients with large ($\geq$ 7cm) clear cell renal cell carcinomas treated with nephron-sparing surgery versus radical nephrectomy: results of a multicenter cohort with long-term follow-up. PLoS ONE **13**(5), e0196427 (2018)
5. AAlAbdulsalam, A.K., Garvin, J.H., Redd, A., Carter, M.E., Sweeny, C., Meystre, S.M.: Automated extraction and classification of cancer stage mentions from unstructured text fields in a central cancer registry. AMIA Summits Transl. Sci. Proc. **2018**, 16 (2018)
6. Bradley, A., MacDonald, L., Whiteside, S., Johnson, R., Ramani, V.: Accuracy of preoperative CT T staging of renal cell carcinoma: which features predict advanced stage? Clin. Radiol. **70**(8), 822–829 (2015)
7. Tan, H.J., Norton, E.C., Ye, Z., Hafez, K.S., Gore, J.L., Miller, D.C.: Long-term survival following partial vs radical nephrectomy among older patients with early-stage kidney cancer. JAMA **307**(15), 1629–1635 (2012)
8. Shah, P.H., et al.: Partial nephrectomy is associated with higher risk of relapse compared with radical nephrectomy for clinical stage T1 renal cell carcinoma pathologically up staged to T3a. J. Urol. **198**(2), 289–296 (2017)

9. Hussain, M.A., Hamarneh, G., Garbi, R.: ImHistNet: Learnable image histogram based DNN with application to noninvasive determination of carcinoma grades in CT scans. In: International Conference on Medical Image Computing and Computer-Assisted Intervention, pp. 1–8. Springer (2019). https://doi.org/10.1007/978-3-030-32226-7_15

10. Clark, K., et al.: The cancer imaging archive (TCIA): maintaining and operating a public information repository. J. Digit. Imaging **26**(6), 1045–1057 (2013)

11. Aerts, H.J.: The potential of radiomic-based phenotyping in precision medicine: a review. JAMA Oncol. **2**(12), 1636–1642 (2016)

12. Zeiler, M.D., Fergus, R.: Visualizing and understanding convolutional networks. In: Fleet, D., Pajdla, T., Schiele, B., Tuytelaars, T. (eds.) ECCV 2014. LNCS, vol. 8689, pp. 818–833. Springer, Cham (2014). https://doi.org/10.1007/978-3-319-10590-1_53

13. Hussain, M.A., Hamarneh, G., Garbi, R.: Noninvasive determination of gene mutations in clear cell renal cell carcinoma using multiple instance decisions aggregated CNN. In: Frangi, A.F., Schnabel, J.A., Davatzikos, C., Alberola-López, C., Fichtinger, G. (eds.) MICCAI 2018. LNCS, vol. 11071, pp. 657–665. Springer, Cham (2018). https://doi.org/10.1007/978-3-030-00934-2_73

# Weakly Supervised Learning Strategy
# for Lung Defect Segmentation

Robin Sandkühler[1]([✉]), Christoph Jud[1], Grzegorz Bauman[1,2], Corin Willers[3],
Orso Pusterla[1,2], Sylvia Nyilas[3], Alan Peters[4], Lukas Ebner[4],
Enno Stranziger[4], Oliver Bieri[1,2], Philipp Latzin[3], and Philippe C. Cattin[1]

[1] Department of Biomedical Engineering, University of Basel, Allschwil, Switzerland
robin.sandkuehler@unibas.ch
[2] Division of Radiological Physics, Department of Radiology,
University of Basel Hospital, Basel, Switzerland
[3] Pediatric Respiratory Medicine, Department of Pediatrics, Inselspital,
Bern University Hospital, University of Bern, Bern, Switzerland
[4] Department of Diagnostic, Interventional and Paediatric Radiology, Inselspital,
Bern University Hospital, University of Bern, Bern, Switzerland

**Abstract.** Through the development of specific magnetic resonance
sequences, it is possible to measure the physiological properties of the
lung parenchyma, e.g., ventilation. Automatic segmentation of pathologies in such ventilation maps is essential for the clinical application. The
generation of labeled ground truth data is costly, time-consuming and
requires much experience in the field of lung anatomy and physiology.
In this paper, we present a weakly supervised learning strategy for the
segmentation of defected lung areas in those ventilation maps. As a weak
label, we use the Lung Clearance Index (LCI) which is measured by a
Multiple Breath Washout test. The LCI is a single global measure for
the ventilation inhomogeneities of the whole lung. We designed a network and a training procedure in order to infer a pixel-wise segmentation
from the global LCI value. Our network is composed of two autoencoder
sub-networks for the extraction of global and local features respectively.
Furthermore, we use self-supervised regularization to prevent the network from learning non-meaningful segmentations. The performance of
our method is evaluated by a rating of the created defect segmentations
by 5 human experts, where over 60% of the segmentation results are
rated with very good or perfect.

## 1 Introduction

Thanks to the development of dedicated image acquisition methods, MRI has
become a new modality allowing for spatial analysis of time-dependent physiological changes of the lung, e.g., ventilation [4]. The ventilation maps are computed from a time-resolved image series and the detection of the corresponding
ventilation frequencies in the image data, after the images are spatially aligned
[3]. An example is shown in Fig. 1. The automatic labeling of defected areas in

these maps is a complex task for naïve methods such as thresholding because the value range depends on the relative signal intensity of the MR images. More sophisticated methods, e.g., supervised segmentation methods require accurate labeled ground truth data, which is difficult to obtain, even for clinical experts.

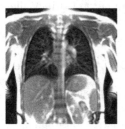 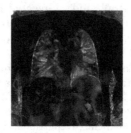 

(a) Morphologic Image        (b) Ventilation Map        (c) Defected Areas

**Fig. 1.** (a) MRI acquisition of a patient with cystic fibrosis, (b) corresponding ventilation maps, and (c) assumed impaired areas.

Compared to supervised methods, unsupervised methods do not require labeled training data. There are several unsupervised learning methods for medical image segmentation. An unsupervised lesion detection using an adversarial auto-encoderder was presented in [5]. The method do not use any labels during training but require a training set of image data with only healthy subjects. A weakly supervised method for the segmentation of brain tumors was shown in [1] by using only one *binary label* for each image (healthy, non-healthy). The methods presented in [7,8] use class level labels of the image contend as a weak label in order to create a semantic object segmentation.

In this paper, we present a first *proof-of-concept* for the segmentation of the defected areas in the ventilation maps using a weakly supervised learning strategy based on the Lung Clearance Index (LCI). The LCI is a single value which expresses the healthiness of the whole lung and corresponds to the global ventilation inhomogeneities [9]. Unlike binary or class labels, the LCI is an *unbounded value* where a value of 6–7 indicates a healthy lung. A higher LCI is correlated to more ventilation inhomogeneities. We designed a network that is able to perform a pixel-wise segmentation using only the LCI value as a weak label during training. Furthermore, we use *self-supervised regularization* to prevent the network from learning a non-meaningful segmentation. The performance of our method is evaluated by a rating of the segmentation results by 5 human experts. Initial results show that over 60% of the segmentation results are scored with very good or perfect.

## 2   Method

In this section, we describe our network design and training procedure in order to segment the defected areas in the lung using only the LCI value as a continuous label. For this, we use the relation

$$\frac{\text{defected lung volume}}{\text{total lung volume}} \propto LCI,$$

which has been proven to be valid [6].

### 2.1 Lung Clearance Index

The Lung Clearance Index (LCI) is a global measure for the ventilation inhomogeneities of the lung, as a result of respiratory diseases like cystic fibrosis or chronic obstructive pulmonary disease [9]. It is defined in lung volume turnovers (TO), i.e., the number of breathing cycles that are necessary in order to clear the lung from a previews inhaled tracer gas. A common method for the determination of the LCI is the Nitrogen Multiple Breath Washout ($N_2$-MBW). Here the patient starts breathing 100 % oxygen, and the remaining nitrogen concentration of the previously breathed ambient air is measured. If the concentration of the $N_2$ is below 2.5 % of the starting concentration the test stops. The LCI is then defined by

$$LCI = \frac{V_{\text{CE}}}{FRC} \qquad FRC = \frac{\text{expired volume } N_2}{c_{\text{start}}^{N_2} - c_{\text{end}}^{N_2}}, \qquad (1)$$

where $V_{\text{CE}}$ is the expired volume during the complete measurement. The LCI for a healthy lung is 6–7 TO. For a more detailed description of the LCI, we refer the reader to [9]. Here, we normalize the LCI between 0 and 1 by assuming a minimum LCI value of 5 and a maximum LCI value of 20.

### 2.2 Ventilation Maps

For the calculation of the ventilation maps a 2D dynamic time series with the ultra-fast steady-state free precession pulse sequence (uf-bSSFP) [4] is acquired during free breathing. The respiratory motion is compensated with a pairwise non-rigid image registration [10] and automated lung segmentation is performed [2]. In the final step, the ventilation maps are calculated using a matrix pencil decomposition as described in [3]. To cover the full chest volume, 8–12 ventilation maps with a thickness of 12 mm at different coronal positions are computed. All maps are stacked together to obtain the final image volume with $N \times 256 \times 256$, where $N$ is the number of acquired slices. This image volume is used as input for the network. We need to process all slices at ones, because the LCI value is related to the complete lung and not to a single slice.

### 2.3 Network Model

An overview of the complete network structure is shown in Fig. 2. Our network model consists of two major parts. The first part is the global autoencoder

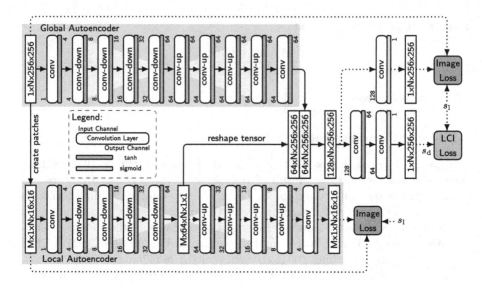

**Fig. 2.** Model for the weakly supervised segmentation of defected lung areas.

(GAE) where the input is the above-described image volume. As the ventilation maps have a slice thickness of 12 mm, neighboring slices can show substantially different content. To overcome this issue, all operations are performed on a single slice only and not across slices. All convolutional layers use a kernel size of $1 \times 3 \times 3$. The conv-down block reduces the spatial dimension by using a strided convolution with a stride of $1 \times 2 \times 2$. The conv-up block increases the spatial resolution by a factor of 2 using bilinear upsampling followed by a convolutional layer. Compared to the classical autoencoder approach the number of feature channels is not reduced in the decoder of the GAE. The input of the second part of the network the local autoencoder (LAE), are overlapping patches of the input volume. For each coronal slice $M$ 2D patches of the input volume with a size of $16 \times 16$ and a stride of 1 are generated. We consider only patches were the region of the patches overlaps with the lung mask. The size of the latent variable of the LAE is set to 64. In contrast to the GAE, the number of feature channels is reduced in the decoder part of the LAE. For the final pixel-wise defect map, all patches of the input volume are encoded using the encoder of the LAE, reshaped and concatenated with the output of GAE. The embeddings of the patches are placed at the center position of the patch in the image volume. In this way, we get a feature map with the spatial dimensions of the input volume and 128 feature channels. The final network output, the pixel-wise defect segmentation $s_d$ is obtained after two convolutional layer and has the final size of $1 \times N \times 256 \times 256$.

## 2.4   Network Training

In order to train the parameter of our network with the LCI as weak label, we define the LCI loss as

$$\mathcal{L}_{\text{LCI}}(s_{\text{d}}, s_{\text{l}}, LCI) = \left( \frac{\sum_{x \in \mathcal{X}}^{|\mathcal{X}|} s_{\text{d}}(x)}{\sum_{x \in \mathcal{X}}^{|\mathcal{X}|} s_{\text{l}}(x)} - LCI \right)^2, \tag{2}$$

where $\mathcal{X} \subset \mathbb{R}^3$ is the domain of the lung mask $s_{\text{l}}$, with $s_{\text{l}}(x) = 1$. The output of our network, i.e. the segmentation of the defect areas of the input ventilation map is defined as $s_{\text{d}} : \mathcal{X} \to [0, 1]$. However, the LCI loss is based on the ratio of the defected lung volume to the whole lung volume and thus not a pixel-wise loss. This can lead to a segmentation result that minimize the LCI loss but do not correspond to the defected areas. We use *self-supervised regularization* during training of our network to prevent the network from overfitting on the LCI loss and learning a non-meaningful segmentation. As shown in Fig. 2, our network contains different paths, some of which are only used for the *self-supervised regularization* during training (dotted) and some are used during training and inference (dense). We use the decoder part of the LAE only during training for the reconstruction of the image patches. With this, we enforce the network to learn an embedding for the classification of the image patch which is strongly related to the image content. The image reconstruction loss for the LAE is defined as

$$\mathcal{L}_{\text{LAE}}(I_{\text{patch}}, \tilde{I}_{\text{patch}}) = \frac{1}{|\mathcal{X}|} \sum_{x \in \mathcal{X}}^{|\mathcal{X}|} \frac{1}{|\mathcal{P}_x|} \sum_{p \in \mathcal{P}_x}^{|\mathcal{P}_x|} (I_{\text{patch}}(x, p) - \tilde{I}_{\text{patch}}(x, p))^2, \tag{3}$$

where $\mathcal{P}_x \subset \mathbb{R}^2$ is the image patch domain at location $x$ of the input image. For the feature regularization of the GAE the same approach is used, but here the output of the GAE is concatenated with the embedding of the LAE before the image is reconstructed. The global reconstruction loss is defined as

$$\mathcal{L}_{\text{GAE}}(I, \tilde{I}) = \frac{1}{|\mathcal{X}|} \sum_{x \in \mathcal{X}}^{|\mathcal{X}|} (I(x) - \tilde{I}(x))^2. \tag{4}$$

The final loss for the training of the network is then given as

$$\mathcal{L} = \mathcal{L}_{\text{LCI}} + \mathcal{L}_{\text{LAE}} + \mathcal{L}_{\text{GAE}}. \tag{5}$$

## 3   Experiments and Results

For our experiments, we use a data set of 35 subjects with 2 examinations per subject on average. We divided our data set in a training set with 28 subjects and in a test set with 7 subjects. In each examination 8–12 dynamic 2D image series were acquired. All examinations were performed on a 1.5 T whole-body MR-scanner (MAGNETOM Aera, Siemens Healthineers, Erlangen, Germany) using

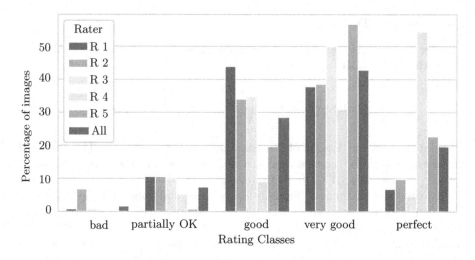

**Fig. 3.** Result of the human expert rating of the presented defect segmentation.

a 12-channel thorax and a 24-channel spine receiver coil array. Each subject was scanned during free breathing with the uf-bSSFP sequence [4]. The main pulse sequence parameters were as follows: field-of-view $375 \times 375 - 425 \times 425 \, \text{mm}^2$, slice thickness $12 \, \text{mm}$, $TE/TR/TA = 0.67 \, \text{ms}/1.46 \, \text{ms}/119 \, \text{ms}$, flip angle $60°$, bandwidth $2056 \, \text{Hz/pixel}$, matrix $128 \times 128$ (interpolated to $256 \times 256$), 160 coronal images, 3.33 images/s, parallel imaging GRAPPA factor of 2. Ventilation maps and the lung segmentation were then computed as described in Sect. 2.2.

Due to the problem of relative values of the ventilation maps caused by the relative values generated by the MR, we normalized each slice independently. We performed a z-normalization followed by clipping of the values at $[-4, 4]$ and a transformation to $[0, 1]$. In the final step, a histogram stretching was performed using the 2 and 98 percentile of the intensities. The normalization was only performed on intensity values inside the lung.

For the evaluation, we applied our method to the 7 subjects of the test set. Because the derivation of pixel-wise manually labeled ground truth remains difficult, we evaluated our method by using a rating of the final defect segmentation by 5 human experts. The rating scheme is defined as the percentage of correct defect segmentation for a given ventilation map: *bad*: 0%–20%, *partially OK*: 21%–40%, *good*: 41%–60%, *very good*: 61%–80%, *perfect*: 81%–100%. For the evaluation the lung ventilation map and the morphological image are available. Each rater scores all 2D segmentation results of the test set, which contains 132 images in total. Rater 1 and 2 are a senior resident radiologist with 20 respectively 10 years of experience. Rater 3 has over 5 years of research experience in the field of MRI lung imaging. Rater 4 is a chest fellow (radiologist) with 4 years of experience in chest imaging. Rater 5 is a physician with 2 years of experience of thorax imaging. The results of the human expert evaluation presented in Fig. 3, show that over 60% of the segmentation results are rated with very

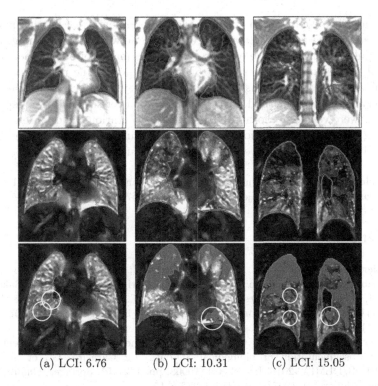

(a) LCI: 6.76          (b) LCI: 10.31          (c) LCI: 15.05

**Fig. 4.** Selected defect segmentation results (red) for different subjects with different LCI values. Top row: morphological image with defect segmentation outline. Middle row: ventilation maps with defect segmentation outline. Bottom row: ventilation maps with defect segmentation overlay. Green shows the outline of the given lung segmentation [2]. Incorrect defect segementations are highlighted with white circles. (Color figure online)

good or perfect. Selected segmentation results of different subjects with different LCIs are shown in Fig. 4. The results of our method demonstrate, that we are able to segment most of the impaired areas with ventilation defects by using *only* the LCI for training. However, in some areas an incorrect segmentation is observed in close approximation to blood vessels as shown in Fig. 4. This might be reasoned by the evidence that the non-ventilated blood vessels are showing the similar characteristics as impaired areas in the ventilation maps.

## 4   Conclusion

We presented a first *proof-of-concept* of our *weakly supervised* learning strategy for the segmentation of defected areas in MRI ventilation maps. We designed a network that is able to generate a pixel-wise segmentation of lung defects in MRI ventilation maps using the LCI value as a weak label. Our network model consists of two major parts for the global and local feature extraction. Both features are then combined to estimate the final segmentation. Furthermore, we use *self-supervised regularization* to prevent the network from learning a non-meaningful segmentation. We evaluated the performance of our method with a rating of the segmentation result by 5 human experts. The results show that over 60% of all segmentations are scored with very good or perfect. However, we observed that our method has a tendency for over-segmentation especially in regions were vessels are located. This over-segmentation could be removed by providing a vessel segmentation as a post-processing step or by adding this to the training procedure, but we will leave this for future work.

**Acknowledgement.** The authors would like to thank the Swiss National Science Foundation for funding this project (SNF 320030_149576).

# References

1. Andermatt, S., Horváth, A., Pezold, S., Cattin, P.: Pathology segmentation using distributional differences to images of healthy origin. In: Crimi, A., Bakas, S., Kuijf, H., Keyvan, F., Reyes, M., van Walsum, T. (eds.) BrainLes 2018. LNCS, vol. 11383, pp. 228–238. Springer, Cham (2019). https://doi.org/10.1007/978-3-030-11723-8_23
2. Andermatt, S., Pezold, S., Cattin, P.: Multi-dimensional gated recurrent units for the segmentation of biomedical 3D-data. In: Carneiro, G., et al. (eds.) LABELS/DLMIA -2016. LNCS, vol. 10008, pp. 142–151. Springer, Cham (2016). https://doi.org/10.1007/978-3-319-46976-8_15
3. Bauman, G., Bieri, O.: Matrix pencil decomposition of time-resolved proton MRI for robust and improved assessment of pulmonary ventilation and perfusion. Magn. Reson. Med. **77**(1), 336–342 (2017)
4. Bauman, G., Pusterla, O., Bieri, O.: Ultra-fast steady-state free precession pulse sequence for fourier decomposition pulmonary MRI. Magn. Reson. Med. **75**(4), 1647–1653 (2016)
5. Chen, X., Konukoglu, E.: Unsupervised detection of lesions in brain MRI using constrained adversarial auto-encoders. arXiv preprint arXiv:1806.04972 (2018)
6. Nyilas, S., et al.: Novel magnetic resonance technique for functional imaging of cystic fibrosis lung disease. Eur. Respir. J. **50**(6) (2017). Article no. 1701464. https://doi.org/10.1183/13993003.01464-2017
7. Papandreou, G., Chen, L.C., Murphy, K.P., Yuille, A.L.: Weakly- and semi-supervised learning of a deep convolutional network for semantic image segmentation. In: International Conference on Computer Vision (2015)
8. Pathak, D., Krahenbuhl, P., Darrell, T.: Constrained convolutional neural networks for weakly supervised segmentation. In: International Conference on Computer Vision (2015)
9. Robinson, P.D., Goldman, M.D., Gustafsson, P.M.: Inert gas washout: theoretical background and clinical utility in respiratory disease. Respiration **78**(3), 339–355 (2009)
10. Sandkühler, R., Jud, C., Pezold, S., Cattin, P.C.: Adaptive graph diffusion regularisation for discontinuity preserving image registration. In: Klein, S., Staring, M., Durrleman, S., Sommer, S. (eds.) WBIR 2018. LNCS, vol. 10883, pp. 24–34. Springer, Cham (2018). https://doi.org/10.1007/978-3-319-92258-4_3

# Gated Recurrent Neural Networks
# for Accelerated Ventilation MRI

Robin Sandkühler[1(✉)], Grzegorz Bauman[1,2], Sylvia Nyilas[3], Orso Pusterla[1,2],
Corin Willers[3], Oliver Bieri[1,2], Philipp Latzin[3], Christoph Jud[1],
and Philippe C. Cattin[1]

[1] Department of Biomedical Engineering, University of Basel, Allschwil, Switzerland
robin.sandkuehler@unibas.ch
[2] Division of Radiological Physics, Department of Radiology,
University of Basel Hospital, Basel, Switzerland
[3] Pediatric Respiratory Medicine, Department of Pediatrics,
Inselspital, Bern University Hospital, University of Bern, Bern, Switzerland

**Abstract.** Thanks to recent advancements of specific acquisition methods and post-processing, proton Magnetic Resonance Imaging became an alternative imaging modality for detecting and monitoring chronic pulmonary disorders. Currently, ventilation maps of the lung are calculated from time-resolved image series which are acquired under free breathing. Each series consists of 140 coronal 2D images containing several breathing cycles. To cover the majority of the lung, such a series is acquired at several coronal slice-positions. A reduction of the number of images per slice enable an increase in the number of slice-positions per patient and therefore a more detailed analysis of the lung function without adding more stress to the patient. In this paper, we present a new method in order to reduce the number of images for one coronal slice while preserving the quality of the ventilation maps. As the input is a time-dependent signal, we designed our model based on Gated Recurrent Units. The results show that our method is able to compute ventilation maps with a high quality using only 40 images. Furthermore, our method shows strong robustness regarding changes in the breathing cycles during the acquisition.

**Keywords:** Ventilation MRI · Gated Recurrent Units

# 1 Introduction

Physiological lung imaging is a vital examination technique for the early detection and monitoring of chronic pulmonary disorders like cystic fibrosis. Due to the very low proton density of the lung parenchyma, the application of proton Magnetic Resonance Imaging (MRI) for functional pulmonary assessment is challenging. Different methods based on the inhalation of hyperpolarized gases during the MRI acquisition were presented in the past [4]. However, broad clinical application of hyperpolarized gas MRI is not feasible as it necessitates specialized

© Springer Nature Switzerland AG 2019
H.-I. Suk et al. (Eds.): MLMI 2019, LNCS 11861, pp. 549–556, 2019.
https://doi.org/10.1007/978-3-030-32692-0_63

equipment and personal. Furthermore, it requires specific breathing maneuvers and the cooperation of the patients, which can not always be granted especially in pediatric subjects.

Recently, rapid acquisition pulse sequences such as ultra-fast balanced steady-state free precession (uf-bSSFP) [3] have shown promise for proton MRI of pulmonary structures and functions. Standard and widely available proton MRI has the potential to become a viable radiation-free alternative imaging modality compared to CT or SPECT to visualize physiological properties of the lung. MR ventilation maps of the lung can be calculated from a coronal time-resolved 2D image series acquired during free breathing. At every breath, the lung expands and contracts creating signal modulations associated with pulmonary ventilation that are detectable by MRI. After nonrigid image registration [8] to align the pulmonary structures in the image series, the corresponding frequency for the ventilation can be detected. Figure 1 shows a representative MR image acquired with the uf-bSSFP sequence and the corresponding ventilation map. The in [2] presented state-of-the-art method for the calculation of ventilation maps (Fig. 1) requires 140 images per coronal slice-position in order to compute the ventilation map. The acquisition time per image series is about one minute. A reduction of the number of images per slice enable an increase in the number of slices per patient within the same examination time. This is important, as an increase of the overall scan time could increase the stress for the patient inside the MR, especially for pediatric patients.

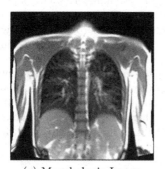 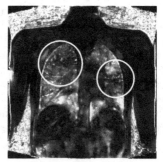

(a) Morphologic Image                    (b) Ventilation Map

**Fig. 1.** (a) Sample coronal image from an MR acquisition with the uf-bSSFP sequence of a patient with cystic fibrosis, and (b) a corresponding ventilation map. The circles mark areas with potential ventilation defects.

In this paper, we present a novel method for the estimation of ventilation maps using an image series composed of only 40 images. We trained a stacked bidirectional Gated Recurrent Units (SB-GRU) to estimate the ventilation maps based on the time-varying intensity signal of the image series. The results show that the presented method can compute accurate ventilation maps using less than a third of the images.

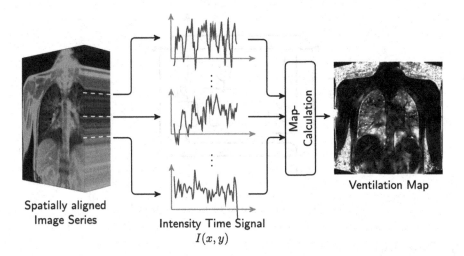

**Fig. 2.** Computation process of MRI ventilation maps.

## 2 Background

MRI image acquisition is performed with a time-resolved 2D uf-bSSFP sequence [3]. This pulse sequence is accelerated thanks to optimized excitation pulses and Cartesian gradient switching patterns, accompanied by partial echo readouts and ramp sampling techniques. As a result echo time (TE) and repetition time (TR) are shortened which improves signal in the lung parenchyma and reduces motion as well as off-resonance artifacts known as banding artifacts. The chest volume was covered using 8 to 12 coronal slices with 140 images per slice position resulting in a total acquisition time of about 10 min per examination.

### 2.1 Ventilation MRI

The ventilation maps are computed according to [2]. In the first step, the respiratory motion in the time-resolved uf-bSSFP data was compensated with a two-dimensional nonrigid image registration algorithm [8]. Subsequently, an automated lung segmentation was performed [1]. After image registration and segmentation, the matrix pencil analysis of the time course was performed voxel-wise to estimate the amplitudes $A_\mathrm{r}$ of the respiratory frequencies of the signal modulations in the lung parenchyma. The estimated amplitudes were used to calculate fractional ventilation maps

$$v_m = \frac{A_\mathrm{r}}{A_\mathrm{DC} + 0.5A_\mathrm{r} - BG} 100[\%], \tag{1}$$

where $A_\mathrm{DC}$ is the amplitude of the baseline signal and $BG$ the background noise. An overview of the calculation process is shown in Fig. 2. For further details, the reader is referred to [2].

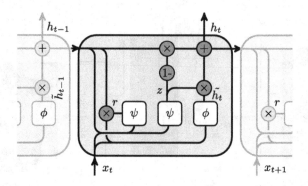

**Fig. 3.** Unrolled gated recurrent unit cell.

# 3 Method

The image series that is acquired for the ventilation maps contains time related information, i.e., the signal intensity changes over time. In order to take this time information into account, we use a Recurrent Neural Network (RNN) for the computation of ventilation maps with only 40 images in a series. We choose 40 images to ensure that the input signal contains at least 2–3 respiratory cycles. Compared to feedforward networks, RNNs contain an internal state and the output of an RNN depends on the current input and the internal state. A simple RNN has the form

$$h_t = \phi(Wx_t + Uh_{t-1}), \tag{2}$$

where $x_t$ is the input, $h_t$ the output of the RNN at time $t$, and $\phi$ is an activation function. Here, the internal state is the last output $h_{t-1}$ of the RNN. The matrices $W$ and $U$ are the learnable weights. Based on the basic RNN (2), several extensions were developed to overcome characteristic issues, e.g., the vanishing gradient problem. A popular RNN extension is the Long Short-Term Memory (LSTM) network [6].

## 3.1 Gated Recurrent Units

A simplified version of the LSTM are GRUs [5]. GRUs show a good performance compared to the LSTM but with fewer parameters. According to [5], a vanilla GRU cell is described by:

$$r_t = \psi\left(W_r x_t + U_r h_{t-1}\right), \tag{3}$$

$$z_t = \psi\left(W_z x_t + U_z h_{t-1}\right), \tag{4}$$

$$\tilde{h}_t = \phi\left(Wx_t + U(r_t \odot h_{t-1}\right), \tag{5}$$

$$h_t = (1 - z) \odot h_{t-1} + z_t \odot \tilde{h}_t. \tag{6}$$

Here, $r$ represents the reset gate, $z$ the update gate, $\tilde{h}$ the proposal state, $h_t$ the output at time $t$, $\phi(\cdot)$ is the hyperbolic tangent, $\psi(\cdot)$ represents the logistic function, and $\odot$ is the Hadamard product. Each gate contains its own learn-able weights $W$ for the input $x_t$ and $U$ for the hidden state $h_{t-1}$. A graphical representation of the Eqs. (3)–(6) is shown in Fig. 3, where the circles describe element wise operations.

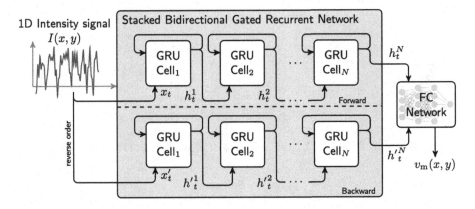

**Fig. 4.** Stacked Bidirectional Recurrent Neural Network architecture for the computation of ventilation maps.

## 3.2 Stacked Bidirectional Gated Recurrent Units

Bidirectional GRUs consists of two separate GRU networks, with a forward and backward direction respectively. In the backward direction, the input sequence is processed in reverse order. This allows an analysis of the time signal independent of the direction of the signal. Furthermore, we use a stacked bidirectional GRU (SB-GRU), in order to model more complex signals. A stacked GRU is defined as a concatenation of a number of single GRU cells, where the input of the current GRU cell is the output of the previous one. In this paper, we used a GRU cell given by

$$r_j = \psi\left(W_r^j x_t + b_{wr}^j + U_r^j h_{t-1}^j + b_{hr}^j\right), \tag{7}$$

$$z_j = \psi\left(W_z^j x_t + b_{wz}^j + U_z^j h_{t-1}^j + b_{hz}^j\right), \tag{8}$$

$$\tilde{h}_t^j = \phi\left(W^j x_t + b_x^j + r_j \odot \left(U^j h_{t-1}^j + b_{\tilde{h}}^j\right)\right), \tag{9}$$

$$h_t^j = (1 - z_j) \odot h_{t-1}^j + z_j \odot \tilde{h}_t^j, \tag{10}$$

where $j$ is the index of a GRU cell and $b$ the corresponding bias. The input of our network is a 1D intensity time signal $I(x, y)$ from the spatially aligned image series as shown in Fig. 2. After the input is processed by the SB-GRU, the output of the forward and the backward GRU are concatenated and applied to a fully connected network with one hidden layer in order to reduce the output to the scalar ventilation map value $v_m(x, y)$. Here $x$ and $y$ are the spatial locations of the image series. A complete 2D ventilation map is created by evaluating the network at each spatial location. The final network is shown in Fig. 4.

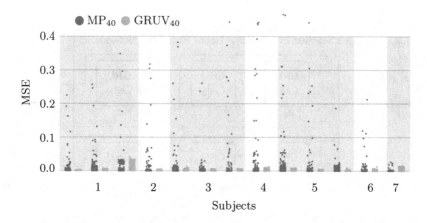

**Fig. 5.** MSE values for the ventilation map calculated with the presented method $GRUV_{40}$ and the state of the art method $MP_{40}$ using a 2D time series with 40 images. Both methods were compared against the ventilation maps of the gold standard matrix pencil method $MP_{140}$ using 140 images.

## 4    Experiments and Results

For our experiments, we used a data set of 84 subjects with an average of two examinations per subject. In each examination, 8–10 dynamic 2D image series at different coronal positions were acquired. We divided our data set into a training set with 70 subjects, an evaluation set with 7 subjects, and a test set with 7 subjects. All examinations were performed on a 1.5 T whole-body MR-scanner (MAGNETOM Aera, Siemens Healthineers, Erlangen, Germany) using a 12-channel thorax and a 24-channel spine receiver coil array. Each subject was scanned during free breathing with the uf-bSSFP sequence [3]. The main pulse sequence parameters were as follows: field-of-view $375 \times 375$–$425 \times 425$ mm$^2$, slice thickness 12 mm, TE/TR/TA = 0.67 ms/1.46 ms/119 ms, flip angle 60°, bandwidth 2056 Hz/pixel, matrix $128 \times 128$ (interpolated to $256 \times 256$), 3.33 images/s, parallel imaging GRAPPA factor 2.

We used 10 stacked GRU cells with a hidden state size of 300 for the forward and the backward GRU. The hidden layer of the fully connected network was set to 1024 with the RELU activation function and the logistic function $\frac{1}{1+\exp(-x)}$ as activation function for the last layer. For the optimization of the network parameters, we used the Adam optimizer [7] with a learning rate of 0.0001.

For the training of the network, we used spatially aligned image series with 140 images. The ventilation maps used as gold standard for the training and the lung segmentation were obtained as described in Sect. 2.1. In each training iteration, a continuous image sequence of 40 images was randomly selected from one slice of the training set. The 1D intensity signals $I(x, y)$ of this sequence were applied to the network. During training, we restrict $x$ and $y$ only to locations inside the lung mask. We use the mean squared error (MSE) loss function to compare the network output with the ground truth during training.

For the evaluation of our method, we used a window of the first 40 images of the complete image series from one coronal slice and computed the ventilation maps using the presented method ($GRUV_{40}$) and the matrix pencil method ($MP_{40}$). Both methods were compared to the gold standard matrix pencil method ($MP_{140}$) [2] which uses 140 images of the series for the computation of the ventilation maps. For the error calculation of the $MP_{40}$ and the $GRUV_{40}$ when compared to the $MP_{140}$ we used MSE metric. To show that our method is robust against breathing variability within the 40 images, the window was shifted for one image and the ventilation maps were computed. This process was repeated until the end of the image series was reached and was done for all coronal slices of each examination. The results for the 7 test subjects are shown in Fig. 5. Each subject contains either one or three examinations. The results show that the $MP_{40}$ and the $GRUV_{40}$ method are able to calculate correct ventilation maps. However, the error variance of our method is much smaller compared to the $MP_{40}$ method. This indicates that our method is robust against breathing variability within the 40 image window. Qualitative results $GRUV_{40}$ are shown in Fig. 6. Here, we can observe a lower amplitude for the map intensities for the $GRUV_{40}$ when compared to the $MP_{140}$ result. The reason for this effect could be the fact that only 1D time signals are used to compute the corresponding ventilation value.

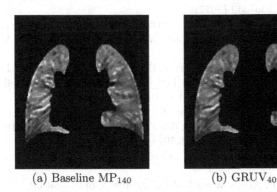

(a) Baseline $MP_{140}$          (b) $GRUV_{40}$

**Fig. 6.** (a) Example MRI ventilation maps of a single slice of the gold standard (140 images), and (b) the presented method GRUV (40 images).

# 5   Conclusion

In this paper, we presented a novel method for the calculation of ventilation maps based on a 2D time-resolved dynamic MRI image series acquired with the uf-bSSFP sequence. Our aim was to calculate ventilation maps which are equivalent to the one calculated with the state of the art method, but with fewer images. In order to encounter the time dependencies in the image series, we designed a network based on SB-GRUs. We show that our method is able to estimate correct ventilation maps for a given image series with only 40 when compared to the current state-of-the-art method. Furthermore, we observe that our method is robust against breathing variabilities inside the 40 images. But, we also discover for some ventilation maps generated with our method a drop of the global intensity amplitude compared to the state-of-the-art method. We believe, we could overcome this issue by taking spatial information into account but we leave this for future work.

**Acknowledgement.** The authors would like to thank the Swiss National Science Foundation for funding this project (SNF 320030-149576).

# References

1. Andermatt, S., Pezold, S., Cattin, P.: Multi-dimensional gated recurrent units for the segmentation of biomedical 3D-data. In: Carneiro, G., et al. (eds.) LABELS/DLMIA -2016. LNCS, vol. 10008, pp. 142–151. Springer, Cham (2016). https://doi.org/10.1007/978-3-319-46976-8_15
2. Bauman, G., Bieri, O.: Matrix pencil decomposition of time-resolved proton MRI for robust and improved assessment of pulmonary ventilation and perfusion. Magn. Reson. Med. **77**(1), 336–342 (2017)
3. Bauman, G., Pusterla, O., Bieri, O.: Ultra-fast steady-state free precession pulse sequence for fourier decomposition pulmonary MRI. Magn. Reson. Med. **75**(4), 1647–1653 (2016)
4. van Beek, E.J., Wild, J.M., Kauczor, H.U., Schreiber, W., Mugler III, J.P., de Lange, E.E.: Functional MRI of the lung using hyperpolarized 3-helium gas. J. Magn. Reson. Imaging **20**(4), 540–554 (2004)
5. Cho, K., van Merrienboer, B., Gülçehre, Ç., Bougares, F., Schwenk, H., Bengio, Y.: Learning phrase representations using RNN encoder-decoder for statistical machine translation. arXiv preprint arXiv:1406.1078 (2014)
6. Hochreiter, S., Schmidhuber, J.: Long short-term memory. Neural Comput. **9**(8), 1735–1780 (1997)
7. Kingma, D.P., Ba, J.: Adam: a method for stochastic optimization. arXiv preprint arXiv:1412.6980 (2014)
8. Sandkühler, R., Jud, C., Pezold, S., Cattin, P.C.: Adaptive graph diffusion regularisation for discontinuity preserving image registration. In: Klein, S., Staring, M., Durrleman, S., Sommer, S. (eds.) WBIR 2018. LNCS, vol. 10883, pp. 24–34. Springer, Cham (2018). https://doi.org/10.1007/978-3-319-92258-4_3

# A Cascaded Multi-modality Analysis in Mild Cognitive Impairment

Lu Zhang[1]([⊠]), Akib Zaman[1], Li Wang[1], Jingwen Yan[2],
and Dajiang Zhu[1]

[1] The University of Texas at Arlington, Arlington, USA
lu.zhang2@mavs.uta.edu
[2] Indiana University-Purdue University Indianapolis, Indianapolis, USA

**Abstract.** Though reversing the pathology of Alzheimer's disease (AD) has so far not been possible, a more tractable goal may be the prevention or slowing of the disease when diagnosed in its earliest stage, such as mild cognitive impairment (MCI). Recent advances in deep modeling approaches trigger a new era for AD/MCI classification. However, it is still difficult to integrate multi-modal imaging data into a single deep model, to gain benefit from complementary datasets as much as possible. To address this challenge, we propose a cascaded deep model to capture both brain structural and functional characteristic for MCI classification. With diffusion tensor imaging (DTI) and functional magnetic resonance imaging (fMRI) data, a graph convolution network (GCN) is constructed based on brain structural connectome and it works with a one-layer recurrent neural network (RNN) which is responsible for inferring the temporal features from brain functional activities. We named this cascaded deep model as Graph Convolutional Recurrent Neural Network (GCRNN). Using Alzheimer's Disease Neuroimaging Initiative (ADNI-3) dataset as a test-bed, our method can achieve 97.3% accuracy between normal controls (NC) and MCI patients.

**Keywords:** Mild Cognitive Impairment · GCN · RNN

## 1 Introduction

Alzheimer's disease (AD) is the most common form of dementia and approximately 10% of people age 65 and older have AD [1]. Given the facts that AD is the only disorder that cannot be prevented or cured, a more tractable goal is to diagnose at its earlier stage - mild cognitive impairment (MCI), as more than 50% people with MCI will convert to AD eventually. To date, the most sensitive AD biomarkers include measures of brain Aβ deposition (amyloid PET) [2] and neurodegeneration (FDG PET) [3]. However, PET can be invasive and may not be feasible or readily available. Thus, non-invasive imaging modalities including MRI (T1 weighted), diffusion tensor imaging (DTI) and resting state fMRI (r-fMRI) are of great interest. There have been a variety of approaches for early diagnosis or classification of AD/MCI, such as voxel-based analysis [4, 5], tract-based spatial statistics (TBSS for DTI) [6, 7], and multi-variate analysis/machine learning-based algorithms [8–10]. Recently, the advances in

© Springer Nature Switzerland AG 2019
H.-I. Suk et al. (Eds.): MLMI 2019, LNCS 11861, pp. 557–565, 2019.
https://doi.org/10.1007/978-3-030-32692-0_64

deep neural network approaches trigger a new era for AD/MCI studies. For example, Convolutional Neural Networks (CNN) [11] was applied on AD classification using structural MRI and PET data. The study in [11] conducted classification of MCI and regression of cognitive scores simultaneously with a multi-channel CNN. Graph Convolutional Network (GCN) [12] was recently proposed to fulfil the MCI conversion with multiple datasets. Despite the advancements made by these methods, most proposed deep models only work with unstructured data in image space, such as voxel intensity. How to leverage the deep models over the brain network has been rarely studied. In addition, brain structure and function are closely related, but it is still difficult to integrate them, via multi-modal imaging data (i.e. DTI and fMRI), into a single deep model, to gain benefit from complementary imaging data as much as possible.

In this work, to capture both brain structural and functional characteristics in MCI patients, we proposed a cascaded GCN and Recurrent Neural Network (RNN) framework to classify MCI via modeling brain spatial and temporal information simultaneously. Brain regions are treated as graph nodes and structural connectome is used as the topological description of the graph. The representative fMRI signal of each brain region composes the feature vector associated with the node. Multiple RNN cells was connected to capture the temporal patterns contained in the structural network. We named this model as Graph Convolutional Recurrent Neural Network (GCRNN). Figure 1 shows the major steps in this work. We use weighted adjacency matrix to store the fiber connectivity of different brain regions and a feature matrix to store the fMRI BOLD signals. During the training process, weighted adjacency matrix and feature matrix are firstly fed into GCN layers to learn the spatial features, then the RNN cells are built on the obtained features to learn temporal patterns in fMRI signals. Finally, a fully connected layer is used to perform the classification. Using Alzheimer's Disease Neuroimaging Initiative (ADNI-3) dataset (116NC/93MCI) as a test-bed, our method can achieve 97.3% accuracy between normal controls (NC) and MCI patients.

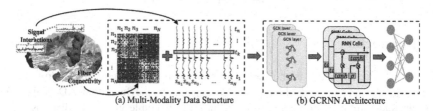

(a) Multi-Modality Data Structure          (b) GCRNN Architecture

**Fig. 1.** The pipeline of the proposed work. (a) We generate two matrices as the input for GCN. Structural connectivity is represented as weighted adjacency matrix to depict the structure of the graph. fMRI signals are formed as feature matrix associated with the nodes. $n_i$ represents the $i^{th}$ brain region, $s_{n_i}$ is the averaged fMRI signal in region $n_i$, and $t_i$ is the value at $i^{th}$ time point. (b) Overview of the proposed GCRNN.

# 2 Method

## 2.1 Dataset

In this work, all the data used was obtained from Alzheimer's Disease Neuroimaging Initiative (ADNI 3) [13]. We began with 661 subjects which have both DTI and rs-fMRI data. The DTI data is 2.0 mm isotropic, TE = 56 ms, TR = 7.2 s, and the gradient directions is 54. For rsfMRI, the range of image resolution in X and Y dimensions was from 2.29 mm to 3.31 mm. The range of slice thickness was from 3.3 mm to 3.4 mm, TE = 30 ms, TR = 3 s, and there were 197 volumes (time points) for each subject.

We applied standard pre-processing procedures including skull removal for both modalities, spatial smoothing, slice time correction, temporal pre-whitening, global drift removal and band pass filtering (0.01–0.1 Hz) for rsfMRI, eddy current correction and fiber tracking via MedINRIA for DTI, registering rsfMRI to DTI space using FLIRT and adopt the Destrieux Atlas [14] for ROI labeling. The brain cortex is partitioned into 148 regions after removing two unknow areas. After the preprocessing and image quality check, we have 209 subjects (116 CN/93 MCI) for experiments.

## 2.2 Multi-modality Data Structure

### 2.2.1 Adjacency Matrix and Feature Matrix

Following the basic brain network approach, we used the Destrieux atlas along with fiber tracking information to reconstruct the brain connectivity matrices, weighted by fiber count and ROI volume. For each brain region, we used the averaged fMRI BOLD signal as the temporal feature. Specifically, we used the adjacency matrix $A \in R^{N \times N}$ to represent the fiber connectivity of different brain regions, $N = 148$ is the number of the brain regions. $A$ is a symmetric matrix, $A_{ij} \in A$ is the number of shared fibers of brain region $i$ and region $j$. The feature matrix $F \in R^{T \times N \times P}$ is used to store the averaged fMRI signal, $T$ is the number of time points, $P$ is the dimension of averaged fMRI signal of one brain region at one time point. By using the adjacency matrix $A$ and feature matrix $F$ simultaneously, we aim to integrate brain spatial and temporal information for MCI diagnosis with our cascaded deep model.

### 2.2.2 Transformation of Adjacency Matrix and Feature Matrix

Before feeding the adjacency matrix and feature matrix into our deep model, we conducted normalization and transformations for two matrices separately. For feature matrix $F$, we normalize it by linear transformation:

$$\vec{Y} = \frac{\vec{X} - X_{min}}{X_{max} - X_{min}}, \tag{1}$$

where $\vec{X}$ is the vector before normalization, $X_{min}$ and $X_{max}$ are the minimum and maximum of $\vec{X}$, $\vec{Y}$ is the new vector.

For adjacency matrix $A$, besides linear transformation using formula (1), we also performed Laplace transformation which has three different forms:

$$L_1 = D - \hat{A} \tag{2}$$

$$L_2 = D^{-1/2}(D - \hat{A})D^{-1/2} \tag{3}$$

$$L_3 = D^{-1}(D - \hat{A}). \tag{4}$$

$\hat{A}$ is the adjacency matrix after linear transformation of $A$, and $D$ is the degree matrix of $\hat{A}$ which is a diagonal matrix: $D_{ii} = \sum_j \hat{A}_{ij}$. The results from Laplace transformation have good properties including: (1) all of them are positive semi-definite (2) 0 is an eigenvalue and the corresponding eigenvectors are constant one vector $1^c$, $D^{-1}1^c$ and $1^c$ respectively (3) they all have n non-negative real-valued eigenvalues. We designed a comparative experiment in Sect. 3.3 to show different performance by using $\hat{A}$, $L_1$, $L_2$, $L_3$ as the adjacency matrix respectively. Here we use the notation $\tilde{A}$ and $\tilde{F}$ represent the adjacency matrix and feature matrix after the normalization and transformation. The input data is $\{X_1, X_2, \ldots, X_T\}$, where $X_t = \{\tilde{A}, \tilde{F}_t\}$ and $\tilde{F} = \{\tilde{F}_1, \tilde{F}_2, \ldots, \tilde{F}_T\}$, $\tilde{F}_t \in R^{N \times P}$.

## 2.3   GCRNN Architecture

The motivation of this work is to design a deep model to integrate brain spatial and temporal information for MCI classification. Graph Convolutional Neural Network (GCN) and Recurrent Neural Network (RNN) have shown their effectiveness in modeling structured data, such as graph and sequence [9, 13]. Here, we used GCN to model brain structural connectivity and RNN to capture temporal pattern of fMRI data. We proposed a Graph Convolutional Recurrent Neural Network (GCRNN) to combine these two powerful models for MCI classification. Because RNN model has two different variants: Long Short-Term Memory (LSTM) and Gated Recurrent Unit (GRU), we will consider both of them and develop two different GCRNN models: GCN-GRU and GCN-LSTM. The overall architectures of the two different GCRNN and the implementation details are shown in Fig. 2.

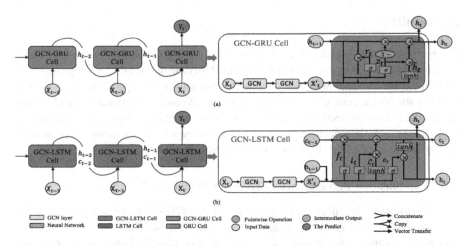

**Fig. 2.** (a) GCRNN with GRU. (b) GCRNN with LSTM. Both of the two GCRNN have the same two-layer GCN. Training process: input data $X_t$ is fitted into GCN layers and obtains the output of GCN, $X_t'$, then $X_t'$ together with $h_{t-1}$ and $c_{t-1}$ are used as input data to fit into a one-layer RNN. According to different RNN, data will be processed differently.

Table 1 is the mathematical definition of GCN-GRU and GCN-LSTM models. Two-layers GCN is defined by formula (5), $W_0$ and $W_1$ are the learnable weights of GCN layer 1 and layer 2 respectively, $\tilde{A}$ and $\tilde{F}$ are the adjacency matrix and feature matrix mentioned in Sect. 2.2.2. $g(\tilde{A}, \tilde{F}_t)$ is the output of the second GCN layer and is also the input of two different RNN models. As the output of GCN, $g(\tilde{A}, \tilde{F}_t)$ contains both topological structure and functional features. LSTMis defined by formula (6)–(11) and GRUis defined by formula (12)–(15). In these formulae, $W_*$ and $b_*$ are the weight and bias of RNN model. Note that GRU and LSTM have different performance when applied to different problems. In order to examine which RNN model works better in GCRNN architecture, we conducted a comparative experiment to compare the performance of the two structures in Table 2.

**Table 1.** The mathematical definition of GCN-GRUand GCN-LSTM models.

| GCN-LSTM | GCN-GRU |
|---|---|
| $g(\tilde{A}, \tilde{F}_t) = ReLU(\tilde{A}ReLU(\tilde{A}\tilde{F}_t W_0)W_1)$ (5) | |
| $f_t = \sigma(W_f \cdot [h_{t-1}, g(\tilde{A}, \tilde{F}_t)] + b_f)$ (6) | $z_t = \sigma(W_z \cdot [h_{t-1}, g(\tilde{A}, \tilde{F}_t)])$ (12) |
| $i_t = \sigma(W_i \cdot [h_{t-1}, g(\tilde{A}, \tilde{F}_t)] + b_i)$ (7) | $r_t = \sigma(W_r \cdot [h_{t-1}, g(\tilde{A}, \tilde{F}_t)])$ (13) |
| $\tilde{C}_t = tanh(W_C \cdot [h_{t-1}, g(\tilde{A}, \tilde{F}_t)] + b_C)$ (8) | $\tilde{h}_t = tanh(W \cdot [r_t * h_{t-1}, g(\tilde{A}, \tilde{F}_t)])$ (14) |
| $C_t = f_t * C_{t-1} + i_t * \tilde{C}_t$ (9) | $h_t = (1 - z_t) * h_{t-1} + z_t * \tilde{h}_t$ (15) |
| $o_t = \sigma(W_o \cdot [h_{t-1}, g(\tilde{A}, \tilde{F}_t)] + b_o)$ (10) | |
| $h_t = o_t * tanh(C_t)$ (11) | |

## 3   Results

We perform binary classification (CN vs. MCI) using GCRNN models and multi-modality data. In order to show the reproducibility of the results, we repeated each experiment for 10 times with the same parameter setting. The performance was evaluated by the best accuracy (Best), worst accuracy (Worst), average accuracy (Ave) and the standard deviation (Stdev) of the 10 runs. To be specific, we have three comparative experiments: (1) classification accuracy (2) influence of brain structural connectivity (3) performance of using different Laplace transformation.

### 3.1   Classification Performance of GCRNN Model

For demonstrating the effectiveness of the proposed GCRNN model, we performed 540 experiments under 27 different model settings with both GCN-LSTM and GCN-GRU. The model setting is defined as: GCN = (number of layers, [feature number of each layer]), RNN = (number of layers, [hidden nodes number of each layer]) and model name. Table 2 displays the results of 220 experiments including two-layer GCN/one-layer RNN, one-layer GCN/one-layer RNN and three-layer GCN/one-layer RNN.

In Table 2, the best results and the corresponding model settings are highlighted in bold. Besides the best results, some items are marked with "*", because except the average accuracy is not the best, they have relatively good performance and stability at the same time. Note that using more hidden nodes in RNN leads to higher accuracy. With the same number of hidden nodes in RNN, the model with two-layer GCN has the best performance comparing to one-layer and three-layer GCN. This suggests that our data might sufficient for current RNN settings. For GCN training, three layers might need more data to retain the accuracy.

**Table 2.** Results of different model settings.

| Model settings | GCN-LSTM-Cell | | | | GCN-GRU-Cell | | | |
|---|---|---|---|---|---|---|---|---|
| | Best | Worst | Ave | Stdev | Best | Worst | Ave | Stdev |
| GCN = (2, [64, 128]) RNN = (1, 1024) | 95.3 | 87.3 | 90.9 | 2.9 | 94.1 | 80.1 | 87.8 | 5.2 |
| **GCN = (2, [32, 64]) RNN = (1, 1024)** | **97.3** | **80.6** | **93.5** | **5.2** | 96.1 | 81.4 | 89.7 | 5.0 |
| GCN = (2, [16, 32]) RNN = (1, 1024) | 96.9 | 72.7 | 87.8 | 7.6 | 91.1 | 76.6 | 83.8 | 4.5 |
| GCN = (2, [64, 128]) RNN = (1, 512) | 98.8 | 58.1 | 77.8 | 11.9 | 93.4 | 61.3 | 75.8 | 11.4 |
| GCN = (2, [32, 64]) RNN = (1, 512) | 94.0 | 73.7 | 82.7 | 5.7 | 93.2 | 56.1 | 76.2 | 10.6 |
| GCN = (2, [16, 32]) RNN = (1, 512) | 96.9 | 53.2 | 84.3 | 13.7 | 86.3 | 58.4 | 68.8 | 8.3 |
| GCN = (2, [64, 128]) RNN = (1, 2048) | 97.2 | 84.5 | 91.3 | 4.1 | 96.5 | 80.9 | 90.9 | 6.5 |
| **GCN = (2, [32, 64]) RNN = (1, 2048)*** | 96.1* | 88.1* | 91.4* | 2.8* | **97.7** | **83.6** | **91.5** | **4.4** |
| GCN = (2, [16, 32]) RNN = (1, 2048) | 92.1 | 83.4 | 87.3 | 2.4 | 91.4 | 81.5 | 87.7 | 3.1 |
| GCN = (1, 64) RNN = (1, 1024) | 91.1 | 82.5 | 87.6 | 2.7 | 93.8 | 83.3 | 88.4 | 4.1 |
| GCN = (3, [32, 64, 128]) RNN = (1, 1024) | 76.1 | 59.6 | 67.6 | 5.3 | 76.1 | 53.1 | 65.0 | 8.6 |

## 3.2 Influence of Brain Structural Connectivity

One major advantage of GCRNN is to use structural connectivity, constructed by counting DTI derived fibers between brain regions, to describe the topology of the graph for GCN. In order to verify the influence of using brain structural network, we make a comparison with the variant that uses all ONE matrix as the adjacency matrix and see how the topology of the graph affects the performance. Note that the all ONE matrix has the same size as brain structural connectivity matrix and it is a complete graph. That is, we assume each pair of brain regions is connected, hence it is unbiased and doesn't introduce any spatial information of brain network during the training. The comparison is under the setting of GCN = (2, [32, 64]) RNN = (1, 1024) with a LSTM and repeated for 10 times. The results are shown in Fig. 3.

From the Fig. 3 we can see that using brain structural connectivity as adjacency matrix has an overwhelming advantage compared to all ONE matrix, which means that the structural connectivity is an effective representation of brain spatial information during GCN training. Moreover, the classification results also suggest that the functional features along with individual brain structures have the potential to capture the intrinsic alterations in MCI patients.

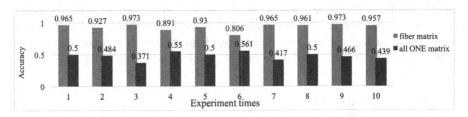

**Fig. 3.** Results of testing influence of brain structural connectivity

## 3.3 Influence of Laplace Transformation

Though Laplace transformation has been applied to a wide range of applications as well as GCN constructions, it is still largely unclear whether it can improve the performance in our binary classification. In this comparative experiment, we used $\hat{A}$ (structural connectivity matrix after linear transformation) $L_1$ $L_2$ and $L_3$ ($\hat{A}$ after three forms of Laplace transformation) which are defined in Sect. 2.2.2, respectively. Our experiment is under the model setting with GCN = (2, [32, 64]) RNN = (1, 1024) with LSTM and repeated for 10 times. The results are shown in Fig. 4.

The results in Fig. 4 show that among three forms Laplace transformation and original matrix $\hat{A}$, the performance of all three forms of Laplace transformation have lower standard deviation (Stdev), thus is relatively stable, and there is no significant difference in best accuracy (Best), worst accuracy (Worst) and average accuracy (Ave) between Laplace transformation and original matrix. So using Laplace transformation will increase the stability of the results in the experiments, but there is no significant improvement in the accuracy.

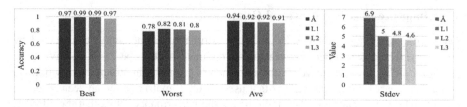

**Fig. 4.** Results of testing influence of Laplace transformation

## 4   Conclusion

In this work, we proposed a cascaded GCN and RNN framework, named as GCRNN, to classify MCI via modeling brain spatial and temporal information simultaneously. Using brain structural connectivity as the graph and fMRI signals as the feature, our cascaded deep model effectively combines GCN and RNN together and achieve 97.7% accuracy for classification of MCI and NC. Note that, besides the considerations of using structural connectivity and different deep architectures, another factor that might influence our result is the length of the fMRI signal used. Previous studies [15] suggested that for resting state fMRI 14 time points (when TR = 2 s) are sufficient to capture functional dynamic patterns. Here, we also examined the influence when adopting different length of fMRI signals. The results are shown in Fig. 5. and it suggests that there is no obvious relationship between length and accuracy in our settings. In the future, this need to be further examined with more samples.

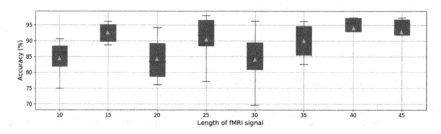

**Fig. 5.** Results of testing length of fMRI signal

**Acknowledgements.** The authors thank Dong Wang for the helpful discussions.

## References

1. Alzheimer's Association: 2019 Alzheimer's Disease Facts and Figures Report. https://www.alz.org/alzheimers-dementia/facts-figures
2. Rowe, C.C., et al.: Amyloid imaging results from the Australian Imaging, Biomarkers and Lifestyle (AIBL) study of aging. Neurobiol. Aging **31**, 1275–1283 (2010)

3. Jagust, W.J., et al.: The Alzheimer's Disease Neuroimaging Initiative positron emission tomography core. Alzheimers Dement. **6**, 221–229 (2010)
4. Ashburner, J., Friston, K.J.: Voxel-based morphometry—the methods. Neuroimage **11**, 805–821 (2000)
5. Thompson, P.M., Apostolova, L.G.: Computational anatomical methods as applied to ageing and dementia. Br. J. Radiol. **80**, S78–S91 (2007)
6. Vemuri, P., et al.: Accelerated vs. unaccelerated serial MRI based TBM-SyN measurements for clinical trials in Alzheimer's disease. Neuroimage **113**, 61–69 (2015)
7. Smith, S.M., et al.: Tract-based spatial statistics: voxelwise analysis of multi-subject diffusion data. Neuroimage **31**, 1487–1505 (2006)
8. Jiang, X., et al.: Intrinsic functional component analysis via sparse representation on Alzheimer's disease neuroimaging initiative database. Brain Connect. **4**, 575–586 (2014)
9. Tong, T., et al.: Multi-modal classification of Alzheimer's disease using nonlinear graph fusion. Pattern Recogn. **63**, 171–181 (2017)
10. Jack Jr., C.R., et al.: The Alzheimer's disease neuroimaging initiative (ADNI): MRI methods. J. Magn. Reson. Imaging: Off. J. Int. Soc. Magn. Reson. Med. **27**(4), 685–691 (2008)
11. Liu, M., Zhang, J., Adeli, E., Shen, D.: Deep multi-task multi-channel learning for joint classification and regression of brain status. In: Descoteaux, M., Maier-Hein, L., Franz, A., Jannin, P., Collins, D.L., Duchesne, S. (eds.) MICCAI 2017. LNCS, vol. 10435, pp. 3–11. Springer, Cham (2017). https://doi.org/10.1007/978-3-319-66179-7_1
12. Parisot, S., et al.: Spectral graph convolutions for population-based disease prediction. In: Descoteaux, M., Maier-Hein, L., Franz, A., Jannin, P., Collins, D.L., Duchesne, S. (eds.) MICCAI 2017. LNCS, vol. 10435, pp. 177–185. Springer, Cham (2017). https://doi.org/10.1007/978-3-319-66179-7_21
13. ADNI: Alzheimer's disease neuroimaging initiative. http://adni.loni.usc.edu/
14. Destrieux, C., et al.: Automatic parcellation of human cortical gyri and sulci using standard anatomical nomenclature. Nuroimage **53**(1), 1–15 (2010)
15. Zhang, X., et al.: Characterization of task-free and task-performance brain states via functional connectome patterns. Med. Image Anal. **17**(8), 1106–1122 (2013)

# Deep Residual Learning for Instrument Segmentation in Robotic Surgery

Daniil Pakhomov[1,3(✉)], Vittal Premachandran[1], Max Allan[2], Mahdi Azizian[2], and Nassir Navab[1,3]

[1] Johns Hopkins University, Baltimore, USA
dpakhom1@jhu.edu
[2] Intuitive Surgical Inc., Sunnyvale, USA
[3] Technische Universität München, Munich, Germany

**Abstract.** Detection, tracking, and pose estimation of surgical instruments provide critical information that can be used to correct inaccuracies in kinematic data in robotic-assisted surgery. Such information can be used for various purposes including integration of pre- and intra-operative images into the endoscopic view. In some cases, automatic segmentation of surgical instruments is a crucial step towards full instrument pose estimation but it can also be solely used to improve user interactions with the robotic system. In our work we focus on binary instrument segmentation, where the objective is to label every pixel as instrument or background and instrument part segmentation, where different semantically separate parts of the instrument are labeled. We improve upon previous work by leveraging recent techniques such as deep residual learning and dilated convolutions and advance both binary-segmentation and instrument part segmentation performance on the EndoVis 2017 Robotic Instruments dataset. The source code for the experiments reported in the paper has been made public (https://github.com/warmspringwinds/pytorch-segmentation-detection).

## 1 Introduction

Robot-assisted Minimally Invasive Surgery (RMIS) overcomes many of the limitations of traditional laparoscopic Minimally Invasive Surgery (MIS), providing the surgeon with improved control over the anatomy with articulated instruments and dexterous master manipulators. In addition to this, 3D-HD visualization on systems such as da Vinci enhances the surgeon's depth perception and operating precision [3]. However, complications due to the reduced field-of-view provided by the surgical camera limit the surgeon's ability to self-localize. Traditional haptic cues on tissue composition are lost through the robotic control system [11].

Overlaying pre- and intra-operative imaging with the surgical console can provide the surgeon with valuable information which can improve decision making during complex procedures [15]. However, integrating this data is a complex

© Springer Nature Switzerland AG 2019
H.-I. Suk et al. (Eds.): MLMI 2019, LNCS 11861, pp. 566–573, 2019.
https://doi.org/10.1007/978-3-030-32692-0_65

task and involves understanding spatial relationships between the surgical camera, operating instruments and patient anatomy. A critical component of this process is segmentation of the instruments in the camera images which can be used to prevent rendered overlays from occluding the instruments while providing crucial input to instrument tracking frameworks [1,12].

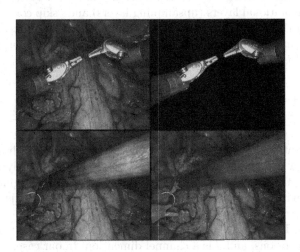

**Fig. 1.** Example frames from RMIS procedures present in the dataset. Left column shows example images frames from the dataset. Right column shows the binary and instrument part segmentation of corresponding images delivered by our method.

Segmentation of surgical tools from tissue backgrounds is an extremely difficult task due to lighting challenges such as shadows and specular reflections, visual occlusions such as smoke and blood (see Fig. 1). Early methods attempted to simplify the problem by modifying the appearance of the instruments [16]. However, this complicates clinical application of the technique as sterilization can become an issue. Segmentation of the instruments using natural appearance is a more desirable approach as it can be applied directly to pre-existing clinical setups. However, this defines a more challenging problem. To solve it, previous work has relied on machine learning techniques to model the complex discriminative boundary. The instrument-background segmentation can be modeled as a binary segmentation problem to which discriminative models, such as Random Forests [4], maximum likelihood Gaussian Mixture Models [12] and Naive Bayesian classifiers [14], all trained on color features, have been applied. More recently, the state-of-the-art has increasingly been defined by Fully Convolutional Networks (FCNs), such as the FCN-8s model [10] adapted for the task of binary segmentation of robotic tools [6] and U-Net [13] which was used for both binary and instrument part segmentation [9].

In this work, we adopt the state-of-art residual image classification Convolutional Neural Network (CNN) [7] for the task of semantic image segmentation by casting it into a FCN. However, the transformed model delivers a prediction map of significantly reduced dimension compared to the input image [10]. To account for that, we reduce in-network downsampling, employ dilated (atrous) convolutions to enable initialization with the parameters of the original classification network, and perform simple bilinear interpolation of the feature maps to obtain the original image size [5,17]. This approach is a powerful alternative to using deconvolutional layers (upsampling layers) and "skip connections" as in FCN-8s model [10] and CSL model [9]. By employing it, we advance the state-of-the-art in binary and instrument part segmentation of tools on the EndoVis 2017 Robotic Instruments dataset [2].

## 2 Method

The goal of this work is to label every pixel of an image $\mathbf{I}$ with one of $C$ semantic classes, representing surgical tool part or background. In case of binary segmentation, the goal is to label each pixel into $C = 2$ classes, namely surgical tool and background. In this work, we also consider a more challenging multi-class segmentation with $C = 4$ classes, namely tool's shaft, wrist and jaws and background.

Each image $\mathbf{I}_i$ is a three-dimensional array of size $h \times w \times d$, where $h$ and $w$ are spatial dimensions, and $d$ is a channel dimension. In our case, $d = 3$ because we use RGB images. Each image $\mathbf{I}_i$ in the training dataset has corresponding annotation $\mathbf{A}_i$ of a size $h \times w \times C$ where each element represents one-hot encoded semantic label $a \in \{0,1\}^C$ (for example, if we have classes 1, 2, and 3, then the one-hot encoding of label 2 is $(0,1,0)^T$).

We aim at learning a mapping from $\mathbf{I}$ to $\mathbf{A}$ in a supervised fashion that generalizes to previously unseen images. In this work, we use CNNs to learn a discriminative classifier which delivers pixel-wise predictions given an input image. Our method is built upon state-of-the-art deep residual image classification CNN (ResNet-18, Sect. 2.1), which we convert into fully convolutional network (FCN, Sect. 2.2).

CNNs reduce the spatial resolution of the feature maps by using pooling layers or convolutional layers with strides greater than one. However, for our task of pixel-wise prediction we would like dense feature maps. We set the stride to one in the last two layers responsible for downsampling, and in order to reuse the weights from a pre-trained model, we dilate the subsequent convolutions (Sect. 2.3) with an appropriate rate. This enables us to obtain predictions that are downsampled only by a factor of $8\times$ (in comparison to the original downsampling of $32\times$).

We then apply bilinear interpolation to regain the original spatial resolution. With an output map of the same resolution as an input image, we perform end-to-end training by minimizing the normalized pixel-wise cross-entropy loss [10].

## 2.1   Deep Residual Learning

Traditional CNNs learn filters that process the input $x_l$ and produce a filtered response $x_{l+1}$, as shown below

$$y_l = g(x_l, w_l), \tag{1}$$

$$x_{l+1} = f(y_l). \tag{2}$$

Here, $g(.,.)$ is a standard convolutional layer with $w_l$ being the weights of the layer's convolutional filters and biases, $f(.)$ is a non-linear mapping function such as the Rectified Linear Unit (ReLU). Recently modifications [7] showed that significant gains in performance can be obtained by employing "residual units" as a building block of a deep CNN, and called such networks Residual Networks (ResNets). Each unit of a ResNet can be expressed in the following general form

$$y_l = h(x_l) + F(x_l, W_l), \tag{3}$$

$$x_{l+1} = f(y_l), \tag{4}$$

where $x_l$ and $x_{l+1}$ are input and output of the $l$-th unit, and $F(.,)$ is a residual function to be learnt. The function $h(.)$ is a simple identity mapping, $h(x_l) = x_l$ and $f(.)$ is a rectified linear unit activation (ReLU) function. As $h(x_l)$ is chosen to be an identity mapping, it is easily realized by attaching an identity skip connection (also known as a "shortcut" connection). In our work, we adopt ResNet-18 architecture which allows us to achieve state-of-the-art performance in tool segmentation.

## 2.2   Fully Convolutional Networks

Deep CNNs (e.g. AlexNet, VGG16, ResNets, etc.) are primarily trained for the task of image classification. However, to obtain the output granularity required for a task such as image segmentation requires converting the CNN's fully connected layers into convolutions with kernels that are equal to their fixed input regions [10] which creates an FCN. An FCN operates on inputs of any size, and produces an output with reduced spatial dimensions [10].

Fully convolutional models deliver prediction maps with significantly reduced dimensions (for both VGG16 and ResNets, the spatial dimensions are reduced by a factor of 32). In the previous work [10], it was shown that adding a deconvolutional layer to learn the upsampling with factor 32 provides a way to get the prediction map of original image dimension, but the segmentation boundaries delivered by this approach are usually too coarse. To tackle this problem, two approaches were recently developed which are based on modifying the architecture. (i) By fusing features from layers of different resolution to make the predictions [9,10]. (ii) By avoiding downsampling of some of the feature maps [5,17] (removing certain pooling layers in VGG16 and by setting the strides to one in certain convolutional layers responsible for the downsampling in ResNets).

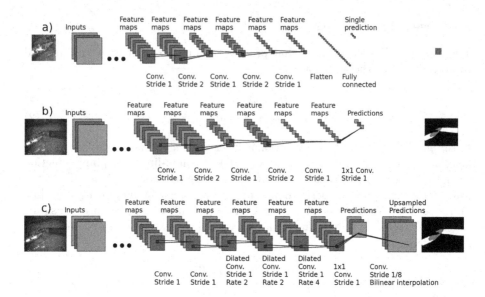

**Fig. 2.** A simplified CNN before and after being converted into an FCN (illustrations (a) and (b) respectively), after reducing downsampling rate with integration of dilated convolutions into its architecture with subsequent bilinear interpolation (illustration (c)). Illustration (a) shows an example of applying a CNN to an image patch centered at the red pixel which gives a single vector of predicted class scores. Illustration (b) shows the fully connected layer being converted into 1 × 1 convolutional layer, making the network fully convolutional, thus enabling a dense prediction. Illustration (c) shows network with reduced downsampling and dilated convolutions that produces outputs that are being upsampled to acquire pixelwise predictions.

However, since the weights in the subsequent layers were trained to work on a downsampled feature map, they need to be adapted to work on the feature maps of a higher spatial resolution. To this end, [5] employs dilated convolutions. In our work, we follow the second approach: we mitigate the decrease in the spatial resolution by using convolutions with strides equal to one in the last two convolutional layers responsible for downsampling in ResNet-18 and by employing dilated convolutions for subsequent convolutional layers (Sect. 2.3).

## 2.3   Dilated Convolutions

In order to account for the problem stated in the previous section, we use dilated (atrous) convolution. Dilated convolution[1] in one-dimensional case is defined as

$$y[i] = \sum_{k=1}^{K} x[i + rk]w[k]$$

---

[1] We follow the practice of previous work and use simplified definition without mirroring and centering the filter [5].

where, $x$ is an input 1D signal, $y$ output signal and $w$ is a filter of size $K$. The rate parameter $r$ corresponds to the dilation factor. The dilated convolution operator can reuse the weights from the filters that were trained on downsampled feature maps by sampling the unreduced feature maps with an appropriate rate.

In our work, since we choose not to downsample in some convolutional layers (by setting their stride to one instead of two), convolutions in all subsequent layers are dilated. This enables initialization with the parameters of the original classification network, while producing higher-resolution outputs. This transformation follows [5] and is illustrated in Fig. 2c.

### 2.4 Training

Given a sequence of images $\{\mathbf{I}_t\}_{t=0}^{n_t}$, and sequence of ground-truth segmentation annotations $\{\mathbf{A}_t\}_{t=0}^{n_t}$, we optimize normalized pixel-wise cross-entropy loss [10] using Adam optimization algorithm [8] with learning rate set to $10^{-4}$ ($n_t$ stands for the number of training examples). Other parameters of Adam optimization algorithm were set to the values suggested in [8].

## 3    Experiments and Results

We test our method on the EndoVis 2017 Robotic Instruments dataset [2]. The training dataset consists of 8 high resolution (1280 × 1024) sequences with 225 frames each that were acquired from a da Vinci Xi surgical system during several different procedures [2]. Each pixel is labeled as either tool's shaft, wrist and jaws or background. The test dataset consists of 8 75-frame sequences sampled immediately after each training sequence and 2 full 300-frame sequences.

**Table 1.** Quantitative results of our method and comparison with previous state-of-the-art in binary segmentation of robotic tools [2].

| | NCT | UB | BIT | MIT | SIAT | UCL | TUM | Delhi | UA | UW | Ours |
|---|---|---|---|---|---|---|---|---|---|---|---|
| Dataset 1 | 0.784 | 0.807 | 0.275 | 0.854 | 0.625 | 0.631 | 0.760 | 0.408 | 0.413 | 0.337 | **0.862** |
| Dataset 2 | 0.788 | 0.806 | 0.282 | 0.794 | 0.669 | 0.645 | 0.799 | 0.524 | 0.463 | 0.289 | **0.855** |
| Dataset 3 | 0.926 | 0.914 | 0.455 | **0.949** | 0.897 | 0.895 | 0.916 | 0.743 | 0.703 | 0.483 | 0.926 |
| Dataset 4 | 0.934 | 0.925 | 0.310 | **0.949** | 0.907 | 0.883 | 0.915 | 0.782 | 0.751 | 0.678 | 0.931 |
| Dataset 5 | 0.701 | 0.740 | 0.220 | 0.862 | 0.604 | 0.719 | 0.810 | 0.528 | 0.375 | 0.219 | **0.877** |
| Dataset 6 | 0.876 | 0.890 | 0.338 | **0.922** | 0.843 | 0.852 | 0.873 | 0.292 | 0.667 | 0.619 | 0.896 |
| Dataset 7 | 0.846 | **0.930** | 0.404 | 0.856 | 0.832 | 0.710 | 0.844 | 0.593 | 0.362 | 0.325 | 0.869 |
| Dataset 8 | 0.881 | 0.904 | 0.366 | 0.937 | 0.513 | 0.517 | 0.895 | 0.562 | 0.797 | 0.506 | **0.939** |
| Dataset 9 | 0.789 | 0.855 | 0.236 | 0.865 | 0.839 | 0.808 | 0.877 | 0.626 | 0.539 | 0.377 | **0.879** |
| Dataset 10 | 0.899 | **0.917** | 0.403 | 0.905 | 0.899 | 0.869 | 0.909 | 0.715 | 0.689 | 0.603 | 0.915 |
| Mean IOU | 0.843 | 0.875 | 0.326 | 0.888 | 0.803 | 0.785 | 0.873 | 0.612 | 0.591 | 0.461 | **0.896** |

Following the terms of the challenge, we excluded the corresponding training set when evaluating on one of the 75-frame sequences.

## 3.1   Results

**Table 2.** Quantitative results of our method and comparison with previous state-of-the-art in the parts based segmentation of robotic tools [2].

|          | NCT   | UB    | BIT   | MIT     | SIAT  | UCL   | TUM     | UA    | UW    | Ours      |
|----------|-------|-------|-------|---------|-------|-------|---------|-------|-------|-----------|
| Dataset 1 | 0.723 | 0.715 | 0.317 | 0.737   | 0.591 | 0.611 | 0.708   | 0.485 | 0.235 | **0.791** |
| Dataset 2 | 0.705 | 0.725 | 0.294 | **0.792** | 0.632 | 0.606 | 0.740 | 0.559 | 0.244 | 0.785   |
| Dataset 3 | 0.809 | 0.779 | 0.319 | **0.825** | 0.753 | 0.692 | 0.787 | 0.640 | 0.239 | 0.805   |
| Dataset 4 | 0.845 | 0.737 | 0.304 | 0.902   | 0.792 | 0.630 | 0.815   | 0.692 | 0.238 | **0.920** |
| Dataset 5 | 0.607 | 0.565 | 0.280 | 0.695   | 0.509 | 0.541 | 0.624   | 0.473 | 0.240 | **0.734** |
| Dataset 6 | 0.731 | 0.763 | 0.271 | 0.802   | 0.677 | 0.668 | 0.756   | 0.608 | 0.235 | **0.832** |
| Dataset 7 | 0.729 | **0.747** | 0.359 | 0.655 | 0.604 | 0.523 | 0.727 | 0.438 | 0.207 | 0.641   |
| Dataset 8 | 0.644 | 0.721 | 0.300 | 0.737   | 0.496 | 0.441 | 0.680   | 0.604 | 0.236 | **0.855** |
| Dataset 9 | 0.561 | 0.597 | 0.273 | 0.650   | 0.655 | 0.600 | **0.736** | 0.551 | 0.221 | 0.660   |
| Dataset 10 | 0.788 | 0.767 | 0.273 | 0.762  | 0.751 | 0.713 | **0.807** | 0.637 | 0.241 | 0.806   |
| Mean IOU | 0.699 | 0.700 | 0.289 | 0.737   | 0.667 | 0.623 | 0.751   | 0.578 | 0.357 | **0.764** |

We report our results for binary and instrument part segmentation in Tables 1 and 2 respectively using standard metric such as Intersection Over Union (IoU). We can see that our method outperforms previous work. Figure 1 shows some qualitative results for both the binary segmentation and the instrument part segmentation tasks.

## 4   Discussion and Conclusion

In this work, we propose a method to perform robotic tool segmentation. This is an important task, as it can be used to prevent rendered overlays from occluding the instruments or to estimate the pose of a tool [1]. We use deep network to model the mapping from the raw images to the segmentation maps. Our use of a state-of-the-art deep network (ResNet-18) with dilated convolutions helps us achieve improvement in binary tool and instrument part segmentation over the previous stat-of-the-art. Our results show the benefit of using deep residual networks for this task and also provide a solid baseline for the future work.

## References

1. Allan, M., et al.: Image based surgical instrument pose estimation with multiclass labelling and optical flow. In: Navab, N., Hornegger, J., Wells, W.M., Frangi, A.F. (eds.) MICCAI 2015. LNCS, vol. 9349, pp. 331–338. Springer, Cham (2015). https://doi.org/10.1007/978-3-319-24553-9_41

2. Allan, M., et al.: 2017 robotic instrument segmentation challenge. arXiv preprint arXiv:1902.06426 (2019)

3. Bhayani, S.B., Andriole, G.L.: Three-dimensional (3D) vision: does it improve laparoscopic skills? An assessment of a 3D head-mounted visualization system. Rev. Urol. **7**(4), 211 (2005)

4. Bouget, D., Benenson, R., Omran, M., Riffaud, L., Schiele, B., Jannin, P.: Detecting surgical tools by modelling local appearance and global shape. IEEE Trans. Med. Imaging **34**(12), 2603–2617 (2015)

5. Chen, L.-C., Papandreou, G., Kokkinos, I., Murphy, K., Yuille, A.L.: DeepLab: semantic image segmentation with deep convolutional nets, atrous convolution, and fully connected CRFs. arXiv preprint arXiv:1606.00915 (2016)

6. García-Peraza-Herrera, L.C., et al.: Real-time segmentation of non-rigid surgical tools based on deep learning and tracking. In: Peters, T., et al. (eds.) CARE 2016. LNCS, vol. 10170, pp. 84–95. Springer, Cham (2017). https://doi.org/10.1007/978-3-319-54057-3_8

7. He, K., Zhang, X., Ren, S., Sun, J.: Deep residual learning for image recognition. In: Proceedings of the IEEE Conference on Computer Vision and Pattern Recognition, pp. 770–778 (2016)

8. Kingma, D., Ba, J.: Adam: a method for stochastic optimization. arXiv preprint arXiv:1412.6980 (2014)

9. Laina, I., et al.: Concurrent segmentation and localization for tracking of surgical instruments. In: Descoteaux, M., Maier-Hein, L., Franz, A., Jannin, P., Collins, D.L., Duchesne, S. (eds.) MICCAI 2017. LNCS, vol. 10434, pp. 664–672. Springer, Cham (2017). https://doi.org/10.1007/978-3-319-66185-8_75

10. Long, J., Shelhamer, E., Darrell, T.: Fully convolutional networks for semantic segmentation. In: Proceedings of the IEEE Conference on Computer Vision and Pattern Recognition, pp. 3431–3440 (2015)

11. Okamura, A.M.: Haptic feedback in robot-assisted minimally invasive surgery. Curr. Opin. Urol. **19**(1), 102 (2009)

12. Pezzementi, Z., Voros, S., Hager, G.D.: Articulated object tracking by rendering consistent appearance parts. In: 2009 IEEE International Conference on Robotics and Automation, ICRA 2009, pp. 3940–3947. IEEE (2009)

13. Ronneberger, O., Fischer, P., Brox, T.: U-Net: convolutional networks for biomedical image segmentation. CoRR, abs/1505.04597 (2015)

14. Speidel, S., Delles, M., Gutt, C., Dillmann, R.: Tracking of instruments in minimally invasive surgery for surgical skill analysis. In: Yang, G.-Z., Jiang, T.Z., Shen, D., Gu, L., Yang, J. (eds.) MIAR 2006. LNCS, vol. 4091, pp. 148–155. Springer, Heidelberg (2006). https://doi.org/10.1007/11812715_19

15. Taylor, R.H., Menciassi, A., Fichtinger, G., Dario, P.: Medical robotics and computer-integrated surgery. In: Siciliano, B., Khatib, O. (eds.) Springer Handbook of Robotics, pp. 1199–1222. Springer, Heidelberg (2008). https://doi.org/10.1007/978-3-540-30301-5_53

16. Tonet, O., Ramesh, T.U., Megali, G., Dario, P.: Tracking endoscopic instruments without localizer: image analysis-based approach. Stud. Health Technol. Inform. **119**, 544–549 (2005)

17. Yu, F., Koltun, V.: Multi-scale context aggregation by dilated convolutions. arXiv preprint arXiv:1511.07122 (2015)

# Deep Learning Model Integrating Dilated Convolution and Deep Supervision for Brain Tumor Segmentation in Multi-parametric MRI

Tongxue Zhou[1,2], Su Ruan[1(✉)], Haigen Hu[1,4], and Stéphane Canu[3]

[1] Université de Rouen Normandie, LITIS - QuantIF, 76183 Rouen, France
`tongxue.zhou@insa-rouen.fr, su.ruan@univ-rouen.fr`
[2] INSA Rouen, LITIS - Apprentissage, 76800 Rouen, France
[3] Normandie Univ, INSA Rouen, UNIROUEN, UNIHAVRE, LITIS, Rouen, France
[4] College of Computer Science and Technology, Zhejiang University of Technology, Hangzhou 310023, China

**Abstract.** Automatic segmentation of brain tumor in magnetic resonance images (MRI) is necessary for diagnosis, monitoring and treatment. Manual segmentation is time-consuming, expensive and subjective. In this paper we present a robust automatic segmentation algorithm based on 3D U-Net. We propose a novel residual block with dilated convolution (res_dil block) and incorporate deep supervision to improve the segmentation results. We also compare the effect of different losses on the class imbalance problem. To prove the effectiveness of our method, we analyze each component proposed in the network architecture and we demonstrate that segmentation results can be improved by these components. Experiment results on the BraTS 2017 and BraTS 2018 datasets show that the proposed method can achieve good performance on brain tumor segmentation.

**Keywords:** Deep learning · Brain tumor segmentation · Residual block · Deep supervision

## 1 Introduction

Brain tumor is one of the most aggressive cancers in the world. Gliomas are the most common brain tumors that arise from glial cells. According to the malignant degree of gliomas [1], they can be categorized into two grades: low-grade gliomas (LGG) and high-grade gliomas (HGG), the former one tend to be benign, grow more slowly with lower degrees of cell infiltration and proliferation, the latter one are malignant, more aggressive and need immediate treatment.

Supported by the Normandie Regional Council via the MoNoMaD project (Grant number: 18P03397/18E01937).

Magnetic resonance imaging (MRI) is a widely used imaging technique to assess these tumors, because it offers a good soft tissue contrast without radiation. The commonly used sequences are T1-weighted, contrast enhanced T1-weighted (T1c), T2-weighted and Fluid Attenuation Inversion Recovery (FLAIR) images. Different sequences can provide complementary information to analyze different subregions of gliomas. For example, T2 and FLAIR highlight the tumor with peritumoral edema, designated "whole tumor". T1 and T1c highlight the tumor without peritumoral edema, designated "tumor core". An enhancing region of the tumor core with hyper-intensity can also be observed in T1c, designated "enhancing tumor core". Therefore applying multi-modal images can reduce the information uncertainty and improve clinical diagnosis and segmentation accuracy.

Over the years, there have been many studies on automatic brain tumor segmentation. Cui et al. [2] proposed a cascaded deep learning convolutional neural network consisting of two subnetworks. The first network is to define the tumor region from a MRI slice and the second network is used to label the defined tumor region into multiple subregions. Zhao et al. [3] integrated fully convolutional neural networks (FCNNs) [4] and Conditional Random Fields (CRFs) to segment brain tumor. Havaei et al. [5] implemented a two-pathway architecture that learns about the local details of the brain as well as the larger context feature. Wang et al. [6] proposed to decompose the multi-class segmentation problem into a sequence of three binary segmentation problems according to the subregion hierarchy. Kamnitsas et al. [7] proposed an efficient fully connected multi-scale CNN architecture named deepmedic that reassembles a high resolution and a low resolution pathway to obtain the segmentation results. Furthermore, they used a 3D fully connected conditional random field to effectively remove false positives. More specifically, U-Net [8] is the most widely used structure in medical image analysis. Such architecture has advantages, following the flexible input image sizes, consideration of spatial information and an end-to-end prediction, leading to lower computational cost and higher representation power. Isensee et al. [9] modified the U-Net to brain tumor segmentation and use data augmentation to prevent the over-fitting. Kamnitsas et al. [10] introduced EMMA, an ensemble of multiple models and architectures including DeepMedic, FCNs and U-Net, and won the first position in BraTS 2017 competition.

However, there are still some challenges on the brain tumor segmentation task. First, the brain anatomy structure varies from patients to patients, making segmentation task more difficult. Second, the tumor contour is fuzzy due to low contrast. Furthermore, the sizes of tumor and background are highly imbalanced, the background is overwhelmingly dominant, resulting in extreme class imbalance for brain tumor segmentation.

Inspired by U-Net, we propose a 3D U-Net brain segmentation network in multi-parametric MRI to address these problems. The main contributions of our method are three folds: (1) A novel 3D MRI brain tumor segmentation network is proposed, which is based on a novel residual block with dilated convolution (res_dil block) to increase the receptive field for getting more semantic information. (2) Deep supervision is employed to integrate multi-level segmentation outputs to improve the final segmentation result. (3) The class imbalance problem is addressed by comparing different loss functions in order to find the best one for our architecture.

## 2    Method

### 2.1    Dataset and Pre-processing

The datasets used in the experiments come from BraTS 2017 and 2018 training sets and validation sets. The training set includes 210 HGG patients and 75 LGG patients. The validation set includes 46 and 66 patients, respectively. Each patient has four image modalities including T1-weighted, contrast enhanced T1-weighted (T1c), T2-weighted and Fluid Attenuation Inversion Recovery (FLAIR) images. All data used in the experiments have been pre-processed with a standard procedure. The N4ITK [11] method is first used to correct the distortion of MRI data and intensity normalization is applied to normalize each modality of each patient. To exploit the spatial contextual information of the image, we used the 3D image and clip and resize the image from $155 \times 240 \times 240$ to $128 \times 128 \times 128$.

### 2.2    Network Architecture

Our network is inspired by the U-Net architecture [8]. Multi-modal images are directly integrated in the original input space channel by channel, which can maximumly reserve the original image information and learn the intrinsic image feature representation. In the encoder and decoder part, res_dil blocks are proposed to increase the receptive field, each block consists of two dilated convolutions with dropout in the middle to alleviate the over-fitting. In order to maintain the spatial information, we use a convolution with stride equals 2 in encoder part to replace pooling operation. Inspired by [8], deep supervision is proposed in the decoder part to integrate different level segmentations to improve the final result. The network architecture is shown in Fig. 1.

The proposed Res_dil block uses dilated convolution that defines the spacing between the values in a kernel [12], which can increase the receptive field. For example, a $3 \times 3$ kernel with a dilation rate of 2 will have the same field of view as a $5 \times 5$ kernel, it can generate different features in this case, as illustrated in Fig. 2. It's likely to require different receptive field when segmenting different regions in an image. For example, large regions may need a large receptive field at the expense of fine details, while small regions may require high resolution local information. Since standard U-Net can't get enough semantic features due to the limited receptive field, inspired by dilated convolution, we use residual block with dilated convolutions (rate = 1, 2, 4) on both encoder part and decoder part to obtain features at multiple scales, shown in Fig. 3. The res_dil block can obtain more extensive local information to help retain information and fill details during training process.

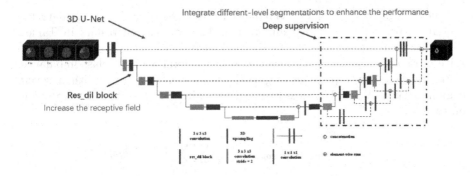

**Fig. 1.** Network architecture.

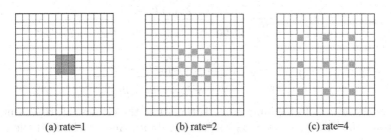

(a) rate=1                    (b) rate=2                    (c) rate=4

**Fig. 2.** Dilated convolution

## 2.3   Solutions for Class Imbalance

Due to the physiological characteristics of brain tumours, the segmentation task has an inherent class imbalance problem. Table 1 illustrates the distribution of the classes in the training data of BraTS 2017. The background is overwhelmingly dominant. So, the choice of the loss functions is crucial to deal with the imbalance problem. We present three different loss functions as follows. The Dice scores for different loss functions on the BraTS 2017 dataset are shown in Table 2.

Category cross entropy loss evaluates individually the class predictions for each pixel and then averages all pixels. Focal tversky loss weights false positives

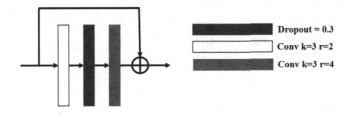

**Fig. 3.** Residual dilated block

and false negatives for highly imbalanced data. Dice loss is to calculate the overlap of prediction and real annotation. The comparison results in Table 2 show that focal tversky loss is may be good for binary classification problems to solve intra-class imbalance. However, it is less helpful for inter-class imbalance. Categorical cross-entropy requires special attention on the dataset with an severe class imbalance. While Dice loss can deal well with the class imbalance problem on the dataset.

$$L_{category\_cross\_entropy} = -\frac{1}{N} \sum_{i=1}^{C} \sum_{j=1}^{N} w_c g_{ic} log p_{ic} \tag{1}$$

$$L_{focal\_tversky} = \sum_{i=1}^{C} (1 - \frac{\sum_{j=1}^{N} p_{ic} g_{ic} + \epsilon}{\sum_{j=1}^{N} p_{ic} g_{ic} + \alpha \sum_{j=1}^{N} p_{i\bar{c}} g_{ic} + \sum_{j=1}^{N} p_{ic} g_{i\bar{c}} + \epsilon})^{1/\gamma} \tag{2}$$

$$L_{dice} = 1 - 2 \frac{\sum_{i=1}^{C} \sum_{j=1}^{N} p_{ic} g_{ic} + \epsilon}{\sum_{i=1}^{C} \sum_{j=1}^{N} p_{ic} + g_{ic} + \epsilon} \tag{3}$$

where $N$ is the set of all examples, $C$ is the set of the classes, $w_c$ represents the weight assigned to the class c, $p_{ic}$ is the probability that pixel $i$ is of the tumor class $c$ and $p_{i\bar{c}}$ is the probability that pixel $i$ is of the non-tumor class $\bar{c}$. The same is true for $g_{ic}$ and $g_{i\bar{c}}$, and $\epsilon$ is a small constant to avoid dividing by 0.

**Table 1.** The distribution of classes on BraTS 2017 training set, NET: Non enhancing tumor, NCR: Necrotic.

| Region | Background | NET/NCR | Edema | Enhancing tumor |
|--------|-----------|---------|-------|-----------------|
| Percentage | 99.12 | 0.28 | 0.40 | 0.20 |

**Table 2.** Comparison with different loss functions on BraTS 2017 training set.

| Loss | Whole tumor | Tumor core | Enhanced tumor |
|------|-------------|------------|----------------|
| Dice | 88.5 | 84.5 | 73.4 |
| Focal tversky loss | 87.9 | 81.1 | 70.0 |
| Categorical cross entropy loss | 42.1 | 51.4 | 44.3 |

# 3    Experiments and Results

## 3.1    Implementation Details

Our network is implemented in Keras with a single Nvidia GPU Quadro P5000 (16G). We trained the network for 200 epochs using both the HGG and LGG datasets simultaneously. We randomly sampled patches of size $128 \times 128 \times 128$ voxels with a batch size of 1. The models are optimized using the Adam optimizer (initial learning rate $= 5e-4$) with a decreasing learning rate factor 0.5 with patience of 10 epochs for 50 epochs.

## 3.2    Experiments Results

Following the challenge, four intra-tumor structures have been grouped into three mutually inclusive tumor regions: (a) whole tumor (WT) that consists of all tumor tissues, (b) tumor core (TC) that consists of the enhancing tumor, necrotic and non-enhancing tumor core, and (c) enhancing tumor (ET). The results are evaluated based on the online evaluation platforms, including dice score, sensitivity, specificity and Hausdorff distance.

**Quantitative Analysis.** We randomly split 20% (57) of the training sets (285) in BRATS 2017 as local validation set. Table 3 shows the contributions of each components in the network on local validation set. We refer to our basic U-Net without res_dil block and deep supervision as base. We can see an increase of dice score, sensitivity and Hausdorff across all tumor regions when we added the proposed strategies gradually. More precisely, we achieve Dice scores of 88.5, 84.5, 73.4 for whole, core and enhancing tumor, respectively. Table 4 shows the results on Brats 2017 and Brats 2018 validation sets. To further verify the effectiveness of the proposed method, we compare the performance of our method with original U-Net and a state-of-the-art U-Net-like network [9] on BraTS 2017 dataset in Table 5. We get the best result of sensitivity and Hausdorff on whole tumor. For tumor core, we achieve the best performance on all evaluation metrics. For enhancing tumor, we obtain the best result of dice and specificity. In general, the proposed method achieves better segmentation result on Dice score than others.

**Table 3.** Results of different strategies on BraTS 2017 training set.

| Strategies | Dice | | | Sensitivity | | | Specificity | | | Hausdorff | | |
|---|---|---|---|---|---|---|---|---|---|---|---|---|
| | WT | TC | ET | WT | TC | ET | WT | TC | ET | WT | TC | ET |
| base | 86.6 | 76.8 | 64.1 | 85.4 | 75.1 | 67.4 | **99.5** | **99.7** | **99.8** | 8.39 | 8.84 | 8.14 |
| base+super | 87.9 | 81.2 | 66.7 | 87.4 | 80.4 | 72.5 | 99.4 | **99.7** | **99.8** | 7.54 | 7.59 | 7.67 |
| base+res_dil | 88.2 | 81.9 | 69.5 | 87.8 | 81.8 | 74.0 | 99.4 | 99.3 | 99.7 | 7.52 | 6.90 | **6.26** |
| base+super+res_dil | **88.5** | **84.5** | **73.4** | **91.7** | **83.1** | **74.3** | 99.1 | **99.7** | 99.7 | **5.81** | **6.47** | 6.81 |

**Table 4.** Results on BraTS 2017 and BraTS 2018. Val: validation set

| Dataset | Dice | | | Sensitivity | | | Specificity | | | Hausdorff | | |
|---|---|---|---|---|---|---|---|---|---|---|---|---|
| | WT | TC | ET | WT | TC | ET | WT | TC | ET | WT | TC | ET |
| BraTS 2017 Val | 86.5 | 75.4 | 65.9 | 86.2 | 75.9 | 68.0 | 99.5 | 99.7 | 99.8 | 9.84 | 6.35 | 9.70 |
| BraTS 2018 Val | 87.3 | 77.9 | 70.5 | 88.5 | 79.1 | 72.6 | 99.4 | 99.7 | 99.8 | 8.06 | 8.81 | 5.60 |

**Table 5.** Quantitative comparison results of different methods on BraTS 2017 dataset

| Methods | Dice | | | Sensitivity | | | Specificity | | | Hausdorff | | |
|---|---|---|---|---|---|---|---|---|---|---|---|---|
| | WT | TC | ET | WT | TC | ET | WT | TC | ET | WT | TC | ET |
| U-Net | 79.1 | 49.9 | 8.0 | 84.6 | 45.9 | 7.3 | 97.6 | 99.4 | 99.7 | 18.8 | 21.1 | 38.0 |
| Isenn et al. [9] | **89.5** | 82.8 | 70.7 | 89.0 | 83.1 | **80.0** | **99.5** | **99.7** | **99.8** | 6.04 | 6.95 | **6.24** |
| Ours | 88.5 | **84.6** | **73.4** | **91.7** | **83.2** | 74.3 | 99.1 | **99.7** | **99.8** | **5.81** | **6.47** | 6.81 |

**Qualitative Analysis.** We randomly select one sample on BraTS 2017 dataset and visualize the segmentation result in Fig. 4. From the results, we can see the orginal U-Net can't segment the enhancing tumor at all and predict many false regions on tumor core and edema. The method in [9] predicts many false positive, especially on necrotic and edema regions and we can see many false edema regions are segmented from the coronal view. However, our method is capable of segmenting large tumor region (necrotic and edema) as well as the difficult region (enhancing tumor). The results show that the proposed method achieves almost the same results as the real annotation. To verify the effectiveness of the proposed method, the relative quantity evaluation results are shown in Table 6. In accordance with the qualitative result, each sample obtains a high dice score on the three brain tumor regions.

**Table 6.** Qualitative results of the segmentation sample

| Sample | Dice | | | Sensitivity | | | Specificity | | | Hausdorff | | |
|---|---|---|---|---|---|---|---|---|---|---|---|---|
| | WT | TC | ET | WT | TC | ET | WT | TC | ET | WT | TC | ET |
| Brats 2017_TCIA_201_1 | 97.1 | 92.9 | 85.2 | 97.5 | 90.1 | 84.6 | 99.6 | 99.8 | 99.6 | 1.41 | 3 | 2.24 |

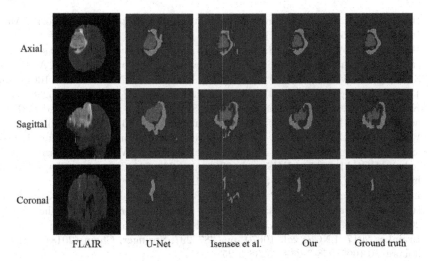

**Fig. 4.** Qualitative comparison of different methods on patient Brats 2017_TCIA_201_1. Edema is shown in green, enhancing tumor in red and necrotic in blue. (Color figure online)

## 4  Conclusion

In this paper, we propose a 3D U-Net brain tumor segmentation in multi-parametric MRI images, where a novel residual block with dilated convolution and a deep supervision are proposed to improve the segmentation result. We compared the results achieved by our method with others. The experimental results on BraTS 2017 and 2018 datasets clearly verify the effectiveness of our method on brain tumor segmentation. In this work, multi-parametric MRI images are simply cascaded to the architecture. In the future, we will focus on how to fuse them effectively to obtain better segmentation.

## References

1. Menze, B.H., et al.: The multimodal brain tumor image segmentation benchmark (BRATS). IEEE Trans. Med. Imaging **34**(10), 1993–2024 (2014)
2. Cui, S., Mao, L., Jiang, J., Liu, C., Xiong, S.: Automatic semantic segmentation of brain gliomas from MRI images using a deep cascaded neural network. J. Healthc. Eng. **2018**, 14 p. (2018). Article no. 4940593. https://doi.org/10.1155/2018/4940593
3. Zhao, X., Yihong, W., Song, G., Li, Z., Zhang, Y., Fan, Y.: A deep learning model integrating FCNNs and CRFs for brain tumor segmentation. Med. Image Anal. **43**, 98–111 (2018)
4. Long, J., Shelhamer, E., Darrell, T.: Fully convolutional networks for semantic segmentation. In: Proceedings of the IEEE Conference on Computer Vision and Pattern Recognition, pp. 3431–3440 (2015)

5. Havaei, M., et al.: Brain tumor segmentation with deep neural networks. Med. Image Anal. **35**, 18–31 (2017)

6. Wang, G., Li, W., Ourselin, S., Vercauteren, T.: Automatic brain tumor segmentation using cascaded anisotropic convolutional neural networks. In: Crimi, A., Bakas, S., Kuijf, H., Menze, B., Reyes, M. (eds.) BrainLes 2017. LNCS, vol. 10670, pp. 178–190. Springer, Cham (2018). https://doi.org/10.1007/978-3-319-75238-9_16

7. Kamnitsas, K., et al.: Efficient multi-scale 3D CNN with fully connected CRF for accurate brain lesion segmentation. Med. Image Anal. **36**, 61–78 (2017)

8. Ronneberger, O., Fischer, P., Brox, T.: U-Net: convolutional networks for biomedical image segmentation. In: Navab, N., Hornegger, J., Wells, W.M., Frangi, A.F. (eds.) MICCAI 2015. LNCS, vol. 9351, pp. 234–241. Springer, Cham (2015). https://doi.org/10.1007/978-3-319-24574-4_28

9. Isensee, F., Kickingereder, P., Wick, W., Bendszus, M., Maier-Hein, K.H.: Brain tumor segmentation and radiomics survival prediction: contribution to the BRATS 2017 challenge. In: Crimi, A., Bakas, S., Kuijf, H., Menze, B., Reyes, M. (eds.) BrainLes 2017. LNCS, vol. 10670, pp. 287–297. Springer, Cham (2018). https://doi.org/10.1007/978-3-319-75238-9_25

10. Kamnitsas, K., et al.: Ensembles of multiple models and architectures for robust brain tumour segmentation. In: Crimi, A., Bakas, S., Kuijf, H., Menze, B., Reyes, M. (eds.) BrainLes 2017. LNCS, vol. 10670, pp. 450–462. Springer, Cham (2018). https://doi.org/10.1007/978-3-319-75238-9_38

11. Avants, B.B., Tustison, N., Song, G.: Advanced normalization tools (ANTS). Insight J. **2**, 1–35 (2009)

12. Yu, F., Koltun, V.: Multi-scale context aggregation by dilated convolutions. arXiv preprint arXiv:1511.07122 (2015)

# A Joint 3D UNet-Graph Neural Network-Based Method for Airway Segmentation from Chest CTs

Antonio Garcia-Uceda Juarez[1,2]($\boxtimes$), Raghavendra Selvan[3], Zaigham Saghir[4], and Marleen de Bruijne[1,3]

[1] Biomedical Imaging Group Rotterdam,
Department of Radiology and Nuclear Medicine, Erasmus MC,
3015 CE Rotterdam, The Netherlands
a.garciauceda@erasmusmc.nl

[2] Department of Pediatric Pulmonology, Erasmus MC-Sophia Children Hospital,
3015 CE Rotterdam, The Netherlands

[3] Department of Computer Science, University of Copenhagen,
2100 Copenhagen, Denmark

[4] Department of Medicine, Section of Pulmonary Medicine, Herlev-Gentofte Hospital,
Copenhagen University Hospital, Kildegårdsvej 28, 2900 Hellerup, Denmark

**Abstract.** We present an end-to-end deep learning segmentation method by combining a 3D UNet architecture with a graph neural network (GNN) model. In this approach, the convolutional layers at the deepest level of the UNet are replaced by a GNN-based module with a series of graph convolutions. The dense feature maps at this level are transformed into a graph input to the GNN module. The incorporation of graph convolutions in the UNet provides nodes in the graph with information that is based on node connectivity, in addition to the local features learnt through the downsampled paths. This information can help improve segmentation decisions. By stacking several graph convolution layers, the nodes can access higher order neighbourhood information without substantial increase in computational expense. We propose two types of node connectivity in the graph adjacency: (i) one predefined and based on a regular node neighbourhood, and (ii) one dynamically computed during training and using the nearest neighbour nodes in the feature space. We have applied this method to the task of segmenting the airway tree from chest CT scans. Experiments have been performed on 32 CTs from the Danish Lung Cancer Screening Trial dataset. We evaluate the performance of the UNet-GNN models with two types of graph adjacency and compare it with the baseline UNet.

**Keywords:** Convolutional neural networks · Graph neural network · Graph convolution · Airway segmentation

© Springer Nature Switzerland AG 2019
H.-I. Suk et al. (Eds.): MLMI 2019, LNCS 11861, pp. 583–591, 2019.
https://doi.org/10.1007/978-3-030-32692-0_67

# 1   Introduction

Since recently, fully convolutional neural networks (CNNs) are the state-of-the-art for many segmentation tasks [1], and in particular the UNet architecture [2] for biomedical image segmentation. The UNet consists of an encoding path, in which high-order features are extracted at several downsampled resolutions, followed by a decoding path, in which these features are leveraged to the full resolution to perform voxel-wise segmentation decisions. An extension of CNNs to graph structured data are Graph neural networks (GNNs) [3,4], which have seen early application for segmenting structures that resemble graphs [8,9]. Initial work of combining CNNs and GNNs was by proposed Shin et al. [9] for 2D vessel segmentation. This was a sequential pipeline in which the CNN was trained for feature extraction prior to applying the GNNs to learn global connectivity.

The segmentation of tree-like structures such as the airways in chest CTs is a complex task, with branches of varying sizes and different orientations while taking into account bifurcations. A comparison of airway extraction methods (prior to CNNs) was performed in the EXACT challenge [5]. The results showed that all methods missed a significant amount of the small, peripheral branches. The UNet has since been applied for airway segmentation in [6,7]. The 3D UNet-based method in [7] is fully automatic and can segment the airways in a full lung in a single pass through the network. However, this method had problems to capture various small terminal branches. Also, the GNNs have been applied to airway extraction as a graph refinement approach in [8]. However, this method was not end-to-end optimised and relied on handcrafted features as input to the graph.

In this paper, we present an end-to-end segmentation approach by combining a 3D UNet with GNNs and evaluate this on extracting the airway tree from chest CTs. This method replaces the two convolutional layers in the deepest level of the baseline UNet by a GNN-based module, comprising graph convolutions. This end-to-end approach simultaneously learns local image features and global information based on graph neighbourhood connectivity.

# 2   Methods

The proposed joint UNet-GNN architecture is described in the following subsections. This approach integrates a GNN module at the deepest level of a baseline 3D UNet, and is schematically shown in Fig. 1 (left). The GNN module uses a graph structure obtained from the dense feature maps resulting from the contracting path of the Unet. Each graph node can be viewed as a "supervoxel" from the downsampled regions with the corresponding vector of features. The connectivity of nodes in such a graph is described by the adjacency matrix and determines the neighbourhood of each node when performing graph convolutions, as shown in Fig. 1 (right). The GNN module learns combinations of the input feature maps based on the graph topology, and outputs another graph with same "supervoxel" nodes as the input graph and the corresponding vector of learnt features for each node. This output are feature maps that are fed to the upsampling path of the UNet.

We have tested two types of node connectivity that are: (i) Predefined and based on a regular neighbourhood, with each node connected to its 26-direct neighbours, and (ii) Dynamically computed during training based on choosing nearest neighbours in the node feature space. Stacking several GNN layers allows nodes to access longer range information beyond the initial neighbourhood, which can improve the segmentation decisions as more complex features that include relevant information from nodes far away in the volume can be used. This is in contrast with CNNs which rely on local feature extraction, and access long range information via successive convolutions and pooling, with a detriment of strong reduction in resolution. This long range access by the GNN module is useful when segmenting tree structures like airways, as information from branches that share some features (shape, orientation, ...) but are further away in the volume can be used when detecting a given branch. The computation of the dynamic graph adjacency is further explained in Sect. 2.2.

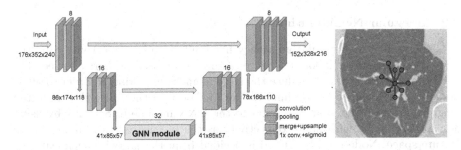

**Fig. 1.** Left: schematics of a UNet-GNN network of 3 levels. Right: illustration of irregular node connectivity for a given voxel in the initial graph.

### 2.1 Graph Neural Network (GNN) Module

The main component of the GNN module is a series of graph convolutional layers [3,4]. This operation can be seen as a generalisation of the cartesian convolution to a graph setting. One of the formulations of graph convolution operation with separate processing of self connections proposed in Kipf et al. [4] is given by the equation,

$$H^{(l+1)} = \sigma\left(H^{(l)}W_0^{(l)} + D^{-1}AH^{(l)}W_1^{(l)}\right) \qquad (1)$$

where $\sigma(\cdot)$ is the rectified linear unit activation function, $H^{(l)} \in \mathbb{R}^{N \times E}$ is the node feature matrix comprising $N$ nodes and $E$ features input to the $l^{\text{th}}$ GNN layer. The learnable GNN filter weights are $W_0^{(l)}, W_1^{(l)} \in \mathbb{R}^{E \times E}$. $A \in \{0,1\}^{N \times N}$ is the binary adjacency matrix, $D$ is the degree matrix derived from $A$ with diagonal entries $D_{ii} = \sum_{j=1}^{N} A_{ij}, \forall i = 1 \ldots N$. The adjacency matrix is largely sparse, with non-zero entries per node corresponding to the size of each node neighbourhood (26 for the regular neighbourhood case above). By processing the adjacency matrix as a sparse tensor, operations in Eq. (1) are done efficiently.

The GNN module in the proposed method has $L = 4$ layers performing the operations in Eq. (1) successively. By stacking several graph convolutions together, each node in the output graph updates its features with information from higher order neighbourhood, which can improve the segmentation decisions. The initial graph features $\mathbf{H}^{(0)}$ are obtained as,

$$\mathbf{H}^{(0)} = f(\mathbf{Z}) \tag{2}$$

where $\mathbf{Z} \in \mathbb{R}^{N \times F}$ is the F-dimensional node feature matrix derived from the UNet and $f(\cdot)$ is a two layered multi-layer perceptron with $F$ input units and $E$ output units and rectified linear units, followed by a normalization layer. The transformation in Eq. (2) allows more complex representations of the input node features useful for the GNN module.

### 2.2   Irregular Neighbourhood

A GNN module with regular adjacency has limited node connectivity comprising only the direct neighbours. This constraint is imposed primarily to keep the adjacency matrix sparse to reduce the large memory footprint. In order to allow nodes in the graph to access information well beyond their directly connected neighbours, we propose an extension to the GNN module in Sect. 2.1 by using a graph adjacency with node connectivity as the $k$ – nearest neighbours in the feature space. Node neighbourhood is decided from the pairwise euclidean distance between nodes from $\mathbf{Z}$ in the $F$ – dimensional feature space. In this work, we set the number of neighbours to $k = 26$. The graph adjacency is dynamically computed during training for every input image in every epoch. This approach, we argue, enables the method to access irregular but meaningful neighbourhoods and utilises the inherent capabilities of using GNN-based learning over irregular neighbourhoods in an improved fashion.

## 3   Experiments

### 3.1   Dataset

We used 32 low-dose CT chest scans from the Danish Lung Cancer Screening Trial [13]. All scans have voxel-resolution of roughly $0.78 \times 0.78 \times 1 \,\mathrm{mm}^3$. The reference segmentations are airway lumen obtained from the method [10] applied on the union of two previous methods [11,12], and corrected by an expert observer.

## 3.2    Network Implementation

The baseline UNet upon which the UNet-GNN approach is built derives from the model in [7] with 3 levels of resolution. Each level in the downsampling/upsampling path is composed of two $3 \times 3 \times 3$ convolutional layers with rectified linear (ReLU) activation, and followed by a $2 \times 2 \times 2$ pooling/upsample layer, respectively. No padding is used in the convolutions in order to reduce the model memory footprint. There are 8 feature maps in the first level, and this is doubled/halved after every pooling/upsampling, respectively. The GNN module in the deepest level has twice as many output features per voxel as input units, i.e. $E = 2F$ in Eqs. (1) and (2). The final layer consists of a $1 \times 1 \times 1$ convolutional layer followed by a sigmoid activation function.

A series of operations to extract the input images from the volume CTs as in [7] are applied. These consist of: (i) crop the CTs to a bounding-box around pre-segmented lung fields, (ii) extract smaller input images in a sliding-window fashion in axial dimension, and (iii) apply image rigid transformation for data augmentation. The model is designed for the largest input images that can fit in GPU memory. This corresponds to a size $176 \times 352 \times 240$ in a batch containing only one image, for a GPU NVIDIA GeForce GTX 1080 Ti with 11 GB memory used in these experiments. The models were implemented in Pytorch framework.

## 3.3    Training the Models

The loss function used for training the network is the dice loss,

$$\mathcal{L} = \frac{2 \sum_{x \in N_L} p(x) g(x)}{\sum_{x \in N_L} p(x) + \sum_{x \in N_L} g(x) + \epsilon} \tag{3}$$

where $p(x), g(x)$ are the predicted voxel-wise airway probability maps and airway ground truth, respectively. The ground truth is masked to the region of interest (ROI): the lungs, indicated by the sub-index $L$, so that only voxels within this region contribute to the loss. This mask removes the trachea and main bronchi from the ground truth, so that training is focused on the smaller branches. The lung segmentation needed for this masking operation is easily computed by a region-growing method in [11]. $\epsilon$ is a tolerance needed when there are no ground truth voxels in the image patch.

To train the networks we use 16 CTs, 4 CTs for model validation/hyperparameter tuning, and the remaining 12 CTs for testing. The Adam optimizer is used with a learning rate that is chosen for each model as large as possible while ensuring convergence of the losses. This was $10^{-4}$ for UNet-GNN models and $5 \times 10^{-5}$ for UNet models. All models are trained until convergence, and we retrieve the model with overall minimum validation loss for testing. As convergence criterion, we monitor the moving average of the validation loss over 50 epochs, and training is stopped when its value (i) increases by more than 5%, or (ii) does not decrease more than 0.1%, over 20 epochs (patience). Training time was approximately 1–2 days, depending on the models, while test time inference takes a few seconds per scan.

## 3.4   Experiments Set-Up

We evaluate four different models: two regular UNets with 3 resolution levels (UNetLev3) and 5 levels (UNetLev5), and two UNet-GNN models each with 3 levels. The UNet-GNN models differ in the type of graph neighbourhood: (i) regular graph adjacency with 26 direct neighbours (UGnnReg), and (ii) dynamic computation of the adjacency matrix (UGnnDyn), with 26 connections per node as described in Sect. 2.2. With our experiments we evaluate: (i) the benefit of the GNN module at deepest level of the UNet when compared to the two convolutional layers of a regular UNet, and (ii) the difference in performance of UNet-GNN models when compared to a more complex model like the UNetLev5.

The models are compared based on (i) Dice overlap coefficient, (ii) airway completeness, (iii) volume leakage, and two centreline distance error measures, (iv) false negative $d_{FN}$ and (v) false positive $d_{FP}$ distances, as in [8]. Completeness is the ratio of ground truth centreline length inside the predictions with respect to ground truth centreline full length, and volume leakage is the ratio of number of false positive voxels with respect to the number of voxels in the ground truth. We refer the reader to [8] for the definition of $d_{FN}$ and $d_{FP}$. Trachea and main bronchi are removed in these measures from both predictions and ground truth.

We compute the ROC curves for all the models using the mean airway completeness and volume leakage measured on the test set, and varying the threshold in the output probability maps used to obtain the final binary segmentations. Further, we compute the operating point with a fixed level of volume leakage (13%) by estimating the correct threshold (with a minimum error $10^{-4}$). This threshold is, for the different models: UNetLev3 (0.1), UNetLev5 (0.04), UGnnReg (0.66), UGnnDyn (0.33). We use the resulting airway segmentations to evaluate the performance measures on the test set. To compare the models, we use the two-sided T-test on two related distributions.

The calculation of the dynamic graph adjacency as described in Sect. 2.2 is computationally expensive, both in memory and run time. In order to fit the model in GPU and reduce the computational cost, the searching space of candidate nodes to compute the node connectivity is constrained to a cube area of at most 5 voxels away from the given node. This limits the range for direct node connections, however long range information is still accessed via the four stacked graph convolutions as described in Sect. 2.1.

## 4   Results and Discussion

The ROC curves for the different models are shown in Fig. 2. The proposed UNet-GNN models and the baseline UNetLev3 show very similar results. In the detailed view, the UGnnReg shows a small improvement, i.e. higher airway completeness for a given volume leakage, over the baseline UNetLev3. Further, the UnetLev5 shows lower completeness than the other models for volume leakage higher than 11%, while the contrary occurs for lower leakage levels.

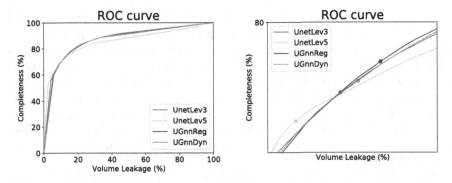

**Fig. 2.** ROC curves for all the models, varying the threshold in the probability maps. Right: detailed view, including the operating points with threshold 0.5.

Performance of the different models on the test set, for an operating point in the ROC curve with 13% volume leakage, is shown in Fig. 3. In dice overlap coefficient, airway completeness and volume leakage, there is no significant difference between the models ($p > 0.1$). Nevertheless, in centreline distance measures, the proposed UNet-GNN models show significantly lower $d_{FN}$ and higher $d_{FP}$ with respect to the baseline UNetLev3: in $d_{FN}$, comparing UGnnDyn ($p = 0.001$) and UGnnReg ($p < 0.01$) with UNetLev3, and in $d_{FP}$, comparing both UNet-GNN models with UNetLev3 ($p < 0.001$). Further, the UNetLev5 shows no significant difference in $d_{FP}$ and $d_{FN}$ with the other models ($p > 0.1$).

The small and significant improvement in distance false negative error $d_{FN}$, with an on par dice overlap and airway completeness, indicates that the proposed UNet-GNN models can segment slightly more complete airway trees,

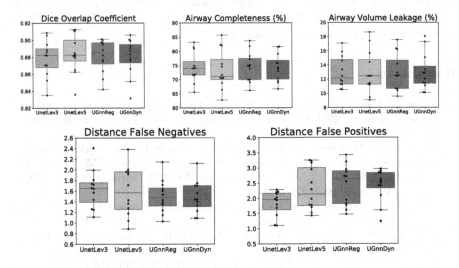

**Fig. 3.** Test set performance measures for the different models.

when compared to the two UNet models, with more and/or longer peripheral branches. This is because the centreline distance measure $d_{FN}$ is not dependent on the scale of airways and provides a uniform measure of accuracy in detecting branches. In contrast, the completeness measure is a binary evaluation of branches with respect to the reference and small improvements in centreline detection may not be reflected in the overall score. On the contrary, the more complex model UNetLev5 does not show any difference in any measure over the baseline UNetLev3. Further, the UNet-GNN models have fewer trainable parameters ($\approx 50k$) than the UNetLev3 ($\approx 90k$) and much less than the UNetLev5 ($\approx 1.4M$).

One aspect that might limit the performance of the proposed UNet-GNN models is that the GNN module is operating only on the deepest level of the UNet, where the image patches have undergone three downsampling operations. A more powerful UNet-GNN model can be formulated by replacing all skip connections in the baseline UNet with GNN modules, each operating at that image resolution level. However, this model has not been experimented with due to the large memory footprint required, which exceeded the available GPU resources at our disposal.

## 5   Conclusions

We presented a joint UNet-GNN based segmentation method with an application to extract airways from chest CTs. By introducing a GNN module with graph convolutions at the deepest level of the UNet the proposed method is able to learn and combine information from a larger region of the image. The proposed UNet-GNN models show a small and significant improvement in the false negative centreline measure over the baseline UNet, with on par dice overlap and airway completeness, for a fixed volume leakage. This indicates that the proposed UNet-GNN models can segment slightly more complete airway trees. Further, this is achieved with fewer trainable parameters.

## References

1. Long, J., Shelhamer, E., Darrell, T.: Fully convolutional networks for semantic segmentation. In: IEEE Conference on Computer Vision and Pattern Recognition (CVPR) (2015)
2. Ronneberger, O., Fischer, P., Brox, T.: U-Net: convolutional networks for biomedical image segmentation. In: Navab, N., Hornegger, J., Wells, W.M., Frangi, A.F. (eds.) MICCAI 2015. LNCS, vol. 9351, pp. 234–241. Springer, Cham (2015). https://doi.org/10.1007/978-3-319-24574-4_28
3. Scarselli, F., Gori, M., Tsoi, A.C., Hagenbuchner, M., Monfardini, G.: The graph neural network model. IEEE Trans. Neural Netw. **20**(1), 61–80 (2009)
4. Kipf, T.N., Welling, M.: Semi-supervised classification with graph convolutional networks. In: International Conference on Learning Representations (2017)
5. Lo, P., et al.: Extraction of airways from CT (EXACT'09). IEEE Trans. Med. Imaging **31**(11), 2093–2107 (2012)

6. Meng, Q., Roth, H.R., Kitasaka, T., Oda, M., Ueno, J., Mori, K.: Tracking and segmentation of the airways in chest CT using a fully convolutional network. In: Descoteaux, M., Maier-Hein, L., Franz, A., Jannin, P., Collins, D.L., Duchesne, S. (eds.) MICCAI 2017. LNCS, vol. 10434, pp. 198–207. Springer, Cham (2017). https://doi.org/10.1007/978-3-319-66185-8_23

7. Juarez, A.G.-U., Tiddens, H.A.W.M., de Bruijne, M.: Automatic airway segmentation in chest CT using convolutional neural networks. In: Stoyanov, D., et al. (eds.) RAMBO/BIA/TIA -2018. LNCS, vol. 11040, pp. 238–250. Springer, Cham (2018). https://doi.org/10.1007/978-3-030-00946-5_24

8. Selvan, R., et al.: Extraction of airways using graph neural networks. In: 1st Conference on Medical Imaging with Deep Learning, Amsterdam (2018)

9. Shin, S.Y., Lee, S., Yon, I.D., Lee, K.M.: Deep vessel segmentation by learning graphical connectivity. ArXiv preprint arXiv:1806.02279 (2018)

10. Petersen, J., et al.: Optimal surface segmentation using flow lines to quantify airway abnormalities in chronic obstructive pulmonary disease. Med. Image Anal. **18**, 531–541 (2014)

11. Lo, P., Sporring, J., Ashraf, H., Pedersen, J.H., de Bruijne, M.: Vessel-guided airway tree segmentation: a voxel classification approach. Med. Image Anal. **14**(4), 527–538 (2010)

12. Lo, P., Sporring, J., Pedersen, J.J.H., de Bruijne, M.: Airway tree extraction with locally optimal paths. In: Yang, G.-Z., Hawkes, D., Rueckert, D., Noble, A., Taylor, C. (eds.) MICCAI 2009. LNCS, vol. 5762, pp. 51–58. Springer, Heidelberg (2009). https://doi.org/10.1007/978-3-642-04271-3_7

13. Pedersen, J., Jesper, H., et al.: The Danish randomized lung cancer CT screening trial overall design and results of the prevalence round. J. Thorac. Oncol. **4**(5), 608–614 (2009)

# Automatic Fetal Brain Extraction Using Multi-stage U-Net with Deep Supervision

Jingjiao Lou[1], Dengwang Li[1($\boxtimes$)], Toan Duc Bui[2], Fenqiang Zhao[2],
Liang Sun[2], Gang Li[2($\boxtimes$)], and Dinggang Shen[2($\boxtimes$)]

[1] Shandong Normal University, Jinan 250358, Shandong, China
dengwang@sdnu.edu.cn
[2] The University of North Carolina at Chapel Hill, Chapel Hill, NC 27599, USA
{gang_li,dgshen}@med.unc.edu

**Abstract.** Fetal brain extraction is one of the most essential steps for prenatal brain MRI reconstruction and analysis. However, due to the fetal movement within the womb, it is a challenging task to extract fetal brains from sparsely-acquired imaging stacks typically with motion artifacts. To address this problem, we propose an automatic brain extraction method for fetal magnetic resonance imaging (MRI) using multi-stage 2D U-Net with deep supervision (DS U-net). Specifically, we initially employ a coarse segmentation derived from DS U-net to define a 3D bounding box for localizing the position of the brain. The DS U-net is trained with deep supervision loss to acquire more powerful discrimination capability. Then, another DS U-net focuses on the extracted region to produce finer segmentation. The final segmentation results are obtained by performing refined segmentation. We validate the proposed method on 80 stacks of training images and 43 testing stacks. The experimental results demonstrate the precision and robustness of our method with the average Dice coefficient of 91.69%, outperforming the existing methods.

**Keywords:** Fetal MRI · Brain extraction · Convolutional neural network

## 1 Introduction

Fetal magnetic resonance imaging (MRI) is instrumental to enhance fetal anatomical evaluation and acquire the conditions of the brain non-invasively. It is thus highly needed to monitor and investigate the development of the fetal brain in the perinatal period. Brain extraction plays an important role for fetal brain MRI reconstruction [1, 2] and analysis [3]. However, in practice, fetal brain extraction is obtained manually, which is extremely time consuming and tedious. Additionally, manual delineation is prone to intra- and inter-observer variability and presents obstacle in large-scale studies. Therefore, it is of great importance to develop an accurate algorithm for automatic extraction/segmentation of the fetal brain in MRI.

As MRI scanning usually takes a long time and is susceptible to motion, both maternal breathing and unpredictable fetal movement can lead to motion artifacts during image acquisition [4]. To mitigate the effects of motion, fetal MRI is typically performed through snapshot imaging methods to acquire two dimensional (2D) slices,

© Springer Nature Switzerland AG 2019
H.-I. Suk et al. (Eds.): MLMI 2019, LNCS 11861, pp. 592–600, 2019.
https://doi.org/10.1007/978-3-030-32692-0_68

such as Single Shot Fast Spin Echo (SSFSE) [5] and Echo-Planar Imaging (EPI) [6]. Typically, a stack of a subject consists of several fast 2D slices acquired one after each other. Stacks of slices acquired in this way are generally artifact free, but may be inconsistent across slices. As a result, extraction of the fetal brain from sparsely acquired stacks typically with motion is a challenging task, often leading to inaccurate results.

Different methodologies have been proposed for automatic fetal brain extraction/segmentation, such as parametric [7], classification [8], and atlas fusion-based techniques [9]. Since brain extraction is a segmentation task, we also use brain segmentation to refer brain extraction in the paper. With successful applications in image processing and analysis, learning-based methods using convolutional neural networks for fetal brain extraction have been proposed increasingly in recent years. Rajchl et al. [10] performed brain extraction using a 3D convolutional neural network (CNN) and conditional random field (CRF). Salehi et al. [11] proposed to use a fully convolutional neural network based on U-Net [12] and directly applied it to the whole input image for fetal brain extraction. Ebner et al. [13] adopted a two-stage method for brain extraction. They firstly localized the fetal brain based on a coarse segmentation by P-Net [14, 15]. Then, they obtained fine segmentation results by the P-Net trained with a multi-scale loss function.

In this paper, we propose an automatic fetal brain extraction method using multi-stage 2D U-Net with deep supervision [16] (DS U-net). Specifically, we initially employ a coarse segmentation produced slice-by-slice from DS U-net to define a 3D bounding box for localizing the position of the brain. The DS U-net is trained with deep supervision loss to acquire more powerful discrimination capability. Afterwards, another DS U-net focuses on the extracted region to perform fine segmentation. Final prediction results are obtained by performing refined segmentation. We validate the proposed approach on 80 stacks of training images and 43 testing stacks. The experimental results demonstrate that the precision and robustness of our method outperforms the existing methods in terms of Dice coefficient.

## 2   Methods

### 2.1   2D U-Net with Deep Supervision

The U-Net is an effective network for various biomedical image segmentation tasks. Generally, it consists of a contracting path and a symmetric expanding path, which enables to capture both rich contextual information and accurate localization information. However, after several layers of down-sampling, the dimensions of the feature maps reduce gradually and become smaller than that of the ground-truth masks. This subsequently makes the error back-propagation ineffective, slows down the convergence rate, and reduces the discrimination capability of the model. Overall, it poses a great challenge to optimization with the presence of vanishing gradient. To alleviate this, we propose an automatic fetal brain extraction method using a 2D U-Net with deep supervision. The loss function from the last layer is defined as:

$$\mathcal{L}(\mathbf{Y}, \mathbf{P}) = \sum_{I_i} -\log p(y_{ij}|x_{ij}) \tag{1}$$

Where $I_i$ represents the $i\text{-}th$ stack, $x_{ij}$ represents the $j$-th voxel of sample $X_i$, $y_{ij}$ represents the target class label corresponding to voxel $x_{ij}$, $p(y_{ij}|x_{ij})$ denotes the probability prediction of $x_{ij}$ after the activation function of softmax.

In order to build a deeply supervised network, we introduce deep supervision to the U-Net architecture from 3 prediction layers. Specifically, the loss function of $d$-th prediction layer is defined as:

$$\mathcal{L}_d(\mathbf{Y}, \mathbf{P}_d) = \sum_{I_i} -\log p_d(y_{ij}|x_{ij}) \tag{2}$$

Finally, the employed loss function of the network is defined and minimized as follows:

$$\mathcal{L} = \mathcal{L}(\mathbf{Y}, \hat{\mathbf{Y}}) + \alpha \mathcal{L}_6(\mathbf{Y}, \mathbf{P}_6) + \beta \mathcal{L}_7(\mathbf{Y}, \mathbf{P}_7) + \gamma \mathcal{L}_8(\mathbf{Y}, \mathbf{P}_8) \tag{3}$$

The balance weights of $\alpha$, $\beta$, and $\gamma$ for deep supervision were initially set as 0.2, 0.3, and 0.4, respectively, and decayed by 10% every 100 epochs. Figure 1 shows the architecture of our 2D U-Net with deep supervision. In this paper, we refer to this network as DS U-Net.

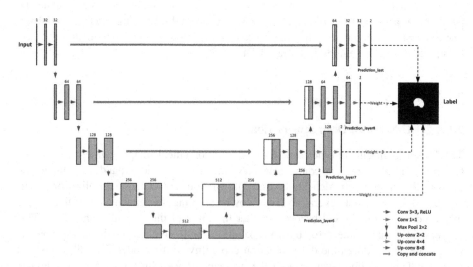

**Fig. 1.** The architecture of the proposed U-Net with deep supervision.

## 2.2    Localization Based on Coarse Segmentation

Since the fetal brain only occupies a small proportion of pixels in fetal MRI slice, sparse and unbalanced data will make the training ineffective. To overcome this, the whole stacks were cropped from $256 \times 256$ to $128 \times 128$ after fetal brain was localized in the first stage. Let $I$ denote an original stack of slices and $I'$ represent the cropped stack after extraction. We utilize the segmentation result of DS U-Net to automatically define a 3D bounding box to cover and localize the position of the fetal brain. Smaller patches of $I'$, which contains a balanced number of positive and negative voxels, are extracted from the whole input of $I$. Figure 2 shows our proposed framework of fetal brain extraction.

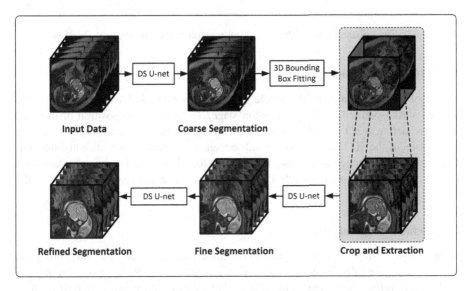

**Fig. 2.** The proposed framework of fetal brain extraction.

In this step, neighborhood information from adjacent slices are selectively used to learn and improve the inference accuracy. Adjacent slices would be selected as additional channels if their similarity, which depends on calculation of Pearson Correlation Coefficient, is greater than a threshold. Let $I_i$ denote the $i\text{-}th$ 2D slice, $I_{i-1}$ represent the $(i\text{-}1)\text{-}th$ slice, and $I_{i+1}$ represent the $(i\text{+}1)\text{-}th$ slice. In our experiment, we used the average value of Pearson Correlation Coefficient of training datasets as the threshold. If the correlation of adjacent slices is below the threshold, the current slice (slice $i$) takes place of adjacent slices (slices $i\pm 1$) to make data tensor has the same channels. Figure 3 shows the utilization of neighborhood information from two adjacent slices.

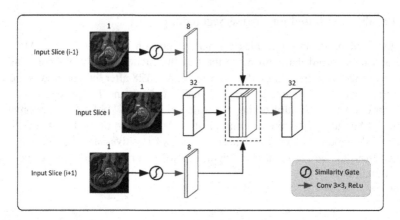

**Fig. 3.** The utilization of neighborhood information in the first layer of DS U-Net.

## 2.3  Fine Segmentation

Instead of direct training on the whole stack of I, another DS U-Net works on the cropped stack acquired in the localization stage. To localize the position of the fetal brain, we define a 3D bounding box based on the coarse segmentation results. The center point of the 3D bounding box is subsequently mapped to each slice and taken as the center point to generate a square region of $128 \times 128$. Finally, the extracted stack of $I'$ is taken as the input of DS U-net to reduce false positives and improve the prediction accuracy.

## 2.4  Refined Segmentation

Rather than using the conventional methodologies, such as morphological closing/opening or fully connected conditional random field (CRF), we consistently use DS U-Net to refine the segmentation results. For every cropped and extracted stack, it generates $128 \times 128$ labels and corresponding intensity images, which only contain pixel values in local patches. As shown in Fig. 4, based on the results of fine segmentation, 2D bounding boxes are defined to fit to the candidate region of the fetal brain in each slice. Local image patches with different size are subsequently generated by expanding a margin of 5 pixels based on the 2D bounding boxes. It is worth noting that, unlike patch-wise training strategy, this method can greatly reduce the computational complexity during training, focus on learning the features of fetal brain, and obtain refined results.

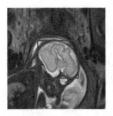
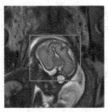
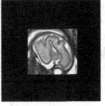

| (a) 2D Bounding Box Fitting | (b) Expended Bounding Box | (c) Image with Local Patch | (d) Final Prediction Result |

**Fig. 4.** Refinement based on fine segmentation. (a) is the fine segmentation result. The green rectangle box represents the 2D bounding box fitting to the segmentation mask. The cross in red represents the mapped center point of the 3D bounding box; (b) is the intensity image with bounding box expanded by margins of 5 pixels; (c) is an image which contains a local patch; (d) is the final prediction result. (Color figure online)

## 3 Experiments and Results

### 3.1 Data and Implement Details

The proposed framework of automatic fetal brain segmentation was trained on 80 stacks and tested on 43 stacks. Ground truth of each case was produced by manual annotation, which was checked and re-edited by two seasoned radiologists. Each subject was acquired through fast 2D snapshot imaging to minimize the effects of motion, with image size of $256 \times 256$ pixels and slice thickness of 3.5 mm. All of the training and testing images were normalized by using mean and standard deviation of training images' intensities. To use the neighborhood information of adjacent slices, we computed the average correlation coefficient of whole datasets and set it as the threshold value of the similarity gate. Specifically, if the correlation coefficient between the input image ($i$-$th$ slice) and adjacent slice (($i\pm1$)-$th$ slice) was greater than the threshold, feature maps of the next slice would be selected as additional channels and concatenated to the primary channels which is generated by the input slice. In order to limit the undue influence of neighbor information, the number of additional channels was set as 8, while the number of primary channels was set as 32. Data augmentation was performed in the stage of fine segmentation and refined segmentation to improve the prediction accuracy.

### 3.2 Localization Results

Table 1 summarizes the localization results of fetal brains based on different methods. It can be seen that Ebner et al. [13] gets a localization result with Intersection over Union (IoU) score of 85.93% and centroid distance of 1.96 mm. While the metric of centroid distance is inferior to P-Net (L), our DS U-Net achieves a better result with IoU of 91.31%. The neighborhood information contributes to a higher localization result, with 5.38% Dice increase. To reduce the inference time and get a fitted 3D bounding box, Ebner et al. [13] first down-sampled the whole stack to the size of $96 \times 96$, and smoothed the coarse segmentation results by performing morphological closing and opening. In contrast, our DS U-Net reduces time in this stage by nearly 27% percent without any pre- and post-processing.

**Table 1.** Quantitative evaluation of fetal brain localization.

| Methods | IoU (%) | Centroid distance (mm) | Stack-level runtime (s) |
|---|---|---|---|
| Ebner et al. [13] | 85.93 ± 0.15 | **1.96** ±1.45 | 1.45 ± 0.55 |
| DS U-Net | **91.31 ± 0.08** | 2.90 ± 3.53 | **1.06 ± 0.44** |

### 3.3   Segmentation Results

Table 2 shows the quantitative evaluation results of fetal brain segmentation using different methods. All reference methods were re-trained on the same data as our proposed one. Trained on our own datasets, the proposed DS U-Net approach outperforms Salehi et al. [11] with an increase of 2.54% in Dice score. After fine segmentation, the prediction results obtained by DS U-Net (Stage 2) achieves a Dice score of 89.07%, with an increase of 1.43% compared to Ebner et al. [13]. Moreover, our final prediction accuracy achieves 91.68% by DS U-Net (Stage 3). Figure 5 shows the extracted brain masks by different methods overlaid on the original fetal brain MR images. We trained the models from scratch. All experiments were performed on a NVIDIA TITAN Xp GPU.

**Table 2.** Quantitative evaluation of different methods for fetal brain segmentations.

| Methods | Dice metric (%) | Hausdorff (mm) | Stack-level runtime (s) |
|---|---|---|---|
| Salehi et al. [11] | 82.42 ± 0.30 | 27.58 ± 16.09 | **0.58 ± 0.39** |
| Ebner et al. [13] | 87.64 ± 0.27 | 14.32 ± 8.73 | 2.48 ± 0.72 |
| DS U-Net | 84.96 ± 0.27 | 19.36 ±10.89 | 1.06 ± 0.44 |
| DS U-Net (Stage 2) | 89.07 ± 0.25 | 14.61 ± 7.14 | 1.73 ± 0.62 |
| DS U-Net (Stage 3) | **91.68 ± 0.22** | **9.78 ± 3.85** | 2.19 ± 0.81 |

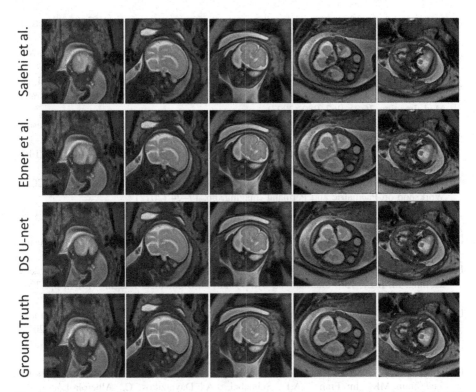

**Fig. 5.** Extracted brain masks of different methods overlaid on the original fetal brain MR images.

## 4  Conclusion

In this work, we propose an automatic brain segmentation method for fetal MRI using 2D U-Net with deep supervision. The network trained with deep supervision loss has more powerful discrimination capability. Moreover, we proposed a three-stage approach to first localize the brain, and then segment the brain, and finally further refine the segmented brain, thus achieving high accuracy. Experimental results demonstrate that the precision and robustness of our method outperforms the existing methods. Our future work will focus on further improving the performance of the framework, increasing the number of annotated data, and applying the method to fetal brain reconstruction.

## References

1. Makropoulos, A., et al.: Automatic whole brain MRI segmentation of the developing neonatal brain. IEEE Trans. Med. Imaging **33**(9), 1818–1831 (2014)
2. Gholipour, A., et al.: Robust super-resolution volume reconstruction from slice acquisitions: application to fetal brain MRI. IEEE Trans. Med. Imaging **29**(10), 1739–1758 (2010)

3. Makropoulos, A., et al.: A review on automatic fetal and neonatal brain MRI segmentation. Neuroimage **170**, 231–248 (2018)
4. Malamateniou, C., et al.: Motion-compensation techniques in neonatal and fetal MR imaging. Am. J. Neuroradiol. **34**(6), 1124–1136 (2013)
5. Jiang, S., et al.: MRI of moving subjects using multislice snapshot images with volume reconstruction (SVR): application to fetal, neonatal, and adult brain studies. IEEE Trans. Med. Imaging **26**(7), 967–980 (2007)
6. Chen, Q., et al.: Fast fetal magnetic resonance imaging techniques. Top. Magn. Reson. Imaging **12**(1), 67–79 (2001)
7. Anquez, J., et al.: Automatic segmentation of head structures on fetal MRI. In: IEEE International Symposium on Biomedical Imaging (ISBI), pp. 109–112. IEEE (2009)
8. Ison M et al.: Fully automated brain extraction and orientation in raw fetal MRI. In: MICCAI Workshop on Paediatric and Perinatal Imaging, pp. 17–24 (2012)
9. Wright, R., et al.: Automatic quantification of normal cortical folding patterns from fetal brain MRI. Neuroimage **91**, 21–32 (2014)
10. Rajchl, M., et al.: Deepcut: Object segmentation from bounding box annotations using convolutional neural networks. IEEE Trans. Med. Imaging **36**(2), 674–683 (2017)
11. Salehi, S.S.M., et al.: Real-time automatic fetal brain extraction in fetal MRI by deep learning. In: IEEE 15th International Symposium on Biomedical Imaging (ISBI), pp. 720–724. IEEE (2018)
12. Ronneberger, O., Fischer, P., Brox, T.: U-Net: convolutional networks for biomedical image segmentation. In: Navab, N., Hornegger, J., Wells, W.M., Frangi, A.F. (eds.) MICCAI 2015. LNCS, vol. 9351, pp. 234–241. Springer, Cham (2015). https://doi.org/10.1007/978-3-319-24574-4_28
13. Ebner, M., et al.: An automated localization, segmentation and reconstruction framework for fetal brain MRI. In: Frangi, A.F., Schnabel, J.A., Davatzikos, C., Alberola-López, C., Fichtinger, G. (eds.) MICCAI 2018. LNCS, vol. 11070, pp. 313–320. Springer, Cham (2018). https://doi.org/10.1007/978-3-030-00928-1_36
14. Wang, G., et al.: Interactive medical image segmentation using deep learning with image-specific fine tuning. IEEE Trans. Med. Imaging **37**(7), 1562–1573 (2018)
15. Wang, G., et al.: DeepIGeoS: a deep interactive geodesic framework for medical image segmentation. IEEE Trans. Pattern Anal. Mach. Intell. (2018)
16. Dou, Q., Chen, H., Jin, Y., Yu, L., Qin, J., Heng, P.-A.: 3D deeply supervised network for automatic liver segmentation from CT volumes. In: Ourselin, S., Joskowicz, L., Sabuncu, M. R., Unal, G., Wells, W. (eds.) MICCAI 2016. LNCS, vol. 9901, pp. 149–157. Springer, Cham (2016). https://doi.org/10.1007/978-3-319-46723-8_18

# Cross-Modal Attention-Guided Convolutional Network for Multi-modal Cardiac Segmentation

Ziqi Zhou[1], Xinna Guo[1], Wanqi Yang[1(✉)], Yinghuan Shi[2(✉)], Luping Zhou[3], Lei Wang[4], and Ming Yang[1]

[1] School of Computer Science, Nanjing Normal University, Nanjing, China
yangwq@njnu.edu.cn
[2] State Key Laboratory for Novel Software Technology, Nanjing University, Nanjing, China
syh@nju.edu.cn
[3] School of Electrical and Information Engineering, University of Sydney, Sydney, Australia
[4] School of Computing and Information Technology, University of Wollongong, Wollongong, Australia

**Abstract.** To leverage the correlated information between modalities to benefit the cross-modal segmentation, we propose a novel cross-modal attention-guided convolutional network for multi-modal cardiac segmentation. In particular, we first employed the cycle-consistency generative adversarial networks to complete the bidirectional image generation (*i.e.*, MR to CT, CT to MR) to help reduce the modal-level inconsistency. Then, with the generated and original MR and CT images, a novel convolutional network is proposed where (1) two encoders learn individual features separately and (2) a common decoder learns shareable features between modalities for a final consistent segmentation. Also, we propose a cross-modal attention module between the encoders and decoder in order to leverage the correlated information between modalities. Our model can be trained in an end-to-end manner. With extensive evaluation on the unpaired CT and MR cardiac images, our method outperforms the baselines in terms of the segmentation performance.

**Keywords:** Multi-modal cardiac segmentation · Cross-modal image synthesis · Cross-modal attention

This work is supported from the National Natural Science Foundation of China (Nos. 61603193, 61673203, 61876087), the Natural Science Foundation of Jiangsu Province (No. BK20171479), Jiangsu Postdoctoral Science Foundation (No. 1701157B), and CCF-Tencent Open Research Fund (RAGR20180114). Wanqi Yang and Yinghuan Shi are co-corresponding authors. Ziqi Zhou and Xinna Guo are co-first authors.

H.-I. Suk et al. (Eds.): MLMI 2019, LNCS 11861, pp. 601–610, 2019.
https://doi.org/10.1007/978-3-030-32692-0_69

# 1  Introduction

According to the report from American Heart Association (AHA) 2019 Heart Disease and Stroke Statistics [1], in the United States in 2019, coronary events are expected to occur in about 1,055,000 individuals, including 720,000 new and 335,000 recurrent coronary events. In this meaning, the early diagnosis and treatment play a significant role in decreasing the mortality and morbidity of the cardiovascular diseases. During the early diagnosis, the physicians usually collect the imaging information from different modalities (*e.g.*, MR, CT) for a full investigation, in which an important prerequisite is accurately segmenting the substructures of the heart from multiple imaging modalities. However, traditional segmentation by manual delineation is very laborious and time-consuming. Therefore, developing automatic methods for whole heart segmentation (WHS) is desperately required.

Although deep convolutional neural networks (CNNs) based methods [2–4] have been widely used for segmenting other organs, their segmentation results on multi-modal WHS are still limited – (1) **inter-patient divergence**: there exists a large appearance divergence between different patients, (2) **inter-modality divergence**: the images between two modalities show very different appearance, *i.e.*, color, contrast, and (3) **complex structure**: different cardiac substructures are interlinked and sometimes overlapped. Also, considering these multi-modal data in real tasks are usually unpaired, the previous methods can hardly capture the correlated information between modalities for segmentation.

To address the above issue, we propose in this paper a novel cross-modal attention-guided convolutional network to guide a robust multi-modal cardiac segmentation. Specifically, our method involves two stages which can be trained in an end-to-end manner:

- In the first stage, a cycle-consistency generative adversarial network (Cycle-GAN) [5] is adopted to generate the fake MR (or CT) images from original CT (or MR) images for a bidirectional image generation. This can ease the issue of limited training samples and also pair the images to help reduce the modal-level inconsistency.
- In the second stage, a novel convolutional network is proposed for segmentation. To simultaneously preserve the specific information and seek a common representation, two separate encoders are firstly used to learn individual features separately, and a common decoder is then employed to learn modal-shareable features for a final consistent segmentation. Moreover, a cross-modal attention is proposed to capture the correlated information between modalities for better segmentation.

The major contribution of our work can be concluded as: (1) employing the CycleGAN for cross-modal image generation to pair the training dataset and reduce the modal-level inconsistency, (2) developing a novel cross-modal attention-guided convolutional network to capture the correlated information between modalities.

**Related Work.** Recently, there have been a few attempts about multi-modal WHS. For example, Dou et al. [6] proposed an unsupervised domain adaptation framework with adversarial learning for cross-modality biomedical image segmentation. Zhang et al. [7] proposed a method that simultaneously learn to translate and segment medical 3D images, which can learn from unpaired data and keep anatomy consistency. However, Zhang et al.'s method suffered from the failure in exploiting the shareable information between modalities because they use two independent segmentors for both modalities during training. In medical image segmentation, there are many deep CNN-based methods proposed to segment other organs, e.g., U-net, V-net, DeepLab. Inspired by the insight to build "fully convolutional" networks (FCN) [8], Ronneberger et al. [2] proposed a architecture called "U-net", which consists of a contracting path to capture context and a symmetric expanding path that enables precise localization. However, these methods cannot effectively overcome the aforementioned limitations.

The novelty and success of the origin GAN [9] has caused the proposal of many variations of GAN. In image-to-image translation, most of the models were developed for specific tasks (e.g., super-resolution, style transfer) [10], until a universal purpose solution, pix2pix, was proposed by Isola et al. [11] with the requirement of abundant paired training examples. However, paired dataset is rarely available and costs intensive labor. To overcome this shortcoming, Cycle-GAN was proposed [5] to transferring unpaired images from source domain to target domain, which have been successfully applied to many applications.

In computer vision, attention mechanism has been used widely in various tasks. For medical image processing, the attention heat map in [12] integrated global branch with local branch for better disease classification, while the attention gate in [3,4] learned to focus on the salient region in Pancreas or other organs. However, they only applied attention mechanism in a single modality. For cross-modal applications, a modality-dependent attention mechanism [13] was proposed to fuse multi-modal information for video description. Also, Ye et al. [14] proposed a cross-modal self-attention module that captures the long-range dependencies between linguistic and visual features. For more similar works that are not the intersection of computer vision and natural language processing, Hong et al. [15] designed a decoupled encoder-decoder architecture with an attention module in order to make segmentation knowledge transferable across categories. However, their objective was to employ segmentation annotations available for different categories to compensate for missing supervision in weakly-annotated images, which is significantly different from our purpose.

## 2   Proposed Method

The section introduces our proposed method. We begin by introducing the overall architecture, and then discuss the formulation of our loss function and the details of our cross-modal attention-guided convolutional network.

The architecture of our method is composed by 2D fully convolutional layers with instance normalization and ReLU for generators or LeakyReLU for discriminators, which were commonly used in GANs to prevent gradient disappearance.

The goal is to pair the training dataset and capture the correlated information between modalities for accurate segmentation. To achieve this, the procedure is further divided into two steps as shown in Fig. 1: (1) synthesizing images between modalities, (2) building attention-guided convolutional segmentation network.

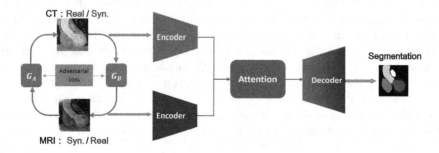

**Fig. 1.** Overview of our proposed method. The original images in both modalities CT and MR pass through their generators $G_A$ and $G_B$ to synthesize corresponding images in the other modality. Original CT (or MR) image and the synthesized images in MR (or CT) generated from it then pass through their own encoder part of a segmentation network, which consists of several downsampling layers. Afterwards, the feature maps outputted from both encoders pass through the attention module together before passing through the shared decoder to get the final segmentation result.

### 2.1    Cross-Modal Image Synthesis

To segment the unpaired images between modalities, we first employ the Cycle-GAN to simultaneously generate the MR-like images from CT and CT-like images from MR, because of the success of CycleGAN on image-to-image translation. Let $A$ and $B$ represent two different modalities (*i.e.*, CT and MR). $x_A$ is a sample from modality $A$, following the distribution $P_A$, and $x_B$ is a sample from modality $B$ with the distribution $P_B$. The two generators $G_A, G_B$ and two discriminators $D_A, D_B$ are jointly learned in an adversarial way. The adversarial loss in modality $A$ can be defined as:

$$\mathcal{L}_{GAN}(G_A, D_A) = \mathbb{E}_{x_A \sim P_A(x_A)}[\log D_A(x_A)] + \mathbb{E}_{x_B \sim P_B(x_B)}[\log(1 - D_A(G_A(x_B)))], \tag{1}$$

where $G_A$ aims to learn a mapping that renders the generated images from $B$ look similar in the images from $A$, while $D_A$ tries to discriminate between the origin images $x_A$ and the synthesis images $G_A(x_B)$. The adversarial loss $\mathcal{L}_{GAN}(G_B, D_B)$ in modality $B$ is similar to the formulation above, so we won't go to details here.

To solve the task of learning generators with unpaired images from two modalities $A$ and $B$, *cycle-consistency loss* is used to guarantee that the generated images is able to return back to the exact data in the original modality.

That is to say, the reconstruction of the synthesized images $G_A(G_B(x_A))$ and $G_B(G_A(x_B))$ are encouraged to be identical to their input $x_A$ and $x_B$ respectively. The *cycle-consistency loss* can be written as:

$$\mathcal{L}_{cyc}(G_A, G_B) = \mathbb{E}_{x_A \sim P_A(x_A)}[\|G_A(G_B(x_A)) - x_A\|_1] \\ + \mathbb{E}_{x_B \sim P_B(x_B)}[\|G_B(G_A(x_B)) - x_B\|_1], \tag{2}$$

where the $L_1$ norm is employed to calculate the reconstruction error over all voxels, showing better visual results than using the $L_2$ norm.

## 2.2 Attention-Guided Multi-modal Cardiac Segmentation

After the image synthesis, we design a convolutional segmentation network, which is shown in the right part of Fig. 1. The network consists of: (1) two separate encoders to learn individual features, (2) an attention module to capture the correlated information between modalities, and (3) a common decoder to learn shareable features between modalities for a final consistent segmentation.

Since both modalities are used to describe the same cardiac organ, we assume that these two modalities may contain several correlated features, which will be useful for cardiac segmentation. Thus, we design a channel-wise attention module between the encoders and the decoder to capture the correlated information between modalities. The attention module takes two individual feature maps with local boundary information of each substructure of the cardiac image as input and outputs a new feature map with the correlated information between modalities into the decoder. The structure of the proposed attention module is shown in Fig. 2. The correlated information will be reflected in the $C_1 \times C_2$ and $C_2 \times C_1$ area of the attention map, while some modal-specific features will be reflected in the $C_1 \times C_1$ and $C_2 \times C_2$ area.

For the encoders and decoder, we apply the encoder-decoder structure of U-net [2]. Specifically, the encoders are implemented by the contracting path of the U-net to learn high-level modality features, while the decoder is implemented by the symmetric expanding path to propagate context information to higher layers and learn the detailed features of segmentation boundaries. On this basis, we employ the cross-entropy loss to design the segmentation loss between segmentation results and ground truth, which can be written as:

$$\mathcal{L}_{seg}(S, G_A, G_B) = \mathbb{E}_{x_A \sim P_A}[L_{ce}(S(G_B(x_A)), y_A)] \\ + \mathbb{E}_{x_B \sim P_B}[L_{ce}(S(G_A(x_B)), y_B)], \tag{3}$$

where $L_{ce}$ refers to the cross-entropy loss. $S$ denotes the segmentation network we design. The segmentation loss can also be used to address this geometrical distortion problem of synthetic images [7].

Given the definitions of the adversarial losses, cycle-consistency loss and segmentation loss above in the two subsections, our full objective can be summarized as:

$$\mathcal{L}(G_A, G_B, D_A, D_B, S) = \mathcal{L}_{GAN}(G_A, D_A) + \mathcal{L}_{GAN}(G_B, D_B) \\ + \lambda \mathcal{L}_{cyc}(G_A, G_B) + \gamma \mathcal{L}_{seg}(S, G_A, G_B), \tag{4}$$

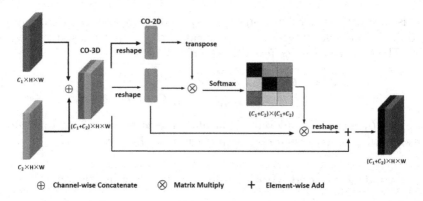

**Fig. 2.** Illustration of our proposed **Channel-Wise Attention Module**. First, two feature maps (3D) from the separate encoders are concatenated into a new feature map with the size of $(C_1 + C_2) \times H \times W$, which is denoted as "CO-3D". Secondly, the "CO-3D" is reshaped into the 2D map with the size of $(C_1 + C_2) \times HW$ called as "CO-2D". Thirdly, "CO-2D" is multiplied with transposed "CO-2D", followed by a softmax function. Thus, we get the channel-wise attention map with the size of $(C_1 + C_2) \times (C_1 + C_2)$. Fourthly, the attention map is multiplied with "CO-2D" and then reshaped into the size of $(C_1 + C_2) \times H \times W$. Finally, the result is element-wisely added by the "CO-3D", and we obtain the final output of our attention module.

where $\lambda$ and $\gamma$ are the coefficients.

**Implementation Details**. For generator, we adopted the U-net architecture [2] without skip connection. For discriminator, we adopted the encoder of U-net and two fully connection layers. We used Adam solver [16] with a learning rate of $2 \times 10^{-4}$ for GAN and $1 \times 10^{-3}$ for segmentation network and closely follow the settings in CycleGAN to train generators with discriminators. Every 2000 iterations, parameters in $G_A, G_B, D_A, D_B$ decayed by 90%, while parameters in $S$ decayed by 10%. $\lambda$ equals to 10 and $\gamma$ equals to 1 in the experiments. In order to accelerate experimenting, we chose to pre-train the $G_A, G_B, D_A, D_B$ separately first for 10000 iterations and then train the whole network jointly for 10000 iterations.

## 3    Experiments

**Dataset and Evaluation Metrics.** We validated our purposed methods on the public dataset of *MICCAI 2017 Multi-Modality Whole Heart Segmentation* (MMWHS) [17], which consists of unpaired 20 MR and 20 CT images derived from 40 patients. The MR and CT data were acquired in different clinical centers. The cardiac structures of the images were manually annotated by radiologists for both MR and CT images. Our segmentors aimed to automatically segment seven cardiac structures including the left ventricle blood cavity (LVC), the right ventricle blood cavity (RVC), the left atrium blood cavity (LAC), the right atrium blood cavity (RAC), the myocardium of the left ventricle (MYO), the ascending aorta (AA) and the pulmonary artery (PA). We randomly split the dataset into training (10 objects) and testing (10 objects), which were fixed throughout all experiments. We applied two-fold cross-validation and repeated the experiment 5 times on each methods to achieve its average precision and standard deviation. We denote CT as modality A data and MR as modality B data.

Because there are some differences in the direction in which the data were acquired, we first adjusted the original dataset in order to unify them at the position of coronal with the assist of a software called *ITK-SNAP*[1]. All labeled parts in the 3D samples were then cropped out and sliced into 2D samples, which turned out into 2534 slices in CT and 2208 in MR. These 2D slices were then resized into the size of 128 × 128. For evaluation metrics, we use DICE (%) as the criterion, which is used for measuring the overlap rate of two segmentation results. A higher DICE indicates a better segment performance.

**Table 1.** Quantitative comparison in percent (%) of segmentation performance on cardiac substructures in CT and MR images between different methods. The highest DICE in each substructure are in bold.

| Modality | Method | FCN [8] | Unet [2] | Zhang [7] | No Atte | Ours |
|---|---|---|---|---|---|---|
| CT images | **AA** | 88.86 ± 0.85 | 92.15 ± 0.81 | 93.82 ± 0.52 | **94.14 ± 0.30** | 94.04 ± 0.26 |
| | **LAC** | 81.98 ± 1.16 | 86.27 ± 2.51 | 84.38 ± 1.26 | 82.86 ± 1.47 | **90.15 ± 0.53** |
| | **LVC** | 88.48 ± 0.81 | 88.28 ± 0.44 | 87.50 ± 0.44 | 86.69 ± 0.96 | **89.97 ± 0.57** |
| | **MYO** | **86.49 ± 0.27** | 84.95 ± 0.62 | 83.93 ± 0.48 | 83.88 ± 0.33 | 85.63 ± 0.30 |
| | **RVC** | 80.73 ± 1.06 | 81.71 ± 0.70 | 82.63 ± 0.46 | 82.48 ± 0.90 | **85.38 ± 0.43** |
| | **RAC** | 80.54 ± 0.84 | 81.18 ± 1.00 | 82.47 ± 0.73 | 82.75 ± 0.62 | **83.57 ± 0.59** |
| | **PA** | 79.12 ± 1.14 | 81.44 ± 1.85 | 81.37 ± 1.23 | 81.27 ± 2.09 | **85.15 ± 0.58** |
| | **AVG** | 83.74 ± 0.65 | 85.14 ± 0.71 | 85.16 ± 0.51 | 84.87 ± 0.63 | **87.70 ± 0.30** |
| MR images | **AA** | 67.41 ± 1.73 | 79.11 ± 0.28 | 79.55 ± 1.01 | 80.43 ± 0.94 | **80.70 ± 1.07** |
| | **LAC** | 72.08 ± 2.28 | 76.51 ± 2.29 | 75.74 ± 1.41 | 75.98 ± 1.61 | **80.44 ± 1.61** |
| | **LVC** | 81.38 ± 0.46 | 85.44 ± 0.58 | 83.08 ± 0.45 | 82.95 ± 0.62 | **88.21 ± 0.73** |
| | **MYO** | 72.55 ± 0.51 | 76.08 ± 1.06 | 75.24 ± 0.62 | 75.23 ± 0.44 | **77.49 ± 0.58** |
| | **RVC** | 72.33 ± 1.16 | 73.13 ± 1.32 | 72.73 ± 0.85 | 72.94 ± 1.22 | **79.45 ± 1.17** |
| | **RAC** | 74.13 ± 1.01 | 78.76 ± 0.85 | 81.03 ± 0.98 | 80.41 ± 0.73 | **81.06 ± 1.66** |
| | **PA** | 65.23 ± 0.96 | 73.50 ± 1.38 | 73.13 ± 0.70 | 72.85 ± 1.40 | **74.60 ± 1.00** |
| | **AVG** | 72.16 ± 0.64 | 77.50 ± 1.01 | 77.21 ± 0.66 | 77.26 ± 0.85 | **80.28 ± 0.86** |

**Results.** To evaluate the performance of our method, we compare it with three related methods and the variant of our method. Specifically, we first evaluate the performance of FCN [8], which is a simple fully convolutional network without expansion in training dataset and exploitation in multiple modalities. U-net [2] is then evaluated on the same dataset separately on each modality. To further validate the effectiveness of our methods, we compare the Zhang *et al.* 's method

---

[1] http://www.itksnap.org/pmwiki/pmwiki.php.

**Table 2.** Statistical comparison of our method with different methods in DICE.

| p-value | FCN [8] | Unet [2] | Zhang [7] | No Atte |
|---|---|---|---|---|
| **Ours_CT** | 0.0007 | 0.0005 | 0.0011 | 0.0003 |
| **Ours_MR** | 0.0002 | 0.0032 | 0.0026 | 0.0064 |

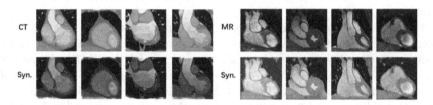

**Fig. 3.** Typical synthesized results of our method. The left two rows are the original CT images and the corresponding synthesis images in MR, and the right two rows are the original MR images and their synthesis CT images, respectively.

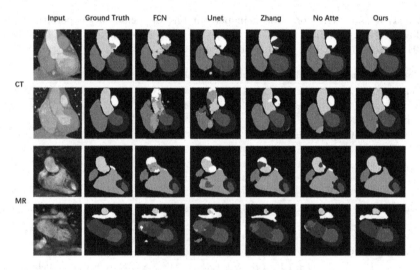

**Fig. 4.** Visualization of segmentation results of different methods on CT (above) and MR (below) images.

[7] on our dataset. For ablation study on attention, we removed the attention module in our method and combine the encoders and decoder directly. This method was called "No Attention", abbreviated as "No Atte".

The quantitative results of these above methods to segment CT and MR images are listed in Table 1. The comparison experiment shows the manifest improvement of segmentation performance on both CT and MR images, which indicates that the proposed method effectively applies our attention module to mine the correlated information between modalities.

In order to demonstrate that our method significantly outperformed rest of the methods, t-test is performed on the 5 independent results of each methods at the 5% significant level. Table 2 shows the $p$-value when our method is compared to each of other methods. If $p$-value is less than 0.05, the compared two methods are considered to be significantly different.

For visualization results, Fig. 3 shows several typical synthesis results from CT or MR. Figure 4 shows some segmentation results of different methods. As can be observed obviously, the synthesized images are similar to real images without manifest geometric distortion, and the segmentation errors of the baselines are largely corrected by our method.

## 4   Conclusion

This paper purposes a novel multi-modal cardiac segmentation method. We address two key problems that limit the success of recent methods on WHS: (1) unpairedness of training images, (2) failure in exploiting the correlated information between modalities. We pioneers apply the attention mechanism on multi-modal segmentation with the assumption that both modalities may have correlated features that can be used to assist the segmentation in the other modality. Extensive experiments validate our assumption and the effectiveness of our approach.

## References

1. Benjamin, E.J., Muntner, P., Alonso, A., et al.: Heart disease and stroke statistics 2019 update: a report from the American Heart Association. Circulation **139**(10), 56–528 (2019)
2. Ronneberger, O., Fischer, P., Brox, T.: U-Net: convolutional networks for biomedical image segmentation. In: Navab, N., Hornegger, J., Wells, W., Frangi, A. (eds.) MICCAI 2015. LNCS, vol. 9351, pp. 234–241. Springer, Cham (2015). https://doi.org/10.1007/978-3-319-24574-4_28
3. Schlemper, J., et al.: Attention gated networks: learning to leverage salient regions in medical images. Med. Image Anal. **53**, 197–207 (2018)
4. Oktay, O., et al.: Attention U-Net: learning where to look for the pancreas. In: International Conference on Medical Imaging with Deep Learning (2018)
5. Zhu, J., Park, T., Isola, P., Efros, A.A.: Unpaired image-to-image translation using cycle-consistent adversarial networks. In: ICCV, pp. 2242–2251 (2017)
6. Dou, Q., Ouyang, C., Chen, C., Chen, H., Heng, P.: Unsupervised cross-modality domain adaptation of ConvNets for biomedical image segmentations with adversarial loss. IJCAI (2018)
7. Zhang, Z., Yang, L., Zheng, Y.: Translating and segmenting multimodal medical volumes with cycle- and shape-consistency generative adversarial network. In: CVPR, pp. 9242–9251 (2018)
8. Shelhamer, E., Long, J., Darrell, T.: Fully convolutional networks for semantic segmentation. In: CVPR, pp. 3431–3440 (2015)
9. Goodfellow, I.J., et al.: Generative adversarial nets. In: NIPS (2014)

10. Yi, Z., Zhang, H., Tan, P., Gong, M.: DualGAN: unsupervised dual learning for image-to-image translation. In: ICCV, pp. 2868–2876 (2017)
11. Isola, P., Zhu, J., Zhou, T., Efros, A.A.: Image-to-image translation with conditional adversarial networks. In: CVPR, pp. 5967–5976 (2017)
12. Guan, Q., Huang, Y., Zhong, Z., Zheng, Z., Zheng, L., Yang, Y.: Diagnose like a radiologist: attention guided convolutional neural network for thorax disease classification. ArXiv abs/1801.09927 (2018)
13. Hori, C., Hori, T., Lee, T., Sumi, K., Hershey, J.R., Marks, T.K.: Attention-based multimodal fusion for video description. In: ICCV, pp. 4203–4212 (2017)
14. Ye, L., Rochan, M., Liu, Z., Wang, Y.: Cross-modal self-attention network for referring image segmentation. In: CVPR (2019)
15. Hong, S., Oh, J., Han, B., Lee, H.: Learning transferrable knowledge for semantic segmentation with deep convolutional neural network. In: CVPR, pp. 3204–3212 (2016)
16. Kingma, D.P., Ba, J.: Adam: a method for stochastic optimization. In: ICLR (2015)
17. Zhuang, X., Shen, J.: Multi-scale patch and multi-modality atlases for whole heart segmentation of MR. Med. Image Anal. **31**, 77–87 (2016)

# High- and Low-Level Feature Enhancement for Medical Image Segmentation

Huan Wang, Guotai Wang$^{(\boxtimes)}$, Zhihan Xu, Wenhui Lei,
and Shaoting Zhang

University of Electronic Science and Technology of China, Chengdu, China
guotai.wang@uestc.edu.cn

**Abstract.** The fully convolutional networks (FCNs) have achieved state-of-the-art performance in numerous medical image segmentation tasks. Most FCNs typically focus on fusing features in different levels to improve the learning ability to multi-scale features. In this paper, we explore an alternative direction to improve network performance by enhancing the encoding quality of high- and low-level features, so as to introduce two feature enhancement modules: (i) high-level feature enhancement module (HFE); (ii) low-level feature enhancement module (LFE). HFE utilizes attention mechanism to selectively aggregate the optimal feature information in high- and low-levels, enhancing the ability of high-level features to reconstruct accurate details. LFE aims to use global semantic information of high-level features to adaptively guide feature learning of bottom networks, so as to enhance the semantic consistency of high- and low-level features. We integrate HFE and LFE into a typical encoder-decoder network, and propose a novel medical image segmentation framework (HLF-Net). On two challenging datasets of skin lesion segmentation and spleen segmentation, we prove that the proposed modules and network can improve the performance considerably.

**Keywords:** Medical image · Segmentation · Feature enhancement · Convolutional networks

## 1 Introduction

Accurate and reliable segmentation of various anatomies from medical images is essential to improve diagnosis and assessment of related diseases. However, it is rather time-consuming to label a large amount of medical images manually. Thus, with the development of fully convolutional network (FCNs) [1], they have achieved state-of-the-art performance for many medical image segmentation tasks [2–4].

Most FCNs have a typical encoder-decoder framework [4]. The high-level semantic information of input images is embedded into the feature maps, and then the decoder uses multiple up-sampling components to restore the original resolution and generate segmentation results. However, when encoding semantic features of images, it is difficult for the encoder to effectively capture global context features of targets because of small local receptive field of bottom networks. Additionally, although the top-level feature maps from encoder may be highly semantic, the ability of decoder to

© Springer Nature Switzerland AG 2019
H.-I. Suk et al. (Eds.): MLMI 2019, LNCS 11861, pp. 611–619, 2019.
https://doi.org/10.1007/978-3-030-32692-0_70

reconstruct accurate details is severely limited to the low feature resolution. Therefore, much work has recently attempted to fuse low-level but high-resolution features from the bottom layers with high-level but low-resolution features from the top layers, which makes decoder generate more accurate segmentation results. Ronneberger et al. [2] proposed Unet which is one of the most representative frameworks of this idea, providing state-of-the-art performance for medical image segmentation tasks.

Although Unet has achieved great success, it also exists some problems. There is a huge gap of semantic level and spatial resolution between high- and low-level features, and the low-level features have complex background noise [5]. Therefore, it is inefficient to integrate the low-level features into high-level features by simple skip connection as used in [2]. Inspired by [6, 7], we introduce high-level features enhancement block (HFE) to optimize the encoding quality of high-level features. HFE adaptively aggregates the optimal feature information in different levels by utilizing the complementary feature information of high- and low-levels. The attention mechanism used in HFE can recalibrate the spatial and channel features of feature maps respectively, and suppress noise from the bottom layers, so as to improve encoding quality of target-related features.

In addition, we believe that not only the detail reconstruction of high-level features requires the high-resolution information from bottom layers, but also the feature encoding of bottom layers requires the guidance of high-level semantic information. With this idea, we construct a semantic embedding module (LFE). LTE adaptively guides the bottom layers to learn the features of effective regions by the global information perception abilities of high-level features, and enhances the semantic consistency of the high- and low-level features. As far as we know, this is the first time to introduce high-level semantic information into bottom layers in the field of medical image segmentation, and to guide the feature learning of the bottom-layer network through global information.

We integrate the proposed feature enhancement modules (HFE & LFE) into a typical encoder-decoder network for medical image segmentation to demonstrate that these two modules are a generic network component to boost performance, so as to propose a novel medical image segmentation framework (HLE-Net). We evaluated our HLE-Net and proposed modules on two challenging datasets of skin lesion segmentation and spleen segmentation. The results show that the proposed methods can achieve competitive performance, and improve segmentation performance considerably.

## 2  Method

We first define a set of convolutional transformations $F_{tr} : X \rightarrow X', X \in R^{H \times W \times C}$, $X' \in R^{H' \times W' \times C'}$, here $H$ and $W$ are spatial height and width, with $C$ and $C'$ being the input and output channels, respectively. The convolution transforms $F_{tr}(\cdot)$ fuse the spatial and channel information in the input feature maps $X$ in the local receptive field, thereby outputting a richer feature representation $X'$. By stacking the convolutional layers and the nonlinear activation function layers, the feature $X'$ will be encoded into higher-level semantic information $U$. In the FCNs, researchers directly fuse low-level features $X$ and high-level features $U$ into $(X + U)$, or directly concatenate $(F_{tr}(X, U))$

by skip connections to obtain high-resolution information from the bottom layers. Although good results have been achieved, there are few studies on further optimizing the encoding quality of high- and low-level features in FCNs. In this study, we focus on using complementary information between high- and low-level features in FCN to enhance the encoding quality of high- and low-level features respectively, and achieve accurate and robust segmentation. We first embed high-level semantic information in the encoder of FCN, then embed the high-resolution features from bottom layers in the decoder, and use the idea of attention mechanism to enhance the efficiency of high- and low-level feature fusion in an adaptive learning way. We will detail the feature enhancement modules (HFE & LFE) proposed in this paper and the corresponding segmentation framework (HLE-Net) in the following parts.

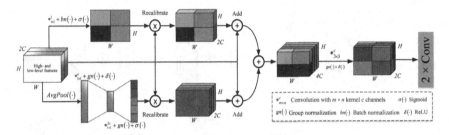

**Fig. 1.** The framework of HFE with spatial and channel attentions.

## 2.1 High-Level Feature Enhancement Module (HFE)

We introduce a high-level feature enhancement module (HFE), which adaptively learns the feature information related to a task through complementary semantic information in high- and low-level features. In addition, HFE emphasizes that different feature channels or different spatial regions in feature maps of different semantic level have different help for tasks. By enhancing relative features and suppressing irrelative features, the encoding quality of high-level features can be greatly improved.

HFE consists of a channel recalibration and a spatial recalibration step. Firstly, we consider the adaptive channel recalibration. Assume that the high- and low-level features $Y = (X, U) = [y_1, y_2, \cdots, y_c, \cdots, y_{2c}]$ are a combination of channels $y_i \in \mathbb{R}^{H \times W}$. We use a global average pooling to compress $y_i$ into a channel descriptor, and generate a channel-wise statistics vector $z \in \mathbb{R}^{1 \times 1 \times 2c}$. The $t$-th element of $z$ is calculated by $z_t = Avgpool(y_i)$. $z$ is processed by a block of two $1 \times 1$ convolution layers that are followed by ReLU and Sigmoid respectively. The output of the Sigmoid is the channel-wise attention coefficient $\tilde{z} = \sigma(z')$. $\tilde{z}$ is used to recalibrate $Y$ to $\tilde{Y}_c = \tilde{z} \otimes Y$, where $\otimes$ denotes element-wise multiplication. Then, we consider spatial adaptive recalibration. By a feature transformation, we use a $1 \times 1$ convolution to compress $Y$ into a single channel feature map $s$, which is followed by Sigmoid to obtain pixel-wise attention coefficient $\tilde{s} = \sigma(s)$. Finally, the feature $\left(\tilde{Y}_s = \tilde{s} \otimes Y\right)$ of spatial recalibration is obtained by element-wise multiplication.

In HFE, the recalibration of spatial and channel features fully considers the guidance of different levels (high- and low-) of semantic information. By stacking HFE and up-sampling components, FCN can gradually refine and reconstruct high-resolution target details and generate accurate segmentation results. However, since the values of the attention coefficient are in the range of 0 to 1, repeated superposition of the HFE will result in a decrease in the value of the deep feature response, thereby affecting the segmentation performance. Here, we use residual connection [8] to improve the feasibility of optimization based on the preservation of original information. Therefore, the output features of channel recalibration and spatial recalibration in HFE is $\tilde{Y}_c = (1 + \tilde{z}) \otimes Y, \tilde{Y}_s = (1 + \tilde{s}) \otimes Y$. Finally, $\tilde{Y}_c$ and $\tilde{Y}_s$ are concatenated and sent to a $3 \times 3$ convolution layer to fuse their respective feature information, and the channel dimension is reduced. The framework of HFE is illustrated in Fig. 1.

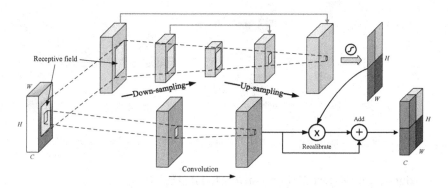

**Fig. 2.** The schematic illustration of the low-level features enhancement module.

## 2.2 Low-Level Feature Enhancement Module (LFE)

In FCN, features in different layers encode information at different levels. The features from bottom layers have rich spatial information, but they suffer from the problem of background noise and semantic ambiguity due to the small local receptive field and lack of guidance of the global context information. The detail reconstruction of the high-level features requires the help of high-resolution information from bottom layers. At the same time, we believe that the feature encoding of the bottom network in FCN requires the guidance of global semantic information to enhance the semantic consistency of high- and low-level features and suppress irrelative background noise. Therefore, the proposed LFE encodes the prior global semantic information of targets into the low-level features in an adaptive learning manner to enhance the semantic encoding ability of the bottom network.

The LFE consists of two branches: a semantic embedded branch and a trunk branch. The trunk branch is responsible for encoding and learning the features associated with the task. The semantic embedded branch is inspired by the excellent segmentation framework [2] and uses a mini encoder-decoder structure. The encoding stage quickly expands the receptive field and encodes global context information by down-sampling. The decoding stage restores spatial resolution through up-sampling and obtains high-level semantic features. Then the global semantic information of high-level features is embedded into the trunk branch to guide its feature encoding and optimize its encoding quality. At the same time, the trunk branch is enhanced to learn the features in the effective region. Specifically, as shown in Fig. 2, in the semantic embedded branch, the input feature maps $X$ obtain a more global receptive field and higher semantic features after two consecutive down-sampling and up-sampling operations. We also add skip connections between down-sampling and up-sampling to fuse information at different scales. Through a $1 \times 1$ convolutional layer, high-level semantic information is encoded into spatial projection map $s', s' \in \mathbb{R}^{H \times W}$. The final semantic embedded map is obtained from a Sigmoid layer. The value of each element in $\sigma(s')$ represents the relative importance of spatial information on the corresponding feature maps. Afterwards, this prior global information is embedded in the trunk branch to optimize its encoding quality through element-wise multiplication. In addition, in order to prevent the decrease of the feature response value of the trunk branch, we also introduce a residual connection. Therefore, the final output feature of LFE is expressed as $\tilde{X} = (1 + \sigma(s')) \otimes F_{tr}(X)$. In the literature [9], a similar structure with LFE is used to introduce a feature attention mechanism throughout the network. However, unlike [9], LFE aims to embed the global context information of the segmentation targets into low-level features through a lighter high-level semantic encoding module to improve the semantic encoding ability of the bottom network.

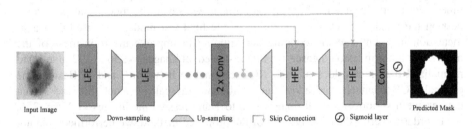

**Fig. 3.** Illustration of the framework of our proposed HLF-Net.

## 2.3 Segmentation Framework Based on Feature Enhancement

The proposed feature enhancement modules can be integrated into the existing segmentation framework to improve their feature learning abilities by replacing standard convolutional layers and skip connection operations. In this work, we integrate HFE and LFE into a typical encoder and decoder structure, and propose a new medical image segmentation network (HLE-Net). As shown in Fig. 3, the encoder network of HLE-Net is composed by superimposed LFEs. Each LFE provides semantic guidance of different levels for the encoding of the bottom network, which gradually enhances and refines the attention to complex targets. Then, the target details are reconstructed by the multi-layer HFEs and the original resolution is restored. Each convolution module consists of a $3 \times 3$ convolutional layer, a group normalization layer [10] and a ReLU layer. In this paper, HLF-Net contains 4 down-sampling and 4 up-sampling operations, and finally obtains the segmentation probability map through the Sigmoid function.

## 3 Experiments

### 3.1 Data and Experimental Setups

We extensively evaluated the proposed approach on ISIC 2017[1] skin lesion segmentation dataset [11] and the spleen segmentation dataset of CT volume images from Memorial Sloan Kettering Cancer Center[2]. In the skin lesion dataset, 2750 dermoscopic images from different clinical centers around the world were included, where 2000 for training, 150 for validation and the last 600 for testing. Our second dataset includes a total of 41 patient data. Due to memory limitations, we split the CT volume images into $512 \times 512$ slices to train the network. We performed data splitting at patient level and used images from 25, 4, 12 patients for training, validation and testing, respectively. Finally, by discarding some slices containing only background from the CT volume images, we obtained a total of 882 training images, 135 validation images, and 380 testing images.

Our HLE-Net is implemented using Pytorch on a Linux system with an Nvidia 1080Ti GPU. During training, we used the dice loss, the Adam optimizer with a learning rate of $1 \times 10^{-4}$ and the batch size of 6, with a learning rate reduction of 0.1 times after every 15 epochs. In each experiment, we saved the model that performed best on the validation set during training as the final test model. We used data augmentation including random copping and flipping to improve the robustness of the model. For the skin lesion dataset, we first re-scaled all images to $256 \times 192$ pixels and normalized the pixel values of each RGB channel to between 0 and 1. Besides the original RGB channels, we added an additional grayscale channel. For the spleen dataset, we first normalized all images to 0 to 1 and resized the images to $256 \times 256$.

In order to verify the effectiveness of the proposed method, we performed ablation studies on the two datasets, and compared HLE-Net with Unet-28 [2], Res-Unet-28. Res-Unet-28 is a modified Unet where each convolution block is replaced by the bottleneck building block used in the ResNet [8]. In order to evaluate our method fairly, the number of basic channels of Unet-28 and Res-Unet-28 is 28 to ensure that the number of parameters is similar to that of HLE-Net. We use the Dice coefficient, the Jaccard index and the Accuracy to evaluate the segmentation performance. Because Accuracy has very little discrimination on spleen dataset, we do not show the Accuracy of spleen segmentation in Table 1.

### 3.2 Results and Discussion

Table 1 shows the results of the different variants of the proposed method (only LFE, only HFE and HLE-Net) on the skin lesion dataset and the spleen dataset, respectively.

---

[1] https://challenge2017.isic-archive.com/.

[2] http://medicaldecathlon.com/.

In addition, the performance of Unet-28, Res-Unet-28 and the scores of the top three in the 2017 Skin Lesion Challenge leaderboard are also shown. It can be seen that the proposed modules considerably improve the segmentation performance of the network on both datasets. This indicates that both LFE and HFE can effectively enhance the encoding quality of the network. We further observe that LFE achieves higher performance than HFE, which confirms our hypothesis that it is more necessary for the feature encoding of the bottom network to require guidance from the global semantic information of high-level features. HLE-Net integrated LFE and HFE has the best performance among all methods. Compared with Unet-28, HLE-Net increases the jaccard index on the spleen dataset and the lesion dataset by 4.5% and 3.4%, respectively. It is also 2.3% higher than the best score on the leaderboard [13].

**Table 1.** Quantitative evaluation of different networks on spleen dataset and ISIC 2017.

| ISIC 2017 | | | | | | | | |
|---|---|---|---|---|---|---|---|---|
| Method | MResNet-Seg [11] | Berseth et al. [12] | Yuan et al. [13] | Unet-28 | Res-Unet-28 | HLE-Net (only HFE) | HLE-Net (only LFE) | HLE-Net |
| Dice | 0.844 | 0.847 | 0.849 | 0.838 | 0.841 | 0.859 | 0.862 | **0.866** |
| Jaccard | 0.760 | 0.762 | 0.765 | 0.754 | 0.755 | 0.777 | 0.783 | **0.788** |
| Accuracy | 0.934 | 0.932 | 0.934 | 0.930 | 0.931 | 0.935 | 0.935 | **0.939** |
| Spleen | | | | | | | | |
| Dice | – | – | – | 0.937 | 0.942 | 0.957 | 0.960 | **0.964** |
| Jaccard | – | – | – | 0.886 | 0.894 | 0.919 | 0.923 | **0.931** |
| Parameters | – | – | – | $5.9 \times 10^6$ | $6.2 \times 10^6$ | $3.6 \times 10^6$ | $3.8 \times 10^6$ | $5.5 \times 10^6$ |

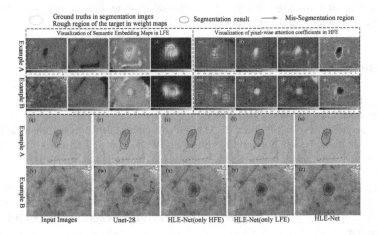

**Fig. 4.** The qualitative segmentation results of two examples (A, B) on ISIC 2017. Each example contains different network segmentation results and the visualization of the weight maps in LFE and HFE. From left to right (a–e–h, i–m–p), feature resolution goes from high to low, then from low to high, and finally restore the original resolution.

The qualitative segmentation results from two examples with different appearance on ISIC 2017 dataset are shown in Fig. 4. For the example A, the lesion area is close to normal skin, so Unet-28 incorrectly predicts normal skin as the lesion area, but HFE improves this situation. LFE further obtains a more accurate segmentation, which proves that improving the encoding quality of the bottom network can improve the segmentation result more effectively. For the example B, the background is very close to the lesion area. Unet-28 cannot accurately locate the lesion area. Gradually refining the attention on the segmentation targets through the attention mechanism can effectively solve this problem. Both LFE and HFE can accurately identify the lesion area, and LFE has a more accurate segmentation result. In addition, we also visualize the semantic embedding maps in LFE and the pixel-wise attention coefficient in HFE. It can be clearly seen that different LFE and HFE exert attention of different degrees on the segmentation targets, and as the network goes from shallow to deep, the concerning areas of LFE and HFE are gradually becoming more refined from blur.

## 4   Conclusion

This paper introduces two modules for feature enhancement for better medical image segmentation performance. LFE aims to encode high-level semantic information into the low-level features to improve the encoding ability of the bottom network. HFE optimizes the fusion efficiency of high- and low-level features using attention mechanism, which provides more high-resolution semantic guidance for high-level features. Based on these two modules, we propose a new medical image segmentation network (HLE-Net). The proposed method has achieved very competitive results in two very different tasks, skin lesion segmentation and spleen segmentation. This proves the effectiveness and wide adaptability of the proposed method. Future work aims to apply the proposed model to 3D segmentation or other segmentation tasks.

## References

1. Long, J., Shelhamer, E., Darrell, T.: Fully convolutional networks for semantic segmentation. In: CVPR, pp. 3431–3440 (2015)
2. Ronneberger, O., Fischer, P., Brox, T.: U-Net: convolutional networks for biomedical image segmentation. In: Navab, N., Hornegger, J., Wells, W.M., Frangi, A.F. (eds.) MICCAI 2015. LNCS, vol. 9351, pp. 234–241. Springer, Cham (2015). https://doi.org/10.1007/978-3-319-24574-4_28
3. Wang, H., Gu, R., Li, Z.: Automated segmentation of intervertebral disc using fully dilated separable deep neural networks. In: Zheng, G., Belavy, D., Cai, Y., Li, S. (eds.) CSI 2018. LNCS, vol. 11397, pp. 66–76. Springer, Cham (2019). https://doi.org/10.1007/978-3-030-13736-6_6
4. Wang, G., Li, W., Ourselin, S., Vercauteren, T.: Automatic brain tumor segmentation using cascaded anisotropic convolutional neural networks. In: Crimi, A., Bakas, S., Kuijf, H., Menze, B., Reyes, M. (eds.) BrainLes 2017. LNCS, vol. 10670, pp. 178–190. Springer, Cham (2018). https://doi.org/10.1007/978-3-319-75238-9_16

5. Zhang, Z., Zhang, X., Peng, C., Xue, X., Sun, J.: ExFuse: enhancing feature fusion for semantic segmentation. In: Ferrari, V., Hebert, M., Sminchisescu, C., Weiss, Y. (eds.) ECCV 2018. LNCS, vol. 11214, pp. 273–288. Springer, Cham (2018). https://doi.org/10.1007/978-3-030-01249-6_17

6. Roy, A.G., Navab, N., Wachinger, C.: Concurrent spatial and channel 'squeeze & excitation' in fully convolutional networks. In: Frangi, A., Schnabel, J., Davatzikos, C., Alberola-López, C., Fichtinger, G. (eds.) MICCAI 2018. LNCS, vol. 11070, pp. 421–429. Springer, Cham (2018). https://doi.org/10.1007/978-3-030-00928-1_48

7. Oktay, O., Schlemper, J., Folgoc, L.L., Lee, M., Heinrich, M.: Attention U-Net: learning where to look for the pancreas. arXiv preprint arXiv:1804.03999 (2018)

8. He, K., Zhang, X., Ren, S., Sun, J.: Deep residual learning for image recognition. In: CVPR, pp. 770–778 (2016)

9. Wang, F., et al.: Residual attention network for image classification. In: CVPR, pp. 3156–3164 (2017)

10. Wu, Y., He, K.: Group normalization. arXiv preprint arXiv:1803.08494 (2018)

11. Bi, L., Kim, J., Ahn, E., Feng, D.: Automatic skin lesion analysis using large-scale dermoscopy images and deep residual networks. arXiv preprint arXiv:1703.04197 (2017)

12. Berseth, M.: ISIC 2017-skin lesion analysis towards melanoma detection. arXiv preprint arXiv:1703.00523 (2017)

13. Yuan, Y.: Automatic skin lesion segmentation with fully convolutional-deconvolutional networks. arXiv:1803.08494 (2017)

# Shape-Aware Complementary-Task Learning for Multi-organ Segmentation

Fernando Navarro[1]([⊠]), Suprosanna Shit[1], Ivan Ezhov[1], Johannes Paetzold[1], Andrei Gafita[3], Jan C. Peeken[2], Stephanie E. Combs[2], and Bjoern H. Menze[1]

[1] Department of Informatics, Technische Universität München, Munich, Germany
fernando.navarro@tum.de
[2] Department of Radiotherapy, Klinikum rechts der Isar, Munich, Germany
[3] Department of Nuclear Medicine, Klinikum rechts der Isar, Munich, Germany

**Abstract.** Multi-organ segmentation in whole-body computed tomography (CT) is a constant pre-processing step which finds its application in organ-specific image retrieval, radiotherapy planning, and interventional image analysis. We address this problem from an organ-specific shape-prior learning perspective. We introduce the idea of complementary-task learning to enforce shape-prior leveraging the existing target labels. We propose two complementary-tasks namely (i) distance map regression and (ii) contour map detection to explicitly encode the geometric properties of each organ. We evaluate the proposed solution on the public VISCERAL dataset containing CT scans of multiple organs. We report a significant improvement of overall dice score from 0.8849 to 0.9018 due to the incorporation of complementary-task learning.

**Keywords:** Multi-task learning · Complementary-task · Multi-organ segmentation

## 1 Introduction

In representation learning, auxiliary-tasks are often designed to leverage *free-of-cost* supervision which is derived from existing *target labels*. The purpose of including auxiliary tasks is not only to learn a shared representation but also to learn efficiently by solving the common *meta-objective*. A group of auxiliary-tasks driven by a common *meta-objective* often have *complementary objectives*. For example, to detect an orange, one can define two sub-tasks: (i) learn only the shape of the orange, and, (ii) learn only the color of the orange. Here, learning the shape and the color complement each other to learn the common *meta-objective*: how an orange looks. In this context, we leverage complementary-tasks learning by jointly optimizing the common *meta-objective* of multiple-tasks.

Solving multiple tasks simultaneously [5] is known to improve each task's performance when compared to learning them independently. Mutual information exchange between multiple tasks such as detection and segmentation drive a

---

F. Navarro and S. Shit—The authors Contributed equally to the work.

© Springer Nature Switzerland AG 2019
H.-I. Suk et al. (Eds.): MLMI 2019, LNCS 11861, pp. 620–627, 2019.
https://doi.org/10.1007/978-3-030-32692-0_71

neural network towards learning a generalized shared representation [6]. A more recent success in multi-task learning is mask-RCNN [4] which benefited from the combined object detection and instance segmentation tasks. Uslu et al. [12] shows that learning vessel interior, centerline, and edges as a set of complementary-tasks improves junction detection in the retinal vasculature. There is a new body of research which aims to efficiently balance losses of different competing tasks [2,5]. In contrast, our main objective is to leverage multiple complementary-tasks which shares a common *meta-objective* and do not need additional annotated targets. Given that medical imaging problems such as multi-organ segmentation have to be solved with limited annotated data, complementary-task learning is a promising alternative solution.

Multiple approaches have been proposed for multi-organ segmentation, which can be classified into registration-based and machine-learning based approaches. In registration-based methods, an atlas is registered to a test volume to obtain the segmentation map. [10,13]. However, this is a time-consuming method and its performance also suffers from inter-subject variability. Alternatively, the state-of-the-art methods for multi-organ segmentation are based on deep learning architectures such as fully convolutional neural networks FCN [9]and U-Net [8]. Deep learning-based methods can successfully segment large anatomical structures but are prone to miss small organs. Recently, Zhao *et al.* [14] have explored the idea of combining both registration-based approaches and deep learning to segment small organs.

However, a contemporary study by Geirhos et al. [3] shows that convolutional neural networks are inherently biased towards texture information over the shape of an object. In human anatomy, all organs have a discriminative shape feature which has not been addressed at its full potential by previous approaches. Our hypothesis is that learning *shape-prior* as a complementary-task improves the performance of the segmentation task. For learning the meta-objective of multi-organ representation, we define two complementary-tasks for shapes-prior learning: (i) inferring geometric shape properties of an organ, and, (ii) detecting the exterior contour of an organ. For the former, we propose the distance transform [1] of shape as geometric shape properties. For the latter, we leverage the binary edge-map of each organ.

In summary, our key contributions in this work are as follows:

- To the best of our knowledge, this is the first work for multi-organ segmentation leveraging complementary-task learning.
- We introduce two complementary-tasks in context of organ-specific shape-prior learning. We show that the inclusion of these complementary-tasks alongside the segmentation task improves its overall performance (Fig. 1).

## 2   Methodology

In this section, we present the proposed complementary-task learning for multi-organ segmentation and, subsequently describe the network architecture and the associated loss functions.

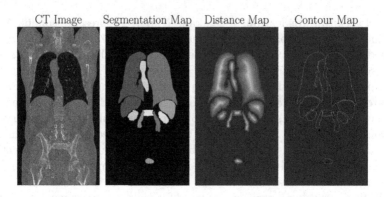

CT Image    Segmentation Map    Distance Map    Contour Map

**Fig. 1.** Target generation for complementary-tasks: *Distance Map* is the cumulative sum of the normalized distance transform of each organs' segmentation map. *Contour Map* is the binary edge of each organ. Shape representation learning is jointly enforced in the distance and contour maps.

In general, learning shape prior is itself a difficult task for a convolutional network due to the variety of shapes in different organs. We identify that the task of learning shape-priors can be broken down into multiple easier and quantifiable sub-task. Motivated by this fact, we propose two complementary-tasks to explicitly enforce shape and anatomical positional prior to the network.

**Learning Distance-Transform:** Euclidean distance transform of a shape is commonly used to find the inscribed circle having the largest radius within an arbitrary shape. It maps a boundary regularity measure of a shape with respect to an interior point. Hence, we argue that the distance transform regression learns geometric properties of shapes. In addition to that, we find that Gaussian heat-map regression is a common task in localizing anatomical landmarks [7]. Parallels can be drawn between Gaussian heat-map regression and Euclidean distance map regression for soft-localization of organ-specific landmarks.

**Learning Organ Contour:** Detecting organ boundaries is the most challenging task for a segmentation network. Hence, we propose to explicitly learn the organ contour as the second complementary-task alongside the distance map regression. The hypothesis is that the distance transform aids the network to accurately localize the organ from the learned anatomical prior whereas contour learning penalizes for boundary miss-classification and thus fine-tunes the organ shape.

**Loss Function:** The loss function consists of three optimization objectives of the corresponding task: segmentation, distance regression, and contour detection. Given the probability $p_l(x)$ of a pixel in location $x$ to belong to class $l$ and the ground truth by $g_l(x)$ the multi-organ segmentation loss $\mathcal{L}_{seg}$ and the contour map loss $\mathcal{L}_{contour}$ are defined as:

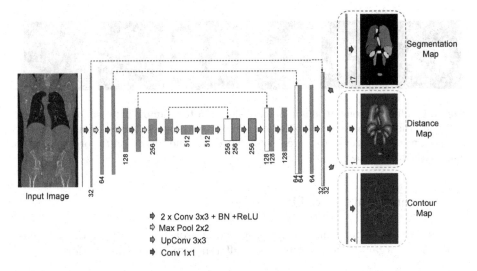

**Fig. 2.** Network architecture for complementary-task learning. The input is a CT slice. The network consists of an encoding and decoding part with skip connections resembling the U-Net architecture with three branches diverging at the end of the last upconvolution. The outputs of the network are the segmentation map, the distance map, and the contour map.

$$\mathcal{L}_{seg}, \mathcal{L}_{contour} = \underbrace{-\sum_x g_l(x)\log p_l(x)}_{\text{Cross-Entropy Loss}} - \underbrace{\frac{2\sum_x p_l(x)g_l(x)}{\sum_x p_l^2(x) + \sum_x g_l^2(x)}}_{\text{Dice Loss}} \qquad (1)$$

where $l = \#$ of organs $+\,1$ in the multi-organ segmentation loss, and $l = 2$ for the contour map. Dice loss is incorporated to handle the class-imbalance. For the distance map regression, the mean square error loss is optimized. Given the estimated distance map $p(x)$ of pixel $x$ and the ground truth value $g(x)$ the distance map loss function $\mathcal{L}_{dist}$ is:

$$\mathcal{L}_{dist} = -\frac{1}{n}\sum_x \left(g(x) - p(x)\right)^2 \qquad (2)$$

where $n = \#$ of pixels and the final loss $\mathcal{L}_{total} = \mathcal{L}_{seg} + \mathcal{L}_{contour} + \mathcal{L}_{dist}$ is given by the summation of all losses.

**Network Architecture:** The network architecture is inspired by encoding-decoding architectures with skip connections [8,9]. A generalized shared feature representation is learned throughout the encoding blocks, the bottleneck, and a part of the decoding blocks of the network. Three different branches are added to the common feature representation to produce three output maps (c.f. Fig. 2).

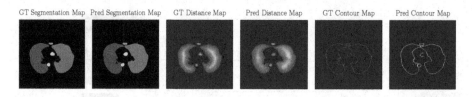

GT Segmentation Map  Pred Segmentation Map    GT Distance Map    Pred Distance Map    GT Contour Map    Pred Contour Map

**Fig. 3.** Qualitative comparison of an axial slice of a test sample between ground truth (GT) and the proposed model prediction (Pred). Our proposed model efficiently learns to (i) segment the organs, (ii) regress on distance map and (iii) detect the organ contour map at the same time.

## 3   Experiments and Discussion

To validate the performance of the proposed approach, we perform the segmentation of 16 organs. The following four different experiments are performed:

- U-Net: baseline using only $\mathcal{L}_{seg}$.
- U-Net + distance: $\mathcal{L}_{seg} + \mathcal{L}_{dist}$.
- U-Net + contour: $\mathcal{L}_{seg} + \mathcal{L}_{contour}$.
- U-Net + distance, contour: $\mathcal{L}_{seg} + \mathcal{L}_{dist} + \mathcal{L}_{contour}$.

**Data-Set:** The data-set used in the experiments consists of CT scans from the gold corpus and silver corpus in VISCERAL dataset [11]. 74 CT scans from the silver corpus data were used for training, the annotations in this set are automatically labeled by fusing the results of multiple algorithms, yielding noisy labels. 23 CT scans from the gold corpus are used for testing, which contains manually annotated labels. Multi-organ segmentation imposes several challenges including the different fields of view (whole-body, thorax), modalities (contrast and non-contrast), severe class-imbalance across the target classes due to the diversity of organ's size and shapes and the capability to generalize when trained with noisy labels.

All models were trained with Adam optimizer with a decaying learning rate initialized at 0.001, mini batch size of 4. The training was continued till validation loss converged. All the experiments were conducted on an NVIDIA Quadro P6000 GPU with 24 GB vRAM. The code was developed in TensorFlow.

To evaluate the overall accuracy of the proposed segmentation approach, we report the average dice score between the ground truth and the predicted segmentation map. Organ-specific dice scores are reported using box plots. We also report the Wilcoxon signed-rank test to find the statistical significance of the results.

**Quantitative Results:** We observe from Table 1 that adding distance task improves the overall dice while adding the contour task alone does not show any improvement. We attribute this behavior to the fact that the training data-set contains noisy labels and therefore the external part of the organs are not exactly

**Table 1.** Quantitative results: mean and standard deviation of the global dice scores shows that complementary-task learning achieves the best result.

| Model | Dice |
|---|---|
| U-Net | 0.8849 ± 0.120 |
| U-Net + distance | 0.8868 ± 0.116 |
| U-Net + contour | 0.8791 ± 0.118 |
| U-Net + distance, contour | **0.9018 ± 0.116** |

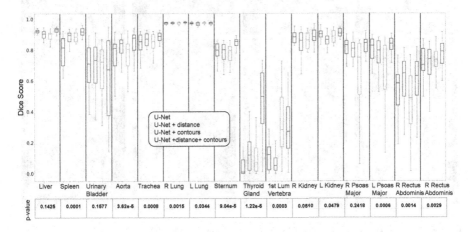

**Fig. 4.** Box plots of different organs show consistent improvement of the dice score using our proposed model (U-Net+distance+contour) over the baseline model (U-net). We also report the *p-value* obtained using Wilcoxon signed-rank statistical test between our proposed model and the baseline. The statistically significant *p-values* < 0.001 are shown in red. (Color figure online)

represented. On the other hand, adding both tasks drives the segmentation network to better generalization resulting in an improvement of 2% compared to the baseline. From the box plots in Fig. 4 we observe that dice score for big organs does not improve significantly compared to the baseline. In contrast, complementary-task learning provides statistically significant improvement for small organs such as the spleen, thyroid gland, and trachea.

**Qualitative Results:** Figure 5 shows a qualitative comparison between the U-Net baseline and the proposed approach. We highlight ROIs with a green box, to show regions where complementary-task learning improves the segmentation. We can visually asses that particularly the small organs results in better segmentation. Additionally, Fig. 3 compares the predicted distance map and the contour map to the ground truth. This confirms that the network is also able to solve the complementary-tasks.

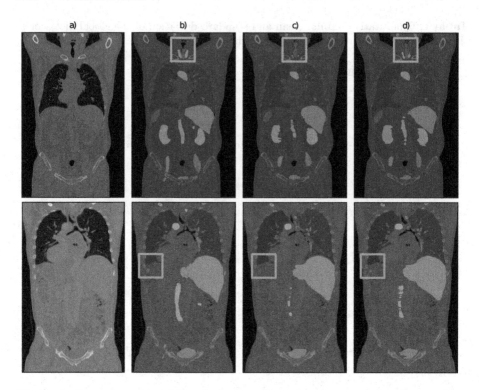

**Fig. 5.** Qualitative results: Each image shows the mid-slice in the coronal view. (a) the input CT slice, (b) ground truth segmentation, (c) prediction form U-Net baseline, (d) complementary-task learning. ROIs are indicated by green box highlighting regions where complementary-tasks learning improves the segmentation. (Color figure online)

## 4    Conclusions

In this work, we have proposed complementary-task learning to provide a novel and alternative solution to the challenging task of multi-organ segmentation. We have validated our method in a public benchmark data set which shows consistent improvement in dice score, especially for the small organs. In medical image segmentation where large data sets are scarce and corresponding dense annotation is expensive, designing complementary-task by leveraging existing target label could be beneficial to learn a generalized representation.

**Acknowledgements.** Fernando Navarro gratefully acknowledge the Deutsche Forschungsgemeinschaft (DFG, German Research Foundation) - GRK for the financial support. Suprosanna Shit and Ivan Ezhov are supported by the Translational Brain Imaging Training Network (TRABIT) under the European Union's 'Horizon 2020' research & innovation programme (Grant agreement ID: 765148). The authors gratefully acknowledge the support of NVIDIA Corporation with the donation of the Titan Xp GPU used for this research.

# References

1. Bischke, B., et al.: Multi-task learning for segmentation of building footprints with deep neural networks. arXiv preprint arXiv:1709.05932 (2017)
2. Chen, Z., et al.: GradNorm: gradient normalization for adaptive loss balancing in deep multitask networks. In: Proceedings of the ICML (2018)
3. Geirhos, R., et al.: ImageNet-trained CNNs are biased towards texture; increasing shape bias improves accuracy and robustness. In: Proceedings of the ICLR (2019)
4. He, K., et al.: Mask R-CNN. In: Proceedings of the IEEE CVPR, pp. 2961–2969 (2017)
5. Kendall, A., et al.: Multi-task learning using uncertainty to weigh losses for scene geometry and semantics. In: Proceedings of the IEEE CVPR, pp. 7482–7491 (2018)
6. Misra, I., et al.: Cross-stitch networks for multi-task learning. In: Proceedings of the IEEE CVPR, pp. 3994–4003 (2016)
7. Payer, C., et al.: Integrating spatial configuration into heatmap regression based CNNs for landmark localization. Med. Image Anal. **54**, 207–219 (2019)
8. Ronneberger, O., Fischer, P., Brox, T.: U-Net: convolutional networks for biomedical image segmentation. In: Navab, N., Hornegger, J., Wells, W.M., Frangi, A.F. (eds.) MICCAI 2015. LNCS, vol. 9351, pp. 234–241. Springer, Cham (2015). https://doi.org/10.1007/978-3-319-24574-4_28
9. Shelhamer, E., et al.: Fully convolutional networks for semantic segmentation. IEEE TPAMI **39**(4), 640–651 (2017)
10. Song, Y., et al.: Progressive multi-atlas label fusion by dictionary evolution. Med. Image Anal. **36**, 162–171 (2017)
11. Jimenez-del Toro, O., et al.: Cloud-based evaluation of anatomical structure segmentation and landmark detection algorithms: VISCERAL anatomy benchmarks. IEEE TMI **35**(11), 2459–2475 (2016)
12. Uslu, F., Bharath, A.A.: A multi-task network to detect junctions in retinal vasculature. In: Frangi, A.F., Schnabel, J.A., Davatzikos, C., Alberola-López, C., Fichtinger, G. (eds.) MICCAI 2018. LNCS, vol. 11071, pp. 92–100. Springer, Cham (2018). https://doi.org/10.1007/978-3-030-00934-2_11
13. Wang, H., et al.: Multi-atlas segmentation with joint label fusion. IEEE TMI **35**(3), 611–623 (2012)
14. Zhao, Y., et al.: Knowledge-aided convolutional neural network for small organ segmentation. IEEE JBHI (2019)

# An Active Learning Approach for Reducing Annotation Cost in Skin Lesion Analysis

Xueying Shi[1]([✉]), Qi Dou[2], Cheng Xue[1], Jing Qin[4], Hao Chen[1,3],
and Pheng-Ann Heng[1,5]

[1] Department of Computer Science and Engineering,
The Chinese University of Hong Kong, Hong Kong, China
xyshi@cse.cuhk.edu.hk
[2] Department of Computing Imperial College London, London SW7 2AZ, UK
[3] Imsight Medical Technology Co., Ltd., Shenzhen, China
[4] Centre for Smart Health, School of Nursing,
The Hong Kong Polytechnic University, Hong Kong, China
[5] Guangdong Provincial Key Laboratory of Computer Vision and Virtual Reality
Technology, Shenzhen Institutes of Advanced Technology,
Chinese Academy of Sciences, Shenzhen, China

**Abstract.** Automated skin lesion analysis is very crucial in clinical practice, as skin cancer is among the most common human malignancy. Existing approaches with deep learning have achieved remarkable performance on this challenging task, however, heavily relying on large-scale labelled datasets. In this paper, we present a novel active learning framework for cost-effective skin lesion analysis. The goal is to effectively select and utilize much fewer labelled samples, while the network can still achieve state-of-the-art performance. Our sample selection criteria complementarily consider both informativeness and representativeness, derived from decoupled aspects of measuring model certainty and covering sample diversity. To make wise use of the selected samples, we further design a simple yet effective strategy to aggregate intra-class images in pixel space, as a new form of data augmentation. We validate our proposed method on data of *ISIC 2017 Skin Lesion Classification Challenge* for two tasks. Using only up to 50% of samples, our approach can achieve state-of-the-art performances on both tasks, which are comparable or exceeding the accuracies with full-data training, and outperform other well-known active learning methods by a large margin.

## 1 Introduction

Skin cancer is among the most common cancers worldwide, and accurate analysis of dermoscopy images is crucial for reducing melanoma deaths [3]. Existing deep convolutional neural networks (CNNs) have demonstrated appealing efficacy for skin lesion analysis, even setting dermatologist-level performance. However, these achievements heavily rely on extensive labelled datasets, which is very expensive,

© Springer Nature Switzerland AG 2019
H.-I. Suk et al. (Eds.): MLMI 2019, LNCS 11861, pp. 628–636, 2019.
https://doi.org/10.1007/978-3-030-32692-0_72

time-consuming and skill-demanding. Recently, with increasing awareness of the impediment from unavailability of large-scale labeled data, researchers have been frequently revisiting the concept of active learning to train CNNs in a more cost-effective fashion [7]. The goal is to learn CNNs with much fewer labelled images, while the model can still achieve the state-of-the-art performance.

Sample selection criteria usually use informativeness or representativeness [4]. Informative samples are the ones which the current model still cannot recognize well. For example, Mahapatra et al. [6] derived uncertainty metrics via a Bayesian Neural Network to select informative samples for chest X-ray segmentation. On the other hand, representativeness measures whether the set of selected samples are diverse enough to represent the underlying distributions of the entire data space. Zheng et al. [12] chose representative samples with unsupervised feature extraction and clusters in latent space. Moreover, rather than only relying on one single criterion, some works actively select samples by integrating both criteria. Yang et al. [9] selected samples which receive low prediction probabilities and have large distances in CNN feature space. Another state-of-the-art method is AIFT [13] (active, incremental fine-tuning), which employed the entropy of CNN predictions for a sample to compute its informativeness as well as representativeness, demonstrating effectiveness on three medical imaging tasks. However, these existing methods derive both criteria based on the same CNN model, which hardly avoid potential correlations within the selected samples. How to exploit such dual-criteria in a more disentangled manner still remains open.

With active sample selection, the data redundancy of unlabelled sample pool is effectively reduced. Meanwhile, we should note that the obtained set of images come with high intra-class variance in color, texture, shape and size [8,11]. Directly using such samples to fine-tune the model may fall into more-or-less hard example mining, and face the risk of over-fitting. Hence, we argue that it is also very critical to more wisely use the compact set of selected samples, for unleashing their value to a large extent. However, sample utilization strategies receive less attention in existing active learning literatures. One notable method is mix-up [10], that augments new training data as pixel-wise weighted addition of two images from different classes. However, mix-up is not suitable for situations where data have large intra-class variance while limited inter-class variance, which is exactly our case at skin lesion analysis.

In this work, we propose a novel active learning method for skin lesion analysis to improve annotation efficiency. Our framework consists of two components, i.e., sample selection and sample aggregation. Specifically, we design dual-criteria to select informative as well as representative samples, so that the selected samples are highly complementary. Furthermore, for effective utilization of the selected samples, we design an aggregation strategy by augmenting intra-class images in pixel space, in order to capture richer and more distinguishable features from these valuable yet ambiguous selected samples. We validate our approach on two tasks with the dataset of *ISIC 2017 Skin Lesion Classification Challenge*. We achieve state-of-the-art performance by using 50% data for task 1 and 40% for task 2 of skin lesion classification tasks. In both tasks, our proposed method

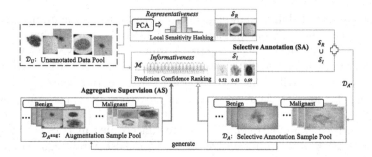

**Fig. 1.** Overview of our proposed active learning framework for skin lesion analysis. In each iteration, from unannotated data pool $\mathcal{D}_U$, we select a worthy-annotation set $\mathcal{D}_{A^*}$ composing representative samples $\mathcal{S}_R$ and informative samples $\mathcal{S}_I$. Moreover, we generate augmentations $\mathcal{D}_{A^{\mathrm{aug}}}$ of all the gathered annotated data pool $\mathcal{D}_A$. Finally, the model is updated by supervised learning with $\mathcal{D}_A \cup \mathcal{D}_{A^{\mathrm{aug}}}$.

consistently outperforms existing state-of-the-art active learning methods by a large margin.

## 2   Methods

Our framework is illustrated in Fig. 1. We first train the ResNet-101 model $\mathcal{M}$ with the annotated set of $\mathcal{D}_A = \{(x_j, y_j)\}_{j=1}^Q$, which is initialized with randomly selected 10% data from the unlabelled sample pool $\mathcal{D}_U = \{x_i\}_{i=1}^T$. Next, we iteratively selecting samples, aggregating samples, and updating the model.

### 2.1   Selective Annotation (SA) with Dual-Criteria

We select samples considering both criteria of informativeness and representativeness. The informativeness is calculated based on the prediction of the trained model. The representativeness is obtained by PCA features and hashing method. In our framework, we call this procedure as *selective annotation (SA)*.

Firstly, we test the unlabelled samples with the current trained model. The images with low prediction confidences computed from the model are selected as informative ones, since they are nearby the decision boundary. The model would present relatively lower confidence when encountering those new "hard" unlabelled samples, which usually have either ambiguous pattern or rare appearance. For each sample, the highest prediction probability across all classes, is regarded as its model certainty. With ranking $\mathcal{D}_U$ according to certainties, the lower certainty indicates stronger informativeness. The selected samples following this aspect of criteria are represented as $\mathcal{S}_I$:

$$\mathcal{S}_I \leftarrow \operatorname*{Rank}_{x_i}(\{\mathcal{M}(x_i)\}, N_I), \tag{1}$$

where $\mathcal{M}(x_i)$ is certainty of current model $\mathcal{M}$ for each sample $x_i$ in $\mathcal{D}_U$, ranking is in ascending order, and the first $N_I$ samples are selected. We set $N_I = 10\% \times N \times$

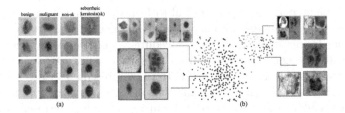

**Fig. 2.** (a) Skin lesion images with limited inter-class variance while large intra-class variance. (b) Embedding of high-level CNN features of the original and augmented samples using t-SNE. The purple and green dots are original and augmented benign data. The blue and yellow dots are original and augmented malignant data. Augmented samples are natural clustering with original ones in the high-level semantic space. (Color figure online)

$\gamma$ where $N$ is the total number of available samples, and $\gamma$ is the sample selection ratio of informativeness criterion. 10% is the hyper-parameter which controls the scale of newly selected samples during each round of sample selection.

Next, considering sample diversity, we desire the added samples present dissimilar appearances, and hence, are representative for the entire dataset. Specifically, we regard feature-level difference as an indicator of sample diversity. To avoid using features from the same CNN as used for informative sample selection, we compute the first principal component of the image as features for data diversity. With the PCA features, we map similar unlabelled items into the same buckets using local sensitivity hashing (LSH), which is for efficient approximate nearest neighbor search. Next, we uniformly fetch samples from each bucket and obtain the set of $\mathcal{S}_R$ as representative samples. This process is formulated as:

$$\mathcal{S}_R \leftarrow \underset{x_i}{\mathrm{UniSample}}(LSH(\{PCA(x_i)\}, K), N_R), \tag{2}$$

where $K = 10$ is our number of buckets in LSH. We set $N_R = 10\% \times N \times (1 - \gamma)$ with $(1 - \gamma)$ being the sample selection ratio of representativeness criterion. As the PCA features are independent of the learned CNN, our obtained $\mathcal{S}_R$ and $\mathcal{S}_I$ are decoupled and highly complementary. With one round of SA, we get the additional labelled set of samples as $\mathcal{D}_{A^*} = \mathcal{S}_I \cup \mathcal{S}_R$ and update $\mathcal{D}_A \leftarrow \mathcal{D}_A \cup \mathcal{D}_{A^*}$.

## 2.2  Aggregative Supervision (AS) with Intra-class Augmentation

In active learning, majority previous efforts have focused on how to select samples, but somehow neglected how to effectively harness them to produce more distinguishable features. As usually the selected training samples are very challenging and ambiguous, it is important to design strategies which can sufficiently unleash the potential values of these newly labelled samples. If just directly using such samples to fine-tune the model, we may encounter high risks of over-fitting, since the updated decision boundary would be curly to fit the ambiguous images.

To enhance the model's capability to deal with those ambiguous samples, we propose to aggregate the images into new form of augmented samples to update the model. In our framework, we call this procedure as *aggregative supervision (AS)*.

Specifically, we aggregate images from the same class in pixel space, by stitching four intra-class images in a 2 × 2 pattern, as presented in Fig. 2(b). Such a concatenation of samples from the same class can provide richer yet more subtle clues for the model to learn more robust features to reduce intra-class variance, especially given the highly ambiguous and limited number of samples obtained from SA process. In a sense that the model aims to discriminate between distributions of benign and malignant images, the proposed sample aggregation scheme can be beneficial to reduce the influence of individual complicated sample on the model, and percolate the underlying pattern inherent in each category. Finally, the aggregated image is resized to the same size as the original resolution, and its label is the same class of those composed images. Generally, our strategy shares the pixel-level augmentation spirit as mix-up [10], while we can avoid overlapping the ambiguous contents of inter-class images with limited appearance difference.

To demonstrate the effectiveness of the proposed aggregation scheme at feature level, we embed the CNN features of the original images and the aggregated images with our intra-class stitching onto a 2D plane using t-SNE, see Fig. 2. We employ the features obtained from the last fully connected layer (before softmax), as these features have strong semantic meanings. Note that these aggregated samples haven't yet been used to train the model. We observe that the aggregated samples naturally group together with the ordinary images within the class, when mapped into the higher-level space with a pre-learned feature extractor (i.e., the CNN model). This demonstrates that our aggregation scheme can provide a new and informative form of training images, offering apparently different view in raw pixel space while maintaining the essential patterns of its category in the highly-abstracted semantic space.

## 3    Experimental Results

**Dataset.** We extensively validate our proposed active learning framework on two different tasks using the public data of *ISIC 2017 Skin Lesion Classification Challenge* [1]. These two tasks hold different aspects of challenges and sample ambiguity characteristics.

Same as the state-of-the-art methods on the leaderboard [2,5], in addition to the 2,000 training images provided by the challenge, we acquired 1,582 more images (histology or expert confirmed studies) from the ISIC archive [1] to build up our available database. In total, we got 3,582 labelled images (2,733 benign and 849 malignant) as our training data pool. We directly utilized the validation set (150 images) and test set (600 images) of the ISIC challenge.

**Implementations.** The luminance and color balance of input images are normalized exploiting color constancy by gray world. Images are resized to 224 × 224 to match input size of pre-trained ResNet-101 model. The images are augmented with rotating by up to 90°, shearing by up to 20°, scaling within [0.8, 1.2], and random flipping horizontally and/or vertically. We use weighted cross-entropy loss with Adam optimizer and initial learning rate as 1e−4. Code will be released.

**Evaluation Metrics.** For quantitative comparisons, our evaluations followed the challenge given metrics, which consist of accuracy (ACC), area under ROC curve (AUC), average precision (AP), sensitivity (SE) and specificity (SP).

**Table 1.** Quantitative evaluations of our proposed active learning framework for skin lesion analysis on two different classification tasks.

| Methods | | Data amount | Extra label | Task 1 | | | | | Task 2 | | | | |
|---|---|---|---|---|---|---|---|---|---|---|---|---|---|
| | | | | ACC | AUC | AP | SE | SP | ACC | AUC | AP | SE | SP |
| Leaderboard | Monty [2] | 100% | ✓ | 0.823 | 0.856 | 0.654 | 0.103 | **0.998** | 0.875 | **0.965** | **0.839** | 0.178 | **0.998** |
| | Popleyi [5] | 100% | x | 0.858 | **0.870** | **0.694** | 0.427 | 0.963 | **0.918** | 0.921 | 0.770 | 0.589 | 0.976 |
| | Full-data (ResNet-101) | 100% | x | **0.863** | 0.821 | 0.590 | **0.496** | 0.952 | 0.903 | 0.941 | 0.773 | **0.856** | 0.912 |
| Selection | Random (Rand) | 50%/40% | x | 0.825 | 0.795 | 0.520 | 0.359 | 0.934 | 0.878 | 0.923 | 0.731 | 0.722 | 0.906 |
| | AIFT [13] | 50%/40% | x | 0.810 | 0.754 | 0.447 | **0.385** | 0.913 | 0.885 | 0.907 | 0.677 | 0.711 | **0.916** |
| | SA (Ours) | 50%/40% | x | **0.847** | **0.800** | **0.575** | 0.368 | **0.963** | 0.903 | **0.938** | 0.784 | 0.844 | 0.914 |
| Aggregation | SA (Ours)+ Mix-up [10] | 50%/40% | x | 0.467 | 0.572 | 0.273 | **0.615** | 0.431 | 0.720 | 0.638 | 0.361 | 0.124 | 0.824 |
| | SA+AS (**Ours**) | 50%/40% | x | **0.860** | **0.831** | **0.600** | 0.479 | **0.952** | **0.908** | **0.934** | **0.755** | **0.756** | **0.935** |

## 3.1 Results of Cost-Effective Skin Lesion Analysis

In our active learning process, based on the initially randomly selected 10% data, we iteratively added training samples until obtaining predictions which cannot be significantly improved ($p > 0.05$) over the accuracy of last round. It turns out that we only need 50% of the data for Task-1 and 40% of the data for Task-2.

The overall performance for Task-1 and Task-2 are representatively presented in Figs. 3(a) and 4(a). In Fig. 3(a), we present the baseline of active learning which is random sample selection (purple). By using our proposed dual-criteria sample selection (green), the accuracy gradually increases and keeps higher than the baseline through different query ratios. Further using our aggregative supervision (red), the accuracy achieves 86.0% when using only 50% samples, which is very close to the accuracy of 86.3% with full-data training (yellow). In Fig. 4(a), by actively querying worth-labelling images, our proposed method can finally exceed the performance of full-data training only using 40% samples. In addition, when comparing with the state-of-the-art method of AIFT (blue) [13], our proposed method can outperform it consistently across all sample query ratios on both tasks. This validates that our deriving dual-criteria in a decoupled way is better than only relying on currently learned network.

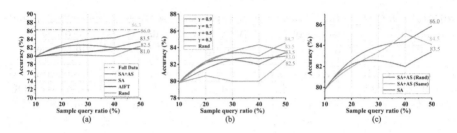

**Fig. 3.** Experimental results of our proposed active learning framework on Task 1. (a) Overall accuracy of different methods at sample query ratios. (b) Ablation study of SA, by adjusting $\gamma$. (c) Ablation study of AS, by changing the choice of stitched images. (Color figure online)

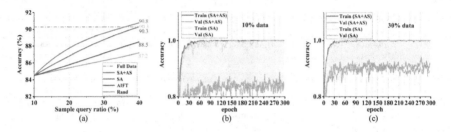

**Fig. 4.** Experimental results of our proposed active learning framework on Task 2. (a) Overall accuracy of different methods at sample query ratios. (b)–(c) Observation of narrowing generalization gap and alleviating over-fitting by our active learning method. (Color figure online)

In Table 1, we categorize the different comparison methods into three groups, i.e., the leading methods in challenge, active learning only with sample selection strategy, and further adding the sample augmentation strategy. The amount of employed annotated data is indicated in *data amount* column. For leaderboard, only rank-2 [2] and rank-4 [5] methods are included, as rank-1 method used non-image information (e.g., sex and age) and rank-3 method used much more extra data besides the ISIC archive ones. Nevertheless, we present the challenge results for demonstrating the state-of-the-art performance of this dataset. We focus on active learning part, with our implemented full-data training as standard bound. From the Table 1, we see that our SA can outperform AIFT [13], and AS can outperform mix-up [10], across almost all evaluation metrics on both tasks. Overall, our proposed method achieves highly competitive results against full-data training and challenge leaderboard, with significantly cost-effective labellings.

## 3.2    Analysis of Components in Active Learning Framework

Firstly, we investigate the impact of hyper-parameter setting in sample selection. We adjust the ratio between $\mathcal{S}_I$ and $\mathcal{S}_R$ by changing the $\gamma$, as shown in Fig. 3(b). Varying the ratio $\gamma$ would bring fluctuation on performance, but even the worst case is much better than random selection. We choose to use $\gamma = 0.7$ as the basis AS process, since it reflects the average-level performance of the SA step.

Secondly, we investigate the practically effective manner to stitch the intra-class samples. As shown in Fig. 3(c), we compare stitching four randomly selected intra-class images and replicating the same image by four times. For aggregative supervision, stitching different intra-class images can outperform replicating the same image, which exactly reflects that our designed augmentation strategy can help to improve performance by suppressing intra-class variance and sample ambiguity.

Finally, the results in Fig. 4(b) and (c) show that our proposed augmentation strategy can alleviate overfitting during model training. The shadow area indicates the generalization gap between the training and validation sets. It unsurprisingly decreases with increasing the data amount from 10% to 30%. With more careful observation, we find that the SA+AS can generally surpass pure SA on validation set, which demonstrates the effectiveness of alleviating over-fitting using our augmented new-style samples.

## 4 Conclusion

This paper presents a novel active learning method for annotation cost-effective skin lesion analysis. We propose a dual-criteria to select samples, and an intra-class sample aggregation scheme to enhance the model. Experimental results demonstrate that using only up to 50% of the labelled samples, we can achieve the state-of-the-art performance on two different skin lesion analysis tasks.

**Acknowledgments.** The work described in this paper was supported by the 973 Program with Project No. 2015CB351706, the National Natural Science Foundation of China with Project No. U1613219 and the Hong Kong Innovation and Technology Commission through the ITF ITSP Tier 2 Platform Scheme under Project ITS/426/17FP.

## References

1. Codella, N.C., et al.: Skin lesion analysis toward melanoma detection: a challenge at the 2017 international symposium on biomedical imaging (ISBI), hosted by the international skin imaging collaboration (ISIC). In: ISBI, pp. 168–172 (2018)
2. Diaz, I.G.: DermaKNet: incorporating the knowledge of dermatologists to convolutional neural networks for skin lesion diagnosis. IEEE J. Biomed. Health Inf. **23**, 547–559 (2018)
3. Esteva, A., et al.: Dermatologist-level classification of skin cancer with deep neural networks. Nature **542**(7639), 115 (2017)
4. Huang, S.J., Jin, R., Zhou, Z.H.: Active learning by querying informative and representative examples. In: NIPS, pp. 892–900 (2010)
5. Lei, B., Jinman, K., Euijoon, A., Dagan, F.: Automatic skin lesion analysis using large-scale dermoscopy image and deep residual networks. arXiv:1703.04197 (2017)

6. Mahapatra, D., Bozorgtabar, B., Thiran, J.-P., Reyes, M.: Efficient active learning for image classification and segmentation using a sample selection and conditional generative adversarial network. In: Frangi, A.F., Schnabel, J.A., Davatzikos, C., Alberola-López, C., Fichtinger, G. (eds.) MICCAI 2018. LNCS, vol. 11071, pp. 580–588. Springer, Cham (2018). https://doi.org/10.1007/978-3-030-00934-2_65

7. Settles, B.: Active learning literature survey. Computer Sciences Technical Report 1648, University of Wisconsin-Madison (2009)

8. Xue, C., Dou, Q., Shi, X., Chen, H., Heng, P.A.: Robust learning at noisy labeled medical images: applied to skin lesion classification. ISBI (2019)

9. Yang, L., Zhang, Y., Chen, J., Zhang, S., Chen, D.Z.: Suggestive annotation: a deep active learning framework for biomedical image segmentation. In: Descoteaux, M., Maier-Hein, L., Franz, A., Jannin, P., Collins, D.L., Duchesne, S. (eds.) MICCAI 2017. LNCS, vol. 10435, pp. 399–407. Springer, Cham (2017). https://doi.org/10.1007/978-3-319-66179-7_46

10. Zhang, H., Cisse, M., Dauphin, Y.N., Lopez-Paz, D.: mixup: beyond empirical risk minimization. In: ICLR (2017)

11. Zhang, J., Xie, Y., Wu, Q., Xia, Y.: Skin lesion classification in dermoscopy images using synergic deep learning. In: Frangi, A.F., Schnabel, J.A., Davatzikos, C., Alberola-López, C., Fichtinger, G. (eds.) MICCAI 2018. LNCS, vol. 11071, pp. 12–20. Springer, Cham (2018). https://doi.org/10.1007/978-3-030-00934-2_2

12. Zheng, H., et al.: Biomedical image segmentation via representative annotation. In: AAAI (2019)

13. Zhou, Z., Shin, J.Y., Zhang, L., Gurudu, S.R., Gotway, M.B., Liang, J.: Fine-tuning convolutional neural networks for biomedical image analysis: Actively and incrementally. In: CVPR, pp. 4761–4772 (2017)

# Tree-LSTM: Using LSTM to Encode Memory in Anatomical Tree Prediction from 3D Images

Mengliu Zhao$^{(\boxtimes)}$ (iD) and Ghassan Hamarneh (iD)

Medical Image Analysis Lab, School of Computing Science,
Simon Fraser University, Burnaby, Canada
{mengliuz,hamarneh}@sfu.ca

**Abstract.** Extraction and analysis of anatomical trees, such as vasculatures and airways, is important for many clinical applications. However, most tracking methods so far intrinsically embedded a first-order Markovian property, where no memory beyond one tracking step was utilized in the tree extraction process. Motivated by the inherent sequential construction of anatomical trees, vis-à-vis the flow of nutrients through branches and bifurcations, we propose Tree-LSTM, the first LSTM neural network to learn to encode such sequential priors into a deep learning based tree extraction method. We also show that mathematically, by using LSTM, the variational lower bound of a higher order Markovian stochastic process could be approximated, which enables the encoding of a long term memory. Our experiments on a CT airway dataset show that, by adding the LSTM component, the results are improved by at least 11% in mean direction prediction accuracy relative to state-of-the-art, and the correlation between bifurcation classification accuracy and evidence is improved by at least 15%, which demonstrate the advantage of a unified deep model for sequential tree structure tracking and bifurcation detection.

## 1 Introduction

Vascular and airway trees, i.e., anatomical trees, of circulatory and respiratory systems are extremely important clinically as they are related to fatal diseases like ischaemic heart disease, stroke, chronic obstructive pulmonary disease, and lower respiratory infection, which were identified as the top four causes of death globally, according to a report from World Health Organization in 2018 [16]. In the field of medical image analysis, anatomical tree extraction from 3D medical imaging data is a crucial task, as accurate extraction of anatomical trees could be further utilized in tasks such as surgery planning [12], early diabetic diagnosis [6], and tumor type classification [2].

Most tree extraction approaches fall into one of the following categories [8,22]: (a) active contour/surface methods (or deformable energy minimizing models), which expand, commonly via a variational framework, a curve or surface to fit the

© Springer Nature Switzerland AG 2019
H.-I. Suk et al. (Eds.): MLMI 2019, LNCS 11861, pp. 637–645, 2019.
https://doi.org/10.1007/978-3-030-32692-0_73

desired vessel/airway boundaries; (b) tracking methods (described below); (c) minimal path approaches, which determine the path of a vessel/airway branch as the route with minimal energy between given points at both ends of the branch; (d) graph based methods, which represent the anatomical tree as a tree graph and model the tree extraction as a combinatorial optimization problem; (e) machine learning and deep learning methods that learn various aspects of the tree extraction process (e.g., bifurcation detection) from training data; and (f) other hybrid methods.

The tracking methods cover a large portion of the tree extraction literature. At a high level, this class of approaches involves starting from one or multiple seed points, followed by iteratively detecting tracking directions, and identifying new candidate branch points (usually along the branch centerline), until the whole tree is tracked. Cetin et al. [3] proposed to use a tensor based direction prediction technique for coronary vessel tracking with a "shape prior" encoding the tube-like geometry of branches. Wang et al. [15] proposed to use Bayesian estimation in the tracking process and the vessel likelihood was estimated iteratively using gradient flux on the cross sectional plane. Lesage et al. [9] proposed to use particle filtering, which adopted the sequential importance sampling technique to sample candidate particles in a recursive way. Lee et al. [7] also proposed to use particle filtering for vessel tracking, only that they leveraged a Chan-Vese model at each prediction. There have also been a rising number of works encoding machine/deep learning techniques [17,20,21] in the tree tracking process.

Examining most tracking methods from the stochastic modelling perspective, we note that they share a common underlying first-order Markovian model assumption, which means the current prediction is only directly affected by the last tracking step (commonly the image features therein), ignoring direct relations with previous points along the tracked trajectory [3,7,9,15,17,20,21]. Even though a perfect Monte-Carlo estimation in the particle filtering approaches is supposed to involve all previous particles for importance sampling, however, in most particle updating scheme implementations [7,9], a first-order Markovian assumption is usually adopted to reduce complexity. Very limited works have tried to encode higher-order Markovian models or global information into the tracking process. Zhao et al. [22] proposed adopting a Bayesian inference formulation to encode branch-wise statistics (tree topology, branch length, and angle geometrical priors), however, in the form of a prior term instead of the interaction among previous predictions.

Deep learning architectures have been explored extensively in recent years in the field of computer vision and medical image analysis in general, and to a lesser degree for anatomical tree extraction. The work of Wu et al. [18] used an AlexNet classifier with PCA and nearest neighbor search to classify whether the current point in a 2D retinal image is a bifurcation. Charbonnier et al. [4] proposed to combine the results of three ConvNets on orthogonal planes to detect leaks in airway segmentation. Wolterink et al. [17] used a seven-layer dilated convolutional neural network (DCNN) to predict coronary vessel directions in 3D patches. Zhao et al. [21] proposed to use a modified V-net [10] for airway direction prediction, by using a custom multi-loss function. Selvan et al. [13] proposed to use a K-nearest neighbour voxel-wise classifier for airway segmentation, then a 10-layer mean field network was used later for tree graph refinement.

Although long short-term memory (LSTM) architectures have been applied to computer vision and medical image analysis problems to perform inference on sequential data by exploiting temporal information in 2D+time and 3D+time data [5,14], no prior work has been done using LSTM for vasculature and airway structure prediction. To the best of our knowledge, the only work that adopted LSTM for anatomical tree analysis is the work of Wu et al. [19], in which they labelled an already segmented abstract representation of a coronary vessel tree using a bidirectional LSTM per branch, whereas the focus of our work is to segment or extract trees form a 3D images.

In this work, we argue that the tree tracking process goes beyond a first-order Markovian and leverage the global information along the pseudo-temporal (sequence) dimension in combination with the proven capabilities of deep networks to automatically learn appearance features. To this end, we propose Tree-LSTM, the first neural network LSTM architecture to learn to encode such sequential priors into a deep learning tree extraction method. Our proposed method is the first work in the field of anatomical tree analysis where: (a) a formal derivation of the higher-order Markovian process is given; (b) an LSTM-equipped convolutional neural network (CNN) is used for approximating the higher-order Markovian process; (c) a novel evaluation method is proposed for inspecting the correlation between bifurcation classification accuracy and sequential image evidence collected along branches. By using the proposed architecture, we show that the bifurcation and direction prediction accuracy could be improved by a large margin.

## 2   Methodology

### 2.1   Problem Definition

Tree tracking is predominantly formulated as a centerline tracking problem, wherein the vessel/airway direction and bifurcation existence at each tracked point is inferred, and used to estimate the next candidate centerline point, and child branches are spawned whenever a bifurcation point is encountered. Specifically, we focus on the inference problem of each tracking step.

Let $C_t$ be a random variable whose value, e.g., branch direction or bifurcation presence, needs to be estimated at the branch centerline point of step $t$. A realization of $C_t$ is denoted $C_t^*$, and $I_t$ be the corresponding image feature learnt from a sequence of image patches. Then the Maximum A Posteriori formulation for estimating $C_t$ is given by:

$$C_t^* = \arg\max_{C_t} P(C_t|C_{t-1}, C_{t-2}, ..., C_1, I_t, I_{t-1}, ..., I_1). \tag{1}$$

In the following, we show that although the maximization of this posterior probability can be intractable (Sect. 2.2), we are able to maximize its variational lower bound instead (Sect. 2.3), a common and effective trick utilized in variational inference [1]. We find the solution to this lower bound problem using LSTM (Sect. 2.4).

## 2.2 Central Theorem

First we prove Lemma 1 and Theorem 1, which essentially state that the optimization in (1) could be reformulated as a simpler optimization (that of the right hand side of (4)).

**Lemma 1.** *If $X$ and $Y$ are conditionally independent variables given $Z$, $P(X)$, $P(Y)$, $P(Z)$ and $P(X,Y)$ are prior probabilities, and $P(Z)$ is constant, then*

$$P(Z|X,Y) \propto P(Z|X)P(Z|Y). \tag{2}$$

*Proof.* By using Bayes' theorem and the definition of conditional independence,

$$P(Z|X,Y) = \frac{P(X,Y|Z) \cdot P(Z)}{P(X,Y)} \propto P(X,Y|Z) = P(X|Z) \cdot P(Y|Z)$$

$$= \frac{P(Z|X) \cdot P(X)}{P(Z)} \cdot \frac{P(Z|Y) \cdot P(Y)}{P(Z)} \propto P(Z|X) \cdot P(Z|Y). \tag{3}$$

$\square$

Please note the proof in (3) does have a strong assumption that $P(Z)$ is constant. However this assumption is intrinsically true in our application, as we use $P(Z)$ to predict the existence of bifurcation or branch direction, modelled by a uniform distribution in the absence of prior knowledge.

Defining $\mathbb{I}_t = \{I_t, I_{t-1}, ..., I_1\}$ and $\mathbb{C}_t = \{C_t, C_{t-1}, ..., C_1\}$, and replacing $X, Y, Z$ with $I_t$, $(\mathbb{I}_{t-1}, \mathbb{C}_{t-1})$, $C_t$, respectively, we attain Theorem 1.

**Theorem 1.** *If $I_t$, $\mathbb{I}_{t-1}$ and $\mathbb{C}_{t-1}$ are conditionally independent given $C_t$, then*

$$P(C_t|I_t, \mathbb{I}_{t-1}, \mathbb{C}_{t-1}) \propto P(C_t|I_t) \cdot P(C_t|\mathbb{I}_{t-1}, \mathbb{C}_{t-1}), \tag{4}$$

i.e, the inference of candidate $C_t$ could be separated into inference from image features at time step $t$ and the inference from all previous states and their respective image features. Since our goal is to find a feasible algorithm to approximate (1), we must approximate $P(C_t|\mathbb{I}_{t-1}, \mathbb{C}_{t-1})$ instead. This could be achieved by calculating its variational lower bound (ELBO) using Jensen's inequality.

## 2.3 ELBO Calculation

We first introduce hidden variables $\mathbb{H}_t = \{h_t, h_{t-1}, ..., h_1\}$ to encode nonobservable variables (i.e., beyond $\mathbb{I}$ and $\mathbb{C}$ of the tracking process). We denote the prior distribution of $\mathbb{H}_{t-1}$ by $q$. Then, since the logarithm function is concave, by Jensen's inequality, $\mathbb{E}(\log(X)) \leq \log(\mathbb{E}(X))$, which we use to arrive at (rewriting $\mathbb{I}_{t-1}, \mathbb{C}_{t-1}$ as $\Theta$ for readability):

$$\log P(C_t|\Theta) = \log \int_{\mathbb{H}_{t-1}} P(C_t, \mathbb{H}_{t-1}|\Theta) = \log \int_{\mathbb{H}_{t-1}} P(C_t, \mathbb{H}_{t-1}|\Theta)\frac{q(\mathbb{H}_{t-1})}{q(\mathbb{H}_{t-1})}$$

$$= \log\left(\mathbb{E}_q\left[\frac{P(C_t, \mathbb{H}_{t-1}|\Theta)}{q(\mathbb{H}_{t-1})}\right]\right) \geq \mathbb{E}_q\left[\log\left(\frac{P(C_t, \mathbb{H}_{t-1}|\Theta)}{q(\mathbb{H}_{t-1})}\right)\right] = \mathcal{LB}. \quad (5)$$

Since $\mathbb{E}_q[\log P(C_t, \mathbb{H}_{t-1}|\Theta)] = \mathbb{E}_q[\log(P(C_t|\mathbb{H}_{t-1}, \Theta) \cdot P(\mathbb{H}_{t-1}|\Theta))]$ and $\log(x/y) = \log x - \log y$, the variational lower bound $\mathcal{LB}$ of (1) can be further simplified to:

$$\mathcal{LB} = \mathbb{E}_q[\log(P(C_t|\mathbb{H}_{t-1}, \Theta))] + \mathbb{Q}(\mathbb{H}_{t-1}, \Theta), \quad (6)$$

where $\mathbb{Q}(\mathbb{H}_{t-1}, \Theta) = \mathbb{E}_q[\log(P(\mathbb{H}_{t-1}|\Theta))] - \mathbb{E}_q[\log(q(\mathbb{H}_{t-1}))]$.

### 2.4 Adopting LSTM

Given their ability to encode sequential data, we adopt LSTM to learn the sequential information within the tracking process. Unlike the memoryless Markovian assumptions, the adoption of the LSTM network naturally encodes all information from previous steps in $h_{t-1}$, which approximates corresponding terms in (4) and (6) as $P(C_t|I_t) \approx P(C_t|I_t, h_{t-1})$ and $P(C_t|\mathbb{H}_{t-1}, \Theta) \approx P(h_{t-1}|\mathbb{H}_{t-1}, \Theta)$. See the proposed architecture in Fig. 1.

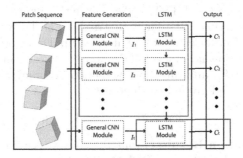

**Fig. 1.** (color figure) Schematic representation of Tree-LSTM. Left column: A sequence of patches from an image. Green box: predicts $P(h_{t-1}|\mathbb{H}_{t-1}, \Theta)$. Red box: predicts $P(C_t|I_t, h_{t-1})$. Right column: final output. (Color figure online)

### 2.5 Implementation Details

We use two CNN implementations, TreeNet [21] and DCNN [17], to extract features $I_t$, which are then fed into the LSTM cell of Sak et al. [11]. We use two fully connected layers (with 1024 and 64 nodes respectively) before the output layer of the network and use the 1024-dim vector as $I_t$. The CNN model is first trained then kept fixed during LSTM training. For the LSTM network, a hidden state vector length of 32 is used with a sequence length $L = 10$. Our model uses a separate LSTM for each task as $C_t$ encodes either the presence of bifurcation ($\mathcal{L}_{\text{CLASS}}$) or the tracking direction ($\mathcal{L}_{\text{DIR}}$), with corresponding losses:

$$\mathcal{L}_{\text{CLASS}} = \sum_{t=1}^{L} |c_t - c_t^g| \qquad \mathcal{L}_{\text{DIR}} = -\sum_{t=1}^{L} \langle \vec{v}_t, \vec{v}_t^g \rangle, \qquad (7)$$

where $c$ is the predicted class ($c = 0$ for single branch, $c = 1$ for bifurcations) and $\vec{v}$ is the predicted direction(s) (1 direction predicted for $c = 1$ and 3 directions predicted for $c = 2$). Superscript $g$ implies ground truth values. We use stochastic gradient descent for optimization with momentum 0.999, exponential decay ratio 0.6, and initial learning rate $1e^{-8}$ for direction prediction and $1e^{-5}$ for bifurcation classification. The implementation is based on TensorFlow v1.12 on Nvidia GTX 1080Ti GPUs.

## 3 Experiments

**Datasets.** We use the EXACT[1] challenge public training dataset with 4-fold cross validation. Three major airway branches – trachea, left main bronchi (LMB) and right main bronchi (RMB) are extracted for evaluation.

**Competing Methods.** For evaluation, we use three state-of-the-art works: Zhao et al. [20] (RF); TreeNet [21]; and DCNN [17] (the last layers of TreeNet and DCNN are modified for classification and regression purposes). To isolate the benefit of adding LSTM, we evaluate the two CNN-based methods, TreeNet and DCNN, without and with LSTM. We change the input patch size to 32 and use the same loss function ([21]) for both TreeNet and DCNN, and remove the middle layer of TreeNet for computational speed up. For evaluation, we measure bifurcation classification accuracy ($\mathcal{ACC}_{CLASS}$) between output class ($c$) and ground truth class ($c^g$), and direction prediction accuracy ($\mathcal{ACC}_{DIR}$) between output direction ($\vec{v}$) and ground truth class ($\vec{v}^g$):

$$\mathcal{ACC}_{\text{CLASS}} = 1 - |c_t - c_t^g| \qquad \mathcal{ACC}_{\text{DIR}} = \langle \vec{v}_t, \vec{v}_t^g \rangle. \qquad (8)$$

**Prediction Evaluation Results.** From Table 1a, we see that TreeNet+LSTM outperforms TreeNet by 21%, and DCNN+LSTM outperforms DCNN by 17%. RF performs better than TreeNet and DCNN alone on almost all cases, and performs no worse than TreeNet+LSTM on the trachea. This is not surprising as RF was designed for the purpose of bifurcation classification whereas TreeNet and DCNN were both designed for direction prediction. From Table 1b, adding LSTM, boosted TreeNet's performance by 11% and DCNN by 18%, on average.

**Assessing LSTM's Ability to Leverage Sequential Data.** In Sect. 2, we hypothesized that LSTM is applicable to higher-order Markovian inference due

---

[1] http://image.diku.dk/exact/.

**Table 1.** Detection accuracy. [†]Not applicable as RF does not predict direction.

| Branch | Trachea | LMB | RMB |
|---|---|---|---|
| RF [20] | 0.74 (±0.49) | 0.67 (±0.45) | 0.61 (±0.45) |
| TreeNet [21] | 0.35 (±0.49) | 0.54 (±0.50) | 0.57 (±0.50) |
| TreeNet+LSTM | 0.61 (±0.39) | 0.74 (±0.44) | 0.75 (±0.44) |
| DCNN [17] | 0.74 (±0.46) | 0.61 (±0.50) | 0.45 (±0.50) |
| DCNN+LSTM | 0.80 (±0.41) | 0.78 (±0.43) | 0.72 (±0.45) |

| Branch | Trachea | LMB | RMB |
|---|---|---|---|
| RF [20] | n/a[†] | n/a[†] | n/a[†] |
| TreeNet | 0.71 (±0.12) | 0.79 (±0.11) | 0.80 (±0.08) |
| TreeNet+LSTM | 0.82 (±0.12) | 0.92 (±0.06) | 0.90 (±0.05) |
| DCNN [17] | 0.76 (±0.15) | 0.57 (±0.21) | 0.84 (±0.13) |
| DCNN+LSTM | 0.87 (±0.12) | 0.93 (±0.05) | 0.92 (±0.07) |

(a) Bifurcation classification accuracy (mean± std)

(b) Direction prediction accuracy (mean± std)

to $P(C_t|\mathbb{H}_{t-1}, \mathbb{I}_{t-1}, \mathbb{C}_{t-1}] \approx P(C_t|h_{t-1}, I_t)$, which suggests the model directly learns information from $\mathbb{H}_{t-1}$ as a whole. To this end, we wish to validate that Tree-LSTM prediction accuracy improves with increased evidence along an $L$-long sequence of patches. So, we define an evidence support measure within the sequence as $\mathcal{B} = \sum_{i=1}^{L} \beta_i$ where $\beta_i = 1$ indicates the presence of a bifurcation in the ground truth data and 0 otherwise. Now, we bin our data based on $\mathcal{B} \in \{1, 2, \cdots, 10\}$ and measure, for every evidence bin, the average bifurcation classification accuracy at the last or $10^{th}$ patch, i.e. $P(C_{10}|\mathbb{H}_9, \mathbb{I}_9, \mathbb{C}_9)$. Table 2 records the correlation values between average bifurcation classification accuracy and evidence, which clearly shows how adding LSTM improves the correlation substantially between ∼15% and 67%. Intuitively speaking, an increased correlation value $\rho$ means, by seeing more evidence in the sequence (e.g., bifurcations found in $\mathbb{C}_9$), the accuracy predicting $C_{10}$ would be increased, which is consistent with our initial assumption in (1).

**Table 2.** Correlation values $\rho$ between average classification accuracy and degree of evidence for different branches. The percentage improvement in $\rho$ when using LSTM (with TreeNet and DCNN) is also reported (calculated as $(\rho_{LSTM} - \rho_{no})/2$, denominator 2 is the max possible change in $\rho$).

| Branch | Trachea | | | | LMB | | | | RMB | | | |
|---|---|---|---|---|---|---|---|---|---|---|---|---|
| Method | TreeNet | | DCNN | | TreeNet | | DCNN | | TreeNet | | DCNN | |
| with LSTM? | No | Yes | No | Yes | No | Yes | No | Yes | No | Yes | No | Yes |
| $\rho$ | 0.09 | 0.61 | 0.12 | 0.91 | 0.50 | 0.81 | 0.10 | 0.67 | −0.26 | 0.87 | −0.52 | 0.83 |
| Improvement | 25.74% | | 39.54% | | 15.98% | | 28.25% | | 56.62% | | 67.24% | |

## 4   Conclusion

To utilize predictions of all previous points along a tracked vessel/airway center-line, we extended the commonly adopted first-order tree branch tracking assumption to a higher-order Markovian process. We estimated the Bayesian variational lower bound of the proposed formulation and used the CNN+LSTM architecture to optimize tracking. We showed the advantage of using LSTM in tracking real clinical data where the proposed method outperformed the state-of-the-art by at least 11%. The improvement in correlation values between bifurcation classification accuracy and amount of branch sequence evidence is improved by at least 15%.

**Acknowledgments.** Partial funding for this project is provided by the Natural Sciences and Engineering Research Council of Canada (NSERC). The authors are grateful to the NVIDIA Corporation for donating a Titan X GPU used in this research.

# References

1. Blei, D.M., et al.: Variational inference: a review for statisticians. J. Am. Stat. Assoc. **112**(518), 859–877 (2017)
2. Caresio, C., et al.: Quantitative analysis of thyroid tumors vascularity: a comparison between 3-D contrast-enhanced ultrasound and 3-D power doppler on benign and malignant thyroid nodules. Med. Phys. **45**(7), 3173–3184 (2018)
3. Cetin, S., et al.: Vessel tractography using an intensity based tensor model with branch detection. TMI **32**(2), 348–363 (2013)
4. Charbonnier, J.P., et al.: Improving airway segmentation in computed tomography using leak detection with convolutional networks. MedIA **36**, 52–60 (2017)
5. Chen, H., et al.: Automatic fetal ultrasound standard plane detection using knowledge transferred recurrent neural networks. In: Navab, N., Hornegger, J., Wells, W.M., Frangi, A.F. (eds.) MICCAI 2015, Part I. LNCS, vol. 9349, pp. 507–514. Springer, Cham (2015). https://doi.org/10.1007/978-3-319-24553-9_62
6. Eladawi, N., et al.: Early diabetic retinopathy diagnosis based on local retinal blood vessels analysis in optical coherence tomography angiography (OCTA) images. Med. Phys. **45**(10), 4582–4599 (2018)
7. Lee, S., et al.: Enhanced particle-filtering framework for vessel segmentation and tracking. CMPB **148**, 99–112 (2017)
8. Lesage, D., et al.: A review of 3D vessel lumen segmentation techniques: models, features and extraction schemes. MedIA **13**(6), 819–845 (2009)
9. Lesage, D., et al.: Adaptive particle filtering for coronary artery segmentation from 3D CT angiograms. CVIU **151**, 29–46 (2016)
10. Milletari, F., et al.: V-Net: fully convolutional neural networks for volumetric medical image segmentation. In: International Conference on 3D Vision, pp. 565–571 (2016)
11. Sak, H., et al.: Long short-term memory recurrent neural network architectures for large scale acoustic modeling. In: International Speech Communication Association (2014)
12. Selle, D., et al.: Analysis of vasculature for liver surgical planning. TMI **21**(11), 1344–1357 (2002)
13. Selvan, R., Welling, M., Pedersen, J.H., Petersen, J., de Bruijne, M.: Mean field network based graph refinement with application to airway tree extraction. In: Frangi, A.F., Schnabel, J.A., Davatzikos, C., Alberola-López, C., Fichtinger, G. (eds.) MICCAI 2018, Part II. LNCS, vol. 11071, pp. 750–758. Springer, Cham (2018). https://doi.org/10.1007/978-3-030-00934-2_83

14. Stollenga, M.F., et al.: Parallel multi-dimensional LSTM, with application to fast biomedical volumetric image segmentation. In: NeurIPS, pp. 2998–3006 (2015)
15. Wang, X., et al.: Statistical tracking of tree-like tubular structures with efficient branching detection in 3D medical image data. Phys. Med. Biol. **57**(16), 5325 (2012)
16. WHO: Global health estimates 2016: deaths by cause, age, sex, by country and by region, 2000–2016. World Health Organization, Geneva (2018)
17. Wolterink, J.M., et al.: Coronary artery centerline extraction in cardiac CT angiography using a CNN-based orientation classifier. MIA **51**, 46–60 (2019)
18. Wu, A., et al.: Deep vessel tracking: a generalized probabilistic approach via deep learning. In: ISBI, pp. 1363–1367 (2016)
19. Wu, D., et al.: Automated anatomical labeling of coronary arteries via bidirectional tree LSTMs. IJCARS **14**(2), 271–280 (2019)
20. Zhao, M., Hamarneh, G.: Bifurcation detection in 3D vascular images using novel features and random forest. In: ISBI, pp. 421–424 (2014)
21. Zhao, M., Hamarneh, G.: TreeNet: multi-loss deep learning network to predict branch direction for extracting 3D anatomical trees. In: Stoyanov, D., et al. (eds.) DLMIA 2018/ML-CDS 2018. LNCS, vol. 11045, pp. 47–55. Springer, Cham (2018). https://doi.org/10.1007/978-3-030-00889-5_6
22. Zhao, M., et al.: Leveraging tree statistics for extracting anatomical trees from 3D medical images. In: Computer and Robot Vision, pp. 131–138 (2017)

# FAIM – A ConvNet Method for Unsupervised 3D Medical Image Registration

Dongyang Kuang[1,2]([✉]) [ID] and Tanya Schmah[2] [ID]

[1] University of Texas, Austin, TX, USA
dykuang@outlook.com
[2] University of Ottawa, Ottawa, Canada

**Abstract.** We present a new unsupervised learning algorithm, "FAIM", for 3D medical image registration. With a different architecture than the popular "U-net" [10], the network takes a pair of full image volumes and predicts the displacement fields needed to register source to target. Compared with "U-net" based registration networks such as VoxelMorph [2], FAIM has fewer trainable parameters but can achieve higher registration accuracy as judged by Dice score on region labels in the Mindboggle-101 dataset. Moreover, with the proposed penalty loss on negative Jacobian determinants, FAIM produces deformations with many fewer "foldings", i.e. regions of non-invertibility where the surface folds over itself. We varied the strength of this penalty and found that FAIM is able to maintain both the advantages of higher accuracy and fewer "folding" locations over VoxelMorph, over a range of hyper-parameters. We also evaluated Probabilistic VoxelMorph [3], both in its original form and with its U-net backbone replaced with our FAIM network. We found that the choice of backbone makes little difference. The original version of FAIM outperformed Probabilistic VoxelMorph for registration accuracy, and also for invertibility if FAIM is trained using an anti-folding penalty. Code for this paper is freely available at https://github.com/dykuang/Medical-image-registration.

**Keywords:** Image registration · Convolutional neural network · Unsupervised registration · Folding penalization

## 1 Introduction

Image registration is a key element of medical image analysis. The spatial deformations required to optimally register images are highly non-linear, especially for regions such as the cerebral cortex, the folding patterns of which can vary significantly between individuals. Most state-of-the-art registration algorithms, such as ANTs [1], use geometric or variational methods that are guaranteed to produce diffeomorphisms, i.e. smooth invertible deformations with a smooth inverse. These algorithms are very computationally intensive and still do not

© Springer Nature Switzerland AG 2019
H.-I. Suk et al. (Eds.): MLMI 2019, LNCS 11861, pp. 646–654, 2019.
https://doi.org/10.1007/978-3-030-32692-0_74

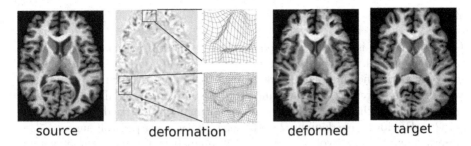

source          deformation          deformed          target

**Fig. 1.** An axial slice of a deformation produced by a CNN method: VoxelMorph-1, with its default $L_2$ regularization parameter $\lambda = 1$ on spatial gradients. The second image in the row shows values of the Jacobian determinant of the predicted deformation, with "folding" locations (negative determinant) marked in red. The deformed grids illustrate parts of the deformation. (Color figure online)

generally find optimal deformations. One general problem is that the optimization problems solved by these algorithms are highly nonconvex. Another is that they treat each pair of images to be registered *de novo*, without any learning.

A revolution is taking place in the last few years in the application of machine learning methods to medical image processing, including registration tasks. Supervised methods for registration, as in [9,12,15], learn from known reference deformations for training data – either actual "ground truth" in the case of synthetic image pairs, or deformations computed by other automatic or semiautomatic methods. Unsupervised methods, as in [2,8,11,14], do not require reference deformations, but instead minimize some cost function modeling the goodness of registration, optionally regularized by a term constraining the deformation. These methods have properties complementary to the standard geometric methods: they are very fast (at test time) and have the ability to learn automatically from data; however the predicted deformations are not guaranteed to be diffeomorphisms. In particular, there are often many regions where one image has been "folded" over itself by a non-invertible transformation. In these regions the Jacobian matrix of the deformation has negative determinant, as shown in Fig. 1. These spatial foldings are not physically possibly and thus constitute registration errors when used in clinical applications. The frequency of this kind of error has limited the adoption of neural network methods in medical image registration.

To address this problem, we propose a new unsupervised image registration algorithm, FAIM (for FAst IMage registration) with an explicit anti-folding regularization. Using the MindBoggle101 dataset [7], we compared FAIM's response on both registration accuracy and anti-folding performance with an U-net [10] based network VoxelMorph [2] and its recent probabilistic variation [3].

## 2  Methods

Our architecture is directly inspired by the spatial transformer network (STN) of Jaderberg et al. [5]. This kind of module is originally developed for 2D images and only affine and thin plate spline transformation were implemented. In some very recent research [2,11], this framework begins to appear in 3D medical image registration. All these works aim to find an optimal parametrized transformation $\phi : \Omega \rightarrow \mathbf{R}^3$, for image domain $\Omega \subset \mathbf{R}^3$, such that the warped volume $S \circ \phi^{-1}(x)$ from a moving/source volume $S(x)$ is well aligned to the fixed/target volume $T(x)$. In our network, we use displacement field $\mathbf{u}(x) : R^3 \rightarrow R^3$ to parametrize the deformation $\phi$ by $S \circ \phi^{-1}(x) = S(x + \mathbf{u}(x))$, which is learned through a spatial deformation module (SDM). That is, SDM will output a 3D vector field of displacements needed for registration defined at each voxel location of the source image. Figure 2 shows the flow chart when the network is in training and a closer look at the SDM.

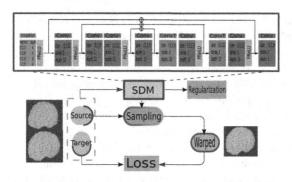

**Fig. 2.** FAIM network architecture.

During training, the pair of moving and target volume are stacked together as the input feeding into SDM. The first layer is inspired by Google's Inception module [13]. The purpose of this layer is trying to compare and capture information at different spatial scales for later registration. PReLU [4] activations are used at the end of each covolutional block except the last layer which uses linear activation to produce displacement fields. The sampling module first generates a deformed grid with the displacements and then use it to sample the source image by interpolation to produce the warped image. We used kernel stride > 1 to reduce the volume size instead of inserting max pooling layers. Transposed convolutional layers are used for upsampling. There are three "add" skip connections between the downsampling and upsampling path to help the gradient flow. Overall, FAIM has only about 70% as many trainable parameters as the U-net architecture used in the original work of VoxelMorph [2].

**Table 1.** Loss and regularization functions used.

$L_{total} = L_{image}(S,T) + \alpha R_1(\mathbf{u}) + \beta R_2(\mathbf{u})$

$L_{image}(S,T) = 1 - CC(S \circ \phi^{-1}, T)$

Regularization: $R_1(\mathbf{u}) = \|D\mathbf{u}\|_2$

Regularization: $R_2(\mathbf{u}) = 0.5 \left( |det(D\phi^{-1})| - det(D\phi^{-1}) \right)$

Losses used in training are all defined in Table 1. The term $L_{image}$ is based on cross correlation (CC) between warped source and target images. The term $R_1$ regularizes the overall smoothness of the predicted displacements. The second regularization term $R_2$ penalizes transformations that have many negative Jacobian determinants. Transformations that have all non-negative Jacobian determinants will not be penalized.

# 3   Experiments

## 3.1   Mindboggle101 Dataset

This dataset, created by Klein et al. [7], is based on a collection of 101 T1-weighted MRIs from healthy subjects. The Freesurfer package (http://www.martinos.org/freesurfer) was used to preprocess all images, and then automatically label the cortex using its DK cortical parcellation atlas. For 54 of the images, including the OASIS-TRT-20 subset, these automatic parcellations were manually edited to follow a custom labeling protocol, DKT. We use the variant DKT25, with 25 cortical regions per hemisphere. Details of data collection and processing, including atlas creation, are described in [7].

In the present paper, we used brain volumes from the following three named subsets of Mindboggle101, for a total of 62 volumes: NKI-RS-22, NKI-TRT-20 and OASIS-TRT-20. These images are already linearly aligned to MNI152 space. We normalized the intensity of each brain volume by its maximum voxel intensity. Each image has dimensions $182 \times 218 \times 182$, which we truncated to $144 \times 180 \times 144$. With this resolution, FAIM has 179,787 trainable parameters, which is about only 70% of VoxelMorph's 259,675 trainable parameters. The Probabilistic VoxelMorph under this setting results in trainable parameters of 266,347 compared with 172,055 when its backbone U-net is replaced by FAIM.

## 3.2   Evaluation Methods

We divide each dataset into sets of training and test sets. The training set consists of all ordered brain volume *pairs*[1] from the union of the NKI-RS-22 and NKI-TRT-20 subsets (1722 pairs in total), and the test set consists of all ordered *pairs* from the OASIS-TRT-20 subset (380 pairs in total). We train FAIM and VoxelMorph on all pairs of images from the training set, and then examine their predicted deformations with pairs of images from the test set. When not otherwise specified, both networks are trained on our training set with the same hyperparameters: Adam optimizer [6] with learning rate $= 10^{-4}$, epochs $=10$ and $\alpha = 1$.

We use predicted deformations to warp corresponding ROI labels from source to target per pair. Registration accuracy is primarily evaluated using the Dice score. It measures the degree of overlap between corresponding regions in the

---

[1] Their corresponding labels are not used in training.

parcellations associated with each image. The quality of the predicted deformations $\phi$ is assessed by the total number of locations where Jacobian determinant $\det\left(\nabla\phi^{-1}(x)\right)$ are negative, $\mathcal{N} := \sum \delta(det(D\phi^{-1}) < 0)$.

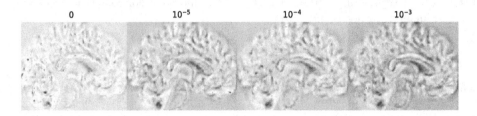

**Fig. 3.** Maps of the Jacobian determinant of the deformation predicted by FAIM, on one slice, for four values of the parameter $\beta$. Red indicates "folding" locations (negative determinant), while blue indicates a positive determinant. (Color figure online)

### 3.3 Results

Figure 3 visualizes the effect of the second regularization term $R_2(\mathbf{u})$ that penalizes "foldings" directly during training. When the regularization is not used, $\beta = 0$, there are multiple locations visible in the transformation whose Jacobian determinants are negative. The number is greatly reduced with $\beta = 10^{-5}$, and almost eliminated at higher $\beta$ values. Numerical results are given in Table 2.

We selected 5 scales of regularization strength $\beta$ from 0 to $10^{-2}$ and trained both FAIM and VoxelMorph under the same hyper-parameters. We summarize the mean Dice score across all predicted ROI labels with their corresponding target labels in the test set and mean $\mathcal{N}$ (i.e. $\overline{\mathcal{N}}$) of all predicted deformations in the test set in Table 2. Note that these Dice scores are all less than 0.54, which is relatively low compared to, for example, [3]. We believe this to be a result of using pairwise registration (instead of registration to an atlas) and using the DKT25 parcellation, with 50 ROIs, which is finer than used in [3]. For comparison, we evaluated ANTs SyN [1] with default parameters, in the same way on the same dataset and obtained the mean Dice score of 0.5139.

**Table 2.** Mean Dice scores and mean number of "folding" locations with different $\beta$ values. For comparison, the mean Dice score for ANTs SyN is 0.5139.

| Mean Dice | $\beta = 0$ | $10^{-5}$ | $10^{-4}$ | $10^{-3}$ | $10^{-2}$ |
|---|---|---|---|---|---|
| VoxelMorph | 0.5066 | 0.5024 | 0.4948 | 0.4791 | 0.4545 |
| FAIM | **0.5330** | **0.5267** | **0.5230** | **0.5126** | **0.4983** |
| Mean $\mathcal{N}$ | $\beta = 0$ | $10^{-5}$ | $10^{-4}$ | $10^{-3}$ | $10^{-2}$ |
| VoxelMorph | 49406 | **1129** | 221 | 77 | 13 |
| FAIM | 59115 | 1215 | **151** | **25** | **2** |

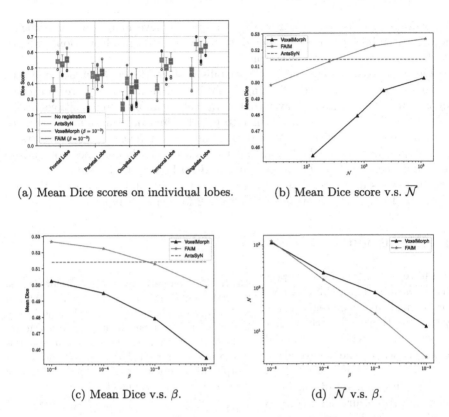

(a) Mean Dice scores on individual lobes.    (b) Mean Dice score v.s. $\overline{\mathcal{N}}$

(c) Mean Dice v.s. $\beta$.    (d) $\overline{\mathcal{N}}$ v.s. $\beta$.

**Fig. 4.** Mean Dice scores, and number of folding locations $\overline{\mathcal{N}}$, for VoxelMorph and FAIM, for different values of hyperparameter $\beta$. All Dice scores are calculated with respect to the DKT25 parcellation, which has 50 ROIs. In (a), these scores are averaged over each lobe individually. In (b) and (c), global mean Dice scores are shown, and the mean Dice score of ANTs SyN is plotted as a horizontal dashed line.

As shown in this table, FAIM has higher registration accuracy for all of the $\beta$ values considered, and also fewer "foldings" in the predicted deformations for $\beta \geq 10^{-4}$. More detailed comparisons are given in Fig. 4. Figure 4(c) suggests this advantage of FAIM in accuracy is consistent across different values of $\beta$, with a mean improvement of approximately 3%. To investigate how the networks balance the two competing tasks of high accuracy and low number of "folding" locations, we plotted mean Dice score against mean number of "folding" locations in Fig. 4(b). In this figure, the flatter curve from FAIM suggests the accuracy of it is more robust with respect to numbers of "folding" locations in its predictions when compared with VoxelMorph. In other words, the higher slope for VoxelMorph shows that to achieve the same gain in reducing number of "foldings", U-net based VoxelMorph has to sacrifice more in registration accuracy. Finally, we check the sensitivity of the control of $\beta$ over negative Jacobian determinants in Fig. 4(d) by visualizing $\overline{\mathcal{N}}$ against $\beta$. The sharper slope of FAIM in this log-log plot reveals that we will have more gain in reducing negative Jacobian determinant per unit increase of the regularization strength $\beta$ when compared with VoxelMorph.

Our final experiment concerns Probabilistic VoxelMorph [3], which does not use an explicit loss to control "foldings", but instead utilizes a "square and scale" algorithm in an integration layer that iteratively computes compositions of the velocity field produced from a U-net to get the final deformation. We replace the backbone U-net with FAIM and examine the differences in their results as summarized in Table 3. We found that the choice of backbone does not make a big difference: the U-net backbone wins in Mean Dice by 0.017, while the FAIM backbone wins in invertibility, with 1271 fewer mean folding locations. We also repeat in Table 3 selected values from Table 2 for better comparisons.

# 4   Discussion

We have developed an unsupervised learning algorithm, FAIM, for 3D medical image registration with an option to directly penalize "foldings", which are spatial locations where the deformation is non-invertible, indicated by a negative determinant of the Jacobian matrix. Our algorithm is similar to the U-net based registration network VoxelMorph of Balakrishnan et al. [2], however our architecture design and loss functions are different. Our anti-folding penalty is similar to (but different from) the penalty used by Zhang et al. [16]. We compared

**Table 3.** Comparison of four architectures: VoxelMorph; FAIM; Probabilistic VoxelMorph with U-net backbone; and Probabilistic Voxel-Morph with FAIM backbone. For VoxelMorph and FAIM, two values of the anti-folding parameter $\beta$ are contrasted. For Probabilistic Voxel-Morph, no anti-folding term in the loss function is used, which corresponds to $\beta = 0$.

| Architecture | Mean Dice | $\overline{\mathcal{N}}$ |
|---|---|---|
| VoxelMorph ($\beta = 0$) | 0.5066 | 49406 |
| VoxelMorph ($\beta = 10^{-2}$) | 0.4545 | 13 |
| FAIM ($\beta = 0$) | **0.5330** | 59115 |
| FAIM ($\beta = 10^{-2}$) | 0.4983 | **2** |
| Prob. VM (U-net) | 0.4740 | 8860 |
| Prov. VM (FAIM) | 0.4572 | 7589 |

FAIM experimentally to VoxelMorph using pairwise registration on the Mind-boggle101 dataset [7]. Our experiments showed that FAIM has advantages in several aspects including: fewer trainable parameters, higher mean registration accuracy (as measured by Dice score), and better invertibility (fewer "foldings"). In particular, in Table 2, FAIM with regularization parameter $\beta = 10^{-2}$ produces deformations that are almost completely invertible (foldings occurring at only 2 voxels per brain on average) while having registration accuracy that is better than VoxelMorph and almost as good as ANTs' SyN. Finally, we evaluated Probabilistic VoxelMorph [3] architectures with different backbones. We found that the choice of backbone makes little difference: using U-net results in a slightly higher mean Dice score, while FAIM results in slightly fewer folding locations and requires fewer trainable parameters.

In summary, we have shown that the FAIM architecture is a promising alternative to U-net in medical image registration, either as a standalone unsupervised registration network or as a component in a larger architecture. In addition, we have shown that, for FAIM, an anti-folding penalty in the training loss function is an effective way to enforce invertibility.

**Acknowledgements.** This work was supported in part by a Discovery Grant from NSERC Canada.

# References

1. Avants, B.B., Tustison, N.J., Song, G., Cook, P.A., Klein, A., Gee, J.C.: A reproducible evaluation of ants similarity metric performance in brain image registration. Neuroimage **54**(3), 2033–2044 (2011)
2. Balakrishnan, G., Zhao, A., Sabuncu, M.R., Guttag, J., Dalca, A.V.: An unsupervised learning model for deformable medical image registration. In: Proceedings of the IEEE Conference on Computer Vision and Pattern Recognition, pp. 9252–9260 (2018)
3. Dalca, A.V., Balakrishnan, G., Guttag, J., Sabuncu, M.R.: Unsupervised learning for fast probabilistic diffeomorphic registration. In: Frangi, A.F., Schnabel, J.A., Davatzikos, C., Alberola-López, C., Fichtinger, G. (eds.) MICCAI 2018, Part I. LNCS, vol. 11070, pp. 729–738. Springer, Cham (2018). https://doi.org/10.1007/978-3-030-00928-1_82
4. He, K., Zhang, X., Ren, S., Sun, J.: Delving deep into rectifiers: surpassing human-level performance on ImageNet classification. In: Proceedings of the IEEE International Conference on Computer Vision, pp. 1026–1034 (2015)
5. Jaderberg, M., Simonyan, K., Zisserman, A., et al.: Spatial transformer networks. In: Advances in Neural Information Processing Systems, pp. 2017–2025 (2015)
6. Kingma, D.P., Ba, J.: Adam: a method for stochastic optimization. arXiv preprint: arXiv:1412.6980 (2014)
7. Klein, A., Tourville, J.: 101 labeled brain images and a consistent human cortical labeling protocol. Front. Neurosci. **6**, 171 (2012)
8. Li, H., Fan, Y.: Non-rigid image registration using fully convolutional networks with deep self-supervision. arXiv preprint: arXiv:1709.00799 (2017)
9. Rohé, M.-M., Datar, M., Heimann, T., Sermesant, M., Pennec, X.: SVF-Net: learning deformable image registration using shape matching. In: Descoteaux, M., Maier-Hein, L., Franz, A., Jannin, P., Collins, D.L., Duchesne, S. (eds.) MICCAI 2017, Part I. LNCS, vol. 10433, pp. 266–274. Springer, Cham (2017). https://doi.org/10.1007/978-3-319-66182-7_31
10. Ronneberger, O., Fischer, P., Brox, T.: U-Net: convolutional networks for biomedical image segmentation. In: Navab, N., Hornegger, J., Wells, W.M., Frangi, A.F. (eds.) MICCAI 2015, Part III. LNCS, vol. 9351, pp. 234–241. Springer, Cham (2015). https://doi.org/10.1007/978-3-319-24574-4_28
11. Shan, S., et al.: Unsupervised end-to-end learning for deformable medical image registration. arXiv preprint: arXiv:1711.08608 (2017)
12. Sokooti, H., de Vos, B., Berendsen, F., Lelieveldt, B.P.F., Išgum, I., Staring, M.: Nonrigid image registration using multi-scale 3D convolutional neural networks. In: Descoteaux, M., Maier-Hein, L., Franz, A., Jannin, P., Collins, D.L., Duchesne, S. (eds.) MICCAI 2017, Part I. LNCS, vol. 10433, pp. 232–239. Springer, Cham (2017). https://doi.org/10.1007/978-3-319-66182-7_27

13. Szegedy, C., et al.: Going deeper with convolutions. In: Proceedings of the IEEE Conference on Computer Vision and Pattern Recognition, pp. 1–9 (2015)

14. Wang, S., Kim, M., Wu, G., Shen, D.: Scalable high performance image registration framework by unsupervised deep feature representations learning. In: Deep Learning for Medical Image Analysis, pp. 245–269. Elsevier (2017)

15. Yang, X., Kwitt, R., Niethammer, M.: Fast predictive image registration. In: Carneiro, G., et al. (eds.) LABELS 2016/DLMIA 2016. LNCS, vol. 10008, pp. 48–57. Springer, Cham (2016). https://doi.org/10.1007/978-3-319-46976-8_6

16. Zhang, J.: Inverse-consistent deep networks for unsupervised deformable image registration. arXiv preprint: arXiv:1809.03443 (2018)

# Functional Data and Long Short-Term Memory Networks for Diagnosis of Parkinson's Disease

Saurabh Garg$^{(\boxtimes)}$ and Martin J. McKeown

Pacific Parkinson's Research Center, University of British Columbia,
Vancouver, Canada
srbh.garg@gmail.com

**Abstract.** Computer-aided diagnostic tools for neurodegenerative and
psychiatric disease and disorders have many practical clinical applications. In this work, we propose a two-component neural network based
on Long Short-Term Memory (LSTM) for the automatic diagnosis of
Parkinson's disease (PD) using whole brain resting-state functional magnetic resonance data. Given the recent findings on structural and functional asymmetry that could be observed in PDs, our proposed architecture consists of two LSTM networks that were designed to facilitate
independent mining of patterns that may differ between the left and right
hemispheres. Under a cross-validation framework, our proposed model
achieved an F1-score of $0.701 \pm 0.055$, which is competitive against an
F1-score of $0.677 \pm 0.033$ achieved by a single LSTM model.

## 1 Introduction

Parkinson's disease is a neuropsychiatric disease associated with progressive disability and chronic symptoms that manifest primarily as tremor, slow movement,
balance problem, rigidity, and walking/gait problems [15,16]. Diagnosis of PD
traditionally depended on the manual observation of symptoms and their longitudinal courses. With clinical symptoms that can be easily confused with those
of at least seven other common disorders [4], its reported diagnostic accuracy is
highly variable. Clinically and etiologically, PD is also a heterogeneous disease,
rendering its neuro-biological underpinnings highly complex [15].

Thanks to the increasing availability of functional magnetic resonance imaging (fMRI), *in vivo* examination of functional neuroanatomy has enabled new
understanding towards this disease. For instance, resting-state (rs) fMRI data
focuses on low-frequency changes in the blood-oxygenation-level-dependent
(BOLD) signal when a subject is at rest. Using rs-fMRI data, Canu et al. [6]
found that patients with PD tend to experience decreased functional connectivity in various brain regions.

**Electronic supplementary material** The online version of this chapter (https://
doi.org/10.1007/978-3-030-32692-0_75) contains supplementary material, which is
available to authorized users.

© Springer Nature Switzerland AG 2019
H.-I. Suk et al. (Eds.): MLMI 2019, LNCS 11861, pp. 655–663, 2019.
https://doi.org/10.1007/978-3-030-32692-0_75

Another research front is the examination of brain asymmetry as observed in PDs [2] and other neuropsychiatric disorders [10]. Clinically, the onset of motor signs in PD is generally asymmetric, notably with asymmetric resting tremor in the upper extremity [2]. Pan et al. [15] have also observed an increased amplitude of low frequency fluctuation (ALFF) in the right ROIs such as the inferior parietal gyrus, but decreased ALFF in the left ROIs such as the inferior parietal gyrus. Structurally, Classen et al. [9] also found that the left nigrostriatal system is more susceptible to early atrophy than that of the right in subjects with PD.

Motivated by the findings made by the aforementioned studies, we hypothesize in this work that deep learning (DL) can be leveraged to analyze and model these patho-physiology brain changes that may depend on the hemispheres in complex ways. We thus propose a DL framework that learns to model the spatiotemporal BOLD changes in the left and right hemispheres via two independently trained Long Short-Term Memory (LSTM) subnetworks. In the literature, there exist a few studies that relate to PD diagnoses, albeit none has proposed to train two LSTM subnetworks to allow for discovery of patterns specific to each brain hemisphere. For instance, Hammerla et al. [7] applied radial basis model on temporal data from wearable sensors to predict disease status of PD. Che et al. [18] also employed multi-class support vector machine (SVM) and logistic regression to predict PD status using clinical similarities learned from LSTM. Kollias et al. [14] employed convolutional and recurrent neural networks to analyze structural MRI and DaT scan.

As we will show in the results, the proposed two-component model achieved consistently better classification performance than its single counterpart for a wide range of model configurations. Furthermore, leveraging the interpretability of LSTM models, we conducted secondary analyses to identify anatomical regions whose fMRI measurements were salient in differentiating PDs from HCs.

## 2   Materials and Methods

### 2.1   Materials

Our dataset was collected from four international sites and includes rs-fMRI data and structural T1-weighted MR data of 92 healthy controls and 282 subjects with PD, which was diagnosed according to the UK brain bank criterion and the MDS clinical diagnostic criterion (MDS-UPDRS) [4]. Mean Age (standard deviation) of the PDs are 64.6 (9.50), while those of the HCs are 58.30 (7.46). The range and mean (standard deviation) of the severity in these subjects as measured using MDS-UPDRS are [4, 82] and 24.99 (14.69), respectively.

### 2.2   Data Processing

All steps below were implemented using the AFNI and SPM8 software packages.

**A. Denoising:** Following standard protocol [12], we first performed pre-processing steps of despiking, slice-timing corrections, and isotropic-reslicing (3 mm in each dimension) on the acquired fMRI data.

**B. Registrations:** We performed motion correction via rigid-body alignment to correct for any major head motion during the acquisition fMRI scan. We then rigidly registered each accompanying structural T1-weighted scan to the motion corrected fMRI volume, and non-linearly registered the transformed T1 scan to a structural MRI atlas (Fig. 1b) that was derived from 2 public atlases, namely, the Desikan-Killiany[1] atlas that consists of 288 brain regions representing the cortex and the HMAT[2] atlas that consists of 12 motor areas.

**C. ROI-calculations:** To reduce the amount of unwanted distortions introduced to our data, segmentation of each fMRI timepoint into anatomical brain regions was performed in the native space by transforming the segmentations of the registered atlases to each fMRI timepoint using the set of transformations obtained in the aforementioned registrations step.

**D. Smoothing:** The fMRI time courses of each position was next detrended; any linear or quadratic trends in the fMRI signal were removed. The time courses were then iteratively smoothed until it reached six FWHM of smoothness. Finally, bandpass-filtering was performed to ensure that the fMRI signals between the recommended frequencies of interest (0.01 Hz to 0.08 Hz) were retained.

**E. Mean time course calculations:** The time courses at all positions within each ROI were then averaged to generate a mean time course per ROI. Each subject data was henceforth represented as a matrix of size $R \times T$, where $R$ was the number of ROIs and $T$ was the number of time-points. Each input sequence spanned roughly 3 min of imaging as commonly done in the literature [12].

### 2.3  Learning of Sequential Data via LSTM

Let $\mathbf{X} \in \mathbb{R}^{R \times T}$ be a data sample from a subject scan extracted using the steps described in Sect. 2.2, $x_t$ be its $t$-th column vector, and $y \in \{0, 1\}$ be its class label, i.e. 0 for HC (1 for PD). The goal in supervised learning is to learn a predictive function $\Phi$ from a labeled set of training set, i.e. $\{X, y\}_{n=1}^{N}$, where $N$ is the number of samples in the training set.

In this work, $\Phi$ is modeled using what is known as the vanilla LSTM, which has been shown to be superior than various other variants such as the Gated Recurrent Unit [13]. In the vanilla LSTM, each memory cell unit has a state and consists of an input gate, output gate, and a forget gate that can save and forget information with a tunable parameter known as *keep probability* $p$ that determines how much information to retain at each training iteration. Layers of LSTM can be stacked on top of one another to achieve multiple levels of data abstractions. After stacking, the final layer consists of a softmax regression layer [13], which outputs the probability of its input sample belonging to the PD class.

---

[1] https://surfer.nmr.mgh.harvard.edu/ftp/articles/desikan06-parcellation.pdf.
[2] https://www.ncbi.nlm.nih.gov/pmc/articles/PMC2034289/.

**Table 1.** Hyper-parameters explored in our work and previous studies for schizophrenia, human connectome project, and autism, respectively. ADD = AdaDelta; ADG = AdaGrad; SC denotes stopping criterion.

| Ref | T | l | u | Optimization | LR | BS | SC | dropout | #Subjs |
|---|---|---|---|---|---|---|---|---|---|
| [11] | 16,64 | 2 | 32 | ADAM | 0.0001 | 64 | 10 epochs | 0.5 | 95 |
| [17] | unknown | 2 | 256 | ADAM | 0.001 | 32 | unknown | ? | 490 |
| [12] | 90 | 1 | 8,16,32,64 | ADD (rho = 0.95) | 1 | ? | 300 epochs | 0.5 | 1100 |
| Our's | 60,90,120 | 2,3,4 | 40,50,60 | ADD,ADG,ADAM | 0.0025, 0.001 | 34 | 200 epochs | 0.3 | 374 |

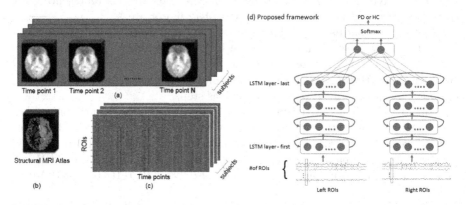

**Fig. 1.** Our proposed framework with two LSTMs. Please refer to main text for details.

## 2.4 Proposed Model

Unlike the standard approach of using a single LSTM that accepts all 200 ROIs as input, we propose to separate the input data $\mathbf{X}$ into left and right data matrices as $\mathbf{X}^L$ and $\mathbf{X}^R$ as motivated in the Sect. 1. For ROIs that could not be assigned to the left or right category such as those belonging to the central region of the brain, we randomly assigned them to the left and the right so that the total volume of these central ROIs are roughly comparable. By chance, the numbers of ROIs assigned to the left and to the right were equal.

Figure 1 shows the proposed two-component LSTM network. The left LSTM was trained with brain ROIs from the left hemisphere and the right LSTM was trained with ROIs from the right hemisphere. The output of each LSTM was then concatenated and then fed into a single fully connected layer with two output nodes, one for each class. The output label was then obtained by using a softmax layer. The different colours portray different mean time courses of the ROIs.

The left and right LSTMs were independently trained in a cross-validation fashion and fine-tuned together in the second stage. $M$ configurations of hyper-parameters were used to train a LSTM network and the optimal set was selected by computing the F1-score over a validation set. Based on literature survey as summarized in Table 1, we narrowed the search range of the key hyper-parameters and derived $M = 12$ configurations determined via grid search with learning rate (LR) set as one of $\{0.0001, 0.0025, 0.005\}$, with batch size (BS) set as one of $\{34, 68\}$ and $p$ as one of $\{0.5, 0.7\}$. Next, we performed fusion of the outputs from the two trained LSTMs by concatenating them with a fully-connected layer. The final output layer consisted of a soft-max layer [13] as explained in the previous subsection. A graphical summary of the proposed framework is given in Fig. 1d.

While some works (e.g. [8]) have shown that stacking multiple layers of LSTMs may improve performance, other works (e.g. [12]) have also reported the contrary, suggesting that the choice of $l$ (the number of layers) is heavily problem-dependent. We thus examine the impact of $l$ in Sect. 3.

### 2.5  Data Augmentation

Our time courses vary in length due to differences in acquisition sites. Accordingly, we cropped the input time courses to a fixed sequence length for all subjects. For each scan, we randomly sampled tokens of length $T$ from the time courses. Our dataset is skewed towards the PD class; to balance the number of classes for the entire dataset, we repeated sampling from the PD class two times and the HC class five times. This yielded an augmented dataset of 858 input sequences, increasing the dataset size by approximately 2.5 fold, giving 53% of PD samples in the training set. We only performed data augmentation for training and validation set but not for testing set. This data augmentation strategy is similar to that performed in previous work [12], except they repeated sampling 10 times and fixed $T$ to 90. Further, our sampling factors differ from theirs because the samples drawn would overlap when our sampling factors is greater than four. For our application, we conjectured that $T$ should be a hyperparameter that could be optimized. We thus explored $T = \{60, 90, 120\}$.

### 2.6  Region-of-Interest Analysis

Once model training converged, weight matrix from the first layer of the trained network for each of the LSTM gates was extracted, yielding four weight matrices (one for input, output, control, and forget gates), each of size $q \times u$. Next, the absolute values of the weights were averaged over all hidden units in the first layer, resulting in four vectors of size $q$. For each of these vectors, we then identified elements (which correspond to ROIs) whose absolute weight was greater than two standard deviation from the mean computed across all elements, i.e. each vector was thresholded to indicate whether or not the corresponding ROI was important for PD-HC classification. The above steps were repeated for every fold of our cross-validation experiments. We report the ROIs that were classified as important in each fold in Sect. 3.

## 3   Results and Discussions

The proposed LSTM-based classification framework was implemented in Keras with TensorFlow background (we used the implementation of [1] that omits the peephole connections). Various variants of the proposed framework were trained by minimizing the binary cross-entropy loss. We empirically explored Adam, AdaDelta and Adagrad optimization algorithms but found that the latter yielded better performance in the preliminary experiments.

For each variant, we performed cross-validation to estimate the average classification performance computed based on F1-score, precision and recall. In each fold, the batch size, keep probability, and learning rate were determined using a validation set (10% of the entire dataset) that does not overlap with the training set nor the test set (10% of the entire dataset).

Table 2 reports the average and standard deviation for each of the performance scores computed on the test set. A more complete table containing trials for $p = 0.5$ and $l = 4$ can be found in the supplementary[3].

As shown on the last two rows, the use of deep learning via LSTM(s) gave superior results when compared to previously proposed methods that used common features extracted from fMRI data and SVM [3,15] or random forest (RF) as the classifier. Interestingly, training a single LSTM using only the left ROIs or using only the right ROIs generally yielded higher mean F1-score than those achieved by the baseline approach of using a single LSTM trained with input data from all 200 ROIs. Our proposed two-component model yielded highest F1-score regardless of $l$ and $u$.

We also included in the comparison variants of a single-model with double[4] the size of hidden units (2× params) of the proposed model. The results of these variants are shown.

We next performed non-parametric Wilcoxon's rank-sum test to examine if the performance of the proposed two-component model is significantly better from the other variants of the same depth ($l$). To increase statistical power, the F1-scores from trials over different hidden sizes $u$ were pooled. For $l = 2$, the best model was close to significance with a p-value of 0.0672. For $l = 3$, the best model was better than the second competing method across all folds, with a statistical significant difference of 0.0265 in p-value. We repeated the same tests with standard LSTM with double the hidden size ("standard-2x"). For $l = 2$, our method was significantly better with a p-value of 0.0060 but for $l = 3$ Wilcoxon's rank sum test did not turn out to be significant with a p-value of 0.1060. When we combined F1-scores from all trials, a one-tail paired t-test showed that our proposed model performed significantly better than the other variants (p-value of 0.0061, 0.0013, respectively).

We next employed the procedure described in Sect. 2.5 to identify the ROIs that are important in discriminating PD from HCs, with a visual presentation shown in the online supplementary. From the figure, one could see that the ROIs are distributed asymmetrically across the brain. Surprisingly, many of the identified ROIs have been shown to be associated with three known networks: default

---

[3] https://github.com/srbhgarg/LSTM_fMRI.git.

[4] With double the hidden size, a total of $m$ parameters were used by the new variant such that $\frac{m}{n} > 1$, and $n$ is the total number of parameters in the proposed two-component variant.

**Table 2.** Shown are the mean and standard deviation of F1-score, precision and recall of various frameworks tested. Compared to baseline approaches, deep learning via LSTM gave better results. The proposed two-component LSTM yielded the highest F1-score when compared to other variants tested, including the single LSTM that examined the same amount of input data (i.e. all ROIs).

| | F1-score | Precision | Recall |
|---|---|---|---|
| $l = 2, u = 40$ | | | |
| Proposed 2-component | **0.6876 ± 0.032331** | 0.73 ± 0.024495 | 0.664 ± 0.064653 |
| Single LSTM - only left ROIs | 0.6826 ± 0.012602 | 0.71 ± 0.041833 | 0.71 ± 0.06364 |
| Single LSTM - only right ROIs | 0.6732 ± 0.017936 | 0.74 ± 0.018708 | 0.658 ± 0.050695 |
| Single LSTM - all ROIs | 0.6694 ± 0.017855 | 0.732 ± 0.023875 | 0.648 ± 0.054037 |
| Single LSTM - 2x params | 0.6578 ± 0.013627 | 0.71 ± 0.05 | 0.624 ± 0.055045 |
| $l = 2, u = 50$ | | | |
| Proposed 2-component | **0.691 ± 0.039906** | 0.738 ± 0.037683 | 0.672 ± 0.068337 |
| Single LSTM - only left ROIs | 0.678 ± 0.035242 | 0.73 ± 0.021213 | 0.642 ± 0.07791 |
| Single LSTM - only right ROIs | 0.6786 ± 0.02411 | 0.728 ± 0.034205 | 0.666 ± 0.068775 |
| Single LSTM - all ROIs | 0.6716 ± 0.016965 | 0.71 ± 0.015811 | 0.654 ± 0.027019 |
| Single LSTM - 2x params | 0.6662 ± 0.013627 | 0.718 ± 0.05 | 0.638 ± 0.055045 |
| $l = 2, u = 60$ | | | |
| Proposed 2-component | **0.6966 ± 0.04217** | 0.72 ± 0.036742 | 0.69 ± 0.046368 |
| Single LSTM - only left ROIs | 0.6748 ± 0.029363 | 0.732 ± 0.0249 | 0.642 ± 0.076289 |
| Single LSTM - only right ROIs | 0.666 ± 0.020298 | 0.718 ± 0.033466 | 0.64 ± 0.051478 |
| Single LSTM - all ROIs | 0.667 ± 0.01164 | 0.704 ± 0.038471 | 0.664 ± 0.021909 |
| Single LSTM - 2x params | 0.661 ± 0.013627 | 0.694 ± 0.05 | 0.64 ± 0.055045 |
| $l = 3, u = 40$ | | | |
| Proposed 2-component | **0.6866 ± 0.023469** | 0.714 ± 0.039749 | 0.72 ± 0.061644 |
| Single LSTM - only left ROIs | 0.6726 ± 0.030146 | 0.708 ± 0.031937 | 0.646 ± 0.056391 |
| Single LSTM - only right ROIs | 0.6716 ± 0.024234 | 0.744 ± 0.018166 | 0.664 ± 0.10597 |
| Single LSTM - all ROIs | 0.6658 ± 0.024519 | 0.714 ± 0.054129 | 0.636 ± 0.065038 |
| Single LSTM - 2x params | 0.6584 ± 0.01743 | 0.736 ± 0.027928 | 0.604 ± 0.055946 |
| $l = 3, u = 50$ | | | |
| Proposed 2-component | **0.6888 ± 0.038003** | 0.742 ± 0.017889 | 0.666 ± 0.065038 |
| Single LSTM - only left ROIs | 0.6718 ± 0.024954 | 0.702 ± 0.040249 | 0.65 ± 0.053852 |
| Single LSTM - only right ROIs | 0.6596 ± 0.017714 | 0.702 ± 0.031937 | 0.63 ± 0.045826 |
| Single LSTM - all ROIs | 0.6634 ± 0.025225 | 0.742 ± 0.016432 | 0.608 ± 0.062209 |
| Single LSTM - 2x params | 0.6736 ± 0.01743 | 0.702 ± 0.027928 | 0.666 ± 0.055946 |
| $l = 3, u = 60$ | | | |
| Proposed 2-component | **0.7012 ± 0.055378** | 0.732 ± 0.05933 | 0.732 ± 0.071903 |
| Single LSTM - only left ROIs | 0.6868 ± 0.030655 | 0.702 ± 0.046583 | 0.702 ± 0.055857 |
| Single LSTM - only right ROIs | 0.6578 ± 0.017627 | 0.73 ± 0.045277 | 0.614 ± 0.069857 |
| Single LSTM - all ROIs | 0.6772 ± 0.032722 | 0.74 ± 0.023452 | 0.644 ± 0.077653 |
| Single LSTM - 2x params | 0.6758 ± 0.01743 | 0.71 ± 0.027928 | 0.652 ± 0.055946 |
| Previous methods | | | |
| SVM + ReHo [3] | 0.5934 ± 0.0483 | 0.5919 ± 0.0427 | 0.5952 ± 0.0556 |
| SVM + ALFF [3] | 0.571 ± 0.039 | 0.553 ± 0.042 | 0.591 ± 0.045 |
| SVM + ALFF + ReHo [3] | 0.6129 ± 0.0212 | 0.6114 ± 0.0296 | 0.6159 ± 0.0316 |
| RF + ReHo [5] | 0.6039 ± 0.11934 | 0.6429 ± 0.2357 | 0.6208 ± 0.2263 |
| RF + ALFF [5] | 0.5376 ± 0.1951 | 0.5255 ± 0.2325 | 0.6153 ± 0.2472 |
| RF + ALFF + ReHo [5] | 0.6445 ± 0.1925 | 0.6674 ± 0.2217 | 0.6658 ± 0.2191 |

mode network, salience network and frontoparietal network. An expanded literature review involving the identified important ROIs as well as a barplot portraying the magnitudes of the weights are provided in the supplementary for readers' interests (Table 3).

**Table 3.** Some of the identified ROIs' relevance to existing literature. Complete table in supplementary. Input, forget, control and output gates are shown in red, green, orange, and blue, respectively.

| ROIs | Functions | Relevance |
|---|---|---|
| Left short insular gyrus | Emotions, cognition | Non-motor symptoms of PD |
| Left superior temporal lobe | Motion perception | Motion perception is impaired in PD |
| Left Posterior ventral cingulate | Cognitive processing, executive performance | Part of default mode network, cognitive impairment in PD |
| Left anterior circular insula | Autonomic processes | Part of salience network, Non-motor symptoms |
| Left postcentral gyrus | sensory receptive area for the sense of touch | sensory deficits like touch and smell in PD |
| Left Thalamus | Relaying motor signals to the cerebral cortex | Motor pathways affected in PD |
| Left superior frontal gyrus | cognitive control and executive control | Part of frontoparietal network |
| Left superior occipital gyrus | Process visual information | Worsened visuo-perceptual processing in Parkinson's disease |
| Left anterior circular insula | subjective emotional experience | Part of salience network, Non-motor symptoms |

## 4   Conclusions

We have applied LSTMs for automatic identification of PDs using resting-state fMRI data. The proposed method performed better than the other evaluated methods. The two-component model was able to automatically learn the ROIs belonging to different networks of the brain that were affected in PD. Future work aims to examine the impact of using bi-directional LSTMs on training time and classification performance.

## References

1. Hochreiter, S., et al.: Long short-term memory. Neural Comput. **9**(8), 1735–1780 (1997)
2. Barrett, M.J., et al.: Handedness and motor symptom asymmetry in Parkinson's disease. J. Neurol. Neurosurg. Psychiatry **82**(10), 1122–1124 (2010)
3. Long, D., et al.: Automatic classification of early Parkinson's disease with multimodal MR imaging. PLoS ONE **7**(11), e47714 (2012)
4. Massano, J., et al.: Clinical approach to Parkinson's disease: features, diagnosis, and principles of management. Cold Spring Harb. perspect. Med. **2**(6), a008870 (2012)

5. Savio, A., Chyzhyk, D., Graña, M.: Computer aided diagnosis of schizophrenia based on local-activity measures of resting-state fMRI. In: Polycarpou, M., de Carvalho, A.C.P.L.F., Pan, J.-S., Woźniak, M., Quintian, H., Corchado, E. (eds.) HAIS 2014. LNCS (LNAI), vol. 8480, pp. 1–12. Springer, Cham (2014). https://doi.org/10.1007/978-3-319-07617-1_1
6. Canu, E., et al.: Brain structural and functional connectivity in Parkinson's disease with freezing of gait. Hum. Brain Mapp. **36**(12), 5064–5078 (2015)
7. Hammerla, N.Y., et al.: PD disease state assessment in naturalistic environments using deep learning. In: AAAI 2015, pp. 1742–1748 (2015)
8. Li, X., et al.: Constructing long short-term memory based deep recurrent neural networks for large vocabulary speech recognition. In: ICASSP. IEEE (2015)
9. Claassen, D.O., et al.: Cortical asymmetry in Parkinson's disease: early susceptibility of the left hemisphere. Brain Behav. **6**(12), e00573 (2016)
10. Kumfor, F., et al.: On the right side? A longitudinal study of left- versus rightlateralized semantic dementia. Brain **139**(3), 986–998 (2016)
11. Dakka, J., et al.: Learning neural markers of schizophrenia disorder using recurrent neural networks. CoRR abs/1712.00512 (2017)
12. Dvornek, N.C., Ventola, P., Pelphrey, K.A., Duncan, J.S.: Identifying autism from resting-state fMRI using long short-term memory networks. In: Wang, Q., Shi, Y., Suk, H.-I., Suzuki, K. (eds.) MLMI 2017. LNCS, vol. 10541, pp. 362–370. Springer, Cham (2017). https://doi.org/10.1007/978-3-319-67389-9_42
13. Greff, K., et al.: LSTM: a search space odyssey. IEEE Trans. Neural Netw. Learn. Syst. **28**(10), 2222–2232 (2017)
14. Kollias, D., et al.: Deep neural architectures for prediction in healthcare. Complex Intell. Syst. **4**(2), 119–131 (2018)
15. Pan, P., et al.: Abnormalities of regional brain function in Parkinson's disease: a meta-analysis of resting state functional magnetic resonance imaging studies. Sci. Rep. **7**, 40469 (2017)
16. Poewe, W., et al.: Parkinson disease. Nat. Rev. Dis. Primers **3**, 17013 (2017)
17. Li, H., et al.: Brain decoding from functional MRI using long short-term memory recurrent neural networks. CoRR abs/1809.05561 (2018)
18. Che, C., et al.: An RNN architecture with dynamic temporal matching for personalized predictions of Parkinson's disease. In: Proceedings of the 2017 SIAM International Conference on Data Mining, pp. 198–206 (2017)

# Joint Holographic Detection and Reconstruction

Florence Yellin[✉], Benjamín Béjar, Benjamin D. Haeffele, Evelien Mathieu, Christian Pick, Stuart C. Ray, and René Vidal

Johns Hopkins University, Baltimore, MD, USA
fyellin1@jhu.edu

**Abstract.** Lens-free holographic imaging is important in many biomedical applications, as it offers a wider field of view, more mechanical robustness and lower cost than traditional microscopes. In many cases, it is important to be able to detect biological objects, such as blood cells, in microscopic images. However, state-of-the-art object detection methods are not designed to work on holographic images. Typically, the hologram must first be reconstructed into an image of the specimen, given a priori knowledge of the distance between the specimen and sensor, and standard object detection methods can then be used to detect objects in the reconstructed image. This paper describes a method for detecting objects directly in holograms while jointly reconstructing the image. This is achieved by assuming a sparse convolutional model for the objects being imaged and modeling the diffraction process responsible for generating the recorded hologram. This paper also describes an unsupervised method for training the convolutional templates, shows that the proposed method produces promising results for detecting white blood cells in holographic images, and demonstrates that the proposed object detection method is robust to errors in estimated focal depth.

**Keywords:** Holography · Convolutional sparse coding · Phase recovery

## 1 Introduction

Lens-free imaging has gained popularity in recent years in the biomedical imaging community, due to its ability to produce wide field of view images for a given magnification with minimal hardware requirements and low cost. Holographic images are acquired by illuminating a specimen with a coherent light source, and the resulting diffraction pattern (hologram) is recorded on an image sensor [3]. The distance between the object (specimen) plane and the hologram (sensor) plane is known as the focal depth, which can vary between experiments due to small shifts in the experimental setup. Recently, the ability to record holographic images of blood cells and use these images to produce an estimate of a sample's

© Springer Nature Switzerland AG 2019
H.-I. Suk et al. (Eds.): MLMI 2019, LNCS 11861, pp. 664–672, 2019.
https://doi.org/10.1007/978-3-030-32692-0_76

cell concentration, has emerged as a promising application for lens-free imaging [7]. Key to estimating cell concentrations from holographic images is being able to accurately detect objects in such images, which is the focus of this paper.

One unique challenge associated with object detection in holograms is that as the signals from individual cells propagate from the object plane to the hologram plane, they interact through a non-linear diffraction process, which is especially apparent in high concentration samples (Fig. 1, bottom left). Thus, traditional methods for detecting cells in images, such as convolutional methods [9], are bound to fail if applied directly to holograms of high cell concentration blood samples. This is highlighted in [8], where the authors attempt to count blood cells directly from holograms via a correlation-based method and observe that they can only accurately count cells in low concentration samples. Furthermore, when using such a method, a large training dataset obtained from multiple depths of focus would be necessary, since the focal depth at testing typically cannot be exactly controlled experimentally. As with many biomedical applications, obtaining data can be expensive, and available training data may be limited.

To address these challenges, state-of-the-art methods for counting objects in holograms rely on a two-step process: First, the holographic image is reconstructed into an image of the object plane, e.g., using [2]. Then, standard object detection methods can be used to detect cells in the reconstructed image. If the reconstruction quality is sufficient, a simple object detection method such as thresholding can reliably be used [10]. While this two-step approach is promising, combining the reconstruction and object detection steps into a single method designed to count objects directly from holograms could potentially improve object detection performance. Furthermore, the focal depth is typically known only approximately, due to experimental variance. If the object detection method is not robust to errors in focal depth, a computationally expensive autofocus step (to compute the focal depth) must be done before reconstructing an image.

This paper presents a method based on convolutional sparse coding for detecting objects directly from holograms, by modeling both the object plane and the diffraction process responsible for producing the holographic images. This is to our knowledge the first method for object detection in holograms that accounts for the non-linear diffraction process, thereby enabling us to count cells directly from holograms, even for high cell concentration samples. We show that our method is robust to large errors in focal depth, potentially alleviating the need to do auto-focusing if the approximate focal depth in the experimental setup is known. We also propose a flexible, unsupervised method for training convolutional templates of the objects being imaged, so that images acquired at any focal depth, even one different than the focal depth of the test images, can be used during training. Finally, we demonstrate that the proposed method can accurately detect white blood cells (WBCs) in holographic images.

## 2    Problem Formulation

We assume that the specimen in the object plane consists of $N$ objects, such as cells, that are similar in appearance, so that the optical wavefront at the object plane, $I \in \mathbb{C}^{M \times M}$, can be expressed as the convolution of $K$ object templates, $\{d_j \in \mathbb{C}^{m \times m}\}_{j=1}^{K}$, with sparse coefficients $\{A_j \in \mathbb{C}^{M \times M}\}_{j=1}^{K}$ (to simplify notation, we assume images and templates are square). We assume each object can be well-approximated by a single template, so that if $I \approx \sum_j d_j \star A_j$, where $\star$ denotes convolution, the locations of the objects resembling the $j^{th}$ template will be given by the support of $A_j$, and the number of objects in the image will be equal to the cardinality of the coefficients' support, $N = \sum_j \|A_j\|_0$.

A hologram $H \in \mathbb{R}^{M \times M}$ records the magnitude of the complex-valued optical wavefront that is formed when the wavefront $I$ in the object plane propagates a distance $z$ to the hologram plane via diffraction. The diffraction process over depth $z$ can be modeled for light with wavenumber $k$ by convolution with the wide angular spectrum transfer function, $T(z)$ [3], whose Fourier transform at frequencies $(k_x, k_y)$ is defined as

$$F[T(z)](k_x, k_y) = \exp\left(iz\sqrt{k^2 - k_x^2 - k_y^2}\right). \tag{1}$$

By combining the model for the wavefront at the object plane with the model for the diffraction process, we can express the holographic image as

$$H \approx \left| T(z) \star \sum_j d_j \star A_j + \mu 1 1^T \right|, \tag{2}$$

where $\mu$ accounts for a constant background illumination in the hologram plane.

## 3   Convolutional Sparse Coding with Phase Recovery

Assume for now that the templates are known. Given a hologram, we would like to find the locations of all objects in the hologram by finding the support of the encodings $A \in \mathbb{C}^{M \times M \times K}$. As a byproduct, we must also find the background $\mu$ and the (not recorded) phase $\theta$ of the complex wavefront at the hologram plane. Specifically, Eq. (2) can also be expressed as $H \circ e^{i\theta} \approx T(z) \star \sum_j d_j \star A_j + \mu 1 1^T$, where $\circ$ denotes element-wise multiplication, the exponential is applied element-wise, and $\theta \in \mathbb{R}^{M \times M}$ is the recovered phase of the hologram [2]. We can then formulate the problem of convolutional sparse coding with phase recovery as

$$\min_{A, \theta, \mu} F(A, \theta, \mu; \{d\}, H, z) \quad \text{s.t.} \quad \|A\|_{0,\infty} \leq 1 \tag{3}$$

$$F(A, \theta, \mu; \{d\}, H, z) = \frac{1}{2}\|H \circ e^{i\theta} - T(z) \star \sum_j d_j \star A_j - \mu 1 1^T\|_F^2 + \lambda \sum_j \|A_j\|_0.$$

We account for prior knowledge that objects in the image are sparse by adding regularization on the $\ell_0$ pseudo-norm of the coefficients, where the parameter $\lambda$ controls the sparsity of the encoding. To capture the fact that we would like the sparsest possible representation for each object in the image, i.e. each object should be approximated by (at most) a single template, we add the additional

**Algorithm 1. (Convolutional sparse coding with phase recovery)**

1: Input focal depth $z$ and templates $\{d\}$, and set $m$ to equal the size of the templates.
2: Initialize $A$ and $\mu$.
3: **while** Not converged **do**
4:     $\theta = \text{angle}\left(T(z) \star \sum_j d_j \star A_j + \mu 11^T\right)$           ▷ Update phase
5:     $\mu = \text{mean}\left(H \circ e^{i\theta} - T(z) \star \sum_j d_j \star A_j\right)$       ▷ Update background
6:     Choose step size $\rho$     ▷ Via backtracking line search, or via Lipschitz constant
7:     $A_j^+ = A_j + \rho d_j \odot \left(\overline{T(z)} \star \left(H \circ e^{i\theta} - \mu 11^T\right) - \sum_l d_l \star A_l\right)$ ▷ Compute for each $j$
8:     $A = M_m\left(H_{\lambda\rho}\left(A^+\right)\right)$               ▷ Update coefficients
9: $N = \sum_j \|A_j\|_0$, $I = \sum_j d_j \star A_j$   ▷ Number objects detected, reconstructed image

constraint on the $\ell_{0,\infty}$ pseudo-norm of the coefficients, introduced in [5]. The $\ell_{0,\infty}$ pseudo-norm promotes sparsity for each patch in $I$, the wavefront at the object plane, and is defined as $\|A\|_{0,\infty} = \max_{i,j} \|P_{i,j}^m A\|_0$, where $P_{ij}^m A$ extracts a patch of size $(2m-1) \times (2m-1) \times K$ from $A$. This patch contains all pixels in the encoding that contribute to the $m \times m$ patch in $I$ centered at $I_{i,j}$.

Note that by solving jointly for the phase and encoding (and background) in Eq. (3), we account for the fact that signals in the object plane combine non-linearly to form the recorded hologram. A naive application of convolutional sparse coding to the hologram would not account for the fact that the hologram records only the magnitude of a complex wavefront. To minimize Eq. (3), we use a hybrid algorithm, summarized in Algorithm 1. We use alternating minimization to update the phase and background with the closed form expressions given in Lines 4 and 5, and we use an approximate proximal gradient descent step to update the coefficients according to Lines 7 and 8, explained below.

To update the coefficients, we split the objective into a differentiable function $h(A) = \frac{1}{2}\|H \circ e^{i\theta} - T(z) \star \sum_j d_j \star A_j - \mu 11^T\|_F^2$, and a non-differentiable function $g(A) = \lambda \sum_j \|A_j\|_0 + I_C(A)$, where $I_C(A)$ is the indicator function that is equal to zero if $A \in C = \{A : \|A\|_{0,\infty} \leq 1\}$ and equal to infinity otherwise. The update for $A$ involves computing a gradient step for $h(A)$, followed by a proximal operator for $g(A)$. In Line 7, we compute the gradient step, where $\odot$ denotes correlation. Note that we utilize the fact that convolution with the transfer function is unitary, so $\|H \circ e^{i\theta} - T(z) \star \sum_j d_j \star A_j - \mu 11^T\|_F^2 = \|\overline{T(z)} \star \left(H \circ e^{i\theta} - \mu 11^T\right) - \sum_j d_j \star A_j\|_F^2$ [2].

Next, we approximate the proximal operator for $g$, which is defined as

$$\text{prox}_g(A) = \arg\min_Y \frac{1}{2}\|Y - A\|_F^2 + \lambda \sum_j \|Y_j\|_0 \quad \text{s.t.} \quad \|Y\|_{0,\infty} \leq 1. \quad (4)$$

Without the $\ell_{0,\infty}$ constraint, the proximal operator in Eq. (4) would be equal to the complex hard-thresholding operator,

$$[H_\lambda(A)]_{i,j,k} = \begin{cases} [A]_{i,j,k} & \text{if } [|A|]_{i,j,k} > \sqrt{2\lambda} \\ 0 & \text{else,} \end{cases} \quad (5)$$

and without the $\ell_0$ term, the proximal operator could be approximated by the non-maximal suppression operator,

$$[M_m(A)]_{i,j,k} = \begin{cases} [A]_{i,j,k} & \text{if } \max_{i,j,k} |P_{i,j}^m A| = [|A|]_{i,j,k} \\ 0 & \text{else.} \end{cases} \quad (6)$$

This can be seen by noticing that if $A$ encodes an image of non-overlapping objects of size $m$, at most a single object will be located in any given $m \times m$ patch in the image. The non-maximal suppression operator suppresses everything other than the maximum element in $A$ that contributes to a given patch in the image. Therefore, for images of non-overlapping objects, the proximal operator of the $\ell_{0,\infty}$ term will almost always be equal to the non-maximal suppression operator. Finally, we observe that the proximal operator in Eq. (4) is in general a hard problem to solve. We conjecture that under certain assumptions, the proximal operator can be computed by composing the non-maximal suppression operator with the complex hard-thresholding operator, as in Line 8. Note that a similar approach has been used to solve a related convex problem in [4].

**Learning Convolutional Templates.** During training, we would like to learn the object templates, given a collection of $S$ holograms, $\{H^i\}_{i=1}^{S}$, obtained at any (known) focal depth(s) $\{z^i\}_{i=1}^{S}$. This is done by minimizing the objective in Eq. (3), but also with respect to the templates $\{d_j\}_{j=1}^{K}$,

$$\min_{\{A^i\},\{\theta^i\},\{\mu^i\},\{d\}} \sum_i F\left(A^i, \theta^i, \mu^i, \{d\}; H^i, z^i\right) \text{ s.t. } \|A^i\|_{0,\infty} \leq 1, \|d_j\|_F = 1, \quad (7)$$

where $A^i$, $\theta^i$, and $\mu^i$ denote the respective coefficients, phase and background corresponding to the $i^{th}$ hologram. As is common in dictionary learning, we constrain the norm of the templates to make the problem well-posed. We use an alternating minimization algorithm: Given the templates, we update the coefficients, phase and background for each hologram according to Algorithm 1. Given the coefficients, phase and background for each hologram, we update the templates using the convolutional dictionary learning method described in [9] (the unitary property of $T(z)$ enables this). Because templates are being learned in the object plane, rather than hologram plane, training and test images need not be acquired at the same focal depth. Also, templates in the object plane are more compact than those in the hologram plane, increasing the efficiency of our method over standard convolutional sparse coding applied directly to holograms.

## 4 Experiments and Results

We applied our method to the task of detecting WBCs in holograms using three types of data: (1) To learn WBC templates, we acquired holograms of **purified WBCs**, meaning WBCs were experimentally extracted from a blood sample containing also red blood cells (RBCs), and then imaged at a focal depth of about $1000\,\mu m$. (2) To verify our ability to detect WBCs, we designed a **tandem-image setup** that allowed us to acquire for a single specimen both fluorescent

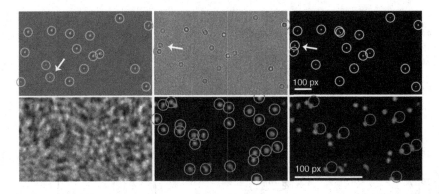

**Fig. 1.** (Top) Crops from a typical fluorescent image (left) and the corresponding holographic image (middle) and its SPR reconstruction (right). (Bottom) Crops from a high concentration sample's hologram (left) and its SPR reconstruction (right, middle). Yellow circles correspond to fluorescent detections, green circles to detections produced by our method, red circles to SPR-Thresh detections and blue circles to CSC detections. Note that both our method and CSC work directly on holograms, and the detections in the bottom (right, middle) panels are overlaid on SPR reconstructions only for visualization purposes. Arrows point out false positive and false negative detections. (Color figure online)

and holographic images with a focal depth of about 400 μm. We used this setup to image blood samples diluted in a lysis buffer, which formed a mixture of WBCs and debris from lysed RBCs. The WBCs were also labeled with a fluorescent dye, so that they would fluoresce while the RBC debris would not. The sample was flown through a microfluidic channel, and the flow was repeatedly stopped to obtain consecutive holographic and fluorescent images. **(3)** We also obtained holograms of a **lysed blood sample** with high WBC concentration.

**Fluorescent Image Processing and Alignment.** We denoised the fluorescent images, resulting in images such as the one shown in Fig. 1 (top left). Next, cells were detected in the denoised images via convolutional sparse coding [6,9], and cells were also detected in the holograms via either the proposed method or one of the baseline methods described below. Correspondences between detections in the two images were established using an affine registration procedure that alternated between estimating the affine transformation given the correspondences, and vice versa. There was still some offset between the sets of detections after alignment, because cells could move slightly between acquiring the fluorescent and holographic images, so we matched points in the two sets of (approximately) aligned detections to each other, where a match was permitted only when points were within a given radius of detection of each other. Additional details about the denoising and alignment procedures can be found in [1].

**Baseline Methods.** We compare our method to two baseline methods. **(1)** The first method counts cells directly from holograms using a standard convolutional sparse coding (CSC) method [9], similar to the method described in [8]. Convo-

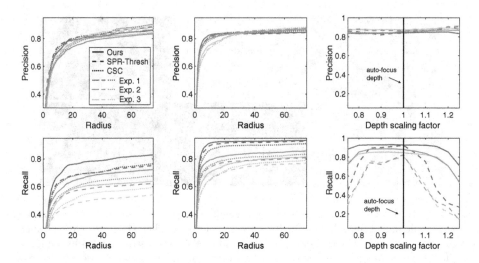

**Fig. 2.** Detection results are shown for our method, SPR-Thresh, and CSC. Precision (top) and recall (bottom) plots are shown for three different experiments as a function of detection radius (left, middle) and depth (right). Depth scaling factor $s$ means methods used $z = s \times z_{GT}$, where $z_{GT}$ is the correct focal distance. Plots in the middle and right columns were obtained after filtering out stationary detections.

lutional templates in the hologram plane were trained using one image from the test dataset. Ideally, the training data should come from a separate dataset, such as the purified WBC dataset, but a limitation of this method is that the training and test data must be obtained at the same focal depth. **(2)** The second baseline method is a two-step process, where we first reconstructed the images using the sparse phase recovery (SPR) method [2] and then thresholded the magnitude of the reconstructed image intensity and filtered the detections based on size (SPR-Thresh). Hyper-parameters for all methods were chosen empirically.

**Cell Detection Results.** After training the convolutional templates, we tested the ability of our method, CSC and SPR-Thresh to detect WBCs on tandem image data obtained from three blood samples, with 49 to 99 image pairs per sample. Note that the templates for our method were trained on the purified WBC dataset, which was acquired at a focal depth of about $500\,\mu m$ greater than that of the test data: Because our method learns templates in the object plane, the focal depth during training and testing need not be the same. For each method and for all images, we performed the alignment and matching described above. Frames with fewer than 20 fluorescent detections were discarded, because the automatic alignment is prone to fail without enough good matches. Sample detections from various methods, after alignment, are shown in Fig. 1 (top).

We then computed precision and recall for each experiment and method as a function of the detection radius, shown in Fig. 2 (left). The precision is similar for all methods and experiments, suggesting there is a fixed percentage of cell-like objects that do not fluoresce but are consistently detected in the hologram, regardless of detection method. However, the recall varies significantly, with our method always out-performing others, suggesting that our method is best-suited to locate hard-to-detect cells. As with any experimental setup, our tandem image setup contain sources of error: Not all WBCs fluoresce (due to variable expression level of proteins targeted by fluorescently labelled antibodies), and clumps of cell debris stuck to the channel may auto-fluoresce, leading to false fluorescent detections. To reduce error due to fluorescent debris stuck to the channel, we filtered out stationary detections; As shown in Fig. 2 (middle), all methods improved significantly, with our method still showing the best performance.

Another advantage of our method is its robustness to errors in focal depth, compared to SPR-Thresh. As the focal depth at which images are reconstructed fluctuates away from the true distance between the sample and sensor, the thresholding method is unable to detect cells in the reconstruction, as evident from the recall plot in Fig. 2 (bottom right). In contrast, our method's performance remains almost constant over a range of about $100\,\mu m$. This is a key advantage of our method, as images acquired by lens-free imaging often have a large field-of-view, so small alignment errors in the experimental setup can result in a large difference in focal depth across the image. Furthermore, we may be able to eliminate the computationally heavy autofocus preprocessing step when the approximate focal depth of the experimental setup is known.

Finally, we qualitatively analyzed the methods' ability to detect cells in high-concentration blood samples. Figure 1 (bottom left) shows a small crop from a hologram of a high cell density sample, where the non-linear interaction of the cell signals is apparent. Because we model the non-linearity in the diffraction process, our method is able to detect the cells reliably in the hologram; However, CSC, which works reasonably well in the low-density regime, is unable to detect cells in the high-concentration sample, as shown in Fig. 1 (bottom middle, right).

## 5 Conclusions

We have proposed a new convolutional method for detecting cells directly in holographic images, which jointly reconstructs the image and detects objects in the hologram. We have shown that our method produces promising results for detecting WBCs in holographic images of lysed blood samples, is robust to errors in the autofocus depth, and is able to handle high-concentration blood samples.

**Acknowledgments.** This work was funded by miDiagnostics.

## References

1. Haeffele, B.D., Pick, C., Lin, Z., Mathieu, E., Ray, S.C., Vidal, R.: An optical model of whole blood for detecting platelets in lens-free images. In: Workshop on Simulation and Synthesis for Medical Imaging (at MICCAI). Springer (2019)

2. Haeffele, B.D., Stahl, R., Vanmeerbeeck, G., Vidal, R.: Efficient reconstruction of holographic lens-free images by sparse phase recovery. In: Descoteaux, M., Maier-Hein, L., Franz, A., Jannin, P., Collins, D.L., Duchesne, S. (eds.) MICCAI 2017. LNCS, vol. 10434, pp. 109–117. Springer, Cham (2017). https://doi.org/10.1007/978-3-319-66185-8_13
3. Kim, M.K.: Digital Holographic Microscopy. Springer, New York (2011). https://doi.org/10.1007/978-1-4419-7793-9
4. Liu, Y., Zhan, Z., Cai, J.F., Guo, D., Chen, Z., Qu, X.: Projected iterative soft-thresholding algorithm for tight frames in compressed sensing magnetic resonance imaging. IEEE Trans. Med. Imaging 35(9), 2130–2140 (2016)
5. Papyan, V., Sulam, J., Elad, M.: Working locally thinking globally: theoretical guarantees for convolutional sparse coding. IEEE Trans. Signal Process. 65(21), 5687–5701 (2017)
6. Plaut, E., Giryes, R.: Matching pursuit based convolutional sparse coding. In: IEEE ICASSP, pp. 6847–6851 (2018)
7. Seo, S., Isikman, S.O., Sencan, I., Mudanyali, O., Su, T.W., Bishara, W., Erlinger, A., Ozcan, A.: High-throughput lens-free blood analysis on a chip. Anal. Chem. 82(11), 4621–4627 (2010)
8. Seo, S., et al.: Lensfree holographic imaging for on-chip cytometry and diagnostics. Lab Chip 9(6), 777–787 (2009)
9. Yellin, F., Haeffele, B., Vidal, R.: Blood cell detection and counting in holographic lens-free imaging by convolutional sparse dictionary learning and coding. In: IEEE International Symposium on Biomedical Imaging, pp. 650–653 (2017)
10. Yellin, F., Haeffele, B., Vidal, R.: Multi-cell classification by convolutional dictionary learning with class proportion priors. In: IEEE Conference on CVPR (2018)

# Reinforced Transformer for Medical Image Captioning

Yuxuan Xiong[1], Bo Du[1(✉)], and Pingkun Yan[2]

[1] School of Computer Science, Wuhan University, Wuhan, China
{xiongyx2017,remoteking}@whu.edu.cn
[2] Department of Biomedical Engineering, Rensselaer Polytechnic Institute,
Troy, NY 12180, USA
yanp2@rpi.edu

**Abstract.** Computerized medical image report generation is of great significance in automating the workflow of medical diagnosis and treatment for reducing health disparities. However, this task presents several challenges, where the generated medical image report should be precise, coherent and contain heterogeneous information. Current deep learning based medical image captioning models rely on recurrent neural networks and only extract top-down visual features, which make them slow and prone to generate incoherent and hard to comprehend reports. To tackle this challenging problem, this paper proposes a hierarchical *Transformer* based medical imaging report generation model. Our proposed model consists of two parts: (1) An *Image Encoder* extracts heuristic visual features by a bottom-up attention mechanism; (2) a non-recurrent *Captioning Decoder* improves the computational efficiency by parallel computation. The former identifies regions of interest via a bottom-up attention module and extracts top-down visual features. Then the *Transformer* based captioning decoder generates a coherent paragraph of medical imaging report. The proposed model is trained by using a self-critical reinforcement learning method. We evaluate the proposed model on publicly available datasets of IU X-ray. The experiment results show that our proposed model has improved the performance in BLEU-1 by more than 50% compared with other state-of-the-art image captioning methods.

## 1 Introduction

Medical imaging has been an essential tool for clinicians to make diagnosis and deliver treatment. With the widely use of various kinds of medical images and the flourish of artificial intelligence/deep learning, some new questions are posed by researchers. Can machines quickly and correctly detect and recognize illness from medical images? Given abundant medical images and other electronic medical record data, can machines automate the process of diagnosis without clinician intervention or maybe just minimal interaction? Automatic medical image analysis is becoming more and more important in the medical world, especially in radiology, which can save labor cost and help to alleviate the situation where the number of experienced medical experts is far below the demand.

© Springer Nature Switzerland AG 2019
H.-I. Suk et al. (Eds.): MLMI 2019, LNCS 11861, pp. 673–680, 2019.
https://doi.org/10.1007/978-3-030-32692-0_77

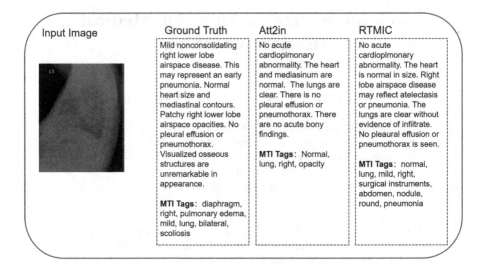

**Fig. 1.** An example of medical imaging report. A complete report includes a brief conclusion of diagnosis as *Impression*, a detailed description of observations in image as *Findings*, and a set of pathological keywords of findings as *MTI tags*.

Automatic medical image captioning is a core technology for automated diagnosis. The goal of medical image captioning is to generate accurate, informative, complete, and coherent medical report. A medical image captioning system first extracts features from medical images (*e.g.* MRI, CT, PET). It then generates report to cover as many pathological findings and normal descriptions as possible in professional languages. An example of report generation is shown in Fig. 1. The process is however very challenging due to a number of reasons. (1) The terminologies used in medical image report need to be very precise; (2) The generated report should be a long coherent paragraph, which is a non-trivial task for the existing image captioning techniques; (3) The medical image report consists of heterogeneous information including *tags*, *findings* and *impression*.

Due to the great success of deep learning in computer vision and video/image captioning, researchers started approaching the problem of medical imaging captioning using deep learning techniques from 2016 [8]. Most deep learning based systems leverage an encoder-decoder framework, in which the encoder (e.g. convolutional neural network (CNN)) extracts visual information and the decoder(e.g. recurrent neural network (RNN)) generates descriptive text. For example, Shin et al. [8] treated the medical imaging annotation problem as a multi-label classification task. They incorporated a cascaded CNN-RNN based captioning model with a joint image/text context cascade mechanism. Their model could only generate individual words providing some details about a detected disease. These words however are not coherent and can be difficult to comprehend. This is caused by the poor information extraction and language modeling capabilities. Later, Zhang et al. [11] proposed a CNN-RNN model enhanced by an auxiliary attention sharpening (AAS) module to automatically generate medical imaging report. They also demonstrate the corresponding attention areas of image descriptions. Their proposed model can generate more natural sentences but the length of each sentence is limited to 59 words. In addition, the content of a generated report is limited to five topics. Recently, Jing et al. [4] invented a hierarchical co-attention based model to generate multi-task medical imaging report, which contains various of heterogeneous data including short labels as Medical Text Indexer (MTI) tags, long paragraph of text as findings, and a summary of findings as impression. Their model can simultaneously attend to image and predict tags while exploring synergistic effects of visual and semantic information. Furthermore, their model can generate long sentence descriptions in reports by incorporating a hierarchical Long Short-Term Memory (LSTM) network. However, the experimental results show that their model was prone to generating false positives because of the interference of irrelevant tags. From there, Li et al. [5] built a hierarchical reinforced medical image report generation agent, which introduced reinforcement learning and template based language generation method into this research filed. However, due to the reliance on RNN model, their model cannot be executed by parallel computation. In addition, the heavy involvement of preprocessing in extracting templates makes the method heuristic and difficult to generalize to other applications.

To get over the above mentioned limitations, there are three main difficulties to be conquered. First, the existing visual encoders for medical imaging captioning are all based on top-down image feature extractors. Such methods cannot figure out the semantic features in medical images that are of great importance for the language generation module to map to pathological terminologies. Second, existing medical imaging reports are mainly generated by RNN-style structures, which may suffer from gradient vanishing and exploding problems when dealing with the long text generation task. Last but not the least, continuous maximum likelihood estimation (MLE) based gradient decent training methods cannot fit with discrete language generation tasks well [7].

In this paper, we propose a novel hierarchical neural network architecture – Reinforced Transformer [9] for Medical Image Captioning (RTMIC) to generate coherent informative medical imaging report. We make an attempt to solve the aforementioned problems from the following three aspects. (1) In order to capture the long distance dependency in images and sentences, we propose to incorporate transformer module into the medical imaging captioning model. This also speeds up the training process by enabling parallel computing in feed-forward layers. (2) We implement bottom-up attention using DenseNet pretrained on Chest-Xray 14 dataset [6]. It helps to detect regions of interest (ROIs) in medical images, which leads to more accurate pathological terminologies in the generated sentences. (3) Since the reinforcement learning based training method can alleviate the problem of exposure bias, it is employed to train the language model. Moreover, the use of reinforcement learning also addresses the discrepancy between MLE based training objective and evaluation metrics of interest.

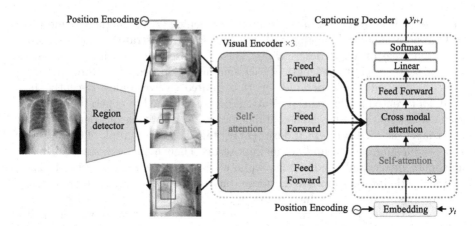

**Fig. 2.** Workflow of the proposed RTMIC model

## 2   Image Captioning

To generate a long coherent medical image report, we first feed the original images into an image encoder. This image encoder is composed of a bottom-up region detector and a top-down visual encoder. The DenseNet based region detector is in charge of extract bottom-up visual features. These bottom-up visual features will help us generate sentences containing more precise pathological terms. Then the top-down visual encoder will extract visual information from detected regions on pixel-wise considering the relationship between different regions. After extracting the visual representation, the captioning decoder will take the output of top-down visual encoder, and generate descriptive sentence for each detected region. In this paper, we focus on generate findings section which lists the radiology observations of each examined image region. Figure 2 provides an overview of the proposed method and the details of each component are presented in the following sections.

### 2.1   Image Encoder

The image encoder in our work consists of a bottom-up region detector and a top-down visual encoder. The extracted semantic visual features will be the input of the following captioning decoder to generate the report.

**Bottom-Up Region Detector.** In our work, a DenseNet-121 [3] based network pretrained on the *Chest X-Ray 14* dataset [10] is used to detect ROIs in a bottom-up attention mechanism. We take an image from set of medical images $\mathbf{I} = (I_j)_{j=1}^{K}$ as the input to the bottom-up region detector. Given an image $I_j$, the output of such network is a variably-sized set of $N$ ROI proposals' feature maps in the last layer of Densenet in the form of a flattened representation vector $V = v_1, v_2, ..., v_N$, where $v_i \in R^D$ and $D = 2048$.

At the same time, the region detector will also output a bounding box grounding the ROI with classification result and some attributes about it. This classification result can be used as the component of MTI tags. We expect such a kind of visual features to inspire the Transformer captioning module generates more precise medical terminologies.

**Top-Down Visual Encoder.** Given the representation vector, we further extract the visual information in proposed ROIs by $Transformer Encoder$, which can be regarded as a pooling operation. Here, we use an visual encoder with 3 stacked sublayer which consists of a self-attention module and a feedforward module. The number of multi-head in each self-attention layer is 8. Each sublayer in visual encoder will take the output $F^l$ from previous sublayer as the input and learns a representation $F^{l+1}$:

$$F^{l+1} = \psi(FFN(Res(F^l)), Res(F^l)) \tag{1}$$

$$\psi(\alpha, \beta) = LayerNorm(\alpha + \beta) \tag{2}$$

$$FFN(x) = max(0, xW_1 + b_1)W_2 + b_2 \tag{3}$$

$$Res(F^l) = \begin{pmatrix} \psi(MA(q(f_1^l), K^l, V^l), \ q(f_1^l))^T \\ ... \\ \psi(MA(q(f_{pro}^l), K^l, V^l), \ q(f_1^l))^T \end{pmatrix} \tag{4}$$

where $\psi(.)$ represents the layer-normalization [1] applied on residual output, $FFN(.)$ is a position-wise feed-forward network consists of two linear transformations with a ReLU activation in between. In Eq. (4), $q$ represents for a query vector in the self-attention mechanism, while $K$ and $V$ stand for key and value vectors, respectively. Notice that the function $MA$ means multi-head self-attention. For the $i$-th query vector $q_i$ corresponding to the $i$-th element in representation vector $V$, calculation process of $MA$ is as below:

$$MA(q_i, K, V) = W^o \begin{pmatrix} head_1 \\ ... \\ head_H \end{pmatrix} \tag{5}$$

$$head_j = Self\_Attention(W_j^q q_i, W_j^K K, W_j^V V) \tag{6}$$

$$Self\_Attention(q_i, K, V) = softmax(\frac{q_i K^T}{\sqrt{d_k}}) \tag{7}$$

where $d_k$ is the dimension of key vector. The number of attention head $H$ in this case equals to 8. $W_j^q, W_j^K, W_j^V \in R^{\frac{d_k}{\#} \times d}$ are the weight matrices of each head projection, and $W^o \in R^{d \times d}$ is a weight matrix averaging the effect of each attention head.

The transformer is a non-recurrent architecture. To describe the order of words in the output sentence, we use a position encoding technology

$$PE_{(pos, 2i)} = \sin(pos/10000^{2i/D}), \tag{8}$$

$$PE_{(pos, 2i+1)} = \cos(pos/10000^{2i/D}), \tag{9}$$

where $D$ is the dimension of input representation vector of a word (in this case, $D = 2048$), $pos$ is the position of a word in a sentence, $2i$ and $2i + 1$ represent the index of the elements in the position encoding vector.

## 2.2  Captioning Decoder

The findings paragraph consists of $M$ sentences $\mathbf{S} = (s_1, s_2, ..., s_M)$. Each sentence is composed by several words $s = (w_{i,1}, w_{i,2}, ..., w_{i,N}), w_{i,j} \in D$, where $i$ is the index of sentences, $j$ is the index of words, and $D$ represents the dictionary of all the output tokens. The captioning decoder takes the output of image encoder as the input. Thus, the decoder also has three stacked sublayers, each of which consists of a self-attention module, cross modal attention module and a feed-forward module. The number of multi-head in each self-attention layer is 8. The proposed ROI is denoted by $(P, S_p, E_p, Width, height)$, where $P$ is the proposal score, $S_p$ and $E_p$ are the start point and end point of ROI, respectively. The visual features can be represented as $\{F_1, ..., F_L\}$, where $L$ is the number of layers in $Transformer$'s encoder. The captioning decoder will generate the description for each proposed ROI. In corresponding decoder with $L$ sub-layers, the computation process of generating the $t$-th word is:

$$Y_{\leqslant t}^{l+1} = \psi(FFN(\phi(Y_{\leqslant t}^l)), \phi(Y_{\leqslant t}^l)) \tag{10}$$

$$\phi(Y_{\leqslant t}^l) = \begin{pmatrix} \psi(MA(q(\Omega(Y_{\leqslant t}^l))_1, K(F^l), V(F^l)), q(\Omega(Y_{\leqslant t}^l))_1)^T \\ \cdots \\ \psi(MA(q(\Omega(Y_{\leqslant t}^l))_t, K(\ddot{F}^i), V(F^l)), q(\Omega(Y_{\leqslant t}^l))_t)^T \end{pmatrix} \tag{11}$$

$$\Omega(Y_{\leqslant t}^l) = \begin{pmatrix} \psi(MA(q(y_1^l), K(Y^l), V(Y^l), q(y_1^l))^T) \\ \cdots \\ \psi(MA(q(y_t^l), K(Y^i), V(Y^l), q(y_t^l))^T) \end{pmatrix} \tag{12}$$

$$p(w_{t+1}|Y_{\leqslant t}^l) = softmax(W^V y_{t+1}^L) \tag{13}$$

where $y_i^j$ indicates the embedding of the $i$-th word in the $j$-th sub-layer, $Y_{\leqslant t}^l = \{y_1^l, ..., y_t^l\}$, $w_{t+1}$ is the probability of each word in the vocabulary for $t + 1$-th timestep, $W^V$ denotes the word embedding matrix whose vocabulary is in the size of $V$. $\omega(.)$ represents the self-attention module in decoder and $\phi(.)$ represents the cross module attention between encoder and decoder.

## 2.3  Reward Module

To solve the problem of discrepancy between MLE based training objective and evaluation metrics of interest and exposure bias, we take self-critical reinforcement learning method to train the $Trasformer$ captioning model, the reward is directly calculated by CIDER metric which is particularly designed for captioning task. The discounted reward function with the discounted factor $\gamma$ can be written as:

$$R(y_t) = \sum_{j=0}^{\infty} \gamma^j CIDER(y_{t+j}). \tag{14}$$

## 3    Experiments

### 3.1    Dataset

In this paper, we use the IU Chest X-ray collection [2] from Open-i to evaluate the performance of RTMIC. This dataset is an authoritative chest x-ray dataset which is widely used to evaluate chest medical imaging processing models. The dataset provides 7,470 chest x-ray images from frontal and lateral-view with 3,955 corresponding radiology reports. The radiology reports consist of four parts: (1) comparison, (2) indication, (3) findings, and (4) impression. To simplify the problem, we only take findings into account here. In experiments, we split the whole dataset into training, validation and test sets with the ratio of 70%, 20% and 10%. For the preprocessing, we first apply data augmentation methods including horizontal flipping, shifting, ratating and center cropping on the original images. Then we down-sample these images into the size of 224 × 224 corresponding to pre-trained DenseNet-121.

**Table 1.** Quantitative evaluation of generated reports on IU X-ray dataset.

| Models | CIDER | BLEU-1 | BLEU-2 | BLEU-3 | BLEU-4 |
|--------|-------|--------|--------|--------|--------|
| CNN-RNN | 0.294 | 0.216 | 0.124 | 0.087 | 0.066 |
| LRCN | 0.284 | 0.223 | 0.128 | 0.089 | 0.067 |
| AdaAtt | 0.295 | 0.220 | 0.127 | 0.089 | 0.068 |
| Att2in | 0.297 | 0.224 | 0.129 | 0.089 | 0.068 |
| RTMIC | 0.323 | 0.350 | 0.234 | 0.143 | 0.096 |

### 3.2    Experiment Results

We take BLEU and CIDER scores as the metric to measure the effectiveness of our proposed model. To simplify the problem, we mainly focus on measure the quality of *findings* in generated medical imaging report. Table 1 shows the comparison of the performance of RTMIC and 4 baselines. It can be seen that our proposed model has a competent performance with the state-of-the-art methods for CIDER. And for the metric BLEU-1, our proposed model has a more than 50% improvement than Att2 [7].

### 3.3    Discussions

According to Fig. 1, it can be seen that for abnormal images, the predicted MTI tags have a lot of overlap with the ground truth. Compared with Att2in [7], RTMIC is able to detect out more pathological features. It suggests that the DenseNet based region detection network really works for inspire the captioning system to generate robust medical report. In this paper, we mainly focus on generating *findings* as is the most important and detailed part of a medical imaging report. As is shown in the middle and right of Fig. 1, except for the last sentence, all the sentences in ground truth are hit correctly by RTMIC, which is a relative promising performance for radiologist. However, there is still a large space for CIDER and BLEU metrics to be improved. Otherwise, in order to prevent the model from being over-fitting, a larger dataset with ground truth is required which is unfortunately rare to be seen.

## 4 Conclusions

In this paper, we have proposed Reinforced Transformer for Medical Image Captioning (RTMIC), a novel Transformer based captioning model to generate long, coherent medical imaging report. RTMIC is the first attempt to combine bottom-up attention mechanism with Transformer based sequence generation model. We take a self-critical reinforcement learning method to update the image encoder, sentence decoder and captioning decoder. The experiments show that RTMIC can achieve the state-of-the-art performance on IU X-Ray dataset.

## References

1. Ba, L.J., Kiros, R., Hinton, G.E.: Layer normalization. CoRR (2016)
2. Demner-Fushman, D., et al.: Preparing a collection of radiology examinations for distribution and retrieval. JAMIA **23**(2), 304–310 (2016)
3. Huang, G., Liu, Z., van der Maaten, L., Weinberger, K.Q.: Densely connected convolutional networks. In: CVPR (2017)
4. Jing, B., Xie, P., Xing, E.P.: On the automatic generation of medical imaging reports. In: Proceedings of the 56th Annual Meeting of the Association for Computational Linguistics, ACL 2018 (2018)
5. Li, Y., Liang, X., Hu, Z., Xing, E.P.: Hybrid retrieval-generation reinforced agent for medical image report generation. NeurIPS **2018**, 1537–1547 (2018)
6. Rajpurkar, P., et al.: CheXNet: radiologist-level pneumonia detection on chest x-rays with deep learning. CoRR abs/1711.05225 (2017)
7. Rennie, S.J., Marcheret, E., Mroueh, Y., Ross, J., Goel, V.: Self-critical sequence training for image captioning. In: CVPR (2017)
8. Shin, H., Roberts, K., Lu, L., Demner-Fushman, D., Yao, J., Summers, R.M.: Learning to read chest x-rays: recurrent neural cascade model for automated image annotation. In: CVPR, pp. 2497–2506 (2016)
9. Vaswani, A., et al.: Attention is all you need. In: NeruIPS (2017)
10. Wang, X., Peng, Y., Lu, L., Lu, Z., Bagheri, M., Summers, R.M.: ChestX-ray8: hospital-scale chest x-ray database and benchmarks on weakly-supervised classification and localization of common thorax diseases. In: CVPR (2017)
11. Zhang, Z., Xie, Y., Xing, F., McGough, M., Yang, L.: MDNet: a semantically and visually interpretable medical image diagnosis network. In: CVPR (2017)

# Multi-Task Convolutional Neural Network for Joint Bone Age Assessment and Ossification Center Detection from Hand Radiograph

Minqing Zhang[1,2], Dijia Wu[1], Qin Liu[1], Qingfeng Li[1,3], Yiqiang Zhan[1], and Xiang Sean Zhou[1(✉)]

[1] Shanghai United Imaging Intelligence Co., Ltd., Shanghai, China
xiang.sean.zhou@united-imaging.com
[2] College of Software Engineering, Southeast University, Jiangsu, China
[3] School of Biomedical Engineering, Southern Medical University, Guangdong, China

**Abstract.** Bone age assessment is a common clinical procedure to diagnose endocrine and metabolic disorders in children. Recently, a variety of convolutional neural network based approaches have been developed to automatically estimate bone age from hand radiographs and achieved accuracy comparable to human experts. However, most of these networks were trained end-to-end, i.e., deriving the bone age directly from the whole input hand image without knowing which regions of the image are most relevant to the task. In this work, we proposed a multi-task convolutional neural network to simultaneously estimate bone age and localize ossification centers of different phalangeal, metacarpal and carpal bones. We showed that, similar to providing attention maps, the localization of ossification centers helps the network to extract features from more meaningful regions where local appearances are closely related to the skeletal maturity. In particular, to address the problem that some ossification centers do not always appear on the hand radiographs of certain bone ages, we introduced an *image-level* landmark presence classification loss, in addition to the conventional *pixel-level* landmark localization loss, in our multi-task network framework. Experiments on public RSNA data demonstrated the effectiveness of our proposed method in the reduction of gross errors of ossification center detection, as well as the improvement of bone age assessment accuracy with the aid of ossification center detection especially when the training data size is relatively small.

## 1 Introduction

Bone age assessment is often used to estimate the maturity of skeletal system in children and diagnose growth disorders. It is usually performed by pediatric radiologists using either Greulich and Pyle (G&P) or Tanner-Whitehouse (TW) method. The G&P method determines bone age by comparing the patient's

© Springer Nature Switzerland AG 2019
H.-I. Suk et al. (Eds.): MLMI 2019, LNCS 11861, pp. 681–689, 2019.
https://doi.org/10.1007/978-3-030-32692-0_78

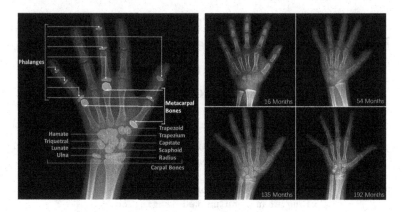

**Fig. 1.** X-ray images of left hand. Left: 20 specific bones as examined in TW method. Right: radiographs scanned from subjects of different age. Note that some carpal bones only appear after certain ages.

radiograph with the atlas of different ages. The TW method examines 20 specific bones as in Fig. 1 and assigns a staging score to each. In both cases, such manual assessment procedures are time-consuming, and subject to observer variation.

A number of automated bone age estimation methods have been developed in the past decades based on various machine learning algorithms, such as Bayesian estimator [4] and fuzzy decision tree [1] However, all these methods relied on manually crafted features and the resulting accuracy was limited. Recently, the convolutional neural network (CNN)-based methods have emerged as powerful solutions to many medical image analysis problems and been applied to bone age assessment with promising results. Spampinato et al. [9] proposed the BoNet which consists of five convolutional and pooling layers and achieved 9.5 month mean absolute error (MAE) on their testing data. Ren et al. [5] adopted the Inception-V3 [10] architecture in their regression CNN and employed Hessian filters to generate attention maps to the network to improve the estimation accuracy. In [3], the hand radiograph was aligned and cropped into three regions with each being used to train a specific CNN model. The ensemble of all regional models yielded the accuracy of 6.10 MAE on public RSNA dataset [7].

Despite the promising results of the CNN-based methods, all these models were trained end-to-end with bone age directly estimated from the input whole hand image. It remains unclear whether really meaningful features are extracted from the most relevant regions of the image, and more importantly, whether the training will become more efficient when provided such information, e.g., locations of the ossification centers where local image appearance determines the bone age as specified in TW.

To answer the questions, we proposed a novel multi-task CNN network based on the U-Net [6], to jointly estimate bone age and localize ossification centers of 20 phalangeal, metacarpal and carpal bones specified in TW as shown in Fig. 1. Both tasks shared the same features extracted by backbone convolutional layers of the network. The bone age estimation was performed using combined features of different resolution levels along the expansive path whereas the ossification center localization was made on the finest level, as shown in Fig. 3. To evaluate the difference, we compared the bone age estimation output from the same network trained *with* and *without* joint ossification center localization on the same testing data. The comparison was repeated multiple times each with different size of training data. The experiment results showed that joint learning of ossification center localization helps improve the accuracy of bone age estimation, and the improvement becomes more evident when the training data size decreases.

In addition, the ossification center localization, which is essentially a multi-landmark detection problem, is challenging in this study because, depending on the bone age, some ossification centers are not always present in the hand radiograph. The regular pixel-level classification formulation is prone to false positives because in our problem, the negative samples consist of not only those pixels off the landmark location, but also the ones on the location while the corresponding landmark is absent. However, the latter occupies only a very small percentage of the whole negative sample space and hence false positives occur. To address this problem, we introduced the image-level landmark presence classification loss into the same network to indicate whether the specific landmark is present in the image. The pixel-level classification results are used to localize the landmark only when the corresponding image-level presence is positive. The experiment results demonstrated the effectiveness of the proposed method especially in the reduction of gross errors such as false positives.

## 2    Method

### 2.1    Preprocessing

To make the bone age estimation model more robust against irrelevant variation of the hand radiographs, such as the texts on the background, the images were first preprocessed to remove such variation as shown in Fig. 2. First, we developed a separate hand segmentation network using U-Net [6], which proved itself very useful for segmentation problems with limited amount of data. The segmentation network was trained with 300 manually annotated hand masks, and the resulting hand masks were then used to remove the background and normalize the pose and intensity of the hand. All images are resized to $512 \times 512$ pixels. Although it can be argued that the size of the hand might be related to the age of the patient, skeletal ages are evaluated by the progression in piphyseal width relative to the metaphyses at different phalanges, carpal bone appearance, and radial or ulnar epiphyseal fusion rather than the size of the hand. The preprocessing pipeline was applied to all the training and testing images used in our experiments.

### 2.2    Network Architecture

The overall network architecture is illustrated in Fig. 3, which consists of the *backbone* network and three task-specific *subnetworks* for the bone age

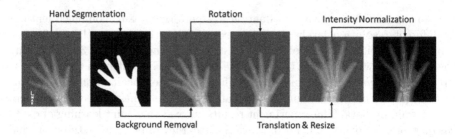

**Fig. 2.** Hand radiograph preprocessing pipeline.

regression (BAR), the ossification center localization, and the ossification center presence classification, respectively. The backbone is a U-Net which consists of a top-down contracting path and a bottom-up expansive path. The contracting path follows repeated application of downsampling blocks and residual blocks, while the expansive path comprises of repeated upsampling blocks and residual blocks. The downsampling block is a $2 \times 2$ convolution with stride 2 and doubles the output channels, and the upsampling block is a $2 \times 2$ transposed convolution with stride 2 and reduces the output channels by half. The residual blocks consist of multiple $3 \times 3$ convolutions with identity shortcut connection [2]. Each convolution in the network is followed by batch normalization and rectified linear unit.

**Landmark Localization Subnet.** The landmark localization subnet takes all feature maps on the finest level of the expansive path of the U-Net as inputs and consists of $1 \times 1$ convolution followed by the softmax layer. The localization loss $\mathcal{L}_{LOC}$ is defined as the focal loss over 21 classes (20 TW ossification centers and background) for all pixels on the input image.

$$\mathcal{L}_{LOC} = \frac{1}{N} \sum_{i=1}^{N} \sum_{c=1}^{C} \alpha_c (1 - p_{i,c})^{\gamma} \log p_{i,c} \delta(y_i = c), \tag{1}$$

where $C = 21$ stands for the number of classes and $N$ for the number of pixels. $y_i$ and $p_{i,c}$ are the class label and the estimated probability for class $c$ of pixel $i$, respectively. The $\delta(.)$ denotes the Dirac delta function. $\alpha_c$ and $\gamma$ represent the weight parameters that control the balance among different classes, as well as between easy and hard examples, respectively.

**Landmark Classification Subnet.** The landmark classification subnet processes the feature maps on the bottom layer of the U-Net. It comprises of $1 \times 1$ convolution and fully connected layer followed by softmax layer. The classification loss $\mathcal{L}_{CLS}$ is defined as binary cross entropy loss over 9 specific ossification centers of the carpal bones, as shown in Fig. 1, because the rest of ossification centers always appear regardless of the skeletal age.

$$\mathcal{L}_{CLS} = \frac{1}{IH} \sum_{i=1}^{I} \sum_{c=1}^{H} -(l_{i,c} \log p_{i,c} + (1 - l_{i,c}) \log(1 - p_{i,c})), \qquad (2)$$

where $H = 9$ stands for the number of landmarks of interest and $I$ for the number of images. $l_{i,c}$ and $p_{i,c}$ is the binary label and the estimated probability of image $i$ containing landmark $c$.

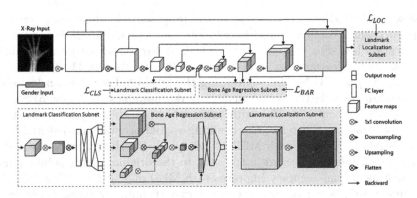

**Fig. 3.** The proposed multi-task U-Net architecture, which comprises of the backbone and three task-specific subnets.

**Bone Age Regression Subnet.** The bone age regression subnet combines feature maps of different resolution along the expansive path of the U-Net. These feature maps are first downsampled to the same resolution as the bottom layer using the same downsampling blocks as defined in the backbone. Following $1 \times 1$ convolution, the features are flattened and concatenated with the gender information and then passed onto the final fully connected layer. Different from previous work, we adopted the relative L1 loss to optimize the BAR module considering that the skeletal appearance difference is more apparent among younger ages. In Eq. 3, $B$ and $\hat{B}$ stands for the ground truth and estimated bone age, respectively. The final multi-task loss is defined as $\mathcal{L} = \mathcal{L}_{LOC} + \mathcal{L}_{CLS} + \mathcal{L}_{BAR}$.

$$\mathcal{L}_{BAR}(B, \hat{B}) = \frac{|B - \hat{B}|}{B}. \qquad (3)$$

## 3 Experiments and Results

Our proposed method was evaluated on the public dataset from the RSNA Pediatric Bone Age Machine Learning Challenge [7]. The dataset contains a total of 12,585 X-ray hand images with age ranging from 1 to 228 months and female to male ratio of 0.84:1. We randomly divided the data into training (10,067), validation (1,259), and testing (1,259) data. Each data consists of a 2D hand radiograph, gender information, bone age label, and 20 ossification center land-mark annotations we added. All models were trained for 1,000 epochs with Adam optimizer (learning rate = 0.0001), using data augmentation of random trans-lation (up to 25 pixels) and rotation (±5°). The same data split and training setting was applied to all the following experiments.

## 3.1   Ossification Classification and Localization Results

First we evaluated the effectiveness of the proposed joint landmark detection framework which combines pixel-level localization loss and image-level presence classification loss. For that purpose, we trained our model without optimizing the bone age regression loss, and compared it with ResNet-34 [2] as well as the same proposed U-Net but optimizing the pixel-level localization loss only. As shown in Table 1, ResNet-34 iteratively downsamples the input $512 \times 512$ image to the bottom $16 \times 16$ feature maps which are then used to predict the landmark locations. Therefore the resulting spatial accuracy of detected land-marks is relatively lower with MED of 2.05 pixel. On the contrary, the U-Net ($\mathcal{L}_{LOC}$) upsamples the feature maps back to the original high resolution thus the resulting spatial accuracy improves with MED of 1.18 pixel. However, it is more prone to gross errors because of the overwhelming negative examples as well as the extremely small percentage of total negative examples that help the model identify the absence of corresponding landmarks as explained above.

Four typical testing results with different ages are shown in Fig. 4 with carpal regions cropped for better visualization. Compared with ResNet-34 (1st row), the landmarks detected by our method (3rd row) are closer to the ground truth with noticeable accuracy improvement pointed by the orange arrow. Compared with U-Net($\mathcal{L}_{LOC}$) (2nd row), the false positive pointed by the yellow arrow and the false negative pointed by the blue arrow are both corrected by our approach.

## 3.2   Bone Age Assessment Results

Next we tested the proposed joint multi-task learning network with simulta-neous landmark detection and bone age estimation, and compared it with the

**Table 1.** Landmark detection results obtained by ResNet-34, U-Net ($\mathcal{L}_{LOC}$), and U-Net ($\mathcal{L}_{LOC}+\mathcal{L}_{CLS}$). FP and FN count the numbers of false positives and false negatives. Mean Euclidean Distance (MED) measures the average distance error of the remaining results in pixel. All numbers are averaged or summed over 20 ossification centers on 1,259 testing data. The CLS. size and LOC. size represent the sizes of the feature maps on the final layer before the classification and localization output, respectively.

| Method | CLS. size | LOC. size | FP | FN | MED (pixel) |
|---|---|---|---|---|---|
| ResNet-34 | – | $16 \times 16$ | 62 | 16 | 2.05 |
| U-Net ($\mathcal{L}_{LOC}$) | – | $512 \times 512$ | 90 | 45 | 1.25 |
| U-Net ($\mathcal{L}_{LOC} + \mathcal{L}_{CLS}$) | $32 \times 32$ | $512 \times 512$ | **54** | **8** | **1.18** |

same network optimizing the bone age estimation loss only. The comparison was repeated three times each with different percentage of training data in order to evaluate the benefit of multi-task under different size of training data available. Also, we chose to compare with the Inception-v3 [10] which outperformed other proposed CNN-based bone age estimation networks as reported in [5]. As shown in Table 2, the joint learning of ossification center detection helps improve the accuracy of bone age estimation, but the improvement drops when the data size increases. We assume that, given enough training data, the deep neural network will eventually extract most useful features and multi-task learning is particularly beneficial when the training data is less than sufficient.

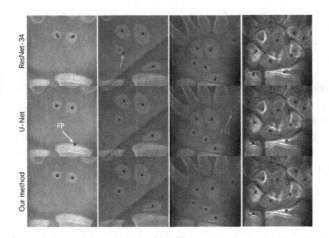

**Fig. 4.** Results obtained by ResNet-34, U-Net($\mathcal{L}_{LOC}$), and U-Net ($\mathcal{L}_{LOC} + \mathcal{L}_{CLS}$) on four test images with different ages. (Green cross: ground truth, Red cross: detection). (Color figure online)

**Table 2.** Bone age estimation results obtained by Inception-V3, U-Net ($\mathcal{L}_{BAR}$), and U-Net ($\mathcal{L}_{BAR} + \mathcal{L}_{CLS} + \mathcal{L}_{LOC}$). In each column, the model was trained with different percentage of training data, and tested on the same 1,259 testing data.

| Network | Parameters | 10% | 50% | 100% |
|---|---|---|---|---|
| Inception-V3 | 23 million | – | – | $6.19 \pm 5.31$ |
| U-Net ($\mathcal{L}_{BAR}$) | 8 million | $11.12 \pm 9.47$ | $6.49 \pm 5.52$ | $5.86 \pm 5.02$ |
| U-Net ($\mathcal{L}_{BAR} + \mathcal{L}_{CLS} + \mathcal{L}_{LOC}$) | 8 million | $9.02 \pm 7.71$ | $5.91 \pm 5.04$ | $\mathbf{5.49 \pm 4.61}$ |

To explain the difference visually, we employed Grad-CAM [8] to produce feature heatmaps which highlight the regions important to the task as learned by the model. In practice, we extracted the feature heatmaps from the last convolutional layer before the fully connected layer of the bone age regression subnet. As shown in Fig. 5, the model with joint learning focused closely around the 20 ossification center regions, which are more relevant to the bone age assessment explaining the accuracy improvement brought by the multi-task learning.

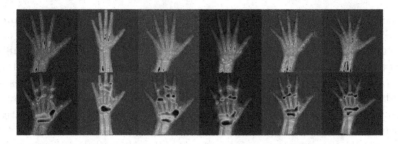

**Fig. 5.** Grad-CAM feature heatmaps generated by models trained with (1st row) and without (2nd row) multi-tasking. Both models were trained with 100% training data.

## 4   Conclusion

In this paper, we proposed a multi-task learning network for joint ossification center detection and bone age estimation. The experiment results showed the advantage of multi-task learning especially when the training data size is small. We also addressed the problem in landmark detection that landmarks are might be absent in the image. By combining both image-level classification loss and pixel-level localization loss, the proposed method improves the detection robustness as well as maintains the detection accuracy.

## References

1. Aja-Fernández, S., de Luis-García, R., Martın-Fernandez, M.A., Alberola-López, C.: A computational TW3 classifier for skeletal maturity assessment a computing with words approach. J. Biomed. Inform. **37**(2), 99–107 (2004)
2. He, K., Zhang, X., Ren, S., Sun, J.: Deep residual learning for image recognition. In: Proceedings of the IEEE Conference on Computer Vision and Pattern Recognition, pp. 770–778 (2016)
3. Iglovikov, V.I., Rakhlin, A., Kalinin, A.A., Shvets, A.A.: Paediatric bone age assessment using deep convolutional neural networks. In: Stoyanov, D., et al. (eds.) DLMIA/ML-CDS -2018. LNCS, vol. 11045, pp. 300–308. Springer, Cham (2018). https://doi.org/10.1007/978-3-030-00889-5_34
4. Mahmoodi, S., Sharif, B.S., Chester, E.G., Owen, J.P., Lee, R.: Skeletal growth estimation using radiographic image processing and analysis. IEEE Trans. Inf. Technol. Biomed. **4**(4), 292–297 (2000)
5. Ren, X., et al.: Regression convolutional neural network for automated pediatric bone age assessment from hand radiograph. IEEE J. Biomed. Health Inform. **23**(5), 2030–2038 (2018)
6. Ronneberger, O., Fischer, P., Brox, T.: U-net: convolutional networks for biomedical image segmentation. In: Navab, N., Hornegger, J., Wells, W.M., Frangi, A.F. (eds.) MICCAI 2015. LNCS, vol. 9351, pp. 234–241. Springer, Cham (2015). https://doi.org/10.1007/978-3-319-24574-4_28
7. RSNA Pediatric Bone Age Challenge (2017). http://rsnachallenges.cloudapp.net/competitions/4

8. Selvaraju, R.R., Cogswell, M., Das, A., Vedantam, R., Parikh, D., Batra, D.: Grad-cam: visual explanations from deep networks via gradient-based localization. In: Proceedings of the IEEE International Conference on Computer Vision, pp. 618–626 (2017)
9. Spampinato, C., Palazzo, S., Giordano, D., Aldinucci, M., Leonardi, R.: Deep learning for automated skeletal bone age assessment in x-ray images. Med. Image Anal. **36**, 41–51 (2017)
10. Szegedy, C., Vanhoucke, V., Ioffe, S., Shlens, J., Wojna, Z.: Rethinking the inception architecture for computer vision. In: Proceedings of the IEEE Conference on Computer Vision and Pattern Recognition, pp. 2818–2826 (2016)

# Author Index